omorrow the Unive

superheterodyne design and the first ever optional SSB module in a portable, this beginning of a legendary tradition led to generation after generation of Satellit series radios, all becoming coveted collector's items.

The Legend. The History. The Pride.

The Satellit 800 Millennium continues the tradition. Our goal was to create the dream. We listened to shortwave enthusiasts from every part of the globe who owned Grundig and other brands. We listened to what they wanted in a high-end shortwave portable: A big, easy to read, beautifully lit display. A large, traditional analog signal strength meter. A tuning knob they could really get a grip on. The option of push-button tuning and direct frequency entry. A tuner with absolutely no audible muting during tuning knob use. We listened. It's here. **The Dream. The Legend. The History. The Tradition.**

The Satellit 800 Millennium.

by GRUNDIG

Lextronix / Grundig, P.O. Box 2307, Menlo Park, CA 94026 • Tel: 650-361-1611 • Fax: 650-361-1724
Shortwave Hotlines: (US) 1-800-872-2228 (CN) 1-800-637-1648 • Web: www.grundigradio.com • Email: grundig@ix.netcom.com

TABLE OF CONTENTS

World Band Radio

TABLE OF CONTENTS

International
Broadcasting
Services, Ltd.

ISSN 0897-0157

OUR READER IS THE MOST IMPORTANT PERSON IN THE WORLD!

Editorial

Editor-in-Chief	Lawrence Magne
Editor	Tony Jones
Assistant Editor	Craig Tyson
Contributing Editors	George Heidelman, Robert Sherwood, John Wagner, Dave Zantow, George Zeller
Consulting Editor	John Campbell
Founder Emeritus	Don Jensen
WorldScan® Contributors	Gabriel Iván Barrera (Argentina), James Conrad (U.S.), David Crystal (Israel), Alok Dasgupta (India), Graeme Dixon (New Zealand), Nicolás Eramo (Argentina), *Jembatan DX*/Juichi Yamada (Japan), Anatoly Klepov (Russia), Marie Lamb (U.S.), *Número Uno*/Jerry Berg (U.S.), *Radio Nuevo Mundo* (Japan), *Relámpago DX*/Takayuki Inoue Nozaki (Japan), Nikolai Rudnev (Russia), Don Swampo (Uruguay), David Walcutt (U.S.)
WorldScan® Software	Richard Mayell
Laboratory	Rob Sherwood
Artwork	Gahan Wilson, cover
Graphic Arts	Bad Cat Design; Mike Wright, layout
Printing	Tri-Graphic Printing, Ottawa

Administration

Publisher	Lawrence Magne
Associate Publisher	Jane Brinker
Offices	IBS North America, Box 300, Penn's Park PA 18943, USA; www.passband.com; Phone +1 (215) 598-9018; Fax +1 (215) 598 3794; mktg@passband.com
Advertising & Media Contact	Jock Elliott, Lightkeeper Communications, 29 Pickering Lane, Troy NY 12180, USA; Phone +1 (518) 271-1761; Fax +1 (518) 271 6131; media@passband.com

Bureaus

IBS Latin America	Tony Jones, Casilla 1844, Asunción, Paraguay; schedules@passband.com; Fax +1 (215) 598 3794
IBS Australia	Craig Tyson, Box 2145, Malaga WA 6062; Fax +61 (8) 9342 9158; addresses@passband.com
IBS Japan	Toshimichi Ohtake, 5-31-6 Tamanawa, Kamakura 247; Fax +81 (467) 43 2167; ibsjapan@passband.com

Library of Congress Cataloging-in-Publication Data

Passport to World Band Radio.
1. Radio Stations, Shortwave—Directories. I. Magne, Lawrence
TK9956.P27 2000 384.54'5 00-22739
ISBN 0-914941-51-8

IC-R75

Pull out the weak signals
30 kHz – 60.0 MHz†

Commercial grade • synchronous AM detection (S-AM) • optional DSP with auto notch filter • all mode • triple conversion • twin passband tuning (PBT) • large front mounted speaker • large display • well spaced keys and dials • 1000 memory channels • up to two optional filters • PC remote control with ICOM software for Windows®.

IC-R10

Advanced performance and features.
500 kHz – 1.3 GHz†

All mode • alphanumeric backlit display • attenuator • 7 different scan modes • beginner mode • 1000 memory channels; band scope • includes AA Ni-Cds and charger.

IC-R2

Excellent audio, tiny package.
500 kHz – 1.3 GHz†

AM, FM, WFM • easy band switching • CTCSS decode • 400 memory channels • priority watch • MIL SPEC 810C/D/E • weather resistant • includes 2 AA Ni-Cds and charger.

IC-R3

See and Hear all the action**. *Coming Soon!*
500 kHz – 2.45 GHz†

www.icomreceivers.com
download frequencies right from the web

ICOM makes it easy to get the frequencies you want. Our database searches your area. You download the frequencies to your computer and easily load them into your ICOM radio. Optional software and PC connection cable required.

log on > download > listen in

DOWNLOAD FREQUENCIES
RIGHT FROM THE WEB

IC-PCR1000

The original "black box" is still best
100 kHz – 1.3 GHz†

AM, FM, WFM, USB, LSB, CW • unlimited memory channels • real time band scope • IF shift • noise blanker • digital AFC • "VSC" voice scan control (when activated, stops only on modulated signals) • attenuator • tunable bandpass filters • AGC function • S meter squelch • CTCSS tone squelch • large selection of tuning steps and scans • external speaker level control • DSP optional • download and demo the latest software for free: <www.icomamerica.com>

IC-R8500

The experts choice
100 kHz - 2.0 GHz†

Commercial grade • all mode • IF shift • noise blanker • audio peak filter (APF) • selectable AGC time constant • digital direct synthesis (DDS) • 1000 memory channels • RS-232C port for PC remote control with ICOM software for Windows®

IC-PCR100

Much like its big brother, but for less
100 kHz – 1.3 GHz†

AM, FM, WFM • many of the same features and performance as the IC-PCR1000 • designed for Windows® 95 or 98 • download and demo the latest free, full version software today:<www.icomamerica.com>

Visit our redesigned website at
www.icomamerica.com

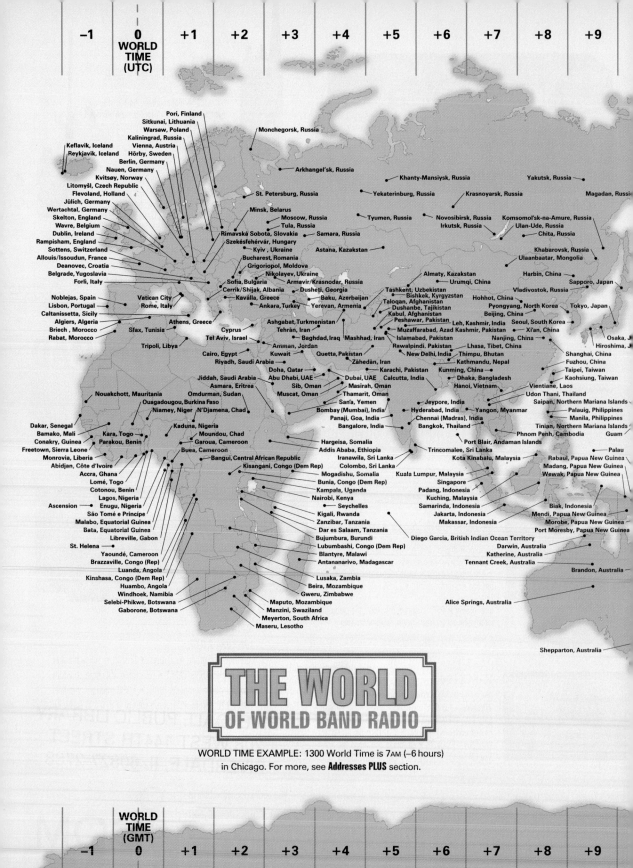

THE WORLD
OF WORLD BAND RADIO

WORLD TIME EXAMPLE: 1300 World Time is 7AM (−6 hours) in Chicago. For more, see **Addresses PLUS** section.

+11   +12   −11   −10   −9   −8   −7   −6   −5   −4   −3   −2

Anchor Point, Alaska, USA

Palana, Russia

Petropavlovsk-Kamchatskiy, Russia

Calgary AB, Canada
Vancouver BC, Canada

Noblesville IN, USA
Toronto ON, Canada
Montréal PQ, Canada
Monticello ME, USA
Greenbush ME, USA
Sackville NB, Canada
St. John's NF, Canada
Halifax NS, Canada
Bethel PA, USA
Red Lion PA, USA
Upton KY, USA
Nashville TN, USA
McCaysville GA, USA
Greenville NC, USA
Newport NC, USA
Cypress Creek SC, USA

Salt Lake City UT, USA
Boulder CO, USA
Delano CA, USA
Rancho Simi CA, USA

Macon GA, USA
Birmingham AL, USA
New Orleans LA, USA
Okeechobee FL, USA
Miami FL, USA
Key West FL, USA
Havana, Cuba

Mesquite NM, USA
Dallas TX, USA

...aha, Kauai Island, Hawai'i, USA
...arbor, Oahu Island, Hawai'i, USA
...alehu, "Big Island," Hawai'i, USA

Mérida, Mexico
México City, Mexico
Chiquimula, Guatemala
Guatemala City, Guatemala
Tegucigalpa, Honduras
Puerto Cabezas, Nicaragua
San José, Costa Rica
Santa Fé de Bogotá, Colombia
Villavicencio, Colombia
Florencia, Colombia
Quito, Ecuador
Tena, Ecuador
Loja, Ecuador
Iquitos, Peru
Yurimaguas, Peru
Cajamarca, Peru

Santo Domingo, Dominican Republic
Roosevelt Roads, Puerto Rico
Anguilla
Antigua
Bonaire, Netherlands Antilles
Caracas, Venezuela
Puerto Ayacucho, Venezuela
Georgetown, Guyana
Paramaribo, Surinam
Montsinéry, French Guiana
Cayenne, French Guiana

Belem, Brazil
Manaus, Brazil

Tarawa, Kiribati

Honiara, Solomon Islands

Guayaramerín, Bolivia
Cobija, Bolivia
Lima, Peru
Cusco, Peru
Arequipa, Peru
La Paz, Bolivia
Santa Cruz, Bolivia
Sucre, Bolivia
Asunción, Paraguay
Villarrica, Paraguay
Encarnación, Paraguay

Porto Velho, Brazil
Salvador, Brazil
Cuiabá, Brazil
Brasília, Brazil
Goiânia, Brazil

Belo Horizonte, Brazil
Rio de Janeiro, Brazil
São Paulo, Brazil
Curitiba, Brazil
Foz do Iguaçu, Brazil
Florianópolis, Brazil
Porto Alegre, Brazil
Artigas, Uruguay
Montevideo, Uruguay
Buenos Aires, Argentina

Port-Vila, Vanuatu

Santiago, Chile

Temuco, Chile

Rangitaiki, New Zealand
Levin, New Zealand

Coyhaique, Chile

Base Esperanza, Antarctica (−3)

−11   +12   −11   −10   −9   −8   −7   −6   −5   −4   −3   −2

SONY

With one fingertip, catch the changing world.

MEMORYSCANNING FUNCTION

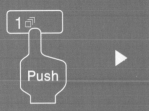

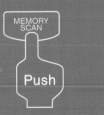

[1] Choose the page-number in which the station you like is preset.

[2] Memory scanning starts, automatically scans 10 frequencies at maximum.

[3] It finds the sensitive frequency.

Memory scan function presents you quick and easy short wave tuning.

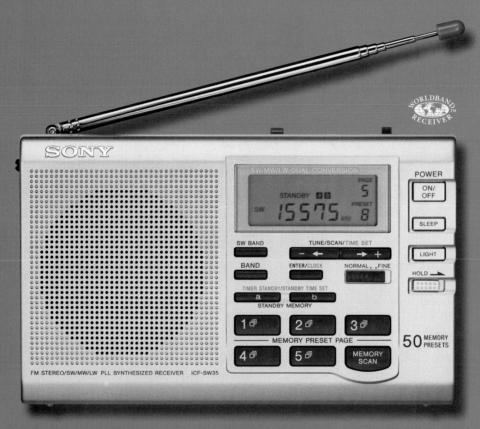

•Automatic memory scanning function searches the sensitive radio frequency among those preinput frequencies. •50 memory presets (10 frequencies in 1 button). •ATT controler can adjust the sensitivity of radio reception. •4 way of tuning-memory scan. auto scan, preset, manual tuning. •Switchable frequency step in SW (1kHz/5kHz). • By 2 indpendent stand-by memories, power will be on at anytime, any channel you like. •60/45/30/15 minutes Sleeptimer.

FM stereo/SW/MW/LW PLL synthesizer receiver **ICF-SW35**

Sony WORLD BAND RECEIVER

SONY

The World Is In Your Hand.

Bring the world closer. For easy, compact, high performance, get Sony's audio cassette case size SW100 World Band Receiver. Sony has packed its extensive radio technology into the new SW100. With a body about the size of an audio cassette case, the SW100 covers virtually all the world's broadcasts, from MW to FM stereo, shortwave, and longwave. ●Large LCD for clear tuning, and easy-to-operate switch layout ●Up to 50 broadcast stations can be preset in memory ●Station name tuning function (you can tune in stations simply by calling stored station names) ●Accurate time for 24 of the world's major cities can be displayed instantly using the built-in world clock ●Dual timer function handles stations that switch broadcast frequencies at different times ●Ample volume with high sound quality despite compact size. Packed with many other advanced features—now available for world travellers.

Radio reception time   World time

SW100

WORLD BAND RECEIVER

FM Stereo/LW/MW/SW
PLL Synthesizer Receiver

ICF-SW100

Bhutan Radio: Living on Thimpu Time

Tiny Bhutan is no ordinary country, not even for the Bhutanese. While most cultures are hooked on gross national product, Bhutan chases after what it calls "gross national happiness."

If happiness were defined only by things, Bhutan would be in trouble. But this landlocked mountain country marches to its own heartbeat, placing emphasis on quality of life.

Here, there is serenity, with freedom from strife and crime.

Radio Brings Bhutan to World

This probably wouldn't have happened if the deeply Buddhist nation weren't so isolated. Air links from its lone airport are minimal, and even then foreign tourists can't enter unless they spend lavishly on an official tour.

World band DXers are better off, as they can eavesdrop on Bhutan in English and other languages. For some this is a fruitless challenge— location and other gremlins conspire to keep it beyond ear's reach. But for others, reception of Bhutan's broadcasts can be a memorable reward for patient and skilled bandscanning.

Radio and TV Share Staff, Facilities

A short walk downtown in the capital of Thimpu, not far from the central market, reveals the compound of the Bhutan Broadcasting Service (BBS). With its traditional Bhutanese architecture and ornate facade, the building is truly handsome, especially when compared to the architectural monoliths that normally house government agencies. Only radio trucks and an antenna next door give away the building's real purpose.

The BBS's newscasts help hold Bhutan together as a unified nation.

M. Guha

The BBS' multi-story broadcasting house is the nerve center for all radio and television operations. It houses three recording and transmission studios, a control room, a newsroom, administrative offices and maintenance areas. Most staffers work using computers and the Internet, as well as up-to-date studio equipment and production techniques.

The BBS is a joint radio and television operation in which most of the 105 staff, facilities and programming are shared for twin-media output. Operations are a daunting task, what with all that needs to be done and the paucity of trained personnel. Each afternoon during peak hours young men and women scurry about in their colorful *gho* and *kira*, giving the station a techno-Alice-in-Wonderland feel.

While most countries chase GNP, Bhutan seeks "gross national happiness."

The BBS broadcasts from facilities sporting traditional architecture, but their equipment is technologically advanced.

M. Guha

The LCD
Big! Bold! Brightly Illuminated 6" by 3½".
Liquid Crystal Display shows all important data:
Frequency, Meter band, Memory position, Time,
LSB/USB, Synchronous Detector and more.

SW, AM and
Aircraft Band and
20 KHz in FM.
• For Fixed-step
Tuning: Big,
responsive
Up/Down tuning
buttons.
• For direct
frequency entry: a responsive, intuitive
numeric keypad.

The Signal Strength Meter
Elegant in its traditional
Analog design, like the
gauges in the world's
finest sports cars. Large.
Well Lit. Easy to read.

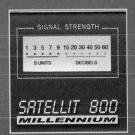

The Frequency Coverage
Longwave, AM and shortwave: continuous
100-30,000 KHz. FM: 87-108 MHz VHF Aircraft
Band: 118-137 MHz.

The Tuning Controls
• For the traditionalist: a smooth, precise tuning
knob, produces no audio muting during use.
Ultra fine-tuning of 50Hz on LSB/USB, 100Hz in

THESE ARE THE SATELLIT 800 MILLENNIUM'S MAJOR FEATURES.
FOR A DETAILED SPECIFICATION SHEET, CONTACT GRUNDIG.

Digital Technology

The Operational Controls
Knobs where you want them; Buttons where they make sense. The best combination of traditional and high-tech controls.

The Sound
Legendary Grundig Audio Fidelity with separate bass and treble controls, big sound from its powerful speaker and FM-stereo with the included high quality headphones.

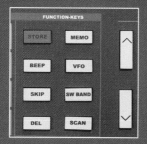

The Technology
Today's latest engineering:
- Dual conversion superheterodyne circuitry.
- PLL synthesized tuner.

The Many Features
- 70 user-programmable memories.
- Two, 24 hour format clocks.
- Two ON/OFF sleep timers.
- Massive, built-in telescopic antenna.
- Connectors for external antennas – SW, AM, FM and VHF Aircraft Band.
- Line-out, headphone and external speaker jacks.

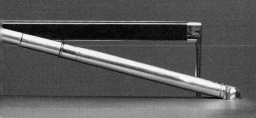

The Power Supply
A 110V AC adapter is included for North America (a 220V AC adapter is available upon request). Also operates on 6 size D batteries. (not included)

Dimensions: 20.5″ L × 9″ H × 8″ W

Weight: 14.50 lbs.

by **GRUNDIG**

Lextronix / Grundig, P.O. Box 2307, Menlo Park, CA 94026 • Tel: 650-361-1611 • Fax: 650-361-1724
Shortwave Hotlines: (US) 1-800-872-2228 (CN) 1-800-637-1648 • Web: www.grundigradio.com • Email: grundig@ix.netcom.com

Kinga Singye, executive head of the BBS, confers with staff after checking over PASSPORT. Singye, a former diplomat, was appointed by the king.

M. Guha

Music Guides Culture

"Bhutan cannot be isolated all the time. We have to move ahead, present what we have, and strike a balance between moderniza- tion and tradition," says Kinga Singye, executive head of the BBS. And striking a balance is what the BBS has done.

Music is a key ingredient. It attracts advertising and is immensely popular— even in neighboring Nepal, Bangladesh and India, judging from letters the station receives. Because there are so few local private studios, the BBS routinely produces commercials for its advertisers. Each news bulletin ends with a roster of public service announcements mixed in with canned music to pep up the mundane insert.

The station also uses music to extend its cultural influence in less visible ways. To promote appropriate songs, the BBS lends out studios at nominal rates to local bands for recording sessions—at times censoring lyrics which might not suit the local palate or official order. To make the offer even more tempting the station provides complimentary electronic drums, guitars, synthesizers and keyboards.

Youth Group First to Broadcast

By 1973 the Bhutanese Civil Wireless Authority was linking the scarcely acces- sible kingdom via Morse code (CW), using a field station in each district. This formed the only communication lifeline before there was widespread telephone and telegraph service. Signals emanated from a 0.4 kW Indian-made BEL communications transmitter owned and maintained by the authority.

The National Youth Association of Bhutan (NYAB) decided to take to the airwaves over the weekends, while the authority took its break. Once that same transmitter was modified for voice, radio broadcasting finally began in Bhutan on November 11, 1973. Radio NYAB, as it was called then, was on the air four hours each Saturday and Sunday between 0000 and 0200 World Time on 7040 kHz. With a transmitter rated at 400 Watts—probably less when used for broadcasts instead of CW—it quickly became a juicy DX catch.

Bhutanese records show that these transmissions were aired in the national language, Dzongkha, along with English.

However, foreign listeners reported also hearing segments in Lhotshampa (Nepali) and Hindi.

Run by Volunteers

This early broadcasting facility consisted of a small space that doubled as studio-cum-control room. The equipment was rudimentary—three-to-four microphones, an audio amplifier and four-to-five Phillips cassette players from Holland. This modest operation was run by a lone engineer, along with a handful of enthusiastic young volunteers. The old building still exists and is presently occupied by the Forest Institute.

Initially that engineer was Thinley Dorji, fresh from India with a telecom degree and brimming with ideas. Still cheerful and optimistic, he nostalgically reminisces, "Every day was a challenge—unlike nowadays, where everything is logic and automation. We had to be really careful of high voltage, as there was always a danger of shock with so many wires strewn around."

Station Moves, Expands

In 1985, Radio NYAB had to relocate to the outskirts of Thimpu, as the Civilian

Radio NYAB aired Bhutan's first broadcasts from here, using a converted 400 Watt Morse-code transmitter. The building is presently occupied by the Forest Institute. M. Guha

Wireless Authority with which it shared the transmission facility had also moved. In the following year, with the advent of a countrywide telephone network, the wireless authority was disbanded.

Consequently, the Royal Government of Bhutan bought a 10 kW Harris tube-type transmitter—Bhutan's first intended solely for broadcast use—although it appears to have operated at half power. Output was increased to six transmitter-hours on weekdays: 1100-1400 World Time on 3395 kHz, using the old transmitter, and 6035

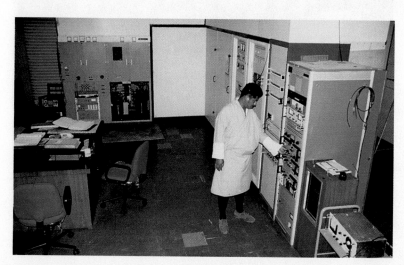

Today, much is changed. The BBS now transmits with sophisticated modern hardware.

M. Guha

Thinley Dorji, Radio NYAB's first engineer, tweaks the station's original transmitter.

M. Guha

kHz. Weekend hours were increased, as well: 0600-0900, using the new Harris sender on 6035 kHz. Two more Bhutanese languages—Sharchopa and Lhotshampa (Nepali)—were thrown in at the same time.

By now the staff numbered twenty. At the new site were three buildings: one each for administration, studios and transmission. That which formerly housed the transmitter has now become a quaint private home, while the others were demolished to make way for vapid new structures. The old CW transmitter is still up and running, thanks to astute maintenance, and will shortly be housed in a museum at the back of the broadcasting house.

BBS Supersedes Radio NYAB

As the royal government realized the need for radio broadcasting to promote social development, it decided to invest in a proper radio setup. It finally got its act together in 1990, when Radio NYAB was reincarnated as the Bhutan Broadcasting Service. An elegant new studio and administrative complex was commissioned in Chubachu, not far from the old site at the edge of Thimpu.

India stepped in to modernize the BBS, with All India Radio engineers and civilian contractors constructing the studio and transmitter site as part of a turnkey project. In 1996, aid from Danida covered the purchase of digital audio equipment.

World Band to Cover Gaps

Bhutan's mountainous terrain tends to disrupt VHF signals. Yet, thanks to an Italian aid package, FM is forming the basis of a nationwide radio network which will leave shortwave to fill in

Radio NYAB's second facility was bulldozed to make way for homes and other new structures.

M. Guha

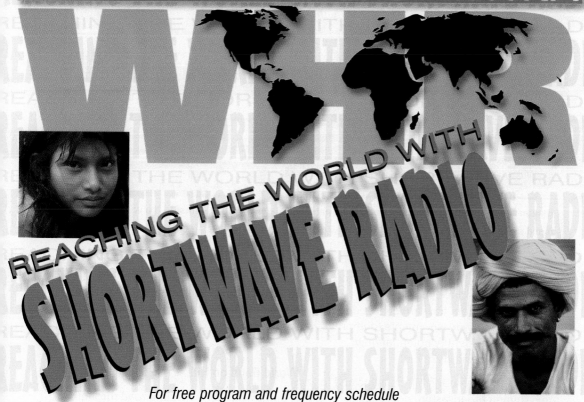

Bhutan's lookalike modern buildings and radio antennas stand in stark contrast to the wild beauty found close by.   M. Guha

coverage gaps. Four FM transmitters of varying powers have been installed, while survey teams from Italy are engaged in signal-strength measurements to improve coverage and identify potential new transmitter locations.

The first of these transmitters is located in the Thimpu broadcasting house itself, ostensibly to feed another transmitter located higher up, atop a hill. It is a suitcase-size 0.25 kW Italian ABS transmitter with enough power to send a reliable signal on 92.0 MHz. The long cable which ran up the hill to the transmitter was accidentally sliced during construction, so feeding transmitters is strictly a wireless operation now.

The largest FM operation is high on another hill, in Dhopchula. This kilowatt ABS transmitter pumps in a powerhouse signal to much of the country on 88.1 MHz. At Takti a fourth transmitter, 0.5 kW, emits a steady signal into southern Bhutan on 98.0 MHz.

World Band on Hill

A bumpy ride up a winding road through thick pine forests takes us to the transmitter site for FM and world band radio. Seductive road signs like "Be gentle on my curves" and "Rest a while" lend a romantic tinge to the idyllic passing countryside.

There is probably no other place quite like this on earth. The transmitter site has a deserted look, giving the impression of a sleeping dragon that needs to be awakened. Throbbing drumbeats from a nearby monastery synergize with the view to produce a contentment worthy of Buddha.

The transmitter site is perched precariously atop Sangayang Hill, which lords over the BBS broadcasting complex and provides a spectacular view of picturesque Thimpu valley. From a distance the facility looks like a quaint collection of Lego huts. The transmission building's architecture and layout are typically Bhutanese, except for the twin shortwave folded-dipole towers and satellite dishes that are out of sync with the landscape's wild beauty.

The station is normally kept locked by the genial *chowkidar*, who opens the door leading to the transmitter hall at the behest of the lone engineer. The place is usually deserted except when the engineer arrives each day to fire up the transmitter.

The BBS' commercial director makes use of the Internet in his work.

M. Guha

Transmitter Ripped Apart

The oblong transmitter hall houses the old Harris shortwave transmitter. This tube-type unit has had its innards ripped apart and is definitely not on standby, as spare parts are costly and difficult to come by. Standing alongside is its replacement, a tough Brown-Boveri/ABB 50kW unit installed in 1992. This German-made transmitter can operate on all world band segments, although for now it only uses 49 and 60 meters. Weekday broadcasts are between 0800 and 1330 World Time on 5030 kHz, although during the final three hours in winter (90 minutes summer) there is co-channel interference from China's first domestic network. Reflecting tradition, the broadcast day is longer on weekends—0400 to 1100 on 6035 kHz. At 1200 weekdays there is an hour in English that starts with ten minutes or so of news, with the station identifying as, "This is the Bhutan Broadcasting Service." Also, news and other fare is aired in Dzongkha, Sharchopa and Lhotshampa (Nepali).

> The station's old Harris shortwave transmitter is no longer on standby.

Deserted news studio of BBS-TV atop Sangayang "transmitter" hill. Evening TV newscasts are aired later over BBS radio.

M. Guha

In the antenna switching room, matrixes are switched by manual levers. There are air-cooled transformers for the four-phase electricity supply, along with an array of batteries for backup power and a seldom used Brown-Boveri dummy load.

The studio-to-transmitter link is a 0.02 kW Italian ABS exciter on 96.0 MHz that feeds an Italian RX-11 FM receiver. Even at such modest power it seconds as a broadcast transmitter which, thanks to its tremendous location, sends a sizable signal to the valley below. There are UN markings on the hardware, indicating that it was part of a UNESCO aid package—a common practice in South Asian countries.

Television's Last Convert

The Bhutanese government's long-standing ban on television came to end on June 2, 1999, the 25th anniversary of King Jigme Singye Wangchuk's coronation. At this point Bhutan became the last country in the world to have its own television station. The advent of television and the Internet were part of King Jigme's silver jubilee, earning him the honorific, "His Majesty, Light of the Cyber Age."

The new station broadcasts only to the capital, Thimpu, using English and Dzong-kha, the national language. Significantly, there are no programs in Lhotshampa—the language of tens of thousands of migrants from Nepal who settled in Bhutan in the last century. A BBS spokesman explains, "Faced with the challenge of converting a radio team to broadcast in both media, we will have to gain experience first and then attempt to grow."

Forbidden Channels Widely Watched

The King has always had reservations about exposing his countrymen to global television abruptly. Yet, in 1999 he let them watch World Cup soccer from France by allowing sports associations to set up their own satellite dishes. Some educational institutions are also given dishes to receive programs considered important for students. Nevertheless, sources close to the King say Wangchuk wants his countrymen to view a national channel for some time before they are finally exposed to global television.

This may be wishful thinking. Long before the station went on the air, many Bhutanese already owned TVs to watch videos or

Thimpu resembles an ancient small town more than a modern capital.

M. Guha

Resident sound wizard Naten Dorji tickles the sliders in a BBS studio.
M. Guha

foreign satellite channels. Still, the new offering has had popular appeal—when over-the-air and cable television were introduced in 1999, television sales increased fourfold. After all, it carries domestic news and weather, as well as local entertainment, much of it in the main native tongue.

The other side of the quaint Sangaygang Hill building houses the television studio and transmission facility which was formerly a storage room. When the powers-that-be wanted a television station, this facility was hurriedly erected in the summer of 1999. The television transmitter is a trunk-size 0.1 kW BEL of ubiquitous Indian origin, complete with a GCEL modulation rack; it operates on channel twelve. A recently procured 1 kW Thomcast transmitter, tuned to channel six, will soon become the primary transmitter, while the older unit will be relegated to standby status.

Radio Repeats TV, Can't Simulcast

Tapes, comely presenters and technicians are ferried in the evening's biting cold to produce the nightly newscast that helps pull the Bhutanese people together. Because of the close proximity and co-siting of radio and television transmitters, simulcasting on both media is impossible without causing mutual interference.

Television will eventually be moved out, but until a studio-to-transmitter link is installed, staffers will continue to work out of a small studio next door.

For now, BBS telecasts are limited to a one-hour show between 1400 and 1500 World Time after the radio operation has finished its nightly run. Video consists of 15 minutes each of news in Dzongkha and English, followed by cultural programs culled from other South Asian nations in an exchange program.

"Happiness" Doomed?

Once basic needs are satisfied, people rarely feel poor unless they witness others who are more prosperous.

With broadcasting and the Internet now part of the Bhutanese culture, the genie of material acquisition is out of the bottle. Sad, perhaps, but the issue appears to be when, not if, "gross national happiness" will cease to survive except as part of a story—the story of how one tiny mountain kingdom for years stood apart from the world so as to better nurture its inner spirit.

Prepared by Manosij Guha in Bhutan, along with Lawrence Magne, Tony Jones, Craig Tyson and the staff of PASSPORT TO WORLD BAND RADIO.

RadioShack Canada has the best selection of high-quality shortwave radios

Shortwave radio enthusiasts take pleasure in listening to programming from all over the world–on the best equipment they can find. At RadioShack Canada, you'll find high-quality Grundig shortwave radios. Grundig is famous for the craftsmanship of their radios. Many hours of planning and crafting goes into each Grundig radio. Crisp, clear sound makes you forget that you're listening to a news program broadcast from Europe or Asia–you'll start to think you're listening to the local FM radio station. Grundig shortwave radios have the features and styles you want–from the Satellit 800 Millennium down to the popular travel sizes with dual alarm functions and more. Come to RadioShack Canada for the best choice in shortwave radios–Grundig.

Grundig Satellit 800 Millennium.
A perfect balance of form and function. Band coverage is complete: shortwave from 100 KHz to 30 MHz, plus AM/FM and VHF aircraft band (118 to 137 MHz). Synchronous detector for superior reception and more. Includes AC adapter and headphones. 2018104

YB300PE shortwave radio.
Features PLL tuning and 24 station presets, titanium-look finish, dynamic micro speaker and external antenna connector. Includes travel cover, AC adapter, earphones and supplementary antenna. 2018103

For radio enthusiasts ...
all around the world.

GRUNDIG

Dual conversion shortwave radio.
Grundig YB400. Features FM/MW/LW/SW bands, PLL synthesized tuner, AM-dual conversion, 40-station memory, dual alarm clock, data monitor and upper and lower side band with BFO. Includes AC adapter, earphones, travel cover and supplementary antenna. 2018100

Ten of the Best: 2001's Top Shows

World band radio is more than just news—it also knows how to have a good time. There are thousands of hours of music and sports, along with drama, comedy and other good stuff you might not come across otherwise.

This article spotlights ten shows especially worth seeking out. Times and days are in World Time, while "winter" and "summer" refer to seasons in the Northern Hemisphere.

"Assignment"
BBC World Service

The best news documentary is the BBC World Service's "Assignment," which focuses on tomorrow's hot topics rather than today's headlines. It covers stories as hard news, but also shows the impact on individuals. As one "Assignment" reporter puts it, "the lives of ordinary people provide the context behind the news."

Whether it's the misery of street children in Morocco or the rise of the political right in Austria, the "Assignment" team delivers ahead of the curve. But be warned: It sometimes disappears for weeks to make way for special BBC documentaries, only to bounce back later. There's no need to change your listening habits—most replacement programs are just as good.

The first opportunity for listeners in *North America* is at 0730 Sunday (local Saturday night in the United States and Canada) on 6175 kHz; with repeats at 1830 Sunday on 17840 kHz, and 0230 Monday on 5975 and 6175 kHz. Thanks to the BBC's scheduling—can anyone figure out their reasoning?—the first two slots are only for western North America, and solely in winter. However, listeners in the western states have another opportunity, via the Asia-Pacific stream, at 1230 Saturday on 9740 kHz.

Europe has two Sunday slots: 0730 on 6195, 9410, 12095, 15565 and 17640 kHz; and eleven hours later, at 1830, on 6195 (winter), 9410 and (summer) 12095 kHz.

In the *Middle East*, try 0430 Saturday and 0730 Sunday on 11760 and 15575 kHz (17640 kHz is also available at 0730); and 1830 Sunday, winter on 9410, 11980 and 12095 kHz, and summer on 12095 and 15575 kHz.

Southern Africa has but one shot: 1830 Sunday on 3255, 6190 and 15400 kHz.

> **The BBC's "Assignment" focuses on tomorrow's hot topics rather than today's headlines.**

Radio Taipei International studios prepare shows heard from Taiwan and through relay facilities. Although it is best known for its news coverage, RTI also offers traditional Chinese entertainment. A high point is the weekly "Jade Bells and Bamboo Pipes." RTI

In *East Asia*, the first airing is at 0430 Saturday on 15280, 17760 and 21660 kHz; with repeats at 1230 Saturday on 6195, 9580, 9740, 11955 and 15280 kHz; and 0730 Sunday on 15360, 17760 and 21660 kHz. Listeners in *Southeast Asia* can choose between 1230 Saturday on 6195 and 9740 kHz, and 0730 Sunday on 9740, 11955, 15360 and 17760 kHz.

Australasia has three opportunities: 1230 Saturday on 9740 kHz; 0730 Sunday on 9580, 11955 and 15360 kHz; and 1830 Sunday on 9740 kHz.

"Jade Bells and Bamboo Pipes"
Radio Taipei International

An exotic title for an exotic program, but a little misleading. Radio Taipei International's window on traditional Taiwanese music features stringed instruments more than jade bells or bamboo pipes.

But that's it for complaints. "Jade Bells" is a thoroughly enjoyable musical half hour which entices Western and Eastern ears, alike. It goes back to when the station was known as the Voice of Free China, and has delighted listeners ever since.

Listeners in *North* and *Central America* can tune in at 0215 Monday (Sunday evening local date) on 5950, 9680 and 11740 kHz, or five hours later, at 0715, on 5950 kHz. The 0715 broadcast is essentially for western North America. All transmissions are via the Family Radio relay in Okeechobee, Florida, so reception is usually good.

For *Europe*, also via the Okeechobee relay, there is just one slot: 2215 Monday, winter on 5810 and 9355 kHz, and summer on 11565 and 15600 kHz.

East Asia gets its chance at 1215 Monday on 7130 kHz, and *Southeast Asia* at 0215 the same day on 11825 and 15345 kHz. In *Australasia*, go for 1215 Monday on 9610 kHz.

"Christian Message from Moscow"
Voice of Russia

Thank God that Gresham's Law hasn't driven out "Christian Message from Moscow." While the world's airwaves are crammed with mediocre religious and related programs, here is a quality offering that stands out. It doesn't even try to convert anybody to anything.

Amsterdam represents some of the finest in both the traditional and the avant garde in European life. Radio Netherlands reflects this breadth of perspectives with its wide-ranging "Documentary" series.

M. Wright

The show's message is Russian Orthodox, little understood outside its home country. No preaching, no readings—just stories about Russian saints and their lives, reports on church developments and superb church music.

It is music for the spiritual senses: Gregorian chants and cathedral choirs; incantations and church bells. These succeed in conveying the spirituality of Russian Orthodoxy, as well as of the Russian people themselves.

Don't tune out if the first couple of minutes sound dry. "Christian Message from Moscow" may start with an item from history or a bishops' report, but it rapidly gets rolling, almost becoming a religious experience in its own right.

For *North America* winter, the first airing is at 0231 Saturday (Friday evening local date) on 7180, 12020, 13665 and 15470 kHz; with a repeat at 0431 Sunday on 7125, 7180, 12010, 12020, 15470, 15595, 17595 and 17660 kHz. In summer, one hour earlier, tune in at 0131 Saturday on 9665, 15595 and 17595 kHz; and 0331 Sunday on 7125, 9665, 15595, 17565, 17650, 17660 and 17690 kHz.

Winter slots for *Europe* are 2031 Saturday on 5940, 5965, 7300, 9890 and 15735 kHz; and 1931 Sunday on 5965, 7340, 9480 and 9890 kHz. Summer times are 1931 Saturday on 9710, 9720, 9775, 9820, 11675, 15485 and 15735 kHz; and 1831 Sunday on 9710, 9720, 9775, 9820 and 11675 kHz.

There is nothing scheduled for the *Middle East*, *Southern Africa* or any part of *Asia*, but listeners in *Southeast Asia* should be able to hear the broadcasts beamed to *Australasia*. These are audible winter Saturdays at 0631 on 15460, 15470, 15525, 17570 and 21790 kHz; and three hours later (at 0931) on 9905, 15460, 15470 and 17495 kHz. Midyear, they air one hour earlier: 0531 on 17625 and 21790 kHz, and 0831 on 15490, 17495 and 17625 kHz.

"Documentary"
Radio Netherlands

Not only PASSPORT holds Radio Netherlands' "Documentary" series in high esteem; it also has garnered prestigious awards at international festivals.

Careful research and first-class production are the hallmarks of Radio Netherlands' small documentary team. Themes are on virtually any topic, offbeat or mainstream—Russia's legal system, the history of rubber, little-known ethnic conflicts, medieval pilgrims, European cowboys. It is radio documentary at its best.

In *North America*, the first airing is at 0000 Thursday (Wednesday evening local date) on 6165 and 9845 kHz. A repeat, mainly for the western United States, goes out a few hours later, at 0500, on 6165 and 9590 kHz. A third slot is available at 0100 Saturday on 6165 and 9845 kHz.

The timing for *Europe* is a little more complicated: winter, 1230 Wednesday and 1200 Friday on 6045 and 9855 kHz; and summer, one hour earlier, on 6045 and 9860 kHz.

For *Southern Africa,* there are two Wednesday slots—at 1800 and 1930—and a repeat at 1900 Friday, all with a rock solid year-round signal on 6020 kHz.

For *East* and *Southeast Asia*, it's a choice between 1000 Wednesday and 1100 Friday, winters on 7260 and 12065 kHz, and summers on 12065 and 13710 kHz. *Australasia* has the same timing, but on 9790 or 9795 kHz.

"Everywoman"
BBC World Service

BBC program planners have made a lot of dumb moves in recent years, but they went a long way towards redeeming themselves when they created "Everywoman." Initially promoted as "for and about women," it would probably have gone on to become just another *au courant* woman's program had someone not added "with men in mind."

Yes, the program really has a substantial listenership among men. It provides an unparalleled insight into women and their world, and is good listening, to boot. Nothing is too sacred or offbeat—goat curry, mental illness, a history of the tiger-hunting poetess

of Bhopal. Traditionally taboo subjects are treated as openly as are anecdotal and humorous items, with no pandering.

Listeners in *North America* have two opportunities to tune in: 0130 Tuesday (Monday evening local American date) on 5975, 6175 and 9590 kHz; and 1530 Wednesday on 9515, 9590 (winter), 11865 (summer), 15220 and 17840 kHz. On the West Coast there's also 1130 Monday on 9740 kHz, which provides good reception despite being targeted at East and Southeast Asia.

Europe is well served, with a first airing (for western parts only) at 1930 Monday on 6195 and 9410 kHz; and repeats at 1430 Tuesday and 0930 Wednesday on 12095 kHz. Farther east, there's also 1730 Monday on 12095 kHz, and 1330 Tuesday (may be one hour later in winter) on 15565 and 17640 kHz.

Shyama Perera hosts "Everywoman" over the BBC World Service. Although it is by, for and about women, many men are regular listeners. BBC World Service

Radio Bulgaria presents the Bulgarian Folk Orchestra and other ensembles over its popular "Folk Studio" each Sunday, with repeats on Monday.

Radio Bulgaria

In the *Middle East*, the first opportunity is at 1730 Monday on 12095 and 15575 kHz, with a repeat at 1330 Tuesday (may be one hour later in winter) on 11760, 15575 and 17640 kHz; and again at 0830 Wednesday on 17640 kHz.

Southern Africa has three options: 1830 Monday on 3255, 6190 and 15400 kHz; 1130 Tuesday on 6190, 11940 and 21470 kHz; and 0830 Wednesday on 6190 and 11940 kHz.

In *East Asia*, choose from 1130 Monday on 6195, 9580, 9740, 11955 and 15280 kHz; 0730 Tuesday on 15360, 17760 and 21660 kHz; and 0330 Wednesday on 15280, 17760 and 21660 kHz. For *Southeast Asia*, it's 1130 Monday on 6195 and 9740 kHz, and 0730 Tuesday on 9740, 11955 and 15360 kHz.

Australasia shares the timings for Southeast Asia: 1130 Monday on 9740 kHz, and 0730 Tuesday on 9580, 11955 and 15360 kHz.

"Folk Studio"
Radio Bulgaria

Part of the thrill of listening to broadcasts from Eastern Europe during the Cold War

was the orgy of folk music which emanated from stations in countries like Bulgaria, Romania and Czechoslovakia. It was one of the few ways producers could genuinely entertain without offending a constipated officialdom.

Those days are past, but Radio Bulgaria continues to feature its people's rich musical heritage. Bulgarian folk music is more than different, it is genuinely exotic at a time when little seems to be fresh or original. No surprise, then, that it has achieved a following among music cognoscenti.

Although there are smatterings of folk music in many Radio Bulgaria broadcasts, the spot to aim for is the 15-minute "Folk Studio" on Sundays and Mondays. Talk is kept to a minimum, so it's nearly all music.

Reception in *North America* is limited mainly to southeastern Canada and eastern and central parts of the United States. Winter, tune in at 0010 and 0310 Monday (local Sunday evening) on 7375 and 9400 kHz; and summer, one hour earlier, on 9400 and 11700 kHz.

Western Europe gets the three remaining slots: winter, choose from 2010 Sunday on

Quality Communications Equipment Since 1942

COMMERCIAL RECEIVERS

TEN-TEC

The Ten-Tec RX-340 is *the* ultimate receiver! Advanced D.S.P. technology at under $4000.

AMATEUR RADIO EQUIPMENT

  ICOM ALINCO

JRC KENWOOD

YAESU

Universal has been selling the finest new and used amateur radio equipment since 1942 and is an authorized sales *and* service center for all major lines.

WIDEBAND RECEIVERS & SCANNERS

AOR ICOM
uniden ALINCO
Bearcat YAESU

Universal offers an extensive line of scanners and wideband receivers from all major manufacturers including AOR, Alinco, ICOM, Yaesu and Uniden-Bearcat. AOR AR8200 and Icom R3 shown.

NOTICE: The Icom R3 has not been approved by the Federal Communications Commission. This device is not and may not be offered for sale or leased until the approval of the F.C.C. has been obtained.

UNIVERSAL M-450v1.5

The **Universal M-450v1.5** reader displays: **RTTY, SITOR, FEC-A, ASCII, SWED-ARQ** and **Weather FAX** (to the printer port) plus the **ACARS** aviation teletype mode. DTMF, CTCSS and DCS are also supported. Features a big two-line, 20 character LCD and parallel port. Operates from 12 VDC or with the supplied AC adapter. No computer or monitor is required. Made in the U.S.A. *#0450* **$399.95**

HUGE FREE CATALOG

The **Universal Communications Catalog** covers everything for the shortwave, amateur and scanner enthusiast. With prices, photos and informative descriptions. This 100 page catalog is **FREE** by bookrate or for $3 by Priority mail (5 IRCs airmail outside N. America). Rising postage costs prevent us from sending this catalog out automatically so request your copy today!

Universal Radio, Inc.
6830 Americana Pkwy.
Reynoldsburg, Ohio
43068-4113 U.S.A.
☎ **800 431-3939** Orders & Prices
☎ 614 866-4267 Information
→ 614 866-2339 FAX Line
✉ dx@universal-radio.com

COMMUNICATIONS RECEIVERS

JRC YAESU

DRAKE

AOR

ICOM

Universal Radio carries an excellent selection of new and used communications receivers. JRC NRD-545 shown.

PORTABLE RECEIVERS

GRUNDIG
SONY
ICOM
SANGEAN

Universal offers over 40 portable receivers from $50 to over $500.
Universal also carries **factory reconditioned Grundig** shortwave radios at a substantial savings over new.

BOOKS

Shortwave Receivers Past & Present *By F. Osterman* This huge 473 page guide covers over 770 receivers from 98 manufacturers, made from 1942-1997. Entry information includes: receiver type, date sold, photograph, size & weight, features, reviews, specifications, new & used values, variants, value rating & availability. Become an instant receiver expert. *#0003* **$24.95**

Passport To Worldband Radio *By L. Magne*
Graphic presentation of all shortwave broadcast stations. Equipment reviews, too. A *must have* book. *#1000* **$19.95**

World Radio TV Handbook
All shortwave broadcast stations organized by country with schedules, addresses, power, etc. *#2000* **$24.95**

Worldwide Aeronautical Frequency Dir. *By R. Evans*
The definitive guide to commercial and military, HF and VHF-UHF aero comms. including ACARS. *#0042* **$19.95**

Guide to Utility Stations *By J. Klingenfuss*
Simply the best guide to non-broadcast stations. 11,600 frequencies CW, SSB, AM, RTTY & FAX. *#4042* **$39.95**

Discover DXing! *By J. Zondlo*
An introduction to DXing AM, FM and TV. *#0019* **$5.95**

Joe Carr's Receiving Antenna Handbook *By J. Carr*
Arguably the best book devoted to receiving antennas for longwave through shortwave. *#3113* **$19.95**

U.S. orders under $100 ship for $4.95, under $500 for $9.95.

Winter slots for *Europe* are at 1831 Tuesday on 5965, 7340, 9480 and 9890 kHz; and 2131 the same day on 5940, 5965, 7300, 9890 and 15735 kHz. Summer times are 1731 and 2031 Tuesday on 9710, 9720, 9775, 9820, 11675 and (2031 only) 15485 and 15735 kHz.

Best winter bet for the *Middle East* and *Southern Africa* is 1831 Tuesday on 7305 kHz; summer, one hour earlier, check 12015 kHz.

For *Southeast Asia* winter, try 1531 Tuesday and Thursday on 9800, 9875 and 11500 kHz; and one hour earlier in summer on 12025 kHz. Unfortunately, this show isn't scheduled for either *East Asia* or *Australasia*, where the audience presumably isn't Godunov.

5845 and 7535 kHz, 2210 Sunday on 7535 and 7545 kHz, and 1210 Monday on 15700 and 17500 kHz; summer times are 1910 and 2110 Sunday on 9400 and 11700 kHz, and 1110 Monday on 15700 and 17500 kHz.

"Music at Your Request"
Voice of Russia

Not all successful shows get wide recognition—some longtime favorites have kept a low profile despite having large listenerships. One example is the Voice of Russia's "Music at Your Request," a 25-minute classical music program that has been gracing the airwaves for years. Even though its offerings include warhorses from the likes of Tchaikovsky and Stravinsky, interpretations are emphatically Slavic.

The station has vast audio archives at its disposal, allowing it to air performances going back decades. Many of these are presentations rarely heard elsewhere.

Winter in *North America*, try 0531 Tuesday (Monday evening local American date) on 7125, 7180, 12010, 12020, 15470, 15595, 17595 and 17660 kHz; and 0231 Friday on 7180, 12020, 13665 and 15470 kHz. In summer, one hour earlier, it's 0431 Tuesday on 7125, 9665, 15595, 17565, 17650, 17660 and 17690 kHz; and 0131 Friday on 9665, 15595 and 17595 kHz.

"One Planet"
BBC World Service

Environmental protection is essential to the quality and existence of life, but so, too, is sustainable development—both economic and human. For those interested in these and related topics, the BBC World Service's "One Planet" is indispensable.

It covers the environment, development, agriculture and just about anything else related to the interaction between humans and their natural world. From locusts in Africa to the Children's Councils of India, its scope is wide and global.

North America has two slots, both with good reception throughout the United States. The program is first aired at 1505 Monday on 9515, 9590 (winter), 11865 (summer), 15220 and 17840 kHz; and the repeat goes out at 0105 Friday (Thursday evening local date) on 5975, 6175 and 9590 kHz.

Much of *Europe* can tune in at 1905 Thursday on 6195 and 9410 kHz, or 1405 Friday on 12095 kHz. In the east of the continent, try 1705 Thursday, 1305 Friday

(possibly one hour later in winter) and 0805 Monday on 15565 and 17640 kHz.

For the *Middle East*, it's 1705 Thursday on 12095 and 15575 kHz; 1305 Friday (possibly one hour later in winter) on 11760, 15575 and 17640 kHz; and a final repeat at 0805 Monday on 17640 kHz.

In *Southern Africa*, tune in at 1805 Thursday on 3255, 6190 and 15400 kHz; 1105 Friday on 6190, 11940 and 21470 kHz; or 0805 Monday on 6190 and 11940 kHz.

East Asia gets three bites: 1105 Thursday on 6195, 9580, 9740, 11955 and 15280 kHz; 0705 Friday on 15360, 17760 and 21660 kHz; and 0305 Monday on 15280, 15360, 17760 and 21660 kHz. For *Southeast Asia*, it's 1105 Thursday on 6195 and 9740 kHz, and 0705 Friday on 9740, 11955 and 15360 kHz.

Australasia has the same slots as Southeast Asia: 1105 Thursday on 9740 kHz, and 0705 Friday on 9580, 11955 and 15360 kHz.

"Folk Box" narrators over the Voice of Russia include (standing) Ivan Sedov, Boris Novikov, Michael Chernikh, (sitting) Irene Larina, Elena Baskakova.   VOR

"Folk Box"
Voice of Russia

Ask world band veterans for their favorite folk music program, and they'll probably say "Folk Box." Originating from when the Voice of Russia was still known as Radio Moscow, this earful spotlights roots music not only from Mother Russia, but also from countries that were once part of the former Soviet Union.

Gentle wedding songs share the stage with guttural gymnastics from Tuvan throat singers, while sublime harmonies compete with rousing Cossack dances. Millions have enjoyed the show over the years, making it an all-time favorite with world band listeners.

In *North America* winter, try 0231 Tuesday (Monday evening local American date) on 7180, 12020, 13665 and 15470 kHz; and 0531

Thursday on 7125, 7180, 12010, 12020, 15470, 15595, 17595 and 17660 kHz. In summer, one hour earlier, it's 0131 Tuesday on 9665, 15595 and 17595 kHz; and 0431 Thursday on 7125, 9665, 15595, 17565, 17650, 17660 and 17690 kHz.

Winter times for *Europe* are 2131 Thursday on 5940, 5965, 7300, 9890 and 15735 kHz; and 1831 Friday on 5965, 7340, 9480 and 9890 kHz. In summer, choose from 1531 Thursday on 9730 kHz; 2031 Thursday on 9710, 9720, 9775, 9820, 11675, 15485 and 15735 kHz; and 1731 Friday on 9710, 9720, 9775, 9820 and 11675 kHz.

Best winter bet for the *Middle East* and *Southern Africa* is 1831 Friday on 7305 kHz; summer, one hour earlier, check 12015 kHz.

For *Southeast Asia* winter, try 1531 Monday on 9800, 9875 and 11500 kHz; and one hour earlier in summer on 12025 kHz. There's nothing for *East Asia*, but *Australasia* has two opportunities: winter, at 0831 Tuesday and 0931 Thursday on 9905, 15460, 15470 and (0831 only) 21790 kHz; and midyear, one hour earlier, on 15490, 17495, 17625 and (0731 only) 21790 kHz.

"Focus on Faith"
BBC World Service

"Focus on Faith" puts the religions of the world and their adherents under a thoughtful spotlight. It peers into the politics of religion, coexistence among religious groups, believers coping with hostile environments, tests of religious faith, and even what it takes to be declared a saint or a martyr.

No topic is too sacred or offbeat. Some of the more unusual subjects have included religious spin doctors, and Halal Kentucky Fried Chicken for Australian Muslims.

Sometimes respectful, sometimes biting , this is a program whose credentials are never in doubt. It is by far the best in its

category—one of a number of offerings that helps world band radio stand apart from the media herd.

Listeners in *North America* have two tries: 0130 Wednesday (Tuesday evening local American date) on 5975, 6175 and 9590 kHz; and 1530 Thursday on 9515, 9590 (winter), 11865 (summer), 15220 and 17840 kHz. For the West Coast, there's also 1130 Tuesday on 9740 kHz, which provides good reception despite being beamed to East and Southeast Asia.

Europe is amply served: 1930 Tuesday (western parts only) on 6195 and 9410 kHz; with repeats at 1430 Wednesday and 0930 Thursday on 12095 kHz. For eastern areas, there's also 1730 Tuesday on 12095 kHz, 1330 Wednesday (may be one hour later in winter) on 15565 and 17640 kHz, and 0830 Thursday on 17640 kHz.

In the *Middle East*, the first opportunity is at 1730 Tuesday on 12095 and 15575 kHz, with a repeat at 1330 Wednesday (may be one hour later in winter) on 11760, 15575 and 17640 kHz; and again at 0830 Thursday on 17640 kHz.

Southern Africa has three choices: 1830 Tuesday on 3255, 6190 and 15400 kHz; 1130 Wednesday on 6190, 11940 and 21470 kHz; and 0830 Thursday on 6190 and 11940 kHz.

In *East Asia*, pick from 1130 Tuesday on 6195, 9580, 9740, 11955 and 15280 kHz; 0730 Wednesday on 15360, 17760 and 21660 kHz; and 0330 Thursday on 15280, 17760 and 21660 kHz. For *Southeast Asia*, it's 1130 Tuesday on 6195 and 9740 kHz, and 0730 Wednesday on 9740, 11955 and 15360 kHz.

Australasia has two slots: 1130 Tuesday on 9740 kHz, and 0730 Wednesday on 9580, 11955 and 15360 kHz.

Prepared by Don Swampo and the staff of PASSPORT TO WORLD BAND RADIO.

GRUNDIG Best in Technolog[y]

Yacht Boy 400 Professional Edition (YB 400PE)

The most powerful compact Radio AM/FM Shortwave Receiver.

"The Best compact shortwave portable we have tested" Lawrence Magne.-Editor in Chief, Passport to World Band Radio.

The Big Breakthrough! Power, performance, and design have reached new heights! The Grundig 400 Professional Edition with its sleek titanium look is packed with features like no other compact radio in the world.

Pinpoint Accuracy! The Grundig 400PE does it all: pulls in AM, FM, FM-Stereo, every shortwave band (even aviation and ship-to-shore)-all with lock-on digital precision.

Ultimate Features! Auto tuning! The Grundig 400PE has auto tuning on shortwave and stops at every signal and lets you listen. With the exceptional sensitivity of the 400PE, you can use the auto tune to catch even the weakest of signals.
Incredible timing features! The Grundig 400PE can send you to sleep listening to your favorite music.
You can set the alarm to wake up to music or the morning traffic report, then switch to BBC shortwave for the world news. The choice is yours!

Powerful Memory! Described as a smart radio with 40 memory positions, the Grundig 400PE remembers your favorites-even if you don't!

Never Before Value! Includes deluxe travel pouch, stereo earphones, owner's manual, external antenna and a 9 volt Grundig AC adapter. Uses 6 AA batteries (not included)

Style • Titanium look

Shortwave, AM and FM • Continuous shortwave from 1.6 - 30 MHz, covering all existing shortwave bands plus FM-stereo, AM and Longwave. • Single sideband (SSB) circuitry allows for reception of two-way communication such as amateur radio, military, commercial, air-to-ground, and ship-to-shore.

Memory Positions • 40 randomly programmable memory positions allow for quick access to favorite stations.

Multi-function Liquid Crystal Display • The LCD simultaneously displays the time, frequency, band, alarm and sleep timer.

Clock, Alarm and Timer • Two alarm modes: Beeper and radio.
• Dual clocks show time in 24 hour format.
• Sleep timer programmable in 15 minute increments.

Dimensions: 7.75" L × 4.5" H × 1.5" W

Compleat Idiot's Guide to Getting Started

Three "Must" Tips to Catch the World

World band radio is your unfiltered connection to what's going on, but it differs from conventional radio. Here are three "must" tips to get started.

"Must" #1: World Time and Day

World band schedules use a single time, *World Time*. After all, world band radio is global, with stations broadcasting around-the-clock from virtually every time zone.

Imagine the chaos if each station used its own local time for scheduling. In England, 9:00 PM is different from nine in the evening in Japan or Canada. How would anybody know when to tune in?

World Time, or Coordinated Universal Time (UTC), is also known as Greenwich Mean Time (GMT) or, in the military, "Zulu." It is announced in 24-hour format, so 2 PM is 1400 ("fourteen hundred") hours.

There are four easy ways to know World Time. First, around North America tune to one of the standard time stations, such as WWV in Colorado and WWVH in Hawaii or CHU in Ottawa. WWV and WWVH are on 5000, 10000 and 15000 kHz, with WWV also on 2500 and 20000 kHz; CHU is on 3330, 7335 and 14670 kHz.

Second, tune to a major international broadcaster, such as the BBC World Service or Voice of America. Most announce World Time at the hour.

Third, on the Internet you can access World Time at various sites, including tycho.usno.navy.mil/what.html and www.nrc.ca/inms/time/cesium.shtml.

Fourth, see the sidebar to set your 24-hour clock. For example, if you live on the East Coast of the United States, *add* five hours winter (four hours summer) to your local time to get World Time. So, if it is 8 PM EST (the 20th hour of the day) in New York, it is 0100 hours World Time.

Once you know the correct World Time, adjust your radio's 24-hour clock. No clock? Get one now unless you enjoy doing weird computations in your head (it's 6:00 PM here, so add five hours to make it 11:00 PM, which on a 24-hour clock converts to 23:00 World Time—but, whoops, it's summer so I should have added four hours instead of five . . .). It will be the best money you've ever spent.

Remember that at midnight a new *World Day* arrives. This can trip up even experienced listeners—sometimes radio stations, too. So if it is 9 PM EST Wednesday in New York, it is 0200 hours World Time *Thursday*. Don't forget to "wind your calendar"!

What happens at midnight, World Time? A new *World Day* arrives, as well.

PASSPORT'S THREE-MINUTE START

No time? Try this:

1. Night time is the right time, so wait until evening when signals are strongest. In a concrete-and-steel building put your radio by a window or balcony.

2. Make sure your radio is plugged in or has fresh batteries. Extend the telescopic antenna fully and vertically. Set the DX/local switch (if there is one) to "DX," but otherwise leave the controls the way they came from the factory.

3. Turn on your radio. Set it to 5900 kHz and begin tuning slowly toward 6200 kHz; you can also try 9400-9900 kHz. You should hear stations from around the world.

Other times? Read "Best Times and Frequencies for 2001."

"Must" #2: How to Find Stations

PASSPORT provides station schedules three ways: by country, time of day and frequency. By-country is best to hear a given station. "What's On Tonight," the time-of-day section, is like *TV Guide* and includes program descriptions from our listening panel. The by-frequency Blue Pages are ideal for when you're dialing around the bands.

World band frequencies are usually given in kilohertz (kHz), but a few stations use Megahertz (MHz). Forget all the techno-babble—the main difference is three decimal places, so 6170 kHz is the same as 6.17 MHz, 6175 kHz identical to 6.175 MHz, and so on. All you need to know is that, either way, it refers to a certain spot on your radio's dial.

You're already used to hearing FM and

SETTING YOUR WORLD TIME CLOCK

PASSPORT's "Addresses PLUS" lets you arrive at the local time in another country by adding or subtracting from World Time. Use that section to determine the time within a country you are listening to.

This box, however, gives it from the other direction—that is, what to add or subtract from your local time to determine World Time at your location. Use this to set your World Time clock.

Wherever in the world you live, you can also use Addresses PLUS, instead of this sidebar, to determine World Time simply by reversing the time difference. For example, Addresses PLUS states that Burundi's local time is "World Time +2." So if you're in Burundi, to set your World Time clock you would take Burundi time *minus* two hours.

WHERE YOU ARE   *TO DETERMINE WORLD TIME*

North America

Newfoundland St. John's NF, St. Anthony NF	Add 3½ hours winter, 2½ hours summer
Atlantic St. John NB, Battle Harbour NF	Add 4 hours winter, 3 hours summer
Eastern New York, Atlanta, Toronto	Add 5 hours winter, 4 hours summer
Central Chicago, Nashville, Winnipeg	Add 6 hours winter, 5 hours summer
Mountain Denver, Salt Lake City, Calgary	Add 7 hours winter, 6 hours summer
Pacific San Francisco, Vancouver	Add 8 hours winter, 7 hours summer
Alaska	Add 9 hours winter, 8 hours summer
Hawaii	Add 10 hours year round

mediumwave AM stations at the same spot on the dial, day and night, or Webcasts at the same URLs. But things are a lot different when you roam the international airwaves.

World band radio is like a global bazaar where a variety of merchants come and go at different times. Similarly, stations routinely enter and leave a given spot—frequency—on the dial throughout the day and night. Where you once tuned in, say, a French station, hours later you might find a Russian or Chinese broadcaster roosting on that same spot.

Or on a nearby perch. If you suddenly hear interference from a station on an adjacent channel, it doesn't mean something is wrong with your radio; it probably means another station has begun broadcasting on a nearby frequency. There are more stations on the air than there is space for

Europe

United Kingdom, Ireland and Portugal	Same time as World Time winter, subtract 1 hour summer
Continental Western Europe; parts of Central and Eastern Continental Europe	Subtract 1 hour winter, 2 hours summer
Estonia, Latvia and Lithuania	Subtract 2 hours year round
Elsewhere in Continental Europe Belarus, Bulgaria, Cyprus, Finland, Greece, Moldova, Romania, Russia (Kaliningradskaya Oblast), Turkey and Ukraine	Subtract 2 hours winter, 3 hours summer

Mideast & Southern Africa

Egypt, Israel, Lebanon and Syria	Subtract 2 hours winter, 3 hours summer
South Africa, Zambia and Zimbabwe	Subtract 2 hours year round

East Asia & Australasia

China, including Taiwan	Subtract 8 hours year round
Japan	Subtract 9 hours year round
Australia: *Victoria, New South Wales, Tasmania*	Subtract 11 hours local summer, 10 local winter (midyear)
Australia: *South Australia*	Subtract 10½ hours local summer, 9½ hours local winter (midyear)
Australia: *Queensland*	Subtract 10 hours year round
Australia: *Northern Territory*	Subtract 9½ hours year round
Australia: *Western Australia*	Subtract 8 hours year round
New Zealand	Subtract 13 hours local summer, 12 hours local winter (midyear)

GRUNDIG Gift Collection

A gift for the auto enthusiast

Maneuver the Porsche Design G2000A Digital Radio Alarm Clock

... to all points around the globe. Wake up to sports and talk radio on AM, soothing stereo (with earphones) on FM or fascinating shortwave from around the world... select from 13 International bands from 2.3 - 7.4 and 9.4 - 26.1 MHz. Punch in any station or lock your favorites into 20 memories... other features include digital clock and alarm with Quartz accuracy... earphones... butter-soft handcrafted leather case. Designed by F. A. Porsche, the G2000A is a pleasure to own and operate. Requires 3 AA batteries (not included).

Dimensions: 5.5" L × 3.5" H × 1.375" W
Weight: 11.52 oz.

A gift for the collector

50th Anniversary Edition Classic 960

AM/FM Stereo Shortwave Radio Nostalgia... remember when a radio was a center piece... handcrafted wooden cabinet ...unforgettable European styling... legendary sound. Those days are back! With the solid-state 960, Grundig's Famous 1950s Classic is updated and improved... two 3" side speakers, left and right, and the 4" front speaker will fill your room with exquisite sound... and let you travel the globe without leaving home... receives shortwave continuously from 2.3-22.3 MHz... additional features include: stereo inputs for CD, tape, VCR, or TV sound.

Dimensions: 15.5" L × 11.25" H × 7" W
Weight: 9 lbs. 9.6 oz.

Traveller II PE (TR2PE)

The world's best-selling travel radio. A compact radio with outstanding performance! This practical and stylish travel companion features AM, FM and five shortwave bands, plus a world clock for 24-time zones and simultaneous display of home and world time in a digital display. Titanium-look finish. Comes with 3 AA batteries, earphones, carrying pouch.

Tuner Frequency Ranges:

FM	88-108 MHz
AM	530-1600KHz
SW Bands	49, 41, 31, 25 and 19 meters

Output:	Micro Speaker or earphones
Batteries:	3 AA (included)
Dimensions:	5.5" L × 3.5" H × 1.25" W
Weight:	9.92 oz.

Mini World 100 PE (Mini).

Grundig's smallest Pocket World Band Radio....Travel with the world in your pocket. Another exciting breakthrough in world band technology. A well built radio that fits in the palm of your hand. AM/FM-Stereo/SW radio with LED indicator, six shortwave broadcast bands, telescopic antenna, earphones and belt clip make listening easy. Comes with soft carrying case.

Tuner Frequency Ranges

FM	88-108MHz
AM	525-1625MHz
SW1	5.80-6.40MHz
SW2	6.90-7.50MHz
SW3	9.40-7.50MHz
SW4	11.65-12.15MHz
SW5	15.00-15.65MHz
SW6	17.50-18.14MHz

Output:	Micro Speaker or Earphones
Batteries:	2 AA (included)
Dimensions:	2.75" L × 4" H × .75" W
Weight:	4.48 oz.

by GRUNDIG

Lextronix / Grundig, P.O. Box 2307, Menlo Park, CA 94026 • Tel: 650-361-1611 • Fax: 650-361-1724
Shortwave Hotlines: (US) 1-800-872-2228 (CN) 1-800-637-1648 • Web: www.grundigradio.com • Email: grundig@ix.netcom.com

WORLD TIME CLOCKS

Because World Time uses 24-hour format, digital clocks are easier to read than analog timepieces with hands. Some radios include a World Time clock that is displayed fulltime—these are best. Many other radios have World Time clocks, but you have to press a button to have time replace frequency in the display.

Basic Models

If your radio has no clock, a separate 24-hour clock is a virtual "must." Here are three affordable choices, listed in order of cost.

MFJ-107B, $9.95. Bare-bones, but this battery-powered LCD "Volksclock" is good enough for many. Seconds not displayed numerically.

MFJ-118, $24.95, is similar to the '107B, but with large (1¼ inches or 32 mm) LCD numerals. Additionally, has an adjustable flip stand and a multilingual 100-year calendar. Seconds not displayed numerically.

> Some radios include a World Time clock that is displayed at all times—these are best.

MFJ-114B/114BX, $54.95; a/k/a **Hamx Business Corp. HX-923D**. If you want your World Time *VISIBLE* and need to see seconds numerically, this wall/desk clock may be for you—but there are caveats. It uses tall (1¾ inches or 44 mm) bright-red LEDs for hours and minutes, half-size LEDs for seconds—better than the usual limited-contrast LCD. Unlike the '107B and '118, the '114B uses a "wall wart" AC adaptor, plus "AA" batteries for backup (the regular '114B model is 120 VAC, the "X" version 220/240 VAC). It also displays the month, day and year for a couple of seconds when you clap twice.

☞ Our sample arrived performing intermittently, the result of two connections not having been soldered and some questionable solder joints. Once ministered to with a soldering iron, it worked properly.

☞ The time display is quite accurate provided you adjust the SCV1 trimmer—an adjust-wait-readjust proposition that can take days before you finally get it "spot on."

☞ The clock emits broadband hash throughout the shortwave spectrum and beyond, so it should be mounted well away from radio antennas.

Sophisticated Timepieces

For those who want only the very best, there are any number of sophisticated 24-hour clocks ranging from under $100 to over $2,000. Nearly all display seconds numerically, and some synchronize the displayed time with one or another of the atomic clock standards.

This desktop clock from Arcron Zeit allows hourly time zone changes to be made for all U.S. and World Times.

Chinese cowboys listen to foreign broadcasts on their Tecsun world band radios. E.A. Hozour

them, so sometimes they try to outshout each other.

Technology to the rescue! To cope with this, purchase a radio with superior adjacent-channel rejection, also known as selectivity, and give preference to radios with synchronous selectable sideband. PASSPORT REPORTS, a major section of this book, tells you which stand out.

One of the most pleasant things about world band radio is cruising up and down the airwaves. Daytime, you'll find most stations above 11500 kHz; night, below 16000 kHz. Tune slowly, savor the sound of foreign tongues alongside English offerings. Enjoy the music, weigh the opinions of other peoples, hear the events that shape their lives and yours.

If a station can't be found or fades out, there is probably nothing wrong with your radio. The atmosphere's sky-high iono-sphere deflects world band signals earthward, whereupon they bounce back up to the ionosphere, and so on like a

dribbled basketball until they get to your radio. This is why world band radio is so unencumbered—its signals don't rely on cables or satellites or the Internet, just layers of ionized gases which have enveloped our planet for millions of years. World band is free from regulation, free from taxes, free from fees—and largely free from ads, as well.

But nature's ionosphere, like the weather, changes constantly, so world band stations have to adjust as best they can. The result is that broadcasters operate in different parts of the world band spectrum, depending upon the time of day and season of the year.

That same changeability can also work in your favor, especially if you like to eaves-drop on signals not intended for your part of the world. Sometimes stations from exotic locales—places you would not ordinarily hear—become surprise arrivals at your radio, thanks to the shifting characteristics of the ionosphere.

BEST TIMES AND FREQUENCIES FOR 2001

With world band, if you dial randomly you're just as likely to get dead air as a program. That's because some world band segments are alive and kicking only by day, while others spring to life at night. Others fare better at certain times of the year.

This guide is most accurate if you're listening from north of Africa or South America. Even then, what you'll actually hear will vary—depending upon your location, where the station transmits from, the time of year and your radio (*see* Propagation in the glossary). Although world band is active around the clock, signals are usually best from an hour or two before sunset until sometime after midnight. Too, try a couple of hours on either side of dawn. **Nighttime** refers to your local hours of darkness, plus dawn and dusk.

Possible Reception Nighttime

2 MHz (120 meters) **2300-2495 kHz**—overwhelmingly domestic stations, with 2496-2504 kHz for time stations only.

Limited Reception Nighttime

3 MHz (90 meters) **3200-3400 kHz**—overwhelmingly domestic stations.

Good-to-Fair in Europe and Asia except Summer Nights; Elsewhere, Limited Reception Nighttime

4 MHz (75 meters) **3900-4050 kHz**—international and domestic stations, primarily not in or beamed to the Americas; 3900-3950 kHz mainly Asian and Pacific transmitters; 3950-4000 kHz also includes European and African transmitters; 4001-4050 kHz currently out-of-band.

Some Reception Nighttime; Regional Reception Daytime

5 MHz (60 meters) **4750-4995 kHz** and **5005-5100 kHz**—mostly domestic stations, with 4996-5004 kHz for time stations only and 5061-5100 kHz currently out-of-band.

Excellent Nighttime; Regional Reception Daytime

6 MHz (49 meters) **5730-6300 kHz**—5730-5899 kHz and 6201-6300 kHz currently out-of-band.

Good Nighttime; Regional Reception Daytime

7 MHz (41 meters) **6890-6990 kHz** and **7100-7600 kHz**—6890-6990 kHz and 7351-7600 kHz currently out-of-band; no American-based transmitters and few transmissions targeted to the Americas.

9 MHz (31 meters) **9250-9995 kHz**—9250-9399 kHz and 9901-9995 kHz currently out-of-band; 9996-10004 kHz for time stations only.

Good Nighttime except Mid-Winter; Some Reception Daytime and Winter Nights; Good Asian and Pacific Reception Mornings in America

11 MHz (25 meters) **11500-12200 kHz**—11500-11599 kHz and 12101-12200 kHz currently out-of-band.

"Must" #3: The Right Radio

Choose carefully, but you shouldn't need a costly set. Avoid cheap radios—they suffer from one or more major defects. With one of the better-rated portables you'll be able to hear much more of what world band has to offer.

Two basics: First, purchase a radio with digital frequency display. Its accuracy and related digital features will make tuning far easier than with outmoded slide-rule tuning. Second, ensure the radio covers at least 4750-21850 kHz with no significant tuning gaps. Otherwise, you may not be able to tune in some stations you'd otherwise be able to hear.

Shoppers in Xinjiang, China, examine radios. E.A. Hozour

You won't need an exotic outside antenna unless you're using a tabletop model. All portables, and to some extent portatops, are designed to work well off the built-in telescopic antenna—or, if you want it to reach a bit further, with several yards or meters of insulated wire clipped on.

If you just want to hear the major stations, you'll do fine with a moderately priced portable. Beyond that, portatop models have a better chance of bringing in faint and difficult signals, and they usually

sound better, too. But most tabletops are costly and complex to operate.

Radio in hand, read or at least glance over your owner's manual—yes, it's worth it. You'll find that, despite a few unfamiliar controls, your new world band receiver isn't all that much different from radios you have used all your life.

_____

Prepared by Jock Elliott, Tony Jones and Lawrence Magne, with David Zantow.

Good Daytime; Good Summer Nighttime

13 MHz (22 meters) **13570-13870 kHz**

15 MHz (19 meters) **15005-15800 kHz**—14996-15004 kHz for time stations only; 15005-15099 kHz currently out-of-band.

Good Daytime; Variable, Limited Reception Summer Nighttime

17 MHz (16 meters) **17480-17900 kHz**

19 MHz (15 meters) **18900-19020 kHz**

21 MHz (13 meters) **21450-21850 kHz**

Some Reception Daytime

25 MHz (11 meters) **25670-26100 kHz**

> There are more stations than there is space, so they try to outshout each other.

Luxurious listening is back–looks like fine furniture, tuned like a musical instrument

The radio that Grundig made famous in the '50s is back–only better thanks to modern technology. Just like the original, this classic has a handmade wooden cabinet which creates that rich, velvety sound. The same exact dimensions, same European styling, same AM/FM/Shortwave versatility . . . all enhanced with solid-state technology.

The 50th Anniversary Edition puts you on the podium with sound that's rich and real. The Grundig Classic 960 has all the features you want in an elegant design. It fits any decor. Get yours today, sit back, get comfortable and start to listen, enjoy the nostalgia.

Grundig Classic-960 AM/FM/shortwave radio. 50th Anniversary edition. A true classic is back, only it's better than ever! Enjoy rich velvety sound with a front and two side speakers in a handcrafted cabinet. Listen to news from around the world or tune into your favourite local radio station. 1218960

Wood cabinet handcrafted by Grundig craftsmen

Quality radios for at home or on the go . . .

GRUNDIG

Grundig MiniWorld 100 PE.
Features AM/FM tuning plus 6 shortwave bands. Has stereo FM output with headphones. Includes stereo earbuds and carrying pouch. 2018102

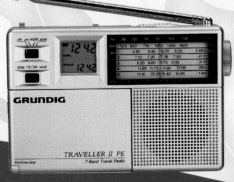

Grundig weather band radio.
Created with legendary Grundig reliability and quality. Features AM/FM/weather band selectable analog tuner and receives three nationally broadcast weather bands. Has large, easy-to-use volume/tuner/selectorcontrols and earphone for private listening. 1218244

Grundig Traveller II PE.
Features AM/FM tuning, 6 shortwave bands, world clock with 24 time zones, simultaneous display of world clock and home time. Includes earbuds and carrying pouch. 2018105

First Tries: Ten Easy Catches

Here are ten powerhouse stations in English. Sure, there are hundreds of other broadcasters on the air, but you can hear these ten transmitter titans almost anywhere. Most have first-rate shows, too. All times are World Time, explained elsewhere in this PASSPORT.

EUROPE
France

Radio France Internationale is one of the classier news-oriented offerings over world band. Alas, the station's use of English is a sensitive point, as they state they don't wish to cater to *les Anglo-Saxons*.

Listeners in western Europe and North America thus have to make do with eavesdropping on signals beamed to other parts of the world.

☞ RECOMMENDED: All programs are first rate.

Central and Eastern Europe: 1200-1300 on 11670, 15155 and 15195 kHz.

Middle East: 1400-1500 on 17620 kHz; also 1600-1730 winter on 11615 kHz and summer on 15210 kHz, though this slot is intended mainly for East Africa.

South Asia: 1400-1500 on 11610 and 17680 kHz. The latter channel also serves *Southeast Asia* and provides adequate reception in parts of *Australia*—better towards the west.

Africa: RFI's broadcasts to Africa have a large audience, and rightly so. Audible at 1600-1700 on 11615, 11995, 12015, 15210 and 17605 (or 17850) kHz; and at 1700-1730 on 11615 (or 17605) and 15210 kHz. The 1200 transmission for Europe is also aired to West Africa on 15540 kHz, and can be heard in much of eastern North America.

Deutsche Welle's quality is a benchmark few stations can match.

Germany

Thanks to solid management, **Deutsche Welle** has successfully preserved its English output in spite of shortsighted budget cuts. Several other languages have suffered or been dropped. Yet, the quality of DW's English broadcasts continues to be a benchmark few stations can hope to match.

☞ RECOMMENDED: "NewsLink."

North and Central America: 0100-0145 winter on 6040, 6145, 9640, 9700 and 9765 kHz; summer on 6040, 9640, 11810 and 13720 kHz. The second edition goes out at 0300-0345: winter on 6045, 9535, 9640, 9700 and 11750 kHz; summer on 9535, 9640, 11810, 13780 and 15105 kHz. The third and final broadcast is at 0500-0545, winter on 5960, 6120, 9670 and 11795 (or 11985) kHz; and summer on 9670, 9785, 11810 and 11985 kHz. This last slot is best for western North America.

Europe: 0600-1900 year-round on 6140 kHz; and 2000-2045 winter on 9725 kHz, replaced summer by 7130 kHz.

East & Southern Africa: 0400-0445 winter—summer in the Southern Hemisphere—on 7280, 9565, 11935 and 11965 kHz; summer on 7225, 9565, 9765 and 13690 kHz. The second slot is available 0900-0945 winter on 11785, 15410, 17860 and 21560 kHz; and summer on 9565 (or 12035), 15210 (or 17800) and 15410 kHz. A third broadcast goes out at 1100-1145 on 15410 and (winter) 11785 kHz; and the fourth and final airing is at 1600-1645 on 9735 and 21775 (or 21780) kHz.

East & Southeast Asia and the Pacific: 0900-0945 winter on 6160, 12055, 15470, 17625, 17770 and 17820 kHz; summer on 6160,

Jonathan Groubert hosts the award-winning "EuroQuest" over Radio Netherlands. RNW

Few countries of any size air so much information about their region than does Radio Nederland Wereldomroep. The university, left, is one of the intellectual centers of Amsterdam. R. Heeder

15105, 15470, 17770, 21680 and 21790 kHz. A second broadcast—nominally to Australasia but also well heard in Southeast Asia—airs at 2100-2145 winter on 9765, 15135 and 17560 kHz; summer on 9670, 9765 and 11915 kHz. There's also an additional transmission for East and Southeast Asia at 2300-2345, winter on 9470, 9815, 13690 and 21790 kHz; summer on 9815, 12055, 13610 and 21790 kHz.

Holland

Radio Nederland—also called **Radio Netherlands**—airs a creative balance of news, opinion and entertainment, with production techniques second to none. What makes the station sparkle is when it plunges into subjects ignored elsewhere; programs on sexual preference and young Europeans' angst pretty much started here, for example. They challenge, too—no empty mental calories. The station also homes in on European news, rather than the same dozen international subjects rehashed by other broadcasters.

☞ RECOMMENDED: "EuroQuest."

North America: Solid reception throughout much of North America at 2330-0125 on 6165 and 9845 kHz. Best slot for western states is the shorter broadcast at 0430-0530 on 6165 and 9590 kHz.

Europe: 1130-1325 winters on 6045 and 9855 kHz, and 1030-1225 summers on 6045 and 9860 kHz.

Southern Africa: 1730-1925 on 6020 kHz.

East and Southeast Asia: 0930-1125 winters on 7260 and 12065 kHz, and summers on 12065 and 13710 kHz.

Australia and the Pacific: 0930-1125 on 9790 or 9795 kHz. Parts of the region are also well served by frequencies for East and Southeast Asia.

Russia

Despite a tendency to follow the official government line, the **Voice of Russia** is far from being the propaganda mouthpiece

JRC NRD-545

Legendary Quality. Digital Signal Processing. Awesome Performance.

With the introduction of the NRD-545, Japan Radio raises the standard by which high performance receivers are judged.

Starting with JRC's legendary quality of construction, the NRD-545 offers superb ergonomics, virtually infinite filter band-width selection, steep filter shape factors, a large color liquid crystal display, 1,000 memory channels, scan and sweep functions, and both double sideband and sideband selectable synchronous detection. With high sensitivity, wide dynamic range, computer control capability, a built-in RTTY demodulator, tracking notch filter, and sophisticated DSP noise control circuitry, the NRD-545 redefines what a high-performance receiver should be.

JRC *Japan Radio Co., Ltd.*

Japan Radio Company, Ltd., Seattle Branch Office —
1011 SW Klickitat Way, Building B, Suite 100, Seattle, WA 98134
Voice: 206-654-5644   Fax: 206-264-1168

Japan Radio Company, Ltd. — Akasaka Twin Tower (main), 17-22,
Akasaka 2-chome, Minato-ku, Tokyo 107, Japan   Fax: (03) 3584-8878

- LSB, USB, CW, RTTY, FM, AM, AMS, and ECSS (Exalted Carrier Selectable Sideband) modes.
- Continuously adjustable bandwidth from 10 Hz to 9.99 kHz in 10 Hz steps.
- Pass-band shift adjustable in 50 Hz steps up or down within a ±2.3 kHz range.
- Noise reduction signal processing adjustable in 256 steps.
- Tracking notch filter, adjustable within ±2.5 kHz in 10 Hz steps, follows in a ±10 kHz range even when the tuning dial is rotated.
- Continuously adjustable AGC between 0.04 sec and 5.1 sec in LSB, USB, CW, RTTY, and ECSS modes.
- 1,000 memory channels that store frequency, mode, bandwidth, AGC, ATT, and (for channels 0–19) timer on/off.
- Built-in RTTY demodulator reads ITU-T No. 2 codes for 170, 425, and 850 Hz shifts at 37 to 75 baud rates. Demodulated output can be displayed on a PC monitor through the built-in RS-232C interface.
- High sensitivity and wide dynamic range achieved through four junction-type FETs with low noise and superior cross modulation characteristics.
- Computer control capability.
- Optional wideband converter unit enables reception of 30 MHz to 2,000 MHz frequencies (less cellular) in all modes.

Beyond the easiest stations to hear are a number with exceptional programming. Finland's broadcasting center produces news and entertainment for and about one of Europe's most unusual people. S. Sarkkinen

of Cold War years, when it was known as Radio Moscow. Popular with listeners, it offers several one-of-a-kind shows—some of which are tops by any broadcasting standard.

☞ RECOMMENDED: "Folk Box."

Eastern North America: 0200-0600 winter on 5940 (0300-0400), 7125 (0400-0600) and 7180 kHz; summer, one hour earlier, it's 9665 kHz at 0100-0500 and 7125 kHz at 0300-0500. During winter afternoons, use frequencies beamed to Europe—some make it to eastern North America.

Western North America: Best bets for winter are: 0200-0400 on 12020, 13665 and 15470 kHz; and 0400-0600 on 12010, 12020, 15470, 15595, 17595 and 17660 kHz. For summer reception, one hour earlier, use 15595 and 17595 kHz at 0100-0300, and 15595, 17565, 17650, 17660 and 17690 kHz at 0300-0500.

Europe: Winter, at 1800-2000, use 5940 (from 1900), 5965, 7340, 9480 and 9890 kHz; for 2000-2200, choose from 5940, 5965, 7300 (from 2100), 9890 and 15735 kHz. In summer, use 9730 kHz at 1500-

1600; then at 1700-1900 it's 7300/7330 (from 1800), 9710, 9720, 9775, 9820 and 11675 kHz. For 1900-2100, look at 9710, 9720, 9775, 9820, 9890 11675, 12070 (till 2000), 15485 (from 2000) and 15735 kHz.

Middle East: 1600-1800 (1500-1700 in summer). Use 4940, 4965 and 4975 kHz during the first hour, especially to the east. Further winter possibilities are 7210 and 9775 kHz at 1600-1700, and 7305 and 9470 kHz during the next hour. In summer, look at 7325 and 12015 kHz at 1500-1600, and 12015 and 15515 kHz at 1600-1700; 12055 kHz may also be available.

Southern Africa: Officially, there's virtually nothing beamed this way, but try 7305 kHz at 1800-2000 winter and 12015 kHz at 1700-1900 summer. These channels are targeted at the Middle East and East Africa, but should make it farther south.

Southeast Asia: 1500-1600 winter on 9800, 9875 and 11500 kHz. In summer, use 0600-0800 on 17655 kHz, 1400-1500 on 12025 kHz, 1500-1600 on 11500 kHz, and 1600-1700 on 12025 kHz. Some of these channels are intended for other regions, but can be well heard in Southeast Asia.

Australasia: 0600-0800 winter on 15460 (from 0630), 15470, 15525, 17495 (from 0700), 17570 and 21790 kHz; and 0800-1000 on 9905 (from 0830), 15460, 15470, 17495 and (till 0900) 21790 kHz. Midyear, 0500-0900 on 15490 (from 0600), 17495 (from 0700), 17625 (from 0530) and (till 0800) 21790 kHz.

Switzerland

Swiss Radio International is widely heard, despite having closed all but one of its transmission sites on Swiss soil. Intelligent use of relays outside Switzerland ensures that its signal reaches all continents.

SRI is heavily committed to news, but its overall output now has a lighter feel. And as always, it is unmistakably Swiss.

☞ RECOMMENDED: Final half hour of one-hour broadcasts.

North America: 0100-0130 and 0400-0500 on 9885 and 9905 kHz.

Europe: Winter at 0500-0530 and 0600-0630 on 9655 kHz; 1100-1130 and 1300-1330 on 9535 kHz; and 2000-2030 on 6165 kHz; summer, one hour earlier, 0400-0430 and 0500-0530 on 9610 kHz; 1000-1030 and 1200-1230 on 15315 kHz; and 1900-1930 on 6110 kHz.

Southern Africa: 0730-0800 winter on 17665 kHz, summer on 21750 kHz; and 2000-2030 winter on 13660 and 13790 kHz, summer on 13710 and 15220 kHz.

East and Southeast Asia: 1100-1200 winter on 9540 and 21770 kHz, summer on 13735 and 21770 kHz; also 1400-1500 winter on 12010 (or 9540) kHz, and summer on 9575 kHz.

Australasia: 0830-0900 on 9885 and 13685 kHz.

Nicolas Lombard, Deputy General Manager of Swiss Radio International. SRI uses transmitters on foreign soil to help ensure high-quality reception.

SRI

United Kingdom

Stations reflect their cultures, and the **BBC World Service** is no exception. Britain's broadcasting jewel has been as important to world band radio as it has been for British influence abroad.

But as Hail Britannia has evolved into Cool Britannia, individualistic excellence has been replaced by imitator's banality. Moreover, the single World Service has been replaced by seven "streams" with a potpourri of shows beamed to different areas—a nightmare for planners and listeners, alike. Even with seven tries, some popular offerings are no longer beamed to North America at prime time.

There are still excellent shows in the BBC lineup, with news programs that are as good or better than those of competing broadcasters. Like the Great Wall of China, there was so much to the original entity that even years of professional lapses haven't manage to bring

Britain's BBC World Service is as important to world band as to British influence abroad.

Charles Haviland interviews a Syrian farmer for the BBC's "One Planet," chosen by PASSPORT as one of the ten best shows on the air.

BBC World Service

it all down. A recent change of top management may yet revive the station's fortunes.

☞ RECOMMENDED: "One Planet."

North America: Winter mornings, easterners can tune in at 1000-1100 on 6195 kHz; 1100-1200 on 5965, 6195 and 15220 kHz (6195 and 15220 kHz carry alternative programs for the Caribbean at 1100-1130 on weekdays); 1200-1400 on 5965, 9515, 9590 (from 1300) and 15220 kHz; 1400-1630 on 9515, 9590 (till 1600) and 17840 kHz; and 1630-1700 on 17840 kHz (also available Saturdays on 9515 kHz). The summer schedule is 1000-1100 on 5965 and 6195 kHz; 1100-1200 on 5965, 6195 and 15220 kHz; 1200-1400 on 9515, 11865 (from 1300) and 15220 kHz; and 1400-1700 on 9515 (till 1630, Sunday through Friday), 11865 (to 1600) and 17840 kHz. In or near the Caribbean area, the schedule is 1000-1100 on 6195 kHz; 1100-1400 on 6195 and 15220 kHz; and 1400-1700 on 17840 kHz. These frequencies are in use year round.

For winter in western North America, use 1100-1200 on 9740 and 15220 kHz; 1200-

1600 on 9515, 9590 (from 1300), 9740, 15220 and (from 1400) 17840 kHz; and 1600-1900 (to 2000, Saturday) on 17840 kHz—9515 kHz is also available till 1630, extended to 1700 on Saturday. In summer, it's 1200-1600 on 9515 (till 1500), 9740, 11865 (from 1300), 15220 and (from 1400) 17840 kHz; and 1600-1800 on 17840 kHz (extended to 2000 on Saturday); 9515 kHz is also available till 1700 Saturday; 1630 on other days. Note that 9740 kHz carries programs for Asia and the Pacific, which are often different from those targeted at North America.

Early evenings in eastern North America—especially down south—use 5975 kHz at 2100-2200. This slot contains the informative "Caribbean Report," aired at 2115-2130 Monday through Friday, and also carried on 11675 and 15390 kHz.

Throughout the evening, most North Americans can listen in at 2200-0500 (0600 in winter) on 5975, 6135, 6175 and 9590 kHz (times vary on each channel). In the southwestern United States and Central America you get a two-hour bonus on 6175 kHz at 0600-0800—one hour earlier in summer.

Europe: A powerhouse 0300-2300 on 6195, 9410, 12095, 15565 and 17640 kHz—times vary for each channel, and 17640 kHz carries the program stream intended for the Mideast.

Middle East: 0300 (0200 in summer)-2100. Key frequencies—times vary according to whether it is winter or summer—are 9410, 11760, 12095, 15575 and 17640 kHz.

Southern Africa: 0300-2200 on, among others, 3255, 6005, 6190, 11765, 11940, 15400, 21470 and 21660 kHz—times vary for each channel.

East and Southeast Asia: 0000-0300 on 6195 (till 0200), 15280, 15360 and (winter) 17760 kHz; 0300-0500 on 15280, 15360, 17760 and 21660 kHz; 0500-1030 on 6195

China Radio International broadcasts in many languages to nearly every part of the world. It makes effective use of overseas relays to help ensure it is heard clearly and reliably. CRI

(from 0900), 9740, 11765 (from 0900), 11955, 15280 (till 0530), 15360, 17760 and 21660 kHz; 1030-1100 on 6195, 9740 and 11955 kHz; 1100-1300 on 6195, 9580, 9740, 11955 and 15280 kHz; 1300-1600 on 5990, 6195 and 9740 kHz; 1600-1700 on 3915, 6195 and 7160 kHz; and 1700-1800 (to Southeast Asia) on 3915 and 7160 kHz. For morning reception, use 2100-2200 on 3915, 5965, 6110 (winter), 6195, 9740 and (summer) 11945 kHz; 2200-2300 on 5965, 6195, 7110 and 11955 kHz; and 2300-2400 on 3915, 5965, 6195, 7110, 11945, 11955 and 15280 kHz. Fancy some alternative programming? Try the stream for South Asia on 15310 kHz, easily audible in Southeast Asia at 1400-1700 winter, and 0900-1700 summer.

Australasia: 0500-0900 on 9580 (0600-0800), 11955 and 15360 kHz; 0900-1100 on 11955 kHz; 1100-1600 and 1800-2000 on 9740 kHz; 2000-2200 on 5975 and 9740 kHz; and 2200-2400 on 11955 kHz. At 2200-2300, 9660 and 12080 kHz are also available for some parts of the region.

ASIA
China

China Radio International may have more transmitting power at its disposal than world band neighbor Radio Japan, but tends to lose out when it comes to selecting suitable frequencies. Overall, though, CRI's signal is well heard in most areas.

One-hour broadcasts are now split into two, with news and current events filling the first 30 minutes, and a more interesting magazine format shaping the second half.

☞ RECOMMENDED: "Music from China."

Eastern North America: 0100-0200 on 9570 kHz, 0300-0400 on 9690 kHz, 0400-0500 on 9730 kHz, 1300-1400 on 9570 kHz, and 2300-2400 on 5990 kHz.

Western North America: 0300-0400 on 9690 kHz, 0400-0500 on 9730 kHz, 0500-0600 (0400-0500 in summer) on 9560 kHz, and 1400-1600 (1300-1500 in summer) on 7405 kHz.

Europe: 2000-2200 winter on 5965 and 9535 kHz (7150 kHz may also be available at 2100-2130), and summer on 11790 and 15110 kHz. A relay via Moscow can be heard winters at 2200-2300 on 7170 kHz, and summers on 9880 kHz.

Middle East: There are no specific broadcasts for this area, but try the 2000 transmission to Europe; also 1900-2100 on 9440 kHz, intended for North Africa.

Southern Africa: 1400-1600 on 13685 and 15125 kHz; 1600-1700 on 7190 and 9565 kHz; 1700-1800 winter on 7150, 7405, 9570 and 9695 kHz; summer on 9570, 9695, 11910 and 13700 kHz; and 2000-2130 on 11735 and 13640 or 15500 kHz.

Asia: (Southeast) 1200-1300 on 9715 and 11980 kHz, and 1300-1400 on 11980 and 15180 kHz; *(South)* 1400-1500 on 11825 and 15110 kHz, and 1500-1600 on 7160 and 9785 kHz. Experimental frequencies of 9700 and 11675 kHz may also be used at 1400.

Australasia: 0900-1100 on 11730 and 15210 kHz; 1200-1300 on 7265 (or 9760), 11675 and 15415 kHz; and 1300-1400 on 11675 and 11900 kHz.

Japan

A strong candidate for the title of Most Improved Station, **Radio Japan** continues to replace its stodgy presentations with lively, stimulating shows. A strong commitment to news and current events is increasingly being complemented by music and general interest programs.

☞ RECOMMENDED: "Music Journey Around Japan."

Eastern North America: Best bets are 1100-1200 on 6120 kHz and 0000-0100 on 6145 (or 11705) kHz, both via a Canadian relay at Sackville, New Brunswick.

Western North America: 0500-0600 on 6110 and 9835 (or 13630) kHz; 0600-0700 on 9835 kHz; 1400-1500 on 9505 kHz; 1700-

1800 on 9505 or 9535 kHz; and 2100-2200 on 17825 kHz.

Europe: 0500-0600 on 5975 kHz; 0500-0700 on 7230 kHz; 1700-1800 on 12000 kHz; 2100-2200 on 6115, 6180 (winter), 9810 (summer) and 9725 kHz.

Middle East: 0100-0200 on 9515 (or 9660) and 11870 kHz, and 1400-1500 on 11880 kHz.

Southern Africa: 1700-1800 on 15355 kHz.

Asia: 0000-0015 on 11815 (or 17810) and 13650 kHz; 0100-0200 on 11860, 15325, 15590 and 17845 kHz; 0500-0600 on 11715, 11760 and 15590 kHz; 0500-0700 on 11840 kHz; 0600-0700 on 11740 kHz; 1000-1200 on 9695 and 15590 kHz; 1400-1600 on 11730 kHz; and 1500-1600 on 7200 (or 9860) and 9750 kHz. Transmissions to Asia are often heard in other parts of the world, as well.

Australasia: 0100-0200 on 17685 kHz; 0300-0400 on 21610 kHz; 0500-0700 and 1000-1100 on 11850 or 21570 kHz; and 2100-2200 on 6035 (or 11920) and 11850 kHz.

NORTH AMERICA
Canada

After years of financial neglect, **Radio Canada International** is reestablishing its role as one of the world's most popular world band stations. Secure funding and extra transmission facilities bode well for its future.

Some of RCI's best programs still originate from the domestic networks of its parent organization, the Canadian Broadcasting Corporation. But the balance is slowly changing as the station regains its international moorings.

☞ RECOMMENDED: "The Mystery Project."

North America: Morning reception is better in eastern North America than farther west, but the evening broadcasts are

GRUNDIG Tunes

SATELLIT 800 MILLENNIUM

The Satellit 800 Millennium. In the history of shortwave receivers, no other manufacturer has maintained a continuously evolving series of high-end portable radios, decade after decade.

Extensive frequency coverage.

- Long wave, AM-broadcast and Shortwave, 100-30,000 KHz, continuous.
- FM broadcast, 87-108 MHz.
- VHF aircraft band, 118-137 MHz.
- Multi-mode reception – AM, FM-stereo, Single Sideband USB/LSB and VHF aircraft band.

The right complement of high-tech features.

- Three built-in bandwidths, using electronically switched IF filters: 6.0, 4.0, 2.3 KHz.
- Synchronous detector for improved quality of AM and USB/LSB signals, minimizes the effects of fading distortion and adjacent frequency interference.
- Selectable AGC in fast and slow mode. Auto Backlight shutoff to conserve battery life. Low Battery Indicator.

Performance engineered for the best possible reception.

- High Dynamic Range, allowing for detection of weak signals in the presence of strong signals.

- Excellent sensitivity and selectivity.

Legendary Grundig audio.

- Outstanding audio quality, with separate bass and treble tone control - in the Grundig tradition.
- FM Stereo with headphones or external amplified stereo speakers.
- Includes high quality stereo headphones.
- Multiple audio outputs: line level output for recording, stereo headphone output.

Information displayed the way it should be.

- Large, illuminated, informational LCD display of operational parameters, measuring a massive 6˝ x 3¹⁄₂˝, easy to read.
- An elegant, calibrated, analog signal strength meter, in the finest tradition.
- Digital frequency display to 100 Hertz accuracy on AM, SW and VHF aircraft bands. 50 Hz when SSB used.

Traditional and high-tech tuning controls.

- A real tuning knob, like on traditional radios, but with ultra-precise digital tuning, with absolutely no audio muting when used.
- A modern, direct-frequency-entry keypad for instant frequency access, and pushbuttons for fixed-step tuning.

Plenty of user programmable memory.

- 70 programmable memories, completely immune to loss due to power interruptions.
- Memory scan feature.

Clocks and timers.

- Dual, 24 hour format clocks.
- Dual programmable timers.

Antenna capabilities that really make sense.

- Built in telescopic antenna for portable use on all bands.
- External antenna connections for the addition of auxiliary antennas, e.g. professionally engineered shortwave antennas; long-wire shortwave antennas; specialized AM broadcast band antennas for enthusiasts of AM DX'ing; FM broadcast band antennas; VHF air band antennas.

Power, dimensions, weight.

- Operation on six internal "D" cell batteries or the included 110V AC adapter (a 220V AC adapter is available upon request).
- Big dimensions and weight. A real radio. 20.5˝ L × 9.4˝ H × 8˝ W., 14.5 lb.

universal radio inc.

6830 Americana Pkwy.
Reynoldsburg, Ohio
43068-4113 U.S.A.

n the World

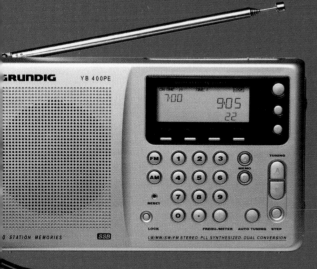

*The most powerful compact
 dio AM/FM Shortwave Receiver.*

*German Look! German Sound!
German Quality! Power and Performance.*

Yacht Boy 400
Professional Edition

werful performance and sleek titanium look design
mbined with sophisticated features make the YB 400 PE a
ue! Covers shortwave, AM, FM-stereo and longwave: SW
-30 MHz, AM 530-1710 KHz, FM 88-108 MHz, LW 150-353
z. SSB circuitry for reception of shortwave single sideband
-way communications, e.g. ham radio, aeronautical and
rine. 2 clocks. 40 memories. Built-in antennas.
ernal SW antenna socket. Includes AC adapter, case,
phones, supplementary SW antenna. Uses 6 AA batteries
t included). Dimensions: 7.75″ L × 4.5″ H × 1.5″ W.
ight: 1 lb. 5 oz.

Yacht Boy 300
Professional Edition

Listen to broadcasts from countries around the
globe on all 13 shortwave international broadcast
bands. Local AM and FM-stereo too. Fully digital
PLL. Direct frequency entry. Auto scan. Push-button
tuning. Clock, alarm and 10 to 90 minute sleep
timer. 24 memories. Titanium color. Easy-read LCD.
Display light. External SW antenna socket. Carrying
strap. Includes AC adapter, case, earphones,
batteries, supplementary SW antenna. Compact.
One year warranty.
Dimensions: 5.75″ L × 3.5″ H × 1.25″ W.
Weight: 12 oz.

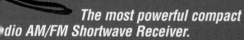

ders & Prices phone: 800 431-3939   Web: dx@universal-radio.com
ormation phone: 614 866-4267   www.DXing.com
x: 614 866-2339   www.universal-radio.com

usually audible throughout much of the United States. Winter, the morning broadcasts go out at 1200-1300 (weekdays), 1300-1400 (daily) and 1400-1500 (weekdays), all on 9640, 13650 and 17710 kHz. There is also a three-hour Sunday broadcast at 1400-1700 on 9640, 13655 and 17710 kHz. In summer the times are one hour earlier: 1100-1400 on 9640, 13650, 17765 and 17820 kHz; and the 1300-1600 Sunday transmission on 13650 and 17800 kHz. During winter, evening broadcasts air at 2300-0100 on 5960 and 9755 kHz (6040, 9535 and 11865 kHz are also available part of the time); 0200-0300 on 6155, 9535, 9755, 9780 and 11865 kHz; and 0300-0330 (0400, weekends) on 6155, 9755 and 9780 kHz. There's an additional 30-minute slot for western North America at 0600-0630 on 5960 and 9670 kHz. The summer schedule is 2200-2400 on 5960, 9755 and 13670 kHz (some programs are also available on 11895, 15305 and 17695 kHz); 0100-0200 on 5960, 9755, 11715, 13670, 15170 and 15305 kHz (only 5960

and 9755 kHz are available 0130-0200 weekday evenings); and 0200-0230 (0300, weekends) on 9755, 11715, 13670, 15170 and 15305 kHz. The final broadcast, for western North America, airs at 0500-0530 on 5995, 9755 and 11830 kHz.

Europe: Winters at 2100-2200 on 5995, 7235, 9770, 9805 and 13650 kHz; and 2200-2300 on 5995, 7235 and 9805 kHz. Summer broadcasts are one hour earlier: 2000-2200 on 5995, 7235 (from 2200), 11690 (till 2100), 13650, 15325, 15470 and 17870 kHz.

Europe and Middle East: 0600-0630 winter on 6045, 6150 and 11905 kHz. Summers, it's one hour earlier on 6145, 7290, 9595 and 15330 kHz. Only some of these channels are audible in the Mideast.

Middle East: 0400-0430 winter on 9505 and 9645 kHz, and summer on 11835, 11975 and 15215 kHz.

Southern Africa: Best bets are 2100-2300 winter (summer in Southern Hemisphere) on 13690, 15325 and (till 2200) 17820 kHz; and 2000-2200 summer on 13670 and 17820 kHz.

Asia: To East Asia at 1200-1230 winter on 6150 and 11730 kHz, and summer on 9660 and 15195 kHz; 1330-1400 on 6150 (winter), 9535 and (summer) 11795 kHz; to South Asia at 1630-1700 on 6140 and 7150 kHz; and to East and Southeast Asia at 2200-2230 winter on 11705 kHz, replaced summer by 17835 kHz.

One of the best shows on the air is the CBC's "Global Village," hosted by Jowi Taylor and aired worldwide over Radio Canada International.   CBC

United States

America's greatest strength is found not in its military might, but in its example. Yet, the U.S. government's best vehicle to convey that example worldwide, the **Voice of America**, has become a demoralized political football. Roundly criticized by listeners for its predominant use of a "rolling news" format, the station has even come under fire from members of the U.S. Senate.

With years of clueless management at the highest levels, the immediate prospects for improvement are not encouraging unless the new White House and Congress take heed. A pity, because the VOA is audible just about everywhere on shortwave.

☞ RECOMMENDED: "Talk to America."

North America: The two best times to listen are at 0000-0200 Tuesday through Saturday—local weekday evenings in the Americas—on 5995, 6130, 7405, 9455, 9775 and 13740 kHz (with 11695 kHz also available at 0000-0100); and 1000-1100 daily on 6165, 7405 and 9590 kHz. This is when the VOA broadcasts to South America and the Caribbean. The African Service can also be heard in parts of North America; try the evening transmission at 1800-2200 on 15580 and (from 2000) 17725 or 17785 kHz.

There's not much for *Europe*, but try 0400-0700 on 7170 kHz, 0500-0700 winter on 11825 kHz, 1500-1700 (1800 in winter) on 15205 kHz, 1700-2100 on 9760 kHz, and 2100-2200 on 6040 and 9760 kHz.

Middle East: 0500-0700 winter on 11825 and 15205 kHz, and 0400-0700 summer on 11965 and 15205 kHz; 1400-1500 (winter) on 15205 kHz; 1500-1700 on 9575 (winter), 9700 (summer) and 15205 kHz; 1700-1800 winter on 6040, 9760 and 15205 kHz; and summer on 9700 and 9760 kHz; 1800-2100 on 9760 kHz (6040 also available winter till 1900); and 2100-2200 on 6040, 9595 (winter) and 9760 kHz.

Southern Africa: 0300-0500 on 6080, 7275 (midyear), 7290, 7340 (to 0330), 7415 (winter), 9575, 9775 (winter, from 0400) and (till 0430) 9885 kHz; 0500-0630 (to 0700 weekends) on 6035 and 12080 kHz; 1600-1800 on 11920 (winter), 12040 (winter), 13710 (till 1700), 15240 (or 15410), 15445 and 17895 kHz; and 1800-2200 on 7415, 11920 (winter, to 2000), 15240 (or 15410), 15445 (midyear, from 1900), 15580 and (till 1900) 17895 kHz.

Today's Voice of America is but a shadow of its former self under Ed Murrow, but excellent shows remain. Arguably the best is "Talk to America," with Carol Pearson.   VOA

East and Southeast Asia: 0800-1000 winter on 11995, 13650 and 15150 kHz; summer on 11930, 13610 and 15150 kHz; 1100-1300 on 6110 (winter), 6160 (summer), 9760, 11705 (winter) and (summer) 15160 kHz; 1300-1500 on 9760, 11705 (winter) and (summer) 15160 kHz; 1900-2000 on 15180 kHz; 2100-2200 on 15185 and 17820 kHz; 2200-2400 on 7215, 9770 (summer), 9890 (winter), 15185, 15290, 15305 (summer) and 17820 kHz; and 0000-0100 on 7215, 9770, 15185, 15290 and 17820 kHz.

Australasia: 1000-1200 on 5985 (winter), 9645 (from 1100), 9770 (midyear) and 15425 kHz; 1200-1500 on 9645 (only to1400 winter) and 15425 kHz; 1900-2000 on 9525 and 11805 (or 11870) kHz; 2100-2200 on 9705 (midyear), 11870 and 17735 (or 17740) kHz; 2200-2400 on 9705 (midyear), 9770 (winter), 11760 and 17735 (or 17740) kHz; and 0000-0100 on 11760 and 17735 (or 17740) kHz.

———————————

Prepared by Don Swampo and the staff of Passport to World Band Radio.

How to Choose a World Band Radio

Some electronic products are almost commodities. With a little common sense you can get what you want without fuss or bother.

Not so world band receivers, which vary greatly from model to model. As usual, money talks, but even that's a fickle barometer. Fortunately, many perform well, and we rate them accordingly. Yet, even among models with comparable star ratings it helps to choose a radio that fits you—not some marketing Everyman.

No Elbow Room

World band radio is a jungle: 1,100 channels, with stations scrunched cheek-by-jowl. It's much more crowded than FM or mediumwave AM, and to make matters worse the international voyage can make signals weak and quavery. To cope, a radio has to perform exceptional electronic gymnastics. Some succeed, others don't.

This is why PASSPORT REPORTS was created. We've tested hundreds of world band products—the good, the bad and the ugly. These evaluations include rigorous hands-on use by listeners, plus specialized lab tests we've developed over the years. These form the basis of PASSPORT REPORTS, and for some premium receivers and antennas there are also soup-to-nuts Radio Database International White Papers®.

Four-Point Checklist

✔ Price. Do you want to hear big stations, or soft voices from exotic lands? Powerful evening signals, or weaker signals by day? Decide, then choose a radio that surpasses your needs by a good notch or so—this helps ensure against disappointment without wasting money.

Once the novelty wears thin, most people give up on cheap radios—they're clumsy to tune and can sound terrible. That's why we don't cover analog-tuned models, but even some digitally tuned models can disappoint.

Most find satisfaction with portables selling for $135-200 in the United States or £90-130 in the United Kingdom with a rating of ✪✪⅞ or more. If you're looking for elite performance, shoot for a portable or portatop rated ✪✪✪¾ or better—at least $350 or £300—or consider a five-star tabletop model.

✔ Location. Signals tend to be strongest in and around Europe, next-strongest in eastern North America. Elsewhere in the Americas, or in Hawaii or Australasia, you'll need a receiver that's unusually sensitive to weak signals—some sort of accessory antenna helps, too.

> Choose a radio that fits you—not some marketing Everyman.

PASSPORT'S STANDARDS

At International Broadcasting Services we have been analyzing shortwave equipment since 1977. Our reviewers, and no one else, write everything in PASSPORT REPORTS. These include our laboratory findings, all of which are done by an independent laboratory recognized as the world's leader. (For more on this, please see the Radio Database International White Paper, *How to Interpret Receiver Lab Tests and Measurements*.)

Our review process is completely separate from equipment advertising, which is not allowed within PASSPORT REPORTS. Our team members may not accept review fees from manufacturers, nor may they "permanently borrow" radios. International Broadcasting Services does not manufacture, sell or distribute world band radios or related hardware.

PASSPORT recognizes superior products regardless of when they first appear on the market. We don't bestow annual awards, but instead designate each exceptional model, regardless of its year of introduction, as *Passport's Choice*.

For apartment dwellers and travelers the Sony AN-LP1 active antenna works well with portables.

> **World band receivers don't test well in stores.**

✔ **Which features?** Divide features between those which affect performance and those that impact operation (see sidebars), but be wary of judging a radio by its features. A radio with few features may outperform one laden with goodies.

✔ **Where to buy?** Whether you buy in a store, by phone or on the Web makes little difference. That's because world band receivers don't test well in stores except in the handful of world band showrooms with proper outdoor antennas. Even then, long-term satisfaction is hard to gauge from a spot test, so visits at different times are advisable.

One thing a store lets you get a feel for is ergonomics—how intuitive a radio is to operate. You can also get a thumbnail idea of world band fidelity by listening to mediumwave AM stations or a superpower world band station.

USEFUL OPERATING FEATURES

Digital frequency readout is a "must" to find stations quickly. A *24-hour World Time clock* helps to know when to tune in; many receivers have them, or you can buy them separately.

Also: direct-access tuning via *keypad* and *presets* ("memories"); and any combination of a *tuning knob*, up/down *slewing* controls or *"signal-seek" scanning* to hunt around for stations. Some radios have handy *one-touch presets* buttons, like a car radio.

Depending on your listening habits, you may be interested in an *on/off timer* or built-in cassette recording. Also, look for an *illuminated display* and a good *signal-strength indicator*. Travelers prefer portables with power-lock switches that keep the radio from going on accidentally, but the lock on some Chinese-made portables doesn't disable the display illumination.

EFFECTIVE PERFORMANCE FEATURES

A signal should not just be audible, but actually sound pleasant. Several features help bring this about—some keep out unwanted sounds, others enhance audio quality. Of course, just because a feature exists doesn't mean it works properly, which is why we check these out in PASSPORT REPORTS.

Full world band coverage from 2300-26100 kHz is best, although 3200-21850 kHz or even 4750-21850 kHz is usually adequate. If coverage is less, look at "Best Times and Frequencies for 2001" elsewhere in this book to ensure that important world band segments are completely covered.

Synchronous selectable sideband greatly enhances adjacent-channel rejection while reducing fading distortion. It is found on some models selling for over $150 or £110.

Especially if a receiver doesn't have synchronous selectable sideband, it helps to have two or more *bandwidths* for superior adjacent-channel rejection. Some premium models incorporate this *and* synchronous selectable sideband—a killer combo. Multiple bandwidths are found on a number of models over $190 or £120.

Multiple conversion or *double conversion* helps reject spurious "image" signals—unwanted growls, whistles, dih-dah sounds and the like. Few models under $100 or £70 have it; nearly all over $150 or £100 do. This borders on a "must" except for casual listening.

High-quality speakers are an aural plus, as are *tone controls*—preferably continuously tunable with separate bass and treble adjustments. For world band reception, *single-sideband* (SSB) reception capability is only marginally relevant, but it is essential for utility or "ham" signals. On costlier models you'll get it whether you want it or not.

Heavy-hitting tabletop models are designed to flush out virtually the most stubborn signal, but they usually require experience to operate and are overkill for casual listening. Among these look for a tunable *notch filter* to zap howls; *passband offset* (a/k/a *passband tuning* and *IF shift*) for superior adjacent-channel rejection and audio contouring, especially in conjunction with synchronous selectable sideband; and multiple *AGC* decay rates. At electrically noisy locations a *noise blanker* is essential; some work much better than others.

> **Be wary of judging a radio by its features. A radio with few features may outperform one laden with goodies.**

Digital signal processing (DSP) is the latest attempt to enhance mediocre signal quality. Until recently it has been much smoke, little fire, but the technology is improving. Watch for more DSP receivers in the years to come, but don't worship at their altar.

With portables and portatops an *AC adaptor* reduces operating costs and may improve weak-signal performance. Some of these are poorly made and cause hum, but most are quite good. With tabletop models an *inboard AC power supply* is preferable but not essential.

Looking a number of years ahead, *digital shortwave transmission* is a question of how and when, not if. Thankfully, digital transmissions are likely to be compatible with existing analog receivers—*in-band, on-channel*—so legacy world band receivers will continue to function properly.

WHEN ANTENNAS HELP

Portables come with built-in telescopic antennas that are fine for evening use in Europe and the east coast of North America.

But during the day or in weak-signal locations, your portable will benefit from more oomph. Among the best in the United States is Radio Shack's ten-buck "SW Antenna Kit" with wire, insulators and other goodies, plus $2 for a claw/alligator clip or other connector.

This antenna may be too long for your radio, but you can always shorten it. Experiment, but as a rough rule of thumb the less costly the portable, the shorter the antenna should be. If you live in an apartment, run the antenna along your balcony or roof and away from the building, then cut off any excess wire. Barring this, try taping a length of wire along a large window.

If the antenna makes a station sound worse, detach it and use the radio's telescopic antenna. Protect the radio's innards by disconnecting any outboard wire antenna when you're not listening—especially when thunder, snow or sand storms are nearby.

Sony Antenna Works Nicely

Sony's active (amplified) AN-LP1 loop antenna helps bring weaker stations out of the mud. It is especially useful if you live in an apartment or townhouse where an outdoor wire antenna isn't feasible.

☞ Don't confuse this with the Sony AN-1 antenna, which is inferior.

☞ The Sony ICF-SW07 portable comes with the AN-LP2 antenna. The 'LP2 isn't sold separately and doesn't replace the AN-LP1, but rather works only with the 'SW07. Except for automated preselector adjustment, it is identical to the AN-LP1.

Antennas Boost Tabletop Performance

Tabletop receivers require an external antenna, either passive or active. Although portatop models don't require an outboard antenna, they usually work better with one.

Active antennas use short rods or wires to snare signals, then amplify those signals electronically. For apartment dwellers they can be a godsend—provided they work right. Our findings on these are given elsewhere in this PASSPORT.

If you have space outdoors, a passive outdoor wire antenna is better, especially when it is designed for world band. Besides not using problematic electronic circuits, a good passive antenna's greater capture length tends to reduce relative disruption by local electrical noise.

Among the best under $100 or £60 are those made by Antenna Supermarket ("Eaves-dropper") and Alpha Delta Communications, direct or from world band vendors. Detailed test results and installation instructions for these and other models are in the Radio Database International White Paper®, *Evaluation of Popular Outdoor Antennas*. Eavesdropper antennas come assembled and are usually equipped with built-in static protectors; unprotected antennas need a separate protector, such as from Alpha Delta. Even then, with any outdoor antenna it is best to disconnect the lead-in if there is lightning nearby. A surge protector for the radio's AC power is good insurance, too. These range from low-cost MOV units to innovative Zero Surge devices.

BRITAIN'S BEST SELLING RADIO MAGAZINES

ARE NOW AVAILABLE WORLDWIDE

TO SUBSCRIBE TO
PRACTICAL WIRELESS OR
SHORT WAVE MAGAZINE JUST
COMPLETE THE FORM BELOW AND
MAIL OR FAX IT THROUGH – OR
CALL US WITH YOUR CREDIT CARD
NUMBER AND WE'LL START YOUR
SUBSCRIPTION IMMEDIATELY.

Practical Wireless

Subscribe to *PW* now and you'll find out why we're
Britain's best selling amateur radio magazine.
We regularly feature:

★ News & reviews of the latest
   equipment
★ Antenna Workshop
★ Radio Scene
★ Radio Basics
★ Focal Point – the world of ATV
★ Valve & Vintage
★ Equipment construction

and much, much more. *PW*
has something for radio
enthusiasts everywhere.

Short Wave Magazine

For everyone, from the newcomer to the
experienced radio monitor, *SWM* is the listeners
magazine with articles and features
written specifically to help
the listener find out what to
buy and where and how to
listen. Regular features
include:

★ News & reviews of the latest
   equipment
★ Utility receiving & decoding
★ Broadcast Stations
★ Bandscan
★ Airband
★ Info in Orbit
★ Scanning

CREDIT CARD ORDERS
+44 (0) 1202 659930
FAX ORDERS
+44 (0) 1202 +659950

PW Publishing Ltd.,
Arrowsmith Court,
Station Approach,
Broadstone,
Dorset BH18 8PW, UK

E-MAIL
orders@pwpublishing.ltd.uk
WEB SITE
http://www.pwpublishing.ltd.uk

On The Road Again

Soon, for a monthly fee, North American drivers will be able to hear the same stations over entire continents, thanks to satellite radio. The fading out of local stations will be a thing of the past, although signals will be subject to blocking by buildings and such.

Yet right now, for no monthly fee, you can drive around enjoying dozens of stations from around the planet— thanks to world band radio. World band blankets entire continents while offering quality programs that don't fade in and out the way ordinary stations do. Whether you're listening to a BBC mystery or Viennese waltzes, world band keeps on trucking.

New Models from Sony

So far, mobile world band hasn't lived up to its potential in North America.

Philips, then Becker, took the plunge in the nineties. Despite heads-up promotion, including fancy PR packets and (un?)coverage in *Playboy*, they found annual unit sales to be in the hundreds—a kernel in the trough compared to portable sales. So both companies stopped production, although in Central Europe some models continue to cover the 49 meter "European band."

Nevertheless, there is a market for world band car radios, so Sony has come to the rescue. It now offers a number of models, but there's a catch: They are available only in parts of Asia and the Middle East, along with Australia and New Zealand. They aren't sold or supported in the Americas or Europe.

Why are world band car radios viable in, say, Australia, where portable sales are modest, while in North America, where portable sales are relatively brisk, car radios haven't caught on? One source suggests that while national advertising and PR are important, neither Philips nor Becker ever followed up by widely distributing to their American car stereo dealers—much less with on-site displays about why world band is so unique on the road.

Sony hasn't made this mistake. In Australia its world band models are found at regular car stereo dealers nationwide. But at Sony of America world band radio is managed separately from auto stereo, so there are internal hurdles to replicating what Sony has done elsewhere.

> **Whether you're listening to a BBC mystery or Viennese waltzes, world band keeps on trucking.**

Firm Sells Worldwide

One online firm, Jacky's Electronics of Dubai (www.jackys.com), exports a goodly number of these radios worldwide via DHL courier. We took the plunge, ordering the digitally tuned XR-C5600X, Sony's latest and top-of-the-line world band car radio. Prices vary with foreign exchange, but it came to a very reasonable $151.47 plus $52.33 shipping, or $203.80 before the $48.69 for local installation. It has a built-in cassette player, while an outboard CD changer or a MiniDisc changer are optional. In Australia it goes for AUS$389 including GST, plus about AUS$95 for installation.

Sony's new XR-C5600X world band stereo sounds as good as it looks, but lacks 10 kHz AM tuning steps.   Sony

World band turns rush hours into Russian hours. With an unparalleled variety of public radio stations, world band comes in whether you're near home or between cities. Corbis

After an initial processing mixup and resulting weeks of delay, our order arrived, insured and in good condition, at our Ohio test location in the United States. Apparently the problem is that Jacky's Website allows for separate credit card and ship-to addresses, which can foul things up. Stick to one address for both, and based on reader comments your order should arrive in a few days. No customs fee was imposed, but in other countries charges may be assessed.

Reasonable World Band Coverage

The country of manufacture was not shown on our receiver or the accompanying box and materials. However, a Perth dealer, Strathfield Car Radios, informed PASSPORT's Australian office that it is made in Thailand.

The great-looking '5600X covers shortwave 2940-7735 (SW1), plus 9500-10140 and 11575-18135 kHz (SW2), the traditional frequency ranges for Sony world band car

radios. This is reasonable coverage, especially for tropical bands aficionados, but there's no getting around omission of the important 9250-9495, 11500-11570, 18900-19020 and 21450-21850 kHz segments. The use of SW1 and SW2 "bands" is also archaic technology that complicates tuning by requiring that a carousel button be pushed every time the SW1/SW2 "boundary" is crossed.

The main bugaboo of world band car radios is electronic noise. Ignition systems, spark plugs, electric motors, microprocessors and other gremlins emit electronic pollution that varies greatly from one car to another, but which always limits DX potential. A good noise blanker would help, but none of the car radios we've tested to date has this.

Best bet is to use a telescopic car antenna, rather than a wire built into the windshield or roof. Also, if your vehicle's engine is not diesel, make sure it has the right ignition wiring and spark plugs.

Outstanding Audio

The presence of electrical noise means that any world band car radio will be used mainly for listening to major stations with reasonably clear signals. This interfaces nicely with the '5600X's single 6 kHz bandwidth and exceptional audio—200 watts into four channels, according to Sony's literature, along with an effective three-stage bass boost. Mated to quality auto stereo speakers, the end result is a delight to the ears so long as adjacent-channel interference isn't substantial. Indeed, first-rate world band signals over this configuration often sound as good as local mediumwave AM stations.

Superior Spurious-Signal Rejection

Other world band car radios PASSPORT has tested have had inexpensive single-conversion circuitry. This results in a proliferation of "image" signals interfering with the desired stations.

Here, the '5600X is well ahead of the curve with double-conversion circuitry, thriftily using the FM's existing 10.7 MHz IF in conjunction with the usual 450 kHz IF used for mediumwave AM. The tuning "hole" between 10145-11570 kHz for the FM's IF is a modest price to pay for improved image rejection.

Other world band car radios have suffered from inadequate front-end selectivity when our test vehicles have been near powerful local transmitters. Not so the '5600X, even when used at locations where there were problems with other models.

Mediocre Ergonomics

The '5600X tunes world band in 5 kHz increments. This means you can't detune the receiver by a kilohertz or two to reduce adjacent-channel interference, or spot-tune off-channel stations. However, in principle 5 kHz tuning should simplify bandscanning.

The reality is less principled. If all you want to hear are strong signals, the scanner will seek out and stop at the next signal automatically—provided it is powerful. Unfortunately, the radio mutes during slewing/scanning, with the VRIT going into warp speed if you hold down the button. This makes bandscanning all but a lost cause unless you press the appropriate slew button repeatedly, like a telegraph operator, to achieve one-channel-per-press tuning. This tuning scheme is far from what it could have been, but eventually you get the knack of it.

There are 36 station presets, including six for mediumwave AM and18 in three banks of six for FM. This leaves only six for the 2940-7735 kHz range, ditto for 9500 kHz and up. For world band, this is slim pickings, so we found ourselves setting one preset for each world band segment, then slewing manually to get to any other desired frequency.

There is no keypad to improve frequency access, but the '5600X comes with a 14-key "card remote commander," a thin calculator-like device that can easily be stowed in a console or glove box. Alas, it has no keypad, either.

The clock is only in 12-hour format—there is no 12/24-hour selector—so it can't be used for World Time. It can be read while the frequency is being displayed, or it can be configured so the frequency and time alternate continuously.

Mediumwave Mystery

The radio comes out of the box covering mediumwave AM from 531-1602 kHz in 9 kHz increments. This is hardly surprising, considering that beyond the Americas these are the norms (American channel

The Becker Mexico was
available until recently. It
covered most of the world
band spectrum, but its
steep price kept it out of
most people's reach.

Bad Cat

spacing is 10 kHz and the band goes to 1700 kHz). But what caught
our attention when we were shopping is that Sony's Singaporean
and Australian Websites both advertised, "Frequency step switch
(XR-C5600X only)."

Indeed, there is a half-inch (13 mm) slot on the bottom of the radio
labeled "9 kHz/10 kHz," although nothing is written about this in the
owner's manual. Yet, despite our best attempts to adjust the radio to
530-1710 kHz in 10 kHz increments, we couldn't, and emails to
various Sony offices worldwide brought responses that they would
look into the problem, although we never heard back.

> Any car stereo
> should have solid
> FM performance,
> but the '5600X
> knocked our
> socks off.

Thinking that perhaps radios from Dubai lacked this feature, we
asked an Australian dealer to go over one of their own '5600X units.
Although their technician makes his living working on Sony car
stereos and virtually disemboweled the radio, he could not figure out
how to obtain 10 kHz spacing.

This greatly limits the coverage and quality of reception in the
Western Hemisphere. Otherwise, mediumwave AM performance is
predictable, with average weak-signal sensitivity and superior
selectivity.

Superb FM

You expect a car stereo receiver to have solid FM performance, but
the '5600X's FM knocked our socks off. Whether in urban areas with
strong stations or along rural routes with fleapowered signals, it

pulled in stations with exceptional aplomb and fidelity, with no noticeable side effects.

The radio's FM tuner automatically switches from stereo to mono if the signal level gets too weak for proper reception. There are also controls to switch manually from stereo to mono, plus a user-selectable narrow FM bandwidth to reduce adjacent-channel interference.

When the radio is set for 9 kHz medium-wave AM tuning increments, it automatically tunes FM in 50 kHz increments. If the nominal 10 kHz AM setting could be made to work, FM would then tune in the more convenient 200 kHz increments found in the Americas. Nevertheless, the 50 kHz setting performs perfectly well, even if it requires four button pushes per channel instead of one.

Worthy Cassette Player

We didn't run any elaborate tests with the cassette player, but with quality tapes it sounds excellent—the various winding/search features perform well, too. The only downside is that you have to flip the front panel down to insert or remove a cassette.

That front panel can also be removed to disable the radio, making it less attractive to thieves. A small plastic case is provided for storage, but because the owner's manual warns about not damaging the panel's connectors we opted to leave it alone. For this, our contrarian behavior has exacted a price: Every time the ignition is turned off, the radio plays a little ditty as a reminder to remove the panel.

Others Models Similar

There are a number of other Sony world band car stereo models available. Although not tested by us, on paper most appear to have world band circuitry comparable to that of the XR-C5600X. The differences apparently lie in non-shortwave features and accessories.

Geographically Limited Support

Sony may be an international organization, but it retails country by country. If you obtain a Sony product abroad, it may be considered "gray market" in your country. So as a practical matter, unless you live where the radio is distributed you're on your own should the receiver need repair or if you have questions. For a list of dealers in Australia, check out Sony's Website at www.sony.com.au/content.asp?go=products.asp. In New Zealand, click on www.sony.co.nz/sonymobile. In Singapore, go to www.sony.com.sg/consumer/mobile/CD_Changer/xr_c5600x.html.

Overall: Best We've Tested

The Philips DC-777 and Becker Mexico were worthy world band car radios in their day, but the Sony XR-C5600X, warts and all, is a keeper. Its coverage and performance are a bit better, it is priced less than was the Becker, and while it's too early to be certain the build quality appears to be better than that of the Philips.

So while you're weighing the merits of satellite car radios, consider the alternative. Thanks to these radios from Sony, world band is on the road again.

_____

This evaluation was prepared by George Zeller, with Craig Tyson and the staff of PASSPORT TO WORLD BAND RADIO.

☞ As we go to press, reader Gary Thorburn has emailed George Zeller indicating that his new Sony XR-C5600X has the frequency step switch missing on other samples, and it works. Hopefully this means Sony has quietly responded to complaints, although for now the situation remains indefinite.

Reach Out and Hear Someone

With a tabletop receiver for world band or a PC for Webcasts, you're stuck in one place. Now, with an FM or AM home transmitter you can hear distant stations around your home on ordinary radios.

Even world band portatops and portables benefit—mowing the lawn with a Walkman sure beats schlepping a portable. FM/AM re-transmission is even handier than Bluetooth, Kima and other evolving technologies, as these need special receiving devices and have limited range.

What You Can—and Can't—Do

"Being legal" on FM without a license is not easy in the United States, where FCC rule 15.239 calls for a field strength not exceeding 250 microvolts/meter measured at a distance of three meters from the transmitter. But in plain English, this translates into having no more than one milliwatt into a short, simple antenna. For mediumwave AM, 100 milliwatts or less into a short antenna apparently will keep you outside the grasp of the Federales.

Kit transmitters appear to fall into a special legal zone in the United States. While a 25 milliwatt assembled FM transmitter is of dubious legality, the 25 milliwatt Ramsey FM-100 kit sells openly, even though Washington is known to keep a strict eye on Ramsey's operations.

Elsewhere, rules vary. In parts of Latin America and the Caribbean low-powered transmitters are virtually ignored, whereas in Saudi Arabia, Singapore, North Korea and some other countries even a fleapowered transmitter might put you in the hoosegow.

Canadian rules are refreshingly rooted in common sense, which helped us in preparing parts of this report. There, so long as you keep any significant signal reasonably confined to within your property— home, business, church or whatever—there's no problem. Bother somebody, there's a problem.

Even if you're operating inside your country's legal power limit, you need to avoid interference to licensed broadcast transmissions. Displeased neighbors can pick up the phone and put you at odds with the law within minutes.

> **FM/AM retransmission is even handier than Bluetooth, Kima and other evolving technologies.**

Bottom Line

We evaluated a number of FM and mediumwave AM transmitters which, unless otherwise indicated, apparently can operate within the rules and regulations of the American FCC, as well as the laws of various other countries. Only FM models scored well.

Tops by a hair is the Ramsey FM-100, which pumps out fully 25 milliwatts. The rub: It's a kit. Ramsey

Easily the best assembled unit is the top-fidelity Decade LX-75S, and the company appears to be unusually responsive to customer issues. Alas, it was recently outlawed for importation into the United States, and you have to pay handsomely for its professional quality of performance. Fortunately, the essentially identical Decade MS-100S operates at legal power and is now available for unlicenced use.

Inexpensive options are awash in short-comings, but thankfully there is another alternative. If you're willing to sacrifice a skosh of fidelity, the NetPlay Radio FMP3 is hard to beat. It sells for much less than anything from Decade, yet has all the features you'll ever need and appears to be reliable.

In that regard, units from three manufacturers had technical difficulties which required service. Decade provided same-day replacement within warranty, while

Realty Electronics repaired our Talking House within two days of having received it.

Ramsey's service brought up the rear. It was much slower, and an $18 labor charge was assessed even though the unit was in-warranty and the problem came about because of ambiguous assembly instructions. However, their telephone tech support is excellent.

FM HOME TRANSMITTERS

✪✪✪✪¾ ☺ *Passport's Choice*
Ramsey FM-100 Kit

Price: $249.95 plus shipping worldwide. Toll-free in the United States and Canada (800) 446-2295, or www.ramseyelectronics.com.

The 25 milliwatt Ramsey FM-100 Kit, apparently legal within the United States, comes with more useful features than any

KITS: WORTH THE EFFORT?

Years ago, the roster of companies offering kits used to be long and distinguished, but none achieved success like Michigan's Heathkit. Their products were often wanting in performance, but Heath had kit building down to a science. If all else failed, you could return the assembled product for quick repair at no charge.

All the old kit companies have vanished, but now and again smaller firms in the United States and England offer kits for various electronic products. All do a reasonable job of explaining assembly, but none fully matches the gold standard set by Heathkit.

Also, soldering has become a lost art. If you have never soldered, buy a low-wattage soldering iron, some rosin-core solder, wire cutters, small needle-nosed pliers and hookup wire. Practice awhile, and your odds for success will improve substantially.

Ramsey kit manuals include a parts placement guide to help during assembly. Circuitry is also explained, so when you're finished you can show others how it works. Construction is based on a series of circuit groups, so you can complete a section in one sitting. Ramsey has anticipated most problems, but if that fails their telephone support, although not toll-free, is excellent.

The Ramsey AM-25 is simpler than the FM-100, but because of ambiguous instructions you should restrict assembly to when the company's tech support is available. We didn't, so were left guessing if something wasn't clear. You can imagine the result, and with Ramsey service is neither quick nor free.

other model tested. It is reasonably priced for all it does, and is among the best performers, to boot.

Tuning is fully PLL synthesized, using easily selected 100 kHz increments, and the frequency is digitally displayed on large LEDs. This stereo/mono transmitter comes with the works: two audio level controls with meter indicators, mic input with level/AGC controls, a limiter to protect against overmodulation, a mixer, a variety of inputs, a power switch and a whip antenna. Unlike other models, it is powered not by an outboard AC adaptor, but rather by an inboard AC power supply that minimizes hum. A number of these features have limited impact on relaying existing program material, which is already processed, but they are important for hobby broadcasting.

Bad news? For buyers within the United States, where Ramsey is located, the FM-100 is nominally available only as a kit, and construction is definitely no cakewalk (*see* box). Thankfully, it comes with reasonable assembly instructions and excellent telephone tech support, but Ramsey is no Heathkit. Figure at least 50 hours—half that if you're an experienced kit-builder— and hope for the best. If you wish to see what's involved, download the manual's PDF file at www.ramseyelectronics.com/scstore/pdf/hmanuals/FM100.pdf.

If your transmitter has a problem and requires service, you have to pay labor charges—usually even within the warranty period. Our limited experience with Ramsey kits also suggests, among other unfortunate things, that the repair turnaround is not all it could be (*see* Ramsey AM-25).

Powerful one-Watt wired and kit versions are available for $399.95 and $329.95, respectively. These are for direct export, or you can inform Ramsey in writing if you plan to export the unit yourself. Also available from Ramsey are optional high-gain FM antennas that allow these

powerful versions to cover more than two miles with the right terrain. In most countries that's all you need to guarantee a visit by an unamused constabulary.

✪✪✪✪½ *Passport's Choice*
Decade LX-75S

Price: *LX-75S transmitter:* US$535.00 plus shipping within Canada and selected other countries; toll-free in North America (888) 428-4323, or www.decade.ca. *AOR TW7030 antenna:* $30.00 in the United States; toll-free in North America (800) 431-3939; www.universal-radio.com.

☞ According to the manufacturer, the new Decade MS-100S is essentially identical to the LX-75S, but operates at one milliwatt and is priced lower. It is completely legal for unlicenced use in the United States, and covers almost any typical home and even into the yard— provided you're using a decent FM radio.

☞ The Decade FM-800 series has variable power, rising in 50 milliwatt steps from a 50 milliwatt minimum to a 1.8 Watt maximum. These Canadian-made units, which sell for around US$1,000, may not be imported into the United States under FCC Part 15 rules, but are allowed in under Part 73—a strange quirk of law, as the

Decade's compact transmitters are of professional caliber.   Decade

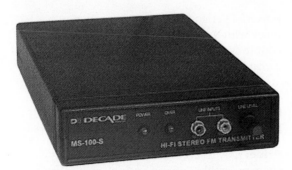

**Best performer for Americans is the Decade MS-100S.
It comes assembled and is fully legal.** Decade

weaker LX-75S is prohibited by both Parts 15 and 73. The catch? The FM-800 series is supposed to be used only by FCC-licensed operators.

The LX-75S from Decade Transmitters is of professional caliber. It is far and away the best assembled transmitter we've come across—FM or AM—with performance to match.

This Canadian-made stereo/mono unit is available throughout Canada and various other parts of the world. Until recently it could also be imported into the United States, but the FCC is no longer allowing it under either Part 15 or Part 73 rules, so it falls into a gray zone which precludes its sales even to licensed broadcasters. Features are not its high point, but it includes a modulation level control for both channels, single-LED overmodulation warning, a bass-boost switch and a power switch. Its 200 kHz tuning increments are ideal for the Americas, although not for Europe and other parts of the world with narrower channel spacing. Changing channels is somewhat inconvenient, as well, and the operating frequency is not displayed.

Audio quality from the '75S is top drawer—the champ among tested models. It excels in feeding even the cleanest Webcasts into excellent audio systems without audible harmonics or spurious responses. Even though it uses an AC adaptor, hum and buzzing are essentially inaudible even without grounding. And while its bass boost may seem like a boom box gimmick, given the quality of most world band programs and Webcasts it can provide genuine fidelity enhancement.

One of the 75S' strongest pluses is that power is adjustable from 1-80 milliwatts—this allows it to cover anything from a house to a city block. Nothing has yet been invented with a signal audible throughout your house and yard, but which suddenly disappears at the property line. Yet, the '75S's precise power gradations come close. It's the best way available to ensure you get what you want without disrupting neighbors.

Government regulations vary, but a sensible solution is to use an unobtrusive antenna like the screw-on AOR TW7030. Law or no law, adjust the power output no higher than you need, choose a frequency at least two channels away from audible stations, and don't blab.

The LX-75S, not much larger than an outboard modem, is solidly constructed. Because it has a low profile, gives off little heat and has no top vents, other things can be stacked on top. This makes it unobtrusive even when desktop space is at a premium.

Factory service is superb. When one of our two units arrived with an inoperative channel, the manufacturer immediately shipped a replacement by prepaid air courier without even waiting for the

**The Decade FM-800's power is adjustable, but cost
and legalities rule it out for most.** Decade

original to be returned. Since then both units have performed flawlessly throughout a year of almost continuous use.

◐◐◐½ ✆
NetPlay Radio FMP3

Price: $189.00 plus shipping worldwide. (818) 879-9785 or www.netplayradio.com.

This American-made stereo unit comes fully assembled, but is priced at much less than the Ramsey FM-100 kit. Its operating frequency is digitally displayed by bright red LEDs, and is easily adjusted by a pair of up/down slew buttons. Frequency steps are 200 kHz—ideal for the Americas, but not for Europe and other parts of the world with narrower channel spacing.

The NetPlay Radio is not equal to the similarly powered Decade MS-100S, but it costs much less. L. Edmond

Unlike the Decade LX-75S, it comes with a built-in telescopic antenna. It also has a power switch and a single four-increment level indicator, with the final LED indicating overmodulation. Our unit has operated for months without so much as a hiccup, and runs cool to the touch.

Power is only 1 mW, but it reaches out surprisingly well, covering almost any typical home and even into the yard— provided you're using a decent FM radio.

Its audio bandwidth and freedom from distortion are audibly inferior to the high professional standard of the Decade unit, but run circles around any AM gear. Even though it uses a 120 VAC AC adaptor, hum and buzzing are scarcely audible, as well. Audio quality thus is more than adequate for retransmission of world band and most Web radio stations.

At under $200, the ready-to-use NetPlay Radio is hard to resist and fully legal.

LOW-COST ALTERNATIVES

Although costlier FM home transmitters provide far and away the best results, for many no amount of excellence is worth upwards of $189. Various analog-tuned "Sound-Feeder" type devices (not tested) are available for $20-30 at outlets like Wal-Mart, Radio Shack, Crutchfield and auto-stereo stores. Most are designed for walkaround CD players so they can be heard over a car's radio, so don't expect much more than 25-30 feet or 9 meters of range.

Another low-cost option is an FM baby monitor—$30-$50—replacing its mic with a female RCA jack. But because these are designed to respond to a child's soft breathing, they tend to overmodulate during broadcast audio peaks.

Among low-cost alternatives, best is a transmitter designed to relay broadcasts and the like. Various FM models have appeared in recent years, including the under-$40 fx-200 (toll-free within North America 800/522-8863 or www.ccrane.com). It radiates for up to 50 feet or 15 meters and is legal within the United States.

Best among AM models is the Talking House T99. It suffers from hum, but this is correctable with a replacement AC adaptor.   Realty Electronics

MEDIUMWAVE AM

For an AM home transmitter to work properly it needs to operate precisely on frequency to avoid heterodyne—whistle—interference with co-channel stations. This rules out low cost analog-tuned models.

All tested AM devices are monaural only and lack such basic operating features as panel-mounted level control and indication. With a Webcast or other stereo feed an outboard mixer can convert stereo audio input to mono. However, as a practical matter the right stereo channel is adequate for input.

All tested models should be set up carefully to minimize hum and buzz, including from your receiver/sound board, cables and connectors—proper grounding sometimes helps. If hum is still more than you can accept, consider replacing the original AC "wall wart" adaptor with a high-quality regulated and filtered adaptor or outboard power supply. If even that is inadequate, use batteries.

Lone Ranger Rides Again

Monaural AM is inherently not a fidelity match for stereo FM, and PASSPORT's ratings reflect this. However, it is good

enough for world band audio. Also, an AM home transmitter is the best way to feed Yesterday USA and other vintage Webcasts, CDs or big band FM stations to your favorite antique radio.

✪✪
Talking House T99

Price: *T99 transmitter:* $299.00 plus shipping in North America; toll-free in the United States (800) 444-8255, or www.talkinghouse.com. *Outboard whip antenna/ATU:* $99.00 plus shipping in North America.

The "Talking House" from Realty Electronics is not just a transmitter; it also comes with a dual-message loop recorder for real-estate agents and homeowners to promote homes to passing automobiles. In our tests this Taiwanese-made unit zero-beated precisely with co-channel North American signals, virtually eliminating the possibility of heterodyne interference. About the size of a laptop PC, the metal-encased T99 is foolproof to operate, although it lacks a power switch.

The tuning synthesizer operates in LED-displayed 10 kHz steps that are easily selected by up/down slew buttons. The operating range is 530-1700 kHz, making it appropriate within the Western Hemisphere, but not in those parts of the world where stations are 9 kHz apart. At 100 mW, its mono-only signal is legal within the U.S. and covers most homes—lawns and all. An optional eight-foot (2.44 meter) external whip antenna/ATU, complete with coaxial cable and fittings, is available to increase range.

You don't expect much in the way of audio fidelity on the AM band, but the T99's audio is designed specifically for speech reproduction. Instead of being broadband, it emphasizes the midrange and high end, with bass coming up woefully short. Even though it sounds clean and intelligible, the overall effect is too telephone-like for listening to music over a worthy antique or other radio.

Alas, that's not all. Like the Ramsey AM-25, the Talking House uses a mediocre AC adaptor which causes hum that's clearly audible even with the T99's limited bass reproduction. A good regulated and bypassed aftermarket adaptor helps alleviate the problem, as does grounding.

Service is excellent. Our unit worked fine for five months before the motor-tuned preselector—inherently a trouble-prone concept—failed to peak properly. The repaired transmitter was on its way to us *gratis* within two days of their having received the original unit.

⭐
Ramsey AM-25 Kit

Price: $129.95 plus shipping worldwide. Toll-free in the United States and Canada (800) 446-2295, or www.ramseyelectronics.com.

If you're handy with a soldering iron, the Ramsey AM-25 Kit is a straightforward monaural AM transmitter kit that's legal within the United States and many other countries. Assembly is an ideal exercise for a rainy day or two, but some components don't correspond exactly to what is indicated in the instructions. That and a couple of ambiguous but important directions make the first-rate tech help line, available weekdays, virtually essential. If you want to know what's required for construction, download the manual's PDF file at www.ramseyelectronics.com/scstore/pdf/hmanuals/am-25.pdf.

The AM-25 nominally tunes 540-1710 kHz. Frequency selection is via an inboard DIP switch rather than the handy up/down PLL tuning found on the Talking House T99. Tuning is in 10 kHz increments, ideal for the Americas but inappropriate for much of

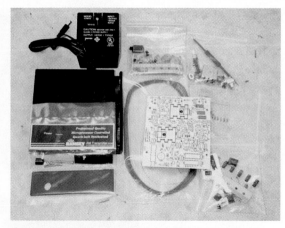

The Ramsey AM25 kit sounds better on paper than it turns out to be in reality.   L. Edmond

the rest of the world, where 9 kHz channel spacing is the norm. The transmitter zero beats precisely with North American co-channel signals, so there's virtually no heterodyne interference.

Alas, channel selection is worse with the AM-25 than with any other unit tested, AM or FM. Besides having to adjust the inboard DIP switch according to a special formula, during assembly you have to choose a frequency segment (e.g. 790-950 kHz), then wind and solder into place three toroid inductors restricted to that range. Changing that range calls for desoldering the original toroids, rewinding them for the new frequency range, then resoldering.

Additionally, although the AM-25's specs call for operation to 1710 kHz we found a distinct and unpleasant rise in distortion above 1600 kHz. We sent the unit back to the factory to be checked out and aligned to Ramsey's satisfaction, but even after that the problem remained.

Where the AM-25 excels is audio bandwidth. Unlike the bass-challenged Talking House T99, the AM-25 has reasonable low-frequency audio reproduction. To this extent it is worth considering for retransmission of musical fare.

Craig Tyson of Australia and New Zealander Graeme Dixon tune a tabletop receiver. A home transmitter allows favorite world band shows to be heard on any FM radio.

C. Tyson

Output power is either 100 milliwatts or one Watt, depending on whether the far leads of resistors R33 and R34 are left uncut and soldered together. Within the United States only the 100 milliwatt alternative is legal, and even then only if the antenna is set up according to the manual's instructions.

At one Watt the AM-25 reaches out very little farther than the Talking House at a tenth the power. However, one of the AM-25's output transistors produces enough heat to melt a spot on the bottom plastic cover. Leaving off the back-panel insert or top cover provides much-needed ventilation, but the bottom plastic cover remains extremely hot no matter what. This is unconscionable—for component life, as well as possibly for fire safety.

Accordingly, the AM-25 is acceptable conditioned on its being operated at its lower-power setting, or if operated at one Watt then only if placed within another and well-ventilated cabinet. Otherwise, it would be prudent to operate it with the cover removed and somebody stationed nearby. Fortunately, a front-panel button makes it easy to turn on and off, unlike some other home transmitters.

The AC adaptor produces enough hum to make listening less pleasurable than it should be. Grounding the transmitter helps, although there is no terminal to facilitate this; best is to use the outer conductor of either RCA socket. Beyond that, what this unit really needs is a properly filtered and bypassed power supply of suitable voltage, amperage and polarity.

If the AM-25 requires service, even within the warranty period you'll probably have to pay a modest labor charge—$18 in our experience—and be patient. Our unit had a problem resulting from a woefully ambiguous instruction, and exclusive of shipping the repair took two weeks.

The Ramsey AM-25 not only can overheat, it lacks even the most fundamental of features, is cumbersome to tune, has flawed instructions, is available only as a kit, distorts above 1600 kHz and has hum. But if you are looking for full bass reproduction in an AM transmitter and are willing to replace the AC adaptor and take suitable precautions, it may make a sensible choice.

Prepared by Thomas Arey, Lawrence Edmond, David Murcoup, Janette Porcelet and the staff of PASSPORT TO WORLD BAND RADIO.

Portables are what most of us spring for, even if we also own something fancier. They are handy, affordable and usually do the trick.

In Europe and the east coast of North America, evening signals come in so well that virtually any well-rated portable should be all you'll need. Even if you live else-where, listen daytime or are into chasing weak signals, a top-ranked portable can do surprisingly well with an outdoor antenna.

World Band on the Go

World band makes for unbeatable outdoor entertainment, as well as a global link when you're away. For these, only a portable will do.

Compact and pocket portables are the radio equivalents of Palm-type handhelds, whereas some larger portables are more like laptop PCs. There are compact models with three or more stars that sell for under the equivalent of $200. These are excellent values for trips—even for home—but even travel warriors should think twice before going smaller. A pocket model makes sense only if weight is paramount and you have a larger radio at home.

Not surprisingly, top-rated portables are also among the largest, but they're not huge. PASSPORT staffers routinely use the Sony ICF-2010 lap portable while globetrotting, for example.

World Band Rebounds in North America

Since the Gulf War there has been a shift in the world band radio landscape in North America, and to a lesser degree Europe and Australasia. All but vanished are cheap analog radios with such dismal performance that they drove newcomers away from world band. At the same time demand has slackened for tabletop and portatop receivers, although this seems to be turning around.

The lion's share of world band radios is now priced from $99.95-499.95, and it is that market segment which is growing. The manufacturer lineup has become more focused, as well, with Sony, Grundig, Sangean and Radio Shack now all but running the show.

Sales emphasis has so far been aimed at the prosperous United States market, with Grundig and, more recently, Sony of America and RadioShack Canada pushing visibly to upgrade world band radio from niche status. Europe and Australia would appear to be next on their target list.

Longwave Useful for Some

The longwave band is still used for some domestic broadcasts in Europe, North Africa and Russia. If you live or travel there, longwave coverage may be a plus. Otherwise, forget it.

Who's the Toughie?

Thankfully, the days of poorly made world band portables appear to be largely behind us. At the same time, truly robust models are becoming harder to find as production and design economies take their toll.

Some Sony models are showing up unusually well, such as the value-priced ICF-SW7600G and the high-performance ICF-2010. Thus far there have been no reliability problems with the complex ICF-SW07, either, although it is still too fresh to have a fully established track record. Early difficulties with the tiny ICF-SW100 series and the larger ICF-SW77 have long since been successfully resolved.

> **The world band landscape has shifted. Mid-priced radios are now the growth market.**

With any brand of world band radio our experience has been that the only models to avoid are those which have been recently introduced and are technologically sophisticated. The ICF-2010, ICF-SW77, ICF-7600G and ICF-SW100 all suffered from significant problems during their first two years or so, but all were appropriately revised and went on to become workhorses.

Until this year, with the introduction of the Chinese-made ICF-SW35, all Sony world band radios were made in Japan. Except for the Yacht Boy 500 and ATS 909, all Grundig and Sangean models are now made in China. That once was enough to put up a caution flag. However, build quality from Chinese plants, although still rarely equal to Japanese or Taiwanese standards, is now much better and continues to improve.

When Looks Count . . .

Radio buffs rarely take appearances into account when deciding on a radio—or at least they won't admit it. But for gift giving or to satisfy an aesthetic impulse, it's nice to own something that looks as good as it sounds.

Taste? The leather-wrapped Grundig 2000 models designed by F.A. Porsche. They make most other radios look like doorstops.

Wow? Sony's ICF-SW07, with its tennis-racquet antenna and clamshell case. The ultimate eyeball grabber.

Retro? The Sony ICF-2010 has Reagan-era panache. It's favored by radiophiles, too, so it qualifies as geek chic.

Aluminum-colored finishes are *au courant*. Most hold up well, but are less forgiving of scratches and wear than dark-plastic models.

Fix It?

Portables aren't meant to be friends for life, and are priced accordingly. Even the most robust model will probably be ready for the landfill after ten years of daily use, while some pedestrian models might give no more than a few years of regular service. At that point, they aren't worth fixing.

Of course, if you own a particularly robust model, listen infrequently, avoid static charges, live where it's pollution-free and dry, and cover the receiver when it's not in use, who knows but that your portable might last a quarter century before sheer age does it in.

If you wind up purchasing a genuinely defective new portable, insist upon an immediate exchange without a restocking fee—manufacturers' repair facilities tend to have a disappointing record. That having been said, Grundig (in Europe and North America) and Sangean America (in the United States and Canada) appear to be providing better service than most, and as mentioned in PASSPORT REPORT's review there is a resident American service expert for the Sony ICF-2010. Still, if quality of service is important to you, consider a portatop or tabletop model, instead.

Many vendors and virtually all world band specialty outlets will cooperate if a just-sold radio turns out to be defective or DOA. While most radios are warrantied for a year, some, such as Radio Shack in certain countries, come only with a 90-day warranty.

Also available are 15-day and other return policies The downside is that those returned units have to wind up some-where. Whether a given outlet puts returned units back in inventory, or resells them as used or for employee purchases, is usually anybody's guess.

Still, you can spot clues. For example, we recently purchased two house-brand units from an electronics chain store in Pennsylvania having a 30-day return policy. One had the plastic bag taped close twice,

WHAT TO LOOK FOR

• **Tuning features.** Digitally tuned models are so superior to analog that these are now the only models tested by PASSPORT. Look for such handy tuning aids as direct-frequency access via keypad, presets (programmable channel memories), up-down tuning via tuning knob and/or slewing keys, band/segment selection, and signal-seek or other scanning. These make the radio easier to tune—no small point, given that a hundred or more channels may be audible at any one time.

• **Audio quality.** Unlike many portatop and tabletop models, portables don't have rich, full audio. However, some are better than others.

• **Adjacent-channel rejection I: *selectivity*.** World band stations are packed together about twice as closely as ordinary mediumwave AM stations, so they tend to slop over and interfere with each other. Radios with superior selectivity are better at rejecting this. However, enhanced selectivity also means less high-end ("treble") audio response and muddier sound. So, having more than one bandwidth allows you to choose between superior selectivity ("narrow bandwidth") when it is warranted, and more realistic audio ("wide bandwidth") when it is not.

• **Adjacent-channel rejection II: *synchronous selectable sideband*.** This is the first major advance in world band listening quality in decades. With powerful stations "out in the clear," it has little audible impact. However, for tougher signals it improves audio quality by minimizing selective-fading distortion, while reducing adjacent-channel interference by selecting the "better half" of a signal.

• **Single-sideband demodulation.** If you are interested in hearing non-broadcast short-wave signals—"hams" and utility signals—single-sideband circuitry is *de rigeur*. Too, the popular low-powered U.S. Armed Forces Radio-Television Service (AFRTS/AFN) can only be heard intelligibly on receivers with single-sideband capability. No portable excels, but those that stand out are cited in PASSPORT REPORTS.

• **Weak-signal sensitivity.** This is important if you live in a weak-signal location or tune to DX or daytime stations. Most portables have more than enough sensitivity to pull in major stations evenings if you're in such places as Europe or North Africa—even Eastern North America.

☞ A simple outboard antenna enhances sensitivity, as well as the signal-to-noise ratio, on nearly any good portable (see sidebar).

• **Ergonomics.** Some radios are easy to use because they don't have complicated features. But even complex models can be designed to operate intuitively.

• **World Time clock.** A World Time clock (24-hour format) is a "must." You can buy these separately, but many radios come with them built in; the best ones display time whether the radio is on or off.

• **AC adaptor.** An outboard AC adaptor is virtually a necessity except on trips. An adaptor provided by the manufacturer is usually best and should be free from hum and noise—Sony's adaptors are particularly good.

☞ Sangean models that come with AC adaptors are often sold without adaptors under other brand names. These "badge engineered" units are not serviced by Sangean.

while the other had batteries in it even though it wasn't supposed to. Perhaps these were opened to demonstrate the radio or for some other innocuous reason, and in fact both radios worked just fine. But in general it is better to get a radio that isn't somebody else's reject.

Manufacturers sometimes go out of their way to avoid this problem. For example, in North America Grundig checks out and repackages radios returned for any reason. They are then sold openly as refurbished units.

Shelling Out

Street prices are given, including European and Australian VAT/GST where applicable. These vary plus or minus, so take them as the general guide they are meant to be. Shortwave specialty outlets and a growing number of other retailers have attractive prices, whereas duty-free shopping is not always a bargain.

We try to stick to plain English, but some specialized terms have to be used. If you come across something that's not clear, check with this edition's glossary.

All Current Models Included

PASSPORT REPORTS evaluates virtually every digitally tuned portable that meets minimum standards of performance. Here, then, are the results of our hands-on and laboratory tests of current models.

What PASSPORT's Ratings Mean

Star ratings: ✪✪✪✪✪ is best. Stars reflect overall performance and meaningful features, plus to some extent ergonomics and build quality. Price, appearance, country of manufacture and the like are not taken into account. To facilitate comparison, the same rating norm is used for professional, tabletop and portatop

models, reviewed elsewhere in this PASSPORT.

A rating of at least ✪✪⅞ should please most who listen to major stations regularly during the evening. However, for casual use on trips virtually any small portable may suffice.

Passport's Choice. La crème de la crème. Our test team's personal picks of the litter—digitally tuned portables we would buy or have bought for our personal use.

✪: A relative bargain, with decidedly more performance than the price would suggest.

How Portables Are Listed

Models are listed by size; and, within size, in order of world band listening suitability. Street prices are given, including VAT where applicable. Models designed for some countries cannot receive single-sideband signals and may have reduced tuning ranges.

Unless otherwise indicated, each digital model has:

- Tuning by keypad, up/down slewing keys, station presets and signal-seek bandscanning.
- Digital frequency readout to nearest kilohertz.
- Coverage of the world band shortwave spectrum from at least 3200-26100 kHz.
- Coverage of the usual 87.5-108 MHz FM band.
- Coverage of the AM (mediumwave) band in selectable 9 and 10 kHz channel increments from about 530-1700 kHz.
- Adequate spurious-signal ("image") rejection.
- No synchronous selectable sideband or single-sideband demodulation. However, when there is synchronous selectable sideband, the unwanted sideband is rejected approximately 25 dB via phasing, not IF filtering.

POCKET PORTABLES
Perfect for Travel, Inappropriate for Home

Pocket portables weigh under a pound, or half-kilogram, and are between the size of an audio cassette jewel box and a handheld calculator. They operate off two to four ordinary small "AA" (UM-3 penlite) batteries. These diminutive models do one job well: provide news and entertainment when you're traveling.

Don't expect much more. Listening to tiny speakers can be tiring, so pocket portables aren't great for everyday listening except through earpieces.

There is also a vast choice among compact models. Their bigger speakers sound better, and they're still small enough for traveling.

Never before has so much performance been shoehorned into such a tiny box. The Sony ICF-SW100 series is an engineering *tour de force*.

✪✪✪
Sony ICF-SW100S

Price: $359.95 in the United States. CAN$599.00 as available in Canada. £199.95 in the United Kingdom.

Pro: Tiny. Superior overall world band performance for size category. High-tech synchronous selectable sideband generally performs well, reducing adjacent-channel interference and selective-fading distortion on world band, longwave and mediumwave AM signals, while adding slightly to weak-signal sensitivity and audio crispness (*see* Con). Single bandwidth, especially when synchronous selectable sideband is used, exceptionally effective at adjacent-channel rejection. Relatively good audio, provided supplied earbuds or outboard audio are used (*see* Con). FM stereo through earbuds. Numerous helpful tuning features, including keypad, two-speed slewing, signal-seek-then-resume scanning (*see* Con), five handy "pages" with ten presets each. Presets can display station name. Tunes in relatively precise 0.1 kHz increments. Good single-sideband performance (*see* Con). Good dynamic range. Worthy ergonomics for size

and features. Illuminated display. Clock for many world cities, which can be made to work as a *de facto* World Time clock (*see* Con). Timer/snooze. Travel power lock. Longwave and Japanese FM bands. Amplified outboard antenna, supplied, in addition to usual built-in antenna, enhances weak-signal reception (*see* Con). Weak-battery indicator; about 16 hours from a set of batteries (*see* Con). High-quality travel case for radio. *Except for North America:* Self-regulating AC adaptor, with American and European plugs, adjusts automatically to all local voltages worldwide.

Con: Tiny speaker, although innovative, has mediocre sound, limited loudness and little tone shaping. Closing clamshell reduces speaker loudness and high-frequency response. Weak-signal sensitivity could be better, although supplied outboard active antenna helps. Expensive. No tuning knob. Clock not readable when station frequency displayed. As "London Time" is used by the clock for World Time, the summertime clock adjustment cannot be used if World Time is to be displayed accurately. Rejection of certain spurious signals ("images"), and 10 kHz "repeats" when synchronous selectable sideband off, could be better. In some urban locations, FM signals from 87.5 to 108 MHz can break through into world band segments with distorted sound, e.g. between 3200 and 3300 kHz. Synchronous selectable sideband tends to lose lock if batteries weak, or if NiCd cells are used. Synchronous selectable sideband alignment can vary with temperature, factory alignment and battery voltage, causing synchronous selectable sideband reception to be slightly more muffled in one sideband than the other. Some readers report BFO pulling causes audio quavering, not found in our test units. Batteries run down faster than usual when radio off. Tuning in 0.1 kHz increments means that non-synchronous single-sideband reception can be mistuned by up to 50 Hz, so audio quality varies. Signal-seek scanner sometimes stops 5 kHz before a strong "real" signal. No meaningful signal-strength indicator. Supplied accessory antenna performs less well than another Sony accessory antenna, the AN-LP1. Mediumwave AM reception only fair. Mediumwave AM channel spacing adjusts peculiarly. Flimsy battery cover. *North America:* AC adaptor only 120 Volts.

☞ In early production samples, the cable connecting the two halves of the "clamshell" case tended to lose continuity with extended use because of a very tight radius and an unfinished edge; this was successfully resolved with a design change in early 1996.

Verdict: The mighty midget. A shoehorning *tour de force*, complete with synchronous selectable sideband and an effective bandwidth filter that, taken together, make this tops in its size class for rejecting adjacent-channel interference. Speaker and, to a lesser extent, weak-signal sensitivity keep it from being all it could have been, and the accessory antenna isn't Sony's latest or best. Yet, this Japanese-

made model still is the handiest pocket portable around, and a nifty gift idea.

✪✪✪
Sony ICF-SW100E

Price: £144.95 in the United Kingdom.

Verdict: This version, not available in North America, nominally includes only a case, tape-reel-type passive antenna and earbuds. Otherwise, it is identical to the Sony ICF-SW100S, above.

Retested for 2001
✪✪✪ ✔ *Passport's Choice*
Sangean ATS 606A, Roberts R617, Radio Shack DX-399, Sangean ATS 606AP, Roberts R876

Price: *ATS 606A:* $139.95 in the United States. CAN$199.00 in Canada. £104.95 in the United Kingdom. AUS$249.00 in Australia. *R617:* £119.95 in the United Kingdom. *DX-399:* $149.99 or less, as available in the United States. *ATS 606AP:* $149.95 as available in the United States. CAN$219.00 as available in Canada. *Sangean AC adaptor for ATS 606A:* $14.95 in the United States. *R876:* £129.95 in the United Kingdom. *ATS 606AP:* $149.95 in the United States. *Sangean AC adaptor for ATS 606A:* $14.95 in the United States.

Pro: Speaker audio quality less bad than most pocket models—comparable to a mediocre-sounding compact model (*see* Con). Speaker audio unusually intelligible. Single bandwidth reasonably effective at adjacent-channel rejection, while providing reasonable audio bandwidth. Weak-signal sensitivity, although not optimum, a bit above average. Various helpful tuning features, including keypad, 54 presets, slewing, signal-seek tuning and meter band selection. Keypad has superior feel and tactile response. Longwave. World Time/local clocks. Illuminated LCD. Alarm. 15/30/45/60-minute snooze. Travel power lock (*see* Con). Multi-level battery strength indicator; also, weak-battery warning. Stereo FM via earphones or earbuds (*see* Con). Above-average FM sensitivity, selectivity, dynamic range and capture ratio. Memory scan (*see* Con). Rubber feet reduce sliding while elevation panel in use. *DX-399:* UL-approved 120/230V AC adaptor, with American and European plugs, adjusts to proper AC voltage automatically. *R876 and ATS 606AP:* UL-approved 120/230V AC adaptor, with American and European plugs, adjusts to proper AC voltage automatically; also ANT-60 reel-in outboard wire antenna. *All Sangean models:* In North America, service provided by Sangean America to models sold under its name. *DX-399:* 30-day money-back period in the United States and Canada; in Canada, product cannot have been opened.

Con: No tuning knob. Audio quality, although superior for size class, lacks low-frequency ("bass") response. Clock readable only when radio is switched off. No meaningful signal-strength indicator. Memory scan doesn't function on short-wave. Keypad not in telephone format. Power lock doesn't disable LCD illumination button. No earphones or earbuds. No carrying strap or handle. On our unit, clock initially refused to be set. *All Sangean models:* Country of manufacture (China) not specified on radio or box. *DX-399:* Box says clock is 12/24 hour, although in reality it is only 24 hour. Warranty only 90 days in the United States and some other countries.

☞ Older Sangean ATS 606P version, made in Taiwan, sometimes still shows up for sale new, usually for under $100. Identical to current ATS 606AP, but tunes in 5 kHz, rather than 1 kHz, increments and has only 45 presets.

Verdict: Easily the best buy in a pocket model—an excellent value. In the land of the deaf, the guy with a hearing aid is king.

The Sangean ATS 606A, sold under a variety of names, is the best value in a pocket portable. It lacks technical sophistication, but has decent audio and is fairly priced.

In that spirit, this model has the best sound among pocket models.

Money aside, choosing between the Sony ICF-SW100 series and this model is a no-brainer. If maximum freedom from adjacent-channel interference and/or smallness of size are paramount, the innovative little Sony wins. If audio quality and ease of use are primary, spring for the Sangean *et al.*

Evaluation of Latest Unit: Production of this model was shifted last year from Taiwan to China, where all Sangean production is expected to take place before long. The first Sangean models to come out of China a few years ago were disappointing, but with the "shakedown cruise" behind them Sangean's China-made products are now much better. In the case of this model, our unit was flawless except that the clocks initially refused to be set.

In the United States Radio Shack introduced the DX-399 in 2000, then apparently chose to withdraw it very shortly thereafter. Its future availability in different parts of the world is not yet known.

Unusual design and above-average audio are
hallmarks of the Grundig Platinum Digital G3D,
also sold as the Grundig Yacht Boy 320.

✪✪
Grundig Platinum Digital G3D, Grundig Yacht Boy 320

Price: *Platinum Digital:* $79.95 in the United
States. CAN$129.00 in Canada. *Yacht Boy
320:* £59.95 in the United Kingdom. *G2ACA
120V AC adaptor:* $12.95 in the United States.

Pro: Superior audio quality for pocket
model. 24-hour clock with alarm and clock
radio. Up/down slew tuning with signal-
seek bandscanning. Illuminated LCD.

The Grundig G4 Executive Traveller fits into its
own wallet, along with passport, currency and
credit cards.

Travel power lock (*see* Con). FM in stereo
through earpieces, not included. *North
America:* Toll-free tech support.

Con: Poor rejection of certain spurious
signals ("images"). Doesn't cover 7400-
9400 kHz world band range, although like
other single-conversion sets it can be
tricked into receiving the lower part of this
range at reduced strength by tuning the
6505-6700 kHz "image" frequencies. Lacks
keypad and tuning knob. Few presets (e.g.,
only five for 2300-7400 kHz range). Tunes
world band only in 5 kHz steps. Even-
numbered frequencies displayed with final
zero omitted; e.g., 5.73 rather than
conventional 5.730 or 5730. So-so adjacent-
channel rejection (selectivity). Unhandy
"SW1/SW2" switch to go between 2300-
7400 kHz and 9400-26100 kHz ranges.
World Time clock not displayed independent
of frequency. Nigh-useless signal-strength
and battery-dead indicators. LCD illumination not disabled when travel power lock
activated. No carrying strap or handle. AC
adaptor extra.

Verdict: Warts and all, this Chinese-made
model is a decent offering at an attractive
price, with audio quality superior to that of
most other pocket models.

✪½
Grundig G4 Executive Traveller

Price: $99.95 in the United States.

Pro: Novel concept—comes with and fits
into luxurious black leather wallet with
room for passport, money, spare batteries,
earbuds and credit cards. Packaged with
batteries and earbuds. Sensitivity to world
band signals at least average for pocket
model. Clock with alarm (see Con). Toll-
free tech support.

Con: Analog radio with a digital frequency
counter, so lacks tuning except by knob.
Does not tune 90, 60, 22, 13 or 11 meter
segments. Frequency counter completely

omits last digit so, say, 9575 kHz appears as either 9.57 or 9.58 MHz. Clock in 12-hour format only. Poor image rejection. Mediocre audio quality. Telescopic antenna does not rotate or swivel. Mediumwave AM lacks weak-signal sensitivity. Pedestrian FM, with spurious signals. On one of our new units the telescopic antenna immediately fell apart.

Verdict: Innovative and stylish. A terrific idea that includes a five-star wallet, but the Chinese-made radio is of a far lesser caliber.

✪½
Tecsun R-818

Same as the Grundig G4 Executive Traveller, above, but sans wallet.

COMPACT PORTABLES
Nice for Travel, Okay for Home

Compact portables are the most popular category because of their intersection of price, performance, size and speaker audio. They tip in at one to two pounds, under a kilogram, and are typically sized $8 \times 5 \times 1.5$ inches, or $20 \times 13 \times 4$ cm. Like pocket models, they feed off "AA" (UM-3 penlite) batteries—but, usually, more of them. They travel almost as well as pocket models, but sound better and usually receive better, too. They can also suffice as home sets.

Sports cars are in vogue once again. You can find models that are priced similarly, look alike, and are of comparable quality. Yet, some will have hard springing, others will be softer. One will have a six-gear box, another an automatic. In short, some are for driving aficionados and will probably cover a mountain road more quickly than others. However, for daily driving others may prefer something simpler and more comfortable.

So it is among the three leading compact portables. The two Sony models have

high-tech synchronous selectable side-band but pedestrian audio, while the Grundig Yacht Boy 400PE has pleasant audio and is simpler to operate. Choose accordingly.

✪✪✪¼ *Passport's Choice*
Sony ICF-SW07

Price: $419.95 in the United States. CAN$699.00 in Canada. £249.95 in the United Kingdom.

Pro: Best non-audio performance among travel portables. Eye popper. High-tech synchronous selectable sideband generally performs very well; reduces adjacent-channel interference and selective-fading distortion on world band, longwave and mediumwave AM signals while adding slightly to weak-signal sensitivity. Unusually small and light for a compact model. Numerous tuning aids, including pushbutton access of frequencies for four stations stored on a replaceable ROM, keypad, two-speed up/down slewing, 20 presets (ten for world band) and "signal-seek, then resume" bandscanning. Clamshell design aids in handiness of operation, and is further helped by

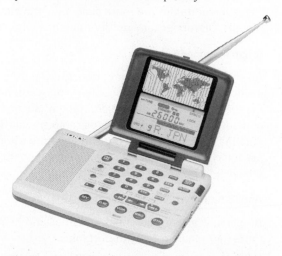

The Sony ICF-SW07 is the best performer among travel-sized radios except for audio. It comes with a full roster of advanced-technology features.

MAKE YOUR PORTABLE "HEAR" BETTER

Regardless of which portable you own, you can boost weak-signal sensitivity on the cheap. How cheap? Nothing, for starters.

Look for "sweet spots" to place your radio: near windows, appliances, telephones, I-beams and the like. If your portable has an AC adaptor, try that, then batteries; sometimes the AC adaptor does better, sometimes not.

Outdoor Antenna Can Help

An outdoor antenna isn't necessary, but it can help. Good news: With compact and smaller portable receivers, simplest is often best. Run several meters or yards of insulated wire to a tree, then clip one end to your set's telescopic antenna with an alligator or claw clip available from Radio Shack and such. It's fast and cheap, yet effective.

Use it only when needed—disconnect it during thunder, snow or sand storms and when the radio is off. And don't touch any antenna during dry weather, as you may discharge static electricity into the radio's vulnerable innards.

Sophisticated outdoor wire antennas? With most portables these can cause "overloading," usually at certain times of the night or day on frequency segments with powerful signals. You'll know this when you tune around and most of what you hear sounds like murmuring in a TV courtroom scene. Remedy: Disconnect the wire, then use the radio's telescopic antenna until you're ready to tune to another frequency segment.

If you are in a weak-signal location, such as central or western North America or Australia, and want stronger signals from a travel-sized portable, best is to erect an inverted-L (so-called "longwire") antenna. These are available at Radio Shack (278-758, $9.99) and other radio specialty outlets, or may be easily constructed from detailed instructions found in the RDI White Paper, PASSPORT *Evaluation of Popular Outdoor Antennas*. Antenna length is not critical, but keep the lead-in wire reasonably short.

However, portables are more susceptible to static damage than are tabletop and portatop models. Disconnect any outdoor antenna when storms are nearby or the radio isn't in use.

Creative Indoor Solutions

All antennas work best out of doors, away from the multitude of electrical noises found inside your home. If your supplementary antenna has to be indoors, run it along the middle of a window with Velcro, tape or suction cups. Another solution, in a reinforced-concrete building which absorbs radio signals, is to affix a long whip or telescopic car antenna outdoors almost horizontally onto a windowsill or balcony rail. Often these are essentially invisible, especially if you're high up, and they can be made even more effective by an active preselector.

Active Antennas Now Practical

Amplified ("active") antennas are small and handy. However, in the past they usually did more harm than good with portables.

The aim of any antenna is a good signal-to-noise ratio, not just raw gain which can overwhelm circuitry. Inexpensive electronic signal-booster devices also tend to fare poorly, although anecdotal evidence suggests that some help in given listening situations. Purchase these on a money-back basis so you can experiment with little risk.

Sony has come up with a surprisingly good active antenna for portables, the eighty dollar AN-LP1. (The "LP" stands for "loop.") It connects to almost any world band portable through its external-antenna socket or by being clipped onto the telescopic antenna. The 'LP1 comes with a variety of adapters for this purpose.

As detailed elsewhere in PASSPORT REPORTS, the AN-LP1 can be used with nearly any portable tested. We have found that it is a superior performer with portatop and tabletop models, as well. A variation, the AN-LP2, is identical except for automatic instead of manual preselection. For now, the 'LP2 only comes bundled with the ICF-SW07 portable and cannot be used with any other radio. However, as sophisticated new Sony models appear presumably they will be designed to work with it.

Both versions use a small amplifier module powered by two "AA" cells, along with a separate loop antenna that looks like the Jolly Green Giant's tennis racket. The two lightweight parts are joined together by over a dozen feet—four meters—of cable which can be reeled into the amplifier module, like a tape measure. The amplifier, in turn, connects to the radio. For traveling, the "tennis racquet" part of the antenna folds so it can fit into a briefcase, handbag or small carry-on.

With a few radios the antenna's circuitry picks up traces of digital hash being emitted by the receiver itself—fundamentally the result of imperfect receiver shielding. Perhaps for this reason, the AN-LP1 is not supposed be used with the Sony ICF-SW77, although in practice the combination appears to work satisfactorily. With the Sony ICF-2010 only a bit of digital hash comes through.

Our tests show that the AN-LP1 provides varying degrees of improvement, depending upon the receiver. As a rough rule of thumb, smaller models benefit more than larger ones, but all show at least some audible improvement. As the ICF-SW07 portable was designed especially to work with the AN-LP2, it really helps with weak signals.

In all, Sony's AN-LP1 and AN-LP2 antennas do yeoman's service with world band radios in need of a modest improvement in weak-signal performance. For many receivers, there's nothing better.

☞ Sony makes other models of active antennas (e.g., AN-1, AN-102). These are passable performers, but the AN-LP1 and AN-LP2 are much better and are priced about the same.

Sometimes different is best, and the Sony AN-LP1 is the best and most different antenna for portable use. A full report appears elsewhere in PASSPORT REPORTS.

illuminated LCD readable from a wide variety of angles. Hump on the rear panel places the keypad at a convenient operating angle. Comes with AN-LP2 outboard "tennis racquet" antenna, effective in enhancing weak-signal sensitivity on world band; this antenna, unlike the AN-LP1, has automatic preselector tuning. Good single sideband performance (*see* Con). Clock covers most international time zones, as well as World Time. Outstanding reception of weak and crowded FM stations, with limited urban FM overloading resolved by variable-level attenuator. FM stereo through earpieces, supplied. Longwave and Japanese FM bands. Above-average reception of mediumwave AM band. Travel power lock. Closing clamshell does not interfere with speaker. Low-battery indicator. Presets information is non-volatile, can't be erased when batteries changed. Two turn-on times for alarm/clock radio. Sixty-minute snooze. Hinged battery cover can't be misplaced. AC adaptor.

Con: Pedestrian audio quality, made worse by the lack of a second, wider, bandwidth and meaningful tone control. Lacks tuning knob. Display shows time and tuned frequency, but not both at the same time. Tuning resolution of 0.1 kHz above 1620 kHz means that non-synchronous single-sideband reception can be mis-tuned by up to 50 Hz, so audio quality varies. Synchronous selectable sideband tends to lose lock if batteries weak, or if NiCd cells are used. Synchronous selectable sideband alignment can vary with temperature, factory alignment and battery voltage, causing synchronous selectable sideband reception to be slightly more muffled in one sideband than the other. No meaningful signal-strength indicator. LCD frequency/ time numbers relatively small for size of display, with only average contrast. AN-LP2 accessory antenna has to be physically disconnected for proper mediumwave AM reception. 1621-1700 kHz portion of American AM band is erroneously treated

as shortwave, although this does not harm reception quality. Low battery indicator misreads immediately after batteries installed; clears up when radio is turned on. Local time shown only in 24-hour format. UTC, or World Time, displays as "London" time even during the summer, when London is an hour off from World Time. DST key can change UTC in error.

☞ A version without the AN-LP2 antenna and certain other accessories may eventually be offered outside North America.

Verdict: Speaker audio aside, this Japanese-made model is the best available for travel—and a killer eyeful.

Retested for 2001

✪✪✪⅛ ☯ *Passport's Choice*
Sony ICF-SW7600G, Sony ICF-SW7600GS

Price: *ICF-SW7600G:* $169.95 in the United States. CAN$299.00 in Canada. £119.95 in the United Kingdom. AUS$449.00 in Australia. ¥2,700 in China. *AC-E60HG 120V AC adaptor:* $19.95 in the United States.

Pro: One of the great values in world band radio. Far and away the least-costly model available with high-tech synchronous selectable sideband; this generally performs well, reducing adjacent-channel interference and selective-fading distortion on world band, longwave and mediumwave AM signals while adding slightly to weak-signal sensitivity (*see* Con). Single bandwidth, especially when synchronous selectable sideband is used, exceptionally effective at adjacent-channel rejection. Robust—superior quality of components and assembly for price class. Numerous helpful tuning features, including keypad, two-speed up/down slewing, presets and "signal-seek, then resume" bandscanning. For those with limited hearing of high-frequency sounds, such as some men over the half-century mark, audio quality may be preferable to that of Grundig Yacht Boy 400PE/400. Single-sideband performance arguably the best of any portable; analog clarifier, combined with LSB/USB switch, allow single-sideband signals (e.g., AFRTS, utility, amateur) to be tuned with uncommon precision, and thus with superior carrier phasing and the resulting natural-sounding audio. World Time clock, easy to set. Reel-in outboard passive antenna accessory. Snooze/timer. Illuminated LCD readable from a wide variety of angles. Travel power lock. Superior reception of difficult mediumwave AM stations. Superior FM capture ratio helps separate co-channel stations. FM stereo through earpieces or headphones. Longwave and Japanese FM bands. Superior battery life. Weak-battery indicator. *ICF-SW7600GS (where available):* Comes with excellent AN-LP1 active antenna to enhance weak-signal reception.

Con: Three switches, including those for synchronous selectable sideband, located unhandily at the side of the cabinet. No tuning knob. Twenty presets, of which only ten function for world band stations. Clock not readable when radio is switched on. No meaningful signal-strength indicator. Synchronous selectable sideband tends to lose lock if batteries weak, or if NiCd cells are used. Synchronous selectable sideband alignment can vary with temperature, factory alignment and battery voltage, causing synchronous selectable sideband reception to be slightly more muffled in one sideband than the other. *ICF-7600G:* Factory AC adaptor a costly extra, although Sony "wall warts" tend to be among the best. No earphones or earpieces. *ICF-SW7600GS:* Not available in the United States or just about anywhere else.

Verdict: So much bang for the buck it's almost ridiculous, even though the Sony ICF-7600G is manufactured in high-cost Japan. Its advanced-tech synchronous

The Sony ICF-7600G is one of the two best values in a compact portable, and the only one near its price that comes with synchronous selectable sideband.

selectable sideband helps greatly in rejecting adjacent-channel interference and selective-fading distortion, even though its audio quality is only *ordinaire.* Top drawer single-sideband reception for a portable, too, along with superior tough-signal FM and mediumwave reception. Years of widespread use show that it is built to last, and is outstandingly priced for all it does so well.

Evaluation of Latest Unit: We've tested numerous ICF-7600G receivers over the years, and each time it was the same story except that quality control kept getting better until they finally got it nailed down a few years back. This time around, alignment was absolutely spot on and everything worked exactly as it should—we even slammed it around a bit, with nary a hiccup.

✪✪✪ ✦ *Passport's Choice*
Grundig Yacht Boy 400PE, Grundig Yacht Boy 400

Price: *400PE:* $199.95 in the United States. CAN$249.00 in Canada. *400PE (refurbished used units, as available):* $139.95 in the United States. CAN$199.00 in Canada. *400, while available:* £129.95 in the United Kingdom. AUS$399.00 in

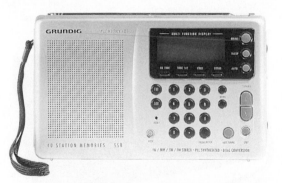

The Grundig Yacht Boy 400PE is one of the most popular and well-liked of world band radios. Affordable and easy to use, with superior sound.

Australia. *400 (refurbished used units), while available:* CAN$149.00 in Canada. £99.95 in the United Kingdom.

Pro: Audio quality tops in size category for those with sharp hearing. Two bandwidths, both well-chosen. Ergonomically superior, a pleasure to operate. A number of helpful tuning features, including keypad, up/down slewing, 40 station presets, "signal seek" frequency scanning and scanning of station presets. Signal-strength indicator. World Time clock with second

time zone, any one of which is shown at all times; however, clock displays seconds only when radio is off. Illuminated display. Alarm/snooze. Tunable BFO allows for superior signal phasing during single-sideband reception. Reel-in outboard wire antenna supplements telescopic antenna. Generally superior FM performance. FM in stereo through headphones. Longwave. *400PE:* 120V AC adaptor. *North America:* Toll-free tech support.

Con: Circuit noise ("hiss") can be slightly intrusive with weak signals. No tuning knob. At many locations there can be breakthrough of powerful AM or FM stations into the world band spectrum. Keypad not in telephone format. No LSB/USB switch.

☞ Refurbished used units reportedly include returns from department stores and other outlets where customers tend to be unfamiliar with world band radio. Everything but the radio itself is supposed to be replaced. Limited availability.

Verdict: An exceptional value in a legendary and pleasant receiver for hearing world band programs. Superior audio quality, dual bandwidths and simplicity of operation set this Chinese-made compact receiver apart—even though circuit noise with weak signals could be lower.

⭐⭐⭐
Sony ICF-SW55, Sony ICF-SW55E

Price: £224.95 as available in the United Kingdom.

Pro: Audio quality. Dual bandwidths. Logical controls. Innovative tuning, with alphabetic identifiers for groups ("pages") of stations; some like this approach. Weak-signal sensitivity a bit better than most. Demodulates single-sideband signals (*see* Con). Reel-in antenna, AC adaptor, earbuds and cord for external DC power. Signal/battery strength indicator. Local

The robust Sony ICF-SW55 has been on the market for several years, but is no longer available except in the United Kingdom.

and World Time clocks, one displayed separately from frequency. Snooze/alarm. Five-event (daily only) timer. Illuminated display. Longwave and Japanese FM.

Con: As we go to press, still available new, mainly in the U.K. Page tuning system cumbersome for some. Spurious-signal rejection in higher segments not commensurate with price. Wide bandwidth rather broad for receiver lacking synchronous selectable sideband. Tuning increments of 0.1 kHz and frequency readout of 1 kHz compromise single-sideband reception. Some readers report BFO pulling causes audio quavering, not found in our test units. Display illumination dim and uneven. High battery consumption.

Verdict: Overpriced, but if you like the Sony ICF-SW55's operating scheme and want a small portable with good audio quality, this veteran model is a respectable performer in its size class. But this Japanese-made unit, now reportedly discontinued, lacks synchronous selectable sideband—a major plus found on newer Sony models.

❊❊❊
Sangean ATS 909, Radio Shack DX-398, Roberts R861

Price: *Sangean:* $259.95 in the United States. CAN$369.00 in Canada. £169.95 in the United Kingdom. AUS$382.00 in Australia. *AC adaptor:* £9.95 in the United Kingdom. *Radio Shack:* $249.99 in the United States; CAN$399.99 in Canada. *Roberts:* £199.95 in United Kingdom.

Pro: Exceptionally wide range of tuning facilities and hundreds of world band presets, including one which works with a single touch. "Page" tuning system uses 29 pages and alphanumeric station descriptors for world band. Two voice bandwidths. Tunes single sideband in unusually precise 0.04 kHz increments, making this one of the best portables for listening to single-sideband signals (*see* Con). Dynamic range

The Sangean ATS 909 is also sold as the Radio Shack DX-398 and Roberts R861. It boasts a sophisticated tuning system and good single-sideband reception.

slightly above average for portable. Travel power lock. 24-hour clock shows at all times, and can display local time in various cities of the world (*see* Con). 1-10 digital signal-strength indicator. Low-battery indicator. Clock radio feature offers three "on" times for three discrete frequencies. Snooze feature. FM is sensitive to weak signals (see Con) and performs well overall, has RDS feature (*see* Con), and is in stereo through earpieces, supplied. Illuminated display. Superior ergonomics, including tuning knob with tactile detents. Longwave. *ATS 909 (North American units):* Superb multivoltage AC adaptor with North American and European plugs. ANT-60 reel-in outboard wire antenna. Sangean service provided by Sangean America to models sold under its name. *DX-398:* 30-day money-back period in the United States and Canada; in Canada, product cannot have been opened.

Con: Tuning knob tends to mute stations during bandscanning (the C. Crane Company offers $20.00/$29.95 modification to remedy this). Large and heavy for a compact. Weak-signal sensitivity not equal to that of better competing models. Signal-seek bandscanning, although flexible and relatively sophisticated, tends to stop on few active shortwave signals. Although scanner can operate out-of-band, reverts to default (in-band) parameters after one pass. Two-second wait between when preset is keyed and station becomes audible. Although synthesizer tunes in 0.04 kHz increments, frequency readout only in 1 kHz increments. Other software oddities; e.g., under certain conditions, alphanumeric station descriptor may stay on full time. Page tuning system cumbersome for some. Audio quality only so-so, not aided by three-level treble-cut tone control. No carrying handle or strap. 24-hour clock set up to display home time, not World Time, although this is easily overcome by not using world-cities-time feature. Clock does not compensate for daylight (summer) time in each displayed city. FM can overload in high-signal-strength environments, causing false "repeat" signals to appear; capture ratio average. RDS, which can automatically display FM-station IDs and update clock, is of limited use, as it requires a stronger signal than it should to activate. Heterodyne interference, possibly related to the digital display, sometimes interferes with reception of strong mediumwave AM signals. Battery consumption well above average; would profit from lower current draw or larger (e.g., "C") cell size. Elevation panel flimsy. *ATS 909:* AC adaptor lacks UL approval. *DX-398:* Warranty only 90 days in the United States and some other countries.

Verdict: A popular Taiwanese-made offering for those seeking a wide range of operating features and relatively precise tuning of single-sideband signals.

✪✪⅞ ✐
Sangean ATS-808A, Roberts R809

Price: *Sangean:* $139.95 in the United States. CAN$199.00 in Canada. £84.95 in the United Kingdom. AUS$299.00 in Australia. *ADP-808 120V AC adaptor:* $10.95 in the United States. *Roberts:* £99.95 in the United Kingdom.

Pro: The best value on the thrifty side of the Sony ICF-SW7600G. Dual bandwidths, a major plus that's exceptional anywhere near this price class (*see* Con). Relatively simple to operate for technology class. Various helpful tuning features include two-speed tuning knob, although only 18 presets for world band. Weak-signal sensitivity a bit better than most. Keypad has exceptional feel and tactile response. Longwave. World Time clock, displayed separately from frequency, and local clock. Alarm/snooze. Seven-level signal strength and battery indicator. Travel power lock. Stereo FM via earpieces, supplied. Superior FM reception.

Con: Fast tuning tends to mute receiver when tuning knob is turned quickly. Narrow bandwidth performance only fair. Spurious-signal ("image") rejection, although above average, not equal to that of top-rated portables. Pedestrian audio quality with two-level tone switch. Display not illuminated. Keypad not in telephone format. No carrying strap or handle. AC adaptor extra. Country of manufacture (now China) not specified on radio or box.

One of the best bargains in a world band portable is the Sangean ATS 808A. In the United Kingdom it is also available as the Roberts R809.

Verdict: This Sangean offering is the best value in an under-$165 world band radio, with relative simplicity of operation and superior overall performance. If you don't need single-sideband capability, the ATS-808A is a better overall choice than the sibling ATS-505, below, for reception of weak or interfered world band signals.

New for 2001

✪✪¾

Sangean ATS 505, Radio Shack DX-402, Roberts R9914, Roberts R9914/BBC World Service

Price: *Sangean:* $129.95 in the United States. CAN$199.00 in Canada. £99.00 in the United Kingdom. AUS$227.00 in Australia. *ADP-808 120V AC Adaptor:* $10.95 in the United States. *Radio Shack:* $149.95 in the United States. *Roberts:* £99.95 in the United Kingdom.

Pro: Numerous helpful tuning features, including two-speed tuning knob, keypad, presets (*see* Con), up/down slewing, meter-band carousel selection, signal-seek band-scan tuning and scanning of presets (*see* Con). Automatic-sorting feature arranges presets in frequency order. Analog clarifier with center detent and stable circuitry allows single-sideband signals to be tuned with uncommon precision and to stay properly tuned, thus allowing for superior audio phasing for a portable (*see* Con). Illuminated LCD. Dual 24/12-hour clocks for World Time and local time. Alarm/snooze. Modest battery consumption. Nine-level battery-reserve indicator. Travel power lock (*see* Con). FM stereo through earbuds, supplied. Longwave. *ATS-505:* In North America, service provided by Sangean America to models sold under its name. *DX-402:* 30-day money-back period in the United States and Canada; in Canada, product cannot have been opened.

Con: Bandwidth slightly wider than appropriate for a single-bandwidth

The new Sangean ATS 505 is not quite the equal of the comparably priced Sangean ATS 808A, but it demodulates single-sideband signals.

receiver (try detuning slightly to reduce 5 kHz world band heterodyne interference). Large for a compact. Only 18 world band presets (divided up between two "pages" with nine presets apiece). Tuning knob tends to mute stations during bandscanning by knob, especially when tuning rate is set to fine (1 kHz); muting with coarse (5 kHz) tuning is much less objectionable. Keys respond slowly, needing to be held down momentarily rather than simply tapped. Stop-listen-resume scanning of presets is slow. Pedestrian overall single-sideband reception because of excessively wide bandwidth and occasional distortion caused by AGC timing. Clock does not display independent of frequency. No meaningful signal-strength indicator. AC adaptor extra. No carrying handle or strap. Country of manufacture (China) not specified on radio or box. Travel power lock does not deactivate LCD illumination key. *Radio Shack:* Warranty only 90 days in the United States and some other countries.

Verdict: The best bet in a low-cost portable which demodulates single-sideband signals, but also consider other models if this feature is not needed.

Evaluation of New Model: World band radio stations almost always transmit in the AM—amplitude modulation—mode, the same used by stations in the medium-wave AM band covered by virtually every radio. Because it has been in existence for nearly a hundred years, this mode is sometimes referred to as "ancient modulation." Nevertheless, because it is easily received by inexpensive receivers it continues to remain hugely popular even into the 21st century.

Even if and when world band transmissions go over to digital, there is at least some chance that it will be an in-band, on-channel (IBOC or iDAB) system. This would allow digital transmissions to be receivable on the hundreds of millions of legacy world band radios scattered around the world.

AM-mode signals have two sidebands, each of which carries the same information as the other; in effect, either of the two sidebands is redundant. So, late in the first half of the 20th century a refined mode was developed in which only one sideband would be transmitted. This single-side-band mode (SSB) is more efficient than AM, but it requires a relatively sophisti-cated receiver and is much fussier to tune.

Tabletop and portatop models excel with SSB, but some portables can do yeoman's service with these signals. These range in price from the $170 Sony ICF-7600G to the $260 Sangean ATS 909 to the $470 Sony ICF-SW77. But below the $170 threshold there has been little in the way of accept-able choice.

Ample Features

Enter the $130 ATS 505, Sangean's newest compact portable—albeit a very large compact portable. It not only demodulates single-sideband signals, but also it includes a plus-or-minus 1.9 kHz analog

clarifier—BFO pitch control—complete with a handy center detent. This allows for precise phasing of the transmitted signal with the receiver's BFO, which must be tuned exactly in phase with the station's signal for voices and music to sound natural. Another plus is that the '505's stable circuitry helps ensure that once a station has been tuned in properly, it won't drift and have to be retuned.

The '505 comes with a two-speed tuning knob—to alter the tuning rate, push in the knob. This is a real plus in this price category, where most digitally tuned receivers have no tuning knob whatsoever. In the fine (1 kHz) setting, the receiver mutes excessively, making bandscanning a frustratingly slow chore. Thankfully, this problem is largely relieved when the coarse (5 kHz) setting is used.

Other useful tuning features include a keypad, 18 world band presets (nine on each of two "pages") plus 27 presets for FM and other bands, up/down frequency slewing, sequential selection of world band segments (49 meters, etc.), and signal-seek bandscanning. Additionally, presets may be scanned, and there is even a sensible feature which allows you to automatically sort presets in frequency order for orderly scanning. This can be useful when you have, say, all nine presets in a given "page" devoted to frequencies of a favorite station so the scanner will search out, in logical frequency order, the active frequencies for that station.

Ergonomically, the '505's tuning configura-tion is good, except that the keys can't be pressed too quickly or the entry may not fully "take." The two-speed tuning knob is an overall advantage, although some find the in-out shifting scheme to be unhandy. The commendably large, illuminated LCD is easy to read head-on or from below, although not from above.

The '505 comes with a travel power lock that, among other things, prevents the radio from being accidentally switched on in a suitcase. As is the case with many Chinese-made receivers, the power lock doesn't disable the illumination key. In recent years Sangean has dropped carrying straps and handles from its line of world band portables, and the '505 is no exception. A radio this size would profit from a simple cloth carrying strap across the top.

The radio is powered by four "AA" cells which, especially if alkaline, rarely need replacement, thanks to the radio's low current drain. As a result, the '505's lack of an AC adaptor is relatively forgivable.

The digital clock covers two time zones in user-selectable 24- or 12-hour format—the chosen format works with both clocks— and it's easy to adjust. Although the clock does not display independent of the displayed frequency, the touch of a key swaps time for frequency on the LCD.

That LCD also includes a handy nine-level battery reserve indicator. Surprisingly, that same 1-9 scale doesn't double as a signal-strength indicator. Instead, a greenish-yellow LED "glow light" tells you when a signal is present—something you already know when you hear a station, so what's the point except perhaps for open carriers? To remind you that the BFO is in the "on" position—the switch, being on the side of the cabinet, is not readily visible—the LED changes over to continuously red when the BFO is on (SSB setting), regardless of whether any signal is present.

Performance

The 505's world band selectivity is typical for its price class, but nonetheless is a far cry from the flexible selectivity of the comparably priced ATS 808A. With the only bandwidth being wider than ideal

TIPS FOR GLOBETROTTING

Airline security and customs are rarely issues in most countries—with the preponderance of laptop computers, world band portables now rarely rate a suspicious glance. A number of PASSPORT editors have traveled unmolested throughout Western Europe, North America and the Caribbean for years, with Sony ICF-2010s in tow.

However, in some other parts of the world officials can be downright ornery. To avoid hassles with these folks:

• Bring a pocket or compact model. Terrorists like big radios.

• Stow your radio in a carry-on bag, not in checked luggage or on your person.

• Take along fresh batteries so you can demonstrate that the radio actually works.

• If asked what the radio is for, say for personal use.

• If traveling in zones of war or civil unrest, or off the beaten path in much of Africa or parts of South America, take along a radio you can afford to lose and which fits inconspicuously in a pocket.

• If traveling to Bahrain, avoid taking a radio which has the word "receiver" on its cabinet. Security personnel may think you're a spy.

Theft? Radios, cameras, binoculars, laptop computers and the like are almost always stolen to be resold. The more worn the item looks—affixing scuffed stickers helps—the less likely it is to be confiscated by corrupt inspectors or stolen by thieves.

when there is no narrow alternative, adjacent-channel heterodyne interference (5 kHz whistle) is commonplace on the '505. Manual "ECSS" (tuning AM-mode signals as though they were SSB) works poorly on this model, but simple detuning by one or two kilohertz often helps reduce interference without creating undue distortion.

Of course, for the half-as-narrow SSB mode, the bandwidth is far too broad, letting in not only the intended signal but also interference and static adjacent to that signal. Too, the AGC timing is not fully appropriate for SSB, resulting in occasional bursts of distortion.

Spurious-signal rejection is quite good, which is a major plus at or near the 505's price point. Many less-costly portables have simple single-conversion circuitry which actually creates extra interference within the receiver, making shortwave listening more aurally challenging than it already is.

Weak-signal sensitivity is decent, but like the Sangean ATS 909 it is not quite equal to that of some other models, such as the Sony ICF-2010 and Sangean's similarly priced ATS-808A (see preceding review). Audio quality is predictable—about

average for its size class and a touch better than that of the '808A. There is a simple three-step switched tone control, like on many other world band portables.

Sangean's ATS 505 and ATS 808A are similarly priced and sized, but are far from the same. The '505 is obviously the choice for those tuning single-sideband signals, but the '808A is more appropriate for general world band listening—especially in weak-signal parts of the world.

New for 2001
✪✪¾ 🅒
Sony ICF-SW35

Price: $89.95 in the United States. CAN$179.95 as available in Canada. £69.95 in the United Kingdom. AUS$259.00 in Australia. *AC-E45HG 120V AC adaptor:* $19.95 in the United States.

Pro: Superior reception quality, with excellent and spurious-signal rejection. Fifty world band presets, which can be scanned within five "pages." Signal-seek-then-resume scanning works unusually well. Two-speed slewing. Illuminated display. World Time and local time clock. Dual-time alarm. Snooze feature (60/45/30/15 minutes). Travel power lock. FM stereo through headphones, not supplied. Weak-battery indicator. Receives longwave and the Japanese FM band.

Con: No keypad or tuning knob. Synthesizer muting and poky slewing degrade bandscanning. Audio quality clear, but lacks low-frequency response ("bass"). Clock not displayed independent of frequency. LCD lacks contrast when viewed from above. AC adaptor, relatively needed, is extra and pricey.

Verdict: The new Sony ICF-SW35 is notable mainly for its superior rejection of spurious image signals that are the bane of nearly all other under-$100 models. This Chinese-made compact lacks a keypad,

New for 2001 is the budget-priced Sony ICF-SW35. Unlike other Sony world band radios, it is manufactured in China.

which is partially overcome by the large number of presets and effective scanning. Overall, a decent low-cost choice if you listen to a predictable roster of stations.

Evaluation of New Model: The new Chinese-made ICF-SW35, which replaces the Japanese-made ICF-SW30, is exceptionally straightforward to operate. There's no keypad or tuning knob, no single-sideband demodulation, no headphones and no AC power supply.

Tuning is limited to two-speed (1 kHz and 5 kHz increments) up/down slewing control, 50 world band presets that can be scanned within five handy "pages," signal-seek-then-resume scanning, and a meter-band carousel. Unlike the earlier 'SW30, it tunes the entire world band range continuously from 2250-26100 kHz.

The sophisticated 50-preset, five-page tuning system is usually found only in receivers costing much more. It is very handy if you listen to the same stations, as it allows you store up to ten quick-access frequencies for up to five stations, then forget it except for occasional seasonal frequency adjustments. Even if the batteries go dead your presets won't erase.

There's a 24-hour two-time-zone clock/alarm, even though you can't see the clock unless the radio is turned off. There's also a travel power lock that also deactivates the LCD light, and FM is in stereo when you listen with headphones. For bedtime, there's a four-level snooze control, plus the radio can be set to turn on at any one given time to function as an alarm, or simply to switch on a favorite program. The telescopic antenna rotates and swivels, and there's an elevation panel so the radio can be operated at a comfortable angle.

Alas, there is no keypad. Bandscanning is further worsened because the slewing controls mute out all but odd bits of what there is to hear. However, no radio under $100 is without some major compromise,

and for many listeners the lack of a keypad is preferable to degraded reception.

Performance is predictable but good, with superior rejection of "image" signals that are otherwise commonplace with nearly all other under-$100 models. It's an enormous plus for making shortwave listening pleasant. Audio quality is crisp and clear, but has mighty little bottom. Selectivity and weak-signal sensitivity are reasonable.

Overall, the Sony ICF-SW35 is a sensible choice in the under-$100 class if you listen to the same stations, but not to hunt and peck through the world band spectrum.

Discontinued, sometimes available
✪✪¾
Grundig Yacht Boy 500

Price: £89.95 in the United Kingdom, while supplies last.

Pro: Attractive layout. Audio-boost circuitry for powerful volume, useful in noisy environments. Forty presets, with

The Yacht Boy 500 represents the last of Grundig's European-made world band radios. It sports avant-garde styling and unusually powerful audio.

alphanumeric names displayed. RDS circuitry for FM. ROM with 90 preassigned channels for nine broadcasters. Two 24-hour clocks, one displays fulltime. Battery-low indicator. FM in stereo via headphones. Travel power lock. Three-increment signal-strength indicator. Analog clarifier with center detent and stable circuitry allows single-sideband signals to be tuned with uncommon precision, thus allowing for superior audio phasing for a portable. Single-sideband reception via handy LSB/USB key. Illuminated display. Timer/snooze. Worldwide dual-voltage AC adaptor and two types of plugs. Audio quality reasonably good. Longwave.

Con: Circuit noise relatively high. Lacks tuning knob. Telescopic antenna tends to get in the way of right-handed users. Volume slider fussy to adjust. Keypad not in telephone format. Stylish key design and layout increase likelihood of wrong key being pushed. Elevation panel and AC adaptor socket flimsy. Factory-preassigned channels relatively complex for beginners to select. Excessive spurious "birdie" signals.

Verdict: Attractive design, with reasonably good performance, powerful audio and a number of worthwhile features are the

For years Radio Shack has carried a series of low-cost digital portables. The DX-396 is its latest and most refined offering—an excellent buy when discounted during special sales.

hallmarks of this, the last of Grundig's European-made (Portugal) digital portables. But better performance and ergonomics can be had in other models for the same price or less.

New for 2001
★★⅝ ✪
Radio Shack DX-396

Price: $99.99 in the United States.

Pro: Superior weak-signal sensitivity, particularly in higher bands used during the daytime. Several handy tuning features, including keypad, 30 presets (10 for world band), slewing, signal-seek scanning, memory scanning and meter-band selection. Two 24/12-hour clocks, one labeled "World Time" (*see* Con). Stereo FM through headphones, not supplied. Travel power lock. Alarm. 15/30/45/60-minute snooze. Weak battery indicator. 30-day money-back period.

Con: Spurious-signal ("image") rejection and dynamic range only fair. Lacks tuning knob. Tunes shortwave only in 5 kHz increments. Clocks don't display when frequency is shown, although pushbutton allows World Time to replace frequency. Signal-strength indicator merely a single LED. AC adaptor extra. Does not tune above 21850 kHz. FM capture ratio just fair. Warranty only 90 days.

☞ According to the manufacturer, the built-in ferrite rod antenna is used not only for mediumwave AM, but also for shortwave 2300-7095 kHz, and there is no external antenna jack. Nevertheless, if an outboard shortwave antenna is clipped to the built-in telescopic antenna it will impact signals below 7100 kHz.

Verdict: This Chinese-made model is a solid low-cost choice for daytime reception, as well as for nighttime listening where signal strengths are substandard. Especially during Radio Shack's periodic sales, the

DX-396 makes an attractively priced entry-level receiver.

✪✪½
Sony ICF-SW40

Price: $119.95 in the United States. £84.95 in the United Kingdom. *AC-E45HG 120V AC adaptor:* $19.95.

Pro: Relatively affordable. Technologically unintimidating for older traditionalists, as its advanced digital tuning circuitry is disguised to look like slide-rule, or analog, tuning. 24-hour clock. Two "on" timers and snooze. Travel power lock. Illuminated LCD. Covers Japanese FM band.

Con: Single bandwidth is relatively wide, reducing adjacent-channel rejection. No keypad. Lacks coverage of 1625-1705 kHz portion of North American mediumwave AM band. AC adaptor, much-needed, is extra and overpriced.

Verdict: If you're turned off by things digital and complex, Sony's Japanese-made ICF-SW40 will feel like an old friend in your hands. Otherwise, forget it.

✪✪½
Sangean ATS 404, Roberts R881

Price: *Sangean:* $99.95 in the United States. CAN$129.00 in Canada. £59.95 in the United Kingdom. AUS$154.00 in Australia. *ADP-808 120V AC adaptor:* $10.95 in the United States. *Roberts:* £79.95 in the United Kingdom.

Pro: Superior weak-signal sensitivity. Several handy tuning features. Stereo FM through earpieces, supplied. Two 24/12-hour clocks display seconds numerically. Alarm/snooze. Travel power lock. Illuminated LCD. Battery indicator.

Con: Poor spurious-signal ("image") rejection. No tuning knob. Overloading, controllable by shortening telescopic

Apparently there are still folks who are intimidated by anything digital. For them, Sony offers the ICF-SW40—digital, but cleverly disguised to seem analog.

antenna on world band and collapsing it on mediumwave AM band. Picks up some internal digital hash. Tunes only in 5 kHz increments. No signal-strength indicator. Frequency and time cannot be displayed simultaneously. Power lock does not disable LCD illumination. No handle or carrying strap. AC adaptor extra. Country of manufacture (China) not specified on radio or box.

Verdict: Value priced.

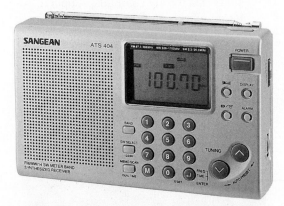

Sangean manufactures several worthy portables, but the compact ATS 404 is not one of them. Still, it is affordable and has above-average sensitivity to weak signals.

A welcome improvement for 2001 is the Grundig Yacht Boy 300PE, which finally tunes all world band segments. It is essentially a rechristened Tecsun PL757.

Revised for 2001
✪✪½
Grundig Yacht Boy 300PE, Tecsun PL757

Price: $99.95 in the United States. CAN$99.95 in Canada.

Pro: Sensitive to weak world band and FM signals. Various helpful tuning features. World Time clock with alarm, clock radio and 10-90 minute snooze (*see* Con). Illuminated LCD (*see* Con). 120V AC adaptor (North America) and supplementary antenna. Travel power lock (*see* Con). Stereo FM through earbuds, supplied. *North America:* Toll-free tech support.

The Radio Shack DX-375 continues to be available, but in much of the world it has been replaced by the DX-396. Differences are minor.

Con: Mediocre spurious-signal ("image") rejection. No tuning knob. Few presets; e.g., only six for 2300-7800 kHz range. Tunes world band only in 5 kHz steps. Even-numbered frequencies displayed with final zero omitted; e.g., 5.73 MHz rather than usual 5730 kHz. Keypad entry of even channels with all digits (e.g., 6 - 1 - 9 - 0, Enter) tunes radio 5 kHz higher (e.g., 6195); remedied by not entering trailing zero (e.g., 6 - 1 - 9, Enter). Unhandy carouseling "MW/SW1/SW2/FM" control required for tuning within 2300-7800 kHz *vs.* 9100-26100 kHz range or *vice versa*. Clock not displayed independent of frequency; button changes which is visible. Nigh-useless signal-strength indicator. LCD illumination not disabled by travel power lock.

Verdict: Except for LCD illumination being permanently enabled, the Chinese-made Grundig Yacht Boy 300PE is priced and sized to be an unusually sensible choice for traveling, as well as for where signals tend to be weak.

Evaluation of Revised Model: Fuller shortwave coverage has finally been implemented in the revised YB-300PE, which now tunes the 7305-7800 and 9100-9495 kHz ranges missing in the original version. The radio also no longer mutes during slew tuning, which makes band-scanning considerably easier and faster. Finally, once-tinny audio now has better low-frequency reproduction, although sound quality is still only middling.

✪✪½
Radio Shack DX-375

Price: CAN$199.99.

Pro: Several handy tuning features. Weak-signal sensitivity a bit above average. Stereo FM through headphones, not supplied. Travel power lock. Timer. 30-day money-back period in Canada; product cannot have been opened.

Con: Mediocre spurious-signal ("image") rejection. Unusually long pauses when tuning from channel to channel. Lacks tuning knob. Doesn't tune 6251-7099 kHz. Tunes only in 5 kHz increments. Antenna swivel sometimes needs tightening. Static discharges may disable microprocessor (usually remediable if batteries removed for a time, then replaced). No World Time clock. Signal-strength indicator only a single LED. AC adaptor extra.

Verdict: Made in China, this is being replaced in some markets by the DX-396 *(see)*.

Someday there will be a first-rate portable that looks as good as it performs. In the meantime, the Grundig Porsche-designed 2000 is the most stylish radio on the market.

✪✪
Grundig G2000A "Porsche Design," Grundig Porsche P2000

Price: *G2000A:* $149.95 in the United States. CAN$199.00 in Canada. *P2000:* £89.95 in the United Kingdom. AUS$219.00 in Australia. *G2ACA 120V AC adaptor:* $12.95 in the United States.

Pro: One of the most functionally attractive world band radios on the market, with generally superior ergonomics that include an effective and handy lambskin protective case. Superior adjacent-channel rejection—selectivity—for price and size class. Keypad (in proper telephone format), handy meter-band carousel control, signal-seek bandscanning and up/down slew tuning. Twenty station presets, of which ten are for world band and the rest for FM and mediumwave AM stations. FM stereo through earpieces, supplied. World Time clock. Timer/snooze/alarm. Illuminated display. Travel power lock. Microprocessor reset control. *North America:* Toll-free tech support.

Con: Mediocre audio quality. Sensitivity mediocre between 9400-26100 kHz, improving slightly between 2300-7400 kHz. Poor spurious-signal ("image") rejection. Does not tune such important world band ranges as 7405-7550 and

9350-9395 kHz. Tunes world band only in 5 kHz steps and displays in nonstandard XX.XX MHz/XX.XX₅ MHz format characteristic of low-cost Chinese radios. No tuning knob. Annoying one-second pause when tuning from one channel to the next. Old-technology SW1/SW2 switch complicates tuning. Protruding power button can get in the way of nearby slew-tuning and meter-carousel keys. Leather case makes it difficult to retrieve folded telescopic antenna. Magnetic catches weak on leather case. No carrying strap. Signal-strength indicator nigh useless. Clock not displayed separately from frequency. AC adaptor extra.

Verdict: This German-styled, Chinese-manufactured portable is the ultimate in tasteful design for men and women alike, although performance is of a lesser caliber.

✪½
Bolong HS-490

Price: ¥360 in China.

Pro: Inexpensive for a model with digital frequency display, ten world band station presets, and ten station presets for

In China the Bolong HS-490 is reportedly the most popular world band radio. Not surprisingly, it is cheap with performance to match.

mediumwave AM and FM. World Time clock (*see* Con). Reel-type outboard passive antenna accessory. AC adaptor. Illuminated display. Alarm/snooze. FM stereo (*see* Con) via earbuds, included.

Con: Seemingly nearly impossible to find outside China. Requires patience to get a station, as it tunes world band only via 10 station presets and multi-speed up/down slewing/scanning. Tunes world band only in 5 kHz steps. Even-numbered frequencies displayed with final zero omitted; e.g., 5.75 rather than conventional 5.750 or 5750. Poor spurious-signal ("image") rejection. So-so adjacent-channel rejection (selectivity). World Time clock not displayed independent of frequency. Does not receive relatively unimportant 6200-7100 kHz portion of world band spectrum. Does not receive 1615-1705 kHz portion of expanded AM band in the Americas. No signal-strength indicator. No travel power lock. Medium-wave AM 9/10 kHz tuning increments not selectable, which may make for inexact tuning in some parts of the world other than where the radio was purchased. FM selectivity and capture ratio mediocre. FM stereo did not trigger on our unit.

Verdict: Made by a joint venture between Xin Hui Electronics and Shanghai Huaxin Electronic Instruments. No prize, but as

good you'll find among the truly cheap, which probably accounts for this model's being the #1 seller among digital world band radios in China.

LAP PORTABLES
Pleasant for Home, Acceptable for Travel

A lap portable is probably your best bet for use primarily around the home and yard, plus on occasional trips. They are large enough to perform well sound better than compact models, yet they are not too big to fit into a carry-on or briefcase. Most take 3-4 "D" (UM-1) or "C" (UM-2) cells, plus they may also use a couple of "AA" (UM-3) cells for memory backup.

These are typically just under a foot wide—that's 30 cm—and weighing in around 3-4 pounds, or 1.3-1.8 kg. For air travel, that's okay if you are a dedicated listener, but a bit much otherwise. Too, larger sets with snazzy controls occasionally attract unwanted attention from suspicious customs and airport-security personnel in some parts of the world (see sidebar).

Two models stand out for most listeners: the Sony ICF-2010 and Sony ICF-SW77, which unfortunately are hard to find outside the United States. They have the same overall rating, but many who favor one don't much care for the other. The Sangean ATS-818 is hardly in the same league, but at its current American pricing it is an attractive option.

Retested for 2001
✪✪✪¾ 📖 *Passport's Choice*
Sony ICF-2010

Price: $349.95 in the United States. CAN$599.00 in Canada, while supplies last. Not distributed by Sony outside the United States, but widely available worldwide by mail order or email from major American world band specialty firms.

Pro: High-tech synchronous selectable sideband, thanks to a Sony proprietary chip with sideband phase canceling; this well-executed feature performs, overall, better than on any other portable in reducing adjacent-channel interference and selective-fading distortion on world band, longwave and mediumwave AM signals while adding slightly to weak-signal sensitivity (*see* Con). This is further aided by two bandwidths (10.4 kHz and 4.3 kHz) which offer a listener-oriented tradeoff between wideband audio fidelity and narrowband adjacent-channel rejection (selectivity). Use of 32 separate one-touch station preset keys in rows and columns is ergonomically the best to be found on any model, portable or tabletop, at any price—simply pushing one key one time brings in your station, a major convenience (*see* Con). Numerous other helpful tuning features. Excellent weak-signal sensitivity above 4 MHz (noise floor typically -131 dBm, sensitivity typically 0.15 microvolts) (*see* Con). Superior dynamic range (DR-20 = 80 dB, DR-5 = 68 dB) and third-order intercept point (IP3-20 = –9 dBm, IP3-5 = –21 dBm). Good overall distortion (under 3.5 percent), although not equal to that of ICF-SW77. Tunes and displays in relatively precise 0.1 kHz increments (*see* Con). Generally superior performance with single-sideband signals (*see* Con). Separate World Time clock displays fulltime and keeps exact time for months on end. Exceptionally robust, with superior quality of construction underscored by huge numbers in use worldwide over the years. First IF rejection 85 dB, excellent. Excellent AGC threshold, 0.6 microvolts. Alarm/snooze, with four-event timer. Illuminated LCD. Travel power lock. Excellent ten-LED digital signal-strength indicator much better than those on most other portables and vastly superior to that of the ICF-SW77; also seconds as a useful indication of battery strength. Superior mediumwave field sensitivity with built-in ferrite-rod antenna, although mediocre with external antenna. Longwave and Japanese FM bands. FM very sensitive to weak signals, making it unusually appropriate for fringe reception in some areas (*see* Con). FM has superior capture ratio to minimize co-channel interference. Superior overall reception of fringe and distant medium-wave AM signals. Some passable reception of air band signals (most versions). Hum-free AC adaptor (center-pin negative, unlike other Sony models).

Con: Distributed by Sony only in the United States; however, routinely exported worldwide from American world band specialty firms. Audio quality only average for size class, with simple three-level treble-cut tone control. Station presets and clock/timer features immediately erase whenever microprocessor/memory batteries are replaced, and also sometimes when set is jostled (changing to a different brand of "AA" batteries may help); this erasing also can happen irregularly on aging units, but for other reasons. Similarly, when the "D" cells lose contact an "Error 3" message appears; there is no other effect, but stretching the battery springs helps. Wide bandwidth unusually wide, especially when synchronous selectable sideband not in use; traveling DXers sometimes prefer the tighter bandwidths of the ICF-SW77, or '2010 replacement bandwidth filters offered by such aftermarket firms as Kiwa, with the tradeoff for less interference being more-muffled audio. Signal-seek bandscanning works poorly. Telescopic antenna swivel gets slack with heavy use, requiring periodic adjustment of tension screw. Synchronous selectable sideband tends to lose lock if batteries weak, or if NiCd cells are used. Synchronous selectable sideband alignment can vary with temperature, factory alignment and battery voltage, causing synchronous selectable sideband reception to be slightly more muffled in one sideband than the other—notably with the narrow bandwidth. Synchronous selectable sideband adds

The Sony ICF-2010 vies for the top spot among world band portables. It is exceptionally robust and comes with 32 one-touch station presets.

slight hiss. Frequency readout often off by 0.3-0.6 kHz in "lower" sync mode; depending upon sample and power source, off by as much as 0.3 kHz otherwise. Lacks up/down slewing controls. Keypad not in telephone format. LCD not clearly visible when radio viewed from above. Tuning resolution in 0.1 kHz increments means that non-synchronous single-sideband reception can be mis-tuned by up to 50 Hz, so audio quality varies. Image rejection, although 62 dB (good), is 18 dB less than on ICF-SW77. Blocking (109 dB) only fair. Weak-signal sensitivity (noise floor –118 dBm, sensitivity 0.75 microvolts) only fair within 120 meter tropical segment. Superior dynamic range invites use of external antennas, which is left connected when storms nearby can cause a transistor to blow; fortunately, it is not difficult for a technician to replace. Only 32 presets offered. In high-signal-strength environments, FM band can overload in high-signal areas, causing false "repeat" signals to appear. FM band's capture ratio only fair, limiting ability to separate co-channel stations. Air band insensitive to weak signals.

☞ The ICF-2010's long carrying strap can be easily converted into a convenient handle either by 1) cutting it shorter, or 2) wrapping over the radio twice (same thing, but twice as strong).

☞ For those seeking to have their ICF-2010 repaired, a helpful source at Sony of America suggests this as Sony's resident repair expert for this model: Steve Ulrich, Sony Service Center, 4300 W. 36½ Street, St. Louis Park MN 55416 USA; +1 (619) 920-8000.

Verdict: With consumer electronic products and PCs, the best is often the newest or the most costly. Not so with world band radios, where the last wave of technological advances occurred between 1976 and 1984. Except for everyday audio quality and urban FM, the '2010 is the favorite portable of most PASSPORT panelists, as well as myriad radio monitors and DXers. It is among the best for rejection of one of world band's major bugaboos, adjacent-channel interference, thanks in large part to its synchronous selectable sideband which performs better than on any other portable. That feature also allows for unusually broadband audio if even one sideband is free from adjacent-channel interference. Alone among sophisticated receivers, it allows dozens of stations to be brought up at the single touch of a key. Although it is costlier to manufacture than newer models—it is made in Japan, and has discrete controls that are too costly for newly designed models—it sells at a surprisingly affordable price because its development costs have been written off. Sony of America emphasizes that they plan to keep this model in their line indefinitely.

Evaluation of Latest Unit: It has been over a decade since we last tested the ICF-2010, but according to Sony nothing has changed in the interim. We checked this out, hoping Sony was wrong and that this seasoned favorite had somehow been made better.

What we found is that Sony is basically correct. Here and there small parts differ slightly, but even this is a stretch. Sony has a winner and is leaving well enough alone.

Still, there are differences. Whether because of age or changed parts, batteries fit tighter than then once did. When the two "AA" cells that power the memory lose contact even for a split second, the presets and clock/timer lose all data and have to be reprogrammed, so it was a pleasant surprise to find that we never lost data when casually jostling the new sample with Eveready Energizer cells. Still, during production Sony could easily add a capacitor to remedy the basic problem without changing the radio in any other way.

The new sample also proved to be slightly more sensitive than in the past to weak signals, especially in the higher reaches of the shortwave spectrum. Alignment for the changeover point from lower to upper sideband with synchronous single sideband was also slightly better: x.8/x.9 kHz for the new, x.6/x.7 kHz for our oldest unit. Of course, both changeover points differ depending on battery freshness. (Similarly, if the AC adaptor is in use the changeover point can shift slightly depending on changes in local AC mains voltage.)

In the final analysis, what may count most is not how the new model fares, but rather how one of our older units has endured for 13 years of merciless use in freezing and tropical climates, several drenchings in the rain, salt spray and heart-stopping falls. The cabinet is worn from finger rubbing; the antenna tip was broken off by a ceiling fan

LAB NUMBERS: TOP TWO PORTABLES

	Sony ICF-2010	Sony ICF-SW77
Max. Sensitivity/Noise Floor	0.15 μV, **S**/–131 dBm, **E** [1]	0.16 μV, **S**/–133 dBm, **E** [2]
Blocking	109 dB, **F**	121 dB, **G**
Shape Factors, voice BWs	1:1.8–1:2.0, **E** - **G**	1:1.9–1:2.0, **E** - **G**
Ultimate Rejection	70 dB, **G**	70 dB, **G**
Front-End Selectivity	**F**	— [3]
Image Rejection	62 dB, **G**	80 dB, **E**
First IF Rejection	85 dB, **E**	80 dB, **E**
Dynamic Range/IP3 (5 kHz)	68 dB, **F**/–21 dBm, **G**	64 dB, **F**/–37 dBm, **F**
Dynamic Range/IP3 (20 kHz)	80 dB, **F**/–9 dBm, **G**	82 dB, **F**/–10 dBm, **G**
Phase Noise	114 dBc, **G**	122 dBc, **E**
AGC Threshold	0.6 μV, **E**	2.0 μV, **G**
Overall Distortion, sync	2.9%, **G**/3.5%, **G** [4]	2.3%, **E**/3.3%, **G** [4]

IBS Lab Ratings: **S** Superb   **E** Excellent   **G** Good   **F** Fair   **P** Poor

(1) Measurements flat from 5-29 MHz, but drop to 0.75 μV, **F**/–118 dBm, **F** at 2 MHz.
(2) Sensitivity varies considerably by frequency at 2 MHz and between 10-29.9 MHz; *viz.*, from 0.16 μV to 1.40 μV, **S** - **G**. Noise floor varies by frequency from –133 dBm to –117 dBm, **E** - **G**. Neither measurement could be made at 5 MHz because of spurious responses, noise and leakage.
(3) Unknown.
(4) Wide/narrow bandwidths.

in Anguilla; the cabinet back has a dent; the controls are full of dirt; and more than a few insects have made its innards their final resting place. Yet, except for the occasional loss of memory data when the radio is vigorously jostled this battlefield veteran continues to soldier on without a hiccup.

This is only one unit out of many, but other '2010 receivers used over the years by PASSPORT reviewers have fared similarly. But the '2010 is not "bulletproof." Although the early '2010 was prone to transistor failure from static electricity via outdoor antennas, even later samples can suffer if the static charge is strong enough. Fortunately, the repair is straightforward.

📄 An *RDI WHITE PAPER* is available for this model.

Retested for 2001
✪✪✪¾
Sony ICF-SW77, Sony ICF-SW77E

Price: $469.95 in the United States. £329.95 as available in the United Kingdom. ¥8,000 in China.

Pro: A rich variety of tuning and other features, including sophisticated "page" tuning that some enjoy but others dislike; includes 162 presets, two-speed tuning knob, signal-seek bandscanning (*see* Con), keypad tuning and meter-band access. Synchronous selectable sideband is exceptionally handy to operate; it significantly reduces selective-fading distortion and adjacent-channel interference on world band, longwave and mediumwave AM signals; although the sync chip part number was changed recently, its performance is virtually unchanged (*see* Con). Two well-chosen bandwidths (6.0 kHz and 3.3 kHz) provide superior adjacent-channel rejection. Excellent image rejection and first-IF rejection, both 80 dB. Excellent-to-superb weak-signal sensitivity (noise floor –133 dBm, sensitivity 0.16 microvolts) in and around lower-middle portion of shortwave spectrum where most listening is done (*see* Con). Superb overall distortion, almost always under one percent. Dynamic range (82 dB) and third-order intercept point (–10 dBm) fairly good and only slightly less than those of the ICF-2010 at 20 kHz separation (*see* Con). Tunes in very precise 0.05 kHz increments; displays in 0.1 kHz increments; these and other factors make this model superior to any other portable for single-sideband reception, although portatop and tabletop models usually fare better yet. Continuous bass and treble tone controls, a rarity. Two illuminated multifunction liquid crystal displays. Separately displayed World Time and local time clocks. Station name appears on LCD when station presets used. 10-level signal-strength indicator (*see* Con). Excellent stability, less than 20 Hz drift after ten-second warmup. Excellent weak-signal sensitivity (noise floor –130 dBm, sensitivity 0.21 microvolts) within little-used 120 meter segment (*see* Con). Flip-up chart for calculating time differences. VCR-type five-event timer controls radio and optional outboard recorder alike. Superior FM audio quality. Stereo FM through earpieces, supplied. Longwave and Japanese FM bands. AC adaptor and reel-in outboard antenna. Hum-free AC adaptor. Rubber strip helps prevent sliding.

Con: "Page" tuning system relatively complex to operate; many find that station presets can't be accessed simply. World band and mediumwave AM audio slightly muffled even when wide bandwidth in use. Synthesizer chugging degrades reception quality during bandscanning by knob. Dynamic range (64 dB) and third-order intercept point (–37 dBm) only fair at 5 kHz separation. Weak-signal sensitivity varies from fair to superb, depending on where between 2 and 30 MHz receiver is being tuned. Synchronous selectable sideband holds lock less well than ICF-2010 model. Synchronous selectable sideband tends to lose lock if batteries weak, or if NiCd cells are used. Synchronous selectable sideband alignment can vary with temperature, factory alignment and battery voltage, causing synchronous selectable sideband reception to be slightly more muffled in one sideband than the other. Signal-seek bandscanning skips over weaker signals. Flimsy 11-element telescopic antenna (the older version of the 'SW77 had nine elements). LCD characters small for size of receiver. Display illumination does not stay on with AC power. Unusual tuning knob design disliked by some. On mediumwave AM band, relatively insensitive, sometimes with spurious sounds during single-sideband reception; this doesn't apply to world band reception, however. Mundane reception of difficult FM signals. Signal-strength indicator grossly overreads, covering only a 20 dB range with maximum reading at only 3 microvolts. AGC threshold, 2 microvolts (good), inferior to that of ICF-2010. Painted surfaces can wear off with heavy use. Getting harder to find outside the United States.

Verdict: The Japanese-made '77 has been a strong contender among portables since it was improved some time back, and for single-sideband reception it is the best portable by a skosh. It's also one of the very few models with continuously tuned bass and treble controls. Ergonomics, however, are a mixed bag, so if you're interested consider trying it out first.

Evaluation of Latest Unit: Sony's ICF-SW77 is priced as a flagship receiver, although most who have used it and the less-costly ICF-2010 wind up slightly preferring the latter. Mainly, this is because the '2010's bandwidth configuration and superior synchronous selectable sideband produce a surprisingly readable signal. On the face of it this may seem surprising, as the 'SW77 has narrower bandwidths and better shaping of the audio, but the end result is audio that is somewhat more

Sony's highest-priced model is the ICF-SW77 with advanced "page" tuning. It is one of only two world band radios with continuous bass and treble tone controls.

muffled no matter how the tone controls are manipulated.

Too, radio enthusiasts need a good signal-strength indicator, which the '2010 has, but is woefully inadequate in the 'SW77. Also, bandscanning on the 'SW77 is compromised by chugging and an unusual tuning knob. And the '2010's front panel looks cluttered for a good reason: It has 32 one-push presets for favorite stations.

Yet, the electrical performance of the 'SW77 is top-drawer—slightly better than that of the '2010 in some categories, even if slightly worse in others. The 'SW77 has more sophisticated features, as well, although the tradeoff is more-complicated operation. But for reception of utility and ham signals the 'SW77 is, hands down, the better receiver, thanks to those tighter bandwidths, superior stability and 50 Hz tuning increments—twice as fine as those of the '2010. FM audio quality is also better than that of the '2010, and is helped by the 'SW77's commendable use of continuous bass and treble tone controls.

Overall, the Sony ICF-SW77 is nothing less than a first-rate portable, and to some—including one of our panelists—it is simply the best.

✪✪½
Sangean ATS-818, Roberts R827

Price: *Sangean:* $174.95 in the United States. CAN$249.00 in Canada. £139.95 in the United Kingdom. *AC adaptor:* £9.95 in the United Kingdom. *Roberts:* £139.95 in the United Kingdom.

Pro: Superior overall world band performance. Numerous tuning features, including 18 world band station presets. Two bandwidths for good fidelity/interference tradeoff. Analog clarifier with center detent and stable circuitry allows single-sideband signals to be tuned with uncommon precision, thus allowing for superior audio phasing for a portable (*see* Con). Illuminated display. Signal-strength indicator. Two 24-hour clocks, one for World Time, with either displayed separately from frequency. Alarm/snooze/timer. Travel power lock. FM stereo through headphones. Longwave. *Sangean (North American units):* AC adaptor.

Con: Tends to mute when tuning knob turned quickly, making bandscanning difficult (the C. Crane Company offers a $20.00/$29.95 modification to remedy this). Wide bandwidth a bit broad for world band reception. Unconfirmed reader reports suggest that the front end is unusually prone to malfunctioning from static discharge into the antenna, such as from fingertips during dry winter periods. Keypad not in telephone format. Touchy variable control for single-sideband fine tuning. Does not come with tape-recorder jack. Country of manufacture (now China) not specified on radio or box.

Verdict: This is a decent, predictable radio—performance and features, alike—although unless modified it is mediocre for bandscanning.

LARGE ("FIELD") PORTABLES
Excellent for Home, Poor for Travel

Large, or "field," shortwave analog portables were common in the days of the Zenith Transoceanic and other bygone tube-type models. Today, smaller digital portables provide improved operation and superior reception except for audio quality.

However, this category is far from gone. Now, large portables are derived from sophisticated tabletop receiver designs. These have superior audio quality, along with the potential to offer exceptional difficult-signal and single-sideband performance. Accordingly, these are now classified as "portatop" receivers—portable versions of tabletop receivers.

PASSPORT's next chapter is devoted to portatop models.

WORLD BAND CASSETTE RECORDERS

What happens if your favorite show comes on at an inconvenient time? Why, tape it, of course, with a world band cassette recorder—just like on your VCR.

Two models are offered, and there's no question which is better: the Sony. Smaller, too, so it is less likely to raise eyebrows among airport security personnel. But there's a whopping price difference over the Sangean.

Sangean replaced its legendary ATS-803A with the ATS-818, shown, as the '803A was unusually costly to manufacture.

✪✪✪⅛ *Passport's Choice*
Sony ICF-SW1000T, Sony ICF-SW1000TS

The Sony ICF-SW1000T is a true world band cassette recorder. It combines advanced-technology reception, true portability and genuine two-event recording.

Price: *ICF-SW1000T:* $449.95 in the United States. CAN$779.00 as available in Canada. £359.95 as available in the United Kingdom. *AC-E30HG 120V AC adaptor:* $19.95.

Pro: Built-in recorder in rear of cabinet, with two events of up to 90 minutes each, selectable in ten-minute increments. Relatively compact for travel, also helpful to avoid airport security hassles. High-tech synchronous selectable sideband; this generally performs well, reducing adjacent-channel interference and selective-fading distortion on world band, longwave and mediumwave AM signals while adding slightly to weak-signal sensitivity (*see* Con). Single bandwidth, especially when synchronous selectable sideband is used, exceptionally effective at adjacent-channel rejection. Numerous helpful tuning features, including keypad, two-speed up/down slewing, 32 presets and signal-seek scanning. Thirty of the 32 presets are within three easy-to-use "pages" so stations can be clustered. Weak-signal sensitivity above average up to about 16 MHz. Demodulates single-sideband signals (*see* Con). World Time clock, easy to set (*see* Con). Snooze feature, 10-90 minutes. Illuminated LCD readable from a wide variety of angles. Travel power lock, also useful to keep recorder from being inadvertently switched on while cabinet being grasped (*see* Con). Easy on batteries. Records on both sides of tape without having to flip cassette (provided FWD is selected along with the "turning-around arrow"). Auto record level (*see* Con). "ISS" switch helps radio avoid interference from recorder's bias circuitry. FM stereo through earphones; earbuds supplied. Longwave and Japanese FM bands. Tape-reel-type outboard passive antenna accessory. Dead-battery indicator. Lapel mic (*see* Con). *ICF-SW1000TS:* Comes with AN-LP1 active antenna system and AC adaptor.

Con: Pedestrian audio quality. Synchronous selectable sideband tends to lose lock if batteries not fresh, or if NiCd cells are used. Synchronous selectable sideband alignment can vary with temperature, factory alignment and battery voltage, causing synchronous selectable sideband reception to be slightly more muffled in one sideband than the other. No tuning knob. Clock not readable when radio switched on except for ten seconds when key is pushed. No meaningful signal-strength indicator, which negates its otherwise obvious role for traveling technical monitors. No recording-level indicator or tape counter. Slow rewind. Fast forward and reverse use buttons that have to be held down. No built-in mic; outboard (lapel) mic is mono. Reception is interrupted for a good two seconds when recording first commences. No pause control. Single lock deactivates controls for radio and recorder alike; separate locks would have been preferable. Tuning resolution of 0.1 kHz allows single-sideband signals to be mis-tuned by up to 50 Hz. Frequency readout to 1 kHz, rather than 0.1 kHz tuning increment. Lacks flip-out elevation panel; instead, uses less handy plug-in elevation tab. FM sometimes overloads. Telescopic antenna exits from the side, which limits tilting choices for

FM. Misleading location of battery springs makes it easy to insert one of the two "AA" radio batteries in the wrong direction, albeit to no ill effect. *ICF-SW1000T:* AC adaptor costs extra. Increasingly hard to find outside United States. *ICF-SW1000TS:* Not available in the United States or most other countries.

Verdict: Strictly speaking, the Sony ICF-SW1000T is the world's only true world band cassette recorder. Made in Japan, this is an innovative little package with surprisingly good battery life and build quality.

★★½ ⊘
Sangean ATS-818ACS, Radio Shack DX-392, Roberts RC828

Price: *Sangean:* $224.95 in the United States. CAN$329.00 in Canada. £139.95 in the United Kingdom. AUS$374.00 in Australia. *AC adaptor:* £9.95 in the United Kingdom. *Radio Shack:* CAN$299.99 in Canada. *Roberts:* £219.95 in the United Kingdom.

Pro: Built-in cassette recorder. Price low relative to competition. Superior overall world band performance. Numerous tuning features, including 18 world band station presets. Two bandwidths for good

Sangean's ATS-818ACS is the value-priced choice for built-in recording of favorite shows.

fidelity/interference tradeoff. Analog clarifier with center detent and stable circuitry allows single-sideband signals to be tuned with uncommon precision, thus allowing for superior audio phasing for a portable (*see* Con). Illuminated display. Signal-strength indicator. Two 24-hour clocks, one for World Time, with either displayed separately from frequency. Alarm/snooze/timer. Travel power lock. Stereo through headphones. Longwave. Built-in condenser mic. *Sangean (North American units):* AC adaptor. *Radio Shack:* 30-day money-back period; conditions may apply.

Con: Recorder has no multiple recording events, just one "on" time (quits when tape runs out). Tends to mute when tuning knob turned quickly, making bandscanning difficult (the C. Crane Company offers a $20.00/$29.95 modification to remedy this). Wide bandwidth a bit broad for world band reception without synchronous selectable sideband. Speaker smaller, with slightly less fidelity, than on regular 818 model without recorder. Unconfirmed reader reports suggest that the front end is unusually prone to malfunctioning from static discharge into the antenna, such as from fingertips during dry winter periods. Keypad not in telephone format. Touchy single-sideband clarifier. Recorder has no level indicator and no counter. Fast-forward and rewind controls installed backwards. Country of manufacture (now China) not specified on radio or box. *Radio Shack:* AC adaptor extra. Warranty only 90 days in the United States and some other countries.

Verdict: A great buy, although recording is only single-event with no timed "off."

The PASSPORT portable-radio review team includes Lawrence Magne and Tony Jones, with laboratory measurements performed independently by Sherwood Engineering. Additional feedback from Craig Tyson and George Zeller.

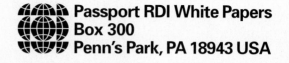

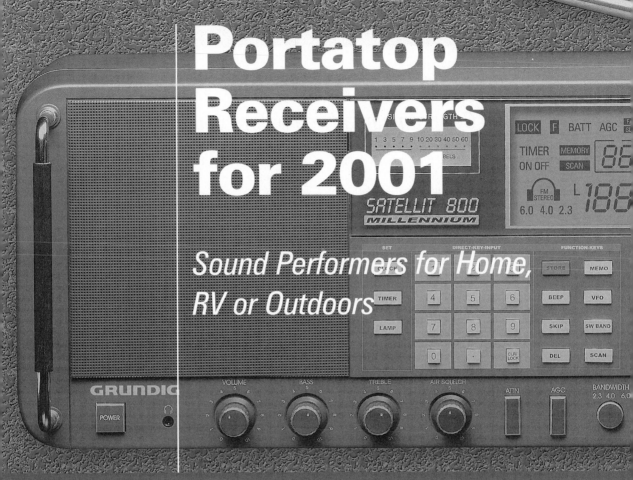

Portatop
Receivers
for 2001

Sound Performers for Home,
RV or Outdoors

Most of us buy a world band radio not for just a room, but for our entire home property. Yet, portables rarely sound as pleasant as tabletop models, nor can most cut the mustard with really tough signals. Solution: Combine various characteristics of portables and tabletops into one high-performance package—a portatop—which can be serviced, like tabletops, for years to come.

Category Launched Years Ago

This category had a bumpy takeoff in 1960 with the Heathkit GC-1/ GC-1A Mohican. This solid-state portatop, which looked advanced on paper, was actually so mediocre that it led one frustrated owner to initiate receiver reviews which eventually became PASSPORT REPORTS.

Other portatop models followed in the late seventies, the best being the Sony ICF-6800W (ultra-sensitive "white" and later "orange" versions), the rugged Sony CRF-1 and the revised version of the Philips/Magnavox D2999. The pricey CRF-1 was for years a favorite among traveling station monitors and eavesdropping officials, but spooks now prefer the inconspicuous Sony ICF-SW100 and other tiny portables.

The CRF-1 was priced beyond the reach of most radio aficionados. For them, the portatop of choice was the '6800W, which to this day continues to be prized for its ability to suck audio from otherwise-inaudible signals. Unfortunately, after so many years the vast majority have ceased to function properly, and few models have been so intractable to service.

Disadvantages Include Size

Drawbacks? Portatops are larger and costlier than portables, and go through batteries with abandon. If you're comfortable with all that, you'll find performance and fidelity approaching those of top-rated tabletop receivers.

Portatops are a great idea, but traditionally have been slow sellers because of pricing. Until recently they were lost in a Bermuda Triangle between the vast market of under-$500 radios for world band listening, and the specialty market of $1,000-up tabletop receivers for DX enthusiasts. Market surveys and experience alike show this to be a difficult zone.

Changes for 2001

For several years Grundig announced it was coming out with a Satellit 900 receiver, but it never materialized. So when Grundig

later announced a forthcoming Satellit 800 and it failed to appear, there were more than a few snickers about this being a real satellite, lost in space.

The S-800 was finally introduced in the spring of 2000, and it was worth the wait. It has turned out to be a milestone receiver—for $500, it offers what used to take around $800 to obtain. The S-800 is based on the costlier Drake SW8, which was formally discontinued on September 15, 2000, although it was available from dealers for some weeks thereafter. Nevertheless, we've included it in this section to provide a benchmark of comparison for Grundig's new offering.

Starting this year, PASSPORT REPORTS is treating receivers as portatops only if they are fully self-contained. Those which have to rely on outboard battery packs, separate active antennas and the like are now included in our section on tabletop models.

What PASSPORT's Ratings Mean

Star ratings: ✪✪✪✪✪ is best. Stars reflect overall performance and meaningful features, plus to some extent ergonomics and build quality. Price, appearance, country of manufacture and the like are not taken into account. With portatop models there is roughly equal emphasis on the ability to flush out tough, hard-to-hear signals, and program-listening quality with stronger broadcasts. To facilitate comparison, the same rating system is used for professional, tabletop and portable models reviewed elsewhere in this PASSPORT.

Passport's Choice. La crème de la crème. Our test team's personal picks of the litter—models we would buy or have bought for our personal use.

✪: A relative bargain, with decidedly more performance than the price would suggest.

Prices: Street, including VAT/GST where applicable. Prices vary plus or minus, so take them as the general guide they are meant to be.

Unless otherwise stated, all portatop models have:

- Digital frequency synthesis and display, using mechanical encoders.
- Full coverage of at least the 155-29999 kHz longwave, mediumwave AM and shortwave spectra—including all world band frequencies—and the usual 87.5-108 MHz FM broadcast band. Models designed for some countries have reduced tuning ranges.
- A wide variety of helpful tuning features, including tuning knob, keypad, up/down slewing and numerous station presets, but no "signal seek" frequency scanning.
- Synchronous selectable sideband to reduce selective-fading distortion, using phase cancellation to attenuate adjacent-channel interference.
- Proper demodulation of utility and "ham" shortwave signals. These include single-sideband (SSB) and CW (Morse code); also, with suitable ancillary devices, radioteletype and radiofax.
- Meaningful signal-strength indication.
- Illuminated display.
- Useful operating manual.

The following two models are variations of the same basic Drake design.

Discontinued
★★★★½ 📖 *Passport's Choice*
Drake SW8

Price: *SW8 (before 11/00):* $799.95 in the United States. CAN$1,219.00 in Canada. *Schematic:* $25 worldwide via the manufacturer.

Pro: Tabletop-model quality of construction. Above-average audio quality with internal speaker or headphones. Excellent-performing synchronous selectable sideband, with just under 30 dB of unwanted-sideband rejection; reduces adjacent-channel interference and selective-fading distortion with world band, long-wave and mediumwave AM signals. Synchronous selectable sideband also boosts recoverable audio from some of the weakest of signals, while reducing overall distortion to 1% from an average of 2% in the ordinary AM mode. Three well-chosen music/voice bandwidths, with excellent skirt selectivity and good-to-excellent ultimate rejection; these bandwidths are selectable independent of mode—or dependent, if the user prefers—and work in concert with the synchronous selectable sideband feature to provide superior adjacent-channel rejection. Slow/fast AGC (*see* Con). Continuous tone control. Numerous helpful tuning aids, including 70 tunable station presets that store many variables (*see* Con); presets may also be scanned (*see* Con). Helpful signal-strength indicator, albeit digital. Single-sideband reception above the portable norm (*see* Con), with excellent frequency stability. Excellent weak-signal shortwave and mediumwave AM sensitivity using external antenna (*see* Con). Superior blocking performance aids consistency of weak-signal sensitivity. Dynamic range ranges from fair at 5 kHz separation to excellent at 20 kHz separation; third-order intercept point is good at 5 kHz separation, excellent at 20 kHz separation. High- and low-impedance inputs for 0.1-30 MHz external antennas. Two-event on/off timer and two 24-hour clocks (*see* Con). FM—mono through speaker, stereo through head-phones—performs well, although capture ratio only average. Covers longwave down to 100 kHz. Covers the 118-137 MHz aeronautical band in the AM mode only and without synchronous selectable sideband; performs about as well as a typical handheld scanner. Superior factory service and tech support, although discontinued models are no longer supported for as long as they used to be. Optional carrying case.

Con: Weak-signal sensitivity, although good, could be slightly better with built-in antenna. Lacks notch filter, adjustable noise blanker and passband tuning. Ergonomics only fair, including pushbuttons that rock on their centers. Key pushes must each be done within three seconds, lest receiver wind up being mis-tuned or placed into an unwanted operating mode. No signal-seek frequency scanning. Single sideband tunes in 50 Hz increments, allowing tuning to be slightly out of phase (up to 25 Hz). Fast AGC sometimes causes distortion with powerful signals; remedied by using slow AGC. Modest birdies; these almost never cause heterodyne interference to world band signals, but on rare occasion they might heterodyne utility, ham and Eastern Hemisphere mediumwave signals. Outboard AC adaptor in lieu of inboard power supply. Telescopic antenna doesn't swivel fully for best FM reception. No built-in ferrite rod antenna for directional longwave and mediumwave AM reception. Clocks don't display when frequency is shown; pushbutton allows time to replace frequency briefly. Both clocks in 24-hour format and don't display seconds numerically; 12-hour format not available for local time."USB" on LCD displays as "LISB," although because of its small size this is essentially invisible. Carrying/elevation handle clunky to adjust, with adjustment stops that can break if handle forced. Optional MS8 outboard speaker not equal to receiver's fidelity potential.

Verdict: Until dealers had virtually run out of stock in late October, 2000, the final version of the Drake SW8 was very nearly everything a top-notch portatop should be: performance only a skosh below that of the fanciest tabletop supersets, yet priced lower, with portability and FM thrown in. Our latest tests suggest that the signal-to-

Drake's SW8 has been refined over several years. It now outperforms all but the top three tabletop models.

noise ratio with the built-in antenna had gotten even better since our last check.

The American-made SW8 was designed and manufactured to the robust standards of radiophile communications hardware, rather than as a consumer electronics offering. This was its trump card, but it also slightly outperformed early production samples of the Grundig Satellit 800 in some respects. Yet, it lacked the S-800's polished ergonomics and superior tonality—and cost $300 more.

An *RDI WHITE PAPER* is available for this model.

New for 2001
★★★★¼ ✪ 🗐 *Passport's Choice*
Grundig Satellit 800

Price: *S-800:* $499.95 including AC adaptor and headset in the United States. CAN$799.99 including AC adaptor and headset in Canada. Price not yet firmed within the United Kingdom. *S-800 (refurbished used units, as available):* $399.95 in the United States.

Grundig's new Satellit 800 is a benchmark receiver, with tabletop performance at a portable price. Unbeatable audio quality, too.

Pro: Outstanding price for level of performance. Superior, room-filling tonal quality by world band, even if not audiophile, standards—whether with the internal speaker, outboard speakers or headphones. Tonal shaping aided by continuous separate bass and treble tone controls, a rarity among world band receivers at any price. Excellent-performing synchronous selectable sideband, with 27 dB of unwanted-sideband rejection; reduces adjacent-channel interference and selective-fading distortion with world band, longwave and mediumwave AM signals. Synchronous selectable sideband also boosts recoverable audio from some of the weakest of signals, and halves overall distortion from 5.3% in the ordinary AM mode to 2.4% from 100-3,000 Hz. Three voice/music bandwidths; wide bandwidth measures from 6.1 to 7.4 kHz, while medium and narrow bandwidths consistently measure 5.5 and 2.6 kHz (*see* Con). Bandwidths have excellent skirt selectivity and good-to-excellent ultimate rejection; all are selectable independent of mode (or dependent, if the user prefers), and work in concert with the synchronous selectable sideband feature to provide superior

adjacent-channel rejection. Slow/fast AGC (*see* Con). Numerous helpful tuning aids, including 70 tunable station presets that store many variables (*see* Con); also, presets may be scanned (*see* Con). Excellent ergonomics, including many dedicated, widely spaced controls and a high-contrast, top/bottom/head-on view LCD with large, bold characters even Mr. Magoo could read (*see* Con). Analog signal-strength indicator reads in useful S1-9/+60 dB standard (*see* Con). Single-sideband reception above the portable norm (*see* Con), with rock-solid frequency stability. High- and low-impedance inputs for 0.1-30 MHz external antennas. Weak-signal shortwave sensitivity with built-in telescopic antenna comparable to that of best-rated portables. Weak-signal shortwave and mediumwave AM sensitivity excellent with external antenna (*see* Con). Weak-signal shortwave sensitivity with an external antenna can be boosted by setting antenna switch to "whip," thus adding preamplification (and, in such locations as Europe evenings, possibly generating overloading as well). Superior blocking performance aids consistency of weak-signal sensitivity. Generally superior dynamic range and third-order intercept point to the extent they can be accurately measured amidst receiver phase noise and such. Two-event on/off timer and two 24-hour clocks (*see* Con). Large, tough telescopic antenna includes spring-loaded detents for vertical, 45-degree and 90-degree swiveling; also rotates freely 360 degrees (*see* Con). Display and signal strength meter illumination is clever—with batteries in use, light automatically comes on for 15 seconds either at the touch of any button or when receiver is knob or slew tuned; 15-second illumination cycle can also be aborted by pushing the light button a second time. FM—mono through built-in speaker, stereo through outboard speakers, headphones and line output—performs well, although capture ratio only average and nearby FM transmitters may cause some overloading. Covers longwave down to 100 kHz. Built-in ferrite rod antenna may be used for 0.1-1.8 MHz. Covers the 118-137 MHz aeronautical band, but only in the AM mode without synchronous selectable sideband; performs about as well as a simple handheld scanner. Excellent, long carrying handle. The only receiver tested that comes with padded, full-size audiophile-style headphones. Comes with AC adaptor—120 VAC or 220 VAC, depending upon where radio is sold; alkaline batteries need changing every 35 hours or so, about 25 cents per hour. Battery-strength indicator (see Con). Rack-type handles protect front panel should radio fall over. Service in and out of one-year warranty is performed by the R.L. Drake Company, long known for superior repairs (see Con). *North America:* Toll-free tech support.

Con: Huge (20 3/8 inches—517 mm—wide) and weighty (15 pounds or 6.8 kg with batteries). Consistency of assembly of early production units not up to par. Plastic cabinet and other components are not in the same radiophile-hardware league as other portatop models. With latest tested sample, difference between wide and middle bandwidths was only 0.6 kHz, much smaller than desirable. Synthesizer phase noise, only fair, slightly impacts reception of weak-signals adjacent to powerful signals and in other circumstances; also, limits ability to make certain laboratory measurements accurately. Lacks notch filter, noise blanker, passband tuning and digital signal processing (DSP). Each key push must each be done within three seconds, lest receiver wind up being mis-tuned or placed into an unwanted operating mode. No signal-seek frequency scanning. Signal-strength indicator greatly underreads, apparently a production component or alignment problem that presumably will be cleared up in due course. Outboard AC adaptor in lieu of inboard power supply. Single sideband tunes in 50 Hz increments, allowing tuning to be slightly out of phase (up to 25 Hz). Fast AGC, handy for bandscanning, sometimes causes distortion with powerful signals; remedied by going to slow AGC when no longer bandscanning. Numerous modest birdies on longwave, mediumwave AM, shortwave and FM bands; although these almost never cause heterodyne interference to world band signals, approximately one time in 250 they might heterodyne utility, ham and Eastern-Hemisphere mediumwave signals. Large, obnoxious spurious signal on 20,000 kHz obscures WWV reception. Ergonomics, although excellent, are not ideal: There are no dedicated buttons for station presets, as are found on the Sony ICF-2010. Tuning knob's ultra-light action, slight wobble and sharp bevel may disappoint those who prefer a less "touchy" knob and some flywheel effect; manufacturer claims wobble will be resolved by using ball bearings in future production. Neither clock displays when frequency is shown; however, pushbutton allows time to replace frequency for three seconds. Both clocks in 24-hour format and don't display seconds numerically; 12-hour format not available for local time. For faint-signal DXing, recoverable audio with an outboard antenna, although good, not fully equal to that of most tabletop and professional models. Using the built-in antenna, sensitivity to weak signals is not of DX caliber in the mediumwave AM band. Slight frontal radiation of digital noise from LCD. No adjustable feet or elevation rod to angle receiver upwards for handy operation. When receiver leaned backward, the telescopic antenna, if angled, spins to the rear. Battery-strength indicator doesn't come on until immediately before radio mutes from low voltage. Misleading location of battery spring clips makes it easy to insert three of the six batteries in the wrong direction, albeit to no ill effect other than the radio won't turn on until the batteries are reinserted correctly. Battery cover may come loose if receiver is bumped in an appropriate manner. Antenna switches located unhandily on rear panel. "USB" on LCD displays as "LISB." No schematic or repair manual available, making service difficult except at Grundig's Drake facility in Ohio—an impractical solution outside North America.

☞ Refurbished used units reportedly include returns from department stores and other outlets where customers tend to be unfamiliar with world band radio. Refurbishing is done at the Drake factory in Ohio, with units being sold, as available, at nearby Universal Radio.

Verdict: The new Grundig Satellit 800 is a benchmark receiver, being the first model ever to offer such a level of near-tabletop performance at portable prices. This Chinese-made model uses circuitry based on the recently discontinued Drake SW8, although it looks like a boom box. Its audio quality and ergonomics are among the best of any world band receiver on the market, regardless of price.

But all is not kudos. Construction consistency was wanting during the "shakedown cruise," with perhaps eight percent of units being returned to dealers for one reason or another. Historically, production quality improves as the learning curve takes effect, and Grundig insists that its efforts at improved QA have already begun to yield results. We will be watching this unfold over the months to come, and if there is signifi-cant improvement over a period of time, a version 3.0 of the S-800 RDI White Paper will be issued. In the meantime,

LAB NUMBERS: TOP TWO PORTATOPS

	Drake SW8	Grundig Satellit 800
Max. Sensitivity/Noise Floor	0.32 µV, Ⓔ/−127 dBm, Ⓖ	0.23 µV, Ⓔ/−129 dBm, Ⓖ[1]
Blocking	125 dB, Ⓔ	132 dB, Ⓔ
Shape Factors, voice BWs	1:1.6–1:1.9, Ⓔ	1:1.5–1:1.9, Ⓔ
Ultimate Rejection	70 dB, Ⓖ	70 dB, Ⓖ
Front-End Selectivity	Ⓕ	Ⓕ
Image Rejection	64 dB, Ⓖ	63 dB, Ⓖ[1]
First IF Rejection	80 dB, Ⓔ	86 dB, Ⓔ[1]
Dynamic Range/IP3 (5 kHz)	67 dB, Ⓕ/-26 dBm, Ⓖ	— [2]
Dynamic Range/IP3 (20 kHz)	92 dB, Ⓔ/+11 dBm, Ⓢ	— [2]
Phase Noise	113 dBc, Ⓖ	111 dBc, Ⓖ[1]
AGC Threshold	0.9 µV, Ⓢ	0.8 µV, Ⓢ
Overall Distortion, sync	1.2%, Ⓔ	2.4%, Ⓔ

IBS Lab Ratings: ⓈSuperb   ⒺExcellent   ⒼGood   ⒻFair   ⒫Poor

(1) Some tested samples measured more poorly.

(2) Customary measurements not possible because of birdies, phase noise and other mixing products. DR/IP3 seemingly comparable to SW8.

your best bet is to buy this receiver on a returnable basis.

Evaluation of New Model: For whatever reason, nearly all world band receivers hit the market doing several things well, yet fall short in one or more important respects. Even PASSPORT's top-rated portable, the Sony ICF-2010, has pedestrian audio quality through the speaker.

One exception is the Drake R8B tabletop receiver. Consider any single variable, and you may find one or more competing models which do better. Yet, it dominates the tabletop receiver market because it does virtually everything well, like a good orchestra.

Evolved from Drake SW8

Drake's recently discontinued SW8 portatop (see preceding review) was no slouch, either—for five years the revised version of this receiver topped PASSPORT REPORTS' ratings for portatops. It also had the singular virtue of being two-thirds the price of the flagship R8B. This didn't go unnoticed by the Grundig, whose North American office signed an agreement of cooperation with Drake in 1997.

The first offspring from this long-term liaison is the Grundig Satellit 800, which first began appearing in limited quantities in mid-2000. This receiver was conceived by Lextronix, a California firm that is the guiding light for world band products from Grundig, a respected German company. In turn, the S-800 was engineered and is serviced by the legendary R.L. Drake Company of Ohio in the United States. Rounding out the international coalition, manufacturing takes place at the same Tecsun plant in China that for years has been turning out various other Grundig world band models.

The Grundig Satellit 800 is a benchmark receiver, the first model to offer near-tabletop performance at portable prices. It is based on the design of the Drake SW8, but incorporates a number of differences and sells at less than two-thirds the price of the SW8. And as if that weren't enough, its ergonomics are among the best of any world band receiver on the market, regardless of price. The result is that the S-800 is not only a receiver of unusual value, it is actually improved over the SW8 in a number of ways, even if not in others.

The attractive pricing has come about because of where the radio is manufactured, albeit with what initially has been substandard consistency of assembly. Among the three units PASSPORT has tested thus far, some performance measurements have varied more than usual from one sample to the next; also, one had a defective signal-strength indicator.

Hiccups during a "shakedown cruise" aren't unusual—many of Sony's sophisticated models came on the market with shortcomings that took months to iron out. In comparison, initial S-800 production, warts and all, has actually gone better, and could be in overdrive by the time you read this. In the meantime, it makes sense to purchase it on a returnable basis in case you get a unit with a problem.

Although the S-800 is exceptionally heavy and large, it can be toted around the house or yard, or taken along in a car or on RV excursions. Forget airplane trips, though—it's like schlepping an extra carry-on and raises suspicious eyebrows during security checks. If you insist on flying with an S-800, bring along six "D" cells to prove to skeptical gumshoes that the radio really works.

Wide Range of Useful Features

The S-800 tunes the full shortwave spectrum, including all world band segments, as well as the mediumwave AM, VHF aeronautical and FM bands. FM usually isn't found in tabletop models, but having it means you don't have to lug along a second radio.

There are several ways to tune: keypad, knob, 70 station presets that store many variables, world-band segment selection, up/down frequency slewing and memory scan. There is also a two-event timer and two 24-hour clocks. Although you can't read the time and frequency at the same moment; pressing a key causes time to replace frequency for three seconds.

Other features include excellent synchronous selectable sideband; a one-level attenuator; continuously variable separate bass and treble controls, rare in world band receivers; a squelch control for the aeronautical band; a massive telescopic antenna for shortwave and FM; a built-in ferrite rod antenna for mediumwave AM and longwave; selectable slow/fast AGC decay; a huge, high-contrast LCD clearly visible from above, head-on and below; an S-9/+60 dB analog signal-strength meter, although for now its readings are greatly understated; and "smart" illumination of the LCD and signal-strength meter.

There is also a plastic tuning knob with a fixed "speed" dimple and variable-rate incremental tuning (VRIT) circuitry—if the knob is turned quickly, the tuning rate increases very slightly. As implemented that speed change is so subtle as to be virtually unnoticeable, which panelists unanimously preferred to a higher speed differential. Holding down the slew buttons produces a similar but appropriately greater shift in tuning speed.

On the back panel are high- and low-impedance antenna connections for the various bands, and useful but unhandy switches for selecting antennas. The "whip" setting allows an external shortwave antenna to make use of the telescopic antenna's preamplifier, boosting weak-signal performance but also risking overloading under some circumstances.

There are also line outputs for recording, an external-speaker jack and a DC power input. The receiver is powered by either six internal "D" batteries—alkaline cells last roughly 35 hours—or a UL-approved 120V AC adaptor (220V for Europe and Australasia), supplied.

Overall Performance Excellent

Overall, performance is excellent—approaching that of the Drake SW8, and better than that of any portable available. Our laboratory findings imply superior dynamic range and related third-order intercept point, although we couldn't make exact measurements because of phase noise from the synthesizer—with all tested samples, the synthesizer has proven to be less quiet than that of the SW8. Overloading thus is unlikely to be a problem in North America and much of the rest of the world, even with a high-gain external antenna.

The S-800 has three voice bandwidths, nominally 6, 4 and 2.3 kHz, but which actually measure 6.1 kHz (7.4 kHz with our earliest sample), 5.5 kHz and 2.6 kHz. The difference between a wide bandwidth of 6.1 kHz and an intermediate bandwidth of 5.5 kHz is so minimal as to be virtually pointless. However, the SW8's bandwidths measured 7.8, 5.2 and 2.6 kHz—close to those of our first Satellit unit. This implies that the S-800's wide bandwidth should be in the 7 kHz to 8 kHz range once production variances get squared away.

At close to these expected measurements, our first S-800 worked very well in rejecting adjacent-channel interference under a wide variety of reception conditions. Moreover, each bandwidth may be selected independent or dependent of mode, as the user commands. Skirt selectivity and ultimate rejection are excellent with all bandwidths.

The telescopic antenna is fully 57 inches or 145 cm long, and looks as tough as a .410

shotgun barrel. This is important, because size enhances weak-signal sensitivity and it is much longer than the SW8's antenna. Because it is so heavy, it would normally flop over if tilted even slightly, so there are spring-loaded detents to hold it vertically— or tilted at either 45 or 90 degrees. If it is too long to be fully extended without hitting the ceiling, it can be compressed slightly.

Excellent blocking performance helps keep weak-signal sensitivity consistent under various conditions. Single-sideband and RTTY reception are aided by the sort of rock-solid stability associated with professional-grade receivers. The AGC threshold—the level of signal needed to activate the AGC—is simply ideal. However, image and IF rejection have thus far varied considerably from sample to sample. Front-end selectivity is fair, but adequate if you don't live near a mediumwave AM transmitter.

Every synthesized receiver has silent "birdie" signals, and the Satellit 800 is no exception, although virtually all are too weak to move the signal meter. Because of their frequencies and other characteristics, these birdies rarely cause interference to on-channel world band or Western Hemisphere mediumwave AM stations. For other applications, they have less than one chance in 250 of being audible on any given utility or ham shortwave frequency, longwave channel or non-American mediumwave channel. However, an obnoxious type of spurious signal, not found on the SW8, appears *inter alia* on 20,000 kHz and disrupts WWV reception.

The S-800's weak-signal sensitivity with an outboard antenna is similar to that of the SW8 and the Sony ICF-2010 portable, and is fairly good even by tabletop receiver standards. Field sensitivity is less with the telescopic antenna, but even then is comparable to that of the highest-rated portables, thanks in no small part to the antenna's length.

FM and Mediumwave Reception

Sensitivity on mediumwave AM measures the same as on shortwave, although field sensitivity is not of DX caliber when the built-in ferrite rod antenna is in use.

Accordingly, we tested two S-800 units with the Terk AM Advantage outboard antenna (Model AM1000, $49.95 plus shipping from www.terk.com, +1-631/543-1900 or 800/942-8375). When connected directly to an external antenna input, the Terk allows signals from roughly 550-1630 kHz to rise in strength considerably, provided it is properly peaked and rotated. However, unlike an external shortwave antenna, an outboard mediumwave AM antenna always works best if the rear antenna switch is never set to "whip," as that introduces more noise than gain.

Unlike with shortwave signals, medium-wave AM stations are often easily nulled by a rotatable loop antenna. This allows at least some distant stations to be heard even when they are co-channel to other audible signals. The Terk or nearly any other outboard loop antenna is far easier to rotate than the entire huge receiver.

The LCD emits slight forward radiation, but not enough to be picked up by the Terk antenna so long as it was placed at either of the receiver's sides. To put this into perspective, this radiation extends out a third as far as it does on the new $4,000 Ten-Tec R340 professional receiver.

Unlike most tabletop models, the S-800 receives FM broadcasts between 87.0 and 108.0 MHz. It comes through as monaural through the built-in speaker, but in stereo through outboard speakers or headphones, as well as the line output. It performs well, although the capture ratio is only average and nearby FM transmitters may cause overloading. FM audio quality is good— better than that of any world band portable, although not up to that of a good boom box or Bose radio.

Superior Tonal Quality

First-class audio quality should be a major concern in the design of any premium radio, especially on world band where proper audio can help overcome the medium's inherent aural challenges. Yet, many otherwise worthy receivers, such as the Sony ICF-2010, suffer from mediocre tonal quality because of lackluster audio circuitry and speakers.

Not so the S-800. Its tonal quality, although hardly of audiophile caliber and lacking a solid bottom, is at the top of the world band pack. It sounds better than virtually any other world band receiver that's not equipped with a Sherwood SE-3—a pricey accessory that costs as much as an entire S-800. However, its average overall distortion from 100-3,000 Hertz is higher than that of the SW8—5.3 percent in the conventional AM reception mode—but it drops to 2.4 percent when synchronous selectable sideband is in use.

Much of the exceptionally pleasant listening quality of the S-800 results from its superior speaker and audio stage, complete with continuously variable bass and treble controls that provide a degree of equalization rarely found on world band receivers. And unlike every other model PASSPORT has tested to date, the S-800 comes not with earbuds or walkaround headphones, but rather with a splendid pair of padded, full-size headphones.

Sync Improves Audio, Interference

The S-800's synchronous selectable sideband performs excellently. Although this is an advanced-tech feature, on this receiver it has been designed so virtually anybody can operate it easily.

Synchronous selectable sideband does much more than reduce overall distortion—this characteristic is more of a welcomed side effect than an intended objective.

What synchronous selectable sideband is designed to do is to knock out "selective" fading distortion by using a stable, receiver-generated carrier in lieu of the received station's transmitted carrier.

Selective fading is not ordinary fading, but rather a specific type which reduces the strength of a signal's carrier relative to that of its sidebands. The greater the relative reduction, the more the station sounds distorted. A receiver-generated carrier eliminates this problem.

But that's not all. Even more important is that synchronous selectable sideband allows the listener to reject the more-interfered of a station's two sidebands which, because they are identical, either one is redundant. This greatly diminishes adjacent-channel interference—one of the great banes of world band listening. With all but very weakest of signals it usually improves the readability of received programs, although because of minor circuit noise from the added circuitry it can be either a plus or a minus with truly faint DX signals.

The synchronous circuitry manages to secure and hold lock on all but the faintest of carriers. Sometimes you can even hear it generate a whistle that falls in pitch as it homes in on its prey, like a heat-seeking missile. The unwanted sideband—the one suffering from adjacent-channel interference—is attenuated via phasing, with a 27 dB reduction on top of the existing rejection from IF filtering. This is not enough to render the unwanted sideband completely inaudible under all circumstances, but at a minimum is enough to eliminate it as a nuisance factor. Sophisticated IF sideband filtering, used on costly tabletop models, is a better technique for deep sideband rejection and AGC triggering, but the S-800's phasing circuit is affordable and performs very well, indeed.

Another advantage of the S-800's synchronous selectable sideband is that if you tune away from the frequency on which it has locked, it will allow you to scan the bands without having to put up with the obnoxious squeals that some synchronous detectors emit unless you switch them off manually. Once you stop tuning, it begins to re-establish lock on the new frequency.

Because synchronous selectable sideband places additional circuitry in the reception chain, the general rule of thumb that it should not be used unless necessary. Indeed, the S-800 operating manual states this outright. However, in practice the S-800's sync circuit works so well that we found ourselves using it virtually all the time because it almost invariably improves the listenability of most programs.

Ergonomics Enhance Operation

The S-800's ergonomics make this receiver a pleasure to operate. One reason is the huge front-panel acreage, which allows for numerous discrete, full-size controls that are widely spaced.

The LCD is a whopping 6¾ by 2¾ inches, or 171 by 70 mm—larger than the entire outsides of some compact portables. The frequency and time appear in bold, high-contrast numerals fully ¾ of an inch, or 19 mm, high. Alas, with such a large LCD you would think the time would be displayed separately from the frequency, but it isn't.

Like the analog signal meter, the LCD is nicely illuminated using heads-up logic that conserves battery power while leaving the light on when it is truly needed, such as when using the tuning knob or slewing controls.

Also clever is the frequency entry, provided you don't pause for long while entering the numbers. Just tap in the frequency, and—voilà—in three seconds it's there, or you

can tune in right away by pressing the decimal key twice. Ergonomics for the station presets are more typical; neither so convoluted as models using "page" presets, nor so straightforward as the one-touch presets found on the Sony ICF-2010.

The initial version of the tuning knob has been pedestrian, lacking any flywheel effect whatsoever. It also has had a slight wobble and a sharp bezel on the outer edge. The manufacturer claims this wobble will disappear once it adds ball bearings to the tuning shaft in future production.

Bottom Line

The Grundig Satellit 800 is a major development in world band receivers, delivering far more in performance than its price suggests. For top-notch listening to world band programs it outperforms any portable or PC-controlled receiver we have tested, regardless of price, and is more pleasant on the ears than most tabletop models.

It also works well with amateur and utility signals. The aeronautical band is a nice bonus, too, performing comparably to a typical handheld scanner.

The S-800 is one of the most straightforward and enjoyable radios to operate we have come across. What's needed to complete this picture is improved quality of assembly. Historically, this has come about over time, and hopefully will have materialized by the time you read this.

An *RDI WHITE PAPER* is available for this model.

The PASSPORT *portatop review team includes Lawrence Magne, Tony Jones, Craig Tyson and George Zeller, with Avery Comarow, George Heidelman and John Wagner. Laboratory measurements by Robert Sherwood.*

Tabletop Receivers for 2001

Tabletop receivers flush out tough game—faint stations swamped by other signals. That's why they are prized by radio aficionados known as "DXers," an old telegraph term meaning long distance.

But tabletop models aren't for everybody, and it shows. Even in prosperous North America and Europe, tabletop unit sales are minimal even while the roster of choices is as great as ever.

Professional models are tempting alternatives to tabletop offerings, and they are built to last. These are reviewed elsewhere in PASSPORT REPORTS, but steep prices keep most buyers away.

If all you want to hear are non-DX signals—daytime stations, say and your portable can't quite hack it, look instead to a portatop model or a better-rated portable. Ironically, with powerful, clean signals certain everyday portables can actually sound better than a number of the costlier receivers. Problem is, most stations aren't powerful or interference-free, much less both.

If you are already using a portable with an outdoor antenna and it is being interfered with by electrical noise from nearby motors, dimmers and such, you probably won't benefit from a tabletop. Its superior circuitry will just boost the local noise right along with distant signals.

Heavy Artillery

Tabletop sets, like portatop and professional models, are heavy artillery for where signals are routinely weak—places like the North American Midwest and West, or Australia and New Zealand. Even elsewhere there can be a problem when world band signals have to follow paths over or near the geomagnetic North Pole. To check, place a string on a globe—a conventional map won't do—between you and from where the received station is transmitted (this is indicated in the Blue Pages). If the string passes near or above latitude 60° north, beware.

> **Tabletop models cost more than portables or portatops, less than professional receivers.**

Daytime Signals Weaker

Since the end of the Cold War many stations have compressed their schedules. Now, many programs—from Eastern European stations, for example—are heard only outside evening prime time.

Daytime signals tend to be weaker, especially when not beamed to your part of the world. However, thanks to the scattering properties of shortwave, you can still eavesdrop on many of these "off-beam" signals. But it's harder, and that's where a highly rated non-portable's longer reach comes in.

Cliff-Dwellers' Choice, but No FM

In high-rise buildings—especially urban—portables can disappoint. Reinforced buildings soak up signals, while local broadcast and cellular transmitters can interfere.

Here, your best bet for tough stations is a good tabletop or portatop model fed by a homebrew insulated-wire antenna along, or just outside, a window or balcony. Also, try an ordinary telescopic car antenna stuck perpendicularly out a window or balcony ledge. If your radio has a built-in preamplifier, all the better. With some portatop models, the built-in preamplifier can be accessed by connecting the external antenna to the receiver's telescopic-antenna input.

You can also try amplified ("active") antennas that have reception elements and amplifiers in separate modules. Another alternative is to amplify the above antennas with an active preselector. A suitable preselector and several active antennas are evaluated elsewhere in this PASSPORT REPORTS.

Most tabletop receivers are pricier than portables, but less expensive than professional supersets. For that money you tend to get not only excellent performance, but also a fairly robust device—tabletop models are not only made better than portables, but also are relatively easy to service and backed up by knowledgeable service facilities. However, what you rarely find in a tabletop is reception of the everyday 87.5-108 MHz FM band—for this coverage, look to a portatop.

Good Antenna Required

Tabletop receiver performance is greatly determined by antenna quality and placement. If you don't live in an apartment, go with a first-rate outdoor wire antenna, like those from Antenna Supermarket and Alpha Delta—usually under $100. A good world band specialty antenna is a must if your tabletop model is to perform properly. For performance findings and specifics for best installation, check with the Radio Database International White Paper, *Popular Outdoor Antennas*, as well as the report on active antennas elsewhere in this PASSPORT REPORTS.

Bargain for 2001

Tabletop receivers are the domain of those for whom money is secondary to performance. Lower-cost models exist, but these are usually lacking in features, performance or both.

However, for now there is a pleasant receiver being sold at a bargain price: the Lowe HF-150. The '150 simply wasn't moving, so its price has been reduced for the time being. Add to that the new Grundig Satellit 800 portatop reviewed

elsewhere in PASSPORT REPORTS, and it's never been a better time to get quality performance at a sensible price.

Complete Findings Now Available

Our unabridged laboratory and hands-on test results for each receiver are too exhaustive to reproduce here. However, they are available for selected models as PASSPORT's Radio Database International White Papers—details on availability are elsewhere in this book.

Tips for Using this Section

Receivers are listed in order of suitability for listening to difficult-to-hear world band stations. Important secondary consideration is given to audio fidelity and ergonomics. Street prices are given, including European and Australian VAT/GST where applicable. Prices vary, so take them as the general guide they are meant to be.

Unless otherwise stated, all tabletop models have:

- Digital frequency synthesis and display.
- Full coverage of at least the 155-29999 kHz longwave, mediumwave AM and shortwave spectra—including all world band frequencies—but no coverage of the FM broadcast band (87.5-108 MHz). Models designed for sale in certain countries have reduced tuning ranges.
- A wide variety of helpful tuning features.
- Synchronous selectable sideband via high-rejection IF filtering (not lower-rejection phasing), which greatly reduces adjacent-channel interference and selective-fading distortion.
  ☞ Many tabletop models can tune to the nearest 10 Hz or even 1 Hz, allowing the user to use the receiver's single-sideband circuitry to manually phase its BFO (internally generated carrier) with the station's transmitted carrier. Called "ECSS" (exalted-carrier, selectable-sideband)

tuning, this can be used in lieu of synchronous selectable sideband. However, in addition to the relative inconvenience of this technique, unlike synchronous detection, which re-phases continually and perfectly, ECSS is always slightly out of phase. This causes at least some degree of harmonic distortion to music and speech, while tuning to the nearest Hertz can generate slow-sweep fading (for this reason, mis-phasing by two or three Hertz may provide better results).

- Proper demodulation of modes used by non-world-band shortwave signals, except for models designed to be sold in certain countries. These modes include single sideband (LSB/USB) and CW ("Morse code"); also, with suitable ancillary devices, radioteletype (RTTY), frequency shift key (FSK) and radiofax (FAX).
- Meaningful signal-strength indication.
- Illuminated display.

What PASSPORT's Rating Symbols Mean

Star ratings: ✪✪✪✪✪ is best. Stars reflect overall performance and meaningful features, plus to some extent ergonomics and build quality. Price, appearance, country of manufacture and the like are not taken into account. With tabletop models there is a slightly greater emphasis on the ability to flush out tough, hard-to-hear signals, as this is one of the main reasons these sets are chosen. To facilitate comparison, the same rating norm is used for professional, portatop and portable models, reviewed elsewhere in this PASSPORT.

Passport's Choice. La crème de la crème. Our test team's personal picks of the litter—models we would buy or have bought for our personal use.

✪: A relative bargain, with decidedly more performance than the price would suggest. However, none of these receivers is cheap.

✪✪✪✪✪ 📄 *Passport's Choice*
Drake R8B

Price: $1,199.00 in the United States. CAN$1,819.00 in Canada. Also available in Germany.

Pro: Superior all-round performance for listening to world band programs and hunting DX catches, as well as utility, amateur and mediumwave AM signals. Mellow, above-average audio quality, especially with suitable outboard speaker or headphones. Selectable-sideband synchronous detector excels at reducing distortion caused by selective fading, as well as at diminishing or eliminating adjacent-channel interference; also has synchronous double sideband. Five well-chosen bandwidths, four suitable for world band. Highly flexible operating controls, including a powerful tunable AF notch filter (tunes to 5,100 Hz AF, but *see* Con) and an excellent passband offset control. Best ergonomics of any five-star model (*see* Con), plus LCD unusually easy to read. Tunes and displays in precise 10 Hz increments. Slow/fast/off AGC with superior performance characteristics. Exceptionally effective noise blanker. Helpful tuning features include 1,000 presets and sophisticated scanning functions; presets can be quickly accessed via tuning knob and slew buttons. Built-in preamplifier. Accepts two antennas, selectable via front panel. Two 24-hour clocks, with seconds displayed numerically and two-event timer (*see* Con). Helpful

Top-selling tabletop receiver is the Drake R8B. It's also the best performer, with superior factory service.

operating manual. Superior factory service, although older models aren't supported for as long as they used to be. Fifteen-day money-back trial period if ordered from factory.

Con: Virtually requires a good outboard speaker for non-headphone listening, but optional Drake MS8 outboard speaker not equal to the receiver's audio potential; try a good amplified computer speaker or high-efficiency passive speaker instead. Some "birdies." Neither clock shows when frequency displayed. Lightweight tuning knob lacks flywheel effect. No IF output. Other-wise-excellent tilt bail difficult to open. Notch filter does not tune below 500 Hz (AF).

Verdict: The American-made Drake R8B is the only non-professional receiver we have ever tested that gets *everything* right, where something important isn't missing or sputtering. This means there's little point spending money on such performance-enhancing accessories as the Sherwood SE-3, although a better (outboard) speaker is worth considering if you want to get the full benefit of the R8B's fidelity potential.

An *RDI WHITE PAPER* is available for this model.

R.L. DRAKE: CHANGING OF THE GUARD

Since 1943 the R.L. Drake Company has been legendary for providing excellent receivers, ham radio gear and other equipment at prices under those of its competitors. For decades this formula led to financial success—Hallicrafters, Hammarlund, Heath, National and other veteran players went belly-up, while Collins abandoned the market. Indeed, in 1993 *Forbes* cited Drake as an example of managerial excellence.

But times have changed, and not for the better. The amateur radio market, once Drake's bread and butter, has nosedived, while Drake's ventures into satellite TV and such have been underwhelming. So on November 1, 1999, the Drake family interests sold the company to four of the company's officers. The SW1 and SW2 receivers were discontinued, and the firm's enviable inventory of spare parts for discontinued models was sold off. Service was restricted to recent models.

The end of an era? Obviously, Drake has dropped its legendary long-term service, but otherwise there are hopeful signs. Four experienced owners are now guiding the ship, so they're unlikely to sit back and let it fade away.

Part of this success strategy is Drake's 1997 working agreement with Lextronix/Grundig. It has already resulted in one new receiver, the Grundig Satellit 800 reviewed in the portatop section of PASSPORT REPORTS. Both firms are tight-lipped about other plans, but it is obvious that other projects are in the works.

This is a propitious marriage of talents. Drake has always had a knack for designing cost-effective shortwave receivers, but has never been a marketing fireball. Lextronix/Grundig, on the other hand, is a marketing superstar, but has lacked shortwave R&D talent. With this new team Grundig can seriously challenge Sony, the other and technically savvy world band superpower.

In the meantime Drake not only continues to manufacture its own high-quality receivers and other products, it also makes its facilities available to produce items for other manufacturers.

✪✪✪✪✪ *Passport's Choice*
AOR AR7030, AOR AR7030 "PLUS"

Price: *AR7030:* CAN$1,995.00 in Canada. £799.00 in the United Kingdom (£680.00 plus shipping for export). AUS$2,820.00 in Australia. *AR7030 PLUS:* $1,399.95 in the United States. CAN$2,895.00 in Canada. £949.00 in the United Kingdom (£765.10 plus shipping for export). AUS$3,150.00 in Australia.

Pro: In terms of sheer performance for program listening, as good a radio as we've ever tested. Except for sensitivity to weak signals (*see* Con), easily overcome, the same comment applies to DX reception. Exceptionally quiet circuitry. Superior audio quality. Synchronous selectable sideband performs quite well for reduced selective-fading distortion and easier rejection of interference. Synchronous detection circuit allows for either selectable-sideband or double-sideband reception. Best dynamic range of any consumer-grade radio we've ever tested. Nearly all other lab measurements are top-drawer. Four voice bandwidths (2.3, 7.0, 8.2 and 10.3 kHz), with cascaded ceramic filters, come standard; up to six, either ceramic or mechanical, upon request (*see* Con). Superior audio quality, so receiver is well suited to listening to programs hour after hour. Advanced tuning and operating features aplenty, including passband tuning. Tunable audio (AF) notch and noise blanker now available, albeit as an option; notch filter extremely effective, with little loss of audio fidelity. Built-in preamplifier (*see* Con). Automatically self-aligns and centers all bandwidth filters for optimum performance, then displays the actual measured bandwidth of each. Remote keypad (*see* Con). Accepts two antennas. IF output. Optional improved processor unit now has 400 memories, including 14-character alphanumeric readout for station names. World Time clock, which displays seconds, calendar and timer/snooze

Tree-type operating logic means you'll either love or hate the AOR AR7030. Recently improved to enhance robustness, it is a sterling performer.

features. Superior mediumwave AM performance. Superior factory service.

Con: Unusually hostile ergonomics, including tree-logic operating scheme, especially in PLUS version. Remote control unit, which has to be aimed carefully at either the front or the back of the receiver, is required to use certain features, such as direct frequency entry; not all panelists were enthusiastic about this arrangement, wishing that a mouse-type umbilical cable had been used instead. Although remote keypad can operate from across a room, the LCD characters are too small to be seen from such a distance. LCD omits certain important information, such as signal strength, when radio in various status modes. Sensitivity to weak signals good, as are related noise-floor measurements, but could be a bit better; a first-rate antenna overcomes this. Because of peculiar built-in preamplifier/attenuator design in which the two are linked, receiver noise rises slightly when preamplifier used in +10 dB position, or attenuator used in -10 dB setting; however, PLUS version remedies this. When six bandwidths used (four standard ceramics, two optional mechanicals), ultimate rejection, although superb with widest three bandwidths, cannot be measured beyond -80/

-85 dB on narrowest three bandwidths because of phase noise; still, ultimate rejection is excellent or better with these narrow bandwidths. Lacks, and would profit from, a bandwidth of around 4 or 5 kHz; a Collins mechanical bandwidth filter of 3.5 kHz (nominal at -3db, measures 4.17 kHz at -6 dB) is an option worth considering. Such Collins filters, in the two optional bandwidth slots, measure as having poorer shape factors (1:1.8 to 1:2) than the standard-slot MuRata ceramic filters (1:1.5 to 1:1.6). LCD emits some digital electrical noise, potentially a problem if an amplified (active) antenna is used with its pickup element (e.g. telescopic rod) placed near the receiver. Minor microphonics (audio feedback), typically when internal speaker is used, noted in laboratory; in actual listening, however, this is not noticeable. Uses outboard AC adaptor instead of built-in power supply.

☞ Mechanical encoders on the '7030 were formerly subject to an above-average failure rate, seemingly because of corrosion on contacts. Starting with serial number 102050, with production as of late July of 1999, AOR has replaced the original Bourns mechanical encoder with a metal-encased version from Alps as follows: AR7030 now uses only Alps mechanical encoders; AR7030 PLUS now uses Alps mechanical and Bourns optical encoders. A conversion kit for earlier units out of warranty is available for £20 plus shipping, although it requires a degree of technical skill to install.

☞ Features of the PLUS version can be incorporated into existing regular models by skilled electronic technicians. Contact the manufacturer or its agents for specifics.

☞ Recently there was a suggestion that it is better to listen to the AR7030 on

LAB NUMBERS: TOP TWO TABLETOPS

	Drake R8B	AOR AR7030
Max. Sensitivity/Noise Floor	0.2 μV, **E**/–131 dBm, **E**	0.2 μV, **E**/–128 dBm, **G**
Blocking	135 dB, **S**	>130 dB, **E**
Shape Factors, voice BWs	1:2.09–1:2.92, **G**	1:1.52–1:1.96, **E**
Ultimate Rejection	80 dB, **E**	90 dB, **S**
Front-End Selectivity	Half octave, **E**	High/low pass, **F**
Image Rejection	85 dB, **E**	>100 dB, **S**
First IF Rejection	>90 dB, **S**	95 dB, **S**
Dynamic Range/IP3 (5 kHz)	75 dB, **G**/–20 dBm, **E**	82 dB, **E**/+1 dBm, **S**
Dynamic Range/IP3 (20 kHz)	89 dB, **G**/+2 dBm, **E**	100 dB, **S**/+28 dBm, **S**
Phase Noise	114 dBc, **G**	130 dBc, **S**
AGC Threshold	0.9 μV, **S**	2.25 μV, **G**
Overall Distortion, sync	0.4%, **S**	2.0%, **E**
Notch filter depth	55 dB, **S**	55 dB, **S**

IBS Lab Ratings: **S** Superb   **E** Excellent   **G** Good   **F** Fair   **P** Poor

headphones using the speaker socket rather than the headphone jack. Our tests show that there is not only no improvement—because the RF gain has to be turned down, weak-signal reception actually becomes worse—but the resulting sound is so loud as to be a hearing hazard.

Verdict: This is definitely not your grandfather's shortwave receiver. The AR7030, designed and manufactured in England, is now an even better performer in its PLUS incarnation. Too, since mid-1999 the company, especially in the PLUS version, has addressed encoder-failure problems that showed up in earlier production; the reliable performance of our improved unit suggests that this has been successful.

Alas, ergonomics, already peculiar and cumbersome in the "barefoot" version, are even more hostile in the PLUS incarnation. This and slightly limited sensitivity to weak signals aside, the '7030 is arguably the best choice for serious DX available on the scotch side of a professional-grade receiver. This is a radio you'll really need to get your hands on for a few days before you'll know whether it's love or hate—or something between.

✪✪✪✪½
Japan Radio NRD-545

Price: $1,799.95 in the United States. CAN$3,299.00 in Canada. £1,299.00 in the United Kingdom. AUS$3,984.00 in Australia. ¥198,000 in Japan.

Pro: Easily upgraded by changing software ROMs. Fully 998 bandwidths provide unprecedented flexibility. Razor-sharp skirt selectivity, especially with voice bandwidths. Outstanding array of tuning aids, including 1,000 presets. Wide array of reception aids, including passband offset, tunable notch and synchronous selectable sideband having good lock. Highly adjustable AGC in all modes requiring BFO.

Most DSP receivers are of professional caliber and priced accordingly. One exception is Japan Radio's NRD-545, with first-class ergonomics.

Tunes in ultra-precise 1 Hz increments; displays in 10 Hz increments. Superior ergonomics, among the best to be found. Some audio shaping. Virtually no spurious radiation of digital "hash." Superior reception of utility signals.

Con: Ultimate rejection only fair, although average ultimate rejection equivalent is 10-15 dB better; this unusual gap results from intermodulation (IMD) inside the digital signal processor. Audio quality is sometimes tough sledding in the unvarnished AM mode—synchronous-AM detector helps clear things up. No AGC adjustment in AM mode or with synchronous selectable sideband, and lone AGC decay rate too fast. Dynamic range only fair. Synchronous selectable sideband sometimes slow to kick in. Notch filter tunes no higher than 2,500 Hz AF. Signal-strength indicator overreads at higher levels. Frequency display misreads by up to 30 Hz. No IF output, nor can one be retrofitted. World Time clock doesn't show when frequency displayed.

Verdict: In many ways Japan Radio's NRD-545 is a remarkable performer, especially for utility and tropical-bands DXing. With its first-class ergonomics it is always a pleasure to operate, but more is needed to make this the ultimate receiver it could and should be.

Icom's IC-R75 now includes some DSP capability. Its synchronous detector is a flop, but it is a bargain for first-rate utility reception.

★★★¼
Icom IC-R75/Icom IC-R75E

Price: *Receiver, including UT-106 DSP unit:* $679.95 in the United States. CAN$1,399.00 in Canada. £699.99 in the United Kingdom. AUS$1,820.00 (AUS$1,650.00 sans DSP) in Australia. *Icom Replacement Bandwidth Filters:* $160-200 or equivalent worldwide. *Sherwood SE-3 Mark III (aftermarket):* $490.00 ($590.00 for deluxe version) including down converter and installation, plus shipping, in the United States. $460.00 ($560.00 for deluxe version) including down converter but not installation, plus shipping, outside the United States.

Pro: Dual passband tuning acts as variable bandwidth and a form of IF shift (*see* Con). Reception of faint signals alongside powerful competing ones aided by excellent ultimate selectivity and good dynamic range. Outstanding rejection of spurious signals. Excellent reception of utility and ham signals, as well as world band signals painstakingly tuned via "ECSS" technique. Tunes and displays in precise 0.001 kHz increments. Two-level preamp allows excellent sensitivity to weak signals. DSP unit with automatic variable notch filter helps improve intelligibility of some tough signals and reduce heterodyne ("whistle") interference. Fairly good ergonomics. Adjustable AGC—fast, slow, off. Pretty good audio with suitable outboard speaker. Effective noise blanker. Two antenna inputs, switchable. Signal-strength indicator unusually linear above S-9, and can be set to hold a peak reading briefly. Audio out jack for recording or feeding low-power FM transmitter to hear world band around the house. Tunes to 60 MHz, including 6 meter VHF ham band.

Con: No synchronous selectable sideband without aftermarket SE-3 installed. Dual passband tuning usually has little impact on received world band signals and is inoperative when synchronous detection is in use. Double-sideband synchronous detector works so poorly as to be virtually useless. DSP's automatic variable notch tends not to work with AM-mode signals not received via "ECSS" technique (tuning AM-mode signals as though they were single sideband). Mediocre audio through internal speaker and no tone controls. Keypad requires frequencies to be entered in MHz format with decimal or trailing zeroes, a pointless inconvenience. Some knobs small. Weird knob adjusts RF gain to 12 o'clock position, then becomes a squelch control. Some distortion in AM mode, but only below 400 Hz AF. Uses outboard AC adaptor in lieu of internal power supply. Can read clock or frequency, but not both at the same time.

☞ The above star rating rises to ★★★½ when the receiver is equipped with the Sherwood SE-3 aftermarket accessory. However, because the 'R75 uses two intermediate frequencies (IFs) for bandwidth filtering, the SE-3's offset has to be tweaked when going from a bandwidth having one IF to another with a different IF.

Verdict: The Icom IC-R75 is a first-rate receiver for unearthing tough utility and ham signals, as well as world band signals received via manual "ECSS" tuning. Even though it is not all it could have been for top-notch world band reception, it is now fully equipped and priced to move—for utility DXing it is a bargain.

★★★★ 📃 ⓒ
Lowe HF-150

Price, without keypad or other options: *HF-150:* to be announced (*see* ☞, below). *Keypad:* £53.00 in the United Kingdom. £45.00 plus shipping for export.

☞ As of the last half of 2000, the HF-150 with AC adaptor was £299.00 in the United Kingdom and £255.00 plus shipping for export via SMC, the current manufacturer (www.smc-comms.com). SMC informs PASSPORT that prices are to increase in the near future, after which our ⓒ rating may or may not apply, depending on the new pricing.

☞ Lowe Electronics (www.lowe.co.uk), the HF-150's original designer and manufacturer, has been selling a onetime batch of these units, which are new. They were originally made by SMC when it had quality control problems, but shortly thereafter were remanufactured by Lowe to Lowe's established standards. The offer is £249.00 including 230V AC adaptor in the United Kingdom, $320.00 plus $35.00 shipping but sans 120V AC adaptor exported to the United States (duty is only occasionally charged). Lowe believes this supply of receivers probably will be exhausted by early 2001. The 120V AC adaptor used for the Palstar R30 series (www.palstarinc.com) reportedly works well with the HF-150; otherwise, try for a regulated adaptor at Radio Shack.

Pro: Top-notch world band and mediumwave AM audio quality, provided a good external speaker or simple headphones are used. Excellent-performing synchronous selectable sideband greatly reduces adjacent-channel interference and selective-fading distortion with world band, long-wave and mediumwave AM signals; also, slightly boosts recoverable audio from weak signals and reduces overall distortion from 1.2% (ordinary AM mode) to a negligible 0.7% (sync). High-rejection 6.5

Rugged, with unbeatable fidelity, the Lowe HF-150 is priced like a portable but performs like a portatop.

and 2.6 kHz bandwidth filters with excellent shape factor (1:1.6). Except for front-end selectivity (*see* Con), all measurements of performance range from good to superb. Exceptionally rugged aluminum housing. Mouse keypad, virtually foolproof and a *de rigeur* option. Sixty presets store frequency and mode. Tunes, but does not display, in exacting 8 Hz increments, unusually precise. Single-sideband reception well above the portable norm.

Con: Grossly inferior front-end selectivity can result in spurious signals if the radio is connected to a significant external antenna and/or used near mediumwave AM transmitters. Clumsy to use as a quasi-portable. Audio only okay through internal speaker; needs high-quality outboard speaker to achieve its considerable audio fidelity potential. No tone controls. Frequency displays no finer than 1 kHz resolution. Lacks lock indicator or similar aid (e.g., finer frequency-display resolution) for handy use of synchronous detector. No tunable notch filter, adjustable noise blanker, passband tuning or signal-strength indicator. Operation of some buttons may confuse initially. Tends to slide around during operation. Lacks elevation feet or tilt bail. On some samples, erratic contact on outboard-speaker socket. Display not illuminated, although Lowe can install backlighting. AC adaptor rather than inboard power supply.

☞ Lowe Electronics no longer makes the receivers which bear its name. The HF-150 is now manufactured by South Midlands Communications in England, while the HF-350 (see) is designed and produced by Palstar in America. Although SMC's initially serious quality control difficulties appear to have been largely resolved, the HF-150's former international sales and service network no longer exists. Also, the superior "Europa" version is no longer available.

☞ Kiwa Electronics (www.kiwa.com/bcb.html) offers a BCB Rejection Filter for $60 which reportedly helps reduce spurious mediumwave AM signals intruding into the shortwave spectrum. Although it has not been tested by us, user reports suggest that it does help, although in some cases it won't completely overcome the problem.

Verdict: The near-portatop Lowe HF-150's exceptional synchronous selectable sideband and audio quality make it an excellent-fidelity choice if you don't live near one or more mediumwave AM transmitters. At the prices in effect as of the last half of 2000, the HF-150 is nothing short of a bargain.

📄 An *RDI WHITE PAPER* is available for this model.

The Icom IC-R8500 cuts the mustard fully as well as other wideband tabletops, yet costs less.

✪✪✪✪
Icom IC-R8500A

Price: *IC-R8500A-02 (no cellular reception):* $1,499.95 in the United States. *IC-R8500A:* $1,799.95 for government use or export in the United States. CAN$2,849.00 in Canada. £1,489.00 in the United Kingdom. AUS$3,195.00 in Australia.

Pro: Wide-spectrum multimode coverage from 0.1-2000 MHz includes longwave, mediumwave AM, shortwave and scanner frequencies all in one receiver. Physically very rugged, with professional-grade cast-aluminum chassis and impressive computer-type innards. Generally superior ergonomics, with generous-sized front panel having large and well-spaced controls, plus outstanding tuning knob with numerous tuning steps. 1,000 presets and 100 auto-write presets have handy naming function. Superb weak-signal sensitivity. Pleasant, low-distortion audio aided by audio peak filter. Passband tuning ("IF shift"). Unusually readable LCD. Tunes and displays in precise 10 Hz increments. Three antenna connections. Clock-timer, combined with record output and recorder-activation jack, make for superior hands-off recording of favorite programs.

Con: No synchronous selectable sideband. Bandwidth choices for world band and other AM-mode signals leap from a very narrow 2.7 kHz to a broad 7.1 kHz with nothing between, where something is most needed; third bandwidth is 13.7 kHz, too wide for world band, and no provision is made for a fourth bandwidth filter. Only one single-sideband bandwidth. Unhandy carousel-style bandwidth selection with no permanent indication of which bandwidth is in use. Poor dynamic range, surprising at this price point. Passband tuning ("IF shift") does not work in the AM mode, used by world band and mediumwave AM-band stations. No tunable notch filter. Built-in speaker mediocre. Uses outboard AC adaptor instead of customary inboard power supply.

☞ The Icom IC-R8500 is available in two similarly priced versions, "02" and "03." The "02" incarnation, sold to the public in the United States, is the same as the "03" version, but does not receive the *verboten* 824-849 and 869-894 MHz cellular bands. In the U.S., the "03" version is available legally only to government-approved organizations, although others reportedly have been bootlegging the "03" version by mail order from Canada. Outside the United States, the "03" version is usually the only one sold.

☞ Also tested with Sherwood SE-3 non-factory accessory, which was outstanding at adding selectable synchronous sideband and provides passband tuning in the AM mode used, among other things, by world band stations. This and replacing the widest bandwidth with a 4 to 5 kHz bandwidth dramatically improve performance on shortwave, mediumwave AM and longwave.

Verdict: The large Icom IC-R8500 is really a scanner that happens to cover world band, rather than *vice versa.* As a standalone world band receiver, it makes little sense, but it is well worth considering if you want worthy scanner and shortwave performance all in one rig.

✪✪✪✪
AOR AR5000+3

Price: *AR5000+3 receiver:* $2,139.95 in the United States. CAN$3,699.00 in Canada. £1,799.00 in the United Kingdom. AUS$4,190.00 in Australia. *Collins 6 kHz mechanical filter (recommended):* $149.95 in the United States. £76.00 in the United Kingdom.

Pro: Ultra-wide-spectrum multimode coverage from 0.1-2,600 MHz includes longwave, mediumwave AM, shortwave and scanner frequencies all in one receiver. Helpful tuning features include fully 2,000 presets. Narrow bandwidth filter and optional Collins wide filter both have

The AOR AR5000+3 is a genuine wideband receiver, but unlike some others it includes features intended to improve world band reception.

superb skirt selectivity (standard wide filter's skirt selectivity unmeasurable because of limited ultimate rejection). Synchronous selectable and double sideband (*see* Con). Front-end selectivity, image rejection, IF rejection, weak-signal sensitivity, AGC threshold and frequency stability all superior. Exceptionally precise frequency readout to nearest Hertz. Most accurate displayed frequency measurement of any receiver tested to date. Superb circuit shielding results in virtually zero radiated digital "hash." IF output (*see* Con). Automatic Frequency Control (AFC) works on AM-mode, as well as FM, signals. Owner's manual, important because of operating system, unusually helpful.

Con: Synchronous detector loses lock easily, especially if selectable sideband feature in use, greatly detracting from the utility of this high-tech feature. Substandard rejection of unwanted sideband with selectable synchronous sideband. Overall distortion rises when synchronous detector used. Ultimate rejection of "narrow" 2.7 kHz bandwidth filter only 60 dB. Ultimate rejection mediocre (50 dB) with standard 7.6 kHz "wide" bandwidth filter, improves to an uninspiring 60 dB when replaced by optional 6 kHz "wide" Collins mechanical filter. Installation of optional Collins filter requires expertise, patience and special equipment. Poor dynamic range. Cumbersome ergonomics. No passband offset. No tunable notch filter. Needs good external speaker for good audio quality. World Time clock does not show when frequency displayed. IF output frequency 10.7 MHz instead of standard 455 kHz.

Verdict: Unbeatable in some respects, inferior in others—it comes down to what use you will be putting the radio. The optional 6 kHz Collins filter is strongly recommended, but it should be installed by your dealer at the time of purchase.

Retested for 2001
✪✪✪✪
Palstar R30, Palstar R30C, Lowe HF-350

Price: *R30:* $495.00 in the United States. *R30C:* $550.00 in the United States. *HF-350:* £375.00 in the United Kingdom.

☞ We tested the standard R30 version. The R30C is identical to the R30, except that a Collins mechanical filter is used for the narrow bandwidth—puzzling, in that the standard version already has superb skirt selectivity and ultimate rejection. The HF-350, like the R30, uses two MuRata ceramic filters, but the wide bandwidth is narrower—nominally 4 kHz, but in practice it could be closer to 5 kHz. Regardless, adjacent-channel interference would be reduced, but at the cost of audio bandwidth.

The Palstar R30/Lowe HF-350 does a limited number of things unusually well. It is much improved over the prototype tested last year.

Pro: Superb skirt selectivity (1:1.4) and ultimate rejection (90 dB); bandwidths measure 7.7 kHz (*see* Con) and 2.7 kHz, using MuRata ceramic filters (*see* Con). Generally good dynamic range. Pleasant audio quality with 7.7 kHz bandwidth (*see* Con). Overall distortion averages 0.5 percent, superb, in single-sideband mode (in AM mode, averages 2.9 percent, good, at 60% modulation and 4.4 percent, fair, at 95% modulation). Without exception, every other performance variable measures either good or excellent in PASSPORT's lab. Features include selectable slow/fast AGC decay; 20-100 Hz/100-500 Hz VRIT (slow/fast variable-rate incremental tuning) knob; 1 MHz slewing; and 100 non-volatile station presets that store frequency, bandwidth, mode, AGC setting and attenuator setting. Analog signal-strength indicator reads in useful S1-9/+60 dB standard and is reasonably accurate (*see* Con). High- and low-impedance antenna inputs. Also operates from ten firmly secured "AA" internal batteries (*see* Con). Lightweight and small (*see* Con). Appears to be robust. Good mediumwave and longwave weak-signal sensitivity. Switchable illumination of LCD and signal-strength indicator. Self-resetting circuit breaker. Optional AA30A and AM-30 active antennas (*see* "Dozen Active Antennas" elsewhere in PASSPORT REPORTS).

Con: No keypad for direct frequency entry (*see* ☞, below). No synchronous selectable sideband. Wide bandwidth slightly broad for a model lacking synchronous selectable sideband, often allowing adjacent-channel (5 kHz) heterodyne whistles to be heard; the HF-350 version's narrower wide bandwidth should resolve this, albeit by reducing audio bandwidth. Lacks features found in "top-gun" receivers, such as tunable notch filter, noise blanker, passband tuning and adjustable RF gain. No visual indication of which bandwidth is being used. No tone controls. Our unit's frequency readout off by 100 Hz. Signal-strength indicator drops about two "S" units when going from wide to narrow bandwidths. Several significant birdies, including one on 20,002 kHz; numerous other and faint birdies don't impact reception. Minor digital "hash" radiates about six inches or 15 centimeters from the front panel. Tiny identical front-panel buttons, including the MEM button which if accidentally pressed can erase a preset. Presets not as intuitive or easy to select as with various other models; lacks frequency information on existing presets during memory storage. Uses AC adaptor instead of built-in power supply. Batteries uniquely difficult to install, requiring partial disassembly of the receiver and care not to damage speaker connections or confuse polarities. Receiver's lightness allows it to slide around, especially when the tuning knob is pushed in to change VRIT increments; the added weight of batteries helps slightly.

☞ Industry scuttlebutt is that Palstar is likely to offer a keypad and outboard speaker as extra-cost options for 2001.

☞ Works best when grounded.

Verdict: Although the Ohio-made Palstar R30 family of receivers is significantly lacking in tuning and performance features, what it sets out to do, it does to a high standard. If you can abide the convoluted battery installation procedure, it can also be used as a quasi-portable.

Nevertheless, this receiver lacks a distinct identity. Although the audio is pleasant, it doesn't have synchronous selectable sideband, which is needed to make it a premium listener's radio like the Lowe HF-150; for now, it even omits tuning features found on portables costing a fraction as much. At the same time, its commendable electronic performance serves a limited purpose because the receiver lacks important features which help snare DX the way sophisticated tabletop models can.

But not everybody fits neatly into these either-or categories. One size doesn't fit all, and to that end the R30's straightforward concept and quality performance adds diversity and choice to the roster of available models.

Current Versions: Nearly each of the negative findings in our test of an R30 prototype last year have been addressed in the final production version—even a tilt bail has been added. Build quality is up to the usual tabletop standard and in some ways better; for example, it uses an optical rather than mechanical encoder to enhance reliability. The possible appearance in 2001 of an optional keypad would improve tuning flexibility.

Discontinued, still available
✪✪✪¾ 📃
Yaesu FRG-100

Price: $599.95 in the United States. CAN$899.00 in Canada. £389.00 in the United Kingdom. AUS$999.00 in Australia. No longer available in Japan.

Pro: Excellent performance in many respects. Includes three bandwidths, a noise blanker, selectable AGC, two attenuators, the ability to select 16 pre-programmed world band segments, two clocks, on-off timers, 52 tunable station presets that store frequency and mode

After a merger Yaesu left certain markets, including world band. The FRG-100 is the last chance to obtain a receiver with this legendary marque.

data, a variety of scanning schemes and an all-mode squelch. A communications-FM module, 500 Hz CW bandwidth and high-stability crystal are optional.

Con: No keypad for direct frequency entry (remediable, see ☞, below). No synchronous selectable sideband. Lacks features found in "top-gun" receivers: passband tuning, notch filter, adjustable RF gain. Simple controls and display, combined with complex functions, can make certain operations confusing. Dynamic range only fair. Uses AC adaptor instead of built-in power supply.

☞ An outboard accessory keypad is virtually a "must" for the FRG-100, and is a no-brainer to attach. Brodier E.E.I. (3 Place de la Fontaine, F-57420 Curvy, France) makes the best one. Reasonably similar is the costlier QSYer—SWL Version, available from Stone Mountain Engineering Company in Stone Mountain GA 30086 USA.

☞ In North America, the FRG-100 is sometimes thought of as having had two versions: the original "A" (American) version and, more recently, the "B", which incorporates one slight improvement. However, although the "A" designator was

ROLL YOUR OWN

During the golden era of kits—the fifties and early sixties—most came from the Heath Company of Benton Harbor, Michigan. These all but vanished after Heath dropped out, but radio kit building has been revived by various American and British firms in recent years.

Weekend Exercise

Most shortwave kits are novelties, but there is one exception: Ten-Tec's 1254 world band radio. This tabletop receiver is actually smaller than some portables, tuning 100 kilohertz through 30 Megahertz. Including shipping it sells for $204 to the continental United States, and US$210 to Hawaii, Alaska and Canada. In the United Kingdom, dealers offer it for £189.95. Parts quality appears to be excellent, and assembly runs at least 24 hours.

The straightforward 1254 has precious little in the way of features to complicate assembly: no keypad, for example, and no signal-strength indicator. No synchronous selectable sideband or tilt bail, either, or LSB/USB settings for single-sideband—much less adjustable AGC or any of the other goodies found on pricey tabletop supersets. It is powered by a simple outboard AC adaptor, and won't accept inboard batteries.

Digitally synthesized tuning is in increments as small as 500 Hz for single sideband and 5 kHz for AM-mode reception, such as world band. Bright red LEDs read out to the nearest 2.5 kHz in the single-sideband mode, the nearest 5 kHz in the AM mode. There is also a fast-tuning rate for the knob, much needed for going from one part of the radio spectrum to another. For tweaking between synthesizer tuning increments, there is an analog clarifier. Rounding out the minimalist roster of features are 15 presets.

Prosaic Performance

Radios in this price class never soar with eagles. The internal speaker is mediocre and phase noise is poor. Front-end selectivity is little better, as is evidenced by false signals within the longwave spectrum. Sensitivity on longwave and mediumwave AM is poor, and the set's digital circuitry radiates hash. AGC decay is somewhat fast for world band.

official, "B" is an informal suffix not actually indicated anywhere on the radio or its documentation.

Verdict: While sparse on features, in many respects the Yaesu FRG-100 succeeds in delivering worthy performance within its price class. Its lack of a keypad for direct frequency entry is now easily remediable (see ☞, above). According to the manufacturer, this model was discontinued in mid-1999. It continues to be available in various countries outside Japan, but even though it is a slow seller supplies should be exhausted soon.

▤ An *RDI WHITE PAPER* is available for this model.

AKD Target HF3, AKD Target HF3M, AKD Target HF3S, AKD Target HF3E, NASA HF-4/HF-4E

Price: *HF-4/HF-4E (not tested):* £149.00 in the United Kingdom. *HF3:* £159.95 in the United Kingdom. *HF3M:* £209.95 in the United Kingdom. *HF3S (not tested):* £159.95 in the United Kingdom. *HF3E (not tested):* £299.00 in the United Kingdom. *NASA AA-30 active antenna (not tested):* £59.95 in the United Kingdom.

Pro: *HF-4/HF-4E, HF3 and HF3M:* Low price. Superior rejection of spurious "image" signals. Third-order intercept point indicates superior strong-signal

The 1254 is a decent overall performer. The lone bandwidth is 5.6 kHz, a good choice for AM-mode reception and with worthy ultimate rejection—70 dB. Also showing up well in PASSPORT's lab are image rejection, sensitivity to weak world band signals, blocking (related to sensitivity), AGC threshold and frequency stability. Dynamic range is fair, yet superior for its price class; first IF rejection is fair, too. Overall distortion averages out as good, and with an external speaker the audio is surprisingly pleasant.

Made to Last

Ten-Tec's sturdy little Model 1254 kit is no DX wonder, and is painfully slim on features; the assembled Sony ICF-SW7600G, for example, is a better overall performer and costs less, to boot. But the 1254 makes for a fun weekend project, especially if you cut your teeth on Heathkits "back when." And the manufacturer's track record for hand-holding means that even if you put "X" where "Y" belongs, in the end the radio will really work.

And when you're through, you'll have something that normally costs far more—a tough little world band receiver that's likely to outlast any plastic portable.

There are several world band receiver kits available, but most are novelties. Not so the sturdy Ten-Tec 1254, attractively priced.

AKD's Target HF3 series, also sold as the NASA HF-4, is unusually affordable in the United Kingdom where it is not subject to import duties.

handling capability. Bandwidths have superb ultimate rejection. *HF-4/HF-4E, HF3M:* Equipped for weatherfax ("WEFAX") reception. *HF-4/HF-4E:* Two AM-mode bandwidths. Illuminated LCD. Configured to accept AA-30 active antenna.

Con: No keypad and variable-rate tuning knob is difficult to control. Broad skirt

selectivity. Single-sideband bandwidth relatively broad. Volume control fussy to adjust. Synthesizer tunes in relatively coarse 1 kHz increments, supplemented by an analog fine-tuning "clarifier" control. Single sideband requires both tuning controls to be adjusted. No synchronous selectable sideband, notch filter or pass-band tuning. Frequency readout off by 2 kHz in single-sideband mode. Uses AC adaptor instead of built-in power supply. No clock, timer or snooze feature. *HF3 and HF3M:* Bandwidths not selectable independent of mode. Only AM-mode bandwidth for world band reception. LCD not illuminated. *HF3:* Only one preset. No elevation feet or tilt bail. When switched on, goes not to the last-tuned frequency and mode but rather to the frequency and mode in the lone preset. *HF3S and HF-4/HF-4E, HF3M:* Only ten presets.

☞ These U.K.-made receivers routinely undergo minor enhancements and designations over time. According to Target, the HF3S is identical to the HF3 but with ten presets, whereas the HF3E is comparable to the HF3M, but with a "quasi-synchronous" detector and illuminated LCD.

Verdict: Surprisingly pleasant world band performance for the price, but frustrating to operate. Yet, these make economic sense in the U.K., where foreign models are relatively costly and neither of Sony's lap portables is even offered. If you would like to own the Target brand, go for the new "M" version; the new "E" version, although not tested, appears to be relatively pricey for what is offered.

★★½
Radio Shack DX-394

Price: CAN$219.99 in Canada. £149.95 in the United Kingdom. AUS$499.95 in Australia.

In some parts of the world the tabletop Radio Shack DX-394 is a steal, selling for less than many digital portables.

Pro: Low price in those parts of the world where the '394 is still sold. Advanced tuning features include 160 tunable presets (*see* Con). Tunes in precise 10 Hz increments. Modest size, light weight and built-in telescopic antenna provide some portable capability. Bandwidths have superior shape factors and ultimate rejection. Two 24-hour clocks, one of which shows independent of frequency display. Five programmable timers. 30/60 minute snooze feature. Noise blanker. In Canada, 30-day money-back period; conditions may apply.

Con: What appear to be four bandwidths turn out to be virtually one bandwidth, and it is too wide for optimum reception of many signals. Bandwidths, such as they are, not selectable independent of mode. No synchronous selectable sideband. Presets cumbersome to use. Poor dynamic range for a tabletop, a potential problem in Europe and other strong-signal parts of the world if an external antenna is used. Overall distortion, although acceptable, higher than desirable.

Verdict: Modest dimensions and equally modest performance, but a great price.

Discontinued, still available
✪✪½
Drake SW1

Price: $199.99 in the United States.

Pro: Exceptionally low price for such a high level of construction quality. Dynamic range, sensitivity to weak signals and certain other performance variables above average for price class. Pleasant audio. Large, bright digital display using LEDs much easier to read indoors than most. Easiest and simplest to use of any tabletop tested, with quality ergonomics. Superior factory service.

Con: Mediocre adjacent-channel rejection (selectivity) from the single bandwidth. No

Well-made with superior factory service, the bare-bones Drake SW1 has been discontinued. Yet, it is still available worldwide from Universal Radio.

features—*nada*, not even a signal-strength indicator—except for tuning. No single sideband. No synchronous selectable sideband. Increments for tuning and frequency display are relatively coarse. Annoying chugging during bandscanning. Uses AC adaptor instead of built-in power supply. Currently available mainly from only one dealer, Universal Radio—an American firm which exports worldwide, although its supplies are dwindling.

Verdict: A tempting price, but where are the features? And why such mediocre selectivity and loud chugging? Still, in many respects, such as the display and quality of construction and service, Drake's American-made SW1 offers solid value at a rock-bottom price. Because of construction quality and service, no other model of world band radio of any type under $400 comes as close to being a "friend for life."

The PASSPORT tabletop-model review team consists of Tony Jones, Lawrence Magne, David Walcutt, David Zantow and George Zeller; also, George Heidelman, Toshimichi Ohtake, Craig Tyson and John Wagner. Laboratory measurements by J. Robert Sherwood.

Black Boxes for The Non-Spy

Spooks use them. Armies use them. Even big fat ships on the sea use 'em.

Why shouldn't you use them, too?

They're "black boxes," receivers with no controls because only computers can operate them. These make sense for the likes of the National Security Agency, so why not for you? Coupling shortwave receivers to PCs allows the performance of each to enhance the capabilities of the other, especially if you tie your radio to databases or other relevant applications.

Problem is, benefits are minor relative to drawbacks, such as convoluted hardware and radio interference from PC hardware. Multi-billion dollar operations are set up to avoid these, but for one person in a home with a PC and radio it's lots tougher than plug-and-play.

Sales reflect this. Although proponents of PC-controlled receivers are enthusiastic and voluble, especially on the Internet, it turns out there's far more smoke than fire. Reliable industry sources report that actual sales levels have been consistently negligible following the initial months after product introduction.

PASSPORT's tests show that only one offering really cuts the mustard for world band: the $295 Ten-Tec RX-320, which earns four stars and is scheduled to remain in Ten-Tec's lineup indefinitely. Runner-up is the three-star Icom IC-PCR1000, which works equally well as a VHF+ scanner; its IC-PCR100 sibling is more rudimentary. The two-star WiNRADiO 1500e was recently replaced by the 1550e that reportedly incorporates some degree of improvement; the 1500e has served much better as a scanner than as a world band receiver.

Given progress in microprocessor and memory technology, it's hard to see PC-controlled receivers as anything more than transitional technology. In time DSP receivers with much of the horsepower of a PC should be able to provide five-star receiver performance with all the features of relevant PC apps—all in one handy, affordable box.

✪✪✪✪ ℮ *Passport's Choice*
Ten-Tec RX-320

Price: *RX-320:* $295 plus shipping worldwide. *Third-party control software:* Free–$99 worldwide.

Pro: Superior dynamic range. Apparently superb bandwidth shape factors (*see* Con). In addition to the supplied factory control software, third-party software is available, often for free, and may improve operation. Up to 34 bandwidths with third-party software. Tunes in extremely precise 1 Hz

increments (10 Hz with tested factory software); displays to the nearest Hertz, and frequency readout is easily user-aligned. Large, easy-to-read digital frequency display and faux-analog frequency bar. For PCs with sound cards, outstanding freedom from distortion aids in providing good audio quality with most but not all cards and speakers. Fairly good audio, but with limited treble, also available through radio for PCs without sound cards. Superb blocking performance helps maintain consistently good world band sensitivity. Passband offset (*see* Con). Spectrum display with wide variety of useful sweep widths (*see* Con). World time on-screen clock (*see* Con). Adjustable AGC decay. Thousands of memories (presets), with first-rate memory configuration, access and sorting—including by station name and frequency. Only PC-controlled model tested which returns to last tuned frequency when PC turned off. Superior owner's manual. Outstanding factory help and repair support.

Con: No synchronous selectable sideband. Some characteristic "DSP roughness" in the audio under certain reception conditions. Synthesizer phase noise measures only fair; among the consequences are that bandwidth shape factors cannot be measured exactly. Some tuning ergonomics only fair as compared with certain standalone receivers. No tunable notch filter. Passband offset doesn't function in AM

Best PC-controlled receiver for world band is Ten-Tec's RX-320. Superior performance, low price, excellent service and a wide choice of software.

mode. Signal-strength indicator, calibrated 0-80, too sensitive, reading 20 with no antenna connected and 30 with only band noise being received. Uses AC adaptor instead of built-in power supply. Spectrum display does not function with some third-party software. Spectrum display only a so-so performer. Marginal front-end selectivity. Mediumwave AM reception below 1 MHz suffers from reduced sensitivity, and long-wave sensitivity is atrocious. Mediocre front-end selectivity also can allow powerful mediumwave AM stations to mix with received shortwave signals. No internal speaker on receiver module. World Time clock tied into computer's clock, which may not be accurate without periodic adjustment.

☞ PASSPORT's four-star rating is for the RX-320 with third-party control software. With factory software the rating is slightly lower.

Verdict: No contest, the American-made Ten-Tec RX-320 is the star of the PC show when it is coupled to solid control software. Unless you live near a mediumwave AM station, this receiver runs circles around most receivers of any sort near its price class.

✪✪✪
Icom IC-PCR1000

Price: *IC-PCR1000:* $399.95 in the United States. CAN$799.00 in Canada. £299.99 in

The Icom IC-PCR1000 covers world band and much more at a fraction of the cost of conventional wideband receivers.

the United Kingdom. AUS$895.00 in Australia. *UT-106 DSP Unit:* $139.95 in the United States.

Pro: Wideband frequency coverage. Spectrum display with many useful sweep widths for shortwave, as well as good real-time performance. Tunes and displays in extremely precise 1 Hz increments. Comes with reasonably performing control software (*see* Con). Excellent sensitivity to weak signals. AGC, adjustable, performs well in AM and single-sideband modes. Nineteen banks of 50 memories each, with potential for virtually unlimited number of memories. Passband offset (*see* Con). Powerful audio with good weak-signal readability and little distortion (*see* Con).

Con: Poor dynamic range. Audio quality, not pleasant, made worse by presence of circuit hiss. No line output to feed PC sound card and speakers, so no alternative to using receiver's audio. No synchronous selectable sideband. Only two AM-mode bandwidths— 8.7 kHz (nominal 6 kHz) and 2.4 kHz (nominal 3 kHz)—both with uninspiring shape factors. Synthesizer phase noise, although not measurable, appears to be only fair; among the effects of this are that bandwidth shape factors cannot be exactly measured. Mediocre blocking slightly limits weak-signal sensitivity when frequency segment contains powerful signals. Tuning ergonomics only fair as compared with some standalone receivers. Automatic tunable notch filter with DSP audio processing (UT-106, not tested) an extra-cost option. Lacks passband offset in AM mode. Uses AC adaptor instead of built-in power supply. Spectrum display mutes audio when single-sideband or CW signal being received. No clock. Mediocre inboard speaker, remediable by using outboard speaker. Sparse owner's manual.

☞ A similar but more rudimentary model, the IC-PCR100, is available worldwide at roughly two-thirds the price of the IC-PCR1000. It has only one (broad) bandwidth.

Verdict: Among tested PC-controlled receivers, the Japanese-made Icom IC-PCR1000 is the most appropriate for wideband frequency coverage and first-rate shortwave spectrum display.

✪✪
WiNRADiO 1500e

Price: $549.95 in the United States. £369.00 in the United Kingdom. DM1,145.00 in Germany. AUS$899.95 in Australia. Exported worldwide for US$664.95 *(sic)* including DHL air shipping from the Australian factory.

Pro: Wideband frequency coverage. AM-mode bandwidth has superb shape factor and good ultimate rejection. Spectrum display with good real-time performance (*see* Con). Tunes in precise 10 Hz incre-ments; display has 1 Hz resolution, but of course can show only tuned 10 Hz incre-ments. Comes with reasonably performing control software (*see* Con). Excellent sensitivity to weak signals, generally best among PC-controlled receivers tested (*see* Con). Passband offset (*see* Con). World time on-screen clock (*see* Con). High quality of assembly and construction.

Con: Dreadful dynamic range, a crucial shortcoming for world band (*see* below). Only one AM-mode bandwidth (6.5 kHz). Audio lacks power quality. No decent line output to feed PC sound card and speak-ers, so receiver's audio has to be used. Microphonics from internal speaker, making outboard speaker *de rigeur*. No synchronous selectable sideband. AGC not adjustable. No tunable notch filter. Poor blocking limits weak-signal sensitivity when band contains powerful signals. Long learning curve due to complexity. Tuning ergonomics only fair as compared with some standalone receivers. Lacks passband offset in AM mode used by virtually all world band stations. Uses AC adaptor instead of built-in power supply.

WiNRADiO makes several "black box" receivers. Those tested have been disappointing for world band, but have fared better as scanners.

Spectrum display of limited utility because of numerous spurious signals (*see* ☞, below). World Time clock tied into computer's clock, which may not be accurate. Comes with 9/25-pin cable and 25/9 adaptor, which doesn't fit onto some laptops, rather than usual 9/9 cable. Sparse owner's manual.

Verdict: As tested, this heavily advertised model is ill suited to world band applica-tions.

☞ The 1500e is being replaced by the similar WR-1550e, which the manufacturer claims has improved dynamic range and spurious-signal rejection. Their official emailed product-release announcement also claims better sensitivity, although the WiNRADiO Website says improved selectivity with no mention of sensitivity.

☞ The pricey WiNRADiO 3100e we tested is very similar to the 1500e, above, but with improved dynamic range and reduced sensitivity to weak shortwave signals. $1,849.95 in the United States, £1,169.00 in the United Kingdom and AUS$2,495.00 in Australia. It being replaced by the WR-3150e with what the manufacturer calls "similar improvements."

Chuck Rippel, Robert Sherwood and David Zantow, with Lawrence Magne.

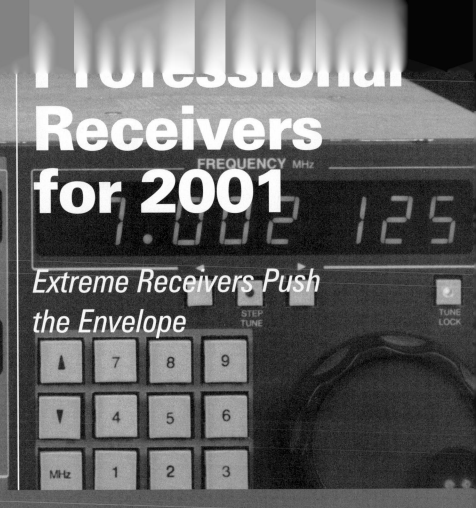

Professional Receivers for 2001

Extreme Receivers Push the Envelope

Professional-grade receivers are for commercial, maritime, surveillance and military duties. These have much in common with the needs of world band listening—differences, too. Some make for better results, others worse. When it all comes together, this is the hardware needed to scale the toughest, most extreme cliffs of DX reception.

Three Types of Receivers

There are numerous categories of professional receivers—indeed, some are made with only one narrow application in mind. But viewed simply, these boil down to three fundamental groups: straightforward for human operation, complex for human operation and no human operation.

The first are designed so laymen can tune "utility" signals with minimal training. After all, if a B-52 takes shrapnel and the radioman is out, the more straightforward a radio is to operate, the more likely it is that other crew members will be able to carry on. Trouble is, simplicity of operation can also result in performance compromises, making these potentially inferior choices for world band cognoscenti.

The second category goes to the other extreme, with features and performance that are "no holds barred." These assume a high degree of operator skill, and are the type of professional receiver we analyze in PASSPORT REPORTS. They are well worth considering if you aren't put off by their complexity of operation and sticker shock.

Simplest of the lot are "black box" professional receivers, which have virtually no controls. These are operated only by computers, often at high-security surveillance centers. We don't cover this arcane topic here, as some of the best models are available only to U.S. Federal agencies or NATO organizations. However, consumer-grade versions are evaluated within the tabletop section of PASSPORT REPORTS.

Major Shared Characteristics

All professional receivers should be physically and electrically robust, with resistance to hostile environments and rough handling, as well as a high mean time between failures (MTBF). Additionally, their components need to be unusually consistent so board swapping and other field repair can be accomplished without disturbing alignment and the like.

Pricey as these receivers are, most professional models are far costlier and some are not even available for sale to the public. But take heart. For world band and utility reception, especially in the Americas, our limited experience suggests that these rarified models are unlikely to outperform

the relatively affordable professional receivers that get five stars in PASSPORT REPORTS. However, at locations, mainly outside the Americas, where extremely high field strengths can pose a problem, the higher processing power of top-end professional receivers may be advantageous.

The two best models tested were developed to replace the nonprofessional Icom IC-R71A for use by the U.S. National Security Agency in offshore surveillance. These folks choose carefully, so hardware that's popular with them has what amounts to a "Good Housekeeping Seal of Approval."

First-Rate Antenna Essential

Top-quality and properly erected antennas are an absolute "must" if these receivers are to reach their full potential. For test results and mounting information, see the Radio Database International White Paper, *Popular Outdoor Antennas*, as well as the analysis of active antennas found elsewhere in this PASSPORT REPORTS.

If reception at your location is already disrupted by electrical noises even when a suitable antenna is in use, a better receiver would be a waste of money. Before buying, try eliminating the source of noise or reorienting your antenna.

Ready for Digital Broadcasts?

It will be years before digital signals supplant everyday analog for world band transmissions. With conventional portable, portatop and tabletop receivers this hardly matters, as these are not intended to be friends for life. Also, when digital broadcasts finally do take to the airwaves they could well be in-band, on channel (IBOC); that is, also receivable on existing analog radios, but without the improved quality of a digital signal.

Professional models are designed to keep humming for decades, not just years. But what happens if digital transmissions begin to appear while your gilt-priced receiver is still in its prime?

Because there aren't yet agreed-upon technical standards for digital world band transmission, manufacturers are in no position to promise future upgrades to receive digital. Nevertheless, among professional models tested by PASSPORT, those that look most promising for eventual digital reception are the Watkins-Johnson WJ-8711A and Ten-Tec RX-340. Indeed, a digital signal output board is already being offered for the '8711A.

Looking Ahead

The Kneisner + Doering KWZ 30 earned nearly five stars in Edition 2000 of PASS-PORT. With inventive circuitry and panzer-tough construction, this limited-production German receiver raised many an eyebrow. It didn't get everything quite right, but it was creative and bold.

For various reasons—not being designed for a target market, sales naivete, growing competition, clunky tree-based operation and some shaky performance variables—the KWZ 30 was discontinued in early 2000. After that, the company concentrated on producing a commercial transceiver.

Nevertheless, the manufacturer says a new receiver is on the drawing board, complete with improved DSP concepts. It is scheduled to come on the market early in 2001, but in the meantime K+D's Hans-J. Kneisner invites interested professional organizations and enthusiasts to submit specifications suggestions and other ideas to him at kdu-bs@t-online.de.

Tips for Using this Section

Professional receivers are listed in order of suitability for listening to difficult-to-hear world band stations. Important secondary consideration is given to audio fidelity, ergonomics and reception of utility signals. We cite actual selling prices as of when we go to press, including European and Australian VAT/GST where applicable.

Unless otherwise stated, all professional models have:

- Digital frequency synthesis and display.
- Full coverage of at least the 155-29999 kHz longwave, mediumwave AM and shortwave spectra—including all world band frequencies—but no coverage of the FM broadcast band (87.5-108 MHz).
- A wide variety of helpful tuning features.
- Synchronous selectable sideband via high-rejection IF filtering (not lower-rejection phasing), which greatly reduces adjacent-channel interference and fading distortion. On some units this is referred to as "SAM" (synchronous AM).

☞ Professional models can tune to the nearest 10 Hz or even 1 Hz, allowing the user to use the receiver's single-side-band circuitry to manually phase its BFO (internally generated carrier) with the station's transmitted carrier. Called "ECSS" (exalted-carrier, selectable-sideband) tuning, this can be used with AM-mode signals in lieu of synchronous selectable sideband. However, in addition to the relative inconvenience of this technique, unlike synchronous detection, which re-phases continually and essentially perfectly, ECSS is always slightly out of phase. This causes at least some degree of harmonic distortion to music and speech, while tuning to the nearest Hertz can generate slow-sweep fading (for this reason, high-pass audio filtering or mis-phasing by two or three Hertz may provide better results).

- Proper demodulation of modes used by non-world-band shortwave signals. These modes include single sideband (LSB/USB and sometimes ISB) and CW ("Morse code"); also, with suitable ancillary devices, radioteletype (RTTY), frequency shift key (FSK) and radiofax (FAX).

- Meaningful signal-strength indication.
- Illuminated display.
- Exceptional build quality, robustness and sample-to-sample consistency.

What PASSPORT's Rating Symbols Mean

Star ratings: ✪✪✪✪✪ is best. Stars reflect overall performance and meaningful features, plus to some extent ergonomics and build quality. Price, appearance, country of manufacture and the like are not taken into account. With professional models there is a strong emphasis on the ability to flush out tough, hard-to-hear signals, as this is usually the main reason these sets are chosen by world band enthusiasts. To facilitate comparison, the same rating system is used for tabletop, portatop and portable models, reviewed elsewhere in PASSPORT REPORTS.

Passport's Choice. *La crème de la crème.* Our test team's personal picks of the litter—models we would buy or have bought for our personal use.

Newly Tested for 2001
✪✪✪✪✪ *Passport's Choice*
Watkins-Johnson WJ-8711A

Price (receiver, factory options): *WJ-8711A:* $5,295.00 plus shipping worldwide. *871Y/SEU DSP Speech Enhancement Unit:* $1,350.00. *8711/PRE Sub-Octave Preselector:* $1,100.00. *871Y/DSO1 Digital Signal Output Unit:* $1,150.00.

Price (aftermarket options): *Ten-Tec #19-0525 cabinet:* $217.24 in the United States. *Sherwood SE-3 MK III accessory:* $495.00 plus shipping worldwide.

Pro: Proven robust. BITE diagnostics and physical layout allows technically qualified users to make most repairs on-site. Users

can upgrade receiver performance over time by EPROM replacement. Exceptional overall performance. Unsurpassed reception of feeble world band DX signals, especially when mated to the Sherwood SE-3 synchronous selectable sideband device and the WJ-871Y/SEU noise-reduction unit (*see* Con). Unusually effective "ECSS" reception (tuning AM-mode signals as though they were single sideband). Superb reception of "utility" (non-AM mode) stations. Generally superior audio quality (*see* Con), especially when used with the Sherwood SE-3 fidelity-enhancing accessory and a worthy external speaker. Unparalleled bandwidth flexibility, with no less than 66 outstandingly high-quality bandwidths. Digital signal processing (DSP). Tunes and displays in ultra-precise 1 Hz increments; trimmer inside radio allows frequency readout to be user-aligned against a known frequency standard, such as WWV/WWVH or a laboratory device. Extraordinary operational flexibility—virtually every receiver parameter is adjustable. One hundred station presets. Synchronous detection, called "SAM" (synchronous AM), reduces selective-fading distortion with world band, mediumwave AM and longwave signals, and works even on very narrow voice bandwidths (*see* Con). Rock stable. Built-in preamplifier. Tunable notch filter. Effective noise blanking. Highly adjustable scanning of both frequency

Watkins-Johnson's WJ-8711A, when loaded with extras, provides world band and utility performance as good as any other receiver tested.

ranges and channel presets. Easy-to-read displays. Large tuning knob. Can be fully and effectively computer and remotely controlled. Passband tuning (see Con). Numerous outputs for data collection and ancillary hardware, including a 455 kHz IF output which makes for instant installation of Sherwood SE-3 accessory (see below) and balanced line outputs (connect to balanced hookup to minimize "hash" radiation). Remote control and dial-up data collection; Windows control software available from manufacturer. Among the most likely of all world band receivers tested to be able to be retrofitted for eventual reception of digital world band broadcasts. Inboard AC power supply senses incoming current and automatically adjusts to anything from 90-264 VAC, 47-

440 Hz—a plus during brownouts or with line voltage or frequency swings. Superior-quality factory service (see Con).

Con: Available only through U.S. manufacturer (+1-301/948-7550). Receiver and factory options have been subjected to a number of price increases since British Aerospace takeover. Mediocre audio in the AM mode; "ECSS" (tuning an AM-mode signal as though it were single sideband) or synchronous detection required to alleviate this. Static and modulation-splash interference sound harsher than with most other models, although this has been improved in the latest version of the receiver's operating software. Complex to operate to full advantage. Synchronous detection not sideband-selectable, so it can't reduce adjacent-channel interference

LAB NUMBERS: TOP TWO PROFESSIONAL RECEIVERS

	Watkins-Johnson WJ-8711A	Ten-Tec RX-340
Max. Sensitivity/Noise Floor	0.13 µV, **S**/–136 dBm, **E**	0.14 µV, **S**/–133 dBm, **E**
Blocking	123 dB, **G**	109 dB, **F**
Shape Factors, voice BWs	1:1.21–1:1.26, **S**	1:1.15–1:1.33, **S**
Ultimate Rejection	>80 dB, **E**	70 dB, **G**
Front-End Selectivity	Wideband, **F**/Half octave, **E**[(1)]	Half octave, **E**
Image Rejection	80 dB, **E**	>100 dB, **S**
First IF Rejection	—[(2)]	>100 dB, **S**
Dynamic Range/IP3 (5 kHz)	74 dB, **G**/–18 dBm, **E**	46 dB, **F**/–55 dBm, **P**
Dynamic Range/IP3 (20 kHz)	99 dB, **S**/+20 dBm, **S**	93 dB, **E**/+9 dBm, **E**
Phase Noise	115 dBc, **G**	113 dBc, **G**
AGC Threshold	0.11 µV, **P**	0.5 µV, **E**/0.13 µV, **P**[(3)]
Overall Distortion, sync	8.2%, **P**	2.6%, **G**
Notch filter depth	58 dB, **S**	58 dB, **S**

IBS Lab Ratings: **S** Superb   **E** Excellent   **G** Good   **F** Fair   **P** Poor

(1) **F** standard/**E** with optional preselector.

(2) Adequate, but could not measure precisely.

(3) Preamp off/on.

(remediable by Sherwood SE-3). Circuitry puts out a high degree of digital noise ("hash"), relying for the most part on the panels for electrical shielding; one consequence is that various versions emanate hash through the rear-panel audio output, signal-strength meter and front-panel headphone jack (this problem is largely avoided when the Sherwood SE-3 is used). Antennas without shielded (e.g., coaxial) feedlines may pick up receiver-generated hash. Passband tuning operates only in CW mode. Jekyll-and-Hyde ergonomics: sometimes wonderful, sometimes awful. Front-panel rack "ears" protrude, with the right "ear" getting in the way of the tuning knob; fortunately, these are easily removed. Mediocre front-end selectivity, remediable by 8711/PRE option. 871Y/ SEU option extremely difficult to install; best to have all options factory-installed. No DC power input. Factory service can take as much as two months. Cabinet extra, available from Ten-Tec. Cumbersome operating manual.

☞ In 1999 Watkins-Johnson was taken over by Marconi, the British electronics goliath, which only months later was swallowed up by British Aerospace. As a result, Watkins-Johnson is now "BAE Systems."

Verdict: The American-made WJ-8711A is, by a hair, the ultimate machine for down-and-dirty world band DXing where money is no object; after all, fully tricked out this is a $9,000 receiver. Had there not been digital hash—and had there been a tone control, passband tuning and synchronous selectable sideband—the '8711A would have been even better, especially for program listening. Fortunately, the Sherwood SE-3 accessory remedies all these problems and improves audio fidelity and DX reception, to boot; the 871Y/SEU complements, rather than competes with, the SE-3 for improving recovered audio. Overall, the WJ-8711A is exceptionally well-suited to demanding aficionados with

suitable financial wherewithal—provided they want an exceptional degree of manual receiver control.

Evaluation of Newly Tested Model: Watkins-Johnson, under its original name—and, during the Cold War, various aliases—is an established supplier of exceptional receivers to a wide range of government agencies. Its spook heritage clearly shows; e.g., at www.sigintel.com/pubpl/webui/ internet_site.view_page?p_page_id=161.

The Watkins-Johnson WJ-8711A is a professional-grade receiver for DXers and program listeners who prefer to optimize reception manually by carefully adjusting a potpourri of controls. There are four displays on the face of the receiver, an analog signal-strength meter, and 44 keys for doing all kinds of good things. This is rounded out by five chunky knobs, plus a large tuning knob. The rack-mounted '8711A measures 19 × 19 inches (482 × 482 mm) including handles, connectors and controls, and 5 1/4 inches (133 mm) high. It doesn't come with or need a cabinet, although one is available from Ten-Tec.

The power supply is internal and fused. Like some PCs, it senses the incoming current and automatically adjusts to anything from 90-264 VAC, 47-440 Hz—a real plus during brownouts or where there are line voltage or frequency swings. There is no DC power input.

Each WJ-8711A is very nearly hand-built, almost a one-of-a-kind, although changes are designed not to impact negatively on field repair. There have been a number of small component changes over the years, in addition to various software upgrades; during the summer of 2000 our main receiver spent weeks at W-J being brought fully up to date. Nevertheless, this means that however closely we analyze and dissect, if you choose to buy one it will almost certainly differ in some respects from our findings.

Exacting Tuning and DX Performance

Tuning and frequency readout is in ultra-precise 1 Hz increments, and unlike some other models it remains extremely accurate throughout the tuned radio spectrum. Should it need tweaking, there is a user-accessible trimmer within the radio to allow it to be adjusted to a known frequency, such as WWV/WWVH, or to a laboratory standard. Step tuning is fully programmable.

There is an armada of no less than 66 well-chosen bandwidths: .056, .063, .069, .075, .081, .088, .094, .100, .113, .125, .138, .150, .163, .175, .188, .200, .225, .250, .275, .300, .325, .350, .375, .400, .450, .500, .550, .600, .650, .700, .750, .800, .900, 1.00, 1.10, 1.20, 1.30, 1.40, 1.50, 1.60, 1.80, 2.00, 2.20, 2.40, 2.60, 2.80, 3.00, 3.20, 3.60, 4.00, 4.40, 4.80, 5.20, 5.60, 6.00, 6.40, 7.20, 8.00, 8.80, 9.60, 10.4, 11.2, 12.0, 12.8, 14.4 and 16.0 kHz. These all have superb shape factors and excellent ultimate rejection, thus offering razor-sharp selectivity.

Dynamic range is worthy, too, and sensitivity to weak signals is unusually good. In short, our laboratory analysis suggests that this receiver has what it takes for flushing out tough signals, and our hands-on tests confirm this.

What's Missing

Yet, this multi-kilobuck receiver omits some goodies found on world band tabletops selling for only a fraction as much. There is no passband tuning (except on CW), no tone control, and the synchronous detection is not sideband selectable.

The '8711A's sophisticated computer circuitry generates digital hash (RFI) that might interfere with the incoming signal in two ways. First, unshielded antenna feedlines may pick up hash radiating from the receiver. So active antennas should be viewed skeptically, especially if their receiving elements are to be located near

the receiver. Second, there is hash generated and then picked up within the receiver itself, but it is very minor.

Accessories Improve DX Reception

Sound quality is generally pleasant when the synchronous detector is switched in—and provided the pedestrian built-in speaker isn't used. Better yet is the exceptional degree of recovered audio using the '8711A with the Sherwood SE-3. This is thanks in part to the SE-3's ability to lock onto even the weakest of station carriers, something not characteristic of ordinary synchronous selectable sideband circuits. Additionally, the SE-3's flutter control can help recover usable audio from chopped-up signals that pass near the magnetic North Pole.

At least as effective for DX, but of little use for other signals, is the optional 871Y/SEU speech enhancement unit. It not only improves faint-signal intelligibility, but also reduces noise from static (QRN). However, it is extremely difficult to install properly, so it should be ordered, factory-installed, when the receiver is purchased.

In practice, the SE-3 and 871Y/SEU complement each other improving recovered audio during reception of faint and difficult DX signals. At times the SE-3 helps, at other times the SEU. Thus configured with this dynamic duo of accessories, the '8711A becomes the proven champ for DX rarities.

Outstanding Performance with Options

The tunable notch filter has a superb 58 dB of attenuation, so it can obliterate any heterodyning signal—within 10 kHz of the received signal, no less. This makes it especially useful for world band use, plus it can be used as something of a tone control by knocking out a narrow range of audio frequencies. This is especially effective if you use it to attenuate the transmitted carrier during synchronous AM reception, then choose a bandwidth to create a sort of an enhanced-audio tone control that needs to be heard to be fully appreciated.

Our lab tests of the '8711A show it to have exceptional performance across the board except for front-end selectivity, which can be remedied by the optional sub-octave preselector. It is easily added, so you can purchase the receiver "barefoot," then install the preselector later if necessary. Our hands-on tests in metro Washington show that the preselector is needed and highly effective when listening in such strong-signal environments as near mediumwave AM transmitters.

For gilt-eared listening to programs, the receiver fares well, but is much better with the Sherwood SE-3 Mk III fidelity-enhancing accessory that connects to the receiver's IF output. The SE-3 also offers continuously tunable selectable sideband. Audio quality is further enhanced by the SE-3's basic tone control.

There is a price to be paid, however, besides the half kilobuck for the Sherwood device. To the already vast array of controls on the '8711A are added a half-dozen on the SE-3. Fortunately, operation of the SE-3 controls is largely intuitive.

All that having been said, the '8711A's state-of-the-art radio performance exacts a price. For one thing, the receiver still makes static sound harsher than on other top-quality models. For another, modulation splash from music and voices on adjacent channels tends to come through more disconcertingly than with "normal" receivers. These aural annoyances can be softened by judicious use of the sophisticated AGC controls, which in additional to having sophisticated choices can be set to any of three predetermined decay rates— or it can be switched off altogether for manual regulation using the RF gain control.

Watkins-Johnson is renowned for exceptional quality of repairs, and the receiver comes with a one-year warranty. For post-warranty service they require a credit card number or a $900 deposit before troubleshooting the receiver and making an estimate; when the actual repair cost is under $900 they refund the difference.

New for 2001
✪✪✪✪✪ *Passport's Choice*
Ten-Tec RX-340

Price: $3,950.00 in the United States. *Ten-Tec #19-0525 cabinet:* $217.24 in the United States. *Sherwood SE-3 MK III accessory:* $495.00 plus shipping worldwide.

Pro: Appears to be robust. BITE diagnostics and physical layout allows technically qualified users to make most repairs on-site. Users can upgrade receiver performance over time by replacing one or another of three socketed EPROM chips. Superb overall performance, including for reception of feeble world band DX signals, especially when mated to the Sherwood SE-3 device; in particular, superlative image and IF rejection, both >100 dB. Few birdies. Generally superior audio quality, especially with a worthy external speaker. Average overall distortion in single-sideband mode a breathtakingly low 0.2 percent; in other modes, under 2.7 percent. Exceptional bandwidth flexibility, with no less than 57 outstandingly high-quality bandwidths having shape factors of 1:1.33 or better; the bandwidth distribution is exceptionally good for world band listening and DXing, along with other activities. Digital signal processing (DSP; *see* Con). Tunes and displays accurately in ultra-precise 1 Hz increments. Extraordinary operational flexibility—virtually every receiver parameter is adjustable; for example, the AGC's various time constants have 118 million possible combinations, plus pushbutton AGC "DUMP to temporarily deactivate AGC (*see* Con). Worthy ergonomics, valuable given the exceptional degree of manual operation; includes easy-to-read displays and large tuning knob with fixed dimple (*see* Con). One hundred station presets; 101 including the scratchpad. Synchronous selectable sideband, called "SAM" (synchronous AM), reduces selective-fading distortion, as well as at diminishing or eliminating adjacent-channel interference, with world band, mediumwave AM and longwave signals (*see* Con). Rock stable. Built-in half-octave preselector comes standard. Built-in preamplifier (*see* Con). Tunable DSP notch filter with exceptional depth of 58 dB (*see* Con). Passband shift (passband tuning) works unusually well (*see* Con). Unusually effective "ECSS" reception (tuning AM-mode signals as though they were single sideband). Superb reception of "utility" (non-AM mode) stations using a wide variety of modes and including fast filters for delay-critical digital modes. Highly adjustable scanning of both frequency ranges and channel presets. Can be fully and effectively computer and remotely controlled. Numerous outputs for data collection and ancillary hardware, including a 455 kHz IF output which makes for instant installation of Sherwood SE-3 accessory. Remote control and dial-up data collection. Among the most likely of all world band receivers tested to be able to be retrofitted for eventual reception of digital world band broadcasts. Noise blanker planned, but no date has been set. Inboard AC power supply senses incoming current and automatically adjusts to anything from 90-264 VAC, 48-440 Hz—a plus during brownouts or with line voltage or frequency swings. Superior-quality factory service, reasonably priced by professional standards, with helpful online/phone tech support.

Con: Sold only in the United States, although Universal Radio exports worldwide and Ten-Tec exports to Canada. DSP microprocessor limitations result in poor dynamic range/IP3 at 5 kHz signal spacing. Blocking, phase noise and ultimate rejection all pretty good, but not of professional caliber. Complex to operate to full advantage. Synchronous selectable sideband loses lock relatively easily. When 10 dB preamplifier turned on, AGC acts on noise unless IF gain reduced by 10 dB. Notch filter tunes only plus or minus 2 kHz and does not work in AM, synchronous AM or ISB modes. Passband shift tunes only plus or minus 2 kHz and does not work in the ISB or synchronous AM modes (remediable with Sherwood SE-3). No AGC off except by holding down DUMP button. No 9 kHz tuning increment, so mediumwave AM tuning outside the Western Hemisphere has to be done using slow 1 kHz increments; presumably this will be remedied soon. Keypad not in telephone format. Some ergonomic clumsiness when going back and forth between the presets and VFO tuning. Emits digital hash in front of receiver, although not elsewhere. No DC power input. Cabinet extra.

Verdict: With an extreme degree of manual control, the Ten-Tec RX-340 is a superb new receiver for those who want no-compromise performance for years to come. It is a sensible value, too—with bells and whistles, it costs half as much as a fully equipped WJ-8711A. But that's a little deceiving, as the '8711A offers certain performance features and options not yet available on the RX-340.

Evaluation of New Model: Ten-Tec has been manufacturing products for amateur radio operators and professional agencies since 1969. Created by Al Kahn, the founder of Electro-Voice, its product line in recent years has grown to become increasingly impressive.

The RX-340, which competes with the costlier WJ-8711A, is derived from Ten-Tec's professional RX-331 "black box" receiver that operates only via external computer control. The '340 rack mounted, but Ten-Tec offers a matching cabinet for tabletop use.

We tested one of the earliest-produced units in great depth. We then made use of a later receiver to evaluate sample-to-sample variation, as consistency from one receiver or part to another facilitates interchangeability in the field. Here, the RX-340 appears to pass muster nicely.

Ten-Tec's new RX-340 provides monster performance for less money than the Watkins-Johnson WJ-8711A. Easily upgraded, with excellent and affordable service.

Manual Operation, Excellent Ergonomics

The '340 is very much a manually operated receiver, even more so than the Watkins-Johnson WJ-8711A. Virtually everything is digital and adjustable, and each of these adjustments has an impact on how well the receiver picks up a signal. So this is no big boy's toy—be prepared for a serious learning curve if you want to tweak the last erg of performance from this sophisticated beauty.

This extreme manual orientation makes it all the more important that the '340 be ergonomically excellent—fortunately, it is. The three two-color fluorescent displays are highly readable, although they would have profited from a dimmer for low ambient light. Each control is nestled amidst related controls, and all fall naturally to hand. Adjustments are made by using individual buttons and an edit knob, but can also be inputted with the keypad.

The front panel and keys should hold up exceptionally well over time and torture—more so than the WJ-8711A, where keypad markings tend to wear off. The various buttons and keys have a solid feel, without the slight wobble of the WJ-8711A's keys. Whenever a button is activated, an internal light comes on—a helpful touch.

Unlike the WJ-8711A, the '340 comes standard with a half-octave preselector that provides excellent front-end selectivity. The '340 also includes a large, illuminated analog signal-strength indicator with relatively fast damping action. This excellent meter simultaneously reads out in ham-oriented "S" units and professional dBm increments. Readings appear to be independent of the IF gain level.

The front panel includes a full-size headphone jack with its own handy audio control. The back panel includes sockets for 50 ohm BNC antenna input, 455 kHz IF output, first mixer out, second mixer out, signal monitor out and external reference in; a full-size mono jack for audio out; an RS-232 port for remote computer control from 75 baud to 38.4 kb; and a 15-pin "D" connector for ancillary audio functions.

The power supply is internal and fused. Like some PCs, it senses the incoming current and automatically adjusts to anything from 90-264 VAC, 48-440 Hz—a real plus during brownouts or where there are line voltage or frequency swings. There is no DC power input.

The internal three-inch (75 mm) speaker faces upward from the top panel. It produces perfectly adequate sound, although a good external speaker helps considerably. When the receiver is operated with the Sherwood SE-3 the internal speaker can be bypassed, anyway.

Vast Array of Tuning Methods

The '340 tunes from 5 kHz or lower through 30 MHz in exacting 1 Hz increments. Sensitivity is consistent throughout, with all noise floor measurements being within 4 dBm. However, sensitivity drops off progressively below 50 kHz. Signals are demodulated in the AM, SAM (synchronous AM), USB, LSB, ISB, CW, CW1 (different offset) and FM modes.

There are 100 tunable presets—101, including the scratchpad—that store frequency, mode and other parameters. However, there is no alphanumeric storage or display of station names. Presets are easily programmed and accessed, although there is some ergonomic clumsiness when going between presets and VFO tuning.

The keypad is not in standard telephone format. Rather, it uses the same "professional receiver" configuration as the WJ-8711A: four rows of buttons that read, from top to bottom, 789/456/123/decimal-0-clear, which is similar to the format used on calculators and numeric keypads. Despite this, the keypad is intuitive, and frequencies can be entered in kHz or MHz by pushing the appropriate button.

The large tuning knob has a fixed dimple, along with nice feel with a pleasant smidgen of flywheel effect. The receiver tunes in 1 Hz, 10 Hz, 50 Hz, 100 Hz, 1 kHz, 5 kHz, 10 kHz and 1 MHz increments. Tuning steps are not programmable, unlike in the WJ-8711A, and there is also no 9 kHz step for mediumwave AM outside the Western Hemisphere. Presumably this was an oversight and will be corrected in the next software upgrade, but in the meantime the slower 1 kHz tuning step can be used.

This radio can be operated by an external computer—hardly surprising, given that the '340 is derived from a model operable only by computer. A vestigial artifact of this is that some of the '340's functions, such as manual AGC control and muting, can only be operated by an external computer.

World band DXers rarely use any scanning function. However, the '340 offers an exceptional menu of scanning options for utility DXers, monitors and others who find scans to be helpful.

The adjustable squelch operates in all modes. A number of scan parameters are adjustable, including dwell time, infinite dwell (stops scanning so long as the signal is active), dead time (how long scanner rests before continuing) and gaze time (time on each vacant frequency). Channels and frequencies can be locked out of scans, and various contents of the presets can be scanned. You can also scan frequency ranges between F1 and F2 frequency limits that you define.

There are controls for a nine-position noise blanker that is planned as a future feature. According to a Ten-Tec spokesperson, no estimated date has yet been set for this.

Fifty-Seven Bandwidths

The potential for superb bandwidth filtering is a high point of any DSP receiver. The '340 has fully 57 bandwidths, with shape factors from 1:1.15 to 1:1.33, about as good as the laws of physics allow. Bandwidths are nominally 100, 120, 150, 170, 200, 220, 250, 300, 350, 400, 450, 500, 600, 700, 800 and 900 Hz, plus 1.0, 1.2, 1.3, 1.4, 1.5, 1.6, 1.7, 1.8, 1.9, 2.0, 2.2, 2.4, 2.6, 2.8, 3.0, 3.2, 3.4, 3.6, 3.8, 4.0, 4.4, 4.8, 5.2, 5.6, 6.0, 6.4, 6.8, 7.2, 7.6, 8.0, 8.8, 9.6, 10.4, 11.2, 12.0, 12.8, 13.6, 14.4, 15.2 and 16.0 kHz. These consistently measure to within three-to-seven percent wider than their nominals, which is very close. The available bandwidths on the '340 are more generous for world band program listening than they are on the WJ-8711A.

No Monkeys Found

All bandwidths have nominal and measured ultimate rejection of 70 dB—good, but far from professional caliber, where 100 dB or greater is considered desirable. Wary of what this might mean, we repeatedly tried to replicate the monkey-chatter problem that occasionally arises on the Japan Radio NRD-545. Fortunately, it did not materialize.

For certain highly specialized utility DXers, there is also a "fast-filter" feature. According to the owner's manual, this offers reduced signal latency and degraded shape factors to facilitate reception of delay-critical digital modes. As world band and most utility DXers don't want degraded shape factors or have an interest in these modes, we didn't evaluate this feature except to verify that, in fact, it works.

Stability is essential to proper reception of most types of utility signals. Our tests found the '340 to be Gibraltar solid, drifting five Hertz or less after a ten-second warmup. Ten-Tec certifies full stability from 0 to 50 degrees Celsius (32-123 Fahrenheit), with reduced stability from minus 10 to 60 degrees Celsius (14-140 Fahrenheit).

Millions of AGC Variations

The receiver comes with three factory-provided AGC decay rates that are easily chosen. However, what makes the AGC stand out is that its attack, hold and decay times are all adjustable—unlike on most other communications receivers, where only the decay may be changed. There are no less than 118,810,000 different AGC combinations! Oddly, amidst this cast of millions there is no discrete AGC off setting, although there is a handy feature which temporarily disables the AGC so long as the "DUMP" button is held down.

The '340 thankfully does not have any perceptible AGC attack distortion. With such receivers as the WJ-8711A, this problem is sometimes aurally apparent on

static bursts and adjacent-channel modulation splash peaks.

Spurious Intrusions Banished

Image and IF rejection are both superb—greater than 100 dB. This borders on perfection, and is especially important for 60 meter DXing to avoid image intrusion from powerhouse signals 910 kHz higher, in the 49 meter segment. Every receiver with synthesized tuning has some birdies, but the '340 has only a dozen or so, mainly around 22 MHz. This is a superb showing, as good as we've ever encountered. During lab tests we came across a local-oscillator impurity feeding one or more of the mixers, but this doesn't seem to be causing any perceptible problem during actual use.

Although the '340 is well shielded, there is hash beaming forward from the front-panel LEDs for up to a yard or meter. This is all but undetectable from the receiver's top, sides and back, so unshielded antenna lead-ins and ancillary connections are essentially unaffected. Loop and other proximity-type active antennas can also be placed close by, so long as they are off to the side.

Strange Dynamic Range

Industry tradition has been to measure dynamic range with signal separation of 20 kHz, but at PASSPORT we have found that 5 kHz separation provides a more meaningful figure for evaluating world band performance. Ten-Tec specs the '340 as having an IP3 of +25 dBm, but because they don't publish the signal spacing—at least they didn't when we were testing—that figure means little.

Because of phase noise, the dynamic range at 20 kHz separation could not be measured in our lab at the voice bandwidth we had specified for testing. However, it could be measured using a 500 Hz (CW) bandwidth. Using this, the '340's 20 kHz dynamic range measures 93 dB, excellent, and the IP3 calculates as being +9 dBm—also excellent, but far from the claimed +25 dBm.

The story doesn't end there. At 100 kHz separation we were able to take a measurement using the specified voice bandwidth. Here, we coincidentally found the same 93 dB dynamic range as at 20 kHz, but instead of an IP3 of +9 dBm it was a superb +21 dBm—very close to the manufacturer's nominal +25 dBm.

The similarity of these dynamic range and IP3 numbers makes it tempting to extrapolate to a conclusion; namely, that the manufacturer's spec is valid at 20 kHz separation—assuming that somehow they, unlike us, were able to make this measurement using a voice-bandwidth filter. However, anything as wide as 100 kHz spacing is a reliable barometer of little more than a receiver's front end; as a measurement of IP3 it is virtually meaningless.

Thus, if it confirms the manufacturer's specification, it also implies that their specification is based on something other than a 20 kHz separation; to wit, 100 kHz.

Curious, we checked with Ten-Tec. They eventually confirmed our suspicion that their published dynamic range numbers result from testing not at 20 kHz separation, but at 100 kHz. According to their spokesperson, "At 20 kHz it gets close to the edges of the roofing filter and doesn't come out as well."

Bottom line, our 20 kHz spacing numbers using a narrow CW bandwidth may be slightly conservative, but they're close to the mark—certainly much more so than DR/IP3 data derived from 100 kHz spacing using a voice bandwidth.

The issue of 20 kHz dynamic range is also important because it leads to a larger

finding: that the RX-340's dynamic range performance is highly stepped, dropping precipitously as signal spacing gets tighter and performance requirements become more critical. At 5 kHz separation, using the same voice bandwidth as was used for our 100 kHz separation measurements, dynamic range plunges to 46 dB and IP3 to -55 dBm.

These disappointing 5 kHz numbers, especially relative to the excellent 20 kHz figures, result from the receiver's microprocessor. It would profit from more power, and Ten-Tec is refreshingly candid about this. A DSP receiver's microprocessor has to perform any number of tasks, and the design engineer's unhappy job is to make judicious tradeoffs. For now, low-end DSP receivers have performance hiccups because affordable microprocessors do not as yet have the necessary power to accomplish all basic and ancillary functions properly. In time, this will improve.

While there is no getting around the implications of the 5 kHz separation numbers, there was no overloading during our field tests in North America. However, European winter DXers using a good antenna and seeking faint signals within 49 meters may be less fortunate when critical situations arise.

Variety of Sensitivity Issues

The '340 comes with a 10 dB preamplifier which boosts the receiver's sensitivity from good (0.4 microvolts) to superb (0.14 microvolts), and the more telling noise floor from good (-123 dBm) to excellent (-133 dBm). But it also causes the receiver's otherwise excellent AGC threshold of 0.5 microvolts to plummet to a poor 0.13 microvolts. This causes the AGC to act on noise, unnecessarily desensitizing the receiver with extremely faint signals—the opposite of the desired effect.

In the absence of a factory-engineered solution, the IF gain can be reduced to "10." Even though this swaps the preamp's RF gain for comparable IF gain, it actually provides a slight net improvement in sensitivity while resolving the AGC threshold problem. Dynamic range is scarcely affected.

In that regard, we unearthed a software bug that, on the surface, may appear to be a sensitivity problem even though it is not. If the IF gain is backed down to 35 instead of 10 as recommended above with the preamp on, then as the bandwidth is adjusted upward, at 4.4 kHz and higher the detected audio and IF output both drop 21 dB. This is caused by the DSP's changing to a different set of program instructions. Ten-Tec's engineers were able to replicate the prob-lem, so presumably it will be fixed soon.

Compounding sensitivity issues is that blocking is only a pedestrian 109 dB, so sensitivity won't be quite so consistent as it could be under varying reception conditions. Phase noise also has a slight impact on weak-signal readability, and on the '340 it measures 113 dBc—good but not outstanding.

When used with the Sherwood SE-3, the '8711A and kindred-but-discontinued HF-1000 have passed muster at a number of DXpeditions, ranking right up there with the legendary Collins HF-2050. Although thus far things look promising, the jury will be out on the '340's "DXability" until it has been put through at least one good winter of use under a wide variety of reception conditions.

The '340 has very pleasant audio. Al-though it lacks any tone controls, average overall distortion is only 1.6 percent in the AM mode and 2.6 percent with SAM. ECSS advocates will be pleased to find that average overall distortion is even less during single-sideband operation, a mere 0.2 percent. Results are similar with the Sherwood SE-3.

Notch Filter and Passband Tuning

The tunable DSP notch filter has a breath-taking 58 dB rejection, pulverizing virtually any heterodyne (whistle) it encounters. Alas, its tuning range is only plus or minus 2 kHz, and it doesn't work in the AM, SAM or ISB modes or with bandwidths above 4 kHz. This compares unfavorably with the 10 kHz tuning range of the WJ-8711A's notch. Other than outboard EQ, there's no obvious fix, either.

The '340's passband tuning (PBT) works unusually well in certain respects. It is an effective means to tune away from adjacent channel interference, as well as to shape the audio. Especially with narrower voice filters this is a real plus—you can get good audio and sharp filtering at the same time.

However, like the notch it tunes only 2 kHz above or below the center frequency. It also does not function in the ISB mode or with the synchronous detector, although the receiver's many bandwidths and other manual controls help overcome this. It can be made to work with synchronous detection by using the '340 in concert with a Sherwood SE-3 accessory, which substitutes its own synchronous detector for that of the receiver. We tried it, as did a friendly colleague, with exceptional results.

Primitive Synchronous Selectable Sideband

Unlike the WJ-8711A, the '340 has syn-chronous selectable sideband—"SAM." This is a huge plus, helping quash adjacent-channel interference, reduce selective-fading distortion and improve audio quality.

Unlike the WJ-8711A, the '340's SAM does not work with filters narrower than 4 kHz, a point of interest only to serious DXers, who usually don't mind reverting to manual ECSS under these circumstances. More important, it loses lock more easily and frequently than do the best of synchronous detectors. This is especially evident with rapidly fading or weak signals, or when there is a powerful adjacent-channel signal. This is resolved to some extent by setting the IF gain to about 30, optimizing the various AGC settings and turning on the preamplifier.

Another and more effective solution is to connect the receiver's IF output to a Sherwood SE-3, which has traditionally been the *ne plus ultra* for synchronous selectable sideband. It performs flawlessly with the '340, while slightly enhancing audio quality.

Putting the BITE on Service

The Built-In Test Equipment (BITE) feature performs a variety of internal diagnostic procedures, and seems to work properly—it was difficult to check this out throughly, as Ten-Tec's instructions were not yet completed during our test period. BITE should allow nearly all failures to be remediable by technically qualified users, using board swaps and the like obtained through the factory's tech support.

Because service is currently available only at the Tennessee factory, BITE is a major plus for users outside North America, especially given the company's excellent tech support. Should off-site repair be preferred, Ten-Tec's service is among the best, and is much more affordable than that of most other professional receiver manufacturers.

Looking Ahead

Ten-Tec refers to the '340 as a work in progress, with refinements in the offing. It plans to make various upgrades in the future, including adding a noise blanker,

having the tunable notch operate in the AM mode, and possibly having the PBT function in the SAM mode. These will be able to be retrofitted simply by the user's replacing one or more of the three socketed EPROM chips. This greatly reduces the risk of obsolescence.

Bottom Line

In San Antonio, Texas, there is an old-time eatery called Earl Abel's with the slogan, "I eat here, too—Earl."

When all the detailed measurements and analyses are said and done, perhaps it is most telling that the main hands-on reviewer for the RX-340 reached deep into his Levi's and ordered one from Universal Radio, along with an SE-3, for his personal use—even though he already has a Watkins-Johnson HF-1000, the erstwhile near-twin to the WJ-8711A.

Because a full DX season is needed to reach certain conclusions, the jury is still out as to whether the RX-340 will be the full equal the very finest rigs with tough DX catches. Otherwise, when mated to the SE-3 this is as good a receiver as we have tested. Even barefoot it is superb.

✪✪✪✪✪ 📄 *Passport's Choice*
Icom IC-R9000L, Icom IC-R9000, Icom IC-R9000A

Price (receiver): $8,499.95 by special order to Federal government purchasers, or for export, in the United States. CAN$15,999.00 in Canada or for export. AUS$19,995.00 by special order in Australia.

Price (aftermarket options): *Three new filter bandwidths, installed by Sherwood:* $499.00. *Synchronous selectable sideband (Sherwood SE-3 with 9 MHz-to-455 kHz IF down converter):* $720.00, installed.

Pro: Exceptional tough-signal performance, especially with faint DX signals that may be unreadable on other top-rated receivers. Flexible, above-average audio for a tabletop model when used with suitable outboard speaker; outstanding audio quality when used with Sherwood SE-3. Tunes and displays frequency in precise 10 Hz increments. Video display of radio spectrum occupancy, a rarely found feature. Sophisticated scanner/timer. Extraordinarily broad and high-quality coverage of radio spectrum, including portions forbidden to be listened to by the general public in the United States. Exceptional assortment of flexible operating controls and sockets. Good ergonomics. Superb reception of utility and ham signals. Superb reception of longwave DX, mediumwave DX, VHF/UHF scanner frequencies and FM broadcasts (monaural). Arguably the best available receiver for TV DX, using the built-in monochrome display. Reliability, originally questionable, found to be above average in recent years. Two 24-hour clocks.

Con: In the United States, available only to Federal agencies, as it receives cellular frequencies; this ban is routinely circumvented by purchasing from Canadian Icom dealers (service is available to any owner within the United States). Not physically robust; one tested sample failed when subjected to ordinary shipment; nonetheless, it has a high MTBF during fixed use, so it appears to be electronically dependable. Power supply runs hot, although over the years this has not caused premature component failure. No synchronous selectable sideband (remediable with Sherwood SE-3). Two AM-mode bandwidths too broad for most world band applications (remediable with Sherwood aftermarket filter option). Both single-sideband bandwidths almost identical. Dynamic range merely adequate. Front-panel controls of only average quality, although robust. Keypad frequency entry only in MHz, decimal and all.

When Newt Gingrich was once overheard on his analog cell phone, Congress outlawed various receivers, including the Icom IC-R9000. Analog phones are fading away, but the law remains on the books.

☞ The five-star rating, above, applies for world band applications only when it is equipped with aftermarket accessory filters and synchronous selectable sideband.

☞ Rack mounted, but an optional cabinet is available for desktop use.

Verdict: The Icom IC-R9000/'R9000A/ 'R9000L are all comparable except that the "L" version's spectrum display uses an LCD instead of a CRT. Our experience confirms what the eye suggests, which is that this is not a receiver designed to take vibration and other physical punishment. Indeed, its high heat would hint at a low MTBF even in fixed applications, but over the years the receiver has proven to be electrically reliable.

With changed AM-mode bandwidth filters—available from at least one world band specialty firm—this receiver is about as good as it gets for DX reception of faint, tough signals throughout the radio spectrum. With the Sherwood SE-3 it is also top drawer for fastidious listening to world band programs. And it shines if you want a visual indication of spectrum occupancy and certain other characteristics of stations within a designated segment of the radio spectrum.

An *RDI WHITE PAPER* is available for this model.

The Japan Radio NRD-301A is all but bulletproof.
With the right accessories its rating becomes a
quarter-point shy of five stars.

✪✪✪✪½
Japan Radio NRD-301A

Price: Under $8,000 in various countries—
actual price varies considerably. *Cabinet
#MPBX10832:* $449.95 if ordered with
receiver, $749.95 if ordered separately, in
the United States. *Aftermarket voice
bandwidth filters:* approximately $150 each,
installed, in the United States. *Sherwood
SE-3:* $495 plus shipping worldwide.

Pro: Uncommonly easy to repair on the
spot—aided by built-in test equipment
(BITE), plug-in circuit boards and a spare-
parts kit. Superior overall performance in
nearly all respects. Superior ergonomics.
Passband shift, operates in AM mode.
Tunes in ultra-precise 1 Hz increments.
Three hundred presets, and VFO operates
from presets' channels. Effective noise
blanker. Adjustable AGC decay. Sophisticated scanning system. AF (audio) filter
narrows high- and low-frequency audio
response. Comes with spare parts for on-
site repair. Operates from a wide range of
AC voltages, using an easily adjusted
inboard power supply and 24 VDC ship's
power. Can be computer controlled. Room
for additional bandwidths. Unlike other
professional models, the actual selling
price varies enormously—shop around, as
attractive pricing can be found.

Con: Usually available only on special
order. Lacks the operating flexibility of
such professional supersets as the
Watkins-Johnson WJ-8711A. Only two
voice bandwidths (*see* Pro), although both
perform nicely and are well chosen. No
keypad tuning, a major omission. No
synchronous selectable sideband (remediable by adding Sherwood SE-3 outboard
accessory, which uses off-tuning to select
sidebands). No tunable notch filter.
Unusual audio, antenna and AC cord
jacks. Signal-strength indicator not
illuminated. Slight whine from LED display
at high brightness after receiver has been
on for over an hour. Slight AC "tingle"
when touching cabinet, remediable by
grounding the receiver or, for receive-only
applications, by removing marine-oriented
C1 and C2 capacitors from across the back
of the AC socket. AC power transformer
runs very hot and sometimes buzzes.
Distribution limited to Japan Radio dealers,
offices, and a few specialty organizations
such as shipyards. Rack mounted, so
cabinet is extra and pricey.

☞ The above star rating is for the receiver
"as is" from the factory. With the addition
of at least one more AM-mode voice filter
and the Sherwood SE-3, the rating improves by a quarter star.

Verdict: Japan Radio's NRD-301A receiver
is exceptional. It is probably fit to be
handed down from one generation to the
next, what with its seemingly bulletproof
construction, ease of repair and superior
overall performance. Yet, as it comes from
the factory it lacks certain features of use
for everyday world band listening and
DXing.

---

*The PASSPORT professional-model review
team consists of Tony Jones, Lawrence
Magne, David Walcutt, David Zantow and
George Zeller, with thanks to Don Nelson
and Craig Tyson. Laboratory measurements
by J. Robert Sherwood.*

WHERE TO FIND IT: INDEX TO DIGITAL RADIOS

PASSPORT REPORTS evaluates nearly every receiver on the market. Here are all digitally tuned models reviewed for this year, with those that are new, revised or retested in **bold**. There are also active antenna reports starting on page 176, with home transmitter reviews from page 78.

Comprehensive PASSPORT® Radio Database International White Papers® are available for the many popular premium receivers and outdoor antennas. Each RDI White Paper®—$6.95 in North America, $9.95 airmail elsewhere—contains virtually all our panel's findings and comments during hands-on testing, as well as laboratory measurements and what these mean to you. These unabridged reports are available from key world band dealers, or you can contact our 24-hour VISA/MC order channels (www.passband.com, autovoice +1 215/598-9018, fax +1 215/598 3794), or write us at PASSPORT RDI White Papers, Box 300, Penn's Park, PA 18943 USA.

🕮 *Radio Database International White Paper®* available.

Dozen Active Antennas: Which Are Best?

Do you listen during the day, when signals are harder to hear? Do you like to flush out weaker, more unusual stations?

If so, a good outboard antenna can be your radio's best friend. Problem is, the most effective world band antennas are passive—unamplified—and need lots of yard space. If you're in an apartment,

hotel or other facility, something else is needed.

That "something else" is an active antenna. These include a small rod ("whip") or wire—the receiving element—to snare signals from the airwaves. But because these elements are so short, the signals they pass on tend to be weak. If something weren't done to overcome this, it would be like powering a car with a golf cart engine.

Price Is Ineffectual Barometer

Active antennas resolve this by electrically amplifying signals before they get to the radio receiver. Although a passive wire antenna has inherent advantages, compact active antennas can do a surprisingly good job. The challenge is to sort out winners from losers.

As we found out over months of testing, price has little relationship to performance. One of the best-rated antennas is among the least costly, while the most expensive model ranks near the bottom—at least for users in most of the world.

We limited our testing to designs likely to perform satisfactorily under a wide range of circumstances. However, various lower-cost amplified antennas exist for portables. In general, the weaker the overall signal strengths at your location, the greater the chances these will work.

Proximate *vs.* Remote Models

There are two basic types of active antennas: proximate and remote. Proximate models (four of the dozen tested) require that the receiving element be located near the receiver, as it is mounted on a control box which must be close to the radio. Remote antennas allow the receiving element to be placed a considerable distance away either indoors or, in most instances, out in the open weather.

Remote models are almost always the better bet, as they allow the receiving element to be placed where electrical noise is low and signals come in best. Proximate models give you no choice unless you are willing to move the entire receiver to where reception happens to be optimum, which may or may not be a pleasant place to listen. Too, many receivers put out some degree of electrical noise, typically radiating from their digital displays,

so it is best to locate a proximate antenna behind or to either side of your receiver.

Preselection *vs.* Broadband

Broadband electronic amplifiers have potential for all sorts of mischief. Some add noise and spurious signals; others may overload a receiver with too much gain.

A partial solution is to have effective preselection. Preselection limits the band of frequencies which get full amplification, and in so doing reduces the odds of spurious signals being created by the antenna or the receiver.

Problem is, preselection adds to construction cost. And because it requires manual tuning, it adds to operating complexity—although it doesn't have to. As indicated in our review of the Sony ICF-SW07 elsewhere in PASSPORT REPORTS, preselection can be automated if the antenna and receiver are designed to work together. So far only the 'SW07 can do this.

Amplified Wire Excellent Alternative

The MFJ-1020B performs only so-so with its built-in antenna, but it does nicely as an active preselector when used with a modest wire antenna. If it is feasible at your location, this option can provide superior performance at an affordable price. A few yards or meters of wire, especially outdoors, act better than a whip for receiving signals.

Because the wire need not be long, it can be super-thin and inconspicious. For this, enameled wire held up by a pair of small insulators is ideal. At the nearer insulator scrape enamel from the last inch or couple of centimeters, solder it to some insulated bell or hookup wire, then run that to the '1020B.

How Much Gain?

With a first-rate receiver and passive outdoor wire antenna, there is rarely any need for electrical gain between the antenna and receiver unless you enjoy pinning signal meters or stressing your receiver's dynamic range.

In principle, a good active antenna should replicate that level of gain—or, better, the signal-to-noise ratio. Too little gain, then overall circuit noise appears, if only from the receiver. Too much gain and the receiver's dynamic range is taxed to no good end.

For this reason we were surprised by the low gain of both RF Systems antennas. These are costly units with a certain mystique, and the Dutch manufacturer has a solid grasp of the theoretical underpinnings behind active antenna design. Yet, other issues aside, both models scarcely boosted signals.

RF Systems defends this practice. They indicated to us in a series of thoughtful communications that it is their intent to use extremely low noise and wide dynamic range in lieu of gain, and they are not alone. At least one of the HF active antennas made by the German firm of Rohde & Schwarz reportedly has a seven-decibel loss, although presumably this is meant to be fitted to R&S receivers costing tens of thousands of dollars—receivers having both appropriate gain and extremely low noise.

There are other circumstances where this may make good sense, although none of our North American testing sites fit these parameters. For example, if there were a powerful transmitter sharing the roof at an embassy, it would help to have low gain to keep both the active antenna and receiver from being swamped. Also, in high-signal parts of the world, such as Europe, the Near East and North Africa, this could be relatively effective if the receiving element were optimally

> **Receivers need a critical mass of signal to overcome their own circuit noise.**

TEST MEASUREMENTS, BROADBAND MODELS

Model	Noise floor peak	MW AM rejection	Max gain	Frequency, MHz	Unity gain at x MHz	Rolloff 30 MHz vs. 5 MHz	Net loss at 30 MHz	IP3 at 14 MHz
Dressler 100 HDX	20 dB	No	>11 dB	1 MHz	—	4 dB	—	>35 dBm[3]
Dressler ARA 60	18 dB	No	>14 dB	—	—	0 dB	—	>35 dBm[3]
Dymek DA100E	21 dB	No	8 dB[2]	5 MHz	19.9 MHz	—	10 dB	21 dBm
MFJ 1024	19 dB	No	9 dB[2]	5 MHz	20.7 MHz	—	10 dB	23 dBm
RF Systems DX 10	5 dB	No	<7 dB	—	—	0 dB	—	>35 dBm[3]
RF Sy DX One Pro	5 dB	Yes[1]	<7 dB	—	—	0 dB	—	>35 dBm[3]
Sony AN-1	5 dB	Yes[1]	4 dB[2]	9.6 MHz	15 MHz	—	11 dB	23 dBm

(1) MW AM attenuation for AN-1: 15 dB at 500 kHz, 10 dB at 1.7 MHz; for DX-One Pro: 4 dB at 500 kHz, 30 to 40 dB from 700-1200 kHz, 1 dB at 1.7 MHz.

(2) Gain measurement was made with 50 ohm termination into head amplifier. Bridging gain not included.

(3) Units with IP3 of >35 dBm are assumed to be greater than +35 dBm. Unable to drive hard enough to get actual value.

erected, the receiver had a superb noise floor, the AGC threshold were superior, and recovered audio was unusually good.

Hypothetical listening situations aside, we could come up with no empirical evidence to support this "less is more" concept. Nearly all receivers need a certain critical mass of signal to overcome their own circuit noise, as well as to trigger the AGC so that fading is smoothed.

Try as we might in our tests in North America, there was no substitute for a given level of gain. No matter how carefully we mounted the RF Systems units, we consistently heard far more useable signals with the simplest of wire antennas, as well as with competing active antennas.

Minimizing Hum

Active antennas work best when powered by battery. This eliminates all possibility of hum and buzzing caused by an AC-to-DC power supply. Problem is, using batteries is not always practical.

Unfortunately, switching over to an AC adaptor isn't a flawless solution, either. Hum and buzzing persisted to a greater or lesser degree throughout our tests of active antennas powered by AC adaptors.

AC adaptors can create hum and buzzing in either of two ways. To being with, if the DC output produced by the AC adaptor is not properly filtered, the resulting ripple can cause hum and buzzing. Most manu-facturers are well aware of this, although some low-quality AC adaptors nonetheless produce impure, hum-prone DC.

However, there's a less-recognized cause for hum and buzzing which persisted throughout our tests of active antennas powered by AC adaptors. Radio signals can cross-modulate into an antenna's power supply, and/or a power supply can radiate signals into the antenna's receiving element. If the adaptor's diode rectifiers and transformer are not properly bypassed to prevent RF hash, received stations may have hum superimposed upon them.

Alas, none of the tested antennas using AC adaptors—regulated or not—managed to keep hum and buzzing completely at bay. Your best practical solution: Keep all AC adaptors as far as possible from the antenna's receiving element.

Testing Procedure

Antenna performance is roughly one part technology, one part geography and geology, plus one part mounting. This report covers the first part, with tips on the third, but in the end all it can accomplish is to boost your odds of success. Much of the outcome depends on where you live and what you do once the antenna arrives.

In addition to being subjected to our roster of lab tests, each antenna has been put through a variety of hands-on listening checks. A number of different portable and tabletop receivers were used at five urban, suburban and rural locations in the Eastern, Midwestern and Western United States. Most of the data from these multiple sources was consistent, but when they weren't we went back to evaluate afresh.

However, except for two models our findings apply to a wide range of listening locations. Within Europe, the Near East and North Africa gain is less important than it is in the Americas and Australasia, whereas third-order intercept performance is more crucial.

Although our findings should apply at your location and with your receiver, there is no escaping the reality that buying an active antenna is something of a craps shoot. Whenever possible buy on a returnable basis, leaving the hardware and packing in pristine condition until you are certain you wish to keep it.

Antenna location and mounting can make all the difference. Experiment with different locations before doing a permanent installation, and if your receiver has multiple antenna inputs don't be afraid to try them all.

Bottom Line

Tops overall is the pricey Dressler ARA 100 HDX. It is a remote model with excellent weather resistance, quality construction, appropriate frequency coverage and superior performance. But the lower-cost Dressler ARA 60 performs almost as well, making it an excellent value.

The cleverly designed Sony AN-LP1 is the bargain of the bunch. At under eighty bucks its overall performance is surpassed only by the pricey Dressler models. It is uniquely portable, too—the only model that makes sense for airline travel. But it is not infallible. Its receiving element isn't weatherproof, so it has to be mounted indoors where reception may not always be best. And its frequency range and uneven gain limit its use for some applications.

The low-cost Ameco TPA works surprisingly well when used with its built-in telescopic antenna. However, as with all proximate models you have to locate your radio where signals come in well. You also have to ensure the antenna doesn't pick up "hash" from your receiver or other indoor sources. But if you want your antenna all in one box, the Ameco is the way to go.

The McKay Dymek/Stoner Dymek DA100E is the latest version of a proven, reliable product that performs well in the Americas and Australasia. The marine version is a good choice for landlubbers and salts, alike, considering the small extra cost.

All models function properly with most portable, portatop and tabletop receivers, but some marriages make more sense than others. The Sony AN-LP1 is designed for use with portables of all sorts, even though it also functions indoors with portatops and tabletops. And even though other remote models work with many portables, because they can be mounted outdoors they are usually better than the AN-LP1 with tabletop receivers.

No tested antenna excels for mediumwave AM or longwave reception, although some do an excellent job of raw signal amplification. Kiwa, Terk, AOR and others make separate directional loop antennas that respond properly to the special conditions found in these bands.

TEST MEASUREMENTS, PRESELECTION MODELS

Model	Oscillate	Gain at frequency in MHz									
		0.5 MHz	1 MHz	2 MHz	3 MHz	5 MHz	10 MHz	15 MHz	20 MHz	25 MHz	30 MHz
Ameco TPA	No	32	23	30	30	21	24	18	17	15	16
MFJ 1020B	No	Won't tune*	15	10	16	21	18	25	25	23	18
Palstar AA30	Yes	40	39	35	28	29	22	15	16	15	15
Sony AN-LP1	No	(see separate chart)									
Vectronics	Yes	35	33	30	25	21	19	15	14	17	18

* The tested MFJ 1020B appears to have a defective lowest frequency inductor; unit does not tune below 530 kHz.

Some gain measurements were made by coupling the signal generator in through a 10 pF capacitor. This decreased loading from the source. Some units worked well with the 10 pF capacitor in series, others did not.

What Passport's Ratings Mean

Star ratings: ✪✪✪✪✪ is best. Stars reflect overall performance and meaningful features, plus to some extent ergonomics and build quality. Price, appearance, country of manufacture and the like are not taken into account.

Passport's Choice. La crème de la crème. Our test team's personal picks of the litter—models we would buy or have bought for our personal use.

₵: A relative bargain, with decidedly more performance than the price would suggest.

Active antennas are listed in descending order of merit. Unless otherwise indicated each has a one-year warranty.

✪✪✪✪¼ *Passport's Choice*
Dressler ARA 100 HDX

Remote, broadband, indoor-outdoor, 0.04-40 MHz

Price: $529.95 in the United States. £325.00 on special order in the United Kingdom.

Pro: Excellent build quality, with fiberglass whip and foam-encapsulated head amplifier to resist the weather (*see* Con). Very good gain below 20 MHz (*see* Con). Outstanding dynamic range/IP3. Superior signal-to-noise ratio. Handy detachable "N" connector on bottom. AC adaptor with regulated DC output is better than most.

Con: Encapsulated design makes most repairs impossible. Above 20 MHz gain

WHERE TO MOUNT A REMOTE ANTENNA

The good news is that if an excellent active antenna is mounted optimally, it can perform very well. The bad news is that if you have room outdoors to mount it optimally, you may also have room for a passive wire antenna that will perform better, yet. Probably cheaper, too.

Still, here are a few practical tips on placement of weather-resistant remote models. As always with antennas, creativity rules—don't be afraid to experiment.

- If you can mount your antenna's receiving element outdoors, use a nonconductive mast or capped PVC pipe, as metal masts or pipes are likely to degrade performance. Optimum height from ground is 10-20 feet or 3-6 meters, but keep in mind that "ground" refers to electrical ground, which includes roofs and the like.

  If this is not feasible, try a nearby tree. This works less well because tree sap is electrically conductive, but is a reasonable fallback, especially with hardwood varieties. Ensure that leaves and branches don't brush against the whip under most weather conditions.

- If remote outdoor mounting is impractical, then place the receiving element out in the fresh air as much as possible. Even if you are in a high-rise building, so long as a window opens or there is a balcony, you can stick your antenna's receiving element away from the building 45 degrees or so, like a wall flagpole. If that is too visible, then try using a string or rope to pull it up by day.

- If all these alternatives are impractical, then at least place the receiving element up against a large window. Glass blocks signals much less than masonry or metal, including insulation foil and aluminum siding.

begins to fall off slightly. RG-58 coaxial cable is of poor quality and should be replaced by user (see ☞, below). Body of antenna runs slightly warm. "N" connector at the head amplifier/antenna element exposed to weather, needs to be inventively sealed by user. Gain control cumbersome to adjust; fortunately, in practice it is rarely needed.

☞ According to the manufacturer's North American representative, both tested Dressler models are soon to be equipped with improved coaxial cable.

Verdict: The Dressler ARA 100 HDX, made in Germany, is an excellent but costly low-noise antenna. Aside from its inferior coaxial cable, which should be replaced by the user (see ☞, above), it is sturdily constructed. It is less complicated to use than the Sony AN-LP1, and comes with an operating range that also makes it the best choice of any antenna tested for tropical bands and utility DXing.

Comments: The two Dressler antennas are excellent, but $240 apart in price. What does that extra money buy?

In listening and lab tests, the gain levels of the ARA 100 HDX and ARA 60 were identical at 7 MHz and 17 MHz, but at 28 MHz the ARA 60's signals were 4.5 dB higher. This appears to be a temporary phenomenon, as the manufacturer indicates that the ARA 60 will shortly be produced with an amplifier chip having slightly less gain. However, in addition to lab findings, on weaker signals some of our panelists felt they heard a slightly better signal-to-noise ratio with the ARA 100 HDX as opposed to the ARA 60.

Of minor note, the body of the ARA 100 HDX runs slightly warm, while the ARA 60 stays cool.

How does the ARA 100 HDX, one of the best models tested, compare to a good passive antenna?

Against a simple 20 meter inverted-V dipole mounted at 35 feet, the ARA 100 HDX, when carefully mounted, performed nigh identically to the dipole within the 20 meter ham band and the 19 meter broadcast band; some stations were modestly stronger on one antenna, weaker on the other. However, when signals were a fraction of a microvolt—truly faint DX—the passive dipole had as much as a 10 dB better signal-to-noise ratio than the Dressler.

This fits in with our earlier findings that a worthy passive wire antenna is inherently quieter than any active model when both are properly erected. However, this may not always have to be. When an East Coast panelist tested an experimental active antenna mounted outdoors in an optimum fashion, he found recovered audio was sometimes better than with a worthy passive wire antenna.

Overloading was a problem only when the antenna was mounted high on a conductive mast. Knowledgeable sources have recommended that active antennas not be mounted on conductive masts, and our tests confirm the wisdom of this advice.

Build quality is excellent except for the coaxial cable provided at the time of our tests. However, the same foam encapsulation which makes the receiving element so robust outdoors also means that it is nigh impossible to repair.

The "N" fitting on the antenna body makes it possible to disconnect the cable after it is installed, which makes it much easier to service. "N" connectors can be weatherproof, but the one which comes with the antenna has only a strain relief boot. It would be prudent to protect this from the weather with Coax Seal or weatherproofing tape.

The same power/interface box is used for both Dressler models. It is compact and, like the rest of the antenna, is very well made. The AC adaptor performed satisfactorily nearly all the time—only one panelist noted slight hum on occasion.

The quality of the included RG-58 coaxial cable is sub-par, consisting of a 100% Mylar shield plus about a 20% copper shield braid. As a result, the connectors cannot take much mechanical stress without failing at the coaxial connector junction. We found this out the hard way when the internal fuse blew as we moved the antenna. The short was intermittent, reappearing after the antenna was mounted 30 feet high. This sort of hassle isn't worth it, especially at this price. The coaxial cable should be replaced with something better before the antenna is set up (first, *see* ☞, above).

When money is no object, the Dressler ARA 100 HDX is a welcome, high-quality alternative if you cannot install a passive inverted-L or trap dipole wire antenna.

✪✪✪✪ *Passport's Choice*
Dressler ARA 60

Remote, broadband, indoor-outdoor, 0.04-60/100 MHz

Price: $289.95 in the United States. £169.00 in the United Kingdom.

Pro: Excellent build quality, with fiberglass whip and foam-encapsulated head amplifier to resist the weather (*see* Con). Very good and consistent gain, even above 20 MHz. Outstanding dynamic range/IP3. AC adaptor with regulated DC output is better than most.

Con: Encapsulated design makes most repairs impossible. Signal-to-noise ratio on some frequencies slightly inferior compared to ARA 100 HDX (*see* ☞, below). RG-58 coaxial cable is of poor quality and permanently attached on antenna end, making user replacement impossible (*see* ☞, below). Gain control

cumbersome to adjust; fortunately, in practice it is rarely needed.

☞ The manufacturer indicates that the ARA 60 will shortly be produced with an amplifier chip having slightly less gain.

☞ According to the manufacturer's North American representative, both tested Dressler models are soon to be equipped with improved coaxial cable.

Verdict: An excellent lower-cost alternative to the ARA 100 HDX. Unless money is no object, the German-made ARA 60 makes the most sense of any model tested for use with tabletop receivers.

Comments: Very similar to the ARA 100 HDX—*see* that model's **Comments** for further details. Even its dynamic range/IP3 and overloading performance are virtually identical.

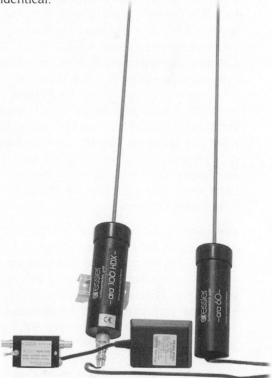

The two best active antennas tested are the ARA 100 HDX and ARA 60, both from the German firm of Dressler.

R. Sherwood

However, unlike its costlier sibling, the ARA 60's coaxial cable is permanently attached to the antenna's body. If for some reason in its lifetime the coaxial cable becomes intermittent at the opening where it goes inside, user repair is out of the question. Too, the body of the tested ARA 60 HDX runs cool even after hours of operation, as it only draws 37 mA compared to 230 mA for the ARA 100 HDX.

◐◐◐½ ◐ *Passport's Choice*
Sony AN-LP1

Remote, manual preselection, indoor/portable, 3.9-4.3 + 4.7-25 MHz

Price: $79.95 in the United States. CAN$179.00 in Canada.

Pro: Very good overall performance, including generally superior gain (*see* Con), especially within world band segments—yet surprisingly free from side effects. Compact folding design for airline and other travel; also handy for hospital, prison or other institutional use where an antenna must be put away periodically. Can be used even with portables that have no antenna input jack (*see* Con). Plug-in filter to reduce local electrical noise (*see* Con). Low battery consumption (*see* Con). Powered by the radio when used with Sony ICF-SW7600G or ICF-SW1000T portables.

Con: Battery operation only—no AC power supply, not even a socket for an AC adaptor. Only remote model tested which can't be mounted outdoors during inclement weather. Functions acceptably on shortwave only between 3.9-4.3 MHz and 4.7-25 MHz, with no mediumwave AM coverage. Gain varies markedly throughout the shortwave spectrum (*see* box), in large part because the preselector's step-tuned resonances lack variable peaking. Preselector bandswitching complicates operation slightly. Consumer-grade plastic construction with no shielding. When clipped onto a telescopic antenna instead of fed through an antenna jack, the lack of a ground connection reduces performance. Plug-in noise filter unit reduces signal strength by several decibels.

☞ Sony recommends that the AN-LP1 not be used with the Sony ICF-SW77 receiver. However, our tests suggest that so long as the control box and loop receiving element are kept reasonably away from the radio, the antenna performs well.

☞ The Sony ICF-SW07 compact portable comes with an AN-LP2 antenna. This is virtually identical in concept and performance to the AN-LP1, except that because it is designed solely for use with the 'SW07 it has automatic preselection. At present the AN-LP2 cannot be used with other radios, even those from Sony.

Verdict: A real winner if the shoe fits. Hands down, this is the best model for world band reception on portables—often an excellent choice for portatop and tabletop models, as well, provided you don't mind battery-only operation. This Japanese-made model has generally excellent gain, low noise and few side effects. The price is right, too.

Yet, inherent in any loop design is limited frequency coverage—90/120 meter DXers needn't apply—and the loop receiving element cannot be mounted permanently outdoors. Too, the lack of variable preselector peaking causes gain to vary greatly by frequency; this especially limits utility DX performance. Otherwise, the Sony AN-LP1 is nothing short of a bargain.

Comments: Our first impression upon unfolding this odd looking antenna was that it couldn't possibly work. But our original impression turned into grudging respect as it racked up worthy performance within its tuning range.

The AN-LP1's gain tends to be considerable, and is decidedly superior to that of

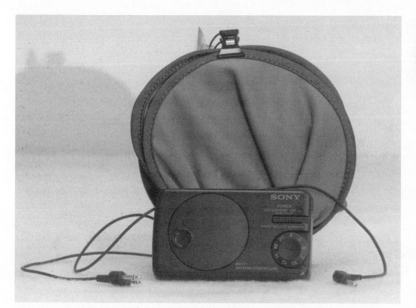

The Sony AN-LP1 is a gem. Affordable and with superior performance, its innovative design works well with portables either at home or on trips—portatops and tabletops, too. R. Sherwood

GAIN VS. FREQUENCY DATA ON SONY AN-LP1		
MHz	Gain (dB)	Preselector setting
3.2	−22	4
3.5	−9	4
3.7	0	4
3.9	9	4
4	19	4
4.06	24	4
4.2	13	4
4.5	4	4
4.5	3	5
4.8	11	5
5	20	5
5.13	28	5
5.3	19	5
5.6	13	5
5.6	9	6
6.2	23	6
6.53	39	6
6.87	31	6
7.3	38	6
7.5	29	6
7.5	39	7
7.6	43	7
8	30	7
8.5	18	7
9	11	7
9	15	10
10.15	24	10
10.47	33	10
11	22	10
11.5	16	10
11.5	16	12
12.93	31	12
13.5	17	12
13.5	11	14
14.5	22	14
15	33	14
15.5	22	14
16	17	14
16	16	16
17	27	16
17.4	33	16
18	25	16
20	15	16
20	22	20
21.7	29	20
22.5	26	20
23	23	20
25	12	20
26.1	8	20

the elder Sony AN-1 with its confusingly similar moniker. Front-end selectivity is excellent, as well, while dynamic range/IP3 is more than adequate. Only once, at a location near local broadcast transmitters, was there a trace of local mediumwave AM breakthrough around 4 MHz.

A preselector switch has to be set to the correct frequency range, after which no peaking is required. This is handier than a continuously variable peaking control, but it is also the antenna's Achilles heel, notably below 6 MHz where "Q" rises. For example, within 60 meters—the 5 MHz tropical segment—gain can be a mighty 28 dB if your receiver is tuned near the antenna's fixed peak; yet, half a Megahertz away it plummets to an anemic 11 dB (*see* box). Fortunately, the antenna is designed to provide good-to-superb gain on nearly all world band frequencies, so this is mainly of concern to utility DXers.

This Sony is the only remote model which cannot be mounted permanently outdoors, as its receiving element is not weatherproofed. That limits its potential to bring in the most signals with the least local noise, but for portable use and window mounting it is nigh ideal.

The AN-LP1 package includes a removable anti-noise filter which plugs into the loop's bottom. This handle-shaped accessory consists of a ferrite choke wrapped by the lead-in cable, and our tests show that it sometimes helps reduce local electrical noise. Great idea, but it also reduces the level of received signals by several decibels. So even though the instruction sheet says to be sure attach the filter unit, if you don't need it, don't use it.

If you like to meet new people, the AN-LP1 comes with an unexpected fringe benefit. When one of our panelists was listening on a Barbados beach, folks from surfers to an English Lord stopped by to inquire about the Sony flyswatter dangling from a palm frond.

✪✪✪ ⬤
Ameco TPA

Proximate, manual preselection, indoor, 0.22-30 MHz

Price: $69.95 in the United States.

Pro: Highest recovered signal with the longest supplied whip of the four proximate models tested. Most pleasant unit to tune to proper frequency. Superior ergonomics, including easy-to-read front panel with good-sized metal knobs (*see* Con). Superior gain below 10 MHz.

Con: Proximate model, so receiving element has to be placed near receiver. Above 15 MHz gain slips to slightly below average. Overloads with external antenna; because gain potentiometer is in the first stage, decreasing gain may increase overloading as current drops through the FET. Preselector complicates operation, compromising otherwise-superior ergonomics. No rubber feet, slides around in use; user-remediable. No AC adaptor. Consumer-grade plastic construction with no shielding. Comes with no printed information on warranty; however, manufacturer states by telephone that it is the customary one year.

Verdict: The Ameco TPA, made in the United States, is the best proximate model tested for bringing in usable signals with the factory-supplied whip—signal recovery was excellent. However, when connected to an external antenna it overloads badly, and reducing gain doesn't help.

Comments: Ameco's classic offering is the cheapest model tested, and with its plastic case and Spartan innards it looks the role. It has no rubber feet, either, so it slides around with use—thankfully, stick-on feet from a hardware store resolve this nicely.

Its use of a manually tuned preselector aside, ergonomics are excellent. It uses large metal knobs with set screws, which along with simple front panel markings made it a pleasure to use.

Don't regard the nominal preselector frequency limits as holy writ. When tuned on the "correct" band, the TPA has far less gain than the Dressler ARA 100 HDX on a variety of frequencies, but it springs to life with the preselector set one "band" lower. Experiment, making sure that the higher gain doesn't result in overloading.

✪✪✪ ⬤
McKay Dymek DX100E, McKay Dymek DA100EM, Stoner Dymek DA100E, Stoner Dymek DA100EM

Remote, broadband, indoor-outdoor-marine, 0.05-30 MHz

Price: *DA100E:* $179.95 in the United States. *DA100EM (marine version, not tested):* $199.95 in the United States.

The best "all in one box" antenna tested is the Ameco TPA. Least costly, too.   R. Sherwood

Pro: Respectable gain and noise. Generally good build quality, with worthy coaxial cable and an effectively sealed receiving element; marine version (not tested) appears to be even better yet. Jack for second antenna when turned off. Minor gain rolloff at higher shortwave frequencies. *DA100EM (not tested):* Fiberglass whip and brass fittings help ensure continued optimum performance.

Con: Slightly higher noise floor compared to other models. Some controls may confuse initially. Dynamic range/IP3 among the lowest of any model tested; for many applications in the Americas this is adequate, but for use near local transmitters, or in Europe and other strong-signal parts of the world, the antenna is best purchased on a returnable basis. *DA100E:* Telescopic antenna allows moisture and avian waste penetration between segments, and thus potential resistance and/or spurious signals; user should seal these gaps with Coax Seal or similar. Telescopic antenna could, in principle, be de-telescoped by birds, ice and the like, although we did not actually encounter this. Warranty only 30 days.

Verdict: The DA100E is a proven "out of the box" choice, with generally excellent weatherproofing and coaxial cable. Because its dynamic range/IP3 is relatively modest, it may be prone to overload, especially in an urban environment or other high-signal-strength location. In principle the extra twenty bucks for the marine version should be a good investment, provided its fiberglass whip is not too visible for your location.

Comments: The American-made DA100 series was conceived in the mid-seventies by California inventor George McKay. The iconoclastic McKay produced other products, including component shortwave and mediumwave AM tuners with oil-rubbed wood trim. A superb passive preselector, too.

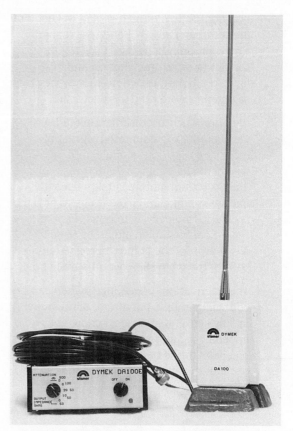

The McKay Dymek DA100E is the latest version of an antenna going back a quarter century. Although the "M" version is for marine applications, it is best for home use, as well. R. Sherwood

His active antennas were labeled "McKay Dymek," but after the McKay Dymek Co. was bought out in 1982 by Stoner Communications, Inc., the name was changed to "Stoner Dymek." But the story doesn't end there. In 1992 Stoner downsized and moved to Oregon, later changing its corporate name to McKay Dymek, Inc. So the antennas are once again being called by their original appellation, although it's a craps shoot whether any given antenna cabinet or packing box gets labeled as "McKay" or "Stoner."

The plastic box that houses the amplifier and antenna is of high quality, with a rear trap door that, although sealed to keep out the weather, can be opened for repairs. However, unless the user uses a good sealant or tape, precipitation and bird fluids are bound to penetrate into the whip segments, shortening the useful life.

With our much-used earlier unit, a DA100D, we eventually encountered a gradual increase in spurious signals until our weathered telescopic antenna was replaced. The DX100EM marine version uses a fiberglass whip, and in so doing avoids this problem. However, with both versions Coax-Seal or similar should be used to weatherproof the point where the female base of the whip slips over the male box.

The attenuation/impedance switch can be confusing at first, but after a bit of study makes sense. It includes a choice of impedances, although with today's receivers this is of little value. Twice on our unit the attenuator/impedance switch

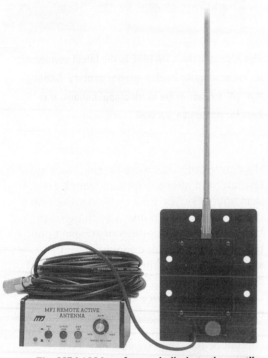

The MFJ 1024 performs similarly to the costlier McKay Dymek DA100E, but suffers from hum and lesser build quality.   R. Sherwood

went beyond its stop. After much fiddling it was returned to normal.

✪✪¼ ∅
MFJ 1024

Remote, broadband, indoor-outdoor, 0.05-30 MHz

Price: $139.95 in the United States. CAN$219.00 in Canada.

Pro: Overall good gain and low noise. A/B selector for quick connection to another receiver. "Aux" input for passive antenna. 30-day money-back guarantee if purchased from manufacturer.

Con: Significant hum with supplied AC adaptor; remedied when we substituted a suitable aftermarket adaptor. Non-standard power socket complicates substitution of AC adaptor; also, adaptor's sub-mini plug can spark when inserted while the adaptor is plugged in. Dynamic range/IP3 among the lowest of any model tested; for many applications in the Americas it is adequate, but for use near local transmitters, or in Europe and other strong-signal parts of the world, antenna is best purchased on a returnable basis. Slightly increased noise floor compared to other models. Telescopic antenna allows moisture and avian waste penetration between segments, and thus potential resistance and/or spurious signals; user should seal these gaps with Coax Seal or similar. Telescopic antenna could, in principle, be de-telescoped by birds, ice and the like after installation, although we did not actually encounter this. Control box/amplifier has no external weather sealing to protect from moisture, although the printed circuit board nominally comes with a water-resistant coating. Coaxial cable to receiver not provided. Mediocre coaxial cable provided between control box and receiving element. On our unit, a coaxial connector came poorly soldered from the factory.

Verdict: The MFJ 1024, made in America, performs almost identically to the Stoner Dymek DA100E, but sells for $40 less. However, that gap lessens if you factor in the cost of a worthy AC adaptor—assuming you can find or alter one to fit the unusual power jack—and the quality of the 1024's coaxial cable is not in the same league.

Comments: The MFJ 1024 and Stoner Dymek DA100E are surprisingly close in performance; see the DA100E's **Comments** for details. However, they are not two peas in a pod. The MFJ has much more gain than the DA100E at 20 MHz, although other gain levels are comparable. Yet, the DA100E has a slightly better noise factor in the 3-6 MHz range, while the 1024 produced a false mediumwave AM harmonic at one test location.

There are handy touches to make daily use less of a hassle. An A/B switch allows alternating the output between two receivers, plus a second antenna can be used when the 1024 is in the "off" position.

But there's a rub. The supplied AC adaptor produces hum aplenty, so all but noncritical users will probably want to obtain an aftermarket regulated power supply with proper filtering. Alas, finding one that works is complicated by the 1024's non-standard power input jack. It takes a sub-mini phone plug, which even with the supplied AC adaptor can spark when the plug is inserted; this can be avoided if the adaptor is unplugged beforehand.

Only time will tell how well the 1024's unusual form of weatherproofing holds up, especially in climates where freezing and thawing take place within the amplifier box. Our own experience and secondhand reports alike indicate that the quality of assembly of MFJ products is well below the industry norm. Nonetheless, our 1024 arrived in proper condition except for one poor solder joint.

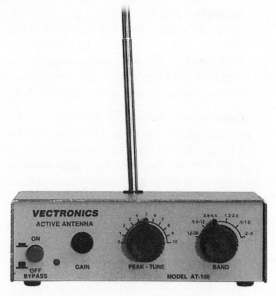

The Vectronics AT-100 works much better with some receivers than with others. R. Sherwood

✪✪½
Vectronics AT-100

Proximate, manual preselection, indoor, 0.3-30 MHz

Price: $79.95 in the United States. CAN$109.00 in Canada.

Pro: Good—sometimes excellent—gain (*see* Con), especially in the mediumwave AM band. Good dynamic range/IP3. Most knobs are commendably large.

Con: Proximate model, so receiving element has to be placed near receiver. No AC power; although it accepts an AC adaptor, the lack of polarity markings complicates adaptor choice (it's center-pin positive). Preselector complicates operation, especially as it is stiff to tune and thus awkward to peak. Our unit oscillated badly with some receivers, limiting usable gain—although it was more stable with other receivers, and thus appears to be a function of the load presented by a given receiver.

Verdict: If ever there were a product that needs to be purchased on a returnable basis, this is it. With one receiver, this American-made model gives welcome gain and worthy performance; with another, it goes into oscillation nearly at the drop of a hat.

Comments: Because of the potential of oscillation, the Vectronics antenna may be a Dr. Jekyll with one configuration, Mr. Hyde with another. Best bet, regardless of receiver, is not to set the gain control to anywhere near wide open with either the attached whip or an external antenna. Otherwise, you may be treated to an earful of wideband noise or heterodynes. Experiment, first placing the gain control at 70 or 80 percent of maximum.

When an amplifier oscillates, it becomes a mixer; in this instance, one fundamental oscillation can appear in the 235 MHz range, mixing up and down in frequency. A second oscillation at 200 kHz may occur when the gain is turned past four o'clock. Harmonics of the 200 kHz fundamental appear well into the lower portion of the shortwave spectrum.

The band and tuning knobs are large, and to that extent are easy to adjust. However the tuning control on our unit was stiff and thus awkward to peak. The gain control has no knob whatsoever, merely a protruding potentiometer shaft. The variable capacitor does not appear to be constructed for vigorous use.

External markings on the cabinet do not indicate the polarity of an external supply, although this can be divined from the supplied schematic—it is center-pin positive. Wrong polarity could damage the semiconductors, as there is no diode polarity protection, so proceed with caution. Also confusing is that the back panel shows 9 VDC, whereas the owner's manual indicates that the operating voltage should be 12 VDC.

⭐⭐
Sony AN-1

Remote, broadband, indoor-outdoor, 0.15-30 MHz

Price: $89.95 in the United States. CAN$149.00 in Canada. £64.95 in the United Kingdom.

Pro: Connects easily to any portable or other receiver, using supplied cables and inductive coupler. Unusually appropriate for low-cost portables lacking an outboard antenna input. Only portable-oriented model tested with weather resistant remote receiving element. Covers entire shortwave spectrum, plus mediumwave AM and longwave. AC adaptor jack, although antenna designed to run on six "AA" batteries. Good quality coaxial cable. Coaxial cable user-replaceable once head unit is disassembled. Switchable high-pass filter helps reduce intrusion of mediumwave AM signals into shortwave spectrum; rolloff begins at 3 MHz. Receiving element's bracket allows for nearly any mounting configuration (*see* Con).

Con: Poor gain, with pronounced reduction as frequency increases. Mediocre mediumwave AM performance. Clumsy but versatile mounting bracket makes installation tedious. No AC adaptor.

The Sony AN-1 lacks gain, but may be mounted outdoors where reception is best.   R. Sherwood

☞ Sony offers a number of active antennas in various world markets. All appear to be similar to the AN-1, except for the unusual AN-LP1 evaluated earlier in this report.

Verdict: The Japanese-made Sony AN-1 has feeble gain, rendering it practically useless on higher frequencies and little better below. However, for outdoor mounting and use on lower frequencies it provides passable performance.

Comments: The AN-1 provides a number of sensible ways to connect it to a receiver— either to a telescopic antenna via a pair of induction coils; or, better, directly plugged into the radio. The receiving element's bracket allows for nearly any mounting configuration, but it is clumsy and might buffalo some folks. All cabling and mounting hardware is provided.

For sets without an antenna jack, the AN-1's coupling boxes work better than the connecting clip used by the AN-LP1 for telescopic antennas. With the proper adaptor the AN-1 will plug into virtually any tabletop radio, as well.

The AN-1 has precious little in the way of gain, especially above 20 MHz. For someone faced with considerable interior electrical noise and who can mount the AN-1 out in the fresh air, away from those noises, the AN-1 can be advantageous. Otherwise, the AN-LP1 is much to be preferred.

The Sony AN-1 covers the mediumwave AM and longwave bands, as well as more of the shortwave spectrum than the Sony AN-LP1. However, mediumwave AM gain is minimal, leaving normally audible stations struggling to overcome circuit noise.

✪✪
Palstar AA30A "Active Antenna Matcher", Palstar AM-30 "Active Antenna Matcher"

Proximate, manual preselection, indoor 0.3-30 MHz

Price: *AA30A:* $65.95 in the United States. *AM-30 (not tested):* £69.95 in the United Kingdom.

Palstar makes a quality receiver, but its matching AA30A active antenna is no great shakes.

R. Sherwood

Pro: Moderate-to-good gain. Tuning control easily peaked. Can be powered directly by the Palstar R30/R30C and Lowe HF-350 tabletop receivers (reviewed elsewhere in PASSPORT REPORTS), an internal battery or an AC adaptor.

Con: Spurious oscillation throughout 14-30 MHz range. Overloads with external antenna. Proximate model, so receiving element has to be placed near receiver. Preselector complicates operation. No AC adaptor.

☞ At present, the AA30A's cabinets are silk screened simply as "AA30," although the accompanying owner's manual refers to the "AA30A."

☞ The Palstar AM-30, not tested, is sold in Europe. It appears to be comparable to the AA30A.

Verdict: Oscillation makes this a dubious choice except for reception below 14 MHz. Manufactured in the United States.

Comments: Inside, the Palstar AA30A and Vectronics AT-100 are remarkably similar. However, the Palstar uses a lower-cost potentiometer and varactor diode in lieu of a tuning capacitor. This provides smooth tuning, but the lower "Q" reduces performance at higher frequencies. Also, a low-cost 2N3904 transistor is used instead of the MPS5179 found in the Vectronics.

With our unit, there was VHF oscillation virtually all the time at nearly any gain, band or preselector setting—frequencies above 14 MHz were particularly impacted by on-frequency oscillation at high gain. When an amplifier oscillates, it becomes a mixer; in this instance, fundamental oscillation is around 250 MHz, mixing up and down in frequency. The fact that it oscillates at VHF with the gain at minimum implies that oscillation is taking place in the output stage.

As an experiment, one of our test engineers tried the Palstar with a "real" tuning capacitor. It performed somewhat better than the unmodified unit above 15 MHz because of the resulting increased "Q."

Some overloading that did not appear on the Vectronics occurred with the Palstar. Backing off the gain does help, more so than it does on the Ameco TPA.

✪✪
MFJ-1020B

Proximate, manual preselection, indoor, 0.3-30 MHz

Price: $79.95 in the United States. CAN$129.00 in Canada.

Pro: Superior dynamic range/IP3. Choice of PL-259 or RCA connections. 30-day money-back guarantee if purchased from manufacturer.

The MFJ-1020B is mediocre because of its proximate receiving element. Yet, it is effective as an active preselector to enhance short outdoor wires and such.

R. Sherwood

Con: Proximate model, so receiving element has to be placed near receiver. Low gain, excessive noise. Preselector complicates operation and tuning capacitor hard to peak. Knobs small and hard to adjust. Confusing markings on front panel. Two manufacturing flaws found on our unit: a defective lowest frequency inductor or switch, as the unit would not tune below 530 kHz; also, crooked front panel. No AC adaptor.

☞ As explained in the introduction to this article, the '1020B works nicely when coupled to a short wire in lieu of the built-in telescopic antenna.

Verdict: The MFJ-1020B, made in the United States, works well as an active preselector for an external antenna, but is uninspiring with its own telescopic antenna.

Comments: Mediocre performance with the built-in antenna, along with questionable ergonomics, make this a dismal choice as an active antenna. If you do purchase a '1020B, figure on replacing the three knobs with larger ones. Those supplied by MFJ are small, making the stiff tuning control disagreeable to adjust. To make matters worse, the front-panel markings make it hard to see which band is being tuned.

Check out the '1020B carefully for defects—ours had two—as it can be returned within 30 days if purchased from the manufacturer.

✪½ *(see story)*
RF Systems DX-One Professional

Remote, broadband, indoor-outdoor, 0.02-54 MHz

Price: $599.95 in the United States. £295.00 in the United Kingdom. AUS$1,170.00 in Australia.

Pro: Outstanding dynamic range/IP3. Very low noise. Outputs for two receivers. Comes standard with switchable high-pass filter to reduce the chances of mediumwave AM signals ghosting into the shortwave spectrum; it is effective below 1.4 MHz (*see* Con); manufacturer offers an optional brick wall filter to cut off the entire mediumwave AM band. Receiving element has outstanding build quality (*see* Con). Coaxial connector at head amplifier is completely shielded from the weather by a clever mechanical design. Operates from either120 or 230 VAC (*see* Con).

Con: Low gain. Control box build quality appears to be lacking. Amplifier appears to be susceptible to static damage, as on the first of our two units it failed; the manufacturer says it was not grounded properly, allowing static to blow the amp, but none of the other tested models suffered such a fate. Modest hum due to AC adaptor's not being thoroughly bypassed. Standard high-pass filter provides only limited rejection of 1.4-1.7 MHz mediumwave AM signals. User must supply own coaxial cable. Control unit has a European-style plug on the 117 VAC American version; user-remediable by purchasing a travel adaptor plug. AC voltage change requires disassembly of AC adaptor, followed by cutting and soldering; no instructions are supplied to explain how this should be done. Warranty only six months.

☞ Star rating is for the Americas and Australasia only. In high-signal parts of the world, such as Europe, the Near East and North Africa, the DX-One Professional could be a sensible choice, provided the receiving element is optimally erected, and the receiver possesses a superior noise floor, AGC threshold and recovered audio. This antenna should be especially attractive in an urban environment, where its high dynamic range/IP3 reduces the chances of overloading caused by a potpourri of local signals.

☞ As we go to press, a message has come in from a Swiss DX-One Professional owner, Ulrich Ruch, who presumably heard about PASSPORT's active antenna

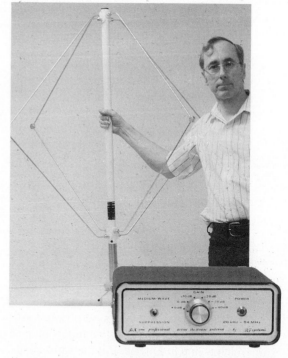

The RF Systems DX-One Professional antenna comes in two parts. The receiving element, held erect by Robert Sherwood, has been nicknamed "The Eggbeater."

T. Miller

tests through RF Systems. Mr. Ruch writes that he complained to the manufacturer about his antenna's low gain—the same problem we encountered in our tests. He says that, as a result, RF Systems modified his antenna, at no cost, to add 4.5 dB gain below 20 MHz and 13 dB above, of which 3 dB was created by eliminating the hybrid splitter. The manufacturer has made no mention to us of such an option, nor can we either confirm it or ascertain its impact on other aspects of performance other than to note that bypassing the splitter should have no deleterious effect. A 4.5 dB gain provides only marginal improvement, but DX-One Pro owners may still wish to pursue this modification if they have no need for the splitter.

Verdict: Clearly not in the running as a high-gain device. However, if the receiving element can be mounted high and outdoors, within suitable environments it should function acceptably as a very low-noise, low-gain antenna. Made in The Netherlands.

Comments: "Eggbeater" describes the DX-One Professional's appearance out of the box, but after assembly it looks more like a weird TV antenna. If you are looking for something unobtrusive to sneak past restrictive covenants, search elsewhere.

The DX-One Pro is easily assembled, and the receiving element is solidly built to withstand the elements for years to come. The base runs slightly warm, like the Dressler ARA 100 HDX.

The user must supply the coaxial feedline between the antenna and the control unit, as well as between the control unit and receiver. The control box's AC power cord comes with a European-style mains plug, which is fine in Europe. But the same plug is also used with the version sold in the Americas, where the user has to either purchase an adaptor or replace the plug.

The control box's build quality appears to be wanting. Our test unit's power-on LED dimmed significantly after being plugged in for just a few minutes; this was traced to an intermittent component after the rectification stage. A colleague owning a separate DX-One Pro has had his unit's control box rotary switch fail after modest use. Yet, even at this antenna's sky-high price the warranty is only six months rather than the usual year.

AC bypass capacitors are used across the rectifiers in the power supply within the control box. Nevertheless, significant hum appeared on many signals. Grounding the antenna's rear ground screw made no discernable difference, but the hum did disappear once we improved the rectifier diode bypassing.

Epoxy "goop" is added inside the control box to keep the S0239 connectors from working loose. Alas, this substance is malodorous—perhaps over time it will become less olfactorily disagreeable.

Gain is modest, especially below 17 MHz, but it improves when mounted optimally. This is especially useful, as the exceptional circuit quietness allows more signal readability than it would were it to have the usual level of circuit noise.

In principle the exotic pickup element, which has both a vertical component and two crossed loops, should provide a degree of polarization diversity, thus reducing fading. Strangely, not only did we find no such result with the usual long-haul shortwave signals, fading actually increased during reception of a close-in (40 miles, 65 kilometers) shortwave signal on 5 MHz.

✪ *(see story)*
RF Systems DX-10

Remote, broadband, indoor-outdoor, 0.1-30 MHz

Price: $289.95 in the United States. £125.00 in the United Kingdom. AUS$490.00 in Australia.

Pro: Outstanding dynamic range/IP3. Very low noise. Very small, unobtrusive design. Well-constructed receiving element.

Con (all versions): Low gain. Weather sealing mediocre on our unit. User must supply coaxial feed line. Warranty only six months.

Con (unique to North American version): *Because of the supplied AC power supply, which lacks rectifier bypass capacitors, there are exceptional problems that would be avoided with a proper power supply:* Buzzes and spurious signals appear throughout the mediumwave AM spectrum, as well as on shortwave to about 4 MHz; lesser hum and buzzing appear throughout the remainder of the tuning range. AC adaptor provided for

North America rated as 100 VAC input, rather than conventional 120 Volts. No substitute AC adaptor can be put into use without cutting the power cord.

☞ Star rating is for North America only, and even then only with the AC power supply being provided at the time our tests were conducted. In high-signal parts of the world, such as Europe, the Near East and North Africa, the DX-10 could be a sensible choice, provided: the 220V AC non-American adaptor (not tested) has proper bypassing, the receiving element is optimally erected, and the receiver possesses a superior noise floor, AGC threshold and recovered audio. This antenna should be especially attractive in an urban environment, where its high dynamic range/IP3 reduces the chances of overloading caused by a potpourri of local signals.

Verdict: The noisy and permanently attached 100 VAC power supply for North America is awful. Assuming that the normally conscientious Dutch manufacturer eventually remedies this, and further assuming the existing 220 VAC power supply is of a high caliber, the DX10 star rating should be comparable to that of the DX-One Professional.

That aside, the minimalist level of gain means that signal pickup is not inspiring— a few yards or meters of wire did just as well in our tests. This is an antenna that makes possible sense only in certain circumstances (see ☞, above).

Comments: One cannot overemphasize the cross-modulation hum and buzzing with the existing North American version. This is the consequence of a mediocre AC power supply, which made the unit only marginally useful below 5 MHz and precious little better above 10 MHz— regardless of geographical location or receiver. When listening with the reference inverted-V dipole nearby, broadband hash from the DX-10's 100 VAC power supply

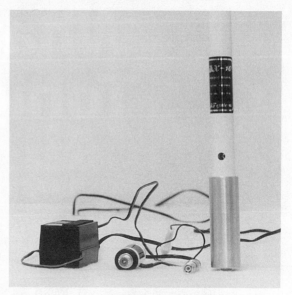

RF Systems' DX-10 flunked because of power supply problems. Assuming this is remedied shortly, it should perform comparably to its costlier DX-One Professional sibling. R. Sherwood

radiated so strongly that one could barely hear S5 stations. Unplugging the DX-10's AC adaptor completely eliminated the buzz.

All this disappears with a proper power supply, which can be provided if you don't mind finding a suitable AC adaptor, cutting and soldering wires, and making sure that the correct polarity is maintained. The manufacturer appears to be caring and technically proficient, so presumably it will eventually provide the American version of the DX-10 with quality AC filtration. If so, its performance would be comparable in nearly all respects to that of the DX-One Professional.

Otherwise, this is a real niche product. For the right situation and with a decent power supply, in principle it could be a sensible choice.

_____

Prepared by Robert Sherwood, with George Heidelman and David Zantow, along with Chuck Rippel; also, Lawrence Magne and Craig Tyson.

What's On Tonight?

PASSPORT's Hour-by-Hour Guide to World Band Shows

World band offers it all, from unparalleled news coverage to old-fashioned propaganda.

However, not everybody is looking for a six-course meal. Some are just interested in a few stations—perhaps from a favorite country or religious ministry. That's where PASSPORT's "Worldwide Broadcasts in English" and "Voices from Home" fit in.

Yet others like to surf the airwaves. They use the Blue Pages to figure out what they've found or what might be causing interference.

PASSPORT's Listening Picks

But many of us simply want to know what's on, when. So here are PASSPORT's listening picks from all over, hour by hour. Most of these shows are pleasant, but the best have icons:

- ■ Station superior, most shows excellent
- ● Show top-notch

Some stations provide schedules, others don't. Yet, even among those that do the information is not always credible or complete. To resolve this, PASSPORT monitors stations around the world to determine schedule activity throughout the year.

Additionally, to be as useful as possible over the months to come, PASSPORT's schedules consist not just of observed activity, but also that which we have creatively opined will take place during the forthcoming year. This predictive material is based on decades of experience and is original from us. Although it is inherently not as exact as real-time data, over the years it has been of tangible value to PASSPORT readers.

The most successful frequencies are given for North America, Western Europe, East Asia and Australasia, plus the Middle East, Southern Africa and Southeast Asia. "Worldwide Broadcasts in English" and the Blue Pages also include secondary and seasonal channels, as well as channels for other parts of the world.

All times are World Time, days are World Day, both explained in "Compleat Idiot's Guide to Getting Started" and PASSPORT's glossary. "Summer" and "winter" refer to seasons in the Northern Hemisphere.

Many stations supplement their programs with newsletters, tourist brochures, magazines, books and other goodies—often free. See "Addresses PLUS" for how these might be obtained.

Royal Bhutanese archers use aluminum arrows to improve accuracy.

M. Guha

PASSPORT monitors stations around the world to determine what's on throughout the year.

The United Nations provides agricultural assistance to rural women in Tajikistan.

RRDPS/UNOPS, Dushanbe

0000–0559
North America—Evening Prime Time
Europe & Mideast—Early Morning
Australasia & East Asia—Midday and Afternoon

00:00

■BBC World Service for the Americas.
Starts with five minutes of *news*, then
Tuesday through Saturday (weekday eve-
nings in the Americas) there's *Meridian* (the
arts). The second half hour is mostly popular
music, except for *World of Music* (Friday) and
15 minutes of soap opera on Wednesday and
Saturday. Weekends, there's Sunday's ●*Play
of the Week* (final part), ●*Sports Roundup* and
Arts in Action; replaced Monday by *World
Briefing*, ●*Sports Roundup* and *The World
Today*. Continuous programming to North
America and the Caribbean on 5975, 6175
and 9590 kHz.

**■BBC World Service for East and
Southeast Asia.** Starts with 20 minutes of
World Briefing, followed by ●*Sports Roundup*.
Except for Sunday, ●*World Business Report*
can then be heard on the half-hour. The final
15-minute slot is taken by ●*Analysis* (Tuesday, Wednesday, Friday and Saturday), ●*From
Our Own Correspondent* (Thursday) and
●*Letter from America* on Monday. The only
30-minute show is *Agenda* at 0030 Sunday.
Audible in East Asia on 15280 and 15360
kHz; and in Southeast Asia on 6195 and
15360 kHz.

Radio Bulgaria. Winter only at this time.
News, music and features. Tuesday through
Saturday (weekday evenings in North
America), the news is followed by *Events and
Developments*, replaced Sunday by *Views
Behind the News* and Monday by the delight-
fully exotic ●*Folk Studio*. The next slot
consists of weekly features. Take your pick
from *Plaza/Walks and Talks* (Monday),
Magazine Economy (Tuesday), *Arts and Artists*
(Wednesday), *History Club* (Thursday), *The
Way We Live* (Friday), *DX Programme* (Satur-
day) and *Answering Your Letters*, a listener
response show, on Sunday. Tuesday through
Sunday, the broadcast ends with *Keyword*

Bulgaria. Sixty minutes to eastern North
America and Central America on 7375 and
9400 kHz. One hour earlier in summer.

Radio Canada International. Winter only
at this time. Tuesday through Saturday
(weekday evenings in North America), it's the
final hour of the CBC domestic service news
program ●*As It Happens*, which features
international stories, Canadian news and
general human interest features. A shortened
Saturday edition is complemented by *C'est la
Vie*. Sundays feature ●*Global Village* (world
music), replaced Monday by another eclectic
music show, *Roots and Wings*, both from the
CBC's domestic output. To North America on
5960 and 9755 kHz. A separate half-hour
broadcast, ●*The World at Six*, can be heard
Tuesday through Saturday on 6040, 9535 and
11865 kHz. All are heard one hour earlier in
summer.

Radio Japan. *News*, then Tuesday through
Saturday (weekday evenings local American
date) it's *44 Minutes* (an in-depth look at
current trends and events in Japan and
elsewhere). This is replaced Sunday by *Hello
from Tokyo*, and Monday by *Weekend Square*.
One hour to eastern North America on 6145
kHz via the powerful relay facilities of Radio
Canada International in Sackville, New
Brunswick. A separate 15-minute news
bulletin for Southeast Asia is aired on any
two frequencies from 11815, 13650 and
17810 kHz.

**Radio Exterior de España ("Spanish
National Radio").** *News*, then Tuesday
through Saturday (local weekday evenings in
the Americas) it's *Panorama*, which features a
recording of popular Spanish music, a
commentary or a report, a review of the
Spanish press, and weather. The remainder
of the program is a mixture of literature,
science, music and general programming.
Tuesday (Monday evening in North America),

Girls return home from school in Bhutan. Instruction is both in English and Dzongkha, their native language. Primary education is one of the success stories of the present king.

M. Guha

there's *Sports Spotlight* and *Cultural Encounters*; Wednesday features *People of Today* and *Entertainment in Spain*; Thursday brings *As Others See Us* and, biweekly, *The Natural World* or *Science Desk*; Friday has *Economic Report* and *Cultural Clippings*; and Saturday offers *Window on Spain* and *Review of the Arts*. The final slot is given over to a language course, *Spanish by Radio*. On the remaining days, you can listen to Sunday's *Hall of Fame* and *Gallery of Spanish Voices*; and Monday's *Visitors' Book*, *Great Figures in Flamenco* and *Radio Club*. Sixty minutes to eastern North America on 6055 kHz.

Global Sound Kitchen, United Kingdom. Part of a four-hour weekend show from the people at Virgin Radio, featuring dance and new music. Saturday and Sunday (Friday and Saturday nights) only. To Europe winter on 3955, 6180 and 7165 kHz, and summer on 3955, 6140 and 7325 kHz. Audible to a certain extent in eastern North America.

Radio For Peace International, Costa Rica. The first 60 minutes of an eight-hour cyclical block of social-conscience and counterculture programming audible in Europe and the Americas on 6970, 15050 and (upper sideband) 21815 kHz.

Radio Pyongyang, North Korea. Strictly of curiosity value only, this broadcasting dinosaur is almost totally removed from

reality. Terms like "Great Leader" and "Beloved Comrade" abound, as do reports on visits to iron factories and other state enterprises. An hour of old-style communist programming to North America on 11710, 13760 and 15180 kHz.

Radio Ukraine International. Summer only at this time. An hour's ample coverage of just about everything Ukrainian, including news, sports, politics and culture. Well worth a listen is ●*Music from Ukraine*, which fills most of the Monday (Sunday evening in the Americas) broadcast. Sixty minutes to Europe on 5905 kHz, to eastern North America on 13590 kHz, and to West Asia on 9640 kHz. One hour later in winter. Budget and technical limitations have reduced audibility of Radio Ukraine International to only a fraction of what it used to be.

Radio Australia. Part of a 24-hour service to Asia and the Pacific, but which can also be heard at this time in parts of North America (better to the west). Begins with world *news*, then Tuesday through Friday there's *Asia Pacific*, replaced Saturday by *Feedback* (a listener-response program), Sunday by *Oz Sounds* and Monday by *Correspondents' Report*. On the half-hour, look for a bit of variety, depending on the day of the week. Monday's *Innovations* deals with the invented and innovative; Tuesday's cultural spot is *Arts*

00:00–01:00

Australia; Wednesday, take a trip up country in *Rural Reporter*; Thursday, it's *Book Talk*; Friday spotlights the environment in *Earthbeat*; and weekends there's Saturday's *Asia Pacific* and Sunday's *Correspondents' Report*. Targeted at Asia and the Pacific on 9660, 12080, 15240, 17580, 17750, 17795 and 21740 kHz. In North America (best during summer) try 17580, 17795 and 21740 kHz; and in East Asia go for 15240 and 17750 kHz. Best bet for Southeast Asia is 17750 kHz.

Radio Prague, Czech Republic. Summer only at this time; see 0100 for specifics. Thirty minutes to eastern North America on 11615 and 13580 kHz. One hour later in winter.

HCJB—Voice of the Andes, Ecuador. Tuesday through Saturday (weekday evenings in North America), you can hear *Insight for Living* and other religious features. This is replaced weekends by Sunday's *Nite Brite Kid's Club* and *Saludos Amigos,* and Monday's *Hour of Decision* and *Mountain Meditations*. To North America on 9745 and (winter) 12015 or (summer) 15115 kHz.

XERMX—Radio México Internacional. Winter only at this time. Consists of a thirty-minute feature. Take your pick from *Mosaic of Mexico* (Tuesday and Saturday—Monday and Friday evenings local American date), *DXperience* (Wednesday and Monday), *Regional Roots and Rhythms* (Thursday), *Mirror of Mexico (*Friday) and Sunday's *Creators of Mexican Art*. Thirty minutes, best heard in western and southern parts of the United States on 9705 kHz. One hour earlier in summer.

Voice of America. The first 60 minutes of a two-hour broadcast to the Caribbean and Latin America which is aired Tuesday through Saturday (weekday evenings in the Americas). *News Now*, a rolling news format covering political, business and other developments. On 5995, 6130, 7405, 9455, 9775, 11695 and 13740 kHz. The final hour of a separate service to East and Southeast Asia and Australasia (see 2200) can be heard on 7215, 9770, 11760, 15185, 15290, 17735 and 17820 kHz.

Radio Thailand. *Newshour.* Not as dry as it used to be, but a little vitality wouldn't be amiss. Thirty minutes to eastern and southern parts of Africa (who listens at this hour?), winter on 9680 kHz and summer on 9690 kHz. A full hour is available for Asia on 9655 and 11905 kHz.

All India Radio. The final 45 minutes of a much larger block of programming targeted at East and Southeast Asia, and heard well beyond. To East Asia on 7410, 9705 and 11620 kHz, and to Southeast Asia on 9950 kHz.

Radio Cairo, Egypt. The final half-hour of a 90-minute broadcast to eastern North America on 9900 kHz. Usually provides good reception. See 2300 for specifics.

Radio New Zealand International. A friendly package of *news* and features sometimes replaced by live sports commentary. Part of a much longer broadcast for the South Pacific, but also heard in parts of North America (especially during summer) on 17675 kHz.

WJCR, Upton, Kentucky. Twenty-four hours of gospel music targeted at North America on 7490 and (at this hour) 13595 kHz. Also heard elsewhere, mainly during darkness hours. For more religious broadcasting at this hour, try **WYFR-Family Radio** on 6085 and 9505 kHz, and **KTBN** on (winter) 7510 or (summer) 15590 kHz. For something a little more controversial, tune to Dr. Gene Scott's University Network, via **WWCR** on 13845 kHz or **KAIJ** on 13815 kHz. Traditionalist Catholic programming can be heard via **WEWN** on 5825 and 9355 (or 13615) kHz.

AFRTS Shortwave, USA. Network news, live sports, music and features in the upper-sideband mode from the Armed Forces Radio & Television Service. Transmitted from modestly powered U.S. Navy stations around the globe. Try 4278.5, 4319, 4993, 5765, 6350, 6458.5, 10320, 10940.5, 12579, 12689.5 and 13362 kHz.

00:30

■**Radio Netherlands.** Opens with a feature, then Tuesday through Saturday (weekday evenings in North America) there's ●*Newsline* (current events). Take your pick from ●*EuroQuest* (Tuesday), ●*A Good Life* (Wednesday), *Dutch Horizons* (Thursday), ●*Research File* (Friday), and Saturday's award-winning ●*Documentary*. Sunday fare consists of ●*Roughly Speaking*, a news bulletin and *Europe Unzipped*; Monday, it's *Aural Tapestry* followed by news and *Wide Angle*. The second of two hours to North America on 6165 and 9845 kHz.

Radio Vilnius, Lithuania. A half hour that's heavily geared to *news* and background reports about events in Lithuania. Of broader appeal is *Mailbag*, aired every other Sunday (Saturday evenings local American date). For a little Lithuanian music, try the next evening, following the news. To eastern North America winter on 6120 (or 6155) kHz, and summer on 9855 kHz.

Voice of the Islamic Republic of Iran. *News*, commentary and features with a strong Islamic slant. Not as anti-American as it used to be. One hour to eastern North America and Central America winter on 6065, 6135 and 9022 kHz, and summer on 9022, 9835 and 11970 kHz. Apart from 9022 kHz, channel usage tends to be a little erratic.

Radio Thailand. *Newshour*. Thirty minutes to central and eastern North America, winter on 13695 kHz and summer on 15395 kHz.

00:50

RAI International—Radio Roma, Italy. *News* and Italian music make up this 20-minute broadcast to North America on 6010, 9675 and 11800 kHz.

01:00

■**BBC World Service for the Americas.** Starts with five minutes of *news*, then it's some of the best of the BBC's output. The best double bill is undoubtedly Tuesday (Monday evening local American date), when ●*Health Matters* shares the stage with ●*Everywoman*. Also recommended are ● *Focus on Faith* (0130 Wednesday), *Sports International* (0105 Thursday), ●*One Planet* and *People and Places* (Friday), and *Discovery* (0105 Saturday). Pick of the remaining days is the long-running *Letter from America* at 0145 Sunday. Continuous programming to North America and the Caribbean on 5975, 6175 and 9590 kHz.

■**BBC World Service for East and Southeast Asia.** Monday through Saturday, there's five minutes of *World News*, replaced Sunday by a half hour of ●*The World Today*. Tuesday through Saturday at 0105, look for ●*Outlook*, one of the BBC's longest running shows. Monday, this gives way to *Talking Point* (a call-in show). On weekdays, the final 15 minutes carry ●*Off the Shelf*, serialized readings from the best of world literature. Continuous to East Asia on 15280 and 15360 kHz, and to Southeast Asia on 6195 and 15360 kHz.

Radio Canada International. Summer only. *News*, followed Tuesday through Saturday (weekday evenings local American date) by *Spectrum* (topics in the news), which in turn is replaced Sunday by *Venture Canada* (business and economics) and the interesting ●*Earth Watch*. On Monday (Sunday evening in North America), *Arts in Canada* is followed by a listener-response program, *The Mailbag*. Sixty minutes to North America on 5960 and 9755 kHz. You can also try 11715, 13670, 15170 and 15305 kHz, but they are only available for the first 30 minutes, except at weekends. One hour later in winter.

■**Deutsche Welle,** Germany. *News*, followed Tuesday through Saturday (weekday evenings in the Americas) by the comprehensive ●*NewsLink*—commentary, interviews, background reports and analysis. This is followed by ●*Insight* (analysis, Tuesday); ●*Man and Environment* (ecology, Wednesday); *Living in Germany* (Thursday), *Spotlight on Sport* (Friday), or Saturday's *German by Radio*. Sunday fare is *Talking Point* and ●*Inside*

01:00–01:00

Europe, replaced Monday by *Religion and Society* and *Arts on the Air*. Forty-five minutes of very good reception in North America and the Caribbean, winter on 6040, 6145, 9640, 9700 and 9765 kHz; and summer on 6040, 9640, 11810 and 13720 kHz.

Radio Slovakia International. *Slovakia Today*, a 30-minute window on Slovakia and its culture. Tuesday (Monday evening in the Americas) there's a variety of short features; the Wednesday spotlight is on tourism and Slovak personalities; Thursday's topic is business and economy; and Friday there's a mix of politics, education and science. Saturday fare includes cultural features, *Slovak Kitchen* and the off-beat *Back Page News*; while Sunday brings the *"Best of"* series. Monday's menu is very much a mixed bag, and includes *Listeners' Tribune* and some enjoyable Slovak music. A friendly half hour to eastern North America and the Caribbean on 5930 and 7230 (or 7300) kHz, and to South America on 9440 kHz.

Radio Budapest, Hungary. Summer only at this time. *News* and features, most of which are broadcast on a non-regular basis. Thirty minutes to North America on 9560 kHz. One hour later in winter.

Radio Prague, Czech Republic. *News*, then Tuesday through Saturday (weekday evenings in the Americas), there's *Current Affairs*. These are followed by one or more features: *Spotlight* (a look at Czech regional affairs, Tuesday); *Talking Point* (issues, Wednesday); *Czechs in History* (Thursday); Friday's *Economic Report*; and Saturday's *Mailbox* (a listener-response program).The Sunday slot is an excellent musical feature (strongly recommended), and Monday there's *A Letter from Prague*, *From the Weeklies* and *Readings from Czech Literature*. Thirty minutes to North

America, better to the East, on 7345 and 9665 (or 11615) kHz.

Swiss Radio International. *World Radio Switzerland*—a workmanlike compilation of news and analysis of world and Swiss events. Somewhat lighter fare on Sunday (Saturday evening in North America), when the biweekly *Capital Letters* (a listener-response program) alternates with *Name Game* (first Sunday) and *Sounds Good* (music and interviews, third Sunday). A half hour to North America and the Caribbean on 9885 and 9905 kHz.

Radio Exterior de España ("Spanish National Radio"). Repeat of the 0000 transmission. One hour to eastern North America on 6055 kHz. Popular with many listeners.

Radio Japan. *News*, then Tuesday through Saturday there's *44 Minutes* (an in-depth look at trends and events in Japan and beyond). This is replaced Sunday by *Hello from Tokyo*, and Monday by *Roundup Asia*. One hour to East Asia on 17845 kHz; to South Asia on 15325 kHz; to Southeast Asia on 11860 and 15590 kHz; to Australasia on 17685 kHz; to South America on 17835 kHz; and to the Mideast on 9515 (or 9660) and 11870 kHz. The broadcast on 17685 kHz may differ somewhat from the other transmissions, and may include alternative features.

Radio For Peace International, Costa Rica. Continues with an eight-hour cyclical block of social-conscience and counterculture programming audible in Europe and the Americas on 6970, 15050 and (upper sideband) 21815 kHz.

China Radio International. Starts with *News,* and Tuesday through Saturday (Monday through Friday evenings in the Americas) is followed by special reports. The rest of the broadcast is devoted to features. Regulars include *People in the Know* (Tuesday), *Sportsworld* (Wednesday), *China*

Horizons (Thursday), *Voices from Other Lands* (Friday), and *Life in China* on Saturday. Sunday's lineup includes *Global Review* and *Listeners' Garden* (has some interesting Chinese music) and the Monday menu offers *Report from Developing Countries* and *In the Spotlight*. One hour to North America on 9570 kHz, via CRI's Cuban relay.

Voice of Vietnam. A relay via the facilities of Radio Canada International. Begins with *news*, then there's *Commentary* or *Weekly Review*, followed by short features and some pleasant Vietnamese music (especially at weekends). Thirty minutes to eastern North America, with reception better to the south. Winter on 9525 kHz and summer on 9695 kHz. Repeated at 0230 on the same channels.

Voice of Russia World Service. Summer only at this hour, and the start of a four-hour block of programming for North America. *News*, then Tuesday through Sunday (Monday through Saturday evenings in North America), there's *Commonwealth Update*, replaced Sunday by *News and Views*, and Monday by *Sunday Panorama* and *Russia in Personalities*. The second half-hour contains some interesting fare, with just about everyone's favorite being Tuesday's ●*Folk Box*. For listeners who like classical music, don't miss Friday's ●*Music at Your Request* (sometimes alternates with *Yours for the Asking*). Pick of the remaining fare is ●*Moscow Yesterday and Today* (Sunday), Wednesday's *Jazz Show*, and Friday's evocative ●*Christian Message from Moscow*. Where to tune? In eastern North America there's 9665 kHz; farther west, shoot for 15595 and 17595 kHz.

Radio Habana Cuba. The start of a two-hour cyclical broadcast to eastern North America, and made up of *news* and features such as *Latin America Newsline*, *DXers Unlimited*, *The Mailbag Show* and ●*The Jazz Place*, interspersed with some lively Cuban music (though not as much as there used to be). To eastern North America on 6000 and 9820 kHz. Also available on 9830 or 11705 kHz upper sideband, though not all radios, unfortunately, can process such signals.

Global Sound Kitchen, United Kingdom. Winter only at this time. The final 60 minutes of a four-hour show featuring dance and new music. Saturday and Sunday (Friday and Saturday nights) only. To Europe winter on 3955, 6180 and 7165 kHz, and summer on 3955, 6140 and 7325 kHz. Audible to a certain extent in eastern North America.

Radio Pyongyang, North Korea. Repeat of the 0000 broadcast; see there for specifics. An hour of old-style communist programming to North America on 11735, 15230 and 17735 kHz.

Radio Australia. *World News*, then a feature. Monday's offering—unusual, to say the least—is *Awaye*, a program dealing with indigenous affairs. This is replaced Tuesday by *Science Show* and Wednesday by *Natural Interest* (topical events). Thursday's presentation is *Background Briefing* (news analysis); Friday brings *Hindsight*; Saturday is given over to *Oz Sounds* and *Arts Australia*; and the Sunday slot belongs to *The Europeans*. Continuous programming to Asia and the Pacific on 9660, 12080, 15240, 15415, 17580, 17750, 17795 and 21725 kHz. In North America (best during summer), try 17580, 17795 and 21725 kHz. Best bets for East Asia are 15240, 15415 and 17750 kHz; in southeastern parts, shoot for 17750 kHz. Some channels carry a separate sports service on winter Saturdays.

Radio Croatia. Summer only at this time, and actually starts two or three minutes into a predominantly Croatian broadcast. Approximately 15 minutes of news from and about Croatia. To eastern North America on 9925 kHz. One hour later in winter.

HCJB—Voice of the Andes, Ecuador. Tuesday through Saturday (weekday evenings in North America) it's *Studio 9*, featuring nine minutes of world and Latin American *news*, followed by 20 minutes of in-depth reporting on Latin America. The second half hour is given over to one of a variety of 30-minute features—including *Inside HCJB* (Tuesday), *Ham Radio Today* (Thursday), *Woman to Woman* (Friday), and the delightful ●*Música del Ecuador* on

01:00–02:00

Saturday. On Sunday (Saturday evening in the Americas), the news is followed by *DX Partyline*, and Monday by *Musical Mailbag*. Continuous programming to North America on 9745 and (winter) 12015 or (summer) 15115 kHz.

Voice of America. The second and final hour of a two-hour broadcast to the Caribbean and Latin America which is aired Tuesday through Saturday (weekday evenings in the Americas). *News Now*, a rolling news format covering political, business and other developments. On the half-hour, a program in "Special" (slow-speed) English is carried on 7405, 9775 and 13740 kHz; with mainstream programming continuing on 5995, 6130 and 9455 kHz.

Radio Ukraine International. Winter only at this time; see 0000 for program details. Sixty minutes of informative programming targeted at Europe, eastern North America and West Asia. Poor reception in most areas due to limited transmitter availability. Try 6020, 9560 and 9610 kHz. One hour earlier in summer.

Radio New Zealand International. A package of *news* and features sometimes replaced by live sports commentary. Part of a much longer broadcast for the South Pacific, but also heard in parts of North America (especially during summer) on 17675 kHz.

Radio Tashkent, Uzbekistan. *News* and features with a strong Uzbek flavor; some exotic music, too. A half hour to West and South Asia and the Mideast, occasionally heard in North America; winter on 5040, 5955, 5975, 7205 and 9540 kHz; and summer on 7190, 9375, 9530 and 9715 kHz.

WJCR, Upton, Kentucky. Continues with country gospel music for North American listeners on 7490 and 13595 kHz. Also with religious programs to North America at this hour are **WYFR-Family Radio** on 6065 and 9505 kHz, **WWCR** on 13845 kHz and **KTBN** on 7510 kHz. For traditionalist Catholic programming, tune to **WEWN** on 5825 and 9355 (or 13615) kHz.

AFRTS Shortwave, USA. Network news, live sports, music and features in the upper-sideband mode from the Armed Forces Radio & Television Service. Transmitted from modestly powered U.S. Navy stations around the globe. Try 4278.5, 4319, 4993, 5765, 6350, 6458.5, 10320, 10940.5, 12579, 12689.5 and 13362 kHz.

01:30

Radio Austria International. Summer only at this time. ●*Report from Austria*, which includes a brief bulletin of *news* followed by a series of current events and human interest stories. Tends to spotlight national and regional issues, and is an excellent source of news about Central Europe. Thirty minutes to the Americas on 9655, 9870 and 13730 kHz. One hour later in winter.

Radio Sweden. Tuesday through Saturday, it's *news* and features in *Sixty Degrees North*, concentrating heavily on Scandinavian topics. Tuesday's accent is on sports; Wednesday has electronic media news; Thursday brings *Money Matters*; Friday features ecology or science and technology; and Saturday offers a review of the week's news. Sunday, there's *Spectrum* (arts) or *Sweden Today* (current events), while Monday's offering is *In Touch with Stockholm* (a listener-response program) or the musical *Sounds Nordic*. Thirty minutes to Asia and Australasia, winter on 9495 kHz and summer on 13625 kHz.

01:45

Radio Tirana, Albania. Summer only at this time. Approximately 15 minutes of *news* and commentary from this small Balkan country. To North America on 6115 and 7160 kHz. One hour later in winter.

02:00

■**BBC World Service for the Americas.** Thirty minutes of ●*The World Today*, then Tuesday through Saturday (weekday eve-

nings in the Americas) there's a quarter hour of ●*World Business Report* followed most days by ●*Analysis* (current events). The exception is Thursday's ●*From Our Own Correspondent* (another edition airs at 0230 Sunday). The Monday slot goes to ●*Assignment* or an alternative documentary. Continuous programming to North America and the Caribbean on 5975, 6135 and 6175 kHz.

■BBC World Service for the Mideast. Summer only at this time. News and current events in *The World Today*. One hour weekdays but reduced to 30 minutes at weekends, when Saturday's *Global Business* and Sunday's ●*From Our Own Correspondent* complete the hour. On 9410 and 11760 kHz.

■BBC World Service for East Asia. Weekdays, the first half hour consists of *News* and an arts show, *Meridian*. In a brutal culture clash, the next 30 minutes are a mixed bag of popular music and soap opera. Weekends there's 30 minutes of *The World Today*, with Saturday's *Global Business* or Sunday's ●*From Our Own Correspondent* completing the hour. Continuous to East Asia on 15280 and 15360 kHz, and to Southeast Asia on 15360 kHz.

Radio Cairo, Egypt. Repeat of the 2300 broadcast, and the first hour of a 90-minute potpourri of *news* and features about Egypt and the Arab world. Fair reception, but often mediocre audio quality. To North America on 9475 kHz.

Radio Argentina al Exterior—R.A.E. Tuesday through Saturday only. *News* and short features spotlighting Argentina and its people. One of only a handful of stations which still give prominence to music from the provinces, and well worth a listen. Tangos, too, for listeners who like nostalgia. Fifty-five minutes to North America on 11710 kHz. Sometimes pre-empted by live soccer commentary in Spanish.

Radio Budapest, Hungary. Winter only at this time; see 0100 for specifics. Thirty minutes to North America on 9835 kHz. One hour earlier in summer.

■Wales Radio International. This time summer Saturdays (Friday evenings American date) only. News and views from the Land of the Red Dragon, and a little music, too. Thirty minutes to North America on 9795 kHz, and one hour later in winter.

Radio Canada International. Starts with *News*, then Tuesday through Saturday (weekday evenings local American date) it's the topical *Spectrum*. Winter Sundays, there's *Venture Canada* (business and economics) and the environmental ●*Earth Watch*, replaced Monday by *The Arts in Canada* and *The Mailbag*. Summer substitutes are Sunday's ●*Vinyl Café* (music and story-telling) and Monday's *Tapestry*. One hour winter to North America on 6155, 9535, 9755, 9780 and 11865 kHz. Summer, it's just 30 minutes Tuesday through Saturday, with a full hour on the remaining days. Choose from 9755, 11715, 13670, 15170 and 15305 kHz.

■Deutsche Welle, Germany. *News*, then Tuesday through Saturday there's the excellent ●*NewsLink*—commentary, interviews, background reports and analysis. The final part of the broadcast consists of a feature. Choose from ●*Insight* (analysis, Tuesday); ●*Man and Environment* (ecology, Wednesday); *Living in Germany* (Thursday); *Spotlight on Sport* (Friday); and Saturday's *German by Radio*. The Sunday offerings are *Weekend Review* and *Mailbag*, replaced Monday by *Weekend Review* (second part) and ●*Marks and Markets*. Forty-five minutes nominally targeted at South Asia, but widely heard elsewhere. Winter on 7285, 9615, 9765 and 11965 kHz; and summer on 9615, 11945 and 11965 kHz.

Radio Bulgaria. Summer only at this time. Starts with *news*, then Tuesday through Saturday (weekday evenings in North America) there's *Events and Developments*, replaced Sunday by *Views Behind the News* and Monday by 15 minutes of Bulgarian exotica in ●*Folk Studio*. Additional features include *Answering Your Letters* (a listener response show, Monday), *Plaza/Walks and Talks* (Tuesday), *Magazine Economy* (Wednesday). *Arts and Artists* (Thursday), *History Club*

(Friday), *The Way We Live* (Saturday) and *DX Programme*, a Sunday show for radio enthusiasts. Wednesday through Monday, the broadcast ends with *Keyword Bulgaria*. Sixty minutes to eastern North America and Central America on 9400 and 11700 kHz. One hour later in winter.

Radio Prague, Czech Republic. Winter only at this time. Repeat of the 0100 broadcast; see there for specifics. A half hour to North America on 6200 and 7345 kHz.

HCJB—Voice of the Andes, Ecuador. A mixed bag of religious programming, depending on the day of the week. Continuous to North America on 9745 and (winter) 12015 or (summer) 15115 kHz.

Radio Croatia. Winter only at this time, and actually starts around 0203. Approximately 15 minutes of news from and about Croatia. To eastern North America on 7280 or 9925 kHz. One hour earlier in summer.

Radio Taipei International, Taiwan. Opens with 15 minutes of *News*, and except for Sunday (when it's *Mailbag Time*), closes with *Let's Learn Chinese*, which has a series of segments for beginning, intermediate and advanced learners. In between, there are either one or two features, depending on which day it is. Monday (Sunday evening in North America) there's the pleasurable and exotic ● *Jade Bells and Bamboo Pipes* (Tai-wanese music); Tuesday brings *People and Trends*; Wednesday's slots are *Taiwan Today* and *Stage and Screen*; Thursday's double bill is *Journey into Chinese Culture* and *Hot Spots*; and Friday's coupling brings together *Taipei Magazine* and *East Meets West*. Weekends, the Saturday spots are taken by *Kaleidoscope* and *Reflection*s, with Sunday's menu featuring *Great Wall Forum* and *Food, Poetry and Others*. One hour to North and Central America on 5950, 9680 and 11740 kHz; and to Southeast Asia on 11825 and 15345 kHz.

Voice of Russia World Service. Winter, the start of a four-hour block of programming to North America; summer, it's the beginning of the second hour. *News*, features and music to suit all tastes. Winter fare includes

Commonwealth Update (0211 Tuesday through Saturday), replaced Sunday by *News and Views* and Monday by *Sunday Panorama*. The second half hour includes ●*Folk Box* (Tuesday), Russian jazz on Wednesday, ●*Music at Your Request* (Friday), ●*Christian Message from Moscow* (Saturday), ●*Moscow Yesterday and Today* (Sunday) and *Timelines* (Monday). In summer, take your pick from *Moscow Mailbag* (0211 Sunday, Monday and Thursday), *Newmarket* (business, same time Wednesday and Saturday), and *Science and Engineering* (0211 Tuesday and Friday). There's a news summary on the half-hour, then ●*Audio Book Club* (Saturday), *Songs from Russia* (Sunday), *This is Russia* (Monday), *Kaleidoscope* (Tuesday), ●*Moscow Yesterday and Today* (Thursday) or Friday's *Russian by Radio*. Note that these days are World Time; locally in North America it will be the previous evening. For eastern North America winter, tune to 7180 kHz; summer, it's 9665 kHz. Listeners in western states should go for 12020, 13665 and 15470 kHz in winter; and 15595 and 17595 kHz in summer.

Radio Habana Cuba. The second half of a two-hour broadcast to eastern North America; see 0100 for program details. On 6000 and 9820 kHz. Also available on 9830 or 11705 kHz upper sideband.

Radio Australia. Continuous programming to Asia and the Pacific, but well heard in parts of North America (especially to the

02:00–03:00

west). Begins with *World News*, then Monday through Friday it's *The World Today* (comprehensive coverage of world events). At 0205 Saturday, look for some incisive scientific commentary in ●*Ockham's Razor*, which is then followed by *Health Report*. These are replaced Sunday by the more sedate *Fine Music Australia* and *Religion Report*. Targeted at Asia and the Pacific on 9660, 12080, 15240, 15415, 15515, 17580, 17750 and 21725 kHz. Best heard in North America (especially during summer) on 17580 kHz. For East and Southeast Asia, choose from 15240, 15415, 17750 and 21725 kHz. Some of these channels carry a separate sports service on summer (midyear) weekends and winter Saturdays.

Radio For Peace International, Costa Rica. Continues with an eight-hour cyclical block of social-conscience and counterculture programming audible in Europe and the Americas on 6970, 15050 and (upper sideband) 21815 kHz.

Radio Korea International, South Korea. Opens with *news* and commentary, followed Tuesday through Thursday (Monday through Wednesday evenings in the Americas) by *Seoul Calling*. Weekly features include *Echoes of Korean Music* and *Shortwave Feedback* (Monday), *Tales from Korea's Past* (Tuesday), *Korean Cultural Trails* (Wednesday), *Pulse of Korea* (Thursday), *From Us to You* (a listener-response program) and *Let's Learn Korean* (Friday), *Let's Sing Together* and *Korea Through Foreigners' Eyes* (Saturday), and Sunday's *Discovering Korea*, *Korean Literary Corner* and *Weekly News*. Sixty minutes to the Americas on 11725, 11810 and 15575 kHz; and to East Asia on 7275 kHz.

Radio Pyongyang, North Korea. Repeat of the 0000 broadcast; see there for specifics. Abominably bad programs, but improvement may be on the way now that the country is beginning to accept outside help. In the meantime, it's one hour of old-fashioned communist programming to North America on 11845 and 13650 kHz.

Radio Romania International. *News*, commentary, press review and features on Romania. Regular spots include Wednesday's *Youth Club* (Tuesday evening, local American date), Thursday's *Romanian Musicians*, and Friday's *Listeners Letterbox* and ●*Skylark* (Romanian folk music). Fifty-five minutes to North America on 9570, 11830 (winter) and (summer) 11940 kHz; to East Asia winter on 9690 and 11740 kHz, and summer on 11885 and 15105 kHz; and to Australasia winter on 9510 and 11940 kHz, and summer on 15380 and 17790 kHz.

Voice of Greece. Actually starts around 0202 Approximately seven minutes of English *news* in a predominantly Greek broadcast. To North America winter on 7450, 9375 and 9420 kHz; and summer on 9420, 12110 and 15630 kHz.

WJCR, Upton, Kentucky. Continues with country gospel music for North American listeners on 7490 kHz. Also with religious broadcasts to North America at this hour are **WYFR**-Family Radio on 6065 and 9505 kHz, **WWCR** on 5935 kHz, **KAIJ** on 5755 kHz, and **KTBN** on 7510 kHz. Traditionalist Catholic programming can be heard via **WEWN** on 5825 kHz.

AFRTS Shortwave, USA. Network news, live sports, music and features in the upper-sideband mode from the Armed Forces Radio & Television Service. Transmitted from modestly powered U.S. Navy stations around the globe. Try 4278.5, 4319, 4993, 5765, 6350, 6458.5, 10320, 10940.5, 12579, 12689.5 and 13362 kHz.

02:30

Radio Austria International. Winter only at this time. ●*Report from Austria*, a popular compilation of news, current events and human interest stories. Good coverage of national and regional issues. Thirty minutes to North America on 7325 kHz. One hour earlier in summer.

Radio Sweden. Tuesday through Saturday (weekday evenings in North America), it's *news* and features in *Sixty Degrees North*, with the accent heavily on Scandinavian topics.

Tuesday's theme is sports; Wednesday has news of the electronic media; Thursday brings *Money Matters*; Friday features ecology or science and technology; and Saturday offers a review of the week's news. Sunday, there's *Spectrum* (arts) or *Sweden Today* (current events), while Monday's offering is *In Touch with Stockholm* (a listener-response program) or the musical *Sounds Nordic*. Thirty minutes to North America on 9495 kHz.

Radio Tirana, Albania. Summer only at this time. Thirty minutes of Balkan news and music to North America on 6115 and 7160 kHz. One hour later during winter.

Radyo Pilipinas, Philippines. Monday through Saturday, the broadcast opens with *Voice of Democracy* and closes with *World News*. These are separated by a daily feature: *Save the Earth* (Monday), *The Philippines Today* (Tuesday), *Changing World* (Wednesday), *Business Updates* (Thursday), *Brotherhood of Men* (Friday), and Saturday's *Listeners and Friends*. Sunday fare consists of *Asean Connection*, *Sports Focus* and *News Roundup*. Approximately one hour to the Mideast on 11805 (winter), 11885 (summer), 15120 and 15270 kHz.

Radio Budapest, Hungary. Summer only at this time. *News* and features, not many of which are broadcast on a regular basis. Thirty minutes to North America on 9835 kHz. One hour later in winter.

Voice of Vietnam. Repeat of the 0100 broadcast; see there for specifics. A relay to eastern North America via the facilities of Radio Canada International, winter on 9525 kHz and summer on 9695 kHz. Reception is better to the south.

02:45

Radio Tirana, Albania. Winter only at this time. Approximately 15 minutes of *news* and commentary from one of Europe's least known countries. To North America on 6115 and 7160 kHz. One hour earlier in summer.

Vatican Radio. Actually starts at 0250. Concentrates heavily, but not exclusively, on issues affecting Catholics around the world. Twenty minutes to eastern North America on 7305 and 9605 kHz.

03:00

■BBC World Service for the Americas. Tuesday through Saturday (weekday evenings in the Americas) there's five minutes of *news*, then a 25-minute feature. Best is Tuesday's ●*Omnibus*, replaced by music or light entertainment on the remaining days. There's another feature at 0330, and ●*Off the Shelf* (readings from the best of world literature) completes the hour. *World Briefing* and ●*Sports Roundup* fill the first 30 minutes on Sunday and Monday, and are followed by ●*Science in Action* and *Westway* (a soap opera), respectively. Continuous programming to North America and the Caribbean on 5975, 6135 and 6175 kHz.

■BBC World Service for Eastern Europe and the Mideast. Starts with *World Briefing* and ●*Sports Roundup*, then Monday through Saturday there's top-notch financial reporting in ●*World Business Report/Review*. The final 15-minute slot goes to ●*Analysis* (Tuesday, Wednesday, Friday and Saturday), *Write On* or *Waveguide* (Monday), and ●*From Our Own Correspondent* on Thursday. A full half hour of ●*Science in Action* airs at 0330 Sunday. To Eastern Europe on 6195 and (summer) 9410 kHz, and to the Mideast on 9410, 11760 and 11955 kHz.

■BBC World Service for Southern Africa. Same as the service for the Mideast until 0330, then Monday through Friday it's *Network Africa*, a fast-moving breakfast show. This is replaced Saturday by *African Quiz* or *This Week and Africa*, and Sunday by *Postmark Africa*. The first 60 minutes of a 19-hour block of programming. On 3255, 6005, 6190 and 7125 kHz.

■BBC World Service for East and Southeast Asia. Monday through Saturday, starts with five minutes of *news*. Best of the features which follow include ●*One Planet* (0305 Monday), *Discovery* (science, same time Tuesday), Wednesday's excellent combo of

03:00–03:00

●*Health Matters* and ●*Everywoman*, Thursday's ●*Focus on Faith* (0330) and Friday's *Sports International* (0305). The Sunday lineup consists of *World Briefing*, ●*Sports Roundup* and ●*Science in Action*. Audible in East Asia on 15280, 15360 (till 0330), 17760 and 21660 kHz. For Southeast Asia there's only 15360 kHz until 0330.

Radio Canada International. Winter only at this time. Starts with *News*, then Tuesday through Saturday (weekday evenings local American date) you can hear *Spectrum* (current events). Weekends, there's a full hour of programs from the domestic service of RCI's parent organization, the Canadian Broadcasting Corporation. Sunday, expect some story-telling amidst a mélange of music in the thoroughly enjoyable ●*Vinyl Café*, while Monday's *Tapestry* is a more serious cultural offering. To eastern North America and the Caribbean on 6155, 9755 and 9780 kHz. One hour earlier in summer.

Radio Croatia. Summer only at this time, and actually starts two or three minutes into a predominantly Croatian broadcast. Approximately 15 minutes of news from and about Croatia. To western North America on 9925 kHz. One hour later in winter.

■**Wales Radio International.** This time winter Saturdays (Friday evenings American date) only. News, interviews and music from the land of harps and Dylan Thomas. Worth a listen for the occasional song from renowned Welsh choirs. Thirty minutes to North America on 9735 kHz, and one hour earlier in summer.

Radio Taipei International, Taiwan. Like the 0200 transmission, the broadcast opens with 15 minutes of *News*, and except for Sunday (when it's *Mailbag Time*), closes with *Let's Learn Chinese*. In between, look for features—one or two, depending on the day of the week. Monday (Sunday evening in North America) there's *Life on the Outside* followed by *Women in Taiwan*; Tuesday's double bill consists of *Taiwan Economic Journal* and *Formosa Oldies*; Wednesday's single feature is *Floating Air*; Thursday's pairing brings together *Soundbite* and *Life*

Unusual; and *Miss Mook's Big Countdown* fills the Friday spotlight. Weekends, look for Saturday's *Carol's Café* and *Taiwan Excursions*, with *Instant Noodles* making up the Sunday menu. To North America on 5950 and 9680 kHz, to East Asia on 11745 kHz; and to Southeast Asia on 11825 and 15345 kHz.

China Radio International. Starts with *News,* then Tuesday through Saturday (weekday evenings in the Americas) there's in-depth reporting. The rest of the broadcast is devoted to features. Regular shows include *People in the Know* (Tuesday), *Sportsworld* (Wednesday), *China Horizons* (Thursday), *Voices from Other Lands* (Friday), and *Life in China* on Saturday. Sunday's lineup includes *Global Review* and *Listeners' Garden* (reports, music and Chinese language lessons), while Monday's broadcast has *Report from Developing Countries* and *In the Spotlight*. One hour to North America on 9690 kHz.

■**Deutsche Welle,** Germany. *News,* then Tuesday through Saturday (weekday evenings in North America) it's ●*NewsLink*—an impressive package of commentary, interviews, background reports and analysis. The final slot is a feature: ●*Insight* (Tuesday), ●*Man and Environment* (Wednesday), *Living in Germany* (Thursday), *Spotlight on Sport* (Friday) and *German by Radio* on Saturday. The Sunday offerings are *Weekend Review* and ●*Spectrum* (science); while Monday brings *Weekend Review* (second part) and *Arts on the Air*. Forty-five minutes to North America and the Caribbean, winter on 6045, 9535, 9640, 9700 and 11750 kHz; and summer on 9535, 9640, 11810, 13780 and 15105 kHz.

Radio Ukraine International. Summer only at this time, and a repeat of the 0000 broadcast See there for specifics). Sixty minutes to Europe and the Mideast on 6020 kHz, to North America on 13590 kHz, and to West Asia on 9640 kHz. One hour later in winter. Generally poor reception due to budget and technical limitations.

Voice of America. Three and a half hours (four at weekends) of continuous programming aimed at an African audience. Monday

Radioworld

through Friday, there's the informative and entertaining ●*Daybreak Africa*, with the remaining airtime taken up by *News Now*—a mixed bag of sports, science, business and other news and features. Although beamed to Africa, this service is widely heard elsewhere, including parts of the United States. Try 6035 (winter), 6080, 6115 (summer), 7105, 7275 (summer), 7290, 7415 (winter), 9575 (winter) and 9885 kHz.

Voice of Russia World Service. Continuous programming to North America at this hour. *News*, then winter it's a listener-response program, *Moscow Mailbag* (Monday, Thursday and Sunday), the business-oriented *Newmarket* (Wednesday and Saturday), or *Science and Engineering* (Tuesday and Friday). At 0331, there's ●*Audio Book Club* (Saturday), *This is Russia* (Monday), *Kaleidoscope* (Tuesday), ●*Moscow Yesterday and Today* (Thursday), *Russian by Radio* (Friday) and *Songs from Russia* on Sunday. Note that these days are World Time, so locally in North America it will be the previous evening. In summer, look for *News and Views* at 0311 Tuesday through Sunday, replaced Monday by *Sunday Panorama* and *Russia in Personalities*. After a brief news summary on the half-hour, there's Sunday's ●*Christian Message from Moscow*, Monday's ●*Audio Book Club*, and a changing roster of features on the remaining days. In eastern North America, choose from 5940 and 7180 kHz in winter, and go for 9665 kHz in summer. In western North America, the situation is a little better—for winter, try 12020, 13665 and 15470 kHz; in summer, take your pick from 15595, 17565, 17650, 17660 and 17690 kHz.

XERMX—Radio México Internacional. Summer only at this time. Tuesday through Saturday (weekday evenings in North America) there's an English summary of the Spanish-language *Antena Radio*, replaced Sunday by *DXperience*, a show for radio enthusiasts. Monday's programming is in Spanish. Thirty minutes to North America on 9705 kHz. One hour later in winter.

Radio Australia. *World News*, then Monday through Friday it's *Australia Talks Back*

(discussion of topical issues). Weekends, look for a novel experience in Saturday's *Book Reading*, which is followed by the out-of-town *Rural Reporter*. The Sunday offerings are *Feedback* (listener-response) and *Correspondents' Reports*. Continuous to Asia and the Pacific on 9660, 12080, 15240, 15415, 15515, 17580, 17750 and 21725 kHz. Also heard in western North America, best on 17580 kHz. In East and Southeast Asia, pick from 15240, 15415, 17750 and 21725 kHz. Some of these channels carry a separate sports service at weekends.

Radio Habana Cuba. Repeat of the 0100 broadcast. To eastern North America on 6000 and 9820 kHz, and also available on 9830 (or 11705) kHz upper sideband.

Radio Thailand. *News Magazine*. Thirty minutes to western North America winter on 15460 kHz, and summer on 15395 kHz. Also available to Asia on 9655 and 11905 kHz, although operation on these channels tends to be somewhat irregular.

HCJB—Voice of the Andes, Ecuador. Predominantly religious programming at this hour. Try *Radio Reading Room* at 0330 Monday (local Sunday evening in North America). Continuous to the United States and Canada on 9745 and (winter) 12015 or (summer) 15115 kHz.

Radio Prague, Czech Republic. Summer only at this time. Repeat of the 0000 broadcast; see 0100 for specifics. A half hour to North America on 7345 and 11615 kHz. This is by far the best opportunity for listeners in western parts. One hour later in winter.

Radio Cairo, Egypt. The final half-hour of a 90-minute broadcast to North America on 9475 kHz.

Radio Bulgaria. Winter only at this time; see 0200 for specifics. A distinctly Bulgarian potpourri of news, commentary, interviews and features, plus a fair amount of music. Not to be missed is the musical ●*Folk Studio* at 0310 Monday (Sunday evening local American date). Sixty minutes to eastern North America and Central America on 7375 and 9400 kHz. One hour earlier in summer.

Radio Japan. *News*, then weekdays there's *Asian Top News*. This is followed by a 35-minute feature. Take your pick from ●*Music Journey Around Japan* (a look at regional music and customs, Monday), Japanese language lessons (Tuesday and Thursday), *Unforgettable Musical Masterpieces* (postwar popular songs with brief historical items of the period, Wednesday), and *Music Beat* (Japanese popular music, Friday). *Weekend Square* fills the Saturday slot, and *Hello from Tokyo* is aired Sunday. Sixty minutes to Australasia on 21610 kHz, and to Central America on 17825 kHz.

Radio New Zealand International. A friendly broadcasting package targeted at a regional audience. Part of a much longer transmission for the South Pacific, but also heard in parts of North America (especially during summer) on 17675 kHz. Often carries commentaries of local sporting events.

Voice of Turkey. Summer only at this time. *News*, followed by *Review of the Turkish Press* and features (some of them unusual) with a strong local flavor. Selections of Turkish popular and classical music complete the program. Fifty minutes to eastern North America on 11655 kHz, to the Mideast on 6155 kHz, and to Southeast Asia and Australasia on 21715 kHz. One hour later during winter.

WJCR, Upton, Kentucky. Continues with country gospel music for North American listeners on 7490 kHz. Also with religious programs to North America at this hour are **WYFR-Family Radio** on 6065 and 9505 kHz, **WWCR** on 5935 kHz, **KAIJ** on 5755 kHz and **KTBN** on 7510 kHz. For traditionalist Catholic fare, try **WEWN** on 5825 kHz.

Radio For Peace International, Costa Rica. Continues with a variety of counterculture and social-conscience features. There is also a listener-response program at 0330 Wednesday (Tuesday evening in the Americas). Audible in Europe and the Americas on 6970, 15050 and (upper sideband) 21815 kHz.

AFRTS Shortwave, USA. Network news, live sports, music and features in the upper-sideband mode from the Armed Forces Radio & Television Service. Transmitted from modestly powered U.S. Navy stations around the globe. Try 4278.5, 4319, 4993, 5765, 6350, 6458.5, 10320, 10940.5, 12579, 12689.5 and 13362 kHz.

03:30

United Arab Emirates Radio, Dubai. *News*, then a feature devoted to Arab and Islamic history or culture. Twenty minutes to North America on 12005, 13675 and 15400 kHz; heard best during the warm-weather months.

Radio Sweden. Repeat of the 0230 transmission; see there for program specifics. Thirty minutes to North America, winter on 9495 kHz and summer on 9495 or 15245 kHz.

Radio Prague, Czech Republic. Summer only at this time. *News*, then Tuesday through Saturday there's *Current Affairs*. These are followed by one or more features: *Spotlight* (a look at Czech regional affairs, Tuesday); *Talking Point* (issues, Wednesday); *Czechs in History* (Thursday); Friday's *Economic Report*; and Saturday's *Mailbox* (a listener-response program).The Sunday slot is an excellent musical feature (strongly recommended), and Monday there's *A Letter from Prague*, *From the Weeklies* and *Readings from Czech Literature*. A half hour to the Mideast and South Asia on 11600 and 15470 kHz. One hour later in winter.

Radio Budapest, Hungary. This time winter only; see 0230 for specifics. Thirty minutes to North America on 9835 kHz. One hour earlier in summer.

Voice of Vietnam. A relay via the facilities of Radio Canada International. Begins with *news*, then there's *Commentary* or *Weekly Review*, followed by short features and some pleasant Vietnamese music (particularly at weekends).A half hour to Central America, and easily heard in the southern United States. On 9795 kHz.

Radio Tirana, Albania. Winter only at this time. *News*, features and lively Albanian

03:30–04:00

music. Thirty minutes to North America on 6115 and 7160 kHz. One hour earlier in summer.

04:00

■BBC World Service for the Americas.

Monday through Friday (Sunday through Thursday evenings in North America), it's 50 minutes of news and current events in *The World Today*, with ●*Sports Roundup* closing the hour. On the remaining days, *The World Today* is cut to 30 minutes, and is followed by Saturday's ●*Assignment* (or another documentary), and Sunday's *Global Business*. Continuous programming to North America and the Caribbean on 5975, 6135 (winter) and 6175 kHz.

■BBC World Service for Europe.

Identical to the service for the Americas except that ●*Weekend* replaces *Assignment* at 0430 Saturday. Continuous to Europe and North Africa on 6195, 9410 and (summer) 12095 kHz.

■BBC World Service for the Mideast.

Similar to the service for the Americas, but *In Praise of God* replaces *Global Business* at 0430 Sunday. Continuous programming on 11760 and 15575 kHz.

■BBC World Service for Southern

Africa. Thirty minutes of ●*The World Today*, followed Monday through Friday by *Network Africa*. Weekends at 0430, look for Saturday's *Talkabout Africa* or Sunday's *African Perspective*. Continues on 3255, 6190, 7125 and (winter) 11765 kHz.

■BBC World Service for East Asia. Same

as to the Americas except for 0430 Sunday, when ●*Omnibus* replaces *Global Business*. Continuous to East Asia on 15280, 17760 and 21660 kHz.

Radio Croatia. Winter only at this time, and actually starts around 0403. Approximately 15 minutes of news from and about Croatia. To western North America on 7285 or 9925 kHz. One hour earlier in summer.

Radio Habana Cuba. Continuous programming to eastern North America and the Caribbean on 6000 and 9820 kHz. Also available on 9830 or 11705 kHz upper sideband.

Radio Vlaanderen Internationaal, Belgium. Tuesday through Saturday (weekdays evenings in North America), starts with *News*, then *Belgium Today*, *Press Review* and features. Take your pick from *Focus on Europe* and *Sports* (Tuesday), *Green Society* (Wednesday), *The Arts* (Thursday and Saturday), *Around Town* (Thursday), *Economics* and *International Report* (Friday) and Saturday's *Tourism*. Closes with *Soundbox*. These are replaced Sunday by *Music from Flanders*, and Monday by *Radio World*, *Tourism*, *Brussels 1043* (a listener-response program) and *Soundbox*. A half hour to western North America winter on 11980 kHz, and summer on 15565 kHz.

Radio Prague, Czech Republic. Winter only at this time. A repeat of the 0100 broadcast, see there for specifics. Thirty minutes to North America on 7345 and 9435 kHz. By far the best opportunity for western parts. One hour earlier in summer.

Swiss Radio International. Repeat of the 0100 broadcast plus an additional 30 minutes of music and interviews in *Rendezvous with Switzerland*. A full hour year-round to North America and the Caribbean on 9885 and 9905 kHz, with the first half hour also available summer to southeastern Europe (one hour later in winter) on 9610 kHz.

Radio Ukraine International. Winter only at this time, and a repeat of the 0100 broadcast. See 0000 for program details. Sixty minutes of informative programming targeted at Europe, North America and West Asia. Generally poor reception due to budget and technical limitations. Try 6020, 9600 and 9610 kHz. One hour earlier in summer.

XERMX—Radio México Internacional. Tuesday through Saturday winter (weekday evenings in North America) there's an English summary of the Spanish-language *Antena Radio*, replaced Sunday by *DXperience*, a show for radio enthusiasts. Monday's programming is in Spanish. The summer lineup consists of *Regional Roots and Rhythms*

(Tuesday), *Mailbox* (Wednesday and Saturday), *Mosaic of Mexico* (Thursday) and *Creators of Mexican Art* on Friday. There are no programs on Sunday or Monday. Thirty minutes to North America on 9705 kHz.

HCJB—Voice of the Andes, Ecuador. Tuesday through Saturday (weekday evenings in North America) it's *Studio 9*, featuring nine minutes of world and Latin American *news*, followed by 20 minutes of in-depth reporting on Latin America. The second half hour is given over to one of a variety of 30-minute features—including *Inside HCJB* (Tuesday), *Ham Radio Today* (Thursday), *Woman to Woman* (Friday), and the unique and enjoyable ●*Música del Ecuador* on Saturday. On Sunday (Saturday evening in the Americas), the news is followed by *DX Partyline*, and Monday by *Musical Mailbag*. Continuous programming to North America on 9745 and (winter) 12015 or (summer) 15115 kHz.

Radio Australia. *World News*, then Monday through Friday it's *The World Today* (in-depth coverage of current events). The weekend fare is also news-oriented, with *Pacific Focus* followed by Saturday's *Asia Pacific* or Sunday's *Week's End*. Continuous to Asia and the Pacific on 9660, 12080, 15240, 15415, 15515, 17580, 17750 and 21725 kHz. Should also be audible in parts of North America (best during summer) on 15515 and 17580 kHz. For East and Southeast Asia, choose from 15240, 15415, 17750 and 21725 kHz. Some channels carry separate sports programming at weekends.

■**Deutsche Welle, Germany.** *News*, followed Tuesday through Saturday by ●*NewsLink* and *Hallo Africa* (except Saturday, when there's *German by Radio*). The Sunday lineup is *Weekend Review* and ●*Inside Europe*, and the Monday menu features *Weekend Review* (second edition) and ●*Marks and Markets*. A 45-minute broadcast aimed primarily at eastern and southern Africa, but also heard in parts of the Mideast. Winter on 7280, 9565, 11935 and 11965 kHz; and summer on 7225, 9565, 9765 and 13690 kHz.

Radio Canada International. *News*, then Tuesday through Saturday it's the topical *Spectrum*. This is replaced Sunday by *Venture Canada* (business and economics), and Monday by a listener-response program, *The Mailbag*. Thirty minutes to the Mideast, winter on 9505 and 9645 kHz; and summer on 11835, 11975 and 15215 kHz.

Voice of America. Directed to Africa and the Mideast, but widely heard elsewhere. *News Now*—a mixed bag of sports, science, business and other news and features. Weekdays on the half-hour, the African service leaves the mainstream programming and carries its own ●*Daybreak Africa*. To North Africa year round on 7170 kHz, and to the Mideast summer on 11965 kHz. The African service is available on 6035 (winter), 6080, 7265 and 7275 (summer), 7415 (winter), 9575, 9775 (winter) and 9885 kHz. Some of these are only available until 0430. Reception of some of these channels is also possible in North America.

Radio Romania International. Similar to the 0200 transmission (see there for specifics). Fifty-five minutes to North America winter on 9570 and 11830 kHz, and summer on 11940 and 15105 kHz.

Voice of Turkey. Winter only at this time. See 0300 for specifics. Fifty minutes to Europe and eastern North America on 6010 and 9655 kHz, to the Mideast on 7240 kHz, and to Southeast Asia and Australasia on 21715 kHz. One hour earlier in summer.

WJCR, Upton, Kentucky. Continues with country gospel music for North American listeners on 7490 kHz. Also with religious programs to North America at this hour are **WYFR-Family Radio** on 6065 and 9505 kHz, **WWCR** on 5935 kHz, **KAIJ** on 5755 kHz and **KTBN** on 7510 kHz. Traditionalist Catholic programming is available via **WEWN** on 5825 kHz.

Kol Israel. Summer only at this time. *News* for 15 minutes from Israel Radio's domestic network. To Europe and eastern North America on 9435 and 15640 kHz, and to Australasia on 17535 kHz. One hour later in winter.

China Radio International. Repeat of the 0300 broadcast; one hour to North America on 9730 and (summer only) 9560 kHz.

04:00–05:00

For decades HCJB's transmitters have reached the entire world from the Ecuadoran Andes. Nevertheless, the station reportedly is considering termination of all programming in 2001 except that intended for South America.   HCJB

Radio New Zealand International.
Continues with regional programming for the South Pacific. Part of a much longer broadcast, which is also heard in parts of North America (especially during summer) on 17675 kHz. Sometimes carries commentaries of local sporting events.

Radio For Peace International, Costa Rica. Part of an eight-hour cyclical block of predominantly social-conscience and counterculture programming. Some of the offerings at this hour include a women's news-gathering service, *WINGS*, (0400 Thursday); a listener-response program (same time Saturday); and *The Far Right Radio Review* (0430 Thursday). Audible in Europe and the Americas on 6970 and 15050 kHz.

Voice of Russia World Service. Continues to North America at this hour. Tuesday through Sunday winter, it's *News and Views*, replaced Monday by *Sunday Panorama* and *Russia in Personalities*. During the second half hour, the Sunday slot is filled by ●*Christian Message from Moscow*, replaced Monday by ●*Audio Book Club*. The rest of the lineup is variable, and often chosen at short notice. The summer schedule has plenty of variety, and includes *Jazz Show* (0431 Monday), ●*Music at Your Request* or *Yours For the Asking* (same time Tuesday), the business-

oriented *Newmarket* (0411 Thursday), *Science and Engineering* (same time Wednesday and Saturday), ●*Folk Box* (0431 Thursday), *Moscow Mailbag* (0411 Tuesday and Friday) and the retrospective ●*Moscow Yesterday and Today* (0431 Sunday). In eastern North America, tune to 7125 and 7180 kHz in winter, and 7125 and 9665 kHz in summer. Best winter bets for the west coast are 12010, 12020, 15470, 15595, 17595 and 17660 kHz; in summer, try 15595, 17565, 17650, 17660 and 17690 kHz.

AFRTS Shortwave, USA. Network news, live sports, music and features in the upper-sideband mode from the Armed Forces Radio & Television Service. Transmitted from modestly powered U.S. Navy stations around the globe. Try 4278.5, 4319, 4993, 5765, 6350, 6458.5, 10320, 10940.5, 12579, 12689.5 and 13362 kHz.

04:30

■**Radio Netherlands.** Tuesday through Saturday (weekday evenings in North America) it's ●*Newsline*, then a feature program. The offerings include the well produced ●*Research File* (science, Tuesday); *Music 52-15* (eclectic, Wednesday); the excellent award-winning ●*Documentary*

(Thursday); *Media Network* (Friday); and ●*A Good Life* (Saturday). The Sunday fare is *Europe Unzipped*, *Insight* and *Aural Tapestry*, replaced Monday by *Sincerely Yours*, a program preview and *Dutch Horizons*. One hour to western North America on 6165 and 9590 kHz.

Radio Austria International. Summer only at this time. ●*Report from Austria*, which includes a brief bulletin of *news*, followed by a series of current events and human interest stories. A popular source of news about Central Europe. Thirty minutes to Europe on 6155 and 13730 kHz. One hour later in winter.

Radio Prague, Czech Republic. Winter only at this time; see 0330 for specifics. Thirty minutes to the Mideast and South Asia on 9865 and 11600 kHz. One hour earlier in summer.

05:00

■BBC World Service for the Americas. Five minutes of *news*, then Tuesday through Saturday (weekday evenings in North America) there's an arts show, *Meridian*. The next half hour consists of a mixed bag of music and light entertainment, except for Friday's ●*Omnibus*. Sunday, the news is followed by *Wright Around the World*, and Monday there's 30 minutes of *The World Today* (news and current events) followed by the first part of ●*Play of the Week* (world theater). Audible in North America (better to the west) on 5975 and 6175 kHz.

■BBC World Service for Europe. Weekdays, a full hour of news in ●*The World Today*. Weekends, the second half hour is replaced by Saturday's *Arts in Action* and Sunday's ●*Science in Action*. Continuous to Europe and North Africa on 6195, 9410 and 12095 kHz.

■BBC World Service for the Mideast. Same as for Europe, except that the 0530 Sunday slot is occupied by *Global Business*.

■BBC World Service for Africa. ●*The World Today*, then weekdays on the half-hour there's a continuation of *Network Africa*. Weekends, the final 30 minutes are filled by

Saturday's *African Quiz* or *This Week and Africa*, and Sunday's *Artbeat*. Continuous programming on 3255 (midyear), 6190, 11765 and (winter) 11940 kHz.

■BBC World Service for East and Southeast Asia and the Pacific. Starts with 30 minutes of ●*The World Today*. Thereafter, it's a mixed bag of features. Longtime favorites are ●*Off the Shelf* (serialized readings from world literature, 0545 weekdays) and ●*Letter from America* (same time Sunday). For a younger audience, there's *Best of the Edge* at 0530 Friday. Continuous to East Asia on 15280 (till 0530), 15360, 17760 and 21660 kHz; and to Southeast Asia on 9740, 11955 and 15360 kHz. In Australasia, choose from 11955 and 15360 kHz.

■Deutsche Welle, Germany. Repeat of the 45-minute 0100 transmission to North America, except that Sunday's *Inside Europe* is replaced by ●*Marks and Markets*; and Monday's *Arts on the Air* gives way to *Cool*. Winter on 5960, 6120, 9670 and 11795 kHz; and summer on 9670, 9785, 11810 and 11985 kHz. This slot is by far the best for western North America.

Radio Exterior de España ("Spanish National Radio"). *News*, then Tuesday through Saturday (local weekday evenings in the Americas) it's *Panorama*, which features a recording of popular Spanish music, a commentary or a report, a review of the Spanish press, and weather. The remainder of the program is a mixture of literature, science, music and general programming. Tuesday (Monday evening in North America), there's *Sports Spotlight* and *Cultural Encounters*; Wednesday features *People of Today* and *Entertainment in Spain*; Thursday brings *As Others See Us* and, biweekly, *The Natural World* or *Science Desk*; Friday has *Economic Report* and *Cultural Clippings*; and Saturday offers *Window on Spain* and *Review of the Arts*. The final slot is given over to a language course, *Spanish by Radio*. On the remaining days, you can listen to Sunday's *Hall of Fame* and *Gallery of Spanish Voices*; and Monday's *Visitors' Book*, *Great Figures in Flamenco* and *Radio Club*. Sixty minutes to the eastern and southern United States on 6055 kHz.

05:00–05:00

Radio Canada International. Summer only at this time. See 0600 for program details. To Europe, Africa and the Mideast on 6145, 7290, 9595, 11710, 13755 and 15330 kHz. One hour later during winter. Also available to western North America and Central America on 5995, 9755 and 11830 kHz.

Vatican Radio. Summer only at this time. Twenty minutes of programming oriented to Catholics. To Europe on 5880 and 7250 kHz. Frequencies may vary slightly. One hour later in winter.

Radio Croatia. Summer only at this time, and actually starts two or three minutes into a predominantly Croatian broadcast. Approximately 15 minutes of news from and about Croatia. To Australasia on 9470 kHz. One hour later in winter.

XERMX—Radio México Internacional. Tuesday through Saturday (weekday evenings local American date) and winter only at this time. Take your pick from *Regional Roots and Rhythms* (Tuesday), *Mailbox* (Wednesday and Saturday), *Mosaic of Mexico* (Thursday) and *Creators of Mexican Art* on Friday. There are no programs on Sunday or Monday. Thirty minutes to North America on 9705 kHz. One hour earlier in summer.

Radio Japan. *News*, then Monday through Friday there's *44 Minutes* (an in-depth look at current trends and events). This is replaced Saturday by *Weekend Square* and Sunday by *Hello from Tokyo*. One hour to Europe on 5975 and 7230 kHz; to East Asia on 11715, 11760 and 11840 kHz; to Southeast Asia on 15590 kHz; to Australasia on 11850 (or 21570) kHz; and to western North America on 6110 and 9835 (or 13630) kHz.

China Radio International. This time winter only. Repeat of the 0300 broadcast; one hour to North America on 9560 kHz via a Canadian relay.

HCJB—Voice of the Andes, Ecuador. Predominantly religious programming at this hour. For a general audience, try Friday's *Inspirational Classics* (Thursday night in North America) or *Saludos Amigos* (same time Sunday). Continuous programming to North America on 9745 and (winter) 12015 or (summer) 15115 kHz.

Voice of America. Continues with the morning broadcast to Africa and the Mideast. *News Now*—a mixed bag of sports, science, business and other news and features. To North Africa on 7170 and (winter only) 5995 and 11805 kHz; to the Mideast on 11825 (winter) or (summer) 11965 kHz; and to the rest of Africa on 5970, 6035, 6080, 7195 (summer), 7295 (winter), 9630 (summer) and 12080 kHz. Some of these channels are audible in parts of North America.

Radio Habana Cuba. Repeat of the 0100 transmission. To western North America on 6000 or 9820 kHz. Also available to Europe on 9830 or 11705 kHz upper sideband.

Voice of Nigeria. Targeted mainly at West Africa, but also audible in parts of Europe and North America, especially during winter. Monday through Friday, opens with the lively *Wave Train* followed by *VON Scope*, a half hour of *news* and press comment. Pick of the weekend programs is ●*African Safari*, a musical journey around the African continent, which can be heard Saturdays at 0500. This is replaced Sunday by five minutes of *Reflections* and 25 minutes of music in *VON Link-Up*, with the second half-hour taken up by *News*. The first 60 minutes of a daily two-hour broadcast on 7255 and (when the transmitter is repaired) 15120 kHz.

Swiss Radio International. *World Radio Switzerland*—news and analysis of Swiss and world events. Some lighter fare on Saturday, when the biweekly *Capital Letters* (a listener-response program) alternates with *Name Game* (first Saturday) and *Sounds Good* (music and interviews, third Saturday). Thirty minutes to southeastern Europe winter on 9655 kHz, and summer on 9610 kHz.

SANGEAN

ATS-909

The **ATS-909** is the flagship of the Sangean line. It packs features and performance into a very compact and stylish package. Coverage includes all long wave, medium wave and shortwave frequencies. FM and FM stereo to the headphone jack is also available. Shortwave performance is enhanced with a wide-narrow bandwidth switch and excellent single side band performance (SSB tuning to 40 Hz steps via fine tuning). Five tuning methods are featured: keypad entry, auto scan, manual up-down tuning, memory recall or manual knob tuning. The alphanumeric memory lets you store 306 presets (260 shortwave, 18 AM, 18 FM and 9 LW plus priority). The three event clock-timer displays even when the radio is tuning and has 42 world city zones stored. The large backlit LCD also features a signal strength and battery bar graph. The ATS-909 will display RDS on PL, PS and CT for station name and clock time in areas where this service is available. Also features a record jack and tone switch. Includes AC adapter, carry case, stereo ear buds, wave guide and Sangean ANT-60 roll-up antenna. 8½" x 5½" x 1½" 2 Lbs. Requires four AA cells (not supplied).

ATS-505

The **Sangean ATS-505** covers long wave 153 - 279 kHz, AM 520-1710, shortwave solid from 1711-29999 kHz plus FM 87.5-108 MHz. The backlit display can show either the frequency or the time (12/24 format). Tune via the tuning knob, Up-Down buttons, automatic tuning, keypad entry or from the 45 memories. The ATS-505 even tunes Morse code and single sideband (SSB) using a separate Clarify knob on the side of the radio. You may press in the tuning knob to select between normal and fine tuning (1 or 10 kHz on AM/LW and 1 or 5 kHz on SW). Other features include: FM stereo to headphone jack, 9/10 kHz AM step, beep on/off, dial lock, stereo-mono switch, alarm by radio or buzzer, auto-scan, auto memory, sleep-timer, tune LED, stereo-mono switch, tilt-stand, external antenna input and 6 VDC jack. With: case, earphones and wave guide. Titanium matte finish. 8.5" x 5.3" x 1.6" Requires four AA cells or ADP-808 AC adapter (both optional).

ATS-818 and ATS-818ACS

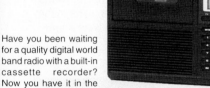

Have you been waiting for a quality digital world band radio with a built-in cassette recorder? Now you have it in the exciting **Sangean ATS-818ACS**. This no-compromise receiver has full dual-conversion shortwave coverage (1.6 - 30 MHz) plus long wave, AM and FM (stereo to headphone jack). A BFO control is included for smooth S.S.B. or CW reception. A big LCD display with dial lamp shows: frequency (1 kHz on SW), 24 hour time, battery indicator and signal strength. The receiver features an RF gain, tone, wide-narrow selectivity, keypad entry, manual tuning knob, plus 54 memories (18 for shortwave). Includes AC adapter, external antenna adapter and wave guide. The recorder has a built-in mic and auto-shutoff. Requires four D cells and three AA cells (not supplied). 11¼" x 7" x 2½" (296x192x68 mm).

The **Sangean ATS-818** is the same as above except with only 45 memories and no cassette recorder. The ATS-818 also includes the AC adapter.

ATS-404

The **Sangean ATS-404** is one of most attractive and capable radios ever offered in the $100 price range. Coverage includes AM, FM and 14 shortwave bands, or continuous shortwave 2.3-26.1 MHz. Tune via the Up-Down buttons, auto tune, keypad entry or from the 45 memories. Other features include: FM stereo to headphone jack, 12/24 hour clock, low-battery indicator, dial lock, 9/10 kHz MW step, dial lamp, stereo-mono switch, alarm by radio or buzzer, sleep-timer, tune LED, tilt-stand and 6 VDC jack. With: case, earphones and wave guide. Silver-gray matte finish. 6½" x 4" x 1½" 10 oz. Requires four AA cells or optional ADP-808 AC adapter.

Universal Radio, Inc.
6830 Americana Pkwy.
Reynoldsburg, Ohio
43068-4113 U.S.A.

☎ **800 431-3939** Orders & Prices
☎ 614 866-4267 Information
→ 614 866-2339 FAX Line
✉ dx@universal-radio.com

The amazing **Sangean DT-300VW** digital radio fits in your shirt pocket yet receives: AM, FM, FM stereo, NOAA weather and VHF TV audio (channels 2 to 13).

www.DXing.com and
www.universal-radio.com

- Visa
- Mastercard
- Discover

- Prices and specs. are subject to change.
- Returns subject to a 15% restocking fee.
- Huge **free catalog** available on request.

Visit our operational showroom near Columbus, Ohio

Radio New Zealand International.
Continues with regional programming for the South Pacific. Part of a much longer broadcast, which is also heard in parts of North America (especially during summer) on 17675 kHz.

Radio Australia. *World News*, then Monday through Friday there's *Pacific Beat* (background reporting on events in the Pacific)—look for a sports bulletin at 0530. Weekends, the news is followed by *Oz Sounds*; then, on the half-hour, it's either Saturday's *Sports Factor* or Sunday's *Media Report*. Continuous to Asia and the Pacific on 9660, 12080, 15240, 15515, 17580, 17750 and 21725 kHz. In North America (best during summer) try 15515 and 17580 kHz. For East Asia, best options are 15240 and 21725 kHz. Some channels carry alternative sports programming at weekends.

Voice of Russia World Service. Winter, the *news* is followed by a wide variety of programs. These include *Jazz Show* (0531 Monday), ●*Music at Your Request* or *Yours For the Asking* (same time Tuesday), the business-oriented *Newmarket* (0511 Thursday), *Science and Engineering* (same time Wednesday and Saturday), ●*Folk Box* (0531 Thursday), *Moscow Mailbag* (0511 Tuesday and Friday), and the retrospective ●*Moscow Yesterday and Today* (0531 Sunday). Tuesday through Saturday summer, there's *Focus on Asia and the Pacific*, replaced Sunday by *Science and Engineering* and Monday by *Moscow Mailbag*. On the half-hour, look for *This is Russia* (Monday and Friday), ●*Audio Book Club* (Sunday), ●*Moscow Yesterday and Today* (Thursday), ●*Christian Message from Moscow* (Saturday) and *Russian by Radio* on Wednesday. Winter only to eastern North America on 7125 and 7180 kHz, and to western parts on 15595, 17565, 17650, 17660 and 17690 kHz. Available summer to Australasia on 17625 (from 0530) and 21790 kHz. If these channels are empty, dial around nearby—the Voice of Russia is not renowned for sticking to its frequencies, but it does tend to use the same world band segments.

block of social-conscience and counterculture programming. Look for some United Nations programs weekdays on the half-hour. Audible in Europe and the Americas on 6970 and 15050 kHz.

Kol Israel. Winter only at this time. *News* for 15 minutes from Israel Radio's domestic network. To Europe and eastern North America on any two channels from 6225, 7410 and 9435 kHz, and to Australasia on 15640 or 17545 kHz. One hour earlier in summer.

WJCR, Upton, Kentucky. Continues with country gospel music for North American listeners on 7490 kHz. Also with religious programs to North America at this hour are **WYFR-Family Radio** on 5985 kHz, **WWCR** on 5935 kHz, **KAIJ** on 5755 kHz and **KTBN** on 7510 kHz. For traditionalist Catholic programming, tune to **WEWN** on 5825 kHz.

AFRTS Shortwave, USA. Network news, live sports, music and features in the upper-sideband mode from the Armed Forces Radio & Television Service. Transmitted from modestly powered U.S. Navy stations around the globe. Try 4278.5, 4319, 4993, 5765, 6350, 6458.5, 10320, 10940.5, 12579, 12689.5 and 13362 kHz.

05:30

Radio Austria International. ●*Report from Austria*; see 0430 for more details. Thirty minutes year-round to western North America on 6015 kHz; and winter only to Europe on 6155 and 13730 kHz, and to the Mideast on 15410 and 17870 kHz.

United Arab Emirates Radio, Dubai. See 0330 for program details. Twenty minutes to East Asia and Australasia on 15435, 17830 and 21700 kHz.

Radio Thailand. Thirty minutes of *news* and short features relayed from one of the station's domestic services. To Europe winter on 15115 kHz, and summer on 15445 or 21795 kHz. Also available to Asia on 9655

0600–1159
Australasia & East Asia—Evening Prime Time
Western North America—Late Evening
Europe & Mideast—Morning and Midday

06:00

■BBC World Service for the Americas.
Except for Monday (Sunday evening in North America), starts with 20 minutes of *World Briefing*, then ●*Sports Roundup*. On the remaining day, it's a continuation of ●*Play of the Week*, which can run to either 0630 or 0700. If the former, you also get 15 minutes of ●*World Business Report* and another fifteen of ●*Letter from America*. Tuesday through Friday, the second half hour is split between ●*World Business Report* and ●*Analysis* (replaced Thursday by ●*From Our Own Correspondent*). The Saturday replacement is ●*People and Politics*, changed Sunday to *Agenda*. Continuous to North America and the Caribbean (better to the west) on 6175 kHz.

■BBC World Service for Europe. Similar to the service for the Americas, except Sunday, when you can hear 20 minutes of *World Briefing* followed by ●*Sports Roundup* and *Agenda* (current events). Continuous to Europe and North Africa on 6195, 9410 and 12095 kHz.

■BBC World Service for Eastern Europe and the Mideast. Tuesday through Saturday, starts with *News*, then the popular ●*Outlook* (except Monday, when there's *Talking Point*, a call-in show). Weekdays, the final 15 minutes are filled by ●*Off the Shelf* (readings from the best of world literature). The Saturday slot goes to *Write On* or *Waveguide*, and Sunday's lineup is *World Briefing*, ●*Sports Roundup* and ●*Agenda* (current events). Continues on 11760, 15565 and 15575 kHz.

■BBC World Service for Southern Africa. Identical to the service for the Mideast at this hour. Continuous programming on 6190, 11765 and 11940 kHz.

■BBC World Service for East and Southeast Asia and the Pacific. Five

minutes of *news*, then Monday through Friday there's an arts show, *Meridian*. The next half hour consists of a mixed bag of music and light entertainment, except for Thursday's ●*Omnibus*. Weekends, starts with *World Briefing* and ●*Sports Roundup*, then it's either Saturday's ●*People and Politics* or Sunday's *Westway* (a soap opera). Continuous to East Asia on 15360, 17760 and 21660 kHz; to Southeast Asia on 9740, 11955 and 15360 kHz; and to Australasia on 9580, 11955 and 15360 kHz.

■Deutsche Welle, Germany. Repeat of the 0400 broadcast. Forty-five minutes to West Africa (and often heard in Europe), winter on 7225, 9565 and 11785 kHz; and summer on 13790, 15275 and 17860 kHz. The same programs also form part of a separate one hour broadcast to Europe on 6140 kHz. The bonus for Europeans is an extra 15-minute feature: *Business German* (Monday), *People in Europe* (Tuesday), *German by Radio* (Wednesday), ●*Insight* (Thursday), ●*Man and Environment* (Friday), *Women on the Move* or *Development Forum* (Saturday) and Sunday's *Around Germany*.

Radio Habana Cuba. Repeat of the 0200 transmission. To western North America on 6000 or 9820 kHz. Also available to Europe on 9830 or 11705 kHz upper sideband.

Radio Canada International. Winter only at this hour. Monday through Friday, there's *First Edition* (current events). This is replaced weekends by a news bulletin followed by Saturday's environmental ●*Earth Watch* or Sunday's *Arts in Canada*. Thirty minutes to Europe, the Mideast and parts of Africa on 6045, 6150 and 11905 kHz. One hour earlier in summer. Also available to western North America and Central America on 5960 and 9670 kHz.

Radio Japan. *News*, then weekdays there's *Asian Top News*. This is followed by a 35-

06:00–06:00

Radio Croatia's announcers bring on-the-spot news and perspectives from the heart of the Balkans.

M. Prezelj

minute feature: ●*Music Journey Around Japan* (a look at regional music and customs, Monday), Japanese language lessons (Tuesday and Thursday), *Unforgettable Musical Masterpieces* (postwar popular songs with historical background information, Wednesday), and *Music Beat* (Japanese popular music, Friday). This last show contains a *Pop Archive* section which goes back at least a couple of decades, so if you're curious to hear the sound of Japanese pops of yesteryear, make a Friday date with Radio Japan. On the remaining days, *Weekend Square* fills the Saturday slot and *Hello from Tokyo* is aired on Sunday. One hour to Europe on 7230 kHz; to East Asia on 11840 kHz; to Southeast Asia on 11740 kHz; to Australasia on 11850 (or 21570) kHz; to western North America on 9835 (or 13630) kHz; and to Hawaii and Central America on 15230 kHz. This last broadcast may differ somewhat from the other transmissions, and may include alternative features.

Radio Croatia. Winter only at this time, and actually starts around 0603. Approximately 15 minutes of news from and about Croatia. To Australasia on 11880 kHz. One hour earlier in summer.

Swiss Radio International. Winter only at this hour. Repeat of the 0500 broadcast; see

there for specifics. A half hour to southeastern Europe on 9655 kHz. One hour earlier in summer.

Voice of America. Final segment of the transmission to Africa and the Mideast. Monday through Friday, the mainstream African service carries just 30 minutes of ●*Daybreak Africa*, with other channels carrying a full hour of *News Now*—a mixed bag of sports, science, business and other news and features. Weekend programming is the same to all areas—60 minutes of *News Now*. To North Africa on 5995 (winter), 7170, 9680 (summer) and 11805 kHz; to the Mideast on 11825 (winter) or (summer) 11965 kHz; and to mainstream Africa on 5970, 6035, 6080, 7195 (summer), 7285 (winter), 9630 (summer), 11950 (winter), 11995 (summer), 12080 and (winter) 15600 kHz. Some of these channels are audible in North America.

Radio Australia. Ten minutes of *News* (five at weekends), then a couple of features. Weekdays, these are separated by a 10-minute sports bulletin on the half-hour. Monday through Friday, the accent is heavily on music, and you get two bites at the same cherry. Each 20-minute show airing at 0610 is repeated at 0640 the following day (except for the Friday slot which is repeated on

Monday). The lineup starts with Monday's *Australian Music Show*, then it's *At Your Request* (Tuesday), *Blacktracker* (Australian aboriginal music, Wednesday), *Australian Country Style* (Thursday), and Friday's *Music Deli*. Weekends bring Saturday's *Feedback* (a listener-response program) and *Arts Australia*, replaced Sunday by the sharp ●*Ockham's Razor* (science talk) and *Correspondents' Report*. Continuous to Asia and the Pacific on 9660, 12080, 15240, 15415, 15515, 17580, 17750 and 21725 kHz. Listeners in western North America should try 17580 kHz. For East and Southeast Asia, best bets are 15240, 15415 and 21725 kHz. Some channels carry an alternative sports program until 0700 on weekends (0800 midyear).

Voice of Nigeria. The second (and final) hour of a daily broadcast intended mainly for listeners in West Africa, but also heard in parts of Europe and North America (especially during winter). Features vary from day to day, but are predominantly concerned with Nigerian and West African affairs. There is a listener-response program at 0600 Friday and 0615 Sunday, and other slots include *Across the Ages* and *Nigeria and Politics* (Monday), *Southern Connection* and *Nigerian Scene* (Tuesday), *West African Scene* (0600 Thursday) and *Images of Nigeria* (0615 Friday). There is a weekday 25-minute program of *news* and commentary on the half-hour, replaced weekends by the more in-depth *Weekly Analysis*. To 0657 on 7255 and (when operating) 15120 kHz.

Radio New Zealand International. Continues with regional programming for the South Pacific. Part of a much longer broadcast, which is also heard in parts of North America (especially during summer) on 17675 kHz.

Voice of Russia World Service. *News*, then winter it's *Focus on Asia and the Pacific* (Tuesday through Saturday), *Science and Engineering* (Sunday), and *Moscow Mailbag* (Monday). On the half-hour, look for *This is Russia* (Monday and Friday), ●*Audio Book Club* (Sunday), ●*Moscow Yesterday and Today* (Thursday), ●*Christian Message from Moscow*

(Saturday) and *Russian by Radio* on Wednesday. In summer, the news is followed by *Science and Engineering* (Monday and Friday), the business-oriented *Newmarket* (Wednesday and Saturday), and a listener-response program, *Moscow Mailbag*, on the remaining days. The lineup for the second half hour includes ●*Moscow Yesterday and Today* (Wednesday), ●*Audio Book Club* (Thursday), *Timelines* (Sunday), *Russian by Radio* (Monday); the eclectic *Kaleidoscope* (Tuesday and Friday) and *This is Russia* on Saturday. Continuous programming to Australasia (and also audible in Southeast Asia). In winter (local summer in Australasia), on 15460 (from 0630), 15470, 15525, 17570 and 21790 kHz; midyear, go for 15490, 17625 and 21790 kHz. If there's nothing on these channels, dial around nearby—frequency usage tends to vary.

Radio For Peace International, Costa Rica. Continues with counterculture and social-conscience programs. Audible in Europe and the Americas on 6970 kHz.

Vatican Radio. Winter only at this time. Twenty minutes with a heavy Catholic slant. To Europe on 4005 and 5880 kHz. One hour earlier in summer. Frequencies may vary slightly.

WJCR, Upton, Kentucky. Continues with country gospel music to North America on 7490 kHz. Also with religious programs for North American listeners at this hour are **WYFR-Family Radio** on 5985 kHz, **WWCR** on 5935 kHz, **KAIJ** on 5755 kHz, **KTBN** on 7510 kHz, and **WHRI-World Harvest Radio** on 5760 and 7315 kHz. Traditionalist Catholic fare is available on 5825 kHz.

Voice of Malaysia. Actually starts at 0555 with opening announcements and program summary, followed by *News*. Then comes *This is the Voice of Malaysia*, a potpourri of news, interviews, reports and music. The hour is rounded off with *Personality Column*. Part of a 150-minute broadcast to Southeast Asia and Australia on 6175, 9750 and 15295 kHz.

HCJB—Voice of the Andes, Ecuador. Predominantly religious programming at this

06:00–07:00

Radio Tashkent is the largest international broadcaster in Central Asia. Its news is prerecorded and meticulously screened before being aired.   M. Guha

hour. A favorite with HCJB listeners is Monday's *Mountain Meditations* (Sunday night in North America). To North America on 9745 and (winter) 12015 or (summer) 15115 kHz. For a separate service to Europe, see the next item.

HCJB—Voice of the Andes, Ecuador. Summer only at this time. Monday through Friday it's *Studio 9*, featuring nine minutes of world and Latin American *news*, followed by 20 minutes of in-depth reporting on Latin America. The second half hour is given over to one of a variety of 30-minute features— including *Inside HCJB* (Monday), *Ham Radio Today* (Wednesday), *Woman to Woman* (Thursday), and the thoroughly enjoyable ●*Música del Ecuador* on Friday. On Saturday, the news is followed by *DX Partyline*, and Monday by *Musical Mailbag*. The first of two hours to Europe on 15160 kHz. One hour later in winter.

AFRTS Shortwave, USA. Network news, live sports, music and features in the upper-sideband mode from the Armed Forces Radio & Television Service. Transmitted from modestly powered U.S. Navy stations around the globe. Try 4278.5, 4319, 4993, 5765, 6350, 6458.5, 10320, 10940.5, 12579, 12689.5 and 13362 kHz.

06:30

Radio Austria International. Winter only at this time. ●*Report from Austria* (see 0430). A half hour via the facilities of Radio Canada International on 6015 kHz, aimed primarily at western North America.

06:40

Radio Romania International. Actually starts at 0641. A 15-minute broadcast to Europe winter on 7105, 9510, 11755 and 15105 kHz; and summer on 9570, 9665, 11885 and 15250 kHz.

07:00

■**BBC World Service for the Americas.** Winter only at this time. Same programs as during the previous hour, except for 0730 Sunday, when ●*Assignment* replaces *Agenda*, and 0700 Monday, when *World Briefing* and ●*Sports Roundup* share the first half hour. To North America and the Caribbean (and better to the west) on 6175 kHz.

■**BBC World Service for Europe.** Tuesday through Saturday, starts with *News*, then the long-running ●*Outlook* (except Monday, when there's *Talking Point*, a call-in show). Weekdays, the final 15 minutes are given to ●*Off the Shelf* (readings from the best of world literature); Saturday, the slot goes to *Write On* or *Waveguide*. Sunday's lineup is *World Briefing*, ●*Sports Roundup* and ●*Assignment* (or an alternative documentary). Continuous to Europe and North Africa on 6195, 9410, 12095 and 15485 kHz.

■**BBC World Service for Eastern Europe and the Mideast.** Five minutes of *News*, then it's either the weekday *Meridian* (an arts program), Saturday's *The Edge* (a 110-minute youth show) or Sunday's *The Alternative* (popular music). Monday through Friday, the second half hour is a mixed bag of mostly popular music, replaced Sunday by ●*Assignment* or its temporary replacement. Continuous programming on 11760, 15565, 15575 and 17640 kHz.

■**BBC World Service for East and Southeast Asia and the Pacific.**
Monday through Saturday, starts with five minutes of *news*, then it's all features. Best of the bunch are *Discovery* (science, 0705 Monday), Tuesday's pairing of ●*Health Matters* and ●*Everywoman*, Wednesday's ●*Focus on Faith* (0730) and Friday's ●*One Planet* (0705). Popular with a younger audience is Saturday's 110-minute youth show, *The Edge*, which follows the news. The Sunday lineup consists of *World Briefing*, ●*Sports Roundup* and ●*Assignment* (or its temporary replacement). Continuous to East Asia on 15360, 17760 and 21660 kHz; to Southeast Asia on 9740, 11955 and 15360 kHz; and to Australasia on 9580, 11955 and 15360 kHz.

■**Deutsche Welle, Germany.** An hour of hybrid programming for Europe. No news, just features—some of which are heard on shortwave at other hours, and some that are normally broadcast only on satellite and the internet. Monday's combo is ●*Spectrum* (science) and *Around Germany*; Tuesday, there's an international joint production, *Women on the Move* (or *Development Forum*) and ●*Insight*; Wednesday is trade oriented, with ●*Marks and Markets*, *Business Germany* and *People in Europe*; Thursday features *Arts on the Air* and ●*Great Performers*; Friday, there's *Cool* and *Focus on Folk*; Saturday, it's ●*Inside Europe*; and Sunday's presentation is *Concert Hour*. On 6140 kHz.

Radio Vlaanderen Internationaal, Belgium. Summer only at this time. Weekdays, starts with *News*, then *Belgium Today*, *Press Review* and features. The lineup includes *The Arts* (Monday and Thursday), *Tourism* (Monday), *Focus on Europe* and *Sports* (Tuesday), *Green Society* (Wednesday), *Around Town* (Thursday), and *Economics* and *International Report* (Friday). Closes with *Soundbox*. These are replaced Saturday by *Music from Flanders*, and Sunday by *Radio World*, *Tourism*, *Brussels 1043* (a listener-response program) and *Soundbox*. A half hour to southern Europe on 5985 kHz. One hour later in winter.

Radio Prague, Czech Republic. Summer only at this time. See 0800 for specifics. Thirty minutes to Europe on 9880 and 11600 kHz. One hour later in winter.

Radio Croatia. Summer only at this time, and actually starts two or three minutes into a predominantly Croatian broadcast. Approximately 15 minutes of news from and about Croatia. To Australasia on 13820 kHz. One hour later in winter.

Radio Slovakia International. *Slovakia Today*, a 30-minute review of Slovakia and its culture. Monday, there's a bag of short features; Tuesday has look at tourism and Slovak personalities; Wednesday's theme is business and economy; and Thursday brings a mix of politics, education and science. Friday offerings include cultural items, cooking recipes and the off-beat *Back Page News*; and Saturday has the *"Best of"* series. Sunday's show is a melange of this and that, and includes *Listeners' Tribune* and some enjoyable Slovak music. A friendly half hour to Australasia on 9440 (summer), 15460, 17550 (or 11990) and (winter) 21705 kHz.

Radio Australia. *World News*, then Monday through Friday it's *Pacific Beat*, news and features for listeners in the Pacific, with a 10-minute sports bulletin on the half-hour. Weekends, the news is followed by *Pacific Focus* and either Saturday's *Week's End* or Sunday's *Rural Reporter*. Continuous to Asia and the Pacific on 9660, 12080, 15240, 15415, 17580, 17750 and 21725 kHz. Listeners in western North America can try 17580 kHz (best during summer), while East Asia is served by 15240, 15415, 17750 and 21725 kHz. For Southeast Asia, take your pick from 15415 and 17750 kHz.

Voice of Malaysia. First, there's a daily feature with a Malaysian theme (except for Thursday, when *Talk on Islam* is aired), then comes a half hour of *This is the Voice of Malaysia* (see 0600), followed by 15 minutes of *Beautiful Malaysia*. Not much doubt about where the broadcast originates! Continuous to Southeast Asia and Australia on 6175, 9750 and 15295 kHz.

07:00–07:00

Radio For Peace International, Costa Rica. Continues with an eight-hour cyclical block of social-conscience and counterculture programming. Audible in Europe and the Americas on 6970 kHz, and sometimes on 15050 kHz.

Voice of Russia World Service. *News,* then a variety of features. The winter lineup includes *Science and Engineering* (Monday and Friday), the business-oriented *Newmarket* (Wednesday and Saturday), and a listener-response program, *Moscow Mailbag,* on the remaining days. During the second half hour, choose from ●*Moscow Yesterday and Today* (Wednesday), ●*Audio Book Club* (Thursday), *Russian by Radio* (Monday), the multifaceted *Kaleidoscope* (Tuesday and Friday), *Timelines* (Sunday) and *This is Russia* on Saturday. Summer, the news is followed by the informative ●*Update* on Tuesday, Thursday and Saturday. Other offerings include *Science and Engineering* (Wednesday), *Moscow Mailbag* (Friday) and Monday's masterpiece, ●*Music and Musicians.* On the half-hour, there's some of the Voice of Russia's best—●*Audio Book Club* (Wednesday), ●*Moscow Yesterday and Today* (Friday), *Songs from Russia* (Sunday), ●*Folk Box* (Tuesday) and *This is Russia* on Thursday. Mondays, it's a continuation of ●*Music and Musicians.* Continuous programming to Australasia (also audible in Southeast Asia). In winter (local summer in Australasia), try 15460, 15470, 15525, 17495, 17570 and 21790 kHz; midyear, go for 15490, 17495, 17625 and 21790 kHz.

WJCR, Upton, Kentucky. Continues with country gospel music for North American listeners on 7490 kHz. Also with religious programs to North America at this hour are **WWCR** on 5935 kHz, **KAIJ** on 5755 kHz, **KTBN** on 7510 kHz, and **WHRI-World Harvest Radio** on 5745 and 9495 kHz. For traditionalist Catholic programming, tune to **WEWN** on 5825 kHz.

Radio New Zealand International.
Continues with regional programming for the South Pacific. Part of a much longer broadcast, which is also heard in parts of North America (especially during summer) on 11720, 15175 or 17675 kHz.

Radio Taipei International, Taiwan. Opens with 15 minutes of *News,* and except for Sunday (when it's *Mailbag Time*), closes with *Let's Learn Chinese.* In between, look for features—one or two, depending on the day of the week. Monday (Sunday evening in North America) there's an opportunity to enjoy Taiwanese music in ● *Jade Bells and Bamboo Pipes.* This is replaced Tuesday by *People* and *Trends,* Wednesday by *Taiwan Today* and *Stage and Screen,* Thursday by *Journey into Chinese Culture* and *Hot Spots*; and Friday by *Taipei Magazine* and *East Meets West.* Weekends, the Saturday spots are taken by *Kaleidoscope* and *Reflections,* with *Great Wall Forum* and *Food, Poetry and Others* making up the Sunday menu. One hour to North America on 5950 kHz and best heard in southern and western parts of the United States.

HCJB—Voice of the Andes, Ecuador. Monday through Friday winter it's *Studio 9,* featuring nine minutes of world and Latin American *news,* followed by 20 minutes of in-depth reporting on Latin America. The second half hour is given over to one of a variety of 30-minute features—including *Inside HCJB* (Monday), *Ham Radio Today* (Wednesday), *Woman to Woman* (Thursday), and the delightful ●*Música del Ecuador* on Friday. On Saturday, the news is followed by *DX Partyline,* and Monday by *Musical Mailbag.* Summer programming is predominantly religious, the one exception being *Saludos Amigos* at 0600 Saturday. To Europe winter on 9780 kHz, and summer on 15160 kHz. A separate block of religious programming to Australasia airs on 11755 kHz.

AFRTS Shortwave, USA. Network news, live sports, music and features in the upper-sideband mode from the Armed Forces Radio & Television Service. Transmitted from modestly powered U.S. Navy stations around the globe. Try 4278.5, 4319, 4993, 5765, 6350, 6458.5, 10320, 10940.5, 12579, 12689.5 and 13362 kHz.

07:30

Swiss Radio International. *World Radio Switzerland*—news and analysis of Swiss and world events. Look for lighter fare on Saturday, when the biweekly *Capital Letters* (a listener-response program) alternates with *Name Game* (first Saturday) and *Sounds Good* (music and interviews, third Saturday). A half hour to North and West Africa winter on 9885 and 13635 kHz, and summer on 15545 and 17685 kHz; also to southern Africa winter on 17665 kHz, and 21750 kHz midyear.

Radio Austria International. Summer only at this time. ●*Report from Austria*, which includes a short bulletin of *news* followed by a series of current events and human interest stories. Good coverage of national and regional issues. Thirty minutes to the Mideast on 15410 and 17870 kHz. Two hours earlier in winter.

KTWR-Trans World Radio, Guam. Starts at 0740 weekdays, 0730 weekends, and closes at 0915. Evangelical programming targeted at Southeast Asia on 15200 kHz.

08:00

■BBC World Service for Europe. Starts with five minutes of *News*, then it's either the weekday *Meridian* (an arts program), Saturday's *The Edge* (a 110-minute youth show) or Sunday's ●*From Our Own Correspondent*. Monday through Friday, the second half hour is a mixed bag of mostly popular music, and Sunday it's *Classical Request*. Continuous to Europe and North Africa on 9410, 12095 and 15485 kHz.

■BBC World Service for Eastern Europe and the Mideast. *News*, then weekdays there's an interesting collection of features: ●*One Planet* and *People and Places* (Monday), *Discovery* and *Essential Guide* (Tuesday), ●*Health Matters* and ●*Everywoman* (Wednesday), *Science View* and ●*Focus on Faith* (Thursday) and *Sports International* and *Pick of the World* on Friday. Saturday airs the final part of *The Edge* (a youth show), replaced Sunday by ●*From Our Own Correspondent*

and *Arts in Action*. Continues on 15565, 15575 and 17640 kHz.

■BBC World Service for East and Southeast Asia and the Pacific. Starts with *news*, then weekdays, a feature: ●*Omnibus* (Monday), alternative pop (Tuesday), *Classical Request* (Wednesday), jazz (Thursday) and light entertainment on Friday. *The Learning Zone* (an educational program) follows on the half-hour. The final part of *The Edge* (a youth show) fills the Saturday slot, with ●*From Our Own Correspondent* and *Arts in Action* the Sunday choices. Continuous to East Asia on 15360, 17760 and 21660 kHz; to Southeast Asia on 9740, 11955 and 15360 kHz; and to Australasia on 11955 and 15360 kHz.

■Deutsche Welle, Germany. A shortwave relay of Deutsche Welle's satellite service. Monday, there's *Cool* and *Focus on Folk*; Tuesday's cultural combo is *Arts on the Air* and ●*Great Performers*; Wednesday's musical spots are *Classical Showcase* and *Hits* (or *Melody Time*); Thursday brings ●*Spectrum* (science), ●*Man and Environment* (ecology) and *Living in Germany*; Friday has *People in Europe*, *Around Germany*, *Business German* and *German History*; Saturday's pairing is ●*Weekend* and *Around Germany*; and Sunday there's an international joint production, *Women on the Move* (or *Development Forum*) and ●*Insight*. An hour of news-free programming for Europe on 6140 kHz.

HCJB—Voice of the Andes, Ecuador. Continuous programming (mostly religious) to Europe and Australasia. To Europe winter on 9780 kHz, and to Australasia year round on 11755 kHz.

Radio Vlaanderen Internationaal, Belgium. This time winter only. See 0700 for specifics. Thirty minutes to southern Europe on 5985 kHz. One hour later in winter.

Radio Croatia. Winter only at this time, and actually starts around 0803. Approximately 15 minutes of news from and about Croatia. To Australasia on 13820 kHz. One hour earlier in summer.

Voice of Malaysia. *News* and commentary, followed Monday through Friday by *Instrumentalia*, which is replaced weekends by *This is the Voice of Malaysia* (see 0600). The final 25 minutes of a much longer transmission targeted at Southeast Asia and Australia on 6175, 9750 and 15295 kHz.

Radio Prague, Czech Republic. *News*, then Tuesday through Saturday there's *Current Affairs*. These are followed by one or more features: *Spotlight* (a look at Czech regional affairs, Tuesday); *Talking Point* (issues, Wednesday); *Czechs in History* (Thursday); Friday's *Economic Report*; and Saturday's *Mailbox* (a listener-response program).The Sunday slot is an excellent musical feature (strongly recommended), and Monday there's *A Letter from Prague*, *From the Weeklies* and *Readings from Czech Literature*. Thirty minutes to Europe on 11600 and 15255 kHz. One hour earlier in summer.

Radio Australia. Part of a 24-hour service to Asia and the Pacific, but which can also be heard at this time throughout much of North America. Begins with a bulletin of *World News*, then Monday through Friday there's an in-depth look at current events in *PM*. Weekends, the news is followed by *Grandstand Wrap*, a roundup of the latest Australian sports action, which gives way to a feature on the half-hour. Saturday, it's *Asia Pacific*, replaced Sunday by *Innovations*. To Asia and the Pacific on 5995, 9710, 12080, 13605, 15240, 15415, 17750 and 21725 kHz. Audible in parts of North America on 13625 and 15240 kHz. Best bets for East and Southeast Asia are 15415, 17750 and 21725 kHz.

WJCR, Upton, Kentucky. Continues with country gospel music to North America on 7490 kHz. Other U.S. religious broadcasters operating at this hour include **WWCR** on 5935 kHz, **KAIJ** on 5755 kHz, **KTBN** on 7510 kHz, and **WHRI-World Harvest Radio** on 5745 and 9495 kHz. Traditionalist Catholic programming can be heard via **WEWN** on 5825 kHz.

Voice of Russia World Service. Winter, *News* is followed by ●*Update* on Tuesday, Thursday and Saturday. Other features

The BBS uses world band newscasts to keep citizens informed throughout mountainous Bhutan. M. Guha

include *Science and Engineering* (Wednesday), *Moscow Mailbag* (Friday) and Monday's outstanding ●*Music and Musicians* (classical music). On the half-hour, there's some of the Voice of Russia's best—●*Audio Book Club* (Wednesday), ●*Moscow Yesterday and Today* (Friday), ●*Folk Box* (Tuesday), *Songs from Russia* (Sunday), *Kaleidoscope* (Saturday), and Thursday's *This is Russia*. In summer, ●*Update* is only available on Wednesday and Friday. It is replaced Monday by *Science and Engineering*, Tuesday by *Focus on Asia*, Thursday by *Newmarket* and Saturday by *Moscow Mailbag*. Sunday's offering is the 45-minute ●*Music and Musicians*—a jewel among classical music shows. Choice pickings from the second half hour include ●*Moscow Yesterday and Today* (Monday), ●*Folk Box* (Thursday) and Saturday's ●*Christian Message from Moscow*. Other slots include *This is Russia* (Wednesday) and Friday's *Jazz Show*. Continuous programming to Australasia (and also audible in Southeast Asia). In winter (local Oz summer), try 9905 (from 0830), 15460, 15470, 17495 and 21790 kHz; midyear, go for 15490, 17495 and 17625 kHz. If there's nothing on these channels, dial around nearby—Moscow's frequencies tend to change more than most.

08:00–09:00

KTWR-Trans World Radio, Guam. Continuation of evangelical programming to Southeast Asia on 15200 kHz, and the start of another ninety-minute block to Australasia on 15330 kHz.

Radio New Zealand International. Continues with regional programming for the South Pacific. Part of a much longer broadcast, which is also heard in parts of North America (especially during summer) on 11720, 15175 or 17675 kHz.

Radio Korea International, South Korea. Opens with *news* and commentary, followed Monday through Wednesday by *Seoul Calling*. Weekly features include *Echoes of Korean Music* and *Shortwave Feedback* (Sunday), *Tales from Korea's Past* (Monday), *Korean Cultural Trails* (Tuesday), *Pulse of Korea* (Wednesday), *From Us to You* (a listener-response program) and *Let's Learn Korean* (Thursday), *Let's Sing Together* and *Korea Through Foreigners' Eyes* (Friday), and Saturday's *Discovering Korea*, *Korean Literary Corner* and *Weekly News Focus*. Sixty minutes to Europe on 13670 kHz, and to Australasia on 9570 kHz.

AFRTS Shortwave, USA. Network news, live sports, music and features in the upper-sideband mode from the Armed Forces Radio & Television Service. Transmitted from modestly powered U.S. Navy stations around the globe. Try 4278.5, 4319, 4993, 5765, 6350, 6458.5, 10320, 10940.5, 12579, 12689.5 and 13362 kHz.

08:30

Radio Austria International. The comprehensive ●*Report from Austria*; see 0430 for more details. A daily half hour in summer, but Saturday only in winter. To East Asia on 21650 kHz, and to Australasia on 21765 kHz.

Swiss Radio International. *World Radio Switzerland*—news and background reports on world and Swiss events. Look for some lighter fare on Saturdays, when *Capital Letters* (a biweekly listener-response program)

alternates with *Name Game* (first Saturday) and *Sounds Good* (third Saturday). To Australasia on 9885 kHz, and to southern Africa on 21770 kHz.

Voice of Armenia. Summer Sundays only. Actually starts at 0840. Twenty minutes of Armenian *news* and culture, mainly of interest to Armenians abroad. To Europe on 15270 kHz. One hour later in winter.

09:00

■**BBC World Service for Europe.** Starts with *News*, then weekdays there's an interesting collection of features: ●*One Planet* and *People and Places* (Monday), *Discovery* and *Essential Guide* (Tuesday), ●*Health Matters* and ●*Everywoman* (Wednesday), *Science View* and ●*Focus on Faith* (Thursday) and *Sports International* and *Pick of the World* on Friday. Saturday brings the final part of *The Edge* (a youth show), replaced Sunday by *Reporting Religion* and *In Praise of God*. Continuous to Europe and North Africa on 12095 and 15485 kHz.

■**BBC World Service for Eastern Europe and the Mideast.** Weekdays, identical to the service for Asia and the Pacific. On the weekends, *World Briefing* is followed by Saturday's ●*Letter from America* and *Global Business*, or Sunday's *Reporting Religion* and ●*People and Politics*. Continuous programming on 11760, 15565, 15575 and 17640 kHz.

■**BBC World Service for East and Southeast Asia and the Pacific.** Monday through Friday there's one hour of *World Update*; weekends, it's *World Briefing* followed by Saturday's ●*Analysis* and *Global Business* or Sunday's *Reporting Religion* and *In Praise of God*. To East Asia on 7245 (summer), 11765, 11945, 15360, 17760 and 21660 kHz; to Southeast Asia on 6195, 9740, 11955 and 15360 kHz; and to Australasia on 11955 kHz.

■**Deutsche Welle,** Germany. *News*, followed Monday through Friday by ●*NewsLink*, and then a feature. Monday, it's

Development Forum or *Women on the Move*; Tuesday brings ●*Insight*; Wednesday has the interesting ●*Man and Environment*; Thursday, there's *Living in Germany*; and Friday's slot is *Spotlight on Sport*. Weekend fare consists of Saturday's *Talking Point* and ●*Marks and Markets*; and Sunday's *Religion and Society* and *Cool*. Forty-five minutes to East and Southeast Asia and Australasia, winter on 6160, 12055, 15470, 17625, 17770 and 17820 kHz; and summer on 6160, 15105, 15470, 17770 and 21680 kHz. For a separate service to Africa, see the next item.

■**Deutsche Welle,** Germany. Similar to the service for Asia and the Pacific, except that Saturday's *Marks and Markets* is replaced by *African Kaleidoscope*. Forty-five minutes to eastern and southern Africa, winter on 11785, 15410 and 21560 kHz; and midyear on 9565 (or 12035), 15210 (or 17800), 15410 and 21790 kHz. For yet another service, to Europe, see the next entry.

■**Deutsche Welle,** Germany. Same as for Asia and the Pacific, but with an extra 15-minute feature: *Business German* (Monday), *German History* (Tuesday), *German by Radio* (Wednesday), ●*Insight* (Thursday), ●*Man and Environment* (Friday), *Women on the Move* or *Development Forum* (Saturday) and Sunday's *Living in Germany*. One hour to Europe on 6140 kHz.

HCJB—Voice of the Andes, Ecuador. Monday through Friday it's *Studio 9*, featuring nine minutes of world and Latin American *news*, followed by 20 minutes of in-depth reporting on Latin America. The second half hour is devoted to a 30-minute feature—including *Inside HCJB* (Monday), *Ham Radio Today* (Wednesday), *Woman to Woman* (Thursday), and the unique ●*Música del Ecuador* on Friday. Saturday, the news is followed by *DX Partyline*, and Sunday by *Musical Mailbag*. Continuous to Australasia on 11755 kHz.

China Radio International. Starts with *News,* then weekdays there are background reports. The rest of the broadcast is devoted to features. Regular shows include *People in the Know* (Monday), *Sportsworld* (Tuesday),

China Horizons (Wednesday), *Voices from Other Lands* (Thursday), and *Life in China* on Friday. The Saturday lineup includes *Global Review* and *Listeners' Garden* (reports, music and Chinese language lessons), and Sunday's broadcast has *Report from Developing Countries* and *In the Spotlight*. One hour to Australasia on 11730 and 15210 kHz.

Radio New Zealand International. Continuous programming for the islands of the South Pacific, where the broadcasts are targeted. On 11720, 15175 or 17675 kHz. Audible in much of North America.

Voice of Russia World Service. Winter only at this time. *News*, followed by ●*Update* on Wednesday and Friday. This is replaced Monday by *Science and Engineering*, Tuesday by *Focus on Asia*, Thursday by *Newmarket* and Saturday by *Moscow Mailbag*. Sunday's offering is the 45-minute ●*Music and Musicians*—not to be missed if you are an aficionado of classical music. Choice pickings from the second half hour include ●*Moscow Yesterday and Today* (Monday), ●*Folk Box* (Thursday) and Saturday's ●*Christian Message from Moscow*. Other slots include *This is Russia* (Wednesday) and Friday's *Jazz Show*. To Australasia (and also audible in Southeast Asia) on 9905, 15460, 15470 and 17495 kHz.

Radio Prague, Czech Republic. Summer only at this time. *News*, then Monday through Friday there's *Current Affairs*, followed by one or more features. Take your pick from *Spotlight* (Monday's look at Czech regional affairs); *Talking Point* (issues, Tuesday); *Czechs in History* (Wednesday); Thursday's *Economic Report*; and Friday's *Mailbox* (a listener-response program). Saturday, there's an excellent musical feature (strongly recommended), and Sunday brings *A Letter from Prague*, *From the Weeklies* and *Readings from Czech Literature*. Thirty minutes to the Mideast and West Africa on 21745 kHz. One hour later in winter.

Radio Australia. *World News*, followed Monday through Friday by *Countrywide* and a five-minute sports bulletin at 0935. The final 20 minutes are devoted to a feature. Monday, it's *Australian Music Show*, replaced Tuesday by *At Your Request,* and Wednesday by *Blacktracker* (Australian aboriginal music). Thursday's *Australian Country Style* shows that country music is alive and well a long way from Nashville, while Friday's *Music Deli* spotlights music from a variety of cultures. These are replaced weekends by Saturday's *Science Show* and Sunday's *Hindsight* (a look at past events). Continuous to Asia and the Pacific on 13605 and 21820 kHz; and heard in North America on 13605 kHz. Listeners in East Asia should try 21820 kHz.

KTWR-Trans World Radio, Guam. Final 15 minutes of evangelical programming to Southeast Asia on 15200 kHz, and the last half hour to Australasia on 15330 kHz.

WJCR, Upton, Kentucky. Continues with country gospel music to North America on 7490 kHz. Other U.S. religious broadcasters operating at this hour include **WWCR** on 5935, **KAIJ** on 5755, **KTBN** on 7510 kHz, and **WHRI-World Harvest Radio** on 5745 and 9495 kHz. Traditionalist Catholic programming is aired via **WEWN** on 5825 kHz.

AFRTS Shortwave, USA. Network news, live sports, music and features in the upper-sideband mode from the Armed Forces Radio & Television Service. Transmitted from modestly powered U.S. Navy stations around the globe. Try 4278.5, 4319, 4993, 5765, 6350, 6458.5, 10320, 10940.5, 12579, 12689.5 and 13362 kHz.

09:30

Radio Austria International. Winter only at this time.●*Report from Austria,* which consists of a short bulletin of *news* followed by a series of current events and human interest stories. Tends to focus on national and regional issues. To East Asia on 21650 kHz, and to Australasia on 21765 kHz. One hour earlier in summer.

■Radio Netherlands. Monday through Friday it's ●*Newsline,* then a feature. Top picks are ●*Research File* (science, Monday), ●*A Good Life* (Friday), and Wednesday's well produced ●*Documentary.* On the remaining

days, you can hear *Music 52-15* (Tuesday) and *Media Network* (Thursday). Weekends, there's a bulletin of *news* followed by Saturday's *Europe Unzipped, Insight* and *Aural Tapestry;* or Sunday's *Sincerely Yours* (a listener-response program) and *Dutch Horizons.* The first of two hours to East and Southeast Asia and Australasia on 7260 (winter), 9790 (winter), 9795 (summer), 12065 and (summer) 13710 kHz. Recommended listening.

Radio Vilnius, Lithuania. Summer only at this time; see 1030 for program specifics. Thirty minutes to western Europe on 9710 kHz. One hour later in winter.

Voice of Armenia. Winter Sundays only. Actually starts at 0940, and mainly of interest to Armenians abroad. Twenty minutes of Armenian *news* and culture. To Europe on 15270 kHz, and one hour earlier in summer.

10:00

■BBC World Service for the Americas. *World Briefing,* ●*Sports Roundup* and (Monday through Friday) ●*World Business Report.* Weekends on the half-hour, there's Saturday's ●*Science in Action* and Sunday's *Agenda.* To eastern North America and the Caribbean on 5965 (summer) and 6195 kHz.

■BBC World Service for Europe. Weekdays, identical to the service for Asia and the Pacific, but weekends there's *World Briefing,* ●*Sports Roundup* and Saturday's ●*Science in Action* or Sunday's ●*Weekend.* Continuous to Europe and North Africa on 12095 and 15485 kHz.

■BBC World Service for Eastern Europe and the Mideast. Starts with a half hour of *World Briefing* (shorter at weekends, when the final ten minutes are taken by ●*Sports Roundup*). The 1030 weekday slot goes to *The Learning Zone,* an educational program. Saturday and Sunday, it's the same as for the Americas. Continues on 11760, 15565, 15575 and 17640 kHz.

■BBC World Service for East and Southeast Asia and the Pacific. Monday through Friday, the format is *World Briefing*, ●*World Business Report* and ●*Sports Roundup*. Weekends, starts with the latest *news*, then it's Saturday's *Jazzmatazz* and *Classic Request* or the Sunday concerts of classical music—not to be missed if you appreciate top-notch performances. Continuous to East Asia on 9740 and (till 1030) 15360, 17760 and 21660 kHz; to Southeast Asia on 6195, 9740, 11955, and (till 1030) 15360 kHz. For Australasia there's 11955 kHz.

■**Deutsche Welle, Germany.** A partial relay of the station's satellite service, consisting of just features. Monday's pairing is ●*Spectrum* (science) and *Around Germany*; Tuesday has an international joint production, *Women on the Move* (or *Development Forum*) and ●*Insight*; Wednesday there's ●*Marks and Markets*, *Business Germany* and *German by Radio*; Thursday features *Arts on the Air* and ●*Great Performers*; and Friday's lineup is *Cool* and *Hits* (or *Melody Time*). Weekends, the Saturday airing is ●*Inside Europe*, replaced Sunday by *Concert Hour*. Sixty minutes to Europe on 6140 kHz.

Radio Australia. *World News*, then weekdays it's *Asia Pacific* and a feature on the half-hour. Monday's slot is given over to *Innovations*, replaced Tuesday by *Arts Australia*, and Wednesday by *Rural Reporter*. Recommendations for a good read can be found in Thursday's *Book Talk*, with Friday spotlighting environmental topics in *Earthbeat*. The weekend lineup consists of Saturday's *Jazz Notes* and *Asia Pacific*, plus Sunday's *Oz Sounds* and *Correspondents' Report*. Continuous to Asia and the Pacific on 11880, 13605, 17750 and 21820 kHz; and heard in North America on 13605 kHz. Listeners in East and Southeast Asia can choose from 11880, 17750 and 21820 kHz. The last frequency can often be heard in Europe.

Swiss Radio International. Summer only at this time. *World Radio Switzerland*—news and analysis of Swiss and world events. Look for something lighter on Saturdays, when the biweekly *Capital Letters* (a listener-response program) alternates with *Name Game* (first Saturday) and *Sounds Good* (third Saturday).

Thirty minutes to southwestern Europe on 15315 kHz. One hour later in winter.

Radio Jordan. Summer only at this time. A 60-minute partial relay of the station's domestic broadcasts, beamed to western Europe and eastern North America on 11690 or 17580 kHz. One hour later in winter.

Radio Prague, Czech Republic. This time winter only. See 0900 for specifics. Thirty minutes to West Africa on 17485 kHz, and to the Mideast and beyond on 21745 kHz. One hour earlier in summer.

Radio Japan. *News*, then Monday through Friday there's *44 Minutes* (an in-depth look at current trends and events). This is replaced Saturday by *Hello from Tokyo*, and Sunday by *Weekend Square*. One hour to South Asia on 15590 kHz, to Southeast Asia on 9695 kHz, and to Australasia on 11850 (or 21570) kHz.

Voice of Vietnam. Begins with *news*, then there's *Commentary* or *Weekly Review* followed by short features and pleasantly exotic Vietnamese music (especially at weekends). Thirty minutes to Southeast Asia on 9840 and 12020 kHz.

Voice of America. The start of the VOA's daily broadcasts to the Caribbean. *News Now*—a mixed bag of sports, science, business and other news and features. On 6165, 7405 and 9590 kHz. For a separate service to Australasia, see the next item.

Voice of America. The ubiquitous *News Now*, but unlike the service to the Caribbean, this is part of a much longer broadcast. To Australasia on 5985, 11720, and 15425 kHz.

China Radio International. Repeat of the 0900 broadcast, but with news updates. One hour to Australasia on 11730 and 15210 kHz.

All India Radio. *News*, then a composite program of commentary, press review and features, interspersed with exotic Indian music. One hour to East Asia on 11585, 15020 and 17840 kHz; and to Australasia on 13700, 15020, 17485 and 17895 kHz.

WJCR, Upton, Kentucky. Continues with country gospel music to North America on

10:00–11:00

Zhou Lian, Tecsun's chief engineer, during a design session at the R.L. Drake Company for the new Grundig Satellit 800. Seated is Drake's Steve Koogler, vice president and head of R&D, with David Powell, chief engineer at Drake, to the right.   Tecsun

7490 kHz. Other U.S. religious broadcasters operating at this hour include **WWCR** on 5935 kHz, **KTBN** on 7510 kHz, **WYFR-Family Radio** on 5950 kHz, and **WHRI-World Harvest Radio** on 6040 and 9495 kHz. For traditionalist Catholic programming, try **WEWN** on 5825 (or 7425) kHz.

HCJB—Voice of the Andes, Ecuador. Sixty minutes of religious programming to Australasia on 11755 kHz.

AFRTS Shortwave, USA. Network news, live sports, music and features in the upper-sideband mode from the Armed Forces Radio & Television Service. Transmitted from modestly powered U.S. Navy stations around the globe. Try 4278.5, 4319, 4993, 5765, 6350, 6458.5, 10320, 10940.5, 12579, 12689.5 and 13362 kHz.

10:30

Radio Korea International, South Korea. Summer only at this time. Starts off with *News*, followed Monday through Wednesday by *Economic News Briefs*. The remainder of the 30-minute broadcast is taken up by a feature: *Shortwave Feedback* (Sunday), *Seoul Calling* (Monday and Tuesday), *Pulse of Korea*

(Wednesday), *From Us to You* (Thursday), *Let's Sing Together* (Friday) and *Weekly News Focus* (Saturday). On 11715 kHz via their Canadian relay, so this is the best chance for North Americans to hear the station. One hour later in winter.

Radio Prague, Czech Republic. This time summer only. Repeat of the 0700 broadcast; see 1130 for program specifics. A half hour to Europe on 9880 and 11615 kHz. One hour later during winter.

■**Radio Netherlands.** The second of two hours targeted at East and Southeast Asia and Australasia. Weekdays, opens with ●*Newsline* (current events), which is replaced weekends by a simple *news* bulletin. The remaining time is given over to features. Quality shows include ●*EuroQuest* (Monday), ●*A Good Life* (Tuesday), ●*Research File* (science, Thursday), ●*Roughly Speaking* (Saturday) and Friday's excellent ●*Documentary*. Other offerings include *Wide Angle* and *Aural Tapestry* (Sunday), *Dutch Horizons* (Wednesday) and Saturday's *Europe Unzipped* and *Insight*. On 7260 (winter), 9790 (winter), 9795 (summer), 12065 and (summer) 13710 kHz. Also available summer to Western Europe on 6045 and 9860 kHz.

Radio Vilnius, Lithuania. Winter only at this time. A half hour that's mostly *news* and background reports about events in Lithuania. Of broader appeal is *Mailbag*, aired every other Sunday. For a little Lithuanian music, try the second half of Monday's broadcast. To western Europe on 9710 kHz. One hour earlier in summer.

Voice of Mongolia. Most days, it's *news*, reports and short features, all with a local flavor. The programs provide an interesting insight into the life and culture of a nation largely unknown to the rest of the world. The entire Sunday broadcast is devoted to exotic Mongolian music. Thirty minutes to Australasia on 12085 kHz.

United Arab Emirates Radio, Dubai. *News*, then a feature dealing with one or more aspects of Arab life and culture. Weekends, there are replies to listeners' letters. To Europe and North Africa on 13675, 15370, 15395 and 21605 kHz.

11:00

■**BBC World Service for the Americas.** Starts with 20 minutes of *World Briefing*, with *British News* making up the half hour. Then comes *Agenda* (Sunday), ●*Letter from America* (Monday), ●*From Our Own Correspondent* (Thursday) and ●*Analysis* on the remaining days. Monday through Saturday, the final slot is filled by ●*Sports Roundup*, except for Friday's *Football Extra* (soccer). Continuous programming to eastern North America and the Caribbean on 5965, 6195 and 15220 kHz. Weekdays, for the first half hour, 6195 and 15220 kHz carry alternative programming for the Caribbean (see next item).

■**BBC World Service for the Caribbean.** A half-hour weekday broadcast consisting of *World News*, *Caribbean Report*, *Sport* and *Caribbean Magazine*. On 6195 and 15220 kHz.

■**BBC World Service for Europe.** Identical to the service for the Americas, except that *Arts in Action* replaces *Agenda* at 1130 Sunday. Continuous to Europe and North Africa on 12095 and 15485 kHz.

■**BBC World Service for Eastern Europe and the Mideast.** *News*, then Monday through Friday there's an arts show, *Meridian*. The next half hour consists of a mixed bag of music and light entertainment, except for Thursday's ●*Omnibus*. On Saturday, the news if followed by *Wright Around the World*, and Sunday fare consists of *World Briefing*, *British News* and *Arts in Action*. Continues on 11760, 15565, 15575 and 17640 kHz.

■**BBC World Service for East and Southeast Asia and the Pacific.** Starts weekdays with five minutes of *news*, then a pair of features: ●*Health Matters* and ●*Everywoman* (Monday), *Science View* and ●*Focus on Faith* (Tuesday), *Sports International* and *Pick of the World* (Wednesday), ●*One Planet* and *People and Places* (Thursday), and *Discovery* and *Essential Guide* on Friday. Some of the BBC's best. Weekends, opens with *World Briefing*, then it's Saturday's ●*Science in Action* or Sunday's *British News* and the first half hour of ●*Play of the Week* (the best in world theater). Continuous to East Asia on 6195, 9580, 9740, 11955 and 15280 kHz; to Southeast Asia on 6195 and 9740 kHz; and to Australasia on 9740 kHz.

Radio Canada International. Summer weekdays only at this time. *World Report* and *Ontario Morning*. Sixty minutes to eastern North America and the Caribbean on 9640, 13650, 17765 and 17820 kHz. One hour later in winter.

Voice of Asia, Taiwan. Opens with 15 minutes of *News*, followed weekdays by *Floating Air* (Monday), *People* and *Trends* (Tuesday); *Taiwan Today* and *Art and Performance* (Wednesday); *Journey into Chinese Culture* and *Hot Spots* (Thursday); and *New Music Lounge* on Friday. The broadcast ends with *Let's Learn Chinese* (except Wednesday, when *English 101* is aired). Weekends, the news is followed by Saturday's *Mabuhay* or Sunday's *Taiwan Excursions*, *Asia Pacific* and *Business Chinese*. One hour to Southeast Asia on 7445 kHz. Some of these programs are also carried by Radio Taipei International.

11:00–11:00

In Afghanistan, mass
transportation includes
the donkey.
M. Guha

■**Deutsche Welle,** Germany. *News*, then weekdays it's ●*NewsLink* and *Hallo Africa* (not Monday). These are replaced Saturday by *Talking Point* and *African Kaleidoscope*, and Sunday by *Religion and Society* and *Cool*. Forty-five minutes to Africa on 15410, 17680, (summer) 17860 (summer) and (winter) 21780 kHz. Best for southern Africa is 15410 kHz. For a separate service to Europe, see the next item.

■**Deutsche Welle,** Germany. Similar to the service for Africa, but with an additional 15-minute feature: *Business German* (Monday), *People in Europe* (Tuesday), *German by Radio* (Wednesday), ●*Insight* (Thursday), ●*Man and Environment* (Friday), *Women on the Move* or *Development Forum* (Saturday) and Sunday's *Around Germany*. One hour to Europe on 6140 kHz.

Radio Australia. *World News*, then weekdays it's *Asia Pacific*, a sports bulletin on the half-hour, and *Countrywide* five minutes later. Weekends, the news is followed by Saturday's *Fine Music Australia* and *Book Reading*, or Sunday's *Jazz Notes* and *Week's End*. Continuous to East Asia and the Pacific on 5995, 6020, 9580, 13605 and 21820 kHz;

and heard in much of North America on 6020, 9580 and 13605 kHz.

Radio Bulgaria. Summer only at this time. Starts with *news*, then Tuesday through Saturday there's *Events and Developments* (preceded Saturday by *In Focus*). The remaining lineup includes *Answering Your Letters* (a listener response show, Sunday), the enjoyable and exotic ●*Folk Studio* (Monday), *Magazine Economy* (Tuesday). *Arts and Artists* (Wednesday), *History Club* (Thursday), *The Way We Live* (Friday) and *DX Programme*, a Saturday show for radio enthusiasts. Tuesday through Sunday, the broadcast ends with *Keyword Bulgaria*. Sixty minutes to Europe on 15700 and 17500 kHz. One hour later during winter.

Radio Ukraine International. Summer only at this time. An hour's ample coverage of just about all things Ukrainian, including news, sports, politics and culture. Well worth a listen is ●*Music from Ukraine*, which fills most of the Sunday broadcast. Sixty minutes to Australasia on 21520 kHz, and one hour later in winter. Tends to be irregular due to financial limitations.

HCJB—Voice of the Andes, Ecuador. First 60 minutes of more than five hours of religious programming to the Americas on 12005 and 15115 kHz.

Voice of America. A mixed bag of sports, science, business and other news and features. To East Asia on 6110 (or 6160), 9760, 11705 (winter) and 15160 kHz, and to Australasia on 5985 (or 9770), 9645, 11720 and 15425 kHz.

Radio Jordan. A 60-minute partial relay of the station's domestic broadcasts, beamed to western Europe and eastern North America on 11690 or 17580 kHz.

Radio Japan. *News*, then weekdays there's *Asian Top News*. This is followed by a 35-minute feature: ●*Music Journey Around Japan* (regional music and customs, Monday), Japanese language lessons (Tuesday and Thursday), *Unforgettable Musical Masterpieces* (postwar Japanese popular songs, Wednesday), and *Music Beat* (Japanese popular music—old and new, Friday). *Roundup Asia* fills the Saturday slot, and is replaced Sunday by *Hello from Tokyo*. One hour to eastern North America on 6120 kHz; to South Asia on 15590 kHz; and to Southeast Asia on 9695 kHz.

Radio Singapore International. A three-hour package for Southeast Asia, and widely heard beyond. Starts with nine minutes of *news* (five at weekends), then Monday through Friday there's *Business and Market Report*, replaced Saturday by *Asia Below the Headlines*, and Sunday by *The Film Programme*. These are followed on the quarter-hour by *Arts Arena* (Monday), *Profile* (Tuesday), and *Star Trax* (Wednesday). A self-denominated lifestyle magazine—*Living*—pairs up with *Afterthought* on Thursday, and the eclectic and informative *Frontiers* fills the Friday slot. Weekends, look for *Regional Press Review* (1120 Saturday) and *Business World* (1115 Sunday). There's a daily

5-minute news bulletin on the half-hour, then one or more short features. Weekdays, take your pick from *Wired Up* (Internet, Monday), *Vox Box* (a radio soapbox, Tuesday), *Reflections* (musings, Wednesday), *The Film Programme* (Thursday), and *The Written Word* (Friday). The hour is rounded off with the 15-minute *Newsline*. Saturday fare consists of *Eco-Watch*, *Comment* and *Business World*; Sunday, there's *Frontiers* and *Regional Press Review*. On 6015 and 6150 kHz.

CBC North-Québec, Canada. Summer only at this time; see 1200 for specifics. Intended for a domestic audience, but also heard in the northeastern United States on 9625 kHz.

Swiss Radio International. *World Radio Switzerland*—news and background reports on world and Swiss events. Some lighter fare on Saturday, when *Capital Letters* (a biweekly listener-response program) alternates with *Name Game* (first Saturday) and *Sounds Good* (music and interviews, third Saturday). On the half-hour, try something more relaxed, *Rendezvous with Switzerland*. To Europe (first 30 minutes and winter only) on 9535 kHz, and a full hour year round to East and Southeast Asia on 9540 (winter), 13735 (summer) and 21770 kHz.

Voice of the Islamic Republic of Iran. The first hour of a 90-minute block of *news*, commentary, features and a little Iranian music. Strongly reflects an Islamic point of view. To West, South and Southeast Asia, but widely heard elsewhere. On 15385, 15430, 15585, 21470 and 21730 kHz.

WJCR, Upton, Kentucky. Continues with country gospel music to North America on 7490 kHz. Other U.S. religious broadcasters operating at this hour include **WWCR** on 5935 (or 15685) kHz, **KTBN** on 7510 kHz, **WYFR-Family Radio** on 5950 and 7355 (or 5850) kHz, and **WHRI-World Harvest Radio** on 6040 and 9495 kHz. Traditionalist Catholic programming can be found on **WEWN** on 5825 (or 7425) kHz.

11:00–11:30

Urban architecture in Thimpu is distinctively Bhutanese, yet it evokes visions of Elizabethan towns.

M. Guha

AFRTS Shortwave, USA. Network news, live sports, music and features in the upper-sideband mode from the Armed Forces Radio & Television Service. Transmitted from modestly powered U.S. Navy stations around the globe. Try 4278.5, 4319, 4993, 5765, 6350, 6458.5, 10320, 10940.5, 12579, 12689.5 and 13362 kHz.

11:30

Radio Korea International, South Korea. Winter only at this time. See 1030 for program details. A half hour on 9650 kHz via their Canadian relay, so a good chance for North Americans to hear the station. One hour earlier in summer.

■**Radio Netherlands.** Winter weekdays, opens with ●*Newsline* (current events), which is replaced weekends by a *news* bulletin. The remaining time is devoted to features. Quality fare includes ●*EuroQuest* (Monday), ●*A Good Life* (Tuesday), ●*Research File* (science, Thursday), ●*Roughly Speaking* (Saturday) and Friday's excellent ●*Documentary*. Other

offerings include *Wide Angle* and *Aural Tapestry* (Sunday), *Dutch Horizons* (Wednesday) and Saturday's *Europe Unzipped* and *Insight*. Summer, Monday through Friday, starts with a feature and ends with ●*Newsline*, replaced weekends by a *news* bulletin and a second feature. Pick of the litter are ●*Research File* (science, Monday), ●*A Good Life* (Friday) and Wednesday's award-winning ●*Documentary*. On the remaining days, you can hear *Music 52-15* (Tuesday), *Media Network* (Thursday), *Aural Tapestry* and *Europe Unzipped* (Saturday) and *Dutch Horizons* and *Sincerely Yours* on Sunday. One hour to western Europe, winter on 6045 and 9855 kHz, and summer on 6045 and 9860 kHz.

Radio Vlaanderen Internationaal, Belgium. Summer only at this time. See 1230 for specifics. Thirty minutes to Europe on 9925 kHz. One hour later in winter. May also be available to East Asia and Australasia on 9865 kHz.

Radio Prague, Czech Republic. Winter only at this time. *News*, then Monday through Friday there's *Current Affairs*, followed by one or more features. Take your pick from *Spotlight* (a Monday look at Czech regional affairs); *Talking Point* (issues, Tuesday); *Czechs in History* (Wednesday); *Economic Report* (Thursday); and Friday's *Mailbox* (a listener-response program). Weekends, Saturday's excellent musical feature (strongly recommended) is replaced Sunday by *A Letter from Prague*, *From the Weeklies* and *Readings from Czech Literature*. Thirty minutes to Europe on 6055 and 11640 kHz, and to East Africa and the Mideast on 21745 kHz. Listeners in the Mideast can also try the same frequency in summer, when the broadcast is targeted at South Asia.

■**Wales Radio International.** Winter Saturdays only at this time. Thirty minutes of news, interviews and music for Australasia on 17625 (or 17650) kHz. One hour later in summer.

Radio Sweden. Summer only at this time; see 1230 for program details. To North America on 18960 kHz.

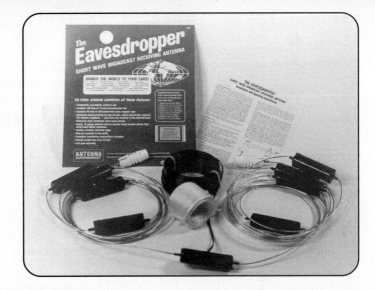

1200–1759
Western Australia & East Asia—Evening Prime Time
North America—Morning
Europe & Mideast—Afternoon and Early Evening

12:00

■BBC World Service for the Americas.
Winter, five minutes of *World News*, then
Monday through Friday there's ●*Outlook*—a
listeners' favorite for over three decades. This
is followed at 1245 by ●*Off the Shelf* (readings
from world literature). The weekend lineup is
World Briefing, British News, ●*World Business
Review* (*Reporting Religion* on Sunday) and
●*Sports Roundup*. In summer, there's the
incomparable ●*Newshour*. Continuous to
North America and the Caribbean on 5965
(winter), 6195, 9515 and 15220 kHz. Weekdays, for the first 20 minutes, 6195 and 15220
kHz carry alternative programming for the
Caribbean (see next item).

■BBC World Service for the Caribbean.
A 20-minute weekday broadcast consisting of
World News, Business and *Caribbean Report*.
On 6195 and 15220 kHz.

■BBC World Service for Europe. Monday
through Friday, similar to the service for Asia
and the Pacific. Weekends, the news is
followed by Saturday's *Wright Around the
World* or Sunday's *The Alternative* (popular
music) and *Global Business*. Continuous to
Europe and North Africa on 12095 and 15485
kHz.

**■BBC World Service for Eastern
Europe and the Mideast.** ●*Newshour*—the
best in news and analysis. Some general
interest items, too. Continuous programming
on 11760, 15565, 15575 and 17640 kHz.

**■BBC World Service for East and
Southeast Asia and the Pacific.** Monday
through Friday, five minutes of *news* are
followed by ●*Outlook* (three decades and still
going strong). The hour ends with a 15-
minute feature. Saturday fare consists of a
news bulletin, some light entertainment and
the excellent ●*Assignment* (or alternative

documentary). Sunday, it's the final part of
●*Play of the Week*, which runs till 1230 or
1300. If the former, *Agenda* takes over the
second half hour. Continuous to East Asia on
6195, 9580, 9740, 11955 and 15280 kHz; to
Southeast Asia on 6195 and 9740 kHz; and to
Australasia on 9740 kHz. Also audible in
western North America on 9740 kHz.

Radio Canada International. Winter
weekdays, you can hear *World Report* and
Ontario Morning; summer, a continuation of
the same, preceded by *RCI News*. Summer
Saturdays, it's Canadian politics in *The House*,
replaced Sunday by ●*Quirks and Quarks* (an
irreverent look at science). Monday through
Friday winter to eastern North America and
the Caribbean on 9640, 13650 and 17710
kHz; and daily in summer on 9640, 13650,
17765 and 17820 kHz. For a separate year-
round service to Asia, see the next item.

Radio Canada International. *News*, then
Monday through Friday it's *Spectrum* (topical
events). Saturday's feature is the environmental *Earth Watch*, and *Arts in Canada*
occupies the Sunday slot. Thirty minutes to
East and Southeast Asia winter on 6150 and
11730 kHz, and summer on 9660 and 15195
kHz.

Radio Tashkent, Uzbekistan. *News* and
commentary, followed by features such as
Life in the Village (Wednesday), a listeners'
request program (Monday), and local music
(Thursday). Heard better in Asia, Australasia
and Europe than in North America. Thirty
minutes winter on 5060, 5975, 6025 and 9715
kHz; and summer on 7285, 9715, 15295 and
17775 kHz.

■Radio France Internationale. The first
30 minutes are made up of *news* and
correspondents' reports, with a review of the
French press rounding off the half hour. The
next 25 minutes are given over to a series of

12:00–12:00

On Easter Sunday, 2000, fire engulfed Radio Nederland Wereldomroep's relay station in Bonaire, Netherlands Antilles. Thanks to a herculean worldwide effort, the 31-year-old facility was fully reactivated within nine days.   RNW

short features, including Sunday's *Every Woman* and *Club 9516* (a listener-response program); Monday's *RFI Europe* and *Arts in France*, Tuesday's *Books* and *Drumbeat* (African culture); and Wednesday's *Power Policy* and *France Today*. On Thursday, look for *Bottom Line* (economics) and *Reach-Out* (humanitarian issues), replaced Friday by *Film Reel* and *Weekend*. Saturday's broadcast includes a French lesson. A fast-moving information-packed hour to central and eastern Europe on 11670, 15155 and 15195 kHz. There's nothing scheduled for North America, but if you live near the east coast, try 15540 kHz, targeted at West Africa via RFI's Gabon relay.

Radio Bulgaria. This time winter only; see 1100 for specifics. Unlike most other stations, Radio Bulgaria continues to feature folk music in its program lineup. Particularly worthy of note is the 15-minute ●*Folk Studio* aired at 1210 Monday. Sixty minutes to Europe on 15700 and 17500 kHz. One hour earlier in summer.

Radio Polonia, Poland. This time summer only. Sixty minutes of news, commentary, features and music—all with a Polish accent. Monday through Friday, it's *News from Poland*—a potpourri of news, reports and interviews. This is followed by an arts program, *Focus*, and *Chart Show* (a cultural clash, Monday); *Day in the Life* and *Request Concert* (Tuesday); *Cookery Corner* and *The Best of Polish Radio* (Wednesday); *Letter from Poland* and *Multimedia Show* (Thursday); and Friday's *Business Week* and *Discovering Chopin* (or an alternative classical music feature). The Saturday broadcast begins with a bulletin of *news*, then there's *Panorama* (investigative reporting) and *Soundcheck*. Sundays, you can hear *The Weeklies, Europe East* and *Postbag*, a listener-response program. To Europe on 6095, 7145, 7270, 9525 and 11820 kHz. One hour later in winter.

Radio Australia. *World News*, then Monday through Thursday it's *Late Night Live* (round-table discussion). On the remaining days you can listen to a relay of the domestic Radio National service. Continuous to Asia and the Pacific on 5995, 6020, 9580, 11650 and 21820 kHz; and well heard in much of North America on 6020, 9580 and 11650 kHz. Listeners in Europe should try 21820 kHz.

Radio Jordan. A 60-minute partial relay of the station's domestic broadcasts, beamed to western Europe and eastern North America on 11690 or 17580 kHz.

Swiss Radio International. Summer only at this time. Repeat of the 1000 broadcast; see there for specifics. Thirty minutes to southwestern Europe on 15315 kHz. One hour later in winter.

Radio Ukraine International. Winter only at this time. See 1100 for specifics. Sixty minutes to Australasia on 21510 kHz, and one hour earlier in summer. Tends to be irregular due to financial limitations.

Radio Korea International, South Korea. Opens with *news* and commentary, followed Monday through Wednesday by *Seoul Calling*. Weekly features include *Echoes of Korean Music* and *Shortwave Feedback* (Sunday), *Tales from Korea's Past* (Monday), *Korean Cultural Trails* (Tuesday), *Pulse of Korea* (Wednesday), *From Us to You* (a listener-response program) and *Let's Learn Korean* (Thursday), *Let's Sing Together* and *Korea Through Foreigners' Eyes* (Friday), and Saturday's *Discovering Korea*, *Korean Literary Corner* and *Weekly News Focus*. Sixty minutes to East Asia on 7285 kHz.

CBC North-Québec, Canada. Part of an 18-hour multilingual broadcast for a domestic audience, but which is also heard in the northeastern United States. Weekend programming at this hour is in English, and features *news* followed by the enjoyably eclectic ●*Good Morning Québec* (Saturday) or *Fresh Air* (Sunday). Starts at this time winter, but summer it is already into the second hour. On 9625 kHz.

HCJB—Voice of the Andes, Ecuador. Continuous religious programming to the Americas on 12005 and 15115 kHz.

Radio Singapore International. Continuous programming to Southeast Asia and beyond. Starts with five minutes of *news*, a weather report, and either the weekday *Front Page* (headlines from local and regional dailies) or instrumental music (Saturday and Sunday). Weekdays, the next 20 minutes are devoted to music. Take your pick from *E-Z*

Beat (Monday and Tuesday), *Classic Gold* (Wednesday and Friday) and *Love Songs* on Thursday. There are two Saturday slots, *Star Trax* and *Currencies*, replaced Sunday by *Comment* and *Profile*. On the half-hour, it's either the weekday *Business and Market Report* or a five-minute news bulletin. The next 25 minutes are given over to features. Monday, it's *The Written Word* and *Business World*; Tuesday, there's *Living* and *Asia Below the Headlines*; and Wednesday's pairing is *Wired Up* and *Frontiers*. Thursday's offerings are *Vox Box* and *Arts Arena*; and Friday brings *Reflections* and *Profile*. Weekends are devoted to repeats of shows aired earlier in the week—Saturday's features are *Arts Arena* and *Wired Up*; and Sunday's lineup is *Living*, *Snapshots*, *Afterthought* and *Currencies*. On 6015 and 6150 kHz.

Radio Taipei International, Taiwan. Opens with 15 minutes of *News*, and except for Sunday (when it's *Mailbag Time*), closes with *Let's Learn Chinese*, which has a series of segments for beginning, intermediate and advanced learners. In between, the weekday lineup is ● *Jade Bells and Bamboo Pipes* (Taiwanese music, Monday), *People and Trends* (Tuesday), *Taiwan Today* and *Stage and Screen* (Wednesday), *Journey into Chinese Culture* and *Hot Spots* (Thursday), and *Taipei Magazine* coupled with *East Meets West* on Friday. Weekends, the Saturday slots are taken by *Kaleidoscope* and *Reflections*, with Sunday's menu featuring *Great Wall Forum* and *Food, Poetry and Others*. One hour to East Asia on 7130 kHz, and to Australasia on 9610 kHz.

Voice of the Islamic Republic of Iran. Final half hour of a 90-minute broadcast with a strong Islamic slant. To West, South and Southeast Asia, but widely heard beyond. On 15385, 15430, 15585, 21470 and 21730 kHz.

Radio Pyongyang, North Korea. One of the last of the old-time communist stations, with quaint terms like "Great Leader" and "Unrivaled Great Man" seemingly destined for immortality. Starts with *"news,"* with much of the remainder of the broadcast devoted to revering the late Kim Il Sung. Abominably bad programs, but worth the occasional

GRUNDIG Satellit 800 Millennium

The World's Most Powerful Radio for the Serious Listener

Grundig Satellit legend continues. The pinnacle
ver three decades of continually evolving
llit series radios, it embodies the dreams
wishes of serious shortwave listeners the
d over. Its continuous frequency coverage of
30,000 KHz means that broadcasts from every
er of the globe are at your finger tips. London,
o, Moscow and many, many more. Listen to
radio operators communicating across the
inent and around the world. Outstanding AM

performance. Beautiful FM-stereo with the included
high quality headphones. And, just for fun, hear
those planes as they take off and land at your local
airport on the VHF 118-136 MHz aircraft band.
Even if you're new to shortwave, you'll find it a
breeze to operate. The experienced hobbyist will
appreciate its host of advanced high-tech features.
Use its built-in antennas, or connect to your
favorite external ones. From its massive, easy-to-
read, fully illuminated 6″ × 3.5″ Liquid Crystal

Display, elegant traditional analog signal strength
meter, modern PLL circuit designs, to the silky
smooth tuning knob which creates absolutely no
audio muting during use, this radio defines the
Grundig tradition. This is the advanced radio for
you. Includes a 110V AC adapter (a 220V AC
adapter is available upon request) and high quality
headphones. Operates on 6 D cells (not included).
20.5″ L × 9.4″ H × 8″ W.

MOST ADVANCED YB 400 PE

BEST VALUE YB 300 PE

TRAVEL WITH PORSCHE G2000A

ance Hi-Tech features, easy to use, exceptional
ormance in Shortwave, AM and FM.
r broadcasts from around the world.
h those hard to receive AM and FM stations
ome. Turn on the SSB and listen to ham
ators. Digital PLL and Display. Direct
uency Entry. Auto Tuning. Manual Step
ng. FM-stereo. 40 memories. 2 Clocks.
ms. Sleep Timer.

ensions: 7.75″ L × 4.5″ H × 1.5″ W

ght: 1 lb. 5 oz.

Hear broadcasts from every continent. Has all
13 shortwave international broadcast bands.
Local AM and FM-stereo too. Fully digital PLL.
Direct frequency entry. Auto scan. Push-button
tuning. Clock, alarm and 10 to 90 minute sleep
timer. 24 memories. Titanium color. Easy-read
LCD. Display light. External SW antenna socket.
Carrying strap. Includes AC adapter, case,
earphones, batteries, supplementary SW antenna.
Compact. One year warranty.
Measures 5.75″ L × 3.5″ H × 1.25″ W
Weight: 12 oz.

The elegance of an original **F.A. Porsche Design**
digital radio alarm clock. The bold Titanium color
finish. The lush, protective natural leather cover.
Perfect for travel with its Dual Clocks, Alarms and
Sleep Timer. Listen to the world on 13 shortwave
bands or to local FM-stereo and AM stations.
20 memories. Modern Digital PLL circuitry with
step tuning and Direct Frequency Entry.
Compact 5.5″ L × 3.5″ H × 1.25″ W. Weight 13 oz.

by GRUNDIG

12:00–13:00

Elderly man meditates on the streets of Thimpu, Bhutan.

M. Guha

listen just to hear how awful they are. One hour to Asia, Africa and North America on 9640, 9850, 9975, 11335 and 13650 kHz. The last three frequencies are best for North America.

Voice of America. A mixed bag of current events, sports, science, business and other news and features. To East Asia on 6110 (or 6160), 9760, 11715, 11705 (winter) and 15160 kHz; and to Australasia on 9645, 11715 and 15425 kHz.

China Radio International. *News*, followed weekdays by in-depth reports. Next come features, including regular shows like *People in the Know* (Monday), *Sportsworld* (Tuesday), *China Horizons* (Wednesday), *Voices from Other Lands* (Thursday) and Friday's *Life in China*. The weekend lineup includes Saturday's *Global Review* and *Listeners' Garden*, and Sunday's *Report from Developing Countries* and *In the Spotlight*. One hour to Southeast Asia on 9715 and 11980 kHz, and to Australasia on 9760, 11675 and 15415 kHz.

WJCR, Upton, Kentucky. Continues with country gospel music to North America on 7490 kHz. Other U.S. religious broadcasters

operating at this hour include **WWCR** on 5935 (or 13845) and 15685 kHz, **KTBN** on 7510 kHz, **WYFR-Family Radio** on 5950, 7355 (or 5850), 11830 (winter) and 11970 (or 17750) kHz, and **WHRI-World Harvest Radio** on 6040 and 9495 kHz. For traditionalist Catholic programming, tune **WEWN** on 5825 (or 7425) kHz.

AFRTS Shortwave, USA. Network news, live sports, music and features in the upper-sideband mode from the Armed Forces Radio & Television Service. Transmitted from modestly powered U.S. Navy stations around the globe. Try 4278.5, 4319, 4993, 5765, 6350, 6458.5, 10320, 10940.5, 12579, 12689.5 and 13362 kHz.

12:15

Radio Cairo, Egypt. The start of a 75-minute package of news, religion, culture and entertainment, much of it devoted to Arab and Islamic themes. The initial quarter hour consists of virtually anything, from quizzes to Islamic religious talks, then there's *news* and commentary, which in turn give way to political and cultural items. To Asia on 17595 kHz.

12:30

Radio Austria International. Summer only at this time. ●*Report from Austria*, a compilation of national and regional news, current events and human interest stories. Thirty minutes to Europe on 6155 and 13730 kHz, with the latter frequency also available for eastern North America. One hour later in winter.

Radio Bangladesh. *News*, followed by Islamic and general interest features and pleasant Bengali music. Thirty minutes to Southeast Asia, also heard in Europe, on 7185 and 9550 kHz. Frequencies may vary slightly.

■**Radio Netherlands.** Winter only at this time. The second of two hours for European listeners. Weekdays, starts with a feature and ends with ●*Newsline* (current events), which is replaced weekends by a *news* bulletin and a second feature. Pick of the litter are ●*Research File* (science, Monday), ●*A Good Life* (Friday) and Wednesday's award-winning ●*Documentary*. On the remaining days, you can hear *Music 52-15* (Tuesday), *Media Network* (Thursday), *Aural Tapestry* and *Europe Unzipped* (Saturday) and *Dutch Horizons* and *Sincerely Yours* on Sunday. On 6045 and 9855 kHz.

Radio Vlaanderen Internationaal, Belgium. Winter only at this time. Weekdays, starts with *News*, then *Belgium Today*, *Press Review* and features. The lineup includes *The Arts* (Monday and Thursday), *Tourism* (Monday), *Focus on Europe* and *Sports* (Tuesday), *Green Society* (Wednesday), *Around Town* (Thursday), and *Economics* and *International Report* (Friday). Closes with *Soundbox*. These are replaced Saturday by *Music from Flanders*, and Sunday by *Radio World*, *Tourism*, *Brussels 1043* (a listener-response program) and *Soundbox*. A half hour to Europe on 9925 kHz. One hour earlier in summer.

Radio Prague, Czech Republic. Winter only at this time. See 1130 for specifics. Thirty minutes to Europe on 6055 kHz, and to Australasia on 21745 kHz.

Voice of Vietnam. Repeat of the 1000 transmission. A half hour to Southeast Asia on 9840 and 12020 kHz. Frequencies may vary slightly.

Radio Thailand. Thirty minutes of *news* and short features. To Southeast Asia and Australasia, winter on 9810 kHz and summer on 9885 kHz. Also available to Asia on 9655 and 11905 kHz, although operation on these channels tends to be somewhat irregular.

Voice of Turkey. This time summer only. Fifty-five minutes of *news*, features and Turkish music beamed to Europe on 17830 kHz, and to Southeast Asia and Australasia on 21540 kHz. One hour later in winter.

Radio Sweden. Monday through Friday, it's *news* and features in *Sixty Degrees North*, concentrating heavily on Scandinavian topics. Monday's accent is on sports; Tuesday has electronic media news; Wednesday, there's *Money Matters*; Thursday features ecology or science and technology; and Friday offers a review of the week's news. Saturday's slot is filled by *Spectrum* (arts) or *Sweden Today*, and Sunday fare consists of *In Touch with Stockholm* (a listener-response program) or the musical *Sounds Nordic*. A year-round half hour to North America on 18960 kHz (may also be available winter on 21810 kHz); and summer to Asia and Australasia on 17505 (or 17900) and 21810 kHz.

Radio Korea International, South Korea. Starts off with *news*, followed Monday through Wednesday by *Economic News Briefs*. The remainder of the broadcast is taken up by a feature: *Shortwave Feedback* (Sunday), *Seoul Calling* (Monday and Tuesday), *Pulse of Korea* (Wednesday), *From Us to You* (Thursday), *Let's Sing Together* (Friday) and *Weekly News Focus* (Saturday). Thirty minutes to East and Southeast Asia on 6055, 9570, 9640 and 13670 kHz.

■Wales Radio International. Summer Saturdays only at this time. News, interviews and local music from Britain's westernmost region. Thirty minutes to Australasia on 17650 kHz, and one hour earlier in winter.

13:00

■BBC World Service for the Americas. Winter, there's ●*Newshour*—news and analysis at its very best. In summer, starts with five minutes of *World News*, then Monday through Friday there's ●*Outlook*—a longtime listeners' favorite. This is followed at 1245 by ●*Off the Shelf* (readings from world literature). The weekend lineup is *World Briefing*, *British News*, ●*World Business Review* (*Reporting Religion* on Sunday) and ●*Sports Roundup*. Sixty minutes to North America and the Caribbean on 5965 (winter), 6195, 9515, 9590 (winter), 11865 (summer) and 15220 kHz.

■BBC World Service for Europe. Five minutes of *news*, then Monday through Friday there's an arts show, *Meridian*. The next half hour consists of a mixed bag of music and light entertainment, except for Thursday's ●*Omnibus*. Weekends, there's a full hour of news and current events in ●*Newshour*. Continuous to Europe and North Africa on 12095 and 15485 kHz.

■BBC World Service for Eastern Europe and the Mideast. Starts with *News*, then it's all features. Pick of the weekday litter are *Discovery* (science, 0705 Monday), Tuesday's pairing of ●*Health Matters* and ●*Everywoman*, Wednesday's ●*Focus on Faith* (0730) and Friday's ●*One Planet* (0705). Weekend fare consists of Saturday's *Jazzmatazz* and ●*People and Politics*, and Sunday's quiz or panel game followed by *Global Business*. Continuous programming on 11760, 15565, 15575 and 17640 kHz.

■BBC World Service for East and Southeast Asia and the Pacific. Fifty minutes of ●*Newshour* (a full hour on weekends), with●*World Business Report* occupying the remaining 10-minute weekday slot. To East Asia on 5990, 6195 and 9740 kHz; to Southeast Asia on 6195 and 9740 kHz; and to Australasia on 9740 kHz. Also audible in western North America on 9740 kHz.

Radio Canada International. Monday through Friday winter, there's a *news* bulletin followed by a continuation of *Ontario Morning*. This is replaced Saturday by *The House* (Canadian politics), and Sunday by a science show, ●*Quirks and Quarks*. In summer, it's the Canadian Broadcasting Corporation's *World Report* and *This Morning*, and weekdays only. Sixty minutes daily to North America and the Caribbean winter on 9640, 13650 and 17710 kHz; and Monday through Friday summer on 9640, 13650, 17765 and 17820 kHz. For an additional service, see the next item.

Radio Canada International. Summer only at this time; see 1400 for program details. Sunday only to North America and the Caribbean on 13650 and 17800 kHz.

Swiss Radio International. Winter only at this time. *World Radio Switzerland*—a workmanlike compilation of news and background reports on world and Swiss events. Look for a change of rhythm on Saturdays, when *Capital Letters* (a biweekly listener-response program) alternates with *Name Game* (first Saturday) and *Sounds Good* (music and interviews, third Saturday). Thirty minutes to southwestern Europe on 9535 kHz, and one hour earlier in summer.

China Radio International. Repeat of the 1200 broadcast; see there for specifics. One hour to western North America summer on 7405 kHz. Also year-round to Southeast Asia on 11980 and 15180 kHz; and to Australasia on 11675 and 11900 kHz. Also available to eastern North America on 9570 kHz, via CRI's Cuban relay.

Radio Polonia, Poland. This time winter only. *News*, commentary, music and a variety of features. See 1200 for specifics. Sixty minutes to Europe on 6095, 7270, 9525 and 11820 kHz. Listeners in southeastern Canada and the northeastern United States should also try 11820 kHz. One hour earlier during summer.

Radio Prague, Czech Republic. Summer only at this time. *News*, then Tuesday through Saturday there's *Current Affairs*. These are followed by one or more features: *Spotlight* (a look at Czech regional affairs, Monday); *Talking Point* (issues, Tuesday); *Czechs in History* (Wednesday); Thursday's *Economic Report*; and Friday's *Mailbox* (a listener-response program).The Saturday slot is an excellent musical feature (strongly recommended), and Sunday there's *A Letter from Prague, From the Weeklies* and *Readings from Czech Literature*. Thirty minutes to Europe on 13580 kHz, and to South Asia (audible in parts of the Mideast) on 17485 kHz.

Radio Jordan. A partial relay of the station's domestic broadcasts, beamed to Europe on 11690 kHz. Continuous till 1630 (1730 in winter).Also audible in parts of eastern North America, especially during winter.

Radio Cairo, Egypt. The final half-hour of the 1215 broadcast, consisting of listener participation programs, Arabic language lessons and a summary of the latest news. To Asia on 17595 kHz.

CBC North-Québec, Canada. Continues with multilingual programming for a domestic audience. *News*, then winter Saturdays it's the second hour of ●*Good Morning Québec*, replaced Sunday by *Fresh Air*. In summer, the news is followed by *The House* (Canadian politics, Saturday) or the highly professional ●*Sunday Morning*. Weekday programs are mainly in languages other than English. Audible in the northeastern United States on 9625 kHz.

Radio Romania International. First afternoon broadcast for European listeners. *News*, commentary, press review, and features about Romanian life and culture, interspersed with lively Romanian folk music. Fifty-five minutes winter on 11940 and 15390 kHz, and summer on 15390 and 17770 kHz. Also targeted at Canada: winter on 15335 and 17735 kHz, and summer on 15250 and 17790 kHz.

Radio Australia. Monday through Friday, there's a quarter-hour of *news* followed by 45 minutes of World Music in ●*The Planet*. Weekends, after five minutes of *news*, look for a relay of the domestic ABC Radio National service. Continuous programming to Asia and the Pacific on 5995, 6020, 9580, 11650 and 21820 kHz; and easily audible in much of North America on 6020, 9580 and 11650 kHz.

Radio Singapore International. The third and final hour of a daily broadcasting package to Southeast Asia and beyond. Starts with a five-minute bulletin of the latest *news*, then most days it's music: *Singapop* (local talent, Monday and Thursday); *Music and Memories* (nostalgia, Tuesday); *Spin the Globe* (world music, Wednesday and Saturday); and *Hot Trax* (new releases, Saturday). *Friends of the Airwaves*, a listener-participation show, occupies the Sunday slot. There's more news on the half-hour, then a short feature. Monday's offering is *Snapshots*, replaced

Tuesday by *Afterthought*. Wednesday and Thursday feature *Eco-Watch*, with the Thursday edition repeated the following Wednesday. The rest of the lineup consists of *Comment* (Friday), *The Written Word* (Saturday) and Sunday's *Reflections*. Weekdays, these are followed by *Newsline*, replaced Saturday by *Regional Press Review*, and Sunday by *Vox Box*. The broadcast ends with yet another five-minute news update. On 6015 and 6150 kHz.

WJCR, Upton, Kentucky. Continues with country gospel music to North America on 7490 kHz. Other U.S. religious broadcasters operating at this hour include **WWCR** on 5935 (or 13845) and 15685 kHz, **KTBN** 7510 kHz, **WYFR-Family Radio** on 11740, 11830, 11970, 13695 and 17750 kHz, and **WHRI-World Harvest Radio** on 6040 and 15105 kHz. Traditionalist Catholic programming is available via **WEWN** on 11875 kHz.

HCJB—Voice of the Andes, Ecuador. A further 60 minutes of religious broadcasting to the Americas on 12005 and 15115 kHz.

Voice of America. A mix of current events and sports, science, business and other news and features. To East Asia on 6110 (or 6160), 9760, 11705 (winter) and 15160 kHz; and to Australasia on 9645 and 15425 kHz. Both areas are also served by 11715 kHz until 1330.

AFRTS Shortwave, USA. Network news, live sports, music and features in the upper-sideband mode from the Armed Forces Radio & Television Service. Transmitted from modestly powered U.S. Navy stations around the globe. Try 4278.5, 4319, 4993, 5765, 6350, 6458.5, 10320, 10940.5, 12579, 12689.5 and 13362 kHz.

13:30

United Arab Emirates Radio, Dubai. *News*, then a feature devoted to Arab and Islamic history and culture. Twenty minutes to Europe and North Africa (also audible in eastern North America) on 13630, 13675, 15395 and 21605 kHz.

13:30–14:00

Radio Austria International. Winter only at this time. ●*Report from Austria* (see 1230 for more details). Thirty minutes to Europe on 6155 and 13730 kHz, and to eastern North America on 13730 kHz. One hour earlier in summer.

Voice of Turkey. This time winter only. *News*, followed by *Review of the Turkish Press* and features (some of them unusual) with a strong local flavor. Selections of Turkish popular and classical music complete the program. Fifty-five minutes to Europe on 17815 kHz, and to Southeast Asia and Australasia on 17685 kHz. One hour earlier in summer.

Radio Canada International. *News*, followed Monday through Friday by *Spectrum* (topical events), Saturday by *Venture Canada*, and Sunday by a listener-response program, *The Mailbag*. To East Asia on 6150 (winter), 9535, and (summer) 11795 kHz.

Radio Sweden. See 1230 for program details. Thirty minutes to North America summer on 18960 kHz. Also to Asia and Australasia winter on 9425 and 17870 (or 17505) kHz, and summer on 17505 kHz.

Voice of Vietnam. Begins with *news*, then there's *Commentary* or *Weekly Review*, followed by short features and pleasant Vietnamese music (particularly at weekends). A half hour to Europe on 7145 (winter), 9730 and (summer) 13740 kHz.

All India Radio. The first half-hour of a 90-minute package of exotic Indian music, regional and international *news*, commentary, and a variety of talks and features of general interest. To Southeast Asia and beyond on 9710, 11620 and 13710 kHz.

Radio Tashkent, Uzbekistan. *News* and commentary, then features. Look for an information and music program on Tuesdays, with more music on Sundays. Apart from Wednesday's *Business Club*, most other features are broadcast on a non-weekly basis. Heard in Asia, Australasia, Europe and

occasionally in North America; winter on 5060, 5975, 6025 and 9715 kHz; and summer on 7285, 9715, 15295 and 17775 kHz.

13:45

Vatican Radio. Twenty minutes of religious and secular programming to Southeast Asia and Australasia on 15500 (summer), 17515 and (winter) 21620 kHz.

14:00

■**BBC World Service for the Americas.** *News*, then weekdays there's 25 minutes of *Meridian* (the arts). The second half hour is truly a culture clash—popular music and (Wednesday and Friday) a soap opera. Weekend programming consists of a five-minute *news* bulletin followed by Saturday's *Sportsworld* or a Sunday call-in show, *Talking Point*. Continuous to North America and the Caribbean on 9515, 9590 (winter), 11865 (summer), 15220 and 17840 kHz.

■**BBC World Service for Europe.** Starts with five minutes of *News*, then come two weekday features, Saturday's live *Sportsworld* or Sunday's *Talking Point* (a call-in show). Best of the bunch are *Discovery* (science, 1405 Monday), Tuesday's pairing of ●*Health Matters* and ●*Everywoman*, Wednesday's ●*Focus on Faith* (1430) and Friday's ●*One Planet* (1405). Continuous to Europe and North Africa on 12095 and 15480 kHz.

■**BBC World Service for Eastern Europe and the Mideast.** Similar to the service for Asia and the Pacific, except for the first half hour weekdays, when *World Briefing* and ●*World Business Report* take the place of *East Asia Today*. Continuous programming on 15565, 15575 and 17740 kHz.

■**BBC World Service for Asia and the Pacific.** The weekday lineup is *East Asia Today*, *British News* and ●*Sports Roundup*. Weekends, starts with *news*, then it's either Saturday's live *Sportsworld* or Sunday's call-in show, *Talking Point*. Continuous to East Asia on 5990, 6195 and 9740 kHz; to Southeast Asia on 6195 and 9740 kHz; and to Australasia on 9740 kHz. Also audible in western North America on 9740 kHz.

Radio Japan. *News*, then Monday through Friday there's *44 Minutes* (an in-depth look at current trends and events). This is replaced Saturday by *Weekend Square*, and Sunday by *Roundup Asia*. One hour to the Mideast on 11880 kHz; to western North America on 9505 kHz; to South Asia on 11730 kHz; and to Southeast Asia on 7200 (or 9860) kHz.

■Radio France Internationale. *News*, press reviews and correspondents' reports, with emphasis on events in Asia and the Mideast. These are followed, on the half-hour, by two or more short features (see the 1200 broadcast for specifics, although there may be one or two minor alterations). An hour of interesting and well-produced programming to the Mideast and beyond on 17620 kHz; and to South and Southeast Asia on 11610 and 17680 kHz. Listeners in western parts of Australia should also get reasonable reception on 17680 kHz.

Voice of Russia World Service. Summer only at this time. Eleven minutes of *News*, followed Monday through Saturday by much of the same in *News and Views*. Making up the list is *Sunday Panorama* and *Russia in Personalities*. On the half-hour, the lineup includes some of the station's better entertainment features. Try ●*Folk Box* (Monday), ●*Music at Your Request* or *Yours For the Asking* (Tuesday and Thursday), and Friday's retrospective ●*Moscow Yesterday and Today*, all of which should please. For different tastes, there's *Jazz Show* (Wednesday), *Kaleidoscope* (Sunday) and Saturday's *Timelines*. Mainly to the Mideast and West Asia at this hour. Try 4940, 4965 and 4975 kHz, plus frequencies in the 11 and 15 MHz world band segments.

Radio Australia. Begins some days with *World News*, and the rest of the time it's a relay of domestic ABC Radio National programming. Continuous to Asia and the Pacific on 5995, 6080, 9500, 9580, 11650 and

11660 kHz (5995, 9580 and 11650 kHz are audible in North America, especially to the west). In East and Southeast Asia, try 6080, 9475 and (from 1430) 11660 kHz.

Swiss Radio International. *World Radio Switzerland*—news and background analysis of Swiss and world events. Some lighter fare on Saturday, when *Capital Letters* (a biweekly listener-response program) alternates with *Name Game* (first Saturday) and *Sounds Good* (music and interviews, third Saturday). After the half-hour, it's music and interviews in *Rendezvous with Switzerland*. Sixty minutes to East and Southeast Asia on 9575 or 12010 kHz; and to West and South Asia winter on 15185 kHz, replaced summer by 17670 kHz.

Radio Prague, Czech Republic. Winter only at this time. Take your pick from *Spotlight* (Monday's look at Czech regional affairs); *Talking Point* (issues, Tuesday); *Czechs in History* (Wednesday); Thursday's *Economic Report*; and Friday's *Mailbox* (a listener-response program). Saturday's musical feature (alternates between classical, folk and jazz) is highly recommended, and is replaced Sunday by *A Letter from Prague*, *From the Weeklies* and *Readings from Czech Literature*. A half hour to eastern North America and East Africa on 21745 kHz.

Voice of America. This time winter only. The first of several hours of continuous programming to the Mideast. *News*, current events and short features covering sports, science, business, entertainment and other topics. On 15205 kHz.

XERMX—Radio México Internacional. Summer only at this time. Monday through Friday, there's an English summary of the Spanish-language *Antena Radio*, replaced Saturday by *Mirror of Mexico*, and Sunday by *Regional Roots and Rhythms*. Thirty minutes, best heard in western and southern parts of the United States on 5985 and 9705 kHz. One hour later in winter.

Radio Taipei International, Taiwan. Opens with 15 minutes of *News*, and except for Sunday, closes with *Let's Learn Chinese*. The rest of the broadcast is devoted to features—one or two, depending on the day of the week. Monday's *Life on the Outside* is followed by *Women in Taiwan*; Tuesday's contrasting double bill consists of *Taiwan Economic Journal* and *Formosa Oldies*; Wednesday's single feature is *Floating Air*; Thursday's pairing brings together *Soundbite* and *Life Unusual*; and *Miss Mook's Big Countdown* fills the Friday spotlight. Weekends, look for Saturday's *Carol's Café* and *Taiwan Excursions*, with *Instant Noodles* and *Mailbag Time* making up the Sunday menu. Sixty minutes to Southeast Asia on 15125 kHz.

China Radio International. Repeat of the 1300 broadcast (see there for specifics), but with updated news coverage. One hour to western North America on 7405 kHz; to South Asia and beyond on two or more channels from 9700, 11675, 11825 and 15110 kHz; and to Africa on 13685 and 15125 kHz.

All India Radio. The final hour of a 90-minute package of regional and international *news*, commentary, features and exotic Subcontinental music. To Southeast Asia and beyond on 9710, 11620 and 13710 kHz.

Radio Canada International. *News* and the Canadian Broadcasting Corporation's Sunday edition of *This Morning*. A three-hour broadcast starting at 1400 winter, and 1300 summer. Sunday only to North America and the Caribbean, winter on 9640, 13655 and 17710 kHz; and summer on 13650 17800 kHz.

HCJB—Voice of the Andes, Ecuador. Another hour of religious fare to the Americas on 12005 and 15115 kHz.

CBC North-Québec, Canada. Continues with multilingual programming for a domestic audience. *News*, followed winter Saturdays by *The House* (Canadian politics). In summer, it's *The Great Eastern*, a magazine for Newfoundlanders. Sundays, there's the excellent ●*Sunday Morning*. Weekday programs are in languages other than English. Audible in the northeastern United States on 9625 kHz.

Radio Jordan. A partial relay of the station's domestic broadcasts, beamed to Europe on 11690 kHz. Continuous till 1630 (1730 in winter).Also audible in parts of eastern North America, especially during winter.

Voice of America. *News* and reports on a variety of topics. To East Asia on 6110 (or 6160), 9760, 11705 (winter) and 15160 kHz; and to Australasia on 15425 kHz.

Radio Thailand. Thirty minutes of tourist features for Southeast Asia and Australasia; winter on 9530 kHz, and summer on 9830 kHz. Also available to Asia on 9655 and 11905 kHz, although operation on these channels tends to be somewhat irregular.

WJCR, Upton, Kentucky. Continues with country gospel music to North America on 7490 kHz. Other U.S. religious broadcasters operating at this hour include **WWCR** on 13845 and 15685 kHz, **KTBN** on 7510 kHz, **WYFR-Family Radio** on 11740, 11830, 11970 (or 17760) and 17750 kHz, and **WHRI-World Harvest Radio** on 6040 and 15105 kHz. For traditionalist Catholic fare, try **WEWN** on 11875 kHz.

CFRX-CFRB, Toronto, Canada. Audible throughout much of the northeastern United States and southeastern Canada during the hours of daylight with a modest, but clear, signal on 6070 kHz. This pleasant, friendly station carries news, sports, weather and traffic reports—most of it intended for a local audience. Call in if you'd like at +1 (514) 790-0600—comments from outside Ontario are welcomed. Weekdays at this hour, you can hear *The Charles Adler Show*.

AFRTS Shortwave, USA. Network news, live sports, music and features in the upper-sideband mode from the Armed Forces Radio & Television Service. Transmitted from modestly powered U.S. Navy stations around the globe. Try 4278.5, 4319, 4993, 5765, 6350, 6458.5, 10320, 10940.5, 12579, 12689.5 and 13362 kHz.

14:30

■**Radio Netherlands.** Monday through Friday it's ●*Newsline* (current events) and a feature. Pick of an excellent pack are

●*Research File* (science, Monday), ●*A Good Life* (Friday) and Wednesday's award-winning ●*Documentary*. Making up the roster are Tuesday's *Music 52-15* and Thursday's *Media Network*. Weekend fare consists of a news bulletin followed by features—Saturday's menu is *Europe Unzipped*, *Insight* and *Aural Tapestry*; Sunday, there's *Sincerely Yours* (a listener response show), a program preview and *Dutch Horizons*. Targeted at South Asia, winter on 12070, 12090 and 15595 kHz; and summer on 9890, 12075 and 15590 kHz.

Radio Sweden. Winter only at this time. Repeat of the 1330 broadcast; see 1230 for program specifics. *News* and features (sometimes on controversial subjects not often discussed on radio), with the accent strongly on Scandinavia. Thirty minutes to North America on 18960 and 21810 kHz, and to Asia and Australasia on 13800 kHz.

15:00

■BBC World Service for the Americas. *News*, then weekdays there's an interesting collection of features: ●*One Planet* and *People and Places* (Monday), *Discovery* and *Essential Guide* (Tuesday), ●*Health Matters* and ●*Everywoman* (Wednesday), *Science View* and ●*Focus on Faith* (Thursday) and *Sports International* and *Pick of the World* on Friday. Aficionados of classical music should not miss Sunday's ●*Concert Hall* (or its substitute), while sports fans are well catered for in the second hour of Saturday's live extravaganza, *Sportsworld*. Continuous programming to North America on 9515, 9590 (winter), 11865 (summer), 15220 and 17840 kHz.

■BBC World Service for Europe. Monday through Friday, it's *World Briefing*, *British News* and ●*Analysis* (except Wednesday, when you can hear ●*From Our Own Correspondent*). Saturday's *Sportsworld* and Sunday's excellent concert of classical music complete the week. Continuous to Europe and North Africa on 9410 (winter), 12095 and 15485 kHz.

■BBC World Service for Eastern Europe and the Mideast. The weekday

lineup is *News*, ●*Outlook* and a 15-minute feature (very much a mixed bag). The Saturday news is followed by a continuation of *Sportsworld*, and Sunday it's time for the BBC's weekly concert of classical music (definitely worth hearing). On 15575 kHz (additional frequencies may be available winter).

■BBC World Service for East and Southeast Asia and the Pacific. *News*, then Monday through Friday, *Meridian* (the arts) and a soap opera or popular music. These are replaced Saturday by *Sportsworld* and Sunday by *The Alternative* (popular music) and ●*Omnibus*. Continuous to East Asia on 5990, 6195 and 9740 kHz; to Southeast Asia on 6195 and 9740 kHz; and to Australasia on 9740 kHz. The ubiquitous 9740 kHz can also be heard in western North America.

China Radio International. See 1300 for program details. Sixty minutes to western North America winter on 7405 kHz, and one hour earlier in summer. Also available year-round to South Asia and beyond on 7160 and 9785 kHz; and to Africa on 13685 and 15125 kHz.

Radio Australia. Continuous programming to Asia and the Pacific. At this hour there's a relay of the domestic ABC Radio National service. To the Pacific on 5995 and 9580 kHz (also well heard in western North America). Additionally available to East and Southeast Asia on 6080, 9475, and 11660 kHz (may also be heard in Europe).

Radio Austria International. Summer only at this time. ●*Report from Austria*, which includes a brief bulletin of *news* followed by a series of current events and human interest stories. Tends to spotlight national and regional issues, and is an excellent source of news about Central Europe. Thirty minutes to western North America on 17865 kHz, via the facilities of Radio Canada International. One hour later in winter.

Voice of America. Continues with programming to the Mideast. A mixed bag of current events and sports, science, business and other news and features. Winter on 9575 and 15205 kHz, and summer on 9700 and 15205 kHz. Also heard in much of Europe.

Radio Canada International. Continues with the Sunday edition of the CBC domestic program *This Morning*. Sunday only to North America and the Caribbean, winter on 9640, 13655 and 17710 kHz; and summer on 13650 and 17800 kHz.

XERMX—Radio México Internacional. Winter weekdays, there's an English summary of the Spanish-language *Antena Radio*, replaced Saturday by *Mirror of Mexico*, and Sunday by *Regional Roots and Rhythms*. The summer lineup consists of *Mirror of Mexico* (Monday), *Creators of Mexican Art* (Tuesday and Friday), *DXperience* (for radio enthusiasts, Thursday), *Mosaic of Mexico* (Saturday) and *Mailbox* (Wednesday and Sunday). Thirty minutes to North America, best heard in western and southern parts of the United States on 5985 and 9705 kHz.

Radio Japan. *News*, then Monday through Friday there's *Asian Top News*. This is followed by a 35-minute feature. Take your pick from ●*Music Journey Around Japan* (regional music and customs. Monday), Japanese language lessons (Tuesday and Thursday), *Unforgettable Musical Masterpieces* (postwar popular songs, Wednesday), and *Music Beat* (Japanese popular music, Friday). *Roundup Asia* fills the Saturday slot, and Sunday's offering is *Hello from Tokyo*. One hour to East Asia on 9750 kHz; to South Asia on 11730 kHz; and to Southeast Asia on 7200 (or 9860) kHz.

Voice of Russia World Service. Predominantly news-related fare for the first half-hour, then a mixed bag, depending on the day and season. At 1531 winter, look for ●*Folk Box* (Monday), *Jazz Show* (Wednesday), ●*Music at Your Request* or *Yours For the Asking* (Tuesday and Thursday), the multifaceted *Kaleidoscope* (Sunday) and Friday's retrospective ●*Moscow Yesterday and Today*. Summer at this time, look for some listener favorites. Take your pick from *This is Russia* (Monday), ●*Moscow Yesterday and Today* (Tuesday's journey into history), ●*Audio Book*

Club (dramatized reading, Wednesday), ●*Folk Box* (Thursday), and *Songs from Russia* on Friday. Weekend fare is split between Saturday's *Kaleidoscope* and Sunday's *Russian by Radio*. Continuous to the Mideast and West Asia on 4940, 4965 and 4975 kHz, as well as frequencies in other world band segments. Winter, look in the 7 and 9 MHz ranges; for summer, try the 7200-7330 and 11900-12070 kHz segments.

HCJB—Voice of the Andes, Ecuador. Continuous religious programming to the Americas on 12005 and 15115 kHz.

Voice of Mongolia. *News*, reports and short features, with Sunday featuring lots of exotic Mongolian music. Thirty minutes to South and Southeast Asia on 9720 (or 12015) and 12085 kHz. Frequencies may vary slightly.

WJCR, Upton, Kentucky. Continues with country gospel music to North America on 7490 and 13595 kHz. Other U.S. religious broadcasters operating at this hour include **WWCR** on 13845 and 15685 kHz, **KTBN** on 7510 (or 15590) kHz, and **WYFR-Family Radio** on 11830 and 17750 (or 17760) kHz. Traditionalist Catholic programming is available from **WEWN** on 11875 kHz.

Radio Jordan. A partial relay of the station's domestic broadcasts, beamed to Europe on 11690 kHz. Continuous till 1630 (1730 in winter). Audible in parts of eastern North America, especially during winter.

CFRX-CFRB, Toronto, Canada. See 1400. Monday through Friday, it's a continuation of *The Charles Adler Show*. Look for *News and Commentary* summer at 1550. Weekend fare consists of *The CFRB Gardening Show* (Saturday) replaced the following day by *CFRB Sunday*. On 6070 kHz.

AFRTS Shortwave, USA. Network news, live sports, music and features in the upper-sideband mode from the Armed Forces Radio & Television Service. Transmitted from modestly powered U.S. Navy stations around the globe. Try 4278.5, 4319, 4993, 5765, 6350, 6458.5, 10320, 10940.5, 12579, 12689.5 and 13362 kHz.

15:30

■**Radio Netherlands.** The second of two hours targeted at South Asia, but heard well beyond. Monday through Friday, starts with a feature and ends with ●*Newsline* (current events). Top choices include ●*EuroQuest* (Monday), ●*A Good Life* (Tuesday), ●*Research File* (science, Thursday) and Friday's ●*Documentary* (winner of several prestigious awards). The weekend format is feature-news-feature. Saturday, you can hear ●*Roughly Speaking* (an award-winning youth program) and *Europe Unzipped*; Sunday, there's *Aural Tapestry* and *Wide Angle*. Winter on 12070, 12090 and 15595 kHz; and summer on 9890, 12075 and 15590 kHz.

Voice of the Islamic Republic of Iran. Sixty minutes of *news*, commentary and features, most of it reflecting the Islamic point of view. To South and Southeast Asia and Australasia on 7115, 9635 and 11775 kHz.

16:00

■**BBC World Service for the Americas.** Winter weekdays, the lineup is *World Briefing*, *British News*, ●*Analysis* (except Wednesday, when you can hear ●*From Our Own Correspondent*) and ●*Off the Shelf* (readings from world literature). In summer, the hour starts with ●*Europe Today*, which is followed by 15 minutes of unmatched financial reporting in ●*World Business Report*, and equally fine reporting in ●*Sports Roundup*. Weekends, a five-minute bulletin of *news* is followed by *Sportsworld* (the Sunday edition may be replaced by other programming during winter). Continuous to North America on 9515 (till 1630 Sunday through Friday, and a full hour on Saturday) and 17840 kHz.

■**BBC World Service for Europe.** Identical to the service for East and Southeast Asia, but weekday programming may be one hour later in winter. Continuous to Europe and North Africa on 9410 (winter), 12095 and 15485 kHz.

■**BBC World Service for Eastern Europe and the Mideast.** *News*, then Monday through Friday, *Meridian* (the arts) and a soap opera or popular music. Weekends, there's live sports. Continuous programming on 15565 and 15575 kHz.

■**BBC World Service for East and Southeast Asia.** Monday through Friday, it's ●*Europe Today*, ●*World Business Report* and ●*Sports Roundup*. Weekends, a five-minute *news* bulletin is followed by live sports. The final hour to East Asia on 6195 kHz; and continuous to Southeast Asia on 3915, 6195 and 7160 kHz.

■**Radio France Internationale.** *News*, press reviews and correspondents' reports, with particular attention paid to events in Africa. These are followed by two or more short features (basically a repeat of the 1200 broadcast, except for weekends when there is more emphasis on African themes). A fast-moving hour to Africa and the Mideast on 11615, 11995, 12015, 15210, 17605 and 17850 kHz. Best for the Mideast is 11615 kHz in winter, and 15210 kHz in summer. For southern Africa, 12015 and 17850 kHz should be more than enough.

United Arab Emirates Radio, Dubai. Starts with a feature on Arab history or culture, then music. Answers listeners' letters at weekends. Thirty minutes to Europe and North Africa (also heard in eastern North America) on 13630, 13675, 15395 and 21605 kHz.

■**Deutsche Welle,** Germany. *News*, then Monday through Friday it's ●*NewsLink* followed by *Africa Report*. Weekends, the Saturday news is followed by *Talking Point* and ●*Spectrum*, with *Religion and Society* and *Arts on the Air* filling the Sunday slots. Forty-five minutes aimed primarily at eastern, central and southern parts of Africa, but also audible outside the continent. Winter on 9735, 11785, 15145, 17800 and 21780 kHz; and summer on 9735, 11810, 15135 and 21695 kHz. For a separate service to South Asia and beyond, see the next entry.

■**Deutsche Welle,** Germany. Similar to the broadcast for Africa (see previous entry), except that *Asia-Pacific Report* replaces *Africa Report*, and *Cool* is aired in place of Sunday's

16:00–16:00

Melazim Koci reads the news in Albanian over RFE-RL.

RFE-RL

Arts on the Air. Nominally to South Asia, but heard well beyond. Winter on 6170, 7225, 7305, 15380 and 17810 kHz; and summer on 6170, 7225, 7305 and 17595 kHz.

Radio Austria International. Winter only at this time. ●*Report from Austria*, news and current events from Central Europe. Thirty minutes to western North America on 17865 kHz, via the facilities of Radio Canada International. One hour earlier in summer.

Radio Korea International, South Korea. Opens with *news* and commentary, followed Monday through Wednesday by *Seoul Calling*. Weekly features include *Echoes of Korean Music* and *Shortwave Feedback* (Sunday), *Tales from Korea's Past* (Monday), *Korean Cultural Trails* (Tuesday), *Pulse of Korea* (Wednesday), *From Us to You* (a listener-response program) and *Let's Learn Korean* (Thursday), *Let's Sing Together* and *Korea Through Foreigners' Eyes* (Friday), and Saturday's *Discovering Korea, Korean Literary Corner* and *Weekly News Focus*. One hour to

East Asia on 5975 kHz, and to the Mideast and much of Africa on 9515 and 9870 kHz.

Radio Pakistan. Fifteen minutes of *news* from the Pakistan Broadcasting Corporation's domestic service. Intended for the Mideast and Africa, but heard well beyond. Try 11570, 15100 and 15725 kHz.

Radio Prague, Czech Republic. Summer only at this time. *News*, then Monday through Friday there's *Current Affairs*. This is followed by *Spotlight* (a look at Czech regional affairs, Monday), *Talking Point* (Tuesday), *Czechs in History* (Wednesday), Thursday's *Economic Report*, and *Mailbox* (a listener-response show) in the Friday slot. The weekend lineup consists of a Saturday musical feature (well worth hearing), and Sunday's *A Letter from Prague, From the Weeklies* and *Readings from Czech Literature*. A half hour to Europe on 5930 kHz, and to East Africa on 21745 kHz. One hour later in winter.

Radio Algiers, Algeria. *News*, then western and Arab popular music, with an occasional feature thrown in. One hour of so-so reception in Europe, and sometimes heard in eastern North America. On 11715 and 15160 kHz.

Radio Australia. Continuous to Asia and the Pacific. At this hour there's a relay of domestic ABC Radio National programs. Beamed to the Pacific on 5995, 9580 and 11650 kHz (also well heard in western North America). Additionally available to East and Southeast Asia on 6080, 9475 and 11660 kHz.

Radio Ethiopia. An hour-long broadcast divided into two parts by the 1630 *news* bulletin. Regular weekday features include *Kaleidoscope* and *Women's Forum* (Monday), *Press Review* and *Africa in Focus* (Tuesday), *Guest of the Week* and *Ethiopia Today* (Wednesday), *Ethiopian Music* and *Spotlight* (Thursday) and *Press Review* and *Introducing Ethiopia* on Friday. For weekend listening, try *Contact* and *Ethiopia This Week* (Saturday), or Sunday's *Listeners' Choice* and *Commentary*. Best heard in parts of Africa and the Mideast, but sometimes audible in Europe. On 7165 and 9560 kHz.

Radio Jordan. A partial relay of the station's domestic broadcasts, beamed to Europe on 11690 kHz. The final half hour in summer, but a full 60 minutes in winter. Audible in parts of eastern North America, especially during winter.

Voice of Russia World Service. *News*, then very much a mixed bag, depending on the day and season. Winter weekdays, there's *Focus on Asia and the Pacific*, with Saturday's *Newmarket* and Sunday's *Moscow Mailbag* making up the week. On the half-hour, choose from *This is Russia* (Monday), ●*Moscow Yesterday and Today* (Tuesday), ●*Audio Book Club* (dramatized reading, Wednesday), the exotic and eclectic ●*Folk Box* (Thursday), and Friday's *Songs from Russia*. Weekend fare is split between Saturday's *Kaleidoscope* and Sunday's *Russian by Radio*. Summer, the news is followed by the business-oriented *Newmarket* (Monday and Thursday), *Science and Engineering* (Tuesday and Sunday), *Moscow Mailbag* (Wednesday and Friday), and Saturday's showpiece, ●*Music and Musicians*. The features after the half-hour tend to be variable. Continuous to the Mideast and West Asia on 4940, 4965 and 4975 kHz, as well as frequencies in other world band segments. Winter, dial around the 7 and 9 MHz ranges (try 7210 and 9775 kHz); in summer, 11 and 15 MHz should give better results (take a look at 12015 and 15515 kHz).

Radio Canada International. Winter only. Final hour of the Sunday edition of CBC's ●*This Morning*. Sunday only to North America and the Caribbean on 9640, 13655 and 17710 kHz.

XERMX—Radio México Internacional. Winter only at this time. Take your pick from *Mirror of Mexico* (Monday), *Creators of Mexican Art* (Tuesday and Friday), *DXperience* (a show for radio enthusiasts, Thursday), *Mosaic of Mexico* (Saturday) and *Mailbox* (Wednesday and Sunday). Thirty minutes to western and southern parts of the United States on 5985 and 9705 kHz. One hour earlier in summer.

China Radio International. Starts with *News*, then weekdays continues with in-depth reports. The remainder of the broadcast is made up of features. Regular shows include *People in the Know* (Monday), *Sportsworld* (Tuesday), *China Horizons* (Wednesday), *Voices from Other Lands* (Thursday) and Friday's *Life in China*. Saturday, there's *Global Review* and *Listeners' Garden* (reports, music and a Chinese language lesson), replaced Sunday by *Report from Developing Countries* and *In the Spotlight*. One hour to eastern and southern Africa on 7190, 9565 and (summer) 9870 kHz.

HCJB—Voice of the Andes, Ecuador. The final half hour of a much longer block of religious programming to the Americas on 12005 and 15115 kHz.

Voice of America. Several hours of continuous programming aimed at an African audience. At this hour, there's a split between mainstream programming and news and features in "Special" (slow-speed) English. The former can be heard on 6035, 13710, 15225 and 15410 kHz, and the "Special" programs on 13600, 15445 and (summer) 17895 kHz. For a separate service to the Mideast, see the next item.

Radio For Peace International, Costa Rica. The first 60 minutes of an eight-hour cyclical block of social-conscience and counterculture programming audible in Europe and the Americas on 15050 and (upper sideband) 21815 kHz.

Voice of America. *News Now*—a mixed bag of news and reports on current events, sports, science, business and more. To the Mideast winter on 9575 and 15205 kHz, and summer on 9700 and 15205 kHz. Also heard in much of Europe.

WJCR, Upton, Kentucky. Continues with country gospel music to North America on 7490 and 13595 kHz. Other U.S. religious broadcasters operating at this hour include **WWCR** on 13845 and 15685 kHz, **KTBN** on 15590 kHz, and **WYFR-Family Radio** on 11830, 15215 (or 15600) and 17750 (or 17760) kHz. Traditionalist Catholic programming can be heard via **WEWN** on 11875 and 13615 kHz.

16:00–17:00

CFRX-CFRB, Toronto, Canada. See 1400. Winter weekdays, it's the final part of *The Charles Adler Show*, with *The CFRB Gardening Show* and *CFRB Sunday* the weekend offerings. Summer, look for *The Motts* Monday through Friday, and ●*The World at Noon* on weekends.

AFRTS Shortwave, USA. Network news, live sports, music and features in the upper-sideband mode from the Armed Forces Radio & Television Service. Transmitted from modestly powered U.S. Navy stations around the globe. Try 4278.5, 4319, 4993, 5765, 6350, 6458.5, 10320, 10940.5, 12579, 12689.5 and 13362 kHz.

16:30

Radio Slovakia International. Summer only at this time; see 1730 for specifics. Thirty minutes of friendly programming to western Europe on 5920, 6055 and 7345 kHz. One hour later in winter.

Radio Canada International. *News*, then Monday through Friday it's *Spectrum* (current events). *Venture Canada* airs on Saturday, and *The Mailbag*, a listener-response program occupies Sunday's slot. A half hour to South Asia and beyond on 6140 and 7150 kHz.

Radio Austria International. Summer only at this time. See 1730 for more details. An informative half-hour in ●*Report from Austria*. Available to Europe on 6155 and 13730 kHz, to the Mideast on 15240 kHz, and to South and Southeast Asia on 17765 kHz. One hour later in winter.

Voice of Vietnam. *News*, then *Commentary* or *Weekly Review* followed by short features and pleasant Vietnamese music (especially at weekends). A half hour to Europe on 7145 (winter), 9730 and (summer) 13740 kHz.

Radio Cairo, Egypt. The first 30 minutes of a two-hour package of Arab music and features reflecting Egyptian life and culture, with *news*, commentary, quizzes, mailbag shows, and answers to listeners' questions. To southern Africa on 15255 kHz.

17:00

■**BBC World Service for the Americas.** Winter weekdays, there's ●*Europe Today*, ●*World Business Report* and ●*Sports Roundup*. These are replaced summer by *World Briefing*, *British News*, ●*Analysis* (except Wednesday, when you can hear ●*From Our Own Correspondent*) and ●*Off the Shelf* (readings from world literature). Weekends, it's a split between news and sports (more sports in winter, and more news in summer). Continuous to western North America on 17840 kHz.

■**BBC World Service for Europe.** Monday through Friday, identical to the service for Southeast Asia, but may be one hour earlier in winter. The Saturday pairing is ●*From Our Own Correspondent* followed by *Agenda*, replaced Sunday by ●*Play of the Week*—the best in world theater. Continuous to Europe and North Africa on 6195 (winter), 9410 (winter) and 15485 kHz

■**BBC World Service for Eastern Europe and the Mideast.** Starts weekdays with five minutes of *news*, then there's a pair of features: ●*Health Matters* and ●*Everywoman* (Monday), *Science View* and ●*Focus on Faith* (Tuesday), *Sports International* and *Pick of the World* (Wednesday), ●*One Planet* and *People and Places* (Thursday), and *Discovery* and *Essential Guide* on Friday. Some of the BBC's best. Saturday's lineup consists of *World Briefing*, *British News* and *Westway* (soap opera); Sunday, it's the first hour of ●*Play of the Week*. On 11980 (winter), 12095 and 15575 kHz.

■**BBC World Service for Southern Africa.** *News*, *Focus on Africa*, and ●*Sports Roundup*. Part of a 19-hour daily service on a variety of channels. At this hour, on 3255, 6190 and 15400 kHz.

■**BBC World Service for Southeast Asia.** The weekday lineup is *News*, ●*Outlook* and a 15-minute feature (very much a mixed bag). Weekends, it's *World Briefing*, *British News*, ●*World Business Review* (Saturday), *Reporting Religion* (Sunday), and ●*Sports Roundup*. The final hour to Southeast Asia, on 3915 and 7160 kHz.

16:00–17:00

Elderly woman circumambulates the Memorial Chorten, one of the holiest shrines in Bhutan. It is believed that this attains nirvana or salvation. M. Guha

Radio Prague, Czech Republic. See 1600 for program specifics. A half hour of *news* and features year round to Europe on 5930 kHz; also winter to West Africa on 17485 kHz, and summer to central and southern Africa on 21745 kHz.

Radio Romania International. *News,* commentary, a press review, and several short features. Music, too. Thirty minutes to Europe winter on 9625 11740, 11940 and 15365 kHz; and summer on 15250, 15390, 17735 and 17805 kHz.

Radio Australia. Continuous programming to Asia and the Pacific. At this hour there's a relay of the domestic ABC Radio National service. Beamed to the Pacific on 5995, 9580 and 11880 kHz (and also heard in western North America). Additionally available to East and Southeast Asia on 6080, 9475 and 9815 kHz.

Radio Polonia, Poland. This time summer only. Monday through Friday, it's *News from Poland*—a compendium of news, reports and interviews. This is followed by *Cookery Corner* and *The Best of Polish Radio* (Monday),

Letter from Poland and *Multimedia Show* (Tuesday), *Day in the Life* and *Discovering Chopin* (Wednesday), *Focus* (the arts in Poland) and *Soundcheck* (Thursday), and Friday's *Business Week* followed by *Postbag*, a listener response show. The Saturday broadcast begins with a bulletin of *news,* then there's *Europe East, The Weeklies* and *Chart Show.* Sundays, it's five minutes of *news* followed by *Panorama* and *Request Concert.* Sixty minutes to Europe on 6000 and 7285 kHz. One hour later during winter.

Radio Jordan. Winter only at this time. The last 30 minutes of a partial relay of the station's domestic broadcasts, beamed to Europe on 11690 kHz.

Voice of Russia World Service. *News,* then it's a mixed bag, depending on the day and season. Winter, the news is followed by the business-oriented *Newmarket* (Monday and Thursday), *Science and Engineering* (Tuesday and Sunday), *Moscow Mailbag* (Wednesday and Friday) and Saturday's 45-minute ●*Music and Musicians.* The choice of features for the second half hour tends to be variable. In summer, the news is followed by

17:00–17:00

With a controlled environment and proper maintenance, transmitters can operate reliably for years. Here, BBS technician makes his rounds.   M. Guha

a series of features: *Moscow Mailbag* (Monday and Thursday), *Newmarket* (Tuesday and Friday), *Science and Engineering* (Wednesday and Saturday), and one of Moscow's musical jewels, ●*Music and Musicians*, on Sunday. On the half-hour, the lineup includes *Kaleido-scope* (Monday), ●*Moscow Yesterday and Today* (Wednesday), *Yours For the Asking* or●*Music at Your Request* (Tuesday), Friday's ●*Folk Box* and Saturday's *Songs from Russia*. To Europe summer on 9710, 9720, 9775, 9820 and 11675 kHz (frequency usage tends to be variable, but 9775 and 11675 kHz are good bets).

Radio For Peace International, Costa Rica. Continues with social-conscience and counterculture programming. Audible in Europe and the Americas on 15050 and (upper sideband) 21815 kHz.

Radio Japan. *News*, then weekdays look for some in-depth reporting in *44 Minutes*.

Saturday's feature is *Hello From Tokyo*, replaced Sunday by *Roundup Asia*. One hour to Europe on 12000 kHz; to southern Africa on 15355 kHz; and to western North America on 9505 (or 9535) kHz.

China Radio International. Repeat of the 1600 transmission; see there for specifics. One hour to eastern and southern parts of Africa winter on 7150, 7405 and 9570 kHz, and summer on 9570, 9675, 11910 and 13700 kHz.

Voice of America. Continuous programming to the Mideast and North Africa. *News*, then Monday through Friday it's the interactive *Talk to America*. Weekends, there's the ubiquitous *News Now*. Winter on 6040, 9760 and 15205 kHz; and summer on 9760, 15135 and 15255 kHz. Also heard in much of Europe. For a separate service to Africa, see the next item.

Voice of America. Programs for Africa. Monday through Saturday, identical to the service for Europe and the Mideast (see previous item). Sunday on the half-hour, look for the entertaining ●*Music Time in Africa*. Audible well beyond where it is targeted. On 6035, 7415, 11920, 11975, 12040, 13710, 15410, 15445 and 17895 kHz, some of which are seasonal. For yet another service (to East Asia and the Pacific), see the next item.

Voice of America. Monday through Friday only. *News*, followed by the interactive *Talk to America*. Sixty minutes to Asia on 5990, 6045, 6110/6160, 7125, 7215, 9525, 9645, 9670, 9770, 11945, 12005 and 15255 kHz, some of which are seasonal. For Australasia, try 9525 and 15255 kHz in winter, and 7150 and 7170 kHz in summer.

■**Radio France Internationale.** An additional half-hour (see 1600) of predominantly African fare. To East Africa and the Mideast on 11615 (winter), 15210 and (summer) 17605 kHz. Occasionally heard in North America.

Radio Cairo, Egypt. See 1630 for specifics. Continues with a broadcast to southern Africa on 15255 kHz.

17:00–18:00

WJCR, Upton, Kentucky. Continues with country gospel music to North America on 7490 and 13595 kHz. Other U.S. religious broadcasters operating at this hour include **WWCR** on 13845 and 15685 kHz, **KTBN** on 15590 kHz, and **WHRI-World Harvest Radio** on 13760 and 15105 kHz.

CFRX-CFRB, Toronto, Canada. See 1400. Winter weekends at this time, there's ●*The World at Noon;* summer, it's *The Mike Stafford Show.* Monday through Friday, look for *The Motts.* On 6070 kHz.

AFRTS Shortwave, USA. Network news, live sports, music and features in the upper-sideband mode from the Armed Forces Radio & Television Service. Transmitted from modestly powered U.S. Navy stations around the globe. Try 4278.5, 4319, 4993, 5765, 6350, 6458.5, 10320, 10940.5, 12579, 12689.5 and 13362 kHz.

17:30

■**Radio Netherlands.** The first of three hours targeted at Africa, and heard well beyond. Monday through Friday, the initial 30 minutes are taken up by ●*Newsline* (current events), with a feature filling the next half hour. Best of a good bunch are ●*Research File* (Monday), ●*Documentary* (Wednesday) and ●*A Good Life* on Friday. For a bit of music, try the eclectic *Music 52-15* aired each Tuesday. Weekend fare consists of a *news* bulletin followed by Saturday's *Europe Unzipped, Insight* and *Aural Tapestry;* and Sunday's *Sincerely Yours* (a listener response show) and *Dutch Horizons.* Sixty minutes on 6020 (best for southern Africa), 7120 (summer) and 11655 kHz.

Radio Austria International. Winter only at this time. ●*Report from Austria,* a half hour of news and human interest stories. Ample coverage of national and regional issues. To Europe on 6155 and 13730 kHz; to the Mideast on 9655 kHz; and to South and Southeast Asia on 13710 kHz. One hour earlier in summer

Radio Slovakia International. Winter only at this time. *Slovakia Today,* a 30-minute look at Slovakia and its people. Tuesday, there's a bag of short features; Wednesday looks at tourism and Slovak personalities; Thursday's slot is given to business and economy; and Friday brings a mix of politics, education and science. Saturday offerings include cultural items, *Slovak Kitchen* and the off-beat *Back Page News;* and Sunday brings the *"Best of"* series. Monday's show is more relaxed, and includes *Listeners' Tribune* and some enjoyable Slovak music. A friendly half hour to western Europe on 5915, 6055 and 7345 kHz. One hour earlier in summer.

Radio Sweden. Summer only at this hour; see 1830 for program specifics. Thirty minutes of Scandinavian fare for Europe, Monday through Saturday on 6065 kHz, and Sunday on 13800 kHz. One hour later during winter.

Radio Vlaanderen Internationaal, Belgium. Summer only at this time. Weekdays, starts with *News,* then *Belgium Today, Press Review* and features. The lineup includes *Focus on Europe* and *Sports* (Monday), *Green Society* (Tuesday), *The Arts* (Wednesday and Friday), *Around Town* (Wednesday), *Economics* and *International Report* (Thursday), and Friday's *Tourism.* Closes with *Soundbox.* These are replaced Saturday by *Music from Flanders,* and Sunday by *Radio World, Tourism, Brussels 1043* (a listener-response program) and *Soundbox.* Thirty minutes to Europe on 5910 and 9925 kHz, to the Mideast on 13710 kHz, and to East Africa on 17590 kHz. This last channel should also be usable in southern Africa. One hour later in winter.

17:45

All India Radio. The first 15 minutes of a two-hour broadcast to Europe, Africa and the Mideast, consisting of regional and international *news,* commentary, a variety of talks and features, press review and exotic Indian music. Continuous till 1945. To Europe on 7410, 9950 and 11620 kHz; to the Mideast on 15200 kHz; and to Africa on 11935, 13750 and 17670 kHz.

1800–2359
Europe & Mideast—Evening Prime Time
East Asia—Early Morning
Australasia—Morning
eastern North America—Afternoon
western North America—Midday

18:00

■BBC World Service for the Americas.
Daily in winter, but summer Saturdays only.
Winter weekdays, starts with five minutes of
news, then ●*Outlook* (general interest) and a
15-minute feature (very much a mixed bag).
Sunday's lineup is *World Briefing*, *News from
Britain* and ●*Assignment* (or alternative
documentary). The year-round Saturday
offering is a two-hour youth show, *The Edge*,
with a break for news on the hour. To
western North America on 17840 kHz.

BBC World Service for Europe. *News*,
then Monday through Friday, *Meridian* (the
arts) and a soap opera or popular music.
These are replaced Saturday by *World
Briefing*, *British News*, *World Business Review*
and *Letter from America*. Sunday, it's the final
part of ●*Play of the Week*. If it ends at 1820,
you also get *British News* and *Assignment* (or
an alternative documentary); if it makes it to
1830, you get just the documentary; and if it
goes the full hour, just sit back and enjoy it!
Continuous to Europe and North Africa on
6195 (winter) and 9410 kHz.

**BBC World Service for Eastern Europe
and the Mideast.** Except Sunday, starts
with 20 minutes of *World Briefing*, with *British
News* making up the half hour. Weekdays, the
next 30 minutes bring ●*World Business Report*
and ●*Analysis* (except 1845 Wednesday, when
it's ●*From Our Own Correspondent*). At the
same time Saturday, there's ●*World Business
Review* and ●*Letter from America*. Sunday, it's
a continuation of ●*Play of the Week*. Continuous programming on 11980 (winter), 12095
and (summer) 15575 kHz.

**■BBC World Service for Southern
Africa.** Starts weekdays with five minutes of
News, then it's a couple of features: ●*Health
Matters* and ●*Everywoman* (Monday), *Science
View* and ●*Focus on Faith* (Tuesday), *Sports
International* and *Pick of the World* (Wednes-
day), ●*One Planet* and *People and Places*
(Thursday), and *Discovery* and *Essential Guide*
on Friday. Not a bad one among them.
Weekends, the first 30 minutes are taken by
World Briefing and *British News*. After the
half-hour, it's Saturday's ●*World Business
Review* and ●*Letter from America* or Sunday's
●*Assignment* (sometimes replaced by an
alternative documentary). Continuous
programming on 3255, 6190 and 15400 kHz.

■BBC World Service for the Pacific.
Identical to the service for Europe. To
Australasia on 9740 kHz.

Radio Kuwait. The start of a three-hour
package of *news*, Islamic-oriented features
and western popular music. Some interesting
features, even if you don't particularly like the
music. There is a full program summary at
the beginning of each transmission, to enable
you to pick and choose. To Europe and
eastern North America on 11990 kHz.

Voice of Vietnam. Begins with *news*, which
is followed by *Commentary* or *Weekly Review*,
short features and some pleasant Vietnamese
music (especially at weekends). A half hour
to Europe on 7145 (winter), 7440 (winter),
9730 and (summer) 12070 and 13740 kHz.
The 7440 and 12070 kHz channels are via
relays in western Russia, and should provide
good reception.

Radio For Peace International, Costa
Rica. Continues with social-conscience and
counterculture programming. Audible in
Europe and the Americas on 15050 and
(upper sideband) 21815 kHz.

18:00–18:30

Elite Royal Bhutan Guards watch over the gates of the Trashi Chhoe Dzong parliament building.

M. Guha

All India Radio. Continuation of the transmission to Europe, Africa and the Mideast (see 1745). *News* and commentary, followed by programming of a more general nature. To Europe on 7410, 9950 and 11620 kHz; to the Mideast on 15200 kHz; and to Africa on 11935, 13750 and 17670 kHz.

Radio Prague, Czech Republic. Winter only at this time. *News*, then Monday through Friday there's *Current Affairs*. The remaining features are *Spotlight* (regional affairs, Monday); *Talking Point* (Tuesday), *Czechs in History* (Wednesday); Thursday's *Economic Report*; and Friday's *Mailbag*, a listener-response show. The Saturday slot goes to a thoroughly enjoyable musical feature, replaced Sunday by *A Letter from Prague*, *From the Weeklies* and *Readings from Czech Literature*. A half hour to Europe on 5930 kHz, and to Australasia on 7315 kHz.

Radio Australia. Friday and Saturday, you can hear a relay of the domestic ABC Radio National service. On the remaining days there's a ten-minute bulletin of world *news*, followed by regional news in *Asia Pacific*. Part of a continuous 24-hour service, and at this

hour beamed to the Pacific on 6080, 7240, 9580, 9815 and 11880 kHz. Additionally available to East and Southeast Asia on 9475 and 9815 kHz. In western North America, try 9580 and 11880 kHz.

Radio Polonia, Poland. This time winter only. See 1700 for program specifics. *News*, features and music reflecting Polish life and culture. Sixty minutes to Europe on 6000 and 7285 kHz. One hour earlier in summer.

Voice of Russia World Service. Predominantly news-related fare during the initial half hour in summer, but the winter schedule offers a more varied diet. Winter, the news is followed by a series of features: *Moscow Mailbag* (Monday and Thursday), *Newmarket* (Tuesday and Friday), *Science and Engineering* (Wednesday and Saturday), and the outstanding ●*Music and Musicians* on Sunday. On the half-hour, the lineup includes *Kaleidoscope* (Monday), ●*Moscow Yesterday and Today* (Wednesday), *Yours For the Asking* or●*Music at Your Request* (Tuesday), *Folk Box* (Friday) and Saturday's *Songs from Russia*. Summer weekdays, the first half hour consists of news followed by ●*Update*. At 1830, weekday features tend to be variable. The Saturday slot is filled by *This is Russia* and Sunday it's ●*Christian Message from Moscow* (an interesting insight into Russian Orthodoxy). Continuous to Europe. Best winter bets are 5965, 7340, 9480 and 9890 kHz; likely summer channels include 7300 (or 7330), 9720, 9775, 9820 and 11675 kHz.

Radio Argentina al Exterior—R.A.E. Monday through Friday only. A freewheeling presentation of news, press review, short features and local Argentinian music. The press review is possibly unique, since the items are often translated on-air as the announcer reads the newspaper in the studio. From the ubiquitous tangos to the music of the provinces, there's plenty to enjoy. Fifty-five minutes to Europe on 15345 kHz.

Voice of America. Continuous programming to the Mideast and North Africa. *News Now*—reports and features on a variety of topics. On 6040 (winter) and 9760 kHz. For a separate service to Africa, see the next item.

Voice of America. Monday through Friday, it's *News Now* and *Africa World Tonight*. Weekends, there's a full hour of the former. To Africa—but heard well beyond—on 7275, 11920, 11975, 12040, 13710, 15410, 15580 and 17895 kHz, some of which are seasonal.

Radio Cairo, Egypt. See 1630 for specifics. The final 30 minutes of a two-hour broadcast to southern Africa on 15255 kHz.

Radio Taipei International, Taiwan. Opens with 15 minutes of *News*, and except for Sunday, closes with *Let's Learn Chinese*. The rest of the broadcast is devoted to features—one or two, depending on the day of the week. Monday's pairing is *Life on the Outside* and *Women in Taiwan*; Tuesday's slots are filled by *Taiwan Economic Journal* and *Formosa Oldies*; Wednesday's single feature is *Floating Air*; Thursday's offerings are *Soundbite* and *Life Unusual*; and the Friday spot is given to *Miss Mook's Big Countdown*. Weekends, look for Saturday's *Carol's Café* and *Taiwan Excursions*, with *Instant Noodles* and *Mailbag Time* making up

the Sunday menu. Sixty minutes to western Europe on 3955 kHz.

WJCR, Upton, Kentucky. Continues with country gospel music to North America on 7490 and 13595 kHz. Other U.S. religious broadcasters operating at this time include **WWCR** on 13845 and 15685 kHz, **KTBN** on 15590 kHz, and **WHRI-World Harvest Radio** on 13760 and 15105 kHz. For traditionalist Catholic programming, tune **WEWN** on 11875 and 13615 kHz.

CFRX-CFRB, Toronto, Canada. Audible throughout much of the northeastern United States and southeastern Canada during the hours of daylight with a modest, but clear, signal on 6070 kHz. This pleasant, friendly station carries news, sports, weather and traffic reports—most of it intended for a local audience. Winter weekdays at this hour, it's *The Motts*; summer, look for *The John Oakley Show*. Weekends feature *The Mike Stafford Show*.

AFRTS Shortwave, USA. Network news, live sports, music and features in the upper-sideband mode from the Armed Forces Radio & Television Service. Transmitted from modestly powered U.S. Navy stations around the globe. Try 4278.5, 4319, 4993, 5765, 6350, 6458.5, 10320, 10940.5, 12579, 12689.5 and 13362 kHz.

18:15

Radio Bangladesh. *News*, followed by Islamic and general interest features; some nice Bengali music, too. Thirty minutes to Europe on 7190 and 9550 kHz, and irregularly on 15520 kHz. Frequencies may be slightly variable.

18:30

■*Radio Netherlands.* The second part of a three-hour block of programming for Africa, but also well heard in parts of North America at this hour. Monday through Friday, the first half hour is occupied by ●*Newsline*, then comes a 30-minute feature. Some excellent

18:30–19:00

shows, including ●*EuroQuest* (Monday), ●*A Good Life* (Tuesday), ●*Research File* (science, Thursday) and Friday's excellent ●*Documentary*. The weekend menu consists of a bulletin of *news* followed by two or more features. Saturday's lineup is *Europe Unzipped, Insight* and ●*Roughly Speaking* (an award-winning youth program), while *Aural Tapestry* and *Wide Angle* are the Sunday offerings. On 6020, 7120 (summer), 9895, 11655, 13700, 17605 and 21590 kHz. The last two frequencies, via a relay in the Netherlands Antilles, are best for North American listeners. In southern Africa, tune to 6020 kHz.

Radio Slovakia International. Summer only at this time; see 1930 for specifics. Thirty minutes of *news* and features with a strong Slovak flavor. To western Europe on 5920, 6055 and 7345 kHz. One hour later in winter.

Radio Vlaanderen Internationaal, Belgium. Winter only at this time. See 1730 for specifics. Thirty minutes to Europe on 5910 and 9925 kHz, to the Mideast on 13600 kHz, and to East Africa (also heard farther south) on 17695 kHz. One hour earlier in summer.

Voice of Turkey. This time summer only. *News*, followed by *Review of the Turkish Press*, then features on Turkish history, culture and international relations, interspersed with enjoyable selections of the country's popular and classical music. Fifty minutes to Western Europe on 9785 and 11765 kHz. One hour later in winter.

Radio Sweden. Winter only at this time. Monday through Friday, it's *news* and features in *Sixty Degrees North*, concentrating heavily on Scandinavian topics. Monday, there's sports; Tuesday spotlights electronic media news; Wednesday has *Money Matters*; Thursday, it's ecology or science and technology; and Friday offers a review of the week's news. Saturday's slot is filled by *Spectrum* (arts) or *Sweden Today*, and Sunday fare consists of *In Touch with Stockholm* (a listener-response program) or the musical *Sounds Nordic*. Thirty minutes to Europe, Monday through Saturday on 6065 kHz, and Sunday on 7345 or 9765 kHz. One hour earlier in summer.

19:00

■**BBC World Service for Europe.** Starts weekdays with five minutes of *news*, then there's a pair of features: ●*Health Matters* and ●*Everywoman* (Monday), *Science View* and ●*Focus on Faith* (Tuesday), *Sports International* and *Pick of the World* (Wednesday), ●*One Planet* and *People and Places* (Thursday), and *Discovery* and *Essential Guide* on Friday. Some of the BBC's best. Weekends, opens with *World Briefing* and ●*Sports Roundup*, then it's either Saturday's soap opera or Sunday's ●*Science in Action*. Continuous to Europe and North Africa on 6195 and 9410 kHz.

■**BBC World Service for Eastern Europe and the Mideast.** Weekdays, starts with *World Briefing* and ●*Sports Roundup*, and ends with ●*Off the Shelf* (readings from world literature). In between, there's a 15-minute feature. On the weekend, a five-minute *news* bulletin is followed by Saturday's *Classical Request* and ●*Omnibus*, or Sunday's *Jazzmatazz* and ●*From Our Own Correspondent*.

■**BBC World Service for Southern Africa.** Monday through Friday, *News* is followed by 25 minutes of *Focus on Africa*. The second half hour is given over to popular music or a soap opera. Weekend programming opens with *World Briefing*, then it's either Saturday's ●*Sports Roundup* and ●*Science in Action* or Sunday's news bulletin followed by *Wright Round the World*. Continuous on 3255, 6190 and 15400 kHz.

■**BBC World Service for the Pacific.** Identical to the service for Europe, except at 1930 Saturday, when ●*World Business Review* and ●*Letter from America* replace *Westway*. To Australasia on 9740 kHz.

Radio Australia. Begins with *World News*, then Sunday through Thursday it's *Pacific Beat* (in-depth reporting on the region). Friday's slots go to ●*Pacific Focus* and *Media Report*, replaced Saturday by the aptly named *Ockham's Razor* (science talk at its sharpest) and *The Sports Factor*. Continuous to Asia and the Pacific on 6080, 7240, 9500, 9580,

9815 and 11880 kHz. Listeners in western North America can try 9580 and 11880 kHz. Best bets for East and Southeast Asia are 9500 kHz (may also be audible in Europe) and 9815 kHz.

Radio Kuwait. See 1800; continuous to Europe and eastern North America on 11990 kHz.

Kol Israel. Summer only at this time. ●*Israel News Magazine*. Twenty-five minutes of even-handed and comprehensive news reporting from and about Israel. To Europe and North America on 11605, 15650 and 17535 kHz; and to Africa and South America on 15640 kHz. One hour later in winter.

All India Radio. The final 45 minutes of a two-hour broadcast to Europe, Africa and the Mideast (see 1745). Starts off with *news*, then continues with a mixed bag of features and Indian music. To Europe on 7410, 9950 and 11620 kHz; to the Mideast on 15200 kHz; and to Africa on 11935, 13750 and 17670 kHz.

Radio Bulgaria. Summer only at this time. Starts with *news*, then Monday through Friday there's *Events and Developments*, replaced Saturday by *Views Behind the News* and Sunday by 15 minutes of Bulgarian exotica in ●*Folk Studio*. Additional features include *Magazine Economy* (Monday), *Arts and Artists* (Tuesday), *History Club* (Wednesday), *The Way We Live* (Thursday) and *DX Programme*, a Friday slot for radio enthusiasts. Saturday is interactive day, with *Answering Your Letters*, a listener response show, and *Walks and Talks* fills the Sunday slot. Monday through Friday, the broadcast ends with *Keyword Bulgaria*. Sixty minutes to Europe on 9400 and 11700 kHz. One hour later during winter.

HCJB—Voice of the Andes, Ecuador. The first of three hours of religious and secular programming targeted at Europe. Monday through Friday it's *Studio 9*, featuring nine minutes of world and Latin American *news*, followed by 20 minutes of in-depth reporting

on Latin America. The final portion is given over to one of a variety of 30-minute features—including *Inside HCJB* (Monday), *Ham Radio Today* (Wednesday), *Woman to Woman* (Thursday) and Friday's exotic and enjoyable ●*Música del Ecuador*. Saturday, the news is followed by *DX Partyline*, and Sunday by *Musical Mailbag*. On 17660 kHz.

Radio Budapest, Hungary. Summer only at this time. *News* and features, few of which are broadcast on a regular basis. Thirty minutes to Europe on 6025 and 7130 kHz. One hour later in winter.

■**Deutsche Welle,** Germany. *News*, then Monday through Friday it's ●*NewsLink* followed by *Africa Report*. Weekends, the Saturday news is followed by *Talking Point* and ●*Spectrum* (science); Sunday, by *Religion and Society* and *Arts on the Air*. Forty-five minutes to Africa, but also well heard in parts of eastern North America. Winter, try 11765, 11785, 11810, 13610, 15135, 15390 and 17810 kHz; in summer, go for 9640, 11785, 11810, 13790, 15390 and 17810 kHz. Best winter options for North America are 11810 and 15135 kHz; and summer, 15390 kHz.

Voice of Russia World Service. *News*, followed winter weekdays by *Commonwealth Update* (news and reports from and about the CIS). Summer, this is replaced Tuesday through Sunday by *News and Views*, and Monday by *Sunday Panorama* and *Russia in Personalities*. Winter weekends at 1930, the Saturday slot is filled by *This is Russia*, replaced Sunday by ●*Christian Message from Moscow*. During the week, the feature lineup tends to be variable. The summer lineup includes ●*Moscow Yesterday and Today* (Monday), *This is Russia* (Tuesday and Sunday), *Kaleidoscope* (Wednesday), ●*Audio Book Club* (Thursday), *Russian by Radio* (Friday) and Saturday's ●*Christian Message from Moscow*. To Europe winter on 5940,

5965, 7340, 9480 and 9890 kHz; for summer, try 9710, 9720, 9775, 9820, 9890, 11675, 12070 or 15735 kHz.

China Radio International. Repeat of the 1600 transmission. One hour to North and West Africa on two or more channels from 6165, 9440, 9565, 9595 and 11750 kHz. Also audible in the Mideast.

Radio Thailand. A 60-minute package of *news*, features and (if you're lucky) enjoyable Thai music. To Northern Europe winter on 9535 kHz, and summer on 7195 kHz. Also available to Asia on 9655 and 11905 kHz, although operation on these channels tends to be somewhat irregular.

Radio Pyongyang, North Korea. Strictly of curiosity value only. An hour of old-style communist programming to North America on 11710 and 13760 kHz.

Radio For Peace International, Costa Rica. Continues with a variety of counterculture and social-conscience features. There is also a listener-response program at 1930 Tuesday. Audible in Europe and North America on 15050 and (upper sideband) 21815 kHz.

Swiss Radio International. This time summer only. World and Swiss *news* and background reports, with some lighter and more general features on Saturdays. Thirty minutes to northern Europe on 6110 kHz. One hour later during winter.

Voice of Vietnam. Repeat of the 1800 transmission (see there for specifics). A half hour to Europe on 7145 (winter), 9730 and (summer) 13740 kHz.

Voice of America. Continuous programming to the Mideast and North Africa. *News Now*—news and reports on a wide variety of topics. On 9760 and (summer) 9770 kHz. Also heard in Europe. For a separate service to Africa, see the next item.

Voice of America. *News Now*, then Monday through Friday it's *World of Music*. Best of the

Kyrgyzstan's capital of Bishkek is thoroughly cosmopolitan, including a national university with classical architecture.

M. Guha

weekend programs is ●*Music Time in Africa* at 1930 Sunday. Continuous to most of Africa on 6035, 7375, 7415, 11920, 11975, 12040, 15410, 15445 and 15580 kHz, some of which are seasonal. For yet another service, to Australasia, see the following item.

Voice of America. Sixty minutes of news and reports covering a variety of topics. One hour to Australasia on 9525, 11870 and 15180 kHz.

Radio Korea International, South Korea. Opens with *news* and commentary, followed Monday through Wednesday by *Seoul Calling*. Weekly features include *Echoes of Korean Music* and *Shortwave Feedback* (Sunday), *Tales from Korea's Past* (Monday), *Korean Cultural Trails* (Tuesday), *Pulse of Korea* (Wednesday), *From Us to You* (a listener-response program) and *Let's Learn Korean* (Thursday), *Let's Sing Together* and *Korea Through Foreigners' Eyes* (Friday), and Saturday's *Discovering Korea*, *Korean Literary Corner* and *Weekly News Focus*. Sixty minutes to East Asia on 5975 and 7275 kHz.

WJCR, Upton, Kentucky. Continues with country gospel music to North America on 7490 and 13595 kHz. Other U.S. religious broadcasters operating at this time include **WWCR** on 13845 and 15685 kHz, **KTBN** on 15590 kHz, and **WHRI-World Harvest**

Radio on 13760 kHz. For traditionalist Catholic programming, try **WEWN** on 11875 and 13615 kHz.

CFRX-CFRB, Toronto, Canada. See 1800. Weekdays at this time, you can hear *The John Oakley Show*; weekends, it's replaced by *The Mike Stafford Show*. On 6070 kHz.

AFRTS Shortwave, USA. Network news, live sports, music and features in the upper-sideband mode from the Armed Forces Radio & Television Service. Transmitted from modestly powered U.S. Navy stations around the globe. Try 4278.5, 4319, 4993, 5765, 6350, 6458.5, 10320, 10940.5, 12579, 12689.5 and 13362 kHz.

19:30

Radio Polonia, Poland. Summer only at this time. Monday through Friday, it's *News from Poland*—news, reports and interviews on the latest events in the country. This is followed by *Cookery Corner* and *The Best of Polish Radio* (Monday), *Letter from Poland* and *Multimedia Show* (Tuesday), *Day in the Life* and *Discovering Chopin* (Wednesday), *Focus* (the arts in Poland) and *Soundcheck* (Thursday), and Friday's *Business Week* followed by *Postbag*, a listener response show. The Saturday broadcast begins with a bulletin of

19:30–20:00

news, then there's *Europe East, The Weeklies* and *Chart Show*. Sundays, look for five minutes of *news* followed by *Panorama* and *Request Concert*. Sixty minutes to Europe on 6035, 7185, 7265 and 9525 kHz. One hour later during winter.

Radio Slovakia International. Winter only at this time. *Slovakia Today*, a 30-minute review of Slovak life and culture. Monday, there's a potpourri of short features; Tuesday spotlights tourism and Slovak personalities; Wednesday is devoted to business and economy; and Thursday brings a mix of politics, education and science. Friday offerings include cultural items, cooking recipes and the off-beat *Back Page News*; and Saturday has the *"Best of"* series. Sunday's show is a melange of this and that, and includes *Listeners' Tribune* and some enjoyable Slovak music. A friendly half hour to Western Europe on 5915, 6055 and 7345 kHz. One hour earlier in summer.

Voice of Turkey. Winter only at this time. See 1830 for program details. Some unusual programming and friendly presentation make this station worth a listen. Fifty minutes to Europe on 6175 and 6180 kHz. One hour earlier in summer.

Voice of the Islamic Republic of Iran. Sixty minutes of *news*, commentary and features from an Islamic point of view. Reflects a way of life not found in western countries. To Europe winter on 7115, 7215 and 9022 kHz, and summer on 9022, 9575 and 11670 kHz. Apart from 9022 kHz, frequency usage tends to be a little erratic.

Radio Vlaanderen Internationaal, Belgium. Summer only at this time. Weekdays, starts with *News*, then *Belgium Today*, *Press Review* and features. The lineup includes *Focus on Europe* and *Sports* (Monday), *Green Society* (Tuesday), *The Arts* (Wednesday and Friday), *Around Town* (Wednesday), *Economics* and *International Report* (Thursday), and Friday's *Tourism*. Closes with *Soundbox*. These are replaced Saturday by *Music from Flanders*, and Sunday by *Radio World*, *Tourism*, *Brussels 1043* (a listener-response program) and *Soundbox*.

Thirty minutes to western Europe on 5960 kHz. There is no corresponding winter broadcast on shortwave.

Radio Sweden. Summer only at this time, and a repeat of the 1730 broadcast. See 1830 for program details. Thirty minutes to Europe on 6065 kHz.

■**Radio Netherlands.** Monday through Friday, starts with a feature and ends with ●*Newsline*, replaced weekends by a *news* bulletin and a second feature. Pick of the litter are ●*Research File* (science, Monday), ●*A Good Life* (Friday) and Wednesday's award-winning ●*Documentary*. On the remaining days, you can hear *Music 52-15* (Tuesday), *Media Network* (Thursday), *Aural Tapestry* and *Europe Unzipped* (Saturday) and *Dutch Horizons* and *Sincerely Yours* on Sunday. The final hour of a three-hour block to Africa on 6020 (best for southern parts), 7120 (summer), 9895, 11655, 13700, 17605 and 21590 kHz. The last two frequencies are heard well in many parts of North America.

RAI International—Radio Roma, Italy. Actually starts at 1935. Approximately 12 minutes of *news*, then some Italian music. Twenty minutes to western Europe winter on 5970, 7285 and 9760 kHz, and summer on 5970, 7290 and 9750 kHz.

19:50

Vatican Radio. Summer only at this time. Twenty minutes of programming oriented to Catholics. To Europe on 4005, 5880 (or 5883) and 7250 kHz. One hour later in winter.

20:00

■**BBC World Service for Europe.** ●*Newshour*, the standard for all in-depth news shows from international broadcasters. One hour to Europe on 6195, 9410 and 12095 kHz.

■**BBC World Service for the Mideast.** Winter only at this time. ●*Newshour*—broadcast to all areas, and deservedly so. On 9410 and 12095 kHz.

■**BBC World Service for Southern Africa.** Fifty minutes of the incomparable ●*Newshour* followed by ten of ●*Sports Roundup*. On 3255, 6190 and 15400 kHz.

■**BBC World Service for the Pacific.** Identical to the service for Europe at this hour. To Australasia on 5975 and 9740 kHz.

■**Deutsche Welle,** Germany. *News*, then Monday through Friday there's the in-depth ●*NewsLink* followed by a feature. Monday, it's *German by Radio*; Tuesday has the ecological ●*Man and Environment*; Wednesday brings ●*Insight*; Thursday, try *Living in Germany*; and Friday's slot is *Spotlight on Sport. Weekend Review* and ●*Weekend* (a European co-production) are aired Saturday, replaced Sunday by a second edition of *Weekend Review* and *Arts on the Air.* Forty-five minutes to Europe winter on 9725 kHz, and summer on 11970 kHz.

Radio Canada International. Summer only at this time. The first of two hours to Europe and beyond. *News,* followed Monday through Friday by *Spectrum* (current events), which is replaced Saturday by *Venture Canada* (business) and ●*Earth Watch* (the environment). The Sunday slots are filled by *Arts in Canada* and *The Mailbag,* a listener-response show. To Europe, Africa and the Mideast on 5995, 11690, 13650, 13670, 15150, 15325, 15470, 17820 and 17870 kHz. Some of these channels are also audible in parts of North America. One hour later during winter.

Radio Damascus, Syria. Actually starts at 2005. *News,* a daily press review, and different features for each day of the week. These can be heard at approximately 2030 and 2045, and include *Arab Profile* and *Palestine Talk* (Monday), *Syria and the World* and *Listeners Overseas* (Tuesday), *Around the World* and *Selected Readings* (Wednesday),

20:00–20:00

From the World Press and Reflections (Thursday), Arab Newsweek and Cultural Magazine (Friday), Welcome to Syria and Arab Civilization (Saturday), and From Our Literature and Music from the Orient (Sunday). Most of the transmission, however, is given over to Syrian and some western popular music. One hour to Europe, often audible in eastern North America, on 12085 and 13610 kHz.

Swiss Radio International. World Radio Switzerland—news and background reports on world and Swiss events. Some lighter fare on Saturdays, when the biweekly Capital Letters (a listener-response program) alternates with Name Game (first Saturday) and Sounds Good (third Saturday). Thirty minutes to northern Europe winter on 6165 kHz (one hour earlier in summer), and year-round to Africa, winter on 9605, 11910, 13660 and 13790 kHz; summer on 13710, 13770, 15220 and 17580 kHz. Easy reception in southern Africa.

Radio Australia. Starts with World News, then Sunday through Thursday there's Pacific Beat (in-depth reporting). Friday fare consists of Oz Sounds and Health Report, and Saturday it's the first of four hours of Australia All Over. Continuous programming to the Pacific on 9580, 9815, 11880 and 12080 kHz; and to East and Southeast Asia on 9500 kHz (may also be audible in Europe). In western North America, try 9580 and 11880 kHz.

Voice of Russia World Service. News, then winter it's News and Views Monday through Saturday, with Sunday Panorama and Russia in Personalities the Sunday offerings. In summer, these are replaced by a variety of features. Take your pick from Science and Engineering (Monday and Thursday), Newmarket (Wednesday and Saturday), Moscow Mailbag (Tuesday and Friday), and the 45-minute ●Music and Musicians on Sunday. Winter on the half-hour, the lineup includes ●Moscow Yesterday and Today (Monday), This is Russia (Tuesday and Sunday), Kaleidoscope (Wednesday), ●Audio Book Club (Thursday), Russian by Radio (Friday) and Saturday's ●Christian Message from Moscow. Best of the summer offerings at this time are Thursday's ●Folk Box and Tuesday's ●Music at Your Request (may alternate with Yours For the Asking). Other features include Songs from Russia (Monday),Friday's Jazz Show and Saturday's Russian by Radio. Continuous to Europe winter on 5940, 5965, 9890 and 15735 kHz; in summer, take a look at 9720, 9775, 9820, 9890, 11675, 15485 and 15735 kHz. Some of these channels are audible in eastern North America.

Radio Kuwait. The final sixty minutes of a three-hour broadcast to Europe and eastern North America (see 1800). Regular features at this time include Theater in Kuwait (2000), Saheeh Muslim (2030) and News in Brief at 2057. On 11990 kHz.

Radio Bulgaria. This time winter only. See 1900 for specifics. Often includes exotic Bulgarian folk music. Sixty minutes to Europe, and sometimes audible in parts of eastern North America, on 5845 and 7535 kHz. One hour earlier during summer.

Radio Budapest, Hungary. Winter only at this time; see 1900 for specifics. Thirty minutes to Europe on 6125 and 7165 kHz. One hour earlier in summer.

Radio Algiers, Algeria. News, then western and Arab popular music, with an occasional feature thrown in. One hour of so-so reception in Europe, and sometimes heard in eastern North America. On 11715 and 15160 kHz.

China Radio International. Starts with News, then weekdays there are special reports. The rest of the broadcast is devoted to features. Regular shows include People in the Know (Monday), Sportsworld (Tuesday), China Horizons (Wednesday), Voices from Other Lands (Thursday), and Life in China on Friday. The Saturday lineup includes Global Review and Listeners' Garden (reports, music and Chinese language lessons), and Sunday's broadcast has Report from Developing Countries and In the Spotlight. One hour to Europe winter on 5965 and 9535 kHz, and summer on 11790 and 15110 kHz. Also available to eastern and southern Africa on 11735 and 13640 (or 15500) kHz; and to North Africa (audible in the Mideast) on 9440 kHz.

GRUNDIG TUNES IN THE WORLD

50th Anniversary Edition Classic 960

Solid wood cabinet… solid-brass trimmed knobs and gold tone dial… the legendary sound and mystique of the original 1950s table top radio. The Classic 960 FM-stereo/AM shortwave radio is updated and improved. Two 3" side speakers, left and right, and the 4" front speaker fill the room with wondrous sound. Travel the world without leaving home… receives shortwave continuously from 2.3-22.3 MHz. Additional features of auxiliary inputs take the audio signal from CD, cassette player or TV and turns it into spacious, roomfilling Grundig sound. Dimensions: 15.5" L x 11.25" H x 7" W. Weight: 9 lbs. 9.6 oz.

LISTENING HAS NEVER BEEN MORE ENJOYABLE...

PORSCHE DESIGN 2000A RADIO ALARM CLOCK
Designed by F.A. Porsche. Wake up to talk radio on AM, soothing stereo (with earphones) on FM or fascinating shortwave from around the world, select from 13 International bands from 2.3-7.4 and 9.4-26.1 MHz. Punch in any station or lock your favorites into 20 memories, supple brown leather snap-on case. Weight: 11.52 oz.

EXECUTIVE TRAVELLER G4 RADIO
Wherever you go, the world goes with you! Nestled inside a luxurious leather travel organizer is the world's smallest AM, FM-stereo, six shortwave band radio with built-in digital quartz clock and travel alarm. The executive Traveler puts everything at your fingertips – passport, travel documents, credit cards, cash and more. Comes with 2 AA batteries and earphones. Radio dimensions: 2.75" L x 4.25" H x .75" W. Weight: 4.48 oz.

PLATINUM DIGITAL G3D
Big on features, the Platinum Digital radio is small enough to fit into a jacket or purse! PLL synthesizer FM/AM (SW1/SW2), FM-stereo with earphones, m-band scan function, 20 user programmable memories, illuminated LCD indicates all operations, auto search up/down, manual tuning up/down, quartz controlled dual alarm clock with sleep timer (10 to 90 minutes) and alarm by buzzer or radio. Uses 3 AA batteries. (not Included) Weighs only 11.52 oz.

TRAVELLER II PE
A proven compact portable with outstanding performance. Stylish titanium look finish combines with practical features for the traveler. AM/FM and five shortwave bands, world clock for 24 time zones and simultaneous display of home and world time in the digital display. Comes with 3 AA batteries, earphones and carrying pouch. Weighs 10.7 oz.

MINI WORLD BAND 100 PE
Smallest Pocket World Band Radio. Travel with the world in your pocket. Another exciting breakthrough in world band technology. A well built radio that fits in the palm of your hand. AM/FM stereo and six shortwave bands with LED indicator. Comes with earphones, belt clip and soft carrying pouch. Weighs 4 oz.

WEATHER BAND G2
Always be prepared with the G2. Take this incredibly powerful AM/FM weather radio with you on all your outdoor activities. This weather resistant radio is your 24 hour hotline to AM, FM, and the national weather service reports and forecasts. Built in speaker and telescopic antenna. Weighs 6 oz.

by **GRUNDIG**

Orders & Prices phone: 800 431-3939
Information phone: 614 866-4267
Fax: 614 866-2339
Web: dx@universal-radio.com
www.DXing.com
www.universal-radio.com

universal radio inc.

6830 Americana Pkwy.
Reynoldsburg, Ohio
43068-4113 U.S.A.

20:00–21:00

Voice of Mongolia. *News*, reports and short features dealing with local topics. Some exotic Mongolian music, too, especially on Sundays. Thirty minutes to Europe on 9720 (or 12015) and 12085 kHz. Frequencies may vary slightly.

Radio Nacional de Angola ("Angolan National Radio"). The first 30 minutes or so consist of a mix of music and short features, then there's *news* near the half-hour. The remainder of the broadcast contains some lively Angolan music. Sixty minutes to Southern Africa on 3354 and 7245 kHz.

Kol Israel. Winter only at this time. Twenty-five minutes of *news* and in-depth reporting from and about Israel. To Europe and North America on any three channels from 6245, 7410, 7510 and 9435 kHz; and to Southern Africa and South America on 15640 kHz. One hour earlier in summer.

HCJB—Voice of the Andes, Ecuador. Continues with a three-hour block of religious and secular programming to Europe, with predominantly religious fare at this hour. On 17660 kHz.

Voice of America. Continuous programming to the Mideast and North Africa. *News*, reports and capsulated features covering everything from politics to entertainment. On 6095 (winter), 9760, and (summer) 9770 kHz. For African listeners there's the weekday *Africa World Tonight*, replaced weekends by *Nightline Africa*, on 6035, 7275, 7375, 7415, 11715, 11855, 15410, 15445, 15580, 17725 and 17755 kHz, some of which are seasonal. Both transmissions are heard well beyond their target areas, including parts of North America.

Radio For Peace International, Costa Rica. Part of an eight-hour cyclical block of predominantly social-conscience and counterculture programming. Some of the offerings at this hour include a women's news-gathering service, *WINGS*, (2030 Wednesday) and a listener-response program (same time Friday). Audible in Europe and North America on 15050 and (upper sideband) 21815 kHz.

WJCR, Upton, Kentucky. Continues with country gospel music to North America on 7490 and 13595 kHz. Other U.S. religious broadcasters which operate at this time include **WWCR** on 13845 and 15685 kHz, **KTBN** on 15590 kHz, and **WHRI-World Harvest Radio** on 13760 kHz. For traditionalist Catholic programming, tune **WEWN** on 11875 and 13615 kHz.

Radio Prague, Czech Republic. Summer only at this time. *News*, then Monday through Friday there's *Current Affairs*. These are followed by Monday's *Spotlight* (a look at the Czech regions), Tuesday's *Talking Point*, Wednesday's *Czechs in History*, Thursday's *Economic Report*, and Friday's listener-response show, *Mailbag*. Look for some excellent entertainment in Saturday's musical feature, which is replaced Sunday by *A Letter from Prague*, *From the Weeklies* and *Readings from Czech Literature*. Thirty minutes to Europe on 5930 kHz, and to Southeast Asia and Australasia on 11600 kHz.

Armenian National Radio/Voice of Armenia. Summer only at this time. Actually starts at 1955, and mainly of interest to Armenians abroad. Twenty minutes of Armenian *news* and culture. To Europe on 9965 kHz. Sometimes audible in eastern North America. One hour later in winter.

CFRX-CFRB, Toronto, Canada. See 1800. Summer weekdays at this time, you can hear ●*The World Today*, three hours of news, interviews, sports and commentary. On 6070 kHz.

AFRTS Shortwave, USA. Network news, live sports, music and features in the upper-sideband mode from the Armed Forces Radio & Television Service. Transmitted from modestly powered U.S. Navy stations around the globe. Try 4278.5, 4319, 4993, 5765, 6350, 6458.5, 10320, 10940.5, 12579, 12689.5 and 13362 kHz.

20:30

Radio Polonia, Poland. This time winter only. See 1930 for program specifics. *News*, music and features, covering multiple aspects of Polish life and culture. Sixty minutes to Europe on 6035, 6095, 7285 and 9525 kHz. One hour earlier in summer.

Radio Sweden. Winter only at this time. See 1830 for program details. Thirty minutes to Europe on 6065 kHz.

Voice of Vietnam. *News*, then it's either *Commentary* or *Weekly Review*, which in turn is followed by short features. Look for some pleasant Vietnamese music towards the end of the broadcast (more at weekends). A half hour to Europe on 7145 (winter), 9730 and (summer) 13740 kHz.

Radio Thailand. Fifteen minutes of *news* targeted at Europe. Winter on 9535 kHz, and summer on 9680 kHz. Also available to Asia on 9655 and 11905 kHz, although operation on these channels tends to be somewhat irregular.

Radio Croatia. Summer only at this time. Approximately 15 minutes of news from and about Croatia. Part of a longer broadcast predominantly in Croatian To the Mideast and southern Africa on 11805 kHz. One hour later in winter.

Voice of Turkey. This time summer only. *News*, followed by *Review of the Turkish Press* and features (some of them unusual) with a strong local flavor. Selections of Turkish popular and classical music complete the program. Fifty minutes to Southeast Asia and Australasia on 9525 kHz. One hour later during winter.

■**Wales Radio International.** Summer Fridays only at this time. News, interviews and music from the Welsh hills and valleys. Worth a listen for the occasional song from renowned Welsh choirs. Thirty minutes to Europe on 7325 kHz, and one hour later in winter.

Radio Habana Cuba. The first half hour of a 60-minute package of *news* (predominantly about Cuba and Latin America), features about the island and its people, and some thoroughly enjoyable Cuban music (though not as much as there used to be). To Europe winter on 9550 kHz and summer on 13750 kHz.

Radio Tashkent, Uzbekistan. Thirty minutes of *news*, commentary and features, with some exotic Uzbek music. To Europe winter on 7105 and 9540 kHz, and summer on 9540 and 9545 kHz.

RAI International—Radio Roma, Italy. Actually starts at 2025. Twenty minutes of *news* and music targeted at the Mideast on 7125 (summer), 7220 (winter), 9710 and 11880 kHz.

20:45

All India Radio. The first 15 minutes of a much longer broadcast, consisting of a press review, Indian music, regional and international *news*, commentary, and a variety of talks and features of general interest. Continuous till 2230. To Western Europe on 7410, 9650 and 9950 kHz; and to Australasia on 7150, 9910, 11620 and 11715 kHz. Early risers in Southeast Asia can try the channels for Australasia.

Vatican Radio. Winter only at this time, and actually starts at 2050. Twenty minutes of predominantly Catholic fare. To Europe on 4005, 5880 and 7250 kHz. Frequencies may vary slightly. One hour earlier in summer.

21:00

■**BBC World Service for the Americas.** *News*, ●*World Business Report/Review* (replaced Sunday by *Global Business*), *Caribbean Report* (weekdays) and ●*Sports Roundup*. Weekdays, the final 15-minute slot (except for Wednesday when ●*From Our Own Correspondent* is aired) is filled by ●*Analysis*. Same time Saturday, there's ●*Letter from America*, which is replaced Sunday by *Reporting Religion*. To the Caribbean on 5975 kHz, and widely heard in eastern and southern parts of the United States. If you prefer *British News* to the Caribbean alternative, try 12095 kHz, targeted at South America.

BBC World Service for Europe. Weekday format is *News*, ●*World Business Report*, ●*Sports Roundup* and ●*Off the Shelf* (readings from world literature). Saturday, the news is followed by *Jazzmatazz* and ●*Omnibus*; Sunday by *The Alternative* (popular music) and light entertainment. Continuous to Europe and North Africa on 6195 and 9410 kHz.

21:00–21:00

BBC World Service for Southern Africa.
The weekday lineup is *News*, ●*World Business Report*, *British News*, ●*Sports Roundup* and ●*Analysis* (replaced Wednesday by ●*From Our Own Correspondent*). Weekends, opens with five minutes of *News*, then Saturday it's ●*World Business Review*, *British News*, ●*Sports Roundup* and ●*Letter from America*. These are replaced Sunday by *Global Business*, ●*Sports Roundup* and *Reporting Religion*. The final 60 minutes of a 19-hour block of programming. On 3255, 6190 and 15400 kHz.

■BBC World Service for East and Southeast Asia and the Pacific. Identical to the mainstream service for the Americas (sans *Caribbean Report*). To East Asia on 5965, 6110 (winter), 6195 and (summer) 11945 kHz; to Southeast Asia on 3915, 6195 and 9740 kHz; and to Australasia on 5975 and 9740 kHz.

Radio Exterior de España ("Spanish National Radio"). *News*, followed Monday through Friday by *Panorama* (Spanish popular music, commentary, press review and weather), then a couple of features: *Sports Spotlight* and *Cultural Encounters* (Monday); *People of Today* and *Entertainment in Spain* (Tuesday); *As Others See Us* and, biweekly, *The Natural World* or *Science Desk* (Wednesday); *Economic Report* and *Cultural Clippings* (Thursday); and *Window on Spain* and *Review of the Arts* (Friday). The broadcast ends with a language course, *Spanish by Radio*. On weekends, there's Saturday's *Hall of Fame*, *Distance Unknown* (for radio enthusiasts) and *Gallery of Spanish Voices*; replaced Sunday by *Visitors' Book*, *Great Figures in Flamenco* and *Radio Club*. One hour to Europe on 6125 kHz, and to Africa on 11775 kHz.

Radio Ukraine International. Summer only at this time. *News*, commentary, reports and interviews, covering multiple aspects of Ukrainian life. Saturdays feature a listener-response program, and most of Sunday's broadcast is a showpiece for Ukrainian music. Sixty minutes to Europe, the Mideast and West Asia on 6020, 9640 and 11950 kHz. One hour later in winter.

Radio Canada International. Winter, the first 60 minutes of a two-hour broadcast;

summer, the last hour of the same. Winter weekdays, *News* is followed by *Spectrum* (current events), which is replaced Saturday by *Venture Canada* and ●*Earth Watch*, and Sunday by *Arts in Canada* and *The Mailbag*, a listener-response program. Monday through Friday summer, it's the CBC domestic service's ●*The World at Six* and ●*As It Happens*. Weekend fare consists of Saturday's ●*Quirks and Quarks,* and Sunday's *Madly Off in All Directions* and *The Inside Track*. To Europe and Africa winter on 5995, 7235, 9770, 9805, 11945, 13650, 13690, 15325 and 17820 kHz; and summer on 5995, 7235, 13650, 13670, 15325, 17820 and 17870 kHz. Some of these are also audible in parts of North America.

Radio Prague, Czech Republic. Winter only at this time. See 2000 for program details. *News* and features reflecting Czech life and culture. A half hour to western Europe (and easily audible in parts of eastern North America) on 5930 kHz, and to South Asia and Australasia on 9435 kHz.

Radio Bulgaria. This time summer only. Starts with *news*, then Monday through Friday there's *Events and Developments*, replaced Saturday by *Views Behind the News* and Sunday by 15 minutes of Bulgarian exotica in ●*Folk Studio*. Additional features include *Walks and Talks* (Monday), *Magazine Economy* (Tuesday), *Arts and Artists* (Wednesday), *History Club* (Thursday), *The Way We Live* (Friday) and *DX Programme*, a Saturday slot for radio enthusiasts. Sunday, look for *Answering Your Letters*, a listener response show. Tuesday through Saturday, the broadcast ends with *Keyword Bulgaria*. Sixty minutes to Europe on 9400 and 11700 kHz. One hour later during winter.

China Radio International. Repeat of the 2000 transmission; see there for specifics. One hour to Europe winter on 5965 and 9535 kHz, and summer on 11790 and 15110 kHz. A 30-minute shortened version is also available to eastern and southern Africa on 11735 and 13640 (or 15500) kHz.

Voice of Russia World Service. Winter only at this time. *News*, then *Science and*

Engineering (Monday and Thursday), the business-oriented *Newmarket* (Wednesday and Saturday), *Moscow Mailbag* (Tuesday and Friday) or Sunday's sublime ●*Music and Musicians*. Best of the second half hour are Thursday's ●*Folk Box* and Tuesday's ●*Music at Your Request* (may alternate with *Yours For the Asking*). Other features include *Songs from Russia* (Monday), Friday's *Jazz Show* and Saturday's *Russian by Radio*. The final hour for Europe on 5940, 5965, 7300, 9890 and 15735 kHz, and one hour earlier in summer. Some of these channels are audible in eastern North America.

Radio Budapest, Hungary. Summer only at this time. *News* and features, most of which are broadcast on a non-regular basis. Thirty minutes to Europe on 6025 kHz. One hour later in winter.

Radio Japan. *News*, then Monday through Friday (Tuesday through Saturday local date in Asia and Australasia) there's *Asian Top News*. This is followed by a 35-minute feature: ●*Music Journey Around Japan* (a look at regional music and customs, Monday), Japanese language lessons (Tuesday and Thursday), *Unforgettable Musical Masterpieces* (postwar popular songs, Wednesday), and *Music Beat* (Japanese popular music, Friday). *Weekend Square* fills the Saturday slot, and *Hello from Tokyo* is aired Sunday. Sixty minutes to Europe on 6115, 6180 (winter), 9725 and (summer) 9810 kHz; to Australasia on 11850 and 11920 (or 6035) kHz; to western North America on 17825 kHz; and to Hawaii on 21670 kHz. The broadcast on 17825 kHz may differ somewhat from the other transmissions, and may include alternative features.

Radio Australia. *World News*, then Sunday through Thursday it's current events in *AM* (replaced Friday by a listener-response program, *Feedback*). Next, on the half-hour, there's a daily feature. Take your pick from *Earthbeat* (environment, Sunday); *Innovations* (the invented and innovative, Monday and Friday); *Arts Australia* (culture, Tuesday) *Rural Reporter* (regional Australia, Wednesday); and *Book Talk* (new books, Thursday). The Saturday slot is filled by the second hour of *Australia All*

Over. Continuous to the Pacific on 7240, 9660, 11880, 12080, 17715 and 21740 kHz; and to East and Southeast Asia (till 2130) on 9500 kHz. Listeners in western North America can try 11880, 17715 and 21740 kHz.

■**Deutsche Welle,** Germany. *News*, then weekdays (Tuesday through Saturday in the target areas) it's ●*NewsLink* followed by a feature. Monday, it's either *Development Forum* or *Women on the Move*; Tuesday, there's a look at ●*Man and Environment*; Wednesday's slot is ●*Insight*; Thursday, there's *Living in Germany*; and Friday's offering is *Spotlight on Sport*. Saturday's slots are *Weekend Review* (first edition) and *Mailbag*, replaced Sunday by *Weekend Review* (second edition) and *Arts on the Air*. Forty-five minutes to Southeast Asia and Australasia, winter on 9765, 15135 and 17560 kHz; and midyear on 9670, 9765 and 11915 kHz. An almost identical broadcast (except that Saturday's *Mailbag* is replaced by *African Kaleidoscope*) goes out simultaneously to West Africa, and is audible in much of eastern North America. Winter on 9615, 9690 and 15410 kHz; and summer on 9875, 11865 and 15135 kHz. In North America, try 15410 kHz in winter and 15135 kHz in summer.

Radio Romania International. *News*, commentary, press review and features. Regular spots include *Youth Club* (Tuesday), *Romanian Musicians* (Wednesday), and Thursday's *Listeners' Letterbox* and ●*Skylark* (Romanian folk music). Fifty-five minutes to Europe winter on 5955, 7195, 7215 and 9690 kHz; and summer on 11740, 11940, 15105 and 15180 kHz.

Radio Korea International, South Korea. Starts with *news*, followed Monday through Wednesday by *Economic News Briefs*. The remainder of the broadcast is taken up by a feature: *Shortwave Feedback* (Sunday), *Seoul Calling* (Monday and Tuesday), *Pulse of Korea* (Wednesday), *From Us to You* (Thursday), *Let's Sing Together* (Friday) and *Weekly News Focus* (Saturday). Thirty minutes to Europe summer on 3980 kHz, and one hour later in winter. Also at this time, a repeat of the 1900 one-hour broadcast to East Asia is beamed to Europe year round on 6480 and 15575 kHz.

21:00–21:30

Radio For Peace International, Costa Rica. Continues at this hour with a potpourri of United Nations, counterculture and other programs. Audible in Europe and North America on 15050 and (upper sideband) 21815 kHz.

HCJB—Voice of the Andes, Ecuador. The final sixty minutes of a three-hour block of predominantly religious programming to Europe on 17660 kHz.

Radio Habana Cuba. The final half hour of a 60-minute package of *news* (predominantly about Cuba and Latin America), short features about Cuba and the Cubans, and some enjoyable Cuban music. To Europe winter on 9550 kHz and summer on 13750 kHz.

Voice of America. For Africa and Australasia, it's *News Now*—a series of reports and features covering a multitude of topics. Also available to the Mideast and North Africa on 6040, 9535 (summer) and 9760 kHz. In Africa, tune to 6035, 7375, 7415, 11715, 11975, 13710, 15410, 15445, 15580 and 17725 kHz (some of which are seasonal); and in Southeast Asia and the Pacific to 11870, 15185 and 17735 kHz.

Global Sound Kitchen, United Kingdom. Summer only at this time. The first 60-minutes of a four-hour weekend show from the people at Virgin Radio, featuring dance and new music. Not for the majority of listeners, but the program has a faithful following among the younger generation. Friday and Saturday to Europe on 3955, 6140 and 7325 kHz.

All India Radio. Continues to Western Europe on 7410, 9650 and 9950 kHz; and to Australasia on 7150, 9910, 11620 and 11715 kHz. Look for some authentic Indian music from 2115 onwards. The European frequencies are audible in parts of eastern North America, while those for Australasia are also heard in Southeast Asia.

Armenian National Radio/Voice of Armenia. Winter only at this time. Actually starts at 2055 and mainly of interest to Armenians abroad. Twenty minutes of Armenian *news* and culture. To Europe on 9965 kHz, and sometimes audible in eastern North America. One hour earlier in summer.

CFRX-CFRB, Toronto, Canada. If you live in the northeastern United States or southeastern Canada, try this pleasant little local station, usually audible for hundreds of miles/kilometers during daylight hours on 6070 kHz. Winter weekdays at this time, you can hear ●*The World Today* (summer, starts at 2000)—three hours of news, sport and interviews.

21:15

Radio Damascus, Syria. Actually starts at 2110. *News*, a daily press review, and a variety of features (depending on the day of the week) at approximately 2130 and 2145. These include *Arab Profile* and *Economic Affairs* (Sunday), *Camera and Masks* and *Selected Readings* (Monday), *Reflections* and *Back on the Stage* (Tuesday), *Listeners Overseas* and *Palestine Talking* (Wednesday), *From the World Press* and *Arab Women in Focus* (Thursday), *Arab Newsweek* and *From Our Literature* (Friday), and *Human Rights* and *Syria and the World* (Saturday). The transmission also contains Syrian and some western popular music. Sixty minutes to North America and Australasia on 12085 and 13610 (or 15095) kHz.

BBC World Service for the Caribbean. *Caribbean Report,* although intended for listeners in the area, can also be clearly heard throughout much of eastern North America. This brief, 15-minute program provides comprehensive coverage of Caribbean economic and political affairs, both within and outside the region. Monday through Friday only, on 5975, 11675 and 15390 kHz.

Radio Cairo, Egypt. The start of a 90-minute broadcast highlighting Arab and Egyptian themes. The initial quarter-hour of general programming is followed by *news*, commentary and political items. This in turn is followed by a cultural program until 2215, when the station again reverts to more general fare. A big signal to Europe on 9990 kHz.

WJCR, Upton, Kentucky. Continuous gospel music to North America on 7490 and 13595 kHz. Other U.S. religious broadcasters operating at this hour include **WWCR** on 13845 and 15685 and kHz, **KTBN** on 15590 kHz, and **WHRI-World Harvest Radio** on 13760 kHz. Traditionalist Catholic programming is available from **WEWN** on 11875 and 13615 kHz.

AFRTS Shortwave, USA. Network news, live sports, music and features in the upper-sideband mode from the Armed Forces Radio & Television Service. Transmitted from modestly powered U.S. Navy stations around the globe. Try 4278.5, 4319, 4993, 5765, 6350, 6458.5, 10320, 10940.5, 12579, 12689.5 and 13362 kHz.

21:30

BBC World Service for the Falkland Islands. *Calling the Falklands* has been running for so long that it has almost ceased to be the broadcasting curiosity it used to be. This twice-weekly transmission for a small community in the South Atlantic consists of news and short features, often on unusual topics. With subjects ranging from Argentinian politics to wayward albatrosses, this is decidedly different from the usual world band fare. Audible for 15 minutes Tuesday and Friday on 11680 kHz, and easily heard in parts of eastern North America.

Radio Croatia. Winter only at this time. Approximately 15 minutes of news from and about Croatia, and part of a longer broadcast predominantly in Croatian. To the Mideast and southern Africa on 9405 or 11605 kHz. One hour earlier in summer.

Radio Austria International. Summer only at this time. Thirty minutes of news and human-interest stories in ●*Report from Austria.* A good source of national and

regional news. To Europe on 5945 and 6155 kHz. One hour later during winter.

Radio Prague, Czech Republic. Summer only at this time. See 2230 for program details. *News* and features dealing with Czech life and culture. A half hour to Australasia on 11600 kHz, and to West Africa on 15545 kHz.

Radio Budapest, Hungary. This time summer only. *News* and features, a few of which are broadcast on a regular basis. Thirty minutes to Europe on 3975 kHz. One hour later in winter.

■**Wales Radio International.** Winter Fridays only at this time. News, interviews and music from the land of harps and Dylan Thomas. Thirty minutes to Europe on 6010 kHz, and one hour earlier in summer.

Radio Tashkent, Uzbekistan. Thirty minutes of *news*, commentary and features, plus some exotic Uzbek music. To Europe winter on 7105 and 9540 kHz, and summer on 9540 and 9545 kHz.

Radio Tirana, Albania. Summer only at this time. *News*, short features and some lively Albanian music. Thirty minutes to Europe on 7160 and 9635 kHz. One hour later in winter.

Voice of the Islamic Republic of Iran. Sixty minutes of *news*, commentary and features with a distinctly Islamic slant. To Australasia on 9745 (winter), 11740 and (summer) 13745 kHz. Frequency usage may vary.

Voice of Turkey. This time winter only. *News*, followed by *Review of the Turkish Press* and features (some of them unusual) with a strong local flavor. Selections of Turkish popular and classical music complete the program. Fifty minutes to Southeast Asia and Australasia on 9525 kHz. One hour earlier in summer.

Radio Sweden. Summer only at this time. Thirty minutes of predominantly Scandinavian fare (see 2230 for specifics). To Europe (and also heard in Africa and the Mideast) on 6065 and 9435 kHz, and to Southeast Asia and Australasia on 15255 kHz.

22:00

■**BBC World Service for the Americas.** Monday through Friday, an hour of news reporting in *The World Today*. Weekends, it's reduced to 30 minutes and followed by Saturday's ●*From Our Own Correspondent* or Sunday's *Agenda*. Continuous programming to North America and the Caribbean on 5975, 6175 and 9590 kHz.

BBC World Service for Europe. News and current events in *The World Today*. Reduced to 30 minutes on Saturday, when it is followed by ●*From Our Own Correspondent*. The final hour of a 19-hour block of programming to Europe and North Africa. On 6195 kHz.

■**BBC World Service for East and Southeast Asia and the Pacific.** Sunday through Thursday (local Asian weekdays), it's a full hour of news and current events in ●*The World Today*. Friday and Saturday, there's 30 minutes of the same, followed by ●*People and Politics* and ●*From Our Own Correspondent*, respectively. Continuous to East Asia on 5965, 6195 and 11955 kHz; to Southeast Asia on 6195, 7110, 9660 and 11955 kHz; and to Australasia on 9660, 11955 and 12080 kHz.

Radio Bulgaria. This time winter only. See 2100 for specifics. News and culture from the Balkans—don't miss ●*Folk Studio* (Bulgarian music) at 2210 Sunday. Sixty minutes to Europe, also heard in parts of eastern North America, on 7535 and 7545 kHz. One hour earlier in summer.

Radio Cairo, Egypt. The second half of a 90-minute broadcast to Europe on 9990 kHz; see 2115 for program details.

China Radio International. Repeat of the 2000 transmission; see there for specifics. One hour to Europe, winter on 7170 kHz and summer on 9880 kHz.

Voice of America. The beginning of a three-hour block of programs to East and Southeast Asia and the Pacific. The ubiquitous *News Now*—news and reports on current events, sports, science, business, entertainment and more. To East and Southeast Asia on 7215, 9705, 9770, 11760, 15185, 15290, 15305, 17735 and 17820 kHz; and to Australasia on 15185, 15305 and 17735 kHz. The first half hour is also available weekday evenings to Africa on 7340, 7375 and 7415 kHz.

Radio Australia. *News*, followed Sunday through Thursday by *AM* (current events). The hour is rounded off with a 20-minute music feature. The lineup starts with Sunday's sampling from different cultures, *Music Deli*, and ends with Thursday's *Australian Country Style*. In-between, choose from *Australian Music Show* (Monday); *At Your Request* (Tuesday); and *Blacktracker* (aboriginal music, Wednesday). Friday's features are *Jazz Notes* and a later-than-usual edition of *AM*; Saturday, it's the third hour of *Australia All Over*. Continuous programming to the Pacific on 17715, 17795 and 21740 kHz. Also audible in parts of western North America.

Radio Taipei International, Taiwan. Opens with 15 minutes of *News*, and except for Sunday (when it's *Mailbag Time*), closes with *Let's Learn Chinese*, which has a series of segments for beginning, intermediate and advanced learners. In between, look for features—one or two, depending on the day of the week: ● *Jade Bells and Bamboo Pipes* (Taiwanese music, Monday), *People* and *Trends* (Tuesday), *Taiwan Today* and *Stage and Screen* (Wednesday), *Journey into Chinese Culture* and *Hot Spots* (Thursday), and *Taipei Magazine* coupled with *East Meets West* on Friday. Weekends, the Saturday offerings are *Kaleidoscope* and *Reflections*, with Sunday's menu featuring *Great Wall Forum* and *Food, Poetry and Others*. Sixty minutes to western Europe, winter on 5810 and 9985 kHz, and summer on 11565 and 15600 kHz.

Radio Tirana, Albania. Winter only at this time. Thirty minutes of news, short features and Albanian music. To Europe on 7130 and 9540 kHz. One hour earlier in summer.

Radio Habana Cuba. Sixty minutes of *news* (mainly about Cuba and Latin America), short features and some Cuban music. To the Caribbean and southern United States on 9550 kHz, and to eastern North America and Europe on (winter) 9505 and (summer) 13720 kHz upper sideband.

Radio Budapest, Hungary. Winter only at this time; see 2100 for specifics. Thirty minutes to Europe on 6025 kHz. One hour earlier in summer.

Voice of Turkey. Summer only at this time. *News*, followed by *Review of the Turkish Press* and features with a strong local flavor. Selections of Turkish popular and classical music complete the program. Fifty minutes to Europe on 7190 and 13640 kHz, and to eastern North America on 13640 kHz. One hour later during winter.

Radio Canada International. This time winter only. The second of two hours to Europe and Africa. Monday through Friday, it's the CBC domestic service's ●*The World at Six* and 30 minutes of ●*As It Happens*. Weekend fare consists of Saturday's popular ●*Quirks and Quarks* (science), replaced Sunday by *Madly Off in All Directions* (mainly of appeal to Canadians abroad) and *The Inside Track*. On 5995, 7235, 9805, 13690 and 15325 kHz. For a separate summer service, see the following item.

Radio Canada International. Summer only at this hour, and a relay of CBC domestic programming. Monday through Friday it's ●*The World at Six*; Saturday and Sunday, *The World This Weekend*. On the half-hour there's the weekday ●*As It Happens*, Saturday's ●*The Mystery Project* or Sunday's *Madly Off in All Directions*. Sixty minutes to North America on 5960, 9755 and 13670 kHz. One hour later in winter. For a separate year-round service to Asia, see the next item.

Radio Canada International. Monday through Friday, it's ●*The World At Six*; Saturday and Sunday summer, *The World This Weekend*. Winter weekends, look for Saturday's ●*Earth Watch* and Sunday's *The Inside Track*. Thirty minutes winter to Southeast Asia on 11705 kHz, and summer on 17835 kHz.

RAI International—Radio Roma, Italy. Approximately ten minutes of *news* followed

22:00–23:00

by a quarter-hour feature (usually music). Twenty-five minutes to East Asia on 9675, 11900 and (summer) 15240 kHz.

Global Sound Kitchen, United Kingdom. Part of a four-hour weekend show from the people at Virgin Radio, featuring dance and new music. Friday and Saturday to Europe, winter on 3955, 6170 and 7165 kHz, and summer on 3955, 6140 and 7325 kHz. Audible to a certain extent in eastern North America.

Radio Korea International, South Korea. Winter only at this hour. Starts with *news*, followed Monday through Wednesday by *Economic News Briefs*. The remainder of the broadcast is taken up by a feature: *Shortwave Feedback* (Sunday), *Seoul Calling* (Monday and Tuesday), *Pulse of Korea* (Wednesday), *From Us to You* (Thursday), *Let's Sing Together* (Friday) and *Weekly News Focus* (Saturday). Thirty minutes to Europe on 3980 kHz, and one hour earlier in summer.

Radio Ukraine International. Winter only at this time. A potpourri of things Ukrainian, with the Sunday broadcast often featuring some excellent music. Sixty minutes to Europe and beyond on 5905, 6020, 6080 and 9560 kHz. Often mediocre reception due to financial and technical limitations. One hour earlier in summer.

Radio For Peace International, Costa Rica. Continues with counterculture and social-conscience programs. Audible in Europe and North America on 15050 and (upper sideband) 21815 kHz.

XERMX—Radio México Internacional. Summer only at this time. Monday through Friday, there's an English summary of the Spanish-language *Antena Radio*, replaced Saturday by *Regional Roots and Rhythms* and Sunday by *Mirror of Mexico*. Best heard in western and southern parts of the United States on 5985 and 9705 kHz. One hour later in winter.

All India Radio. The final half-hour of a transmission to Western Europe and Australasia, consisting mainly of news-related fare. To Europe on 7410, 9650 and 9950 kHz; and to Australasia on 7150, 9910, 11620 and 11715 kHz. Frequencies for Europe are audible in parts of eastern North America, while those for Australasia are also heard in Southeast Asia.

WJCR, Upton, Kentucky. Continues with country gospel music to North America on 7490 and 13595 kHz. Other U.S. religious broadcasters heard at this hour include **WWCR** on 13845 kHz, **KAIJ** on 13815 kHz, **KTBN** on 15590 kHz, and **WHRI-World Harvest Radio** on 5745 kHz. For traditionalist Catholic programming, try **WEWN** on 9355 and 13615 kHz.

CFRX-CFRB, Toronto, Canada. See 2100.

AFRTS Shortwave, USA. Network news, live sports, music and features in the upper-sideband mode from the Armed Forces Radio & Television Service. Transmitted from modestly powered U.S. Navy stations around the globe. Try 4278.5, 4319, 4993, 5765, 6350, 6458.5, 10320, 10940.5, 12579, 12689.5 and 13362 kHz.

22:30

Radio Sweden. Winter only at this time. Monday through Friday, it's *news* and features in *Sixty Degrees North*, concentrating heavily on Scandinavian topics. Monday's theme is sports; Tuesday brings the latest in electronic media news; Wednesday, there's *Money Matters*; Thursday features ecology or science and technology; and Friday offers a review of the week's news. Saturday's slot is filled by *Spectrum* (arts) or *Sweden Today*, and Sunday fare consists of *In Touch with Stockholm* (a listener-response program) or the musical *Sounds Nordic*. Thirty minutes to Europe on 6065 and 7325 kHz. One hour earlier in summer.

Radio Austria International. Winter only at this time. The informative and well-presented ●*Report from Austria*. Ample coverage of national and regional issues. Thirty minutes to Europe on 5945 and 6155 kHz. One hour earlier in summer.

Radio Budapest, Hungary. Winter only at this time. *News* and features, few of which are broadcast on a regular basis. Thirty minutes to Europe on 3975 kHz. One hour earlier in summer.

Radio Vlaanderen Internationaal, Belgium. Summer only at this time. Weekdays, starts with *News*, then *Belgium Today*, *Press Review* and features. The lineup includes *Focus on Europe* and *Sports* (Monday), *Green Society* (Tuesday), *The Arts* (Wednesday and Friday), *Around Town* (Wednesday), *Economics* and *International Report* (Thursday), and Friday's *Tourism*. Closes with *Soundbox*. These are replaced Saturday by *Music from Flanders*, and Sunday by *Radio World*, *Tourism*, *Brussels 1043* (a listener-response program) and *Soundbox*. Thirty minutes to North America winter on 13670 kHz, and summer on 15565 kHz.

Radio Prague, Czech Republic. *News*, then Monday through Friday there's *Current Affairs*, followed by one or more features. Early in the week there's *Spotlight* (a Monday look at the Czech regions), Tuesday's *Talking Point* (issues), and Wednesday's *Czechs in History*. The Thursday airing is *Economic Report*, and *Mailbag* fills the Friday slot. Saturday's offering is a highly enjoyable musical feature, replaced Sunday by *A Letter from Prague*, *From the Weeklies* and *Readings from Czech Literature*. A half hour to eastern North America winter on 7345 kHz, and summer on 11600 and 15545 kHz; also to West Africa winter on 9435 kHz.

22:45

All India Radio. The first 15 minutes of a much longer broadcast, consisting of Indian music, regional and international *news*, commentary, and a variety of talks and features of general interest. Continuous till 0045. To East Asia on 7410, 9950 and 11620 kHz; and to Southeast Asia on 9705 kHz.

Vatican Radio. Twenty minutes of religious and secular programming to East and Southeast Asia and Australasia on 7305, 9600 and 11830 kHz, some of them seasonal.

23:00

■**BBC World Service for the Americas.** Monday through Friday, opens with five minutes of *news*. Next comes the popular and long-running ●*Outlook*, and the hour is rounded off with a 15-minute feature (very much a mixed bag). Saturday brings ●*Play of the Week* (world theater), replaced Sunday by *The World Today* and *Classical Request*. Continuous to North America and the Caribbean on 5975, 6175 and 9590 kHz.

■**BBC World Service for East and Southeast Asia and the Pacific.** Sunday through Thursday (weekday mornings in Asia), it's the second hour of *The World Today*, a breakfast news show for the region. On the remaining days there's 30 minutes of the same, followed by Friday's *Global Business* or Saturday's *Arts in Action*. Continuous to East Asia on 5965, 6035, 6195, 11945, 11955 and 15280 kHz; to Southeast Asia on 3915, 6195, 7110 and 11955 kHz; and to Australasia on 11955 kHz.

Voice of Turkey. Winter only at this hour. See 2200 for program details. Fifty minutes to Europe on 6135 and 9655 kHz, and to eastern North America on 9655 kHz. One hour earlier in summer.

■**Deutsche Welle,** Germany. Repeat of the 2100 broadcast to Southeast Asia and Australasia (see there for specifics). Forty-five minutes to South and Southeast Asia, winter on 6010, 9815 and 13690 kHz; and summer on 9715, 9815 and 11965 kHz.

Radio Australia. *World News*, followed Monday through Thursday by *Asia Pacific* (replaced Friday by *Book Reading*, and Sunday by *Correspondents' Reports*). On the half-hour, look for a feature. *Media Report* occupies the Sunday slot, and is replaced Monday by *The Sports Factor*. Then come Tuesday's *Health Report*, Wednesday's *Law Report*, Thursday's *Religion Report*, and Friday's *Week's End*. Not very original, but you know what you're getting. Saturday, there's the fourth and final hour of *Australia All Over*. Continuous to the Pacific on 9660, 12080, 17715, 17795 and 21740 kHz. Listen-

23:00–23:30

ers in western North America should try the last three channels, especially in summer.

Radio Canada International. Summer weekdays, the final hour of ●*As It Happens* (a shorter edition on Fridays is complemented by *C'est la Vie*); winter, the first 30 minutes of the same, preceded by the up-to-the-minute *news* program ●*World at Six*. Summer weekends, look for ●*Global Village* (world music, Saturday) and *Roots and Wings* (eclectic music, Sunday). These are replaced winter by *The World This Weekend* (both days), ●*Mystery Project* (Saturday) and *The Inside Track* (Sunday). To eastern North America on 5960 and 9755 kHz, with 13670 kHz also available in summer. For the rest of North America and the Caribbean, try some additional weekend frequencies: 6040, 9535 and 11865 kHz in winter; and 11895, 15305 and 17695 kHz in summer.

China Radio International. Starts with *News*, and weekdays continues with in-depth reports. The remainder of the broadcast is made up of features. Regular shows include *People in the Know* (Monday), *Sportsworld* (Tuesday), *China Horizons* (Wednesday), *Voices from Other Lands* (Thursday) and Friday's *Life in China*. Saturday, there's *Global Review* and *Listeners' Garden* (reports, music and a Chinese language lesson), replaced Sunday by *Report from Developing Countries* and *In the Spotlight*. Sixty minutes to the Caribbean and southern United States on 5990 kHz, via CRI's Cuban relay.

Radio For Peace International, Costa Rica. The final 60 minutes of a continuous eight-hour block of United Nations, counter-culture, social-conscience and New Age programming. Audible in Europe and the Americas on 15050 and (upper sideband) 21815 kHz. A repeat eight-hour broadcast starts at 0000.

Radio Cairo, Egypt. The first hour of a 90-minute broadcast featuring Arab and Egyptian themes. Music, too. There are also quizzes, mailbag shows, and answers to listeners' questions. Now uses 500 kilowatts and much improved audio. Easy reception in eastern North America on 9900 kHz.

Radio Romania International. *News*, commentary and features, plus some enjoyable Romanian music. Fifty-five minutes to Europe on 7195 (winter), 9690 and (summer) 11830 kHz; also to eastern North America winter on 9570 and 11940 kHz, and summer on 11775 and 15105 kHz.

Global Sound Kitchen, United Kingdom. Continues with dance and new music for a European audience. Friday and Saturday only, winter on 3955, 6170 and 7165 kHz, and summer on 3955, 6140 and 7325 kHz. Audible to some extent in eastern North America.

Radio Bulgaria. Summer only at this time. *News*, music and features. Monday through Friday (weekday evenings in North America), the news is followed by *Events and Developments*, replaced Saturday by *Views Behind the News* and Sunday by the enjoyable and exotic ●*Folk Studio*. The next slot consists of weekly features. Take your pick from *Plaza/Walks and Talks* (Sunday), *Magazine Economy* (Monday), *Arts and Artists* (Tuesday), *History Club* (Wednesday), *The Way We Live* (Thursday), *DX Programme* (Friday) and *Answering Your Letters*, a listener response show, on Saturday. Monday through Saturday, the broadcast ends with *Keyword Bulgaria*. Sixty minutes to eastern North America on 9400 and 11700 kHz. One hour later during winter.

XERMX—Radio México Internacional. Winter weekdays, there's an English summary of the Spanish-language *Antena Radio*, replaced Saturday by *Regional Roots and Rhythms* and Sunday by *Mirror of Mexico*. The summer lineup features *Mosaic of Mexico* (Monday and Friday), *DXperience* (a show for radio enthusiasts, Tuesday and Sunday), *Regional Roots and Rhythms* (Wednesday), *Mirror of Mexico* (Thursday) and Saturday's *Creators of Mexican Art*. Thirty minutes to North America on 9705 kHz, and best heard in western and southern parts of the United States.

Voice of America. Continues with programs aimed at East Asia and the Pacific on the same frequencies as at 2200.

WJCR, Upton, Kentucky. Continuous country gospel music to North America on 7490 and

13595 kHz. Other U.S. religious broadcasters heard at this time include **WWCR** on 13845 kHz, **KAIJ** on 13815 kHz, **KTBN** on 15590 kHz, and **WHRI-World Harvest Radio** on 5745 kHz. For traditionalist Catholic programming, tune **WEWN** on 9355 and 13615 kHz.

AFRTS Shortwave, USA. Network news, live sports, music and features in the upper-sideband mode from the Armed Forces Radio & Television Service. Transmitted from modestly powered U.S. Navy stations around the globe. Try 4278.5, 4319, 4993, 5765, 6350, 6458.5, 10320, 10940.5, 12579, 12689.5 and 13362 kHz.

23:30

■**Radio Netherlands.** *News*, followed Monday through Friday by ●*Newsline*, then a feature program. Select offerings include the well produced ●*Research File* (science, Monday); *Music 52-15* (eclectic, Tuesday); the outstanding ●*Documentary* (Wednesday); *Media Network* (Thursday); and ●*A Good Life*

(Friday). The Saturday offerings are *Europe Unzipped*, *Insight* and *Aural Tapestry*, replaced Sunday by *Sincerely Yours*, a program preview and *Dutch Horizons*. The first of two hours to North America on 6165 and 9845 kHz.

Radio Prague, Czech Republic. Winter only at this time; see 2230 for program specifics. A half hour to eastern North America on 7345 and 9345 kHz.

All India Radio. Continuous programming to East and Southeast Asia. A potpourri of *news*, commentary, features and exotic Indian music. To East Asia on 7410, 9950 and 11620 kHz; and to Southeast Asia on 9705 kHz.

Voice of Vietnam. *News*, then *Commentary* or *Weekly Review*. These are followed by short features and some pleasant Vietnamese music. A half hour to Southeast Asia (often heard in Europe) on 9840 and 12020 kHz. Frequencies may vary slightly.

———————————————

Prepared by Don Swampo and the staff of PASSPORT TO WORLD BAND RADIO.

Addresses PLUS—2001

Station Email and Postal Addresses . . . PLUS Websites, Webcasts, Who's Who, Phones, Faxes, Bureaus, Future Plans, Items for Sale, Giveaways . . . PLUS Summer and Winter Times in Each Country!

PASSPORT usually shows how stations reach out to you, but Addresses PLUS flips things around—it shows how you can reach out to stations. It also reveals ways besides world band that stations can inform and entertain you.

"Applause" Replies

When radio broadcasting was in its infancy, listeners sent in "applause" cards to inform stations about reception and program quality. To say "thanks," stations would reply with a letter or illustrated card verifying ("QSLing") that the station the listener reported hearing was, in fact, theirs. While they were at it, some would also throw in a free souvenir—a station calendar, perhaps, or a pennant or sticker.

This is still being done today to some extent. You can see how to provide technical feedback by looking under Verification in the glossary farther back in this book, then making use of Addresses PLUS for contact specifics.

Some stations sell stuff, too—usually radios, CDs, publications, clothing, tote bags, caps, watches, clocks, pens, knives, letter openers, lighters, refrigerator magnets and keyrings.

One-eyed bell ringer in Thimpu, Bhutan.
M. Guha

Paying Postfolk

Most stations reply to listener correspondence—even email—through the postal system. That way, they can send out printed schedules, verification cards and other "hands-on" souvenirs. Big stations usually do so for free, but smaller ones often want to be reimbursed for postage costs.

Most effective, especially for Latin American and Indonesian stations, is to enclose some unused (mint) stamps from the station's country. These are available from Plum's Airmail Postage, 12 Glenn Road, Flemington NJ 08822 USA, phone +1 (908) 788-1020, fax +1 (908) 782 2612. One way to help ensure your return-postage stamps will be put to the intended use is to affix them onto a pre-addressed return airmail envelope. The result is a self-addressed stamped envelope, or SASE as it is referred to in Addresses PLUS.

You can also prompt reluctant stations by donating one or more U.S. dollars, preferably hidden from prying eyes by a piece of foil-covered carbon paper or the like. Registration helps, too, as cash tends to get stolen. Additionally, International Reply Coupons (IRCs), which recipients may exchange locally for air or surface stamps, are available at many post offices worldwide. Thing is, they're relatively costly, are not fully effective, and aren't accepted by postal authorities in some countries.

Some stations provide free cards and stickers. Others sell native recordings and products.

Bhutan has but one primitive airport—Paro. Anything more elaborate would encourage greater contact with the outside world.
M. Guha

Stamp Out Crime

Yes, even in 2001 mail theft is a problem in several countries. We identify these, and for each one offer proven ways to help avoid theft. Remember that some postal employees are stamp collectors, and in certain countries they freely steal mail with unusual stamps. When in doubt, use everyday stamps or, even better, a postal meter or PC-generated postage. Another option is to use an aerogram.

¿Que Hora Es?

World Time, explained elsewhere in this book, is essential if you want to find out when your favorite station is on. But if you want to know what time it is in any given country, World Time and Addresses PLUS work together to give you local times within each country.

So that you don't have to wrestle with seasonal changes in your own time, we give local times for each country in terms of hours' difference from World Time, which stays the same year-round. For example, if you look below under "Algeria," you'll see that country is World Time +1;

that is, one hour ahead of World Time. So, if World Time is 1200, the local time in Algeria is 1300 (1:00 PM). On the other hand, México City is World Time -6; that is, six hours behind World Time. If World Time is 1200, in México City it's 6:00 AM.

Times shown in parentheses are for the middle of the year—roughly April-October; specific dates of seasonal-time changeovers for individual countries can be obtained (U.S. callers only) by dialing the OAG toll-free (800) 342-5624 during working hours, or (worldwide) fax +1 (630) 574 6565. On the Web, go to www.webexhibits.org/daylightsaving/g.html.

Spotted Something New?

Has something changed since we went to press? A missing detail? Please let us know! Your update information, especially photocopies of material received from stations, is highly valued. Contact the IBS Editorial Office, Box 300, Penn's Park, PA 18943 USA, fax +1 (215) 598 3794, email addresses@passband.com.

Muchas gracias to the kindly folks and helpful organizations mentioned at the end of this chapter for their tireless cooperation in the preparation of this section. Without you, none of this would have been possible.

Using PASSPORT's Addresses PLUS Section

Stations included: All stations are listed if known to reply, however erratically. Also, new stations which possibly may reply to correspondence from listeners.

Leased-time programs: Private organizations/NGOs that lease air time, but which possess no world band transmitters of their own, are usually not listed. However, they may be reached via the stations over which they are heard.

Postal addresses. Communications addresses are given. These sometimes differ from the physical transmitter locations given in the Blue Pages.

Email addresses and Websites. Given in Internet format. Periods, commas and semicolons at the end of an address listing are normal sentence punctuation, not part of the address, and "http://" is used only when there is no "www."

Phone and fax numbers. To help avoid confusion, telephone numbers are given with hyphens, fax numbers without. All are configured for international dialing once you add your country's International access code (011 in the United States and Canada, 010 in the United Kingdom, and so on). For domestic dialing within countries outside the United States, Canada and the Caribbean, replace the country code (1-3 digits preceded by a "+") by a zero.

Giveaways. If you want freebies, say so politely in your correspondence. These are usually available until supplies run out.

Webcasting. World band stations which simulcast and/or provide archived

programming over the Internet are indicated by 🕮.

Unless otherwise indicated, stations:

- Reply regularly within six months to most listeners' correspondence in English.

- Provide, upon request, free station schedules and verification ("QSL") postcards or letters (see "Verification" in the glossary for further information). We specify when other items are available for free or for purchase.

- Do not require compensation for postage costs incurred in replying to you. Where compensation is required, details are provided.

Local times. These are given in difference from World Time. For example, "World Time -5" means that if you subtract five hours from World Time, you'll get the local time in that country. Thus, if it were 1100 World Time, it would be 0600 local time in that country. Times in (parentheses) are for the middle of the year—roughly April-October. For exact changeover dates, see above explanatory paragraph.

Afghan rebels operate broadcasts over world band radio. They may be reached by mail through friendly intermediaries. M. Guha

AFGHANISTAN   World Time +4:30

NOTE: Postal service to this country is sometimes suspended.

ISLAMIC EMIRATE OF AFGHANISTAN (under Taliban control)

Radio Voice of Shari'ah, Afghan Radio TV, P.O. Box 544, Ansari Wat, Kabul, Afghanistan, via Pakistan (while direct postal service is unavailable)—under normal conditions, replace "Afghanistan, via Pakistan" with "Islamic Emirate of Afghanistan." Phone: +92 (91) 287-454. Fax: +92 (81) 447 300. Email: (English Service) english.program@usa.net. External telephone links are currently suspended, except for a limited service provided by Pakistan Telecom. Contact: Abdul Rahman Nasseri, Department of Planning and Foreign Relations; Ahmad Shoaib Sharafi, English Program Producer; or Ahmad Neyazmand, Director of Foreign Relations. Correspondence in Dari, Farsi, Pashto or Urdu preferred, but reception reports in English are sometimes verified, especially when directed to Mr. Nasseri. Given the erratic postal system that operates via Pakistan, replies may take several months.

NEW YORK OFFICE: Representative of the Islamic Emirate of Afghanistan to the United Nations, 55/16 Main Street, Flushing NY, USA. Phone: +1 (718) 359-0457; (Newsline) +1 (718) 762-8095. Fax: +1 (718) 661 2721. Email: AMujahid@aol.com. Web: www.taleban.com. Contact: Mulawi Abdul Hakeem Mujahid; or Noorullah Zadran.

ISLAMIC REPUBLIC OF AFGHANISTAN (Northern Afghanistan, pro-Rabbani, pro-Masud)

Takhar Radio, Operations Complex, Taloqan, Takhar Province, Northern Afghanistan, via Dushanbe, Tajikistan. Phone: +873 76201256 (c/o Abdul Ghani). Contact: (administration) Sayd Habib, Director; Habib Inayatullah, Deputy Director; (technical) Mohammed Taher Ramin, Engineer. Although there is no official verification policy, reception reports are welcomed. Correspondence in English, Dari or Farsi is best directed to Mr. Arayanfar at the embassy in Dushanbe (*see,* below), though listeners in North America may prefer sending their correspondence c/o the Afghan Mission to the United Nations.

TAJIKISTAN ADDRESS: Embassy of Afghanistan, ul. Pushkina, Dushanbe, Tajikistan. Phone: +7 (3772) 216-418 or +7 (3772) 216-072. Fax: +7 (3772) 216 394. Contact: Shamsul Haq Arayanfar, Cultural Attaché.

USA ADDRESS: Mission of Afghanistan to the United Nations, 360 Lexington Avenue, 11th Floor, New York NY 10010 USA. Phone: +1 (212) 972-1212/3. Fax: +1 (212) 972 1216. Email: afghangovernment@afghangovernment.org. Web: www.afghangovernment.org.

ALBANIA   World Time +1 (+2 midyear)

▣Radio Tirana, External Service, Rruga Ismail Qemali Nr. 11, Tirana, Albania. Phone: (general) +355 (42) 23-239; (Phone/fax, Technical Directorate) +355 (42) 26203. Fax: (External Service) +355 (42) 23650; (Technical Directorate) +355 (42) 27 745. Email: (general) radiotirana@radiotirana.net; radiotirana@interalb.net; (Technical Directorate) 113566.3011@compuserve.com; or dcico@artv.tirana.al. Web: (general) www.radiotirana.net; http://rtsh.sil.at; (RealAudio from Radio Tirana 1, domestic service) http://rtsh.sil.at/online.htm. Contact: Bardhyl Pollo, Director of External Services; Adriana Bislea, English Department; Marjeta Thoma; Pandi Skaka, Producer; or Diana Koci; (Technical Directorate) Irfan Mandija, Chief of Radio Broadcasting, Technical Directorate; Hector Karanxha; or Rifat Kryeziu, Director of Technical Directorate; (Frequency Management) Mrs. Drita Cico, Head of RTV Monitoring Center. May send free stickers and postcards. Replies from the station are again forthcoming, but it is advisable to include return postage ($1 should be enough).

Trans World Radio—*see* Monaco.

ALGERIA   World Time +1 (+2 midyear)

Radio Algiers International—same details as "Radio Algérienne," below.

▣Radio Algérienne (ENRS)

NONTECHNICAL AND GENERAL TECHNICAL: 21 Boulevard des Martyrs, Algiers 16000, Algeria. Phone: (Direction Générale) +213 (2) 230-821; (Direction Commerciale) +213 (2) 590-700; (head of international relations) +213 (2) 594-266; (head of technical direction) +213 (2) 692-867. Fax: +213 (2) 605 814. Email: radioalg@ist.cerist.dz. Web: (includes RealAudio) www.algerian-radio.dz. Contact: (nontechnical) L. Zaghlami; Chaabane Lounakil, Head of International Arabic Section; Mrs. Zehira Yahi, Head of International Relations; or Relations Extérieures; (technical) M. Lakhdar Mahdi, Head of Technical Direction. Replies irregularly. French or Arabic preferred, but English accepted.

FREQUENCY MANAGEMENT OFFICE: Télédiffusion d'Algérie, Centre Nsdal, Bouzareah 1850, Algeria. Phone: +213 (2) 904-512; or +213 (2) 901-717. Fax: +213 (2) 901 499 or +213 (2) 901 522. Email: tda@ist.cerist.dz. Contact: Slimane Djemmatene; or Karim Zitouni.

ANGOLA   World Time +1

Emissora Provincial de Benguela (if reactivated), C.P. 19, Benguela, Angola. Contact: Simão Martins Cuto, Responsável Administrativo; Carlos A. A. Gregório, Diretor; or José Cabral Sande. $1 or return postage required. Replies irregularly.

Emissora Provincial de Moxico (if reactivated), C.P. 74,

Luena, Angola. Contact: Paulo Cahilo, Diretor. $1 or return postage required. Replies to correspondence in Portuguese. Other **Emissora Provincial** stations (if reactivated)—same address, etc., as Rádio Nacional, below.

Rádio Ecclésia (when operating), Rua Comandante Bula 118, São Paulo, Luanda, Angola; or C.P. 3579, Luanda, Angola. Phone: (general) +244 (2) 443-041; (studios) +244 (2) 445-484. Fax: +244 (2) 443 093. Email: ecclesia@snet.co.ao. Web: http://ecclesia.snet.co.ao/noticias.htm. A Catholic station founded in 1954 and which broadcast continuously from March 1955 until closed by presidential decree in 1978. Reestablished in March 1997, when it was granted a permit to operate on FM. Experimented with shortwave transmissions via Radio Nederland facilities during July 2000, but these were terminated for technical reasons. Eventually hopes to resume shortwave broadcasts via its own transmitter, if and when the current tight regulations in Angola are relaxed.

Rádio Nacional de Angola, C.P. 1329, Luanda, Angola. Fax: +244 (2) 391 234. Email: (technical) rochapinto@rna.so Web: (includes RealAudio) www.rna.ao; if the audio link doesn't work, try www.netangola.com/p/default.htm. At the time we went to press, the RealAudio service was suspended pending an agreement between the station and its ISP. Contact: Júlio Mendonça, Diretor dos Serviços de Programas; Lourdes de Almeida, Chefe de Secção; or Manuel Rabelais, Diretor Geral; (technical) Cândido Rocha Pinto, Diretor dos Serviços Técnicos. Formerly replied occasionally to correspondence, preferably in Portuguese, but replies have been more difficult recently. $1, return postage or 2 IRCs most helpful.

ANTARCTICA World Time –3 Base Antárctica Esperanza

Radio Nacional Arcángel San Gabriel—LRA36, Base Esperanza, 9411 Antártida Argentina, Argentina. Phone/Fax: +54 (2964) 421 519. Email:lra36@topmail.com.ar; esc38ant@satlink.com (do not include attachments). Contact: Tte. Cnel. Fernando García Pinasco, Jefe de Base Esperanza; Carlos Alberto Drews, Director. Return postage required. Replies to correspondence in Spanish, and sometimes to correspondence in English and French, depending upon who is at the station. If no reply, try sending your correspondence (but don't write the station's name on the envelope) and 2 IRCs via the helpful Gabriel Iván Barrera, Casilla 2868, 1000 Buenos Aires, Argentina.

ANGUILLA World Time –4

Caribbean Beacon, Box 690, Anguilla, British West Indies. Phone: +1 (264) 497-4340. Fax: +1 (264) 497 4311. Contact: Monsell Hazell, Chief Engineer. $2 or return postage helpful. Relays Dr. Gene Scott's University Network—see USA.

ANTIGUA World Time –4

BBC World Service—Caribbean Relay Station, P.O. Box 1203, St. John's, Antigua. Phone: +1 (268) 462-0994. Fax: +1 (268) 462 0436. Contact: (technical) David George. Nontechnical correspondence should be sent to the BBC World Service in London (see).

Deutsche Welle—Relay Station Antigua—same address and contact as BBC World Service, above. Nontechnical correspondence should be sent to Deutsche Welle in Germany (see).

ARGENTINA World Time –3

"De Colección," Casilla 96, 1900 La Plata, Argentina. Phone: +54 (221) 4270-507; or +54 (221) 4216-607. Contact: Jorge Bourdet, Editor. Program from a medium wave station in the city of La Plata, aired local Sunday evenings to Antarctica in the SSB mode (try 15820 kHz, upper sideband); also heard via WRMI, USA and at least one Italian shortwave broadcaster. Include 2 IRCs when writing.

Radiodifusión Argentina al Exterior—RAE, Casilla de Correos 555, Correo Central, 1000 Buenos Aires, Argentina. Phone/fax: +54 (11) 4325-6368. Fax: +54 (11) 4325 9433. Email: RNA@mecom.ar. Contact: (general) John Anthony Middleton, Head of English Team; María Dolores López; or Sandro Cenci, Chief, Italian Section; (administration) Señorita Perla Damuri, Directora; (technical) Gabriel Iván Barrera, DX Editor; or Patricia Menéndez. Free paper pennant and tourist literature. Return postage or $1 appreciated.

Radio La Colifata—LT22, Casilla 17, 1640 -Martínez (B.A.), Argentina. Email: colifata@interactive.com.ar. Contact: Alfredo Olivera, Director General; or Norberto Pugliese, Producción onda corta. Verifies reception reports and replies to correspondence in Spanish. Return postage (2 IRCs) required. Normally transmits only on FM, from its location in the Dr. J. T. Borda Municipal Neuropsychiatric Hospital, but occasionally has special programs broadcast via stations like WRMI, USA. Programs are produced by residents of the hospital.

Radio Nacional Buenos Aires, Maipú 555, 1006 Buenos Aires, Argentina. Phone: +54 (11) 4325-9100. Fax: (general) +54 (11) 4325 9433; (technical) +54 (11) 4325 5742. Contact: Patricia Ivone Barral, Directora Nacional; Patricia Claudia Dinale de Jantus, Directora Administrativa; or María Eugenia Baya Casal, Directora Operativa. $1 helpful. Prefers correspondence in Spanish, and usually replies via RAE (see, above). If no reply, try sending your correspondence (but don't write the station's name on your envelope) and 1 IRC via the helpful Gabriel Iván Barrera, Casilla 2868, 1000 Buenos Aires, Argentina.

Radio Pasteur, Casilla 1852 Correo Central, 1000 Buenos Aires, Argentina. Phone/Fax: (Morales) +54 (11) 4503 6317. Email: radio-pasteur@iname.com or (Morales) morales.arg @sicoar.com. Contact: Claudio Morales. A radio production by students of a journalism workshop in Buenos Aires. Features sports, arts, culture and entertainment. Also looks at ecology and the environment, customs and traditions, plus social and human rights in Argentina. Letters and reception reports welcome. Return postage helpful.

ARMENIA World Time +3 (+4 midyear)

Armenian Radio—see Voice of Armenia for details.

Armenian National Radio/Voice of Armenia, Radio Agency, Alek Manoukyan Street 5, 375025 Yerevan, Armenia. Phone: +374 (2) 558-010. Fax: +374 (2) 551 513. Contact: V. Voskanian, Deputy Editor-in-Chief; R. Abalian, Editor-in-Chief; Armenag Sansaryan, International Relations Bureau; Laura Baghdassarian, Deputy Manager, Radioagency; or Dr. Levon V. Ananikian, Director. Free postcards and stamps. Replies slowly. Announces as both Armenian National Radio and Voice of Armenia, so the exact status of the external service is unclear.

Radio Intercontinental, Vardanants 28, No. 34, Yerevan 70, Armenia. If a reply from the station is not forthcoming, try writing direct to the program you heard.

The audio editor's job at the BBS has an unusual wrinkle—the same audio processed for television is broadcast later over FM and world band radio.
M. Guha

ASCENSION   World Time exactly

BBC World Service—Atlantic Relay Station, English Bay, Ascension (South Atlantic Ocean). Fax: +247 6117. Contact: (technical) Jeff Cant, Staff Manager; M.R. Watkins, A/Assistant Resident Engineer; or Mrs. Nicola Nicholls, Transmitter Engineer. Nontechnical correspondence should be sent to the BBC World Service in London (*see*).

Radio Japan, Radio Roma and Voice of America via BBC Ascension Relay Station—All correspondence should be directed to the regular addresses in Japan, Italy and USA (*see*).

AUSTRALIA   World Time +11 (+10 midyear) Victoria (VIC), New South Wales (NSW), Australian Capital Territory (ACT) and Tasmania (TAS); +10:30 (+9:30 midyear) South Australia (SA); +10 Queensland (QLD); +9:30 Northern Territory (NT); +8 Western Australia (WA)

Australian Broadcasting Corporation Northern Territory HF Service—ABC Radio 8DDD Darwin, Administrative Center for the Northern Territory Shortwave Service, ABC Box 9994, GPO Darwin NT 0820, Australia. Phone: +61 (8) 8943-3222; (engineering) +61 (8) 8943-3209. Fax: +61 (8) 8943 3235 or +61 (8) 8943 3208. Contact: (general) Tony Bowden, Branch Manager; (administration) Carole Askham, Administrative Officer; (technical) Peter Camilleri or Yvonne Corby. Free stickers and postcards. "Traveller's Guide to ABC Radio" for $1. T-shirts US$20. Three IRCs or return postage helpful.

Australian Defence Forces Radio (when active), Department of Defence, EMU (Electronic Media Unit) ANZAC Park West, APW 1-B-07, Reid, Canberra, ACT 2601, Australia. Phone: +61 (2) 6266-6669. Fax: +61 (2) 6266 6565. Contact: (general) Adam Iffland, Presenter; (technical) Hugh Mackenzie, Managing Presenter; or Brian Langshaw. SAE and 2 IRCs needed for a reply. Station broadcasts irregularly, and replies to verification inquiries only.

BBC World Service via Radio Australia—For verification direct from the Australian transmitters, contact John Westland, Director of English Programs at Radio Australia (*see*). Nontechnical correspondence should be sent to the BBC World Service in London (*see*).

📻Radio Australia—ABC

STUDIOS AND MAIN OFFICES: GPO Box 428G, Melbourne VIC 3001, Australia. Phone: ("Openline" voice mail for listeners' messages and requests) +61 (3) 9626-1825; (switchboard) +61 (3) 9626-1800; (English programs) +61 (3) 9626-1922; (marketing manager) +61 (3) 9626 1723. Fax and Faxpoll: (general) +61 (3) 9626 1899; (engineering) +61 (3) 9626 1917. Email: (general) english@ra.abc.net.au; (marketing manager) mccaig.anne@abc.net.au; (Radio Australia transmissions and programs) raelp@radioaus.abc.net.au; (Pacific Services) rapac@radioaus.abc.net.au; (Internet and Web Coordinator) naughton.russell@a2.abc.net.au. Web: (includes RealAudio) www.abc.net.au/ra/ (RealAudio in English also at www.wrn.org/ondemand/australia.html). Contact: (general) John Westland, Head, English Language Programming; Roger Broadbent, Producer "Feedback"; Tony Hastings, Director of Programs; Caroline Bilney, Information Officer; Anne McCaig, Marketing Manager; or Jean-Gabriel Manguy, General Manager; (technical) Nigel Holmes, Transmission Manager, Transmission Management Unit. Free stickers and sometimes pennants and souvenirs available. On-air language courses available in Chinese, Indonesian, Khmer and Vietnamese. Course notes available at cost price. Radio Australia will attempt to answer listener's letters even though this will largely depend on the availability of resources and a reply may no longer be possible in all cases. All reception reports received by Radio Australia will now be forwarded to the Australian Radio DX Club for assessment and checking. ARDXC will forward completed QSLs to Radio Australia for mailing. For further information, contact John Westland, Director of English Programs at Radio Australia (Email: westland.john@a2.abc.net.au); or John Wright, Secretary/Editor, ARDXC (Email: dxer@fl.net.au). Plans to add new aerials and re-locate 250 kW transmitters.

NEW YORK BUREAU, NONTECHNICAL: Room 2260, 630 Fifth Avenue, New York NY 10020 USA. Phone: (representative) +1 (212) 332-2540; or (correspondent) +1 (212) 332-2545. Fax: +1 (212) 332 2546. Contact: Maggie Jones, North American Representative.

LONDON BUREAU, NONTECHNICAL: 54 Portland Place, London W1N 4DY, United Kingdom. Phone: +44 (20) 7631-4456. Fax: (administration) +44 (20) 7323 0059, (news) +44 (20) 7323 1125. Contact: Robert Bolton, Manager.

BANGKOK BUREAU, NONTECHNICAL: 209 Soi Hutayana off Soi Suanplu, South Sathorn Road, Bangkok 10120, Thailand. Fax: +66 (2) 287 2040. Contact: Nicholas Stuart.

SAN FRANCISCO OFFICE, SCHEDULES: 2654 17th Avenue, San Francisco CA 94116 USA. Phone: +1 (415) 564-9968. Email: GPoppin@aol.com. Contact: George Poppin. This address, a volunteer office, only provides Radio Australia schedules to listeners. All other correspondence should be sent directly to the main office in Melbourne.

Radio Christian Voice

As we went to press, this new station was about to commence test transmissions via Radio Australia's Darwin relay station. Phone: +61 (8) 8981-6591. Fax: +61 (8) 8981 2846. Web: www.christianvision.org. Contact: Andrew Flynn, Acting Chief Engineer (replacement expected shortly). Also, *see* entry under Chile for Radio Voz Cristiana and further contact details.

Radio VNG (official time station)

PRIMARY ADDRESS: National Standards Commission, P.O. Box 282, North Ryde, NSW 1670, Australia. Toll-free telephone number (Australia only) (1800) 251-942. Phone: +61 (2) 9888-3922. Fax: +61 (2) 9888 3033. Email: rbrittain@nsc.gov.au. Contact: Dr. Richard Brittain, Secretary, National Time Committee. Station offers a free 16-page booklet about VNG and free promotional material. Free stickers and postcards. One IRC or $1 helpful. May be forced to close down if sufficient funding is not found by June 30th 2002.

ALTERNATIVE ADDRESS: VNG Users Consortium, GPO Box 1090, Canberra, ACT 2601, Australia. Fax: +61 (2) 6249 9355. Contact: Dr. Marion Leiba, Honorary Secretary. Three IRCs appreciated.

AUSTRIA   World Time +1 (+2 midyear)

☎Radio Austria International

MAIN OFFICE: Argentinierstrasse 31, A-1040 Vienna, Austria. Phone: (management) +43 (1) 87878-12130; (answering machine/listener's service) +43 (1) 87878-13636; (technical) +43 (1) 87878-12629. Fax: (management) +43 (1) 87878 14404; (technical) +43 (1) 87878 12773; (listener's service) +43 (1) 87878 14404. Email: (frequency schedules, comments, reception reports) roi.service@orf.at; (intermedia programme) intermedia@orf.at; (Internet programming service) roi@orf.at; (frequency management) hfbc@orf.at. Web: (general, including RealAudio) www.roi.orf.at; (RealAudio news in German) www.wrn.org/ondemand/austria.html. Contact: (general) Vera Bock, Listener's Service; "Postbox"/"Hörerbriefkasten/Flash des Ondes" listeners' letters shows; Wolf Harranth, Editor, "Intermedia"; (management) Roland Machatschke, Director; or Michael Kerbler, Deputy Director, Head of German Department & Director of Programs; (English Department) David Ward; (French Department) Lucien Giordani; (Spanish Department) Jacobo Naar-Carbonell; (Internet Programming Service) Marianne Veit or Oswald Klotz; (technical) Ing. Ernst Vranka, Frequency Manager; Ing. Klaus Hollndonner, Chief Engineer; or Listener's Service. Free stickers and program schedule twice a year, as well as quiz prizes. Mr. Harranth seeks collections of old verification cards and letters for the highly organized historical archives he is maintaining.

WASHINGTON NEWS BUREAU: 1206 Eaton Ct. NW, Washington DC 20007 USA. Phone: +1 (202) 822-9570. Contact: Eugen Freund.

AZERBAIJAN   World Time +3 (+4 midyear)

Azerbaijani Radio—*see* Radio Dada Gorgud for details.

Radio Dada Gorgud (Voice of Azerbaijan), Medhi Hüseyin küçäsi 1, 370011 Baku, Azerbaijan. Phone: +994 (12) 398-585. Fax: +994 (12) 395 452. Contact: Mrs. Tamam Bayatli-Öner, Director; or Kamil Mamedov, Director of Division of International Relations. May run station contests at various times during the year. Free postcards, and occasionally, books. $1 or return postage helpful. Replies irregularly to correspondence in English.

BAHRAIN   World Time +3

Radio Bahrain (if reactivated), Broadcasting and Television, Ministry of Information, P.O. Box 702, Al Manāmah, Bahrain. Phone: (Arabic Service) +973 781-888; (English Service) +973 629-085. Fax: (Arabic Service) +973 681 544; (English Service) +973 780 911. Web: www.gna.gov.bh/brtc/radio.html. Contact: A. Suliman (for Director of Broadcasting). $1 or IRC required. Replies irregularly.

BANGLADESH   World Time +6

Bangladesh Betar

NONTECHNICAL CORRESPONDENCE: External Services, Bangladesh Betar, Shahbagh Post Box No. 2204, Dhaka 1000, Bangladesh; (physical address) Betar Bhaban Sher-e-Bangla Nagar, Agargaon Road, Dhaka 1207, Bangladesh. Phone: (general) +880 (2) 865-294; (Rahman Khan) +880 (2) 863-949; (external services) +880 (2) 868-119. Fax: +880 (2) 862 021. Contact: Mrs. Dilruba Begum, Director, External Services; Ashfaque-ur Rahman Khan, Director -Programmes; or (technical) Muhammed Nazrul Islam, Station Engineer. $1 helpful. For further technical contacts, *see* below.

TECHNICAL CORRESPONDENCE: National Broadcasting Authority, NBA Bhaban, 121 Kazi Nazrul Islam Avenue, Shahabagh, Dhaka 1000, Bangladesh. Phone: +880 (2) 500-143/7, +880 (2) 500-490, +880 (2) 500-810, +880 (2) 505-113 or +880 (2) 507-269; (Shakir) +880 (2) 818-734; (Das) +880 (2) 500-810. Fax: +880 (2) 817 850; (Shakir) +880 (2) 817 850. Email: dgradio@drik.bgd.toolnet.org. Contact: Syed Abdus Shakir, Chief Engineer; (reception reports) Manoranjan Das, Station Engineer, Dhaka; or Muhammed Romizuddin Bhuiya, Senior Engineer (Research Wing). Verifications not common from this office.

BELARUS   World Time +2 (+3 midyear)

Belarusian Radio—*see* Radio Belarus, below, for details.

Radio Grodno (Hrodna)—contact via Radio Belarus, below.

Radio Mogilev (Mahiliou)—contact via Radio Belarus, below.

Radio Belarus/Radio Minsk, ul. Krasnaja 4, 220807 Minsk, Belarus. Phone: (domestic Belarusian Radio) +375 (17) 239-5810; (external services, general) +375 (17) 239-5830; (English Service) +375 (17) 239-5831; (German Service) +375 (17)

239-5875. Fax: (all services) +375 (17) 236 6643. Email: there's an online form at the station's Website, but messages must be limited to 2000 characters. Web: (includes several music files in MP3) www.tvr.by. Contact: Irina Polozhentseva, English Program Editor; Jürgen Eberhardt, Editor, German Service. Free Belarus stamps.

BELGIUM   World Time +1 (+2 midyear)

📻**RTBF-International**, B-1044 Brussels, Belgium. Phone: +32 (2) 737-4024. Fax: +32 (2) 737 3032. Email: relint.r@rtbf.be. Web: (RTBF-International) www.rtbf.be/ri/; ("La Première") www.rtbf.be/premiere/; (RealAudio) www.rtbf.be/jp/. Contact: Jean-Pol Hecq, Directeur des Relations Internationales (or "Head, International Service" if writing in English). Broadcasts are essentially a relay of news and information programs from the domestic channel "La Première" of RTBF (Radio-Télévision Belge de la Communauté Française) via facilities of Deutsche Telekom (see) in Jülich, Germany. Return postage not required. Accepts email reports.

📻**Radio Vlaanderen Internationaal (RVI)**
NONTECHNICAL AND GENERAL TECHNICAL: B-1043 Brussels, Belgium; (English Section) RVI Brussels Calling, B-1043 Brussels, Belgium. Phone: +32 (2) 741-5611, +32 (2) 741-3806/7 or +32 (2) 741-3802. Fax: (administration and Dutch Service) +32 (2) 732 6295; (other language services) +32 (2) 732 8336. BBS: +32 (3) 825-3613. Email: info@rvi.be. Web: (text and RealAudio) www.rvi.be; (RealAudio in English, French, German and Dutch) www.wrn.org/ondemand/belgium.html. Contact (general) Deanne Lehman, Producer, "Brussels 1043" letterbox program; Liz Sanderson, Head, English Service; Maryse Jacob, Head, French Service; Martina Luxen, Head, German Service; or Wim Jansen, Station Manager; (general technical) Frans Vossen, Producer, "Radio World." Sells RVI T-shirts (large/extra large) for 400 Belgian francs. Remarks and reception reports can also be sent c/o the following diplomatic addresses:
NIGERIA EMBASSY: Embassy of Belgium, 1A, Bak Road, Ikoyi-Island, Lagos, Nigeria.
ARGENTINA EMBASSY: Embajada de Bélgica, Defensa 113 - 8% Piso, 1065 Buenos Aires, Argentina.
FREQUENCY MANAGEMENT OFFICE: BRTN, August Reyerslaan 52, B-1043 Brussels, Belgium. Phone: +32 (2) 741-5020. Fax: +32 (2) 741 5567. Email: (De Cuyper) hector.decuyper@vrt.be. Contact: Hector De Cuyper, Frequency Manager.

TIPS FOR EFFECTIVE CORRESPONDENCE

Write to be read. Be interesting and helpful from the recipient's point of view, yet friendly without being chummy. Comments on specific programs are almost always appreciated, even if you are sending in what is basically a technical report.

Incorporate language courtesies. Using the broadcaster's tongue is always a plus—Addresses PLUS indicates when it is a requirement—but English is usually the next-best bet. When writing in any language to Spanish-speaking countries, remember that what gringos think of as the "last name" is actually written as the penultimate name. Thus, Juan Antonio Vargas García, which can also be written as Juan Antonio Vargas G., refers to Sr. Vargas; so your salutation should read, *Estimado Sr. Vargas*.

What's that "García" doing there, then? That's *mamita's* father's family name. Latinos more or less solved the problem of gender fairness in names long before Anglos.

But, wait—what about Portuguese, used by all those stations in Brazil? Same concept, but in reverse. *Mamá's* father's family name is penultimate, and the "real" last name is where English-speakers are used to it, at the end.

In Chinese, the "last" name comes first. However, when writing in English, Chinese names are sometimes reversed for the benefit of *weiguoren*—foreigners. Use your judgement. For example, "Li" is a common Chinese last name, so if you see "Li Dan," it's "Mr. Li." But if it's "Dan Li"—and certainly if it's been Westernized into "Dan Lee"—he's already one step ahead of you, and it's still "Mr. Li" (or Lee). Less widely known is that the same can also occur in Hungarian. For example, "Bartók Béla" for Béla Bartók.

If in doubt, fall back on the ever-safe "Dear Sir" or "Dear Madam," or use email, where salutations are not expected. And be patient—replies by post usually take weeks, sometimes months. Slow responders, those that tend to take many months to reply, are cited in Addresses PLUS, as are erratic repliers.

BENIN   World Time +1

Office de Radiodiffusion et Télévision du Benin, Boite Postale 366, Cotonou, Bénin. Phone: +229 300-481, +229 301-096 or +229 301-347. Fax: +229 302 184. Web: http://elodia.intnet.bj/bol/ortb.htm. Contact: (Cotonou) Damien Zinsou Ala Hassa; Emile Desire Ologoudou, Directeur Generale; or Leonce Goohouede; (technical) Anastase Adjoko, Chef de Service Technique. Return postage, $1 or IRC required. Replies irregularly and slowly to correspondence in French.
PARAKOU REGIONAL STATION: ORTB-Parakou, Boite Postale 128, Parakou, Benin. Phone: +229 610-773. Fax: +229 610-881. Contact: (general) J. de Matha, Le Chef de la Station; (technical) Léon Donou, Chef des Services Techniques. Return postage required. Replies tend to be extremely irregular, and a safer option is to send correspondence to the Cotonou address.

BHUTAN   World Time +6

Bhutan Broadcasting Service
STATION: Department of Information and Broadcasting, Ministry of Communications, P.O. Box 101, Thimphu, Bhutan. Phone: +975 (2) 323-071/72. Fax: +975 (2) 323 073. Email: bbsnews@druknet.net.bt. Contact: (general) Thinley Tobgay Dorji, Coordinator, News and Current Affairs Division; Narda Gautam; Kinga Singye, Executive Head; or Sonam Tshong, Executive Director; (technical) Sonam Tobgyal, Station Engineer; or Technical Head. Two IRCs, return postage or $1 required. Replies irregularly; correspondence to the U.N. Mission (*see* following) may be more fruitful.
UNITED NATIONS MISSION: Permanent Mission of the Kingdom of Bhutan to the United Nations, Two United Nations Plaza, 27th Floor, New York NY 10017 USA. Fax: +1 (212) 826 2998. Contact: Mrs. Kunzang C. Namgyel, Third Secretary; Mrs. Sonam Yangchen, Attaché; Ms. Leki Wangmo, Second Secretary; or Hari K. Chhetri, Second Secretary. Free newspapers and booklet on the history of Bhutan.

BOLIVIA   World Time –4

NOTE ON STATION IDENTIFICATIONS: Many Bolivian stations listed as "Radio..." may also announce as "Radio Emisora..." or "Radiodifusora..."
Galaxia Radiodifusión—*see* Radio Galaxia, below.
Hitachi Radiodifusión—*see* Radio Hitachi, below.
Paititi Radiodifusión—*see* Radio Paititi, below.
Radio Abaroa, Calle Nicanor Gonzalo Salvatierra 249, Riberalta, Beni, Bolivia. Contact: René Arias Pacheco, Director. Return postage or $1 required. Replies occasionally to correspondence in Spanish.
Radio Animas, Chocaya, Animas, Potosí, Bolivia. Contact: Julio Acosta Campos, Director. Return postage or $1 required. Replies irregularly to correspondence in Spanish.
Radio Camargo—*see* Radio Emisoras Camargo, below.
Radio Carlos Palenque (if reactivated), Casilla de Correo 8704, La Paz, Bolivia. Phone: +591 (2) 354-418, +591 (2) 375-953, +595 (2) 324-394 or +595 (2) 361-176. Fax: +591 (2) 356 785. Contact: Rodolfo Beltrán Rosales, Jefe de Prensa de "El Metropolicial." Free postcards and pennants. $1 or return postage necessary.
Radio Centenario "La Nueva"
MAIN OFFICE: Casilla 818, Santa Cruz de la Sierra, Bolivia. Phone: +591 (3) 529-265. Fax: +591 (3) 524 747. Email: mision.eplabol@scbbs-bo.com. Contact: Napoleón Ardaya B.,

Director. May send a calendar. Free stickers. Return postage or $1 required. Audio cassettes of contemporary Christian music and Bolivian folk music $10, including postage; CDs of Christian folk music $15, including postage. Replies to correspondence in English and Spanish.
U.S. BRANCH OFFICE: LATCOM, 1218 Croton Avenue, New Castle PA 16101 USA. Phone: +1 (412) 652-0101. Fax: +1 (412) 652 4654. Contact: Hope Cummins.
Radio Eco
MAIN ADDRESS: Correo Central, Reyes, Ballivián, Beni, Bolivia. Contact: Gonzalo Espinoza Cortés, Director. Free station literature. $1 or return postage required. Replies to correspondence in Spanish.
ALTERNATIVE ADDRESS: Rolmán Medina Méndez, Correo Central, Reyes, Ballivián, Bolivia.
Radio Eco San Borja (San Borja la Radio), Correo Central, San Borja, Ballivián, Beni, Bolivia. Contact: Gonzalo Espinoza Cortés, Director. Free station poster promised to correspondents. Return postage appreciated. Replies slowly to correspondence in Spanish.
Radio El Mundo (when operating), Casilla 1984, Santa Cruz de la Sierra, Bolivia. Phone: +591 (3) 464-646. Fax: +591 (3) 465 057. Contact: Freddy Banegas Carrasco, Gerente; Lic. José Luis Vélez Ocampo C., Director; or Lic. Juan Pablo Sainz, Gerente General. Free stickers and pennants. $1 or return postage required. Replies irregularly to correspondence in Spanish.
Radio Emisora Dos de Febrero (if reactivated), Calle Vaca Diez 400, Rurrenabaque, Beni, Bolivia. Contact: John Arze von Boeck. Free pennant, which is especially attractive. Replies occasionally to correspondence in Spanish.
Radio Emisora Galaxia—*see* Radio Galaxia, below.
Radio Emisora Padilla—*see* Radio Padilla, below.
Radio Emisora San Ignacio, Calle Ballivián s/n, San Ignacio de Moxos, Beni, Bolivia. Contact: Carlos Salvatierra Rivero, Gerente y Director. $1 or return postage necessary.
Radio Emisora Villamontes—*see* Radio Villamontes, below.
Radio Emisoras Camargo, Casilla 09, Camargo, Provincia Nor-Cinti, Bolivia. Contact: Pablo García B., Gerente Propietario. Return postage or $1 required. Replies slowly to correspondence in Spanish.
Radio Emisoras Minería—*see* Radiodifusoras Minería.
Radio Estación Frontera—*see* Radio Frontera, below.
Radio Fides, Casilla 9143, La Paz, Bolivia. Fax: +591 (2) 379 030. Email: rafides@caoba.entelnet.bo (rafides@wara.bolnet.bo may also work). Web: www.fides2001.com. Contact: Pedro Eduardo Pérez Iribarne, Director; Felicia de Rojas, Secretaria; Roberto Carrasco Guzmán, Gerente de Ventas y RR HH; or Roxana Beltrán C. Replies occasionally to correspondence in Spanish.
Radio Frontera (if reactivated), Casilla 179, Cobija, Pando, Bolivia. Contact: Lino Miahuchi von Ancken, CP9AR. Free pennants. $1 or return postage necessary. Replies to correspondence in Spanish.
Radio Galaxia (if reactivated), Calle Beni s/n casi esquina Udarico Rosales, Guayaramerín, Beni, Bolivia. Contact: Dorián Arias, Gerente; Héber Hitachi Banegas, Director; or Carlos Arteaga Tacaná, Director-Dueño. Return postage or $1 required. Replies to correspondence in Spanish.
Radio Grigotá (when operating), Casilla 203, Santa Cruz de la Sierra, Bolivia. Phone/fax: +591 (3) 326-443. Fax: +591 (3) 362 795. Contact: (general) Víctor Hugo Arteaga B., Director General; (technical) Tania Martins de Arteaga, Gerente Administrativo. Free stickers, pins, pennants, key rings and

posters. $1 or return postage required. Replies occasionally to correspondence in English, French, Portuguese and Spanish. May replace old Philips transmitter.

Radio Hitachi (Hitachi Radiodifusión) (if reactivated), Calle Sucre 20, Guayaramerín, Beni, Bolivia. Contact: Héber Hitachi Banegas, Director. Return postage of $1 required.

Radio Illimani, Casilla 1042, La Paz, Bolivia. Phone: +591 (2) 376-364. Fax: +591 (2) 359 275. Email: illimani@communica.gov.bo. Contact: Gabriel Astorga Guachala. $1 required, and your letter should be registered and include a tourist brochure or postcard from where you live. Replies irregularly to friendly correspondence in Spanish.

Radio Integración, Casilla 1722, La Paz, Bolivia. Contact: Lic. Manuel Liendo Rázuri, Gerente General; Benjamín Juan Carlos Blanco Q., Director Ejecutivo; or Carmelo de la Cruz Huanca, Comunicador Social. Free pennants. Return postage required.

Radio Juan XXIII [Veintitrés], Avenida Santa Cruz al frente de la plaza principal, San Ignacio de Velasco, Santa Cruz, Bolivia. Phone: +591 (962) 2087. Phone/Fax: +591 (962) 2188. Contact: Pbro. Elías Cortezón, Director; or María Elffy Gutiérrez Méndez, Encargada de la Discoteca. Return postage or $1 required. Replies occasionally to correspondence in Spanish.

Radio La Cruz del Sur, Casilla 1408, La Paz, Bolivia. Email: cruzdel-sur@mail.zuper.net. Contact: Presbítero Reyes Baltazar Quispe, Director. Pennant $1 or return postage. Replies slowly to correspondence in Spanish.

Radio La Palabra, Parroquia de Santa Ana de Yacuma, Beni, Bolivia. Phone: +591 (848) 2117. Contact: Padre Yosu Arketa, Director. Return postage necessary. Replies to correspondence in Spanish.

Radio La Plata, Casilla 276, Sucre, Bolivia. Phone: +591 (64) 31-616. Fax: +591 (64) 41 400. Contact: Freddy Donoso Bleichner, Director Ejecutivo.

Radio Loyola (when operating), Casilla 40, Sucre, Bolivia. Phone: +591 (64) 62-213 or +591 (64) 54-248. Fax: +591 (64) 62 618. Contact: (general) Lic. José Weimar León G., Director; (technical) Tec. Norberto Rosales. Free stickers and pennants. Replies occasionally to correspondence in English, Italian and Spanish. Considering replacing 19-year old transmitter.

Radio Mallku (formerly Radio A.N.D.E.S.), Casilla No. 16, Uyuni, Provincia Antonio Quijarro, Departamento de Potosí, Bolivia. Phone: +591 (693) 2145. Owners: La Federación Unica de Trabajadores Campesinos del Altiplano Sud. Contact: Erwin Freddy Mamani Machaca, Jefe de Prensa y Programación. Spanish preferred. Return postage in the form of two U.S. dollars appreciated, as the station depends on donations for its existence.

Radio Mauro Núñez, Centro de Estudios para el Desarrollo de Chuquisaca (CEDEC), Casilla 196, Sucre, Bolivia. Phone: +591 (64) 25-008. Fax: +591 (64) 32 628. Contact: Jorge A. Peñaranda Llanos; Ing. Raúl Ledezma, Director Residente "CEDEC"; José Peneranda; or Jesús Urioste. Replies to correspondence in Spanish.

Radio Minería—*see* Radiodifusoras Minería.

Radio Mosoj Chaski, Casilla 4493, Cochabamba, Bolivia. Phone: +591 (42) 220-641 or +591 (42) 220-644. Fax: +591 (42) 251 041. Email: chaski@bo.net. Web: http://tunari.socs.utsedu.au/rmc/. Contact: Eldon Porter, Gerente.

Radio Movima, Calle Baptista No. 24, Santa Ana de Yacuma, Beni, Bolivia. Contact: Rubén Serrano López, Director; Javier Roca Díaz, Director Gerente; or Mavis Serrano, Directora. Return postage or $1 required. Replies irregularly to correspondence in Spanish.

Radio Nacional de Huanuni, Casilla 681, Oruro, Bolivia. Contact: Rafael Linneo Morales, Director General; or Alfredo Murillo, Director. Return postage or $1 required. Replies irregularly to correspondence in Spanish.

Radio Norte, Calle Warnes 195, 2do piso del Cine Escorpio, Montero, Santa Cruz, Bolivia. Phone: +591 (92) 20-970. Fax: +591 (92) 21 062. Contact: Leonardo Arteaga Ríos, Director.

Radio Padilla, Padilla, Chuquisaca, Bolivia. Contact: Moisés Palma Salazar, Director. Return postage or $1 required. Replies to correspondence in Spanish.

Radio Paitití, Casilla 172, Guayaramerín, Beni, Bolivia. Contact: Armando Mollinedo Bacarreza, Director; Luis Carlos Santa Cruz Cuéllar, Director Gerente; or Ancir Vaca Cuéllar, Gerente-Propietario. Free pennants. Return postage or $3 required. Replies irregularly to correspondence in Spanish.

⛺Radio Panamericana, Casilla 5263, La Paz, Bolivia; (physical address) Av. 16 de Julio, Edif. 16 de Julio, Of. 902, El Prado, La Paz, Bolivia. Phone: +591 (2) 324-606, +591 (2) 325-239 or +591 (2) 358-945. Fax: +591 (2) 392 353. Email: pana@panamericana-bolivia.com. Web: (includes RealAudio) www.panamericana-bolivia.com. Contact: Daniel Sánchez Rocha, Director. Replies irregularly, with correspondence in Spanish preferred. $1 or 2 IRCs helpful.

Radio Perla del Acre (if reactivated), Casilla 7, Cobija, Departamento de Pando, Bolivia. Return postage or $1 required. Replies irregularly to correspondence in Spanish.

Radio Pío XII [Doce], Siglo Veinte, Potosí, Bolivia. Phone: +591 (58) 20-250. Fax: +591 (58) 20 544. Email: radiopio@nogal.oru.entelnet.bo. Contact: Pbro. Roberto Durette, OMI, Director General; or René Paco, host of "Los Pikichakis" program (aired Saturdays at 2300-0100 World Time). Return postage necessary. As mail delivery to Siglo Veinte is erratic, latters may be sent instead to: Casilla 434, Oruro, Bolivia; to the attention of Abenor Alfaro Castillo, periodista de Radio Pío XX (Phone: +591 (52) 76-163).

Radio San Gabriel, Casilla 4792, La Paz, Bolivia. Phone: +591 (2) 414-371. Phone/fax: +591 (2) 411 174. Email: rsg@fundayni.rds.org.bo. Contact: Hno. José Canut Saurat, Director General; or Sra. Martha Portugal, Dpto. de Publicidad. $1 or return postage helpful. Free book on station, Aymara calendars and *La Voz del Pueblo Aymara* magazine. Replies fairly regularly to correspondence in Spanish. Station of the Hermanos de la Salle Catholic religious order.

Radio San Miguel, Casilla 102, Riberalta, Beni, Bolivia. Phone: +591 (852) 8268 or +591 (852) 8363. Fax: +591 (852) 8268. Contact: Félix Alberto Rada Q., Director; or Gerin Pardo Molina, Director. Free stickers and pennants; has a different pennant each year. Return postage or $1 required. Replies irregularly to correspondence in Spanish. Feedback on program "Bolivia al Mundo" (aired 0200-0300 World Time) especially appreciated.

Radio Santa Ana, Calle Sucre No. 250, Santa Ana de Yacuma, Beni, Bolivia. Contact: Mario Roberto Suárez, Director; or Mariano Verdugo. Return postage or $1 required. Replies irregularly to correspondence in Spanish.

Radio Santa Cruz, Emisora del Instituto Radiofónico Fé y Alegría (IRFA), Casilla 672 (or 3213), Santa Cruz, Bolivia. Phone: +591 (3) 521-814. Fax: +591 (3) 532 257. Email: infacruz@roble.scz.entelnet.bo. Contact: Padre Francisco Flores, S.J., Director General; Srta. María Yolanda Marco E., Secretaria; Señora Mirian Suárez, Productor, "Protagonista Ud."; or Lic. Silvia Nava S. Free pamphlets, stickers and pennants. Return postage required. Replies to correspondence in English, French and Spanish.

Radio Sararenda (when operating), Casilla 7, Camiri, Santa Cruz, Bolivia. Phone: +595 (952) 2121. Contact: Freddy Lara Aguilar, Director; or Kathy Arenas, Administradora. Free stickers and photos of Camiri. Replies to correspondence in Spanish.

Radio Villamontes, Avenida Méndez Arcos No. 156, Villamontes, Departamento de Tarija, Bolivia. Contact: Gerardo Rocabado Galarza, Director. $1 or return postage required.

Radio Yura (La Voz de los Ayllus), Yura, Provincia Quijarro, Departamento de Potosí, Bolivia. Email: canal18@cedro.pts.entelnet.bo. Contact: Rolando Cueto F., Director.

Radiodifusoras Integración—see Radio Integración.

Radiodifusoras Minería, Casilla de Correo 247, Oruro, Bolivia. Phone: +591 (52) 77-736. Contact: Dr. José Carlos Gómez Espinoza, Gerente Propietario; or Srta. Costa Colque Flores, Responsable del programa "Minería Cultural." Free pennants. Replies to correspondence in Spanish.

Radiodifusoras Trópico, Casilla 60, Trinidad, Beni, Bolivia. Contact: Eduardo Avila Alberdi, Director. Replies slowly to correspondence in Spanish. Return postage required for reply.

BOTSWANA   World Time +2

Radio Botswana, Private Bag 0060, Gaborone, Botswana. Phone: +267 352-541 or +267 352-861. Fax: +267 357 138. Contact: (general) Ted Makgekgenene, Director; or Monica Mphusu, Producer, "Maokaneng/Pleasure Mix"; (technical) Kingsley Reetsang, Principal Broadcasting Engineer. Free stickers, pennants and pins. Return postage, $1 or 2 IRCs required. Replies slowly and irregularly.

Voice of America/IBB—Botswana Relay Station
TRANSMITTER SITE: Voice of America, Botswana Relay Station, Moepeng Hill, Selebi-Phikwe, Botswana. Phone: +267 810-932. Contact: Station Manager. This address for specialized technical correspondence only. All other correspondence should be directed to the regular VOA or IBB addresses (see USA).

BRAZIL   World Time –1 (–2 midyear) Atlantic Islands; –2 (–3 midyear) Eastern, including Brasília and Rio de Janeiro, plus the town of Barra do Garças; –3 (–4 midyear) Western; –5 Acre. Most, if not all, northern states keep midyear time year round.

NOTE: Postal authorities recommend that, because of the level of theft in the Brazilian postal system, correspondence to Brazil be sent only via registered mail.

Emissora Rural A Voz do São Francisco, C.P. 8, 56300-000 Petrolina PE, Brazil. Contact: Maria Letecia de Andrade Nunes. Return postage necessary. Replies to correspondence in Portuguese.

Rádio Alvorada (Londrina), Rua Senador Souza Naves 9, 9 Andar, 86010-921 Londrina PR, Brazil. Contact: Padre José Guidoreni, Diretor; Padre Manuel Joaquim; or Sonia López. Pennants $1 or return postage. Replies to correspondence in Portuguese.

Rádio Alvorada (Parintins), Rua Governador Leopoldo Neves 516, 69151-440 Parintins AM, Brazil. Contact: Raimunda Ribeira da Motta, Diretora; or M. Braga. Return postage required. Replies occasionally to correspondence in Portuguese.

Rádio Alvorada (Rio Branco), Avenida Ceará 2150—Altos de Gráfica Globo, 69900-470 Rio Branco AC, Brazil. Occasionally replies to correspondence in Portuguese.

☞**Rádio Araguaia**—FM sister-station to Rádio Anhanguera (see next entry) and often relayed via the latter's shortwave outlet. Web: (general) www.opopular.com.br/araguaia/; (RealAudio) www2.opopular.com.br/radio.htm. Usually identifies as "Araguaia FM."

Rádio Anhanguera, BR-157 Km. 1103, Zona Rural, 77804-970 Araguaína TO, Brazil. Return postage required. Occasionally replies to correspondence in Portuguese. Often airs programming from sister-station Rádio Araguaia, 97.1 FM (see previous item) or from the Rede Somzoomsat satellite network.

☞**Rádio Anhanguera**, C.P. 13, 74823-000 Goiânia GO, Brazil. Web: (RealAudio only) www2.opopular.com.br/radio.htm. Contact: Rossana F. da Silva; or Eng. Domingo Vicente Tinoco. Return postage required. Replies to correspondence in Portuguese. Although—like its namesake in Araguaína (see, above)—a member of the Sistema de Rádio da Organização Jaime Câmara, this station is also an affiliate of the CBN network and often identifies as "CBN Anhanguera," especially when airing news programming.

Rádio Aparecida, Avenida Getulio Vargas 185, 12570-000 Aparecida SP, Brazil; or C.P. 14547, 03698-970 Aparecida SP, Brazil. Phone: +55 (12) 565-1133. Fax: +55 (12) 565 1138. Email: (nontechnical) radioaparecida@redemptor.com.br. Web: www.radioaparecida.com.br. Contact: Padre C. Cabral; Savio Trevisan, Departamento Técnico; Cassiano Alves Macedo, Producer, "Encontro DX"; Ana Cristina Carvalho, Secretária da Direção; Padre Cesar Moreira; or João Climaco, Diretor Geral. Return postage or $1 required. Replies occasionally to correspondence in Portuguese.

☞**Rádio Bandeirantes**, C.P. 372, Rua Radiantes 13, Morumbi, 01059-970 São Paulo SP, Brazil. Fax: +55 (11) 3743 5391. Email: rbradio@band.com.br. Web: (includes RealAudio) www.radiobandeirantes.com.br. Contact: Samir Razuk, Diretor Geral; Carlos Newton; or Salomão Esper, Superintendente. Free stickers, pennants and canceled Brazilian stamps. $1 or return postage required.

Rádio Baré, Avenida Santa Cruz Machado 170 A, 69010-070 Manaus AM, Brazil. Contact: Fernando A.B. Andrade, Diretor Programação e Produção. The Diretor is looking for radio catalogs.

Rádio Brasil, C.P. 625, 13000-000 Campinas, São Paulo SP, Brazil. Contact: Wilson Roberto Correa Viana, Gerente. Return postage required. Replies to correspondence in Portuguese.

Rádio Brasil Central, C.P. 330, 74001-970 Goiânia GO, Brazil. Contact: Ney Raymundo Fernández, Diretor Administrativo; Sergio Rubens da Silva; or Arizio Pedro Soárez, Diretor Gerente. Free stickers. $1 or return postage required. Replies to correspondence in Portuguese.

Rádio Brasil Tropical, C.P. 405, 78005-970 Cuiabá MT, Brazil (street address: Rua Joaquim Murtinho 1456, 78020-830 Cuiabá MT, Brazil). Phone: +55 (65) 321-6882 or +55 (65) 321-6226. Fax: +55 (65) 624 3455. Email: rcultura@nutecnet.com.br. Contact: Klécius Antonio dos Santos, Diretor Comercial; or Roberto Ferreira, Gerente Comercial. Free stickers. $1 required. Replies to correspondence in Portuguese. Shortwave sister-station to Rádio Cultura de Cuiabá (see).

Rádio Caiari, Av. Carlos Gomes 932, 78900-030 Porto Velho RO, Brazil. Contact: Carlos Alberto Diniz Martins, Diretor Geral. Free stickers. Return postage helpful. Replies irregularly to correspondence in Portuguese.

This building once housed Radio NYAB, Bhutan's first radio station. It operated on world band at very low power.
M. Guha

🖼Rádio Canção Nova, C.P. 57, 12630-000 Cachoeira Paulista SP, Brazil; (physical address) Rua João Paulo II s/n, Alto da Bela Vista, 12630-000 Cachoeira Paulista SP, Brazil. Phone: +55 (12) 560-2022. Fax: +55 (12) 561 2074. Email: (general) radio@cancaonova.org.br; (Director) adriana@ cancaonova.org.br. Web: (includes RealAudio) www.cancaonova.org.br/cnova/radio/. Contact: (general) Benedita Luiza Rodrigues; Ana Claudia de Santana; or Valera Guimarães Massafera, Secretária; (administration) Adriana Pereira, Diretora da Rádio. Free stickers, pennants and station brochure sometimes given upon request. May send magazines. $1 helpful.

Rádio Capixaba, C.P. 509, 29000-000 Vitória ES, Brazil; or (street address) Av. Santo Antônio 366, 29025-000 Vitória ES, Brazil. Contact: Jairo Gouvea Maia, Diretor; or Sr. Sardinha, Técnico. Replies occasionally to correspondence in Portuguese.

🖼**Rádio Clube de Ribeirao Preto** (if reactivated), Ribeirao Preto SP, Brazil. Phone/fax: +55 (16) 610-3511. Email: scc@clube.com.br; clubeam@clube.com.br. Web: (includes RealAudio) www.clube.com.br.

Rádio Clube de Rondonópolis (when active), C.P. 190, 78700-000 Rondonópolis MT, Brazil. Contact: Canário Silva, Departamento Comercial; or Saúl Feliz, Gerente-Geral. Return postage helpful. Replies to correspondence in Portuguese.

Rádio Clube do Pará, C.P. 533, 66000-000 Belém PA, Brazil. Contact: Edyr Paiva Proença, Diretor Geral; or José Almeida Lima de Sousa. Return postage required. Replies irregularly to correspondence in Portuguese.

Radio Clube Paranaense, Rua Rockefeller 1311, Prado Velho, 80230-130 Curitiba PR, Brazil. Phone: +55 (41) 332-4255 or +55 (41) 332-6644. Contact: Vicente Mickosz, Superintendente.

Rádio Clube Varginha, C.P. 102, 37000-000 Varginha MG, Brazil. Contact: Juraci Viana. Return postage necessary. Replies slowly to correspondence in Portuguese.

Rádio Coari—*see* Rádio Educação Rural-Coari.

Rádio Copacabana, Rua Visconde Inhauma 37, 12 Andar, Rio de Janeiro. Phone: +55 (21) 233-9269 or +55 (21) 263-8567. Replies slowly to correspondence in Portuguese.

Rádio Cultura Araraquara, Avenida Feijó 583 (Centro), 14801-140 Araraquara SP, Brazil. Phone: +55 (16) 232-3790. Fax: +55 (16) 232 3475. Email: cultura@techs.com.br. Web: www.techs.com.br/cultura/. Contact: Antonio Carlos Rodrigues dos Santos, Gerente Comercial. Return postage required. Replies slowly to correspondence in Portuguese.

Rádio Cultura de Campos, C.P. 79, 28100-970 Campos RJ, Brazil. $1 or return postage necessary. Replies to correspondence in Portuguese.

Rádio Cultura de Cuiabá—AM sister-station of Rádio Brasil Tropical (*see*) and whose programming is partly relayed by RBT. Email: rcultura@nutecnet.com.br. Web: www.solunet.com.br/rcultura/.

Rádio Cultura de Foz do Iguaçu (Onda Corta), C.P. 84, 85852-520 Foz do Iguaçu PR, Brazil. Phone: +55 (45) 574-3010. Contact: Pastor Francisco Pires dos Santos, Gerente-Geral; or Sandro Souza. Return postage necessary. Replies to correspondence in Portuguese. Observation: since 1999 this station has been identifying as "Rádio Cultura Filadelfia" (*see*), and announcing a different address and phone number to that listed above. It is unknown if this reflects a change of ownership or whether the station is leasing its airtime to the Filadelfia evangelical organization.

Rádio Cultura do Pará, Avenida Almirante Barroso 735, 66090-000 Belém PA, Brazil. Phone: +55 (91) 228-1000. Fax: +55 (91) 226 3989. Contact: Ronald Pastor; or Augusto Proença. Return postage required. Replies irregularly to correspondence in Portuguese.

Rádio Cultura Filadelfia, Rua Antonio Barbosa 1353, C.P. 89, 85851-090 Foz do Iguaçu PR, Brazil. Phone: +55 (45) 523-2930. Also, *see* Rádio Cultura de Foz do Iguaçu (Onda Corta), above.

Rádio Cultura Ondas Tropicais, Rua Barcelos s/n Praça 14, 69020-060 Manaus AM, Brazil. Phone: +55 (92) 633-3857/2030. Fax: +55 (92) 633 3332. Contact: Luíz Fernando de Souza Ferreira; or Maria Jerusalem dos Santos, Chefe da Divisão de Rádio. Replies to correspondence in Portuguese. Return postage appreciated. Station is part of the FUNTEC, Fundação Televisão e Rádio Cultura do Amazonas network.

Rádio Cultura São Paulo, Rua Cenno Sbrighi 378, 05099-900 São Paulo, Brazil. Phone: +55 (11) 3611-2140, +55 (11) 3874-3080, +55 (11) 3874-3086. Fax: +55 (11) 3611 1914. Email: (general) radio@tvcultura.com.br; (Cultura AM, relayed on 9615 and 17815 kHz) radioam@tvcultura.com.br; (Cultura FM, relayed on 6170 kHz) radiofm@tvcultura.com.br; (technical) tecnica@tvcultura.com.br. Web: www.tvcultura.com.br. Contact: Thais de Almeida Dias, Chefe de Produção e Programação; Sra. Maria Luíza Amaral Kfouri, Chefe de Produção; or Valvenio Martins de Almeida, Coordenador de Produção. $1 or return postage required. Replies slowly to postal correspondence in Portuguese. May respond to English messages sent to the "radio" and "tecnica" email addresses, above.

Rádio Difusora Acreana, Rua Benjamin Constant 161, 69908-520 Rio Branco AC, Brazil. Contact: Washington Aquino, Diretor Geral. Replies irregularly to correspondence in Portuguese.

Rádio Difusora Cáceres, C.P. 297, 78200-000 Cáceres MT, Brazil. Contact: Sra. Maridalva Amaral Vignardi. $1 or return postage required. Replies occasionally to correspondence in Portuguese.

Rádio Difusora de Aquidauana, C.P. 18, 79200-000 Aquidauana MS, Brazil. Phone: +55 (67) 241-3956 or +55 (67) 241-3957. Contact: Primaz Aldo Bertoni, Diretor; or João Stacey. Free tourist literature and used Brazilian stamps. $1 or return postage required. This station sometimes identifies during the program day as "Nova Difusora," but its sign-off announcement gives the official name as "Rádio Difusora, Aquidauana."

Rádio Difusora de Londrina, C.P. 1870, 86000-000 Londrina PR, Brazil. Contact: Walter Roberto Manganoti, Gerente. Free tourist brochure, which sometimes seconds as a verification. $1 or return postage helpful. Replies irregularly to correspondence in Portuguese.

Rádio Difusora de Roraima, Avenida Capitão Ene Garcez 830, 69304-000 Boa Vista RR, Brazil. Phone: +55 (95) 623-1871, +55 (95) 623-2085 or +55 (95) 623-2131. Contact: Francisco G. França, Diretor Gerente; Galvão Soares, Diretor Geral; Benjamin Monteiro, Locutor; or Francisco Alves Vieira. Return postage required. Replies occasionally to correspondence in Portuguese.

Rádio Difusora do Amazonas (if reactivated), C.P. 311, 69000-000 Manaus AM, Brazil. Contact: J. Joaquim Marinho, Diretor. Joaquim Marinho is a keen collector and especially interested in Duck Hunting Permit Stamps, stamp booklets and stamp sheets. Will reply to correspondence in Portuguese or English. $1 or return postage helpful.

Rádio Difusora Jataí, C.P. 33 (or Rua de José Carvalhos Bastos 542), 75800-000 Jataí GO, Brazil. Contact: Zacarías Faleiros, Diretor Gerente.

Rádio Difusora Macapá, C.P. 2929, 68900-000 Macapá AP, Brazil. Contact: Paulo Roberto Rodrigues, Gerente; Francisco de Paulo Silva Santos; Rui Lobato; or Eng. Arquit. Benedito Rostan Costa Martins, Diretor. $1 or return postage required. Replies irregularly to correspondence in Portuguese. Sometimes provides stickers, key rings and—on rare occasions—T-shirts.

Rádio Difusora Poços de Caldas, C.P. 937, 37701-970 Poços de Caldas MG, Brazil; or (street address) Rua Rio Branco 681 primeiro andar, 37701-001 Poços de Caldas MG, Brazil. Phone/fax: +55 (35) 722-1530. Email: difusora@pocos-net.com.br. Web: www.pocos-net.com.br/difusora/. Contact: Marco Aurelio C. Mendoça, Diretor; or Dr. Wanderley de Mello, Gerente. $1 or return postage required. Replies to correspondence in Portuguese.

Rádio Difusora "6 de Agosto," Rua Pio Nazário 31, 69930-000 Xapuri AC, Brazil. Contact: Francisco Evangelista de Abreu. Replies to correspondence in Portuguese.

Rádio Difusora Taubaté (when active), Rua Dr. Sousa Alves 960, 12020-030 Taubaté SP, Brazil. No contact details available at press time.

Rádio Educação Rural—Campo Grande, C.P. 261, 79002-233 Campo Grande MS, Brazil. Phone: +55 (67) 384-3164, +55 (67) 382-2238 or +55 (67) 384-3345. Contact: Ailton Guerra, Gerente-Geral; Angelo Venturelli, Diretor; or Diácono Tomás Schwamborn. $1 or return postage required. Replies to correspondence in Portuguese.

Rádio Educação Rural—Coari, Praça São Sebastião 228, 69460-000 Coari AM, Brazil. Contact: Lino Rodrigues Pessoa, Diretor Comercial; Joaquim Florencio Coelho, Diretor Administrador da Comunidade Salgueiro; or Elijane Martins Correa. $1 or return postage helpful. Replies irregularly to correspondence in Portuguese.

☞**Rádio Educadora da Bahia**, Centro de Rádio, Rua Pedro Gama 413/E, Alto Sobradinho Federação, 40230-291 Salvador BA, Brazil. Phone: +55 (71) 339-1180. Fax: +55 (71) 339 1170. Web: (includes RealAudio) www.educadora.com.br. Contact: Elza Correa Ramos; or Walter Sequieros R. Tanure. $1 or return postage required. May send local music CD. Replies to correspondence in Portuguese.

Rádio Educadora de Bragança, Rua Barão do Rio Branco 1151, 68600-000 Bragança PA, Brazil. Contact: José Rosendo de S. Neto; Zelina Cardoso Gonçalves; or Adelino Borges, Aux. Escritório. $1 or return postage required. Replies to correspondence in Portuguese.

Rádio Educadora de Guajará Mirim, Praça Mario Correa No.90, 78957-000 Guajará Mirim RO, Brazil. Contact: Padre Isidoro José Moro. Return postage helpful. Replies to correspondence in Portuguese.

Rádio Educadora de Limeira, C.P. 105, 13480-970 Limeira SP, Brazil. Email: (Bortolan) bab@zaz.com.br. Contact: Bruno Arcaro Bortolan, Gerente.

☞**Rádio Gaúcha**, Avenida Ipiranga 1075 2do andar, Azenha, 90169-900 Porto Alegre RS, Brazil. Phone: +55 (51) 223-6600. Email: (general) gaucha@rdgaucha.com.br; (technical) gilberto.kussler@rdgaucha.com.br. Web: (includes RealAudio) www.rdgaucha.com.br:8080/index2.htm. Contact: Marco Antônio Baggio, Gerente de Jornalismo/Programação; Armindo Antônio Ranzolin, Diretor Gerente; Gilberto Kussler, Gerente Técnico; Geraldo Canali. Replies occasionally to correspondence, preferably in Portuguese.

Rádio Gazeta, Avenida Paulista 900, 01310-940 São Paulo SP, Brazil. Fax: +55 (11) 285 4895. Contact: Shakespeare Ettinger, Supervisor Geral de Operação; Bernardo Leite da Costa; José Roberto Mignone Cheibub, Gerente Geral; or Ing. Aníbal Horta Figueiredo. Free stickers. $1 or return postage necessary. Replies to correspondence in Portuguese. Currently leasing all its airtime to the "Deus é Amor" Pentecostal church, but has been observed in the past to sometimes carry its own programming on at least one of its three shortwave channels.

Rádio Globo, Rua do Russel 434-Glória, 22213-900 Rio de Janeiro RJ, Brazil. Email: (administration) gerenciaamrio@radioglobo.com.br. Web: (includes RealAudio) www.radioglobo.com.br/globorio/. Contact: Marcos Libretti, Diretor Geral. Replies irregularly to correspondence in Portuguese. Return postage helpful.

Rádio Globo, Rua das Palmeiras 315, 01288-900 São Paulo SP, Brazil. Email: (Rapussi) margarete@radioglobo.com.br. Web: (includes RealAudio) www.radioglobo.com.br/globosp/. Contact: Ademar Dutra, Locutor, "Programa Ademar Dutra"; Margarete Rapussi; Guilherme Viterbo; or José Marques. Replies to correspondence, preferably in Portuguese.

Rádio Guaíba, Rua Caldas Junior 219, 90019-900 Porto Alegre RS, Brazil. Phone: +55 (51) 224-3755 or +55 (51) 224-4555. Email: guaiba@cpovo.net. Web: (includes RealAudio) www.cpovo.net/radio/. Return postage helpful.

Rádio Guarani, Avenida Assis Chateaubriand 499, Floresta, 30150-101 Belo Horizonte MG, Brazil. Web: (includes RealAudio) www.guarani.com.br/index.html. Contact: Junara Belo, Setor de Comunicações. Replies slowly to correspondence in Portuguese. Return postage helpful.

Rádio Guarujá
STATION: C.P. 45, 88000-000 Florianópolis SC, Brazil. Contact: Mario Silva, Diretor; Joana Sempre Bom Braz, Assessora de Marketing e Comunicação; or Rosa Michels de Souza. Return postage required. Replies irregularly to correspondence in Portuguese.
NEW YORK OFFICE: 45 West 46 Street, 5th Floor, Manhattan, NY 10036 USA.

Rádio Inconfidência, C.P. 1027, 30650-540 Belo Horizonte MG, Brazil. Fax: +55 (31) 296 3070. Email: inconfidencia@plugway.com.br. Web: (includes RealAudio) www.plugway.com.br/inconfidencia/. Contact: Isaias Lansky, Diretor; Manuel Emilio de Lima Torres, Diretor Superintendente; Jairo Antolio Lima, Diretor Artístico; or Eugenio Silva. Free stickers and postcards. May send CD of Brazilian music. $1 or return postage helpful.

Rádio Integração (when active), Rua Alagoas 270, 69980-000 Cruzeiro do Sul AC, Brazil. Contact: Oscar Alves Bandeira, Gerente. Return postage helpful.

Rádio IPB AM, Rua Itajaí 473, Bairro Antonio Vendas, 79041-270 Campo Grande MS, Brazil. Contact: Iván Páez Barboza, Diretor Geral (hence, the station's name, "IPB"); Pastor Laercio Paula das Neves, Dirigente Estadual; Agenor Patrocinio S., Locutor; Pastor José Adão Hames; or Kelly Cristina Rodrigues da Silva, Secretária. Return postage required. Replies to correspondence in Portuguese. Most of the airtime is leased to the "Deus é Amor" Pentecostal church.

Rádio Itatiaia, Rua Itatiaia 117, 31210-170 Belo Horizonte MG, Brazil. Fax: +55 (31) 446 2900. Email: itatiaia@itatiaia.com.br. Web: (includes RealAudio) www.itatiaia.com.br. Contact: Lúcia Araújo Bessa, Assistente da Diretória; or Claudio Carneiro.

Rádio Jornal "A Crítica" (when active), C.P. 2250, 69061-970 Manaus AM, Brazil; or Av. Andre Araujo s/n, Aleixo, 69060-001 Manaus AM, Brazil. Contact: Sr. Cotrere, Gerente.

Rádio Liberal, C.P 498, 66017-970 Belém PA, Brazil; (physical address) Av. Nazaré 350. 66035-170 Belém PA, Brazil. Phone: +55 (91) 244-6000 or +55 (91) 241-1330. Fax: +55 (91) 224 5240. Email: radio@radioliberal.com.br. Web: (includes RealAudio from the station's FM outlet) www.radioliberal.com.br. Contact: Flavia Vasconcellos; Advaldo Castro, Diretor de Programação AM; João Carlos Silva Ribeiro, Coordenador de Programação AM.

Rádio Marumby, C.P. 296, 88010-970 Florianópolis SC, Brazil; Rua Angelo Laporta 841, C. P. 62, 88020-600 Florianópolis SC, Brazil; or (missionary parent organization) Gideões Missionários da Última Hora—GMUH, Ministério Evangélico Mundial, Rua Joaquim Nunes 244, C.P. 4, 88340-000 Camboriú SC, Brazil. Email: (GMUH parent organization) gmuh@gmuh.com.br. Web: www.gmuh.com.br/Radio/Marumby.htm. Contact: Davi Campos, Diretor Artístico; Dr. Cesario Bernardino, Presidente, GMUH; Pb. Claudiney Nunes, Coordenador Rádio e Jornalismo; or Jair Albano, Diretor. $1 or return postage required. Free diploma and stickers. Replies to correspondence in Portuguese.

Rádio Marumby, Curitiba—*see* Rádio Novas de Paz, Curitiba, below.

Rádio Meteorologia Paulista, C.P. 91, 14940-970 Ibitinga, São Paulo SP, Brazil. Contact: Roque de Rosa, Diretora. Replies to correspondence in Portuguese. $1 or return postage required.

Rádio Missões da Amazônia, Travessa Ruy Barbosa 142, 68250-000 Obidos PA, Brazil. Contact: Max Hamoy; Edérgio de Moras Pinto; or Maristela Hamoy. Return postage required. Replies occasionally to correspondence in Portuguese.

Rádio Mundial, Av. Paulista 2198-Térreo, Cerqueira Cesar, 01310-300 São Paulo, Brazil. Phone: +55 (11) 253-0082. Phone/Fax: +55 (11) 283 5833. Email: webmaster@radiomundial.com.br; radiomundial@radiomundial.com.br. Web: (includes Windows Media) www.radiomundial.com.br. Contact: (nontechnical) Luci Rothschild de Abreu, Diretora Presidente.

Rádio Nacional da Amazônia, SCRN 702/3 Bloco B Lote 16/18, Ed. Radiobrás, 70323-900 Brasília DF, Brazil. Fax: +55 (61) 321 7602. Web: (general) www.radiobras.gov.br/institucional/radioamz.htm; (NetShow audio) www.radiobras.gov.br/radios/radios.htm. Contact: (general) Luíz Otavio de Castro Souza, Diretor; Fernando Gómez da Câmara, Gerente de Escritório; or Januario Procopio Toledo, Diretor. Free stickers, but no verifications.

Rádio Nacional São Gabriel da Cachoeira, Avenida Alvaro Maia 850, 69750-000 São Gabriel da Cachoeira AM, Brazil. Contact: Luíz dos Santos França, Gerente; or Valdir de Souza Marques. Return postage necessary. Replies to correspondence in Portuguese.

Rádio Novas de Paz, Avenida Paraná 1896, 82510-000 Curitiba PR, Brazil; or C.P. 22, 80000-000 Curitiba PR, Brazil. Phone: +55 (41) 257-4109. Contact: João Falavinha Ienzen, Gerente. $1 or return postage required. Replies irregularly to correspondence in Portuguese.

Rádio Nova Visão
STUDIOS: Rua do Manifesto 1373, 04209-001 São Paulo SP, Brazil. Contact: José Eduardo Dias, Diretor Executivo. Return postage required. Replies to correspondence in Portuguese. Free stickers. Relays Rádio Trans Mundial fulltime.
TRANSMITTER: C.P. 551, 97000-000 Santa Maria RS, Brazil; or C.P. 6084, 90000-000 Porto Alegre RS, Brazil. Reportedly issues full-data verifications for reports in Portuguese or German, upon request, from this location. If no luck, try contacting, in English or Dutch, Tom van Ewijck, via email at egiaroll@mail.iss.lcca.usp.br. For further information, see the entry for Rádio Trans Mundial.

Rádio Oito de Setembro, C.P. 8, 13690-000 Descalvado SP, Brazil. Contact: Adonias Gomes. Replies to corrrespondence in Portuguese.

Rádio Pioneira de Teresina, Rua 24 de Janeiro 150 sul/centro, 64001-230 Teresina PI, Brazil. Phone: +55 (86) 222-

8121. Fax: +55 (86) 222 8122. Email: pioneira@ranet.com.br. Contact: Luíz Eduardo Bastos; or Padre Tony Batista, Diretor. $1 or return postage required. Replies slowly to correspondence in Portuguese.

Rádio Progresso (when operating), Estrada do Belmont s/n, Bº Nacional, 78903-400 Porto Velho RO, Brazil. Return postage required. Replies occasionally to correspondence in Portuguese.

Rádio Record
STATION: C.P. 7920, 04084-002 São Paulo SP, Brazil. Email: radiorecord@rederecord.com.br. Web: www.rederecord.com.br (click on "Rádio"). Contact: Mário Luíz Catto, Diretor Geral. Free stickers. Return postage or $1 required. Replies occasionally to correspondence in Portuguese.
NEW YORK OFFICE: 630 Fifth Avenue, Room 2607, New York NY 10111 USA.

Rádio Relógio, Rua Paramopama 131, Ribeira, Ilha do Governador, 21930-110 Rio de Janeiro RJ, Brazil. Phone: +55 (21) 467-0201 or +55 (21) 467-4656. Email: relogio@radiorelogio.com.br. Web: www.radiorelogio.com.br. Replies occasionally to correspondence in Portuguese.

Rádio RGS—see Rádio Rio Grande do Sul, below.

Rádio Ribeirão Preto, C.P. 1252, 14025-000 Ribeirão Preto SP, Brazil (physical address: Av. 9 de Julho 600, 14025-000 Ribeirão Preto SP, Brazil). Phone/fax: +55 (16) 610-3511. Contact: Lucinda de Oliveira, Secretária; Luis Schiavone Junior; or Paulo Henríque Rocha da Silva. Replies to correspondence in Portuguese.

Rádio Rio Grande do Sul, Rede Pampa de Comunicação, Rua Orfanatrófio 711, 90840-440 Porto Alegre RS, Brazil. Phone: +55 (51) 233-8311. Fax: +55 (51) 233-4500. Email: pampa@pampa.com.br. All the station's shortwave outlets carry programming from Sistema LBV Mundial (see), to where all program and reception related correspondence should be sent.

Rádio Rio Mar, Rua José Clemente 500, 69010-070 Manaus AM, Brazil. Replies to correspondence in Portuguese. Contact: Jairo de Sousa Coelho, Diretor de Programação e Jornalismo. $1 or return postage helpful.

Rádio Rural Santarém, Rua São Sebastião 622, 68005-090 Santarém PA, Brazil. Contact: João Elias B. Bentes, Gerente Geral; or Edsergio de Moraes Pinto. Replies slowly to correspondence in Portuguese. Free stickers. Return postage or $1 required.

Rádio Trans Mundial, Caixa Postal 18300, 04626-970 São Paulo SP, Brazil. Phone: +55 (11) 533-3533. Fax: +55 (11) 533 5271. Email: transmun@sp.dglnet.com.br; ("Amigos do Rádio" DX-program) amigosdoradio@transmundial.com.br. Web: www.transmundial.com.br. Contact: José Eduardo Dias, Diretor; or Rudolf Grimm, programa "Amigos do Rádio." Sells religious books and cassettes of religious music (from choral to bossa nova). Prices, in local currency, can be found at the Website (click on "catálogo"). Program provider for Rádio Nova Visão—see, above.

Rádio Tupi, Avenida Nadir Dias Figueiredo 1329, 02110-901 São Paulo SP, Brazil. Contact: Alfredo Raymundo Filho, Diretor Geral; Montival da Silva Santos; or Elia Soares. Free stickers. Return postage required. Replies occasionally to correspondence in Portuguese.

Rádio Universo/Rádio Tupi, C.P. 7133, 80000-000 Curitiba PR, Brazil. Contact: Luíz Andreu Rúbio, Diretor. Replies occasionally to correspondence in Portuguese. Rádio Universo's program time is rented by the "Deus é Amor" Pentecostal church, and is from the Rádio Tupi network. Identifies on the air as "Radio Tupi, Sistema Universo de Comunicação" or, more often, just as "Radio Tupi."

Rádio Verdes Florestas, C.P. 53, 69981-970 Cruzeiro do Sul AC, Brazil. Contact: Marlene Valente de Andrade. Return postage required. Replies occasionally to correspondence in Portuguese.

Rádio Voz do Coração Imaculado, C.P. 354, 75001-970 Anápolis GO, Brazil. A new station which appeared in 1999, broadcasting via the transmitter formerly used by Rádio Carajá.

Sistema LBV Mundial, Legião da Boa Vontade, Av. Sérgio Tomás 740, Bom Retiro, 01131-010 São Paulo SP, Brazil; or Rua Doraci 90, Bom Retiro, 01134-020 São Paulo SP, Brazil. Phone: 3225-4500. Fax: +55 (11) 3225 4639. Web: (general) http://sistema.lbv.org; (LBV parent organization, includes RealAudio) www.lbv.org. Contact: André Tiago, Diretor; Sandra Albuquerque, Secretária; or Gizelle Almeida, Gerente do Dept. de Rádio. Replies slowly to correspondence in all main languages. Program provider for Radio Rio Grande do Sul (see).
NEW YORK OFFICE: 383 5th Avenue, 2nd Floor, New York NY 10016 USA. Phone: +1 (212) 481-1004. Fax: +1 (212) 481 1005. Email: lgw2000@aol.com.

Voz de Libertação. Ubiquitous programming originating from the "Deus é Amor" Pentecostal church's Rádio Universo (1300 kHz) in São Bernardo do Campo, São Paulo, and heard over several shortwave stations, including Rádio Universo, Curitiba (see) and Rádio Gazeta, São Paulo (see). A RealAudio feed is available at the "Deus é Amor" Website, www.ipda.org.br.

Voz do Coração Imaculado—see Rádio Voz do Coração Imaculado.

BULGARIA   World Time +2 (+3 midyear)

Bulgarian National Radio, 4 Dragan Tsankov Blvd., 1040 Sofia, Bulgaria. Phone: +359 (2) 652-871. Fax: (weekdays) +359 (2) 657 230. Web: (includes RealAudio) www.nationalradio.bg. Contact: Borislav Djamdjiev, Director; Iassen Indjev, Executive Director; or Martin Minkov, Editor-in-Chief.

Radio Bulgaria
NONTECHNICAL AND TECHNICAL: P.O. Box 900, BG-1000, Sofia, Bulgaria. Phone: (general) +359 (2) 661-954 or +359 (2) 854-633; (Managing Director) +359 (2) 854-604. Fax: (general, usually weekdays only) +359 (2) 871 060, +359 (2) 871 061 or +359 (2) 650 560; (Managing Director) +359 (2) 946 1576; or +359 (2) 988 5103; (Frequency Manager) +359 (2) 963 4464. Email: rcorresp1@fon15.bnr.acad.bg; or rbul1@nationalradio.bg. Web: (RealAudio in English, French and Russian) www.nationalradio.bg/real.htm. Contact: (general) Mrs. Iva Delcheva, English Section; Kristina Mihailova, In Charge of Listeners' Letters, English Section; Christina Pechevska, Listeners' Letters, English Section; Svilen Stoicheff, Head of English Section; (administration and technical) Anguel H. Nedyalkov, Managing Director; (technical) Atanas Tzenov, Director. Replies regularly, but sometimes slowly. Return postage helpful, as the station is financially overstretched due to the economic situation in the country. For concerns about frequency usage, contact BTC, below, with copies to Messrs. Nedyalkov and Tzenov of Radio Bulgaria.
FREQUENCY MANAGEMENT AND TRANSMISSION OPERATIONS: Bulgarian Telecommunications Company (BTC), Ltd., 8 Totleben Blvd., 1606 Sofia, Bulgaria. Phone: +359 (2) 88-00-75. Fax: +359 (2) 87 58 85 or +359 (2) 80 25 80. Contact: Roumen Petkov, Frequency Manager; or Mrs. Margarita Krasteva, Radio Regulatory Department.

🔊**Radio Horizont**—a service of Bulgarian National Radio (*see*, above).

Radio Varna, 22 blv. Primorski, 9000 Varna, Bulgaria. Replies irregularly. Return postage required. If no reply is forthcoming, try sending an email to rcorresp1@bnr.acad.bg.

BURKINA FASO World Time exactly

Radiodiffusion-Télévision Burkina, B.P. 7029, Ouagadougou, Burkina Faso. Phone: +226 310-441. Contact: (general) Raphael L. Onadia or M. Pierre Tassembedo; (technical) Marcel Teho, Head of Transmitting Centre. Replies irregularly to correspondence in French. IRC or return postage helpful.

BURMA—*see* MYANMAR.

BURUNDI World Time +2

La Voix de la Révolution, B.P. 1900, Bujumbura, Burundi. Phone: +257 22-37-42. Fax: +257 22 65 47 or +257 22 66 13. Email: rtnb@cbinf.com. Contact: (general) Grégoire Barampumba, Head of News Section; or Frederic Havugiyaremye, Journaliste; (administration) Gérard Mfuranzima, Le Directeur de la Radio; or Didace Baranderetse, Directeur Général de la Radio; (technical) Abraham Makuza, Le Directeur Technique. $1 required.

CAMBODIA World Time +7

National Radio of Cambodia
STATION ADDRESS: 106 Preah Kossamak Street, Monivong Boulevard, Phnom Penh, Cambodia. Phone: +855 (23) 423-369 or +855 (23) 422-869. Fax: + 855 (23) 427 319. Contact: (general) Miss Hem Bory, English Announcer; Kem Yan, Chief of External Relations; or Touch Chhatha, Producer, Art Department; (administration) In Chhay, Chief of Overseas Service; Som Sarun, Chief of Home Service; Van Sunheng, Deputy Director General, Cambodian National Radio and Television; or Ieng Muli, Minister of Information; (technical) Oum Phin, Chief of Technical Department. Free program schedule. Replies irregularly and slowly. Do not include stamps, currency, IRCs or dutiable items in envelope. Registered letters stand a much better chance of getting through.

CAMEROON World Time +1

NOTE: Any CRTV outlet is likely to be verified by contacting via registered mail, in English or French with $2 enclosed, James Achanyi-Fontem, Head of Programming, CRTV, B.P. 986, Douala, Cameroon.

Cameroon Radio Television Corporation (CRTV)—Bafoussam (if reactivated), B.P. 970, Bafoussam (Ouest), Cameroon. Contact: (general) Boten Celestin; (technical) Ndam Seidou, Chef Service Technique. IRC or return postage required. Replies irregularly in French to correspondence in English or French.

Cameroon Radio Television Corporation (CRTV)—Bertoua (if reactivated), B.P. 230, Bertoua (Eastern), Cameroon. Rarely replies to correspondence, preferably in French. $1 required.

Cameroon Radio Television Corporation (CRTV)—Buea, P.M.B., Buea (Sud-Ouest), Cameroon. Contact: Ononino Oli Isidore, Chef Service Technique. Three IRCs, $1 or return postage required.

Cameroon Radio Television Corporation (CRTV)—Douala (if reactivated), B.P. 986, Douala (Littoral), Cameroon. Contact: (technical) Emmanual Ekite, Technicien. Free pennants. Three IRCs or $1 required.

Cameroon Radio Television Corporation (CRTV)—Garoua, B.P. 103, Garoua (Nord/Adamawa), Cameroon. Contact: Kadeche Manguele. Free cloth pennants. Three IRCs or return postage required. Replies irregularly and slowly to correspondence in French.

🔊**Cameroon Radio Television Corporation (CRTV)—Yaoundé**, B.P. 1634, Yaoundé (Centre-Sud), Cameroon. Phone: +237 214-035, +237 208-037. Fax: +237 204 340. Email: crtv@crtv.cm. Web: (includes RealAudio and MP3) www.crtv.cm. Contact: (technical or nontechnical) Prof. Gervais Mendo Ze, Directeur-Général; (technical) Eyebe Tanga, Directeur Technique. $1 required. Replies slowly (sometimes extremely slowly) to correspondence in French.

CANADA World Time −3:30 (−2:30 midyear)
Newfoundland; −4 (−3 midyear) Atlantic; −5 (−4 midyear) Eastern, including Quebec and Ontario; −6 (−5 midyear) Central; except Saskatchewan; −6 Saskatchewan; −7 (−6 midyear) Mountain; −8 (−7 midyear) Pacific, including Yukon

BBC World Service via RCI/CBC—For verification direct from RCI's CBC shortwave transmitters, contact Radio Canada International (*see* below). Nontechnical correspondence should be sent to the BBC World Service in London (*see*).

🔊**Canadian Broadcasting Corporation (CBC)—English Programs**, P.O. Box 500, Station A, Toronto, Ontario, M5W 1E6, Canada. Phone: (Audience Relations) +1 (416) 205-3700. Email: cbcinput@toronto.cbc.ca. Web: (includes RealAudio) www.radio.cbc.ca. CBC prepares some of the programs heard over Radio Canada International (*see*).

LONDON NEWS BUREAU: CBC, 43-51 Great Titchfield Street, London W1P 8DD, England. Phone: +44 (20) 7412-9200. Fax: +44 (20) 7631 3095.

PARIS NEWS BUREAU: CBC, 17 avenue Matignon, F-75008 Paris, France. Phone: +33 (1) 4421-1515. Fax: +33 (1) 4421 1514.

WASHINGTON NEWS BUREAU: CBC, National Press Building, Suite 500, 529 14th Street NW, Washington DC 20045 USA. Phone: +1 (202) 383-2900. Contact: Jean-Louis Arcand, David Hall or Susan Murray.

🔊**Canadian Broadcasting Corporation (CBC)—French Programs**, Société Radio-Canada, C.P. 6000, succ. centre-ville, Montréal, Québec, H3C 3A8, Canada. Phone: (Audience Relations) +1 (514) 597-6000. Email: (comments on programs) auditoire@montreal.radio-canada.ca. Welcomes correspondence sent to this address but may not reply due to shortage of staff. Web: (includes RealAudio) www.radio-canada.ca. CBC prepares some of the programs heard over Radio Canada International (*see*).

CBC Northern Quebec Shortwave Service—*see* Radio Canada International, below.

🔊**CFRX-CFRB**
MAIN ADDRESS: 2 St. Clair Avenue West, Toronto, Ontario, M4V 1L6, Canada. Phone:(main switchboard) +1 (416) 924-5711; (talk shows switchboard) +1 (416) 872-1010; (news centre) +1 (416) 924-6717; (CFRB information access line) +1 (416) 872-2372. Fax: (main fax line) +1 (416) 323 6830; (CFRB news fax line) +1 (416) 323 8616. Email: (comments) CFRBcomments@cfrb.com; (news) news@cfrb.com; (nontechnical) opsmngr@cfrb.com; (technical) ian.sharp@cfrb.com.

Web: (includes Windows Media) www.cfrb.com. Contact: (nontechnical) Steve Kowch, Operations Manager; (technical) Ian Sharp. Reception reports should be sent to verification address, below.

VERIFICATION ADDRESS: Ontario DX Association, P.O. Box 161, Station 'A', Willowdale, Ontario, M2N 5S8, Canada or by email: odxa@compuserve.com. Information about CFRB/CFRX can be seen on the ODXA Website Web: www.odxa.on.ca. General information about CFRB/CFRX reception may be directed to the QSL Manager, Steve Canney, VA3SC. A free CFRB/CFRX information sheet and an ODXA brochure is enclosed with your verification card. Reports are processed quickly if sent to this address.

CFVP-CKMX, AM 1060, Standard Broadcasting, P.O. Box 2750, Station 'M', Calgary, Alberta, T2P 4P8, Canada. Phone: (general) +1 (403) 240-5800; (news) +1 (403) 240-5844; (technical) +1 (403) 240-5867. Fax: (general and technical) +1 (403) 240 5801; (news) +1 (403) 246 7099. Contact: (general) Gary Russell, General Manager; or Beverley Van Tighem, Exec. Ass't.; (technical) Ken Pasolli, Technical Director.

CHNX-CHNS (when operating), P.O. Box 400, Halifax, Nova Scotia, B3J 2R2, Canada. Phone: +1 (902) 422-1651. Fax: +1 (902) 422 5330. Email: (general, including reception reports) chns@ns.sympatico.ca; (reception reports only) chnx@post.com. Contact: Garry Barker, General Manager; (programs) Troy Michaels, Operations Manager; (technical) Mark Olson, Station Engineer; (reception reports) Scott Snailham, Production Assistant. Program schedules, stickers and small souvenirs sometimes available. Return postage or $1 helpful. Replies irregularly.

CHU, Time and Frequency Standards, Bldg. M-36, National Research Council, Ottawa, Ontario, K1A 0R6, Canada. Phone: (general) +1 (613) 993-5186; (administration) +1 (613) 993-1003 or +1 (613) 993-2704. Fax: +1 (613) 993 1394. Email: time@nrc.ca. Web: www.cisti.nrc.ca/inms/time/ctse.html. Contact: Dr. Rob Douglas; Dr. Jean-Simon Boulanger, Group Leader; or Ray Pelletier, Technical Officer. Official standard frequency and World Time station for Canada on 3330, 7335 and 14670 kHz. Brochure available upon request. Those with a personal computer, Bell 103 compatible modem and appropriate software can get the exact time, from CHU's cesium clock, via the telephone; details available upon request, or direct from the Website.

CKZN, CBC Newfoundland and Labrador, P.O. Box 12010, Station 'A', St. John's, Newfoundland, A1B 3T8, Canada. Phone: +1 (709) 576-5155. Fax: +1 (709) 576 5099. Email: (administration) radiomgt@stjohns.cbc.ca. Web: (includes RealAudio) www.stjohns.cbc.ca. Contact: (general) Heather Elliott, Communications Officer; (technical) Shawn R. Williams, Manager, Transmission and Distribution; Keith Durnford, Station Engineer; or Jerry Brett, Transmitter Department. Free CBC sticker and verification card with the history of Newfoundland included. Don't enclose money, stamps or IRCs with correspondence, as they will only have to be returned. Relays CBN (St. John's, 640 kHz) except at 1000-1330 World Time (one hour earlier in summer) when programming comes from CFGB Goose Bay.

CFGB ADDRESS: CBC Radio, Box 1029 Station 'C', Happy Valley, Goose Bay, Labrador, Newfoundland A0P 1C0, Canada.

CKZU-CBU, CBC, P.O. Box 4600, Vancouver, British Columbia, V6B 4A2, Canada—for verification of reception reports, mark the envelope, "Attention: Engineering." Toll-free telephone (U.S and Canada only) 1-800-961-6161. Phone: (general) +1 (604) 662-6000; (engineering) +1 (604) 662-6060.

Fax: +1 (604) 662 6350. Email: (general) webmaster @vancouver.cbc.ca; (Newbury) newburyd@vancouver.cbc.ca. Web: (includes RealAudio) www.vancouver.cbc.ca. Contact: (general) Public Relations; (technical) Dave Newbury, Transmission Engineer.

Radio Canada International

NOTE: (CBC Northern Quebec Service) The following RCI address, fax and email information for the Main Office and Transmission Office is also valid for the CBC Northern Quebec Shortwave Service, provided you make your communication to the attention of the particular service you seek to contact.

MAIN OFFICE: P.O. Box 6000, Montréal, Quebec, H3C 3A8, Canada; or (street address) 1400 boulevard René Lévesque East, Montréal, Québec, H2L 2M2, Canada. Phone: (general) +1 (514) 597-7500; (Audience Relations, Ms. Maggy Akerblom) +1 (514) 597-7555; (Communications, Marketing and Research) +1 (514) 597-7659. Fax: (general) +1 (514) 597 7076; (Audience Relations) +1 (514) 597 7760; (Communications, Marketing and Research) +1 (514) 597 6607. Email: rci@montreal.radio-canada.ca. Web: (includes RealAudio) www.rcinet.ca. Contact: (general) Maggy Akerblom, Director of Audience Relations; Stéphane Parent, Producer/Host "Le courrier mondial"; or Mark Montgomery, Producer/Host "The Maple Leaf Mailbag"; (Communications, Marketing and Research) Ms. Hélène Robillard-Frayne, Director; (administration) Robert O'Reilly, Executive Director; or Ms. Joy Sellers, Programming and Operations; (technical—verifications) Bill Westenhaver. Free stickers. T-shirts, baseball caps, lapel pins, keyholders and briefcases available for sale; write to the above address for a free illustrated flyer giving prices and ordering information.

TRANMISSION OFFICE: 1400 boulevard René Lévesque East, Montréal, Québec, H2L 2M2, Canada. Phone: +1 (514) 597-769/20. Fax: +1 (514) 284 2052. Email: (Théorêt) gtheoret @montreal.radio-canada.ca; (Bouliane) jboulian @montreal.radio-canada.ca. Contact: (general) Gérald Théorêt, Manager, Frequency Management; or Ms. Nicole Vincent, Frequency Management; (administration) Jacques Bouliane, Coordinator, Plant Engineering. This office only for informing about transmitter-related problems (interference, modulation quality, etc.), especially by fax. Verifications not given out at this office; requests for verification should be sent to the main office, above.

TRANSMITTER SITE: CBC, P.O. Box 6131, Sackville New Brunswick, E4L 1G6, Canada. Phone: +1 (506) 536-2690/1. Fax: +1 (506) 536 2342. Contact: Raymond Bristol, Plant Manager Transmitting Stations. All correspondence not concerned with transmitting equipment should be directed to the appropriate address in Montréal, above. Free tours given during normal working hours.

RCI MONITORING STATION: P.O. Box 322, Station C, Ottawa, Ontario, K1Y 1E4, Canada. Phone: +1 (613) 831-2801. Fax: +1 (613) 831 0343. Contact: Derek Williams, Manager Monitoring Station.

Radio Monte-Carlo Middle East (via Radio Canada International)—*see* France.

Shortwave Classroom, G.L. Comba Public School, P.O. Box 580, Almonte, Ontario, K0A 1A0, Canada. Phone: +1 (613) 256-2735. Fax: +1 (613) 256 3107. Contact: Neil Carleton, Organizer. *The Shortwave Classroom* newsletter, three times per year, for "$10 and an accompanying feature to share with teachers in the newsletter." Ongoing nonprofit volunteer project of teachers and others to use shortwave listening in the classroom to teach about global perspectives, media studies, world geography, languages, social studies and other subjects. Interested teachers and parents worldwide are invited to make contact.

CENTRAL AFRICAN REPUBLIC   World Time +1

Radio Centrafrique, Radiodiffusion-Télévision Centrafricaine, B.P. 940, Bangui, Central African Republic. Contact: (technical) Jacques Mbilo, Le Directeur des Services Techniques; or Michèl Bata, Services Techniques. Replies on rare occasions to correspondence in French; return postage required.

Radio Ndeke Luka, c/o PNUD, Av. de l'Indépendance, B.P. 872, Bangui, Central African Republic. Operated by the Hirondelle Foundation, and successor to the UN-run Radio MINURCA.

CHAD   World Time +1

Radiodiffusion Nationale Tchadienne—N'djamena, B.P. 892, N'Djamena, Chad. Web: www.tit.td/rnt/. Contact: Djimadoum Ngoka Kilamian; or Ousmane Mahamat. Two IRCs or return postage required. Replies slowly to correspondence in French.

Radiodiffusion Nationale Tchadienne—Radio Moundou (when operating), B.P. 122, Moundou, Logone, Chad. Contact: Dingantoudji N'Gana Esaie.

CHILE   World Time –3 (–4 midyear)

Radio Esperanza

OFFICE: Casilla 830, Temuco, Chile. Phone/fax: +56 (45) 240-161. Contact: (general) Juanita Cárcamo, Departamento de Programación; Eleazar Jara, Dpto. de Programación; Ramón P. Woerner K., Publicidad; or Alberto Higueras Martínez, Locutor; (verifications) Rodolfo Campos, Director; Juanita Carmaco M., Dpto. de Programación; (technical) Juan Luis Puentes, Dpto. Técnico. Free pennants, stickers, bookmarks and tourist information. Two IRCs, $1 or 2 U.S. stamps appreciated. Replies, often slowly, to correspondence in Spanish or English.

STUDIO: Calle Luis Durand 03057, Temuco, Chile. Phone/fax: +56 (45) 240-161.

Radio Santa María, Apartado 1, Coyhaique, Chile. Phone: +56 (67) 23-23-98, +56 (67) 23-20-25 or +56 (67) 23-18-17. Fax: +56 (67) 23 13 06. Contact: Pedro Andrade Vera, Coordinador. $1 or return postage required. May send free tourist cards. Replies to correspondence in Spanish and Italian.

Radio Triunfal Evangélica (when operating), Calle Las Araucarias 2757, Villa Monseñor Larrain, Talagante, Chile. Phone: +56 (1) 815-4765. Contact: Fernando González Segura, Obispo de la Misión Pentecostal Fundamentalista. Two IRCs required. Replies to correspondence in Spanish.

Radio Voz Cristiana, Casilla 490-3, Santiago, Chile. Phone: (engineering) +56 (2) 855-7046. Fax: +56 (2) 855 7053. Email: (engineering) vozing@interaccess.cl; or aflynn@interaccess.cl; (administration) vozcrist@interaccess.cl. Web: www.christianvision.org/christian-vision/chile.htm; (includes Windows Media) www.vozcristiana.com. Contact: (technical) Andrew Flynn, Chief Engineer. Free program and frequency

schedules. Sometimes sends small souvenirs. All QSL requests should be sent to the Miami Address. May extend broadcasting targets beyond Latin America.

INTERNATIONAL OFFICE: Christian Vision, Ryder Street, West Bromwich, West Midlands B70 0EJ, United Kingdom. Contact: Terry Bennett, Regional Manager for the Americas.

MIAMI ADDRESS: P.O. Box 2889, Miami FL 33144 USA. Phone: +1 (305) 231-7704. Fax: +1 (305) 231 7447. Email: cv-usa@msn.com. Contact: (nontechnical) Mark Gallado.

CHINA   World Time +8; still nominally +6 ("Urümqi Time") in the Xinjiang Uighur Autonomous Region, but in practice +8 is observed there, as well.

NOTE: China Radio International, the Central People's Broadcasting Station and certain regional outlets reply regularly to listeners' letters in a variety of languages. If a Chinese regional station does not respond to your correspondence within four months—and many will not, unless your letter is in Chinese or the regional dialect—try writing them c/o China Radio International.

Central People's Broadcasting Station (CPBS)—China National Radio, Zhongyang Renmin Guangbo Diantai, P.O. Box 4501, Beijing 100866, China. Phone: +86 (10) 6851-2435 or +86 (10) 6851-5522. Fax: +86 (10) 6851 6630. Email: cnr@shcei.com.cn. Web: (includes RealAudio) http://cnr.net.cn/. Contact: Wang Changquan, Audience Department, China National Radio. Tape recordings of music and news $5 plus postage. CPBS T-shirts $10 plus postage; also sells ties and other items with CPBS logo. No credit cards. Free stickers, pennants and other small souvenirs. Return postage helpful. Responds regularly to correspondence in English and Standard Chinese (Mandarin). Although in recent years this station has officially been called "China National Radio" in English-language documents, all on-air identifications in Standard Chinese continue to be "Zhongyang Renmin Guangbo Diantai" (Central People's Broadcasting Station). CPBS-1 also airs Chinese-language programs co-produced by CPBS and Radio Canada International.

China Huayi Broadcasting Company, P.O. Box 251, Fuzhou, Fujian 350001, China. Contact: Lin Hai Chun, Announcer; or Wu Gehong. Replies to correspondence in English and Chinese. On-air, announces in English as "Corporation" but the correct translation from the Chinese name is "Company."

China National Radio—see Central People's Broadcasting Station (CPBS), above.

China Radio International

MAIN OFFICE, NON-CHINESE LANGUAGES SERVICE: 16A Shijingshan Street, Beijing 100040, China; or P.O. Box 4216, CRI-2 Beijing 100040 China. Phone: (Director's office) +86 (10) 6889-1676; (Audience Relations.) +86 (10) 6889-1617 or +86 (10) 6889-1652; (English newsroom) +86 (10) 6889-1619; (current affairs) +86 (10) 6889-1588; (Technical Director) +86 (10) 6609-2577. Fax: (Director's office) +86 (10) 6889 1582; (English Service) +86 (10) 6889 1378 or +86 (10) 6889 1379; (Audience Relations) +86 (10) 6851 3175; or (administration) +86 (10) 6851 3174. Email: (English Service) crieng@cri.com.cn; or msg@cri.com.cn; (Chinese Service) chn@cri.com.cn; (Ger-

man Service) ger@box.cri.com.cn; (Spanish Service) servispa@box.cri.com.cn; ("Voices from Other Lands" program) voices@box.cri.com.cn. Web: (official, including RealAudio) www.cri.com.cn; (unofficial, but regularly updated) http://pw2.netcom.com/~jleq/cril.htm. Contact: Ms. Qi Guilin, Director of Audience Relations, English Service; Shang Chunyan, "Listener's Letterbox"; Xu Ming, Editor; or Xia Jixuan, Director of English Service; (technical) Wang Guoqing, Technical Director; (administration) Li Dan, President, China Radio International; Wang Guoqing, Cong Yingmin and Wong Rufeng, Deputy Directors, China Radio International. Free bimonthly *Messenger* newsletter for loyal listeners, pennants, stickers, desk calendars, pins and handmade papercuts. Sometimes, China Radio International holds contests and quizzes, with the overall winner getting a free trip to China. T-shirts for $8. Two-volume, 820-page set of *Day-to-Day Chinese* language-lesson books $15, including postage worldwide; a 155-page book, *Learn to Speak Chinese: Sentence by Sentence*, plus two cassettes for $15. Two chinese music tapes for $15. Various other books (on arts, medicine, Chinese idioms etc.) in English available from Audience Relations Department, English Service, China Radio International, 100040 Beijing, China. Payment by postal money order to Mr. Li Yi. Every year, the Audience Relations Department will renew the mailing list of the *Messenger* newsletter. CRI is also relayed via shortwave transmitters in Canada, Cuba, France, French Guiana, Mali, Russia and Spain.
FREQUENCY PLANNING DIVISION: Radio and Television of People's Republic of China, 2 Fuxingmenwai Street, Beijing 100866, China; or P.O. Box 2144, Beijing 100866, China. Phone: (Wang Xiulan) +86 (10) 6609-2080 or +86 (10) 6609-2627; (Yang Minmin) +86 (10) 6609-2070. Fax: +86 (10) 6801 6436 or +86 (10) 6609 2176. Email: (Wang Xiulan) plc2000@btamail.net.cn; (Yang Minmin & Li Guohua) pdc@abrs.chinasartft. Contact: Ms. Wang Xiulan; Ms. Li Guohua; Ms. Yang Minmin; or Zheng Shuguang.
MAIN OFFICE, CHINESE LANGUAGES SERVICE: China Radio International, Beijing 100040, China. Prefers correspondence in Chinese (Mandarin), Cantonese, Hakka, Chaozhou or Amoy.
ARLINGTON NEWS BUREAU: 2000 South Eads Street APT#712, Arlington VA 22202 USA. Phone: +1 (703) 521-8689. Contact: Mr. Zhenbang Dong.
CHINA (HONG KONG) NEWS BUREAU: 387 Queen's Road East, Room 1503, Hong Kong, China. Phone: +852 2834-0384. Contact: Ms. Zhang Jiaping.
JERUSALEM NEWS BUREAU: Flat 16, Hagdud Ha'ivri 12, Jerusalem 92345, Israel. Phone: +972 (2) 566-6084. Contact: Mr. H. Yi.
LONDON NEWS BUREAU: 13B Clifton Gardens, Golders Green, London NW11 7ER, United Kingdom. Phone: +44 (20) 8458-6943. Contact: Ms. Xu Huazhen
NEW YORK NEWS BUREAU: 630 First Avenue #35K, New York NY 10016 USA. Fax: +1 (212) 889 2076. Contact: Mr Li.
SYDNEY NEWS BUREAU: Unit 53, Block A15 Herbert Street, St. Leonards NSW 2065, Australia. Phone: +61 (2) 9436-1493. Contact: Mr. Shi Chungyong.
SAN FRANCISCO OFFICE, SCHEDULES: 2654 17th Avenue, San Francisco CA 94116 USA. Phone: +1 (415) 564-9968. Email: GPoppin@aol.com. Contact: George Poppin. This address, a volunteer office, only provides CRI schedules to listeners. All other correspondence should be sent directly to the main office in Beijing.
Fujian People's Broadcasting Station, 2 Gutian Lu, Fuzhou, Fujian 350001, China. $1 or IRC helpful. Contact: Audience Relations. Replies occasionally and usually slowly.

Prefers correspondence in Chinese.
Gansu People's Broadcasting Station, 226 Donggang Xilu, Lanzhou 730000, China. Phone: +86 (931) 841-1054. Fax: +86 (931) 882 5834. Contact: Li Mei. IRC helpful.
Guangxi Foreign Broadcasting Station, 12 Min Zu Avenue, Nanning, Guangxi 530022, China. Phone: +86 (771) 585-4191, +86 (771) 585-4256 or +86 (771) 585-4403. Email: 101@gxfbs.com or 103@gxfbs.com; (Thanh Mai) thanhmai@gxfbs.com. Web: www.gxfbs.com. Contact: Thanh Mai, Vietnamese Section. Free stickers and handmade papercuts. IRC helpful. Replies irregularly. Broadcasts in Vietnamese and Cantonese to listeners in Vietnam.
Guangxi People's Broadcasting Station, 75 Min Zu Avenue, Nanning, Guangxi 530022, China. Email: gxbs@public.nn.gx.cn. Web: www.gxpbs.com. IRC helpful. Replies irregularly.
Guizhou People's Broadcasting Station, 259 Qingyun Lu, Guiyang, Guizhou 550002, China.
Heilongjiang People's Broadcasting Station, 181 Zhongshan Lu, Harbin, Heilongjiang 150001, China. Phone: +86 (451) 262-7454. Fax: +86 (451) 289 3539. $1 or return postage helpful.
Honghe People's Broadcasting Station, 32 Jianshe Donglu, Gejiu, Yunnan 661400, China. Contact: Shen De-chun, Head of Station; or Mrs. Cheng Lin, Editor-in-Chief. Free travel brochures.
Hubei People's Broadcasting Station, 563 Jiefang Dadao, Wuhan, Hubei 430022, China.
Hunan People's Broadcasting Station, 27 Yuhua Lu, Changsha, Hunan 410007, China.
Jiangxi People's Broadcasting Station, 111 Hongdu Zhong Dadao, Nanchang, Jiangxi 330046, China. Email: gfzq@public.nc.jx.cn. Contact: Tang Ji Sheng, Editor, Chief Editor's Office. Free gold/red pins. Replies irregularly. Mr. Tang enjoys music, literature and stamps, so enclosing a small memento along these lines should help assure a speedy reply.
Nei Menggu (Inner Mongolia) People's Broadcasting Station, 19 Xinhua Darjie, Hohhot, Nei Menggu 010058, China. Contact: Zhang Xiang-Quen, Secretary; or Liang Yan. Replies irregularly.
Qinghai People's Broadcasting Station, 96 Kunlun Lu, Xining, Qinghai 810001, China. Contact: Liqing Fangfang; or Ghou Guo Liang, Director, Technical Department. $1 helpful.
Sichuan People's Broadcasting Station, 119-1 Hongxing Zhonglu, Chengdu, Sichuan 610017, China. Replies occasionally.
Voice of Jinling (Jinling zhi Sheng), P.O. Box 268, Nanjing, Jiangsu 210002, China. Fax: +86 (25) 413 235. Contact: Strong Lee, Producer/Host, "Window of Taiwan." Free stickers and calendars, plus Chinese-language color station brochure and information on the Nanjing Technology Import and Export Corporation. Replies to correspondence in Chinese and to simple correspondence in English. $1, IRC or 1 yuan Chinese stamp required for return postage.
Voice of Pujiang (Pujiang zhi Sheng), P.O. Box 3064, Shanghai 200002, China. Phone: +86 (21) 6208-2797. Fax: +86 (21) 6208 2850. Contact: Jiang Bimiao, Editor and Reporter.
Voice of the Strait (Haixia zhi Sheng), People's Liberation Army Broadcasting Centre, P.O. Box 187, Fuzhou, Fujian 350012, China. Email: hxzs@mail.radiohx.com. Web: (includes RealAudio) www.radiohx.com. Replies irregularly.
Wenzhou People's Broadcasting Station, 19 Xianxue Qianlu, Wenzhou, Zhejiang 325000, China.

Xilingol People's Broadcasting Station, Xilin Dajie, Xilinhot, Nei Menggu 026000, China.

Xinjiang People's Broadcasting Station, 84 Tuanjie Lu, Urümqi, Xinjiang 830044, China. Contact: Zhao Ji-shu. Free tourist booklet, postcards and used Chinese stamps. Replies to correspondence in Chinese and to simple correspondence in English.

Xizang People's Broadcasting Station, 180 Beijing Zhonglu, Lhasa, Xizang 850000, China. Contact: Lobsang Chonphel, Announcer. Free stickers and brochures. Enclosing an English-language magazine may help with a reply.

Yunnan People's Broadcasting Station, 73 Renmin Xilu, Central Building of Broadcasting and TV, Kunming, 650031 Yunnan, China. Contact: Sheng Hongpeng or F.K. Fan. Free Chinese-language brochure on Yunnan Province, but no QSL cards. $1 or return postage helpful. Replies occasionally.

Zhejiang People's Broadcasting Station, 11 Wulin Xiang, Moganshan Lu, Hangzhou, Zhejiang 310005, China.

CHINA (TAIWAN) World Time +8

⬛**Central Broadcasting System (CBS)**, 55 Pei'an Road, Tachih, Taipei 104, Taiwan, Republic of China. Phone: +886 (2) 2591-8161. Fax: +886 (2) 2585 0741. Email: cbs@cbs.org.tw. Web: www.cbs.org.tw; www.cbs-taipei.org; (RealAudio) www.cbs.org.tw/cbsns.html. Contact: Lee Ming, Deputy Director. Free stickers.

China Radio, 21 Chang Chun Road 7th Floor, Taipei 10413, Taiwan. Email: (Adams) readams@usa.net. Contact: Richard E. Adams, Station Director. Verifies reception reports. A religious broadcaster, sometimes referred to as "True Light Station," transmitting via leased facilities in Petropavlovsk-Kamchatskiy, Russia.

⬛**Radio Taipei International**, P.O. Box 24-38, Taipei 106, Taiwan, Republic of China. Phone: +886 (2) 2591-8161. Fax: +886 (2) 2598 2254. Email: (nontechnical) prog@cbs.org.tw. Web: (broadcast schedules) www.cbs.org.tw/eng/engb.html; (RealAudio) www.cbs.org.tw/indexenglish.html; (RealAudio program schedule) www.cbs.org.tw/program/Program.htm; www.cbs.org.tw/NewRadio/NewRadio.asp. Contact: (general) Daniel Dong, Chief, Listeners' Service Section; Paula Chao, Producer, "Mailbag Time";Yea-Wen Wang; or Phillip Wong, "Perspectives"; (administration) John C.T. Feng, Director; or Dong Yu-Ching, Deputy Director; (technical) Wen-Bin Tsai, Engineer, Engineering Department; Tai-Lau Ying, Engineering Department; Tien-Shen Kao; or Huang Shuh-shyun, Director, Engineering Department. Free stickers, caps, shopping bags, annual diary, "Let's Learn Chinese" language-learning course materials, booklets and other publications, and Taiwanese stamps. T-shirts $5. The station's programs are relayed to the Americas via WYFR's transmitters in Okeechobee, Florida, USA (see).

OSAKA NEWS BUREAU: C.P.O. Box 180, Osaka Central Post Office, Osaka 530-091, Japan.

TOKYO NEWS BUREAU: P.O Box 21, Azubu Post Office, Tokyo 106, Japan.

SAN FRANCISCO NEWS BUREAU: P.O. Box 192793, San Francisco CA 94119-2793 USA.

⬛**Voice of Asia**, P.O. Box 24-777, Taipei, Taiwan, Republic of China. Phone: +886 (2) 2771-0151, X-2431. Fax: +886 (2) 2751 9277. Web: same as for Radio Taipei International, above. Contact: (general) Vivian Pu, Co-Producer, with Isaac Guo of "Letterbox"; or Ms. Chao Mei-Yi, Deputy Chief; (technical)

Engineering Department. Free shopping bags, inflatable globes, coasters, calendars, stickers and booklets. T-shirts $5.

CLANDESTINE

Clandestine broadcasts are often subject to abrupt change or termination. Being operated by anti-establishment political and/or military organizations, these groups tend to be suspicious of outsiders' motives. Thus, they are more likely to reply to contacts from those who communicate in the station's native tongue, and who are perceived to be at least somewhat favorably disposed to their cause. Most will provide, upon request, printed matter on their cause, though not necessarily in English.

For more detailed information on clandestine stations, refer to the annual publication, *Clandestine Stations List*, about $10 or 10 IRCs postpaid by air, published by the Danish Shortwave Clubs International, Tavleager 31, DK-2670 Greve, Denmark; phone (Denmark) +45 4290-2900; fax (via Germany) +49 6371 71790; email 100413.2375@compuserve.com; its expert editor, Finn Krone of Denmark, may be reached at (email) Krone@dk-online.dk. For CIA media contact information, *see* USA. Also available on the Internet, *The Clandestine Radio Intel Webpage,* specializing in background information on these stations and organized by region and target country. The page can be accessed via: www.qsl.net/yb0rmi/cland.htm. Another informative Web page specializing in Clandestine Radio information and containing a biweekly report on the latest news and developments affecting the study of clandestine radio is *Clandestine Radio Watch* and it can be found at www.geocities.com/capecanaveral/2594/geo-cla.htm.

⬛**"Democratic Voice of Burma"** ("Democratic Myanmar a-Than")
STATION: DVB Radio, P.O. Box 6720, St. Olavs Plass, N-0130 Oslo, Norway. Phone: +47 (22) 20-0021. Phone/fax: +47 (22) 36-2525. Email: euburma@online.no; dvbburma@online.no. Web: (includes RealAudio) www.communique.no/dvb/. Contact: (general) Dr. Anng Kin, Listener Liaison; Aye Chan Naing, Daily Editor; or Thida, host for "Songs Request Program"; (administration) Harn Yawnghwe, Director; or Daw Khin Pyone, Manager; (technical) Saw Neslon Ku, Studio Technician; or Technical Dept. Free stickers and booklets to be offered in the near future. Norwegian kroner requested for a reply, but presumably Norwegian mint stamps would also suffice. Programs produced by Burmese democratic movements, as well as professional and independent radio journalists, to provide informational and educational services for the democracy movement inside and outside Burma. Opposes the current Myanmar government. Transmits via the facilities of Radio Norway International, among others.

AFFINITY GROUPS Web:
BURMA NET. Email: (BurmaNet News editor, Free Burma Coalition, USA) strider@igc.apc.org; (Web coordinator, Free Burma Coalition, USA) freeburma@pobox.com. Web: (BurmaNet News, USA) http://sunsite.unc.edu/freeburma/listservers.html.
FREE BURMA COALITION. Email: justfree@ix.netcom.com. Web: http://danenet.wicip.org/fbc/.

"National Radio of the Democratic Saharan Arab Republic"—*see* Radio Nacional de la República Arabe Saharaui Democrática, Western Sahara.

"Radio Free Iraq"—*see* USA.

"Radio Independence Bougainville," 2 Griffith Avenue, Roseville NSW 2069, Australia. Phone/fax: +61 (2) 9417-1066.

Radio Free Asia's antenna diplexer in Saipan became operational in September, 1999. As a gesture to host nations, RFA's other transmission sites are usually not made public.
H. Creech

Contact: Sam Voron, Australian Director. $5, AUS$5 or 5 IRCs required. Station is operated from Panguna, Central Bougainville by the pro independence forces of the Meekamui Defence Force led by Fransis Ona. Opposed to the Papua New Guinea government.

"Radio Anternacional," BM Box 1499, London WC1N 3XX, United Kingdom. Phone: +44 (771) 461-1099. Email: radio7520@yahoo.com. Web: (includes Windows Media) www.anternacional.org. Contact: Ms. Azar Majedi. A broadcast in Persian sponsored by the Committee for Humanitarian Assistance to Iranian Refugees (CHAIR)—see below— and aired via transmitting facilities in Moldova.
SPONSORING ORGANIZATION: Committee for Humanitarian Assistance to Iranian Refugees (CHAIR), GPO, P.O. Box 7051, New York NY 10116 USA. Phone: +1 (212) 747-1046. Fax: +1 (212) 425 7260. Email: info@chair.org. Web: www.chair.org.

"Radio Kurdistan"—see Iraq.

"Radio Nacional de la República Arabe Saharaui Democrática"—see Western Sahara.

"Radio Rainbow" ("Kestedamena rediyo ye selamena yewendimamach dimtse"), c/o RAPEHGA, P.O. Box 140104, D-53056 Bonn, Germany. Contact: T. Assefa. Supposedly operated by an Ethiopian opposition group called Research and Action Group for Peace in Ethiopia and the Horn of Africa. Broadcasts via hired shortwave transmitters in Germany.

"Radio Sedaye Iran"—see KRSI, USA.

"Radio Voice of Liberty and Renewal," ("Idha'at sawt al-hurriyah wa al-tajdid, sawt quwwat al-tahaluf al-sudaniyyah, sawt al-intifadah al-sha'biyyah al-musallahah"). Web: (Sudan Alliance Forces) www.safsudan.com. The Sudan Alliance Forces are an opposition guerrilla army of ex-government northern soldiers, affiliated to the Asmara, Eritrea-based National Democratic Alliance (NDA). Opposes the current Sudanese government. Also identifies as "Voice of the Sudan Alliance Forces" and "Voice of the Popular Armed Uprising."

"Radio Voice of the Mojahed"—see "Voice of the Mojahed," below.

"Republic of Iraq Radio, Voice of the Iraqi People" ("Idha'at al-Jamahiriya al-Iraqiya, Saut al-Sha'b al-Iraqi"), Broadcasting Service of the Kingdom of Saudi Arabia, P.O. Box 61718, Riyadh 11575, Saudi Arabia. Phone: +966 (1) 442-5170. Fax: +966 (1) 402 8177. Contact: Suliman A. Al-Samnan, Director of Frequency Management. Anti-Saddam Hussein "black" clandestine supported by CIA, British intelligence, the Gulf Cooperation Council and Saudi Arabia. The name of this station has changed periodically since its inception during the Gulf crisis. Via transmitters in Saudi Arabia.
SPONSORING ORGANIZATION: Iraqi National Congress, 17 Cavendish Square, London W1M 9AA, United Kingdom. Phone: +44 (20) 7665-1812; (office in Arbil, Iraq) +873 (682) 346-239. Fax: +44 (20) 7665 1201; (office in Arbil, Iraq) +873 (682) 346 240. Email: pressoffice@inc.org.uk. Web: www.inc.org.uk.

"Voice of China" ("Zhongguo zhi Yin"), P.O. Box 273538, Concord CA 94527 USA; or (sponsoring organization) Foundation for China in the 21st Century, P.O. Box 11696, Berkeley CA 94701 USA. Contact: Bang Tai Xu, Director. Mainly "overseas Chinese students" interested in the democratization of China. Financial support from the Foundation for China in the 21st Century. Has "picked up the mission" of the earlier Voice of June 4th, but has no organizational relationship with it. Transmits via facilities of the Central Broadcasting System, Taiwan (see).

"Voice of Democratic Eritrea" ("Sawt Eritrea al-Dimuqratiya-Sawtu Jabhat al-Tahrir al-Eritrea") (when active), ELF-RC, P.O. Box 200434, D-53134 Bonn, Germany. Phone: +49 (228) 356-181. Email: (Eritrean political opposition) meskerem@erols.com. Web: (includes RealAudio) http:users.erols.com/meskerem/. Contact: Seyoum O. Michael, Member of Executive Committee, ELF-RC. Station of the Eritrean Liberation Front-Revolutionary Council, hostile to the government of Eritrea. Transmits via facilities in Jülich, Germany.

"Voice of Iranian Kurdistan," KDPI, c/o AFK, Boite Postale 102, F-75623 Paris Cedex 13, France. Phone: +33 (1) 4585-6431. Fax: +33 (1) 4585 2093. Email: (Democratic Party of Iranian Kurdistan parent organization) pdkiran@club-internet.fr. Web: www.pdk-iran.org. Anti-Iranian government.

"Voice of Iraqi Kurdistan"—see Iraq.

"Voice of Jammu Kashmir Freedom" ("Sada-i Hurriyat-i Jammu Kashmir"), P.O. Box 102, Muzaffarabad, Azad Kashmir, via Pakistan. Favors Azad Kashmiri independence from India; pro-Moslem, sponsored by the Kashmiri Mojahedin organization. Believed to transmit via facilities in Pakistan.

"Voice of Liberty and Renewal"—*see* "Radio Voice of Liberty and Renewal," above.

"Voice of National Salvation" ("Gugugui Sori Pangsong"), Grenier Osawa 107, 40 Nando-cho, Shinjuku-ku, Tokyo, Japan. Phone: + 81 (3) 5261-0331. Fax: +81 (3) 5261 0332. Email: (National Salvation Front) kuguk@alles.or.jp. Web: (National Salvation Front parent organization) www.alles.or.jp/~kuguk/ . Pro-North Korea, pro-Korean unification; supported by North Korean government. On the air since 1967, but not always under the same name. Via North Korean transmitters located in Pyongyang, Haeju and Wongsan.

📻"Voice of Oromo Liberation" ("Segalee Bilisummaa Oromoo"), Postfach 510610, D-13366 Berlin, Germany; or SBO, Prinzenallee 81, D-13357 Berlin, Germany. Phone: +49 (30) 494-1036. Fax: +49 (30) 494 3372. Email: SBO13366@aol.com. Web: (includes RealAudio) www.oromoliberationfront.org. Contact: Taye Teferah, European Coordinator. Occasionally replies to correspondence in English or German. Return postage required. Station of the Oromo Liberation Front of Ethiopia, an Oromo nationalist organization transmitting via facilities in Germany and, irregularly, elsewhere.

OROMO LIBERATION FRONT USA OFFICE: P.O. Box 73247, Washington DC 20056 USA. Phone: +1 (202) 462-5477. Fax: +1 (202) 332 7011.

"Voice of Palestine, Voice of the Palestinian Islamic Revolution" ("Saut al-Filistin, Saut al-Thowrah al-Islamiyah al-Filistiniyah")—for many years considered a clandestine station, but is now officially listed as part of the Arabic schedule of the Voice of the Islamic Republic of Iran, over whose transmitters the broadcasts are aired. *See* "Iran" for potential contact information. Supports the Islamic Resistance Movement, Hamas, which is anti-Arafat and anti-Israel.

"Voice of Peace and Brotherhood,"—*see* "Radio Rainbow," above.

"Voice of Rebellious Iraq" ("Sawt al-Iraq al-Tha'ir"), P.O. Box 11365/738, Tehran, Iran; P.O. Box 37155/146, Qom, Iran; or P.O. Box 36802, Damascus, Syria. Anti-Iraqi regime, supported by the Shi'ite-oriented Supreme Assembly of the Islamic Revolution of Iraq, led by Mohammed Baqir al-Hakim. Supported by the Iranian government and transmitted from Iranian soil. Hostile to the Iraqi government.

SPONSORING ORGANIZATION: Supreme Council for Islamic Revolution in Iraq (SCIRI), 27a Old Gloucester St, London WC1N 3XX, United Kingdom. Phone: +44 (20) 7371-6815. Fax: +44 (20) 7371 2886. Email: 101642.1150@compuserve.com. Web: http://ourworld.compuserve.com/homepages/sciri/.

"Voice of Sudan," NDA, 16 Camaret Court, Lorne Gardens, London W11 4XX, United Kingdom. Phone: (Asmara studio) +291 (1) 184-027. Email: sudanvoice@umma.org. Web: www.umma.org/nda/sudanvoice.html. Contact: Abdullahi Elmahdi, Secretary General, National Democratic Alliance. Broadcasts on behalf of the National Democratic Alliance (*see*, below), which is opposed to the present Sudanese government. Studios and transmitters located in Asmara, Eritrea.

NATIONAL DEMOCRATIC ALLIANCE (NDA): (Headquarters) Asmara, Eritrea. Phone: +291 (1) 127-641. Fax: +291 (1) 127 632. Email: nda@umma.org. (U.K. Office) Phone: +44 (1344) 874-123. Fax: +44 (1344) 628 077. Email: aelmahdi@cygnet.co.uk. (Egypt Office) Phone: +20 (2) 591-9408. Fax: +20 (2) 593 2908 or +20 (2) 271 5979. Web: www.umma.org/nda/; http://members.xoom.com/_XOOM/nda_soa/index.html.

"Voice of the Communist Party of Iran" ("Seda-ye Hezb-e Komunist-e Iran"), B.M. Box 2123, London WC1N 3XX, United Kingdom. Email: ib@cpiran.org. Web: www.cpiran.org. Sponsored by the Communist Party of Iran (KOMALA, formerly Tudeh).

📻"Voice of the Democratic Path of Ethiopian Unity," Finote Democracy, P.O. Box 88675, Los Angeles CA 90009 USA. Email: efdpu@finote.org. Web: (includes RealAudio) www.finote.org. Transmits via Jülich, Germany.

EUROPE ADDRESS: Finote Democracy, Postbus 10573, 1001 EN, Amsterdam, Holland.

"Voice of the Iranian Revolution" ("Aira Dangi Shurashi Irana")—*see* "Voice of the Communist Party of Iran," above, for details.

"Voice of the Islamic Revolution in Iraq"—*see* "Voice of Rebellious Iraq," above, for contact information. Affiliated with the Shi'ite-oriented Supreme Assembly for Islamic Revolution in Iraq, led by Mohammed Baqir al-Hakim. Transmits via the facilities of Islamic Republic of Iran Broadcasting.

📻"Voice of the Mojahed" ("Seda-ye Mojahed ast")

PARIS BUREAU: Mojahedines de Peuple d'Iran, 17 rue des Gords, F-95430 Auvers-sur-Oise, France; or Mojahed, c/o CCI, 147 rue St. Martin, F-75003 Paris, France. Fax: +33 (1) 4271-5627. Email: (People's Mojahedin Organization of Iran parent organization) Mojahed@mojahedin.org. Web: (RealAudio) www.iran.mojahedin.org/Pages/seda/; (People's Mojahedin Organization of Iran parent organization) www.iran.mojahedin.org. Contact: Majid Taleghani. Station replies very irregularly and slowly. Pre-prepared verification cards and SASE helpful, with correspondence in French or Persian almost certainly preferable. Sponsored by the People's Mojahedin Organization of Iran (OMPI) and the National Liberation Army of Iran.

OTHER BUREAUS: Voice of the Mojahed, c/o Heibatollahi, Postfach 502107, 50981 Köln, Germany; M.I.S.S., B.M. Box 9720, London WC1N 3XX, United Kingdom; P.O. Box 951, London NW11 9EL, United Kingdom; or P.O. Box 3133, Baghdad, Iraq (Contact: B. Moradi, Public Relations).

"Voice of the Kurdistan People"—*see* Iraq.

"Voice of the Popular Armed Uprising,"—*see* "Radio Voice of Liberty and Renewal," above.

"Voice of the Sudan Alliance Forces,"—*see* "Radio Voice of Liberty and Renewal," above.

"Voice of the Worker"

WORKER-COMMUNIST PARTY OF IRAN PARENT ORGANIZATION: Email: wpi@wpiran.org. Web: www.wpiran.org.

"Voice of the Worker Communist Party of Iraq" ("Aira dangi kizb-e cummunist-e kargar-e iraqa"), WCPI Radio, Zargata, Sulaimania, Iraq. Email: radio@wpiraq.org. Web: (WCPI parent organization) www.wpiraq.org; http://users.cybercity.dk/~bsq1433/home.html.

WCPI CANADIAN OFFICE: P.O. Box 491, Domains Postal Station, North York, Ontario M3C 2T4, Canada.

WCPI GERMAN OFFICE: A.K.P.I., Postfach 160244, D-10336 Berlin, Germany.

WCPI UNITED KINGDOM OFFICE: P.O. Box 7962, London SE1 2ZG United Kingdom.

📻"Voice of Tibet," Welhavensgate 1, N-0166 Oslo, Norway. Phone: (administration) +47 2211-4980; (studio) +47 2211-1209. Fax: +47 2211 5474. Email: mail@vot.org; or voti@online.no; (Alme) votibet@yahoo.com. Web: (includes RealAudio) www.vot.org; (text only) www.voti.com. Contact: Øystein Alme, Project Manager [sometimes referred to as "Director"]; or Chophel Norbu, Journalist. Joint venture of the

Norwegian Human Rights House, Norwegian Tibet Committee and World-View International. Programs, which are produced in Oslo, Norway, and elsewhere, focus on Tibetan culture, education, human rights and news from Tibet. Opposed to Chinese control of Tibet. Those seeking a verification for this program should enclose a prepared card or letter. Return postage helpful. Broadcasts via transmitters in Central Asia.

"Voz de la Resistencia"
Email: (FARC-EP parent organization) farc-ep @comision.internal.org; or elbarcino@laneta.apc.org (updated transmission schedules and QSLs available from this address, but correspond in Spanish). Web: www.resistencianacional.org/ radio.htm; (FARC-EP parent organization) http:// burn.ucsd.edu/~farc-ep/. Program of the Fuerzas Armadas Revolucionarias de Colombia - Ejercito del Pueblo.

"World Falun Dafa Radio"
Email: A Chinese online email form is available at the station's Website, but nothing in English. Web: www.falundafaradio.org. Given the secrecy surrounding this station's activities, all that is known is that the programs are produced in the USA and broadcast via leased facilities in Central Asia. Supports the Falun Dafa (Falun Gong) spiritual movement outlawed by the Chinese authorities.

COLOMBIA World Time –5

NOTE: Colombia, the country, is always spelled with two o's. It should never be written as "Columbia."

Armonías del Caquetá, Apartado Aéreo 71, Florencia, Caquetá, Colombia. Phone: +57 (88) 352-080. Contact: Padre Alvaro Serna Alzate, Director. Replies occasionally and slowly to correspondence in Spanish. Return postage required.

Caracol Arauca—see La Voz del Cinaruco.

Caracol Colombia
MAIN OFFICE: Apartado Aéreo 9291, Santafé de Bogotá, D.C., Colombia. Phone: +57 (1) 337-8866. Fax: +57 (1) 337 7126. Web: (includes RealAudio) www.caracol.com.co/webasp2/ homeneo.asp. Contact: Hernán Peláez Restrepo, Jefe Cadena Básica; Efraín Jiménez, Director de Operaciones; or Oscar López M., Director Musical. Free stickers. Replies to correspondence in Spanish and English.
MIAMI OFFICE: 2100 Coral Way, Miami FL 33145 USA. Phone: +1 (305) 285-2477 or +1 (305) 285-1260. Fax: +1 (305) 858 5907.

Caracol Florencia (when active), Apartado Aéreo 465, Florencia, Caquetá, Colombia. Phone: +57 (88) 352-199. Contact: Guillermo Rodríguez Herrera, Gerente; or Vicente Delgado, Operador. Replies occasionally to correspondence in Spanish.

Caracol Villavicencio—see La Voz de los Centauros.

Colmundo Bogotá, Diagonal 58 No. 26-29, Santafé de Bogotá, Colombia; or Apartado Aéreo 36750, Santafé de Bogotá, Colombia. Fax: +57 (1) 217 9358. Contact: María Teresa Gutiérrez, Directora Gerente; Marcela Aristizábal, Presidente; Jorge Eliecer Hernández, Gerente Nacional de Programación; Carlos Arturo Echeverry, Chief Engineer; or Néstor Chamorro, Presidente de la Red Colmundo. Email: colradio@latino.net.co.Actively seeks reception reports from abroad, preferably in Spanish. Free stickers and program schedule.

Ecos del Atrato, Apartado Aéreo 196, Quibdó, Chocó, Colombia. Phone: +57 (49) 711-450. Contact: Absalón Palacios Agualimpia, Administrador. Free pennants. Replies to correspondence in Spanish.

Ecos del Orinoco (when active), Gobernación del Vichada, Puerto Carreño, Vichada, Colombia.

La Voz de la Selva—see Caracol Florencia.

La Voz de los Centauros (Caracol Villavicencio), Cra. 31 No. 37-71 Of. 1001, Villavicencio, Meta, Colombia. Phone: +57 (986) 214-995. Fax: +57 (986) 623 954. Contact: Carlos Torres Leyva, Gerencia; or Olga Arenas, Administradora. Replies to correspondence in Spanish.

La Voz del Cinaruco (if reactivated), Calle 19 No. 19-62, Arauca, Colombia. Contact: Efrahim Valera, Director. Pennants for return postage. Replies rarely to correspondence in Spanish; return postage required.

La Voz del Guaviare, Carrera 22 con Calle 9, San José del Guaviare, Colombia. Phone: +57 (986) 840-153/4. Fax: +57 (986) 840 102. Contact: Luis Fernando Román Robayo, Director General. Replies slowly to correspondence in Spanish.

La Voz del Llano, Calle 41B No. 30-11, Barrio La Grama, Villavicencio, Meta, Colombia. Phone:+57 (986) 624-102. Fax: +57 (986) 625 045. Contact: Manuel Buenaventura, Director; or Edgar Valenzuela Romero. Replies occasionally to correspondence in Spanish. $1 or return postage necessary.

La Voz del Río Arauca
STATION: Carrera 20 No. 19-09, Arauca, Colombia. Phone: +57 (818) 52-910. Contact: Jorge Flórez Rojas, Gerente; Luis Alfonso Riaño, Locutor; or Mario Falla, Periodista. $1 or return postage required. Replies occasionally to correspondence in Spanish; persist.
BOGOTÁ OFFICE: Cra. 10 No. 14-56, Of. 309/310, Santafé de Bogotá, D.C., Colombia.

La Voz del Yopal (when active), Calle 9 No. 22-63, Yopal, Casanare, Colombia. Phone: +57 (87) 558-382. Fax: +57 (87)

557 054. Contact: Pedro Antonio Socha Pérez, Gerente; or Marta Cecilia Socha Pérez, Subgerente. Return postage necessary. Replies to correspondence in Spanish.

Ondas del Meta (when active), Calle 41B No. 30-11, Barrio La Grama, Villavicencio, Meta, Colombia. Phone: +57 (986) 626-783. Fax: +57 (986) 625 045. Contact: Yolanda Plazas Agredo, Administradora. Free tourist literature. Return postage required. Replies irregularly and slowly to correspondence in Spanish. Plans to reactivate from a new antenna site.

Ondas del Orteguaza, Calle 16, No. 12-48, piso 2, Florencia, Caquetá, Colombia. Phone: +57 (88) 352-558. Contact: Sandra Liliana Vásquez, Secretaria; Señora Elisa Viuda de Santos; or Henry Valencia Vásquez. Free stickers. IRC, return postage or $1 required. Replies occasionally to correspondence in Spanish.

Radio Auténtica, Calle 38 No. 32-41, piso 7, Edif. Santander, Villavicencio, Meta, Colombia. Phone: +57 (986) 626-780. Phone/fax: +57 (986) 624 507. Contact: (general) Pedro Rojas Velásquez; or Carlos Alberto Pimienta, Gerente; (technical) Sra. Alba Nelly González de Rojas, Administradora. Sells religious audio cassettes for 3,000 pesos. Return postage required. Replies slowly to correspondence in Spanish.

Radiodifusora Nacional de Colombia
MAIN ADDRESS: Edificio Inravisión, CAN, Av. Eldorado, Santafé de Bogotá, D.C., Colombia. Phone: +57 (1) 222-0415. Fax: +57 (1) 222 0409 or +57 (1) 222 8000. Email: radio_oc @inravision.com.co; radiodifusora@hotmail.com. Web: (includes online reception report form) www.inravision.com.co/ radiodifusora/onda/. Contact: Janeth Jiménez M., Coordinadora de Onda Corta; or Dra. Athala Morris, Directora. Free lapel badges, membership in Listeners' Club and monthly program booklet.

⧉RCN (Radio Cadena Nacional)
MAIN OFFICE: Apartado Aéreo 4984, Santafé de Bogotá, D.C., Colombia. Phone: +57 (1) 314-7070. Fax: +57 (1) 285 0121 or +57 (1) 288 6130. Email: rcn@impsat.net.co. Web: (RealAudio, news and correspondence) www.rcn.com.co. Contact: Antonio Pardo García, Gerente de Producción y Programación. Will verify all correct reports for stations in the RCN network. Spanish preferred and return postage necessary.

Radio Melodía (Cadena Melodía) (when active), Apartado Aéreo 58721, Santafé de Bogotá, D.C., Colombia; or Apartado Aéreo 19823, Santafé de Bogotá, D.C., Colombia. Phone: +57 (1) 217-0423, +57 (1) 217-0720, +57 (1) 217-1334 or +57 (1) 217-1452. Fax: +57 (1) 248 8772. Contact: Gerardo Páez Mejía, Vicepresidente; Elvira Mejía de Pérez, Gerente General; or Gracilla Rodríguez, Asistente Gerencia. Stickers and pennants. $1 or return postage.

Radio Mira, Apartado Aéreo 165, Tumaco, Nariño, Colombia. Phone: +57 (27) 272-452. Contact: Padre Jairo Arturo Ochoa Zea. Return postage required.

Radio Super (Ibagué) (when active), Parque Murillo Toro 3-31, P. 3, Ibagué, Tolima, Colombia. Phone: +57 (982) 611-652 or +57 (982) 637-004. Fax: +57 (82) 611 471. Contact: Fidelina Caycedo Hernández; or Germán Acosta Ramos, Locutor Control. Free stickers. Return postage or $1 helpful. Replies irregularly to correspondence in Spanish.

CONGO (DEMOCRATIC REPUBLIC) (formerly Zaïre) World Time +1 Western, including Kinshasa; +2 Eastern

Radio Bukavu (when active), B.P. 475, Bukavu, Democratic Republic of the Congo. Contact: Jacques Nyembo-Kibeya; Kalume Kavue Katumbi; or Baruti Lusongela, Directeur. $1 or return postage required. Replies slowly. Correspondence in French preferred.

Radio CANDIP Bunia (formerly La Voix du Peuple, and prior to that, Radio CANDIP), B.P. 373, Bunia, Democratic Republic of Congo. Letters should preferably be sent via registered mail. $1 or return postage required. Correspondence in French preferred.

Radio Kisangani (when active), B.P. 1745, Kisangani, Democratic Republic of the Congo. Contact: (general) Lumeto lue Lumeto, Directeur Regional; or Lumbutu Kalome, Directeur Inspecteur; (technical) Lukusa Kowumayi Branly, Technicien. $1 or 2 IRCs required. Correspondence in French preferred. Mail to this station may be interfered with by certain staff members. Try sending letters to Lumbutu Kalome at his private address: 10ᵉ Avenue 34, Zone de la Tshopo, Kisangani, Democratic Republic of the Congo. Registering letters may also help. Replies to North American listeners sometimes are mailed via the Oakland, California, post office.

Radio Lubumbashi (when active), B.P. 7296, Lubumbashi, Democratic Republic of the Congo. Contact: Senga Lokavu, Chef du Service de l'Audiovisuel; Bébé Beshelemu, Directeur; or Mulenga Kanso, Chef du Service Logistique. Letters should be sent via registered mail. $1 or 3 IRCs helpful. Correspondence in French preferred.

Radio-Télévision Nationale Congolaise, B.P. 3171, Kinshasa-Gombe, Democratic Republic of the Congo. Contact: Faustin Mbula, Ingenieur Technicien. Letters should be sent via registered mail. $1 or 3 IRCs helpful. Correspondence in French preferred

CONGO (REPUBLIC)   World Time +1

Radiodiffusion Nationale Congolaise (also announces as "Radio Liberté," "Radio Nationale" or "Radio Congo"), Radiodiffusion-Télévision Congolaise, B.P. 2241, Brazzaville, Congo. Contact: (general) Antoine Ngongo, Rédacteur en chef; (administration) Alphonse Bouya-Dimi, Directeur; or Zaou Mouanda. $1 required. Replies irregularly to letters in French sent via registered mail.

COSTA RICA   World Time –6

Faro del Caribe—TIFC
MAIN OFFICE: Apartado 2710, 1000 San José, Costa Rica. Phone: +506 (226) 2573 or +506 (226) 2618. Fax: +506 (227) 1725. Email: al@casa-pres.go.cr. Web: www.cristo.net/faro/ faro.html. Contact: Carlos A. Rozotto Piedrasanta, Director Administrativo; or Mauricio Ramires; (technical) Minor Enrique, Station Engineer. Free stickers, pennants, books and bibles. $1 or IRCs helpful.
U.S. OFFICE, NONTECHNICAL: Misión Latinoamericana, P.O. Box 620485, Orlando FL 32862 USA.

Radio 88 Estéreo (when operating), Apartado 827-8000, Pérez Zeledón, Costa Rica. Phone: +506 257-8585, +506 771-6094 or (phone/fax) +506 771-6093. Fax: +506 771 5539. Contact: Juan Vega, Director.

Radio Casino, Apartado 287, 7301 Puerto Limón, Costa Rica. Phone: +506 758-0029. Fax: +506 758 3029. Contact: Edwin Zamora, Departamento de Notícias; or Luis Grau Villalobos, Gerente; (technical) Ing. Jorge Pardo, Director Técnico; or Geraldo Moya, Técnico.

Radio Exterior de España—Cariari Relay Station, Cariari de Pococí, Costa Rica. Phone: +506 767-7308, +506 767-7311. Fax: +506 225 2938.

📻Radio For Peace International (RFPI)
MAIN OFFICE: Apartado 88, Santa Ana, Costa Rica. Phone: +506 249-1821. Fax: +506 249 1095. Email: info@rfpi.org; rfpicr@sol.racsa.co.cr. Web: (includes RealAudio) www.rfpi.org. Contact: (general) Debra Latham, General Manager of RFPI, Editor of *VISTA* and co-host of "RFPI Mailbag"; (programming) Joe Bernard, English Program Coordinator; Willie Barrantes, Director, Spanish Department; or Ms. Sabine Kapuschinski, Host of German program; (nontechnical or technical) James Latham, Station Manager. Replies sometimes slow in coming because of the mail. Quarterly *VISTA* newsletter, which includes schedules and program information, $40 annual membership ($50 family/organization) in "Friends of Radio for Peace International"; station commemorative T-shirts and rainforest T-shirts $20; thermo mugs $10 (VISA/MC). Actively solicits listener contributions. Free online verification of email reports, but $1 or 3 IRCs required for verification by QSL card. Limited number of places available for volunteer broadcasting and journalism interns; those interested should send résumé. RFPI was created by United Nations Resolution 35/55 on December 5, 1980.
U.S. OFFICE, NONTECHNICAL: P.O. Box 20728, Portland OR 97294 USA. Phone: +1 (503) 252-3639. Fax: +1 (503) 255 5216. Contact: Dr. Richard Schneider, Chancellor CEO, University of Global Education (formerly World Peace University). Newsletter, T-shirts and so forth, as above. University of the Air courses (such as "Earth Mother Speaks" and "History of the U.N.") $25 each, or on audio cassette $75 each (VISA/MC).

Radio Reloj, Sistema Radiofónico H.B., Apartado 341, 1000 San José, Costa Rica. Contact: Roger Barahona, Gerente; or Francisco Barahona Gómez. Can be very slow in replying. $1 required.

Radio Universidad de Costa Rica, Apartado 1-06, 2060 Universidad de Costa Rica, San Pedro de Montes de Oca, San José, Costa Rica. Phone: (general) +506 207-4727; (studio) +506 225-3936. Fax: +506 207 5459. Email: radioucr@cariari.ucr.ac.cr. Web: http://cariari.ucr.ac.cr/~radioucr/radioucr/. Contact: Marco González Muñoz; Henry Jones, Locutor de Planta; or Nora Garita B., Directora. Marco González is a radio amateur, call-sign TI3AGM. Free postcards, station brochure and stickers. Replies slowly to correspondence in Spanish or English. $1 or return postage required.

University Network—*see* entry under "USA," later in this section.

CÔTE D'IVOIRE   World Time exactly

Radiodiffusion Télévision Ivoirienne (if reactivated), B.P. 191, Abidjan 1, Côte d'Ivoire. Phone: +225 324-800. Email: rti@rti.ci. Web: www.rti.ci. Correspondence in French preferred, but English accepted.

CROATIA   World Time +1 (+2 midyear)

📻Croatian Radio (Hrvatska Radio-Televizija)
MAIN OFFICE: Hrvatska Radio-Televizija (HRT), Prisavlje 3, HR-10000 Zagreb, Croatia. Phone: (operator) +385 (1) 616-3366; (technical) +385 (1) 616-3355; or +385 (1) 616-3428. Fax: (general) +385 (1) 616 3308; (technical) +385 (1) 616 3347. Email: (Editor-in-Chief) i.lucev@hrt.hr; (technical) z.klasan@hrt.hr. Web: (general) www.hrt.hr/; (program guide) www.hrt.hr/hr/program/; (RealAudio) www.hrt.hr/hr/audio/. Contact: (general) Ivanka Lucev; (technical) Zelimir Klasan. This station of HRT, is the domestic (first) national radio programme, transmitted via HRT Deanovec shortwave station, for listeners in Europe and the Mediterranean.
WASHINGTON NEWS BUREAU: Croatian-American Association, 2020 Pennsylvania Avenue NW., Suite 287, Washington DC 20006 USA. Phone: +1 (202) 429-5543. Fax: +1 (202) 429 5545. Email: 73150.3552@compuserve.com. Web: www.hrnet.org/CAA/. Contact: Frank Brozovich, President.

Radio Croatia (Radio Hrvatska), Hrvatski Informativni Centar/Radio Hrvatska, Meduliceva 13, HR-10000 Zagreb, Croatia. Phone: (A. Beljo) +385 (1) 484-6121; or (M. Risek) +385 (1) 484-8630. Fax: (general) +385 (1) 484 8634; or (Phone/fax, technical (M. Prezelj) +49 (69) 636 210. Email: (general) radio@hic.hr; (M. Risek) marica.risek@hic.hr; or (E. Candrlic) eliana.candrlic@hic.hr; (technical) (M. Prezelj) prezelj@t-online.de. Web: www.hic.hr. Contact: (general) Ante Beljo, HIC Managing Director; Marica Risek, Head of Electronic Media; or Eliana Candrlic, Editor-in-Chief; (technical) Milan Prezelj. Sells books on Croatian heritage from Website at www.hic.hr/books/. All technical correspondence should be sent to: Milan Prezelj, Franz-Lenbach-Str.10, D-60596 Frankfurt, Germany. This station is operated by the Hrvatski Informativni Centar (HIC) in Zagreb and is the shortwave foreign service, mainly for Croatian expatriates, transmitted via Deutsche Telekom's Jülich station.

CUBA   World Time –5 (–4 midyear)

Radio Habana Cuba, P.O. Box 6240, Habana, Cuba 10600. Phone: (general) +53 (7) 784-954 or +53 (7) 334-272; (English and Spanish Departments) +53 (7) 791-053; (French Department) +53 (7) 785-444; (Coro) +53 (7) 814-243 or (home) +53 (7) 301-794. Fax: (general) +53 (7) 783 518; (English and Spanish Departments) +53 (7) 795 007; (French Department) +53 (7) 705 810. Email: radiohc@ip.etecsa.cu. Web: www.radiohc.cu (if an error message appears, try www.radiohc.cu/programacion.html, and use the links from there). Contact: (general) Lourdes López, Head of Correspondence Dept.; Jorge Miyares, English Service; or Mike La Guardia, Senior Editor; (administration) Ms. Milagro Hernández Cuba, General Director; (technical) Arnaldo Coro Antich, ("Arnie Coro"), Producer, "DXers Unlimited"; or Luis Pruna Amer, Director Técnico. Free wallet and wall calendars, pennants, stickers, keychains and pins. DX Listeners' Club. Free sample *Granma International* newspaper. Contests with various prizes, including trips to Cuba.

Radio Rebelde, Departamento de Relaciones Públicas, Apartado 6277, Habana 10600, Cuba; or (street address) Calle 23 No. 258 entre L y M, El Vedado, Habana, Cuba 10600. For technical correspondence (including reception reports), substitute "Servicio de Onda Corta" in place of "Departamento de Relaciones Públicas." Reception reports can also be emailed to Radio Habana Cuba's Arnie Coro (arnie@radiohc.org) for forwarding to Radio Rebelde. Phone: +53 (7) 334-269. Fax: +53 (7) 323 514. Email: (nontechnical) rebelde@ceniai.inf.cu. Web: www2.cuba.cu/RRebelde/; www.ceniai.inf.cu/RRebelde/; www.ceniai.inf.cu/noticias/rebelde/. Contact: Daimelis Monzón; Noemí Cairo Marín; Iberlise González Padua; or Marisel Ramos Soca (all from "Relaciones Públicas"); or Jorge Luis Más Zabala, Director, Relaciones Públicas. Replies slowly, with correspondence in Spanish preferred.

CYPRUS   World Time +2 (+3 midyear)

Bayrak Radio—BRT International (when operating), BRTK Campus, Dr. Fazil Küçük Boulevard, P.O. Box 417, Lefkosa - T.R.N.C., via Mersin 10, Turkey. Phone: (general) +90 (392) 225-5555; (public relations office) +90 (392) 228-0577. Fax: (general) +90 (392) 225 2918; (news dept.) +90 (392) 225 4991. Email: (general) brt@cc.emu.edu.tr; (technical, including reception reports) tosun@cc.emu.edu.tr. Web: (includes RealAudio) www.emu.edu.tr/~brt/. Contact: Mustafa Tosun, Head of Transmission Department.

BBC World Service—East Mediterranean Relay Station, P.O. Box 209, Limassol, Cyprus. Contact: Steve Welch. This address for technical matters only. Other correspondence should be sent to the BBC World Service in London (see).

Cyprus Broadcasting Corporation, Broadcasting House, P.O. Box 4824, 1397 Nicosia, Cyprus; or (physical address) RIK Street, Athalassa, Nicosia, Cyprus. Phone: +357 (2) 422-231. Fax: +357 (2) 314 050 or +357 (2) 335 010. Email: rik@cybc.com.cy. Web: (includes RealAudio) www.cybc.com.cy/. Contact: (general) Pavlos Soteriades, Director General; or Evangella Gregoriou, Head of Public and International Relations; (technical) Andreas Michaelides, Director of Technical Services. Free stickers. Replies occasionally, sometimes slowly. IRC or $1 helpful.

CZECH REPUBLIC   World Time +1 (+2 midyear)

Radio Prague, Czech Radio, Vinohradská 12, 12099 Prague 2, Czech Republic. Phone: (general) +420 (2) 2409-4608; (Czech Department) +420 (2) 2422-2236; (English Department) +420 (2) 2422-2211; (Internet) +420 (2) 2421 5456. Phone/fax: (Oldrich Cip, technical) +420 (2) 2271-5005. Fax: (nontechnical and technical) +420 (2) 2421 8239 or +420 (2) 2422 2236; (English Department) +420 (2) 2421 8349. Email: (general) cr@radio.cz; (Director) Miroslav.Krupicka@radio.cz; (English Department) english@radio.cz; (Program Director) David.Vaughan@radio.cz; (free news texts) robot@radio.cz, writing "Subscribe English" (or other desired language) within the subject line; (technical, chief engineer) cip@radio.cz. Web: (text and RealAudio in English, German, Spanish and French) www.radio.cz; www.prague.org; (text) ftp://ftp.radio.cz; gopher://gopher.radio.cz. Contact: (general) Markéta Atanasová; David Vaughan, Program Director; Libor Kubik, Head of English Section; (administration) Miroslav Krupička, Director; (technical, all programs) Oldrich Čip, Chief Engineer. Free stickers, key chains, and calendars. Samples of *Welcome to the Czech Republic* and *Czech Life* available upon request from Orbis, Vinohradská 46, 120 41 Prague, Czech Republic.

RFE-RL—*see* USA.

DENMARK   World Time +1 (+2 midyear)

Radio Danmark
MAIN OFFICE: Radioavisen, Rosenørns Allé 22, DK-1999

Frederiksberg C, Denmark. Phone: (office, including voice mail, voice schedules in Danish and schedule by return fax) +45 3520-5784. Fax: + 45 3520 5781. Email: (schedule and program matters) rdk@dr.dk; (technical matters and reception reports) rdktek@dr.dk. Web: (includes RealAudio) www.dr.dk/rdk/. Contact: (general) Malene Friis Schultz, Audience Communications; or Bjorn Schionning; (technical) Erik Køie, Technical Adviser. Replies to correspondence in English, German, French, Norwegian, Swedish or Danish. Cassette tapes (not returned), short RealAudio or MP3 email files accepted. Will verify all correct reception reports; although not necessary, return postage ($1 or one IRC) appreciated. Uses transmitting facilities of Radio Norway International. All broadcasts are in Danish, and are aired at xx.30-xx.55 24 hours a day. "Tune In" letterbox program aired last Saturday/Sunday of the month, hourly 24 times from 16.37 UTC (summer; winter 17.37 UTC). *TRANSMISSION MANAGEMENT AUTHORITY:* Tele Danmark, NIA-Broadcast, Telegade 2, DK-2630 Taastrup, Denmark. Phone: +45 4334-5746. Fax: +45 4371 1143. Email: ihl@tdk.dk. Contact: Ib H. Lavrsen, Senior Engineer.
NORWEGIAN OFFICE, TECHNICAL: Details of reception quality may also be sent to the Engineering Department of Radio Norway International (see), which operates the transmitters currently used by Radio Danmark.

DOMINICAN REPUBLIC   World Time –4

Emisora Onda Musical (when active), Pablo Hincado 204 Altos, Apartado Postal 860, Santo Domingo, Dominican Republic. Contact: Mario Báez Asunción, Director. Replies occasionally to correspondence in Spanish. $1 helpful.

Radio Amanecer Internacional, Apartado Postal 4680, Santo Domingo, Dominican Republic. Phone: +1 (809) 688-5600, +1 (809) 688-5609, +1 (809) 688-8067. Fax: +1 (809) 227 1869. Email: amanecer@tricom.net. Web: www.tricom.net/amanecer/. Contact: (general) Señora Ramona C. de Subervi, Directora; (technical) Sócrates Domínguez. $1 or return postage required. Replies slowly to correspondence in Spanish.

Radio Barahona (when active), Apartado 201, Barahona, Dominican Republic; or Gustavo Mejía Ricart No. 293, Apto. 2-B, Ens. Quisqueya, Santo Domingo, Dominican Republic. Contact: (general) Rodolfo Z. Lama Jaar, Administrador; (technical) Ing. Roberto Lama Sajour, Administrador General. Free stickers. Letters should be sent via registered mail. $1 or return postage helpful. Replies to correspondence in Spanish.

Radio Cristal Internacional, Apartado Postal 894, Santo Domingo, Dominican Republic; or (street address) Calle Pepillo Salcedo No. 18, Altos, Santo Domingo, Dominican Republic. Phone: +1 (809) 565-1460 or +1 (809) 566-5411. Fax: +1 (809) 567 9107. Contact: (general) Fernando Hermón Gross, Director de Programas; or Margarita Reyes, Secretaria; (administration) Darío Badía, Director General; or Héctor Badía, Director de Administración. Seeks reception reports. Return postage of $2 appreciated.

Radio Villa, Apartado 804, Santo Domingo, Dominican Republic. Fax: +1 (809) 541 1088. Contact: Roberto Vargas, Director. Free pennants, postcards, coins and taped music. Roberto likes collecting stamps and coins.

ECUADOR   World Time –5 (–4 sometimes, in times of drought); –6 Galapagos

NOTE: According to HCJB's "DX Party Line," during periods of drought, such as caused by "El Niño," electricity rationing causes periods in which transmitters cannot operate because of inadequate hydroelectric power, as well as spikes which occasionally damage transmitters. Accordingly, many Ecuadorian stations tend to be irregular, or even entirely off the air, during drought conditions.

NOTE: According to veteran Dxer Harald Kuhl in Hard-Core-DX of Kotanet Communications Ltd., IRCs are exchangeable only in the cities of Quito and Guayaquil. Too, overseas airmail postage is very expensive now in Ecuador; so when in doubt, enclosing $2 for return postage is appropriate.

Emisoras Jesús del Gran Poder (if reactivated), Casilla 17-01-133, Quito, Ecuador. Phone: +593 (2) 513-077. Contact: Mariela Villarreal; Padre Angel Falconí, Gerente; or Hno. Segundo Cuenca OFM.

Emisoras Luz y Vida, Casilla 11-01-222, Loja, Ecuador. Phone: +593 (7) 570-426. Contact: Hermana (Sister) Ana Maza Reyes, Directora; or Lic. Guida Carrión H., Directora de Programas. Return postage required. Replies irregularly to correspondence in Spanish.

Escuelas Radiofónicas Populares del Ecuador, Calles Juan de Velasco 2060 y Guayaquil, Casilla Postal 06-01-341, Riobamba, Ecuador. Phone: (administration) +593 (3) 961-608; (radio) +593 (3) 960-221. Fax: +593 (3) 961 625. Email: admin @esrapoec.ecuanex.net.ec. Web: www.exploringecuador.com/erpe/. Contact: Juan Pérez Sarmiento, Director Ejecutivo; or María Ercilia López, Secretaria. Free pennants and key rings. "Chimborazo" cassette of Ecuadorian music for 10,000 sucres plus postage; T-shirts for 12,000 sucres plus postage; and caps with station logo for 8,000 sucres plus postage. Return postage helpful. Replies to correspondence in Spanish.

⊡HCJB World Radio, The Voice of the Andes

STATION: Casilla 17-17-691, Quito, Ecuador. Phone: (general) +593 (2) 266-808 (X-4441, 1300-2200 World Time Monday through Friday, for the English Dept.); (phone/fax, Frequency Management) +593 (2) 267-098 (X-5216). Fax: (general) +593 (2) 447 263. Email: (Frequency Management) irops @hcjb.org.ec or dweber@hcjb.org.ec; (language sections) format is language@hcjb.org.ec; so to reach, say, the Japanese Department, it would be japanese@hcjb.org.ec. Web: (includes RealAudio and online reception report form) www.hcjb.org. Contact: (general) English [or other language] Department; (administration) Jim Estes, Director of Broadcasting; Alex Saks, Station Manager; Curt Cole, Programme Director, or Allen Graham, Director of English Language Service; (technical) Douglas Weber, Frequency Manager. Free religious brochures, calendars, stickers and pennants; free email *The Andean Herald* newsletter. *Catch the Vision* book $8, postpaid. IRC or unused U.S. or Canadian stamps appreciated for airmail reply.

INTERNATIONAL HEADQUARTERS: HCJB World Radio, Inc., P.O. Box 39800, Colorado Springs CO 80949-9800 USA. Phone: +1 (719) 590-9800. Fax: +1 (719) 590 9801. Email: info@hcjb.org. Contact: Andrew Braio, Public Information; (administration) Richard D. Jacquin, Director, International Operations. Various items sold via U.S. address—catalog available. This address is not a mail drop, so listeners' correspondence, except those concerned with purchasing HCJB items, should be directed to the usual Quito address.

ENGINEERING CENTER: 2830 South 17th Street, Elkhart IN 46517 USA. Phone: +1 (219) 294-8201. Fax: +1 (219) 294 8391. Email: info@hcjbeng.org. Web: www.hcjbeng.org/. Contact: Dave Pasechnik, Project Manager; or Bob Moore, Engineering. This address only for those professionally concerned with the design and manufacture of transmitter and antenna equipment. Listeners' correspondence should be directed to the usual Quito address.

REGIONAL OFFICES: Although HCJB has over 20 regional offices throughout the world, the station wishes that all listener correspondence be directed to the station in Quito, as the regional offices do not serve as mail drops for the station.

"EDXP NEWSREPORTS" : Web: www.members.tripod.com/-bpadula/edxp.html. Special news reports concentrating on shortwave broadcasts to and from Asia, the Far East, Australia, the Pacific and the Indian sub-continent, compiled by EDXP and aired once a month on the third Saturday (UTC) and repeated on the following Sunday via HCJB during the *"DX Partyline"* English program. Special EDXP QSLs will be offered for the shortwave releases (not for RealAudio). Reports of the EDXP feature should be sent to: Bob Padula, EDXP QSL Service, 404 Mont Albert Road, Surrey Hills, Victoria 3127, Australia. Return postage appreciated. Outside of Australia, 1 IRC or $1; within Australia, four 45c Australian stamps. Email reports welcome at edxp@bigpond.com, and verified with Web-delivered animated QSLs.

La Voz de Saquisilí—Radio Libertador, Calle 24 de Mayo, Saquisilí, Cotopaxi, Ecuador. Phone: +593 (3) 721-035. Contact: Arturo Mena Herrera, Gerente-Propietario, who may also be contacted via his son-in-law, Eddy Roger Velástegui Mena, who is studying in Quito (Email: eddyv@uio.uio.satnet.net). Reception reports actively solicited, and will be confirmed with a special commemorative QSL card. Return postage, in the form of $2 or mint Ecuadorian stamps, appreciated; IRCs difficult to exchange. Spanish strongly preferred.

La Voz del Napo, Misión Josefina, Tena, Napo, Ecuador. Phone: +593 (6) 886-422. Contact: Ramiro Cabrera, Director.

Free pennants and stickers. $2 or return postage required. Replies occasionally to correspondence in Spanish.

La Voz del Río Tarqui (when operating), Manuel Vega 653 y Presidente Córdova, Cuenca, Ecuador. Phone: +593 (7) 822-132. Contact: Sra. Alicia Pulla Célleri, Gerente. Replies irregularly to correspondence in Spanish. Has ties with station WKDM in New York.

La Voz del Upano
STATION: Vicariato Apostólico de Méndez, Misión Salesiana, 10 de Agosto s/n, Macas, Ecuador. Phone: +593 (7) 700-186. Contact: P. Domingo Barrueco C., Director. Free pennants and calendars. On one occasion, not necessarily to be repeated, sent tape of Ecuadorian folk music for $2. Otherwise, $2 required. Replies to correspondence in Spanish.
QUITO OFFICE: Procura Salesiana, Equinoccio 623 y Queseras del Medio, Quito, Ecuador. Phone: +593 (2) 551-012.

Radio Bahá'í ("La Emisora de la Familia"), Casilla 10-02-1464, Otavalo, Imbabura, Ecuador. Phone: +593 (6) 920-245. Fax: +593 (6) 922 504. Contact: (general) William Rodríguez Barreiro, Coordinador; or Juan Antonio Reascos, Locutor; (technical) Ing. Tom Dopps. Free information about the Bahá'í faith, which teaches the unity of all the races, nations and religions, and that the Earth is one country and mankind its citizens. Free pennants. Return postage appreciated. Replies regularly to correspondence in English or Spanish. Enclosing a family photo may help getting a reply. Station is property of the Instituto Nacional de Enseñanza de la Fe Bahá'í (National Spiritual Assembly of the Bahá'ís of Ecuador). Although there are many Bahá'í radio stations around the world, Radio Bahá'í in Ecuador is the only one on shortwave.

Radio Buen Pastor—see Radio "El Buen Pastor."

Radio Centinela del Sur (C.D.S. Internacional), Casilla 11-01-106, Loja, Ecuador; or (studios) Olmedo 11-56 y Mercadillo, Loja, Ecuador. Phone: +593 (7) 561-166 or +593 (7) 570-211. Fax: +593 (7) 562 270. Contact: (general) Marcos G. Coronel V., Director de Programas; or José A. Coronel V., Director del programa "Ovación"; (technical) José A. Coronel Illescas, Gerente General. Return postage required. Replies occasionally to correspondence in Spanish.

Radio Centro, Casilla 18-01-574, Ambato, Ecuador. Phone: +593 (3) 822-240 or +593 (3) 841-126. Fax: +593 (3) 829 824. Contact: Luis Alberto Gamboa Tello, Director Gerente; or Lic. María Elena de López. Free stickers. Return postage appreciated. Replies to correspondence in Spanish.

Radiodifusora Cultural Católica La Voz del Upano—see La Voz del Upano, above.

Radiodifusora Cultural, La Voz del Napo—see La Voz del Napo, above.

Radio "El Buen Pastor," Asociación Cristiana de Indígenas Saraguros (ACIS), Reino de Quito y Azuay, Correo Central, Saraguro, Loja, Ecuador. Phone: +593 (2) 00-146. Contact: (general) Dean Pablo Davis, Sub-director; Segundo Poma, Director; Mark Vogan, OMS Missionary; Mike Schrode, OMS Ecuador Field Director; Juana Guamán, Secretaria; or Zoila Vacacela, Secretaria; (technical) Miguel Kelly. $2 or return postage in the form of mint Ecuadorian stamps required, as IRCs are difficult to exchange in Ecuador. Station is keen to receive reception reports; may respond to English, but correspondence in Spanish preferred. $10 required for QSL card and pennant.

Radio Federación Shuar (Shuara Tuntuiri), Casilla 17-01-1422, Quito, Ecuador. Phone/fax: +593 (2) 504-264. Contact: Manuel Jesús Vinza Chacucuy, Director; Yurank Tsapak Rubén Gerardo, Director; or Prof. Albino M. Utitiaj P., Director

de Medios. Return postage or $2 required. Replies irregularly to correspondence in Spanish.

Radio Interoceánica, Santa Rosa de Quijos, Cantón El Chaco, Provincia de Napo, Ecuador. Contact: Byron Medina, Gerente; or Ing. Olaf Hegmuir. $2 or return postage required, and donations appreciated (station owned by Swedish Covenant Church). Replies slowly to correspondence in Spanish or Swedish.

Radio Jesús del Gran Poder—see Emisoras Jesús del Gran Poder, above.

Radio La Voz del Río Tarqui—see La Voz del Rio Tarqui.

Radio Luz y Vida—see Emisoras Luz y Vida, above.

Radio Nacional Espejo (when operating), Casilla 17-01-352, Quito, Ecuador. Phone: +593 (2) 21-366. Email: (Marco Caicedo) mcaicedo@hoy.net. Contact: Marco Caicedo, Gerente; Steve Caicedo; or Mercedes B. de Caicedo, Secretaria. Replies irregularly to correspondence in English and Spanish.

Radio Nacional Progreso, Casilla V, Loja, Ecuador. Contact: José A. Guamán Guajala, Director del programa "Círculo Dominical." Replies irregularly to correspondence in Spanish, particularly for feedback on "Círculo Dominical" program aired Sundays from 1100 to 1300. Return postage required.

Radio Oriental, Casilla 260, Tena, Napo, Ecuador. Phone: +593 (6) 886-033 or +593 (6) 886-388. Contact: Luis Enrique Espín Espinosa, Gerente General. $2 or return postage helpful. Reception reports welcome.

Radio Quito, Casilla 17-21-1971, Quito, Ecuador. Phone/fax: +593 (2) 508-301. Email: radioquito@elcomercio.com. Contact: Xavier Almeida, Gerente General; or José Almeida, Subgerente. Free stickers. Return postage normally required, but occasionally verifies email reports. Replies slowly, but regularly.

Sistema de Emisoras Progreso—see Radio Nacional Progreso, above.

EGYPT   World Time +2 (+3 midyear)

WARNING: MAIL THEFT. Feedback from PASSPORT readership indicates that money is sometimes stolen from envelopes sent to Radio Cairo.

📻**Egyptian Radio**, P.O. Box 1186, 11511 Cairo, Egypt. Email: rtu@idsc.gov.eg. Web: (RealAudio) www.sis.gov.eg/realpg/html/adfront9.htm (if you encounter difficulty loading the page, try one of the mirror sites: www.uk.sis.gov.eg/; www.us.sis.gov.eg/). For additional details, see Radio Cairo, below.

Radio Cairo
NONTECHNICAL: P.O. Box 566, Cairo 11511, Egypt. Phone: +20 (2) 677-8945. Fax: +20 (2) 575 9553. Contact: Mrs. Amal Badr, Head of English Programme; Mrs. Sahar Kalil, Director of English Service to North America and Producer, "Questions and Answers"; or Mrs. Magda Hamman, Secretary. Free stickers, postcards, stamps, maps, papyrus souvenirs, calendars and External Services of Radio Cairo book. Free booklet and individually tutored Arabic-language lessons with loaned textbooks from Kamila Abdullah, Director General, Arabic by Radio, Radio Cairo, P.O. Box 325, Cairo, Egypt. Arabic-language religious, cultural and language-learning audio and video tapes from the Egyptian Radio and Television Union sold via Sono Cairo Audio-Video, P.O. Box 2017, Cairo, Egypt; when ordering video tapes, inquire to ensure they function on the television standard (NTSC, PAL or SECAM) in your country. Once replied regularly, if slowly, but recently replies have been increasingly scarce. Comments welcomed about

audio quality—*see TECHNICAL*, below. Avoid enclosing money (*see WARNING*, above). A new 500 kW shortwave transmitter is to be brought into service in the near future to improve reception.

TECHNICAL: Broadcast Engineering Department, 24th Floor—TV Building (Maspiro), Egyptian Radio and Television Union, P.O. Box 1186, 11151 Cairo, Egypt. Phone: +20 (2) 347-6521 or +20 (2) 574-6840. Phone/fax: (propagation and monitoring office, set to automatically receive faxes outside normal working hours; otherwise, be prepared to request a switchover from voice to fax) +20 (2) 578-9461. Fax: +20 (2) 578 9310. Email: (general) rtu@idsc.gov.eg; (Lawrence) niveenl @hotmail.com; (Eldine) gihanessam@hotmail.com. Contact: Dr. Eng. Abdoh Fayoumi, Head of Propagation and Monitoring; Mrs. Hoda Helmy; Gihan Essam Eldine; Mrs. Rokaya M. Kamel; or Niveen W. Lawrence, Director of Shortwave Department. Comments and suggestions on audio quality and level especially welcomed.

ENGLAND—*see* UNITED KINGDOM.

EQUATORIAL GUINEA World Time +1

Radio Africa
TRANSMISSION OFFICE: Apartado 851, Malabo, Isla Bioko, Equatorial Guinea.
U.S. OFFICE FOR CORRESPONDENCE AND VERIFICATIONS: Pan American Broadcasting, 20410 Town Center Lane #200, Cupertino CA 95014 USA. Phone: +1 (408) 996-2033; (toll-free, within the United States) 1-800-726-2620. Fax: +1 (408) 252 6855. Email: pabcomain@aol.com. Web: www.radiopanam.com. Contact: (listener correspondence) Terry Kraemer; (general) Carmen Jung, Office and Sales Administrator; or James Manero. $1 in cash or unused U.S. stamps, or 2 IRCs, required for reply.
Radio East Africa—same details as "Radio Africa," above.
Radio Nacional de Guinea Ecuatorial—Bata ("Radio Bata"), Apartado 749, Bata, Río Muni, Equatorial Guinea. Phone: +240 (8) 2592. Fax: +240 (8) 2093. Contact: José Mba Obama, Director. If no response try sending your letter c/o Spanish Embassy, Bata, enclosing $1 for return postage. Spanish preferred.
Radio Nacional de Guinea Ecuatorial—Malabo ("Radio Malabo"), Apartado 195, Malabo, Isla Bioko, Equatorial Guinea. Phone: +240 (9) 2260. Fax: (general) +240 (9) 2097; (technical) +240 (9) 3122. Contact: (general) Román Manuel Mané-Abaga, Jefe de Programación; Ciprano Somon Suakin; or Manuel Sobede, Inspector de Servicios de Radio y TV; (technical) Hermenegildo Moliko Chele, Jefe Servicios Técnicos de Radio y Televisión. $1 or return postage required. Replies irregularly to correspondence in Spanish.

ERITREA World Time +3

⬛Voice of the Broad Masses of Eritrea (Dimtsi Hafash), Ministry of Information, Radio Division, P.O. Box 872, Asmara, Eritrea; or Ministry of Information, Technical Branch, P.O. Box 243, Asmara, Eritrea. Phone: +291 (1) 119-100. Fax: +291 (1) 120 138. Web: (RealAudio) www.visafric.com/Dimtsi_hafash.htm. Contact: Ghebreab Ghebremedhin; or Mehreteab Tesfagiorgis, Technical Director, Engineering Division. Return postage or $1 helpful. Free information on history of the station and about Eritrea.

ETHIOPIA World Time +3

⬛Radio Ethiopia: (external service) P.O. Box 654; (domestic service) P.O. Box 1020—both in Addis Ababa, Ethiopia (address your correspondence to "Audience Relations"). Phone: (main office) +251 (1) 116-427 or +251 (1) 551-011; (engineering) +251 (1) 200-948. Fax: +251 (1) 552 263. Email: there is no direct email address for the station (all correspondence should be sent to the postal address, above) but the Webmaster of the US-based site may be contacted at radioethiopia@usa.net. Web: (includes RealAudio) www.angelfire.com/biz/radioethiopia/. Contact: (external service, general) Kahsai Tewoldemedhin, Program Director; Ms. Woinshet Woldeyes, Secretary, Audience Relations; Ms. Ellene Mocria, Head of Audience Relations; or Yohaness Ruphael, Producer, "Contact"; (administration) Kasa Miliko, Head of Station; (technical) Terefe Ghebre Medhin or Zegeye Solomon. Free stickers and tourist brochures. Poor replier.
Radio Fana (Radio Torch), P.O. Box 30702, Addis Ababa, Ethiopia. Phone: +251 (1) 516-777. Email: radio-fana@telecom.net.et. Contact: Mulugeta Gessese, General Manager; Mesfin Alemayehu, Head, External Relations; or Girma Lema, Head, Planning and Research Department. Station is autonomous and receives its income from non-governmental educational sponsorship. Seeks help with obtaining vehicles, recording equipment and training materials.
Voice of Peace, Inter-Africa Group, P.O. Box 1631, Addis Ababa, Ethiopia. A humanitarian broadcast partially funded by UNICEF, seeking peace and reconciliation among warring factions in central and eastern Africa. Via Radio Ethiopia (*see*, above).
Voice of the Tigray Revolution, P.O. Box 450, Mek'ele, Tigray, Ethiopia. Contact: Fre Tesfamichael, Director. $1 helpful.

FINLAND World Time +2 (+3 midyear)

⬛YLE Radio Finland
MAIN OFFICE: Box 78, FIN-00024 Yleisradio, Finland. Phone: (general, 24-hour English speaking switchboard for both Radio Finland and Yleisradio Oy) +358 (9) 14801; (international information) +358 (9) 1480-3729; (administration) +358 (9) 1480-4320 or +358 (9) 1480-4316; (Technical Customer Service) +358 (9) 1480-3213; (comments on programs) +358 (9) 1480-5490. Fax: (general) +358 (9) 148 1169; (international information) +358 (9) 1480 3391; (Technical Affairs) +358 (9) 1480 3588. Email: (general) rfinland@yle.fi or rfinland@aol.com; (comments on programs) christina.rockstroh@yle.fi; (German section) stefan.tschirpke@yle.fi; (Yleisradio Oy parent organization) fbc@yle.fi. To contact individuals, the format is firstname.lastname@yle.fi; so to reach, say, Pertti Seppä, it would be pertti.seppa@yle.fi. Web: (includes RealAudio in Finnish, Swedish, English, German, French, Russian and Classic Latin) www.yle.fi/fbc/radiofin.html; (stored news audio in Finnish, Swedish, English, German, French and Russian) www.wrn.org/ondemand/finland.html; (online reception form) www.yle.fi/sataradio/receptionreport.html. Contact—Radio Finland: (English) Eddy Hawkins; (Finnish and Swedish) Pertti Seppä; (German and French) Dr. Stefan Tschirpke; (Russian) Timo Uotila and Mrs. Eija Laitinen; (administration) Juhani Niinistö, Head of External Broadcasting; (comments on programs) Mrs. Christina Rockstroh, Organizer, foreign language external programming. Contact—Yleisradio Oy parent organization: (general) Marja Salusjärvi, Head of International PR; (administration) Arne Wessberg, Managing Director; or Tapio Siikala, Director for Domestic and Interna-

It's still winter in May, with sunshine near midnight at this regional station in Lapland.

S. Soininen

tional Radio. Sometimes provides free stickers and small souvenirs, as well as tourist and other magazines. Replies to correspondence. Radio Finland will verify reception reports directly if sent to: Radio Finland, Attention: Raimo Mäkelä, PL 113, FIN-28101 Pori, Finland (Email: raimo.makela@pp.inet.fi). Also, *see* Transmission Facility, below. YLE Radio Finland external broadcasting is a part of YLE and not a separate administrative unit. Radio Finland itself is not a legal entity.

NUNTII LATINI (Program in Latin): P.O. Box 99, FIN-00024 Yleisradio, Finland. Fax: +358 (9) 1480 3391. Email: nuntii.latini@yle.fi. Web: www.yle.fi/fbc/nuntii.html. Six years of Nuntii Latini now available in books I to III at US$30 each from: Bookstore Tiedekirja, Kirkkokatu 14, FIN-00170 Helsinki, Finland; fax: +358 (9) 635 017. VISA/MC/EURO.

NETWORK PLANNING: Digita, P.O. Box 135, FIN-00521 Helsinki, Finland. Phone: +358 (9) 1480-7287. Fax: +358 (9) 148 5260. Email: esko.huuhka@digita.fi or kari.hautala @digita.fi. Contact: Esko Huuhka, Head of Network Planning; or Kari Hautala, Monitoring Engineer.

TRANSMISSION FACILITY: Digita Shortwave Centre, Makholmantie 79, FIN-28660 Pori, Finland. Web: (Digita Oy) www.digita.fi. Contact: Ms. Marjatta Jokinen; or Myitta Tiki. Issues full-data verification cards for good reception reports, and provides free illustrated booklets about the transmitting station.

NORTH AMERICAN OFFICE—LISTENER and MEDIA LIAISON: P.O. Box 462, Windsor CT 06095 USA. Phone: +1 (860) 688-5540 or +1 (860) 688-5098. Phone/fax: (24-hour toll-free within U.S. and Canada for recorded schedule and voice mail) 1-800-221-9539. Fax: +1 (860) 688 0113. Email: yleus@aol.com. Contact: John Berky, YLE Finland Transcriptions. Free *YLE North America* newsletter. This office does not verify reception reports.

Scandinavian Weekend Radio, P.O. Box 35, FIN-40321, Jyväskylä, Finland. Phone: +358 (50) 564-3054. Fax: +358 (14) 242 380. Email: (general) info@swradio.net; (technical) esa.saunamaki@swradio.net; (reception reports) online report form at the station's Website. Web: www.swradio.net. Two IRCs or $2 required for verification card.

FRANCE   World Time +1

📻 Radio France Internationale (RFI)

MAIN OFFICE: B.P. 9516, F-75016 Paris Cedex 16, France. Phone: (general) +33 (1) 42-30-22-22; (International Affairs and Program Placement) +33 (1) 44-30-89-31 or +33 (1) 44-30-89-49; (Service de la communication) +33 (1) 42-30-29-51; (Audience Relations) +33 (1) 44-30-89-69/70/71; (Media Relations) +33 (1) 42-30-29-85; (Développement et de la communication) +33 (1) 44-30-89-21; *(Fréquence Monde)* +33 (1) 42-30-10-86; (English Department) +33 (1) 42-30-30-62; (Spanish Department) +33 (1) 42-30-30-48. Fax: (general) +33 (1) 42 30 30 71; (International Affairs and Program Placement) +33 (1) 44 30 89 20; (Audience Relations) +33 (1) 44 30 89 99; (other nontechnical) +33 (1) 42 30 44 81; (English Department) +33 (1) 42 30 26 74; (Spanish Department) +33 (1) 42 30 46 69. Web: (general) www.rfi.fr/; (RealAudio and StreamWorks in French, English, Spanish and Portuguese) www.francelink.com/radio_stations/rfi/. Contact: Simson Najovits, Chief, English Department; J.P. Charbonnier, Producer, "Lettres des Auditeurs"; Joël Amar, International Affairs/Program Placement Department; Arnaud Littardi, Directeur du développement et de la communication; Nicolas Levkov, Rédactions en Langues Etrangères; Daniel Franco, Rédaction en français; Mme. Anne Toulouse, Rédacteur en chef du Service Mondiale en français; Christine Berbudeau, Rédacteur en chef, *Fréquence* **Monde**; or Marc Verney, Attaché de Presse; (administration) Jean-Paul Cluzel, Président-Directeur Général; (technical) M. Raymond Pincon, Producer, "Le Courrier Technique." Free *Fréquence* **Monde** bi-monthly magazine in French upon request. Free souvenir keychains, pins, lighters, pencils, T-shirts and stickers have been received by some—especially when visiting the headquarters at 116 avenue du Président Kennedy, in the chichi 16th Arrondissement. Can provide supplementary materials for "Dites-moi tout" French-language course; write to the attention of Mme. Chantal de Grandpre, "Dites-moi tout." "Le Club des Auditeurs" French-language listener's club ("Club 9516" for English-language listeners); applicants must provide name, address and two passport-type photos, whereupon they will receive a membership card and the club bulletin. RFI exists primarily to defend and promote Francophone culture, but also provides meaningful information and cultural perspectives in non-French languages.

TRANSMISSION OFFICE, TECHNICAL: TéléDiffusion de France, Direction de la Production et des Méthodes, Shortwave service, 10 rue d'Oradour sur Glane, 75732 Paris Cedex 15, France. Phone: (Bochent) +33 (1) 5595-1369; or (Meunier) +33 (1) 5595-1161. Fax: +33 (1) 5595 2137. Email: (Bochent) 101317.2431 @compuserve.com; or danielbochent@compuserve.com; (Meunier) a_meunier@compuserve.com. Contact: Daniel Bochent, Head of short wave service; Alain Meunier, Michel Penneroux, Business Development Manager AM-HF; Mme Annick Daronian or Mme Sylvie Greuillet (short wave service). This office is for informing about transmitter-related problems (interference, modulation quality), and also for reception reports and verifications.

UNITED STATES PROMOTIONAL, SCHOOL LIAISON, PROGRAM PLACEMENT AND CULTURAL EXCHANGE OFFICES:
NEW ORLEANS: Services Culturels, Suite 2105, Ambassade de France, 300 Poydras Street, New Orleans LA 70130 USA. Phone: +1 (504) 523-5394. Phone/fax: +1 (504) 529-7502. Contact: Adam-Anthony Steg, Attaché Audiovisuel. This office promotes RFI, especially to language teachers and others in the educational community within the southern United States, and arranges for bi-national cultural exchanges. It also sets up RFI feeds to local radio stations within the southern United States.
NEW YORK: Audiovisual Bureau, Radio France Internationale, 972 Fifth Avenue, New York NY 10021 USA. Phone: +1 (212) 439-1452. Fax: +1 (212) 439 1455. Contact: Gérard Blondel or Julien Vin. This office promotes RFI, especially to language teachers and others within the educational community outside the southern United States, and arranges for bi-national cultural exchanges. It also sets up RFI feeds to local radio stations within much of the United States.
NEW YORK NEWS BUREAU: 1290 Avenue of the Americas, New York NY 10019 USA. Phone: +1 (212) 581-1771. Fax: +1 (212) 541 4309. Contact: Ms. Auberi Edler, Reporter; or Bruno Albin, Reporter.
WASHINGTON NEWS BUREAU: 529 14th Street NW, Suite 1126, Washington DC 20045 USA. Phone: +1 (202) 879-6706. Contact: Pierre J. Cayrol.
SAN FRANCISCO OFFICE, SCHEDULES: 2654 17th Avenue, San Francisco CA 94116 USA. Phone: +1 (415) 564-9968. Email: GPoppin@aol.com. Contact: George Poppin. This address, a volunteer office, only provides RFI schedules to listeners. All other correspondence should be sent directly to the main office in Paris.

⬛Radio Monte Carlo-Middle East

MAIN OFFICE: Radio Monte Carlo-Moyen Orient, 116 avenue du président Kennedy, F-75116 Paris, France; or B.P. 371, Paris 16, France. Email: contact@rmc-mo.com. Web: (includes RealAudio) www.rmc-mo.com. A station of the RFI group whose programs are produced in Paris and aired via a medium wave (AM) transmitter in Cyprus; also via FM in France and parts of the Middle East. Some Arabic programs are also broadcast on shortwave to North America via Radio Canada International's Sackville facilitiies, and to North Africa as part of the RFI Arabic broadcasts.
CYPRUS ADDRESS: P.O. Box 2026, Nicosia, Cyprus. Contact: M. Pavlides, Chef de Station. Reception reports have sometimes been verified via this address.

⬛**Tamil-Oli Radio**, Radio Asia, 79 rue Rateau, F-93120 La Courneuve, France. Phone: +33 (1) 4311-2773. Fax: +33 (1) 4311 2772. Email: info@trt.net. Web: (includes RealAudio) www.trt.net. First broadcast on shortwave in 1999 via Madagascar. Transmissions were discontinued after several months, but later resumed (in August 2000) from Deutsche Telekom's Jülich facilities.
LONDON ADDRESS: Tamil Radio and Television, 727 London Road, Thornton Heath, CR7 6AU, United Kingdom. Phone: +44 (20) 8689-7503. Fax: +44 (20) 8683 4445.
Voice of Orthodoxy—*see* Voix de l'Orthodoxie, below.
Voix de l'Orthodoxie, B.P. 416-08, F-75366 Paris Cedex 08, France. Email: irinavo@wanadoo.fr. Contact: Michel Solovieff, General Secretary. An organization that has long broadcast religious programming to Russia via shortwave transmitters in various countries, most recently via Deutsche Telekom (Germany) and Kazakstan. Verifies reception reports, including those written in English.
RUSSIAN OFFICE: Nab. Leitenanta Shmidta 39, St. Petersburg 199034, Russia.

FRENCH GUIANA   World Time −3

Radio France Internationale/Swiss Radio International—Guyane Relay Station, TDF, Montsinéry, French Guiana. Contact: (technical) Chef des Services Techniques, RFI Guyane. All correspondence concerning non-technical matters should be sent directly to the main addresses (*see*) for Radio France International in France and Swiss Radio International in Berne. Can consider replies only to technical correspondence in French.
⬛**RFO Guyane**, 43 bis, rue du Docteur-Gabriel-Devèze, B.P. 7013 - Cayenne Cedex, French Guiana. Phone: +595 299-900 or +594 299-907. Fax: +594 299 958. Web: (includes Quick-Time audio) www.rfo.fr/guyane/guyane.htm. Contact: (administration) George Chow-Toun, Directeur Régional; (editorial) Claude Joly, Rédacteur en Chef; (technical) Charles Diony, Directeur Technique. Free stickers. Replies occasionally and sometimes slowly; correspondence in French preferred, but English often okay.

GABON   World Time +1

Afrique Numéro Un, B.P. 1, Libreville, Gabon. Fax: +241 742 133. Email: africagc@club-internet.fr. Web: www.africa1.com/. Contact: (general) Gaston Didace Singangoye; or A. Letamba, Le Directeur des Programmes; (technical) Mme. Marguerite Bayimbi, Le Directeur [sic] Technique. Free calendars and bumper stickers. $1, 2 IRCs or return postage helpful. Replies very slowly.
RTV Gabonaise, B.P. 10150, Libreville, Gabon. Contact: André Ranaud-Renombo, Le Directeur Technique, Adjoint Radio. Free stickers. $1 required. Replies occasionally, but slowly, to correspondence in French.

GEORGIA   World Time +4

Georgian Radio, TV-Radio Tbilisi, ul. M. Kostava 68, Tbilisi 380071, Republic of Georgia. Phone: (domestic service) +995 (32) 368-362; (external service) +995 (32) 360-063. Fax: +995 (32) 955 137. Contact: (external service) Helena Apkhadze, Foreign Editor; Tamar Shengelia; Mrs. Natia Datuaschwili, Secretary; or Maya Chihradze; (domestic service) Lia Uumlaelsa, Manager; or V. Khundadze, Acting Director of Television and Radio Department. Replies erratically and slowly, in part due to financial difficulties. Return postage or $1 helpful.

Republic of Abkhazia Radio, Abkhaz State Radio and TV Co., Aidgylara Street 34, Sukhum 384900, Republic of Abkhazia; however, as of press time, according to the station there is a total embargo on mail to the Republic of Abkhazia. Phone: +995 (881) 24-867 or +995 (881) 25-321. Fax: +995 (881) 21 144. Contact: G. Amkuab, General Director; or Yury Kutarba, Deputy General Director. A 1992 uprising in northwestern Georgia drove the majority of ethnic Georgians from the region. This area remains virtually autonomous from Georgia.

GERMANY   World Time +1 (+2 midyear)

Adventist World Radio, the Voice of Hope

Postfach 100252, D-64202 Darmstadt, Germany. Phone: (Frequency Management Office) +49 (6151) 953-151. Fax: (Frequency Management Office) +61 (6151) 953 152. Email: english@awr.org; or (Dedio) 102555.257@compuserve.com. Web: (includes online order form for cassettes, Cds and videos) www.stimme-der-hoffnung.de. Contact: (Frequency Management Office) Claudius Dedio, Frequency Coordinator. All listener mail should be sent to AWR, 39 Brendon Street, London W1, United Kingdom. *See* under Italy for further AWR mail information. Also, *see* other AWR listings under Guam, Guatemala, Kenya, Madagascar, United Kingdom and USA.

▣ Bayerischer Rundfunk, Rundfunkplatz 1, D-80300 München, Germany. Phone: +49 (89) 5900-01. Fax: +49 (89) 5900 2375. Email: info@br-online.de. Web: (includes RealAudio) www.br-online.de. Contact: Dr. Gualtiero Guidi; or Jutta Paue, Engineering Adviser. Free stickers and 250-page program schedule book.

Christliche Wissenschaft (Christian Science), Radiosendungen, E. Bethmann, P.O. Box 7330, D-22832 Norderstedt, Germany. A program aired fortnightly via Deutsche Telekom, Jülich.

Deutsche Telekom—*see* "Shortwave Radio Station Jülich—Deutsche Telekom AG."

▣ Deutsche Welle, Radio and TV International

MAIN OFFICE: Raderbergguertel 50, D-50968 Cologne, Germany. Phone: (general) +49 (221) 389-2001/2; (listeners' mail) +49 (221) 389-2500; (Program Distribution) +49 (221) 389-2731; (technical) +49 (221) 389-3221 or +49 (221) 389-3208;(Technical Advisory, Horst Scholz) +49 (221) 389-3201; (Frequency Manager, Peter Pischalka) +49 (221) 389-3228; (Public Relations) +49 (221) 2041. Fax: (general) +49 (221) 389 4155, +49 (221) 389 2080 or +49 (221) 389 3000; (listeners' mail) +49 (221) 389 2510; (English Service, general) +49 (221) 389 4599; (English Service, Current Affairs) +49 (221) 389 4554; (Public Relations) +49 (221) 389 2047; (Program Distribution) +49 (221) 389 2777; (Technical Advisory) +49 (221) 389 3200 or +49 (221) 389 3240. Email: (general) online@dwelle.de; (specific individuals or programs) format is firstname.lastname @dw.gmd.de, so to reach, say, Harald Schuetz, it would be harald.schuetz@dw.gmd.de (if this fails, try the format firstname@dwelle.de); (Program Distribution) 100302.2003 @compuserve.com; (technical) (Pischalka) 100565.1010 @compuserve.com; (Schall) nschall@dwelle.de; (Scholz) 100536.2173@compuserve.com. Web: (general) www.dwelle.de/; (German program, including RealAudio) www.dwelle.de/dpradio/Welcome.html; (non-German languages, including RealAudio) www.dwelle.de/language.html. Contact: (general) Ursula Fleck-Jerwin, Audience Mail Department; Dr. Ralf Siepmann, Director of Public Relations; Dr.

Burkhard Nowotny, Director of Media Department; Harald Schuetz; or ("German by Radio" language course) Herrad Meese; (administration) Dieter Weirich, Director General; (technical—head of engineering) Peter Senger, Chief Engineer; (technical—Radio Frequency Department) Peter Pischalka, Frequency Manager; or Horst Scholz, Head of Transmission; (technical—Transmission Management/Technical Advisory Service) Mrs. Silke Bröker; Norbert Schall; Horst Scholz; Jürgen Hortenbach; or B. Klaumann, Transmission Management. Free pennants, stickers, key chains, pens, *Deutsch—warum nicht?* language-course book, *Germany—A European Country and its People* book. Free 40 page booklet *"Radio Worlds/Worlds of Radios"* featuring radio related articles and stories from different countries. Available from PR and Marketing. Local Deutsche Welle Listeners' Clubs in selected countries. Operates via shortwave transmitters in Germany, Antigua, Canada, Madagascar, Portugal, Russia, Rwanda and Sri Lanka. Deutsche Welle is sheduled to move from Cologne to Bonn in the near future.

ELECTRONIC TRANSMISSION OFFICE FOR PROGRAM PREVIEWS: Infomedia, 25 rue du Lac, L-8808 Arsdorf, Luxembourg. Phone: +352 649-270. Fax: +352 649 271. This office will electronically transmit Deutsche Welle program previews to you upon request; be sure to provide either a dedicated fax number or an email address so they can reply to you.

BRUSSELS NEWS BUREAU: International Press Center, 1 Boulevard Charlemagne, B-1040 Brussels, Belgium.

U.S./CANADIAN LISTENER CONTACT OFFICE: 2800 South Shirlington Road, Suite 901, Arlington VA 22206-3601 USA. Phone: +1 (703) 931-6644.

RUSSIAN LISTENER CONTACT OFFICE: Nemezkaja Wolna, Abonentnyj jaschtschik 596, Glawpotschtamt, 190000 St. Petersburg, Russia.

TOKYO NEWS BUREAU: C.P.O. Box 132, Tokyo 100-91, Japan.

WASHINGTON NEWS BUREAU: P.O. Box 14163, Washington DC 20004 USA. Fax: +1 (202) 526 2255. Contact: Adnan Al-Katib, Correspondent.

Deutschlandfunk, Raderberggürtel 40, D-50968 Köln, Germany. Phone: +49 (221) 345-0. Fax: +49 (221) 345-4802. Web: www.dradio.de/dlf/themen/.

DeutschlandRadio-Berlin, Hans-Rosenthal-Platz, D-10825 Berlin Schönberg, Germany. Phone: +49 (30) 8503-0. Fax: +49 (30) 8503 6168. Email: dlrb@dlf.de; online@dlf.de. Web: www.dradio.de/dlrb/index.html. Contact: Dr. Karl-Heinz Stamm; or Ulrich Reuter. Correspondence in English accepted. Sometimes sends stickers, pens, magazines and other souvenirs.

▣ Evangeliums-Rundfunk—*see* Monaco (Trans World Radio).

Lutherische Stunde, Postfach 1162, D-27363 Sottrum, Germany; or (street address) Clüversborstel 14, D-27367 Sottrum, Germany. Religious program sometimes aired over world band facilities in Europe. Verifies reception reports in German, and may also reply to correspondence in English.

Missionswerk Werner Heukelbach, D-51702 Bergneustadt 2, Germany. Contact: Manfred Paul. Religious program heard via the Voice of Russia. Replies to correspondence in English and German.

▣ Mitteldeutscher Rundfunk, Kantstrasse 71-73, Leipzig, Germany. Phone: +49 (341) 300-0. Fax: +49 (341) 300-5544. Email: (technical) techhot@mdr.de; for nontechnical correspondence, use the online email form at the station's Website. Web: (includes RealAudio) www.mdr.de. Free stickers, lapel pins, booklets and pamphlets. Relayed on shortwave during the night hours via the transmitter of Bayerischer Rundfunk. Replies to correspondence in English and German; return postage not required.

Shortwave Radio Station Jülich—Deutsche Telekom AG

JÜLICH ADDRESS: Rundfunksendestelle Jülich, Merscher Höhe D-52428 Jülich, Germany. Phone: +49 (2461) 697-310; (Technical Engineer) +49 (2461) 697-330; (Technical Advisor and Sales Management) +49 (2461) 697-350. Fax: (all offices) +49 (2461) 697 372. Email: (Hirte) guenter.hirte@telekom.de; (Goslawski) roman.goslawski@telekom.de; (Brodowsky) walter.brodowsky@telekom.de; (Weyl) ralf.weyl@telekom.de. Contact: Günter Hirte, Head of Shortwave Radio Station Jülich; Roman Goslawski, Technical Engineer; (technical) Walter Brodowsky, Technical Advisor; or (nontechnical) Ralf Weyl, Sales Management. Reception reports accepted by mail or fax, and should be clearly marked to the attention of Walter Brodowsky.

KÖLN ADDRESS: Niederlassung 2 Köln, Service Centre Rundfunk, D-50482 Köln Germany. Phone: (Kraus) +49 (221) 575-4000; (Hufschlag) +49 (221) 575-4011. Fax: +49 (221) 575 4090. Email: info@dtag.de. Web: www.dtag.de; www.telekom.de. Contact: Egon Kraus, Head of Broadcasting Service Centre; or Josef Hufschlag, Customer Advisor for High Frequency Broadcasting. This organization operates transmitters on German soil used by Deutsche Welle, as well as those leased to various non-German world band stations.

📻**Radio Santec**, Marienstrasse 1, D-97070 Würzburg, Germany. Phone: (0800-1600 Central European Time, Monday through Friday) +49 (931) 3903-264. Fax: +49 (931) 3903 195. Email: info@radio-santec.com. Web: (includes RealAudio) www.radio-santec.com. Reception reports verified with QSL cards only if requested. Radio Santec, constituted as a separate legal entity in 1999, is the radio branch of Universelles Leben (*see*, below).

📻**Südwestrundfunk**, Neckarstrasse 230, D-70190 Stuttgart, Germany. Phone +49 (711) 929-0. Fax: +49 (711) 929 2600. Email: (general) info@swr-online.de; (technical) technik@swr-online.de. Web: (includes RealAudio) www.swr-online.de. *SWR BADEN-BADEN:* Hans-Bredow-Strasse, D-76530 Baden-Baden, Germany. Phone: +49 (7221) 929-0. This station is the result of a merger between Süddeutscher Rundfunk and Südwestfunk. Based in Stuttgart, transmissions under the new banner commenced in September 1998.

📻**Universelles Leben** (Universal Life)

HEADQUARTERS: Postfach 5643, D-97006 Würzburg, Germany. Phone: +49 (931) 3903-0. Fax: (general) +49 (931) 3903 233. Email: info@universelles-leben.org. Web: (includes RealAudio) www.universelles-leben.org. Contact: Janet Wood, English Dept; "Living in the Spirit of God" listeners' letters program; or Johanna Limley. Free stickers, publications and occasional small souvenirs. Produces "The Word, The Cosmic Wave" (Das Wort, die kosmische Welle) transmitted via the Voice of Russia, Deutsche Telekom (Jülich, Germany) and various other world band stations. Replies to correspondence in English, German or Spanish. Also, *see* Radio Santec, above. *SALES OFFICE:* Das WORT GmbH, Im Universelles Leben, Max-Braun-Str. 2, D-97828 Marktheidenfeld/Altfeld, Germany. Phone: +49 (9391) 504-135. Fax: +49 (9391) 504 133. Email: info@das-wort.com. Web: www.das-wort.com. Sells books, audio cassettes and videos related to broadcast material. *NORTH AMERICAN BUREAU:* Universal Life, The Inner Religion, P.O. Box 651, Guilford CT 06437 USA. Phone: +1 (203) 458-7771. Fax: +1 (203) 458 0713.

GHANA   World Time exactly

WARNING—CONFIDENCE ARTISTS: Attempted correspondence with Radio Ghana may result in requests, perhaps resulting from mail theft, from skilled confidence artists for money, free electronic or other products, publications or immigration sponsorship. To help avoid this, correspondence to Radio Ghana should be sent via registered mail.

📻**Ghana Broadcasting Corporation**, Broadcasting House, P.O. Box 1633, Accra, Ghana. Phone: +233 (21) 221-161. Fax: +233 (21) 221 153 or +233 (21) 773 227. Email: gbc@ghana.com. Web: (includes RealAudio) www.gbc.com.gh; (2000 UTC English news in RealAudio) www.ghanaclassifieds.com. Contact: (general) Mrs. Maud Blankson-Mills, Director of Corporate Affairs; (administration) Cris Tackie, Acting Director of Radio; (technical) K.D. Frimpong, Director of Engineering; or E. Heneath, Propagation Department. Replies tend to be erratic, and reception reports are best sent to the attention of the Propagation Engineer, GBC Monitoring Station. Enclosing an IRC, return postage or $1 and registering your letter should improve the chances of a reply.

GREECE   World Time +2 (+3 midyear)

📻**Foni tis Helladas** (Voice of Greece)

NONTECHNICAL: Hellenic Radio-Television, ERA-5, The Voice of Greece, 432 Mesogion Av., 153-42 Athens, Greece. Phone: + 30 (1) 606-6298, +30 (1) 606-6308 or +30 (1) 606-6310. Fax: +30 (1) 606 6309. Email: (program reports) fonel@hol.gr; era5@leon.nrcps.ariadne-t.grc. Web: (transmission schedule in English) http://ert.ntua.gr/programs/era5/indexeng.htm; (RealAudio in Greek) http://ert.nua.gr; (RealAudio, other languages) http://ert.nua.gr/news/foreignnews.htm. Contact: Angeliki Barka, Head of Programmes. Free tourist literature. *TECHNICAL:* Elliniki Radiophonia—ERA-5, General Technical Directorate, ERT/ERA Hellenic Radio Television SA, Mesogion 402, 15342 Athens, Greece. Phone: (Angelogiannis) +30 (1) 606-6255; (Vorgias) +30 (1) 606-6263; or +31 (1) 606-6264. Fax: +30 (1) 606 6243. Email: (Angelogiannis) dangelogiannis @ert.gr; or dangelogiannis@yahoo.com. Contact: (general) Ing. Dionysios Angelogiannis, Planning Engineer; or Sotiris Vorgias, Planning Engineer; (administration) Th. Kokossis, General Director; or Nicolas Yannakakis, Director. Technical reception reports may be sent via mail, fax or email. Taped reports not accepted.

Radiophonikos Stathmos Makedonias—ERT-3, Angelaki 2, 546 21 Thessaloniki, Greece. Phone: +30 (31) 244-979. Fax: +30 (31) 236 370. Email: charter3@compulink.gr. Contact: (general) Mrs. Tatiana Tsioli, Program Director; or Lefty Kongalides, Head of International Relations; (technical) Dimitrios Keramidas, Engineer. Free booklets and other small souvenirs.

GUAM   World Time +10

Adventist World Radio, the Voice of Hope—KSDA

AWR-Asia, P.O. Box 8990, Agat, Guam 96928 USA. Phone: +1 (671) 565-2000. Fax: +1 (671) 565 2983. Email: english@awr.org. Web: www.awr.org. Contact: Elvin Vence, Chief Engineer. All listener mail to: AWR, 39 Brendon Street, London W1, United Kingdom. Also, *see* AWR listings under Germany, Guatemala, Italy, Kenya, Madagascar, United Kingdom and USA.

Trans World Radio—KTWR

MAIN OFFICE, NONTECHNICAL: P.O. Box CC, Agana, Guam 96910 USA. Phone: (main office) +1 (671) 477-9701; (engineering) +1 (671) 828-8637. Fax: (main office) +1 (671) 477 2838; (engineering) +1 (671) 828-8636. Email: (administration) estortro@twr.org; (technical) cwhite@twr.org; or dgregson@twr.org. Web: (schedule) www.gospelcom.net/twr/broadcasts/guam.htm. Contact: (general) Karen Zeck, Listener Correspondence; Byron Tyler, Producer, "Friends in Focus" listeners' questions program; Janette McSurk; or Mrs. Kathy Greggowski; (administration) Edward Stortro, Station Director; (technical) Chuck White, Chief Engineer; or (Frequency Management) D. Gregson. Also, *see* USA. Free small publications.

FREQUENCY COORDINATION OFFICE: 1868 Halsey Drive, Asan, Guam 96922-1505 USA. Phone: +671 828-8637. Fax: +1 (671) 828 8636. Email: ktwrfreq@twr.hafa.net.gu. Contact: George Zensen, Chief Engineer. This office will also verify email reports with a QSL card.

AUSTRALIAN OFFICE: Trans World Radio ANZ, 2-6 Albert Street, Blackburn, Victoria 3130, Australia; or P.O. Box 390, Box Hill, Victoria 3128, Australia. Phone: +61 (3) 9878-5922. Fax: +61 (3) 9878 5944. Email: info@twradio.org. Web: www.twradio.org. Contact: John Reeder, National Director.

CHINA (HONG KONG) OFFICE: TWR-CMI, P.O. Box 98697, Tsimshatsui Post Office, Kowloon, Hong Kong. Phone: +852 2780-8336. Fax: +852 2385 5045. Email: (general) info@twr.org.hk; (Ko) simon_ko@compuserve.com; (Lok) joycelok@compuserve.com. Web: www.twr.org.hk. Contact: Simon Ko, Acting Area Director; or Joyce Lok, Programming/Follow-up Director.

NEW DELHI OFFICE: P.O. Box 4310, New Delhi-110 019, India. Contact: N. Emil Jebasingh, Vishwa Vani; or S. Stanley.

SINGAPORE OFFICE: Trans World Radio Asia Pacific Office, 2A Martaban Road, Singapore 328627. Phone: +65 251-1887. Fax: +65 251 1846. Email: (Spieker) 76573.1147 @compuserve.com; (Flaming) vflaming@mbox3.singnet.com.sg. Contact: Edmund Spieker, Acting Regional Director; or Vic Flaming, Regional Services Director.

TOKYO OFFICE: Pacific Broadcasting Association, C.P.O. Box 1000, Tokyo 100-91, Japan. Phone +81 (3) 3295-4921. Fax: +81 (3) 3233 2650. Email: pba@path.ne.jp. Contact: (administration) Nobuyoshi Nakagawa.

GUATEMALA   World Time –6

Adventist World Radio, the Voice of Hope—Unión Radio, Apartado de Correo 51-C, Guatemala City, Guatemala. Phone: +502 365-2509. Fax:+502 365 9076. Email: uniradio@infovia.com.gt; mundi@guate.net. Free tourist and religious literature and Guatemalan stamps. Return postage (3 IRCs or $1) appreciated. Correspondence in Spanish preferred. Also, *see* AWR listings under Germany, Guam, Italy, Kenya, Madagascar, United Kingdom and USA.

La Voz de Guatemala—TGW (when active), 18 Calle 6-70 2do piso, Zona 1, 01001 Guatemala City, Guatemala. Phone: +502 232-3321. Fax: +502 251 9873.

La Voz de Nahualá, Nahualá, Sololá, Guatemala. Phone: +502 763-0115. Contact: (technical) Juan Fidel Lepe Juárez, Técnico Auxiliar; or F. Manuel Esquipulas Carrillo Tzep. Return postage required. Correspondence in Spanish preferred.

Radio Buenas Nuevas, 13020 San Sebastián, Huehuetenango, Guatemala. Contact: Israel G. Rodas Mérida, Gerente. $1 or return postage helpful. Free religious and sta-

tion information in Spanish. Sometimes includes a small pennant. Replies to correspondence in Spanish.

Radio Chortís, Centro Social, 20004 Jocotán, Chiquimula, Guatemala. Contact: Padre Juan María Boxus, Director. $1 or return postage required. Replies irregularly to correspondence in Spanish.

Radio Cultural—TGNA, Apartado de Correo 601, Guatemala City, Guatemala. Phone: +502 471-0807. Contact: Mariela Posadas, QSL Secretary; or Wayne Berger, Chief Engineer. Free religious printed matter. Return postage or $1 appreciated.

Radio Cultural Coatán, San Sebástian Coatán, Huehuetenango, Guatemala. Contact: Domingo Hernández, Director; or Virgilio José, Locutor.

Radio K'ekchi—TGVC, 3ra Calle 7-15, Zona 1, 16015 Fray Bartolomé de las Casas, Alta Verapaz, Guatemala; (Media Consultant) David Daniell, Asesor de Comunicaciones, Apartado Postal 25, Bulevares MX, 53140 Mexico. Phone: (station) +502 950-0299; (Daniell, phone/fax) +52 (5) 572-9633. Fax: +502 950 0398. Email: (Daniell) DPDaniell@aol.com. Contact: (general) Gilberto Sun Xicol, Gerente; Ancelmo Cuc Chub, Director; or Mateo Botzoc, Director de Programas; (technical) Larry Baysinger, Ingeniero Jefe. Free paper pennant. $1 or return postage required. Replies to correspondence in Spanish.

Radio Mam, Acu'Mam, Cabricán, Quetzaltenango, Guatemala. Contact: Porfirio Pérez, Director. Free stickers and pennants. $1 or return postage required. Replies irregularly to correspondence in Spanish. Donations permitting (the station is religious), they would like to get a new transmitter to replace the current unit, which is failing.

Radio Maya de Barillas—TGBA, 13026 Villa de Barillas, Huehuetenango, Guatemala. Contact: José Castañeda, Pastor Evangélico y Gerente. Free pennants and pins. Station is very interested in receiving reception reports. $1 or return postage required. Replies occasionally to correspondence in Spanish and Indian languages.

Radio Tezulutlán—TGTZ, Apartado de Correo 19, 16901 Cobán, Guatemala. Phone: Contact: Sergio W. Godoy, Director; or Hno. Antonio Jacobs, Director Ejecutivo. Pennant for donation to specific bank account. $1 or return postage required. Replies to correspondence in Spanish.

Radio Verdad, Apartado Postal 5, Chiquimula, Guatemala. Contact: Dr. Edgar Amílcar Morales, Gerente.

GUINEA   World Time exactly

Radiodiffusion-Télévision Guinéenne, B.P. 391, Conakry, Guinea. If no reply is forthcoming from this address, try sending your letter to: D.G.R./P.T.T., B.P. 3322, Conakry, Guinea. Phone/fax: +224 451-408. Contact: (general) Yaoussou Diaby, Journaliste Sportif; Boubacar Yacine Diallo, Directeur Général/ORTG; or Seny Camara; (administration) Momo Toure, Chef Services Administratifs; (technical, studio) Mbaye Gagne, Chef de Studio; (technical, overall) Direction des Services Techniques. Return postage or $1 required. Replies very irregularly to correspondence in French.

GUYANA   World Time –3

Voice of Guyana, Guyana Broadcasting Corporation, Broadcasting House, P.O. Box 10760, Georgetown, Guyana. Phone: +592 (2) 58734, +592 (2) 58083 or +592 (2) 62691. Fax: +592 (2) 58756, but persist as the fax machine appears to be switched off much of the time. Contact: (general) Indira Anandjit, Personnel Assistant; or M. Phillips; (technical) Roy Marshall, Senior Technician; or Shiroxley Goodman, Chief

Engineer. $1 or IRC helpful. Sending a spare sticker from another station helps assure a reply. Note that when the station's medium wave transmitter is down because of a component fault, parts of the shortwave unit are sometimes 'borrowed' until spares become available. As a result, the station is sometimes off shortwave for several weeks at a time.

HOLLAND (NETHERLANDS) World Time +1 (+2 midyear)

InfoRadio, P.O. Box 140, 5590 AC Heeze, Netherlands. Email: inforadio@club.tip.nl. Web: (includes online reception report form) www.inforadio.nl. Return postage ($1 or 2 IRCs) required. A private broadcaster with a weekly half-hour program for Dutch vacationers in Europe and the Americas. June through August via Deutsche Telekom's Jülich facility and WRMI, USA (see).

Radio Nederland Wereldomroep (Radio Netherlands)
MAIN OFFICE: P.O. Box 222, 1200 JG Hilversum, Netherlands. Phone: (general) +31 (35) 672-4211; (English Language Service) +31 (35) 672-4242; (24-hour listener Answerline) +31 (35) 672-4222. Fax: (general) +31 (35) 672 4207, but indicate destination department on fax cover sheet; (English Language Service) +31 (35) 672 4239. Email: (English Language Service) letters@rnw.nl. ("Media Network") media@rnw.nl; (Webcasting) pepijn.kalis@rnw.nl. Web: (general) www.rnw.nl (online publications are listed in the section "Real Radio"); (RealAudio) www.rnw.nl/distrib/realaudio/. Contact: (management) Lodewijk Bouwens, Director General; Jonathan Marks, Director of Programmes; Jan Hoek, Director of Finance and Logistics; Mike Shaw, Head of English Language Service; Ginger da Silva, Network Manager English; (listener correspondence) Helma Brugma, English Correspondence; or Veronica Wilson, Host of listener-contact programme: "Sincerely Yours" (include your telephone number or email address). Full-data verification card for reception reports, following guidelines in the RNW folder, "Writing Useful Reception Reports," available free and on the Internet. Semi-annual On Target newsletter also free upon request, as are stickers and booklets. Other language departments have their own newsletters. The Radio Netherlands Music Department produces concerts heard on many NPR stations in North America, as well as a line of CDs, mainly of classical, jazz, world music and the Euro Hit 40. Most of the productions are only for rebroadcasting on other stations, but recordings on the NM Classics label are for sale. More details are available at the RNW Website. Visitors welcome, but must call in advance.
PROGRAMME DISTRIBUTION, NETWORK AND FREQUENCY PLANNING: P.O. Box 222, 1200 JG Hilversum, Netherlands. Phone: +31 (35) 672-4825, +31 (35) 672-4424 or +31 (35) 672-4427. Fax: +31 (35) 672 4429. Email: rocus.dejoode@rnw.nl; ehard.goddijn; jan.willem.drexhage.rne.nl. Contact: Rocus de Joode; Ehard Goddijn; or Jan Willem Drexhage, Head of Programme Distribution.
NORTH AMERICAN OPERATION: 316 Eisenhower Parkway, Livingston, NJ 07039 USA. Phone: toll-free in the USA 1-800-797-1670; or +1 (973) 533-6761. Fax: +1 (973) 533 6762. Email: lee.martin@rnw.nl. Contact: Lee Martin, Manager of Client Services. This bureau markets Radio Netherlands radio and television productions in English and Spanish for the North American market. These programs are available to stations on satellite and CD.
NEW DELHI OFFICE: (local correspondence only) P.O. Box 5257, Chanakya Puri Post Office, New Delhi, 110 021, India.

Forwards mail from Indian listeners to Holland every three weeks.

HONDURAS World Time –6

La Voz de la Mosquitia (when operating)
STATION: Puerto Lempira, Dpto. Gracias a Dios, Honduras. Contact: Sammy Simpson, Director; or Larry Sexton. Free pennants.
U.S. OFFICE: Global Outreach, Box 1, Tupelo MS 38802 USA. Phone: +1 (601) 842-4615. Another U.S. contact is Larry Hooker, who occasionally visits the station, and who can be reached at +1 (334) 694-7976.

La Voz Evangélica—HRVC
MAIN OFFICE: Apartado Postal 3252, Tegucigalpa, M.D.C., Honduras. Phone: +504 234-3468/69/70. Fax: +504 233 3933. Email: hrvc@infanet.hn. Contact: (general) Srta. Orfa Esther Durón Mendoza, Secretaria; Tereso Ramos, Director de Programación; Alan Maradiaga; or Modesto Palma, Jefe, Depto. Tráfico; (technical) Carlos Paguada, Director del Dpto. Técnico; (administration) Venancio Mejía, Gerente; or Nelson Perdomo, Director. Free calendars. Three IRCs or $1 required. Replies to correspondence in English, Spanish, Portuguese and German.
REGIONAL OFFICE, SAN PEDRO SULA: Apartado 2336, San Pedro Sula, Honduras. Phone: +504 557-5030. Contact: Hernán Miranda, Director.
REGIONAL OFFICE, LA CEIBA: Apartado 164, La Ceiba, Honduras. Phone: +504 443-2390. Contact: José Banegas, Director.
Radio Costeña—relays Radio Ebenezer (1220 kHz medium wave), and all correspondence should be sent to the latter's address: Radio Ebenezer 1220 AM, Apartado 3466, San Pedro Sula, Honduras. Email: ebenezer@globalnet.hn; or pastor@ebenezer.hn. Web: www.ebenezer.hn. Contact: Germán Ponce, Gerente. According to a Swedish DXer, a reply was received from Iván Franco at casasps@yahoo.com, but it's not known what relation this person has with the station.
Radio HRET
STATION: Primera Iglesia Bautista, Domicilio Conocido, Puerto Lempira, Gracias a Dios 33101, Honduras. Fax: +504 898 0018. Contact: Leonardo Alvarez López, Locutor y Operador; or Desiderio Williams, Locutor y Operador. Return postage necessary. Replies, sometimes slowly, to correspondence in Spanish.
NONTECHNICAL ENGLISH CORRESPONDENCE: David Daniell, Asesor de Comunicaciones, Apartado Postal 25, Bulevares, MX-53140, Mexico. Email: DPDaniell@aol.com. Replies to correspondence in English and Spanish.
TECHNICAL ENGLISH CORRESPONDENCE: Larry Baysinger, 8000 Casualwood Ct., Louisville KY 40291 USA. Replies to correspondence in English and Spanish, but calls not accepted.
Radio HRMI, La Voz de Misiones Internacionales
STATION: Apartado Postal 20583, Comayaguela, M.D.C., Honduras. Phone: +504 233-9029. Contact: Wayne Downs, Director. $1 or return postage helpful.
U.S. OFFICE: IMF World Missions, P.O. Box 6321, San Bernardino CA 92412, USA. Phone +1 (909) 370-4515. Fax: +1 (909) 370 4862. Email: JKPIMF@msn.com. Contact: Dr. James K. Planck, President; or Gustavo Roa, Coordinator.
Radio Litoral, Apartado Postal 878, La Ceiba, Provincia Atlántida, Honduras. Contact: José A. Mejía, Gerente-Propietario. Free postcards. 1$ or return postage required. Replies to correspondence in Spanish.
Radio Luz y Vida—HRPC, Apartado 303, San Pedro Sula, Honduras. Phone: +504 654-1221. Fax: +504 557 0394. Con-

News director Ralph Kurtenbach is one of the personalities regularly heard over HCJB in Quito, Ecuador. This inspirational station has attracted a worldwide following for many years. HCJB

tact: C. Paul Easley, Director; Cristóbal "Chris" Fleck; Ubaldo Zaldívar; or, to have your letter read over the air, "English Friendship Program." Return postage or $1 appreciated.

HUNGARY   World Time +1 (+2 midyear)

📻**Radio Budapest**

STATION OFFICES: Bródy Sándor utca 5-7, H-1800 Budapest, Hungary. Phone: (general) +36 (1) 328-7339, +36 (1) 328-8328, +36 (1) 328-7357 +36 (1) 328-8588, +36 (1) 328-7710 or +36 (1) 328-7723; (voice mail, English) +36 (1) 328-8320; (voice mail, German) +36 (1) 328-7325; (administration) +36 (1) 328-7503 or +36 (1) 328-8415; (technical) +36 (1) 328-7226 or +36 (1) 328-8923. Fax: (general) +36 (1) 328 8517; (administration) +36 (1) 328 8838; (technical) +36 (1) 328 7105. Email: (Radio Budapest, English) ango11@kaf.radio.hu; (Radio Budapest, German) nemetl@kaf.radio.hu; (Hungarian Information Resources) avadasz@bluemoon.sma.com; (technical) (Füszlás) Fuszfasla@muszak.radio.hu. Web: (general) www.kaf.radio.hu/index.html; (RealAudio in English, German, Hungarian and Russian) www.wrn.org/ondemand/hungary.html. Contact: (English Language Service) Ágnes Kevi, Correspondence; Charles Taylor Coutts, Producer, "Gatepost" (listeners' letters' program) and Head of English Language Service; Louis Horváth, DX Editor; or Sándor Laczkó, Editor; (administration) Antal Réger, Director, For-

eign Broadcasting; Dr. Zsuzsa Mészáros, Vice-Director, Foreign Broadcasting; János Szirányi, President, Magyar Rádió; or János Simkó, Vice President, Magyar Rádió; (technical) László Füszfás, Deputy Technical Director, Magyar Rádió; Külföldi Adások Főszerkesztősége; or Lajos Horváth, Műszaki Igazgatcsá; (Hungarian Information Resources) Andrew Vadasz. Free Budapest International periodical, stickers, pennants, stamps and printed tourist and other material. Also, for those whose comments or program proposals are used over the air, T-shirts, baseball-style caps and ballpoint pens. RBSWC DX News bulletin free to all Radio Budapest Shortwave Club members. Advertisements considered.

COMMUNICATION AUTHORITY: P.O. Box 75, H-1525 Budapest, Hungary. Phone: +36 (1) 457-7178. Fax: +36 (1) 457 7120 or 36 (1) 356 5520. Email: czuprak@hif.hu. Contact: Ernö Czuprák.

TRANSMISSION AUTHORITY: Ministry of Transport, Communications and Water Management, P.O. Box 87, H-1400 Budapest, Hungary. Phone: +36 (1) 461-3390. Fax: +36 (1) 461 3392. Email: horvathf@cms.khvm.hu. Contact: Ferenc Horváth, Frequency Manager, Radio Communications Engineering Services.

ICELAND   World Time exactly

📻**Ríkisútvarpid**, International Relations Department, Efstaleiti 1, IS-150 Reykjavík, Iceland. Phone: +354 515-3000. Fax: +354 515 3010. Email: isradio@ruv.is. Web: (includes RealAudio) www.ruv.is/utvarpid/. Contact: Dóra Ingvadóttir, Head of International Relations; or Markús Öern Antonsson, Director.

INDIA   World Time +5:30

WARNING—MAIL THEFT: Several Passport readers report that letters to India containing IRCs and other valuables have disappeared en route when not registered. Best is either to register your letter or to send correspondence in an unsealed envelope, and without enclosures.

📻**All India Radio**

NOTE: The facility "New Broadcasting House" is being built to supplement the existing Broadcasting House on Parliament Street. It is to be used by the domestic and external services, alike, and is scheduled to be in full operation by 2001.

ADMINISTRATION: Directorate General of All India Radio, Akashvani Bhawan, 1 Sansad Marg, New Delhi-110 001, India. Phone: (general) +91 (11) 371-0006; (Engineer-in-Chief) +91 (11) 371-0058; (Frequency Management) +91 (11) 371-0145 or +91 (11) 371-4062; (Director General) +91 (11) 371-0300 or +91 (11) 371-4061; (CEO) +91 (11) 338-8159; (programming) +91 (11) 371-5411, (voice mail, English) +91 (11) 376-1166, (Hindi) +91 (11) 376-1144. Fax: +91 (11) 371 1956. Email: faair@giasdl01.vsnl.net.in or (Bhatnagar, Frequency Assignments) akb@air.org.in. Contact: (general) Rajeeva Ratna Shah, Director General & CEO; (technical) H.M. Joshi, Engineer-in-Chief; or A.K. Bhatnagar, Director - Frequency Assignments.

AUDIENCE RESEARCH: Audience Research Unit, All India Radio, Press Trust of India Building, 2nd floor, Sansad Marg, New Delhi-110 001, India. Phone: +91 (11) 371-0033. Contact: S.K. Khatri, Director.

CENTRAL MONITORING SERVICES: Central Monitoring Services, All India Radio, Ayanagar, New Delhi-100 047, India. Phone: (Director) +91 (11) 680-1763 or +91 (11) 680-2955; (Control Room) +91 (11) 680-2362. Fax: +91 (11) 680 2679, +91 (11) 680 2362 or +91 (11) 680 2955. Contact: P. Mazumdar, Director.

INTERNATIONAL MONITORING STATION—MAIN OFFICE: International Monitoring Station, All India Radio, Dr. K.S. Krishnan Road, Todapur, New Delhi-110 012, India. Phone: (general) +91 (11) 581-461;(administration) +91 (11) 680-2306; (Frequency Planning) +91 (11) 573-5936 (Chhabra) or +91 (11) 573-5937 (Malviya). Contact: D.P. Chhabra or R.K. Malviya, Assistant Research Engineers—Frequency Planning.

NEWS SERVICES DIVISION: News Services Division, Broadcasting House, 1 Sansad Marg, New Delhi-110 001, India. Phone: +91 (11) 371-0084 or +91 (11) 373-1510. Contact: Harish Awasthi, Director General—News.

RESEARCH AND DEVELOPMENT: Office of the Chief Engineer R&D, All India Radio, 14-B Ring Road, Indraprastha Estate, New Delhi-110 002, India. Phone: (general) +91 (11) 331-1711, +91 (11) 331-1762, +91 (11) 331-3532 or +91 (11) 331-3574; (Chief Engineer) +91 (11) 331 8329 or +91 (11) 373-6255. Fax: +91 (11) 331 8329 or +91 (11) 331 6674. Email: rdair@giasdl01.vsnl.net.in. Web: www.air.kode.net. Contact: A.S. Guin, Chief Engineer.

TRANSCRIPTION AND PROGRAM EXCHANGE SERVICES: Akashvani Bhawan, 1 Sansad Marg, New Delhi-110 001, India. Phone: +91 (11) 371-7927. Contact: Dr. Gangesh Gunjan, Director.

All India Radio—Aizawl, Radio Tila, Tuikhuahtlang, Aizawl-796 001, Mizoram, India. Phone: +91 (3652) 2415. Contact: (technical) D.K. Sharma, Station Engineer; or T.R. Rabha, Station Engineer.

All India Radio—Bangalore
HEADQUARTERS: see All India Radio—External Services Division.
AIR OFFICE NEAR TRANSMITTER: P.O. Box 5096, Bangalore-560 001, Karnataka, India. Phone: +91 (80) 261-243. Contact: (technical) C. Iyengar, Superintending Engineer.

All India Radio—Bhopal, Akashvani Bhawan, Shamla Hills, Bhopal-462 002, Madhya Pradesh, India. Phone: +91 (755) 540-041. Contact: (technical) C. Lal, Station Engineer.

All India Radio—Calcutta, G.P.O. Box 696, Calcutta—700 001, West Bengal, India. Phone: +91 (33) 248-9131. Contact: (technical) R.N. Dam, Superintending Engineer.

All India Radio—Chennai
EXTERNAL SERVICES: see All India Radio—External Services Division.
DOMESTIC SERVICE: Kamrajar Salai, Mylapore, Chennai-600 004, Tamil Nadu, India. Phone: +91 (44) 845-975. Contact: (technical) S. Bhatia, Superintending Engineer.

All India Radio—External Services Division
MAIN ADDRESS: Broadcasting House, 1 Sansad Marg, P.O. Box 500, New Delhi-110 001, India. Phone: (general) +91 (11) 371-5411; (Director) +91 (11) 371-0057. Contact: (general) P.P. Setia, Director of External Services; or S.C. Panda, Audience Relations Officer; (technical) S.A.S. Abidi, Assistant Director Engineering (F.A.). Email (Research Dept.): rdair@giasdl01.vsnl.net.in; (comments on programs) air@kode.net. Web: (includes RealAudio in English and other languages) www.allindiaradio.com; http://air.kode.net; (unofficial, but contains updated schedule information) www.angelfire.com/in/alokdg/air.html. Free monthly *India Calling* magazine and stickers. Replies erratic. Except for stations listed below, correspondence to domestic stations is more likely to be responded to if it is sent via the External Services Division; request that your letter be forwarded to the appropriate domestic station.
VERIFICATION ADDRESS: Prasar Bharati Corporation of India, Akashvani Bhawan, Room 204, Sansad Marg, New Delhi-110 001, India; or P.O. Box 500, New Delhi-110 001, India. Fax:

+91 (11) 372 5212 or +91 (11) 371 4697. Email: faair@giasdl01.vsnl.net.in. Contact: A.K. Bhatnagar, Director, Frequency Assignments.

All India Radio—Gangtok, Old MLA Hostel, Gangtok—737 101, Sikkim, India. Phone: +91 (359) 22636. Contact: (general) Y.P. Yolmo, Station Director; (technical) Deepak Kumar, Station Engineer.

All India Radio—Gorakhpur
NEPALESE EXTERNAL SERVICE: see All India Radio—External Services Division.
DOMESTIC SERVICE: Post Bag 26, Gorakhpur-273 001, Uttar Pradesh, India. Phone: +91 (551) 337-401. Contact: (technical) Dr. S.M. Pradhan, Superintending Engineer.

All India Radio—Guwahati, P.O. Box 28, Chandmari, Guwahati-781 003, Assam, India. Phone: +91 (361) 540-135. Contact: (technical) P.C. Sanghi, Superintending Engineer.

All India Radio—Hyderabad, Rocklands, Saifabad, Hyderabad-500 004, Andhra Pradesh, India. Phone: +91 (40) 234-904. Contact: (technical) N. Srinivasan, Superintending Engineer.

All India Radio—Imphal, Palau Road, Imphal-795 001, Manipur, India. Phone: +91 (385) 20-534. Contact: (technical) M. Jayaraman, Superintending Engineer.

All India Radio—Itanagar, Naharlagun, Itanagar-791 110, Arunachal Pradesh, India. Phone: +91 (3781) 4485. Contact: J.T. Jirdoh, Station Director; or Suresh Naik, Superintending Engineer. Verifications direct from station are difficult, as engineering is done by staff visiting from the Regional Engineering Headquarters at AIR—Guwahati (see); that address might be worth contacting if all else fails.

All India Radio—Jaipur, 5 Park House, Mirza Ismail Road, Jaipur-302 001, Rajasthan, India. Phone: +91 (141) 366-623. Contact: (technical) S.C. Sharma, Station Engineer.

All India Radio—Jammu—*see* Radio Kashmir—Jammu.

All India Radio—Jeypore, Jeypore-764 005, Orissa, India. Phone: +91 (685) 422-524. Contact: P. Subramanium, Assistant Station Engineer.

All India Radio—Kohima, Kohima-797 001, Nagaland, India. Phone: +91 (3866) 2121. Contact: (technical) K.G. Talwar, Superintending Engineer; K.K Jose, Assistant Engineer; or K. Morang, Assistant Station Engineer. Return postage, $1 or IRC helpful.

All India Radio—Kurseong, Mehta Club Building, Kurseong-734 203, Darjeeling District, West Bengal, India. Phone: +91 (3554) 350. Contact: (general) George Kuruvilla, Assistant Director; (technical) R.K. Sinha, Chief Engineer.

All India Radio—Leh—*see* Radio Kashmir—Leh.

All India Radio—Lucknow, 18 Vidhan Sabha Marg, Lucknow-226 001, Uttar Pradesh, India. Phone: +91 (522) 244-130. Contact: R.K. Singh, Superintending Engineer. This station now appears to be replying via the External Services Division, New Delhi.

All India Radio—Mumbai
EXTERNAL SERVICES: see All India Radio—External Services Division.
COMMERCIAL SERVICE (VIVIDH BHARATI): All India Radio, P.O. Box 11497, 101 M K Road, Mumbai-400 0020, Maharashtra, India. Phone: (general) +91 (22) 203-1341 or +91 (22) 203-594; (director) +91 (22) 203-7702. Fax: +91 (22) 287 6040. Contact: Vijayalakshmi Sinha, Director.
DOMESTIC SERVICE: P.O. Box 13034, Mumbai-400 020, Maharashtra, India. Phone: +91 (22) 202-9853. Contact: S. Sundaram, Superintending Engineer; or Lak Bhatnagar, Supervisor, Frequency Assignments. Return postage helpful.

All India Radio—New Delhi, P.O. Box 70, New Delhi-110 011, India. Phone: (general) +91 (11) 371-0113. Contact: (technical) G.C. Tyagi, Superintending Engineer. $1 helpful.

All India Radio—Panaji

HEADQUARTERS: see All India Radio—External Services Division, above.

AIR OFFICE NEAR TRANSMITTER: P.O. Box 220, Altinho, Panaji-403 001, Goa, India. Phone: +91 (832) 5563. Contact: (technical) V.K. Singhla, Station Engineer; or G.N. Shetti, Assistant Engineer.

All India Radio—Port Blair, Dilanipur, Port Blair-744 102, South Andaman, Andaman and Nicobar Islands, Union Territory, India. Phone: +91 (3192) 20-682. Contact: (technical) Yuvraj Bajaj, Station Engineer. Registering letter appears to be useful. Don't send any cash with your correspondence as it appears to be a violation of their foreign currency regulations.

All India Radio—Ranchi, 6 Ratu Road, Ranchi-834 001, Bihar, India. Phone: +91 (651) 302-358. Contact: (technical) H.N. Agarwal, Superintending Engineer.

All India Radio—Shillong, P.O. Box 14, Shillong-793 001, Meghalaya, India. Phone: +91 (364) 224-443 or +91 (364) 222-781. Contact: (general) C. Lalsaronga, Director NEIS; (technical) H.K. Agarwal, Superintending Engineer. Free booklet on station's history.

All India Radio—Simla, Choura Maidan, Simla-171 004, Himachal Pradesh, India. Phone: +91 (177) 4809. Contact: (technical) B.K. Upadhayay, Superintending Engineer; or P.K. Sood, Assistant Station Engineer. Return postage helpful.

All India Radio—Srinagar—*see* Radio Kashmir—Srinagar.

All India Radio—Thiruvananthapuram, P.O. Box 403, Bhakti Vilas, Vazuthacaud, Thiruvananthapuram-695 014, Kerala, India. Phone: +91 (471) 65-009. Contact: (technical) K.M. Georgekutty, Station Engineer.

Ministry of Information and Broadcasting, Main Secretariat, A-Wing, Shastri Bhawan, New Delhi-110 001, India. Phone: (general) +91 (11) 338-4340, +91 (11) 338-4782 or +91 (11) 379-338; (Information and Broadcasting Secretary) +91 (11) 338-2639. Fax: +91 (11) 338 3513, +91 (11) 338 7823, +91 (11) 338 4785, +91 (11) 338 7617 or +91 (11) 338 1043. Contact: (general) N.P. Nawani, Information and Broadcasting Secretary; (administration) C.M. Ibrahim, Minister for Information and Broadcasting.

Radio Kashmir—Jammu, Begum Haveli, Old Palace Road, Jammu-180 001, Jammu and Kashmir, India. Phone: +91 (191) 544-411. Fax: +91 (191) 546 658. Contact: (technical) S.K. Sharma, Station Engineer.

Radio Kashmir—Leh, Leh-194 101, Ladakh District, Jammu and Kashmir, India. Phone: +91 (1982) 2263. Contact: (technical) L.K. Gandotar, Station Engineer.

Radio Kashmir—Srinagar, Sherwani Road, Srinagar-190 001, Jammu and Kashmir, India. Phone: +91 (194) 71-460. Contact: L. Rehman, Station Director.

Radio Tila—*see* All India Radio—Aizawl.

Trans World Radio

STUDIO: P.O. Box 4407, L-15, Green Park, New Delhi-110 016, India. Phone: +91 (11) 685-2568, +91 (11) 685-5674 or +91 (11) 686-1319. Fax: +91 (11) 686 8049. Email: emiljeba@nda.vsnl.net.in. Web: www.gospelcom.net/twr/zsa.index.htm. Contact: N. Emil Jebasingh, Director. This office is used for program production and answering listeners' correspondence, and does not have its own transmission facilities.

ON-AIR ADDRESS: P.O. Box 5, Andhra Pradesh, India.

INDONESIA
World Time +7 Western: Waktu Indonesia Bagian Barat (Jawa, Sumatera); +8 Central: Waktu Indonesia Bagian Tengal (Bali, Kalimantan, Sulawesi, Nusa Tenggara); +9 Eastern: Waktu Indonesia Bagian Timur (Papua, Maluku)

NOTE: Except where otherwise indicated, Indonesian stations, especially those of the Radio Republik Indonesia (RRI) network, will reply to at least some correspondence in English. However, correspondence in Indonesian is more likely to ensure a reply.

Kang Guru II Radio English, Indonesia Australia Language Foundation, Kotak Pos 6756 JKSRB, Jakarta 12067, Indonesia. Email: kangguru@denpasar.wasantara.net.id. Contact: Walter Slamer, Kang Guru Project Manager. This program is aired over various RRI outlets, including Jakarta and Sorong. Continuation of this project, currently sponsored by Australia's AusAID, will depend upon whether adequate supplementary funding can be made available.

Radio Pemerintah Daerah Kabupaten TK II—RPDK Ende, Jalan Panglima Sudirman, Ende, Flores, Nusa Tenggara Timor, Indonesia. Contact: (technical) Thomas Keropong, YC9LHD. Return postage required.

Radio Pemerintah Daerah Kabupaten TK II—RPDK Manggarai, Ruteng, Flores, Nusa Tenggara Timur, Indonesia. Contact: Simon Saleh, B.A. Return postage required.

Radio Pemerintah Daerah Kabupaten Daerah TK II—RSPDKD Ngada, Jalan Soekarno-Hatta, Bjawa, Flores, Nusa Tenggara Tengah, Indonesia. Phone: +62 (384) 21-142. Contact: Drs. Petrus Tena, Kepala Studio.

Radio Republik Indonesia—RRI Ambon, Jalan Jendral Akhmad Yani 1, Ambon 97124, Maluku, Indonesia. Contact: Drs. H. Ali Amran or Pirla C. Noija, Kepala Seksi Siaran. A very poor replier to correspondence in recent years. Correspondence in Indonesian and return postage essential.

Radio Republik Indonesia—RRI Banda Aceh (when operating), Kotak Pos 112, Banda Aceh 23243, Aceh, Indonesia. Contact: Parmono Prawira, Technical Director; or S.H. Rosa Kim. Return postage helpful.

Radio Republik Indonesia—RRI Bandar Lampung, Kotak Pos 24, Bandar Lampung 35213, Indonesia. Phone: +62 (721) 52-280. Fax: +62 (721) 62 767. Contact: M. Nasir Agun, Kepala Stasiun; Hi Hanafie Umar; Djarot Nursingaih, Tech. Transmission; Drs. Soewadji, Kepala Seksi Siaran; Drs. Zulhaqqi Hafiz, Kepala Sub Seksi Periklanan; or Asmara Haidar Manaf. Return postage helpful. Replies in Indonesian to correspondence in English or Indonesian.

Radio Republik Indonesia—RRI Bandung (when operating), Stasiun Regional 1, Kotak Pos 1055, Bandung 40122, Jawa Barat, Indonesia. Contact: Drs. Idrus Alkaf, Kepala Stasiun; Mrs. Ati Kusmiati; or Eem Suhaemi, Kepala Seksi Siaran. Return postage or IRC helpful.

Radio Republik Indonesia—RRI Banjarmasin (when operating), Stasiun Nusantara 111, Kotak Pos 117, Banjarmasin 70234, Kalimantan Selatan, Indonesia. Contact: Jul Chaidir, Stasiun Kepala; or Harmyn Husein. Free stickers. Return postage or IRCs helpful.

Radio Republik Indonesia—RRI Bengkulu, Stasiun Regional 1, Kotak Pos 13 Kawat, Kotamadya Bengkulu 38227, Indonesia. Contact: Drs. Drs. Jasran Abubakar, Kepala Stasiun. Free picture postcards, decals and tourist literature. Return postage or 2 IRCs helpful.

Radio Republik Indonesia—RRI Biak, Kotak Pos 505, Biak 98117, Papua, Indonesia. Contact: Butje Latuperissa, Kepala Seksi Siaran; or Drs. D.A. Siahainenia, Kepala Stasiun. Correspondence in Indonesian preferred.

Radio Republik Indonesia—RRI Bukittinggi (when operating), Stasiun Regional 1 Bukittinggi, Jalan Prof. Muhammad Yamin 199, Aurkuning, Bukittinggi 26131, Propinsi Sumatera Barat, Indonesia. Fax: +62 (752) 367 132. Contact: Mr. Effendi, Sekretaris; Zul Arifin Mukhtar, SH; or Samirwan Sarjana Hukum, Producer, "Phone in Program." Replies to correspondence in Indonesian or English. Return postage helpful.

Radio Republik Indonesia—RRI Denpasar (when operating), Kotak Pos 3031, Denpasar 80233, Bali, Indonesia. Contact: Drs. Utiek Ruktiningsih, Kepala Stasiun. Replies slowly to correspondence in Indonesian. Return postage or IRCs helpful.

Radio Republik Indonesia—RRI Dili (when operating), Stasiun Regional 1 Dili, Jalan Kaikoli, Kotak Pos 103, Dili 88000, Timor-Timur, Indonesia. Contact: Harry A. Silalahi, Kepala Stasiun; Arnoldus Klau; or Paul J. Amalo, BA. Return postage or $1 helpful. Replies occasionally to correspondence in Indonesian.

Radio Republik Indonesia—RRI Fak Fak, Jalan Kapten P. Tendean, Kotak Pos 54, Fak-Fak 98612, Papua, Indonesia. Contact: Bahrun Siregar, Kepala Stasiun; Aloys Ngotra, Kepala Seksi Siaran; Drs. Tukiran Erlantoko; or Richart Tan, Kepala Sub Seksi Siaran Kata. Station plans to upgrade its transmitting facilities with the help of the Japanese government. Return postage required. Replies occasionally.

Radio Republik Indonesia—RRI Gorontalo, Jalan Jendral Sudirman 30, Gorontalo 96115, Sulawesi Utara, Indonesia. Fax: +62 (435) 821 590/91. Contact: Drs. Muhammad. Assad, Kepala Stasiun; or Saleh S. Thalib, Technical Manager. Return postage helpful. Replies occasionally, preferably to correspondence in Indonesian.

⌨ **Radio Republik Indonesia—RRI Jakarta**
STATION: Stasiun Nasional Jakarta, Kotak Pos 356, Jakarta 10110, Daerah Khusus Jakarta Raya, Indonesia. Web: (RealAudio via cyberstation Syahreza Radio) www.hway.net/syahreza/rri.htm. Contact: Drs. Beni Koesbani, Kepala Stasiun. Return postage helpful. Replies irregularly.
"DATELINE" ENGLISH PROGRAM: see Kang Guru II Radio English.
"U.N. CALLING ASIA" ENGLISH PROGRAM: Program via RRI Jakarta Programa Ibukota Satu, every Sunday. Contact address same as United Nations Radio (see).

Radio Republik Indonesia—RRI Jambi
STATION: Jalan Jendral A. Yani 5, Telanaipura, Jambi 36122, Propinsi Jambi, Indonesia. Contact: M. Yazid, Kepala Siaran; H. Asmuni Lubis, BA; or Byamsuri, Acting Station Manager. Return postage helpful.

Radio Republik Indonesia—RRI Jayapura, Kotak Pos 1077, Jayapura 99200, Papua, Indonesia. Contact: Harry Liborang, Direktorat Radio; Hartono, Bidang Teknik; or Dr. David Alex Siahainenia, Kepala. Return postage of $1 helpful. Replies to correspondence in Indonesian or English.

Radio Republik Indonesia—RRI Kendari, Kotak Pos 7, Kendari 93111, Sulawesi Tenggara, Indonesia. Contact: H. Sjahbuddin, BA; Muniruddin Amin, Programmer; or Drs. Supandi. Return postage required. Replies slowly to correspondence in Indonesian.

Radio Republik Indonesia—RRI Kupang (Regional I), Jalan Tompello 8, Kupang 85225, Timor, Indonesia. Contact: Drs. P.M. Tisera, Kepala Stasiun; Qustigap Bagang, Kepala Seksi Siaran; or Said Rasyid, Kepala Studio. Return postage helpful. Correspondence in Indonesian preferred. Replies occasionally.

Radio Republik Indonesia—RRI Madiun (when operating), Jalan Mayor Jendral Panjaitan 10, Madiun 63133, Jawa Timur, Indonesia. Fax: +62 (351) 4964. Contact: Imam Soeprapto, Kepala Seksi Siaran. Replies to correspondence in English or Indonesian. Return postage helpful.

Radio Republik Indonesia—RRI Makassar, Jalan Riburane 3, Makassar, 90174, Sulawesi Selatan, Indonesia. Contact: H. Kamaruddin Alkaf Yasin, Head of Broadcasting Department; L.A. Rachim Ganie; Ashan Muhammad, Kepala Bidang Teknik; or Drs. Bambang Pudjono. Return postage, $1 or IRCs helpful. Replies irregularly and sometimes slowly.

Radio Republik Indonesia—RRI Malang (when operating), Kotak Pos 78, Malang 65140, Jawa Timur, Indonesia; or Jalan Candi Panggung No. 58, Mojolangu, Malang 65142, Indonesia. Contact: Drs.Tjutju Tjuar Na Adikorya, Kepala Stasiun; Ml. Mawahib, Kepala Seksi Siaran; or Dra Hartati Soekemi, Mengetahui. Return postage required. Free history and other booklets. Replies irregularly to correspondence in Indonesian.

Radio Republik Indonesia—RRI Manado, Kotak Pos 1110, Manado 95124 Propinsi Sulawesi Utara, Indonesia. Fax: +62 (431) 63 492. Contact: Costher H. Gulton, Kepala Stasiun; or Untung Santoso, Kepala Seksi Teknik. Free stickers and postcards. Return postage or $1 required. Replies occasionally to correspondence in Indonesian.

Radio Republik Indonesia—RRI Manokwari, Regional II, Jalan Merdeka 68, Manokwari 98311, Papua, Indonesia. Contact: Nurdin Mokogintu. Return postage helpful.

Radio Republik Indonesia—RRI Mataram (when operating), Stasiun Regional I Mataram, Jalan Langko 83 Ampenan, Mataram 83114, Nusa Tenggara Barat, Indonesia. Phone: +62 (364) 33-713 or +62 (364) 21-355. Contact: Drs. Hamid Djasman, Kepala; or Bochri Rachman, Ketua Dewan Pimpinan Harian. Free stickers. Return postage required. With sufficient return postage or small token gift, sometimes sends tourist information and Batik print. Replies to correspondence in Indonesian.

Radio Republik Indonesia—RRI Medan, Jalan Letkol Martinus Lubis 5, Medan 20232, Sumatera, Indonesia. Phone: +62 (61) 324-222/441. Fax: +62 (61) 512 161. Contact: Kepala Stasiun, Ujamalul Abidin Ass; Drs. S. Parlin Tobing, SH, Produsennya, "Kontak Pendengar"; Drs. H. Suryanta Saleh; or Suprato. Free stickers. Return postage required. Replies to correspondence in Indonesian.

Radio Republik Indonesia—RRI Merauke, Stasiun Regional 1, Kotak Pos 11, Merauke 99611, Papua, Indonesia. Contact: (general) Drs. Buang Akhir, Direktor; Achmad Ruskaya B.A., Kepala Stasiun, Drs.Tuanakotta Semuel, Kepala

Seksi Siaran; or John Manuputty, Kepala Subseksi Pemancar; (technical) Daf'an Kubangun, Kepala Seksi Tehnik. Return postage helpful.

Radio Republik Indonesia—RRI Nabire (when operating), Kotak Pos 110, Jalan Merdeka 74 Nabire 98811, Papua, Indonesia. Contact: Muchtar Yushaputra, Kepala Stasiun. Free stickers and occasional free picture postcards. Return postage or IRCs helpful.

Radio Republik Indonesia—RRI Padang, Kotak Pos 77, Padang 25111, Sumatera Barat, Indonesia. Phone: +61 (751) 28-363. Contact: H. Hutabarat, Kepala Stasiun; or Amir Hasan, Kepala Seksi Siaran. Return postage helpful.

Radio Republik Indonesia—RRI Palangkaraya, Jalan M. Husni Thamrin 1, Palangkaraya 73111, Kalimantan Tengah, Indonesia. Phone: +62 (514) 21-779. Fax: +62 (514) 21 778. Contact: Andy Sunandar; Drs.Amiruddin; S. Polin; A.F. Herry Purwanto; Meyiwati SH; Supardal Djojosubrojo, Sarjana Hukum; Gumer Kamis; or Ricky D. Wader, Kepala Stasiun. Return postage helpful. Will respond to correspondence in Indonesian or English.

Radio Republik Indonesia—RRI Palembang, Jalan Radio 2, Km. 4, Palembang 30128, Sumatera Selatan, Indonesia. Contact: Drs. H. Mursjid Noor, Kepala Stasiun; H.Ahmad Syukri Ahkab, Kepala Seksi Siaran; or H.Iskandar Suradilaga. Return postage helpful. Replies slowly and occasionally.

Radio Republik Indonesia—RRI Palu, Jalan R.A. Kartini 39, Palu 94112, Sulawesi Tengah, Indonesia. Phone: +62 (451) 21-621. Contact: Akson Boole; Nyonyah Netty Ch. Soriton, Kepala Seksi Siaran; Gugun Santoso; Untung Santoso, Kepala Seksi Teknik; or M. Hasjim, Head of Programming. Return postage required. Replies slowly to correspondence in Indonesian.

Radio Republik Indonesia—RRI Pekanbaru (when operating), Kotak Pos 51, Pekanbaru 28113, Kepulauan Riau, Indonesia. Phone: +62 (761) 22-081. Fax: +62 (761) 23 605. Contact: (general) Hendri Yunis, ST, Kepala Stasiun, Ketua DPH; Arisun Agus, Kepala Seksi Siaran; Drs. H. Syamsidi, Kepala Supag Tata Usaha; or Zainal Abbas. Return postage helpful.

Radio Republik Indonesia—RRI Pontianak, Kotak Pos 1005, Pontianak 78117, Kalimantan Barat, Indonesia. Contact: Ruddy Banding, Kepala Seksi Siaran; Achmad Ruskaya, BA; Drs. Effendi Afati, Producer, "Dalam Acara Kantong Surat"; Subagio, Kepala Sub Bagian Tata Usaha; Augustwus Campek; Rahayu Widati; Suryadharma, Kepala Sub Seksi Programa; or Muchlis Marzuki B.A. Return postage or $1 helpful. Replies some of the time to correspondence in Indonesian (preferred) or English.

Radio Republik Indonesia—RRI Samarinda, Kotak Pos 45, Samarinda, Kalimantan Timur 75110, Indonesia. Phone: +62 (541) 43-495. Fax: +62 (541) 41 693. Contact: Siti Thomah, Kepala Seksi Siaran; Tyranus Lenjau, English Announcer; S. Yati; Marthin Tapparan; or Sunendra, Kepala Stasiun. May send tourist brochures and maps. Return postage helpful. Replies to correspondence in Indonesian.

Radio Republik Indonesia—RRI Semarang (when operating), Kotak Pos 1073, Semarang 50241, Jawa Tengah, Indonesia. Phone: +62 (24) 316 501. Contact: Djarwanto, SH; Drs. Sabeni, Doktorandus; Drs. Purwadi, Program Director; Dra. Endang Widiastuti, Kepala Sub Seksi Periklanan Jasa dan Hak Cipta; Bagus Giarto, Kepala Seksi Siaran; or Mardanon, Kepala Teknik. Return postage helpful.

Radio Republik Indonesia—RRI Serui, Jalan Pattimura Kotak Pos 19, Serui 98213, Papua, Indonesia. Contact: Agus

Raunsai, Kepala Stasiun; J. Lolouan, BA, Kepala Studio; Ketua Tim Pimpinan Harian, Kepala Seksi Siaran; Yance Yebi-Yebi; Natalis Edowai; Albertus Corputty; or Drs. Jasran Abubakar. Replies occasionally to correspondence in Indonesian. IRC or return postage helpful.

Radio Republik Indonesia—RRI Sibolga (when operating), Jalan Ade Irma Suryani, Nasution No. 11, Sibolga 22513, Sumatera Utara, Indonesia. Contact: Mrs. Laiya, Mrs. S. Sitoupul or B.A. Tanjung. Return postage required. Replies occasionally to correspondence in Indonesian.

Radio Republik Indonesia—RRI Sorong
STATION: Kotak Pos 146, Sorong 98414, Papua, Indonesia. Phone: +62 (951) 21-003, +62 (951) 22-111, or +62 (951) 22-611. Contact: Drs. Sallomo Hamid; Tetty Rumbay S., Kasubsi Siaran Kata; Mrs. Tien Widarsanto, Resa Kasi Siaran; Ressa Molle; Mughpar Yushaputra, Kepala Stasiun; or Linda Rumbay. Return postage helpful. Replies to correspondence in English. *"DATELINE" ENGLISH PROGRAM: See* Kang Guru II Radio English.

Radio Republik Indonesia—RRI Sumenep (when operating), Jalan Urip Sumoharjo 26, Sumenep 69411, Madura, Jawa Timur, Indonesia. Contact: Dian Irianto, Kepala Stasiun. Return postage helpful.

Radio Republik Indonesia—RRI Surabaya, Stasiun Regional 1, Kotak Pos 239, Surabaya 60271, Jawa Timur, Indonesia. Phone: +62 (31) 41-327. Fax: +62 (31) 42 351. Contact: Zainal Abbas, Kepala Stasiun; Usmany Johozua, Kepala Seksi Siaran; Drs. E. Agus Widjaja, MM, Kasi Siaran; or Ny Koen Tarjadi. Return postage or IRCs helpful.

Radio Republik Indonesia—RRI Surakarta (when operating), Kotak Pos 40, Surakarta 57133, Jawa Tengah, Indonesia. Contact: H. Tomo, B.A., Head of Broadcasting; or Titiek Sudartik, SH., Kepala. Return postage helpful.

Radio Republik Indonesia—RRI Tanjungpinang, Stasiun RRI Regional II Tanjungpinang, Kotak Pos 8, Tanjungpinang 29123, Kepulauan Riau, Indonesia. Contact: M. Yazid, Kepala Stasiun; Wan Suhardi, Produsennya, "Siaran Bahasa Melayu"; or Rosakim, Sarjana Hukum. Return postage helpful. Replies occasionally to correspondence in Indonesian or English.

Radio Republik Indonesia—RRI Ternate, Jalan Sultan Khairun, Kedaton, Ternate 97720 (Ternate), Maluku Utara, Indonesia. Contact: (general) Abd. Latief Kamarudin, Kepala Stasiun; (technical) Rusdy Bachmid, Head of Engineering; or Abubakar Alhadar. Return postage helpful.

Radio Republik Indonesia Tual (when operating), Watden, Pulau Kai, Tual 97661 Maluku, Indonesia.

Radio Republik Indonesia—RRI Wamena, RRI Regional II, Kotak Pos 10, Wamena, Papua 99511, Indonesia. Contact: Yoswa Kumurawak, Penjab Subseksi Pemancar. Return postage helpful.

Radio Republik Indonesia—RRI Yogyakarta, Jalan Amat Jazuli 4, Kotak Pos 18, Yogyakarta 55224, Jawa Tengah, Indonesia. Fax: +62 (274) 2784. Contact: Phoenix Sudomo Sudaryo; Tris Mulyanti, Seksi Programa Siaran; Martono, ub. Kabid Penyelenggaraan Siaran; Mr. Kadis, Technical Department; or Drs. H. Hamdan Sjahbeni, Kepala Stasiun. IRC, return postage or $1 helpful. Replies occasionally to correspondence in Indonesian or English.

Radio Siaran Pemerintah Daerah TK II—RSPD Halmahera Tengah, Soasio, Jalan A. Malawat, Soasio, Maluku Tengah 97812, Indonesia. Contact: Drs. S. Chalid A. Latif, Kepala Badan Pengelola.

Radio Siaran Pemerintah Daerah TK II—RSPD Sumba Timur, Jalan Gajah Mada 10 Hambala, Waingapu, Nusa

Tenggara Timur 87112, Indonesia. Contact: Simon Petrus, Penanggung Jawab Operasional. Replies slowly and rarely to correspondence in Indonesian.

Voice of Indonesia, Kotak Pos 1157, Jakarta 10001, Daerah Khusus Jakarta Raya, Indonesia. Phone: +62 (21) 720-3467, +62 (21) 355-381 or +62 (21) 349-091. Fax: +62 (21) 345 7132. Contact: Anastasia Yasmine, Head of Foreign Affairs Section. Free stickers and calendars. Very slow in replying.

IRAN   World Time +3:30 (+4:30 midyear)

Voice of the Islamic Republic of Iran
MAIN OFFICE: IRIB External Services, P.O. Box 19395-6767, Tehran, Iran; or P.O. Box 19395-3333, Tehran, Iran. Phone: (IRIB Public Relations) +98 (21) 204-001/2/3 and +98 (21) 204-6894/5. Fax: (external services) +98 (21) 205 1635, +98 (21) 204 1097 or + 98 (21) 291 095; (IRIB Public Relations) +98 (21) 205 3305/7; (IRIB Central Administration) +98 (21) 204 1051; (technical) +98 (21) 654 841. Email: (general) webmaster @irib.com; irib@dci.iran.com; (Research Centre) iribrec @dci.iran.com. Web: (includes RealAudio) www.irib.com/. Contact: (general) Hamid Yasamin, Public Affairs; Ali Larijani, Head; or Hameed Barimani, Producer, "Listeners Special"; (administration) J. Ghanbari, Director General; or J. Sarafraz, Deputy Managing Director; (technical) M. Ebrahim Vassigh, Frequency Manager. Free seven-volume set of books on Islam, magazines, calendars, book markers, tourist literature and postcards. Verifications require a minimum of two days' reception data, plus return postage. Station is currently asking their listeners to send in their telephone numbers so that they can call and talk to them directly. Upon request they will even broadcast your conversation on air. You can send your phone number to the postal address above or you can fax it to: + 98 (21) 205 1635. If English Service doesn't reply, then try writing the French Service in French.
ENGINEERING ACTIVITIES, TEHRAN: IRIB, P.O. Box 15875-4344, Tehran, Iran. Phone: +98 (21) 2196-6127. Fax: +98 (21) 204 1051, +98 (21) 2196 6268 or +98 (21) 172 924. Contact: Mrs. Niloufar Parviz.
ENGINEERING ACTIVITIES, HESSARAK/KARAJ: IRIB, P.O. Box 155, Hessarak/Karaj, Iran. Phone: (Mohsen Amiri) +98 (21) 216-3745;(Frequency Control & Design Burea) +98 (21) 216-3762. Fax: (Mohsen Amiri) +98 (21) 216 3799; or (Frequency Design Bureau) +98 (21) 201 3649. Email: rezairib @dci.iran.com; (Mohsen Amiri) moazzami@irib.com; or (Majid Farahmandnia) farahmand@irib.com. Contact: Mohsen Amiri, Manager of Shortwave Transmitters Affair; M. Ebrahim Vasigh; or Majid Farahmandnia, Manager, Frequency Control and Design Bureau.
BONN BUREAU, NONTECHNICAL: Puetzsir. 34, 53129 Bonn, Postfach 150 140, D-53040 Bonn, Germany. Phone: +49 (228) 231-001. Fax: +49 (228) 231 002.
LONDON BUREAU, NONTECHNICAL: c/o WTN, IRIB, The Interchange Oval Road, Camden Lock, London NWI, United Kingdom. Phone: +44 (20) 7284-3668. Fax: + 44 (20) 7284 3669.
PARIS BUREAU, NONTECHNICAL: 27 rue de Liège, escalier B, 1ᵉ étage, porte D, F-75008 Paris, France. Phone: + 33 (1) 4293-1273. Fax: +33 (1) 4293 0513.

Mashhad Regional Radio, P.O. Box 555, Mashhad Center, Jomhoriye Eslame, Iran. Contact: J. Ghanbari, General Director.

IRAQ   World Time +3 (+4 midyear)

Radio Iraq International (Idha'at al-Iraq al-Duwaliyah)
MAIN OFFICE: P.O. Box 8145 CN.12222, Baghdad, Iraq; if no reply try, P.O. Box 8125, Baghdad, Iraq; or P.O. Box 7728, Baghdad, Iraq. Contact: M. el Wettar. All state broadcasting facilities in Iraq are currently suffering from operational difficulties.
INDIA ADDRESS: P.O. Box 3044, New Delhi 110003, India.

Radio Kurdistan ("Aira ezgay kurdistana, dangi hizbi socialisti democrati kurdistan"). Email: kurdish6065@aol.com. Station is run by the Kurdistan Socialist Democratic Party, a member of the Democratic Alliance of Kurdistan which is a made up of five parties under the leadership of the Patriotic Union of Kurdistan (PUK).

Voice of Iraqi Kurdistan ("Aira dangi Kurdestana Iraqa") (when active). Sponsored by the Kurdistan Democratic Party-Iraq (KDP), led by Masoud Barzani, and the National Democratic Iraqi Front. Broadcasts from its own transmitting facilities, reportedly located in the Kurdish section of Iraq. To contact the station or to obtain verification of reception reports, try going via one of the following KDP offices:
KURDISTAN-SALAHEDDIN CENTRAL MEDIA AND CULTURE OFFICE: Phone: +873 (761) 610-320. Fax: +873 (761) 610 321. Email: kdppress@aol.com.
KDP LONDON OFFICE: KDP International Relations Committee-London, P.O. Box 7725, London SW1V 3ZD, United Kingdom. Phone: +44 (20) 7931-7764. Fax: +44 (20) 7931 7765. Email: KdpEurope@aol.com; 106615.1017@compuserve.com.
KDP MADRID OFFICE: PDK Comité de Relaciones Internacionales-España, Avenida Papa Negro, 20-1º-105ª, E-28043 Madrid, Spain. Phone: +34 (91) 759-9475. Fax: +34 (91) 300 1638. Email: pdk@futurnet.es. Web: http://usuarios.futurnet.es/p/pdk/.
KDP WASHINGTON OFFICE: KDP International Relations Committee-Washington, 1015 18th Street, NW, Suite 704, Washington DC 20036 USA. Phone: +1 (202) 331-9505. Fax: +1 (202) 331 9506. Email: Kdpusa@aol.com. Contact: Namat Sharif, Kurdistan Democratic Party.
KDP-CANADA OFFICE: Phone: +1 (905) 387-3759. Fax: +1 (905) 387 3756. Email: kdpcanada@hotmail.com. Web: www.geocities.com/Paris/Gallery/3209/.
KDP-DENMARK OFFICE: Postbox 437, DK-3000 Helsingor, Denmark; or Postbox 551, DK-2620 Albertslund, Denmark. Phone/Fax: +45 5577 9761. Email: kdpDenmark@hotmail.com. Web: http://members.tripod.com/kdpDenmark/.
KDP-SWEDEN OFFICE: Box 2017, SE-14502 Norsborg, Sweden. Phone: +46 (8) 361-446. Fax: +46 (8) 367 844. Email: taha_barwary@hotmail.com; party@kdp.pp.se. Web: www.kdp.pp.se. Contact: Alex Atroushi, who will verify email reports sent to the "party" address.

Voice of the Kurdistan People ("Aira dangi kurdistana"). Email: said@aha.ru or webmaster@puk.org. Web: www.aha.ru/~said/dang.htm; (PUK parent organization) www.puk.org. Official radio station of the Patriotic Union of Kurdistan (PUK) led by Jalal Talabani. Originally called "Voice of the Iraqi Revolution."
PUK-GERMAN OFFICE: Patriotische Union Kurdistan (PUK), Postfach 21 0231, D-10502 Berlin, Germany. Contact: Salah Rashid. Replies to correspondence in English and German, and verifies reception reports.

IRELAND   World Time exactly (+1 midyear)

Radio Telefis Éireann, Broadcasting Developments, RTÉ, Dublin 4, Ireland. Phone: (general) +353 (1) 208-3111; (Broadcasting Developments) +353 (1) 208-2350. Audio services available by phone include concise news bulletins: (United

States, special charges apply) +1 (900) 420-2411; (United Kingdom) +44 (891) 871-116; (Australia) +61 (3) 552-1140; and concise sports bulletins: (United States, special charges apply) +1(900) 420-2412; (United Kingdom) +44 (891) 871-117; (Australia) +61 (3) 552-1141. Fax: (general) +353 (1) 208 3082; (Broadcasting Developments) +353 (1) 208 3031. Email: (Hayde) haydej@rte.ie. Web: (general, includes RealAudio) www.rte.ie/radio/; (RealAudio, some programs) www.wrn.org/ondemand/ireland.html. Contact: Julie Hayde; or Bernie Pope, Reception. IRC appreciated. Offers a variety of video tapes (mostly PAL, but a few "American Standard"), CDs and audio casettes for sale from RTÉ Commercial Enterprises Ltd, Box 1947, Donnybrook, Dublin 4, Ireland; (phone) +353 (1) 208-3453; (fax) +353 (1) 208 2620. A full list of what's on offer can be viewed at www.rte.ie/lib/store.html#music. Regular transmissions via facilities of Merlin Communications International (see United Kingdom) in Ascension, Canada, Singapore and the United Kingdom—see next item—and irregularly via these and other countries for sports or election coverage.

RTÉ Overseas (Shortwave)—a half-hour information bulletin from RTÉ's (see, above) domestic Radio 1, relayed on shortwave. Web: www.rte.ie/radio/worldwide.html. Same contact details as RTÉ above.

ISRAEL World Time +2 (+3 midyear)

Bezeq, The Israel Telecommunication Corp Ltd, Engineering and Planning Division, Radio and T.V. Broadcasting Section, P.O. Box 62081, Tel-Aviv 61620, Israel. Phone: +972 (3) 626-4562 or +972 (3) 626-4500. Fax: +972 (3) 626 4558/59. Email: (Oren) moshe_oren@bezeq.co.il; mosheor @bezeq.com. Web: www.bezeq.co.il. Contact: Moshe Oren, Frequency Manager. Bezeq is responsible for transmitting the programs of the Israel Broadcasting Authority (IBA), which *inter alia* parents Kol Israel. This address only for pointing out transmitter-related problems (interference, modulation quality, network mixups, etc.), especially by fax, of transmitters based in Israel. Verifications not given out at this office; requests for verification should be sent to the English Department of Kol Israel (see below).

◨Galei Zahal (Israel Defence Forces Radio), Zahal, Military Mail No. 01005, Israel. Phone: +972 (3) 512-6666. Fax: +972 (3) 512 6760. Email: ofer@glz.co.il. Web: (includes Windows Media) www.glz.co.il. Israeli law allows the Galei Zahal, as well as the Israel Broadcasting Authority, to air broadcasts beamed to outside Israel. Occasionally heard on Kol Israel frequencies when the latter is affected by industrial action; also more regularly on out-of-band channels via unknown transmitters.

Israel Radio International—see Kol Israel, below.

◨Kol Israel (Israel Radio, the Voice of Israel)
STUDIOS: Israel Broadcasting Authority, P.O. Box 1082, Jerusalem 91010, Israel. Phone: (general) +972 (2) 302-222; (Engineering Dept.) +972 (2) 535-051; (administration) +972 (2) 248-715; Hebrew voice mail for Reshet Bet expatriate program) +972 (3) 765-1929. Fax: (English Service) +972 (2) 530 2424; (Engineering Dept.) +972 (2) 388 821; (other) +972 (2) 248 392 or +972 (2) 302 327. Email: (general) ask@israel-info.gov.il; (correspondence relating to reception problems, only) engineering@israelradio.org; (Reshet Bet program for Israelis abroad) radio1@iba.org.il. Web: (schedule, RealAudio) www.israelradio.org; (IBA parent organization, including RealAudio in Hebrew and Arabic) www.iba.org.il. Contact:

Edmond Sehayeq, Head of Programming, Arabic, Persian and Yemenite broadcasts; Yishai Eldar,
Reporter, English News Department; Steve Linde, Head of English News Department; or Sara Gabbai, Head of Western Broadcasting Department; (administration) Shmuel Ben-Zvi, Director; (technical, frequency management) Raphael Kochanowski, Director of Liaison and Coordination, Engineering Dept. Various political, religious, tourist, immigration and language publications. IRC required for reply. Announces in English as "Israel Radio International" but continues to refer to itself as "Kol Israel" in other languages, such as French and Spanish.
SAN FRANCISCO OFFICE, SCHEDULES: 2654 17th Avenue, San Francisco CA 94116 USA. Phone: +1 (415) 564-9968. Email: GPoppin@aol.com. Contact: George Poppin. This address, a volunteer office, only provides Kol Israel schedules. All other correspondence should be sent directly to the main office in Jerusalem.

ITALY World Time +1 (+2 midyear)

Adventist World Radio, the Voice of Hope, AWR Europe, Casella Postale 383, I-47100 Forlì, Italy. Phone: +39 (0543) 766-655. Fax: +39 (0543) 768 198. Email: english@awr.org. Web: www.awr.org. Contact: Erika Gysin, Listener Mail Services; (technical) Brook Powers, Chief Engineer. English listener mail to: AWR, 39 Brendon Street, London W1, United Kingdom. Free religious printed matter, stickers and program schedules. Return postage, IRCs or $1 appreciated. Airs "Radio Magazine," a DX program produced by Dario Villani. AWR has a license to operate the station at Forlì, as well as a new facility which is soon to be built near Argenta. Also, see AWR listings under Germany, Guam, Guatemala, Kenya, Madagascar, United Kingdom and USA.

◨Italian Radio Relay Service, IRRS-Shortwave, Nexus-IBA, C.P. 10980, 20100 Milano, Italy; or alternatively, to expedite cassette deliveries only: NEXUS-IBA, Attn. Anna Boschetti, P.O. Box 11028, I-20110 Milano, Italy. Phone: +39 (02) 266-6971. Fax: +39 (02) 7063 8151. Email: (general) info@nexus.org; ("Hello There" program, broadcast on special occasions only) ht@nexus.org; (reception reports of test transmissions) reports@nexus.org; (International Public Access Radio, a joint venture of IRRS and WRMI, USA) IPAR@nexus.org; (Alfredo Cotroneo) aec@nexus.org; (Ron Norton) ron@nexus.org. Web: (general) www.nexus.org; (RealAudio) www.nexus.org/IRN/index.html; (schedules) www.nexus.org/NEXUS-IBA/Schedules; (International Public Access Radio) www.nexus.org/IPAR; (Internet Services) www.nexus.org/NEXUS-IBA/Services/index-english.html. Contact: (general) Ms. Anna S. Boschetti, Verification Manager; Alfredo E. Cotroneo, President and Producer of "Hello There"; (technical) Ron Norton. Due to recent funding cuts, this station cannot assure a reply to all listener's mail. Email correspondence and reception reports by email are answered promptly and at no charge. A number of booklets and sometimes stickers and small souvenirs are available for sale, but check their Website for further details. Two IRCs or $1 helpful.

Radio Europe, P.O. Box 12, 20090 Limito di Pioltello, Milan, Italy. Phone: +39 (02) 3931-0347. Fax: +39 (02) 8645 0149. Email: 100135.54@compuserve.com. Contact: Dario Monferini, Foreign Relations Director; or Alex Bertini, General Manager. Pennants $5 and T-shirts $25. $30 for a lifetime membership to Radio Europe's Listeners' Club. Membership includes T-shirt, poster, stickers, flags, gadgets, and so forth, with a

DXers from Italy and Baltic States visit Radio Finland International's Russian Service. From left, Andrew Kuznetson, Valentin Jershov, Simo S. Soininen, Klaudia Gröndahl, Roberto Pavenello and Dario Monferini.   S. Soininen

monthly drawing for prizes. Application forms available from station. Sells airtime for $20 per hour. Two IRCs or $1 return postage appreciated.

Radio Maria Network Europe, Spoleto relay (when active), Via Turati 7, 22036 Erba, Italy. Fax: +39 (031) 611 288. Web: www.cta.it/aziende/r_maria/info.htm.

📻**Radio Roma-RAI International** (external services)

MAIN OFFICE: External/Foreign Service, Centro RAI, Saxa Rubra, 00188 Rome, Italy; or P.O. Box 320, Correspondence Sector, 00100 Rome, Italy. Phone: +39 (06) 33-17-2360. Fax: +39 (06) 33 17 18 95 or +39 (06) 322 6070. Email: raiinternational @rai.it. Web: (shortwave) www.raiinternational.rai.it/radio/indexoc.htm. Contact: (general) Rosaria Vassallo, Correspondence Sector; or Augusto Milana, Editor-in-Chief, Shortwave Programs in Foreign Languages; Esther Casas, Servicio Español; (administration) Angela Buttiglione, Managing Director; or Gabriella Tambroni, Assistant Director. Free stickers, banners, calendars and *RAI Calling from Rome* magazine. Can provide supplementary materials, including on VHS and CD-ROM, for Italian-language video course, "Viva l' italiano," with an audio equivalent soon to be offered, as well. Is constructing "a new, more powerful and sophisticated shortwave transmitting center" in Tuscany; when this is activated, RAI International plans to expand news, cultural items and music in Italian and various other language services—including Spanish, Portuguese, Italian, plus new services in Chinese and Japanese. Responses can be very slow. Pictures of RAI's Shortwave Center at Prato Smeraldo can be found at www.mediasuk.org/rai/.

SHORTWAVE FREQUENCY MONITORING OFFICE: RAI Monitoring Station, Centro di Controllo, Via Mirabellino 1, 20052 Monza (MI), Italy. Phone: +39 (039) 388-389. Phone/fax (ask for fax): +39 (039) 386-222. Email: cqmonza@rai.it. Contact: Signora Giuseppina Moretti, Frequency Management; Lucia Luisa La Franceschina; or Mario Ballabio.

ENGINEERING OFFICE, ROME: Via Teulada 66, 00195 Rome, Italy. Phone: +39 (06) 331-70721. Fax: +39 (06) 331 75142 or +39 (06) 372 3376. Email: isola@rai.it. Contact: Clara Isola.

ENGINEERING OFFICE, TURIN: Via Cernaia 33, 10121 Turin, Italy. Phone: +39 (011) 810-2293. Fax: +39 (011) 575 9610. Email: allamano@rai.it. Contact: Giuseppe Allamano.

NEW YORK OFFICE, NONTECHNICAL: 1350 Avenue of the Americas—21st floor, New York NY 10019 USA. Phone: +1 (212) 468-2500. Fax: +1 (212) 765 1956. Contact: Umberto

Bonetti, Deputy Director of Radio Division. RAI caps, aprons and tote bags for sale at Boutique RAI, c/o the aforementioned New York address.

SAN FRANCISCO OFFICE, SCHEDULES: 2654 17th Avenue, San Francisco CA 94116 USA. Phone: +1 (415) 564-9968. Email: GPoppin@aol.com. Contact: George Poppin. This address, a volunteer office, only provides RAI schedules to listeners. All other correspondence should be sent directly to the main office in Rome.

Radio Speranza, Modena (when operating), Largo San Giorgio 91, 41100 Modena, Italy. Phone/fax: +39 (059) 230-373. Email: ter7769@iperbole.bologna. Contact: Padre Cordioli Luigi, Missionario Redentorista. Free Italian-language newsletter. Replies enthusiastically to correspondence in Italian. Return postage appreciated.

RTV Italiana-RAI (domestic services)

CALTANISSETTA: Radio Uno, Via Cerda 19, 90139 Palermo, Sicily, Italy. Contact: Gestione Risorse, Transmission Quality Control. $1 required.

ROME: Centro RAI, Saxa Rubra, 00188 Rome, Italy. Fax: +39 (06) 322 6070. Email: grr@rai.it. Web (experimental): (general) http:www.rai.it/; (RealAudio) www.rai.it/grr.

Tele Radio Stereo, Roma, Via Bitossi 18, 00136 Roma, Italy. Fax: + 39 (06) 353 48300.

IVORY COAST—*see* Côte d'Ivoire

JAPAN   World Time +9

NHK Fukuoka, 1-1-10 Ropponmatsu, Chuo-ku, Fukuoka-shi, Fukuoka 810-77, Japan.

NHK Osaka, 3-43 Bamba-cho, Chuo-ku, Osaka 540-01, Japan. Fax: +81 (6) 6941 0612. Contact: (technical) Technical Bureau. IRC or $1 helpful.

NHK Sapporo, 1-1-1 Ohdori Nishi, Chuo-ku, Sapporo 060-8703, Japan. Fax: +81 (11) 232 5951. Sometimes sends postcards, stickers or other small souvenirs.

NHK Tokyo/Shobu-Kuki, JOAK, 3047-1 Oaza-Sanga, Shobu-cho, Minamisaitama-gun, Saitama 346-0104, Japan. Fax: +81 (3) 3481 4985 or +81 (480) 85 1508. IRC or $1 helpful. Replies occasionally. Letters should be sent via registered mail.

📻**Radio Japan/NHK World** (external service)

MAIN OFFICE: NHK World, Nippon Hoso Kyokai, Tokyo 150-

8001, Japan. Phone: +81 (3) 3465-1111. Fax: (general) +81 (3) 3481 1350; ("Hello from Tokyo" and Production Center) +81 (3) 3465 0966. Email: (general) info@intl.nhk.or.jp; ("Hello from Tokyo" program) hello@intl.nhk.or.jp. Web: includes RealAudio) www.nhk.or.jp/rjnet/. Contact: (administration) Isao Kitamoto, Deputy Director General; Hisashi Okawa, Senior Director International Planning; (general) Yoshiki Fushimi; H. Kawamoto, English Service; or K. Terasaka, Programming Division. Free *Radio Japan News* publication, sundry other small souvenirs and language-course materials.
ENGINEERING ADMINISTRATION DEPART-MENT: Nipon Hoso Kyokai, Tokyo 150-8001, Japan. Phone: +81 (3) 5455-5395 or +81 (3) 5455-2288. Fax: +81 (3) 3485 0952. E-mail: yoshimi@eng.nhk.or.jp or kurasima@eng.nhk.or.jp. Contact: Tetsuya Itsuk or Toshiki Kurashima.
HONG KONG OFFICE: Phone: +852 2577-5999.
LONDON OFFICE: Phone: +44 (20) 7334-0909.
LOS ANGELES OFFICE: Phone: +1 (310) 816-0300.
NEW YORK OFFICE: Phone: +1 (212) 755-3907.
SINGAPORE OFFICE: Phone: + 65 225-0667.

Radio Tampa/NSB

MAIN OFFICE: Nihon Shortwave Broadcasting, 9-15 Akasaka 1-chome, Minato-ku, Tokyo 107-8373, Japan. Fax: +81 (3) 3583 9062. Email: web@tampa.co.jp. Web: (in Japanese only) www.tampa.co.jp. Contact: H. Nagao, Public Relations; M. Teshima; Ms. Terumi Onoda; or H. Ono. Sending a reception report may help with a reply. Free stickers and Japanese stamps. $1 or 2 IRCs helpful.
NEW YORK NEWS BUREAU: 1325 Avenue of the Americas #2403, New York NY 10019 USA. Fax: +1 (212) 261 6449. Contact: Noboru Fukui, reporter.

JORDAN   World Time +2 (+3 midyear)

Radio Jordan, P.O. Box 909, Amman, Jordan; or P.O. Box 1041, Amman, Jordan. Phone: (general) +962 (6) 477-4111; (International Relations) +962 (6) 477-8578; (English Service) +962 (6) 475-7410 or +962 (6) 477-3111; (Arabic Service) +962 (6) 463-6454; (Saleh) +962 (6) 474-8048; (Al-Areeny) +962 (6) 475-7404. Fax: +962 (6) 478 8115. Email: (general) general@jrtv.gov.jo; (programs) rj@jrtv.gov.jo; (schedule) feedback@jrtv.gov.jo; (technical) eng@jrtv.gov.jo. Web: www.jrtv.com/radio.htm. Contact: (general) Jawad Zada, Director of English Service and Producer of "Mailbag"; Mrs. Firyal Zamakhshari, Director of Arabic Programs; or Qasral Mushatta; (administrative) Hashem Khresat, Director of Radio; Mrs. Fatima Massri, Director of International Relations; or Muwaffaq al-Rahayifah, Director of Shortwave Services; (technical) Fawzi Saleh, Director of Engineering; or Yousef Al-Areeny, Director of Radio Engineering. Free stickers. Replies irregularly and slowly. Enclosing $1 helps.

KAZAKSTAN   World Time +6 (+7 midyear)

NOTE: Although "Kazakstan" is now considered to be the official spelling, "Kazakhstan" is still widely used both inside

and outside the country. What happens eventually is anyone's guess, but for the time being, both versions are acceptable.
Kazak Radio, 175A Zheltoksan Street, 480013 Almaty, Kazakstan. Phone: (general) +7 (3272) 637-694, +7 (3272) 633-716 or +7 (3272) 631-207; (international service, when operational) +7 (3272) 627-733; (Director) +7 (3272) 628-639; (Kassymzhanova) +7 (3272) 636-895; (Abdelanov) +7 (3272) 636-895; (technical) +7 (3272) 634-878. Fax: + 7 (3272) 650 387. Note that the country and city codes are scheduled to be changed in the near future, and the current +7 (3272) should then become +997 (327). Email: kazradio @astel.kz (if the message comes back as undeliverable, try kazradio@asdc.kz). Contact: (administration) Torehan Rysbekovich Daniyarov, Director; or Dr. Choi Young Gun, Director International Service (when operating); (correspondence in English) Ms. Gaukhar Kassymzhanova, producer/announcer; (correspondence in French) Dias Abdelanov, producer/announcer; (technical) Aleksander Zaporogets, Technical Director. Part of the facilities and personnel were moved to the new capital—Astana—during 1999, and Kazak Radio's operations have been considerably interrupted as a result. The station welcomes correspondence in Russian or Kazakh. Letters in English and French are best sent to the contacts listed above. Replies to correspondence in German are erratic as there is only a part-time staff.

TRANSMISSION FACILITIES: Republican Enterprise of Post and Communications, Republic Ministry of Transport, Communication and Tourism, 86 Ablai Khan Batyr, Almaty, Kazakstan. Phone: +7 (3272) 627-366. Fax: +7 (3272) 627 527. Email: KAZPOST@mail.banknet.kz. Contact: Orazaly Santaevich Erhanov, Director General.

KENYA   World Time +3

Adventist World Radio, The Voice of Hope, AWR Africa, P.O. Box 42276, Nairobi, Kenya. Phone: +254 (2) 573-277. Fax: +254 (2) 568 433. Web: www.awr.org. Contact: (general) Samuel Misiani, Regional Director. Free home Bible study guides, program schedule and other small items. Return postage (IRCs or 1$) appreciated. This office will sometimes verify reception reports direct, but replies are slow. Also, *see* AWR listings under Germany, Guam, Guatemala, Italy, Madagascar, United Kingdom and USA.
Kenya Broadcasting Corporation, P.O. Box 30456, Harry Thuku Road, Nairobi, Kenya. Phone: +254 (2) 334-567. Fax: +254 (2) 220 675. Email: (general) kbc@swiftkenya.com; (management) mdkbc@swiftkenya.com; (technical services) kbctechnical@swiftkenya.com. Web: (general) www.kbc.co.ke; (RealAudio) www.africaonline.co.ke/AfricaOnline/netradio.html. Contact: (general) Henry Makokha, Liaison Office; (administration) Simeon N. Anabwani, Managing Director; (technical) Nathan Lamu, Senior Principal Technical Officer; Augustine Kenyanjier Gochui; Lawrence Holnati, En-

gineering Division; or Daniel Githua, Assistant Manager Technical Services (Radio). IRC required. Replies irregularly.

KIRIBATI World Time +12

Radio Kiribati (when operating), P.O. Box 78, Bairiki, Tarawa, Republic of Kiribati. Phone: +686 21187. Fax: +686 21096. Email: bpa@tskl.net.ki. Contact: (general) Atiota Bauro, Programme Organiser; Mrs. Otiri Laboia; Batiri Bataua, News Editor; or Moia Tetoa, Radio Manager; (technical) Tooto Kabwebwenibeia, Broadcast Engineer; Martin Ouma Ojwach, Senior Superintendent of Electronics; or T. Fakaofo, Technical Staff. Cassettes of local songs available for purchase. $1 or return postage required for a reply (IRCs not accepted).

KOREA (DPR) World Time +9

Radio Pyongyang, External Service, Korean Central Broadcasting Station, Pyongyang, Democratic People's Republic of Korea (not "North Korea"). Phone and fax numbers valid only in those countries with direct telephone service to North Korea. Free book for German speakers to learn Korean, sundry other publications, pennants, calendars, newspapers, artistic prints and pins. Do not include dutiable items in your envelope. Replies are irregular, as mail from countries not having diplomatic relations with North Korea is sent via circuitous routes and apparently does not always arrive. Indeed, some PASSPORT readers continue to report that mail to Radio Pyongyang in North Korea results in their receiving anti-communist literature from *South* Korea, which indicates that mail interdiction has not ceased. One way around the problem is to add "VIA BEIJING, CHINA" to the address, but replies via this route tend to be slow in coming. Another gambit is to send your correspondence to an associate in a country—such as China, Ukraine or India—having reasonable relations with North Korea, and ask that it be forwarded. If you don't know anyone in these countries, try using the good offices of the following person: Willi Passman, Oberhausener Str. 100, D-45476, Mülheim, Germany. Send correspondence in a sealed envelope without any address on the back. That should be sent inside another envelope. Include 2 IRCs to cover the cost of forwarding.

Regional Korean Central Broadcasting Stations—Not known to reply, but a long-shot possibility is to try corresponding in Korean to: Korean Central Broadcasting Station, Ministry of Posts and Telecommunications, Chongsung-dong (Moranbong), Pyongyang, Democratic People's Republic of Korea. Fax: +850 (2) 812 301 (valid only in those countries with direct telephone service to North Korea). Contact: Chong Ha-chol, Chairman, Radio and Television Broadcasting Committee.

KOREA (REPUBLIC) World Time +9

Korean Broadcasting System (KBS), 18 Yoido-dong, Youngdungpo-gu, Seoul, Republic of Korea 150-790. Phone: +82 (2) 781-2410. Fax: +82 (2) 761 2499. Email: webmaster @kbs.co.kr. Web: (includes RealAudio) http://kbs.co.kr.

Radio Korea International

MAIN OFFICE: Overseas Service, Korean Broadcasting System, 18 Yoido-dong, Youngdungpo-gu, Seoul, Republic of Korea 150-790. Phone: (general) +82 (2) 781-3650/60/70; (English Service) +82 (2) 781-3674/75/76; (Russian Service) +82 (2) 781-3714. Fax: +82 (2) 781 3694/95/96; or (toll-free fax lines available for overseas listeners) (United States) 1-888-229-2312; (United Kingdom) 0800-89-5993; (Canada) 1-888-211-

5865; (Australia) 1-800-142-644. Email: rki@kbs.co.kr. Web: (includes RealAudio) www.rki.kbs.co.kr. Contact: Cho Won-Suk, Executive Director; Ms. Shin Joo-Ok, Director Division 1; or Ms. Han Hee-Joo, Director Division 2, and is also the Producer/Co-Host of *Multiwave Feedback* show. QSLs, time/frequency schedule, station stickers, calendars, *Let's Learn Korean* book and a wide variety of other small souvenirs. *History of Korea* is available via Internet (see URL, above) and on CD-ROM (upon request).

"EDXP NEWS REPORTS" : Web: www.members.tripod.com/-bpadula/edxp.html. Special news reports concentrating on shortwave broadcasts to and from Asia, the Far East, Australia, the Pacific and the Indian sub-continent, compiled by EDXP and aired once a week on a Sunday (UTC) during the Radio Korea International *"Multiwave Feedback"* program in English. Special EDXP QSLs will be offered for the shortwave releases (not for RealAudio). Reports of the EDXP feature should be sent to: Bob Padula, EDXP QSL Service, 404 Mont Albert Road, Surrey Hills, Victoria 3127, Australia. Return postage appreciated. Outside of Australia, 1 IRC or $1; within Australia, four 45c Australian stamps. Email reports welcome at edxp@bigpond.com, and verified with Web-delivered animated QSLs.

KUWAIT World Time +3

Ministry of Information, P.O. Box 193, 13002 Safat, Kuwait. Phone: +965 241-5301. Fax: +965 243 4511. Web: www.moinfo.gov.kw. Contact: Sheik Nasir Al-Sabah, Minister of Information.

FREQUENCY SECTION: Ministry of Information, P.O. Box 967 13010 Safat, Kuwait. Phone: +965 243-6193 or +965 241-7830. Fax: +965 241 5498. Contact: Ms. Wesam Najaf, Head of Frequency Section; or Ahmad Alawdhi, Communication Engineer.

Radio Kuwait, P.O. Box 397, 13004 Safat, Kuwait; (technical) Department of Frequency Management, P.O. Box 967, 13010 Safat, Kuwait. Phone: (general) +965 242-3774; (technical) +965 241-0301, +965 242-1422. Fax: (general) +965 245 6660; (technical) +965 241 5946. Email: (technical, including reception reports) kwtfreq@hotmail.com; (frequency matters) kwtfreq@ncc.moc.kw; (general) radiokuwait@radiokuwait.org. Web: (technical) www.moinfo.gov.kw/ENG/FREQ/; (RealAudio) www.radiokuwait.org/. Contact: (general) Manager, External Service; (technical) Nasser M. Al-Saffar, Frequency Manager; or Wessam Najaf. Sometimes gives away stickers, calendars, pens or key chains.

KYRGYZSTAN World Time +5 (+6 midyear)

Kyrgyz Radio, Kyrgyz TV and Radio Center, 59 Jash Gvardiya Boulevard, 720300 Bishkek, Kyrgyzstan. Phone: (general) +996 (312) 253-404 or +996 (312) 255-741; (Director) +996 (312) 255-700 or +996 (312) 255-709; (Assemov) +996 (312) 650-7341 or +996 (312) 255-703; (Atakanova) +996 (312) 251-927; (technical) +996 (312) 257-771. Fax: +996 (312) 257 952. Note that from a few countries, the dialing code is still the old +7 (3312). Email: trk@kyrnet.kg. Contact: (administration) Mrs. Baima J. Sutenova, Vice-Chairman - Kyrgyz Radio; or Eraly Ayilchiyev, Director; (general) Talant Assemov, Editor - Kyrgyz/Russian/German news; Gulnara Abdulaeva, Announcer - Kyrgyz/Russian/German news; Nargis Atakanova, Announcer - English news; (technical) Mirbek Uursabekov, Technical Director. Kyrgyz and Russian preferred, but correspondence in English and German can also be processed. For quick processing of reception reports, use email in German to Talant Assemov. Reports are regularly verified and verifications are usually signed by Mrs. Sutenova.
TRANSMISSION FACILITIES: Ministry of Transport and Communications, 42 Issanova Street, 720000 Bishkek, Kyrgyzstan. Phone: +996 (312) 216-672. Fax: +996 (312) 213 667. Contact: Jantoro Satybaldiyev, Minister. The shortwave transmitting station is located at Krasny-Retcha (Red River), a military encampment in the Issk-Ata region, about 40 km south of Bishkek.

LAOS World Time +7

Lao National Radio, Luang Prabang (when active), Luang Prabang, Laos; or B.P. 310, Vientiane, Laos. Return postage required (IRCs not accepted). Replies slowly and very rarely. Best bet is to write in Laotian or French directly to Luang Prabang, where the transmitter is located.
Lao National Radio, Vientiane, Laotian National Radio and Television, B.P. 310, Vientiane, Laos. Phone: +856 (21) 212-429. Fax: +856 (21) 212 430. Contact: Khoun Sounantha, Manager-in-Charge; Bounthan Inthasai, Director General; Mrs. Vinachine, English/French Sections; Ms. Mativarn Simanithone, Deputy Head, English Section; or Miss Chanthery Vichitsavanh, Announcer, English Section who says, "It would be good if you send your letter unregistered, because I find it difficult to get all letters by myself at the post. Please use my name, and 'Lao National Radio, P.O. Box 310, Vientiane, Laos P.D.R.' It will go directly to me." Sometimes includes a program schedule and Laotian stamps when replying. The external service of this station is currently off shortwave.

LEBANON World Time +2 (+3 midyear)

◘**Voice of Charity**, Rue Fouad Chéhab, B.P. 850, Jounieh, Lebanon. Phone: +961 (9) 914-901 or +961 (9) 918-090. Email: radiocharity@opuslibani.org.lb. Web: (includes RealAudio) www.radiocharity.org.lb/. Contact: Frère Elie Nakhoul, Managing Director. Program aired via facilities of Vatican Radio

from a station founded by the Order of the Lebanese Missionaries. Basically, a Lebanese Christian educational radio program. Replies to correspondence in English, French and Arabic, and verifies reception reports.
◘**Voice of Lebanon** (if reactivated), P.O. Box 165271, Al-Ashrafiyah, Beirut, Lebanon; or (street address) Radio Voice of Lebanon Bldg., Bachir Gémayel Avenue, Beirut, Lebanon. Phone: +961 (1) 201-380 or +961 (1) 323-458. Fax: +961 (1) 219 290. Email: vdl@cyberia.net.lb. Web: (includes RealAudio) www.vdl.com.lb. Contact: Sheik Simon El-Khazen, General Manager. $1 required. Replies occasionally to correspondence in French or Arabic. Operated by the Phalangist organization.
LESOTHO World Time +2
Radio Lesotho, P.O. Box 552, Maseru 100, Lesotho. Phone: +266 323-561. Fax: +266 310 003. Contact: (general) Mamonyane Matsaba, Acting Programming Director; or Sekhonyana Motlohi, Producer, "What Do Listeners Say?"; (administration) Ms. Mpine Tente, Principal Secretary, Ministry of Information and Broadcasting; or Molahlehi Letlotlo, Director; (technical) Lebohang Monnapula, Chief Engineer; Basia Maraisane, Transmitter Engineer; or Motlatsi Monyane, Studio Engineer. Return postage necessary.

LIBERIA World Time exactly

NOTE: Mail sent to Liberia may be returned as undeliverable.
ELBC (if reactivated), Liberian Broadcasting System, P.O. Box 10-594, 1000 Monrovia 10, Liberia. Phone: +231 224-984 or +231 222-758.
Radio ELWA, c/o SIM Liberia, 08 B.P. 886, Abidjan 08, Côte d'Ivoire. Contact: Moses T. Nyantee, Station Manager; or Chief Technician.
Radio Liberia International, Liberian Communications Network/KISS, P.O. Box 1103, 1000 Monrovia 10, Liberia. Phone: +231 226-963 or +231 227-593. Fax: (during working hours) +231 226 003. Contact: Issac P. Davis, Engineer-in-Charge/QSL Coordinator. $5 required for QSL card.
Radio Veritas, P.O. Box 3569, Monrovia, Liberia. Phone: +231 226-979. Contact: Steve Kenneh, Manager.
Star Radio (if granted a new license for shortwave operation), Sekou Toure Avenue, Mamba Point, Monrovia, Liberia. Phone: +231 226-820, +231 226-176 or +231 227-390. Fax: +231 227 360. Email: libe@atge.automail.com. Web: (Star Radio Daily News) www.hirondelle.org/. Contact: James Morlue, Station Manager. Star radio is staffed by Liberian journalists and managed by a Swiss NGO, Fondation Hirondelle, which can be contacted at: 3 Rue Traversière, CH 1018-Lausanne, Switzerland; (phone) +41 (21) 647-2805; (fax) +41 (21) 647 4469; (email) info@hirondelle.org.

LIBYA World Time +1 (+2 midyear)

Libyan Jamahiriyah Broadcasting (frequency management only), Box 333, Soug al Jama, Tripoli, Libya. Phone: +218 (21) 361-4508. Fax: +218 (21) 489 4240. Contact: Youssef Moujrab; Salah Zayani; or Abdessalem Zaglem.
Voice of Africa/Voice of Libya, P.O. Box 4677, Tripoli, Libya. Phone: +218 (21) 444-0112, +218 (21) 444-9106 or +218 (21) 444-9872. Fax: +218 (21) 444 9875. This, the external service of Libyan Jamahiriyah Broadcasting, seems to be going through an identity crisis. It has been heard identifying as both "Voice of Africa" and "Voice of Libya" in its English and French programs, while in Arabic it uses the same identification as for the domestic service.

MALTA OFFICE: P.O. Box 17, Hamrun, Malta. Replies tend to be more forthcoming from this address than direct from Lybia.

LITHUANIA World Time +2 (+3 midyear)

Lietuvos Radijo ir Televizijos Centras (LRTC), Sausio 13-osios 10, LT-2044 Vilnius, Lithuania. Phone: +370 (2) 459-397. Fax: +370 (2) 451 738. Email: admin@lrtc.lt. Web: www.lrtc.lt. Contact: A. Vydmontas, Director General. This organization operates the transmitters used by Lithuanian Radio.

▣Lithuanian Radio
STATION: Lietuvos Radijas, S. Konarskio 49, LT-2674 Vilnius MTP, Lithuania. Phone: (general) +370 (2) 333-182; (Grumadiene) +370 (2) 334-471; (Vilciauskas) +370 (2) 233-503. Fax: (general) +370 (2) 263 282; (Technical Director) +370 (2) 232 465. Email: format is initial.lastname@rtv.lrtv.ot.lt, so to contact, say, Juozas Algirdas Vilciauskas, it would be jvilciauskas@rtv.lrtv.ot.lt. Web: (includes RealAudio) www.lrtv.lt/lt_lr.htm. Contact: (general) Mrs. Kazimiera Mazgeliene, Programme Director; or Guoda Litvaitiene, International Relations; (technical) Juozas Algirdas Vilciauskas, Technical Director.
ADMINISTRATION: Lietuvos Nacionalinis Radijas ir Televizija (LNRT), Konarskio 49, LT-2674 Vilnius MTP, Lithuania. Phone: (general) +370 (2) 263-383; (Director General) +370 (2) 263-292. Fax: +370 (2) 263 282. Email: (Ilginis) ailginis@rtv.lrtv.ot.lt. Web: www.lrtv.lt/lt_lrtv.htm. Contact: Arvydas Ilginis, Director General.
STATE RADIO FREQUENCY SERVICE: Algirdo str. 27, LT-2006 Vilnius, Lithuania. Phone: +370 (2) 231-550; or +370 (2) 261-177. Fax: +370 (2) 261 564. Email: (Medeisis) medeisis@radio.lt; (Norkunas) enorkuna@radio.lt; (Cesna) acesna@radio.lt. Contact: Arturas Medeisis, Head of Division of Strategic Planning; Augutis Cesna, Deputy Head of EMC Division; or Eugenijus Norkunas, Director.
▣Radio Vilnius, Lietuvos Radijas, Konarskio 49, LT-2674 Vilnius, Lithuania. Phone: +370 (90) 71297. Fax: +370 (2) 233 526. Email: ravil@rtv.lrtv.ot.lt. Web: (includes RealAudio) *see* Lithuanian Radio, above. Contact: Ms. Rasa Lukaite, "Letterbox"; Audrius Braukyla, Editor-in-Chief; or Ilonia Rukiene, Head of English Department. Free stickers, pennants, Lithuanian stamps and other souvenirs. Transmissions to North America are via the facilities of Deutsche Telekom in Germany (*see*).

MADAGASCAR World Time +3

Adventist World Radio, the Voice of Hope
ADMINISTRATION: B.P. 700, Antananarivo, Madagascar. Phone: +261 (2022) 404-65.
STUDIO: B.P. 460, Antananarivo, Madagascar.
TECHNICAL AND NON-TECHNICAL (e.g. comments on programs)—see USA and Italy. AWR Broadcasts in Malagasy and French on leased airtime from Radio Nederland's Madagascar Relay. Reception reports concerning these broadcasts are best sent to the AWR Italian office. Also, *see* AWR listings under Germany, Guam, Guatemala, Italy, Kenya, United Kingdom and USA.
Radio Madagasikara, B.P. 442, Antananarivo 101, Madagascar. Email: radmad@dts.mg. Web: http://takelaka.dts.mg/radmad/. Contact: Mlle. Rakotonirina Soa Herimanitia, Secrétaire de Direction, a young lady who collects stamps; Mamy Rafenomanantsoa, Directeur; or J.J. Rakotonirina, who

has been known to request hi-fi catalogs. $1 required, and enclosing used stamps from various countries may help. Tape recordings accepted. Replies slowly and somewhat irregularly, usually to correspondence in French.
Radio Nederland Wereldomroep—Madagascar Relay, B.P. 404, Antananarivo, Madagascar. Contact: (technical) Rahamefy Eddy, Technische Dienst; or J.A. Ratobimiarana, Chief Engineer. Nontechnical correspondence should be sent to Radio Nederland Wereldomreop in Holland (*see*).

MALAWI World Time +2

Malawi Broadcasting Corporation, P.O. Box 30133, Chichiri, Blantyre 3, Malawi. Phone: +265 671-222. Fax: +265 671 257 or +265 671 353. Email: dgmbc@malawi.net. Contact: (general) Wilson Bankuku, Director General; J.O. Mndeke; or T.J. Sineta; (technical) Edwin K. Lungu, Controller of Transmitters; Phillip Chinseu, Engineering Consultant; or Joseph Chikagwa, Director of Engineering. Return postage or $1 helpful.

MALAYSIA World Time +8

Asia-Pacific Broadcasting Union, P.O. Box 1164, Pejabat Pos Jalan Pantai Bahru, 59700 Kuala Lumpur, Malaysia; or (street address) 2nd Floor, Bangunan IPTAR, Angkasapuri, 50614 Kuala Lumpur, Malaysia. Phone: (general) +60 (3) 2282-3592; (Programme Department)+60 (3) 2282-2480; (Technical Department) +60 (3) 2282-3108. Fax: +60 (3) 2282 5292. Email: sg@abu.org.my; se2@abu.org.my; or tech@abu.org.my. Web: www.abu.org.my/. Contact: Hugh Leonard, Secretary-General; or Sharad Sadhu, Senior Engineer, Technical Department.
Radio Malaysia Kota Kinabalu, RTM, 88614 Kota Kinabalu, Sabah, Malaysia. Contact: Benedict Janil, Director of Broadcasting; Hasbullah Latiff; or Mrs. Angrick Saguman. Registering your letter may help. $1 or return postage required.
▣Radio Malaysia, Kuala Lumpur
MAIN OFFICE: RTM, Angkasapuri, Bukit Putra, 50614 Kuala Lumpur, Peninsular Malaysia, Malaysia. Phone: +60 (3) 2282-5333 or +60 (3) 2282-4976. Fax: +60 (3) 2282 4735, +60 (3) 2282 5103 or +60 (3) 2282 5859. Email: sabariah@rtm.net.my. Web: (general) www.asiaconnect.com.my/rtm-net/; (RealAudio, live) www.asiaconnect.com.my/rtm-net/live/; (RealAudio, archives) www.asiaconnect.com.my/rtm-net/online/index.html. Contact: (general) Madzhi Johari, Director of Radio; (technical) Ms. Aminah Din, Deputy Director Engineering (Radio); Abdullah Bin Shahadan, Engineer, Transmission and Monitoring; or Ong Poh, Chief Engineer. May sell T-shirts and key chains. Return postage required.
TRANSMISSION OFFICE: Controller of Engineering, Department of Broadcasting (RTM), 43009 Kajang, Selangor Darul Ehsan, Malaysia. Phone: +60 (3) 8736-1530. Fax: +60 (3) 8736 1227. Email: rtmkjg@po.jaring.my. Contact: Jeffrey Looi.
Radio Malaysia Sarawak (Kuching), RTM, Broadcasting House, Jalan P. Ramlee, 93614 Kuching, Sarawak, Malaysia. Phone: +60 (82) 248-422. Fax: +60 (82) 241 914. Contact: (general) Yusof Ally, Director of Broadcasting; Mohd. Hulman Abdollah; or Human Resources Development; (technical, but also nontechnical) Colin A. Minoi, Technical Correspondence; (technical) Kho Kwang Khoon, Deputy Director of Engineering. Return postage helpful.
Radio Malaysia Sarawak (Miri), RTM, Miri, Sarawak, Malaysia. Contact: Clement Stia. $1 or return postage helpful.

Radio Malaysia Sarawak (Sibu), RTM, Jabatan Penyiaran, Bangunan Penyiaran, 96009 Sibu, Sarawak, Malaysia. Contact: Clement Stia, Divisional Controller, Broadcasting Department. $1 or return postage required. Replies irregularly and slowly.
Voice of Islam—Program of the Voice of Malaysia (*see*), below.
Voice of Malaysia, Suara Malaysia, Wisma Radio, P.O. Box 11272-KL, 50740 Angkasapuri, Kuala Lumpur, Malaysia. Phone: +60 (3) 2282-5333. Fax: +60 (3) 2282 5514. Contact: (general) Mrs. Mahani bte Ujang, Supervisor, English Service; Hajjah Wan Chuk Othman, English Service; (administration) Santokh Singh Gill, Director; or Mrs. Adilan bte Omar, Assistant Director; (technical) Lin Chew, Director of Engineering. Free calendars and stickers. Two IRCs or return postage helpful. Replies slowly and irregularly.

MALDIVES   World Time +5

Voice of Maldives (when reactivated), Ministry of Information, Arts and Culture, Moonlight Higun, Malé 20-06, Republic of Maldives. Phone: (administration and secretaries) +960 321-642; (Director General) +960 322-577; (Director of Programs) +960 322-746; (Duty Officer) +960 322-841; (programme section) +960 322-842; (studio 1) +960 325-151; (studio 2) +960 323-416; (newsroom) +960 322-253, +960 324-506 or + 960 324-507; (office assistant/budget secretary) +960 320-508; (FM Studio) +960 314-217; (technical, office) +960 322-444 or +960 320-941; (residence) +960 323-211. Fax: +960 328 357 or +960 325 371. Email: informat@dhivehinet.net.mv. Contact: Maizan Ahmed Manik, Director General of Engineering. Long inactive on the world bands, the station is hoping to resume shortwave broadcasts sometime in the future with a newly installed 10 kilowatt transmitter on the island of Mafushi.

MALI   World Time exactly

Radiodiffusion Télévision Malienne, B.P. 171, Bamako, Mali. Phone: +223 21-20-19 or +223 21-24-74. Fax: +223 21 42 05. Email: (Traore) cotraore@sotelma.ml. Contact: Karamoko Issiaka Daman, Directeur des Programmes; (administration) Abdoulaye Sidibe, Directeur General; (Technical) Nouhoum Traore. $1 or IRC helpful. Replies slowly and irregularly to correspondence in French. English is accepted.

MALTA   World Time +1 (+2 midyear)

◙**Voice of the Mediterranean (Radio Melita)**, St Francis Ravelin, Floriana, VLT 15, Malta; or P.O. Box 143, Valetta, CMR 01, Malta. Phone: +356 220-950, +356 240-421 or +356 248-080. Fax: +356 241 501. Email: vomradio@vom-malta.org.mt. Web: (includes RealAudio) www.vom-malta.org.mt. Contact: (administration) Dr. Richard Vella Laurenti, Managing Director; (German Service and listener contact) Ingrid Huettmann; M. Delu. Letters and reception reports welcomed May send blank QSL cards, stickers and bookmarks.

MAURITANIA   World Time exactly

Office de Radiodiffusion-Télévision de Mauritanie, B.P. 200, Nouakchott, Mauritania. Phone: +222 (2) 52287. Fax: +222 (2) 51264. Email: rm@mauritania.mr. Contact: Madame Amir Feu; Lemrabott Boukhary; Madame Fatimetou Fall Dite Ami, Secretaire de Direction; Mr. El Hadj Diagne; or Mr. Hane Abou. Return postage or $1 required. Rarely replies.

MEXICO   World Time –6 (–5 midyear) Central, including D.F.; –7 (–6 midyear) Mountain; –8 (–7 midyear) Pacific

Candela FM—XEQM (when operating), Apartado Postal 217, 97001-Mérida, YUC, Mexico. Phone: +52 (99) 236-155. Fax: +52 (99) 280 680. Contact: Lic. Bernardo Laris Rodríguez, Director General del Grupo RASA Mérida. Replies irregularly to correspondence in Spanish.
La Hora Exacta—XEQK (when operating), Real de Mayorazgo 83, Barrio de Xoco, 03330-México 13, D.F., Mexico. Phone: +52 (5) 628-1731, +52 (5) 628-1700 Ext. 1648 or 1659. Fax: +52 (5) 604-8292. Web: www.imer.gob.mx (click on the corresponding icon). Contact: Lic. Santiago Ibarra Ferrer, Gerente.
La Jarocha—XEFT (if reactivated), Apartado Postal 21, 91701-Veracruz, VER., Mexico. Phone: +52 (29) 322-250. Contact: C.P. Miguel Rodríguez Sáez, Sub-Director; or Lic. Juan de Dios Rodríguez Díaz, Director. Free tourist guide to Veracruz. Return postage, IRC or $1 probably helpful. Likely to reply to correspondence in Spanish.
Radio Educación—XEPPM, Apartado Postal 21-940, 04021-México 21, D.F., Mexico. Phone: (general) +52 (5) 559-6169. Fax: +52 (5) 575 6566. Web: www.cnca.gob.mx/cnca/buena/radio/temas.html. Contact: (general) Lic. Susana E. Mejía Vázquez, Jefe del Dept. de Audiencia y Evaluación; María Teresa Moya Malfavón, Directora de Producción y Planeación; Felicita Vázquez Nava, Secretaria; or Angélica Cortés, locutora; (administration) Luis Ernesto Pi Orozco, Director General; (technical) Ing. Gustavo Carreño López, Subdirector, Dpto. Técnico. Free stickers, calendars, station photo and a copy of a local publication, *Audio Tinta Boletín Informativo*. Return postage or $1 required. Replies, sometimes slowly, to correspondence in English, Spanish, Italian or French.
Radio Huayacocotla—XEJN
STATION ADDRESS: "Radio Huaya," Dom. Gutiérrez Najera s/n, Apartado Postal 13, 92600-Huayacocotla, VER, Mexico. Phone: +52 (775) 80067. Fax: +52 (775) 80178. E-mail: framos@uibero.uia.mx. Web: www.sjsocial.org/Radio/huarad.html. Contact: Martha Silvia Ortiz López, Coordinadora. Return postage or $1 helpful. Replies irregularly to correspondence in Spanish.
◙**Radio México Internacional—XERMX**, Instituto Méxicano de la Radio, Apartado Postal 21-300, 04021-México 21, D.F., Mexico. Phone: +52 (5) 604-7846 or +52 (5) 628-1720. Fax: +52 (5) 628 1710. E-mail: rmi@eudoramail.com. Web: www.imer.gob.mx (click on the appropriate icon); http://hello.to/rmi. Contact: Lic. Martín Rizo Gavira, Gerente; or Juan Josi Miroz, host "Mailbag Program." Free stickers, post cards and stamps. Sometimes free T-shirts and CDs. Welcomes correspondence, including inquiries about Mexico, in Spanish, English and French. $1 helpful. A bilingual reception report form can be downloaded and printed from the website.
Radio Mil—XEOI, NRM, Avda. Insurgentes Sur 1870, Col. Florida, 01030-México 20 D.F., Mexico; or Apartado Postal 21-1000, 04021-México 21, D.F., Mexico (this address for reception reports on the station's shortwave broadcasts). Phone: (station) +52 (5) 662-1000 or +52 (5) 662-1100; (Núcleo Radio Mil network) +52 (5) 662-6060, +52 (5) 663-0739 or +52 (5) 663 0590. Fax: (station) +52 (5) 662 0974; (Núcleo Radio Mil network) +52 (5) 662 0979. E-mail: info@nrm.com.mx. Web: www.nrm.com.mx/estaciones/radiomil/. Contact: Lic. Guillermo D. Salas Vargas, Vicepresidente Ejecutivo del Núcleo Radio Mil; Lic. Javier Trejo Garay, Gerente; or Zoila Quintanar Flores. Free stickers. $1 or return postage required.

Radio Transcontinental de América—XERTA, Apartado Postal 653, 06002 México 1, D.F., Mexico; or Torre "Latinoamericana" (Desp. 3706), 06007-México 1, D.F., Mexico. Phone: +52 (5) 510-9896. Fax: +52 (5) 510 3326. Contact: Roberto Najera Martínez, Presidente de Radio Transcontinental de América.

📻**Radio Universidad Autónoma de México (UNAM)—XEYU**, Adolfo Prieto 133, Colonia del Valle, 03100-México 12, D.F., Mexico. Phone: +52 (5) 523-2633. E-mail: radiounam@www.unam.mx. Web: (includes RealAudio) www.unam.mx/radiounam/. Contact: (general) Lic. Malena Mijares Fernández, Directora General de Radio UNAM; (technical) Ing. Gustavo Carreño, Departamento Técnico. Free tourist literature and stickers. $1 or return postage required. Replies irregularly to correspondence in Spanish.

MOLDOVA   World Time +2 (+3 midyear)

Radio Moldova International

GENERAL CORRESPONDENCE: If direct mail service is available from your location, try Maison de la Radio, Miorița str. 1, 277028 Chișinău, Moldova. Phone: +373 (2) 721-792, + (373) (2) 723-369, +373 (2) 723-379 or +373 (2) 723-385. Fax: +373 (2) 723 329 or +373 (2) 723 307. Contact: Constantin Marin, International Editor-in-Chief; Alexandru Dorogan, General Director of Radio Broadcasting; Constantin Rotaru, Director General; Daniel Lacky, Editor, English Service; Veleriu Vasilica, Head of English Department; Iurie Moraru, Director of Spanish Department; or Raisa Gonciar. Transmits via facilities of Radio România International. Free stickers and calendars.
RECEPTION REPORTS: RMI-Monitoring Action, P.O. Box 9972, 277070 Chișinău-70, Moldova.

MONACO   World Time +1 (+2 midyear)

Trans World Radio

STATION: B.P. 349, MC-98007 Monte-Carlo, Monaco-Cedex. Phone: +377 (92) 16-56-00. Fax: +377 (92) 16 56 01. URL (transmission schedule): www.gospelcom.net/twr/broadcasts/europe.htm. Contact: (general) Mrs. Jeanne Olson; (administration) Richard Olson, Station Manager; (Technical) *See VIENNA OFFICE, TECHNICAL* below. Free paper pennant. IRC or $1 helpful. Also, *see* USA.
GERMAN OFFICE: Evangeliums-Rundfunk, Postfach 1444, D-35573 Wetzlar, Germany. Phone: +49 (6441) 957-0. Fax: +49 (6441) 957-120. Email: erf@erf.de; or siemens@arf.de. Web: (includes RealAudio) www.erf.de. Contact: Jürgen Werth, Direktor.
HOLLAND OFFICE, NONTECHNICAL: Postbus 176, NL-3780 BD Voorthuizen, Holland. Phone: +31 (0) 34-29-27-27. Fax: +31 (0) 34 29 67 27. Contact: Beate Kiebel, Manager Broadcast Department; or Felix Widmer.
VIENNA OFFICE, TECHNICAL: Postfach 141, A-1235 Vienna, Austria. Phone: +43 (1) 863-1233 or +43 (1) 863-1247. Fax: +43 (1) 863 1220. Email: (Menzel) 100615.1511 @compuserve.com; (Schraut) eurofreq@twr.org; bschraut @twr.org; or 101513.2330@compuserve.com; (Dobos) kdobos@twr-europe.at. Contact: Helmut Menzel, Director of Engineering; Bernhard Schraut, Frequency Manager; Charles K. Roswell; or Kalman Dobos, Frequency Coordinator.
SWISS OFFICE: Evangelium in Radio und Fernsehen, Witzbergstrasse 23, CH-8330 Pfäffikon ZH, Switzerland. Phone: +41 (951) 0500. Fax: +41 (951) 0540. Email: erf@erf.ch. Web: www.erf.ch.

MONGOLIA   World Time +8

Mongolian Radio (Postal and email addresses same as Voice of Mongolia, *see* below). Phone: (administration) +976 (1) 323-520 or +976 (1) 328-978; (editorial) +976 (1) 329-766; (MRTV parent organization) +976 (1) 326-663. Fax: +976 (1) 327 234. Email: radiomongolia@magicnet.mn. Web: www.mol.mn/mrtv/MONGRAD.html. Contact: A. Buidakhmet, Director.

📻**Voice of Mongolia**, C.P.O. Box 365, Ulaanbaatar 13, Mongolia. Phone: +976 (1) 321-624 or (English Section) +976 (1) 327-900. Fax: +976 (1) 323 096 or (English Section) +976 (1) 327 234. Email: (general) radiomongolia@magicnet.mn; or (International Relations Office) mrtv@magicnet.mn. Web: (includes RealAudio) www.mongol.net/vom/. Contact: (general) Mrs. Narantuya, Chief of Foreign Service; D. Batbayar, Mail Editor, English Department; N. Tuya, Head of English Department; Dr. Mark Ostrowski, Consultant, MRTV International Relations Department; or Ms. Tsegmid Burmaa, Japanese Department; (administration) Ch. Surenjav, Director; (technical) Ing. Ganhuu, Chief of Technical Department. Correspondence should be directed to the relevant language section and 2 IRCs or 1$ appreciated. Sometimes very slow in replying. Accepts taped reception reports, preferably containing five-minute excerpts of the broadcast(s) reported, but cassettes cannot be returned. Free pennants, postcards, newspapers and Mongolian stamps.

MOROCCO   World Time exactly

📻**Radio Medi Un**

MAIN OFFICE: B.P. 2055, Tanger, Morocco (physical location: 3, rue Emsallah, 90000 Tanger, Morocco). Phone/fax: +212 (9) 936-363 or +212 (9) 935-755. Email: (general) medi1@medi1.com; (technical) technique@medi1.com. Web: (with RealAudio) www.medi1.com; www.medi1.co.ma. Contact: J. Dryk, Responsable Haute Fréquence. Two IRCs helpful. Free stickers. Correspondence in French preferred.
PARIS BUREAU, NONTECHNICAL: 78 Avenue Raymond Poincaré, F-75016 Paris, France. Phone: +33 (1) 45-01-53-30. Correspondence in French preferred.

Radio Mediterranée Internationale—*see* Radio Medi Un.

📻**Radiodiffusion-Télévision Marocaine**, 1 rue El Brihi, Rabat, Morocco. Phone: +212 (7) 766-881/83/85, +212 (7) 701-740; or +212 (7) 201-404. Fax: +212 (7) 722 047, or +212 (7) 703 208. Email: rtm@rtm.gov.ma; (technical) hammouda @rtm.gov.ma. Web: (general) www.rtm.gov.ma; (radio) www.rtm.gov.ma/Radiodiffusion/Radiodiffusion.htm; (RealAudio) www.maroc.net/rc/live.htm. Contact: (nontechnical and technical) Ms. Naaman Khadija, Ingénieur d'Etat en Télécommunication; Rahal Sabir; (technical) Tanone Mohammed Jamaledine, Technical Director; Hammouda Mohamed, Engineer; or N. Read. Correspondence welcomed in English, French, Arabic or Berber.

Voice of America/IBB—Morocco Relay Station, Briech. Phone: (office) +212 (9) 93-24-81. Fax: +212 (9) 93 55 71. Contact: Station Manager. These numbers for urgent technical matters only. Otherwise, does not welcome direct correspondence; *see* USA for acceptable VOA and IBB Washington addresses and related information.

MOZAMBIQUE   World Time +2

Rádio Maputo (when active)—*see* Radio Moçambique, below.
Rádio Moçambique, Rua da Rádio no. 2, Caixa Postal 2000, Maputo, Mozambique. Phone: +258 (1) 421-814, +258 (1) 429-

Radio Netherlands' Ann Blair Gould with daughter. On October 26, 2000, the station dropped "Media Network," successor to the popular "DX-Jukebox" started in 1959. RNW

826 or +258 (1) 429-836. Fax: +258 (1) 421 816. Contact: (general) João B. de Sousa, Administrador de Produção; Izidine Faquira, Diretor de Programas; Orlanda Mendes, Produtor, "Linha Direta"; (technical) Eduardo Rufino de Matos, Administrador Técnico; or Daniel Macabi, Diretor Técnico. Free medallions and pens. Cassettes featuring local music $15. Return postage, $1 or 2 IRCs required. Replies to correspondence in Portuguese or English.

MYANMAR (BURMA)   World Time +6:30

Radio Myanmar
STATION: GPO Box 1432, Yangon-11181, Myanmar; or Pyay Road, Yangon-11041, Myanmar. Contact: Ko Ko Htway, Director of Radio.

NAGORNO-KARABAGH   World Time +3 (+4 midyear)

Voice of Justice, Tigranmetz Street 23a, Stepanakert, Nagorno-Karabagh. Contact: Michael Hajiyan, Station Manager. Replies to correspondence in Armenian, Azeri, Russian and German.

NAMIBIA   World Time +2 (+1 midyear)

Radio Namibia/Namibian Broadcasting Corporation, P.O. Box 321, Windhoek 9000, Namibia. Phone: (general) +264 (61) 291-3111; (studio, during "Chat Show" and "Openline") +264 (61) 236-381. Fax: (general) +264 (61) 217 760; (Duwe, technical) +264 (61) 231 881. Email: (Tyson) robin@imlt.org.na. Web: (National Radio) http://natradio.imlt.org.na. Contact: (nontechnical) Robin Tyson, Manager, National Radio; (technical) P. Schachtschneider, Manager, Transmitter Maintenance; Joe Duwe, Chief Technician. Free stickers.

NEPAL   World Time +5:45

📻**Radio Nepal**, P.O. Box 634, Singha Durbar, Kathmandu, Nepal. Phone: (general) +977 (1) 223-910; (engineering) +977 (1) 225-467. Fax: +977 (1) 221 952. Email: rne@rne.wlink.com.np; radio@rne.wlink.com.np; (engineering) radio@engg.wlink.com.np. Web: (include RealAudio in English and Nepali) www.catmando.com/news/radio-nepal/; www.catmando.com/radio-nepal/. Contact: (general) M.P. Acharya, Executive Director; M.P. Adhikari, Deputy Executive Director; Jayanti Rajbhandari, Director - Programming; or S.K. Pant, Producer, "Listener's Mail"; (technical) Ram Sharan Kharki, Director - Engineering. 3 IRCs necessary, but station urges that neither mint stamps nor cash be enclosed, as this invites theft by Nepalese postal employees.

NETHERLANDS—see Holland

NETHERLANDS ANTILLES   World Time –4

Radio Nederland Wereldomroep—Bonaire Relay, P.O. Box 45, Kralendijk, Netherlands Antilles. Contact: Leo Kool, Manager. Nontechnical correspondence should be sent to Radio Nederland Wereldomreop in Holland (see).

NEW ZEALAND   World Time +13 (+12 midyear)

📻**Radio New Zealand International (Te Reo Irirangi O Aotearoa, O Te Moana-nui-a-kiwa)**, P.O. Box 123, Wellington, New Zealand. Phone: +64 (4) 474-1437. Fax: +64 (4) 474 1433 or +64 (4) 474 1886. Email: info@rnzi.com. Web: (general) www.rnzi.com; (RealAudio) www.audionet.co.nz/ranz.html (can also be accessed via a link at the rnzi.com Website). Contact: Florence de Ruiter, Listener Mail; Myra Oh, Producer, "Mailbox"; or Walter Zweifel, News Editor; (administration) Ms. Linden Clark, Manager; (technical) Adrian Sainsbury, Technical Manager. Free stickers, schedule/flyer about station, map of New Zealand and tourist literature available. English/Maori T-shirts for US$20; Sweatshirts $40; interesting variety of CDs, as well as music cassettes and spoken programs, in Domestic "Replay Radio" catalog (VISA/MC). Three IRCs for verification, one IRC for schedule/catalog.

Radio Reading Service—ZLXA, P.O. Box 360, Levin 5500, New Zealand. Phone: (general) +64 (6) 368-2229; (engineering) +64 (25) 985-360. Fax: +64 (6) 368 7290. Email: (general) nzrpd@xtra.co.nz; (Bell) ABell@radioreading.org; (Little) Alittle@radioreading.org; (Stokoe) BStokoe@radioreading.org. Web: www.radioreading.org. Contact: (general) Ash Bell, Manager/Station Director; (administration) Allen J. Little, Executive President; (technical, including reception reports) Brian Stokoe. Operated by volunteers 24 hours a day, seven days a week. Station is owned by the "New Zealand Radio for the Print Disabled Inc." Free brochure, postcards and stickers. $1, return postage or 3 IRCs appreciated.

NICARAGUA   World Time –6

Radio Miskut, Barrio Pancasan, Puerto Cabezas, R.A.A.N., Nicaragua. Phone: +505 (282) 2443. Fax: +505 (267) 3032. Contact: Evaristo Mercado Pérez, Director de Operación y de Programas; or Abigail Zúñiga Fagoth. T-shirts $10, and *Resumen Mensual del Gobierno y Consejo Regional* and *Revista Informativa Detallada de las Gestiones y Logros* $10 per copy.

Station has upgraded to a new shortwave transmitter and is currently improving its shortwave antenna. Replies slowly and irregularly to correspondence in English and Spanish. $2 helpful, as is registering your letter.

NIGER World Time +1

La Voix du Sahel, O.R.T.N., B.P. 361, Niamey, Niger. Fax: +227 72 35 48. Contact: (general) Adamou Oumarou; Issaka Mamadou; Zakari Saley; Souley Boubacou; or Mounkaïla Inazadan, Producer, "Inter-Jeunes Variétés"; (administration) Oumar Tiello, Directeur; (technical) Afo Sourou Victor. $1 helpful. Correspondence in French preferred. Correspondence by males with this station may result in requests for certain unusual types of magazines and photographs.

NIGERIA World Time +1

WARNING—MAIL THEFT: For the time being, correspondence from abroad to Nigerian addresses has a relatively high probability of being stolen.
WARNING—CONFIDENCE ARTISTS: For years, now, correspondence with Nigerian stations has sometimes resulted in letters from highly skilled "pen pal" confidence artists. These typically offer to send you large sums of money, if you will provide details of your bank account or similar information (after which they clean out your account). Other scams are disguised as tempting business proposals; or requests for money, free electronic or other products, publications or immigration sponsorship. Persons thus approached should contact their country's diplomatic offices. For example, Americans should contact the Diplomatic Security Section of the Department of State [phone +1 (202) 647-4000], or an American embassy or consulate.
Radio Nigeria—Enugu, P.M.B. 1051, Enugu (Anambra), Phone: +234 (42) 254-137. Fax: +234 (42) 255354. Nigeria. Contact: Louis Nnamuchi, Assistant Director Technical Services. Two IRCs, return postage or $1 required. Replies slowly.
Radio Nigeria—Ibadan, Broadcasting House, P.M.B. 5003, Ibadan, Oyo State, Nigeria. Phone: +234 (22) 241-4093 or +234 (22) 241-4106. Fax: +234 (22) 241 3930. Contact: V.A. Kalejaiye, Technical Services Department; Rev. Olukunle Ajani, Executive Director; Nike Adegoke, Executive Director; or Dare Folarin, Principal Public Affairs Officer. $1 or return postage required. Replies slowly.
Radio Nigeria—Kaduna, P.O. Box 250, Kaduna (Kaduna), Nigeria. Contact: Yusuf Garba, Ahmed Abdullahi, R.B. Jimoh, Assistant Director Technical Service; or Johnson D. Allen. May send sticker celebrating 30 years of broadcasting. $1 or return postage required. Replies slowly.
Radio Nigeria—Lagos, P.M.B. 12504, Ikoyi, Lagos, Nigeria. Phone: +234 (1) 269-0301. Fax: +234 (1) 269 0073. Contact: Willie Egbe, Assistant Director for Programmes; Babatunde Olalekan Raji, Monitoring Unit. Two IRCs or return postage helpful. Replies slowly and irregularly.
Voice of Nigeria, P.M.B. 40003 Falomo Post Office, Ikoyi, Lagos, Nigeria. Phone: +234 (1) 269-3078/3245/3075/. Fax: +234 (1) 269 1944. Contact: (general) Alhaji Lawal Yusuf Saulawa, Director of Programming; Mrs. Stella Bassey, Deputy Director Programmes; Alhaji Mohammed Okorejior, Acting Director News; or Livy Iwok, Editor; (administration) Taiwo Alimi, Director General; Abubakar Jijiwa, Chairman; Frank Iloye, Station Manager; or Dr. Walter Ofonagoro, Minister of Information; (technical) J.O. Kurunmi, Deputy Director Engineering Services; O.I. Odumsi, Acting Director, Engineering;

or G.C. Ugwa, Director Engineering. Replies from station tend to be erratic, but continue to generate unsolicited correspondence from supposed "pen pals" (*see WARNING—CONFIDENCE ARTISTS*, above); faxes, which are much less likely to be intercepted, may be more fruitful. Two IRCs or return postage helpful.

NORTHERN MARIANA ISLANDS World Time +10

Far East Broadcasting Company—Radio Station KFBS Saipan
MAIN OFFICE: FEBC, P.O. Box 209, Saipan, Mariana Islands MP 96950 USA. Phone: (main office) +1 (670) 322-3841. Fax: +1 (670) 322 3060. Email: febc@itecnmi.com. Web: www.febc.org. Contact: Chris Slabaugh, Field Director; Irene Gabbie, QSL Secretary; Mike Adams; or Robert Springer, Director. Replies sometimes take months. Also, *see* FEBC Radio International, USA.

NORWAY World Time +1 (+2 midyear)

⊠Radio Norway International (Utenlandssendingen)
MAIN OFFICE, NONTECHNICAL: Utenlandssendingen, NRK, N-0340 Oslo, Norway. Phone: (general) + 47 (23) 048-441 or +47 (23) 048-444; (Norwegian-language 24-hour recording of schedule information +47 (23) 048-008 (Americas, Europe, Africa), +47 (23) 048-009 (elsewhere). Fax: (general) +47 (23) 047 134 or +47 (22) 605 719. Email: radionorway@nrk.no. Web: (includes RealAudio) www.nrk.no/radionyheter/radionorway/. Contact: (general) Kirsten Ruud Salomonsen, Head of External Broadcasting; or Grethe Breie, Consultant; (technical) Gundel Krauss Dahl, Head of Radio Projects. Free stickers and flags.
WASHINGTON NEWS BUREAU: Norwegian Broadcasting, 2030 M Street NW, Suite 700, Washington DC 20036 USA. Phone: +1 (202) 785-1481 or +1 (202) 785-1460. Contact: Bjorn Hansen or Gunnar Myklebust.
SINGAPORE NEWS BUREAU: NRK, 325 River Valley Road #01-04, Singapore.
FREQUENCY MANAGEMENT OFFICE: Statens Teleforvaltning, Dept. TF/OMG, Revierstredet 2, P.O. Box 447 Sentrum, N-0104 Oslo, Norway. Phone: +47 (22) 824-889 or +47 (22) 824-878. Fax: +47 (22) 824 891 or +47 (22) 824 790. Contact: Erik Johnsbråthen, Frequency Manager; or Ayumu Ohta.

OMAN World Time +4

BBC World Service—Eastern Relay Station (BERS), P.O. Box 23, Wilayat Masirah, Post Code 414, Sultanate of Oman. Technical correspondence should be sent to "Senior Transmitter Engineer"; nontechnical goes to the BBC World Service in London (*see* United Kingdom). Construction of a new transmission complex is under way at Al-Ashkhara and will eventually replace the current facilities at Masirah, built in 1966.
⊠Radio Sultanate of Oman, Ministry of Information, P.O. Box 600, Muscat, Post Code 113, Sultanate of Oman. Phone: +968 602-494 or +968 603-222. Fax: (general) +968 602 055 or +968 602 831; (technical) +968 604 629; or +968 607 239. Email: (technical) sjnornani@omantel.net.om; or abulukman@hotmail.com. Web: (RealAudio only) www.oman-tv.gov.om/. Contact: (Directorate General of Technical Affairs) Abdallah Bin Saif Al-Nabhani, Acting Chief Engineer; Rashid Haroon Al-Jabry, Head of Radio Maintenance; Salim Al-

Nomani, Director of Frequency Management; or Ahmed Mohamed Al-Balushi, Head of Studio's Engineering. Replies regularly, and responses are from one to two weeks. $1, return postage or 3 IRCs helpful.

PAKISTAN   World Time +5

Azad Kashmir Radio, Muzaffarabad, Azad Kashmir, Pakistan. Contact: (technical) M. Sajjad Ali Siddiqui, Director of Engineering; or Liaquatullah Khan, Engineering Manager. Registered mail helpful. Rarely replies to correspondence.

☎**Pakistan Broadcasting Corporation**—same address, fax and contact as "Radio Pakistan," below. Email: cnoradio@isb.comsats.net.pk. Web: (includes RealAudio) www.radio.gov.pk.

Radio Pakistan, P.O. Box 1393, Islamabad 44000, Pakistan. Email: same as for Pakistan Broadcasting Corporation, above. Phone: +92 (51) 921-0689. Fax: +92 (51) 920-1861. Web: www.radio.gov.pk/exter.html. Contact: (technical) Ahmed Nawaz, Senior Broadcast Engineer, Room No. 324, Frequency Management Cell; Syed Abrar Hussain, Controller of Frequency Management; Syed Asmat Ali Shah, Senior Broadcasting Engineer; or Nasirahmad Bajwa, Frequency Management. Free stickers, pennants and *Pakistan Calling* magazine. May also send pocket calendar. Very poor replier. Plans to replace two 50 kW transmitters with 500 kW units if and when funding is forthcoming.

PALAU   World Time +9

KHBN—Voice of Hope, P.O. Box 66, Koror, Palau 96940, Pacific Islands. Phone: +680 488-2162. Fax: (main office) +680 488 2163; or (engineering) +680 544 1008. Email: (general) hamadmin@palaunet.com; or (engineering) khbntx @palaunet.com. Web: www.intertvnet.net/~highorg/stations/asia_china/. Contact: (general) Regina Subris, Station Manager; (technical) Ernie Fontanilla, Engineer. Free stickers and publications. IRC requested. Also, *see* KVOH—Voice of Hope/ High Adventure Ministries, USA.

PAPUA NEW GUINEA   World Time +10

NOTE: Stations are sometimes off the air due to financial or technical problems which can take weeks or months to resolve.

National Broadcasting Corporation of Papua New Guinea, P.O. Box 1359, Boroko NCD, Papua New Guinea. Phone: + 675 325-5949 or +675 325-6779. Fax: +675 325 0796 or +675 325 6296. Contact: (general) Renagi R. Lohia, CBE, Managing Director and C.E.O.; or Ephraim Tammy, Director, Radio Services; (technical) Bob Kabewa, Sr. Technical Officer; or F. Maredey, Chief Engineer. Two IRCs or return postage helpful. Replies irregularly.

Radio Bougainville, P.O. Box 35, Buka, North Solomons Province (NSP), Papua New Guinea. Contact: A.L. Rumina, Provincial Programme Manager; Ms. Christine Talei, Assistant Provincial Manager; or Aloysius Laukai, Senior Programme Officer. Replies irregularly.

Radio Central (when operating), P.O. Box 1359, Boroko, NCD, Papua New Guinea. Contact: Steven Gamini, Station Manager; Lahui Lovai, Provincial Programme Manager; or Amos Langit, Technician. $1, 2 IRCs or return postage helpful. Replies irregularly.

Radio Eastern Highlands (when operating), P.O. Box 311, Goroka, EHP, Papua New Guinea. Contact: Tonko Nonao, Program Manager; Ignas Yanam, Technical Officer; or Kiri Nige, Engineering Division. $1 or return postage required. Replies irregularly.

Radio East New Britain (when operating), P.O. Box 393, Rabaul, ENBP, Papua New Guinea. Contact: Esekia Mael, Station Manager; or Oemas Kumaina, Provincial Program Manager. Return postage required. Replies slowly.

Radio East Sepik, P.O. Box 65, Wewak, E.S.P., Papua New Guinea. Contact: Elias Albert, Assistant Provincial Program Manager; or Luke Umbo, Station Manager.

Radio Enga, P.O. Box 300, Wabag, Enga Province, Papua New Guinea. Phone: +675 547-1213. Contact: (general) John Lyein Kur, Station Manager; or Robert Papuvo, (technical) Gabriel Paiao, Station Technician.

Radio Gulf (when operating), P.O. Box 36, Kerema, Gulf, Papua New Guinea. Contact: Robin Wainetta, Station Manager; or Timothy Akia, Provincial Program Manager.

Radio Madang, P.O. Box 2138, Madang, Papua New Guinea. Phone: +675 852-2415. Fax: +675 852 2360. Contact: (general) Damien Boaging, Senior Programme Officer; Geo Gedabing, Provincial Programme Manager; Peter Charlie Yannum, Assistant Provincial Programme Manager; or James Steve Valakvi, Senior Programme Officer; (technical) Lloyd Guvil, Technician.

Radio Manus, P.O. Box 505, Lorengau, Manus, Papua New Guinea. Phone: +675 470-9029. Fax: +675 470 9079. Contact: (technical and nontechnical) John P. Mandrakamu, Provincial Program Manager. Station is seeking the help of DXers and broadcasting professionals in obtaining a second hand, but still usable broadcasting quality CD player that could be donated to Radio Manus. Replies regularly. Return postage appreciated.

Radio Milne Bay(when operating), P.O. Box 111, Alotau, Milne Bay, Papua New Guinea. Contact: (general) Trevor Webumo, Assistant Manager; Simon Muraga, Station Manager; or Raka Petuely, Program Officer; (technical) Philip Maik, Technician. Return postage in the form of mint stamps helpful.

Radio Morobe, P.O. Box 1262, Lae, Morobe, Papua New Guinea. Fax: +675 472 6423. Contact: Ken L. Tropu, Assistant Program Manager; Peter W. Manua, Program Manager; Kekalem M. Meruk, Assistant Provincial Program Manager; or Aloysius R. Nase, Station Manager.

Radio New Ireland, P.O. Box 140, Kavieng, New Ireland, Papua New Guinea. Contact: Otto A. Malatana, Station Manager; or Ruben Bale, Provincial Program Manager. Return postage or $1 helpful.

Radio Northern (when operating), Voice of Oro, P.O. Box 137, Popondetta, Oro, Papua New Guinea. Contact: Roma Tererembo, Assistant Provincial Programme Manager; or Misael Pendaia, Station Manager. Return postage required.

Radio Sandaun, P.O. Box 37, Vanimo, Sandaun Province, Papua New Guinea. Contact: (nontechnical) Gabriel Deckwalen, Station Manager; Zacharias Nauot, Acting Assistant Manager; Celina Korei, Station Journalist; Elias Rathley, Provincial Programme Manager; Mrs. Maria Nauot, Secretary; (technical) Paia Ottawa, Technician. $1 helpful.

Radio Simbu, P.O. Box 228, Kundiawa, Chimbu, Papua New Guinea. Phone: +675 735-1038 or +675 735-1082. Fax: +675 735 1012. Contact: (general) Jack Wera, Manager; Tony Mill Waine, Provincial Programme Manager; Felix Tsiki; or Thomas Ghiyandiule, Producer, "Pasikam Long ol Pipel." Cassette recordings $5. Free two-Kina banknotes.

Radio Southern Highlands (when operating), P.O. Box 104, Mendi, SHP, Papua New Guinea. Contact: (general) Andrew

Meles, Provincial Programme Manager; Miriam Piapo, Programme Officer; Benard Kagaro, Programme Officer; Lucy Aluy, Programme Officer; or Nicholas Sambu, Producer, "Questions and Answers"; (technical) Ronald Helori, Station Technician. $1 or return postage helpful; or donate a wall poster of a rock band, singer or American landscape.

Radio Western, P.O. Box 23, Daru, Western Province, Papua New Guinea. Contact: Robin Wainetti (Manager); (technical) Samson Tobel, Technician. $1 or return postage required. Replies irregularly.

Radio Western Highlands (when operating), P.O. Box 311, Mount Hagen, WHP, Papua New Guinea. Contact: (technical) Esau Okole, Technician. $1 or return postage helpful. Replies occasionally. Often off the air because of theft, armed robbery or inadequate security for the station's staff.

Radio West New Britain, P.O. Box 412, Kimbe, WNBP, Papua New Guinea. Fax: +675 983 5600. Contact: Valuka Lowa, Provincial Station Manager; Darius Gilime, Provincial Program Manager; Lemeck Kuam, Producer, "Questions and Answers"; or Esekial Mael. Return postage required.

PARAGUAY   World Time –3 (–4 midyear)

La Voz del Chaco Paraguayo, Filadelfia, Dpto. de Boquerón, Chaco, Paraguay. Contact: Erwin Wiens, Director; or Arnold Boschmann, Director de Programación. This station, currently only on mediumwave AM, hopes to add a world band transmitter within the 60-meter (5 MHz) band. Although the station is located above the Tropic of Capricorn, and therefore eligible to use the tropical bands, the telecommunications authorities in Asunción, south of the line, have never supported broadcasting on tropical band frequencies within Paraguay.

Radio Encarnación (when operating), Gral. Artigas casi Gral. B. Caballero, Encarnación, Paraguay. Phone: (general) +595 (71) 4376 or +595 (71) 3345; (press) +595 (71) 4120. Fax: +595 (71) 4099. $1 or return postage helpful.

Radio Guairá (when operating), Alejo García y Presidente Franco, Villarrica, Paraguay. Phone: +595 (541) 2385 or +595 (541) 3411. Fax: +595 (541) 2130. Contact: (general) Lídice Rodríguez Vda. de Traversi, Propietaria; (technical) Enrique Traversi. Welcomes correspondence in Spanish. $1 or return postage helpful.

Radio Nacional del Paraguay, Blas Garay 241 entre Yegros e Iturbe, Asunción, Paraguay. Phone: +595 (21) 449-213. Fax: +595 (21) 332 750. Contact: Efraín Martínez Cuevas, Director. Free tourist brochure. $1 or return postage required. Replies, sometimes slowly, to correspondence in Spanish.

PERU   World Time –5 year-round in Loreto, Cusco and Puno. Other departments sometimes move to World Time –4 for a few weeks of the year.

NOTE: Obtaining replies from Peruvian stations calls for creativity, tact, patience—and the proper use of Spanish, not form letters and the like. There are nearly 150 world band stations operating from Perú on any given day. While virtually all of these may be reached simply by using as the address the station's city, as given in the Blue Pages, the following are the only stations known to be replying—even if only occasionally—to correspondence from abroad.

Emisoras JSV—see Radio JSV.

Estación C, Casilla de Correo 210, Moyobamba, San Martín, Peru. Contact: Porfirio Centurión, Propietario.

Estación Tarapoto (if reactivated), Jirón Federico Sánchez 720, Tarapoto, Peru. Phone: +51 (94) 522-709. Contact: Luis Humberto Hidalgo Sánchez, Gerente General; or José Luna Paima, Announcer. Replies occasionally to correspondence in Spanish.

Estación Wari, Calle Nazareno 108, Ayacucho, Peru. Phone: +51 (64) 813-039. Contact: Walter Muñoz Ynga I., Gerente.

Estación X (Equis) (when operating), Plaza de Armas No. 106, Yurimaguas, Provincia de Alto Amazonas, Loreto, Peru. Contact: Franklin Coral Sousa, Director Propietario, who may also be contacted at his home address: Jirón Mariscal Castilla No. 104, Yurimaguas, Provincia de Alto Amazonas, Loreto, Peru.

Frecuencia Líder (Radio Bambamarca), Jirón Jorge Chávez 416, Bambamarca, Hualgayoc, Cajamarca, Peru. Phone: (office) +51 (74) 713-260; (studio) +51 (74) 713-249. Contact: (general) Valentín Peralta Diaz, Gerente; Irma Peralta Rojas; or Carlos Antonio Peralta Rojas; (technical) Oscar Lino Peralta Rojas. Free station photos. *La Historia de Bambamarca* book for 5 Soles; cassettes of Peruvian and Latin American folk music for 4 Soles each; T-shirts for 10 Soles each (sending US$1 per Sol should suffice and cover foreign postage costs, as well). Replies occasionally to correspondence in Spanish. Considering replacing their transmitter to improve reception.

Frecuencia San Ignacio, Jirón Villanueva Pinillos 330, San Ignacio, Cajamarca, Peru. Contact: Franklin R. Hoyos Cóndor, Director Gerente; or Ignacio Gómez Torres, Técnico de Sonido. Replies to correspondence in Spanish. $1 or return postage necessary.

Frecuencia VH—see Radio Frecuencia VH.

La Super Radio San Ignacio (when operating), Avenida Víctor Larco 104, a un costado del campo deportivo, San Ignacio, Distrito de Sinsicap, Provincia de Otuzco, La Libertad, Peru.

La Voz de Anta, Distrito de Anta, Provincia de Acobamba, Departamento de Huancavelica. Phone: +51 (64) 750-201.

La Voz de la Selva—see Radio La Voz de la Selva.

La Voz de San Juan—see Radio La Voz de San Juan.

La Voz del Campesino—see Radio La Voz del Campesino.

La Voz del Marañon—see Radio La Voz del Marañon.

Ondas del Suroriente—see Radio Ondas del Suroriente, below.

Radio Adventista Mundial—La Voz de la Esperanza, Jirón Dos de Mayo No. 218, Celendín, Cajamarca, Peru. Contact: Francisco Goicochea Ortiz, Director; or Lucas Solano Oyarce, Director de Ventas.

Radio Altura (Cerro de Pasco), Casilla de Correo 140, Cerro de Pasco, Pasco, Peru. Phone: +51 (64) 721-875, +51 (64) 722-398. Contact: Oswaldo de la Cruz Vásquez, Gerente General. Replies to correspondence in Spanish.

Radio Altura (Huarmaca), Antonio Raymondi 3ra Cuadra, Distrito de Huarmaca, Provincia de Huancabamba, Piura, Peru.

Radio Amauta del Perú, (when operating), Jirón Manuel Iglesias s/n, a pocos pasos de la Plazuela San Juan, San Pablo, Cajamarca, Nor Oriental del Marañón, Peru.

Radio América (if reactivated), Montero Rosas 1099, Santa Beatriz, Lima, Peru. Phone: +51 (1) 265-3841/2/3. Fax: +51 (1) 265 3844. Contact: Liliana Sugobono F., Directora; or Jorge Arriola Viván, Promociones y Marketing.

Radio Amistad, Manzana I-11, Lote 6, Calle 22, Urbanización Mariscal Cáceres, San Juan de Lurigancho, Lima, Peru. Phone: +51 (1) 392-3640. Email: radioamistad@peru.com. Contact: Manuel Mejía Barboza. Accepts email reception reports.

Radio Ancash, Casilla de Correo 221, Huaraz, Peru. Phone: +51 (44) 721-381,+51 (44) 721-359, +51 (44) 721-487, +51 (44) 722-512. Fax: +51 (44) 722 992. Contact: Armando Moreno Romero, Gerente General. Replies to correspondence in Spanish.

Radio Andahuaylas, Jr. Ayacucho No. 248, Andahuaylas, Apurímac, Peru. Contact: Sr. Daniel Andréu C., Gerente. $1 required. Replies irregularly to correspondence in Spanish.

Radio Andina (Huancabamba), Huáscar 201, Huancabamba, Piura, Peru. According to an on-air announcement, the station is expected to move to Avenida Ramón Castilla 254. Phone: +51 (74) 473-104. Contact: Manuel Campos Ojeda, Director.

Radio Andina (Huancayo), Real 175, Huancayo, Junín, Peru. Phone: +51 (64) 231-123. Replies infrequently to correspondence in Spanish.

Radio Apurímac (when operating), Jirón Cusco 206 (or Ovalo El Olivo No. 23), Abancay, Apurímac, Peru. Contact: Antero Quispe Allca, Director General.

Radio Arcángel San Miguel—*see* Radio San Miguel Arcángel.

Radio Arequipa, Avenida Unión 215, 3er piso, Distrito Miraflores, Arequipa, Peru. May identify as "Radio Arequipa Bethel" when carrying religious programming from the "Movimiento Misionero Mundial" evengelistic organization.

Radio Atlántida
STATION: Jirón Arica 441, Iquitos, Loreto, Peru. Phone: +51 (94) 234-452, +51 (94) 234-962. Contact: Pablo Rojas Bardales.
LISTENER CORRESPONDENCE: Sra. Carmela López Paredes, Directora del prgrama "Trocha Turística," Jirón Arica 1083, Iquitos, Loreto, Peru. Free pennants and tourist information. $1 or return postage required. Replies to most correspondence in Spanish, the preferred language, and some correspondence in English. "Trocha Turística" is a bilingual (Spanish and English) tourist program aired weekdays 2300-2330.

Radio Ayaviri (La Voz de Melgar) (when operating), Apartado Postal 8, Ayaviri, Puno, Peru. Fax: +51 (54) 320 207, specify on fax "Anexo 127." Contact: (general) Sra. Corina Llaiqui Ochoa, Administradora; (technical) José Aristo Solórzano Mendoza, Director. Free pennants. Sells audio cassettes of local folk music for $5 plus postage; also exchanges music cassettes. Correspondence accepted in English, but Spanish preferred.

Radio Bahía, Jirón Alfonso Ugarte 309, Chimbote, Ancash, Peru. Phone: +51 (44) 322-391. Contact: Margarita Rossel Soria, Administradora; or Miruna Cruz Rossel, Administradora.

Radio Bambamarca—*see* Frecuencia Líder, above.

Radio Bolívar, Correo Central, Bolívar, Provincia de Bolívar, Departamento de La Libertad, Peru. Contact: Julio Dávila Echevarría, Gerente. May send free pennant. Return postage helpful.

Radio Cajamarca, Jirón La Mar 675, Cajamarca, Peru. Phone: +51 (44) 921-014. Contact: Porfirio Cruz Potosí.

Radio Chanchamayo, Jirón Tarma 551, La Merced, Junín, Peru.

Radio Chaski, Baptist Mid-Missions, Apartado Postal 368, Cusco, Peru; or Alameda Pachacútec s/n B-5, Cusco, Peru. Phone: +51 (84) 225-052. Contact: Andrés Tuttle H., Gerente.

Radio Chincheros, Jirón Apurímac s/n, Chincheros, Departamento de Apurímac, Peru.

Radio Chota, Jirón Anaximandro Vega 690, Apartado Postal 3, Chota, Cajamarca, Peru. Phone: +51 (44) 771-240. Contact: Aladino Gavidia Huamán, Administrador. $1 or return postage required. Replies slowly to correspondence in Spanish.

Radio Comas Televisión, Avenida Estados Unidos 327, Urbanización Huaquillay, km 10 de la Avenida Túpac Amaru, Distrito de Comas, Lima, Peru. Phone: +51 (1) 525-0859. Fax: +51 (1) 525 0094. Email: rtcomas@protelsa.com.pe; rtcomas @terra.com.pe. Web: http://homepages.go.com/homepages/ r/a/d/radio_cantogrande/. Contact: Edgar Saldaña R.; Juan Rafael Saldaña Reátegui (Relaciones Públicas) or Gamaniel Francisco Chahua, Productor-Programador General.

Radio Concordia (if reactived), Av. La Paz 512-A, Arequipa, Peru. If a reply is not forthcoming, try: Miguel Grau s/n Mz.2 Lt. 1, Arequipa, Peru. Phone: +51 (54) 446-053. Contact: Pedro Pablo Acosta Fernández. Free stickers. Return postage required.

Radio Continental (if reactivated), Av. Independencia 56, Arequipa, Peru. Phone: +51 (54) 213-253. Contact: J. Antonio Umbert D., Director General; or Leonor Núñez Melgar. Free stickers. Replies slowly to correspondence in Spanish.

◩**Radio CORA**, Compañía Radiofónica Lima, S.A., Paseo de la República 144, Centro Cívico, Oficina 5, Lima 1, Peru. Phone: +51 (1) 433-5005, +51 (1) 433-1188, +51 (1) 433-0848. Fax: +51 (1) 433 6134. Email: cora@peru.itete.com.pe; cora@lima.business.com.pe. Web: (includes RealAudio) www.radiocora.com.pe. Contact: (general) Juan Ramírez Lazo, Propietario y Director Gerente; Dra. Lylian Ramírez M., Directora de Prensa y Programación; Juan Ramírez Lazo, Director Gerente; or Srta. Angelina María Abie; (technical) Srta. Sylvia Ramírez M., Directora Técnica. Free station sticky-label pads, bumper stickers and may send large certificate suitable for framing. Audio cassettes with extracts from their programs $20 plus $2 postage; women's hair bands $2 plus $1 postage. Two IRCs or $1 required. Replies slowly to correspondence in English, Spanish, French, Italian and Portuguese.

Radio Cristal, Jirón Ucayali s/n, a un costado de la Carretera Marginal de la Selva, San Hilarión, Provincia de Picota, Región San Martín, Peru. Contact: Señora Marina Gaona, Gerente; or Lucho García Gaona.

Radio Cultural Amauta, Cahuide 278, Apartado Postal 24, Huanta, Ayacucho, Peru. Phone: +51 (64) 832-153. Contact: Vicente Saico Tinco.

Radio Cusco, Apartado Postal 251, Cusco, Peru. Phone: (general)+51 (84) 225-851; (management) +51 (84) 232-457. Fax: +51 (84) 223 308. Contact: Sra. Juana Huamán Yépez, Administradora; or Raúl Siú Almonte, Gerente General; (technical) Benjamín Yábar Alvarez. Free pennants, postcards and key rings. Audio cassettes of Peruvian music $10 plus postage. $1 or return postage required. Replies irregularly to correspondence in English or Spanish. Station is looking for folk music recordings from around the world to use in their programs.

Radio del Pacífico, Apartado Postal 4236, Lima 1, Peru. Phone: +51 (1) 433-3275. Fax: +51 (1) 433 3276. Email: postmast@pacifico.com.pe. Contact: J. Petronio Allauca, Secretario, Departamento de Relaciones Públicas; or P.G. Ferreyra. $1 or return postage required. Replies occasionally to correspondence in Spanish.

Radio El Sol (Lima) (when active), Avenida Uruguay 355, 7%, Lima Peru. Phone: +51 (1) 330-0713, +51 (1) 424-6107. Rarely replies, and only to correspondence in Spanish.

Radio El Sol (Pucará), Avenida Jaén s/n, Distrito de Pucará, Jaén, Cajamarca, Peru.

Radio El Sol de los Andes, Jirón 2 de Mayo 257, Juliaca, Peru. Phone: +51 (54) 321-115. Fax: +51 (54) 322-981. Contact: Armando Alarcón Velarde.

Radio Estación Uno, Barrio Altos, Distrito de Pucará, Provincia Jaén, Nor Oriental del Marañón, Peru.

Radio Estudio 2000, Distrito Miguel Pardo Naranjos, Provincia de Rioja, Departamento de San Martín, Peru.

Radio Frecuencia VH ("La Voz de Celendín"; "RVC"), Jirón José Gálvez 1030, Celendín, Cajamarca, Peru. Contact: Fernando Vásquez Castro, Propietario.

Radio Frecuencia San Ignacio—*see* Frecuencia San Ignacio.

Radio Horizonte (Chachapoyas), Apartado Postal 69 (or Jirón Amazonas 1177), Chachapoyas, Amazonas, Peru. Phone: +51 (74) 757-793. Fax: +51 (74) 757 004. Contact: Sra. Rocío García Rubio, Ing. Electrónico, Directora; Percy Chuquizuta Alvarado, Locutor; María Montaldo Echaiz, Locutora; Marcelo Mozambite Chavarry, Locutor; Ing. María Dolores Gutiérrez Atienza, Administradora; Juan Nancy Ruíz de Valdez, Secretaria; Yoel Toro Morales, Técnico de Transmisión; or María Soledad Sánchez Castro, Administradora. Replies to correspondence in English, French, German and Spanish. $1 required.

Radio Horizonte (Chiclayo), Jirón Incanato 387 Altos, Distrito José Leonardo Ortiz, Chiclayo, Lambayeque, Peru. Phone: +51 (74) 252-917. Contact: Enrique Becerra Rojas, Owner and General Manager. Return postage required.

Radio Hualgayoc, Jirón San Martín s/n, Hualgayoc, Cajamarca, Peru. Contact: Máximo Zamora Medina, Director Propietario.

Radio Huamachuco (if reactivated), Jirón Bolívar 937, Huamachuco, La Libertad, Peru. Contact: Manuel D. Gil Gil, Director Propietario.

Radio Huanta 2000, Jirón Gervacio Santillana 455, Huanta, Peru. Phone: +51 (64) 932-105. Fax: +51 (64) 832 105. Contact: Ronaldo Sapaico Maravi, Departamento Técnico; or Sra. Lucila Orellana de Paz, Administradora. Free photo of staff. Return postage or $1 appreciated. Replies to correspondence in Spanish.

Radio Huarmaca, Av. Grau 454 (detrás de Inversiones La Loretana), Distrito de Huarmaca, Provincia de Huancabamba, Región Grau, Peru. Contact: Simón Zavaleta Pérez. Return postage helpful.

Radio Ilucán, Jirón Lima 290, Cutervo, Región Nororiental del Marañón, Peru. Phone: +51 (44) 737-010, +51 (44) 737-231. Contact: José Gálvez Salazar, Gerente Administrativo. $1 required. Replies occasionally to correspondence in Spanish.

Radio Imagen, Casilla de Correo 42, Tarapoto, San Martín, Peru; Jirón San Martín 328, Tarapoto, San Martín, Peru; or Apartado Postal 254, Tarapoto, San Martín, Peru. Phone: +51 (94) 522-696. Contact: Adith Chumbe Vásquez, Secretaria; or Jaime Ríos Tapullima, Gerente General. Replies irregularly to correspondence in Spanish. $1 or return postage helpful.

Radio Integración, Av. Seoane 200, Apartado Postal 57, Abancay, Departamento de Apurimac, Peru. Contact: Zenón Hernán Farfán Cruzado, Propietario.

Radio Internacional del Perú (when operating), Jirón Bolognesi 532, San Pablo, Cajamarca, Peru.

Radio Jaén (La Voz de la Frontera), Calle Mariscal Castilla 439, Jaén, Cajamarca, Peru. Contact: Luis A. Vilchez Ochoa, Administrador.

Radio JSV, Jirón Aguilar 742-744, Huánuco, Peru. Phone: +51 (64) 512-930. Return postage required.

Radio Juliaca (La Decana), Jirón Ramón Castilla 949, Apartado Postal 67, Juliaca, San Román, Puno, Peru. Phone: +51 (54) 321-372. Fax: +51 (54) 332-386. Contact: Robert Theran Escobedo, Director.

Radio JVL, Jirón Túpac Amaru 105, Consuelo, Distrito de San Pablo, Provincia de Bellavista, Departamento de San Martín, Peru. Contact: John Wiley Villanueva Lara—a student of electronic engineering—who currently runs the station, and whose initials make up the station name. Replies to correspondence in Spanish. Return Postage required.

Radio La Hora, Av. Garcilaso 180, Cusco, Peru. Phone: +51 (84) 225-615, +51 (84) 231-371. Contact: (general) Edmundo Montesinos G., Gerente; (reception reports) Carlos Gamarra Moscoso, who is also a DXer. Free stickers, pins, pennants and postcards of Cusco. Return postage required. Replies to correspondence in Spanish. Reception reports are best sent direct to Carlos Gamarra's home address: Av. Garcilaso 411, Wanchaq, Cusco, Peru. The station hopes to increase transmitter power to 2 kw if and when the economic situation improves.

Radio La Inmaculada, Parroquia La Inmaculada Concepción, Frente de la Plaza de Armas, Santa Cruz, Provincia de Santa Cruz, Departamento de Cajamarca, Peru. Phone: +51 (74) 714-051. Contact: Reverendo Padre Angel Jorge Carrasco, Gerente; or Gabino González Vera, Locutor.

Radio Lajas, Jirón Rosendo Mendívil 589, Lajas, Chota, Cajamarca, Nor Oriental del Marañón, Peru. Contact: Alfonso Medina Burga, Gerente Propietario.

Radio La Merced, Junín 163, La Merced, Junín, Peru. Phone: +51 (64) 531-199. Occasionally replies to correspondence in Spanish.

Radio La Oroya, Calle Lima 190, Tercer Piso Of. 3, Apartado Postal 88, La Oroya, Provincia de Yauli, Departamento de Junín, Peru. Phone: +51 (64) 391-401. Fax: +51 (64) 391 440. Email: rlofigu@net.cosapidata.com.pe. Web: www.cosapidata.com.pe/empresa/rlofigu/rlofigu.htm. Contact: Jacinto Manuel Figueroa Yauri, Gerente-Propietario. Free pennants. $1 or return postage necessary. Replies to correspondence in Spanish.

Radio La Voz, Andahuaylas, Apurímac, Peru. Contact: Lucio Fuentes, Director Gerente.

Radio La Voz de Chiriaco, Jirón Ricardo Palma s/n, Chiriaco, Distrito de Imaza, Provincia de Bagua, Departamento de Amazonas, Peru. Contact: Hildebrando López Pintado, Director; Santos Castañeda Cubas, Director Gerente; or Fidel Huamuro Curinambe, Técnico de Mantenimiento. $1 or return postage helpful.

Radio La Voz de Cutervo (if reactivated), Jirón María Elena Medina 644-650, Cutervo, Cajamarca, Peru.

Radio La Voz de Huamanga (if reactivated), Calle El Nazareno, 2do Pasaje No. 161, Ayacucho, Peru. Phone: +51 (64) 812-366. Contact: Sra. Aguida A. Valverde Gonzales. Free pennants and postcards.

Radio La Voz de la Selva, Jirón Abtao 255, Casilla de Correo 207, Iquitos, Loreto, Peru. Phone: +51 (94) 265-245. Fax: +51 (94) 264 531. Email: lvsradio@tvs.com.pe. Contact: Julia Jauregui Rengifo, Directora; Marcelino Esteban Benito, Director; Pedro Sandoval Guzmán, Announcer; or Mery Blas Rojas. Replies to correspondence in Spanish.

Radio La Voz de las Huarinjas, Barrio El Altillo s/n, Huancabamba, Piura, Peru. Phone: +51 (74) 473-126 or +51 (74) 473-259. Contact: Alfonso García Silva, Gerente Director (also the owner of the station); or Bill Yeltsin, Administrador. Replies to correspondence in Spanish.

Radio La Voz de Oxapampa, Av. Mullenbruck 469, Oxapampa, Pasco, Peru. Contact: Pascual Villafranca Guzmán, Director Propietario.

Radio La Voz de San Juan, 28 de Julio 420, Lonya Grande, Provincia de Utcubamba, Región Nororiental del Marañón, Peru. Contact: Prof. Víctor Hugo Hidrovo; or Edilberto Ortiz Chávez, Locutor. Formerly known as Radio San Juan.

Vatican Radio's transmission facilities are used not only for papal communication, but also to relay broadcasts from Swiss Radio International.
VR

Radio La Voz de Santa Cruz (if reactivated), Av. Zarumilla 190, Santa Cruz, Cajamarca, Peru.

Radio La Voz del Campesino, Av. Ramón Castilla s/n en la salida a Chiclayo, Huarmaca, Provincia de Huancabamba, Piura, Peru. Contact: Hernando Huancas Huancas.

Radio La Voz del Marañón (if reactivated), Jirón Bolognesi 130, Barrio La Alameda, Cajamarca, Nor Oriental del Marañón, Peru. Contact: Eduardo Díaz Coronado.

Radio Libertad de Junín, Cerro de Pasco 528, Apartado Postal 2, Junín, Peru. Phone: +51 (64) 344-026. Contact: Mauro Chaccha G., Director Gerente. Replies slowly to correspondence in Spanish. Return postage necessary.

Radio Líder, Portal Belén 115, 2do piso, Cusco, Peru. Contact: Mauro Calvo Acurio, Propietario.

Radio Lircay (when operating), Barrio Maravillas, Lircay, Provincia de Angaraes, Huancavelica, Peru.

Radio Los Andes (Huamachuco) (if reactivated), Pasaje Damián Nicolau 108-110, 2do piso, Huamachuco, La Libertad, Peru. Phone: +51 (44) 441-240 or +51 (44) 441-502. Fax: +51 (44) 441 214. Contact: Monseñor Sebastián Ramis Torerns.

Radio Los Andes (Huarmaca), Huarmaca, Provincia de Huancabamba, Región Grau, Peru. Contact: William Cerro Calderón.

Radio Luz y Sonido, Apartado Postal 280, Huánuco, Peru; (physical address) Jirón Dos de Mayo 1286, Oficina 205, Huánuco, Peru. Phone: +51 (64) 512-394 or +51 (64) 518-500. Fax: +51 (64) 511 985. Email: luz.sonido@hys.com.pe. Web: www.hys.com.pe/page/luzysonido/. Contact: (technical) Jorge Benavides Moreno; (nontechnical) Pedro Martínez Tineo, Director Ejecutivo; Lic. Orlando Bravo Jesús; or Seydel Saavedra Cabrera, Operador/Locutor. Return postage or $2 required. Replies to correspondence in Spanish, Italian and Portuguese. Sells video cassettes of local folk dances and religious and tourist themes.

Radio Madre de Dios, Daniel Alcides Carrión 385, Apartado Postal 37, Puerto Maldonado, Madre de Dios, Peru. Phone: +51 (84) 571-050. Fax: +51 (84) 571 018 or +51 (84) 573 542. Contact: (administration) Padre Rufino Lobo Alonso, Director; (general) Alcides Arguedas Márquez, Director del programa "Un Festival de Música Internacional," heard Mon-

days 0100 to 0200 World Time. Sr. Arguedas is interested in feedback for this letterbox program. Replies to correspondence in Spanish. $1 or return postage appreciated.

Radio Majestad, Calle Real 1033, Oficina 302, Huancayo, Junín, Peru.

Radio Marañón (if reactivated), Apartado Postal 50, Jaén, Cajamarca, Peru. Phone: +51 (44) 731-147, +51 (44) 732-580. Fax: +51 (44) 733 464. Email: (director) tavaral @telemail.telematic.edu.pe. Contact: Padre Luis Távara Martín, S.J., Director. Return postage necessary. May send free pennant. Replies slowly to correspondence in Spanish.

Radio Marginal, San Martín 257, Tocache, San Martín, Peru. Phone: +51 (94) 551-031. Rarely replies.

Radio Máster, Jirón 20 de Abril 308, Moyobamba, Departamento de San Martín, Peru. Contact: Américo Vásquez Hurtado, Director

Radio Melodía, San Camilo 501, Arequipa, Peru. Phone: +51 (54) 232-071, +51 (54) 232-327, +51 (54) 285-152. Fax: +51 (54) 237 312. Contact: Hermogenes Delgado Torres, Director; or Señora Elba Alvarez de Delgado. Replies to correspondence in Spanish.

Radio Mi Frontera, Calle San Ignacio 520, Distrito de Chirinos, Provincia de San Ignacio, Región Nor Oriental del Marañón, Peru.

Radio Moderna, Jirón Arequipa 323, 2do piso, Celendín, Cajamarca, Peru.

Radio Mundial Adventista, Colegio Adventista de Titicaca, Casilla 4, Juliaca, Peru. Currently on mediumwave only, but is expected to add shortwave sometime in the future.

Radio Mundo, Calle Tecte 245, Cusco, Peru. Phone: + 51 (84) 232-076. Fax: +51 (84) 233 076. Contact: Valentín Olivera Puelles, Gerente. Free postcards and stickers. Return postage necessary. Replies slowly to correspondence in Spanish.

Radio Municipal de Cangallo (when active), Concejo Provincial de Cangallo, Plaza Principal No. 02, Cangallo, Ayacucho, Peru. Contact: Nivardo Barbarán Agüero, Encargado Relaciones Públicas.

Radio Nacional del Perú
ADMINISTRATIVE OFFICE: Avenida José Gálvez 1040 Santa Beatriz, Lima, Peru. Fax: +51 (14) 433 8952. Contact: Henry

Aragón Ibarra, Director General; or Rafael Mego Carrascal, Jefatura de la Administración. Replies occasionally, by letter or listener-prepared verification card, to correspondence in Spanish. Return postage required.
STUDIO ADDRESS: Av. Petit Thouars 447, Lima, Peru.

Radio Naylamp, Avenida Andrés Avelino Cáceres 800, Lambayeque, Peru. Phone: +51 (74) 283-353. Contact: Dr. Juan José Grández Vargas, Director Gerente; or Delicia Coronel Muñoz, who is interested in receiving postcards and the like. Free stickers, pennants and calendars. Return postage necessary.

Radio Nor Andina, Jirón José Gálvez 602, Celendín, Cajamarca, Peru. Contact: Misael Alcántara Guevara, Gerente; or Víctor B. Vargas C., Departamento de Prensa. Free calendar. $1 required. Donations (registered mail best) sought for the Committee for Good Health for Children, headed by Sr. Alcántara, which is active in saving the lives of hungry youngsters in poverty-stricken Cajamarca Province. Replies irregularly to casual or technical correspondence in Spanish, but regularly to Children's Committee donors and helpful correspondence in Spanish.

Radio Nor Peruana, Emisora Municipal, Jirón Ortiz Arrieta 588, 1er. piso del Concejo Provincial de Chachapoyas, Chachapoyas, Amazonas, Peru. Contact: Carlos Poema, Administrador; or Edgar Villegas, program host for "La Voz de Chachapoyas," (Sundays, 1100-1300).

Radio Nueva Sensación, Cadena Radial Nuevo Siglo, Panamericana Norte km. 361, Urbanización Ricardo Palma, Chiclayo, Peru.

Radio Onda Imperial, Calle Sacsayhuamán K-10, Urbanización Manuel Prado, Cusco, Peru. Phone: +51 (84) 232-521, +51 (84) 233-032.

Radio Ondas del Huallaga, Jirón Leoncio Prado 723, Apartado Postal 343, Huánuco, Peru. Phone: +51 (64) 511-525, +51 (64) 512-428. Contact: Flaviano Llanos Malpartida, Representante Legal. $1 or return postage required. Replies to correspondence in Spanish.

Radio Ondas del [Río] Marañón, Jirón Amazonas 315, Distrito de Aramango, Provincia de Bagua, Departamento de Amazonas, Región Nororiental del Marañón, Peru. Contact: Agustín Tongod, Director Propietario. "Rio"—river—is sometimes, but not always, used in on-air identification.

Radio Ondas del Río Mayo, Jirón Huallaga 348, Nueva Cajamarca, San Martín, Peru. Phone: +51 (94) 556-006. Contact: Edilberto Lucío Peralta Lozada, Gerente; or Víctor Huaras Rojas, Locutor. Free pennants. Return postage helpful. Replies slowly to correspondence in Spanish.

Radio Ondas del Suroriente, Jirón Ricardo Palma 510, Quillabamba, La Convención, Cusco, Peru.

Radio Oriente, Vicariato Apostólico, Avenida Progreso 114, Yurimaguas, Loreto, Peru. Phone: +51 (94) 352-156. Fax: +51 (94) 352 128. Contact: (general) Sra. Elisa Cancino Hidalgo; or Juan Antonio López-Manzanares M., Director; (technical) Pedro Capo Moragues, Gerente Técnico. $1 or return postage required. Replies occasionally to correspondence in English, French, Spanish and Catalan.

Radio Origen, Acobamba, Departamento de Huancavelica, Peru.

Radio Paccha (if reactivated), Calle Mariscal Castilla 52, Paccha, Provincia de Chota, Departamento de Cajamarca, Peru.

Radio Panorama
STATION: Centro-poblado Recopampa, Distrito de Sorochuco, Provincia de Celendín, Departamento de Cajamarca, Región Autónoma del Marañón, Peru. Phone: +51 (44) 820-321. This

is a public phone booth, so the person who answers may not necessarily work at the station! Contact: Segundo Ayala Brione, Propietario.
ADDRESS OF SISTER STATION, RADIO LA VOZ DE LOS ANDES: Plaza de Armas, Distrito de Sorochuco, Provincia de Celendín, Departamento de Cajamarca, Región Autónoma del Marañón, Peru.

Radio Paucartambo, Emisora Municipal
STATION ADDRESS: Paucartambo, Cusco, Peru.
STAFFER ADDRESS: Manuel H. Loaiza Canal, Correo Central, Paucartambo, Cusco, Peru. Return postage or $1 required.

Radio Perú ("Perú, la Radio")
STUDIO ADDRESS: Jirón Atahualpa 191, San Ignacio, Región Nororiental del Marañón, Peru.
ADMINISTRATION: Avenida San Ignacio 493, San Ignacio, Región Nororiental del Marañón, Peru. Contact: Oscar Vásquez Chacón, Director General; or Idelso Vásquez Chacón, Director Propietario. Sometimes relays the FM outlet, "Estudio 97."

Radio Quillabamba, Jirón Ricardo Palma 432, Apartado Postal 76, Quillabamba, La Convención, Cusco, Peru. Phone: +51 (84) 281-002. Fax: +51 (84) 281 771. Contact: Padre Francisco Javier Panera, Director. Replies very irregularly to correspondence in Spanish.

Radio Real, Av. Ramón Castilla casi Limón y Nieto, Parque Leoncio Prado, Huarmaca, Provincia de Huancabamba, Piura, Peru.

Radio Regional, Jirón Grau s/n frente al Colegio Nuestra Señora del Carmen, Celendín, Cajamarca, Peru.

Radio Reina de la Selva, Jirón Ayacucho 944, Plaza de Armas, Chachapoyas, Región Nor Oriental del Marañón, Peru. Phone: +51 (74) 757-203. Contact: José David Reina Noriega, Gerente General; or Jorge Oscar Reina Noriega, Director General. Replies irregularly to correspondence in Spanish. Return postage necessary.

Radio San Antonio, Parroquia San Antonio de Padua, Plaza Principal s/n, Callalli, Departamento de Arequipa, Peru.

Radio San Francisco Solano, Parroquia de Sóndor, Calle San Miguel No. 207, Distrito de Sóndor, Huancabamba, Piura, Peru. Contact: Reverendo Padre Manuel José Rosas Castillo, Vicario Parroquial. Station operated by the Franciscan Fathers. Replies to correspondence in Spanish. $1 helpful.

Radio San Ignacio, Jirón Victoria 277, San Ignacio, Región Nororiental del Marañón, Peru. Contact: César Colunche Bustamante, Director Propietario; or his son, Fredy Colunche, Director de Programación.

Radio San Juan, Distrito de Aramango, Provincia de Bagua, Departamento de Amazonas, Región Nororiental del Marañón, Peru.

Radio San Juan, 28 de Julio 420, Lonya Grande, Provincia de Utcubamba, Región Nororiental del Marañón, Peru. Contact: Prof. Víctor Hugo Díaz Hidrovo; or Edilberto Ortiz Chávez, Locutor.

Radio San Miguel, Av. Huayna Cápac 146, Huánchac, Cusco, Peru. Contact: Sra. Catalina Pérez de Alencastre, Gerente General; or Margarita Mercado. Replies to correspondence in Spanish.

Radio San Miguel Arcángel, Jirón Bolívar 356, a media cuadra de la Plaza de Armas, Provincia de San Miguel, Cajamarca, Peru.

Radio San Miguel de El Faique, Distrito de El Faique, Provincia de Huancabamba, Departamento de Piura, Peru.

Radio San Nicolás, Jirón Amazonas 114, Rodríguez de Mendoza, Peru. Contact: Juan José Grández Santillán, Gerente;

or Violeta Grández Vargas, Administradora. Return postage necessary.

Radio Santa Rosa, Jirón Camaná 170, Casilla 4451, Lima 01, Peru. Phone: +51 (1) 427-7488. Fax: +51 (1) 426 9219. Email: santarosa@viaexpresa.com.pe. Web: www.viaexpresa.com.pe/santarosa/santarosa.htm. Contact: Padre Juan Sokolich Alvarado, Director; or Lucy Palma Barreda. Free stickers and pennants. $1 or return postage necessary. 180-page book commemorating station's 35th anniversary $10. Replies to correspondence in Spanish.

Radio Santiago, Municipalidad Distrital de Río Santiago, Puerto Galilea, Provincia de Condorcanqui, Amazonas, Peru. Contact: Juan Tuchia Oscate, Alcalde Distrital; Sara Sánchez Cubas, Locutora Comercial; or Guillermo Gómez García, Director. Free pennants and postcards. Return postage necessary. Replies to correspondence in Spanish.

Radio Satélite, Jirón Cutervo No. 543, Provincia de Santa Cruz, Cajamarca, Peru. Phone: +51 (74) 714-074, +51 (74) 714-169. Contact: Sabino Llamo Chávez, Gerente. Free tourist brochure. $1 or return postage required. Replies to correspondence in Spanish.

Radio Selecciones, Chuquibamba, Provincia de Condesuyos, Arequipa, Peru.

Radio Sicuani, Jirón 2 de Mayo 212, Sicuani, Canchis, Cusco, Peru; or Apartado Postal 45, Sicuani, Peru. Phone: +51 (84) 351-136 or +51 (84) 351-698. Fax: +51 (84) 351 697. Email: cecosda@mail.cosapidata.com.pe. Contact: Mario Ochoa Vargas, Director.

Radio Soledad, Centro Minero de Retama, Distrito de Parcoy, Provincia de Pataz, La Libertad, Peru. Contact: Vicente Valdivieso, Locutor. Return postage necessary.

Radio Sudamérica, Jirón Ramón Castilla 491, tercer nivel, Plaza de Armas, Cutervo, Cajamarca, Peru. Phone: +51 (74) 736-090 or +51 (74) 737-443. Contact: Jorge Luis Paredes Guerra, Administrador; or Amadeo Mario Muñoz Guivar, Propietario.

Radio Superior (Bolívar), Jirón San Martín 229, Provincia de Bolívar, Departamento de La Libertad, Peru.

Radio Tacna, Aniceto Ibarra 436, Casilla de Correo 370, Tacna, Peru. Phone: +51 (54) 714-871. Fax: +51 (54) 723 745. Email: radiotac@principal.unjbg.edu.pe. Web: http://principal.unjbg.edu.pe/radio/radta.html. Contact: (nontechnical and technical) Ing. Alfonso Cáceres Contreras, Sub-Gerente/Jefe Técnico; (administration) Yolanda Vda. de Cáceres C., Directora Gerente. Free stickers and samples of *Correo* local newspaper. $1 or return postage helpful. Audio cassettes of Peruvian and other music $2 plus postage. Replies irregularly to correspondence in English and Spanish.

Radio Tawantinsuyo, Av. Sol 806, Cusco, Peru. Phone: +51 (84) 226-955, +51 (84) 228-411. Has a very attractive QSL card, but only replies occasionally to correspondence, which should be in Spanish.

Radio Tarma, Jirón Molino del Amo 167, Apartado Postal 167, Tarma, Peru. Phone/fax: +51 (64) 321 167 or +51 (64) 321 510. Contact: Mario Monteverde Pomareda, Gerente General. Sometimes sends 100 Inti banknote in return when $1 enclosed. Free stickers. $1 or return postage required. Replies irregularly to correspondence in Spanish.

Radio Tayacaja, Correo Central, Distrito de Pampas, Tayacaja, Huancavelica, Peru. Phone: +51 (64) 22-02-17, Anexo 238. Contact: (general) J. Jorge Flores Cárdenas; (technical) Ing. Larry Guido Flores Lezama. Free stickers and pennants. Replies to correspondence in Spanish. Hopes to replace transmitter.

Radio Tingo María (when operating), Jirón Callao 115 (or Av. Raimondi No. 592), Casilla de Correo 25, Tingo María, Leoncio Prado, Departamento de Huánuco, Peru. Contact: Gina A. de la Cruz Ricalde, Administradora; or Ricardo Abad Vásquez, Gerente. Free brochures. $1 required. Replies slowly to correspondence in Spanish.

Radio Tropical, Casilla de Correo 31, Tarapoto, Peru. Phone: +51 (94) 522-083, +51 (94) 524-689. Fax: +51 (94) 522 155. Contact: Mery A. Rengifo Tenazoa, Secretaria; or Luis F. Mori Reátegui, Gerente. Free stickers, occasionally free pennants, and station history booklet. $1 or return postage required. Replies occasionally to correspondence in Spanish.

Radio Unión, Apartado Postal 833, Lima 27, Peru; or (street address) Avenida Central 717 - Piso 12, San Isidro, Lima 27, Peru. Phone: +51 (1) 440-2093. Fax: +51 (1) 440 7594. Email: runion@amauta.rcp.net.pe. Contact: Carlos A. González Solimano, Director Gerente; Juan Zubiaga Santiváñez, Gerente; Natividad Albizuri Salinas, Secretaria; or Juan Carlos Sologuren, Dpto. de Administración, who collects stamps. Free satin pennants and stickers. IRC required, and enclosing used or new stamps from various countries is especially appreciated. Replies irregularly to correspondence and tape recordings, with Spanish preferred.

Radio Uno, Av. Balta 1480, 3er piso, frente al Mercado Modelo, Chiclayo, Peru. Phone: +51 (74) 224-967. Contact: Luz Angela Romero, Directora del noticiero "Encuentros"; Plutarco Chamba Febres, Director Propietario; Juan Vargas, Administrador; or Filomena Saldívar Alarcón, Pauta Comercial. Return postage required.

Radio Victoria, Jr.Reynel 320, Mirones Bajo, Lima 1, Peru. Phone: +51 (1) 336-5448. Fax: +51 (1) 427 1195. Email: soermi@mixmail.com. Contact: Marta Flores Ushinahua. This station is owned by the Brazilian-run Pentecostal Church "Dios Es Amor," with local headquarters at Av. Arica 248, Lima; phone: +51 (1) 330-8023. Their program "La Voz de la Liberación" is produced locally and aired over numerous Peruvian shortwave stations.

Radio Virgen del Carmen ("RVC"), Jirón Virrey Toledo 466, Huancavelica, Peru. Phone: +51 (64) 752-740. Contact: Rvdo. Samuel Morán Cárdenas, Gerente.

Radiodifusoras Huancabamba, Calle Unión 409, Huancabamba, Piura, Peru. Phone: +51 (74) 473-233. Contact: Federico Ibáñez M., Director.

Radiodifusoras Paratón, Jirón Alfonso Ugarte 1090, contiguo al Parque Leoncio Prado, Huarmaca, Provincia de Huancabamba, Piura, Peru. Contact: Prof. Hernando Huancas Huancas, Gerente General; or Prof. Rómulo Chincay Huamán, Gerente Administrativo.

PHILIPPINES   World Time +8

NOTE: Philippine stations sometimes send publications with lists of Philippine young ladies seeking "pen pal" courtships.

DUR2—Philippine Broadcasting Service (when operating), Bureau of Broadcasting Services, Media Center, Bohol Avenue, Quezon City, Philippines. Relays DZRB Radio ng Bayan and DZRM Radio Manila.

☞Far East Broadcasting Company—FEBC Radio International (External Service)

MAIN OFFICE: P.O. Box 1, Valenzuela, Metro Manila, Philippines 0560. Phone: (general) +63 (2) 292-5603 or +63 (2) 292-9403; (frequency management) +63 (2) 292-5603. Fax: +63 (2) 292 9430; +63 (2) 291 4982, but lacks funds to provide faxed replies; (Frequency Management) +63 (2) 294 0859.

Email: febcomphil@febc.org.ph; (Peter McIntyre) pm@febc.jfm.org.ph; (Larry Podmore) lpodmore@febc.jmf.org.ph; (Peter Hsu) phsu@febc.org. Web: www.febc.org; www.febc.ph. Contact: (general) Peter McIntyre, Manager, International Operations Division; (administration) Carlos Peña, Managing Director; (engineering) Ing. Renato Valentin, Frequency Manager; Larry Podmore, IBG Chief Engineer; or Peter Hsu, International Frequency Manager. Free stickers and calendar cards. Three IRCs appreciated for airmail reply. Plans to add a new 100 kW shortwave transmitter.

NEW DELHI BUREAU, NONTECHNICAL: c/o FEBA, Box 6, New Delhi-110 001, India.

Far East Broadcasting Company (Domestic Service), Bgy. Bayanan Baco Radyo DZB2, c/o ONF Calapan, Orr. Mindoro, Philippines 5200. Contact: (general) Dangio Onday, Program Supervisor/OIC; (technical) Danilo Flores, Broadcast Technician.

Radyo Pilipinas, the Voice of Democracy, Philippine Broadcasting Service, 4th Floor, PIA Building, Visayas Avenue, Quezon City 1100, Metro Manila, Philippines. Phone: (general) +63 (2) 924-2620; +63 (2) 920-3963; or +63 (2) 924-2548; (engineering) +63 (2) 924-2268. Fax: +63 (2) 924 2745. Contact: (nontechnical) Evelyn Salvador Agato, Officer-in-Charge; Mercy Lumba; Leo Romano, Producer, "Listeners and Friends"; or Richard G. Lorenzo, Production Coordinator; (technical) Danilo Alberto, Supervisor; or Mike Pangilinan, Engineer. Free postcards and stickers.

Radio Veritas Asia

STUDIOS AND ADMINISTRATIVE HEADQUARTERS: P.O. Box 2642, Quezon City, 1166 Philippines. Phone: +63 (2) 939-0011 to14, +63 (2) 939-4465, +63 (2) 939-7476 or +63 (2) 939-4692. Fax: (general) +63 (2) 938 1940; (Frequency and Monitoring) +63 (2) 939 7556. Email: (Program Dept.) veritas @mnl.sequel.net; (technical) info@radio-veritas.org.ph; or fmrva@pworld.net.ph. Web: www.radio-veritas.org.ph; www.pworld.net.ph/user/fmrva/. Contact: (administration) Ms. Erlinda G. So, Manager; (general) Ms. Cleofe R. Labindao, Audience Relations Supervisor; Mrs. Regie de Juan Galindez; or Msgr. Pietro Nguyen Van Tai, Program Director; (technical) Ing. Floremundo L. Kiguchi, Technical Director; Ing. Honorio L. Llavore, Assistant Technical Director; or Frequency and Monitoring Department. Free caps, T-shirts, stickers, pennants, rulers, pens, postcards and calendars. Return postage appreciated. *TRANSMITTER SITE:* Radio Veritas Asia, Palauig, Zambales, Philippines. Contact: Fr. Hugo Delbaere, CICM, Technical Consultant.

BRUSSELS BUREAUS AND MAIL DROPS: Catholic Radio and Television Network, 32-34 Rue de l' Association, B-1000 Brussels, Belgium; or UNDA, 12 Rue de l'Orme, B-1040 Brussels, Belgium.

Voice of Friendship—*see* FEBC Radio International.

PIRATE

Pirate radio stations are usually one-person operations airing home-brew entertainment and/or iconoclastic viewpoints. In order to avoid detection by the authorities, they tend to appear irregularly, with little concern for the niceties of conventional program scheduling. Most are found in Europe chiefly on weekends, and mainly during evenings in North America, often just above 6200 kHz, just below 7000 kHz and just above 7375 kHz. These *sub rosa* stations and their addresses are subject to unusually abrupt change or termination, sometimes as a result of forays by radio authorities.

Two worthy sources of current addresses and other information on American pirate radio activity are: *The Pirate Radio Directory*, by Andrew Yoder and George Zeller [Tiare Publications, P.O. Box 493, Lake Geneva WI 53147 USA, U.S. toll-free phone 1-800-420-0579; or for specific inquiries, contact author Zeller directly: (fax) +1 (216) 696 0770; (email) George.Zeller @acclink.com], an excellent annual reference; and A*C*E, P.O. Box 12112, Norfolk VA 23541 USA (email: pradio@erols.com; Web: www.frn.net/ace/), a club which publishes a periodical ($20/year U.S., US$21 Canada, $27 elsewhere) for serious pirate radio enthusiasts.

For Europirate DX news, try:

SRSNEWS, Swedish Report Service, Ostra Porten 29, SE-442 54 Ytterby, Sweden. Email: srs@ice.warp.slink.se. Web: www-pp.kdt.net/jonny/index.html.

Pirate Connection, P.O. Box 4580, SE-203 20 Malmoe, Sweden; or P.O. Box 7085, Kansas City, Missouri 64113, USA. Phone: (home, Sweden) +46 (40) 611-1775; (mobile, Sweden) +46 (70) 581-5047. Email: etoxspz@eto.ericsson.se, xtdspz@lmd.ericsson.se or spz@exallon.se. Web: www-pp.hogia.net/jonny/pc. Six issues annually for about $23. Related to SRSNEWS, above.

Pirate Chat, 21 Green Park, Bath, Avon, BA1 1HZ, United Kingdom.

FRS Goes DX, P.O. Box 2727, NL-6049 ZG Herten, Holland. Email: FRSH@pi.net; or peter.verbruggen@tip.nl. Web: http://home.pi.net/~freak55/home.htm.

Free-DX, 3 Greenway, Harold Park, Romford, Essex, RM3 OHH, United Kingdom.

FRC-Finland, P.O. Box 82, FIN-40101 Jyvaskyla, Finland.

Pirate Express, Postfach 220342, Wuppertal, Germany.

For up-to-date listener discussions and other pirate-radio information on the Internet, the usenet URLs are: alt.radio.pirate and rec.radio.pirate.

POLAND   World Time +1 (+2 midyear)

Radio Maryja, ul. Żwirki i Wigury 80, PL-87-100 Toruń, Poland. Phone: (general) +48 (56) 655-2361; (studio) +48 (56) 655-2333, +48 (56) 655-2366. Fax: +48 (56) 655 2362. Email: radio @radiomaryja.pl; (Kabulska) anna.kabulska@radiomaryja.pl. Web: (includes RealAudio) www.radiomaryja.pl; (Windows Media only) http://nyas.radiomaria.org/mediaserver/index.htm (click the Poland button on the world map). Contact: Father Tadeusz Rydzk, Dyrektor; Father Jacek Cydzik; or Anna Kabulska, Secretary. Polish preferred, but also replies to correspondence in English. Transmits via facilities in Samara, Russia.

Radio Polonia

STATION: External Service, P.O. Box 46, PL-00-977 Warsaw, Poland. Phone: (general) +48 (22) 645-9305 or +48 (22) 444-123; (English Section) +48 (22) 645-9262; (German Section) +48 (22) 645-9333; (placement liaison) +48 (2) 645-9002. Fax: (general and administration) +48 (22) 645 5917 or +48 (22) 645 5919; (placement liaison) +48 (2) 645 5906. Email (general): piatka@radio.com.pl; (Polish Section) polonia @radio.com.pl; (English Section) english.section @radio.com.pl; (German Section) deutsche.redaktion @radio.com.pl. Web: www.radio.com.pl/polonia/; (RealAudio in English and Polish) www.wrn.org/ondemand/poland.html. Contact: (general) Rafał Kiepuszewski, Head, English Section and Producer, "Postbag"; Peter Gentle, Presenter, "Postbag"; or Ann Flapan, Corresponding Secretary; (administration) Jerzy M. Nowakowski, Managing Director; Wanda Samborska, Managing Director; Bogumiła Berdychowska, Deputy Managing Director; or Maciej Lętowski, Executive Manager. On-air Polish language course with free printed material. Free stickers, pens, key rings and possibly T-shirts depending on financial cutbacks. DX Listeners' Club.

TRANSMISSION AUTHORITY: PAR (National Radio-communication Agency), ul. Kasprzaka 18/20, PL-01-211 Warsaw, Poland. Phone: +48 (22) 608-8139/40, +48 (22) 608-8174 or +48 (22) 608-8191. Fax: +48 (22) 608 8195. Email: the format is initial.last name@par.gov.pl, so to reach, say, Filomena Grodzicka, it would be f.grodzicka@par.gov.pl. Contact: Mrs. Filomena Grodzicka, Head of BC Section; Lukasz Trzos; Mrs. Katalin Jaros; Ms. Urszula Rzepa or Jan Kondej. Responsible for coordinating Radio Polonia's frequencies.

Radio Racja

SHORTWAVE: Email: r101@user.unibel.by. Web: www.racja.pl. BIALYSTOK FM STATION: Osrodek Radiowy w Bialymstoku, ul. Ciapla 1/7. PL-15-472 Bialystok, Poland. Contact: Wiktor Stachwiuk, Director.

Broadcasts in Belarusian and is opposed to President Lukashenko. The shortwave broadcasts are a joint Minsk-Warsaw production, and transmitted from Warsaw. The Bialystok station is part of the same organization, but has different programs which are intended for the Belarusian community in eastern Poland.

PORTUGAL   World Time exactly (+1 midyear); Azores World Time –1 (World Time midyear)

📻**RDP Internacional—Rádio Portugal**, Apartado 1011, 1001 Lisbon, Portugal; (street address) Av. Eng. Duarte Pacheco 26, 1070-110 Lisbon, Portugal. Phone: (general) +351 (21) 382-0000; (engineering) +351 (21) 382-2000. Fax: (general) +351 (21) 382 0165; (engineering) +351 (21) 387 1381. Email: (general) rdpinternacional@rdp.pt; (director) marquesalmeida@rdp.pt; (reception reports and listener correspondence) isabelsaraiva@rdp.pt, or christianehaupt@rdp.pt; (frequency management) teresaabreu@rdp.pt, or paulacarvalho@rdp.pt. Web: (includes Windows Media) www.rdp.pt/internacional/. Contact: (administration) José Manuel Nunes, Chairman; Isabel Saraiva or Christiane Haupt, Listener's Service Department; or Jaime Marques de Almeida, Director; (technical) Eng. Francisco Mascarenhas, Technical Director; Teresa Abreu, Frequency Manager; or Ms. Paula Carvalho. Free stickers. May also send literature from the Portuguese National Tourist Office.

Radio Trans Europe (transmission facilities), 6° esq., Rua Braamcamp 84, 1200 Lisbon, Portugal. Transmitter located at Sines.

QATAR   World Time +3

Qatar Broadcasting Service, P.O. Box 3939, Doha, Qatar. Phone: (director) +974 86-48-05; (under secretary) +974 864-823; (engineering) +974 864-518; (main Arabic service audio feed) +974 895-895. Fax: +974 822 888 or +974 831 447. Contact: Jassim Mohamed Al-Qattan, Head of Public Relations. May send booklet on Qatar Broadcasting Service. Occasionally replies, and return postage helpful.

TECHNICAL OFFICE: Qatar Radio and Television Corporation, P.O. Box 1836, Doha, Qatar. Phone: +974 831-443, +974 864-057 or +974 894-613. Fax: +974 831 447. Contact: Hassan Al-Mass or Issa Ahmed Al-Hamadi, Head of Frequency Management.

ROMANIA   World Time +2 (+3 midyear)

📻**Radio România Actualitati**, Societatea Româna de Radiodifuziune, 60-62 Berthelot St., RO-70747 Bucharest, Romania. Phone: +40 (1) 615-9350. Fax: +40 (1) 223 2612. Web: (RealAudio only) www.ituner.com.

📻**Radio România International**

STATION: 60-62 Berthelot St., RO-70747 Bucharest, Romania; P.O. Box 111, RO-70756 Bucharest, Romania; or Romanian embassies worldwide. Phone: (general) +40 (1) 222-2556, +40 (1) 303-1172, +40 (1) 303-1488 or +40 (1) 312-3645; (English Department) +40 (1) 303-1357; (engineering) +40 (1) 303-1193. Fax: (general) +40 (1) 223 2613 [if no connection, try via the office of the Director General of Radio România, but mark fax "Pentru RRI"; that fax is +40 (1) 222 5641]; (Engineering Services) +40 (1) 312 1056/7 or +40 (1) 615 6992. Email: (general) rri@rri.ro; (English Service) engl@rri.ro; (Nisipeanu) emisie@radio.ror.ro; (Ianculescu) rianculescu@rri.ro. Web: (includes RealAudio) www.rri.ro. Contact: (communications in English or Romanian) Dan Balamat, "Listeners' Letterbox"; or Ioana Masariu, Coordinating Producer, English Service; (radio enthusiasts' issues, English only) "DX Mailbox," English Department; (communications in French or Romanian) Doru Vasile Ionescu, Deputy General Director; (listeners' letters) Giorgiana Zachia; or Dan Dumitrescu; (technical) Sorin Floricu; Radu Ianculescu, Frequency Monitoring Engineer; or Marius Nisipeanu, Engineering Services. Free stickers, pennants, posters, pins and assorted other items. Can provide supplementary materials for "Romanian by Radio" course on audio cassettes. Listeners' Club. Annual contests. Replies slowly but regularly. Concerns about frequency management should be directed to the PTT (see below), with copies to the Romanian Autonomous Company (see farther below) and to a suitable official at RRI.

TRANSMISSION AND FREQUENCY MANAGEMENT, PTT: General Directorate of Regulations, Ministry of Communications, 14a Al. Libertatii, R-70060 Bucharest, Romania. Phone: +40 (1) 400-1312 or +40 (1) 400-177. Fax: +40 (1) 400 1230. Email: sfloricu@radio.ror.ro. Contact: Mrs. Elena Danila, Head of Frequency Management Department.

TRANSMISSION AND FREQUENCY MANAGEMENT, AUTONOMOUS COMPANY: Romanian Autonomous Company for Radio Communications, 14a Al. Libertatii, R-70060 Bucharest, Romania. Phone: +40 (1) 400-1072. Fax: +40 (1) 400 1228 or +40 (1) 335 5965. Contact: Mr. Marian Ionitá.

RUSSIA   (Times given for republics, oblasts and krays):

- World Time +2 (+3 midyear) Kaliningradskaya;
- World Time +3 (+4 midyear) Arkhangel'skaya (incl. Nenetskiy), Astrakhanskaya, Belgorodskaya, Bryanskaya, Ivanovskaya, Kaluzhskaya, Karelia, Kirovskaya, Komi, Kostromskaya, Kurskaya, Lipetskaya, Moscovskaya, Murmanskaya, Nizhegorodskaya, Novgorodskaya, Orlovskaya, Penzenskaya, Pskovskaya, Riazanskaya, Samarskaya, Sankt-Peterburgskaya, Smolenskaya, Tambovskaya, Tulskaya, Tverskaya, Vladimirskaya, Vologodskaya, Volgogradskaya, Voronezhskaya, Yaroslavskaya;
- World Time +4 (+5 midyear) Checheno-Ingushia, Chuvashia, Dagestan, Kabardino-Balkaria, Kalmykia, Krasnodarskiy, Mari-Yel, Mordovia, Severnaya Osetia, Stavropolskiy, Tatarstan, Udmurtia;
- World Time +5 (+6 midyear) Bashkortostan, Chelyabinskaya,

Kurganskaya, Orenburgskaya, Permskaya, Yekaterinburgskaya, Tyumenskaya;

- World Time +6 (+7 midyear) Altayskiy, Omskaya;
- World Time +7 (+8 midyear) Kemerovskaya, Krasnoyarskiy (incl. Evenkiyskiy), Novosibirskaya, Tomskaya, Tuva;
- World Time +8 (+9 midyear) Buryatia, Irkutskaya;
- World Time +9 (+10 midyear) Amurskaya, Chitinskaya, Sakha (West);
- World Time +10 (+11 midyear) Khabarovskiy, Primorskiy, Sakha (Center), Yevreyskaya;
- World Time +11 (+12 midyear) Magadanskaya (exc. Chukotskiy), Sakha (East), Sakhalinskaya;
- World Time +12 (+13 midyear) Chukotskiy, Kamchatskaya, Koryakskiy;
- World Time +13 (+14 midyear) all points east of longtitude 172.30 E.

VERIFICATION OF STATIONS USING TRANSMITTERS IN ST. PETERSBURG AND KALININGRAD: Transmissions of certain world band stations—such as the Voice of Russia, Radio Rossii and China Radio International—when emanating from transmitters located in St. Petersburg and Kaliningrad, may be verified directly from: World Band Verification QSL Service, Centre for Broadcasting and Radio Communications No. 2 (CRR-2), ul. Akademika Pavlova 13A, 197376 St. Petersburg, Russia. Fax: +7 (812) 234 2971 during working hours. Contact: Mikhail V. Sergeyev, Chief Engineer; or Mikhail Timofeyev, verifier. Free stickers. Two IRCs required for a reply, which upon request includes a copy of "Broadcast Schedule," which gives transmission details (excluding powers) for all transmissions emanating from three distinct transmitter locations: Kaliningrad-Bolshakovo, St. Petersburg and St. Petersburg-Popovka. This organization—which has 26 shortwave, three longwave, 15 mediumwave AM and nine FM transmitters—relays broadcasts for clients for the equivalent of about $0.70-1.00 per kW/hour.

Government Radio Agencies

C.I.S. FREQUENCY MANAGEMENT ENGINEERING OFFICE: The Main Centre for Control of Broadcasting Networks, 7 Nikolskaya Str., 103012 Moscow, Russia. Phone: +7 (095) 298-3302. Fax: +7 (095) 956 7546 or +7 (095) 921 1624. Email: (Titov) titov@mccbn.ru; or titov@nsl.ru. Web: www.mccbn.ru. Contact: (general) Mrs. Antonia Ostakhova, Interpreter, Mrs. Nina Bykova; or Ms. Margarita Ovetchkina; (administration) Anatoliy T. Titov, Chief Director. This office is responsible for the operation of radio broadcasting in the Russian Federation, as well as for frequency usage of transmitters throughout much of the C.I.S. Correspondence should be concerned only with significant technical observations or engineering suggestions concerning frequency management improvement—not regular requests for verifications. Correspondence in Russian preferred, but English accepted.

CENTRE FOR BROADCASTING AND RADIO COMMUNICATIONS NO. 2 (GPR-2)—see VERIFICATION OF STATIONS USING TRANSMITTERS IN ST. PETERSBURG AND KALININGRAD, above.

STATE RADIO COMPANY: AS Radioagency Co., Pyatnitskaya 25, 113326 Moscow, Russia. Phone: (Khlebnikov and Petrunicheva) +7 (095) 233-6474; (Komissarova) +7 (095) 233-6660; (Staviskaia) +7 (095) 233-7003. Fax: (Khlebnikov, Petrunicheva and Komissarova) +7 (095) 233 1342; (Staviskaia) +7 (095) 230 2828 or +7 (095) 233 7648. Contact: Valentin Khlebnikov, Mrs. Maris Petrunicheva, Mrs. Lyudmila Komissarova or Mrs. Rachel Staviskaia.

STATE TRANSMISSION AUTHORITY: Russian Ministry of Tele-communication, ul. Tverskaya 7, 103375 Moscow, Russia. Phone: +7 (095) 201-6568. Fax: +7 (095) 292 7086 or +7 (095) 292 7128. Contact: Anatoly C. Batiouchkine.

STATE TV AND RADIO COMPANY: Russian State TV and Radio Company, ul. Yamskogo 5, Polya 19/21, 125124 Moscow, Russia. Phone: +7 (095) 213-1054, +7 (095) 213-1054 or +7 (095) 250-0511. Fax: +7 (095) 250 0105. Contact: Ivan Sitilenlov.

Adygey Radio (Radio Maykop), ul. Zhukovskogo 24, 352700 Maykop, Republic of Adygeya, Russia. Contact: A.T. Kerashev, Chairman. English accepted but Russian preferred. Return postage helpful.

Amur Radio, GTRK Amur, per Svyatitelya Innokentiya 15, 675000 Blagoveschensk, Russia. Contact: V.I. Kal'chenko, Chief Engineer.

Arkhangel'sk Radio, GTRK "Pomorye," ul. Popova 2, 163000 Arkhangel'sk, Arkhangel'skaya Oblast, Russia; or U1PR, Valentin G. Kalasnikov, ul. Suvorov 2, kv. 16, Arkhangel'sk, Arkhangel'skaya Oblast, Russia. Replies irregularly to correspondence in Russian.

Bashkortostan Radio, ul. Gafuri 9/1, 450076 Ufa, Bashkortostan, Russia. Phone: +7 (3472) 220-943 or +7 (3472) 223-820. Fax: +7 (3472) 232 545. Web: http://info.ufanet.ru/radio/bashkort.htm. Replies irregularly to correspondence in Russian.

Buryat Radio, Dom Radio, ul. Erbanova 7, 670013 Ulan-Ude, Republic of Buryatia, Russia. Contact: Z.A. Telin; Mrs. M.V. Urbaeva, 1st Vice-Chairman; or L.S. Shikhanova.

Chita Radio (if reactivated), ul. Kostushko-Grigorovicha 27, 672090 Chita, Chitinskaya Oblast, Russia. Contact: (technical) V.A. Klimov, Chief Engineer; V.A. Moorzin, Head of Broadcasting; or A.A. Anufriyev.

Evenkiyskaya Radio, ul. 50 let Oktyabrya 28, 663370 Tura, Evenkiyskiy Avt. Okrug, Russia. Contact: B. Yuryev, Engineer. Replies to correspondence in Russian.

Islamskaya Volna (Islamic Wave), Islamic Center of Moscow Region, Moscow Jami Mosque, Vypolzov per. 7, 129090 Moscow, Russia; or Pyatnitskaya ulitsa 25, 133326 Moscow, Russia. Phone: +7 (095) 233-6423/6, +7 (095) 233-6629 or +7 (095) 281-4904. Contact: Sheikh Ravil Gainutdin. Return postage necessary.

Kabardino-Balkar Radio (Radio Nalchik), ul. Nogmova 38, 360000 Nalchik, Republic of Kabardino-Balkariya, Russia. Contact: Kamal Makitov, Vice-Chairman. Replies to correspondence in Russian.

Kala Atouraya (Voice of Assyria) (when active), ul.Pyatnitskaya 25, 113326 Moscow. Contact: Marona Arsanis, Chief Editor; or Roland T. Bidjamov, Editor. Return postage helpful. Replies irregularly.

Kamchatka Radio, RTV Center, Dom Radio, ul. Sovietskaya 62-G, 683000 Petropavlovsk-Kamchatskiy, Kamchatskaya Oblast, Russia. Contact: A. Borodin, Chief OTK; or V.I. Aibabin. $1 required. Replies in Russian to correspondence in Russian or English. Currently inactive on shortwave, apart from a special program for fishermen—*see* next item.

Kamchatka Rybatskaya—a special program for fishermen off the coasts of China, Japan and western North America; *see* "Kamchatka Radio," above, for contact details.

Khabarovsk Radio, RTV Center, ul. Lenina 71, 680013 Khabarovsk, Khabarovskiy Kray, Russia; or Dom Radio, pl. Slavy, 682632 Khabarovsk, Khabarovskiy Kray, Russia. Contact: (technical) V.N. Kononov, Glavnyy Inzhener.

Khanty-Mansiysk Radio, Dom Radio, ul. Mira 7, 626200 Khanty-Mansiysk, Khanty-Mansyiskiy Avt. Okrug,

Tyumenskaya Oblast, Russia. Contact: (technical) Vladimir Sokolov, Engineer.

Koryak Radio, ul. Obukhova 4, 684620 Palana, Koryakskiy Khrebet, Russia.

Krasnoyarsk Radio, Krasnoyarskaya GTRK, "Tsentr Rossii," ul. Mechnikova 44A, 666001 Krasnoyarsk 28, Krasnoyarskiy Kray, Russia. Contact: Valeriy Korotchenko; or Anatoliy A. Potehin, RAØAKE. Free local information booklets in English/ Russian. Replies in Russian to correspondence in English or Russian. Return postage helpful.

Magadan Radio, RTV Center, ul. Kommuny 8/12, 685013 Magadan, Magadanskaya Oblast, Russia. Contact: Viktor Loktionov or V.G. Kuznetsov. Return postage helpful. May reply to correspondence in Russian.

Mariy Radio, Mari Yel, ul. Osipenko 50, 424014 Yoshkar-Ola, Russia.

Mayak—*see* Radiostantsiya Mayak.

Murmansk Radio, Sopka Varnichnaya, 183042 Murmansk, Murmanskaya Oblast, Russia; or RTV Center, Sopka Varnichaya, 183042 Murmansk, Murmanskaya Oblast, Russia. Phone: +7 (8152) 561-527. Phone/Fax: +7 (8152) 459-770. Fax: +7 (8152) 231 913. Email: tvmurman@sampo.ru; tvmurman@sampo.karelia.ru; murmantv@com.mels.ru. Web: www.sampo.ru/~tvmurman/radio/rmain.html. Contact: D. Perederi (chairman).

Perm Radio, Permskaya Gosudarstvennaya Telekinoradiokompaniya, ul. Technicheskaya 21, 614600 Perm, Permskaya Oblast, Russia; or ul. Krupskoy 26, 614060 Perm, Permskaya Oblast, Russia. Contact: M. Levin, Senior Editor; or A. Losev, Acting Chief Editor.

Qala Atouraya—*see* Kala Atouraya.

Radio Maykop—*see* Adygey Radio, above.

Radio Mix-Master, Office 1, ul. Oktyabr'skaya 20/1, 677027 Yakutsk, Respublika Sakha, Russia. Phone: +7 (4112) 420-302.

Radio Nalchik—*see* Radio Kabardino-Balkar, above.

Radio Rossii (Russia's Radio), Room 121, ul. Yamskogo 5-A, Polya 19/21, 125124 Moscow, Russia. Phone: +7 (095) 213-1054, +7 (095) 250-0511 or +7 (095) 251-4050. Fax: +7 (095) 250 0105, +7 (095) 233 6449 or +7 (095) 214 4767. Web: (Windows Media) http://rtr.relline.ru/radiorus. Contact: Sergei Yerofeyev, Director of International Operations [sic]; or Sergei Davidov, Director. Free English-language information sheet. For verification of reception from transmitters located in St. Petersburg and Kaliningrad, *see NOTE*, above, shortly after the country heading, "RUSSIA."

Radio Samorodinka, P.O. Box 898, Center, 101000 Moscow, Russia. Contact: Lev Stepanovich Shiskin, Editor. This station may be licensed as other than a regular broadcaster.

Radiostantsiya Mayak, ul. Pyatnitskaya 25, 113326 Moscow, Russia. Phone: +7 (095) 950-6767. Fax: +7 (095) 959 4204. Email: inform@radiomayak.ru. Web: (includes Windows Media) www.radiomayak.ru. Although no longer operating officially on shortwave from Russia, the station's programs can still be heard on the world bands via outlets such as Belarussian Radio's Program 2, Turkmen Radio, and one or two regional stations in western Siberia. Unofficially, Mayak broadcasts are also aired over certain military transmitters in Belarus which operate in the 2, 3 and 5 MHz bands. Correspondence in Russian preferred, but English increasingly accepted.

Radiostantsiya Tikhiy Okean ("Radio Station Pacific Ocean") (if reactivated), RTV Center, ul. Uborevieha 20A, 690000 Vladivostok, Primorskiy Kray, Russia.

Sakha Radio, GTRK Respubliki Sakha, ul. Ordzhonikidze 48, 677007 Yakutsk, Respublika Sakha, Russia. Contact: (general) Alexandra Borisova; Lia Sharoborina, Advertising Editor; or Albina Danilova, Producer, "Your Letters"; (technical) Sergei Bobnev, Technical Director. Russian books $15; audio cassettes $10. Free station stickers and original Yakutian souvenirs. Replies to correspondence in English.

Sakhalin Radio, GTRK "Sakhalin," ul. Komsomolskaya 211, 693000 Yuzhno-Sakhalinsk, Sakhalinskaya Oblast, Russia. Phone/fax: +7 (42422) 35286. Email: gtrk@sakhalin.ru. Web: http://gtrk.sakhalin.ru. Contact: V. Belyaev, Chairman of Sakhalinsk RTV Committee.

Tyumen' Radio, RTV Center, ul. Permyakova 6, 625013 Tyumen', Tyumenskaya Oblast, Russia. Contact: (technical) V.D. Kizerov, Engineer, Technical Center. Sometimes replies to correspondence in Russian. Return postage helpful.

📻Voice of Russia, ul. Pyatnitskaya 25, Moscow 113326, Russia. Phone: (International Relations Department) +7 (095) 233-7801; (Deputy Editor-in-Chief) +7 (095) 950-6980 or +7 (095) 950-6586; (Programmes Directorate) +7 (095) 233-6793; (Commercial Dept.) +7 (095) 233-7934; (Audience Research) +7 (095) 233-6278; (Chairman's Secretariat) +7 (095) 233-6331; (News Directorate) +7 (095) 233-6513; (Technical Department) +7 (095) 950-6115. Fax: (Chairman's Secretariat) +7 (095) 230 2828; (Editor-in-Chief) +7 (095) 950 5693; (World Service) +7 (095) 233 7693; (Russian Service) +7 (095) 950 6116; (International Relations Department) +7 (095) 233 7648; (News Directorate) +7 (095) 233 7567; (technical) +7 (095) 233 1342. Email: (general) letters@vor.ru; (administrative) chairman@vor.ru. Web: (general) www.vor.ru; (RealAudio in English, German, Russian and Spanish) www.wrn.org/ ondemand/russia.html. Listeners with a computer equipped with a sound card can send a voice mail to the station via the Internet (detailed instructions are available at the Voice of Russia Website). Contact: (English Service—listeners' questions to be answered over the air) Joe Adamov; (English Service—all other general correspondence) Ms. Olga Troshina, Mrs. Tanya Stukova; Elena Prolovskaya; or Elena Osipova, World Service, Letters Department; (general correspondence, all languages) Victor Kopytin, Director of International Relations Department; Vladimir Zhamkin, Editor-in-Chief; Yevgeny Nilov, Deputy Editor-in-Chief; Anatoly Morozov, Deputy Editor-in-Chief; (Japanese) Yelena Sopova, Japanese Department; (verifications, all services) Mrs. Eugenia Stepanova, c/o English Service; (Russian Service) Pavel Mikhailov, who also speaks English; (administration) Yuri Minayev, First Deputy Chairman, Voice of Russia; Armen Oganesyan, Chairman, World Service, Voice of Russia; (technical) Valentin Khleknikov, Frequency Coordinator; Leonid Maevski, Engineering Services; Rachel Staviskaya, Technical Department; or Maria Petrunicheva, Engineering Services. To get in touch with other language services, contact the International Relations Department. Because of budget restrictions, the Voice of Russia may sometimes be unable to answer correspondence except by email. It is therefore advisable to include an email address (if you have one) when writing to the station. For verification of reception from transmitters located in St. Petersburg and Kaliningrad, *see NOTE*, above, shortly after the country heading, "RUSSIA." For verification of broadcasts from transmitters in Khabarovsk, you can also write directly to the Voice of Russia, Dom Radio, Lenina 4, Khabarovsk 680020, Russia. For engineering correspondence concerning frequency management problems, besides "technical," preceding, *see NOTE* on C.I.S. Frequency Management towards the beginning of this "Russia" listing. Free stickers, booklets and sundry other souvenirs occasionally available upon re-

This Soviet-era spa— *turbaza*—serves radio staffers in rural Kyrgyzstan. M. Guha

quest. Sells audio cassettes of Russian folk and classical music, as well as a Russian language-learning course. Although not officially a part of the Voice of Russia, an organization selling Russian art and handcrafts that sprung from contacts made with the Voice of Russia is "Cheiypouka," Box 266, Main St., Stonington ME 04681 USA; phone +1 (207) 367-5021.

Voice of Assyria—see Qala Atouraya, above.

Voice of Tatarstan, ul. Maksima Gor'kogo 15, 420015 Kazan, Tatarstan, Russia. Phone: (general) +7 (8432) 384-846; (editorial) +7 (8432) 367-493. Fax: +7 (8432) 361-283. Email: root@gtrkrt.kazan.su; postmaster@ stvcrt.kazan.su. Contact: Hania Hazipovna Galinova.

ADDRESS FOR RECEPTION REPORTS: QSL Manager, P.O. Box 134, 420136 Kazan, Tatarstan, Russia. Contact: Ildus Ibatullin, QSL Manager. Offers an honorary diploma in return for 12 correct reports in a given year. The diploma costs 2 IRCs for Russia and 4 IRCs elsewhere. All reports to the QSL Manager address listed above. Accepts reports in English and Russian.

RWANDA   World Time +2

Deutsche Welle—Relay Station Kigali—Correspondence should be directed to the main offices in Cologne, Germany *(see)*.

Radio Rwanda, B.P. 404, Kigali, Rwanda. Fax: +250 (7) 6185. Contact: Marcel Singirankabo. $1 required. Rarely replies, with correspondence in French preferred.

SAO TOME E PRINCIPE   World Time exactly

Voice of America/IBB—São Tomé Relay Station, P.O. Box 522, São Tomé, São Tomé e Príncipe. Contact: Manuel Neves, Transmitter Plant Technician. Replies direct if $1 included with correspondence, otherwise all communications should be directed to the usual VOA or IBB addresses in Washington (*see* USA).

SAUDI ARABIA   World Time +3

Broadcasting Service of The Kingdom of Saudi Arabia, P.O. Box 61718, Riyadh-11575, Saudi Arabia. Phone: (general)

+966 (1) 404-2795; (administration) +966 (1) 442-5493. Fax: (general) +966 (1) 402 8177. Contact: (general) Mutlaq A. Albegami, European Service Manager. Free travel information and book on Saudi history. For technical contacts including Engineering and Frequency Management *see* entry below.

Saudi Arabian Radio & Television, P.O. Box 8525, Riyadh-11492, Saudi Arabia. Phone: (technical & frequency managementl) +966 (1) 442-5170. Fax: (technical & frequency management) +966 (1) 404 1692. Email: alsamnan@yahoo.com. Contact: Suleiman Al-Samnan, Director of Engineering; Suleiman Al-Kalifa, General Manager; Suleiman Al Haidari, Engineer; or Youssef Dhim.

SENEGAL   World Time exactly

⊠Radiodiffusion Télévision Sénégalaise (when active), B.P. 1765, Dakar, Senegal. Phone: +221 23-63-49. Fax: + 221 22 34 90. Email: rts@primature.sn. Web: (includes live NetShow audio) www.primature.sn/rts/. Contact: (technical) Joseph Nesseim, Directeur des Services Techniques; or Mme. Elisabeth Ndiaye. Free stickers and Senegalese stamps. Return postage, $1 or 2 IRCs required; as Mr. Nesseim collects stamps, unusual stamps may be even more appreciated. Replies to correspondence in French.

SEYCHELLES   World Time +4

BBC World Service—Indian Ocean Relay Station, P.O. Box 448, Victoria, Mahé, Seychelles; or Grand Anse, Mahé, Seychelles. Phone: +248 78-269. Fax: +248 78 500. Contact: (administration) Peter J. Loveday, Station Manager; (technical) Peter Lee, Resident Engineer; Nigel Bird, Resident Engineer; or Steve Welch, Assistant Resident Engineer. Nontechnical correspondence should be sent to the BBC World Service in London (*see*).

Far East Broadcasting Association—FEBA Radio
MAIN OFFICE: P.O. Box 234, Mahé, Seychelles, Indian Ocean. Phone: (main office) +248 282-2000 Fax: +248 242-146. Email: mmaillet@feba.org.sc. Web: www.feba.org.uk. Contact: (general) Hugh Barton, Seychelles Director; (technical) Richard Whittington, Schedule Engineer; or Andy Platts, Head of En-

gineering; (reception reports) N. Nugashe, QSL Secretary; or Doreen Dugathe. Free stickers, pennants and station information sheet. $1 or one IRC helpful. Also, *see* FEBC Radio International—USA and United Kingdom.

CANADA OFFICE: 6850 Antrim Avenue, Burnaby BC, V5J 4M4 Canada. Fax: +1 (604) 430 5272. Email: dpatter@axionet.com. *INDIA OFFICE:* FEBA India, P.O. Box 2526, 7 Commissariat Road, Bangalore-560 025, India. Fax: +91 (80) 584 701. Email: 6186706@mcimail.com. Contact: Peter Muthl Raj.

SIERRA LEONE   World Time exactly

Sierra Leone Broadcasting Service, New England, Freetown, Sierra Leone. Phone: +232 (22) 240-123; +232 (22) 240-173; +232 (22) 240-497 or 232 (22) 241-919. Fax: +232 (22) 240 922. Contact: Cyril Juxon-Smith, Officer in Charge; or Henry Goodaig Hjax, Assistant Engineer.

SINGAPORE   World Time +8

BBC World Service—Far Eastern Relay Station, 26 Olive Road, Singapore. Phone: + 65 260-1511. Fax: +65 253 8131. Contact: (technical) Far East Resident Engineer. Nontechnical correspondence should be sent to the BBC World Service in London (*see*).

📻**Radio Corporation of Singapore**, Farrer Road, P.O. Box 968, Singapore 912899; or (physical location) Caldecott Broadcast Centre, Caldecott Hill, Andrew Road, Singapore 299939. Phone: +65 251-8166, +65 251-8622 or +65 359-7340. Fax: +65 254 8062, +65 256 1995, +65 256 9533, +65 256 9556 or +65 256 9338. Email: (general) info@rcs.com.sg; (Engineering Dept.) engineering@rcs.com.sg. Web: (general) www.rcs.com.sg; (RealAudio) http://rcslive.singnet.com.sg. Contact: (general) Lillian Tan, Public Relations Division; Lim Heng Tow, Manager, International and Community Relations; Tan Eng Lai, Promotion Executive; Hui Wong, Producer/Presenter; or Lucy Leong; (administration) Anthony Chia, Director General; (technical) Asaad Sameer Bagharib, V.P. Engineering; or Lee Wai Meng. Free regular and Post-It stickers, pens, umbrellas, mugs, towels, wallets and lapel pins. Do not include currency in envelope.

Radio Nederland via Singapore—All correspondence should be directed to the regular address in Holland (*see*).

Radio Japan via Singapore—All correspondence should be directed to the regular address in Japan (*see*).

📻**Radio Singapore International**, Farrer Road, P.O. Box 5300, Singapore 912899, Singapore; or (physical address) Caldecott Broadcast Centre, Annex Building Level 1, Andrew Road, Singapore 299939. Phone: (general) + 65 251-8622. Fax: +65 259 1357 or +65 259 1380. Email: info@rsi.com.sg; or english@rsi.com.sg. Web: (includes RealAudio) www.rsi.com.sg. Contact: (general) Mrs. Sakuntala Gupta, Programme Manager, English Service; (technical) Mr Lim Wing Kee, RSI Engineering. Free souvenir T-shirts and key chains to selected listeners. Do not include currency in envelope.

SLOVAKIA   World Time +1 (+2 midyear)

📻**Radio Slovakia International**, Mýtna 1, P.O. Box 55, 81755 Bratislava 15, Slovakia. Phone: (Editor-in-Chief) +421 (7) 5727-3730; (English Service) +421 (7) 5727-3736 or +421 (7) 5727-2737; (technical) +421 (7) 5727-3251. Fax: +421 (7) 5249 6282 or +421 (7) 5249 8247; (technical) +421 (7) 5249 7659. Email: (English Section) englishsection@slovakradio.sk; for other languages, the format is rsi_language@slovakradio.sk (e.g. rsi_german@slovakradio.sk). Web: (general)

www.slovakradio.sk/rsi.html; (RealAudio in English) www.wrn.org/ondemand/slovakia.html. Contact: Oxana Ferjenčíková, Director of English Broadcasting; (administration) PhDr. Karol Palkovič, Head of External Broadcasting; or Dr. Slavomira Kubickova, Head of International Relations; (technical) Ms. Edita Chocholatá, Frequency Manager; Jozef Krátky, Ing. May exchange stamps, recipes and coins. Free pennants, pocket calendars, T-shirts (occasionally) and other souvenirs and publications.

SOLOMON ISLANDS   World Time +11

Solomon Islands Broadcasting Corporation, P.O. Box 654, Honiara, Solomon Islands. Phone: +677 20051. Fax: +677 23159. Contact: (general) Julian Maka'a, Producer, "Listeners From Far Away"; Cornelius Teasi; or Silas Hule; (administration) Johnson Honimae, General Manager; (technical) John Babera, Chief Engineer. IRC or $1 helpful. Problems with the domestic mail system may cause delays.

SOMALIA   World Time +3

Radio Gaalkacyo, 2 Griffith Avenue, Roseville NSW 2069, Australia. Phone/fax: +61 (2) 9417-1066. Contact: Sam Voron, Australian Director. $5, AUS$5 or 5 IRCs required. Station is operated from Gaalkacyo in the Mudug region of northeastern Somalia by the Somali International Amateur Radio Club. Seeks volunteers and donations of radio equipment and airline tickets.

SOMALILAND   World Time +3

NOTE: "Somaliland," claimed as an independent nation, is diplomatically recognized only as part of Somalia.

Radio Hargeisa, P.O. Box 14, Hargeisa, Somaliland, Somalia. Contact: Sulayman Abdel-Rahman, announcer. Most likely to respond to correspondence in Somali or Arabic.

SOUTH AFRICA   World Time +2

BBC World Service via South Africa—For verification direct from the South African transmitters, contact Sentech (*see* below). Nontechnical correspondence should be sent to the BBC World Service in London (*see*).

📻**Channel Africa**, P.O. Box 91313, Auckland Park 2006, South Africa. Phone: (executive editor) +27 (11) 714-2255; + 27 (11) 714-2551 or +27 (11) 714-3942; (technical) +27 (11) 714-3409. Fax: (executive editor) +27 (11) 482 3506; + 27 (11) 714 2546, +27 (11) 714 4956 or +27 (11) 714 6377; (technical) +27 (11) 714 5812. Email: (general) africancan@channelafrica.org; (news desk) news.africa@channelafrica.org. Web: (RealAudio in English, French and Portuguese, plus text) www.channelafrica.org; (RealAudio in English) www.wrn.org/ondemand/southafrica.html. Contact: (general) Tony Machilika, Head of English Service; Robert Michel, Head of Research and Strategic Planning; or Noeleen Vorster, Corporate Communications Manager; (technical) Mrs. H. Meyer, Supervisor Operations; or Lucienne Libotte, Technology Operations. T-shirts $11 and watches $25. Prices do not include shipping and handling. Free *Share* newsletter from the Department of Foreign Affairs, stickers and calendars. Reception reports are best directed to Sentech (*see* below), which operates the transmission facilities.

📻**Radiosondergrense (Radio Without Boundaries)**, Posbus 91312, Auckland Park 2006, South Africa; or SABC, P.O. Box 2551, Cape Town 8000, South Africa. Phone: (general) +27 (89) 110-2525; (live studio on-air line) +27 (89) 110-4553; (station manager) +27 (11) 714-2702. Fax: (general) +27 (11) 714 6445; (station manager) +27 (11) 714 3472. Email: (general) info@rsg.co.za; (Myburgh) myburghs@sabc.co.za. Web: (includes RealAudio) www.rsg.co.za. Contact: Sarel Myburgh, Station Manager. Reception reports are best directed to Sentech (see below), which operates the shortwave transmission facilities. A domestic service of the South African Broadcasting Corporation (see below), and formerly known as Afrikaans Stereo. The shortwave operation is scheduled to be eventually replaced by a satellite and FM network.

Sentech (Pty) Ltd, Shortwave Services, Private Bag X06, Honeydew 2040, South Africa. Phone: (general) +27 (11) 475-5600; (shortwave) +27 (11) 475-1596; (Otto) +27 (11) 471-4658 or +27 (11) 471-4537. Fax: (general) +27 (11) 475 5112; (Otto) +27 (11) 471 4758 or +27 (11) 471 4754. Email: (general) comms@sentech.co.za; (Otto) ottok@sentech.co.za; (Smuts) smutsn@sentech.co.za. Web: (general) www.sentech.co.za; (schedules, unofficial) http://home.mweb.co.za/an/andre46/. Contact: Mr. Neël Smuts, Managing Director; Rodgers Gamuti, Client Manager; or Kathy Otto, HF Coverage Planner. Sentech issues its own verification cards, and is the best place to send reception reports for world band stations broadcasting via South African facilities.

⌨South African Broadcasting Corporation
ADMINISTRATION AND GENERAL TECHNICAL MATTERS: Private Bag X1, Auckland Park 2006, South Africa. Phone: (Head Office) +27 (11) 714-9111; (information) +27 (11) 714-9797; (technical) +27 (11) 714-3409. Fax: (general) +27 (11) 714 4086 or +27 (11) 714 5055; (technical) +27 (11) 714 3106 or +27 (11) 714 5812. Web: (includes RealAudio) www.sabc.co.za. Contact: (administration) Mrs. Charlotte Mampane, Chief Executive, Radio. Reception reports are best directed to Sentech (see, above), which operates the transmission facilities.
RADIO PROGRAMME SALES: Private Bag X1, Auckland Park 2006, South Africa. Phone: (general enquiries) +27 (11) 714-5681, +27 (11) 714-6039 or +27 (11) 714-4044; (actuality programs) +27 (11) 714-4709; (music) +27 (11) 714-4315. Fax: +27 (11) 714 3671. Email: botham@sabc.co.za; snymane @sabc.co.za; or corbinm@sabc.co.za. Offers a wide range of music, book readings, radio drama, comedy and other types of programs.

Trans World Radio Africa
NONTECHNICAL CORRESPONDENCE: Trans World Radio—South Africa, Private Bag 987, Pretoria 0001, South Africa. Phone: +27 (12) 807-0053. Fax: +27 (12) 807 1266. Web: www.gospelcom.net/twr/ttatlow/Welcome.htm; (schedule) www.gospelcom.net/twr/broadcasts/africa.htm.
TECHNICAL CORRESPONDENCE: Reception reports and other technical correspondence are best directed to Sentech (see, above) or to TWR's Swaziland office (see). Also, see USA.

SPAIN   World Time +1 (+2 midyear)

⌨Radio Exterior de España (Spanish National Radio)
MAIN OFFICE: Apartado de Correos 156.202, E-28080 Madrid, Spain. Phone: (general) +34 (91) 346-1081/1083; (Audience Relations) +34 (91) 346-1149. Fax: +34 (91) 346 1815. Email: (Director) dir_ree.rne@rtve.es; (Spanish programming) audiencia.ree.rne@rtve.es; (foreign language programming, including English) lenguas_extranjeras.rne@rtve.es. Web: (includes RealAudio and Windows Media) www.rtve.es/rne/ree/. Contact: (nontechnical) Pilar Salvador M., Nuria Alonso Veiga, Head of Information Service; Alejo Garcia, Director;

Ricardo H. Calvo, Webmaster; or Penelope Eades, Foreign Language Programmer; (technical) Relaciones con la Audiencia. Free stickers, calendars, pennants and tourist information. Reception reports can be sent to: Radio Exterior de España, Relaciones con la Audiencia, Sección DX, Apartado de Correos 156.202, E-28080 Madrid, Spain.
TRANSCRIPTION SERVICE: Radio Nacional de España, Servicio de Transcripciones, Apartado 156.200, Casa de la Radio (Prado del Rey), E-28223 Madrid, Spain.
HF FREQUENCY PLANNING OFFICE: Prado del Rey. Pozuelo de Alarcom, E-28223 Madrid, Spain. Phone: +34 (91) 346-1276 or +34 (91) 346-1978. Fax: +34 (91) 346 1402. Email: (Huerta) plan_red.rne@rtve.es; or (Almarza) planif_red2.rne@rtve.es. Contact: José M. Huerta, Frequency Manager; or Fernando Almarza.
NOBLEJAS TRANSMITTER SITE: Centro Emisor de RNE en Onda Corta, Ctra. Dos Barrios s/n, E-45350 Noblejas-Toledo, Spain.
COSTA RICA RELAY FACILITY—see Costa Rica.
RUSSIAN OFFICE: P.O Box 88, 109044 Moscow, Russia.
WASHINGTON NEWS BUREAU: National Press Building, 529 14th Street NW, Suite 1288, Washington DC 20045 USA. Phone: +1 (202) 783-0768. Contact: Luz María Rodríguez.

SRI LANKA   World Time +6:00

Deutsche Welle—Relay Station Sri Lanka, 92/2 D.S. Senanayake Mawatha, Colombo 08, Sri Lanka. Phone: +94 (1) 699-449. Fax: +94 (1) 699 450. Contact: R. Groschkus, Resident Engineer. Nontechnical correspondence should be sent to Deutsche Welle in Germany (see).

Radio Japan/NHK, c/o SLBC, P.O. Box 574, Torrington Square, Colombo 7, Sri Lanka. This address for technical correspondence only. General nontechnical listener correspondence should be sent to the usual Radio Japan address in Japan. News-oriented correspondence may also be sent to the NHK Bangkok Bureau (see Radio Japan, Japan).

Sri Lanka Broadcasting Corporation (also announces as "Radio Sri Lanka" in the external service), P.O. Box 574, Independence (Torrington) Square, Colombo 7, Sri Lanka. Phone: (general) +94 (1) 697-491 or +94 (1) 697-493; (Director General) +94 (1) 696-140. Fax: (general) +94 (1) 697 150 or +94 (1) 698 576; (Director General) +94 (1) 695 488; (Sooryia, phone/fax) +94 (1) 696 1311. Email: slbc@sri.lanka.net; slbcweb@sri.lanka.net. Web: www.infolanka.com/people/sisira/slbc.html. Contact: (general) N. Jayhweera, Director - Audience Research; or Icumar Ratnayake, Controller, "Mailbag Program"; (SLBC administration) Eric Fernando, Director General; Newton Gunaratne, Deputy Director-General; (technical) H.M.N.R. Jayawardena, Engineer - Training and Frequency Management; Wimala Sooriya, Deputy Director - Engineering; or A.M.W. Gunaratne, Station Engineer, Ekala.

Voice of America/IBB—Iranawila Relay Station.
ADDRESS: International Broadcasting Bureau, Sri Lanka Transmission Station, c/o U.S. Embassy, 210 Galle Road, Colombo 3, Sri Lanka. Contact: Gary Wise, Station Manager. Nontechnical correspondence should be sent to the VOA address in Washington.

SUDAN   World Time +3

⌨Sudan National Radio Corporation, P.O. Box 572, Omdurman, Sudan. Phone: +249 (11) 553-151 or +249 (11) 552-100. Email: snrc@sudanmail.net. Web: (includes RealAudio) www.sudanradio.net. Contact: (general) Mohammed Elfatih El Sumoal; (technical) Abbas Sidig, Di-

Radio Tashkent's listener's mail department is papered over with letters and cards.
M. Guha

rector General, Engineering and Technical Affairs; Mohammed Elmahdi Khalil, Administrator, Engineering and Technical Affairs; Saleh Al-Hay; or Adil Didahammed, Engineering Department. Replies irregularly. Return postage necessary.

SURINAME   World Time –3

Radio Apintie, Postbus 595, Paramaribo, Suriname. Phone: +597 40-05-00. Fax: +597 40 06 84. Email: apintie@sr.net. Web: www.apintie.sr. Contact: Charles E. Vervuurt, Director. Free pennant. Return postage or $1 required. Email reception reports preferred, since local mail service is unreliable.

SWAZILAND   World Time +2

Swaziland Commercial Radio
NONTECHNICAL CORRESPONDENCE: P.O. Box 5569, Rivonia 2128, Transvaal, South Africa. Phone: +27 (11) 884-8400. Fax: +27 (11) 883 1982. Contact: Fernando Vaz-Osiori; Rob Vickers, Manager—Religion. IRC helpful. Replies irregularly.
TECHNICAL CORRESPONDENCE: P.O. Box 99, Amsterdam 2375, South Africa. Contact: Guy Doult, Chief Engineer.
SOUTH AFRICA BUREAU: P.O. Box 1586,Alberton 1450, Republic of South Africa. Phone: +27 (11) 434-4333. Fax: +27 (11) 434 4777.

Trans World Radio—Swaziland
MAIN OFFICE: P.O. Box 64, Manzini, Swaziland. Phone: +268 505-2781/2/3. Fax: +268 505 5333. Email: (James Burnett, Regional Engineer and Frequency Manager) jburnett@twr.org; (Chief Engineer) sstavrop@twr.org; (Mrs. L. Stavropoulos, DX Secretary) lstavrop@twr.org; (Greg Shaw, Follow-up Department) gshaw@twr.org. URL (transmission schedule): www.gospelcom.net/twr/broadcasts/africa.htm. Contact: (general) Greg Shaw, Follow-up Department; G.J. Alary, Station Director; or Joseph Ndzinisa, Program Manager; (technical) Mrs. L. Stavropoulos, DX Secretary; Chief Engineer; or James Burnett, Regional Engineer. Free stickers, postcards and calendars. A free Bible Study course is available. May swap canceled stamps. $1, return postage or 3 IRCs required. Also, see USA.
AFRICA REGIONAL OFFICE: P.O. Box 4232,Kempton Park 1610, South Africa. Contact: Stephen Boakye-Yiadom, African Regional Director.

CÔTE D'IVOIRE OFFICE: B.P. 2131, Abidjan 06, Côte d'Ivoire.
KENYA OFFICE: P.O. Box 21514 Nairobi, Kenya.
MALAWI OFFICE: P. O. Box 52 Lilongwe, Malawi.
SOUTH AFRICA OFFICE: P.O. Box 36000, Menlo Park 0102, South Africa.
ZIMBABWE OFFICE: P.O. Box H-74, Hatfield, Harare, Zimbabwe.

SWEDEN   World Time +1 (+2 midyear)

IBRA Radio (program)
MAIN OFFICE: International Broadcasting Association, Box 396, SE-105 36 Stockholm, Sweden. Phone: +46 (8) 619-2540; Fax: +46 (8) 619 2539. Email: hq@ibra.se; or ibra@ibra.se. Web: www.ibra.se/; www.ibra.org/. Contact: Mikael Stjernberg, Public Relations Manager; or Helene Hasslof. Free pennants and stickers. IBRA Radio is heard as a program over various world band stations, including Trans World Radio (Monaco); and also airs broadcasts via transmitters in Russia and the CIS. Accepts emailed reception reports.
CYPRUS OFFICE: P.O. Box 7420, 3315 Limassol, Cyprus. Contact: Rashad Saleem. Free schedules, calendars and stickers.

Radio Sweden
MAIN OFFICE: SE-105 10 Stockholm, Sweden. Phone: (general) +46 (8) 784-7200, +46 (8) 784-7207, +46 (8) 784-7288 or +46 (8) 784-5000; (listener voice mail) +46 (8) 784-7287; (technical department) +46 (8) 784-7286. Fax: (general) +46 (8) 667 6283; (polling to receive schedule) +46 8 660 2990. Email: (general) info@rs.sr.se; (schedule on demand) english@rs.sr.se; (Roxström) sarah.roxstrom@rs.sr.se; (Hagström) nidia.hagstrom@rs.sr.se; (Wood) george.wood@rs.sr.se; (Beckman, technical manager) rolf-b@stab.sr.se. Web: (general) www.sr.se/rs/; (online reception report form) www.sr.se/rs/english/qsl.htm; (RealAudio multilingual archives) www.sr.se/rs/listen/; (RealAudio daily broadcast in English) www.sr.se/rs/english/sounds/ (replace "english" by "svenska" to hear the Swedish broadcasts). FTP versions of Radio Sweden's daily broadcasts (all languages) are available at www.sr.se/ftp/rs/. Contact: (general) Nidia Hagström, Host, "In Touch with Stockholm" [include your telephone number]; Sarah Roxström, Head, English Service; Greta Grandin, Program Assistant, English Service; George Wood, Producer, MediaScan; Olimpia Seldon, Assistant to the Director; or Char-

lotte Adler, Public Relations and Information; (administration) Finn Norgren, Director General; (technical) Rolf Erik Beckman, Head, Technical Department; or Anders Baecklin, Editor, Technical Administration. T-shirts (two sizes) $12 or £8. Payment for T-shirts may be made by international money order, Swedish postal giro account No. 43 36 56-6 or internationally negotiable bank check.

NEW YORK NEWS BUREAU: Swedish Broadcasting, 825 Third Avenue, New York, New York NY 10022 USA. Phone: +1 (212) 688-6872 or +1 (212) 643-8855. Fax: +1 (212) 594 6413. Contact: Elizabeth Johansson.

WASHINGTON NEWS BUREAU: Swedish Broadcasting, 2030 M Street NW, Suite 700, Washington DC 20036 USA. Phone: +1 (202) 785-1727. Contact: Folke Rydén, Lisa Carlsson or Steffan Ekendahl.

TRANSMISSION AUTHORITY: TERACOM, Svensk Rundradio AB, P.O. Box 17666, SE-118 92 Stockholm, Sweden. Phone: (general) +46 (8) 555-420-00; (Nilsson) +46 (8) 555-420-66. Fax: (general) +46 (8) 555-420-01; (Nilsson) +46 (8) 555 420 60. Email: (general) info@teracom.se; (Nilsson) magnus.nilsson@teracom.se. Web: www.teracom.se. Contact: (Frequency Planning Dept.—Head Office): Magnus Nilsson; (Engineering) H. Widenstedt, Chief Engineer. Free stickers; sometimes free T-shirts to those monitoring during special test transmissions. Seeks monitoring feedback for new frequency usages.

SWITZERLAND   World Time +1 (+2 midyear)

European Broadcasting Union, Case Postal 67, CH-1218 Grand-Saconnex, Geneva, Switzerland. Phone: +41 (22) 717-2111 or +41 (22) 717-2221. Fax: +41 (22) 798 5897 or +41 (22) 717 2481. Email: ebu@ebu.ch. Web: www.ebu.ch. Contact: Jean-Bernard Munch, Secretary-General; or Robin Levey, Strategic Information Service Database Manager. Umbrella organization for broadcasters in 49 European and Mediterranean countries.

International Telecommunication Union, Place des Nations, CH-1211 Geneva 20, Switzerland. Phone: (Fonteyne) +41 (22) 730-5983; or Pham) +41 (22) 730-6136. Fax: +41 (22) 730 5785. Contact: Jacques Fonteyne or Hai Pham. Email: (schedules and reference tables) Brmail@itu.int; (Fonteyne) jacques.fonteyne@itu.int; or (Pham) pham.hai@itu.int. Web: www.itu.ch. The ITU is the world's official regulatory body for all telecommunication activities, including world band radio. Offers a wide range of official multilingual telecommunication publications in print and/or digital formats.

Mitternachtsruf, Postfach 290, Eichholzstrasse 38, CH-8330 Pfaffikon, Switzerland. Contact: Jonathan Malgo or Paul Richter. Verifies reports with a QSL card. Free stickers and promotional material. Religious program sometimes aired over world band facilities in Europe.

GERMAN OFFICE: Postfach 62, D-79807 Lottstetten, Germany.

U.S. OFFICE: P.O. Box 4389, W. Columbia, SC 29171 USA.

Swiss Radio International

MAIN OFFICE: Giacomettistrasse 1, CH-3000 Berne 15, Switzerland. Phone: (general) +41 (31) 350-9222; (English Department) +41 (31) 350-9790; (French Department) +41 (31) 350-9555; (German Department) +41 (31) 350-9535; (Italian Department) +41 (31) 350-9531; (Frequency Management) +41 (31) 350-9734. Fax: (general) +41 (31) 350 9569; (administration) +41 (31) 350 9744 or +41 (31) 350 9581; (Communication and Marketing) +41 (31) 350 9544; (Programme Department) +41 (31) 350 9569; (English Department) +41 (31)

350 9580; (French Department) +41 (31) 350 9664; (German Department) +41 (31) 350 9562; (Italian Department) +41 (31) 350 9678; (Frequency Management) +41 (31) 350 9745. Email: (general) format is language@sri.ch (e.g. english@sri.ch, german@sri.ch); (marketing) marketing@swissinfo.org; (technical) technical@swissinfo.org; (Frequency Management): ulrich.wegmueller@sri.ch. Web: (including RealAudio in English) www.sri.ch; www.swissinfo.org; http:// mobile.swissinfo.org. Contact: (general) Diana Zanotti, English Department; Marlies Schmutz, Listeners' Letters, German Programmes; Thérèse Schafter, Listeners' Letters, French Programmes; Esther Niedhammer, Listeners' Letters, Italian Programmes; Beatrice Lombard, Promotion; Giovanni D'Amico, Audience Officer; (administration) Ulrich Kündig, General Manager; Nicolas Lombard, Deputy General Manager; Walter Fankhauser, Head, Communication and Marketing Services; Rose-Marie Malinverni, Head, Editorial Co-ordination Unit; Ron Grünig, Head, English Programmes; James Jeanneret, Head, German Programmes; Philippe Zahne, Head, French Programmes; Fabio Mariani, Head, Italian Programmes; (technical) Paul Badertscher, Head, Engineering Services; Ulrich Wegmüller, Frequency Manager; or Bob Zanotti. Free station flyers, posters, stickers and pennants. Sells CDs of Swiss music, plus audio and video (PAL/NTSC) cassettes; also, Swiss watches and clocks, microphone lighters, briefcases, umbrellas, letter openers, books, T-shirts, sweatshirts and Swiss Army knives. VISA/EURO/AX or cash, but no personal checks. For catalog, write to SRI Enterprises, c/o the above address, fax +41 (31) 350 9581, or email shopping@sri.srg-ssr.ch.

WASHINGTON NEWS BUREAU: 2030 M Street NW, Washington DC 20554 USA. Phone: (general) +1 (202) 775-0894 or +1 (202) 429-9668; (French-language radio) +1 (202) 296-0277; (German-language radio) +1 (202) 7477. Fax: +1 (202) 833 2777. Contact: Christophe Erbeck, reporter.

SYRIA   World Time +2 (+3 midyear)

Radio Damascus, Syrian Radio and Television, Ommayad Square, Damascus, Syria. Phone: +963 (11) 221-7653. Fax: +963 (11) 222 2692. Contact: Mr. Afaf, Director General; Mr. Adnan Al-Massri; Adnan Salhab; Lisa Arslanian; or Mrs. Wafa Ghawi. Free stickers, paper pennants and *The Syria Times* newspaper. Replies can be highly erratic, but as of late have been more regular, if sometimes slow.

TAHITI—*see* FRENCH POLYNESIA.

TAJIKISTAN   World Time +5

Radio Tajikistan, Chapaev Street 31, 734025 Dushanbe, Tajikistan; or English Service, International Service, Radio Tajikistan, P.O. Box 108, 734025 Dushanbe, Tajikistan. Phone: (Director) +7 (3772) 210-877 or +7 (3772) 277-417; (English Department) +7 (3772) 277-417; (Ramazonov) +7 (3772) 277-667 or +7 (3772) 277-347. Fax: +7 (3772) 211 198. Note that the country and city codes are scheduled to be changed in the near future, so the current +7 (3772) should them become +992 (372). Email: treng@td.silk.org. Contact: (administration) Mansur Sultanov, Director - Tajik Radio; Nasrullo Ramazonov, Foreign Relations Department. Correspondence in Russian or Tajik preferred. There is no official policy for verification of listeners' reports, so try sending reception reports and correspondence in English to the attention of Mr. Ramazonov, who is currently the sole English speaker at the station. Caution should be exercised when contacting him via email, as it is his personal account and he is charged for both incoming and outgoing mail. In addition, all email is routinely monitored and censored. Return postage of 5$ has been requested on at least one occasion, but enclosing currency notes is risky due to the high level of postal theft in the country. IRCs are not exchangeable, so including small souvenirs with your letter may help produce a reply.

TRANSMISSION FACILITIES: Television and Radiocommunications Ltd., ul. Internationalskaya 85, 734001 Dushanbe, Tajikistan. Phone: +7 (3772) 244-646. Fax: +7 (3772) 212 517. Email: nodir@uralnet.ru. Contact: Rakhmatillo Masharipovich Masharipov, Director General.

Tajik Radio, ul. Chapaeva 31, 734025 Dushanbe, Tajikistan. Contact information as for Radio Tajikistan, above.

TANZANIA   World Time +3

Radio Tanzania, Nyerere Road, P.O. Box 9191, Dar es Salaam, Tanzania. Phone: +255 (51) 860-760. Fax: +255 (51) 865 577. Email: radiotanzania@raha.com. Contact: (general) Abdul Ngarawa, Director of Broadcasting; Mrs. Edda Sanga, Controller of Programs; Ms. Penzi Nyamungumi, Head of English Service and International Relations Unit; or Ahmed Jongo, Producer, "Your Answer"; (technical) Taha Usi, Chief Engineer; or Emmanuel Mangula, Deputy Chief Engineer. Replies to correspondence in English.

Voice of Tanzania Zanzibar, Department of Broadcasting, Radio Tanzania Zanzibar, P.O. Box 2503, Zanzibar, Tanzania (if this address brings no reply, try P.O. Box 1178); (Muombwa, personal address) P.O. Box 2068, Zanzibar, Tanzania. Phone: +255 (54) 231-088. Fax: + 255 (54) 257 207. Contact: (general) Yusuf Omar Chunda, Director Department of Information and Broadcasting; Ndaro Nyamwolha; Ali Bakari Muombwa; Abdulrah'man M. Said; N. Nyamwochd, Director of Broadcasting; Khalid Hassan. Rajab; or Kassim S. Kassim; (technical) Nassor M. Suleiman, Maintenance Engineer. $1 return postage helpful.

THAILAND   World Time +7

BBC World Service—Asia Relay Station, P.O. Box 20, Muang, Nakhon Sawan 60000, Thailand. Contact: Jaruwan Meesaurtong, Personal Assistant. Verifies reception reports.
Radio Thailand World Service, 236 Vibhavadi Rangsit Highway, Din Daeng, Huaykhwang, Bangkok 10400, Thailand. Phone: +66 (2) 277-1814, +66 (2) 274-9098. Phone/fax: +66 (2) 277-6139, +66 (2) 274-9099. Email: amporns@mozart.inet.co.th. Web: (includes RealAudio) www.prd.go.th/prdnew/eng/radio_e/index.html. Contact: Mrs. Amporn Samosorn, Chief of External Services; or Patra Lamjiack. Free pennants. Replies irregularly, especially to those who persist.

TOGO   World Time exactly

Radio Lomé, B.P. 434, Lomé, Togo. Phone: + 228 212-492. Contact: (nontechnical) Batchoudi Malúlaba or Geraldo Isidine. Return postage, $1 or 2 IRCs helpful. French preferred but English accepted.

TUNISIA   World Time +1

Radiodiffusion Télévision Tunisienne, 71 Avenue de la Liberté, TN-1070 Tunis, Tunisia. Phone: +216 (1) 801-177.

Fax: +216 (1) 781 927. Email: info@radiotunis.com. Web: (includes RealAudio) www.radiotunis.com/news.html. Contact: Mongai Caffai, Director General; Mohamed Abdelkafi, Director; Kamel Cherif, Directeur; Masmoudi Mahmoud; Mr. Bechir Betteib; or Smaoui Sadok, Le Sous-Directeur Technique. Replies irregularly and slowly to correspondence in French or Arabic. $1 helpful. For reception reports try: Le Chef de Service du Controle de la Récepcion de l'Office National de la Télédiffusion, O.N.T, Cité Ennassim I, Bourjel, B.P. 399, TN-1080 Tunis, Tunisia. Phone: +216 (1) 801-177. Fax: +216 (1) 781 927. Email: ont.@ati.tn. Contact: Abdesselem Slim.

TURKEY   World Time +2 (+3 midyear)

Meteoroloji Sesi Radyosu (Voice of Meteorology), T.C. Tarim Bakanliği, Devlet Meteoroloji İsleri, Genel Müdürlüğü, P.K. 401, Ankara, Turkey. Phone: +90 (312) 359-7545, X-281. Fax: +90 (312) 314 1196. Contact: (nontechnical) Gühekin Takinalp; Recep Yilmaz, Head of Forecasting Department; or Abdullah Gölpinar; (technical) Mehmet Örmeci, Director General. Free tourist literature. Return postage helpful.

Türkiye Polis Radyosu (Turkish Police Radio), T.C. İçişleri Bakanliği, Emniyet Genel Müdürlüğü, Ankara, Turkey. Contact: Fatih Umutlu. Tourist literature for return postage. Replies irregularly.

Voice of Turkey (Turkish Radio-Television Corporation External Service)
MAIN OFFICE, NONTECHNICAL: TRT External Services Department, TRT Sitesi, Turan Güneş Blv., Or-An Çankaya, 06450 Ankara, Turkey; or P.K. 333, Yenişehir, 06443 Ankara, Turkey. Phone: (general) +90 (312) 490-9800/9801; (English Service) +90 (312) 490-9842. Fax: +90 (312) 490 9835/45/46. Email: (general) infotsr@tsr.gov.tr; (Turkish broadcasts) turkceyayin@tsr.gov.tr; (English Service) englishservice@tsr.gov.tr; same format applies for Arabic, French, German and Russian services, e.g. germanservice@tsr.gov.tr. Web: (general) www.tsr.gov.tr; (RealAudio) www.trt.net.tr. Contact: (English and non-technical) Mr. Osman Erkan, Chief, English Service and Host of, "Letterbox"; or Ms. Reshide Morali, Announcer "DX Corner"; (other languages) Mr. Rafet Esit, Director, Foreign Languages Section; (administration) Mr. Danyal Gurdal, Head, External Services Department. Technical correspondence, such as on reception quality should be directed to: Ms. Sedef Somaltin *see* next entry below. On-air language courses offered in Arabic and German, but no printed course material. Free stickers, pennants, women's embroidery artwork swatches and tourist literature.
MAIN OFFICE, TECHNICAL (FOR EMIRLER AND ÇAKIRLAR TRANSMITTER SITES AND FOR FREQUENCY MANAGEMENT): TRT Teknik Yardimcilik, TRT Sitesi, Kat: 5/C, Oran, 06450 Ankara, Turkey. Phone: +90 (312) 490-1730/2. Fax: +90 (312) 490 1733. Email: utis@turnet.net.tr or utis2@trt.net.tr; (Tekeli) vural.tekeli@trt.net.tr. Contact: Mr. Vural Tekeli, TRT Head of Engineering; Ms. Sedef Somaltin; or Turgay Cakimci, Chief Engineer, International Technical Relations Service.
SAN FRANCISCO OFFICE, SCHEDULES: 2654 17th Avenue, San Francisco CA 94116 USA. Phone: +1 (415) 564-9968. Email: GPoppin@aol.com. Contact: George Poppin. This address, a volunteer office, only provides TRT schedules to listeners. All other correspondence should be sent directly to Ankara.

TURKMENISTAN   World Time +5

Radio Turkmenistan, National TV and Radio Broadcasting Company, Mollanepes St. 3, 744000 Ashgabat, Turkmenistan.

Phone: +993 (12) 251-515. Fax: +993 (12) 251 421. Contact: (administration) Yu M. Pashaev, Deputy Chairman of State Television and Radio Company; (technical) G. Khanmamedov; Kakali Karayev, Chief of Technical Department; or A.A Armanklichev, Deputy Chief, Technical Department. This country is currently under strict censorship and media people are closely watched. A lot of foreign mail addressed to a particular person may attract the attention of the security services. Best is not to address your mail to particular individuals but to the station itself.

UGANDA   World Time +3

Radio Uganda
GENERAL OFFICE: P.O. Box 7142, Kampala, Uganda. Phone: +256 (41) 257-256. Fax: +256 (41) 256 888. Email: ugabro@infocom.co.ug. Contact: (general) Charles Byekwaso, Controller of Programmes; Machel Rachel Makibuuka; or Mrs. Florence Sewanyana, Head of Public Relations. $1 or return postage required. Replies infrequently and slowly.
ENGINEERING DIVISION: P.O. Box 2038, Kampala, Uganda. Phone: +256 (41) 256-647. Contact: Leopold B. Lubega, Principal Broadcasting Engineer; or Rachel Nakibuuka, Secretary. Four IRCs or $2 required. Enclosing a self addressed envelope may also help to get a reply.

UKRAINE   World Time +2 (+3 midyear)

WARNING-MAIL THEFT: For the time being, letters to Ukrainian stations, especially containing funds or IRCs, are more likely to arrive safely if sent by registered mail.
Government Transmission Authority: RRT/Concern of Broadcasting, Radiocommunication and Television, 10 Dorogajtshaya St., 254112 Kyiv, Ukraine. Phone: +380 (44) 226-2262 or +380 (44) 444-6900. Fax: +380 (44) 440 8722; or +380 (44) 452 6784. Email: ak@cbrt.freenet.kiev.ua. Contact: Mr. Mykola Kyryliuk, Technical Operations & Management; Alexej M. Kurilov; Alexey Karpenko; Alexander Serdiuk; Nikolai P. Kiriliuk, Head of Operative Management Service; or Mrs. Liudmila Deretskaya, Interpreter. This agency is responsible for choosing the frequencies used by Radio Ukraine International.
Radio Ukraine International, Kreshchatik str., 26, 252001 Kyiv, Ukraine. Phone: +380 (44) 228-2534, +380 (44) 229-1757, +380 (44) 229-1883 or (phone/fax) +380 (44) 228-7356. Fax: +380 (44) 229 4585 or +380 (44) 229 3477. Email: vsru@nrcu.gov.ua;   mo@ukrradio.ru.kiev.ua.   Web: www.nrcu.gov.ua/eng/program/vsru/vsru.html. Contact: (administration) Inna Chichinadze, Vice-Director of RUI; (technical) Anatolii Ivanov, Frequency Coordination, Engineering Services, Ukrainian Radio. Free stickers, calendars and Ukrainian stamps.

UNITED ARAB EMIRATES   World Time +4

UAE Radio from Abu Dhabi, Ministry of Information and Culture, P.O. Box 63, Abu Dhabi, United Arab Emirates. Phone:

+971 (2) 451-000. Fax: (Ministry of Information and Culture) +971 (2) 452 504. Contact: (technical) Ibrahim Rashid, Director General, Technical Department; or Fauzi Saleh, Chief Engineer. Free stickers, postcards and stamps. Do not enclose money with correspondence.
FREQUENCY MANAGEMENT: Abu Dhabi Radio, P.O. Box 63, Abu Dhabi, United Arab Emirates. Phone: +971 (2) 436-849. Fax: +971 (2) 451 155 or +971 (2) 450 205. Email: waleed_alzaabi@ebc.co.ae. Contact: Mr. Samir Iskander, Senior Engineer; or Mr. Waleed Al-Zaabi, Chief Engineer.
SHORTWAVE TRANSMITTER STATION: P.O. Box 3966, Abu Dhabi, United Arab Emirates. Phone: +971 (2) 406-2149 or +971 (2) 644-1936. Fax: +971 (2) 406 2149. Contact: Bahaaeldin Abdelrazek, Head of Transmitter Station.

UAE Radio in Dubai, P.O. Box 1695, Dubai, United Arab Emirates. Phone: +971 (4) 370-255. Fax: +971 (4) 374 111, +971 (4) 370 283 or +971 (4) 371 079. Contact: Ms. Khulud Halaby; or Sameer Aga, Producer, "Cassette Club Cinarabic"; (technical) K.F. Fenner, Chief Engineer—Radio; or Ahmed Al Muhaideb, Assistant Controller, Engineering. Free pennants. Replies irregularly.

UNITED KINGDOM   World Time exactly (+1 midyear)

Adventist World Radio, the Voice of Hope, AWR, 39 Brendon Street, London W1, United Kingdom. Phone: +44 (1344) 401-401. Fax: +44 (1344) 401 419. Email: english@awr.org. Web: www.awr.org. Contact: Bert Smit, European Regional Director; or Victor Hulbert, Director English Listener Mail. All mail addressed to AWR and written in English is processed at this address. Also, *see* AWR listings under Germany, Guam, Guatemala, Italy, Kenya, Madagascar and USA.
BBC Monitoring, Caversham Park, Reading RG4 8TZ, United Kingdom. Phone: (main) +44 (118) 947-2742; (Foreign Media Unit—Broadcast Schedules/monitoring) +44 (118) 946-9261; Marketing Department) +44 (118) 946-9289. Fax: (Foreign Media Unit) +44 (118) 946 1993; (Marketing Department) +44 (118) 946 3823. Email: (Marketing Department) marketing@mon.bbc.co.uk; (Foreign Media Unit/World Media) fmu@mon.bbc.co.uk; (Kenny) dave_kenny@mon.bbc.co.uk; (publications and real time services) marketing @mon.bbc.co.uk. Web: www.monitor.bbc.co.uk. Contact: (administration) Andrew Hills, Director of Monitoring; (Foreign Media Unit) Chris McWhinnie, Editor "World Media," Broadcast Schedules; Dave Kenny, Chief Sub Editor, "World Media," Broadcast Schedules; or Peter Feuilherade; (Publication Sales) Stephen Innes, Marketing. BBC Monitoring produces the weekly publication *World Media* which reports political, economic, legal, organisational, programming and technical developments in the world's electronic media. Its reports are based on material broadcast or published by radio and TV stations, news agencies, Websites and publications; other information issued but not necessarily broadcast by such sources and by other relevant bodies; and information obtained by BBC Monitoring's own observations of foreign media. Available on yearly subscription, costing £410.00. Price excludes postage overseas. *World Media* is also available online through

the Internet or via a direct dial-in bulletin board at an annual cost of £425.00. Broadcasting Schedules, issued weekly by email at an annual cost of £99.00. VISA/MC/AX. The Technical Operations Unit provides detailed observations of broadcasts on the long, medium, short wave, satellite bands and Internet. This unit provides tailored channel occupancy observations, reception reports, and updates the *MediaNet* source information database (constantly updated on over 100 countries) and the *Broadcast Research Log* (a record of broadcasting developments compiled daily). BBC Monitoring works in conjunction with the Foreign Broadcast Information Service (*see* USA).

BBC World Service

MAIN OFFICE, NONTECHNICAL: Bush House, Strand, London WC2B 4PH, United Kingdom. Phone: (general) +44 (20) 7240-3456; (Press Office) +44 (20) 7557-2947/1; (International Marketing) +44 (20) 7557-1143. Fax: (Audience Relations) +44 (20) 7557 1258; ("Write On" listeners' letters program) +44 (20) 7436 2800; (Audience and Market Research) +44 (20) 7557 1254; (International Marketing) +44 (20) 7557 1254. Email: (general listener correspondence) worldservice.letters @bbc.co.uk; ("Write On") writeon@bbc.co.uk. Web: (general, including RealAudio) www.bbc.co.uk/worldservice/; (entertainment and information) www.beeb.com. Contact: Patrick Condren, Presenter, of "Write On"; Alan Booth, Controller, Marketing & Communications; or Mark Byford, Chief Executive. Offers *BBC On Air* magazine (*see* below). Also, *see* Antigua, Ascension, Oman, Seychelles, Singapore and Thailand. The present facility at Masirah, Oman, is scheduled to be replaced in 2001 by a new site at Al-Ashkharah, also in Oman, and is to include four 300 kW shortwave transmitters. Does not verify reception reports due to budget limitations.
SAN FRANCISCO OFFICE, SCHEDULES: 2654 17th Avenue, San Francisco CA 94116 USA. Phone: +1 (415) 564-9968. Email: GPoppin@aol.com. Contact: George Poppin. This address, a volunteer office, only provides BBC World Service schedules to listeners. All other correspondence should be sent directly to the main office in London.
TECHNICAL: See Merlin Communications International, below.
BBC World Service—Publication and Product Sales
BBC WORLD SERVICE SHOP, Bush House Arcade, Strand, London WC2B 4PH, United Kingdom. Phone: +44 (20) 7557-2576. Fax: +44 (20) 7240 4811. Sells numerous audio/video (video PAL/VHS only) cassettes, publications, portable world band radios, T-shirts, sweatshirts and other BBC souvenirs available by mail order to UK addresses only.
BBC ON AIR monthly program magazine, Room 310 NW, Bush House, Strand, London WC2B 4PH, United Kingdom. Phone: (editorial office) +44 (20) 7557-2211; (Circulation Manager) +44 (20) 7557-2855; (advertising) +44 (20) 7557-2873; (subscription voice mail) +44 (20) 7557-2211. Fax: +44 (20) 7240 4899. Email: on.air.magazine@bbc.co.uk. Contact: (editorial) Dionne St. Hill, Editor; (subscriptions) Rosemarie Reid, Circulation Manager; (advertising) Adam Ford. Subscription $32 or £20 per year. VISA/MC/AX/Barclay/EURO/Access, Postal Order, International Money Draft or cheque in pounds sterling.

Commonwealth Broadcasting Association, CBA Secretariat, 17 Fleet Street, London EC4Y 1AA, United Kingdom. Phone: +44 (20) 7583-5550. Fax: +44 (20) 7583 5549. Email: (general) cba@cba.org.uk; (Smith) elizabeth@cba.org.uk. Web: www.oneworld.org/cba/. Contact: Elizabeth Smith, Secretary-General; Colin Lloyd, Manager—Training and Development; or Hilary Clucas, Administrator. Publishes the annual *Commonwealth Broadcaster Directory* and the quarterly *Commonwealth Broadcaster* (online subscription form available).

Far East Broadcasting Association (FEBA), Ivy Arch Road, Worthing, West Sussex BN14 8BX, United Kingdom. Phone: +44 (1903) 237-281. Fax: +44 (1903) 205 294. Email: reception@febaradio.org.uk; or (Richard Whittington) dwhittington@febaradio.org.uk. Web: www.feba.org.uk. Contact: Tony Ford or Richard Whittington, Schedule Engineer. This office is the headquarters for FEBA worldwide.

Global Sound Kitchen, G-One Ltd, 50 Lisson Street, London, NW1 5DF. Phone: +44 (20) 7453-1610. Email: studio@globalsoundkitchen.com. Web: (includes RealAudio and Windows Media) www.globalsoundkitchen.com. Contact: Claire Marshall. For further contact information (including where to send reception reports), *see* Virgin Radio. A service produced by the Ginger Media Group (operators of Virgin Radio in the U.K.) and transmitted via facilities of Merlin Communications International (*see*).

High Adventure Radio (Voice of Hope), P.O. Box 109, Hereford HR4 9XR, United Kingdom. Email: mail@highadventure.net. Web: www.intertvnet.net/~highorg/stations/europe/. Broadcasts via transmitters of Deutsche Telekom (*see*) in Jülich, Germany. Also, *see* KVOH—High Adventure Radio, USA.

IBC-Tamil, P.O. Box 1505, London SW8 2ZH, United Kingdom. Phone: +44 (20) 7787-8000. Fax: +44 (20) 7787 8010. Contact: A.C. Tarcisius, Managing Director; S. Shivaranjith, Manager; or Public Relations Officer.

London Radio Service (LRS), The Interchange, Oval Road, London NW1 7DZ, United Kingdom. Phone: +44 (20) 7453-7500. Fax: +44 (20) 7413 0072. Email: tayris@lrs.co.uk. Web: (includes RealAudio) www.lrs.co.uk. Contact: Tim Ayris, Marketing Officer. An award-winning producer and syndicator of news and feature programs in English, Arabic, Russian, Spanish and Portuguese, LRS is a service of Associated Press Television News on behalf of the Foreign and Commonwealth Office. Broadcasts on shortwave in English and Spanish via WWCR, USA (*see*).

Merlin Communications International Limited, 20 Lincoln's Inn Fields, London WC2A 3ES, United Kingdom. Phone: +44 (20) 7969-0000. Fax: +44 (20) 7396 6223; (Nicola Wallbridge) +44 (20) 7396 6223. Email: marketing @merlincommunications.com; (frequency-related matters) sfm@mercom.co.uk. Web: www.merlincommunications.com; www.mercom.co.uk. Contact: Fiona Lowry, Chief Executive; Rory Maclachlan, Comercial Director; Richard Hurd, Business Development Manager, Transmission Sales; Ciaran Fitzgerald, Head of BBC Customer Services; Anver Anderson, Head of Satellite Sales; or Michelle Franks, Communications Assistant. Merlin has a ten year contract with the BBC World Service to provide a full range of complex programme transmission and distribution services from 11 strategic sites to over 100 countries worldwide. International customers include Radio Canada International, Voice of America, NHK, Radio Telefis Eireann, HCJB World Radio and Swiss Radio International. Does not verify reception reports.

Virgin Radio, 1 Golden Square, London, W1R 4DJ, United Kingdom. Phone: +44 (20) 7434-1215. Fax: +44 (20) 7437 2498. Email: (reception reports) lee.roberts@ginger.com. Contact: Lee Roberts, Director. Snail mail reception reports for all Virgin Radio/Ginger Media productions and services aired on shortwave should be sent to: Lee Roberts, c/o Virgin Radio, at the above address.

Wales Radio International, Preseli Radio Productions, Pros Kairon, Crymych, Pembrokeshire, SA41 3QE, Wales, United Kingdom. Phone: +44 (1437) 563-361. Fax: +44 (1239)

831 390. Email: jenny@wri.cymru.net. Web: (includes RealAudio) http://wri.cymru.net. Contact: Jenny O'Brien. A weekly broadcast via the facilities of Merlin Communications International (*see*).

☞**World Radio Network Ltd**, Wyvil Court, 10 Wyvil Road, London SW8 2TY, United Kingdom. Phone: +44 (20) 7896-9000. Fax: + 44 (20) 7896 9007. Email: (general) online@wrn.org; wrn@cityscape.co.uk; (Cohen) jeffc@wrn.org. Web: www.wrn.org. Contact: Karl Miosga, Managing Director; Jeffrey Cohen, Director of Development; Tim Ashburner, Director of Technical Operations; or Simon Spanswick, Director of Corporate Affairs. Sells numerous items such as Polo T-shirts, baseball caps, pen knives and watches. Ask for WRN collection catalogue for further details. VISA/MC. Webcasts using RealAudio and Media Player, plus program placement via satellite in various countries for nearly two dozen international broadcasters.

UNITED NATIONS   World Time –5 (–4 midyear)

☞**United Nations Radio**, Secretariat Building, Room S-850-M, United Nations, New York NY 10017 USA; or write to the station over which UN Radio was heard. Phone: +1 (212) 963-5201. Fax: +1 (212) 963 1307. Email: (general) unradio@un.org; (comments on programs) audio-visual@un.org; (reception reports) smithd@un.org. Web: (general) www.un.org/av/radio; (RealAudio) www.wrn.org/ondemand/unitednations.html; www.internetbroadcast.com/unhome.htm. Contact: (general) Sylvester E. Rowe, Chief, Radio and Video Service; or Ayman El-Amir, Chief, Radio Section, Department of Public Information; (reception reports) David Smith; (technical and nontechnical) Sandra Guy, Secretary. Free stamps and *UN Frequency* publication. Reception reports (including those sent by email) are verified with a QSL card.
GENEVA OFFICE: Room G209, Palais des Nations, CH-1211 Geneva 10, Switzerland. Phone: +41 (22) 917-4222. Fax: +41 (22) 917 0123.
PARIS OFFICE: UNESCO Radio, 7 Place de Fontenoy, F-75007 Paris, France. Fax: +33 (1) 45 67 30 72. Contact: Erin Faherty, Executive Radio Producer.

URUGUAY   World Time –3

Emisora Ciudad de Montevideo, Canelones 2061, 11200 Montevideo, Uruguay. Phone: +598 (2) 402-0142. Fax: +598 (2) 402 0700. Contact: Aramazd Yizmeyian, Director General. Free stickers. Return postage helpful.
La Voz de Artigas (when operating), Av. Lecueder 483, 55000 Artigas, Uruguay. Phone: +598 (772) 2447 or +598 (772) 3445. Fax: +598 (772) 4744. Contact: (general) Sra. Solange Murillo Ricciardi, Co-Propietario; or Luis Murillo; (technical) Roberto Murillo Ricciardi. Free stickers and pennants. Replies to correspondence in English, Spanish, French, Italian and Portuguese.
Radiodifusion Nacional—*see* S.O.D.R.E., below.
☞**Radio Monte Carlo**, Av. 18 de Julio 1224 piso 1, 11100 Montevideo, Uruguay. Phone: +598 (2) 901-4433 or +598 (2) 908-3987. Fax: +598 (2) 901 7762. Email: cx20@netgate.com.uy. Web: (includes RealAudio) http://netgate.com.uy/cx20/. Contact: Ana Ferreira de Errázquin, Secretaria, Departamento de Prensa de la Cooperativa de Radioemisoras; Alexi Haysaniuk, Jefe Técnico; Déborah Ibarra, Secretaria; Emilia Sánchez Vega, Secretaria; or Ulises Graceras. Correspondence in Spanish preferred.

☞**Radio Oriental**—Same mailing address as Radio Monte Carlo, above. Phone: +598 (2) 901-4433 or +598 (2) 900-5612. Fax: +598 (2) 901 7762. Email: cx12@netgate.com.uy. Web: (includes RealAudio) http://netgate.com.uy/cx12/. Correspondence in Spanish preferred.
S.O.D.R.E., Radiodifusión Nacional, Casilla 1412, 11000 Montevideo, Uruguay. Phone: +598 (2) 916-1933. Email: info @sodre.gub.uy. Web: www.sodre.gub.uy. Contact: (administration) Dr. Jorge Mascheroni, Director de Radiodifusión Nacional; (publicity) Daniel Ayala González, Publicidad; (technical) Francisco Escobar, Dpto. Técnico. Reception reports may also be sent to the "Radioactividades" program (*see*, below).
MEDIA PROGRAM: "Radioactividades," Casilla 7011, 11000 Montevideo, Uruguay. Fax: +598 (2) 575 4640. Email: radioact@chasque.apc.org. Web: www.chasque.apc.org/radioact/. Contact: Daniel Muñoz Faccioli.

USA   World Time –4 Atlantic, including Puerto Rico and Virgin Islands; –5 (–4 midyear) Eastern, excluding Indiana; –5 Indiana, except northwest and southwest portions; –6 (–5 midyear) Central, including northwest and southwest Indiana; –7 (–6 midyear) Mountain, except Arizona; –7 Arizona; –8 (–7 midyear) Pacific; –9 (–8 midyear) Alaska, except Aleutian Islands; –10 (–9 midyear) Aleutian Islands; –10 Hawaii; –11 Samoa

☞**Adventist World Radio, the Voice of Hope**
HEADQUARTERS OFFICE: 12501 Old Columbia Pike, Silver Spring MD 20904 USA. Email: english@awr.org. Web: www.awr.org. Send all letters and reception reports to: AWR, 39 Brendon Street, London W1, United Kingdom.
INTERNATIONAL RELATIONS: Box 29235, Indianapolis IN 46229 USA. Phone/fax: +1 (317) 891-8540. Contact: Dr. Adrian M. Peterson, International Relations Coordinator. Provides publications with regular news releases and technical information. Sometimes issues special verification cards. QSL stamps and certificates also available from this address in return for reception reports.
DX PROGRAM: "Wavescan," prepared by Adrian Peterson; aired on all AWR facilities and other stations. Also available in RealAudio at the AWR Website, www.awr.org. Also, *see* AWR listings under Germany, Guam, Guatemala, Italy, Kenya, Madagascar and United Kingdom.
☞**AFNL-American Farsi NetLink**, 7417 Van Nuys Blvd., Van Nuys CA 91405 USA. Phone: +1 (818) 988-4241; (toll-free within the United States) 1-800-547-9986. Fax: +1 (818) 781 3666. Email: afnl@pacbell.net. Web: (includes MP3) www.afnl.com. A satellite broadcaster which commenced shortwave broadcasts via Moldova during summer 2000.
☞**AFRTS-Armed Forces Radio and Television Service (Shortwave)**, Naval Media Center, NDW Anacostia Annex, 2713 Mitscher Road SW, Washington DC 20373-5819 USA. For verification of reception, be sure to mark the envelope, "Attn: Short Wave Reception Reports." Email: (verifications) qsl@mediacen.navy.mil. Web: (AFRTS parent organization) www.afrts.osd.mil; (2-minute news clips in RealAudio): www.defenselink.mil/news/radio/; (Naval Media Center) www.mediacen.navy.mil. The Naval Media Center is responsible for all AFRTS broadcasts aired on shortwave.
BBC World Service via WYFR—Family Radio. For verification direct from WYFR's transmitters, contact WYFR—Family Radio (*see* below). Nontechnical correspondence should be sent to the BBC World Service in London (*see*).

Broadcasting Board of Governors (BBG), 330 Independence Avenue SW, Room 3360, Washington DC 20547 USA. Phone: +1 (202) 401-3736. Fax: +1 (202) 401 3376. Contact: (general) Kathleen Harrington, Public Relations; (administration) Mark Nathanson, Chairman. The BBG, created in 1994 and headed by nine members nominated by the President, is the overseeing agency for all official non-military United States international broadcasting operations, including the VOA, RFE-RL, Radio Martí and Radio Free Asia.

FEBC Radio International

INTERNATIONAL HEADQUARTERS: Far East Broadcasting Company, Inc., P.O. Box 1, La Mirada CA 90637 USA. Phone: +1 (310) 947-4651. Fax: +1 (310) 943 0160. Email: 3350911@mcimail.com; febc-usa@xc.org; or febc@febc.org. Web: www.febc.org. Operates world band stations in the Northern Mariana Islands, the Philippines and the Seychelles. Does not verify reception reports from this address.

RUSSIAN OFFICE: P.O. Box 2128, Khabarovsk 680020, Russia. Email: russia@febc.org.

UNITED KINGDOM OFFICE: FEBA Radio, Ivy Arch Road, Worthing, West Sussex BN14 8BX, United Kingdom. Phone: +44 (903) 237-281. Fax: +44 (903) 205 294. Email: reception@feba.org.uk. Web: www.feba.org.uk.

Federal Communications Commission, 1919 M Street NW, Washington DC 20554 USA. Phone: +1 (202) 418-0200. Fax: +1 (202) 418 0232. Email: (general) fccinfo@fcc.gov; (Public Services Division) psd@fcc.gov; (specific individuals) format is initiallastname@fcc.gov, so to reach, say, Tom Polzin it would be tpolzin@fcc.gov. Web: (general) www.fcc.gov/; (high frequency operating schedules) www.fcc.gov/ib/pnd/neg/ hf_web/seasons.html; (FTP) ftp://ftp.fcc.gov/pub/. Contact: (consumer information) Martha Contee, Director, Public Services Division; (International Bureau, technical) Thomas E. Polzin.

Fundamental Broadcasting Network, Grace Missionary Baptist Church, 520 Roberts Road, Newport NC 28570 USA. Phone: +1 (252) 223-6088; (toll-free, within the United States) 1-800-245-9685; (Robinson) +1 (252) 223-4600. Web: (text) www.clis.com/fbn/; (RealAudio) www.worthwhile.com/fbn/. Email: fbn@bmd.clis.com. Alternative address: Morehead City NC 28557 USA. Phone: +1 (252) 240-1600. Fax: +1 (252) 726 2251. Contact: Pastor Clyde Eborn; (technical) David Robinson, Chief Engineer. Verifies reception reports if 1 IRC or (within USA) an SASE is included. Accepts email reports. Plans to eventually broadcast in Chinese, French, Russian and Spanish in addition to English.

George Jacobs and Associates, Inc., 8701 Georgia Avenue, Suite 711, Silver Spring MD 20910 USA. Phone: +1 (301) 587-8800. Fax: +1 (301) 587 8801. Email: gja@gjainc.com; or gjainc_20910@yahoo.com. Web: www.gjainc.com/. Contact: (technical) Bob German or Mrs. Anne Case; (administration) George Jacobs, P.E. This firm provides frequency management and other engineering services for a variety of private U.S. and other world band stations and brokers time on worldwide shortwave, AM, FM, satellite and cable systems for international broadcasters.

Good News Hour, Good News World Radio, P.O. Box 895, Fort Worth TX 76101 USA. Phone: +1 (817) 226-6100 or +1 (817) 275-3334. Email: hope@goodnewsworld.org. Web: (includes RealAudio) www.goodnewsworld.org/content/ broadcasts.htm. Contact: Robert Mawire, President; Jeannine Kuhnell. Welcomes reception reports both to postal and email addresses. Free literature available. A program from Good News Ministries broadcast via the transmitters of Deutsche Telekom *(see)* in Jülich, Germany.

Herald Broadcasting Syndicate—Shortwave Broadcasts (all locations), Shortwave Broadcasts, P.O. Box 1524, Boston MA 02117-1524 USA. Phone: (general, toll-free within U.S.) 1-800-288-7090 or (general elsewhere) +1 (617) 450-2929 [with either number, extension 2060 to hear recorded frequency information, or 2929 for Shortwave Helpline and request printed schedules and information]. Fax: +1 (617) 450 2283. Web: (includes RealAudio) www.tfccs.com/GV/CSPS/ HERALD/bdcst/bdcst.html. Contact: Catherine Aitken-Smith, Director of International Broadcasting, Herald Broadcasting Syndicate (representative for station activity in Boston). Free schedules and information about Christian Science. *The Christian Science Monitor* newspaper and a full line of Christian Science books are available from: 1 Norway Street, Boston MA 02115 USA. *Science and Health with Key to the Scriptures* by Mary Baker Eddy is available in English $14.95 paperback ($16.95 in French, German, Portuguese or Spanish paperback; $24.95 in Czech or Russian hardcover) from Science and Health, P.O. Box 1875, Boston MA 02117 USA.

Herald Broadcasting Syndicate—WSHB Cypress Creek, 1030 Shortwave Lane, Pineland SC 29934 USA. Phone: (general) +1 (803) 625-5551; (station manager) +1 (803) 625-5555; (engineer) +1 (803) 625-5554. Fax: +1 (803) 625 5559. Email: (Station Manager) evansc@wshb.com, or cee@hargray.com; (Chief Engineer) centgrafd@wshb.com; (QSL coordinator) riehmc@wshb.com. Web: www.tfccs.com/GV/shortwave/ shortwave_schedule.html. Contact: (technical) Damian Centgraf, Chief Engineer; C. Ed Evans, Senior Station Manager; or Cindy Riehm, QSL Coordinator. Free station stickers when available. Visitors welcome from 9 to 4 Monday through Friday; for other times, contact transmitter site beforehand to make arrangements. This address is for technical feedback on South Carolina transmissions only; other inquiries should be directed to Shortwave Broadcasts, P.O. Box 1524, Boston MA 02117-1524 USA.

International Broadcasting Bureau (IBB)—Reports to the Broadcasting Board of Governors *(see)*, and includes, among others, the Voice of America, RFE-RL, Radio Martí and Radio Free Asia. IBB Engineering (Office of Engineering and Technical Operations) provides broadcast services for these stations. Contact: (administration) Brian Conniff, Director; or Joseph O'Connell, Director of External Affairs; (technical) George Woodard, Director of Engineering. Web: www.ibb.gov/ ibbpage.html.

FREQUENCY AND MONITORING OFFICE, TECHNICAL: USIA/IBB/EOF: Spectrum Management Division, International Broadcasting Bureau (IBB), Room 4611 Cohen Bldg., 330 Independence Avenue SW, Washington DC 20547 USA. Phone: +1 (202) 619-1669. Fax: +1 (202) 619 1680. Email: (scheduling) dferguson@ibb.gov; (monitoring) bw@his.com. Web: (general) http://monitor.ibb.gov; (email reception report form) http://monitor.ibb.gov/now_you_try_it.html. Contact: Dan Ferguson (dferguson@ibb.gov); or Bill Whitacre (bw@his.com).

KAIJ

ADMINISTRATION OFFICE: Two-if-by-Sea Broadcasting Co., 22720 SE 410th St., Enumclaw WA 89022 USA. Phone/fax: (Mike Parker, California) +1 (818) 606-1254; (Washington State office, if and when operating) +1 (206) 825 4517. Contact: Mike Parker (mark envelope, "please forward"). Relays programs of Dr. Gene Scott's University Network *(see)*. Replies occasionally. *STUDIO:* Faith Center, 1615 S. Glendale Avenue, Glendale CA 91025 USA. Phone: +1 (818) 246-8121. Contact: Dr. Gene Scott, President.

TRANSMITTER: RR#3 Box 120, Frisco TX 75034 USA (physical location: Highway 380, 3.6 miles west of State Rt. 289, near Denton TX). Phone: +1 (214) 346-2758. Contact: Walt Green or Fred Bithell. Station encourages mail to be sent to the administration office, which seldom replies, or the studio (*see* above).

KJES—King Jesus Eternal Savior

STATION: The Lord's Ranch, 230 High Valley Road, Vado NM 88072 USA. Phone: +1 (505) 233-2090. Fax: +1 (505) 233 3019. Email: KJES@aol.com. Contact: Michael Reuter, Manager. $1 or return postage appreciated.

SPONSORING ORGANIZATION: Our Lady's Youth Center, P.O. Box 1422, El Paso TX 79948 USA. Phone: +1 (915) 533-9122.

KNLS—New Life Station

OPERATIONS CENTER: 605 Bradley Ct., Franklin TN 37067 USA (letters sent to the Alaska transmitter site are usually forwarded to Franklin). Phone: +1 (615) 371-8707 ext.140. Fax: +1 (615) 371 8791. Email: knls@aol.com. Web: www.knls.org. Contact: (general) Dale Ward, Executive Producer; L. Wesley Jones, Director of Follow-Up Teaching; or Mike Osborne, Senior Producer, English Language Service; (technical) F.M. Perry, Frequency Coordinator. Free *Alaska Calling!* newsletter and station pennants. Free spiritual literature and bibles in Russian, Mandarin and English. Free Alaska books, tapes, postcards and cloth patches. Two free DX books for beginners. Special, individually numbered, limited edition, verification cards issued for each new transmission period to the first 200 listeners providing confirmed reception reports. Stamp and postcard exchange. Return postage appreciated.

TRANSMITTER SITE: P.O. Box 473, Anchor Point AK 99556 USA. Phone: +1 (907) 235-8262. Fax: +1 (907) 235 2326. Contact: (technical) Kevin Chambers, Chief Engineer.

▣KRSI—Radio Sedaye Iran. Moved from Santa Monica to Beverly Hills during summer 2000, and no address or phone information available by the time we went to press. Email: krsi@glancing.com. Web: (includes Windows Media) www.krsi.com. Normally operates via a closed broadcasting system and the Internet, but started shortwave broadcasts from Moldova during 2000.

▣KTBN—Trinity Broadcasting Network:

GENERAL CORRESPONDENCE: P.O. Box A, Santa Ana CA 92711 USA. Phone: +1 (714) 832-2950. Fax: +1 (714) 730 0661. Email: tbntalk@tbn.org or comments@tbn.org. Web: (Trinity Broadcasting Network, including RealAudio) www.tbn.org; (KTBN) www.tbn.org/ktbn.html. Contact: Dr. Paul F. Crouch, Managing Director; Jay Jones, Producer, "Music of Praise"; or Programming Department. Monthly TBN newsletter. Free booklets, stickers and small souvenirs sometimes available.

TECHNICAL CORRESPONDENCE: Engineering/QSL Department, 2442 Michelle Drive, Tustin CA 92780-7015 USA. Phone: +1 (714) 665-2145. Fax: +1 (714) 730 0661. Email: lreyes@tbn.org. Contact: Laura Reyes, QSL Manager; or Ben Miller, Vice President of Engineering. Responds to reception reports. Write to : Trinity Broadcasting Network, Attention: Superpower KTBN Radio QSL Manager, Laua Reyes, 2442 Michelle Drive, Tustin CA 92780 USA. Return postage (IRC or SASE) helpful. Although a California operation, KTBN's shortwave transmitter is located at Salt Lake City, Utah.

KVOH—High Adventure Global Broadcasting Network

MAIN OFFICE: P.O. Box 100, Simi Valley CA 93062 USA. Phone: +1 (805) 520-9460; toll-free (within USA) 1-800-517-HOPE. Fax: +1 (805) 520 7823. Email: kvoh@highadventure.net. Web: www.highadventure.org. Contact: (listeners' correspondence) Pat Kowalick, "Listeners' Letterbox"; (nontechnical) Ralph

McDevitt, Program Manager; (administration, High Adventure Ministries) George Otis, President and Chairman; (administration, KVOH) Paul Johnson, General Manager, KVOH; (technical) Paul Hunter, Director of Engineering. Free program schedules and *Voice of Hope* book. Sells books, audio and video cassettes, T-shirts and world band radios. Booklist available on request. VISA/MC. Also, *see* Palau and United Kingdom. Return postage (IRCs) required. Replies as time permits.

CORRESPONDENCE RELATING TO BROADCASTS TO SOUTH ASIA: P.O. Box 100, Simi Valley, Los Angeles CA 93062 USA

WESTERN AUSTRALIA OFFICE, NONTECHNICAL: 79 Sycamore Drive, Duncraig WA 6023, Australia. Phone: +61 (9) 9345-1777. Fax: +61 (9) 9345 5407. Contact: Caron or Peter Hedgeland.

CANADA OFFICE, NONTECHNICAL: Box 425, Station 'E', Toronto, M6H 4E3 Canada. Phone/fax: +1 (900) 898-5447. Contact: Don McLaughlin, Director.

PALAU OFFICE, NONTECHNICAL: P.O. Box 66, Koror, Palau 96940, Pacific Islands. Phone: +680 488-2162. Fax: +680 488 2163. Contact: Rolland Lau.

SINGAPORE OFFICE, NONTECHNICAL: 265 B/C South Bridge Road, Singapore 058814, Singapore. Phone: + 65 221-2054. Fax: +65 221 2059. Contact: Cyril Seah.

U.K. OFFICE: P.O. Box 109, Hereford HR4 9XR, United Kingdom. Phone: +44 (1432) 359-099 or (mobile) +44 (0589) 078-444. Fax: +44 (1432) 263 408. Email: mail@highadventure.net. Web: www.highadventure.org/europe1.html. Contact: Peter Darg, Director. This office verifies reports of Voice of Hope ("European Beacon") broadcasts via Jülich, Germany.

▣KWHR-World Harvest Radio:

ADMINISTRATION OFFICE: see WHRI, USA, below.

TRANSMITTER: Although located 6 _ miles southwest of Naalehu, 8 miles north of South Cape, and 2000 feet west of South Point (Ka La) Road (the antennas are easily visible from this road) on Big Island, Hawaii, the operators of this rural transmitter site maintain no post office box in or near Naalehu, and their telephone number is unlisted, Best bet is to contact them via their administration office (*see* WHRI, below), or to drive in unannounced (it's just off South Point Road) the next time you vacation on Big Island.

Leinwoll (Stanley)—Telecommunication Consultant, 305 E. 86th Street, Suite 21S-W, New York NY 10028 USA. Phone: +1 (212) 987-0456. Fax: +1 (212) 987 3532. Email: stanL00011@aol.com. Contact: Stanley Leinwoll, President. This firm provides frequency management and other engineering services for some private U.S. world band stations, but does not correspond with the general public.

National Association of Shortwave Broadcasters, P.O. Box 8700, Cary NC 27512 USA. Phone: +1 (919) 460-3750. Fax: +1 (919) 460 3702. Email: nasbmem@rocketmail.com. Web: www.shortwave.org. Contact: Glenn W. Sink, Secretary-Treasurer. Association of most private U.S. world band stations, as well as a group of other international broadcasters, equipment manufacturers and organizations related to shortwave broadcasting. Includes committees on various subjects, such as digital shortwave radio. Interfaces with the Federal Communications Commission's International Bureau and other broadcasting-related organizations to advance the interests of its members. Publishes *NASB Newsletter* for members and associate members; free sample upon request on letterhead of an appropriate organization. Annual one-day convention held near Washington DC's National Airport early each spring; non-members wishing to attend should contact the Secretary-Treasurer in advance; convention fee typically $50 per person.

Overcomer Ministry ("Voice of the Last Day Prophet of God"), P.O. Box 691, Walterboro SC 29488 USA. Phone: (0900-1700 local time, Sunday through Friday) +1 (803) 538-3892. Email: brotherstair@overcomerministry.com. URLs (including RealAudio): www.overcomerministry.com; www.soundwaves2000.com/ocm99/default.htm. Contact: Brother R.G. Stair. Sample "Overcomer" newsletter and various pamphlets free upon request. Sells a Sangean shortwave radio for $50, plus other items of equipment and various publications at appropriate prices. Via Deutsche Telekom, Germany; and WINB, WRNO and WGTG, USA.

Que Huong Radio, 2670 S. White Rd. #165, San Jose CA 95148 USA. Phone: +1 (408) 223-3130; (toll-free within the United States) 1-888-313-1120. Fax: +1 (408) 223-3131. Email: quehuong@quehuongmedia.com or qhradio@aol.com. Web: www.quehuongmedia.com. A Californian Vietnamese station operating on Medium Wave/AM, and which airs some of its programs on shortwave via the facilities of World Harvest Radio (*see*) and a leased transmitter in Central Asia.

Radio Free Asia, Suite 300, 2025 M Street NW, Washington DC 20036 USA. Phone: (general) +1 (202) 530-4900; (programming) +1 (202) 530-4907; (president) +1 (202) 457-4901; (vice-president) +1 (202) 536 4902; (technical) +1 (202) 530-4958. Fax: +1 (202) 530 7794 or +1 (202) 721 7468. Email: (individuals) the format is lastnameinitial@rfa.org; so to reach, say, David Baden, it would be badend@rfa.org; (language sections) the format is language@www.rfa.org; so to contact, say, the Cambodian section, address your message to khmer@www.rfa.org; (general) Webmaster@www.rfa.org. Web: (includes audio in Audio Active format) www.rfa.org. Contact: (administration) Richard Richter, President; Craig Perry, Vice President; Daniel Southerland, Executive Editor; (technical) David Baden, Director of Technical Operations. RFA, originally created in 1996 as the Asia Pacific Network, is funded as a private nonprofit U.S. corporation by a grant from the Broadcasting Board of Governors (*see*), a politically bipartisan body appointed by the President. The purpose of RFA is to deliver accurate and timely news, information, and commentary, and to provide a forum for a variety of opinions and voices from within Asian countries. RFA focuses on events occurring in those countries. RFA seeks to promote the rights of freedom of opinion and expression—including the freedom to seek, receive and impart information and ideas through any medium regardless of frontiers.
CHINA OFFICE: P.O. Box 28840, Hong Kong, China.
JAPAN OFFICE: P.O. Box 49, Central Post Office, Tokyo 100-91, Japan.

Radio Free Europe-Radio Liberty/RFE-RL
PRAGUE HEADQUARTERS: Vinohradská 1, 110 00 Prague 1, Czech Republic. Phone: +420 (2) 2112-1111; (president) +420 (2) 2112-3000; (news desk) +420 (2) 2112-3629; (public relations) +420 (2) 2112-3012; (technical operations) +420 (2) 2112-3700; (broadcast operations) +420 (2) 2112-3550; (affiliate relations) +420 (2) 2112-2539. Fax: +420 (2) 2112 3013; (president) +420 (2) 2112 3002; (news desk) +420 (2) 2112 3613; (public relations) +420 (2) 2112 2995; (technical operations) +420 (2) 2112 3702; (broadcast operations) +420 (2) 2112 3540; (affiliate operations) +420 (2) 2112 4563. Email: the format is lastnameinitial@rferl.org; so to reach, say, David Walcutt, it would be walcuttd@rferl.org. Web: (general, including RealAudio) www.rferl.org/; (broadcast services) www.rferl.org/bd. Contact: Thomas A. Dine, President; Kestutis Girnius, Managing Editor, News and Current Affairs; Luke Springer, Deputy Director, Technology; Jana Horakova,

Public Relations Coordinator; Uldis Grava, Marketing Director; or Christopher Carzoli, Broadcast Operations Director.
WASHINGTON OFFICE: 1201 Connecticut Avenue NW, Washington DC 20036 USA. Phone: +1 (202) 457-6900; (newsdesk) +1 (202) 457-6950; (technical) +1 (202) 457-6963. Fax: +1 (202) 457 6992; (news desk) +1 (202) 457 6997; (technical) +1 (202) 457 6913. Email and Web: *see* above. Contact: Jane Lester, Secretary of the Corporation; or Paul Goble, Director of Communications and Technology; (news) Oleh Zwadiuk, Washington Bureau Chief; (technical) David Walcutt, Broadcast Operations Liaison. A private non-profit corporation funded by a grant from the Broadcasting Board of Governors, RFE/RL broadcasts in 21 languages (but not English) from transmission facilities now part of the International Broadcasting Bureau (IBB), *see*.

Radio Free Iraq—a service of Radio Free Europe-Radio Liberty (*see*, above). Web: (includes RealAudio) www.rferl.org.bd/iq/index.html.

Radio Martí, Office of Cuba Broadcasting, 4201 N.W. 77th Avenue, Miami FL 33166 USA. Phone: +1 (305) 437-7000. Fax: +1 (305) 437 7016. Email: (Spanish) rcotta@ocb.ibb.gov; (English) webmaster@ocb.ibb.gov. Web: (includes RealAudio) www.ibb.gov/marti/. Contact: (general) Herminio San Ramón, Director, Office of Cuba Broadcasting; Roberto Rodríguez-Tejera, Director, Radio Martí; Martha Yedra, Director of Programs; or William Valdez, Director, News; (technical) Michael Pallone, Director of Technical Operations.

Trans World Radio, International Headquarters, P.O. Box 8700, Cary NC 27512-8700 USA. Phone: +1 (919) 460-3700. Fax: +1 (919) 460 3702. Email: info2@twr.org. Web: (includes RealAudio) www.gospelcom.net/twr/main.shtml. Contact: (general) Jon Vaught, Public Relations; Richard Greene, Director, Public Relations; Joe Fort, Director, Broadcaster Relations; or Bill Danick; (technical) Glenn W. Sink, Assistant Vice President, International Operations. Free "Towers to Eternity" publication for those living in the U.S. Technical correspondence should be sent to the office nearest the country where the transmitter is located—Guam, Monaco or Swaziland. For information on TWR offices in Asia and Australasia, refer to the entry under "Guam."
CANADIAN OFFICE: P.O. Box 444, Niagara Falls ON, L2E 6T8 Canada. Web: http://twrcan.ca.

University Network, P.O. Box 1, Los Angeles CA 90053 USA. Phone: (toll-free within U.S.) 1-800-338-3030; (elsewhere, call collect) +1 (818) 240-8151. Email: drgenescott @mail.drgenescott.org. Web: (includes VDO and RealAudio) www.drgenescott.org/. Contact: Dr. Gene Scott. Sells audio and video tapes and books relating to Dr. Scott's teaching. Free copies of *The Truth About* and *The University Cathedral Pulpit* publications. Transmits over KAIJ and WWCR (USA); Caribbean Beacon (Anguilla, West Indies); the former AWR facilities in Cahuita, Costa Rica; and facilities in Samara, Russia.

USA Radio Network, 2290 Springlake #107, Dallas TX 75234 USA. Email: (general) newsroom@usaradio.com; (complaints/suggestions) tradup@usaradio.com; (technical) david@usaradio.com. Web: (includes RealAudio) www.usaradio.com. Does not broadcast direct on shortwave, but some of its news and other programs are heard via KWHR, WHRA, WHRI and WWCR, USA.

Voice of America—All Transmitter Locations
MAIN OFFICE: 330 Independence Avenue SW, Washington DC 20237 USA. If contacting the VOA directly is impractical, write c/o the American Embassy or USIS Center in your country. Phone: (to hear VOA-English live) +1 (202) 619-1979; (Office

of External Affairs) +1 (202) 619-2358 or +1 (202) 619-2039; (Audience Mail Division) +1 (202) 619-2770; (Africa Division) +1 (202) 619-1666 or +1 (202) 619-2879; ("Communications World") +1 (202) 619-3047; (Office of Research) +1 (202) 619-4965; (administration) +1 (202) 619-1088. Fax: (general information for listeners outside the United States) +1 (202) 376 1066; (Public Liaison for listeners within the United States) +1 (202) 619 1241; (Office of External Affairs) +1 (202) 205 0634 or +1 (202) 205 2875; (Africa Division) +1 (202) 619 1664; ("Communications World," Audience Mail Division and Office of Research) +1 (202) 619 0211; (administration) +1 (202) 619 0085; ("Communications World") +1 (202) 619 2543. Email: (general business) pubaff@ibb.gov; (reception reports and schedule requests) letters@voa.gov; (reception reports from outside the United States) qsl@voa.gov; (reception reports from within the United States) qsl-usa@voa.gov; ("Communications World") cw@voa.gov; (Office of Research) gmackenz @usia.gov; ("VOA News Now") newsnow@voa.gov; (VOA Special English) special@voa.gov. Web: (including RealAudio) www.voa.gov; www.ibb.gov. Contact: Sanford J. Ungar, Director; Mrs. Betty Lacy Thompson, Chief, Audience Mail Division, B/K. G759A Cohen; Larry James, Director, English Programs Division; Leo Sarkisian; Rita Rochelle, Africa Division; Kim Andrew Elliott, Producer, "Communications World"; or George Mackenzie, Audience Research Officer; (reception reports) Mrs. Irene Greene, QSL Desk, Audience Mail Division, Room G-759-C. Free stickers and calendars. If you're an American and miffed because you can't receive these goodies from the VOA, don't blame the station—they're only following the law. The VOA occasionally hosts international broadcasting conventions, and as of 1996 has been accepting limited supplemental funding from the U.S. Agency for International Development (AID). Also, see Ascension, Botswana, Greece, Morocco, Philippines, São Tomé e Príncipe, Sri Lanka and Thailand.

Voice of America/IBB—Delano Relay Station, Rt. 1, Box 1350, Delano CA 93215 USA. Phone: +1 (805) 725-0150. Fax: +1 (805) 725 6511. Contact: (technical) Brent Boyd, Manager. Nontechnical correspondence should be sent to the VOA address in Washington.

Voice of America/IBB—Greenville Relay Station, P.O. Box 1826, Greenville NC 27834 USA. Phone: +1 (919) 752-7115. Fax: +1 (919) 752 5959. Contact: (technical) Bruce Hunter, Manager. Nontechnical correspondence should be sent to the VOA address in Washington.

⬛WBCQ—"The Planet," 97 High Street, Kennebunk ME 04043 USA. Email: wbcq@gwi.net. Web: (includes MP3) http:/ /theplanet.wbcq.net/. Contact: Allan H. Weiner; Elayne Star, Office Manager; or Scott Becker. Verifies reception reports if 1 IRC or (within USA) an SASE is included.

⬛WEWN—EWTN Global Catholic Radio
TRANSMISSION FACILITY AND STATION MAILING ADDRESS: 1500 High Road, P.O. Box 176, Vandiver AL 35176 USA.
ENGINEERING AND MARKETING OFFICES: 5817 Old Leeds Rd., Irondale AL 35210 USA.
Phone: (general) +1 (205) 271-2900; (Station Manager) +1 (205) 271-2943; (Chief Engineer) +1 (205) 271-2959; (Marketing Manager) +1 (205) 271-2982; (Program Director, English) +1 (205) 271-2944; (Program Director, Spanish) +1 (205) 271-2900 ext. 2073; (Frequency Manager) +1 (205) 271-2900 ext. 2017. Fax: (general) +1 (205) 271 2926; (Marketing) +1 (205) 271 2925; (Engineering) +1 (205) 271 2953. Email: (general) wewn@ewtn.com. To contact individuals, the format is initiallastname@ewtn.com; so to reach, say, Thom Price, it

would be tprice@ewtn.com. Web: (EWTN parent organization) www.ewtn.com; (WEWN, including RealAudio) www.ewtn.com/wewn/. Contact: (general) Thom Price, Director of English Programming; or Doug Archer, Director of Spanish Programming; (marketing) Bernard Lockhart, Radio Marketing Manager; (administration) William Steltemeier, President; or Frank Leurck, Station Manager; (technical) Terry Borders, Vice President Engineering; Joseph A. Dentici, Frequency Manager; or Dennis Dempsey, Chief Engineer. Listener correspondence welcomed; responds to correspondence on-air and by mail. Free bumper stickers, program schedules and (sometimes) other booklets or publications. Sells numerous religious books, CDs, audio and video cassettes, T-shirts, sweatshirts and various other religious articles; list available upon request (VISA/MC). IRC or return postage appreciated for correspondence. Although a Catholic entity, WEWN is not an official station of the Vatican, which operates its own Vatican Radio (see). Rather, WEWN reflects the activities of Mother M. Angelica and the Eternal Word Foundation, Inc. Donations and bequests accepted by the Eternal Word Foundation.

WGTG—With Glory To God, Box 1131, Copperhill TN 37317-1131 USA. Phone/fax: +1 (706) 492-5944. Email: wgtg@ellijay.com. Web: www.wgtg.org. Contact: (general)

Roseanne Frantz, Program Director; (technical) Dave Frantz, Chief Engineer. WGTG is a family-run station partly supported by listener donations. Usually not interested in reception reports, but if you provide 5 hours of programming details, a self addressed envelope, and return postage or 2 IRCs you might get a response. Offers airtime at $50 per hour. Plans to add another transmitter and three new antennas, and upgrade its existing transmitters to 120 kW each.

WHRA-World Harvest Radio:
ADMINISTRATION OFFICE: see WHRI, USA, below.
TRANSMITTER: Located in Greenbush, Maine, but all technical and other correspondence should be sent to WHRI (*see* next entry).

WHRI—World Harvest Radio, WHRI/WHRA/KWHR, LeSEA Broadcasting, P.O. Box 12, South Bend IN 46624 USA. Phone: +1 (219) 291-8200. Fax: (station) +1 (219) 291 9043. Email: whr@lesea.com; (Joe Brashier) jbrashier@lesea.com; (Joe Hill) jhill@lesea.com. URLs (including RealAudio): www.whr.org/; (LeSEA Broadcasting parent organization) www.lesea.com/. Contact: (listener contact) Loren Holycross; (general) Pete Sumrall, Vice President; or Joe Hill, Operations Manager; (programming or sales) Joe Hill or Joe Brashier; (technical) Douglas Garlinger, Chief Engineer. World Harvest Radio T-shirts available from 61300 S. Ironwood Road, South Bend IN 46614 USA. Return postage appreciated.
"EDXP NEWS REPORTS" : Web: www.members.tripod.com/-bpadula/.html. Special news reports concentrating on shortwave broadcasts to and from Asia, the Far East, Australia, the Pacific and the Indian sub-continent, compiled by EDXP and aired on the first Friday of each month, (UTC) and repeated on the following Saturday and Sunday within the *"Dxing with Cumbre"* program, over the World Harvest Radio shortwave and RealAudio Networks. Special EDXP QSLs will be offered for the shortwave releases (not for RealAudio). Reports of the EDXP feature should be sent to: Bob Padula, EDXP QSL Service, 404 Mont Albert Road, Surrey Hills, Victoria 3127, Australia. Return postage appreciated. Outside of Australia, 1 IRC or $1; within Australia, four 45c Australian stamps. Email reports welcome at: edxp@bigpond.com, and verified with Web-delivered animated QSLs.

WINB—World International Broadcasters, WINB, World International Broadcasters, P.O. Box 88, Red Lion PA 17356 USA. Phone: (all departments) +1 (717) 244-5360. Fax: +1 (717) 246 0363. Email: info@winb.com. Web: www.winb.com. Contact: (general) Mrs. Sally Spyker, Manager; (sales) Hans Johnson; (technical) Fred W. Wise, Technical Director; or John H. Norris, Owner. Return postage helpful outside United States. No giveaways or items for sale.

WJCR—Jesus Christ Radio, P.O. Box 91, Upton KY 42784 USA. Phone: +1 (502) 369-8614. Email: (general) wjcrfm@earthlink.net; (engineering) LarryBaysinger@usa.net. Web: www.wjcr.com. Contact: (general) Pastor Don Powell, President; Gerri Powell; Trish Powell; or A.L. Burile; (technical) Louis Tate, Chief Engineer. Free religious printed matter. Return postage or $1 appreciated. Actively solicits listener contributions.

WMLK—Assemblies of Yahweh, P.O. Box C, Bethel PA 19507 USA. Toll free telephone (U.S only) 1-800-523-3827; (elsewhere) +1 (717) 933-4518 or +1 (717) 933-4880. Email: AOY@avana.net. Web: www.assembliesof yahweh.com/Log.htm. Contact: (general) Elder Jacob O. Meyer, Manager and Producer of "The Open Door to the Living World"; (technical) Gary McAvin, Engineer. Free *Yahweh* magazine, stickers and religious material. Bibles, audio and video (VHS) tapes and religious paperback books offered. Enclosing return postage ($1 or IRCs) helps speed things up.

World Beacon, 2251 St. John's Bluff Road, Jacksonville FL 32246 USA; (alternative address) 8133 Baymeadows Way, Jacksonville FL 32556 USA. Phone: +1 (904) 642-8902. Fax: +1 (904) 642-8916. Email: (general) info@wordbeacon.net; (reception reports) reception@worldbeacon.net. Web: (includes MP3) www.worldbeacon.net; (AMG parent organization) www.affiliatedmedia.com. Contact: Scott Westerman, President; Jeff Johnson, Program Director. A mission service of Affiliated Media Group. Currently broadcasts via transmitters of Merlin Communications International (*see*) in the U.K. and Sentech (*see*) in South Africa.
AFRICA OFFICE: World Beacon-African Service, Box 651525, Benmore, Postal Code 2010, South Africa.

WRMI—Radio Miami International, 175 Fontainebleau Blvd., Suite 1N4, Miami FL 33172 USA; or P.O. Box 526852, Miami FL 33152 USA. Phone: (general) +1 (305) 559-9764; (Engineering) +1 (305) 827-2234. Fax: (general) +1 (305) 559 8186; (Engineering) +1 (305) 819 8756. Email: info@wrmi.net. Web: www.wrmi.net. Contact: (technical and nontechnical) Jeff White, General Manager/Sales Manager; (technical) Indalecio "Kiko" Espinosa, Chief Engineer. Free station stickers and tourist brochures. Sells "public access" airtime to nearly anyone to say virtually anything for $1 or more per minute. Radio Miami Internacional also acts as a broker for Cuban exile programs aired via U.S. station WHRI.

WRNO, Box 100, New Orleans LA 70181 USA; or 4539 I-10 Service Road North, Metairie LA 70006 USA. Phone: +1 (504) 889-2424. Fax: +1 (504) 889 0602. Web: www.noconnect.com/commerc/wrno/wrno.htm. Contact: Paul Heingarten, Operations Manager. Single copy of program guide for 2 IRCs or an SASE. Stickers available for SASE. T-shirts available for $10. Sells World Radio radios. Carries programs from various organizations; these may be contacted either directly or via WRNO. Correct reception reports verified for 2 IRCs or an SASE.

WSHB—*see* Herald Broadcasting Syndicate, above.

WTJC, Fundamental Broadcasting Network, 520 Roberts Road, Newport NC 28570 USA.Phone: +1 (252) 223-4600 (8:00 AM-4:00 PM Eastern Time). Fax: +1 (252) 223 2201. Email: fbn@clis.com. Web: (general) www.clis.com.fbn/; (RealAudio) www.worthwhile.com/fbn/. Contact: Michael Ebron, General Manager; or David Robinson, FBN Missionary Engineer. Station is operated by FBN, a religious and educational non-commercial broadcasting network.

WWBS, P.O. Box 18174. Macon GA 31209 USA. Phone: +1 (912) 477-3433. Email: (general) wwbsradio@aol.com. Contact: Charles C. Josey; or Joanne Josey. Include return postage if you want your reception reports verified.

WWCR—World Wide Christian Radio, F.W. Robbert Broadcasting Co., 1300 WWCR Avenue, Nashville TN 37218 USA. Phone: (general) +1 (615) 255-1300. Fax: +1 (615) 255 1311. Email: (general) wwcr@aol.com; (head of operations) wwcrl@aol.com; ("Ask WWCR" program) askwwcr@aol.com. Web: www.wwcr.com. Contact: (general) Chuck Adair, Sales Representative; (administration) George McClintock, K4BTY, General Manager; Adam W. Lock, Sr., WA2JAL, Head of Operations; or Dawn Parton, Program Director; (technical) D. Reming, Chief Engineer. Free program guide, updated monthly. Free stickers and small souvenirs sometimes available. Return postage helpful. For items sold on the air, contact the producers of the programs, and *not* WWCR. Replies as time permits. Carries programs from various political organizations, which may be contacted directly.

WWV/WWVB (official time and frequency stations), Time and Frequency Division, NIST, 325 Broadway, Boulder CO 80303 USA. Phone: +1 (303) 497-3276. Fax: +1 (303) 497 6461. Email: nist.radio@boulder.nist.gov; (Lowe) lowe@boulder.nist.gov. Web: www.boulder.nist.gov/timefreq/wwv/. Contact: John Lowe. Along with branch sister station WWVH in Hawaii (see below), WWV and WWVB are the official time and frequency stations of the United States, operating over longwave (WWVB) on 60 kHz, and over shortwave (WWV) on 2500, 5000, 10000, 15000 and 20000 kHz.

WWVH (official time and frequency station), NIST—Hawaii, P.O. Box 417, Kekaha, Kauai HI 96752 USA. Phone: +1 (808) 335-4361; (live audio) +1 (808) 335-4363. Fax: +1 (808) 335 4747. Contact: (technical) Dean T. Okayama, Engineer-in-Charge. Email: None planned. Along with headquarters sister stations WWV and WWVB (see preceding), WWVH is the official time and frequency station of the United States, operating on 2500, 5000, 10000 and 15000 kHz.

WYFR—Family Radio

NONTECHNICAL: Family Stations, Inc., 290 Hegenberger Road, Oakland CA 94621 USA; or P.O. Box 2140 Oakland CA 94621-9985 USA. Phone: (toll-free, U.S. only) 1-800-543-1495; (elsewhere) +1 (510) 568-6200; (engineering) +1 (510) 568-6200 ext. 240. Fax: (main office) +1 (510) 568-6200; (engineering) +1 (510) 562 1023. Email: (general) famradio@familyradio.com; (shortwave department) shortwave@familyradio.com. Web: (Family Radio Network, including RealAudio) www.familyradio.com; (WYFR) www.familyradio.com/short-wave/swlinks.html; (foreign-language broadcasts in RealAudio) www.familyradio.com/foreign.htm. Contact: (general) Harold Camping, General Manager; or Thomas Schaff, Shortwave Program Manager; (technical) Dan Elyea, Station Manager; or Shortwave Department. Free gospel tracts (33 languages), books, booklets, quarterly Family Radio News magazine and frequency schedule. 2 IRCs helpful.

BELARUS OFFICE: B.A International, Chapaeva Street #5, 220600 Minsk, Belarus.

INDIA OFFICE: Family Radio, c/o Rev. Alexander, Tekkali 532201 Andra Pradesh India.

TECHNICAL: WYFR—Family Radio, 10400 NW 240th Street, Okeechobee FL 34972 USA. Phone: +1 (941) 763-0281. Fax: +1 (941) 763 1034. Contact: Dan Elyea, Engineering Manager; or Edward F. Dearborn, Assistant Engineer Manager.

UZBEKISTAN World Time +5

WARNING—MAIL THEFT: Due to increasing local mail theft, Radio Tashkent suggests that those wishing to correspond should try using one of the drop-mailing addresses listed below.

Radio Tashkent, 49 Khorazm Street, 700047 Tashkent, Uzbekistan. Phone: (Head of International Service) +998 (71) 133-8920; (Correspondence Section) +998 (71) 139-9657; (Shekhar) +998 (71) 139-0752 or +998 (71) 139-9521. Fax: +998 (71) 144 0021. Email: (Shekhar) alex@kirsh.silk.org. Contact: Sherzat Gulyamov, Head of International Service; Mrs. Alfia Ruzmatova, Head of Correspondence Section; Babur Turdieav, Head of English Service; Alok Shekhar, Announcer - Hindi Service. Correspondence is welcomed in English, German, Russian, Uzbek and nine other languages broadcast by Radio Tashkent. Reception reports are verified with colorful QSL cards. Free pennants, badges, wallet calendars and postcards. Books in English by Uzbek writers are apparently available for purchase. Station offers free membership to the "Salum Aleikum Listeners' Club" for regular listeners.

LONDON OFFICE: 72 Wigmore Street, London W18 9L, United Kingdom.

FRANKFURT OFFICE: Radio Taschkent, c/o Uzbekistan Airways, Merkurhaus, Raum 215, Hauptbahnhof 10, D-60329 Frankfurt, Germany.

BANGKOK OFFICE: 848-850 Ramapur Road, Bangkok 10050, Thailand.

TRANSMISSION FACILITIES: Pochta va Telekommunikasiyalar Agentligi, Aleksey Tolstoy küçä 1, 700000 Tashkent, Uzbekistan. Phone: +998 (71) 133-6645. Fax: +998 (71) 144 2603. Contact: Fatrullah Fazullahyev, Director General.

Uzbek Radio, Khorazm küçä 49, 700047 Tashkent, Uzbekistan. Phone: (general) +998 (71) 144-1210; (Director) +998 (71) 133-8920 or 998 (71) 139-9636; (technical) +998 (71) 136-2290. Fax: (general) +998 (71) 144 0021; (Director) +998 (71) 133 8920. Email: uzradio@eanetways.com. Contact: (administration) Fakhriddin N. Nizom, Director; (technical) Komoljon Rajapov, Chief Engineer.

VANUATU World Time +12 (+11 midyear)

Radio Vanuatu, Information and Public Relations, Private Mail Bag 049, Port Vila, Vanuatu. Phone: +678 22999 or +678 23026. Fax: +678 22026. Email: vbtcnews@vanuatu.com. Web: www.vbtc.com.vu/Radio/radio.html. Contact: Jonas Cullwick, General Manager; Ambong Thompson, Head of Programmes; or Allan Kalfabun, Sales and Marketing Consultant, who is interested in exchanging letters and souvenirs from other countries; (technical) K.J. Page, Principal Engineer; Marianne Berukilkilu, Technical Manager; or Willie Daniel, Technician.

VATICAN CITY STATE World Time +1 (+2 midyear)

Radio Vaticana (Vatican Radio)

MAIN AND PROMOTION OFFICES: 00120 Città del Vaticano,

Vatican City State. Phone: (general) +39 (06) 6988-3551; (Director General) +39 (06) 6988-3945; (Programme Director) +39 (06) 6988-3996; (Publicity and Promotion Department) +39 (06) 6988-3045; (technical, general) +39 (06) 6988-4897; (frequency management) +39 (06) 6988-5258. Fax: (general) +39 (06) 6988 4565; (frequency management) +39 (06) 6988 5062. Email: sedoc@vatiradio.va; (Director General) dirigen@vatiradio.va; (frequency management) mc6790@mclink.it; (technical direction, general) sectec@vatiradio.va; (Programme Director) dirpro@vatiradio.va; (Publicity and Promotion Department) promo@vatiradio.va; (English Section) englishpr@vatiradio.va, (French Section) magfra@vatiradio.va; (German Section) deutsch@vatiradio.va; (Japanese Section) japan@vatiradio.va. Web: (general, including multilingual news and live broadcasts in RealAudio) www.vatican.va/news_services/radio/; (RealAudio in English and other European languages, plus text) www.wrn.org/vatican-radio/. Contact: (general) Elisabetta Vitalini Sacconi, Promotion Office and schedules; Eileen O'Neill, Head of Program Development, English Service; Fr. Lech Rynkiewicz S.J., Head of Promotion Office; Fr. Federico Lombardi, S.J., Program Director; Solange de Maillardoz, Head of International Relations; Sean Patrick Lovett, Head of English Service; or Veronica Scarisbrick, Producer, "On the Air;" (administration) Fr. Pasquale Borgomeo, S.J., Director General; (technical) Umberto Tolaini, Frequency Manager, Direzione Tecnica; Sergio Salvatori, Assistant Frequency Manager, Direzione Tecnica; Fr. Eugenio Matis S.J., Technical Director; or Giovanni Serra, Frequency Management Department. Correspondence sought on religious and programming matters, rather than the technical minutiae of radio. Free station stickers and paper pennants. Music CDs $13; *Pope John Paul II: The Pope of the Rosary* double CD/cassette $19.98 plus shipping; "Sixty Years...a Single Day" PAL video on Vatican Radio for 15,000 lire, including postage, from the Promotion Office.

INDIA OFFICE: Loyola College, P.B. No 3301, Chennai-600 03, India. Fax: +91 (44) 825 7340. Email: (Tamil) tamil@vatiradio.va; (Hindi) hindi@vatiradio.va; (English) india@vatiradio.va.

REGIONAL OFFICE, INDIA: Pastoral Orientation Centre, P.B. No 2251, Palarivattom, India. Fax: +91 (484) 336 227. Email: (Malayalam) malayalam@vatiradio.va.

JAPAN OFFICE: 2-10-10 Shiomi, Koto-ku, Tokyo 135, Japan. Fax: +81 (3) 5632 4457.

POLAND OFFICE: Warszawskie Biuro Sekcji Polskiej Radia Watykanskiego, ul. Skwer Ks. Kard. S, Warsaw, Poland. Phone: +48 (22) 838-8796.

VENEZUELA   World Time −4

Ecos del Torbes, Apartado 152, San Cristóbal 5001-A, Táchira, Venezuela. Phone: +58 (76) 438-244 or (studio): +58 (76) 421-949. Contact: (general) Licenciada Dinorah González Zerpa, Gerente; Simón Zaidman Krenter; (technical) Ing. Iván Escobar S., Jefe Técnico.

Observatorio Cagigal—YVTO, Apartado 6745, Armada 84-DHN, Caracas 103, Venezuela. Phone: +58 (2) 481—2761. Email: armdhn@ven.net. Contact: Jesús Alberto Escalona, Director Técnico; or Gregorio Pérez Moreno, Director. $1 or return postage helpful.

Radio Amazonas, Av. Simón Bolívar 4, Puerto Ayacucho 7101, Amazonas, Venezuela; or if no reply try Francisco José Ocaña at: Urb. 23 de Enero, Calle Nicolás Briceño, No. 18-266, Barinas 5201-A, Venezuela. Contact: Luis Jairo, Director; or Santiago

Sangil Gonzales, Gerente. Francisco José Ocaña is a keen collector of U.S. radio station stickers. Sending a few stickers with your letter as well as enclosing $2 may help.

Radio Nacional de Venezuela (when operating), Final Calle Las Marías, El Pedregal de Chapellín, 1050 Caracas, Venezuela. If this fails, try: Director de la Onda Corta, Sr. Miguel Angel Cariel, Apartado Postal 3979, Caracas 1010-A, Venezuela. Phone: +58 (2) 745-166. Email: rnb2000@hotmail.com. Web: www.venezuela.gov.ve/OCI/radio1.htm. Contact: Miguel Angel Cariel, Director de la Onda Corta. The transmitter site is actually located at Campo Carabobo, near Valencia, some three hours drive from Caracas.

Radio Occidente (if reactivated), Carrera 4a. No. 6-46, Tovar 5143, Mérida, Venezuela.

Radio Táchira, Apartado 152, San Cristóbal 5001-A, Táchira, Venezuela. Phone: +58 (76) 430-009. Contact: Desirée González Zerpa, Directora; Sra. Albertina, Secretaria; or Eleázar Silva Malavé, Gerente.

Radio Valera, Av. 10 No. 9-31, Valera 3102, Trujillo, Venezuela. Phone: +58 (71) 53-744. Contact: Gladys Barroeta; or Mariela Leal. Replies to correspondence in Spanish. Return postage required. This station has been on the same world band frequency for almost 50 years, which is a record for Latin America. If no response try via Antonio J. Contín. *(see* Radio Frontera, above).

VIETNAM   World Time +7

Bac Thai Broadcasting Service—contact via Voice of Vietnam—Overseas Service, below.

Lai Chau Broadcasting Service—contact via Voice of Vietnam—Overseas Service, below.

Lam Dong Broadcasting Service, Da Lat, Vietnam. Contact: Hoang Van Trung. Replies slowly to correspondence in Vietnamese, but French may also suffice.

Son La Broadcasting Service, Son La, Vietnam. Contact: Nguyen Hang, Director. Replies slowly to correspondence in Vietnamese, but French may also suffice.

Voice of Vietnam—Domestic Service (Đài Tiếng Nói Việt Nam, TNVN)—Addresses and contact numbers as for all sections of Voice of Vietnam—Overseas Service, below. Contact: Phan Quang, Director General.

▣Voice of Vietnam—Overseas Service

TRANSMISSION FACILITY (MAIN ADDRESS FOR NONTECHNICAL CORRESPONDENCE AND GENERAL VERIFICATIONS): 58 Quán Sú, Hànôi, Vietnam. Phone: +84 (4) 824-0044 or +84 (4) 825-5669. Fax: +84 (4) 826 1122. Email: qhqt.vov@hn.vnn.vn. Web: (English text) www.vov.org.vn/docs1/english/; (Vietnamese text and RealAudio in English and Vietnamese) www.vov.org.vn. Contact: Tran Mai Hanh, Director General; Mr. Pham Van Ly; or Ms. Hoang Minh Nguyet, Director of International Relations. Free paper pennant and, occasionally upon request, Vietnamese stamps. $1 helpful, but IRCs apparently of no use. Replies slowly. Try not to send stamps on correspondence to Vietnam. They're often cut off the envelopes and the station doesn't receive the letters. Machine-franked envelopes stand a better chance of getting through. *STUDIOS (NONTECHNICAL CORRESPONDENCE AND GENERAL VERIFICATIONS):* 45 Ba Trieu Street, Hànôi, Vietnam. Phone: (director) +84 (4) 825-7870; or (newsroom) +84 (4) 825-5761 or +84 (4) 825-5862. Fax: +84 (4) 826 6707. Email: btdn.vov@hn.vnn.vn. Contact Dinh The Loc, Director. TECHNICAL CORRESPONDENCE: Office of Radio Reception Quality, Central Department of Radio and Television Broadcast Engineering, Vietnam General Corporation of Posts and Telecommunications, Hànôi, Vietnam.

Yen Bai Broadcasting Station—contact via Voice of Vietnam, Overseas Service, above.

WESTERN SAHARA   World Time exactly

Radio Nacional de la República Arabe Saharaui Democrática, Directeur d'Information, Frente Polisario, B.P. 10, El-Mouradia, 16000 Algiers, Algeria; or c/o Ambassade de la République Arabe Saharaui Démocratique, 1 Av. Franklin Roosevelt, 16000 Algiers, Algeria. Phone (Algeria): +213 (2) 747-907. Fax, when operating (Algeria): +213 (2) 747 984. Web: (includes a RealAudio recording made in the station's studios) http://web.jet.es/rasd/amateur4.htm. Contact: Mohamed Lamin Abdesalem; Mahafud Zein; or Sneiba Lehbib. Two IRCs helpful. Pro-Polisario Front, and supported by the Algerian government.

YEMEN   World Time +3

⊠**Republic of Yemen Radio**, Ministry of Information, P.O. Box 2182 (or P.O. Box 2371), Sana'a, Yemen. Phone: +967 (1) 230-654. Fax: +967 (1) 230 761. Web: (RealAudio only) www.althawra.com. Contact: (general) English Service; (administration) Mohammed Dahwan, General Director of Sana'a Radio; (technical) Ali Al-Tashi, Technical Director; Mr. Adel Affara; or Abdulrahman Al-Haimi.

YUGOSLAVIA   World Time +1 (+2 midyear)

Radiotelevizija Srbije, Hilendarska 2/IV, 11000 Beograd, Serbia, Yugoslavia. Phone: +381 (11) 322-1850 or +381 (11) 321-1119. Fax: +381 (11) 324 8808. Email: (Simic) momcilo.simic@ties.itu.int or msimic@iname.com. Web: www.rts.co.yu. Contact: Momcilo Simic.

⊠**Radio Beograd**, Hilandarska 2a, 11000 Beograd, Serbia, Yugoslavia. Phone: +381 (11) 324-8888 or +381 (11) 324-9337. Web: (includes RealAudio) www.radiobeograd.co.yu. A service of Radiotelevizija Srbije (*see*, above). Currently inactive on shortwave, after its transmitter was destroyed by NATO forces in 1999. Some of its programs are also relayed by Radio Yugoslavia (*see*, below).

⊠**Radio Yugoslavia** (when operating), Hilendarska 2/IV, P.O. Box 200, 11000 Beograd, Serbia, Yugoslavia. Phone: +381 (11) 324-4455. Fax: +381 (11) 323 2014. Email: radioyu@bits.net. Web: (includes RealAudio) www.radioyu.org. Contact: (general) Nikola Ivanovic, Director; Aleksandar Georgiev; Aleksandar Popovic, Head of Public Relations; Pance Zafirovski, Head of Programs; or Slobodan Topovi_, Producer, "Post Office Box 200/Radio Hams' Corner"; (technical) B. Miletic, Operations Manager of HF Broadcasting; Technical Department; or Rodoljub Medan, Chief Engineer. Free pennants, stickers, pins and tourist information. $1 helpful. In August 2000, the Bosnian authorities ordered Radio Yugoslavia to abandon its shortwave transmitting facility at Bijeljina. At the time we went to press, the station had still not found alternative facilities.

ZAMBIA   World Time +2

Radio Christian Voice

STATION: Private Bag E606, Lusaka, Zambia. Phone: +260 (1) 274-251. Fax: +260 (1) 274 526. Email: cvoice@zamnet.zm. Contact: Andrew Flynn, Head of Transmission; Philip Haggar, Station Manager; Beatrice Phiri; or Lenganji Nanyangwe, Assistant to Station Manager. Free calendars and stickers pens, as available. Free religious books and items under selected circumstances. Sells T-shirts and sundry other items. $1 or 2 IRCs appreciated for reply. This station broadcasts Christian teachings and music, as well as news and programs on farming, sport, education, health, business and children's affairs. *U. K. OFFICE:* Christian Vision, Ryder Street, West Bromwich, West Midlands, B70 0EJ, United Kingdom. Phone:+44 (121) 522-6087. Fax: +44 (121) 522 6083. Email: 100131.3711 @compuserve.com. Web: www.christianvision.org/.

MIAMI OFFICE: Christian Vision USA, 15485 Eagle Nest Lane, Suite 220, Miami Lakes, FL 33014 USA.

Radio Zambia, ZNBC Broadcasting House, P.O. Box 50015, Lusaka 10101, Zambia. Phone: (general) +260 (1) 254-989; (Public Relations) +260 (1) 254-989, X-216; (engineering) +260 (1) 250-380. Fax: +260 (1) 254 317 or +260 (1) 250 5424. Email: zambroad@zamnet.zm. Contact: (general) Keith M. Nalumango, Director of Programmes; or Lawson Chishimba, Public Relations Manager; (administration) Duncan H. Mbazima, Director-General; (technical) Patrick Nkula, Director of Engineering. Free *Zamwaves* newsletter. Sometimes gives away stickers, postcards and small publications. $1 required, and postal correspondence should be sent via registered mail. Tours given of the station Tuesdays to Fridays between 9:00 AM and noon local time; inquire in advance. Used to reply slowly and irregularly, but seems to be better now.

ZIMBABWE   World Time +2

⊠**Zimbabwe Broadcasting Corporation**, P.O. Box HG444, Highlands, Harare, Zimbabwe; or P.O. Box 2271, Harare, Zimbabwe. Phone: +263 (4) 498-664 or +263 (4) 498-620. Fax: +263 (4) 498 624 or +263 (4) 498 608. Email: zbc@africaonline.co.zw. Web: (general) www.africaonline.co.zw/zbc/; (Windows Media) www.zbc.co.zw. Contact: (general) Charles Warikandwa; P.Chitava; or Luke Z. Chikani; (administration) Edward Moyo, Director General; or Thomas Mandigora, Director of Programmes; (technical) Sam Barrbis, I. Magoryo or Cloud Nyamundanda (engineers). $1 helpful.

CREDITS: Craig Tyson (Australia), Editor, with Tony Jones (Paraguay). Also, Marie Lamb (USA) and Lawrence Magne (USA). Special thanks to colleagues Gabriel Iván Barrera (Argentina), David Crystal (Israel),Graeme Dixon (New Zealand), Gary Neal (USA), Fotios Padazopulos (USA) and George Poppin (USA); also the following organizations for their support and cooperation Cumbre DX/Hans Johnson (USA), Jembatan DX/Juichi Yamada (Japan), Número Uno (USA), Radio Nuevo Mundo/Tetsuya Hirahara (Japan), Relámpago DX/Takayuki Inoue Nozaki (Japan/Latin America) and RUS-DX/Anatoly Klepov (Russia).

Worldwide Broadcasts in English— 2001

Country-by-Country Guide to Best-Heard Stations

Dozens of countries reach out to us in English, and this section gives the times and frequencies where you're likely to hear them. If you want to know which shows are on hour-by-hour, check out "What's On Tonight."

• **When and where:** "Best Times and Frequencies," earlier in this edition, pinpoints where each world band segment is found and gives tuning tips. Best is late afternoon and evening, when most programs are beamed your way. Tune world band segments within the 5730-10000 kHz range in winter, 5730-15800 kHz during summer. Around breakfast, you can also explore segments within the 5730-17900 kHz range for fewer but intriguing catches.

- **Strongest (and weakest) frequencies:** Frequencies shown in italics—say, *6175* kHz—tend to be best, as they are from transmitters that may be located near you. Frequencies with no target zones are typically for domestic coverage, so they are unlikely to be heard unless you're in or near that country.

Program Times

Some stations shift broadcast times by one hour midyear, typically April through October. These are indicated by ⬜ (one hour earlier) and ➡ (one hour later). Frequencies used seasonally are labeled 🅂 for summer (midyear, typically April through October), and 🅆 for winter. Stations may also extend their hours of transmission, or air special programs, for national holidays, emergencies or sports events.

Times and days of the week are in World Time, explained in "Setting Your World Time Clock" earlier in this edition, as well as in PASSPORT's glossary.

Indigenous Music

Broadcasts in other than English? Turn to the next section, "Voices from Home," or the Blue Pages. Keep in mind that stations for kinsfolk abroad sometimes carry delightful chunks of native music. They make for enjoyable listening, regardless of language.

Schedules for Entire Year

To be as useful as possible over the months to come, PASSPORT's schedules consist not just of observed activity, but also that which we have creatively opined will take place during the forthcoming year. This predictive material is based on decades of experience and is original from us. Although inherently not as exact as real-time data, over the years it's been of tangible value to PASSPORT readers.

Copy editor works over item for the evening BBS news. M. Guha

> **The best time for English programs is in the late afternoon and evening.**

ALBANIA

RADIO TIRANA
0230-0245 &
0330-0400 [↹] 6115 (N America), 7160 (E North
Am)
2130-2200 [S] 7160 (W Europe)
2230-2300 [W] 7130 (W Europe)

ALGERIA

RADIO ALGERIENNE—(Europe)
1600-1700 &
2000-2100   11715 & 15160

ARGENTINA

RADIO ARGENTINA AL EXTERIOR-RAE
0200-0300   Tu-Sa 11710 (Americas)
1800-1900   M-F 15345 (Europe & N Africa)

ARMENIA

VOICE OF ARMENIA
0940-1000 [↹] Su 4810 (E Europe, Mideast &
W Asia), Su 15270 (Europe)
2055-2115 [↹] M-Sa 4810 (E Europe, Mideast &
W Asia), M-Sa 9965 (Europe)

AUSTRALIA

RADIO AUSTRALIA
0000-0100   21740 (Pacific & N America)
0000-0200   17795 (Pacific & W North Am)
0000-0500   17750 (E Asia & SE Asia)
0000-0700   15240 (Pacific & E Asia)
0000-0800   9660 (Pacific), 17580 (Pacific &
W North Am)
0000-0900   12080 (S Pacific)
0100-0500   15415 (E Asia & SE Asia)
0100-0900   21725 (Pacific & E Asia)
0200-0700   15515 (Pacific & N America)
0600-0900   15415 & 17750 (E Asia & SE Asia)
0700-0800   15240 (Pacific, E Asia & W North
Am)
0800-0900   5995 & 9710 (Pacific), 15240
(Pacific & W North Am)
0800-1200   13605 (Pacific & W North Am)
0900-1000   Sa/Su 11550 (SE Asia), Sa/Su
11880 & Sa/Su 17750 (E Asia &
SE Asia)
0900-1400   21820 (Asia & Europe)
1000-1100   11880 & 17750 (E Asia & SE Asia)
1100-1400   5995 (Pacific), 6020 (Pacific &
W North Am)
1100-2130   9580 (Pacific & N America)
1200-1700   11650 (Pacific & W North Am)
1330-1900   9475 (E Asia & SE Asia)
1400-1800   5995 (Pacific & W North Am), 6080
(E Asia & SE Asia)

1430-1700   11660 (E Asia & SE Asia)
1700-2100   9815 (Pacific & E Asia)
1700-2200   11880 (Pacific & W North Am)
1800-2000   6080 (Pacific & E Asia), 7240
(Pacific)
1900-2130   9500 (E Asia & SE Asia)
2000-2200   12080 (S Pacific)
2100-2200   7240 & 9660 (Pacific)
2100-2400   17715 (Pacific & W North Am),
21740 (Pacific & N America)
2200-2400   17795 (Pacific & W North Am)
2300-2400   9660 (Pacific), 12080 (S Pacific)

AUSTRIA

RADIO AUSTRIA INTERNATIONAL
0130-0200   [S] 9655 (E North Am), [S] 9870 &
[S] 13730 (S America)
0230-0300   [W] 7325 (E North Am)
0430-0500   [S] 6155 (Europe), [S] 13730 (E
Europe)
0530-0600   *6015* (W North Am), [W] 6155
(Europe), [W] 13730 (E Europe),
[W] 15410 & [W] 17870 (Mideast)
0630-0700   [W] *6015* (W North Am)
0730-0800   [S] 15410 & [S] 17870 (Mideast)
0830-0900   [S] 21650 & [W] Sa 21650 (E Asia),
[S] 21765 & [W] Sa 21765
(Australasia)
0930-1000   [W] 21650 (E Asia), [W] 21765
(Australasia)
1230-1300   [S] 6155 (Europe), [S] 13730 (W
Europe & E North Am)
1330-1400   [W] 6155 (Europe), [W] 13730 (W
Europe & E North Am)
1600-1630 [↹] *17865* (W North Am)
1630-1700   [S] 6155 (Europe), [S] 13730 (S
Europe & W Africa), [S] 15240
(Mideast), [S] 17765 (S Asia &
SE Asia)
1730-1800   [W] 6155 (Europe), [W] 9655 (Mideast),
[W] 13710 (S Asia & SE Asia),
[W] 13730 (S Europe & W Africa)
1830-1900   [S] 13730 (E Africa & S Africa)
2130-2200   [S] 5945 & [S] 6155 (Europe),
[S] 13730 (N Africa & W Africa)
2230-2300   [W] 5945 & [W] 6155 (Europe),
[W] 13730 (N Africa & W Africa)

BANGLADESH

BANGLADESH BETAR
1230-1300   7185 & 9550 (SE Asia)
1530-1545   15520 (Mideast & Europe)
1745-1815 &
1815-1900   7185, 9550 & 15520 (Irr) (Europe)

BELARUS

RADIO BELARUS/RADIO MINSK

0300-0330 ⬅	M/W/F-Su 6070 (W Europe & Atlantic), M/W/F-Su 7210 (N Europe)
2030-2100 & 2130-2200 ⬅	Tu/Th 7105 (Europe), Tu/Th 7210 (N Europe)

BELGIUM

RADIO VLAANDEREN INTERNATIONAAL

0400-0430	[W] *11980* & [S] *15565* (W North Am)
0800-0830 ⬅	5985 (S Europe)
1130-1200	[S] *9865* (E Asia & Australasia)
1230-1300 ⬅	9925 (Europe)
1730-1800	[S] *13710* (E Europe & Mideast), [S] *17590* (C Africa & E Africa)
1830-1900 ⬅	5910 (S Europe), 9925 (E Europe)
1830-1900	[W] *13600* (E Europe & Mideast), [W] *17695* (C Africa & E Africa)
1930-2000	[S] *5960* (W Europe)
2230-2300	[W] *13670* & [S] *15565* (N America)

BULGARIA

RADIO BULGARIA

0000-0100 ⬅	9400 (E North Am)
0000-0100	[W] 7375 (E North Am)
0200-0300	[S] 11700 (E North Am)
0300-0400 ⬅	9400 (E North Am)
0300-0400	[W] 7375 (E North Am)
1200-1300 ⬅	15700 & 17500 (Europe)
1900-2000	[S] 9400 & [S] 11700 (Europe)
2000-2100	[W] 5845 & [W] 7535 (Europe)
2100-2200	[S] 9400 & [S] 11700 (Europe)
2200-2300	[W] 7535 & [W] 7545 (Europe)
2300-2400	[S] 11700 (E North Am)

CANADA

CANADIAN BROADCASTING CORP—(E North Am)

0000-0300 ⬅	Su 9625
0200-0300 ⬅	Tu-Sa 9625
0300-0310 & 0330-0609 ⬅	M 9625
0400-0609 ⬅	Su 9625
0500-0609 ⬅	Tu-Sa 9625
1200-1255 ⬅	M-F 9625
1200-1505 ⬅	Sa 9625
1200-1700 ⬅	Su 9625
1600-1615 & 1700-1805 ⬅	Sa 9625
1800-2400 ⬅	Su 9625
1945-2015, 2200-2225 & 2240-2330 ⬅	M-F 9625

The shortwave transmission facility at Minsk, Belarus, includes transmitters of up to 250 kW. They feed a number of directional curtain antennas, shown.

A. Mujunen

CFRX-CFRB, Toronto—(E North Am)

24 Hr	6070

CFVP-CKMX, Calgary—(W North Am)

0600-0400 ⬅	6030

CHNX-CHNS, Halifax—(E North Am)

24 Hr	6130

CKZN, St John's NF—(E North Am)

24 Hr	6160

CKZU-CBU, Vancouver—(W North Am)

24 Hr	6160

RADIO CANADA INTERNATIONAL

0000-0030	[W] Tu-Sa 6040 (C America), [W] Tu-Sa 9535 & [W] Tu-Sa 11865 (C America & S America)
0000-0100 ⬅	9755 (E North Am & C America)
0000-0100	[W] 5960 (E North Am)
0100-0130	[S] 11715, [S] 13670, [S] 15170 & [S] 15305 (C America & S America)
0100-0200	[S] 5960 (E North Am)
0130-0200	[S] Su/M 11715, [S] Su/M 13670, [S] Su/M 15170 & [S] Su/M 15305 (C America & S America)

0200-0230	**S** 11715, **S** 13670, **S** 15170 & **S** 15305 (C America & S America)
0200-0300 ◄	9755 (E North Am & C America)
0200-0300	**W** 9535 & **W** 11865 (C America & S America)
0200-0330	**W** 6155 (E North Am & C America), **W** 9780 (W North Am)
0230-0300	**S** Su/M 11715, **S** Su/M 13670, **S** Su/M 15170 & **S** Su/M 15305 (C America & S America)
0300-0330 ◄	9755 (E North Am & C America)
0330-0400 ◄	Su/M 9755 (E North Am & C America)
0330-0400	**W** Su/M 6155 (E North Am & C America), **W** Su/M 9780 (W North Am)
0400-0430	**W** 9505 (Mideast), **W** M-F 9535 (Africa), **W** 9645 (Mideast), **W** M-F 9690 (C Africa & E Africa), **W** M-F 11795 (E Africa), **S** 11835 & **S** 11975 (Mideast), **S** M-F 13765 (C Africa & E Africa), **S** 15215 (Mideast), **S** M-F 15345 (C Africa & E Africa)
0500-0530	**S** 5995 (W North Am), **S** 6145 (Europe), **S** 7290 (W Europe), **S** 9595 (Europe), **S** 9755 (W North Am), **S** 11710 (W Europe & W Africa), **S** 11830 (W North Am), **S** 13755 (W Africa), **S** 15330 (N Africa & Mideast)
0600-0630	**W** 5960 (W North Am), **W** 6045 (Europe), **W** 6150 (Europe & Mideast), **W** 9670 (W North Am), **W** M-F 9780 (W Africa), **W** M-F 11710 (Africa), **S** M-F 11715 (W Africa), **W** 11905 (Mideast & E Africa), **S** M-F 13755 (W Africa), **W** M-F 15325 (Africa), **S** M-F 15330 & **S** M-F 17820 (W Africa)
1100-1200	**S** M-F 17765 & **S** M-F 17820 (E North Am & C America)
1200-1230	**W** 6150 & **S** 9660 (E Asia), **W** 11730 (E Asia & S Asia), **S** 15195 (E Asia & SE Asia)
1200-1300 ◄	M-F 9640 (E North Am), M-F 13650 (E North Am & C America)
1200-1300	**W** M-F 17710 (C America & S America), **S** 17765 & **S** 17820 (E North Am & C America)
1300-1400 ◄	9640 (E North Am), 13650 (E North Am & C America)
1300-1400	**W** 17710 (C America & S America), **S** M-F 17765 & **S** M-F 17820 (E North Am & C America)
1300-1600	**S** Su 13650 & **S** Su 17800 (E North Am & C America)
1330-1400	**W** 6150, 9535 & **S** 11795 (E Asia)
1400-1500 ◄	M-F 9640 (E North Am), M-F 13650 (E North Am & C America)
1400-1500	**W** Su-F 17710 (C America & S America)
1400-1700	**W** Su 9640 (E North Am), **W** Su 13655 (E North Am & C America)
1430-1500	**W** 11980 (S Europe & W Africa), **W** 17820 (W Africa)
1500-1700	**W** Su 17710 (C America & S America)
1630-1700	6140 (S Asia), 6550 (E Asia), 7150 (S Asia)
2000-2100	**S** 11690 & **S** 13650 (Europe), **S** 15470 (W Africa), **S** 17820 (Africa)
2000-2200	**S** 13670 (N Africa & W Africa), **S** 15325 & **S** 17870 (Europe)
2100-2200 ◄	5995 (W Europe & N Africa)
2100-2200	**S** 7235 (Europe), **W** 9770 (W Europe), **W** 11945 (W Africa), 13650 (Europe), 17820 (Africa)
2100-2300	**W** 7235 & **W** 9805 (W Europe & N Africa), **W** 13690 (Africa), **W** 15325 (W Africa & S Africa)
2200-2230	**W** 11705 (E Asia & SE Asia), **S** 15305 (C America & S America), **S** 17695 (E North Am & C America), **S** 17835 (E Asia & SE Asia)
2200-2300	**S** 5960 (E North Am), **W** 5995 (N Africa), **S** 5995 (W Europe & N Africa)
2200-2400	**S** 13670 (C America & S America)
2300-2330	**W** 6040 (C America), **W** 9535, **W** 11865, **S** 11895 & **S** 15305 (C America & S America), **S** 17695 (E North Am & C America)
2300-2400 ◄	9755 (E North Am & C America)
2300-2400	5960 (E North Am)
2330-2400	**W** Sa/Su 6040 (C America), **W** Sa/Su 9535, **W** Sa/Su 11865, **S** Sa/Su 11895 & **S** Sa/Su 15305 (C America & S America), **S** Sa/Su 17695 (E North Am & C America)

CHINA

CHINA RADIO INTERNATIONAL

0100-0200	9570 (E North Am)
0300-0400	9690 (N America & C America)
0400-0500	9730 (W North Am)
0500-0600 ◄	9560 (N America)
0900-1100	11730 & 15210 (Australasia)
1200-1300	7265/9760 (Australasia), 9715 (SE Asia), 15415 (Australasia)
1200-1400	11675 (Australasia), 11980 (SE Asia)
1300-1400	9570 (E North Am), 11900 (Australasia), 15180 (SE Asia)

Brothers at play in rural Bhutan, where foreigners are a rarity. M. Guha

1400-1500	9700, 11675, 11825 & 15110 (S Asia)
1400-1600 ▱	7405 (W North Am)
1400-1600	*13685* (E Africa), *15125* (W Africa & C Africa)
1500-1600	7160 & 9785 (S Asia)
1600-1700	9565 (S Africa), 9870/7190 (E Africa)
1700-1800	🆆 7150 (E Africa), 7405 & 9570 (E Africa & S Africa), 🆆 9745 (N Africa), 🆂 11910 (E Africa)
1900-2000	🆂 11750 (N Africa & Mideast), 🆂 13650 (Mideast & W Asia)
1900-2100	🆆 6165 (Mideast & N Africa), 9440 & 9695/11750 (N Africa)
2000-2130	*11735* & *13640/15500* (E Africa & S Africa)
2000-2200	🆆 5965, 🆆 9535, 🆂 11790 & 🆂 15110 (Europe)
2200-2300	🆆 7170 & 🆂 *9880* (Europe)
2300-2400	*5990* (C America)

CHINA (TAIWAN)
RADIO TAIPEI INTERNATIONAL
0200-0300	*5950* (E North Am), *11740* (C America)
0200-0400	*9680* (W North Am), 11825 & 15345 (SE Asia)
0300-0400	*5950* (N America & C America), 11745 (E Asia)
0700-0800	*5950* (W North Am & C America)
1200-1300	7130 (E Asia), 9610 (Australasia)
1400-1500	15125 (SE Asia)

1600-1845	🆆 *15695* (Europe)
1800-1900	*3955* (W Europe)
2200-2300	🆆 *5810*, 🆆 *9355*, 🆂 *11565* & 🆂 *15600* (Europe)

VOICE OF ASIA—(SE Asia)
1100-1200	7445

COSTA RICA
RADIO FOR PEACE INTERNATIONAL—(N America)
0000-0630	6970 & 15050
0630-0645	Su-F 6970 & Su-F 15050
0645-0800	6970
0645-1430	15050
0800-1200	Sa/Su 6970
1430-1445	Su-F 15050
1445-2230	15050
2230-2245	Sa-Th 15050
2245-2400	15050

CROATIA
RADIO CROATIA
0100-0115	🆂 *9925* (E North Am)
0200-0215	🆆 *7280/9925* (E North Am)
0300-0315	🆂 *9925* (W North Am)
0400-0415	🆆 *7285/9925* (W North Am)
0500-0515	🆂 *9470* (Australasia)
0600-0615	🆆 *11880* (Australasia)
0800-0815 ▱	*13820* (Australasia)
2030-2045	🆂 *11805* (Mideast & S Africa)
2130-2145	🆆 *9405/11605* (Mideast & S Africa)

CUBA

RADIO HABANA CUBA

0100-0500	6000 (E North Am), 9820 (N America)
0100-0700	11705 USB (E North Am & Europe)
0500-0700	9550/6000 & 9820 (W North Am)
2030-2130	W 9620, S 13660 USB & S 13750 (Europe & E North Am)
2230-2330	9550 (C America)

CZECH REPUBLIC

RADIO PRAGUE

0000-0030	S 11615 (N America), S 13580 (C America)
0100-0130	7345, W 9665 & S 11615 (N America)
0200-0230	W 6200 & W 7345 (N America)
0300-0330	S 7345 (N America), S 11615 (W North Am & C America)
0330-0400	S 11600 (Mideast), S 15470 (Mideast & S Asia)
0400-0430	W 7345 (N America), W 9435 (W North Am & C America)
0430-0500	W 9865 (Mideast), W 11600 (Mideast & S Asia)
0700-0730	S 9880 (W Europe)
0800-0830 ⬛	11600 (W Europe)
0800-0830	W 15255 (W Europe)
0900-0930	S 21745 (S Asia & W Africa)
1000-1030	W 17485 (W Africa), W 21745 (Mideast & S Asia)
1030-1100	S 9880 (N Europe), S 11615 (N Europe & W Europe)
1130-1200	W 11640 (N Europe), S 21745 (S Asia), W 21745 (E Africa & Mideast)
1230-1300 ⬛	6055 (Europe)
1230-1300	W 21745 (S Asia & Australasia)
1300-1330	S 13580 (N Europe), S 17485 (S Asia)
1400-1430	W 21745 (E North Am & E Africa)
1600-1630	S 21745 (E Africa)
1700-1730 ⬛	5930 (W Europe)
1700-1730	W 17485 (W Africa & C Africa), S 21745 (C Africa)
1800-1830 ⬛	5930 (W Europe)
1800-1830	W 7315 (E Europe, Asia & Australasia)
2000-2030	S 11600 (S Asia & Australasia)
2100-2130 ⬛	5930 (W Europe)
2100-2130	W 9430 (S Asia & Australasia)
2130-2200	S 11600 (S Asia & Australasia), S 15545 (W Africa)
2230-2300	W 7345 (N America), W 9435 (W Africa), S 11600 & S 15545 (N America)
2330-2400	W 7345 & W 9435 (N America)

ECUADOR

HCJB-VOICE OF THE ANDES

0000-0400	9745 (E North Am)
0000-0700	W 12015 & S 15115 (N America)
0000-1530	21455 USB (Europe & Australasia)
0400-0700	9745 (W North Am)
0600-0800	S 15160 (Europe)
0700-0900	W 9780 (Europe)
0700-1100	11755 (Australasia)
1100-1630	12005 (C America), 15115 (N America & S America)
1530-1630	W 21455 USB (Europe & Australasia)
1900-2200	17660 (Europe), W 21455 USB (Europe & Australasia)

EGYPT

RADIO CAIRO

0000-0030	9900 (E North Am)
0200-0330	9475 (N America)
1215-1330	17595 (S Asia)
1630-1830	15255 (S Africa)
2030-2200	15375 (W Africa)
2115-2245	9990 (Europe)
2300-2400	9900 (E North Am)

AND NOW THAT WAS THANK YOU FOR JOINING US WE HAVE A SPECIAL SHOW THIS EVENING WE NOW BRING YOU A SPECIAL TONIGHT ON OUR SHOW

ETHIOPIA
RADIO ETHIOPIA

1030-1100	M-F 5990, M-F 7110, M-F 9704
1600-1700	7165/7175 & 9560 (E Africa)

FRANCE
RADIO FRANCE INTERNATIONALE

1200-1300	11670, 15155 & 15195 (E Europe), *15540* (W Africa)
1400-1500	*5220* (E Asia), *11610* (S Asia), *17620* (Mideast), 17680 (S Asia & SE Asia)
1600-1700	11615 (Irr) (N Africa), *11995* (W Africa), *12015* (S Africa), 17850 (C Africa & S Africa)
1600-1730	[W] 11615 & [S] 15210 (Mideast), [W] 15210 & [S] 17605 (E Africa)

GERMANY
DEUTSCHE WELLE

0100-0145	[S] *6040* (N America), [W] *6040* & [W] 6145 (N America & C America), [S] *9640* (E North Am), [W] *9640* (E North Am & C America), [W] *9700* (E North Am), [W] *9765* (N America), [S] *11810* (W North Am), [S] *13720* (E North Am & C America)
0200-0245	[W] 7285, *9615*, [W] 9765, [S] 11945 & *11965* (S Asia)
0300-0345	[W] *6045* (N America), *9535* (W North Am), [S] *9640* (E North Am), [W] *9640* (E North Am & C America), [W] *9700* (N America), [W] *11750* & [S] *11810* (W North Am), [S] *13780* (E North Am & C America), [S] *15105* (W North Am)
0400-0445	[S] *7225* (E Africa & S Africa), [W] *7280* & 9565 (S Africa), [S] *9765* & [W] *11935* (E Africa & S Africa), [W] *11965* (S Africa), [S] *13690* (E Africa & S Africa)
0500-0545	[W] 5960, [W] *6120*, 9670, [S] *9785*, [W] *11795/11985*, [S] 11810 & [S] *11985* (W North Am)
0600-0645	[W] *7225*, [W] 9565, [W] 11785 & [S] *13790* (W Africa), [S] *15275* & [S] 17860 (W Africa & C Africa)
0600-1900	6140 (Europe)
0900-0945	*6160* (Australasia), [W] *11785* (E Africa & S Africa), [S] *12035/9565* (E Africa), [W] *12055* (E Asia), [S] *15105* (SE Asia & Australasia), [S] *15210/17800* & 15410 (S Africa), 15470 (E Asia), [W] *17625* (Australasia), 17770 (SE Asia & Australasia), [S] *17800/21775* (W Africa), [W] *17820* (SE Asia & Australasia), [W] *17860* (S Africa),
1100-1145	[W] 21560 (E Africa), [S] 21680 (SE Asia & Australasia), [S] 21790 (E Africa & S Africa) [S] *11785* (E Africa & S Africa), *15410* (S Africa), [S] 17680 (W Africa & C Africa), *17800/17860* & [W] *21780* (W Africa)
1600-1645	*6170* & *7225* (S Asia), *9735* (E Africa & S Africa), [S] *11665/11810* (S Africa), [W] 15380 (S Asia), [W] *15455* (S Africa), [S] *17595* & [W] *17810* (S Asia), [S] *21775* & [W] *21780* (E Africa & S Africa)
1900-1945	[W] 11765 (E Africa), [S] *11785/11965* (S Africa), *11810/11805* (C Africa & W Africa), [W] 13610 & [S] 13720 (W Africa), [W] *15135* & [S] *15390* (W Africa & C Africa), [W] *15390* (S Africa), *17810* (E Africa)
2000-2045	[S] 7130 & [W] *9725* (W Europe)
2100-2145	[W] *9615* (W Africa), [S] *9670* (SE Asia & Australasia), [W] *9690* (C Africa & S Africa), 9765 (Australasia), [S] *9875* & [S] *11865* (W Africa), [S] *11915* (SE Asia & Australasia), [S] *15135* (W Africa & C America), [W] *15135* (SE Asia & Australasia), [W] *15410* (W Africa & Americas), [W] *17560* (SE Asia & Australasia), [W] *17835* (W Africa)
2300-2345	[W] *9470* (E Asia), 9815, [S] *12055* & [S] *13610* (S Asia & SE Asia), [W] *13690* (SE Asia), [S] *21790* (S Asia & SE Asia), [W] *21790* (E Asia)

GHANA
GHANA BROADCASTING CORPORATION

0530-0900	4915, 6130/3366
0900-1200	Sa/Su//Holidays 4915
0900-1700	6130
1200-1700	M-F 6130
1200-2400	4915
1700-2400	3366

GREECE
FONI TIS HELLADAS

0200-0210	[W] 7450, [W] 9375, 9420, 12105/12110 & [S] 15630 (N America)
1900-1930	7475 & 9375 (Europe)

GUAM
KTWR-TRANS WORLD RADIO

0730-0740	Sa/Su 15200 (SE Asia)
0740-0915	15200 (SE Asia)
0800-0930	15330 (Australasia & S Pacific)
1430-1630	15330 (S Asia)

GUYANA

VOICE OF GUYANA
24 Hr	5950/3290

HOLLAND

RADIO NETHERLANDS
0000-0125	*6165* (N America), *9845* (E North Am)
0430-0530	*6165 & 9590* (W North Am)
0930-1125	**W** *12065* (SE Asia), **S** *13710* (E Asia & SE Asia)
0930-1130	**W** *7260* (E Asia & Australasia), **W** *9790 &* **S** *9795* (Australasia), **S** *12065* (E Asia)
1030-1225	**S** *9860* (W Europe)
1130-1325 ◪	*6045* (W Europe)
1130-1325	**W** *9855* (W Europe)
1430-1625	**S** *9890,* **W** *12070,* **S** *12075,* **W** *12090,* **S** *15590 &* **W** *15595* (S Asia)
1730-2025	*6020* (S Africa), **S** *7120* (E Africa), **S** *11655* (W Africa), **W** *11655* (E Africa)
1830-2025	*9895, 13700, 17605 & 21590* (W Africa)
2330-2400	*6165* (N America), *9845* (E North Am)

HUNGARY

RADIO BUDAPEST
0100-0130	**S** 9560 (N America)
0200-0230	**W** 9835 (N America)
0230-0300	**S** 9835 (N America)
0330-0400	**W** 9835 (N America)
1900-1930	**S** 7130 (W Europe)
2000-2030 ◪	6025 (Europe)
2000-2030	**W** 7165 (W Europe)
2200-2230 ◪	6025 (Europe)
2230-2300 ◪	3975 (Europe)

INDIA

ALL INDIA RADIO
0000-0045	7410 (E Asia), 9705 (SE Asia), 9950 & 11620 (E Asia), 13625 (SE Asia)
1000-1100	11585 (E Asia), 13700 (Australasia), 15020 (E Asia & Australasia), 17485 (Australasia), 17840 (E Asia), 17895 (Australasia)
1330-1500	9710, 11620 & 13710 (SE Asia)
1745-1945	7410, 9950 & 11620 (Europe), 11935 (E Africa), 13750 (N Africa & W Africa), 15200 (Mideast & W Asia), 17670 (E Africa)
2045-2230	7150 (Australasia), 7410 & 9650 (Europe), 9910 (Australasia), 9950 (Europe), 11620 & 11715 (Australasia)
2245-2400	7410 (E Asia), 9705 (SE Asia), 9950 & 11620 (E Asia), 13625 (SE Asia)

INDONESIA

VOICE OF INDONESIA
0100-0200	9525 (E Asia, SE Asia & Pacific), 11785 (Mideast & S Asia)
0800-0900	9525 (E Asia, SE Asia & Pacific), 11785 (Australasia)
2000-2100	15150 (Europe)

IRAN

VOICE OF THE ISLAMIC REPUBLIC
0030-0130	**W** 6065 (C America), **W** 6135 (E North Am & C America), 9022 (C America), **S** 9835 (E North Am & C America), **S** 11970 (C America)
1100-1230	15385, 15430 & 15585 (W Asia & S Asia), 21470 & 21730 (S Asia & SE Asia)
1530-1630	7115 & 9635 (S Asia, SE Asia & Australasia), 11775 (S Asia & SE Asia)
1930-2030	**W** 6180 (Europe), **W** 7215 (W Europe), 9022 & **S** 9575 (Europe), **S** 11670 (W Europe)
2130-2230	**W** 9745 & 11740 (Australasia), **S** 13745 (S Asia, SE Asia & Australasia)

IRELAND

RTE OVERSEAS
0130-0200	*6155* (C America)
1000-1030	*11740* (Australasia)
1800-1830	**W** *9895 &* **S** *15315* (Mideast)
1830-1900	**W** *13640 &* **S** *13725* (N America), *21630* (C Africa & S Africa)

ISRAEL

KOL ISRAEL
0400-0415	**S** 15640 (Europe & N America), **S** 17535 (Australasia)
0500-0515 ◪	9435 (W Europe & E North Am)
0500-0515	**W** 6220/7410 (W Europe & E North Am), **W** 17545/15640 (Australasia)
1900-1925	**S** 17535 (C America)
2000-2025 ◪	11605 (W Europe & E North Am), 15640 (S Africa), 15650 (W Europe & E North Am)
2000-2025	**W** 9435 (W Europe & E North Am)

ITALY

RADIO ROMA-RAI INTERNATIONAL
0050-0110	6010 & 9675 (N America), 11800 (N America & C America)
0425-0440	5975, **W** 7120 & **S** 7150 (S Europe & N Africa)
1935-1955	5970, **W** 7285, **S** 7290, **S** 9750 & **W** 9760 (W Europe)

2025-2045   **S** 7125, **W** 7220, 9710 & 11880 (Mideast)

2200-2225   9675, 11900 & **S** 15240 (E Asia)

JAPAN
RADIO JAPAN/NHK

0000-0015   11815/17810 & 13650 (SE Asia)

0000-0100   *6145* (E North Am)

0100-0200   *9515/9660* & 11870 (Mideast), 15325 (S Asia), 15590 (SE Asia), 17685 (Australasia), 17835 (S America), 17845 (E Asia)

0300-0400   17825 (C America), 21610 (Australasia)

0500-0600   *5975* (W Europe), *6110* (W North Am & C America), 11715 & 11760 (E Asia), 15590 (SE Asia)

0500-0700   *7230* (Europe), 9835/13630 (W North Am), 11840 (E Asia), 11850/ 21570 (Australasia)

0600-0700   *11740* (SE Asia), 15230 (Pacific, C America & S America)

1000-1100   11850/21570 (Australasia)

1000-1200   9695 (SE Asia), 15590 (S Asia)

1100-1200   *6120* (E North Am)

1400-1500   9505 (W North Am), *11880* (Mideast)

1400-1600   7200/9860 (SE Asia), 11730 (S Asia)

1500-1600   9750 (E Asia)

1700-1800   9505/9535 (W North Am), 12000 (Europe), *15355* (S Africa)

2100-2200   *6035/11920* (Australasia), *6115* (W Europe), **W** *6180*, 9725 & **S** *9810* (Europe), 11850 (Australasia), *11855* (C Africa), 17825 (W North Am), 21670 (Pacific)

JORDAN
RADIO JORDAN—(W Europe & E North Am)

1100-1300 **□**   17580

1300-1730 **□**   11690

KOREA (DPR)
RADIO PYONGYANG

0000-0100   11710, 13760 & 15180 (N America & C America)

0100-0200   11735, 15230 & 17735 (N America & C America)

0200-0300   11845 & 13650 (N America & C America)

1200-1300   11335 & 13650 (N America & C America)

1900-2000   11710 & 13760 (N America & C America)

KOREA (REPUBLIC)
RADIO KOREA INTERNATIONAL

0200-0300   7275 (E Asia), 11725 & 11810 (S America), 15575 (N America)

0800-0900   9570 (Australasia), 13670 (Europe)

1030-1100   **S** *11715* (E North Am)

1130-1200   **W** *9650* (E North Am)

1300-1400   9570 (SE Asia), 9640 (E Asia), 13670 (SE Asia)

1600-1700   5975 (E Asia), 9515 & 9870 (Mideast & Africa)

1900-2000   5975 (E Asia), 7275 (Europe)

2100-2130   **S** *3970* & 6480 (Europe)

2100-2200   15575 (Europe)

2200-2230   **W** *3975* (Europe)

KUWAIT
RADIO KUWAIT

0500-0800   15110 (S Asia & SE Asia)

1800-2100   11990 (Europe & E North Am)

LIBERIA
LIBERIAN COMMUNICATIONS NETWORK

0450-0800   6100/5100

0800-1800   6100

1800-2400   5100/5000

LITHUANIA
RADIO VILNIUS

0030-0100   **W** *6120/6155* & **S** *9855* (E North Am)

0930-1000 **□**   9710 (W Europe)

MALAYSIA
VOICE OF MALAYSIA

0500-0700 &

0700-0830   6175 & 9750 (SE Asia), 15295 (Australasia)

MALTA
VOICE OF THE MEDITERRANEAN

0700-0730 **□**   M-Sa *7150* (Europe & N Africa)

0900-1000 **□**   Su *11770* (Europe)

1900-2000   **S** Sa-Th *12060* (Europe & N Africa)

2000-2100   **W** Sa-Th *7440* (Europe)

MEXICO
RADIO MEXICO INTERNACIONAL—(W North Am & C America)

0000-0030 **□**   9705

0400-0430 **□**   Tu-Su 9705

0500-0530 **□**   Tu-Sa 9705

1500-1530,
1600-1630 &
2300-2330 **□**   5985 & 9705

MOLDOVA

RADIO MOLDOVA INTERNATIONAL
1200-1225	**S**	M-F *15315* (E North Am)
1300-1325	**W**	M-F *11580* (E North Am)
2130-2155 **▣**		M-F *7520* (Europe)

MONACO

TRANS WORLD RADIO—(W Europe)
0745-0755 **▣**	Sa/Su *9755*
0755-0920 **▣**	*9755*
0920-0935 **▣**	Sa/Su *9755*
0935-0950 **▣**	Su *9755*

MONGOLIA

VOICE OF MONGOLIA
1030-1100	12085 (E Asia & SE Asia)
1500-1530	**W** 9720 & **S** 12015 (E Asia & SE Asia), 12085 (S Asia)
2000-2030	**W** 9720, **S** 12015 & 12085 (Europe)

NEPAL

RADIO NEPAL
0215-0225 &	
1415-1425	5005, 7165/3230

NEW ZEALAND

RADIO NEW ZEALAND INTERNATIONAL—
(Pacific)
0000-0705	17675
0705-1015	15175/17675
1650-1850	6095/6145 (Irr), M-F 11695/11725
1850-2400	17675

NIGERIA

VOICE OF NIGERIA
0500-0700,	
1000-1100,	
1500-1700 &	
1900-2100	7255 (Africa)

OMAN

RADIO SULTANATE OF OMAN
0300-0400	15355 (E Africa)
1400-1500	15140 (Mideast & Europe)

PAPUA NEW GUINEA

NBC
0000-0730	9675
0730-0900	9675/4890
0900-1200	4890
1200-1930	M-Sa 4890
1930-2200	M-Sa 9675/4890
2200-2400	9675

PHILIPPINES

RADYO PILIPINAS—(Mideast)
0230-0330	**W** 11805, **S** 11885, 15120 & 15270

POLAND

RADIO POLONIA
1300-1400 **▣**	6095, 7270 & 9525 (W Europe), 11820 (W Europe & E North Am)
1800-1900 **▣**	6000 & 7285 (W Europe)
1930-2030	**S** 7185 & **S** 7265 (W Europe)
2030-2125 **▣**	6035 (W Europe)
2030-2125	**W** 6095 (W Europe)
2030-2130 **▣**	9525 (W Europe)
2030-2130	**W** 7285 (W Europe)

RUSSIA

VOICE OF RUSSIA
0100-0400	**S** 17595 (W North Am)
0100-0500	**S** *9665* (E North Am), **S** 15595 (W North Am)
0200-0400	**W** 13665 (W North Am)
0200-0600	**W** *7180* (E North Am), **W** 12020 & **W** 15470 (W North Am)
0300-0400	**W** 5940 (E North Am)
0300-0500	**S** 17565, **S** 17650 & **S** 17690 (W North Am)
0400-0500	17595 (W North Am)
0400-0600 **▣**	*7125* (E North Am), 17660 (W North Am)
0400-0600	**W** 12010 & **W** 15595 (W North Am)
0500-0600	**W** 17595 (W North Am)
0530-1000	**S** 17625 (Australasia)
0600-0800	**W** 15470, **W** 15525 & **W** 17570 (Australasia)
0600-0900 **▣**	21790 (Australasia)
0600-0900	**S** 15490 (E Asia & Australasia)
0630-1000	**W** 15460 (Australasia)
0700-0900	*17495* (SE Asia & Australasia)
0830-1000	**W** 9905 (Australasia)
0900-1000	**W** *17495* (SE Asia & Australasia)
1500-1600	*11500* (SE Asia)
1500-1700 **▣**	*4940, 4965* & *4975* (W Asia & S Asia)
1600-1700	**S** *11675* (N Europe)
1700-2000	**S** 9710 (Europe)
1700-2100	**S** 9775 (Europe)
1700-2200	**W** 9890 (N Europe)
1800-1900	**W** W/Th/Sa-M 5940 & **W** W/Th/Sa-M 5965 (N Europe)
1800-2100	**S** *11675* (N Europe)
1800-2200	**W** 7340 (Europe)
1900-2000	**W** 5920, **W** 7205 & **S** 12070 (Europe)
1900-2200	**W** 5940 & **W** 5965 (N Europe)
2000-2200 **▣**	*15735* (S America)
2100-2200	**W** 7300 (Europe)

SEYCHELLES

FEBA RADIO

0345-0400	F 11885 (E Africa)
0815-0900	F 15460 (S Asia)
1245-1300	F 15535 (Mideast & E Africa)
1500-1600	11600 (S Asia)
1630-1700	Su 11605 (S Asia)

SINGAPORE

RADIO SINGAPORE INTERNATIONAL—(SE Asia)

1100-1400	6150 & 9590

RADIO CORPORATION OF SINGAPORE

1400-1600 & 2300-1100	6150

SLOVAKIA

RADIO SLOVAKIA INTERNATIONAL

0100-0130	5930 & 7230/7300 (E North Am & C America), 9440 (S America)
0700-0730	[S] 9440, 15460, 17550/11990 & [W] 21705 (Australasia)
1630-1700	[S] 5920 (W Europe)
1730-1800 ⬅	6055 & 7345 (W Europe)
1730-1800	[W] 5915 (W Europe)
1830-1900	[S] 5920 (W Europe)
1930-2000 ⬅	6055 & 7345 (W Europe)
1930-2000	[W] 5915 (W Europe)

SOLOMON ISLANDS

SOLOMON ISLANDS BROADCASTING CORP

0000-0030	M-F 5020
0000-0230	Sa 5020
0030-0230	Su 5020
0100-0800	M-F 5020
0500-0800	Sa 5020, Su 5020
0815-1100	Su 5020
0830-0900	M-F 5020
0845-1100	Sa 5020
0915-0930, 0945-1100 & 1930-2030	M-F 5020
1945-2400	Sa 5020
2000-2015 & 2030-2330	Su 5020
2045-2400	M-F 5020

SOUTH AFRICA

CHANNEL AFRICA

0300-0330	[S] 6035 & [W] 9525 (E Africa & C Africa)
0400-0430	5955 (S Africa)
0500-0530	[S] 11720 & [W] 15215 (W Africa)
0600-0630	15215 (W Africa)
1300-1455	Sa/Su 11720 (S Africa), Sa/Su 17780 (E Africa), Sa/Su 21725 (W Africa)
1500-1530	17770 & [S] 17870 (E Africa)
1600-1630	9525 (S Africa)
1700-1730	[S] 17860 & [W] 17870 (W Africa)
1800-1830	17870 (W Africa)

SPAIN

RADIO EXTERIOR DE ESPAÑA

0000-0200 & 0500-0600	6055 (N America & C America)
1900-2000	[S] M-F 15285 (Europe)
2000-2100	M-F 9595 (N Africa & W Africa), [W] M-F 9680 (Europe)
2100-2200	[S] Sa/Su 9595 (N Africa & W Africa), [S] Sa/Su 9840 (Europe)
2200-2300	[W] Sa/Su 9595 (N Africa & W Africa), [W] Sa/Su 9680 (Europe)

SRI LANKA

SRI LANKA BROADCASTING CORPORATION

0030-0430	6005, 9730 & 15425 (S Asia)
1030-1130	11835 (SE Asia & Australasia), 17850 (E Asia)
1230-1600	6005, 9730 & 15425 (S Asia)
1900-2000	[W] Sa *5975* & [S] Sa *6010* (Europe)

SWAZILAND

TRANS WORLD RADIO

0430-0500	3200 (S Africa)
0430-0605	[S] 6100 (S Africa)
0430-0700	4775 (S Africa)
0500-0600	[S] 3200 (S Africa)
0505-0735	9500 (E Africa)
0605-0735	6100 & [W] 9650 (S Africa)
0700-0735	[S] 4775 (S Africa)
0735-0805	[S] Sa/Su 4775 & Sa/Su 6100 (S Africa), Sa/Su 9500 (E Africa), [W] Sa/Su 9650 (S Africa)
1600-1830	9500 (E Africa)
1730-1745	M-Th 3200 (S Africa)
1745-2015	3200 (S Africa)

European pastry shop? No, this haven for sweets and bread is in none other than the bowels of Bhutan. M. Guha

SWEDEN

RADIO SWEDEN

0130-0200	**W** 9495 & **S** 13625 (E Asia & Australasia)
0230-0300	9495 (N America)
0330-0400	9495/15245 (N America)
1230-1300 ⇦	18960 & **W** 21810 (N America)
1430-1500 ⇦	18960 (N America)
1730-1800	**S** Su 13800 (W Europe)
1830-1900 ⇦	M-Sa 6065 (Europe & Mideast)
1830-1900	**W** Su 9765 (Europe & Mideast)
2030-2100 ⇦	6065 (Europe)
2130-2200	**S** 9430 (Europe & Africa)
2230-2300 ⇦	6065 (Europe)
2230-2300	**W** 7325 (S Europe & W Africa)

SWITZERLAND

SWISS RADIO INTERNATIONAL

0100-0130	9885 & *9905* (N America & C America)
0400-0430	**S** *9610* (E Europe)
0400-0500	9885 & *9905* (N America & C America)
0500-0530	**S** *9610* & **W** *9655* (E Europe)
0600-0630	**W** *9655* (E Europe)
0730-0800	**W** *9885* (W Africa), **W** *13635* & **S** *15545* (N Africa), **W** 17665 (C Africa & S Africa), **S** *17685* (N Africa & W Africa), **S** 21750 (C Africa & S Africa)
0830-0900	*9885* (Australasia), 21770 (C Africa & S Africa)
1000-1030	**S** *15315* (W Europe)
1100-1130	**W** *9535* (W Europe)
1100-1200	**W** *9540* & **S** *13735* (E Asia), 21770 (S Asia & SE Asia)
1200-1230	**S** *15315* (W Europe)
1300-1330	**W** *9535* (W Europe)
1400-1500	**S** *9575* & **W** *12010* (E Asia & SE Asia), **W** 15185 & **S** 17670 (W Asia & S Asia)
1600-1615	**S** *9575* (E Asia & SE Asia)
1900-1930	**S** *6110* (N Europe)
2000-2030	**W** *6165* (N Europe), **W** *9605* (N Africa & W Africa), **W** *11910* (E Africa), **W** 13660 (C Africa & S Africa), **S** *13710* (S Africa), **S** 13770 (E Africa), **W** *13790* (S Africa), **S** *15220* (C Africa & S Africa), **S** *17580* (N Africa & W Africa)

SYRIA

RADIO DAMASCUS

2005-2105	12085 & 13610 (Europe)
2110-2210	12085 (N America), 13610 (Australasia)

THAILAND

RADIO THAILAND

0000-0030	**W** 9680 & **S** 9690 (E Africa)
0000-0100	9655 (Irr) & 11905 (Irr) (Asia)
0030-0100	**W** 13695 & **S** 15395 (E North Am)
0300-0330	9655 (Irr) & 11905 (Irr) (Asia), **S** 15395 & **W** 15460 (W North Am)
0530-0600	9655 (Irr) & 11905 (Irr) (Asia), **W** 15115 & **S** 21795/15445 (Europe)
1230-1300	9655 (Irr) (Asia), **W** 9810 & **S** 9885 (SE Asia & Australasia), 11905 (Irr) (Asia)
1400-1430	**W** 9530 & **S** 9830 (SE Asia & Australasia)

1900-2000	**S** 7195 & **W** 9535 (N Europe), 9655 (Irr) & 11905 (Irr) (Asia)
2030-2045	**W** 9535 (Europe), 9655 (Irr) (Asia), **S** 9680 (Europe), 11905 (Irr) (Asia)

TURKEY

VOICE OF TURKEY

0300-0350	**S** 6155 (Mideast), **S** 11655 (Europe & N America), **S** 21715 (S Asia, SE Asia & Australasia)
0400-0450	**W** 6010 (Europe & N America), **W** 7240 (Mideast), **W** 9655 (Europe & N America), **W** 21715 (S Asia, SE Asia & Australasia)
1230-1325	**S** 17830 (Europe), **S** 21540 (S Asia, SE Asia & Australasia)
1330-1425	**W** 17685 (S Asia, SE Asia & Australasia), **W** 17815 (Europe)
1830-1920	**S** 9785 & **S** 11765 (Europe)
1930-2020	**W** 6175 & **W** 6180 (Europe)
2130-2220 ◧	9525 (S Asia, SE Asia & Australasia)
2200-2250	**S** 13640 (Europe & E North Am)
2200-2300	**S** 7190 (Europe)
2300-2350	**W** 6135 (Europe), **W** 9655 (Europe & E North Am)

UNITED ARAB EMIRATES

UAE RADIO IN DUBAI

0330-0350	12005, 13675 & 15400 (E North Am & C America)
0530-0550	15435 (Australasia), 17830 (E Asia), 21700 (Australasia)
1030-1050	13675 (Europe), 15370 (N Africa), 15395 & 21605 (Europe)
1330-1350 & 1600-1630	13630 (N Africa), 13675, 15395 & 21605 (Europe)

UNITED KINGDOM

BBC WORLD SERVICE

0000-0030	*3915* (SE Asia), *11945* (E Asia)
0000-0045	*7105/7110* (SE Asia)
0000-0200	*5965* (S Asia), *6195* (SE Asia), *9590* (N America), *12095* (S America)
0000-0300	*11955* (S Asia), *15280* (E Asia), *15310* (S Asia)
0000-0330	*15360* (SE Asia)
0000-0400	*6175* (N America)
0000-0700	*5975* (N America & C America)
0030-0045	*6080* (SE Asia), *9600* (E Asia)
0030-0100	*17790* (E Asia)
0100-0300	9915 (S America)
0200-0400	*6135* (W North Am & C America)
0300-0400	*6005* (W Africa & S Africa) & *12095* (E Africa)

0300-0500	*3255* (S Africa), **S** *11955* (S Asia)
0300-0530	*15280* (E Asia)
0300-0730	6195 (Europe)
0300-0800	*11760* (Mideast)
0300-0815	*15310* (S Asia)
0300-2200	*6190* (S Africa), 9410 (Europe)
0330-0400	**S** *9610* & **W** *15420* (E Africa)
0330-0500	*11955* & *17760* (E Asia)
0400-0500	**W** *6135* (W North Am & C America), **W** *11765* (S Africa), **S** 12095 (Europe), **W** *12095* & **S** *17640* (E Africa)
0400-0630	*15420* (E Africa)
0400-0700	*7160* (W Africa & C Africa)
0400-0730	*6005* (W Africa), *15575* (Mideast & W Asia)
0500-0600	**S** *3255* (S Africa)
0500-0630	*17885* (E Africa)
0500-0700	*11765* (S Africa), *17640* (E Africa)
0500-0800 ◧	*6175* (W North Am & C America)
0500-0900	*11955* (Australasia)
0500-0915	*15360* (SE Asia & Australasia), **W** *17760* (E Asia & SE Asia)
0500-1100	*9740* (SE Asia)
0500-2000	12095 (Europe)
0530-1030	*21660* (SE Asia)
0600-0800	*17790* (S Asia) & 9580 (Australasia)
0600-1500	15565 (Europe)
0600-1700	*11940* (S Africa)
0630-0700	15420 & 17885 (E Africa)
0700-0800	**W** *5975* (N America & C America), *11765* (W Africa)
0700-0900	Sa/Su *17885* (E Africa)
0700-1500	17640 (E Europe & C Asia)
0700-1800	15485 (W Europe & N Africa)
0715-1000	*15400* (W Africa & S Africa)
0730-0800	**W** 6195 (Europe), **W** *11835* (W Africa)
0730-0900	Sa/Su *15575* (Mideast & W Asia)
0730-1000	*17830* (W Africa & C Africa)
0800-0810	*17790* (S Asia)
0815-0900	*15310* (S Asia)
0900-1000	*6065, 9580, 11765, 11945* & *11955* (E Asia), *15190* (S America)
0900-1100	*15310* & *17790* (S Asia)
0900-1400	*11760* (Mideast), *17885* (E Africa)
0900-1500	*15575* (Mideast & W Asia)
0900-1530	17705 (N Africa)
0900-1615	*6195* (SE Asia)
0915-1000	*15280* (E Asia)
0915-1030	**S** *15360* (SE Asia), **W** *15360* (Australasia), *17760* (E Asia & SE Asia)
1000-1100	**S** *5965* (E North Am), Sa/Su *15400* (W Africa), Sa/Su *17830* (W Africa & C Africa)
1000-1130	Sa/Su *15190* (S America)
1000-1400	*6195* (C America & N America)

1100-1130	*15400* (W Africa), *17790* (S America)
1100-1200	*5965* (E North Am)
1100-1300	*9580, 11955 & 15280* (E Asia), *17785* (S Asia)
1100-1400	*15220* (Americas), *15310* (S Asia)
1100-1600	*9740* (SE Asia & Australasia)
1100-1700	*21660* (S Africa)
1100-2100	*17830* (W Africa & C Africa)
1200-1400	**W** *5965* (E North Am)
1200-1615	*9515* (N America)
1300-1400	**W** *17785* (S Asia)
1300-1415	*15420* (E Africa)
1300-1600	**W** *9590* (N America), **S** *11865* (W North Am)
1300-1615	*5990* (E Asia)
1300-1700	*11750* (S Asia)
1330-1345	*15105* (W Africa), *17810* (W Africa & C Africa), *21640* (W Africa)
1400-1415	*11860, 17880 & 21490* (E Africa)
1400-1600	*15220* (N America)
1400-1700	*15310* (S Asia), *17840* (Americas), *21470* (E Africa)
1500-1530	*11860, 15420 & 21490* (E Africa)
1500-1700	*15400* (W Africa), 15575 (Europe & Mideast)
1500-1830	*5975* (S Asia)
1600-1745	*3915 & 7160* (SE Asia)
1600-1800	**W** 6195 (Europe), *9740* (S Asia)
1615-1700	**W** *6195* (SE Asia), **S** 9510 (S Asia), Sa *9515* (N America), *15420* (E Africa)
1700-1830	**S** *6095* (Mideast & W Asia), *9510* (S Asia)
1700-1900	**S** *11860* (E Africa), *15400* (W Africa & S Africa), **W** *15420* (E Africa), **S** 15575 (Europe), **W** *17840* (W North Am)
1700-2200	*3255* (S Africa), **W** *11980* (Mideast)
1800-1830	**S** *9740* (S Asia), **W** *9740* (Australasia)
1800-2300	6195 (Europe)
1830-2100	*9630* (E Africa)
1830-2200	*6005* (E Africa), *9740* (Australasia)
1900-2000	**S** *5975* (Mideast & W Asia)
1900-2100	**S** *11835 &* **W** *15400* (S Africa)
1900-2300	15400 (W Africa)
1930-2000	**S** *11835* (W Africa)
2000-2200	*5975* (Australasia)
2000-2300	11835 (W Africa)
2100-2130	M-F *11675 &* M-F *15390* (C America)
2100-2200	*3915* (SE Asia), **W** *6110* (E Asia), **S** *11945* (E Asia)
2100-2400	*5965* (E Asia), *5975* (N America & C America), *6195* (SE Asia), *12095* (S America)
2130-2145	Tu/F 11680 (Atlantic & S America)
2200-2300	*9660* (SE Asia), *12080* (S Pacific)
2200-2400	*6175* (N America), *7110* (SE Asia), *9590* (N America), 9915 (S America), *11955* (SE Asia & Australasia)
2300-2400	*3915* (SE Asia), *6035, 11945,* **W** *15280 &* **W** *17790* (E Asia)
2330-2345	5875 (SE Asia)

GLOBAL SOUND KITCHEN

0000-0100	**S** Sa/Su 6140 (Europe), **S** Sa/Su 7325 (W Europe)
0000-0200 ◄	Sa/Su 3955 (Europe)
0000-0200	**W** Sa/Su 6180 (Europe), **W** Sa/Su 7165 (W Europe)
2100-2400	**S** F/Sa 6140 (Europe), **S** F/Sa 7325 (W Europe)
2200-2400 ◄	F/Sa 3955 (Europe)
2200-2400	**W** F/Sa 6170 (Europe), **W** F/Sa 7165 (W Europe)

WALES RADIO INTERNATIONAL

0200-0230	**S** Sa 9795 (N America)
0300-0330	**W** Sa 9735 (N America)
1130-1200	**W** Sa 17625 (Australasia)
1230-1300	**S** Sa 17650 (Australasia)
2030-2100	**S** F 7325 (Europe)
2130-2200	**W** F 6010 (Europe)

UNITED NATIONS

UNITED NATIONS RADIO

1730-1745	M-F *6125* (S Africa), M-F *15265* (E Africa), M-F *17710* (W Africa & C Africa)

USA

ADVENTIST WORLD RADIO

0130-0200	**W** *7235 &* **S** *11600* (W Asia & S Asia)
0300-0330	**S** *6015 &* **W** *9835* (E Africa)
0500-0530	*5960 & 6015* (S Africa)
0930-1000	**W** *7230/9610 &* **S** *9610* (Europe)
1000-1100	*11660/11560* (E Asia)
1030-1100	*11795* (E Asia)
1230-1300	**W** *7230/11700 &* **S** *9610* (Europe), **W** *15225 &* **S** *15330* (SE Asia)
1330-1400	**S** *11705* (E Asia), **S** *11750* (S Asia), **W** *11755* (E Asia), **W** *15225* (S Asia)
1430-1500	**S** *9355 &* **W** *9385* (S Asia), **W** *13720 &* **S** *17525* (W Asia & S Asia)
1600-1700	*9355* (S Asia)
1730-1800	**W** *7455,* **W** *7560,* **S** *11560 &* **S** *11965* (Mideast & W Asia), *12130* (E Africa)
1800-1830	*5960 & 6100* (S Africa)
2030-2100	**W** *9640* (N Africa & W Africa), *9745* (C Africa & E Africa), **S** *15560* (N Africa & W Africa)
2130-2200	**S** *11980,* **W** *11985 &* **S** *15550* (E Asia)

AFRTS—ARMED FORCES RADIO & TV SERVICE

24 Hr	4279 USB (N America & C America), *4319/12579* USB (S Asia), *4993/10941* USB (Europe & N Africa), *5765/13362* USB (Pacific), *6350/10320* USB, 6459 USB (C America), 12690 USB (Americas)

FAMILY RADIO—(S Asia)

0100-0200	⬛ *11750* & ⬛ *15060*
1305-1505	*11550*

HERALD BROADCASTING

0000-0057	W/F-M 9430 (E North Am), M/W/F 15285 (C America & S America)
0100-0157	9430 (N America), M 15285 (C America & S America)
0200-0257	M/Th 7535 (W North Am & C America), Su/M 9430 (N America)
0300-0357	⬛ M 7535 & ⬛ M 11930 (E Europe)
0400-0457	⬛ M/Tu/Th/Sa 12020 & ⬛ M/Tu/Th/Sa 15195 (E Africa & C Africa)
0500-0557	⬛ M 7535 (E Europe), ⬛ 9840 (S Africa), ⬛ M 11930 (E Europe), ⬛ 12020 (S Africa)
0600-0657	⬛ M/W/F/Sa 7535 & ⬛ M/W/F/Sa 13650 (W Africa & C Africa)
0700-0757	⬛ Tu/Th 7535 & ⬛ Tu/Th 13650 (W Africa)
0800-0857	⬛ Sa/Su 7535 (Europe), Sa-Th 9845 (Australasia), ⬛ Sa/Su 9860 (Europe)
0900-0957	⬛ Tu/Th 7535 & ⬛ Tu/Th 9860 (Europe)
1000-1057	M/W/Th 6095 (E North Am), Su 9455 (S America)
1000-1100	Th-Tu *11870* (E Asia)
1100-1157	Tu/F-Su 6095 (E North Am), M 11660 (C America & S America)
1200-1257	M/W/Th 6095 (E North Am), Sa 11660 (C America & S America)
1200-1300	⬛ *5915* & ⬛ *9875* (E Asia & SE Asia), ⬛ *9880* & ⬛ *17635* (SE Asia)
1300-1357	Sa-Th 9430 (N America), Tu/F 9455 (W North Am & C America)
1300-1400	⬛ *7460* & ⬛ *9940* (S Asia)
1600-1657	Sa 18910 (E Africa)
1700-1800	Tu/Th/Sa 18910 (C Africa)
1800-1857	Su 15665 (E Europe), Su/W 18910 (S Africa)
1900-1957	Su/Tu/Th 15665 (E Europe), 18910 (S Africa)
2000-2057	⬛ Su/M/W/F 15665 & ⬛ Su/M/W/F 18910 (Africa)
2100-2157	⬛ W/Sa-M 11550 & ⬛ W/Sa-M 15665 (W Europe), ⬛ F 15665 & ⬛ F 18910 (W Africa & C Africa)
2200-2257	⬛ Su/Th 7510 & ⬛ Su/Th 13770 (W Europe), W/Su 15285 (S America)
2300-2357	⬛ Su/W 7510 & ⬛ Su/W 13770 (S Europe & W Africa), Su 15285 (S America)

KAIJ—(N America)

0000-0200	5755/13815
0200-1200	5755
1200-1400	5755/13815
1400-2400	13815

KJES

0100-0230	7555 (W North Am)
1300-1400	11715 (N America)
1400-1500	11715 (W North Am)
1800-1900	15385 (Australasia)

KNLS-NEW LIFE STATION—(E Asia)

0800-0900	⬛ 9615 & ⬛ 11765
1300-1400	⬛ 7365 & ⬛ 9615

KTBN—(E North Am)

0000-0100	⬛ 7510 & ⬛ 15590
0100-1500	7510
1500-1600	⬛ 7510 & ⬛ 15590
1600-2400	15590

KVOH-VOICE OF HOPE—(C America)

0300-0600	9975

ODXA's Steve Canney alongside CFRX's kilowatt transmitter in Toronto. He verifies reception reports and maintains the equipment's operating environment.

S. Canney

In this Radio Free Asia studio, programs are prepared for audiences where the flow of news is otherwise restricted.

K. Zaffina

KWHR-WORLD HARVEST RADIO

0000-0100	M-Sa 17510 (E Asia)
0100-0400	17510 (E Asia)
0400-1000	17780 (E Asia)
0500-0700	M-F 11565 (Australasia)
0700-1045	11565 (Australasia)
1000-1030	Su-F 9930 (E Asia & SE Asia)
1030-1200	9930 (E Asia & SE Asia)
1045-1600	Sa/Su 11565 (Australasia)
1300-1400 &	
1600-1800	9930 (E Asia & SE Asia)
1800-2000	�winter 9930 (E Asia & SE Asia), �s 17510 (E Asia)
2000-2100	M-F 17510 (E Asia)
2330-2400	M-Sa 17510 (E Asia)

UNIVERSITY NETWORK

24 Hr	*5030* (C America), *6150* (C America & S America), *9725* (N America), *11870* (S America), *13750* (C America)
0800-1200 ◖	*17590* (S Asia)
1230-1600 ◖	*17795* (S Asia)

VOA-VOICE OF AMERICA

0000-0100	*7215*, �s *9770* & �w *9890* (SE Asia), Tu-Sa 11695 (C America & S America), *11760* (SE Asia), *15185* (SE Asia & S Pacific), *15290* (E Asia), *17740* (E Asia & S Pacific), *17820* (E Asia)
0000-0200	Tu-Sa 5995, Tu-Sa 6130, Tu-Sa 7405, Tu-Sa 9455, Tu-Sa 9775 & Tu-Sa 13740 (C America & S America)

0100-0300	*7115*, �w *7200*, �s *9635*, �w *9850*, 11705, �s *11725*, �s *13650*, *15250*, �w *15300*, *17740* & *17820* (S Asia)
0300-0330	M-F *4960* (W Africa & C Africa), *7340* (C Africa & E Africa)
0300-0400	�w *6035* & �s *6115* (E Africa & S Africa), *7105* (S Africa)
0300-0430	*9885* (Africa)
0300-0500	*6080* (S Africa), �s *7275* (Africa), *7290* (C Africa & E Africa), �w *7415* (Africa), 9575 (W Africa & S Africa), �s *17685* (E Africa & S Africa)
0400-0500	�s *7265* (S Africa & E Africa)
0400-0600	�w *9775* (C Africa & E Africa)
0400-0700	�w *7170* & �s *9530* (N Africa), �s *11965* (Mideast), *15205* (Mideast & S Asia)
0500-0600	�w *9700* (N Africa & W Africa)
0500-0630	*5970* (W Africa & C Africa), 6035 (W Africa & S Africa), *6080*, �s *7195* & �w *7295* (W Africa), *12080* (Africa), �s *13670* (C Africa)
0500-0700	�w *11825* (Mideast)
0600-0630	�w *11805* & �s *11995* (E Africa & S Africa), �w *15600* (C Africa & E Africa)
0600-0700	�w *5995*, �s *9680*, �s *11805* & �w *11930* (N Africa)
0630-0700	Sa/Su *5970* (W Africa & C Africa), Sa/Su 6035 (W Africa & S Africa), Sa/Su *6080*, �s Sa/Su *7195* & �w Sa/Su *7295* (W Africa), �w Sa/Su 11805 & �s Sa/Su *11995* (E Africa &

S Africa), Sa/Su *12080* (Africa), **S** Sa/Su *13670* (C Africa), **W** Sa/Su *15600* (C Africa & E Africa)

0700-0730	**W** Sa 6873 (Europe)
0800-1000	**S** *11930*, **W** *11995*, **S** *13610*, *13615*, **W** *13650* & *15150* (E Asia)
1000-1100	6165, **W** 7370, **S** 7405 & 9590 (C America)
1000-1200	**W** 5985 & **S** 9770 (Pacific & Australasia), *11720* (E Asia & Australasia), **W** *15250* (E Asia)
1000-1300	**S** *15240* (E Asia)
1000-1500	*15425* (SE Asia & Pacific)
1100-1300	**W** *6110* & **S** *6160* (SE Asia)
1100-1400	9645 (SE Asia & Australasia)
1100-1500	9760 (E Asia, S Asia & SE Asia), **W** *11705* & **S** *15160* (E Asia)
1200-1300	**W** *9780* (E Asia)
1200-1330	**W** *11715* (E Asia & Australasia)
1300-1400	**W** *11920* (S Asia), **W** *21550* (S Asia & SE Asia)
1300-1800	**W** *6110* & **S** *6160* (S Asia & SE Asia)
1400-1430	Su 18275 (Europe)
1400-1500	**W** *21555* & **W** *21840* (S Asia)
1400-1800	*7125*, *7215* & *9645* (S Asia), **W** *15205* (Mideast & S Asia), **S** *15255* (Mideast)
1500-1600	**S** *9590* & **W** *9760* (S Asia & SE Asia), **W** *9760* (E Asia, S Asia & SE Asia), *9845* & *12040* (E Asia), **S** *15235* (SE Asia & Australasia), **W** *15460* (SE Asia)
1500-1700	**W** *9575* (Mideast & S Asia), **S** *15205* (Europe, N Africa & Mideast)
1500-1800	**S** *9700* (Mideast), **W** *15395* (S Asia)
1600-1700	*6035* (W Africa), *9760* (S Asia & SE Asia), *13600* (C Africa & E Africa), *13710* (Africa), *15225* (S Africa), **S** *15410* (Africa)
1600-1800	**W** *12040* & *15445* (E Africa), *17895* (Africa)
1600-2000	**W** *11920* (E Africa)
1600-2200	**W** *15240* (Africa)
1700-1800	M-F *5990* & M-F *6045* (E Asia), **S** M-F *7150* (E Asia & S Pacific), **S** M-F *7170* (Australasia), **W** M-F *9525* (E Asia, SE Asia & S Pacific), **S** M-F *9550* & **W** M-F *9670* (E Asia & SE Asia), **S** M-F *9770* (E Asia), **W** M-F *9795* (S Asia & SE Asia), **W** M-F *12005* (SE Asia), **S** M-F *15255* (E Asia & Australasia)
1700-1900	**W** *6040* (N Africa & Mideast)
1700-2100	**S** *9760* (N Africa & Mideast), **W** *9760* (Mideast & S Asia)
1700-2200	**S** *15410* (Africa)
1730-1800	**W** *13680* (S Africa)
1800-1900	**S** *7415* (Africa), **S** *9770* (Mideast), **S** *17895* (Africa)
1800-2100	**W** *9565* (Mideast & S Asia)
1800-2200	*6035* (W Africa), *11975* (C Africa & E Africa), **W** *13710* (Africa), *15580* (W Africa)
1830-1900	**W** Sa/Su *9845*, **S** Sa/Su *11690*, **W** Sa/Su *13675*, **S** Sa/Su *13740*, **W** Sa/Su *15445* & **S** Sa/Su *15525* (E Africa)
1900-1930	**W** Sa *4950* (W Africa & C Africa)
1900-2000	**W** *5965*, **S** *6160* & **S** *7260* (Mideast), *9525* (Australasia), **S** *9550*, **S** *9680* & **W** *9785* (Mideast), M-F *9840* (S Asia), **W** *11720* & **S** *11780* (Mideast), **S** *11805* (S Pacific), **W** *11870* (Austra sia), **S** M-F *11970* (SE Asia), **W** M-F *11970* (E Asia), **S** M-F *12015* (S Asia), **W** *13640*, **S** *13690*, **S** *13725* & **W** *13725* (Mideast), *15180* (Pacific), **W** *15205* (Mideast), **S** M-F *15235* (SE Asia), **W** M-F *15410* (E Asia)
1900-2100	**S** *9770* (N Africa & Mideast)
1900-2200	**S** *7375* (Africa), *7415* (E Africa & S Africa), **S** *15445* (Africa)
1930-2030	*4950* (W Africa & C Africa)
2000-2030	*11855* (W Africa)
2000-2100	**S** *17745* & **W** *17885* (W Africa & C Africa)
2000-2200	*6095* (Mideast), 17725/17785 (Africa)
2030-2100	Sa/Su *4950* (W Africa & C Africa)
2100-2200	*6040* (Mideast), **S** *9535* (N Africa & Mideast), **W** *9595* (Mideast & S Asia), *9760* (E Europe & Mideast), *11870* (Australasia)
2100-2400	**S** *9705* (SE Asia), *15185* (SE Asia & S Pacific), 17735/17740 (E Asia & S Pacific), *17820* (E Asia)
2200-2230	M-F *6035* (W Africa), **S** M-F *7340* & **S** M-F *7375* (Africa), M-F *7415* (E Africa & S Africa), **W** M-F *11655* (Africa), M-F 11975 (C Africa & E Africa), **W** M-F *13710* (Africa)
2200-2400	*7215* & **S** *9770* (SE Asia), **W** *9770* (SE Asia & Australasia), **W** *9890* & *11760* (SE Asia), *15290* (E Asia), *15305* (E Asia & SE Asia)
2300-2400	**W** *7140*, **S** *7190*, **S** *7200*, *9545*, *11925*, **S** *13775* & **W** *15395* (E Asia)
2330-2400	**W** *7130*, **S** *7225*, **S** *7260*, **W** *9620*, *11805*, **S** *13735*, **W** *13745* & *15205* (SE Asia)

WBCQ-"THE PLANET"—(N America)

0000-0100	▭	9330 USB
0000-0600	▭	7415

0100-0700 ◰	Su-F 9330 USB	
0600-0715 ◰	Tu-Su 7415	
2100-2200 ◰	7415 (Irr)	
2200-2400 ◰	7415 & Su-F 9330 USB	

WEWN

0000-0200	▣ 5825 (E North Am), ▥ 5825 (N America & C America), ▥ 9355 (Europe), ▣ 13615 (W North Am & C America)
0200-1000	5825 (N America & C America)
1000-1100	▥ 7465 & ▣ 15745 (Europe)
1000-1300	▥ 5825 & ▣ 7425 (N America & C America)
1100-2100	15745 (Europe)
1300-1600	11875 (N America & C America)
1600-2200	11875 (E North Am)
1600-2400	13615 (W North Am & C America)
2100-2200	▥ 9975 & ▣ 15745 (Europe)
2200-2400	9385 (E North Am), 9975 (Europe)

WGTG

0000-0100 ◰	6890/12172 USB (W North Am)
0000-0200 ◰	5085/9320 USB (W North Am & C America)
0100-0700 ◰	6890 USB (W North Am)
0200-0700 ◰	5085 USB (W North Am & C America)
1300-2100 ◰	9400 USB (W North Am & C America)
1300-2400 ◰	12172 USB (W North Am)
1700-2400	▣ 12170 (W North Am)
2100-2300 ◰	9320/9400 USB (W North Am & C America)
2300-2400 ◰	5085/9320 USB (W North Am & C America)

WHRA-WORLD HARVEST RADIO

0000-0500	7580 (Europe & Mideast)
0500-1000	▥ 7435 & ▣ 11565 (Africa)
1600-2300 ◰	17650 (Africa)
2200-2300	▣ 7580 (Europe & Mideast)
2300-2400	7580 (Europe & Mideast)

WHRI-WORLD HARVEST RADIO

0000-1000	5745 (E North Am)
0045-0300	M 7315 (C America)
0300-1000	7315 (C America)
1000-1045	M-Sa 9495 (N America & C America)
1000-1500	6040 (E North Am)
1045-1300	9495 (N America & C America)
1300-1700	15105 (C America)
1500-1600	▥ 6040 (E North Am), ▣ 13760 (E North Am & W Europe)
1600-1715	13760 (E North Am & W Europe)
1700-1800	▣ 9495 (N America & C America), ▥ 15105 (C America)
1715-1730	M-Sa 13760 (E North Am & W Europe)
1730-2000	13760 (E North Am & W Europe)
1800-2400	9495 (N America & C America)
2000-2400	5745 (E North Am)

WINB-WORLD INTERNATIONAL BROADCASTERS—(C America & W North Am)

0000-0230	12160
0230-0330	Su/M 12160
1330-1400	Su 13570
1400-1500	Sa/Su 13570
1500-2300	13570
2300-2400	13570/12160

WJCR

24 Hr	7490 (E North Am), 13595 (W North Am)

WMLK—(Europe, Mideast & N America)

0400-0900 &	
1700-2200	Su-F 9465

WORLD BEACON

0430-0630	*6115* (S Africa)
1530-1600	M-F *6145* (S Africa)
1600-1800	*6145* (S Africa)
1800-1900	*17665* (W Africa)
1800-2200	*3230* (S Africa), *9675* (Africa)
1900-2200	*11640* (W Africa)
2100-2200	*7360* (Europe)

WTJC—(N America)

24 Hr	9370

WWCR

0000-0100	3215/9475 (E North Am)
0000-0200	5935/13845 & 13845 (E North Am)
0000-0400	7435 (E North Am)
0000-1300	5070 (E North Am)
0100-0400	3215 (E North Am)
0200-1200	5935 (E North Am)
0400-0500	▥ 3215 (E North Am)
0400-0600	▥ 2390/7435 (E North Am)
0500-1000 ◰	3210 (E North Am)
0600-1200 ◰	2390 (E North Am)
1000-1100 ◰	Su-F 7435 (E North Am)
1000-1100	▣ Su-F 9475 (E North Am)
1100-1200	▥ Su-F 12160 (E North Am & Europe)
1100-1300	▣ 15685 (E North Am & Europe)
1100-1400 ◰	7435 (E North Am)
1200-1300	▥ 12160 (E North Am & Europe)
1200-1400	5935/13845 (E North Am)
1300-1400	▥ 5070 & ▣ 9475 (Irr) (E North Am), ▣ 12160 (E North Am & Europe)
1300-2100	15685 (E North Am & Europe)
1400-2100	9475 (E North Am)
1400-2200	12160 (E North Am & Europe)
1400-2400	13845 (E North Am)
2100-2145	▣ Sa/Su 15685 (E North Am & Europe)
2100-2200	▥ 15685/9475 (E North Am)
2145-2200	▣ 15685 (E North Am & Europe)
2200-2245	▣ 9475 & ▥ Sa/Su 9475 (E North Am)
2200-2400	5070/12160 (E North Am & Europe), 7435 (E North Am)
2245-2300	9475 (E North Am)
2300-2400	3215/9475 & 9475 (E North Am)

WYFR-FAMILY RADIO

0000-0100	6085 (E North Am)
0000-0445	9505 (W North Am)
0100-0445	6065 (E North Am)
0400-0445	9985 (Europe)
0445-0600	[S] 9985 (Europe)
0500-0600	[W] 11550 & [S] 11580 (Europe)
0500-0700	5985 (W North Am)
0600-0745	7355 (Europe)
0700-0800	[W] 9985 (W Africa), [W] 11580 (C Africa & S Africa), [S] 13695 (W Africa), [S] 15170 (C Africa & S Africa)
1000-1245	5950 (E North Am)
1100-1245	[S] 5850 & [W] 7355 (W North Am)
1200-1300	[W] 11830 (W North Am)
1200-1345	[W] 11970 (C America)
1200-1700	[S] 17750 (W North Am & C America)
1300-1500	[W] 11740 & [S] 11970 (E North Am)
1300-1700	11830 (W North Am)
1400-1700	[W] 17760 (W North Am & C America)
1600-1700	[S] 15600 (W North Am), 21525 (C Africa & S Africa)
1600-1800	[W] 17510 & [S] 21455 (Europe)
1600-1845	[W] 15695 (Europe)
1600-2145	[S] 18980 (Europe)
1604-1700	[W] 15215 (W North Am)
1900-2145	[W] 11565 (Europe)
2000-2200	[W] 7355 (Europe)
2000-2245	[W] 15565 & [S] 17845 (W Africa), [W] 21525 (C Africa & S Africa)
2100-2245	[S] 15120 (C Africa & S Africa)
2200-2345	11740 (W North Am)

UZBEKISTAN

RADIO TASHKENT

0100-0130	[W] 5040 & 5060 (C Asia), [W] 5955 (S Asia), [W] 5975 (Mideast & W Asia), [W] 7105 (W Asia), [S] 7190 (Mideast & W Asia), [W] 7205 (Mideast), [S] 9375 (W Asia), [W] 9540 (Mideast & W Asia), [S] 9715 (Mideast & S Asia)
1200-1230 & 1330-1400	[W] 5060 & [W] 5975 (S Asia), [W] 6025 & [S] 7285 (W Asia & S Asia), 9715 & [S] 15295 (S Asia), [S] 17775 (S Asia & SE Asia)
2030-2100 & 2130-2200	[W] 7105 (W Asia), 9540 (Mideast & W Asia), [S] 9545 (W Asia)

VATICAN STATE

VATICAN RADIO

0140-0200	[W] 7335, [S] 9650 & [S] 11935 (S Asia)
0250-0310	7305 (E North Am) & 9605 (E North Am & C America)
0600-0620 ⬅	4005 (Europe), 5880 (W Europe)
0730-0745 ⬅	M-Sa 4005 (Europe), M-Sa 5880 (W Europe), M-Sa 7250 & M-Sa 9645 (Europe), M-Sa 11740 (W Europe & N Africa), M-Sa 15210/15215 (Mideast)
1120-1130 ⬅	M-Sa 7250 (Europe), M-Sa 11740 (W Europe), M-Sa 15210 (Mideast)
1615-1630	[S] 7250 (N Europe), [S] 11810 (Mideast)
1715-1730 ⬅	4005 (Europe), 5880 & 9645 (W Europe)
2050-2110 ⬅	4005 & 5880 (Europe)
2245-2305	7305 (E Asia), 9600 & 11830 (Australasia)

Fakhriddin Nizom, director of Radio Tashkent, with PASSPORT. M. Guha

VIETNAM

VOICE OF VIETNAM

0100-0130 & 0230-0300	[W] *9525* & [S] *9695* (E North Am)
0330-0400	*9795* (C America)
1000-1030 & 1230-1300	9840 & 12020 (SE Asia)
1330-1400 & 1630-1700	[W] 7145, 9730 & [S] 13740 (Europe)
1800-1830	[W] 7145, [W] *7440*, 9730, [S] *12070* & [S] 13740 (Europe)
1900-1930 & 2030-2100	[W] 7145, 9730 & [S] 13740 (Europe)
2330-2400	9840 & 12020 (SE Asia)

Voices from Home—2001

Country-by-Country Guide to Native Broadcasts

For some listeners, English offerings are merely icing on the cake. Their real interest is in eavesdropping on broadcasts for *nativos*—the home folks. These can be enjoyable regardless of language, especially when they offer traditional music.

Some you'll hear, many you won't, depending on your location and receiving equipment. Keep in mind that native-language broadcasts are sometimes weaker than those in English, so you may need more patience and better hardware. PASSPORT REPORTS shows which radios and antennas work best.

When to Tune

Some broadcasts come in better during the day within world band segments from 9300 to 21850 kHz. However, signals from Latin

America and Africa peak near or during darkness, especially from 4700 to 5100 kHz. See "Best Times and Frequencies" for specifics.

Times and days of the week are in World Time, explained in "Setting Your World Time Clock" and PASSPORT's glossary; for local times in each country, see "Addresses PLUS." Midyear, some stations are an hour earlier (◧) or later (◧) because of daylight saving time, typically April through October. Those used only seasonally are labeled ◲ for summer (midyear) and ◲ for winter (January, etc.). Stations may also extend their hours for holidays, emergencies or sports events.

Frequencies in *italics* may be best, as they come from relay transmitters that might be near you. Frequencies with no target zones are usually for domestic coverage, so they are the least likely to be heard unless you're in or near that country.

BBS presents the evening news.   M. Guha

Schedules for Entire Year

To be as useful as possible over the months to come, PASSPORT's schedules consist not just of observed activity, but also that which we have creatively opined will take place during the forthcoming year. This predictive material is based on decades of experience and is original from us. Although inherently not as exact as real-time data, over the years it's been of tangible value to PASSPORT readers.

Signals from Latin America and Africa peak near or during darkness.

ALBANIA—Albanian

RADIO TIRANA
0000-0600 ▣	6090 & 7270 (N America)
0400-0900 ▣	6100 (Europe)
0800-1100 ▣	7110 (Europe)
0900-1400 ▣	9585/9760 (W Europe)
1000-1500 ▣	7150 (Europe)
1500-1800 ▣	5985 (S Europe), 7270 (Europe)
1800-2300 ▣	6100 (Europe)
1900-2200	**S** 9575 (Europe)
2000-2300 ▣	7295 (Europe)
2000-2300	**W** 9750 (Europe)

ARGENTINA—Spanish

RADIO ARGENTINA AL EXTERIOR-RAE
1200-1400	M-F 11710 (S America)
2200-2400	M-F 9690 (S America), M-F 15345 (Europe & N Africa)

RADIO NACIONAL
0000-0230	Tu-Sa 9690 (Irr) (S America)
0000-0300	11710 (Irr) (S America), 15345 (Irr) (Americas)
0000-0400	Su/M 6060 (S America)
0900-1200	6060 (S America), 15345 (Americas)
1200-2400	Sa/Su 6060 (S America)
1700-2400	M-F 6060 (Irr) & 11710 (Irr) (S America)
1800-2400	Sa/Su 15345 (Europe & N Africa)

ARMENIA—Armenian

VOICE OF ARMENIA
0300-0345 &	
0400-0430 ▣	9965 (S America)
0815-0900 ▣	Su 4810 (E Europe, Mideast & W Asia), Su 15270 (Europe)
1930-2015 ▣	M-Sa 4810 (E Europe, Mideast & W Asia), M-Sa 9965 (Europe)

AUSTRIA—German

RADIO AUSTRIA INTERNATIONAL
0000-0030 &	
0100-0130	**W** 7325 & **S** 9655 (E North Am), 9870 & 13730 (S America)
0200-0230	**W** 7325 (E North Am), 9870 (C America), 13730 (S America)
0200-0300	**S** 9655 (E North Am)
0230-0300	**S** 9870 (C America), **S** 13730 (S America)
0300-0330	9870 (C America), 13730 (S America)
0400-0430	6155 (Europe), 13730 (E Europe)
0430-0500	**W** 6155 (Europe), **W** 13730 (E Europe)
0500-0530	*6015* (W North Am), 6155 (Europe), 13730 (E Europe), 15410 & 17870 (Mideast)
0530-0600	**S** 6155 (Europe), **S** 13730 (E Europe), **S** 15410 & **S** 17870 (Mideast)
0600-0630	*6015* (W North Am), 6155 (Europe), 13730 (E Europe), 15410 & 17870 (Mideast)
0630-0700	**W** 6155 (Europe), **W** 13730 (E Europe), **W** 15410 & **W** 17870 (Mideast)
0700-0730	6155 (Europe), 13730 (E Europe), 15410 & 17870 (Mideast)
0730-0800	**S** 6155 (Europe), **S** 13730 (E Europe)
0800-0830	21650 (E Asia), 21765 (Australasia)
0800-1100	13730 (N Europe)
0800-1130	6155 (Europe)
0830-0900	**W** Su-F 21650 (E Asia), **W** Su-F 21765 (Australasia)
0900-0930	21650 (E Asia), 21765 (Australasia)
0930-1000	**S** 21650 (E Asia), **S** 21765 (Australasia)
1000-1100	21650 (E Asia), 21765 (Australasia)
1100-1130	13730 (W Europe & E North Am)
1130-1200	**W** 6155 (Europe), **W** 13730 (W Europe & E North Am)
1200-1230 &	
1300-1330	6155 (Europe), 13730 (W Europe & E North Am)
1400-1430	6155 (Europe), 13730 (S Europe & W Africa)
1430-1500	**S** 6155 (Europe), **S** 13730 (S Europe & W Africa)
1500-1630	6155 (Europe), 13730 (S Europe & W Africa), **S** 15240 (Mideast), **S** 17765 (S Asia & SE Asia)
1500-1730	**W** 9655 (Mideast), **W** 13710 (S Asia & SE Asia)
1630-1700	**W** 6155 (Europe), **W** 13730 (S Europe & W Africa)
1700-1730	6155 (Europe), 13730 (S Europe & W Africa)
1700-1800	**S** 17765 (S Asia & SE Asia)
1700-1900	**S** 15240 (Mideast)
1800-1830	5945 & 6155 (Europe), **W** 9655 (Mideast), 13730 (E Africa & S Africa)
1830-1900	**S** 5945 & **S** 6155 (Europe)
1900-1930	5945 & 6155 (Europe), 13730 (E Africa & S Africa)
1930-2000	**S** Sa 5945, **W** 5945 & **S** Sa 6155 (Europe), **W** 13730 (E Africa & S Africa)
1930-2030	6155 (Europe)
2000-2030	**W** 5945 (Europe), 13730 (E Africa & S Africa)
2030-2100	**W** Sa 5945 & **W** Sa 6155 (Europe), **S** 13730 (E Africa & S Africa)
2100-2130 &	
2200-2230	5945 & 6155 (Europe), 13730 (N Africa & W Africa)

2230-2300	🅂 5945 & 🅂 6155 (Europe), 🅂 13730 (N Africa & W Africa)
2300-2400	6155 (Europe), 9870 & 13730 (S America)

BANGLADESH—Bangla

BANGLADESH BETAR

1200-1530	15520 (Mideast & Europe)
1540-1600	15520 (Mideast & Europe)
1630-1730	7185 & 9550 (Mideast), 15520 (Mideast & Europe)
1710-1740	15520 (Mideast & Europe)
1915-2000	7185, 9550 & 15520 (Irr) (Europe)

BELGIUM

RADIO VLAANDEREN INTERNATIONAAL
Dutch

0430-0500	🅆 *11980* & 🅂 *15565* (W North Am)
0600-0700	🅂 13710 (E Europe & Mideast)
0600-0800 ➡	5985 (S Europe)
0600-0900 ➡	9925 (Europe)
0700-0800	🅂 13710 (S Europe & W Africa), 🅆 13740/11690 (E Europe & Mideast)
0800-0830	🅆 11690 (S Europe & W Africa)
1000-1100	🅂 Su 17690 (C Africa & E Africa)
1100-1130	🅂 13710 (S Europe & W Africa)
1100-1200 ➡	Su 21630 (C Africa & E Africa)
1100-1200	🅆 Su 17695 (C Africa & E Africa)
1200-1230 ➡	9925 (Europe)
1200-1230	*9865* (E Asia & Australasia), 🅆 13760 (S Europe), 🅆 *17685* & 🅂 *17690* (SE Asia & Australasia), 21630 (C Africa & E Africa)
1300-1600	🅂 Su 13710 (S Europe & W Africa), 🅂 Su 21630 (C Africa & E Africa)
1400-1700 ➡	Su 9925 (Europe)
1400-1700	🅆 Su 13740 (S Europe & W Africa), 🅆 Su 21820 (C Africa & E Africa)
1600-1630	🅂 13710 (E Europe & Mideast)
1700-1730 ➡	9925 (Europe)
1700-1730	🅆 11780 (E Europe), 🅂 13710 (S Europe & W Africa)
1800-1830 ➡	5910 (S Europe), 9925 (Europe)
1800-1830	🅆 *11780* (W Europe)
1800-1900	🅂 *7195* (S Africa), 🅂 *13710* (E Europe & Mideast), 🅂 *17590* (C Africa & E Africa)
1900-2000 ➡	5910 & 9925 (S Europe), 15365 (Africa)
1900-2000	🅆 *13600* (E Europe & Mideast), 🅆 *13645* (S Africa), 🅆 *17695* (C Africa & E Africa)
2000-2100 ➡	Sa 5910 & Sa 9925 (S Europe), Sa 15365 (Africa)
2100-2200 ➡	5910 (S Europe), 9925 (S Europe & W Africa)
2300-2330	🅆 *13670* & 🅂 *15565* (N America)

French

1630-1645	🅂 9925 (Europe)
1900-1915	🅂 *5960* (W Europe)

RTBF INTERNATIONAL
French

0400-0530 ➡	M-F *9490* (C Africa)
0400-0800	🅂 9970/9965 (S Europe)
0530-0600 ➡	*9490* (C Africa)
0600-0812 ➡	*17580* (C Africa)
0800-1700	9970/9965 (S Europe)
0812-0906 ➡	Sa/Su *17580* (C Africa)
0906-1100 ➡	Sa *17580* (C Africa)
1100-1200 ➡	M-Sa *21565* (C Africa)
1200-1217 ➡	*21565* (C Africa)
1217-1306 ➡	M-F *21565* (C Africa)
1600-1700 ➡	Su-F *17570* (C Africa)
1700-1715	🅂 9970/9965 (S Europe)
1700-1812 ➡	*17570* (C Africa)

BRAZIL—Portuguese

RADIO BANDEIRANTES
24 Hr	6090, 9645, 11925

RADIO BRASIL CENTRAL
0200-0600 ➡	4985 (Irr)
0600-0200 ➡	4985
0600-0330 ➡	11815

RADIO CULTURA SAO PAULO
0000-0200 ➡	6170, 9615, 17815
0700-2400 ➡	9615, 17815
0800-2400 ➡	6170

RADIO NACIONAL DA AMAZONIA
0700-2300 ➡	6180/11780

BULGARIA—Bulgarian

RADIO BULGARIA

0000-0100	🅂 9500 & 🅂 11600 (S America), 🅂 11700 (E North Am)
0100-0200 ➡	9400 (E North Am)
0100-0200	🅆 5900 (S America), 🅆 7375 (E North Am), 🅆 9415 (S America)
0300-0400	🅂 7500 (E Europe & W Asia)
0400-0500 ➡	5900 (E Europe & W Asia)
0400-0500	🅆 7400 (E Europe & W Asia)
1200-1500	🅂 7300 (Europe)
1300-1600 ➡	13600 (Europe)
1300-1600	🅆 7500 (S Europe & Mideast)
1500-1600	🅂 13600 (Mideast)
1500-1800	🅂 9900 & 🅂 11700 (E Europe & W Asia)
1600-1700 ➡	17500 (S Africa)
1600-1700	🅆 9400 (Mideast)
1600-1900	🅆 5865 & 🅆 7465 (E Europe & W Asia)
1800-1900	🅂 6000 (S Europe)
1800-2100	🅂 7400 (Mideast), 🅂 7500 (Europe)
1900-2000	🅆 5855 (S Europe)
1900-2200	🅆 7500 (Mideast), 🅆 7545 (Europe)

CANADA—French

CANADIAN BROADCASTING CORP—(E North Am)

0100-0300 ◪	M 9625
0300-0400 ◪	Su 9625 & Tu-Sa 9625
1300-1310 &	
1500-1555 ◪	M-F 9625
1700-1715 ◪	Su 9625
1900-1945 ◪	M-F 9625
1900-2310 ◪	Sa 9625

RADIO CANADA INTERNATIONAL

0000-0030	🅢 Tu-Sa 11895, 🅢 Tu-Sa 13670, 🅢 Tu-Sa 15170 & 🅢 Tu-Sa 15305 (C America & S America)
0000-0100	🅢 5960 (E North Am)
0100-0130	🅦 9535 & 🅦 11865 (C America & S America)
0100-0200 ◪	9755 (E North Am & C America)
0100-0200	🅦 5960 (E North Am)
0130-0200	🅦 Su/M 9535 & 🅦 Su/M 11865 (C America & S America)
0230-0300	🅢 Tu-Sa 11715, 🅢 Tu-Sa 13670, 🅢 Tu-Sa 15170 & 🅢 Tu-Sa 15305 (C America & S America)
0300-0330	🅦 *6025*, 🅦 *9505*, 🅢 *11835* & 🅢 *11940* (Mideast)
0330-0400 ◪	Tu-Sa 9755 (E North Am & C America)
0330-0400	🅦 Tu-Sa 6155 (E North Am & C America), 🅦 Tu-Sa 9780 (W North Am)
0430-0500	🅦 M-F *9690* (C Africa & E Africa), 🅦 M-F *11795* (E Africa), 🅢 M-F 13765 & 🅢 M-F *15345* (C Africa & E Africa)
0530-0600	🅢 5995 (W North Am), 🅢 *6145* (Europe), 🅢 *7290* (W Europe), 🅢 *9595* (Europe), 🅢 9755 (W North Am), 🅢 11710 (W Europe & W Africa), 🅢 11830 (W North Am), 🅢 13755 (W Africa), 🅢 *15330* (N Africa & Mideast)
0630-0700	🅦 5960 (W North Am), 🅦 6045 (Europe), 🅦 *6150* (Europe & Mideast), 🅦 9670 (W North Am), 🅦 M-F 9780 (W Africa), 🅦 M-F *11710* (Africa), 🅢 M-F 11715 (W Africa), 🅦 *11905* (Mideast & E Africa), 🅢 M-F 13755 (W Africa), 🅦 M-F *15325* (Africa), 🅢 M-F *15330* & 🅢 M-F *17820* (W Africa)
1200-1300	🅢 15305 (E North Am & C America)
1230-1300	🅦 *6150* & 🅢 *9660* (E Asia), 🅦 *11730* (E Asia & S Asia), 🅢 *15195* (E Asia & SE Asia)
1300-1400 ◪	11855 (E North Am & C America)
1300-1400	🅦 15425 (C America)
1300-1600	🅢 Su 15305 (E North Am & C America)
1400-1700	🅦 Su 17795 (E North Am & C America)
1500-1600	🅦 *17820* (W Africa)
1800-1900	🅢 13650 (Europe), 🅢 17820 (Africa)
1800-2000	🅢 *13670* (N Africa & W Africa), 🅢 21570 (W Europe)
1800-2200	🅢 17695 (Europe)
1900-2000	🅢 *7235* (W Europe), 13650 & 🅢 15325 (Europe), 🅢 15470 (W Africa), 17820 (Africa)
1900-2100	🅦 15325 (W Africa & S Africa)
2000-2100 ◪	*5995* (W Europe & N Africa)
2000-2100	🅦 *7235* (W Europe & N Africa), 🅦 9770 (W Europe), 🅦 *9805* (W Europe & N Africa), 🅦 11730 (W Europe), 🅦 11945 (W Africa), 🅦 13650 (Europe), 🅦 13690 & 🅦 17820 (Africa)
2030-2100	🅢 M-F *17735* & 🅢 M-F 17805 (W Africa), 🅢 M-F 21570 (W Europe)
2130-2200	🅦 M-F *9670* (W Africa), 🅦 M-F 11755 (W Europe), 🅦 M-F *11890* (W Africa), 🅢 11920 (E North Am & C America), 🅢 15305 (C America & S America), 🅦 M-F 17875 (Africa)
2230-2300 ◪	9755 (E North Am & C America)
2230-2300	🅢 5960 (E North Am), 🅦 *11705* (E Asia & SE Asia), 🅢 15305 (C America & S America), 🅢 17695 (E North Am & C America), 🅢 *17835* (E Asia & SE Asia)

CHINA

CENTRAL PEOPLE'S BROADCASTING STATION
Chinese

0000-0004	🅦 6015, 🅦 6160/6175, 🅦 9380, 🅢 11100, 🅢 11935, 🅢 15710
0000-0030	🅦 7345, 🅢 12080, 🅢 15550
0000-0100	5880, 5915, 5955, 5975, 5980, 5990, 🅦 6110, 6125, 🅦 9775, 🅦 9845, 🅢 11000, 🅢 11960, 🅢 17550, 🅢 17700
0000-0103	🅦 9710/9170, 🅢 15880
0000-0130	7210, 11630, 12000, 12045
0000-0200	🅦 9830, 🅦 11925, 🅢 15390, 🅢 17580, 🅢 17605
0000-0600	6030, 7200, 7230, 9625, 9645, 9675, 9810, 11610/11780, 11660, 11670, 11800, 12030, 15480, 15500, 15540
0000-1130	17625
0000-1200	17890
0030-0130	11710
0030-0330	11720
0030-0600	15550
0055-0613	11680/11100, 11935, 15710

0100-0600	11960, 17550, 17700
0130-0600	12080
0200-0600	9500, 11740, 15390, 17580, 17605
0230-0600	15570
0355-0603	15880
0355-0604	11000
0600-0855	W-M 6030, W-M 7230, W-M 9645, W-M 9675, W-M 11630, W-M 11960, W-M 12000, W-M 12030, W-M 12045, W-M 15390, W-M 15480, W-M 15550, W-M 17550, W-M 17580, W-M 17605
0600-0955	Th/Sa-Tu 7200, Th/Sa-Tu 9500, Th/Sa-Tu 9625, Th/Sa-Tu 9810, Th/Sa-Tu 11610/11780, Th/Sa-Tu 11660, Th/Sa-Tu 11670, Th/Sa-Tu 11740, Th/Sa-Tu 11800, Th/Sa-Tu 12080, Th/Sa-Tu 15500, Th/Sa-Tu 15540, Th/Sa-Tu 15570, Th/Sa-Tu 17625, Th/Sa-Tu 17700
0603-0955	Th-Tu 15880
0604-0955	W-M 11000
0855-0930	11960
0855-1000	9645, 15550
0855-1100	9675, 17605
0855-1130	15390, 17550
0855-1200	11630, 12045, 17580
0855-1230	15480
0855-1300	12000
0855-1400	12030
0855-1730	6030, 7230
0930-1300	[W] 6110, [S] 11960
0955-1030	15500
0955-1100	11000, 15570, 17700
0955-1130	11610/11780, 17625
0955-1200	9500, 9810, 11740, 12080
0955-1300	[S] 11660, 15880
0955-1330	11800, 15540
0955-1400	9380, [S] 11670
0955-1602	7200, 9625
0955-2400	[W] 6015, [W] 6160/6175, [S] 11100, [S] 11935
1000-1230	[W] 7345, [S] 15550
1000-1330	[W] 6055, [S] 9645
1000-1400	[W] 4850
1000-1730	7210
1030-1602	[W] 5010, [S] 15500
1100-1200	[W] 5030, [S] 9675
1100-1300	[W] 9775, [S] 15570, [S] 17605, [S] 17700
1100-1400	[W] 9830
1100-1730	5880, 5955, 5975, 5980, 5990, 6125, 9800
1100-1804	[S] 11000
1130-1300	[W] 9655
1130-1330	[W] 9845, [S] 17550
1130-1400	[S] 15390
1130-1602	[W] 7140, 9745, [S] 11610/11780
1200-1400	[W] 11925, [S] 17580
1200-1602	[W] 5163, [S] 9810
1200-1730	5030, 7290
1230-1730	5320, 7345
1300-1602	[W] 6090, 9775, [S] 11660
1300-1730	6110, 9655
1300-1804	9710/9170
1330-1602	[W] 3290, 11730, [S] 11800
1330-1730	6055, 9845
1400-1602	4850
1400-1730	[W] 7305, 7415/7180, 9830, 11925
1400-2300	[W] 5090, [W] 6070, [S] 9380
2000-2200	6055, 7290
2000-2230	5320
2000-2300	6110, 7345, 7415/7180, 9655, 9830, 9845, 11925, 11960
2000-2330	5030
2000-2400	5880, 5915, 5955, 5975, 5980, 5990, 6030, 6125, 7210, 7230, 11630, 12000, 12045
2055-2400	9710/9170
2100-2230	[W] 3290, [S] 11800
2100-2300	[W] 4850, 5010, 6090, 9745, 9775, [S] 11670, [W] 11730, [S] 15540
2100-2330	[W] 5163, [W] 7140, [S] 9810, [S] 11610/11780
2100-2400	7200, 9625
2200-2400	[W] 6055, [W] 7290, [S] 9645, [S] 11000, [S] 17890
2230-2400	11800, 15480
2300-2400	[W] 5010, [W] 6110, [W] 7345, [W] 9380, [W] 9655, [W] 9745, [W] 9775, [W] 9830, [W] 9845, 11660, 11670, [W] 11925, [S] 11960, 12030, [S] 15390, [S] 15500, 15540, [S] 15550, [S] 15710, [S] 17550, [S] 17580, [S] 17625, [S] 17700
2330-2400	9675, 9810, 11610/11780, [S] 12080, [S] 17605

CHINA RADIO INTERNATIONAL
Chinese

0200-0300	*9570* (E North Am), *9690* (N America & C America), 15435 (S America)
0300-0400	*9720* (W North Am)
0900-1000	6165 (E Asia), 9690, 9945, 11700 & 15440 (Australasia)
0900-1100	6010 & 11685 (SE Asia), [W] 11875 (Australasia), 12015 & 17785 (SE Asia)
1200-1300	*9570* (E North Am)
1200-1400	9580 (Australasia), 9755, 11685, 15260 & 17785 (SE Asia)
1500-1600	7170 & [S] 8260 (E Asia), 11740 (SE Asia), 15300 (S Asia)
1730-1830	5250 (E Asia), [W] 7110 (Europe), [W] 7160 (Mideast), [W] 7255 (E Europe), 9645 (Africa), [S] 11825 (Europe), [S] 13650 (Mideast & W Asia), [S] 15165 (Europe)

2000-2100	**W** 7120 (Mideast), 7185 (Europe), **W** 7245 (Mideast), 7525 (E Europe), **W** 9685 & **S** 9710 (Mideast), 9730 (E Europe & W Asia), **S** 11650 (E Europe), **S** 11750 (N Africa & Mideast), **S** 13650 (Mideast & W Asia)
2230-2300	*15500* (E Africa)
2230-2330	6140, **W** 7130 & 7335 (SE Asia), **S** 8260 (E Asia), 9755, 11945, **S** 12065, 15100, **S** 15135, 15260, 15300 & 15400 (SE Asia)
2230-2400	*11975* (N Africa)
2300-2400	*7170* (W Africa & C Africa)

Cantonese

1000-1100	11915 (SE Asia), 15440 (Australasia)
1100-1200	11685, 11720 & 17785 (SE Asia)
1200-1300	**W** 9590 & **S** 15125 (E North Am)
1700-1800	**W** 7220 (S Asia & E Africa), 7265 (E Africa & S Africa), 9675 (W Asia), 9690 (S Asia), 9770 & **S** 11675 (E Africa)
1900-2000	**W** 7255 (E Europe), 9730 (E Europe & W Asia)
2330-2400	6140, **W** 7130, 7335, 9755, 11945, **S** 12065, 15100, **S** 15135, 15260, 15300 & 15400 (SE Asia)

CHINA (TAIWAN)

CENTRAL BROADCASTING SYSTEM-CBS
Chinese

0000-0100	9610 (E Asia), 15125
0000-0200	3335 & 9630 (E Asia)
0000-0400	7150 (E Asia)
0000-0500	6040 (E Asia)
0100-0400	9280 (E Asia)
0200-1000	11970 (E Asia)
0300-0600	9610 (E Asia)
0400-0700	11775 (E Asia)
0400-0900	6180 (E Asia)
0400-1000	11840 (E Asia)
0400-1600	11725 (SE Asia)
0400-2400	6085 & 7105/7108 (E Asia)
0700-0900	7285 (E Asia)
0700-2400	3335 (E Asia)
0800-1000	15125
0900-1000	7285 (E Asia)
0900-1100	6180 (E Asia)
0900-1800	9630 (E Asia)
0900-2400	6040 & 7150 (E Asia)
1000-1100	7285 (E Asia)
1100-1200	9610
1100-1800	11775 & 11840 (E Asia)
1100-2400	6180 (E Asia)
1400-1500	9610
1400-1800	9690 (E Asia)

1500-1700	15125
2100-2400	9630 (E Asia)
2200-2400	*5950* (E North Am), 9610 (E Asia), 11725 (SE Asia), 11860, 15125, *15440* (W North Am & C America)

RADIO TAIPEI INTERNATIONAL
Amoy

0000-0100	11550 (E Asia), *15440* (W North Am & C America)
0200-0300	11550 (SE Asia)
0200-0400	11915 (E Asia)
0500-0600	11745 (SE Asia)
1000-1100	7130 & 11745 (E Asia), 15125 & 15345 (SE Asia)
1300-1400	7130 (E Asia), 11860 (SE Asia)
2100-2200	11745 (Australasia)

Chinese

0100-0200	**W** *11825*, *15215* & **S** *17845* (S America)
0400-0500	*5950* (N America & C America), 7130 (SE Asia), *9680* (W North Am), 11825, 15270 & 15345 (SE Asia)
0700-0800	7130 (SE Asia)
0900-1000	7445 (SE Asia), 9610 (Australasia), 11745 (E Asia), 11915 (SE Asia)
1200-1300	11745 (E Asia), 15270 (SE Asia)
1900-2000	**W** *9355* (Europe), 9955 (Mideast & N Africa), **S** *15600*, **S** *17750* & **W** *17760* (Europe)
2300-2400	*3975* (W Europe)

Cantonese

0000-0500	9690 (E Asia)
0100-0200	*5950* (E North Am), *7520* (Europe), 11550 (SE Asia), *15440* (W North Am & C America)
0300-0400	*11740* (C America)
0500-0600	*5950* (N America & C America), *9680* (W North Am), 11825 (SE Asia), 11915 (E Asia), 15270 & 15345 (SE Asia)
0900-1200	15270 (SE Asia)
0900-1400	9690 (E Asia)
1000-1100	7445 (SE Asia), 9610 (Australasia), 11915 (SE Asia)
1300-1400	9765 & 15345 (SE Asia)

VOICE OF ASIA
Chinese

0300-0700	7285 (SE Asia)
0700-1100	9280 (E Asia)
1100-1300	15125 (SE Asia)
1300-1500	7445 (SE Asia)

COLOMBIA—Spanish

CARACOL COLOMBIA
24 Hr	5077

RADIODIFUSORA NACIONAL DE COLOMBIA
1100-1700	Su 4955/9635
1700-0445	4955/9635

CROATIA—Croatian

CROATIAN RADIO—(Europe)
0400-0600	7365 & 9830
0500-0700 ◲	6165
0600-0605	[S] Su 7365, [W] 7365 & [S] Su 9830
0605-0700	7365 & 9830
0700-0705 ◲	Su 6165
0700-0705	[S] M-Sa 7365, [W] Su 7365, [S] M-Sa 9830 & [W] Su 9830
0705-0800 ◲	6165
0705-0800	7365 & 9830
0800-0805 ◲	M-Sa 6165
0800-0805	[S] 7365, [W] M-Sa 7365, [S] 9830 & [W] M-Sa 9830
0805-0900	7365
0805-1200	9830
0805-1300 ◲	6165
0900-1200	13830
0900-1300	[W] 7365
1200-1205	[W] 9830 & [W] 13830
1205-1300	9830 & 13830
1300-1305	[S] 9830 & [S] 13830
1305-1700	9830
1305-1800	[W] 7365 & 13830
1305-1830 ◲	6165
1500-1830	[W] 7185
1700-1730	[S] 9830
1800-1805	[W] 13830
1805-1900	13830
1900-1905	[S] 13830
1905-2100	13830

RADIO CROATIA
0015-0200 ◲	*9925 (S America)*
0115-0300	[S] *9925 (E North Am)*
0215-0400	[W] *7280/9925 (E North Am)*
0315-0500	[S] *9925 (W North Am)*
0415-0600	[W] *7285/9925 (W North Am)*
0515-0700	[S] *9470 (Australasia)*
0615-0800	[W] *11880 (Australasia)*
0815-1000 ◲	*13820 (Australasia)*
2000-2030 & 2045-2100	[S] *11805 (Mideast & S Africa)*
2100-2130 & 2145-2200	[W] *9405/11605 (Mideast & S Africa)*

CUBA—Spanish

RADIO HABANA CUBA
0000-0100	6000 (E North Am), 9820 (N America)
0000-0300	11970 (S America)
0000-0500	5965 (C America), 6070 (C America & W North Am), 9505 (S America), 11760 (Americas), 15230 (S America)
0200-0500	9550 (E North Am)
1100-1400	6000 (C America)
1100-1500	11760 (C America)

1200-1400	15340 (S America)
1200-1500	6070 (C America & W North Am), 9550 (C America)
2100-2300	[W] 9820 (Europe & N Africa), 9830 USB (E North Am & Europe), 11760 & [S] 13680 (Europe & N Africa)

RADIO REBELDE
24 Hr	5025
0300-0400	6120 (C America)
1100-1400	6140 & 9600 (C America)

CYPRUS—Greek

CYPRUS BROADCASTING CORP—(Europe)
2215-2245	F-Su 6180, F-Su 7205 & F-Su 9760

CZECH REPUBLIC—Czech

RADIO PRAGUE
0030-0100	[W] 7345 (N America), [W] 11615 (S America)
0130-0200	[S] 7345 (N America), [S] 11615 (S America)
0230-0300	[W] 6200 & [S] 7345 (N America), [W] 7345 (S America), [S] 11615 (W North Am & C America)
0330-0400	[W] 7345 (N America), [W] 9435 (W North Am & C America)
0830-0900	[S] 11600 (W Europe), [S] 21745 (E Africa & Mideast)
0930-1000	[W] 15255 (W Europe), [S] 21745 (S Asia & W Africa), [W] 21745 (E Africa & Mideast)
1030-1100	[W] 17485 (W Africa), [W] 21745 (Mideast & S Asia)
1100-1130	[S] 21745 (S Asia)
1200-1230	[W] 11640 (N Europe), [W] 21745 (S Asia & Australasia)

Zhou Lian of Tecsun, Ltd., and CEO Esmail Amid-Hozour of Grundig/Lextronix visit Fred Osterman (tie) at Universal Radio to discuss the new Grundig Satellit 800 portatop receiver.

Tecsun

1330-1400 ▣	6055 (Europe), 7345 (W Europe)	0330-0355	🅂 *7465* (Mideast), 🅆 *7465* (W North Am), 🅆 *7485* (Mideast), 🅆 *9945* (E Africa), 🅂 *11635* (W North Am), 🅂 *13800* (Mideast & E Africa)
1330-1400	🅂 13580 (N Europe), 🅂 17485 (S Asia)		
1430-1500	🅆 21745 (E North Am & E Africa)		
1530-1600	🅂 21745 (E Africa)	0430-0455	🅂 *7465* (Europe), 🅆 *7465* (W North Am), 🅆 *7485* (Mideast), 🅂 *9475* (E Europe & Mideast), 🅆 *9945* (E Europe & E Africa), 🅂 *11635* (W North Am), 🅂 *13800* (Mideast & E Africa)
1630-1700 ▣	5930 (W Europe)		
1630-1700	🅆 17485 (W Africa & C Africa)		
1730-1800	🅂 5930 (E Europe, SE Asia & Australasia), 🅂 21745 (C Africa)		
1830-1900	🅆 5930 (W Europe), 🅆 7315 (E Europe, Asia & Australasia)	0530-0555	🅆 *5965* & 🅂 *7465* (Europe), 🅆 *7485* (E Europe & W Asia), 🅂 *11615* (Mideast), 🅂 *13800* (Africa)
1930-2000	🅂 11600 (S Asia & Australasia)		
2030-2100 ▣	5930 (W Europe)	0630-0655	🅆 *5965* (W Europe), 🅂 *7180* (Europe), 🅆 *7180* & 🅂 *9590* (W Europe), 🅆 *9590* (W Africa), 🅂 *13800* (W Africa & Australasia), 🅆 *13800* (Africa), 🅂 *15705* (Africa & Australasia)
2030-2100	🅆 9430 (S Asia & Australasia)		
2100-2130	🅂 11600 (S Asia & Australasia), 🅂 15545 (W Africa)		
2200-2230	🅆 5930 (W Europe), 🅆 9435 (S Europe & S America)		
2330-2400	🅂 11615 (N America), 🅂 17485 (S America)	0730-0755	🅂 *7180* (Europe), 🅆 *7180* (W Europe), 🅂 *9590* (Europe), 🅆 *9590* (W Europe), 🅂 *15705* (W Africa & Australasia)

DENMARK—Danish

RADIO DANMARK

0030-0055	🅆 *9935* (SE Asia), 🅆 *9945* (E North Am & C America), 🅂 *11635* (N America), 🅂 *13800* (E North Am & C America), 🅂 *13805* (SE Asia & Australasia)	0830-0855	🅆 *15705* (Australasia), 🅂 *18910* (S America & Australasia), 🅂 *18950* (Mideast), 🅆 *18950* (E Asia & Australasia)
		0930-0955	🅆 *15705* (Australasia), 🅂 *18910* (S America & Australasia), 🅆 *18950* (E Asia & Australasia), 🅆 *21725* (Mideast), 🅂 *21755* (E Asia)
0130-0155	🅆 *7465* (E North Am & C America), 🅆 *7495* (S Asia), 🅆 *9945* & 🅂 *9985* (N America), 🅂 *11635* (E North Am & C America), 🅂 *13800* (S Asia)	1030-1055	*13800* (Europe), 🅆 *21725* (S America), 🅂 *21755* (W Africa & S America)
0230-0255	🅆 *7465* (E North Am & C America), 🅆 *7490* (S Asia), 🅆 *9590* (N America), 🅂 *13800* (S Asia)	1130-1155	🅂 *13800* (Europe), 🅆 *13800* (W Europe), 🅂 *15735* (E North Am & C America), 🅆 *21760* (S America)

1230-1255	▣ *13800* (E Asia), ◼ *15735* (N America), ▣ *15735* (Europe), ◼ *17535* (E Asia), ▣ *18910* (SE Asia & Australasia), *18950* (E North Am & C America), ◼ *21755* (SE Asia & Australasia)
1330-1355	*9590* (Europe), ▣ *13800* (E Asia), ◼ *15735* (N America), ◼ *17535* (E Asia), ▣ *18910* (SE Asia & Australasia), ▣ *18950* (N America), ◼ *21755* (SE Asia & Australasia)
1430-1455	▣ *15705* (Mideast & S Asia), ◼ *17505* (W North Am), ◼ *18950* (S Asia), ▣ *18950* (N America)
1530-1555	*13800* (S Asia), ▣ *15705* (Mideast), ◼ *15735* (Mideast & S Asia), ▣ *15735* & ◼ *17505* (W North Am)
1630-1655	▣ *9590* (E Europe & W Asia), ◼ *12080* (Europe), ◼ *13800* (Mideast & S Asia), ▣ *13800* (E Africa), ▣ *18950* (W North Am), ◼ *21730* (Mideast & E Africa)
1630-1700	◼ *21755* (E North Am & C America)
1730-1755	▣ *7485* (Europe), ▣ *9985* (E Europe & W Asia), ◼ *12080* (Europe), ▣ *15705* (E Africa), ◼ *15735* (Mideast), ◼ *17505* (N America), ▣ *18950* (E North Am & C America), ◼ *21730* (Mideast & E Africa)
1830-1855	▣ *5960* & ◼ *7485* (Europe), ▣ *9985* & ◼ *13800* (Australasia), ▣ *13800* & ◼ *13810* (Africa), ▣ *18950* (E North Am & C America)
1930-1955	◼ *7485* (W Europe), ▣ *7485* (Europe), *13800* (Africa), ◼ *15705* (Australasia), ▣ *15705* & ◼ *17505* (W North Am)
2030-2055	▣ *7465* (Australasia), ◼ *7485* (W Europe), ▣ *7485* (Europe), ◼ *9985* (Australasia)
2130-2155	▣ *7465* (Australasia), ▣ *7485* (W Europe), ◼ *11610* (Australasia)
2230-2255	▣ *9415* (S America), ▣ *9480* (E Asia), ◼ *11625* (S America), ◼ *15735* (E Asia)
2330-2355	▣ *7465* (S America), ▣ *9480* (E Asia), ▣ *9580* & ◼ *9935* (SE Asia & Australasia), ▣ *9945* & ◼ *13805* (E North Am & C America), ◼ *15735* (E Asia)
2330-2400	◼ *11625* (S America)

ECUADOR—Spanish

HCJB-VOICE OF THE ANDES

0000-0100	15140 (N America & S America)
0000-0500	6050 (S America)
0100-0500	15140 (C America & W North Am)

0700-0730	▣ 9765 & ◼ 11875 (Europe)
0900-1100	◼ 9780 & ▣ 11960 (S America)
1100-1300	11960 (C America)
1100-1500	15140 (S America)
1100-2400	6050 (S America)
1300-1500	17670/17690 (C America & W North Am)
1630-1900	▣ 21455 USB (Europe & Australasia)
2100-2300	15140 (S America)
2130-2230	▣ 12025, 15550, ◼ 17795 & ◼ 21470 (Europe)
2300-2400	15140 (N America & S America), 21455 USB (Europe & Australasia)

EGYPT—Arabic

EGYPTIAN RADIO

0000-0030 ◼	9700 (N Africa), 11665 (C Africa & E Africa), 15285 (Mideast)
0150-2400 ◼	12050 (Europe & E North Am)
0200-2200 ◼	9755 (N Africa & Mideast)
0300-0600 ◼	9855 (N Africa & Mideast)
0300-2400 ◼	15285 (Mideast)
0350-0700 ◼	9620 & 9770 (N Africa)
0350-2400 ◼	9800 (Mideast)
0600-1400 ◼	11980 (N Africa & Mideast)
0700-1100 ◼	15115 (W Africa)
0700-1400 ◼	15475 (E Africa)
0700-1500 ◼	11785 (N Africa)
1100-2400 ◼	9850 (N Africa & Mideast)
1245-1900 ◼	17670 (N Africa)
1800-2400 ◼	9700 (N Africa)
1900-2400 ◼	11665 (C Africa & E Africa)

RADIO CAIRO

0000-0045	15590 (C America & S America), 17770 (S America)
0030-0430	9900 (E North Am)
1015-1215	17745 (Mideast & W Asia)
1100-1130	17800 (E Africa & S Africa)
1300-1600	15220 (C Africa)
2000-2200	11990 (Australasia)
2330-2400	17770 (S America)
2345-2400	15590 (C America & S America)

FRANCE

RADIO FRANCE INTERNATIONALE
French

0000-0030	▣ *15440* & ◼ *17710* (SE Asia)
0000-0100	▣ 9805 & ◼ 11660 (S Asia & SE Asia), ▣ *12025* (SE Asia), *15200* (S America), ◼ *15535* (SE Asia)
0100-0200	▣ *15440* & ◼ *17710* (S Asia)
0130-0200	▣ 9790 (C America), ▣ 9800 (S America), *9800* & *11665* (C America), ◼ 11995 (S America)
0200-0230	*15200* (S America)

0300-0400	[W] 5915 (Mideast & E Africa), [S] 5925 (C Africa & E Africa), [W] 5925 (S Africa), [W] 5945 (E Europe & Mideast), 9550 (Mideast), [S] 9825, [S] 11700 & [S] 13610 (E Africa)
0300-0500	[W] 7315 (Mideast), 11995 (E Africa)
0300-0600	9790 (Africa), [W] 9845 (E Africa)
0300-0700	7135 (Africa)
0330-0500	[S] 9745 (E Europe)
0400-0445	[S] 7280 (E Europe)
0400-0500	[W] 3965 (N Africa), 4890 (C Africa), [S] 5925 (N Africa), [W] 9805 (C Africa), 11850 (Mideast), [W] 11910, 13610 (Irr) & [S] 15155 (E Africa)
0400-0600 ▭	11685 (Mideast)
0400-0600	[W] 9550 (Mideast), 11700 (C Africa & S Africa), [S] 15135 (E Africa), [S] 15605 (Mideast & W Asia)
0430-0445	[W] 5990 (E Europe)
0430-0500 ▭	7280 (E Europe)
0430-0600 ▭	6045 (E Europe)
0500-0600	6175 (C Africa), [W] 11995 & [W] 13610 (E Africa), [W] 15155 (S Africa), [S] 15300 (C Africa & S Africa), 15605 (N Africa & Mideast), [S] 17800 (E Africa)
0500-0700	[W] 11700 (C Africa & S Africa), [W] 15155 & [S] 17620 (E Africa)
0600-0700	[W] 5925 (N Africa), [W] 6175 (E Europe), 9790 (N Africa & W Africa), [S] 9790 (C Africa), [W] 15135 (Mideast), 15300 (C Africa & S Africa), 15315 (Irr) (W Africa), [S] 17650 (Mideast), 17800 (E Africa), [S] 17850 (C Africa & S Africa), [S] 21620 (E Africa)
0600-0800	11700 (N Africa & W Africa)
0700-0800	[W] 7135 (N Africa), [W] 9790 (N Africa & W Africa), 9790 (C Africa), 9805 (E Europe), [W] 11975 (N Europe), [S] 15300 (N Africa & W Africa), [W] 15300 (C Africa & S Africa), 15315, 15605 & [S] 17620 (W Africa), 17850 (C Africa & S Africa)
0700-1130	11670 (E Europe)
0800-0900	[S] 15315, 17620 & [W] 21685 (W Africa)
0800-1000	15300 (N Africa & W Africa), [W] 21580 (C Africa & S Africa)
0800-1600	11845 (N Africa)
0900-0930	[W] 9715 & [S] 11670 (S America)
0900-1000	[W] 17620 (W Africa)
0900-1200	21620 (E Africa)
0900-1300	25820 (E Africa)
0900-1600	21685 (W Africa)
1000-1100	15155 (E Europe), 15300 (W Africa), 17850 (C Africa & S Africa)
1000-1600	21580 (C Africa & S Africa)
1030-1100	15435 (S America)
1030-1200	[W] 7140 & [S] 9830 (E Asia), [W] 9830, [S] 11890 & [S] 15215 (SE Asia)
1100-1130	[W] 17610 (Irr) (E North Am & C America)
1100-1200	6175 (W Europe & Atlantic), 11600 (SE Asia), [W] 11670, 13640 & 15515 (C America), [S] 17570 (E North Am & C America), 21755 (S Africa)
1100-1300	[S] 17620 (W Africa)
1100-1400	15300 (N Africa & W Africa)
1130-1200	[W] 17610 (E North Am & C America)
1200-1400	9790 (C Africa)
1230-1300	15515 & 17860 (C America)
1300-1330	17860 (C America)
1300-1400	17620 (W Africa), 21645 (C America)
1330-1400	M-Sa 17860 (C America)
1400-1500	17650 (Mideast)
1400-1600	15300 (W Africa)
1500-1600	[W] 15605 (Mideast & W Asia), 17605 & 17620 (E Africa), [S] 17650 (Mideast), 17850 (C Africa & S Africa), 21620 (E Africa)
1600-1700	6090 (SE Asia), 11700 (N Africa), [S] 15300 (W Africa), [W] 17605 & [S] 21620 (E Africa)
1600-1800	[W] 15300 (Africa), [S] 21580 (C Africa & S Africa)
1700-1800	[W] 5960 (N Europe), [S] 11670 (E Europe), 11700 (Irr) (N Africa), [S] 15300 (N Africa & W Africa), [S] 17620 (W Africa & E Africa)
1700-2000	[W] 11965 (W Africa)
1730-1800	[W] 11615 & [S] 15210 (Mideast), 15210 & [S] 17605 (E Africa)
1800-1900	[W] 5900 (E Europe), [W] 5970 (N Europe), [W] 11615 (N Africa), [S] 17620 (E Africa)
1800-2000	[W] 9790 (N Africa & W Africa), [S] 11615 (W Africa), 11705 (Africa), [W] 11995 (E Africa), 15300 (Africa), [S] 15460 (E Africa)
1800-2200	7160 (C Africa), 11955 (W Africa)
1900-2000	[W] 3965 (Europe), [W] 6175 (N Europe), [W] 7315 (N Africa), [W] 9485 (E Africa), [S] 11670 (E Europe), [S] 17620 (W Africa)
2000-2100	[W] 6175 (N Africa), [S] 15300 (Africa)
2000-2200	[W] 5960 (S Europe), 7315 (N Africa), 9485 (E Africa), 9790 (N Africa & W Africa), [W] 9790 (C Africa & S Africa), 11995 (E Africa)
2100-2200	[W] 3965 (N Africa), [S] 5915 (E Europe), 6175 (N Africa), [S] 9805 (E Europe), [S] 15300 (C Africa & S Africa)
2200-2300	[W] 9790 (W Africa)

2230-2300	*17620* (S America)
2300-2400	**W** 9805 & **S** 11660 (S Asia & SE Asia), **W** *12025* (SE Asia), **W** *12075* (E Asia), **W** *15440*, **S** *15535*, **S** *15595* & **S** *17710* (SE Asia)
2330-2400	**W** 9790 (C America), **W** 9800 (S America), **S** 11670 (C America), **S** 11995, *15200* & *17620* (S America)

RADIO MONTE CARLO—(N America)
Arabic

0300-0320	**S** *6040*
0400-0420 ⬌	*9755*
0400-0420	**W** *5960*

GABON—French

AFRIQUE NUMERO UN

0500-2300	9580 (C Africa)
0700-1600	17630 (W Africa)
1600-1900	15475 (W Africa & E North Am)

RTV GABONAISE

0500-0800	7270/4777
0800-1600	7270
1600-2100	4777

GERMANY—German

BAYERISCHER RUNDFUNK

24 Hr	6085

DEUTSCHE WELLE

0000-0155	**W** *13750* (SE Asia & Australasia), **S** *17875* (SE Asia)
0000-0200	6075 (Europe), 6100 (N America), **S** 7130 (N Africa & S America), 9545, **S** 9730, **W** *11785* & **S** *13780* (S America), **W** *15105* (W Africa & C America), **S** *15275* (C America), **W** *15275* (S Asia & SE Asia), *15410* (S America), **S** *17860* (SE Asia)
0000-0355	**S** *11785* (C America), **W** *13780* (W Africa & C America)
0000-0400	**W** 7130 (S Europe & S America)
0000-0600	3995 (Europe)
0200-0300	**S** 9735 (N America)
0200-0400	**W** 6100 (C America), **W** 6145 (N America & C America), **S** 11795 (E Africa), *15205* (S Asia)
0200-0555	**W** 9545 (Mideast & W Asia)
0200-0600	6075 (Europe & N America), **S** 6100 (N America)
0300-0555	**S** 9735 (E Europe & N America)
0400-0555	**W** 9735 (Mideast & Africa), **S** 13780 (Africa)
0400-0600	**W** *6100* (W North Am), **W** 6145 (N America & C America), **W** *7225* (S Europe), **W** *9650* & **S** *9700* (S Africa)
0500-0600	**S** 9735 (Australasia)
0600-0800	**W** 3995 & 6075 (Europe), *11985* (Australasia), **S** 21600 (E Africa & S Africa)
0600-1000	*9690*, 9735 & 11795 (Australasia), 11865 (E Europe & W Asia), **S** 17845 & *21640* (SE Asia & Australasia), **W** 21780 (Africa)
0600-1800	13780 (S Europe & Mideast)
0600-2000	9545 (S Europe)
0800-1355	**W** 25740 (S Asia & SE Asia)
0800-1600	6075 (Europe)
0900-1155	*15135* (C Africa & E Africa)
1000-1355	**S** *21640* (E Asia), **S** 21680 (E Europe & Asia), **S** 21790 (S Asia & SE Asia), **W** *21790* (E Asia), 21840 (Mideast)
1000-1400	**W** *5905*, **W** *7400* & **S** *9900* (E Asia), **S** *13720* & **W** *15490* (S Asia & SE Asia), **S** 17560 (W Africa), **W** 17845 (Mideast, S Asia & SE Asia), **S** *17845* (SE Asia & Australasia)
1100-1300	**S** *15275* (W Europe)
1200-1400	*15135* (S Africa), **W** *17570* (W Europe), **W** 17650 (E Europe), **S** *17730* & **W** *17765* (S America)
1200-1600	**W** *9480* & **S** *15480* (W Asia & C Asia)
1200-1700	*17730* (N America)
1400-1555	**W** 15275 (S Europe & Mideast), **W** 21790 (S Asia)
1400-1600	17845 (S Asia & SE Asia)
1400-1700	**W** *15285* (N America & C America), *17765* (S America), **S** *17875* (N America)

1400-1755	**W** *15135* (Mideast), **S** 15275 (S Asia), **S** *21560* (Mideast)
1400-1800	*9655* (S Asia), **S** 17845 (Mideast)
1600-1755	**W** 15275 & **S** 17845 (S Asia & SE Asia)
1600-1800	6075 (Europe), **W** 11795 (S Asia)
1800-2000	**W** 3995 (Europe), **S** 13780 (S Europe & Mideast)
1800-2155	*9735* (S Africa), **S** *11765* & **W** *15275* (SE Asia & Australasia)
1800-2200	6075 (Europe & E Africa), **S** 7185 (Africa), **S** 11795 (E Africa & S Africa), **W** 11795 & **S** 15275 (W Africa & S America), *17860* (W Africa & Americas)
2000-2200	**S** 9545 (W Africa & S America), **W** 9545 (S Europe), *17810* (N America & S America)
2000-2400	3995 (Europe)
2200-2355	**W** *11840* (E Asia), **S** *15250* (E Asia & SE Asia), *17860* (C America)
2200-2400	**W** *5925* (E Asia), 6075 (Europe), **S** 6100 (E North Am), **W** *7375* (E Asia), 9545 (S America), **W** 9545 (C America), **W** 9715 (S Asia & SE Asia), **S** 9730 (S America), **S** *11785* (C America), **W** *11785* (S America), *11795* (E Asia), **S** 11895 (SE Asia), **S** *13690* (S Asia & SE Asia), **S** *13780* (S America), **W** *13780* & **W** *15105* (W Africa & C America), **S** *15275* (C America), **W** *15275* (S Asia & SE Asia), *15410* (S America)

DEUTSCHLANDFUNK—(Europe)

24 Hr	6190

DEUTSCHLANDRADIO—(Europe)

24 Hr	6005

SUDWESTRUNDFUNK—(Europe)

24 Hr	7265
0455-2305 ⬚	6030

GREECE—Greek

FONI TIS HELLADAS

0000-0200 &	
0210-0350	**W** 7450, **W** 9375, 9420, 12105/12110 & **S** 15630 (N America)
0400-0525	**W** 7450, 9425/9420, **W** 11645 & 15650 (Mideast)
0600-0750	7450, **S** 9425 & 11645 (Europe & Australasia)
0700-0800	*9775* (Australasia)
0900-0950	*9775* (Australasia), 15415/15630 (E Asia), 15650 (Australasia)
0900-1000	*9770* (Australasia)
1000-1135	9425 & 9915 (Mideast)
1200-1230	**W** 9420 (Mideast), **W** 11645 & **W** 15650 (Africa)
1200-1350	15630 (Europe & N America)
1200-1800	*15455* (N America)
1400-1430	**S** 9420, 11645 & **S** 15630 (Mideast)
1500-1600	**W** 7450 (Europe), **S** 9375, 9420 & 11645 (E Europe)
1800-1850	11645 & 15150 (Africa)
1800-1900	**W** 7450, **W** 9395, **W** 9425 & **W** 11595 (Europe)
1800-2150	*17705* (N America)
1900-2100	**W** 9420 (Europe)
1900-2150	7450 (Europe), **S** 9420 (Europe, N America & Australasia)
2000-2150	*17565* (S America)
2100-2250	9425 (Australasia)
2200-2350	**S** 9395 (C America & S America), 11595 (S America)
2300-2350	**S** 9425 (C America & Australasia)

RADIOFONIKOS STATHMOS MAKEDONIAS

0600-0800 ⬚	7430 (Europe)
0600-2300 ⬚	9935 (Europe), 11595 (Mideast)
1300-2300 ⬚	7430/7455 (Europe)

HOLLAND—Dutch

RADIO NEDERLAND

0000-0025	**S** *7280* (SE Asia), **W** *7280* & **S** *9590* (SE Asia & Australasia), **W** *9590*, **W** *15560*, **W** *17570* & **S** *17590* (SE Asia)
0130-0225	**W** 6020 & **S** 11730 (E North Am & C America), *15315* (S America)
0330-0425	*6165* (N America), *9590* (W North Am), **S** *9845* & **W** *9860* (E Africa), *15560* (Mideast)
0600-0700 ⬚	7130 (Europe)
0600-0700	**W** 5945 (S Europe)
0600-1800 ⬚	5955 (W Europe), 9895 (S Europe)
0700-0800	**W** 9715, **S** 9820 & 11655 (Australasia)
0700-0900 ⬚	11935 (S Europe)
0800-1100	**S** 13700 (S Europe)
0930-1015	M-Sa *6020* (C America)
1030-1125	*9720* (Australasia), *13820* (E Asia), *17575* (Australasia), *21480* (SE Asia)
1100-1300	13700 (S Europe)
1300-1700	**S** 13700 (S Europe)
1330-1425	**W** *5930*, **W** *7375* & **S** *9890* (E Asia & SE Asia), **S** *12065* (SE Asia & Australasia), **S** *13695* (E Asia & SE Asia), **W** 13700 (Mideast & S Asia), **W** *13820* (SE Asia & Australasia), *17580* & *21480* (S Asia)
1600-1800	**W** 13700 (S Europe & W Africa)
1630-1725	*6020* (S Africa), *11655* (E Africa)
1730-1825	**S** 9895 & **S** 13700 (S Europe & Mideast), **S** 15560 (S Africa & E Africa), **S** *21590* (W Africa)

1830-1925	11695 (Mideast & E Africa), 15315 (W Africa)
2030-2125	*5835* (Europe), 6015 (S Europe), *6015* (S Africa), 6020 (S Europe), *6020* (S Africa), *7120* (C Africa & W Africa), 9895 (S Europe, N Africa & Mideast), 11655 (W Africa), *11655* (W Africa & C Africa), *15315 & 17605* (W Africa), *21590* (W Africa & C Africa)
2130-2225	*6020* (C America), 9895 (C America & S America), 9895 (E North Am), 11730 (C America & S America), 13700 (S America), *13700 &* *15155* (E North Am), *15315* (S America)
2330-2400	*7280* (SE Asia), *7280 &* *9590* (SE Asia & Australasia), *9590*, *15560*, *17570 &* *17590* (SE Asia)

HUNGARY—Hungarian

RADIO BUDAPEST

0000-0100	M 9560 (S America), 9800 (N America), M 11990 (S America)
0100-0200	9835 (N America)
0130-0230	9835 (N America)
0230-0330	9835 (N America)
0700-1800	7135 (Europe)
0900-1300	6025 (Europe)
1100-1200	21560 (Australasia)
1200-1300	Su 21560 (Australasia)
1300-1400	M-Sa 6025 (Europe)
1400-1500	Sa-Th 6025 (Europe)
1500-1530	M-Sa 6025 (Europe)
1900-2000	3975 & 6025 (Europe)
1900-2000	9685/11890 (Australasia)
2000-2100	17690 (N America)
2100-2200	3975 & 6025 (Europe)
2100-2200	9840 (N America), 11890 (Australasia)
2200-2300	11870 & 15455 (S America)
2300-2400	9560, Su 11870, 11990 & Su 15455 (S America)

INDIA—Hindi

ALL INDIA RADIO

0315-0415	13695 (E Africa), 15075 (Mideast & W Asia), 15185 & 17715 (E Africa)
0430-0530	15075, 15185 & 17715 (E Africa)
1615-1730	7410 (Mideast & W Asia), 9950 (E Africa), 12025 (Mideast & W Asia), 13770 (W Asia & Mideast), 17670 (E Africa)
1945-2045	7410 & 9950 (Europe)
2300-2400	9910, 11740 & 13795 (SE Asia)

IRAN—Persian

VOICE OF THE ISLAMIC REPUBLIC

0000-0630	15084 (Europe & C America)
0130-0400	7275 (W Asia & S Asia)
0730-1200	15084 (Europe & C America), 15215 (W Asia), 15365 (W Asia & S Asia)
1030-1100	15115 (E Asia)
1030-1130	17785 (Europe)
1030-1200	13695 (W Asia)
1300-2400	15084 (Europe & C America)
1530-1730	7270 (W Asia & S Asia)
1730-1830	9765 (Europe)
2030-2130	7105 (W Europe), 9775 (Australasia)

ISRAEL

KOL ISRAEL
Arabic

| 0400-2215 | 5915 (Mideast & N Africa), 9815 (Mideast), 12140/15430/15480 (Mideast) |

Hebrew

0000-0330	11585 (W Europe & E North Am)
0000-0400	15760 (Europe & N America)
0000-0600	7525 (W Europe & N America), 9345 & 15640 (W Europe & E North Am)
0330-0430	11585 (W Europe & E North Am)
0400-0600	15760 (W Europe & E North Am)
0430-0600	11590 (W Europe & E North Am)
0500-0600	17545 (Europe & N America)
0600-1900	15760 (W Europe & E North Am), 17545 (Europe & N America)

1600-1800	11590 (W Europe & E North Am)
1800-2400	11585 (W Europe & E North Am)
1900-1945 ■	15650 (Europe & N America)
1900-2200	🅦 9345 (W Europe & E North Am)
1900-2400	🅦 5790 (W Europe & N America),
	🅢 15615 (W Europe & E North Am)
2100-2215 ■	15640 (S America)
2100-2215	🅦 17535 (S America)
2200-2400	🅦 9345 (W Europe & E North Am)
2215-2400	🅢 15640 (W Europe & E North Am)

Yiddish

1700-1725 ■	9435 & 11605 (Europe), 15640 (E Europe), 15650 (N Africa)
1700-1725	🅦 17535 (Europe & N America)
1800-1825 ■	9435 (Europe), 15640 (E Europe)
1800-1825	🅦 17535 (Europe & N America)

ITALY—Italian
RADIO ROMA-RAI INTERNATIONAL

0000-0050	6010 & 9675 (N America), 9840 & 11755 (S America), 11800 (N America & C America)
0130-0230	*6110* (S America), *11765* (C America)
0130-0305	6010 & 9675 (N America), 9840 & 11755 (S America), 11800 (E North Am & C America)
0415-0425	5975, 🅦 7120 & 🅢 7150 (S Europe & N Africa)
0435-0510	15250 & 17780 (E Africa)
0600-1300	9670 (Europe & N Africa), 11800 (E Europe), 17710 & 21520 (E Africa)
1000-1100	*11920* (Australasia)
1250-1350	Su 17780 (Irr) (N America), Su 21535 (Irr) (S America), Su 21710 (Irr) (C Africa & S Africa)
1300-1350	Su 21520 (Irr) (E Africa)
1345-1630	Su 9670 (N Europe)
1350-1630	Su 17780 (N America), Su 21520 (E Africa), Su 21535 (S America), Su 21710 (C Africa & S Africa)
1400-1430	M-Sa 17780 (N America), M-Sa 21520 (E North Am)
1500-1525	M-Sa 9670 (S Europe & N Africa), 11880 (Mideast)
1555-1625	7240 (W Europe), M-Sa 9670 (Europe), 11880 (W Europe)
1630-1730	🅦 Su 9670 (Irr) (N Europe)
1700-1800	9670 & 11910 (S Europe & N Africa), 15220/15230 (C Africa & S Africa), *15320* (S Africa), 17660 (C Africa & S Africa)
1830-1905	🅦 15250, 17780 & 🅢 21520 (N America)
2230-2400	6010 & 9675 (N America), 9840 & 11755 (S America), 11800 (N America & C America)

RAI-RADIOTELEVISIONE ITALIANA

0000-0003,	
0012-0103,	
0112-0203,	
0212-0303,	
0312-0403 &	
0412-0500 ■	6060 (Europe, Mideast & N Africa)
0500-2300 ■	6060 & 9515 (Europe, N Africa & Mideast)
0500-2300	7175 (Europe, Mideast & N Africa)
2300-2400 ■	6060 (Europe, Mideast & N Africa)

JAPAN—Japanese
RADIO JAPAN/NHK

0200-0300	*11860* (SE Asia), 17825 (C America), 17845 (E Asia), 21610 (Australasia)
0200-0400	*5960* (E North Am), 11870 (Mideast), 15325 (S Asia), 17685 (Australasia), 17810/17875 (W North Am), 17835 (S America)
0200-0500	11840 (E Asia), 15590 (SE Asia)
0300-0400	*9515/9540* (Mideast), *9660* (S America), *11890* (S Asia)
0700-0800	6145, 6165 & 11840 (E Asia)
0700-0900	17860 (SE Asia)
0700-1000	9685/15230 (Pacific, C America & S America), *11740* (SE Asia), 11850/21570 & *11920* (Australasia)
0800-1000	*9530* (S America), 9835 (W North Am), *11710* (Europe), 12030 (C America), 🅦 *15230* (Mideast), 15590 (S Asia), *17650* (W Africa), 🅢 *21550* (Mideast)
0800-1500	9750 (E Asia)
0900-1500	11815 (SE Asia)
1300-1500	*11705* (E North Am)
1500-1700	9505/9535 (W North Am), 11895 (C America), *12045* (S Asia)
1600-1700	9750 (E Asia), 11730 (S Asia), 🅢 *15145* & 🅦 *21630* (E Africa)
1600-1800	7140 (Australasia)
1600-1900	6035 (E Asia), 7200/9860 (SE Asia)
1700-1800	🅦 *9750* & 🅢 *15115* (Europe), *21600* (S America), *21630* (E Africa)
1700-1900	*6175* (W Europe), 9835 (Pacific), *11880* (Mideast)
1800-1900	*15355* (S Africa)
1900-2100	6165 (E Asia)
1900-2400	11910/9790 (E Asia), 13680/17810 (SE Asia)
2000-2100	*6035/11920* & 11850 (Australasia)
2000-2200	7225/11665 (SE Asia)
2200-2300	*6110* (E North Am), *6115* (W Europe), 9725 (Europe), *11895* (C America), *15220* (S America), 17825 (W North Am)

RADIO TAMPA

0000-0800	3925, 9760
0000-1000	6115
0000-1300	3945
0000-1730	6055, 9595
0800-1500 &	
2030-2300	3925
2030-2400	6055, 9595
2300-2400	3925, 3945, 6115, 9760

JORDAN—Arabic

RADIO JORDAN

0000-0205	▣	6105 (Irr) (Mideast)
0000-0210	▣	11930 (W Europe & E North Am), 15435 (S America)
0000-0600	▣	11810 (Mideast & S Asia)
0400-0600	▣	9630/13630 (Mideast & E Africa)
0400-0700	▣	15435 (W Europe)
0600-0900	▣	11835/11960 (E Europe)
0830-1615	▣	11810 (Mideast, S Asia & Australasia)
1000-1300	▣	15290 (N Africa & C America)
1300-1625	▣	13630 (Mideast & E Africa)
1600-2155	▣	6105 (Mideast)
1630-2055	▣	7155 (E Europe)
1800-2155	▣	9830 (W Europe)
2155-2400	▣	6105 (Irr) (Mideast)
2200-2400	▣	11810 (Mideast & S Asia), 11930 (W Europe & E North Am), 15435 (S America)

KOREA (REPUBLIC)—Korean

RADIO KOREA INTERNATIONAL

0000-0100	5975 (E Asia), 15575 (N America)
0100-0200	7275 (E Asia), 11725 (S America)
0300-0400	7275 (E Asia), 11725 & 11810 (S America), 15575 (N America)
0700-0800	7550 & *9535* (Europe), 9570 (Australasia)
0900-1000	7550 (S America)
0900-1100	5975 & 7275 (E Asia), 9570 (Australasia), 13670 (Europe)
1100-1130	*6145* (E North Am), 9580 (S America), 9640 (E Asia), *9650* (E North Am)
1200-1300	7285 (E Asia)
1700-1900	5975 (E Asia), 7550 & 15575 (Europe)
2100-2200	5975 (E Asia), 9640 (SE Asia)
2300-2400	5975 (E Asia), 15575 (N America)

KUWAIT—Arabic

RADIO KUWAIT

0000-0530	11675 (W North Am)
0200-1305	6055 & 15495 (Mideast)
0400-0805	15505 (E Europe & W Asia)
0445-0500 &	
0800-0930	15110 (S Asia & SE Asia)

0815-1740	15505 (W Africa & C Africa)
0900-1000	17885 (E Asia)
0930-1605	13620 (Europe & E North Am)
1200-1505	17885 (E Asia)
1310-2130	9880 (Mideast)
1315-1600	15110 (S Asia & SE Asia)
1615-1800	11990 (Europe & E North Am)
1745-2130	15505 (Europe & E North Am)
1745-2400	15495 (W Africa & C Africa)
1800-2400	9855 (Europe & E North Am)
2145-2400	11675 (W North Am)

LIBYA—Arabic

RADIO JAMAHIRIYA-VOICE OF AFRICA

0000-0445	▣	15415/17725 (Africa)
1115-2400	▣	15415/17725 (Africa)

LITHUANIA—Lithuanian

LITHUANIAN RADIO

0900-0930 &		
1030-1200	▣	9710 (W Europe)
1330-1345	▣	9555 (E Europe)
1345-1355	▣	M-F 9555 (E Europe)

RADIO VILNIUS

0000-0030		▣ *6120/6155* & ▣ *9855* (E North Am)
1000-1030	▣	9710 (W Europe)

MEXICO—Spanish

RADIO EDUCACION

0000-0830	▣	6185
0830-0900	▣	Th-Tu 6185
0900-1200	▣	6185

RADIO MEXICO INTERNACIONAL—(W North Am & C America)

0030-0100	▣	Su/Tu/Th/Sa 9705
0100-0400	▣	9705
0400-0430	▣	M 9705
0430-0500	▣	9705
0530-0600	▣	W/F 9705
1300-1500 &		
1530-1600	▣	5985 & 9705
1630-1700	▣	Su/M/W/F 5985 & Su/M/W/F 9705
1900-2300 &		
2330-2400	▣	5985 & 9705

RADIO MIL

24 Hr	6010

MOROCCO

RADIO MEDI UN—(Europe & N Africa)
French & Arabic

0500-0200	9575

RTV MAROCAINE
Arabic

0000-0500		▣ 7185 & ▣ 11920 (N Africa & Mideast)

0900-2200	15345 (N Africa & Mideast)
1100-1500	15335 (Europe)
2200-2400	[W] 7160 & [S] 15335 (Europe)

NORWAY—Norwegian

RADIO NORWAY INTERNATIONAL

0000-0030	[W] 9935 (SE Asia), [W] 9945 (E North Am & C America), [S] 11635 (N America), [S] 13800 (E North Am & C America), [S] 13805 (SE Asia & Australasia)
0100-0130	[W] 7465 (E North Am & C America), [W] 7495 (S Asia), [W] 9945 (N America), [S] 11635 (E North Am & C America), [S] 13800 (S Asia)
0200-0230	[W] 7465 (E North Am & C America), [W] 7490 (S Asia), [W] 9590 (N America), [S] 13800 (S Asia)
0300-0330	[S] 7465 (Mideast), [W] 7465 (W North Am), [W] 7485 (Mideast), [W] 9945 (E Africa), [S] 11635 (W North Am), [S] 13800 (Mideast & E Africa)
0400-0430	[S] 7465 (Europe), [W] 7465 (W North Am), [W] 7485 & [S] 9475 (Mideast), [W] 9945 (E Europe & E Africa), [S] 11635 (W North Am), [S] 13800 (Mideast & E Africa)
0500-0530	[W] 5965 & [S] 7465 (Europe), [W] 7485 (E Europe & W Asia), [S] 11615 (Mideast), [S] 13800 (Africa)
0600-0630	[W] 5965 (W Europe), [S] 7180 (Europe), [W] 7180 & [S] 9590 (W Europe), [W] 9590 (W Africa), [S] 13800 (W Africa & Australasia), [W] 13800 (Africa), [S] 15705 (Africa & Australasia)
0700-0730	[S] 7180 (Europe), [W] 7180 (W Europe), [S] 9590 (Europe), [W] 9590 (W Europe), [S] 15705 (W Africa & Australasia)
0800-0830	[W] 15705 (Australasia), [S] 18910 (S America & Australasia), [S] 18950 (Mideast), [W] 18950 (E Asia & Australasia)
0900-0930	[W] 15705 (Australasia), [S] 18910 (S America & Australasia), [W] 18950 (E Asia & Australasia), [W] 21725 (Mideast), [S] 21755 (E Asia)
1000-1030	13800 (Europe), [W] 21725 (S America), [S] 21755 (W Africa & S America)
1100-1130	[S] 13800 (Europe), [W] 13800 (W Europe), [S] 15735 (E North Am & C America), [W] 21760 (S America)
1200-1230	[W] 13800 (E Asia), [S] 15735 (N America), [W] 15735 (Europe), [S] 17535 (E Asia), [W] 18910 (SE Asia & Australasia), 18950 (E North Am & C America), [S] 21755 (SE Asia & Australasia)
1300-1330	9590 (W Europe), [W] 13800 (E Asia), [S] 15735 (N America), [S] 17535 (E Asia), [W] 18910 (SE Asia & Australasia), [W] 18950 (N America), [S] 21755 (SE Asia & Australasia)
1400-1430	[W] 15705 (Mideast & S Asia), [S] 17505 (W North Am), [W] 18910 (N America), [S] 18950 (S Asia)
1500-1530	[S] 13800 (S Asia), [W] 15705 (Mideast), [S] 15735 (Mideast & S Asia), [W] 15735 & [S] 17505 (W North Am)
1600-1630	[W] 9590 (E Europe & W Asia), [S] 12080 (Europe), [S] 13800 (Mideast & S Asia), [W] 13800 (E Africa), [W] 18950 (W North Am), [S] 21730 (Mideast & E Africa), [S] 21755 (E North Am & C America)
1700-1730	[W] 7485 (Europe), [W] 9985 (E Europe & W Asia), [S] 12080 (Europe), [W] 15705 (E Africa), [S] 15735 (Mideast), [S] 17505 (N America), [W] 18950 (E North Am & C America), [S] 21730 (Mideast & E Africa)
1800-1830	[W] 5960 & [S] 7485 (Europe), [W] 9985 & [S] 13800 (Australasia), [W] 13800 & [S] 13810 (Africa), [W] 18950 (E North Am & C America)
1900-1930	[S] 7485 (W Europe), [W] 7485 (Europe), 13800 (Africa), [S] 15705 (Australasia), [W] 15705 & [S] 17505 (W North Am)
2000-2030	[W] 7465 (Australasia), [S] 7485 (W Europe), [W] 7485 (Europe), [S] 9985 (Australasia)
2100-2130	[W] 7465 (Australasia), [W] 7485 (W Europe), [S] 11610 (Australasia)
2200-2230	[W] 9415 (S America), [W] 9480 (E Asia), [S] 11625 (S America), [S] 15735 (E Asia)
2300-2330	[W] 7465 (S America), [W] 9480 (E Asia), [W] 9580 & [S] 9935 (SE Asia & Australasia), [W] 9945 (E North Am & C America), [S] 11625 (S America), [S] 13805 (E North Am & C America), [S] 15735 (E Asia)

OMAN—Arabic

RADIO SULTANATE OF OMAN

0000-0200	9735 (Mideast)
0200-0300	15355 (E Africa)
0200-0400	6085 (Mideast)
0400-0500	[W] 15355 & [S] 17590 (E Africa)
0400-0600	9515 (Mideast)
0500-0600	17590 (E Africa)
0600-0800	[W] 17590 (E Africa), [S] 17610 (Mideast)
0600-1400	13640 (Mideast)
0800-1000	17610 (Mideast)
1400-1800	15375 (Mideast & E Africa)

1500-1700	15140 (Mideast & Europe)
1700-1800	**S** 15140 (Mideast & Europe)
1700-2000	**W** 11805 (Europe)
1800-2000	11890 (Mideast & E Africa), **S** 15355 (E Africa)
2000-2200	6085 (Mideast)
2000-2400	9735 (Mideast)

PARAGUAY—Spanish

RADIO NACIONAL DEL PARAGUAY

0700-1700 **➡**	9735 (S America & E North Am)
1700-2000 **➡**	9735 (Irr) (S America)
2000-0300 **➡**	9735 (S America & E North Am)

POLAND—Polish

RADIO POLONIA

0700-0800	**S** 5995 (Europe)
1200-1225 **◧**	7270 (W Europe), 7285 (E Europe)
1630-1730 **◧**	6035 (W Europe), 7285 (E Europe)
2200-2255 **◧**	6035 (E Europe), 6095 (W Europe)
2200-2300 **◧**	7270 (E Europe)

PORTUGAL—Portuguese

RDP INTERNACIONAL-RADIO PORTUGAL

0000-0200	**S** Tu-Sa 13660 (S America)
0000-0300 **◧**	Tu-Sa 9715 (E North Am), Tu-Sa 11655 (W North Am), Tu-Sa 13700 (C America)
0000-0300	**W** Tu-Sa 12030/11980 & **W** Tu-Sa 13770 (S America)
0500-0700	**S** M-F 15555 (W Europe)
0500-0900	**S** M-F 11950 (W Europe)
0600-0800 **◧**	Tu-Sa 15585 (W North Am)
0600-0800	**W** M-F 11675 (Europe)
0600-1300 **◧**	M-F 9815 (W Europe), M-F 11960 (Europe)
0600-1300	**W** M-F 15140 (W Europe)
0645-0800	**S** M-F 11850 (Europe)
0700-1200	**S** 15555 (W Europe)
0700-1400	**S** Sa/Su 12020/9840 (Europe), **S** Sa/Su 13610 (W Europe)
0745-0900	**W** M-F 11660 (Europe)
0800-1100 **◧**	Sa/Su 21655 (W Africa & S America), Sa/Su 21830 (E Africa & S Africa)
0800-1500	**W** Sa/Su 11875 (Europe), **W** Sa/Su 12020 & **W** Sa/Su 15575 (W Europe)
0930-1100 **◧**	Sa/Su 11995 (Europe)
1100-1300 **◧**	21655 & M-F 21725 (W Africa & S America), 21830 (E Africa & S Africa)
1200-1600	**S** Sa/Su 15555 (W Europe)
1200-2000	**S** Sa/Su//Holidays 15180 (E North Am), **S** Sa/Su//Holidays 17615 (C America)
1300-1500	**S** M-F 17760 (Mideast & S Asia)
1300-1700 **◧**	Sa/Su 21655 (W Africa & S America), Sa/Su 21800 (S America)
1300-1800 **◧**	Sa/Su 21830 (E Africa & S Africa)
1300-2100	**W** Sa/Su//Holidays 15540 (N America), **W** Sa/Su//Holidays 17745 (C America)
1400-1600	**S** Sa/Su 13770 (S Europe), **W** M-F 15490 (Mideast & S Asia)
1500-2100	**W** Sa/Su 13660 (Europe), **W** Sa/Su 13790 (W Europe)
1600-1900	**S** 13770 (S Europe), **S** 15555 (W Europe), **S** M-F 17650 (S Europe)
1700-2000 **◧**	M-F 13625/13585 (S Europe), 17680 (E Africa & S Africa), 21655 (W Africa & S America), 21800 (S America)
1700-2000	**W** M-F 11800 (W Europe), **W** M-F 11860 (Europe)
1900-2000	**S** Sa/Su 13770 (S Europe)
1900-2300	**S** 11945 (Irr) (S Africa), **S** 13720 (Irr) (W Europe), **S** 13770 (Irr) (C America), **S** 15555 (Irr) (W Europe)
2000-2300 **◧**	17680 (Irr) (E Africa & S Africa)
2000-2300	**S** 15180 (Irr) (E North Am)
2000-2400 **◧**	M-F 13625/13585 (Irr) (S Europe), Sa/Su 21655 (Irr) (W Africa & S America), 21800 (Irr) (S America)
2000-2400	**W** M-F 11675 (Irr) (S Europe), **W** M-F 11800 (Irr) (W Europe), **W** M-F 11860 (Irr) (Europe), **W** 13770 (Irr) (C America)
2100-2400	**W** 15540 (Irr) (N America)
2300-2400	**S** Tu-Sa 13660 (S America)

All Radio Tashkent programs are taped in advance, then carefully scrutinized for content.   M. Guha

QATAR—Arabic

QATAR BROADCASTING SERVICE

0000-0245	9570 (Irr) & 11655 (Irr) (Mideast & N Africa)
0245-0704	**W** 7210 & **S** 17770 (Mideast & N Africa)
0245-2125	9570 (Mideast & N Africa)
0704-1304	**W** 15285/11820 & **S** 17880 (Mideast & N Africa)
1304-1704	**W** 11750 & **S** 17575 (Europe)
1704-2125	**W** 11655 & **S** 17895 (Europe)
2125-2400	9570 (Irr) & 11655 (Irr) (Mideast & N Africa)

RUSSIA—Russian

VOICE OF RUSSIA

0100-0300	**S** 9480 & **S** 12070 (S America), **S** 17565, **S** 17650, **S** 17690 & **S** 21755 (W North Am)
0200-0400 **◻**	7125 (E North Am), 17660 (W North Am)
0200-0400	**W** 7350 & **S** 9890 (S America), **W** 12010, **W** 15595 & **W** 17595 (W North Am)
1300-1500	**W** 7155 (E Asia), **W** 7170 (E Asia & SE Asia)
1800-1900	**W** 5920 & **W** 7205 (Europe)
1800-2000	**S** 11980 (Europe)
1900-2000	**S** 15455 & **S** 9710 (Europe)
2000-2100	**W** 7310 & **W** 7380 (Europe), **S** 9450 (Europe & N Africa), **S** 9710 & **S** 12070 (Europe)
2000-2200	**W** 6205 (S Europe & N Africa), **W** 7205, **W** 7320 & **W** 9905 (Europe)

SAUDI ARABIA—Arabic

BROADCASTING SERVICE OF THE KINGDOM

0300-0600	9578 (Mideast & E Africa), 11818 (N Africa), 15170 (E Europe & W Asia), 15435 (W Asia), 21495 (C Asia)
0600-0800	17895 (C Asia)
0600-0900	15380 (Mideast), 17560 (W Asia), 17760 (N Africa)
0600-1500	21505 (N Africa), 21705 (W Europe)
0600-1700	11855 (Mideast & E Africa)
0900-1200	11935 (Mideast), 17880 (SE Asia), 21495 (E Asia & SE Asia)
1200-1400	15380 (Mideast), 21495 (SE Asia)
1200-1500	17560 (W Asia), 17895 (N Africa)
1200-1600	17760 (N Africa)
1500-1800	11948/11913 (W Asia), 13690/13610 & 15275 (W Asia), 15435 (W Europe)
1600-1800	11708 (N Africa), 15205/15345 (W Europe), 17560 (C Africa & W Africa)
1700-2200	9578 (Mideast & E Africa)
1800-2100	11948 (W Asia)

1800-2300	9555 (N Africa), 9870 & 11820 (W Europe), 11935 (N Africa), 15230/15275 (C Africa & W Africa)

SINGAPORE—Chinese

RADIO SINGAPORE INTERNATIONAL—(SE Asia)

1100-1400	6000 & 9560

RADIO CORPORATION OF SINGAPORE

1400-1600 & 2300-1100	6000

SLOVAKIA—Slovak

RADIO SLOVAKIA INTERNATIONAL

0130-0200	5930 & 7230/7300 (E North Am & C America), 9440 (S America)
0730-0800	**S** 9440, 15460, 17550/11990 & **W** 21705 (Australasia)
1530-1600	**S** 5920 (W Europe)
1630-1700 **◻**	6055 & 7345 (W Europe)
1630-1700	**W** 5915 (W Europe)
1900-1930	**S** 5920 (W Europe)
2000-2030 **◻**	6055 & 7345 (W Europe)
2000-2030	**W** 5915 (W Europe)

SPAIN

RADIO EXTERIOR DE ESPAÑA
Galician, Catalan and Basque

1340-1355	**S** M-F 9765 (C America), **S** M-F 15585 (Europe), **S** M-F 17595 (N America & C America), **S** M-F 21540 (C Africa & S Africa), **S** M-F 21570 (S America), **S** M-F 21610 (Mideast)
1440-1455	**W** M-F 15585 (Europe), **W** M-F 17595 (N America & C America), **W** M-F 21540 (C Africa & S Africa), **W** M-F 21570 (S America), **W** M-F 21610 (Mideast)

Spanish

0000-0100	**W** Su/M 9765 (C America), **W** Su/M 11880 (C America & S America), **W** Su/M 15170 (W North Am & C America)
0000-0200	**S** 11680 & **W** 11945 (S America)
0000-0400	**S** 6020 (C America)
0000-0500	**W** 6125 (S America), 9540 (N America & C America), 9620 & **S** 15160 (S America)
0100-0400	**W** Tu-Sa 3210 & **W** Tu-Sa 5970 (C America)
0100-0500	**W** Tu-Sa 9630 (C America)
0200-0500	6055 (N America & C America)
0200-0600	**S** 6125 (W North Am & C America), **S** 9765 (C America & S America)
0500-0700	**S** 9710 (Europe), **W** 11890 & **S** 17665 (Mideast)

0600-0800	■ 9705 (Europe)
0600-0900 ⬛	12035 (Europe)
0700-0900	17770 & 21610 (Australasia)
0800-0900	■ 15585 (Europe)
0800-1000	M-F 21570 (S America)
0900-1340	15585 (Europe), 21540 (C Africa & S Africa), 21610 (Mideast)
1000-1200	*9660* (E Asia), ■ M-F 21700 (C America)
1000-1340	21570 (S America)
1100-1200	■ M-F *9765* (C America)
1100-1400	■ M-F *5970* & M-F *11815* (C America), ■ M-F *15170* (W North Am & C America)
1200-1340	■ Su-F *9765* (C America)
1200-1400	*5220* (E Asia), *11910* (SE Asia)
1200-2000	Sa/Su 21700 (C America & S America)
1300-1340	M-F 17595 (N America & C America)
1340-1355	■ Su *9765* (C America), ■ Sa/Su 15585 & ■ 15585 (Europe), ■ M-F 17595 (N America & C America), ■ Sa/Su 21540 & ■ 21540 (C Africa & S Africa), ■ Sa/Su 21570 & ■ 21570 (S America), ■ 21610 & ■ Sa/Su 21610 (Mideast)
1355-1440	15585 (Europe), M-F 17595 (N America & C America), 21540 (C Africa & S Africa), 21570 (S America), 21610 (Mideast)
1400-1700	■ Sa/Su *15170* (W North Am & C America)
1400-1800	■ Sa/Su *9765* (C America), ■ Sa/Su *15125* (C America & S America)
1400-2300	■ Su *9765* (C America)
1440-1455	■ 15585 & ■ Sa/Su 15585 (Europe), ■ M-F 17595 (N America & C America), ■ Sa/Su 21540 & ■ 21540 (C Africa & S Africa), ■ 21570 & ■ Sa/Su 21570 (S America), ■ 21610 & ■ Sa/Su 21610 (Mideast)
1455-1700	15585 (Europe), 21570 (S America), ■ 21610 (Mideast)
1500-1600	■ Su *17850* (W North Am & C America)
1500-1700	■ 21770 (Mideast)
1500-1900	17755 (C Africa & S Africa)
1600-1700	M-Sa 15375 (W Africa & C Africa)
1600-2300	■ Sa/Su *17850* (W North Am & C America)
1700-1800	■ Sa/Su *17850* (W North Am & C America)
1700-1900	17715 (S America)
1700-2000	Sa/Su 9665 (Europe)
1700-2300	7275 (Europe)
1800-2100	M-F 21700 (Irr) (C America & S America)

1800-2200	■ *15125* (C America & S America), ■ *17850* (W North Am & C America)
1800-2400	■ *9765* (C America)
1900-2100	Su 17755 (C Africa & S Africa)
1900-2300	15110 (N America & C America)
2000-2100	Sa 9665 (Europe), Sa 21700 (C America & S America)
2200-2300	7270 (N Africa & W Africa)
2200-2400	■ *11880* (C America & S America), ■ *15170* (W North Am & C America)
2300-2400	■ 6125 (S America), 9540 (N America & C America), 9620, ■ 11680, ■ 11945 & ■ 15160 (S America)

SWITZERLAND
SWISS RADIO INTERNATIONAL
French

0200-0230	9885 & *9905* (N America & C America)
0430-0500	■ *9610* (E Europe)
0500-0530	9885 (N America & C America)
0530-0600	■ 9655 (E Europe)
0600-0630	■ 9885 (W Africa), ■ *13635* & ■ *15545* (N Africa), ■ 17665 (C Africa & S Africa), ■ *17685* (N Africa & W Africa), ■ 21750 (C Africa & S Africa)
1000-1030	*9885* (Australasia), 21770 (C Africa & S Africa)
1100-1130	■ *15315* (W Europe)
1200-1230	■ 9535 (W Europe)
1230-1300	■ *9540* & ■ *13735* (E Asia), 21770 (S Asia & SE Asia)
1530-1600	■ 9575 & ■ *12010* (E Asia & SE Asia), ■ 15185 & ■ 17670 (W Asia & S Asia)
1800-1815	■ *9605*, ■ *13790* & ■ *15220* (Mideast), ■ 15555 (Mideast & E Africa), ■ *17640* (Mideast), ■ 21720 (Mideast & E Africa)
1830-1900	■ *6110* (N Europe)
1930-2000	■ *6165* (N Europe)
2100-2130	■ 9605 (N Africa & W Africa), ■ *11910* (E Africa), ■ 13660 (C Africa & S Africa), ■ *13710* (S Africa), ■ 13770 (E Africa), ■ *13790* (S Africa), ■ *15220* (C Africa & S Africa), ■ *17580* (N Africa & W Africa)
2200-2230	9885, ■ *11660* & ■ *11905* (S America)

German

0030-0100 &	
0330-0400	9885 & *9905* (N America & C America)
0530-0600	■ *9610* (E Europe)

0630-0700	**W** *9655* (E Europe), **W** *9885* (W Africa), **W** *13635* & **S** *15545* (N Africa), **W** 17665 (C Africa & S Africa), **S** *17685* (N Africa & W Africa), **S** 21750 (C Africa & S Africa)
0930-1000	*9885* (Australasia), 21770 (C Africa & S Africa)
1030-1100	**S** *15315* (W Europe)
1130-1200	**W** *9535* (W Europe)
1200-1230	**W** 9540 & **S** *13735* (E Asia), 21770 (S Asia & SE Asia)
1500-1530	**S** *9575* & **W** *12010* (E Asia & SE Asia), **W** 15185 & **S** 17670 (W Asia & S Asia)
1730-1800	**S** *6110* (N Europe)
1830-1900	**W** *6165* (N Europe)
2030-2100	**W** *9605* (N Africa & W Africa), **W** *11910* (E Africa), **W** 13660 (C Africa & S Africa), **S** *13710* (S Africa), **S** 13770 (E Africa), **W** *13790* (S Africa), **S** *15220* (C Africa & S Africa), **S** *17580* (N Africa & W Africa)
2230-2300	9885, **W** *11660* & **S** *11905* (S America)

Italian

0300-0330	9885 & *9905* (N America & C America)
0530-0545	9885 (N America & C America)
0600-0630	**S** *9610* (E Europe)
0700-0730	**W** *9655* (E Europe), **W** *9885* (W Africa), **W** *13635* & **S** *15545* (N Africa), **W** 17665 (C Africa & S Africa), **S** *17685* (N Africa & W Africa), **S** 21750 (C Africa & S Africa)
0900-0930	*9885* (Australasia), 21770 (C Africa & S Africa)
1130-1200	**S** *15315* (W Europe)
1230-1300	**W** *9535* (W Europe)
1300-1330	**W** 9540 & **S** *13735* (E Asia), 21770 (S Asia & SE Asia)
1630-1700	**W** *9605*, **W** *13790* & **S** *15220* (Mideast), **W** 15555 (Mideast & E Africa), **S** *17640* (Mideast), **S** 21720 (Mideast & E Africa)
1800-1830	**S** *6110* (N Europe)
1830-1900	**W** *9605* (N Africa & W Africa), **W** *11910* (E Africa), **W** 13660 (C Africa & S Africa), **S** 13770 (E Africa), **S** *15220* (C Africa & S Africa), **S** *17580* (N Africa & W Africa)
1900-1930	**W** *6165* (N Europe)
2300-2330	9885, **W** *11660* & **S** *11905* (S America)

SYRIA—Arabic

RADIO DAMASCUS—(S America)

2215-2315	12085 & 13610

SYRIAN BROADCASTING SERVICE

0600-1600	□	13610
0600-1700	□	12085

THAILAND—Thai

RADIO THAILAND

0000-1605	4830 (Irr), 6070, 7115
0100-0200	9655 (Irr) & 11905 (Irr) (Asia), **W** 13695 & **S** 15395 (E North Am)
0330-0430	9655 (Irr) & 11905 (Irr) (Asia), **S** 15395 & **W** 15460 (W North Am)
1000-1100	**W** 7285 & **S** 11805 (SE Asia & Australasia)
1330-1400	**W** 7145 (E Asia), 9655 (Irr) & 11905 (Irr) (Asia), **S** 11955 (E Asia)
1800-1900	9655 (Irr) (Asia), **S** 9690 & **W** 11855 (Mideast), 11905 (Irr) (Asia)
2045-2115	**W** 9535 (Europe), 9655 (Irr) (Asia), **S** 9680 (Europe), 11905 (Irr) (Asia)
2200-2400	4830 (Irr), 6070, 7115

TUNISIA—Arabic

RADIO TUNISIENNE

0200-0500	9720/12005 (N Africa & Mideast)
0400-0600	7275 (W Europe)
0400-0700	7110 (N Africa)
1200-1400	17735 (N Africa & Mideast)
1200-1700	**W** 15450 (N Africa & Mideast)
1400-1700	11730 (W Europe), **S** 17735 (N Africa & Mideast)
1400-1900	11655 (N Africa)
1700-2100	9720/12005 (N Africa & Mideast)
1700-2300	7225 (W Europe)
1900-2300	7110 (N Africa)

TURKEY—Turkish

VOICE OF TURKEY

0000-0300		**S** 21715 (W Asia, S Asia & Australasia)
0000-0400		**S** 5960 (Mideast), **S** 11885 (Europe & N America)
0000-0500	□	5980 (Europe)
0000-0500		**W** 6120 (Mideast), **W** 7300 (Europe & N America)
0000-0800	□	9445 (Europe & E North Am), 9460 (Europe, E North Am & C America)
0300-0400		**W** 21715 (S Asia, SE Asia & Australasia)
0400-0500		**S** 21715 (S Asia, SE Asia & Australasia)
0400-0700		**S** 11910 (Europe), **S** 21540 (W Asia & C Asia)
0400-0900		**S** 11750 (Mideast), **S** 17600 (Mideast & W Asia)
0500-0800		**W** 11620 (Europe), **W** 17690 (W Asia & C Asia)

0500-1000	ⓦ 9560 (W Asia, S Asia & Australasia), ⓦ 11925 (Mideast), ⓦ 17570 (W Asia)
0500-1300	21715 (W Asia, S Asia & Australasia)
0500-1700 ▣	11955 (Mideast)
0800-0900 ▣	11690 (Mideast & W Asia)
0800-1700 ▣	15350 (Europe)
0800-2200 ▣	9460 (Europe)
1100-1600 ▣	F 15615 (N Africa)
1300-1600	ⓢ 13655 & ⓦ 15370 (S Asia, SE Asia & Australasia)
1600-2200	9560 (W Asia, S Asia & Australasia)
1600-2400	ⓢ 5960 (Mideast)
1700-2200	ⓢ 7220 (N Africa & W Africa)
1700-2400 ▣	5980 (Europe)
1700-2400	ⓦ 6120 (Mideast)
1800-2300	ⓦ 7110 (N Africa & W Africa)
1900-2200	ⓢ 11910 (Europe)
2000-2050	ⓦ 7190 (Europe)
2200-2400 ▣	9445 (Europe & E North Am), 9460 (Europe, E North Am & C America)
2200-2400	ⓦ 7135 (Mideast & W Asia), ⓢ 11885 (Europe & N America), ⓢ 15325 (S Asia, SE Asia & Australasia)
2300-2400	ⓦ 7300 (Europe & N America)

UNITED ARAB EMIRATES—Arabic

UAE RADIO FROM ABU DHABI

0200-0400	6180 (Mideast), ⓦ 11770 & ⓢ 17665 (E Asia)
0200-0600	21630 (Australasia)
0200-0700	21735 (E Asia)
0400-0600	11945 (Mideast)
0600-1000	21630 (Europe)
0600-1300	15310 (Mideast)
0700-1600	21735 (N Africa)
0900-1300	ⓦ 17760 & ⓢ 17835 (E Asia)
1000-1800	ⓦ 15255 & ⓢ 15265 (Europe)
1300-1600	15315 (Australasia)
1300-2200	9605 (Mideast)
1600-2000	13755 (N Africa)
1800-2200	11710 (Europe)
2000-2200	17760 (N Africa)

UAE RADIO IN DUBAI

0000-0200	11950 (Irr), 13675 (Irr) (E North Am & C America)
0230-0330	12005, 13675 & 15400 (E North Am & C America)
0400-0530	15435 (Australasia), 17830 (E Asia), 21700 (Australasia)
0600-1030	13675, 15395 & 21605 (Europe)
1050-1200	15370 (N Africa)
1050-1330	13675, 15395 & 21605 (Europe)
1200-1330	13630 (N Africa)
1350-1600	13630 (N Africa), 13675, 15395 & 21605 (Europe)

Buddhist monks enjoy complete freedom in Bhutan, unlike in some other countries. M. Guha

1630-2050	11950 (Europe), 13630 (N Africa), 13675 & 15395 (Europe)
2050-2400	11950 (Irr), 13675 (Irr) (E North Am & C America)

VENEZUELA—Spanish

ECOS DEL TORBES

0900-0400	4980
1200-2200	9640

RADIO NACIONAL—(C America)

0000-0100,	
0300-0400,	
1100-1200,	
1400-1500,	
1800-1900 &	
2100-2200	9540 (Irr)

RADIO TACHIRA

1000-1400 &	
2100-0400	4830

VIETNAM—Vietnamese

VOICE OF VIETNAM

0000-0100	ⓦ 7145, 9730 & ⓢ 13740 (C Africa)
0130-0230	ⓦ 9525 & ⓢ 9695 (E North Am)
0400-0500	9795 (W North Am)
1700-1800	ⓦ 7145, 9730 & ⓢ 13740 (Europe)
1830-1930	ⓦ 7440 & ⓢ 12070 (Europe)
1930-2030	ⓢ 12030 (Europe)
2030-2130	ⓦ 7390 (Europe)

WESTERN SAHARA

RADIO NACIONAL DE LA RASD

Arabic

1900-2400	7450

Spanish

1800-1900	7450

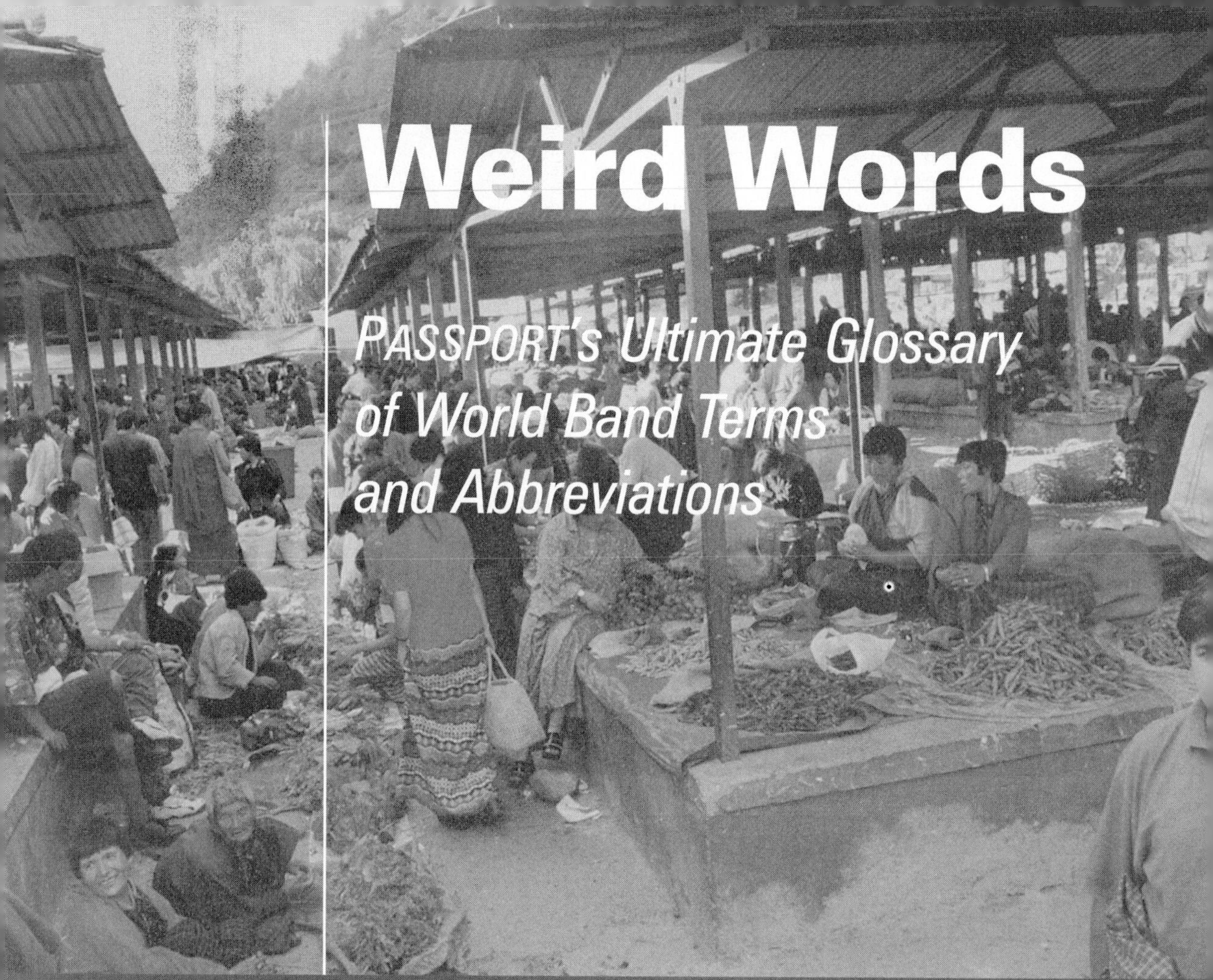

Weird Words

*PASSPORT's Ultimate Glossary
of World Band Terms
and Abbreviations*

All sorts of terms and abbreviations are used in world band radio. Some are specialized and benefit from explanation; several are foreign words that need translation; and yet others are simply adaptations of everyday usage.

Here, then, is PASSPORT's A-Z guide to what's what in world band buzzwords—including what each one means. For a thorough writeup on nomenclature used in evaluating how well a world band radio performs, see the Radio Database International White Paper, *How to Interpret Receiver Specifications and Lab Tests.*

Active Antenna. An antenna that electronically amplifies signals. Active antennas are typically mounted indoors, but some models can also be mounted outdoors. Active antennas take up relatively little space, but their amplification circuits may introduce certain types of problems that can result in unwanted sounds being heard. *See* Passive Antenna.

Adjacent-Channel Rejection. *See* Selectivity.

AGC. *See* Automatic Gain Control.

Alt. Freq. Alternative frequency or channel. Frequency or channel that may be used in place of the regularly scheduled one.

Amateur Radio. *See* Hams.

AM Band. The local radio band, which currently runs from 520 to 1611 kHz (530–1705 kHz in the Western Hemisphere), within the Medium Frequency (MF) range of the radio spectrum. Outside North America, it is usually called the mediumwave (MW) band. However, in parts of Latin America it is sometimes called, by the general public and a few stations, *onda larga*—longwave—strictly speaking, a misnomer.

Amplified Antenna. *See* Active Antenna.

Analog Frequency Readout. Needle-and-dial or "slide-rule" tuning, greatly inferior to synthesized tuning for scanning the world band airwaves. *See* Synthesizer.

Audio Quality. At PASSPORT, audio quality refers to what in computer testing is called "benchmark" quality. This means, primarily, the freedom from distortion of a signal fed through a receiver's entire circuitry—*not* just the audio stage—from the antenna input through to the speaker terminals. A lesser characteristic of audio quality is the audio bandwidth needed for pleasant world band reception of music. Also, *see* Enhanced Fidelity.

Automatic Gain Control (AGC). Smooths out fluctuations in signal strength brought about by fading, a regular occurrence with world band signals.

AV. A Voz—Portuguese for "The Voice." In PASSPORT, this term is also used to represent "The Voice of."

Bandwidth. A key variable that determines selectivity (*see*), bandwidth is the amount of radio signal at –6 dB a radio's circuitry will let pass, and thus be heard. With world band channel spacing at 5 kHz, the best single bandwidths are usually in the vicinity of 3 to 6 kHz. Better radios offer two or more selectable bandwidths: at least one of 5 to 7 kHz or so for when a station is in the clear, and one or more others between 2 to 4 kHz for when a station is hemmed in by other signals next to it. Proper selectivity is a key determinant of the aural quality of what you hear, and some newer models of tabletop receivers have dozens of bandwidths.

Baud. Measurement of the speed by which radioteletype (*see*), radiofax (*see*) and other digital data are transmitted. Baud is properly written entirely in lower case, and thus is abbreviated as b (baud), kb (kilobaud) or Mb (Megabaud). Baud rate standards are usually set by the international CCITT regulatory body.

BC. Broadcasting, Broadcasting Company, Broadcasting Corporation.

Birdie. A silent spurious signal, similar to a station's open carrier, created by circuit interaction within a receiver. The fewer and weaker the birdies within a receiver's tuning range, the better.

Broadcast. A radio or television transmission meant for the general public. *Compare* Utility Stations, Hams.

BS. Broadcasting Station, Broadcasting Service.

Cd. Ciudad—Spanish for "City."

Channel. An everyday term to indicate where a station is supposed to be located on the dial. World band channels are spaced exactly 5 kHz apart. Stations operating outside this norm are "off-channel" (for these, PASSPORT provides resolution to better than 1 kHz to aid in station identification).

Chugging, Chuffing. The sound made by some synthesized tuning systems when the tuning knob is turned. Called "chugging" or "chuffing," as it is suggestive of the rhythmic "chug, chug" sound of a steam engine or "chugalug" gulping.

Cl. Club, Clube.

Cult. Cultura, Cultural.

Default. The setting at which a control of a digitally operated electronic device, including many world band radios, normally operates, and to which it will eventually return (e.g., when the radio is next switched on).

Digital Frequency Display, Digital Tuning. *See* Synthesizer.

Digital Signal Processing (DSP). Where computer-type circuitry and software are used to perform radio circuit functions traditionally done using analog circuits. Used on certain world band receivers; also, available as an add-on accessory for audio processing only.

Dipole Antenna. *See* Passive Antenna.

Domestic Service. *See* DS.

DS. Domestic Service—Broadcasting intended primarily for audiences in the broadcaster's home country. However, some domestic programs are beamed on world band to expatriates and other kinfolk abroad, as well as interested foreigners. *Compare* ES.

DSP. *See* Digital Signal Processing.

DX, DXers, DXing. From an old telegraph term "to DX"; that is, to communicate over a great distance. Thus, DXers are those who specialize in finding distant or exotic stations that are considered to be rare catches. Few world band listeners are considered to be regular DXers, but many others seek out DX stations every now and then—usually by bandscanning, which is greatly facilitated by PASSPORT's Blue Pages.

Dynamic Range. The ability of a receiver to handle weak signals in the presence of strong competing signals within or near the same world band segment (*see* World Band Spectrum). Sets with inferior dynamic range sometimes "overload," especially with external antennas, causing a mishmash of false signals up and down—and even beyond—the segment being received.

Earliest Heard (or Latest Heard). See key at the bottom of each Blue Page. If the PASSPORT monitoring team cannot establish the definite sign-on (or sign-off) time of a station, the earliest (or latest) time that the station could be traced is indicated by a left-facing or right-facing "arrowhead flag." This means that the station almost certainly operates beyond the time shown by that "flag." It also means that, unless you live relatively close to the station, you're unlikely to be able to hear it beyond that "flagged" time.

EBS. Economic Broadcasting Station, a type of station found in China.

ECSS. Exalted-carrier selectable sideband, a term no longer in general use, yet sometimes mis-used when it does appear. Properly used, it refers to the manual tuning of a conventional AM-mode signal using the receiver's single-sideband circuitry to zero-beat the receiver's BFO with the transmitted signal's carrier. *See* Synchronous Detector.

Ed, Educ. Educational, Educação, Educadora.

Electrical Noise. *See* Noise.

Em. Emissora, Emisora, Emissor, Emetteur—in effect, "station" in various languages.

Enhanced Fidelity. Radios with good audio performance and certain types of high-tech circuitry can improve the fidelity of world band signals. Among the newer fidelity-enhancing techniques is synchronous detection (*see*), especially when coupled with selectable sideband. Another potential technological advance to improve fidelity is digital world band transmission, which is actively being researched and tested.

EP. Emissor Provincial—Portuguese for "Provincial Station."

ER. Emissor Regional—Portuguese for "Regional Station."

Ergonomics. How handy and comfortable—intuitive—a set is to operate, especially hour after hour.

ES. External Service—Broadcasting intended primarily for audiences abroad. *Compare* DS.

External Service. *See* ES.

F. Friday.

Fax. *See* Radiofax.

Feeder, Shortwave. A utility transmission from the broadcaster's home country to a relay site or placement facility some distance away. Although these specialized transmissions carry world band programming, they are not intended to be received by the general public. Many world band radios can process these quasi-broadcasts anyway. Feeders operate in lower sideband (LSB), upper sideband (USB) or independent sideband (termed ISL if heard on the lower side, ISU if heard on the upper side) modes. Nearly all shortwave feeders have now been replaced by satellite and Internet audio feeders. *See* Single Sideband, Utility Stations.

In Taliban-controlled Afghanistan young women are forbidden from attending school. Girls are more fortunate in rebel-controlled parts of the country, where segregated education is provided to both sexes. Here, Muslim students' attire ranges from varying degrees of traditional to thoroughly modern.
M. Guha

Frequency. The standard term to indicate where a station is located on the dial—regardless of whether it is "on-channel" or "off-channel" (*see* Channel). Measured in kilohertz (kHz) or Megahertz (MHz), which differ only in the placement of a decimal; e.g., 5975 kHz is the same as 5.975 MHz. Either measurement is equally valid, but to minimize confusion PASSPORT and most stations designate frequencies only in kHz.

Frequency Synthesizer. *See* Synthesizer, Frequency.

Front-End Selectivity. The ability of the initial stage of receiving circuitry to admit only limited frequency ranges into succeeding stages of circuitry. Good front-end selectivity keeps signals from other, powerful bands or segments from being superimposed upon the frequency range you're tuning. For example, a receiver with good front-end selectivity will receive only shortwave signals within the range 3200-3400 kHz. However, a receiver with mediocre front-end selectivity might allow powerful local mediumwave AM stations from 520-1700 kHz to be heard "ghosting in" between 3200 and 3400 kHz, along with the desired shortwave signals. Obviously, mediumwave AM signals don't belong on shortwave. Receivers with inadequate front-end selectivity can benefit from the addition of a preselector (*see*).

GMT. Greenwich Mean Time—*See* World Time.

Hams. Government-licensed amateur radio hobbyists who *transmit* to each other by radio, often by single sideband (*see*), within special amateur bands. Many of these bands are within the shortwave spectrum (*see*). This is the same spectrum used by world band radio, but world band and ham radio, which laymen sometimes confuse with each other, are two very separate entities. The easiest way is to think of hams as making something like phone calls, whereas world band stations are like long-distance versions of ordinary FM or mediumwave AM stations.

Harmonic, Harmonic Radiation, Harmonic Signal. Usually, an unwanted weak spurious repeat of a signal in multiple(s) of the fundamental, or "real," frequency. Thus, the third harmonic of a mediumwave AM station on 1120 kHz might be heard faintly on 4480 kHz within the world band spectrum. Stations almost always try to minimize harmonic radiation, as it wastes energy and spectrum space. However, in rare cases stations have been known to amplify a harmonic signal so they can operate inexpensively on a second frequency. Also, *see* Subharmonic.

Hash. Electrical noise. *See* Noise.

High Fidelity. *See* Enhanced Fidelity.

IBS. International Broadcasting Services, Ltd., publishers of *Passport to World Band Radio* and other international broadcasting publications.

Image. A common type of spurious signal found on low-cost radios where a strong signal appears at reduced strength, usually on a frequency 900 kHz or 910 kHz lower down. For example, the BBC on 5975 kHz might repeat on 5075 kHz, its "image frequency." *See* Spurious-Signal Rejection.

Independent Sideband. *See* Single Sideband.

Interference. Sounds from other signals, notably on the same ("co-channel") frequency or nearby channels, that are disturbing the one you are trying to hear. Worthy radios reduce interference by having good selectivity (*see*). Nearby television sets and cable television wiring may also generate a special type of radio interference called TVI, a "growl" usually heard every 15 kHz or so.

International Reply Coupon (IRC). Sold by selected post offices in most parts of the world, IRCs amount to official international "scrip" that may be exchanged for postage in most countries of the world. Because they amount to an international form of postage repayment, they are handy for listeners trying to encourage foreign stations to write them back. However, IRCs are very costly for the amount in stamps that is provided in return. Too, some countries are not forthcoming about "cashing in" IRCs. Specifics are provided in the Addresses PLUS section of this book.

International Telecommunication Union (ITU). The regulatory body, headquartered in Geneva, for all international telecommunications, including world band radio. Sometimes incorrectly referred to as the "International Telecommunications Union." In recent years, the ITU has become increasingly ineffective as a regulatory body for world band, with much of its former role having been taken up by groups of affiliated international broadcasters voluntarily coordinating their schedules a number of times each year.

Internet Radio. *See* Web radio.

Inverted-L Antenna. *See* Passive Antenna.

Ionosphere. *See* Propagation.

IRC. *See* International Reply Coupon.

Irr. Irregular operation or hours of operation; i.e., schedule tends to be unpredictable.

ISB. Independent sideband. *See* Single Sideband.

ISL. Independent sideband, lower. *See* Feeder.

ISU. Independent sideband, upper. *See* Feeder.

ITU. *See* International Telecommunication Union.

Jamming. Deliberate interference to a transmission with the intent of discouraging listening. Jamming is practiced much less now than it was during the Cold War.

Keypad. On a world band radio, like a computer, a keypad can be used to control many variables. However, unlike a computer, the keypad on most world band radios consists of ten numeric or multifunction keys, usually supplemented by two more keys, as on a telephone keypad. Keypads are used primarily so you can enter a station's frequency for reception, and the best keypads have real keys (not a membrane) in the standard telephone format of 3×4 with "zero" under the "8" key. Many keypads are also used for presets, but this means you have to remember code numbers for stations (e.g., BBC 5975 kHz is "07"); handier radios either have separate keys for presets, or use LCD-displayed "pages" to access presets.

kHz. Kilohertz, the most common unit for measuring where a station is on the world band dial. Formerly known as "kilocycles per second," or kc/s. 1,000 kilohertz equals one Megahertz.

Kilohertz. See kHz.

kW. Kilowatt(s), the most common unit of measurement for transmitter power (see).

LCD. Liquid-crystal display. LCDs, if properly designed, are fairly easily seen in bright light, but require illumination under darker conditions. LCDs, typically gray on gray, also tend to have mediocre contrast, and sometimes can be read from only a certain angle or angles, but they consume nearly no battery power.

LED. Light-emitting diode. LEDs are very easily read in the dark or in normal room light, but consume battery power and are hard to read in bright light.

Location. The physical location of a station's transmitter, which may be different from the studio location. Transmitter location is useful as a guide to reception quality. For example, if you're in eastern North America and wish to listen to the Voice of Russia, a transmitter located in St. Petersburg will almost certainly provide better reception than one located in Siberia.

Longwave Band. The 148.5–283.5 kHz portion of the low-frequency (LF) radio spectrum used in Europe, the Near East, North Africa, Russia and Mongolia for domestic broadcasting. As a practical matter, these longwave signals, which have nothing to do with world band or other shortwave signals, are not usually audible in other parts of the world.

Longwire Antenna. See Passive Antenna.

LSB. Lower Sideband. See Feeder, Single Sideband.

LV. La Voix, La Voz—French and Spanish for "The Voice." In PASSPORT, this term is also used to represent "The Voice of."

M. Monday.

Mediumwave Band, Mediumwave AM Band. See AM Band.

Megahertz. See MHz.

Memory, Memories. See Preset.

Meters. An outdated unit of measurement used for individual world band segments of the shortwave spectrum. The frequency range covered by a given meters designation—also known as "wavelength"—can be gleaned from the following formula: *frequency (kHz) = 299,792 ÷ meters*. Thus, 49 meters comes out to a frequency of 6118 kHz—well within the range of frequencies included in that segment (see World Band Spectrum). Inversely, meters can be derived from the following: *meters = 299,792 ÷ frequency (kHz)*.

MHz. Megahertz, a common unit to measure where a station is on the dial. Formerly known as "Megacycles per second," or Mc/s. One Megahertz equals 1,000 kilohertz.

Mode. Method of transmission of radio signals. World band radio broadcasts are almost always in the analog AM mode, the same mode used in the mediumwave AM band (see). The AM mode consists of three components: two "sidebands" and one "carrier." Each sideband contains the same programming as the other, and the carrier carries no programming, so a few stations have experimented with the single-sideband (SSB) mode. SSB contains only one sideband, either the lower sideband (LSB) or upper sideband (USB), and a reduced carrier. It requires special radio circuitry to be demodulated, or made intelligible, which is the main reason SSB has not succeeded, and is not expected to succeed, as a world band mode. There are yet other modes used on shortwave, but not for world band. These include CW (Morse-type code), radiofax, RTTY (radioteletype) and narrow-band FM used by utility and ham stations. Narrow-band FM is not used for music, and is different from usual FM. See Single Sideband, ISB, ISL, ISU, LSB and USB.

N. New, Nueva, Nuevo, Nouvelle, Nacional, National, Nationale. *Nac. Nacional.* Spanish and Portuguese for "National."

Nat, Natl, Nat'l. National, Nationale.

Noise. Static, buzzes, pops and the like caused by the earth's atmosphere (typically lightning), and to a lesser extent by galactic noise. Also, electrical noise emanates from such man-made sources as electric blankets, fish-tank heaters, heating pads, electrical and gasoline motors, light dimmers, flickering light bulbs, non-incandescent lights, computers and computer peripherals, office machines, electrical fences, and faulty electrical utility wiring and related components.

Other. Programs are in a language other than one of the world's primary languages.

Overloading. See Dynamic Range.

Passive Antenna. An antenna that is not electronically amplified. Typically, these are mounted outdoors, although the "tape-measure" type that comes as an accessory with some portables is usually strung indoors. For world band reception, virtually all outboard models for consumers are made from wire, rather than rod-type or tubular elements. The two most common designs are the inverted-L (so-called "longwire") and trapped dipole (either horizontal or sloper). These antennas are preferable to active antennas (see), and are reviewed in detail in the Radio Database International White Paper, PASSPORT *Evaluation of Popular Outdoor Antennas (Unamplified)*.

PBS. People's Broadcasting Station.

PLL (Phase-Locked Loop). With world band receivers, a PLL circuit means that the radio can be tuned digitally, often using a number of handy tuning techniques, such as a keypad and presets (see).

Power. Transmitter power *before* amplification by the antenna, expressed in kilowatts (kW). The present range of world band powers is 0.01 to 1,000 kW.

Power Lock. See Travel Power Lock.

PR. People's Republic.

Preselector. A device—typically outboard, but sometimes inboard—that effectively limits the range of frequencies which can enter a receiver's circuitry or the circuitry of an active antenna (see); that is, which improves front-end selectivity (see). For example, a preselector may let in the range 15000-16000 kHz, thus helping ensure that your receiver or active antenna will encounter no problems within that range caused by signals from, say, 5800-6200 kHz or local mediumwave AM signals (520-1705 kHz). This range usually can be varied, manually or automatically, according to the frequency to which the receiver is being tuned. A preselector may be passive (unamplified) or active (amplified).

Preset. Allows you to select a station pre-stored in a radio's memory. The handiest presets require only one push of a button, as on a car radio.

Propagation. World band signals travel, like a basketball, up and down from the station to your radio. The "floor" below is the earth's surface, whereas the "player's hand" on high is the *ionosphere*, a gaseous layer that envelops the planet. While the earth's surface remains pretty much the same from day to day, the ionosphere—nature's own passive "satellite"—varies in how it propagates radio signals, depending on how much sunlight hits the "bounce points." Thus, some world band segments do well mainly by day, whereas others are best by night. During winter there's less sunlight, so the "night bands" become unusually active, whereas the "day bands" become correspondingly less useful (see World Band Spectrum). Day-to-day changes in the sun's weather also cause short-term changes in world band radio reception; this explains why some days you can hear rare signals.

Additionally, the 11-year sunspot cycle has a long-term effect on propagation. Currently, the sunspot cycle is at a vigorous phase. This means that the upper world band segments will remain unusually lively over the coming years.

PS. Provincial Station, Pangsong.

Pto. Puerto, Porto.

QSL. See Verification.

R. Radio, Radiodiffusion, Radiodifusora, Radiodifusão, Radiophonikos, Radiostantsiya, Radyo, Radyosu, and so forth.

**PASSPORT's Jane Brinker explains world band radio
to David Cox at the BEA book convention in
Los Angeles.**   L. Magne

Radiofax, Radio Facsimile. Like ordinary telefax (facsimile by
telephone lines), but by radio.

Radioteletype (RTTY). Characters, but not illustrations, transmitted by radio. *See* Baud.

RDI. Radio Database International, a registered trademark of
International Broadcasting Services, Ltd.

Receiver. Synonym for a radio, but sometimes—especially when
called a "communications receiver"—implying a radio with superior tough-signal or utility-signal performance.

Reduced Carrier. *See* Single Sideband.

Reg. Regional.

Relay. A retransmission facility, often highlighted in "Worldwide
Broadcasts in English" and "Voices from Home" in PASSPORT's
WorldScan® section. Relay facilities are generally considered to be
located outside the broadcaster's country. Being closer to the target audience, they usually provide superior reception. *See* Feeder.

Rep. Republic, République, República.

RN. See R and N.

RS. Radio Station, Radiostantsiya, Radiostudiya, Radiophonikos
Stathmos.

RT, RTV. Radiodiffusion Télévision, Radio Télévision, and so forth.

RTTY. *See* Radioteletype.

S. As an icon ☒: aired summer (midyear) only. As an ordinary letter:
San, Santa, Santo, São, Saint, Sainte. Also, South.

Sa. Saturday.

Scan, Scanning. Circuitry within a radio that allows it to
bandscan or memory-scan automatically.

Segments. *See* Shortwave Spectrum.

Selectivity. The ability of a radio to reject interference (*see*) from
signals on adjacent channels. Thus, also known as adjacent-
channel rejection, a key variable in radio quality. Also, *see* "Bandwidth" and "Synchronous Detector".

Sensitivity. The ability of a radio to receive weak signals; thus,
also known as weak-signal sensitivity. Of special importance if
you're listening during the day, or if you're located in such parts of
the world as Western North America, Hawaii and Australasia, where
signals tend to be relatively weak.

Shortwave Spectrum. The shortwave spectrum—also known
as the High Frequency (HF) spectrum—is, strictly speaking, that
portion of the radio spectrum from 3-30 MHz (3,000-30,000 kHz).
However, common usage places it from 2.3-30 MHz (2,300-30,000
kHz). World band operates on shortwave within 14 discrete seg-

ments between 2.3-26.1 MHz, with the rest of the shortwave spectrum being occupied by hams (*see*) and utility stations (*see*). Also,
see the detailed "Best Times and Frequencies" article elsewhere in
this edition.

Sideband. *See* Mode.   .

Single Sideband, Independent Sideband. Spectrum- and
power-conserving modes of transmission commonly used by utility
stations and hams. Very few broadcasters use, or are expected
ever to use, these modes. Many world band radios are already
capable of demodulating single-sideband transmissions, and some
can even process independent-sideband signals. Certain single-
sideband transmissions operate with a minimum of carrier reduction, which allows them to be listened to, albeit with some
distortion, on ordinary radios not equipped to demodulate single
sideband. Properly designed synchronous detectors (*see*) may prevent such distortion. *See* Feeder, Mode.

Site. *See* Location.

Slew Controls. Elevator-button-type up and down controls to
tune a radio. On many radios with synthesized tuning, slewing is
used in lieu of tuning by knob. Better is when slew controls are
complemented by a tuning knob, which is more versatile.

Sloper Antenna. *See* Passive Antenna.

SPR. Spurious (false) extra signal from a transmitter actually operating on another frequency. One such type is harmonic (*see*).

Spurious-Signal Rejection. The ability of a radio receiver not
to produce false, or "ghost," signals that might otherwise interfere
with the clarity of the station you're trying to hear. *See* Image.

St, Sta, Sto. Abbreviations for words that mean "Saint."

Static. *See* Noise.

Su. Sunday.

Subharmonic. A harmonic heard at 1.5 or 0.5 times the operating frequency. This anomaly is caused by the way signals are generated within vintage-model transmitters, and thus cannot take
place with modern transmitters. For example, the subharmonic of
a station on 3360 kHz might be heard faintly on 5040 or 1680 kHz.
Also, *see* Harmonic.

Sunspot Cycle. *See* Propagation.

Synchronous Detector. World band radios are increasingly
coming equipped with this high-tech circuit that greatly reduces
fading distortion. Better synchronous detectors also allow for selectable sideband; that is, the ability to select the less-interfered of
the two sidebands of a world band or other AM-mode signal. *See*
Mode.

Synchronous Selectable Sideband. *See* Synchronous Detector.

Synthesizer, Frequency. Simple radios often use archaic needle-
and-dial tuning that makes it difficult to find a desired channel or
to tell which station you are hearing, except by ear. Other models
utilize a digital frequency synthesizer to tune to signals without
your having to hunt and peck. Among other things, such synthesizers allow for push-button tuning and presets, and display the
exact frequency digitally—pluses that make tuning to the world
considerably easier. Virtually a "must" feature.

Target. Where a transmission is beamed.

Th. Thursday.

Travel Power Lock. Control to disable the on/off switch to prevent a radio from switching on accidentally.

Transmitter Power. *See* Power.

Trapped Dipole Antenna. *See* Passive Antenna.

Tu. Tuesday.

Universal Day. *See* World Time.

Universal Time. *See* World Time.

URL. Universal Resource Locator; i.e., the Internet address for a
given Webpage.

USB. Upper Sideband. *See* Feeder, Single Sideband.

UTC. Coordinated Universal Time. *See* World Time.

Utility Stations. Most signals within the shortwave spectrum are
not world band stations. Rather, they are utility stations—radio
telephones, ships at sea, aircraft and the like—that transmit strange
sounds (growls, gurgles, dih-dah sounds, etc.) point-to-point and
are not intended to be heard by the general public. *Compare* Broadcast, Hams and Feeders.

v. Variable frequency; i.e., one that is unstable or drifting because of a transmitter malfunction or, less often, to avoid jamming or other interference.

Verification. A "QSL" card or letter from a station verifying that a listener indeed heard that particular station. In order to stand a chance of qualifying for a verification card or letter, you need to provide the station heard with, at a minimum, the following information in a three-number "SIO" code, in which "SIO 555" is best and "SIO 111" is worst:

- **S**ignal strength, with 5 being of excellent quality, comparable to that of a local mediumwave AM station, and 1 being inaudible or at least so weak as to be virtually unintelligible. 2 (faint, but somewhat intelligible), 3 (moderate strength) and 4 (good strength) represent the signal-strength levels usually encountered with world band stations.
- **I**nterference from other stations, with 5 indicating no interference whatsoever, and 1 indicating such extreme interference that the desired signal is virtually drowned out. 2 (heavy interference), 3 (moderate interference) and 4 (slight interference) represent the differing degrees of interference more typically encountered with world band signals. If possible, indicate the names of the interfering station(s) and the channel(s) they are on. Otherwise, at least describe what the interference sounds like.
- **O**verall quality of the signal, with 5 being best, 1 worst.
- In addition to providing SIO findings, you should indicate which programs you've heard, as well as comments on how you liked or disliked those programs. Refer to the "Addresses PLUS" section of this edition for information on where and to whom your report should be sent, and whether return postage should be included.
- Because of the time involved in listening, few stations wish to receive tape recordings of their transmissions.

Vo. Voice of.

W. As an icon ⬛: aired winter only. As a regular letter: Wednesday.

Wavelength. See Meters.

Weak-Signal Sensitivity. See Sensitivity.

Webcasting. See Web Radio.

Web Radio, Webcasting. Broadcasts aired to the public over the World Wide Web. These thousands of stations worldwide include existing FM, mediumwave AM and world band stations simulcasting over the Web ("Webcasting"), or Web-only "stations."

World Band Radio. Similar to regular mediumwave AM band and FM band radio, except that world band stations can be heard over enormous distances and thus often carry news, music and entertainment programs created especially for audiences abroad. Some world band stations have audiences of up to 120 million each day. Some 600 million people worldwide are believed to listen to world band radio.

World Band Spectrum. See "Best Times and Frequencies" elsewhere in this edition.

World Day. See World Time.

World Time. Also known as Coordinated Universal Time (UTC), Greenwich Mean Time (GMT) and Zulu time (Z). With nearly 170 countries on world band radio, if each announced its own local time you would need a calculator to figure it all out. To get around this, a single international time—World Time—is used. The difference between World Time and local time is detailed in the "Addresses PLUS" section of this edition, the "Compleat Idiot's Guide to Getting Started" and especially in the last page of this edition. It is also determined simply by listening to World Time announcements given on the hour by world band stations—or minute by minute by WWV and WWVH in the United States on such frequencies as 5000, 10000 and 15000 kHz, or CHU in Canada on 3330, 7335 and 14670 kHz. A 24-hour clock format is used, so "1800 World Time" means 6:00 PM World Time. If you're in, say, North America, Eastern Time is five hours behind World Time winters and four hours behind World Time summers, so 1800 World Time would be 1:00 PM EST or 2:00 PM EDT. The easiest solution is to use a 24-hour clock set to World Time. Many radios already have these built in, and World Time clocks are also available as accessories. World Time also applies to the days of the week. So if it's 9:00 PM (21:00) Wednesday in New York during the winter, it's 0200 *Thursday* World Time.

WS. World Service.

Printed in Canada

PASSPORT's Blue Pages— 2001

Channel-by-Channel Guide to World Band Schedules

If you scan the world band airwaves, you'll discover lots more stations than those aimed your way. That's because shortwave signals are capriciously scattered by the heavens, so you can often hear stations not targeted to your area.

Blue Pages Help Identify Stations

But just dialing around can be frustrating if you don't have a "map"—PASSPORT's Blue Pages. Let's say that you've stumbled across something Asian-sounding on 7410 kHz at 2035 World Time. The Blue Pages show All India Radio beamed to Western Europe, with a hefty 500 kW of power from Bangalore. These clues suggest this is probably what you're hearing, even if you're not in Europe. You can also see that English from India will begin on that same channel in about ten minutes.

Schedules for Entire Year

Times and days of the week are in World Time; for local times in each country, see "Addresses PLUS." Some stations are shown as one hour earlier (◧) or later (◨) midyear—typically April through October. Stations may also extend their hours for holidays, emergencies or sports events.

To be as useful as possible over the months to come, PASSPORT's schedules consist not just of observed activity, but also that which we have creatively opined will take place during the forthcoming year. This predictive material is based on decades of experience and is original from us. Although inherently not as exact as real-time data, over the years it's been of tangible value to PASSPORT readers.

Guide to Blue Pages Format

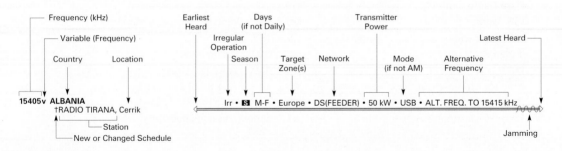

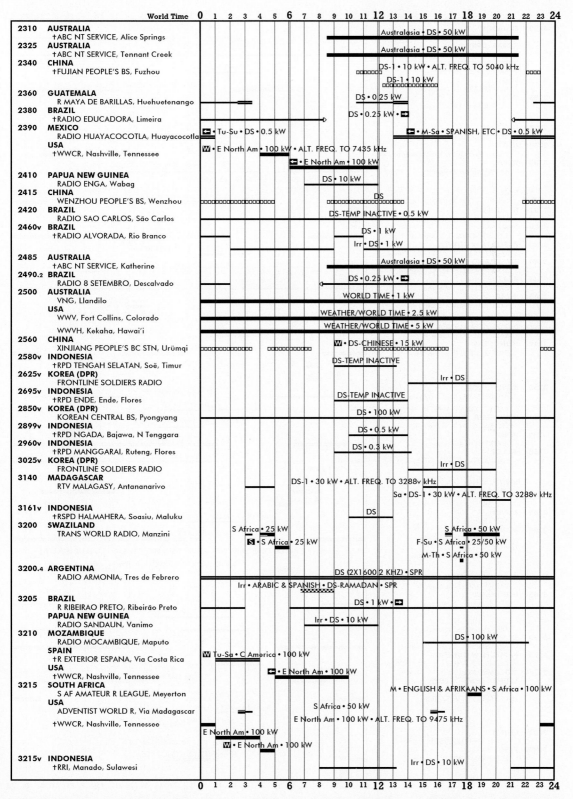

World Time	0 1 2 3 4 5 6 7 8 9 10 11 12 13 14 15 16 17 18 19 20 21 22 23 24
2310 AUSTRALIA †ABC NT SERVICE, Alice Springs	Australasia • DS • 50 kW
2325 AUSTRALIA †ABC NT SERVICE, Tennant Creek	Australasia • DS • 50 kW
2340 CHINA †FUJIAN PEOPLE'S BS, Fuzhou	DS-1 • 10 kW • ALT. FREQ. TO 5040 kHz DS-1 • 10 kW
2360 GUATEMALA R MAYA DE BARILLAS, Huehuetenango	DS • 0.25 kW
2380 BRAZIL †RADIO EDUCADORA, Limeira	DS • 0.25 kW • ▭▶
2390 MEXICO RADIO HUAYACOCOTLA, Huayacocotla	◀▭ • Tu-Su • DS • 0.5 kW ▭◀ • M-Sa • SPANISH, ETC • DS • 0.5 kW
USA †WWCR, Nashville, Tennessee	W • E North Am • 100 kW • ALT. FREQ. TO 7435 kHz ◀▶ • E North Am • 100 kW
2410 PAPUA NEW GUINEA RADIO ENGA, Wabag	DS • 10 kW
2415 CHINA WENZHOU PEOPLE'S BS, Wenzhou	DS
2420 BRAZIL RADIO SAO CARLOS, São Carlos	DS-TEMP INACTIVE • 0.5 kW
2460v BRAZIL †RADIO ALVORADA, Rio Branco	DS • 1 kW Irr • DS • 1 kW
2485 AUSTRALIA †ABC NT SERVICE, Katherine	Australasia • DS • 50 kW
2490.2 BRAZIL RADIO 8 SETEMBRO, Descalvado	DS • 0.25 kW • ▭▶
2500 AUSTRALIA VNG, Llandilo	WORLD TIME • 1 kW
USA WWV, Fort Collins, Colorado	WEATHER/WORLD TIME • 2.5 kW
WWVH, Kekaha, Hawai'i	WEATHER/WORLD TIME • 5 kW
2560 CHINA XINJIANG PEOPLE'S BC STN, Urümqi	W • DS-CHINESE • 15 kW
2580v INDONESIA †RPD TENGAH SELATAN, Soë, Timur	DS-TEMP INACTIVE
2625v KOREA (DPR) FRONTLINE SOLDIERS RADIO	Irr • DS
2695v INDONESIA †RPD ENDE, Ende, Flores	DS-TEMP INACTIVE
2850v KOREA (DPR) KOREAN CENTRAL BS, Pyongyang	DS • 100 kW
2899v INDONESIA †RPD NGADA, Bajawa, N Tenggara	DS • 0.5 kW
2960v INDONESIA †RPD MANGGARAI, Ruteng, Flores	DS • 0.3 kW
3025v KOREA (DPR) FRONTLINE SOLDIERS RADIO	Irr • DS
3140 MADAGASCAR RTV MALAGASY, Antananarivo	DS-1 • 30 kW • ALT. FREQ. TO 3288v kHz Sa • DS-1 • 30 kW • ALT. FREQ. TO 3288v kHz
3161v INDONESIA †RSPD HALMAHERA, Soasiu, Maluku	DS
3200 SWAZILAND TRANS WORLD RADIO, Manzini	S Africa • 25 kW / S Africa • 50 kW S • S Africa • 25 kW / F-Su • S Africa • 25/50 kW M-Th • S Africa • 50 kW
3200.4 ARGENTINA RADIO ARMONIA, Tres de Febrero	DS (2X1600 2 KHZ) • SPR Irr • ARABIC & SPANISH • DS-RAMADAN • SPR
3205 BRAZIL R RIBEIRAO PRETO, Ribeirão Preto	DS • 1 kW • ▭▶
PAPUA NEW GUINEA RADIO SANDAUN, Vanimo	Irr • DS • 10 kW
3210 MOZAMBIQUE RADIO MOCAMBIQUE, Maputo	DS • 100 kW
SPAIN †R EXTERIOR ESPANA, Via Costa Rica	W Tu-Sa • C America • 100 kW
USA †WWCR, Nashville, Tennessee	◀▭ • E North Am • 100 kW
3215 SOUTH AFRICA S AF AMATEUR R LEAGUE, Meyerton	M • ENGLISH & AFRIKAANS • S Africa • 100 kW
USA ADVENTIST WORLD R, Via Madagascar	S Africa • 50 kW E North Am • 100 kW • ALT. FREQ. TO 9475 kHz
†WWCR, Nashville, Tennessee	E North Am • 100 kW W • E North Am • 100 kW
3215v INDONESIA †RRI, Manado, Sulawesi	Irr • DS • 10 kW

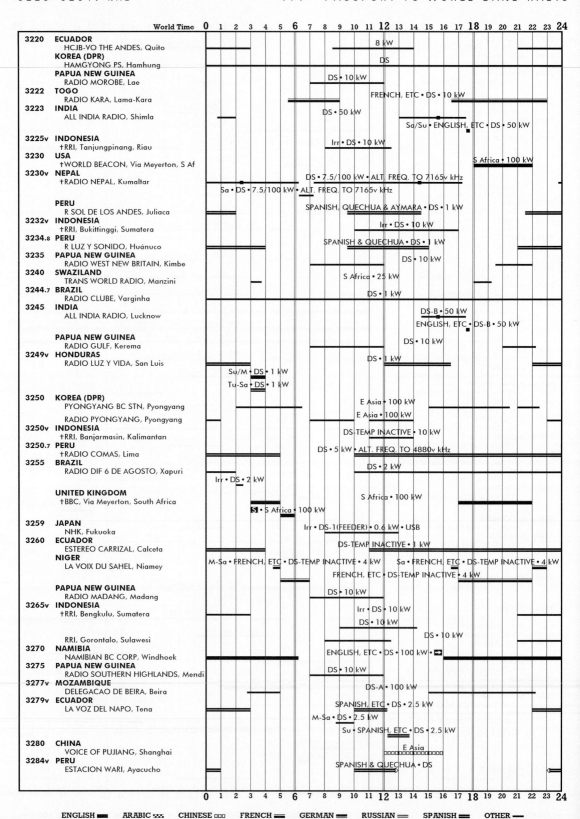

3220	ECUADOR	
	HCJB-VO THE ANDES, Quito	8 kW
	KOREA (DPR)	
	HAMGYONG PS, Hamhung	DS
	PAPUA NEW GUINEA	
	RADIO MOROBE, Lae	DS • 10 kW
3222	TOGO	
	RADIO KARA, Lama-Kara	FRENCH, ETC • DS • 10 kW
3223	INDIA	
	ALL INDIA RADIO, Shimla	DS • 50 kW
		Sa/Su • ENGLISH, ETC • DS • 50 kW
3225v	INDONESIA	
	†RRI, Tanjungpinang, Riau	Irr • DS • 10 kW
3230	USA	
	†WORLD BEACON, Via Meyerton, S Af	S Africa • 100 kW
3230v	NEPAL	
	†RADIO NEPAL, Kumaltar	DS • 7.5/100 kW • ALT. FREQ. TO 7165v kHz
		Sa • DS • 7.5/100 kW • ALT. FREQ. TO 7165v kHz
	PERU	
	R SOL DE LOS ANDES, Juliaca	SPANISH, QUECHUA & AYMARA • DS • 1 kW
3232v	INDONESIA	
	†RRI, Bukittinggi, Sumatera	Irr • DS • 10 kW
3234.8	PERU	
	R LUZ Y SONIDO, Huánuco	SPANISH & QUECHUA • DS • 1 kW
3235	PAPUA NEW GUINEA	
	RADIO WEST NEW BRITAIN, Kimbe	DS • 10 kW
3240	SWAZILAND	
	TRANS WORLD RADIO, Manzini	S Africa • 25 kW
3244.7	BRAZIL	
	RADIO CLUBE, Varginha	DS • 1 kW
3245	INDIA	
	ALL INDIA RADIO, Lucknow	DS-B • 50 kW
		ENGLISH, ETC • DS-B • 50 kW
	PAPUA NEW GUINEA	
	RADIO GULF, Kerema	DS • 10 kW
3249v	HONDURAS	
	RADIO LUZ Y VIDA, San Luis	DS • 1 kW
		Su/M • DS • 1 kW
		Tu-Sa • DS • 1 kW
3250	KOREA (DPR)	
	PYONGYANG BC STN, Pyongyang	E Asia • 100 kW
	RADIO PYONGYANG, Pyongyang	E Asia • 100 kW
3250v	INDONESIA	
	†RRI, Banjarmasin, Kalimantan	DS-TEMP INACTIVE • 10 kW
3250.7	PERU	
	†RADIO COMAS, Lima	DS • 5 kW • ALT. FREQ. TO 4880v kHz
3255	BRAZIL	
	RADIO DIF 6 DE AGOSTO, Xapuri	DS • 2 kW
		Irr • DS • 2 kW
	UNITED KINGDOM	
	†BBC, Via Meyerton, South Africa	S Africa • 100 kW
		S • S Africa • 100 kW
3259	JAPAN	
	NHK, Fukuoka	Irr • DS-1(FEEDER) • 0.6 kW • USB
3260	ECUADOR	
	ESTEREO CARRIZAL, Calceta	DS-TEMP INACTIVE • 1 kW
	NIGER	
	LA VOIX DU SAHEL, Niamey	M-Sa • FRENCH, ETC • DS-TEMP INACTIVE • 4 kW Sa • FRENCH, ETC • DS-TEMP INACTIVE • 4 kW
		FRENCH, ETC • DS-TEMP INACTIVE • 4 kW
	PAPUA NEW GUINEA	
	RADIO MADANG, Madang	DS • 10 kW
3265v	INDONESIA	
	†RRI, Bengkulu, Sumatera	Irr • DS • 10 kW
		DS • 10 kW
	RRI, Gorontalo, Sulawesi	DS • 10 kW
3270	NAMIBIA	
	NAMIBIAN BC CORP, Windhoek	ENGLISH, ETC • DS • 100 kW • ➡
3275	PAPUA NEW GUINEA	
	RADIO SOUTHERN HIGHLANDS, Mendi	DS • 10 kW
3277v	MOZAMBIQUE	
	DELEGACAO DE BEIRA, Beira	DS-A • 100 kW
3279v	ECUADOR	
	LA VOZ DEL NAPO, Tena	SPANISH, ETC • DS • 2.5 kW
		M-Sa • DS • 2.5 kW
		Su • SPANISH, ETC • DS • 2.5 kW
3280	CHINA	
	VOICE OF PUJIANG, Shanghai	E Asia
3284v	PERU	
	ESTACION WARI, Ayacucho	SPANISH & QUECHUA • DS

ENGLISH ▬   ARABIC ░░░   CHINESE ▫▫▫   FRENCH ══   GERMAN ▬   RUSSIAN ═   SPANISH ▬   OTHER ▬

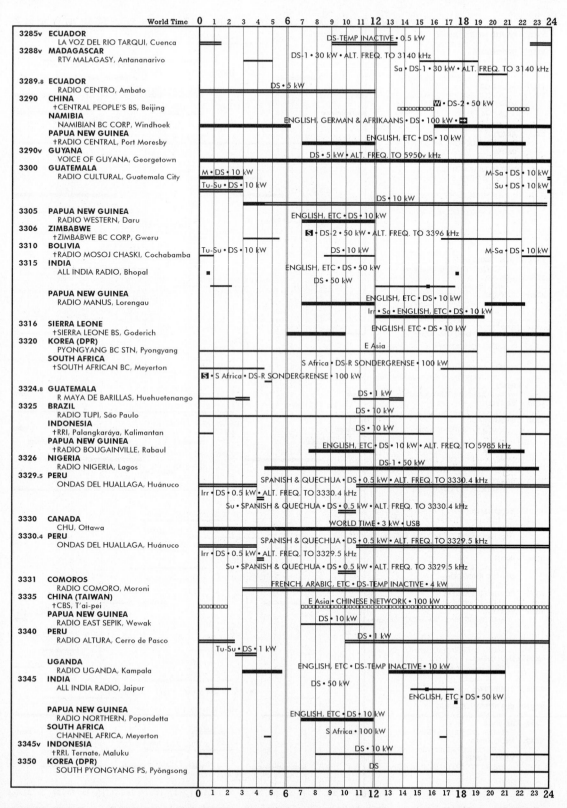

World Time 0 1 2 3 4 5 6 7 8 9 10 11 12 13 14 15 16 17 18 19 20 21 22 23 24

3285v ECUADOR
LA VOZ DEL RIO TARQUI, Cuenca — DS-TEMP INACTIVE • 0.5 kW

3288v MADAGASCAR
RTV MALAGASY, Antananarivo — DS-1 • 30 kW • ALT. FREQ. TO 3140 kHz
Sa • DS-1 • 30 kW • ALT. FREQ. TO 3140 kHz

3289.8 ECUADOR
RADIO CENTRO, Ambato — DS • 5 kW

3290 CHINA
†CENTRAL PEOPLE'S BS, Beijing — W • DS-2 • 50 kW

NAMIBIA
NAMIBIAN BC CORP, Windhoek — ENGLISH, GERMAN & AFRIKAANS • DS 100 kW • 🔲

PAPUA NEW GUINEA
†RADIO CENTRAL, Port Moresby — ENGLISH, ETC • DS • 10 kW

3290v GUYANA
VOICE OF GUYANA, Georgetown — DS • 5 kW • ALT. FREQ. TO 5950v kHz

3300 GUATEMALA
RADIO CULTURAL, Guatemala City — M • DS • 10 kW   M-Sa • DS • 10 kW
Tu-Su • DS • 10 kW   Su • DS • 10 kW
DS • 10 kW

3305 PAPUA NEW GUINEA
RADIO WESTERN, Daru — ENGLISH, ETC • DS • 10 kW

3306 ZIMBABWE
†ZIMBABWE BC CORP, Gweru — S • DS-2 • 50 kW • ALT. FREQ. TO 3396 kHz

3310 BOLIVIA
†RADIO MOSOJ CHASKI, Cochabamba — Tu-Su • DS • 10 kW   DS • 10 kW   M-Sa • DS • 10 kW

3315 INDIA
ALL INDIA RADIO, Bhopal — ENGLISH, ETC • DS • 50 kW
DS • 50 kW

PAPUA NEW GUINEA
RADIO MANUS, Lorengau — ENGLISH, ETC • DS • 10 kW
Irr • Sa • ENGLISH, ETC • DS • 10 kW

3316 SIERRA LEONE
†SIERRA LEONE BS, Goderich — ENGLISH, ETC • DS • 10 kW

3320 KOREA (DPR)
PYONGYANG BC STN, Pyongyang — E Asia

SOUTH AFRICA
†SOUTH AFRICAN BC, Meyerton — S Africa • DS-R SONDERGRENSE • 100 kW
S • S Africa • DS-R SONDERGRENSE • 100 kW

3324.8 GUATEMALA
R MAYA DE BARILLAS, Huehuetenango — DS • 1 kW

3325 BRAZIL
RADIO TUPI, São Paulo — DS • 10 kW

INDONESIA
†RRI, Palangkaráya, Kalimantan — DS • 10 kW

PAPUA NEW GUINEA
†RADIO BOUGAINVILLE, Rabaul — ENGLISH, ETC • DS • 10 kW • ALT. FREQ. TO 5985 kHz

3326 NIGERIA
RADIO NIGERIA, Lagos — DS-1 • 50 kW

3329.5 PERU
ONDAS DEL HUALLAGA, Huánuco — SPANISH & QUECHUA • DS • 0.5 kW • ALT. FREQ. TO 3330.4 kHz
Irr • DS • 0.5 kW • ALT. FREQ. TO 3330.4 kHz
Su • SPANISH & QUECHUA • DS • 0.5 kW • ALT. FREQ. TO 3330.4 kHz

3330 CANADA
CHU, Ottawa — WORLD TIME • 3 kW • USB

3330.4 PERU
ONDAS DEL HUALLAGA, Huánuco — SPANISH & QUECHUA • DS • 0.5 kW • ALT. FREQ. TO 3329.5 kHz
Irr • DS • 0.5 kW • ALT. FREQ. TO 3329.5 kHz
Su • SPANISH & QUECHUA • DS • 0.5 kW • ALT. FREQ. TO 3329.5 kHz

3331 COMOROS
RADIO COMORO, Moroni — FRENCH, ARABIC, ETC • DS-TEMP INACTIVE • 4 kW

3335 CHINA (TAIWAN)
†CBS, T'ai-pei — E Asia • CHINESE NETWORK • 100 kW

PAPUA NEW GUINEA
RADIO EAST SEPIK, Wewak — DS • 10 kW

3340 PERU
RADIO ALTURA, Cerro de Pasco — DS • 1 kW
Tu-Su • DS • 1 kW

UGANDA
RADIO UGANDA, Kampala — ENGLISH, ETC • DS-TEMP INACTIVE • 10 kW

3345 INDIA
ALL INDIA RADIO, Jaipur — DS • 50 kW
ENGLISH, ETC • DS • 50 kW

PAPUA NEW GUINEA
RADIO NORTHERN, Popondetta — ENGLISH, ETC • DS • 10 kW

SOUTH AFRICA
CHANNEL AFRICA, Meyerton — S Africa • 100 kW

3345v INDONESIA
†RRI, Ternate, Maluku — DS • 10 kW

3350 KOREA (DPR)
SOUTH PYONGYANG PS, Pyŏngsong — DS

0 1 2 3 4 5 6 7 8 9 10 11 12 13 14 15 16 17 18 19 20 21 22 23 24

SEASONAL S OR W   1-HR TIMESHIFT MIDYEAR 🔲 OR 🔲   JAMMING / OR /\   EARLIEST HEARD ◁   LATEST HEARD ▷   NEW FOR 2001 †

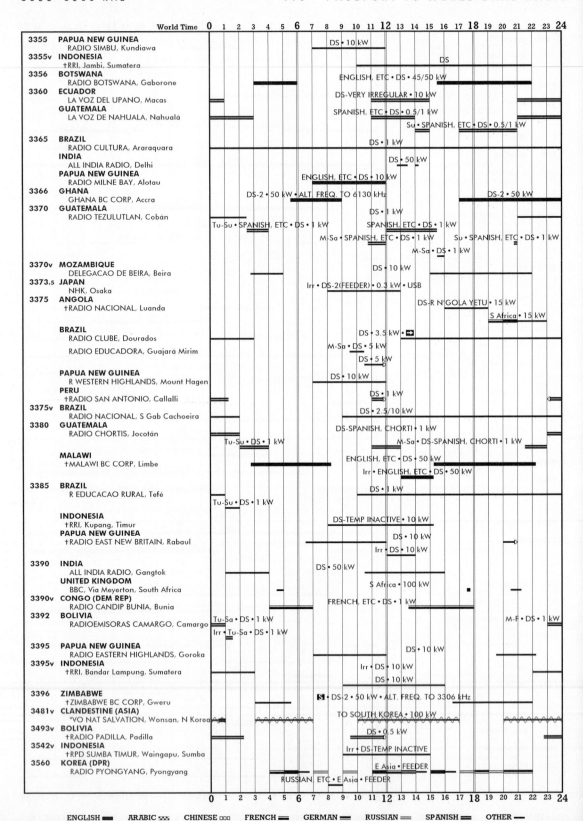

| World Time | 0 | 1 | 2 | 3 | 4 | 5 | 6 | 7 | 8 | 9 | 10 | 11 | 12 | 13 | 14 | 15 | 16 | 17 | 18 | 19 | 20 | 21 | 22 | 23 | 24 |

3355 PAPUA NEW GUINEA
RADIO SIMBU, Kundiawa — DS • 10 kW

3355v INDONESIA
†RRI, Jambi, Sumatera — DS

3356 BOTSWANA
RADIO BOTSWANA, Gaborone — ENGLISH, ETC • DS • 45/50 kW

3360 ECUADOR
LA VOZ DEL UPANO, Macas — DS-VERY IRREGULAR • 10 kW

GUATEMALA
LA VOZ DE NAHUALA, Nahualá — SPANISH, ETC • DS • 0.5/1 kW
Su • SPANISH, ETC • DS • 0.5/1 kW

3365 BRAZIL
RADIO CULTURA, Araraquara — DS • 1 kW

INDIA
ALL INDIA RADIO, Delhi — DS • 50 kW

PAPUA NEW GUINEA
RADIO MILNE BAY, Alotau — ENGLISH, ETC • DS • 10 kW

3366 GHANA
GHANA BC CORP, Accra — DS-2 • 50 kW • ALT. FREQ. TO 6130 kHz   DS-2 • 50 kW

3370 GUATEMALA
RADIO TEZULUTLAN, Cobán — DS • 1 kW
Tu-Su • SPANISH, ETC • DS • 1 kW   SPANISH, ETC • DS • 1 kW
M-Sa • SPANISH, ETC • DS • 1 kW   Su • SPANISH, ETC • DS • 1 kW
M-Sa • DS • 1 kW

3370v MOZAMBIQUE
DELEGACAO DE BEIRA, Beira — DS • 10 kW

3373.5 JAPAN
NHK, Osaka — Irr • DS-2(FEEDER) • 0.3 kW • USB

3375 ANGOLA
†RADIO NACIONAL, Luanda — DS-R N'GOLA YETU • 15 kW
S Africa • 15 kW

BRAZIL
RADIO CLUBE, Dourados — DS • 3.5 kW • ▶

RADIO EDUCADORA, Guajará Mirim — M-Sa • DS • 5 kW
DS • 5 kW

PAPUA NEW GUINEA
R WESTERN HIGHLANDS, Mount Hagen — DS • 10 kW

PERU
†RADIO SAN ANTONIO, Callalli — DS • 1 kW

3375v BRAZIL
RADIO NACIONAL, S Gab Cachoeira — DS • 2.5/10 kW

3380 GUATEMALA
RADIO CHORTIS, Jocotán — DS-SPANISH, CHORTI • 1 kW
Tu-Su • DS • 1 kW   M-Sa • DS-SPANISH, CHORTI • 1 kW

MALAWI
†MALAWI BC CORP, Limbe — ENGLISH, ETC • DS • 50 kW
Irr • ENGLISH, ETC • DS • 50 kW

3385 BRAZIL
R EDUCACAO RURAL, Tefé — DS • 1 kW
Tu-Su • DS • 1 kW

INDONESIA
†RRI, Kupang, Timur — DS-TEMP INACTIVE • 10 kW

PAPUA NEW GUINEA
†RADIO EAST NEW BRITAIN, Rabaul — DS • 10 kW
Irr • DS • 10 kW

3390 INDIA
ALL INDIA RADIO, Gangtok — DS • 50 kW

UNITED KINGDOM
BBC, Via Meyerton, South Africa — S Africa • 100 kW

3390v CONGO (DEM REP)
RADIO CANDIP BUNIA, Bunia — FRENCH, ETC • DS • 1 kW

3392 BOLIVIA
RADIOEMISORAS CAMARGO, Camargo — Tu-Sa • DS • 1 kW   M-F • DS • 1 kW
Irr • Tu-Sa • DS • 1 kW

3395 PAPUA NEW GUINEA
RADIO EASTERN HIGHLANDS, Goroka — DS • 10 kW

3395v INDONESIA
†RRI, Bandar Lampung, Sumatera — Irr • DS • 10 kW
DS • 10 kW

3396 ZIMBABWE
†ZIMBABWE BC CORP, Gweru — 🅂 • DS-2 • 50 kW • ALT. FREQ. TO 3306 kHz

3481v CLANDESTINE (ASIA)
"VO NAT SALVATION, Wonsan, N Korea — TO SOUTH KOREA • 100 kW

3493v BOLIVIA
†RADIO PADILLA, Padilla — DS • 0.5 kW

3542v INDONESIA
†RPD SUMBA TIMUR, Waingapu, Sumba — Irr • DS-TEMP INACTIVE

3560 KOREA (DPR)
RADIO PYONGYANG, Pyongyang — E Asia • FEEDER
RUSSIAN, ETC • E Asia • FEEDER

| | 0 | 1 | 2 | 3 | 4 | 5 | 6 | 7 | 8 | 9 | 10 | 11 | 12 | 13 | 14 | 15 | 16 | 17 | 18 | 19 | 20 | 21 | 22 | 23 | 24 |

ENGLISH ▬▬   ARABIC ⌇⌇⌇   CHINESE □□□   FRENCH ═══   GERMAN ▬▬   RUSSIAN ══   SPANISH ▬▬   OTHER ▬▬

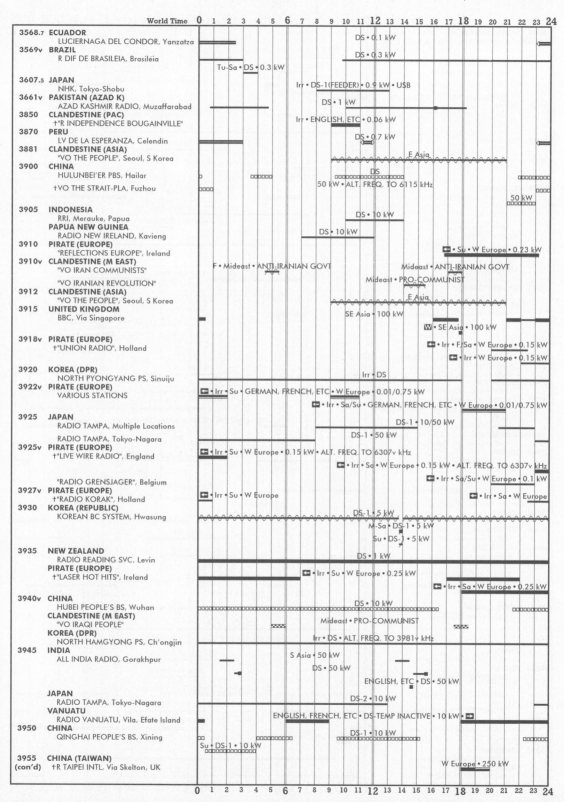

World Time	0 1 2 3 4 5 6 7 8 9 10 11 12 13 14 15 16 17 18 19 20 21 22 23 24
3568.7 **ECUADOR** LUCIERNAGA DEL CONDOR, Yanzatza	DS • 0.1 kW
3569v **BRAZIL** R DIF DE BRASILEIA, Brasiléia	DS • 0.3 kW / Tu-Sa • DS • 0.3 kW
3607.5 **JAPAN** NHK, Tokyo-Shobu	Irr • DS-1(FEEDER) • 0.9 kW • USB
3661v **PAKISTAN (AZAD K)** AZAD KASHMIR RADIO, Muzaffarabad	DS • 1 kW
3850 **CLANDESTINE (PAC)** †"R INDEPENDENCE BOUGAINVILLE"	Irr • ENGLISH, ETC • 0.06 kW
3870 **PERU** LV DE LA ESPERANZA, Celendin	DS • 0.7 kW
3881 **CLANDESTINE (ASIA)** "VO THE PEOPLE", Seoul, S Korea	E Asia
3900 **CHINA** HULUNBEI'ER PBS, Hailar	DS
†VO THE STRAIT-PLA, Fuzhou	50 kW • ALT. FREQ. TO 6115 kHz / 50 kW
3905 **INDONESIA** RRI, Merauke, Papua	DS • 10 kW
PAPUA NEW GUINEA RADIO NEW IRELAND, Kavieng	DS • 10 kW
3910 **PIRATE (EUROPE)** "REFLECTIONS EUROPE", Ireland	Su • W Europe • 0.23 kW
3910v **CLANDESTINE (M EAST)** "VO IRAN COMMUNISTS"	F • Mideast • ANTI-IRANIAN GOVT / Mideast • ANTI-IRANIAN GOVT
"VO IRANIAN REVOLUTION"	Mideast • PRO-COMMUNIST
3912 **CLANDESTINE (ASIA)** "VO THE PEOPLE", Seoul, S Korea	E Asia
3915 **UNITED KINGDOM** BBC, Via Singapore	SE Asia • 100 kW / W • SE Asia • 100 kW
3918v **PIRATE (EUROPE)** †"UNION RADIO", Holland	Irr • F/Sa • W Europe • 0.15 kW / Irr • W Europe • 0.15 kW
3920 **KOREA (DPR)** NORTH PYONGYANG PS, Sinuiju	Irr • DS
3922v **PIRATE (EUROPE)** VARIOUS STATIONS	Irr • Su • GERMAN, FRENCH, ETC • W Europe • 0.01/0.75 kW / Irr • Sa/Su • GERMAN, FRENCH, ETC • W Europe • 0.01/0.75 kW
3925 **JAPAN** RADIO TAMPA, Multiple Locations	DS-1 • 10/50 kW
RADIO TAMPA, Tokyo-Nagara	DS-1 • 50 kW
3925v **PIRATE (EUROPE)** †"LIVE WIRE RADIO", England	Irr • Su • W Europe • 0.15 kW • ALT. FREQ. TO 6307v kHz / Irr • Sa • W Europe • 0.15 kW • ALT. FREQ. TO 6307v kHz / Irr • Sa/Su • W Europe • 0.1 kW
"RADIO GRENSJAGER", Belgium	
3927v **PIRATE (EUROPE)** †"RADIO KORAK", Holland	Irr • Su • W Europe / Irr • Sa • W Europe
3930 **KOREA (REPUBLIC)** KOREAN BC SYSTEM, Hwasung	DS-1 • 5 kW / M-Sa • DS-1 • 5 kW / Su • DS-1 • 5 kW
3935 **NEW ZEALAND** RADIO READING SVC, Levin	DS • 1 kW
PIRATE (EUROPE) †"LASER HOT HITS", Ireland	Irr • Su • W Europe • 0.25 kW / Irr • Sa • W Europe • 0.25 kW
3940v **CHINA** HUBEI PEOPLE'S BS, Wuhan	DS • 10 kW
CLANDESTINE (M EAST) "VO IRAQI PEOPLE"	Mideast • PRO-COMMUNIST
KOREA (DPR) NORTH HAMGYONG PS, Ch'ongjin	Irr • DS • ALT. FREQ. TO 3981v kHz
3945 **INDIA** ALL INDIA RADIO, Gorakhpur	S Asia • 50 kW / DS • 50 kW / ENGLISH, ETC • DS • 50 kW
JAPAN RADIO TAMPA, Tokyo-Nagara	DS-2 • 10 kW
VANUATU RADIO VANUATU, Vila, Efate Island	ENGLISH, FRENCH, ETC • DS-TEMP INACTIVE • 10 kW
3950 **CHINA** QINGHAI PEOPLE'S BS, Xining	DS-1 • 10 kW / Su • DS-1 • 10 kW
3955 **CHINA (TAIWAN)** (con'd) †R TAIPEI INTL, Via Skelton, UK	W Europe • 250 kW

| | 0 1 2 3 4 5 6 7 8 9 10 11 12 13 14 15 16 17 18 19 20 21 22 23 24 |

SEASONAL 🅢 OR 🅦   1-HR TIMESHIFT MIDYEAR ⬅ OR ➡   JAMMING / OR ∧   EARLIEST HEARD ◁   LATEST HEARD ▷   NEW FOR 2001 †

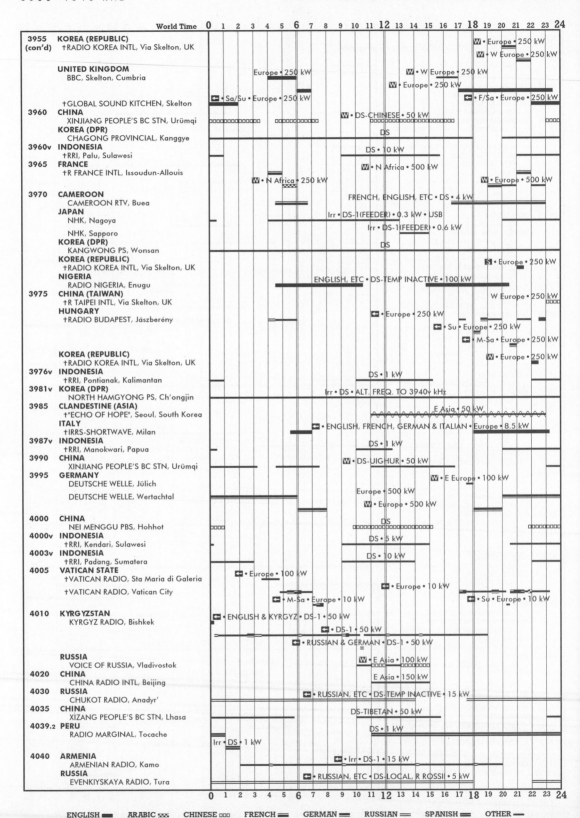

| | | ENGLISH ▬ | ARABIC ∷∷ | CHINESE ▫▫▫ | FRENCH ▭▭ | GERMAN ▬ | RUSSIAN ═ | SPANISH ▬ | OTHER ▬ |

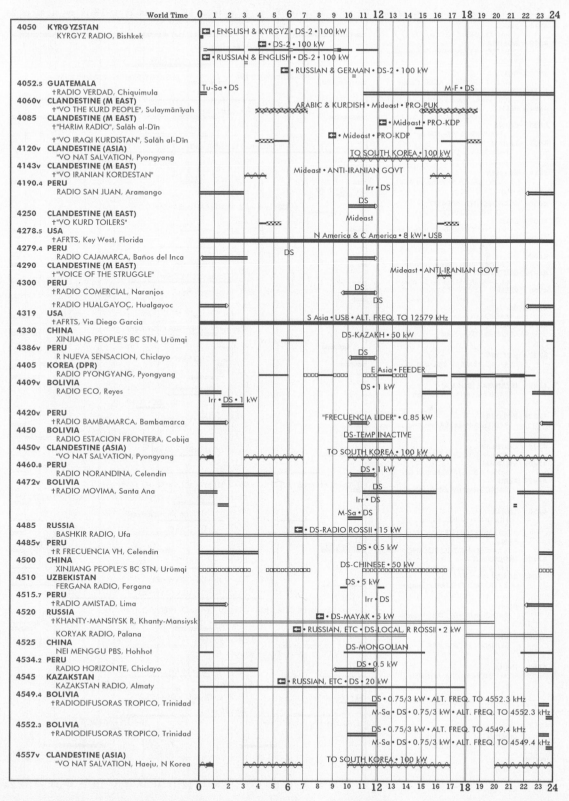

World Time	0 1 2 3 4 5 6 7 8 9 10 11 12 13 14 15 16 17 18 19 20 21 22 23 24

4050 KYRGYZSTAN
KYRGYZ RADIO, Bishkek
· ENGLISH & KYRGYZ · DS-2 · 100 kW
· DS-2 · 100 kW
· RUSSIAN & ENGLISH · DS-2 · 100 kW
· RUSSIAN & GERMAN · DS-2 · 100 kW

4052.5 GUATEMALA
†RADIO VERDAD, Chiquimula
Tu-Sa · DS   M-F · DS

4060v CLANDESTINE (M EAST)
†"VO THE KURD PEOPLE", Sulaymānīyah
ARABIC & KURDISH · Mideast · PRO-PUK

4085 CLANDESTINE (M EAST)
†"HARIM RADIO", Salāh al-Dīn
· Mideast · PRO-KDP

†"VO IRAQI KURDISTAN", Salāh al-Dīn
· Mideast · PRO-KDP

4120v CLANDESTINE (ASIA)
"VO NAT SALVATION, Pyongyang
TO SOUTH KOREA · 100 kW

4143v CLANDESTINE (M EAST)
†"VO IRANIAN KORDESTAN"
Mideast · ANTI-IRANIAN GOVT

4190.4 PERU
RADIO SAN JUAN, Aramango
Irr · DS

4250 CLANDESTINE (M EAST)
†"VO KURD TOILERS"
DS
Mideast

4278.5 USA
†AFRTS, Key West, Florida
N America & C America · 8 kW · USB

4279.4 PERU
RADIO CAJAMARCA, Baños del Inca
DS

4290 CLANDESTINE (M EAST)
†"VOICE OF THE STRUGGLE"
Mideast · ANTI-IRANIAN GOVT

4300 PERU
†RADIO COMERCIAL, Naranjos
DS

†RADIO HUALGAYOC, Hualgayoc
DS

4319 USA
†AFRTS, Via Diego Garcia
S Asia · USB · ALT. FREQ. TO 12579 kHz

4330 CHINA
XINJIANG PEOPLE'S BC STN, Urümqi
DS-KAZAKH · 50 kW

4386v PERU
R NUEVA SENSACION, Chiclayo
DS

4405 KOREA (DPR)
RADIO PYONGYANG, Pyongyang
E Asia · FEEDER

4409v BOLIVIA
RADIO ECO, Reyes
DS · 1 kW
Irr · DS · 1 kW

4420v PERU
†RADIO BAMBAMARCA, Bambamarca
"FRECUENCIA LIDER" · 0.85 kW

4450 BOLIVIA
RADIO ESTACION FRONTERA, Cobija
DS-TEMP INACTIVE

4450v CLANDESTINE (ASIA)
"VO NAT SALVATION, Pyongyang
TO SOUTH KOREA · 100 kW

4460.8 PERU
RADIO NORANDINA, Celendin
DS · 1 kW

4472v BOLIVIA
†RADIO MOVIMA, Santa Ana
DS
Irr · DS
M-Sa · DS

4485 RUSSIA
BASHKIR RADIO, Ufa
· DS-RADIO ROSSII · 15 kW

4485v PERU
†R FRECUENCIA VH, Celendin
DS · 0.5 kW

4500 CHINA
XINJIANG PEOPLE'S BC STN, Urümqi
DS-CHINESE · 50 kW

4510 UZBEKISTAN
FERGANA RADIO, Fergana
DS · 5 kW

4515.7 PERU
†RADIO AMISTAD, Lima
Irr · DS

4520 RUSSIA
†KHANTY-MANSIYSK R, Khanty-Mansiysk
· DS-MAYAK · 5 kW

KORYAK RADIO, Palana
· RUSSIAN, ETC · DS-LOCAL, R ROSSII · 2 kW

4525 CHINA
NEI MENGGU PBS, Hohhot
DS-MONGOLIAN

4534.2 PERU
RADIO HORIZONTE, Chiclayo
DS · 0.5 kW

4545 KAZAKSTAN
KAZAKSTAN RADIO, Almaty
· RUSSIAN, ETC · DS · 20 kW

4549.4 BOLIVIA
†RADIODIFUSORAS TROPICO, Trinidad
DS · 0.75/3 kW · ALT. FREQ. TO 4552.3 kHz
M-Sa · DS · 0.75/3 kW · ALT. FREQ. TO 4552.3 kHz

4552.3 BOLIVIA
†RADIODIFUSORAS TROPICO, Trinidad
DS · 0.75/3 kW · ALT. FREQ. TO 4549.4 kHz
M-Sa · DS · 0.75/3 kW · ALT. FREQ. TO 4549.4 kHz

4557v CLANDESTINE (ASIA)
"VO NAT SALVATION, Haeju, N Korea
TO SOUTH KOREA · 100 kW

0 1 2 3 4 5 6 7 8 9 10 11 12 13 14 15 16 17 18 19 20 21 22 23 24

SEASONAL ⑤ OR Ⓦ   1-HR TIMESHIFT MIDYEAR ◨ OR ◧   JAMMING / OR ∧   EARLIEST HEARD ◁   LATEST HEARD ▷   NEW FOR 2001 †

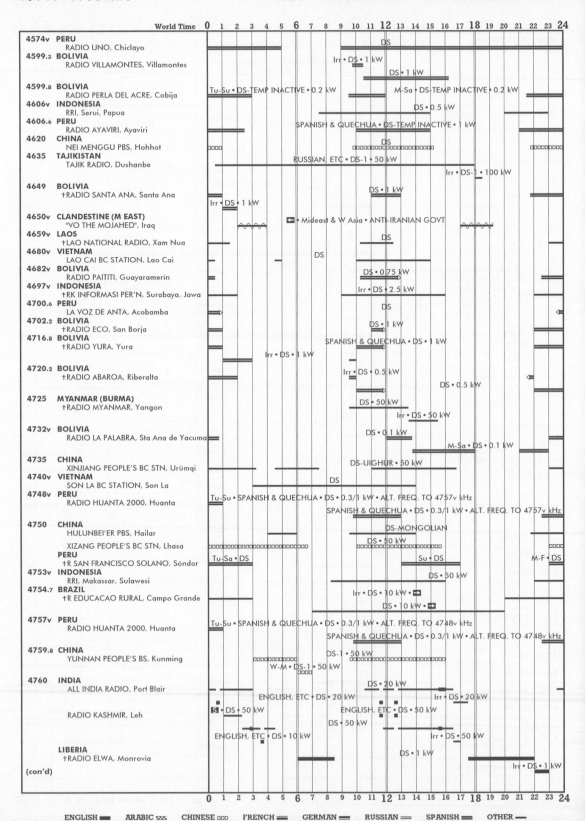

World Time 0 1 2 3 4 5 6 7 8 9 10 11 12 13 14 15 16 17 18 19 20 21 22 23 24

Freq	Country / Station	Details
4574v	**PERU** RADIO UNO, Chiclayo	DS
4599.3	**BOLIVIA** RADIO VILLAMONTES, Villamontes	Irr • DS • 1 kW / DS • 1 kW
4599.8	**BOLIVIA** RADIO PERLA DEL ACRE, Cobija	Tu-Su • DS-TEMP INACTIVE • 0.2 kW M-Sa • DS-TEMP INACTIVE • 0.2 kW
4606v	**INDONESIA** RRI, Serui, Papua	DS • 0.5 kW
4606.6	**PERU** RADIO AYAVIRI, Ayaviri	SPANISH & QUECHUA • DS-TEMP INACTIVE • 1 kW
4620	**CHINA** NEI MENGGU PBS, Hohhot	DS
4635	**TAJIKISTAN** TAJIK RADIO, Dushanbe	RUSSIAN, ETC • DS-1 • 50 kW Irr • DS-1 • 100 kW
4649	**BOLIVIA** †RADIO SANTA ANA, Santa Ana	DS • 1 kW Irr • DS • 1 kW
4650v	**CLANDESTINE (M EAST)** "VO THE MOJAHED", Iraq	▷• Mideast & W Asia • ANTI-IRANIAN GOVT
4659v	**LAOS** †LAO NATIONAL RADIO, Xam Nua	DS
4680v	**VIETNAM** LAO CAI BC STATION, Lao Cai	DS
4682v	**BOLIVIA** RADIO PAITITI, Guayaramerin	DS • 0.75 kW
4697v	**INDONESIA** †RK INFORMASI PER'N, Surabaya, Jawa	Irr • DS • 2.5 kW
4700.6	**PERU** LA VOZ DE ANTA, Acobamba	DS
4702.2	**BOLIVIA** †RADIO ECO, San Borja	DS • 1 kW
4716.8	**BOLIVIA** †RADIO YURA, Yura	SPANISH & QUECHUA • DS • 1 kW Irr • DS • 1 kW
4720.2	**BOLIVIA** †RADIO ABAROA, Riberalta	Irr • DS • 0.5 kW DS • 0.5 kW
4725	**MYANMAR (BURMA)** †RADIO MYANMAR, Yangon	DS • 50 kW Irr • DS • 50 kW
4732v	**BOLIVIA** RADIO LA PALABRA, Sta Ana de Yacuma	DS • 0.1 kW M-Sa • DS • 0.1 kW
4735	**CHINA** XINJIANG PEOPLE'S BC STN, Urümqi	DS-UIGHUR • 50 kW
4740v	**VIETNAM** SON LA BC STATION, Son La	DS
4748v	**PERU** RADIO HUANTA 2000, Huanta	Tu-Su • SPANISH & QUECHUA • DS 0.3/1 kW • ALT. FREQ. TO 4757v kHz SPANISH & QUECHUA • DS • 0.3/1 kW • ALT. FREQ. TO 4757v kHz
4750	**CHINA** HULUNBEI'ER PBS, Hailar	DS-MONGOLIAN
	XIZANG PEOPLE'S BC STN, Lhasa	DS • 50 kW
	PERU †R SAN FRANCISCO SOLANO, Sóndor	Tu-Sa • DS Su • DS M-F • DS
4753v	**INDONESIA** RRI, Makassar, Sulawesi	DS • 50 kW
4754.7	**BRAZIL** †R EDUCACAO RURAL, Campo Grande	Irr • DS • 10 kW • ▷ DS • 10 kW • ▷
4757v	**PERU** RADIO HUANTA 2000, Huanta	Tu-Su • SPANISH & QUECHUA • DS • 0.3/1 kW • ALT. FREQ. TO 4748v kHz SPANISH & QUECHUA • DS • 0.3/1 kW • ALT. FREQ. TO 4748v kHz
4759.8	**CHINA** YUNNAN PEOPLE'S BS, Kunming	DS-1 • 50 kW W-M • DS-1 • 50 kW
4760	**INDIA** ALL INDIA RADIO, Port Blair	DS • 20 kW ENGLISH, ETC • DS • 20 kW Irr • DS • 20 kW
	RADIO KASHMIR, Leh	DS • 50 kW ENGLISH, ETC • DS • 50 kW DS • 50 kW ENGLISH, ETC • DS • 10 kW Irr • DS • 50 kW
	LIBERIA †RADIO ELWA, Monrovia	DS • 1 kW Irr • DS • 1 kW
(con'd)		

World Time 0 1 2 3 4 5 6 7 8 9 10 11 12 13 14 15 16 17 18 19 20 21 22 23 24

ENGLISH ▬▬   ARABIC ∿∿∿   CHINESE □□□   FRENCH ▬▬   GERMAN ▬▬   RUSSIAN ══   SPANISH ══   OTHER ▬

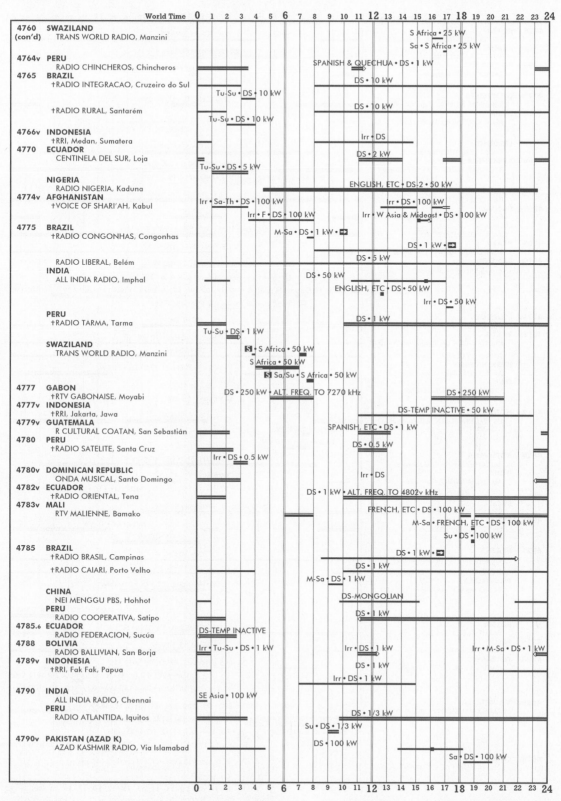

World Time

Freq	Country / Station	Schedule
4760 (con'd)	**SWAZILAND** — TRANS WORLD RADIO, Manzini	S Africa • 25 kW; Sa • S Africa • 25 kW
4764v	**PERU** — RADIO CHINCHEROS, Chincheros	SPANISH & QUECHUA • DS • 1 kW
4765	**BRAZIL** — †RADIO INTEGRACAO, Cruzeiro do Sul	DS • 10 kW; Tu-Su • DS • 10 kW
	†RADIO RURAL, Santarém	DS • 10 kW; Tu-Su • DS • 10 kW
4766v	**INDONESIA** — †RRI, Medan, Sumatera	Irr • DS
4770	**ECUADOR** — CENTINELA DEL SUR, Loja	DS • 2 kW; Tu-Su • DS • 5 kW
	NIGERIA — RADIO NIGERIA, Kaduna	ENGLISH, ETC • DS • 2 • 50 kW
4774v	**AFGHANISTAN** — †VOICE OF SHARI'AH, Kabul	Irr • Sa-Th • DS • 100 kW; Irr • DS • 100 kW; Irr • F • DS • 100 kW; Irr • W Asia & Mideast • DS • 100 kW
4775	**BRAZIL** — †RADIO CONGONHAS, Congonhas	M-Sa • DS • 1 kW • ➡; DS • 1 kW • ➡
	RADIO LIBERAL, Belém	DS • 5 kW
	INDIA — ALL INDIA RADIO, Imphal	DS • 50 kW; ENGLISH, ETC • DS • 50 kW; Irr • DS • 50 kW
	PERU — †RADIO TARMA, Tarma	DS • 1 kW; Tu-Su • DS • 1 kW
	SWAZILAND — TRANS WORLD RADIO, Manzini	🅂 • S Africa • 50 kW; S Africa • 50 kW; 🅂 • Sa/Su • S Africa • 50 kW
4777	**GABON** — †RTV GABONAISE, Moyabi	DS • 250 kW • ALT. FREQ. TO 7270 kHz; DS • 250 kW
4777v	**INDONESIA** — †RRI, Jakarta, Jawa	DS-TEMP INACTIVE • 50 kW
4779v	**GUATEMALA** — R CULTURAL COATAN, San Sebastián	SPANISH, ETC • DS • 1 kW
4780	**PERU** — †RADIO SATELITE, Santa Cruz	DS • 0.5 kW; Irr • DS • 0.5 kW
4780v	**DOMINICAN REPUBLIC** — ONDA MUSICAL, Santo Domingo	Irr • DS
4782v	**ECUADOR** — †RADIO ORIENTAL, Tena	DS • 1 kW • ALT. FREQ. TO 4802v kHz
4783v	**MALI** — RTV MALIENNE, Bamako	FRENCH, ETC • DS • 100 kW; M-Sa • FRENCH, ETC • DS • 100 kW; Su • DS • 100 kW
4785	**BRAZIL** — †RADIO BRASIL, Campinas	DS • 1 kW • ➡; DS • 1 kW
	†RADIO CAIARI, Porto Velho	M-Sa • DS • 1 kW
	CHINA — NEI MENGGU PBS, Hohhot	DS-MONGOLIAN
	PERU — RADIO COOPERATIVA, Satipo	DS • 1 kW
4785.6	**ECUADOR** — RADIO FEDERACION, Sucúa	DS-TEMP INACTIVE
4788	**BOLIVIA** — RADIO BALLIVIAN, San Borja	Irr • Tu-Su • DS • 1 kW; Irr • DS • 1 kW; Irr • M-Sa • DS • 1 kW
4789v	**INDONESIA** — †RRI, Fak Fak, Papua	DS • 1 kW; Irr • DS • 1 kW
4790	**INDIA** — ALL INDIA RADIO, Chennai	SE Asia • 100 kW
	PERU — RADIO ATLANTIDA, Iquitos	DS • 1/3 kW; Su • DS • 1/3 kW
4790v	**PAKISTAN (AZAD K)** — AZAD KASHMIR RADIO, Via Islamabad	DS • 100 kW; Sa • DS • 100 kW

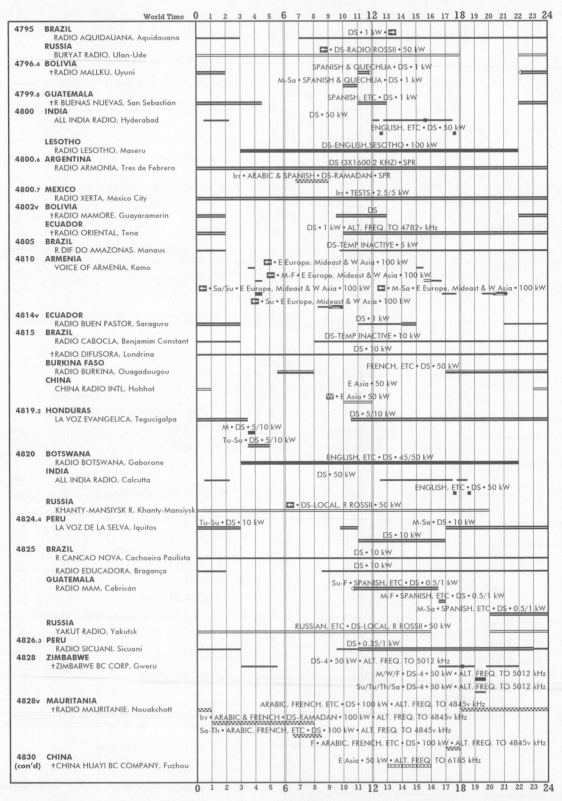

| | World Time | 0 1 2 3 4 5 6 7 8 9 10 11 12 13 14 15 16 17 18 19 20 21 22 23 24 |

4795 BRAZIL RADIO AQUIDAUANA, Aquidauana — DS • 1 kW • ▯▷

RUSSIA BURYAT RADIO, Ulan-Ude — ◁▯ • DS-RADIO ROSSII • 50 kW

4796.4 BOLIVIA †RADIO MALLKU, Uyuni — SPANISH & QUECHUA • DS • 1 kW / M-Sa • SPANISH & QUECHUA • DS • 1 kW

4799.8 GUATEMALA †R BUENAS NUEVAS, San Sebastián — SPANISH, ETC • DS • 1 kW

4800 INDIA ALL INDIA RADIO, Hyderabad — DS • 50 kW / ENGLISH, ETC • DS • 50 kW

LESOTHO RADIO LESOTHO, Maseru — DS-ENGLISH,SESOTHO • 100 kW

4800.6 ARGENTINA RADIO ARMONIA, Tres de Febrero — DS (3X1600 2 KHZ) • SPR / Irr • ARABIC & SPANISH • DS-RAMADAN • SPR

4800.7 MEXICO RADIO XERTA, México City — Irr • TESTS • 2.5/5 kW

4802v BOLIVIA †RADIO MAMORE, Guayaramerin — DS

ECUADOR †RADIO ORIENTAL, Tena — DS • 1 kW • ALT. FREQ. TO 4782v kHz

4805 BRAZIL R DIF DO AMAZONAS, Manaus — DS-TEMP INACTIVE • 5 kW

4810 ARMENIA VOICE OF ARMENIA, Kamo — ◁▯ • E Europe, Mideast & W Asia • 100 kW / ◁▯ • M-F • E Europe, Mideast & W Asia • 100 kW / ▯ • Sa/Su • E Europe, Mideast & W Asia • 100 kW / ◁▯ • M-Sa • E Europe, Mideast & W Asia • 100 kW / ◁▯ • Su • E Europe, Mideast & W Asia • 100 kW

4814v ECUADOR RADIO BUEN PASTOR, Saraguro — DS • 1 kW

4815 BRAZIL RADIO CABOCLA, Benjamim Constant — DS-TEMP INACTIVE • 10 kW

†RADIO DIFUSORA, Londrina — DS • 10 kW

BURKINA FASO RADIO BURKINA, Ouagadougou — FRENCH, ETC • DS • 50 kW

CHINA CHINA RADIO INTL, Hohhot — E Asia • 50 kW / W • E Asia • 50 kW

4819.2 HONDURAS LA VOZ EVANGELICA, Tegucigalpa — DS • 5/10 kW / M • DS • 5/10 kW / Tu-Su • DS • 5/10 kW

4820 BOTSWANA RADIO BOTSWANA, Gaborone — ENGLISH, ETC • DS • 45/50 kW

INDIA ALL INDIA RADIO, Calcutta — DS • 50 kW / ENGLISH, ETC • DS • 50 kW

RUSSIA KHANTY-MANSIYSK R, Khanty-Mansiysk — ◁▯ • DS-LOCAL, R ROSSII • 50 kW

4824.4 PERU LA VOZ DE LA SELVA, Iquitos — Tu-Su • DS • 10 kW / M-Sa • DS • 10 kW / DS • 10 kW

4825 BRAZIL R CANCAO NOVA, Cachoeira Paulista — DS • 10 kW

RADIO EDUCADORA, Bragança — DS • 10 kW

GUATEMALA RADIO MAM, Cabricán — Su-F • SPANISH, ETC • DS • 0.5/1 kW / M-F • SPANISH, ETC • DS • 0.5/1 kW / M-Sa • SPANISH, ETC • DS • 0.5/1 kW

RUSSIA YAKUT RADIO, Yakutsk — RUSSIAN, ETC • DS-LOCAL, R ROSSII • 50 kW

4826.3 PERU RADIO SICUANI, Sicuani — DS • 0.35/1 kW

4828 ZIMBABWE †ZIMBABWE BC CORP, Gweru — DS-4 • 50 kW • ALT. FREQ. TO 5012 kHz / M/W/F • DS-4 • 50 kW • ALT. FREQ. TO 5012 kHz / Su/Tu/Th/Sa • DS-4 • 50 kW • ALT. FREQ. TO 5012 kHz

4828v MAURITANIA †RADIO MAURITANIE, Nouakchott — ARABIC, FRENCH, ETC • DS • 100 kW • ALT. FREQ. TO 4845v kHz / Irr • ARABIC & FRENCH • DS-RAMADAN • 100 kW • ALT. FREQ. TO 4845v kHz / Sa-Th • ARABIC, FRENCH, ETC • DS • 100 kW • ALT. FREQ. TO 4845v kHz / F • ARABIC, FRENCH, ETC • DS • 100 kW • ALT. FREQ. TO 4845v kHz

4830 CHINA (con'd) †CHINA HUAYI BC COMPANY, Fuzhou — E Asia • 50 kW • ALT. FREQ. TO 6185 kHz

| | 0 1 2 3 4 5 6 7 8 9 10 11 12 13 14 15 16 17 18 19 20 21 22 23 24 |

ENGLISH ▬ ARABIC ▨ CHINESE ▫▫▫ FRENCH ▭ GERMAN ▬ RUSSIAN ═ SPANISH ▭ OTHER ▬

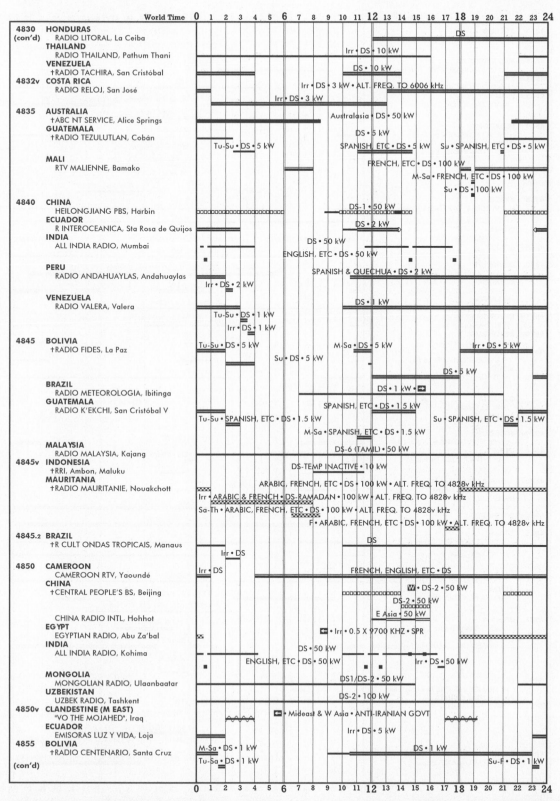

| World Time | 0 | 1 | 2 | 3 | 4 | 5 | 6 | 7 | 8 | 9 | 10 | 11 | 12 | 13 | 14 | 15 | 16 | 17 | 18 | 19 | 20 | 21 | 22 | 23 | 24 |

4830 **HONDURAS**
(con'd) RADIO LITORAL, La Ceiba — DS
THAILAND
RADIO THAILAND, Pathum Thani — Irr • DS • 10 kW
VENEZUELA
†RADIO TACHIRA, San Cristóbal — DS • 10 kW
4832v COSTA RICA
RADIO RELOJ, San José — Irr • DS • 3 kW • ALT. FREQ. TO 6006 kHz
Irr • DS • 3 kW

4835 **AUSTRALIA**
†ABC NT SERVICE, Alice Springs — Australasia • DS • 50 kW
GUATEMALA
†RADIO TEZULUTLAN, Cobán — DS • 5 kW
Tu-Su • DS • 5 kW — SPANISH, ETC • DS • 5 kW — Su • SPANISH, ETC • DS • 5 kW
MALI
RTV MALIENNE, Bamako — FRENCH, ETC • DS • 100 kW
M-Sa • FRENCH, ETC • DS • 100 kW
Su • DS • 100 kW

4840 **CHINA**
HEILONGJIANG PBS, Harbin — DS-1 • 50 kW
ECUADOR
R INTEROCEANICA, Sta Rosa de Quijos — DS • 2 kW
INDIA
ALL INDIA RADIO, Mumbai — DS • 50 kW
ENGLISH, ETC • DS • 50 kW
PERU
RADIO ANDAHUAYLAS, Andahuaylas — SPANISH & QUECHUA • DS • 2 kW
Irr • DS • 2 kW
VENEZUELA
RADIO VALERA, Valera — DS • 1 kW
Tu-Su • DS • 1 kW
Irr • DS • 1 kW

4845 **BOLIVIA**
†RADIO FIDES, La Paz — Tu-Su • DS • 5 kW — M-Sa • DS • 5 kW — Irr • DS • 5 kW
Su • DS • 5 kW
DS • 5 kW
BRAZIL
RADIO METEOROLOGIA, Ibitinga — DS • 1 kW •
GUATEMALA
RADIO K'EKCHI, San Cristóbal V — SPANISH, ETC • DS • 1.5 kW
Tu-Su • SPANISH, ETC • DS • 1.5 kW — Su • SPANISH, ETC • DS • 1.5 kW
M-Sa • SPANISH, ETC • DS • 1.5 kW
MALAYSIA
RADIO MALAYSIA, Kajang — DS-6 (TAMIL) • 50 kW
4845v INDONESIA
†RRI, Ambon, Maluku — DS-TEMP INACTIVE • 10 kW
MAURITANIA
†RADIO MAURITANIE, Nouakchott — ARABIC, FRENCH, ETC • DS • 100 kW • ALT. FREQ. TO 4828v kHz
Irr • ARABIC & FRENCH • DS-RAMADAN • 100 kW • ALT. FREQ. TO 4828v kHz
Sa-Th • ARABIC, FRENCH, ETC • DS • 100 kW • ALT. FREQ. TO 4828v kHz
F • ARABIC, FRENCH, ETC • DS • 100 kW • ALT. FREQ. TO 4828v kHz
4845.2 BRAZIL
†R CULT ONDAS TROPICAIS, Manaus — DS
Irr • DS

4850 **CAMEROON**
CAMEROON RTV, Yaoundé — Irr • DS — FRENCH, ENGLISH, ETC • DS
CHINA
†CENTRAL PEOPLE'S BS, Beijing — W • DS-2 • 50 kW
DS-2 • 50 kW
CHINA RADIO INTL, Hohhot — E Asia • 50 kW
EGYPT
EGYPTIAN RADIO, Abu Za'bal — • Irr • 0.5 X 9700 KHZ • SPR
INDIA
ALL INDIA RADIO, Kohima — DS • 50 kW
ENGLISH, ETC • DS • 50 kW — Irr • DS • 50 kW
MONGOLIA
MONGOLIAN RADIO, Ulaanbaatar — DS1/DS-2 • 50 kW
UZBEKISTAN
UZBEK RADIO, Tashkent — DS-2 • 100 kW
4850v CLANDESTINE (M EAST)
"VO THE MOJAHED", Iraq — • Mideast & W Asia • ANTI-IRANIAN GOVT
ECUADOR
EMISORAS LUZ Y VIDA, Loja — Irr • DS • 5 kW
4855 **BOLIVIA**
†RADIO CENTENARIO, Santa Cruz — M-Sa • DS • 1 kW — DS • 1 kW
Tu-Sa • DS • 1 kW — Su-F • DS • 1 kW
(con'd)

| | 0 | 1 | 2 | 3 | 4 | 5 | 6 | 7 | 8 | 9 | 10 | 11 | 12 | 13 | 14 | 15 | 16 | 17 | 18 | 19 | 20 | 21 | 22 | 23 | 24 |

SEASONAL 🅂 OR 🅆 1-HR TIMESHIFT MIDYEAR ⬅ OR ➡ JAMMING / OR ∧ EARLIEST HEARD ◁ LATEST HEARD ▷ NEW FOR 2001 †

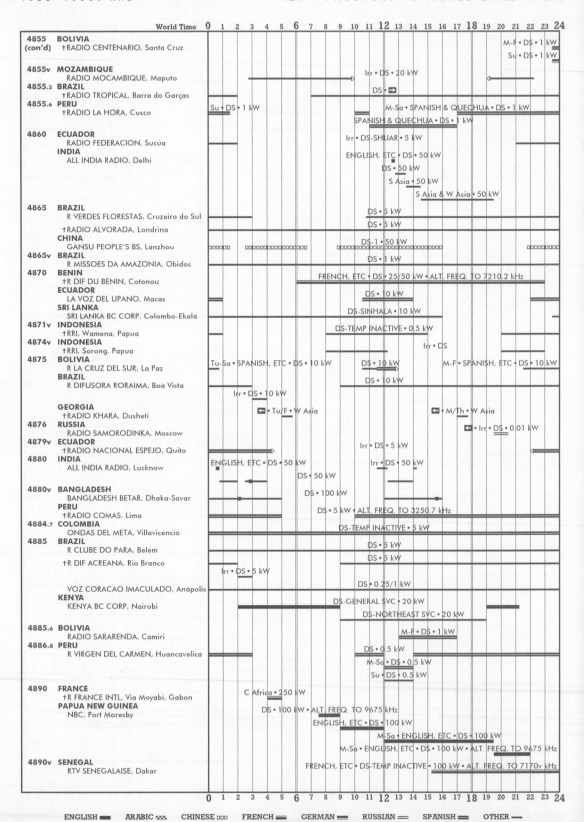

ENGLISH ▬   ARABIC ⌇⌇⌇   CHINESE ▫▫▫   FRENCH ▭▭   GERMAN ▬▬   RUSSIAN ══   SPANISH ▭▭   OTHER ▬

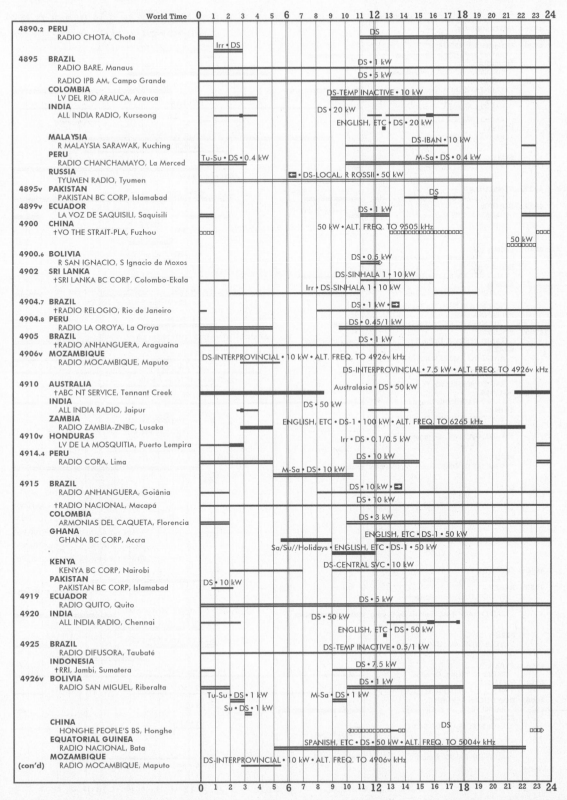

4890.2	**PERU**	
	RADIO CHOTA, Chota	DS
		Irr • DS
4895	**BRAZIL**	
	RADIO BARE, Manaus	DS • 1 kW
	RADIO IPB AM, Campo Grande	DS • 5 kW
	COLOMBIA	
	LV DEL RIO ARAUCA, Arauca	DS-TEMP INACTIVE • 10 kW
	INDIA	
	ALL INDIA RADIO, Kurseong	DS • 20 kW
		ENGLISH, ETC • DS • 20 kW
	MALAYSIA	
	R MALAYSIA SARAWAK, Kuching	DS-IBAN • 10 kW
	PERU	
	RADIO CHANCHAMAYO, La Merced	Tu-Su • DS • 0.4 kW M-Sa • DS • 0.4 kW
	RUSSIA	
	TYUMEN RADIO, Tyumen	⬅ • DS-LOCAL, R ROSSII • 50 kW
4895v	**PAKISTAN**	
	PAKISTAN BC CORP, Islamabad	DS
4899v	**ECUADOR**	
	LA VOZ DE SAQUISILI, Saquisili	DS • 1 kW
4900	**CHINA**	
	†VO THE STRAIT-PLA, Fuzhou	50 kW • ALT. FREQ. TO 9505 kHz
		50 kW
4900.6	**BOLIVIA**	
	R SAN IGNACIO, S Ignacio de Moxos	DS • 0.5 kW
4902	**SRI LANKA**	
	†SRI LANKA BC CORP, Colombo-Ekala	DS-SINHALA 1 • 10 kW
		Irr • DS-SINHALA 1 • 10 kW
4904.7	**BRAZIL**	
	†RADIO RELOGIO, Rio de Janeiro	DS • 1 kW • ➡
4904.8	**PERU**	
	RADIO LA OROYA, La Oroya	DS • 0.45/1 kW
4905	**BRAZIL**	
	†RADIO ANHANGUERA, Araguaína	DS • 1 kW
4906v	**MOZAMBIQUE**	
	RADIO MOCAMBIQUE, Maputo	DS-INTERPROVINCIAL • 10 kW • ALT. FREQ. TO 4926v kHz
		DS-INTERPROVINCIAL • 7.5 kW • ALT. FREQ. TO 4926v kHz
4910	**AUSTRALIA**	
	†ABC NT SERVICE, Tennant Creek	Australasia • DS • 50 kW
	INDIA	
	ALL INDIA RADIO, Jaipur	DS • 50 kW
	ZAMBIA	
	RADIO ZAMBIA-ZNBC, Lusaka	ENGLISH, ETC • DS-1 • 100 kW • ALT. FREQ. TO 6265 kHz
4910v	**HONDURAS**	
	LV DE LA MOSQUITIA, Puerto Lempira	Irr • DS • 0.1/0.5 kW
4914.4	**PERU**	
	RADIO CORA, Lima	DS • 10 kW
		M-Sa • DS • 10 kW
4915	**BRAZIL**	
	RADIO ANHANGUERA, Goiânia	DS • 10 kW • ➡
	†RADIO NACIONAL, Macapá	DS • 10 kW
	COLOMBIA	
	ARMONIAS DEL CAQUETA, Florencia	DS • 3 kW
	GHANA	
	GHANA BC CORP, Accra	ENGLISH, ETC • DS-1 • 50 kW
		$a/Su//Holidays • ENGLISH, ETC • DS-1 • 50 kW
	KENYA	
	KENYA BC CORP, Nairobi	DS-CENTRAL SVC • 10 kW
	PAKISTAN	
	PAKISTAN BC CORP, Islamabad	DS • 10 kW
4919	**ECUADOR**	
	RADIO QUITO, Quito	DS • 5 kW
4920	**INDIA**	
	ALL INDIA RADIO, Chennai	DS • 50 kW
		ENGLISH, ETC • DS • 50 kW
4925	**BRAZIL**	
	RADIO DIFUSORA, Taubaté	DS-TEMP INACTIVE • 0.5/1 kW
	INDONESIA	
	†RRI, Jambi, Sumatera	DS • 7.5 kW
4926v	**BOLIVIA**	
	RADIO SAN MIGUEL, Riberalta	DS • 1 kW
		Tu-Su • DS • 1 kW M-Sa • DS • 1 kW
		Su • DS • 1 kW
	CHINA	
	HONGHE PEOPLE'S BS, Honghe	DS
	EQUATORIAL GUINEA	
	RADIO NACIONAL, Bata	SPANISH, ETC • DS • 50 kW • ALT. FREQ. TO 5004v kHz
	MOZAMBIQUE	
(con'd)	RADIO MOCAMBIQUE, Maputo	DS-INTERPROVINCIAL • 10 kW • ALT. FREQ. TO 4906v kHz

World Time 0 1 2 3 4 5 6 7 8 9 10 11 12 13 14 15 16 17 18 19 20 21 22 23 24

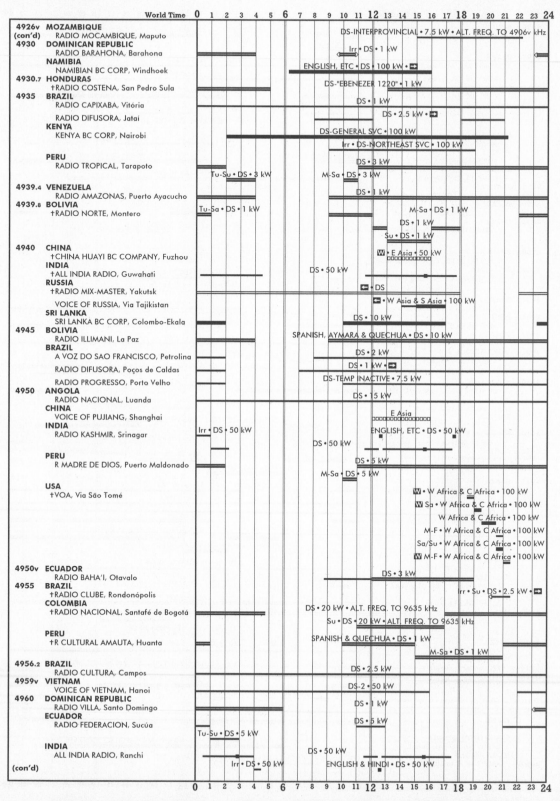

Freq	Country / Station	Notes
4926v	MOZAMBIQUE	
(con'd)	RADIO MOCAMBIQUE, Maputo	DS-INTERPROVINCIAL • 7.5 kW • ALT. FREQ. TO 4906v kHz
4930	DOMINICAN REPUBLIC	
	RADIO BARAHONA, Barahona	Irr • DS • 1 kW
	NAMIBIA	
	NAMIBIAN BC CORP, Windhoek	ENGLISH, ETC • DS 100 kW •
4930.7	HONDURAS	
	†RADIO COSTENA, San Pedro Sula	DS-"EBENEZER 1220" • 1 kW
4935	BRAZIL	
	RADIO CAPIXABA, Vitória	DS • 1 kW
	RADIO DIFUSORA, Jataí	DS • 2.5 kW •
	KENYA	
	KENYA BC CORP, Nairobi	DS-GENERAL SVC • 100 kW
		Irr • DS-NORTHEAST SVC • 100 kW
	PERU	
	RADIO TROPICAL, Tarapoto	DS • 3 kW
		Tu-Su • DS • 3 kW / M-Sa • DS • 3 kW
4939.4	VENEZUELA	
	RADIO AMAZONAS, Puerto Ayacucho	DS • 1 kW
4939.8	BOLIVIA	
	†RADIO NORTE, Montero	Tu-Sa • DS • 1 kW / M-Sa • DS • 1 kW
		DS • 1 kW
		Su • DS • 1 kW
4940	CHINA	
	†CHINA HUAYI BC COMPANY, Fuzhou	W • E Asia • 50 kW
	INDIA	
	†ALL INDIA RADIO, Guwahati	DS • 50 kW
	RUSSIA	
	†RADIO MIX-MASTER, Yakutsk	• DS
	VOICE OF RUSSIA, Via Tajikistan	• W Asia & S Asia • 100 kW
	SRI LANKA	
	SRI LANKA BC CORP, Colombo-Ekala	DS • 10 kW
4945	BOLIVIA	
	RADIO ILLIMANI, La Paz	SPANISH, AYMARA & QUECHUA • DS • 10 kW
	BRAZIL	
	A VOZ DO SAO FRANCISCO, Petrolina	DS • 2 kW
	RADIO DIFUSORA, Poços de Caldas	DS • 1 kW •
	RADIO PROGRESSO, Porto Velho	DS-TEMP INACTIVE • 7.5 kW
4950	ANGOLA	
	RADIO NACIONAL, Luanda	DS • 15 kW
	CHINA	
	VOICE OF PUJIANG, Shanghai	E Asia
	INDIA	
	RADIO KASHMIR, Srinagar	ENGLISH, ETC • DS • 50 kW
		Irr • DS • 50 kW
		DS • 50 kW
	PERU	
	R MADRE DE DIOS, Puerto Maldonado	DS • 5 kW
		M-Sa • DS • 5 kW
	USA	
	†VOA, Via São Tomé	W • W Africa & C Africa • 100 kW
		W Sa • W Africa & C Africa • 100 kW
		W Africa & C Africa • 100 kW
		M-F • W Africa & C Africa • 100 kW
		Sa/Su • W Africa & C Africa • 100 kW
		W M-F • W Africa & C Africa • 100 kW
4950v	ECUADOR	
	RADIO BAHA'I, Otavalo	DS • 3 kW
4955	BRAZIL	
	†RADIO CLUBE, Rondonópolis	Irr • Su • DS • 2.5 kW •
	COLOMBIA	
	†RADIO NACIONAL, Santafé de Bogotá	DS • 20 kW • ALT. FREQ. TO 9635 kHz
		Su • DS • 20 kW • ALT. FREQ. TO 9635 kHz
	PERU	
	†R CULTURAL AMAUTA, Huanta	SPANISH & QUECHUA • DS • 1 kW
		M-Sa • DS • 1 kW
4956.2	BRAZIL	
	RADIO CULTURA, Campos	DS • 2.5 kW
4959v	VIETNAM	
	VOICE OF VIETNAM, Hanoi	DS-2 • 50 kW
4960	DOMINICAN REPUBLIC	
	RADIO VILLA, Santo Domingo	DS • 1 kW
	ECUADOR	
	RADIO FEDERACION, Sucúa	DS • 5 kW
		Tu-Su • DS • 5 kW
	INDIA	
	ALL INDIA RADIO, Ranchi	DS • 50 kW
(con'd)		Irr • DS • 50 kW / ENGLISH & HINDI • DS • 50 kW

0 1 2 3 4 5 6 7 8 9 10 11 12 13 14 15 16 17 18 19 20 21 22 23 24

ENGLISH ▬▬   ARABIC ▨▨   CHINESE ▢▢▢   FRENCH ══   GERMAN ▬▬   RUSSIAN ═══   SPANISH ▬▬   OTHER ▬

World Time   0 1 2 3 4 5 6 7 8 9 10 11 12 13 14 15 16 17 18 19 20 21 22 23 24

Freq	Country / Station	Schedule / Notes
4960 (con'd)	**INDIA** — ALL INDIA RADIO, Ranchi	ENGLISH, ETC • DS • 50 kW
	USA — VOA, Via São Tomé	M-F • W Africa & C Africa • 100 kW / W Africa & C Africa • 100 kW
	VANUATU — RADIO VANUATU, Vila, Efate Island	ENGLISH, FRENCH, ETC • DS • 10 kW • ALT. FREQ. TO 7260 kHz • ⇨
4960.5	**HONDURAS** — RADIO HRET, Puerto Lempira	Tu-Su • DS-TEMP INACTIVE / DS-TEMP INACTIVE
4965	**BRAZIL** — RADIO ALVORADA, Parintins	DS • 5 kW
	NAMIBIA — NAMIBIAN BC CORP, Windhoek	ENGLISH, GERMAN & AFRIKAANS • DS • 100 kW • ⇨
	RUSSIA — †VOICE OF RUSSIA, Via Tajikistan	⇦ • W Asia & S Asia • 100 kW
	ZAMBIA — †RADIO CHRISTIAN VOICE, Lusaka	S Africa • 100 kW / S Africa • 100 kW • ALT. FREQ. TO 9865 kHz
4970	**CHINA** — XINJIANG PEOPLE'S BC STN, Ürümqi	DS-KAZAKH • 50 kW • ALT. FREQ. TO 5440 kHz
	INDIA — ALL INDIA RADIO, Shillong	DS • 50 kW / ENGLISH, ETC • DS • 50 kW / Irr • DS • 50 kW
4971v	**PERU** — RADIO IMAGEN, Tarapoto	DS • 1 kW / M-Sa • DS • 1 kW
4975	**BRAZIL** — RADIO MUNDIAL, São Paulo	DS • 1 kW • ⇨ / M-Sa • DS • 1 kW • ⇨ / Su • DS • 1 kW • ⇨ M-F • DS • 1 kW • ⇨ / Sa/Su • DS • 1 kW • ⇨
	CHINA — FUJIAN PEOPLE'S BS, Jianyang	DS-1 • 10 kW
	RUSSIA — VOICE OF RUSSIA, Via Tajikistan	⇦ • W Asia & S Asia • 100 kW
	TAJIKISTAN — RADIO TAJIKISTAN, Dushanbe	W Asia & C Asia • 100 kW • ALT. FREQ. TO 7245 kHz
4975v	**COLOMBIA** — †ONDAS DEL ORTEGUAZA, Florencia	DS-TODELAR • 1 kW
4975.2	**PERU** — RADIO DEL PACIFICO, Lima	DS • 5 kW / Su/M • DS • 5 kW M-Sa • DS • 5 kW / Tu-Sa • DS • 5 kW
4976	**UGANDA** — RADIO UGANDA, Kampala	ENGLISH, ETC • DS-RED CHANNEL • 10 kW
4980	**VENEZUELA** — †ECOS DEL TORBES, San Cristóbal	DS • 10 kW
4980v	**CHINA** — †XINJIANG PEOPLE'S BC STN, Ürümqi	DS-MONGOLIAN • 50 kW
4985	**BRAZIL** — †R BRASIL CENTRAL, Goiânia	DS • 10 kW • ⇨ / Irr • DS • 10 kW • ⇨
4990	**CHINA** — HUNAN PEOPLE'S BS, Changsha	DS-1 • 10 kW
	INDIA — ALL INDIA RADIO, Itanagar	DS • 50 kW
	NIGERIA — RADIO NIGERIA, Lagos	ENGLISH, ETC • DS-TEMP INACTIVE • 50 kW
4991	**BOLIVIA** — RADIO ANIMAS, Animas	Tu-Su • DS • 1 kW / M-F • SPANISH & QUECHUA • DS • 1 kW ⇢ Sa • DS • 1 kW / M-Sa • SPANISH & QUECHUA • DS • 1 kW
	SURINAME — RADIO APINTIE, Paramaribo	DS • 0.05/0.35 kW • ALT. FREQ. TO 5005.7 kHz / Tu-Su • DS • 0.05/0.35 kW • ALT. FREQ. TO 5005.7 kHz
4991v	**PERU** — RADIO ANCASH, Huaraz	SPANISH & QUECHUA • DS • 5 kW / Irr • SPANISH & QUECHUA • DS • 5 kW
4993	**USA** — †AFRTS, Via Sigonella, Italy	Europe & N Africa • USB • ALT. FREQ. TO 10940.5 kHz
4995.6	**PERU** — RADIO ANDINA, Huancayo	DS • 1 kW / Tu-Su • DS • 1 kW M-Sa • DS • 1 kW / Irr • Tu-Su • DS • 1 kW
5000	**LIBERIA** — LIBERIAN COMM'S NETWORK, Totota	ENGLISH, ETC • DS-"RADIO LIBERIA" • 10 kW • ALT. FREQ. TO 5100 kHz
(con'd)	**USA** — WWV, Fort Collins, Colorado	WEATHER/WORLD TIME • 10 kW

0 1 2 3 4 5 6 7 8 9 10 11 12 13 14 15 16 17 18 19 20 21 22 23 24

SEASONAL Ⓢ OR Ⓦ   1-HR TIMESHIFT MIDYEAR ⇦ OR ⇨   JAMMING / OR /\   EARLIEST HEARD ◁   LATEST HEARD ▷   NEW FOR 2001 †

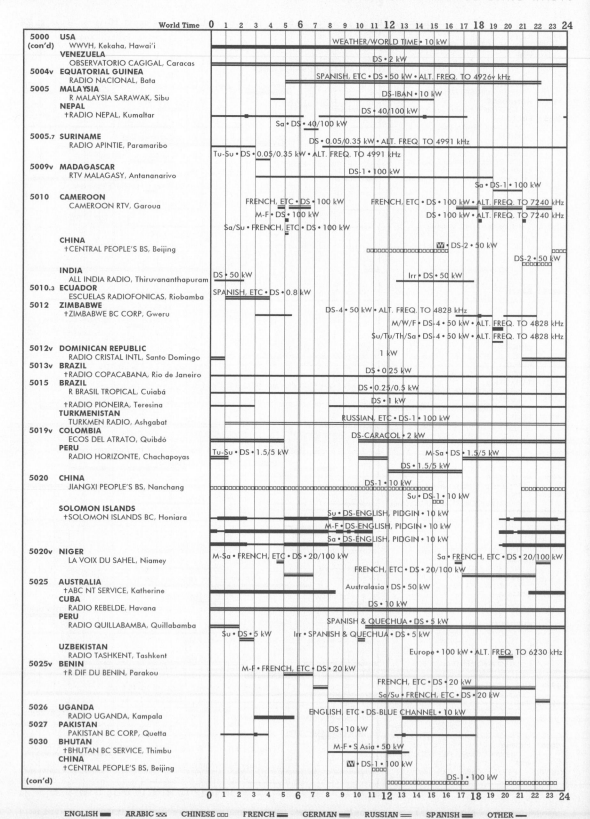

World Time		0	1	2	3	4	5	6	7	8	9	10	11	12	13	14	15	16	17	18	19	20	21	22	23	24

5000 (con'd) **USA** — WWVH, Kekaha, Hawai'i — WEATHER/WORLD TIME • 10 kW

VENEZUELA — OBSERVATORIO CAGIGAL, Caracas — DS • 2 kW

5004v EQUATORIAL GUINEA — RADIO NACIONAL, Bata — SPANISH, ETC • DS • 50 kW • ALT. FREQ. TO 4926v kHz

5005 MALAYSIA — R MALAYSIA SARAWAK, Sibu — DS-IBAN • 10 kW

NEPAL — †RADIO NEPAL, Kumaltar — DS • 40/100 kW — Sa • DS • 40/100 kW

5005.7 SURINAME — RADIO APINTIE, Paramaribo — DS • 0.05/0.35 kW • ALT. FREQ TO 4991 kHz — Tu-Su • DS • 0.05/0.35 kW • ALT. FREQ. TO 4991 kHz

5009v MADAGASCAR — RTV MALAGASY, Antananarivo — DS-1 • 100 kW — Sa • DS-1 • 100 kW

5010 CAMEROON — CAMEROON RTV, Garoua — FRENCH, ETC • DS • 100 kW — FRENCH, ETC • DS • 100 kW • ALT. FREQ. TO 7240 kHz — M-F • DS • 100 kW — DS • 100 kW • ALT. FREQ. TO 7240 kHz — Sa/Su • FRENCH, ETC • DS • 100 kW

CHINA — †CENTRAL PEOPLE'S BS, Beijing — Ⓦ • DS-2 • 50 kW — DS-2 • 50 kW

INDIA — ALL INDIA RADIO, Thiruvananthapuram — DS • 50 kW — Irr • DS • 50 kW

5010.3 ECUADOR — ESCUELAS RADIOFONICAS, Riobamba — SPANISH, ETC • DS • 0.8 kW

5012 ZIMBABWE — †ZIMBABWE BC CORP, Gweru — DS-4 • 50 kW • ALT. FREQ. TO 4828 kHz — M/W/F • DS-4 • 50 kW • ALT. FREQ. TO 4828 kHz — Su/Tu/Th/Sa • DS-4 • 50 kW • ALT. FREQ. TO 4828 kHz

5012v DOMINICAN REPUBLIC — RADIO CRISTAL INTL, Santo Domingo — 1 kW

5013v BRAZIL — †RADIO COPACABANA, Rio de Janeiro — DS • 0.25 kW

5015 BRAZIL — R BRASIL TROPICAL, Cuiabá — DS • 0.25/0.5 kW

†RADIO PIONEIRA, Teresina — DS • 1 kW

TURKMENISTAN — TURKMEN RADIO, Ashgabat — RUSSIAN, ETC • DS-1 • 100 kW

5019v COLOMBIA — ECOS DEL ATRATO, Quibdó — DS-CARACOL • 2 kW

PERU — RADIO HORIZONTE, Chachapoyas — Tu-Su • DS • 1.5/5 kW — M-Sa • DS • 1.5/5 kW — DS • 1.5/5 kW

5020 CHINA — JIANGXI PEOPLE'S BS, Nanchang — DS-1 • 10 kW — Su • DS-1 • 10 kW

SOLOMON ISLANDS — †SOLOMON ISLANDS BC, Honiara — Su • DS-ENGLISH, PIDGIN • 10 kW — M-F • DS-ENGLISH, PIDGIN • 10 kW — Sa • DS-ENGLISH, PIDGIN • 10 kW

5020v NIGER — LA VOIX DU SAHEL, Niamey — M-Sa • FRENCH, ETC • DS • 20/100 kW — Sa • FRENCH, ETC • DS • 20/100 kW — FRENCH, ETC • DS • 20/100 kW

5025 AUSTRALIA — †ABC NT SERVICE, Katherine — Australasia • DS • 50 kW

CUBA — RADIO REBELDE, Havana — DS • 10 kW

PERU — RADIO QUILLABAMBA, Quillabamba — SPANISH & QUECHUA • DS • 5 kW — Su • DS • 5 kW — Irr • SPANISH & QUECHUA • DS • 5 kW

UZBEKISTAN — RADIO TASHKENT, Tashkent — Europe • 100 kW • ALT. FREQ. TO 6230 kHz

5025v BENIN — †R DIF DU BENIN, Parakou — M-F • FRENCH, ETC • DS • 20 kW — FRENCH, ETC • DS • 20 kW — Sa/Su • FRENCH, ETC • DS • 20 kW

5026 UGANDA — RADIO UGANDA, Kampala — ENGLISH, ETC • DS-BLUE CHANNEL • 10 kW

5027 PAKISTAN — PAKISTAN BC CORP, Quetta — DS • 10 kW

5030 BHUTAN — †BHUTAN BC SERVICE, Thimbu — M-F • S Asia • 50 kW

CHINA — †CENTRAL PEOPLE'S BS, Beijing — Ⓦ • DS-1 • 100 kW — DS-1 • 100 kW

(con'd)

		0	1	2	3	4	5	6	7	8	9	10	11	12	13	14	15	16	17	18	19	20	21	22	23	24

ENGLISH ▬ ARABIC ▨▨▨ CHINESE □□□ FRENCH ═ GERMAN ▬ RUSSIAN ═ SPANISH ▬ OTHER ▬

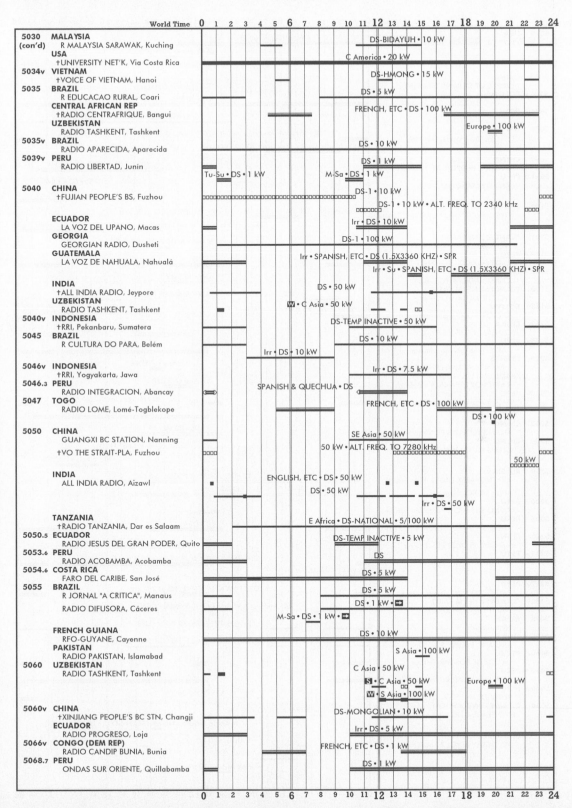

World Time 0 1 2 3 4 5 6 7 8 9 10 11 12 13 14 15 16 17 18 19 20 21 22 23 24

Freq	Country / Station	Details
5030 (con'd)	MALAYSIA — R MALAYSIA SARAWAK, Kuching	DS-BIDAYUH • 10 kW
	USA — †UNIVERSITY NET'K, Via Costa Rica	C America • 20 kW
5034v	VIETNAM — †VOICE OF VIETNAM, Hanoi	DS-HMONG • 15 kW
5035	BRAZIL — R EDUCACAO RURAL, Coari	DS • 5 kW
	CENTRAL AFRICAN REP — †RADIO CENTRAFRIQUE, Bangui	FRENCH, ETC • DS • 100 kW
	UZBEKISTAN — RADIO TASHKENT, Tashkent	Europe • 100 kW
5035v	BRAZIL — RADIO APARECIDA, Aparecida	DS • 10 kW
5039v	PERU — RADIO LIBERTAD, Junín	DS • 1 kW / Tu-Su • DS • 1 kW / M-Sa • DS • 1 kW
5040	CHINA — †FUJIAN PEOPLE'S BS, Fuzhou	DS-1 • 10 kW / DS-1 • 10 kW • ALT. FREQ. TO 2340 kHz
	ECUADOR — LA VOZ DEL UPANO, Macas	Irr • DS • 10 kW
	GEORGIA — GEORGIAN RADIO, Dusheti	DS-1 • 100 kW
	GUATEMALA — LA VOZ DE NAHUALA, Nahualá	Irr • SPANISH, ETC • DS (1.5X3360 KHZ) • SPR / Irr • Su • SPANISH, ETC • DS (1.5X3360 KHZ) • SPR
	INDIA — †ALL INDIA RADIO, Jeypore	DS • 50 kW
	UZBEKISTAN — RADIO TASHKENT, Tashkent	W • C Asia • 50 kW
5040v	INDONESIA — †RRI, Pekanbaru, Sumatera	DS-TEMP INACTIVE • 50 kW
5045	BRAZIL — R CULTURA DO PARA, Belém	DS • 10 kW / Irr • DS • 10 kW
5046v	INDONESIA — †RRI, Yogyakarta, Jawa	Irr • DS • 7.5 kW
5046.3	PERU — RADIO INTEGRACION, Abancay	SPANISH & QUECHUA • DS
5047	TOGO — RADIO LOME, Lomé-Togblekope	FRENCH, ETC • DS • 100 kW / DS • 100 kW
5050	CHINA — GUANGXI BC STATION, Nanning	SE Asia • 50 kW
	†VO THE STRAIT-PLA, Fuzhou	50 kW • ALT. FREQ. TO 7280 kHz / 50 kW
	INDIA — ALL INDIA RADIO, Aizawl	ENGLISH, ETC • DS • 50 kW / DS • 50 kW / Irr • DS • 50 kW
	TANZANIA — †RADIO TANZANIA, Dar es Salaam	E Africa • DS-NATIONAL • 5/100 kW
5050.5	ECUADOR — RADIO JESUS DEL GRAN PODER, Quito	DS-TEMP INACTIVE • 5 kW
5053.6	PERU — RADIO ACOBAMBA, Acobamba	DS
5054.6	COSTA RICA — FARO DEL CARIBE, San José	DS • 5 kW
5055	BRAZIL — R JORNAL "A CRITICA", Manaus	DS • 5 kW
	RADIO DIFUSORA, Cáceres	DS • 1 kW • ⇨ / M-Sa • DS • 1 kW • ⇨
	FRENCH GUIANA — RFO-GUYANE, Cayenne	DS • 10 kW
	PAKISTAN — RADIO PAKISTAN, Islamabad	S Asia • 100 kW
5060	UZBEKISTAN — RADIO TASHKENT, Tashkent	C Asia • 50 kW / S • C Asia • 50 kW / Europe • 100 kW / W • S Asia • 100 kW
5060v	CHINA — †XINJIANG PEOPLE'S BC STN, Changji	DS-MONGOLIAN • 10 kW
	ECUADOR — RADIO PROGRESO, Loja	Irr • DS • 5 kW
5066v	CONGO (DEM REP) — RADIO CANDIP BUNIA, Bunia	FRENCH, ETC • DS • 1 kW
5068.7	PERU — ONDAS SUR ORIENTE, Quillabamba	DS • 1 kW

0 1 2 3 4 5 6 7 8 9 10 11 12 13 14 15 16 17 18 19 20 21 22 23 24

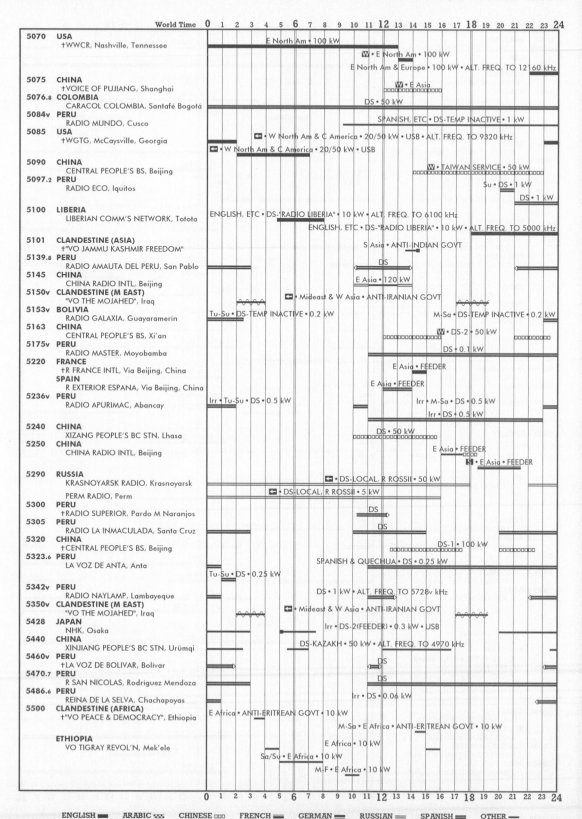

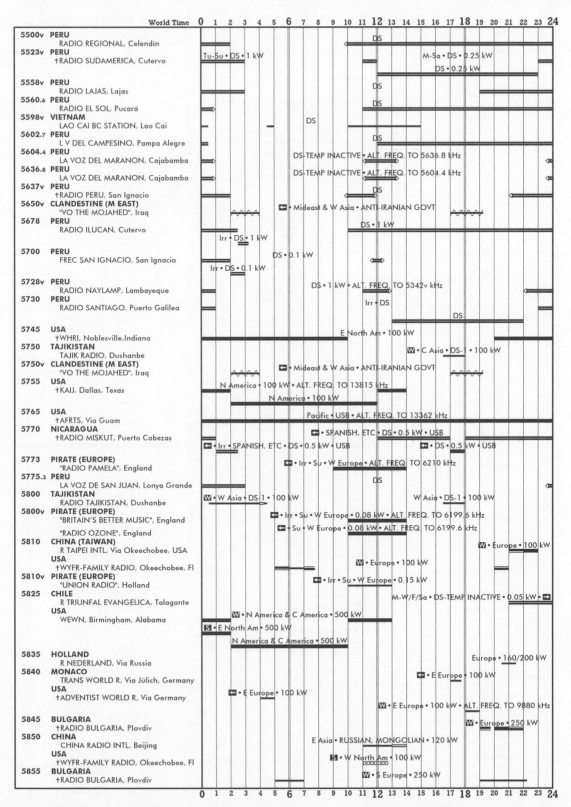

World Time 0 1 2 3 4 5 6 7 8 9 10 11 12 13 14 15 16 17 18 19 20 21 22 23 24

5500v PERU
RADIO REGIONAL, Celendin
DS

5523v PERU
†RADIO SUDAMERICA, Cutervo
Tu-Su • DS • 1 kW
M-Sa • DS • 0.25 kW
DS • 0.25 kW

5558v PERU
RADIO LAJAS, Lajas
DS

5560.6 PERU
RADIO EL SOL, Pucará
DS

5598v VIETNAM
LAO CAI BC STATION, Lao Cai
DS

5602.7 PERU
L V DEL CAMPESINO, Pampa Alegre
DS

5604.4 PERU
LA VOZ DEL MARANON, Cajabamba
DS-TEMP INACTIVE • ALT. FREQ. TO 5636.8 kHz

5636.8 PERU
LA VOZ DEL MARANON, Cajabamba
DS-TEMP INACTIVE • ALT. FREQ. TO 5604.4 kHz

5637v PERU
†RADIO PERU, San Ignacio
DS

5650v CLANDESTINE (M EAST)
"VO THE MOJAHED", Iraq
• Mideast & W Asia • ANTI-IRANIAN GOVT

5678 PERU
RADIO ILUCAN, Cutervo
DS • 1 kW
Irr • DS • 1 kW

5700 PERU
FREC SAN IGNACIO, San Ignacio
DS • 0.1 kW
Irr • DS • 0.1 kW

5728v PERU
RADIO NAYLAMP, Lambayeque
DS • 1 kW • ALT. FREQ. TO 5342v kHz

5730 PERU
RADIO SANTIAGO, Puerto Galilea
Irr • DS
DS

5745 USA
†WHRI, Noblesville, Indiana
E North Am • 100 kW

5750 TAJIKISTAN
TAJIK RADIO, Dushanbe
W • C Asia • DS-1 • 100 kW

5750v CLANDESTINE (M EAST)
"VO THE MOJAHED", Iraq
• Mideast & W Asia • ANTI-IRANIAN GOVT

5755 USA
†KAIJ, Dallas, Texas
N America • 100 kW • ALT. FREQ. TO 13815 kHz
N America • 100 kW

5765 USA
†AFRTS, Via Guam
Pacific • USB • ALT. FREQ. TO 13362 kHz

5770 NICARAGUA
†RADIO MISKUT, Puerto Cabezas
• SPANISH, ETC • DS • 0.5 kW • USB
• Irr • SPANISH, ETC • DS • 0.5 kW • USB
• DS • 0.5 kW • USB

5773 PIRATE (EUROPE)
"RADIO PAMELA", England
• Irr • Su • W Europe • ALT. FREQ. TO 6210 kHz

5775.3 PERU
LA VOZ DE SAN JUAN, Lonya Grande
DS

5800 TAJIKISTAN
RADIO TAJIKISTAN, Dushanbe
W • W Asia • DS-1 • 100 kW
W Asia • DS-1 • 100 kW

5800v PIRATE (EUROPE)
"BRITAIN'S BETTER MUSIC", England
• Irr • Su • W Europe • 0.08 kW • ALT. FREQ. TO 6199.6 kHz

"RADIO OZONE", England
• Su • W Europe • 0.08 kW • ALT. FREQ. TO 6199.6 kHz

5810 CHINA (TAIWAN)
R TAIPEI INTL, Via Okeechobee, USA
W • Europe • 100 kW

USA
†WYFR-FAMILY RADIO, Okeechobee, Fl
W • Europe • 100 kW

5810v PIRATE (EUROPE)
"UNION RADIO", Holland
• Irr • Su • W Europe • 0.15 kW

5825 CHILE
R TRIUNFAL EVANGELICA, Talagante
M-W/F/Sa • DS-TEMP INACTIVE • 0.05 kW •

USA
WEWN, Birmingham, Alabama
W • N America & C America • 500 kW
S • E North Am • 500 kW
N America & C America • 500 kW

5835 HOLLAND
R NEDERLAND, Via Russia
Europe • 160/200 kW

5840 MONACO
TRANS WORLD R, Via Jülich, Germany
• E Europe • 100 kW

USA
†ADVENTIST WORLD R, Via Germany
• E Europe • 100 kW
W • E Europe • 100 kW • ALT. FREQ. TO 9880 kHz

5845 BULGARIA
†RADIO BULGARIA, Plovdiv
W • Europe • 250 kW

5850 CHINA
CHINA RADIO INTL, Beijing
E Asia • RUSSIAN, MONGOLIAN • 120 kW

USA
†WYFR-FAMILY RADIO, Okeechobee, Fl
S • W North Am • 100 kW

5855 BULGARIA
†RADIO BULGARIA, Plovdiv
W • S Europe • 250 kW

0 1 2 3 4 5 6 7 8 9 10 11 12 13 14 15 16 17 18 19 20 21 22 23 24

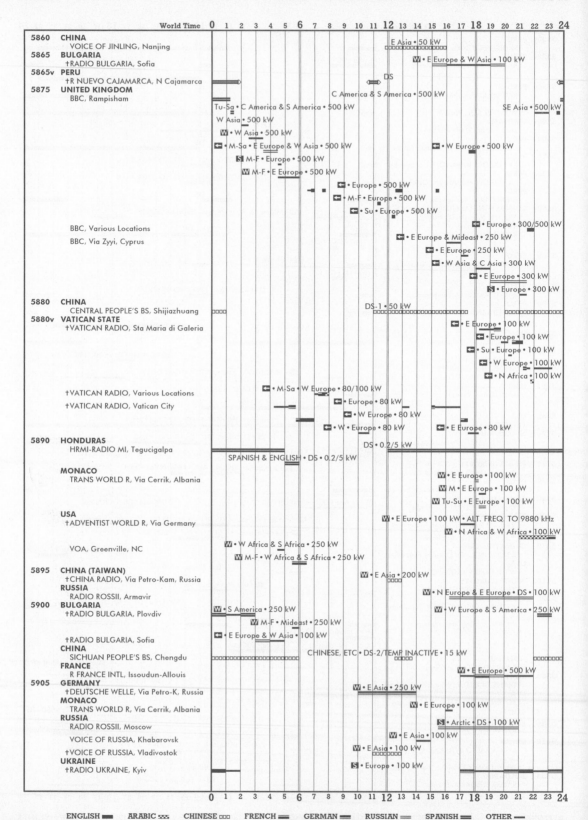

5860	**CHINA**	
	VOICE OF JINLING, Nanjing	E Asia • 50 kW
5865	**BULGARIA**	
	†RADIO BULGARIA, Sofia	W • E Europe & W Asia • 100 kW
5865v	**PERU**	
	†R NUEVO CAJAMARCA, N Cajamarca	DS
5875	**UNITED KINGDOM**	
	BBC, Rampisham	C America & S America • 500 kW
		Tu-Sa • C America & S America • 500 kW · SE Asia • 500 kW
		W Asia • 500 kW
		W • W Asia • 500 kW
		M-Sa • E Europe & W Asia • 500 kW · W Europe • 500 kW
		S M-F • Europe • 500 kW
		W M-F • E Europe • 500 kW
		• Europe • 500 kW
		• M-F • Europe • 500 kW
		• Su • Europe • 500 kW
	BBC, Various Locations	• Europe • 300/500 kW
	BBC, Via Zyyi, Cyprus	• E Europe & Mideast • 250 kW
		• E Europe • 250 kW
		• W Asia & C Asia • 300 kW
		• E Europe • 300 kW
		S • Europe • 300 kW
5880	**CHINA**	
	CENTRAL PEOPLE'S BS, Shijiazhuang	DS-1 • 50 kW
5880v	**VATICAN STATE**	
	†VATICAN RADIO, Sta Maria di Galeria	• E Europe • 100 kW
		• Europe • 100 kW
		• Su • Europe • 100 kW
		• W Europe • 100 kW
		• N Africa • 100 kW
	†VATICAN RADIO, Various Locations	• M-Sa • W Europe • 80/100 kW
	†VATICAN RADIO, Vatican City	• Europe • 80 kW
		• W Europe • 80 kW
		• W • Europe • 80 kW · E Europe • 80 kW
5890	**HONDURAS**	
	HRMI-RADIO MI, Tegucigalpa	DS • 0.2/5 kW
		SPANISH & ENGLISH • DS • 0.2/5 kW
	MONACO	
	TRANS WORLD R, Via Cerrik, Albania	W • E Europe • 100 kW
		W M • E Europe • 100 kW
		W Tu-Su • E Europe • 100 kW
	USA	
	†ADVENTIST WORLD R, Via Germany	W • E Europe • 100 kW • ALT. FREQ. TO 9880 kHz
		W • N Africa & W Africa • 100 kW
	VOA, Greenville, NC	W • W Africa & S Africa • 250 kW
		W M-F • W Africa & S Africa • 250 kW
5895	**CHINA (TAIWAN)**	
	†CHINA RADIO, Via Petro-Kam, Russia	W • E Asia • 200 kW
	RUSSIA	
	RADIO ROSSII, Armavir	W • N Europe & E Europe • DS • 100 kW
5900	**BULGARIA**	
	†RADIO BULGARIA, Plovdiv	W • S America • 250 kW · W • W Europe & S America • 250 kW
		W M-F • Mideast • 250 kW
	†RADIO BULGARIA, Sofia	• E Europe & W Asia • 100 kW
	CHINA	
	SICHUAN PEOPLE'S BS, Chengdu	CHINESE, ETC • DS-2/TEMP INACTIVE • 15 kW
	FRANCE	
	R FRANCE INTL, Issoudun-Allouis	W • E Europe • 500 kW
5905	**GERMANY**	
	†DEUTSCHE WELLE, Via Petro-K, Russia	W • E Asia • 250 kW
	MONACO	
	TRANS WORLD R, Via Cerrik, Albania	W • E Europe • 100 kW
	RUSSIA	
	RADIO ROSSII, Moscow	S • Arctic • DS 100 kW
	VOICE OF RUSSIA, Khabarovsk	W • E Asia • 100 kW
	†VOICE OF RUSSIA, Vladivostok	W • E Asia • 100 kW
	UKRAINE	
	†RADIO UKRAINE, Kyiv	S • Europe • 100 kW

World Time 0 1 2 3 4 5 6 7 8 9 10 11 12 13 14 15 16 17 18 19 20 21 22 23 24

ENGLISH ▬ ARABIC ▨ CHINESE ▫▫▫ FRENCH ▬ GERMAN ▭ RUSSIAN ═ SPANISH ▬ OTHER ▬

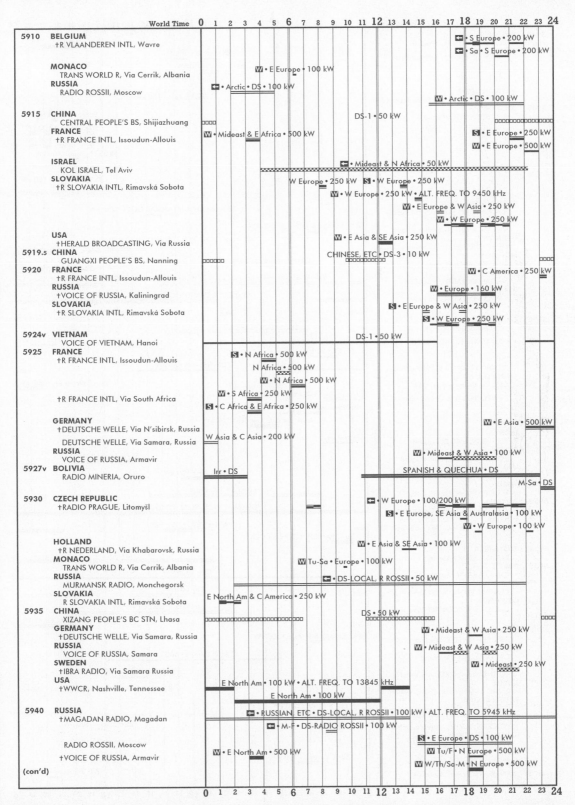

World Time 0 1 2 3 4 5 6 7 8 9 10 11 12 13 14 15 16 17 18 19 20 21 22 23 24

5910 BELGIUM
†R VLAANDEREN INTL, Wavre — • S Europe • 200 kW; • Sa • S Europe • 200 kW

MONACO
TRANS WORLD R, Via Cerrik, Albania — [W] • E Europe • 100 kW

RUSSIA
RADIO ROSSII, Moscow — • Arctic • DS • 100 kW; [W] • Arctic • DS • 100 kW

5915 CHINA
CENTRAL PEOPLE'S BS, Shijiazhuang — DS-1 • 50 kW

FRANCE
†R FRANCE INTL, Issoudun-Allouis — [W] • Mideast & E Africa • 500 kW; [S] • E Europe • 250 kW; [W] • E Europe • 500 kW

ISRAEL
KOL ISRAEL, Tel Aviv — • Mideast & N Africa • 50 kW

SLOVAKIA
†R SLOVAKIA INTL, Rimavská Sobota — W Europe • 250 kW; [S] • W Europe • 250 kW; [W] • W Europe • 250 kW • ALT. FREQ. TO 9450 kHz; [W] • E Europe & W Asia • 250 kW; [W] • W Europe • 250 kW

USA
†HERALD BROADCASTING, Via Russia — [W] • E Asia & SE Asia • 250 kW

5919.5 CHINA
GUANGXI PEOPLE'S BS, Nanning — CHINESE, ETC • DS-3 • 10 kW

5920 FRANCE
†R FRANCE INTL, Issoudun-Allouis — [W] • C America • 250 kW

RUSSIA
†VOICE OF RUSSIA, Kaliningrad — [W] • Europe • 160 kW

SLOVAKIA
†R SLOVAKIA INTL, Rimavská Sobota — [S] • E Europe & W Asia • 250 kW; [S] • W Europe • 250 kW

5924v VIETNAM
VOICE OF VIETNAM, Hanoi — DS-1 • 50 kW

5925 FRANCE
†R FRANCE INTL, Issoudun-Allouis — [S] • N Africa • 500 kW; N Africa • 500 kW; [W] • N Africa • 500 kW
†R FRANCE INTL, Via South Africa — [W] • S Africa • 250 kW; [S] • C Africa & E Africa • 250 kW

GERMANY
†DEUTSCHE WELLE, Via N'sibirsk, Russia — [W] • E Asia • 500 kW
DEUTSCHE WELLE, Via Samara, Russia — W Asia & C Asia • 200 kW

RUSSIA
VOICE OF RUSSIA, Armavir — [W] • Mideast & W Asia • 100 kW

5927v BOLIVIA
RADIO MINERIA, Oruro — Irr • DS; SPANISH & QUECHUA • DS; M-Sa • DS

5930 CZECH REPUBLIC
†RADIO PRAGUE, Litomyšl — • W Europe • 100/200 kW; [S] • E Europe, SE Asia & Australasia • 100 kW; [W] • W Europe • 100 kW

HOLLAND
†R NEDERLAND, Via Khabarovsk, Russia — [W] • E Asia & SE Asia • 100 kW

MONACO
TRANS WORLD R, Via Cerrik, Albania — [W] Tu-Sa • Europe • 100 kW

RUSSIA
MURMANSK RADIO, Monchegorsk — • DS-LOCAL, R ROSSII • 50 kW

SLOVAKIA
R SLOVAKIA INTL, Rimavská Sobota — E North Am & C America • 250 kW

5935 CHINA
XIZANG PEOPLE'S BC STN, Lhasa — DS • 50 kW

GERMANY
†DEUTSCHE WELLE, Via Samara, Russia — [W] • Mideast & W Asia • 250 kW

RUSSIA
VOICE OF RUSSIA, Samara — [W] • Mideast & W Asia • 250 kW

SWEDEN
†IBRA RADIO, Via Samara Russia — [W] • Mideast • 250 kW

USA
†WWCR, Nashville, Tennessee — E North Am • 100 kW • ALT. FREQ. TO 13845 kHz; E North Am • 100 kW

5940 RUSSIA
†MAGADAN RADIO, Magadan — • RUSSIAN, ETC • DS-LOCAL, R ROSSII • 100 kW • ALT. FREQ. TO 5945 kHz; • M-F • DS-RADIO ROSSII • 100 kW
RADIO ROSSII, Moscow — [S] • E Europe • DS • 100 kW
†VOICE OF RUSSIA, Armavir — [W] • E North Am • 500 kW; [W] Tu/F • N Europe • 500 kW; [W] W/Th/Sa-M • N Europe • 500 kW

(con'd)

0 1 2 3 4 5 6 7 8 9 10 11 12 13 14 15 16 17 18 19 20 21 22 23 24

SEASONAL [S] OR [W] — 1-HR TIMESHIFT MIDYEAR OR — JAMMING / OR ∧ — EARLIEST HEARD ◁ — LATEST HEARD ▷ — NEW FOR 2001 †

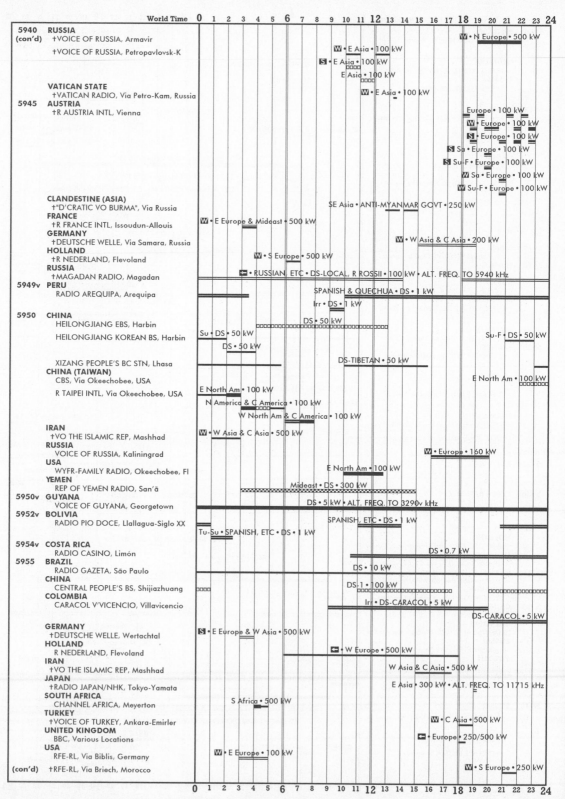

World Time 0 1 2 3 4 5 6 7 8 9 10 11 12 13 14 15 16 17 18 19 20 21 22 23 24

5940 RUSSIA
(con'd) †VOICE OF RUSSIA, Armavir
⬛ • N Europe • 500 kW

†VOICE OF RUSSIA, Petropavlovsk-K
Ⓦ • E Asia • 100 kW
Ⓢ E Asia • 100 kW
E Asia • 100 kW

VATICAN STATE
†VATICAN RADIO, Via Petro-Kam, Russia
Ⓦ • E Asia • 100 kW
5945 AUSTRIA
†R AUSTRIA INTL, Vienna
Europe • 100 kW
Ⓦ • Europe • 100 kW
Ⓢ • Europe • 100 kW
Ⓢ Sa • Europe • 100 kW
Ⓢ Su-F • Europe • 100 kW
Ⓦ Sa • Europe • 100 kW
Ⓦ Su-F • Europe • 100 kW

CLANDESTINE (ASIA)
†"D'CRATIC VO BURMA", Via Russia
SE Asia • ANTI-MYANMAR GOVT • 250 kW
FRANCE
†R FRANCE INTL, Issoudun-Allouis
Ⓦ • E Europe & Mideast • 500 kW
GERMANY
†DEUTSCHE WELLE, Via Samara, Russia
Ⓦ • W Asia & C Asia • 200 kW
HOLLAND
†R NEDERLAND, Flevoland
Ⓦ • S Europe • 500 kW
RUSSIA
†MAGADAN RADIO, Magadan
⬛ • RUSSIAN, ETC • DS-LOCAL, R ROSSII • 100 kW • ALT. FREQ. TO 5940 kHz
5949v PERU
RADIO AREQUIPA, Arequipa
SPANISH & QUECHUA • DS • 1 kW

Irr • DS • 1 kW
5950 CHINA
HEILONGJIANG EBS, Harbin
DS • 50 kW
HEILONGJIANG KOREAN BS, Harbin
Su • DS • 50 kW
Su-F • DS • 50 kW
DS • 50 kW

XIZANG PEOPLE'S BC STN, Lhasa
DS-TIBETAN • 50 kW
CHINA (TAIWAN)
CBS, Via Okeechobee, USA
E North Am • 100 kW
R TAIPEI INTL, Via Okeechobee, USA
E North Am • 100 kW
N America & C America • 100 kW
W North Am & C America • 100 kW

IRAN
†VO THE ISLAMIC REP, Mashhad
Ⓦ • W Asia & C Asia • 500 kW
RUSSIA
VOICE OF RUSSIA, Kaliningrad
Ⓦ • Europe • 160 kW
USA
WYFR-FAMILY RADIO, Okeechobee, Fl
E North Am • 100 kW
YEMEN
REP OF YEMEN RADIO, San'ā
Mideast • DS • 300 kW
5950v GUYANA
VOICE OF GUYANA, Georgetown
DS • 5 kW • ALT. FREQ. TO 3290v kHz
5952v BOLIVIA
RADIO PIO DOCE, Llallagua-Siglo XX
SPANISH, ETC • DS • 1 kW
Tu-Su • SPANISH, ETC • DS • 1 kW

5954v COSTA RICA
RADIO CASINO, Limón
DS • 0.7 kW
5955 BRAZIL
RADIO GAZETA, São Paulo
DS • 10 kW
CHINA
CENTRAL PEOPLE'S BS, Shijiazhuang
DS-1 • 100 kW
COLOMBIA
CARACOL V'VICENCIO, Villavicencio
Irr • DS-CARACOL • 5 kW
DS-CARACOL • 5 kW

GERMANY
†DEUTSCHE WELLE, Wertachtal
Ⓢ • E Europe & W Asia • 500 kW
HOLLAND
R NEDERLAND, Flevoland
⬛ • W Europe • 500 kW
IRAN
†VO THE ISLAMIC REP, Mashhad
W Asia & C Asia • 500 kW
JAPAN
†RADIO JAPAN/NHK, Tokyo-Yamata
E Asia • 300 kW • ALT. FREQ. TO 11715 kHz
SOUTH AFRICA
CHANNEL AFRICA, Meyerton
S Africa • 500 kW
TURKEY
†VOICE OF TURKEY, Ankara-Emirler
Ⓦ • C Asia • 500 kW
UNITED KINGDOM
BBC, Various Locations
⬛ • Europe • 250/500 kW
USA
RFE-RL, Via Biblis, Germany
Ⓦ • E Europe • 100 kW
(con'd) †RFE-RL, Via Briech, Morocco
Ⓦ • S Europe • 250 kW

0 1 2 3 4 5 6 7 8 9 10 11 12 13 14 15 16 17 18 19 20 21 22 23 24

ENGLISH ▬▬   ARABIC ⧓⧓⧓   CHINESE □□□   FRENCH ▬▬   GERMAN ▬▬   RUSSIAN ══   SPANISH ▬▬   OTHER ▬▬

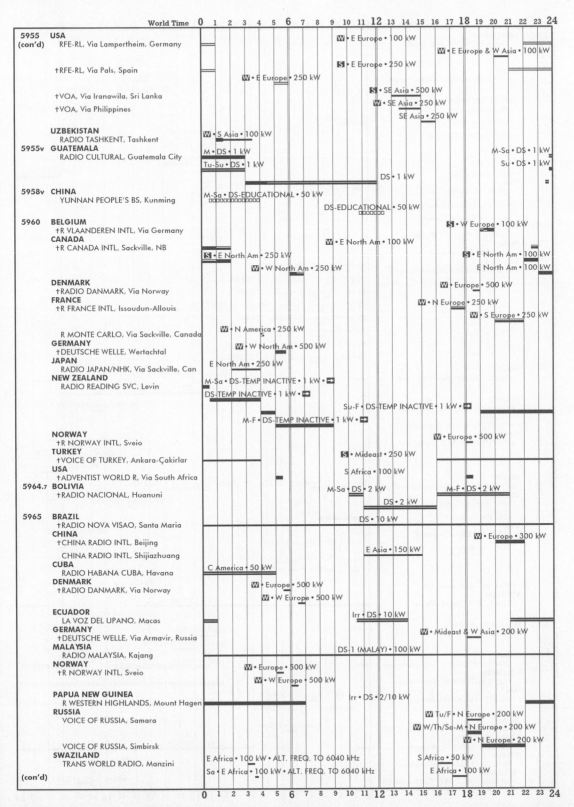

| World Time | 0 | 1 | 2 | 3 | 4 | 5 | 6 | 7 | 8 | 9 | 10 | 11 | 12 | 13 | 14 | 15 | 16 | 17 | 18 | 19 | 20 | 21 | 22 | 23 | 24 |

5955 **USA**
(con'd)   RFE-RL, Via Lampertheim, Germany — **W** • E Europe • 100 kW; **W** • E Europe & W Asia • 100 kW

†RFE-RL, Via Pals, Spain — **S** • E Europe • 250 kW; **W** • E Europe • 250 kW

†VOA, Via Iranawila, Sri Lanka — **S** • SE Asia • 500 kW

†VOA, Via Philippines — **W** • SE Asia • 250 kW; SE Asia • 250 kW

UZBEKISTAN
RADIO TASHKENT, Tashkent — **W** • S Asia • 100 kW

5955v **GUATEMALA**
RADIO CULTURAL, Guatemala City — M • DS • 1 kW; M-Sa • DS • 1 kW; Tu-Su • DS • 1 kW; Su • DS • 1 kW; DS • 1 kW

5958v **CHINA**
YUNNAN PEOPLE'S BS, Kunming — M-Sa • DS-EDUCATIONAL • 50 kW; DS-EDUCATIONAL • 50 kW

5960 **BELGIUM**
†R VLAANDEREN INTL, Via Germany — **S** • W Europe • 100 kW

CANADA
†R CANADA INTL, Sackville, NB — **W** • E North Am • 100 kW; **S** • E North Am • 250 kW; **S** • E North Am • 100 kW; E North Am • 100 kW; **W** • W North Am • 250 kW

DENMARK
†RADIO DANMARK, Via Norway — **W** • Europe • 500 kW

FRANCE
†R FRANCE INTL, Issoudun-Allouis — **W** • N Europe • 250 kW; **W** • S Europe • 250 kW

R MONTE CARLO, Via Sackville, Canada — **W** • N America • 250 kW

GERMANY
†DEUTSCHE WELLE, Wertachtal — **W** • W North Am • 500 kW

JAPAN
RADIO JAPAN/NHK, Via Sackville, Can — E North Am • 250 kW

NEW ZEALAND
RADIO READING SVC, Levin — M-Sa • DS-TEMP INACTIVE • 1 kW • ➡; DS-TEMP INACTIVE • 1 kW • ➡; Su-F • DS-TEMP INACTIVE • 1 kW • ➡; M-F • DS-TEMP INACTIVE • 1 kW • ➡

NORWAY
†R NORWAY INTL, Sveio — **W** • Europe • 500 kW

TURKEY
†VOICE OF TURKEY, Ankara-Çakirlar — **S** • Mideast • 250 kW

USA
†ADVENTIST WORLD R, Via South Africa — S Africa • 100 kW

5964.7 **BOLIVIA**
†RADIO NACIONAL, Huanuni — M-Sa • DS • 2 kW; M-F • DS • 2 kW; DS • 2 kW

5965 **BRAZIL**
†RADIO NOVA VISAO, Santa Maria — DS • 10 kW

CHINA
†CHINA RADIO INTL, Beijing — **W** • Europe • 300 kW

CHINA RADIO INTL, Shijiazhuang — E Asia • 150 kW

CUBA
RADIO HABANA CUBA, Havana — C America • 50 kW

DENMARK
†RADIO DANMARK, Via Norway — **W** • Europe • 500 kW; **W** • W Europe • 500 kW

ECUADOR
LA VOZ DEL UPANO, Macas — Irr • DS • 10 kW

GERMANY
†DEUTSCHE WELLE, Via Armavir, Russia — **W** • Mideast & W Asia • 200 kW

MALAYSIA
RADIO MALAYSIA, Kajang — DS-1 (MALAY) • 100 kW

NORWAY
†R NORWAY INTL, Sveio — **W** • Europe • 500 kW; **W** • W Europe • 500 kW

PAPUA NEW GUINEA
R WESTERN HIGHLANDS, Mount Hagen — Irr • DS • 2/10 kW

RUSSIA
VOICE OF RUSSIA, Samara — **W** Tu/F • N Europe • 200 kW; **W** W/Th/Sa-M • N Europe • 200 kW; **W** • N Europe • 200 kW

VOICE OF RUSSIA, Simbirsk

SWAZILAND
TRANS WORLD RADIO, Manzini — E Africa • 100 kW • ALT. FREQ. TO 6040 kHz; S Africa • 50 kW; Sa • E Africa • 100 kW • ALT. FREQ. TO 6040 kHz; E Africa • 100 kW

(con'd)

| | 0 | 1 | 2 | 3 | 4 | 5 | 6 | 7 | 8 | 9 | 10 | 11 | 12 | 13 | 14 | 15 | 16 | 17 | 18 | 19 | 20 | 21 | 22 | 23 | 24 |

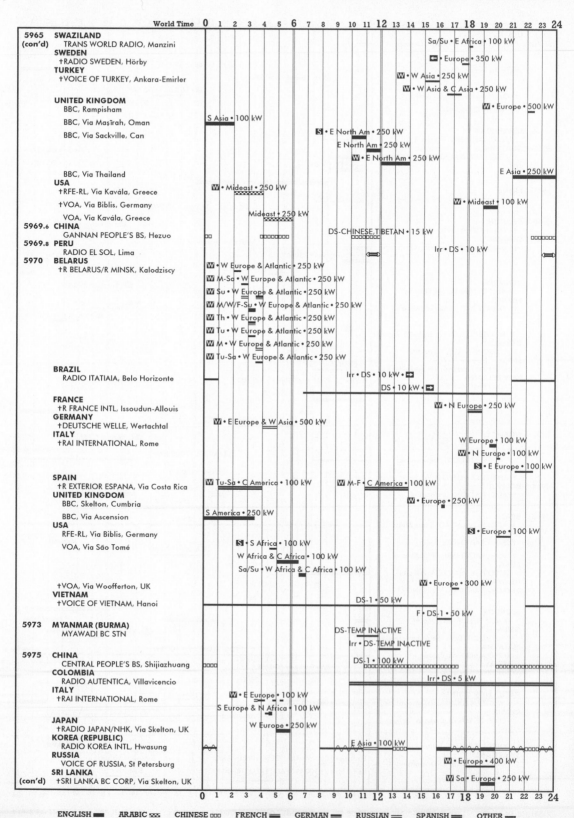

| | World Time | 0 | 1 | 2 | 3 | 4 | 5 | 6 | 7 | 8 | 9 | 10 | 11 | 12 | 13 | 14 | 15 | 16 | 17 | 18 | 19 | 20 | 21 | 22 | 23 | 24 |

5965
(con'd) SWAZILAND
    TRANS WORLD RADIO, Manzini — Sa/Su • E Africa • 100 kW
    SWEDEN
    †RADIO SWEDEN, Hörby — ◀ • Europe • 350 kW
    TURKEY
    †VOICE OF TURKEY, Ankara-Emirler — W • W Asia • 250 kW / W • W Asia & C Asia • 250 kW
    UNITED KINGDOM
     BBC, Rampisham — W • Europe • 500 kW
     BBC, Via Maşīrah, Oman — S Asia • 100 kW
     BBC, Via Sackville, Can — S • E North Am • 250 kW / E North Am • 250 kW / W • E North Am • 250 kW
     BBC, Via Thailand — E Asia • 250 kW
    USA
    †RFE-RL, Via Kavála, Greece — W • Mideast • 250 kW
    †VOA, Via Biblis, Germany — W • Mideast • 100 kW
    VOA, Via Kavála, Greece — Mideast • 250 kW
5969.6 CHINA
    GANNAN PEOPLE'S BS, Hezuo — DS-CHINESE,TIBETAN • 15 kW
5969.8 PERU
    RADIO EL SOL, Lima — Irr • DS • 10 kW
5970 BELARUS
    †R BELARUS/R MINSK, Kalodziscy — W • W Europe & Atlantic • 250 kW
     W M-Sa • W Europe & Atlantic • 250 kW
     W Su • W Europe & Atlantic • 250 kW
     W M/W/F-Su • W Europe & Atlantic • 250 kW
     W Th • W Europe & Atlantic • 250 kW
     W Tu • W Europe & Atlantic • 250 kW
     W M • W Europe & Atlantic • 250 kW
     W Tu-Sa • W Europe & Atlantic • 250 kW
    BRAZIL
    RADIO ITATIAIA, Belo Horizonte — Irr • DS • 10 kW / DS • 10 kW
    FRANCE
    †R FRANCE INTL, Issoudun-Allouis — W • N Europe • 250 kW
    GERMANY
    †DEUTSCHE WELLE, Wertachtal — W • E Europe & W Asia • 500 kW
    ITALY
    †RAI INTERNATIONAL, Rome — W Europe • 100 kW / W • N Europe • 100 kW / S • E Europe • 100 kW
    SPAIN
    †R EXTERIOR ESPANA, Via Costa Rica — W Tu-Sa • C America • 100 kW / W M-F • C America • 100 kW
    UNITED KINGDOM
     BBC, Skelton, Cumbria — W • Europe • 250 kW
     BBC, Via Ascension — S America • 250 kW / S • Europe • 100 kW
    USA
     RFE-RL, Via Biblis, Germany — S • S Africa • 100 kW
     VOA, Via São Tomé — W Africa & C Africa • 100 kW / Sa/Su • W Africa & C Africa • 100 kW
    †VOA, Via Woofferton, UK — W • Europe • 300 kW
    VIETNAM
    †VOICE OF VIETNAM, Hanoi — DS-1 • 50 kW / F • DS-1 • 50 kW
5973 MYANMAR (BURMA)
    MYAWADI BC STN — DS-TEMP INACTIVE / Irr • DS-TEMP INACTIVE
5975 CHINA
    CENTRAL PEOPLE'S BS, Shijiazhuang — DS-1 • 100 kW
    COLOMBIA
    RADIO AUTENTICA, Villavicencio — Irr • DS • 5 kW
    ITALY
    †RAI INTERNATIONAL, Rome — W • E Europe • 100 kW / S Europe & N Africa • 100 kW
    JAPAN
    †RADIO JAPAN/NHK, Via Skelton, UK — W Europe • 250 kW
    KOREA (REPUBLIC)
    RADIO KOREA INTL, Hwasung — E Asia • 100 kW
    RUSSIA
    VOICE OF RUSSIA, St Petersburg — W • Europe • 400 kW
    SRI LANKA
(con'd) †SRI LANKA BC CORP, Via Skelton, UK — W Sa • Europe • 250 kW

| | 0 | 1 | 2 | 3 | 4 | 5 | 6 | 7 | 8 | 9 | 10 | 11 | 12 | 13 | 14 | 15 | 16 | 17 | 18 | 19 | 20 | 21 | 22 | 23 | 24 |

ENGLISH ▬   ARABIC ▨   CHINESE ▫▫▫   FRENCH ▬   GERMAN ▬   RUSSIAN ═   SPANISH ▬   OTHER ▬

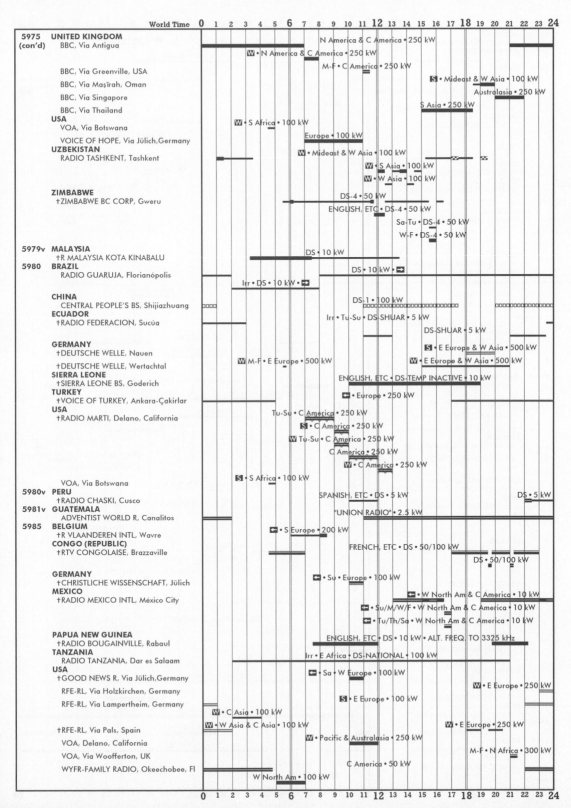

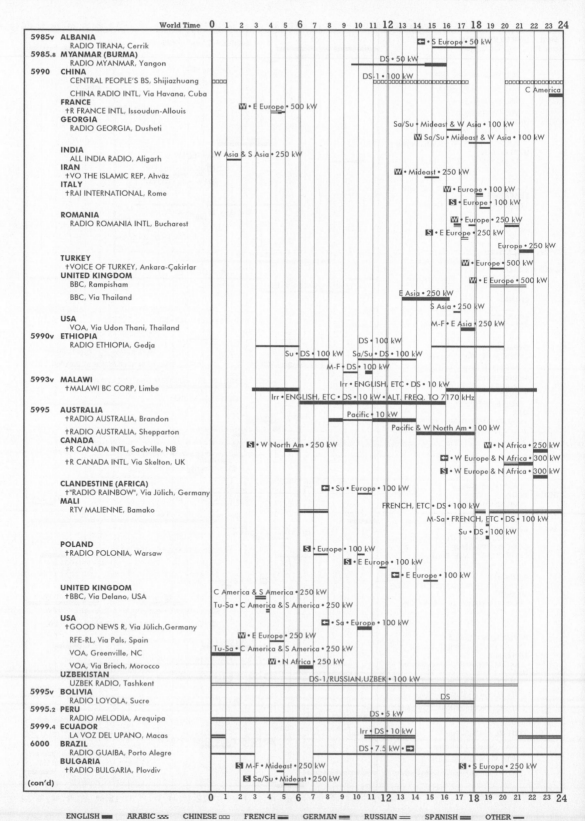

| | World Time | 0 | 1 | 2 | 3 | 4 | 5 | 6 | 7 | 8 | 9 | 10 | 11 | 12 | 13 | 14 | 15 | 16 | 17 | 18 | 19 | 20 | 21 | 22 | 23 | 24 |

5985v ALBANIA
RADIO TIRANA, Cerrik — ⏴ • S Europe • 50 kW

5985.8 MYANMAR (BURMA)
RADIO MYANMAR, Yangon — DS • 50 kW

5990 CHINA
CENTRAL PEOPLE'S BS, Shijiazhuang — DS-1 • 100 kW
CHINA RADIO INTL, Via Havana, Cuba — C America

FRANCE
†R FRANCE INTL, Issoudun-Allouis — W • E Europe • 500 kW

GEORGIA
RADIO GEORGIA, Dusheti — Sa/Su • Mideast & W Asia • 100 kW
W Sa/Su • Mideast & W Asia • 100 kW

INDIA
ALL INDIA RADIO, Aligarh — W Asia & S Asia • 250 kW

IRAN
†VO THE ISLAMIC REP, Ahväz — W • Mideast • 250 kW

ITALY
†RAI INTERNATIONAL, Rome — W • Europe • 100 kW
S • Europe • 100 kW

ROMANIA
RADIO ROMANIA INTL, Bucharest — W • Europe • 250 kW
S • E Europe • 250 kW
Europe • 250 kW

TURKEY
†VOICE OF TURKEY, Ankara-Çakirlar — W • Europe • 500 kW

UNITED KINGDOM
BBC, Rampisham — W • E Europe • 500 kW
BBC, Via Thailand — E Asia • 250 kW
S Asia • 250 kW

USA
VOA, Via Udon Thani, Thailand — M-F • E Asia • 250 kW

5990v ETHIOPIA
RADIO ETHIOPIA, Gedja — DS • 100 kW
Su • DS • 100 kW   Sa/Su • DS • 100 kW
M-F • DS • 100 kW

5993v MALAWI
†MALAWI BC CORP, Limbe — Irr • ENGLISH, ETC • DS • 10 kW
Irr • ENGLISH, ETC • DS • 10 kW • ALT. FREQ. TO 7170 kHz

5995 AUSTRALIA
†RADIO AUSTRALIA, Brandon — Pacific • 10 kW
†RADIO AUSTRALIA, Shepparton — Pacific & W North Am • 100 kW

CANADA
†R CANADA INTL, Sackville, NB — S • W North Am • 250 kW   W • N Africa • 250 kW
†R CANADA INTL, Via Skelton, UK — ⏴ • W Europe & N Africa • 300 kW
S • W Europe & N Africa • 300 kW

CLANDESTINE (AFRICA)
†"RADIO RAINBOW", Via Jülich, Germany — ⏴ • Su • Europe • 100 kW

MALI
RTV MALIENNE, Bamako — FRENCH, ETC • DS • 100 kW
M-Sa • FRENCH, ETC • DS • 100 kW
Su • DS • 100 kW

POLAND
†RADIO POLONIA, Warsaw — S • Europe • 100 kW
S • E Europe • 100 kW
⏴ • E Europe • 100 kW

UNITED KINGDOM
†BBC, Via Delano, USA — C America & S America • 250 kW
Tu-Sa • C America & S America • 250 kW

USA
†GOOD NEWS R, Via Jülich, Germany — ⏴ • Sa • Europe • 100 kW
RFE-RL, Via Pals, Spain — W • E Europe • 250 kW
VOA, Greenville, NC — Tu-Sa • C America & S America • 250 kW
VOA, Via Briech, Morocco — W • N Africa • 250 kW

UZBEKISTAN
UZBEK RADIO, Tashkent — DS-1/RUSSIAN, UZBEK • 100 kW

5995v BOLIVIA
RADIO LOYOLA, Sucre — DS

5995.2 PERU
RADIO MELODIA, Arequipa — DS • 5 kW

5999.4 ECUADOR
LA VOZ DEL UPANO, Macas — Irr • DS • 10 kW

6000 BRAZIL
RADIO GUAIBA, Porto Alegre — DS • 7.5 kW • ⏴

BULGARIA
†RADIO BULGARIA, Plovdiv — S M-F • Mideast • 250 kW   S • S Europe • 250 kW
S Sa/Su • Mideast • 250 kW

(con'd)

| | 0 | 1 | 2 | 3 | 4 | 5 | 6 | 7 | 8 | 9 | 10 | 11 | 12 | 13 | 14 | 15 | 16 | 17 | 18 | 19 | 20 | 21 | 22 | 23 | 24 |

ENGLISH ▬   ARABIC ⌇⌇⌇   CHINESE ▫▫▫   FRENCH ▬▬   GERMAN ▬▬   RUSSIAN ═   SPANISH ▬   OTHER ▬

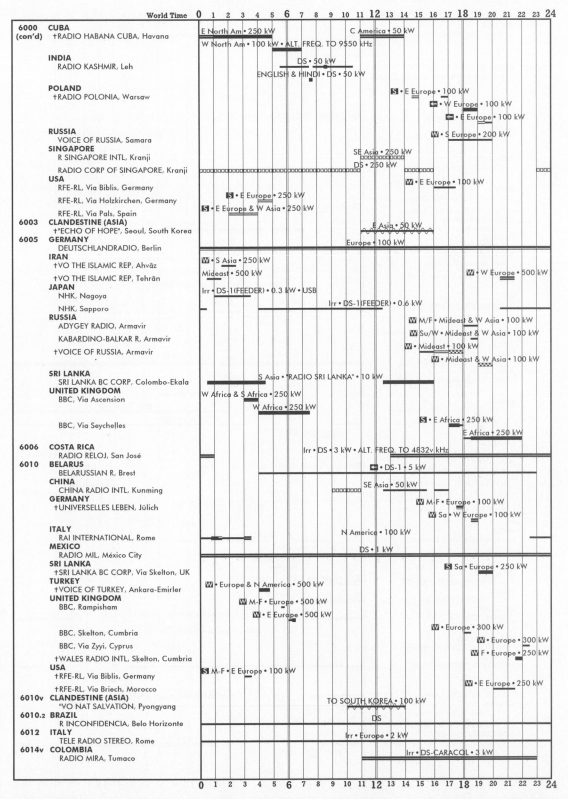

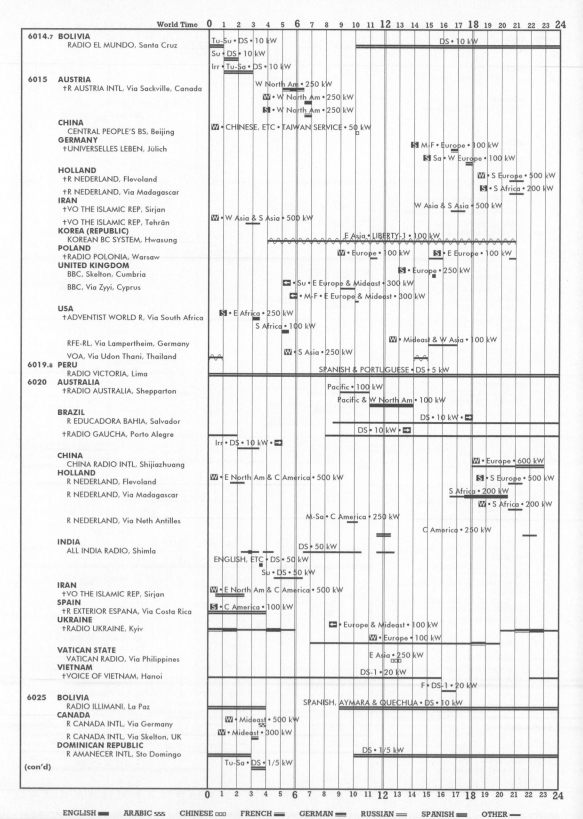

World Time 0 1 2 3 4 5 6 7 8 9 10 11 12 13 14 15 16 17 18 19 20 21 22 23 24

6014.7 BOLIVIA
  RADIO EL MUNDO, Santa Cruz
  Tu-Su • DS • 10 kW   DS • 10 kW
  Su • DS • 10 kW
  Irr • Tu-Sa • DS • 10 kW

6015 AUSTRIA
  †R AUSTRIA INTL, Via Sackville, Canada
    W North Am • 250 kW
    W • W North Am • 250 kW
    S • W North Am • 250 kW
  CHINA
    CENTRAL PEOPLE'S BS, Beijing
    W • CHINESE, ETC • TAIWAN SERVICE • 50 kW
  GERMANY
    †UNIVERSELLES LEBEN, Jülich
    S M-F • Europe • 100 kW
    S Sa • W Europe • 100 kW
  HOLLAND
    †R NEDERLAND, Flevoland
    W • S Europe • 500 kW
    †R NEDERLAND, Via Madagascar
    S • S Africa • 200 kW
  IRAN
    †VO THE ISLAMIC REP, Sirjan
    W Asia & S Asia • 500 kW
    †VO THE ISLAMIC REP, Tehrān
    W • W Asia & S Asia • 500 kW
  KOREA (REPUBLIC)
    KOREAN BC SYSTEM, Hwasung
    E Asia • LIBERTY-1 • 100 kW
  POLAND
    †RADIO POLONIA, Warsaw
    W • Europe • 100 kW   S • E Europe • 100 kW
  UNITED KINGDOM
    BBC, Skelton, Cumbria
    S • Europe • 250 kW
    BBC, Via Zyyi, Cyprus
    ← • Su • E Europe & Mideast • 300 kW
    ← • M-F • E Europe & Mideast • 300 kW
  USA
    †ADVENTIST WORLD R, Via South Africa
    S • E Africa • 250 kW
    S Africa • 100 kW
    RFE-RL, Via Lampertheim, Germany
    W • Mideast & W Asia • 100 kW
    VOA, Via Udon Thani, Thailand
    W • S Asia • 250 kW
6019.8 PERU
    RADIO VICTORIA, Lima
    SPANISH & PORTUGUESE • DS • 5 kW
6020 AUSTRALIA
    †RADIO AUSTRALIA, Shepparton
    Pacific • 100 kW
    Pacific & W North Am • 100 kW
  BRAZIL
    R EDUCADORA BAHIA, Salvador
    DS • 10 kW • →
    †RADIO GAUCHA, Porto Alegre
    DS • 10 kW • →
    Irr • DS • 10 kW • →
  CHINA
    CHINA RADIO INTL, Shijiazhuang
    W • Europe • 600 kW
  HOLLAND
    R NEDERLAND, Flevoland
    W • E North Am & C America • 500 kW
    S • S Europe • 500 kW
    R NEDERLAND, Via Madagascar
    S Africa • 200 kW
    W • S Africa • 200 kW
    R NEDERLAND, Via Neth Antilles
    M-Sa • C America • 250 kW
    C America • 250 kW
  INDIA
    ALL INDIA RADIO, Shimla
    DS • 50 kW
    ENGLISH, ETC • DS • 50 kW
    Su • DS • 50 kW
  IRAN
    †VO THE ISLAMIC REP, Sirjan
    W • E North Am & C America • 500 kW
  SPAIN
    †R EXTERIOR ESPANA, Via Costa Rica
    S • C America • 100 kW
  UKRAINE
    †RADIO UKRAINE, Kyiv
    ← • Europe & Mideast • 100 kW
    W • Europe • 100 kW
  VATICAN STATE
    VATICAN RADIO, Via Philippines
    E Asia • 250 kW
  VIETNAM
    †VOICE OF VIETNAM, Hanoi
    DS-1 • 20 kW
    F • DS-1 • 20 kW
6025 BOLIVIA
    RADIO ILLIMANI, La Paz
    SPANISH, AYMARA & QUECHUA • DS • 10 kW
  CANADA
    R CANADA INTL, Via Germany
    W • Mideast • 500 kW
    R CANADA INTL, Via Skelton, UK
    W • Mideast • 300 kW
  DOMINICAN REPUBLIC
    R AMANECER INTL, Sto Domingo
    DS • 1/5 kW
    Tu-Sa • DS • 1/5 kW

(con'd)

0 1 2 3 4 5 6 7 8 9 10 11 12 13 14 15 16 17 18 19 20 21 22 23 24

ENGLISH ▬   ARABIC ⦚⦚⦚   CHINESE □□□   FRENCH ══   GERMAN ▭▭   RUSSIAN ═   SPANISH ▭   OTHER ▬

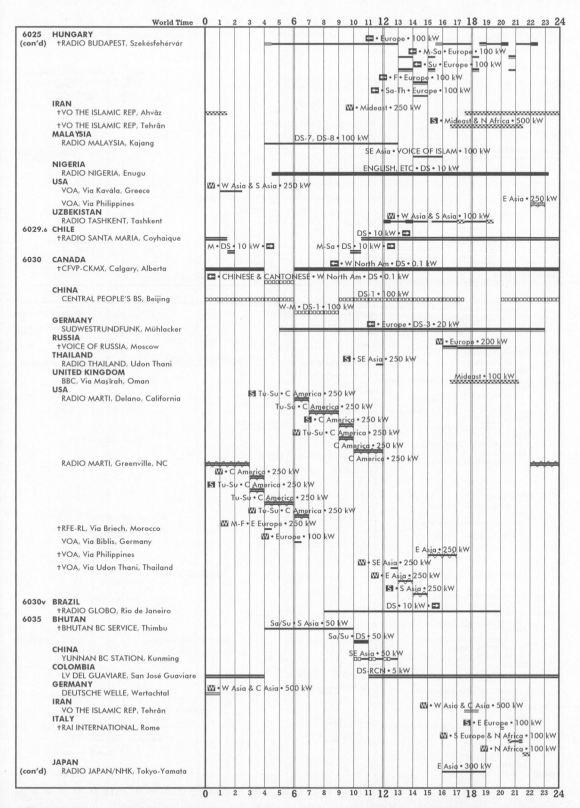

World Time   0 1 2 3 4 5 6 7 8 9 10 11 12 13 14 15 16 17 18 19 20 21 22 23 24

6025 HUNGARY
(con'd) †RADIO BUDAPEST, Szekésfehérvár
  • Europe • 100 kW
  • M-Sa • Europe • 100 kW
  • Su • Europe • 100 kW
  • F • Europe • 100 kW
  • Sa-Th • Europe • 100 kW

IRAN
  †VO THE ISLAMIC REP, Ahvāz   W • Mideast • 250 kW
  †VO THE ISLAMIC REP, Tehrān   S • Mideast & N Africa • 500 kW
MALAYSIA
  RADIO MALAYSIA, Kajang   DS-7, DS-8 • 100 kW
  SE Asia • VOICE OF ISLAM • 100 kW

NIGERIA
  RADIO NIGERIA, Enugu   ENGLISH, ETC • DS • 10 kW
USA
  VOA, Via Kavála, Greece   W • W Asia & S Asia • 250 kW
  VOA, Via Philippines   E Asia • 250 kW
UZBEKISTAN
  RADIO TASHKENT, Tashkent   W • W Asia & S Asia • 100 kW
6029.6 CHILE
  †RADIO SANTA MARIA, Coyhaique   DS • 10 kW •
   M • DS • 10 kW •   M-Sa • DS • 10 kW •

6030 CANADA
  †CFVP-CKMX, Calgary, Alberta   • W North Am • DS • 0.1 kW
   • CHINESE & CANTONESE • W North Am • DS • 0.1 kW
CHINA
  CENTRAL PEOPLE'S BS, Beijing   DS-1 • 100 kW
   W-M • DS-1 • 100 kW
GERMANY
  SUDWESTRUNDFUNK, Mühlacker   • Europe • DS-3 • 20 kW
RUSSIA
  †VOICE OF RUSSIA, Moscow   W • Europe • 200 kW
THAILAND
  RADIO THAILAND, Udon Thani   S • SE Asia • 250 kW
UNITED KINGDOM
  BBC, Via Maṣīrah, Oman   Mideast • 100 kW
USA
  RADIO MARTI, Delano, California   S • Tu-Su • C America • 250 kW
   Tu-Su • C America • 250 kW
   S • C America • 250 kW
   W • Tu-Su • C America • 250 kW
   C America • 250 kW
   C America • 250 kW

  RADIO MARTI, Greenville, NC   W • C America • 250 kW
   S • Tu-Su • C America • 250 kW
   Tu-Su • C America • 250 kW
   W • Tu-Su • C America • 250 kW
  †RFE-RL, Via Briech, Morocco   W • M-F • E Europe • 250 kW
  VOA, Via Biblis, Germany   W • Europe • 100 kW
  †VOA, Via Philippines   E Asia • 250 kW
  †VOA, Via Udon Thani, Thailand   W • SE Asia • 250 kW
   W • E Asia • 250 kW
   S • S Asia • 250 kW

6030v BRAZIL
  †RADIO GLOBO, Rio de Janeiro   DS • 10 kW •
6035 BHUTAN
  †BHUTAN BC SERVICE, Thimbu   Sa/Su • S Asia • 50 kW
   Sa/Su • DS • 50 kW

CHINA
  YUNNAN BC STATION, Kunming   SE Asia • 50 kW
COLOMBIA
  LV DEL GUAVIARE, San José Guaviare   DS-RCN • 5 kW
GERMANY
  DEUTSCHE WELLE, Wertachtal   W • W Asia & C Asia • 500 kW
IRAN
  VO THE ISLAMIC REP, Tehrān   W • W Asia & C Asia • 500 kW
ITALY
  †RAI INTERNATIONAL, Rome   S • E Europe • 100 kW
   W • S Europe & N Africa • 100 kW
   W • N Africa • 100 kW

JAPAN
(con'd) RADIO JAPAN/NHK, Tokyo-Yamata   E Asia • 300 kW

0 1 2 3 4 5 6 7 8 9 10 11 12 13 14 15 16 17 18 19 20 21 22 23 24

SEASONAL S OR W   1-HR TIMESHIFT MIDYEAR ⇦ OR ⇨   JAMMING / OR ∧   EARLIEST HEARD ◁   LATEST HEARD ▷   NEW FOR 2001 †

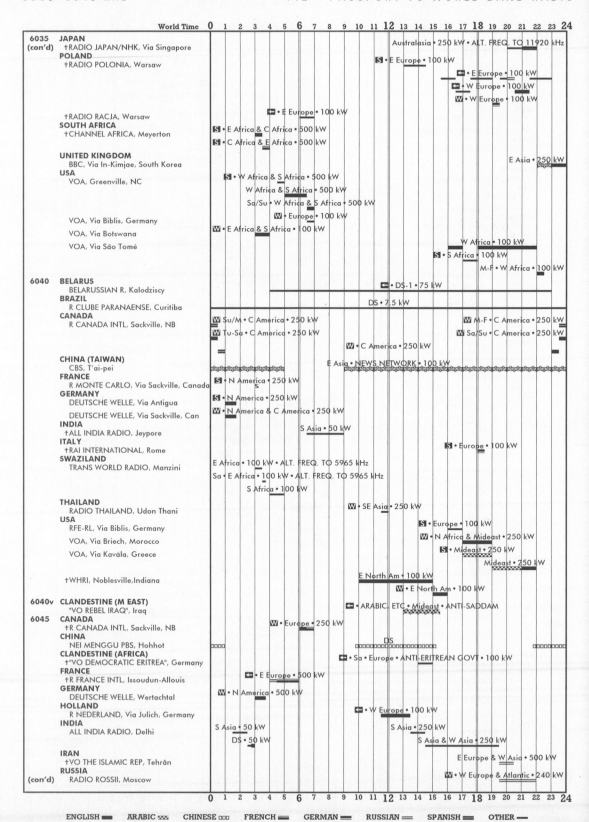

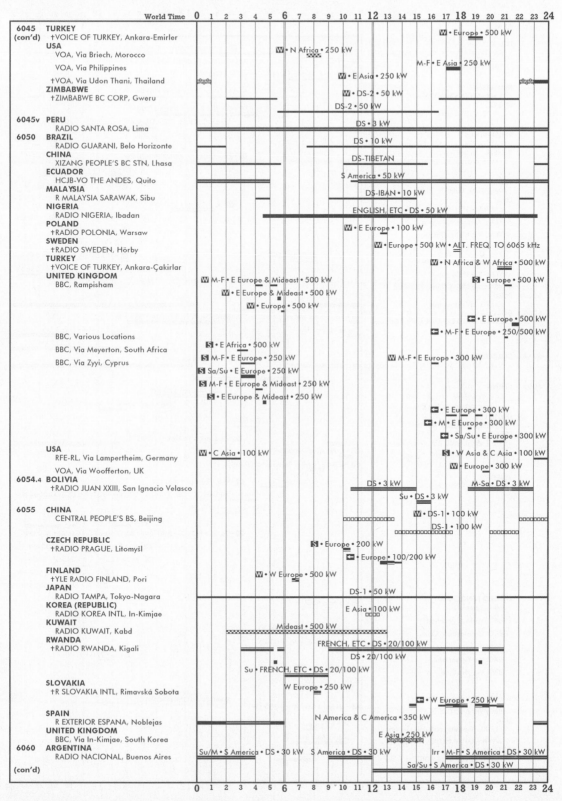

World Time 0 1 2 3 4 5 6 7 8 9 10 11 12 13 14 15 16 17 18 19 20 21 22 23 24

6045 TURKEY
(con'd) †VOICE OF TURKEY, Ankara-Emirler — W • Europe • 500 kW
    USA
      VOA, Via Briech, Morocco — W • N Africa • 250 kW
      VOA, Via Philippines — M-F • E Asia • 250 kW
      †VOA, Via Udon Thani, Thailand — W • E Asia • 250 kW
    ZIMBABWE
      †ZIMBABWE BC CORP, Gweru — W • DS-2 • 50 kW / DS-2 • 50 kW

6045v PERU
    RADIO SANTA ROSA, Lima — DS • 3 kW
6050 BRAZIL
    RADIO GUARANI, Belo Horizonte — DS • 10 kW
    CHINA
      XIZANG PEOPLE'S BC STN, Lhasa — DS-TIBETAN
    ECUADOR
      HCJB-VO THE ANDES, Quito — S America • 50 kW
    MALAYSIA
      R MALAYSIA SARAWAK, Sibu — DS-IBAN • 10 kW
    NIGERIA
      RADIO NIGERIA, Ibadan — ENGLISH, ETC • DS • 50 kW
    POLAND
      †RADIO POLONIA, Warsaw — W • E Europe • 100 kW
    SWEDEN
      †RADIO SWEDEN, Hörby — W • Europe • 500 kW • ALT. FREQ. TO 6065 kHz
    TURKEY
      †VOICE OF TURKEY, Ankara-Çakirlar — W • N Africa & W Africa • 500 kW
    UNITED KINGDOM
      BBC, Rampisham — W M-F • E Europe & Mideast • 500 kW / S • Europe • 500 kW
        W • E Europe & Mideast • 500 kW
        W • Europe • 500 kW
         ⇦ • E Europe • 500 kW
         ⇦ • M-F • E Europe • 250/500 kW
      BBC, Various Locations
      BBC, Via Meyerton, South Africa — S • E Africa • 500 kW
      BBC, Via Zyyi, Cyprus — S M-F • E Europe • 250 kW / W M-F • E Europe • 300 kW
        S Sa/Su • E Europe • 250 kW
        S M-F • E Europe & Mideast • 250 kW
        S • E Europe & Mideast • 250 kW
         ⇦ • E Europe • 300 kW
         ⇦ • M • E Europe • 300 kW
         ⇦ • Sa/Su • E Europe • 300 kW
    USA
      RFE-RL, Via Lampertheim, Germany — W • C Asia • 100 kW / S • W Asia & C Asia • 100 kW
      VOA, Via Woofferton, UK — W • Europe • 300 kW
6054.4 BOLIVIA
    †RADIO JUAN XXIII, San Ignacio Velasco — DS • 3 kW / M-Sa • DS • 3 kW
      Su • DS • 3 kW
6055 CHINA
    CENTRAL PEOPLE'S BS, Beijing — W • DS-1 • 100 kW
      DS-1 • 100 kW
    CZECH REPUBLIC
      †RADIO PRAGUE, Litomyšl — S • Europe • 200 kW / ⇦ • Europe • 100/200 kW
    FINLAND
      †YLE RADIO FINLAND, Pori — W • W Europe • 500 kW
    JAPAN
      RADIO TAMPA, Tokyo-Nagara — DS-1 • 50 kW
    KOREA (REPUBLIC)
      RADIO KOREA INTL, In-Kimjae — E Asia • 100 kW
    KUWAIT
      RADIO KUWAIT, Kabd — Mideast • 500 kW
    RWANDA
      †RADIO RWANDA, Kigali — FRENCH, ETC • DS • 20/100 kW
      DS • 20/100 kW
      Su • FRENCH, ETC • DS • 20/100 kW
    SLOVAKIA
      †R SLOVAKIA INTL, Rimavská Sobota — W Europe • 250 kW
       ⇦ • W Europe • 250 kW
    SPAIN
      R EXTERIOR ESPANA, Noblejas — N America & C America • 350 kW
    UNITED KINGDOM
      BBC, Via In-Kimjae, South Korea — E Asia • 250 kW
6060 ARGENTINA
    RADIO NACIONAL, Buenos Aires — Su/M • S America • DS • 30 kW / S America • DS • 30 kW / Irr • M-F • S America • DS • 30 kW
      Sa/Su • S America • DS • 30 kW

(con'd)

0 1 2 3 4 5 6 7 8 9 10 11 12 13 14 15 16 17 18 19 20 21 22 23 24

SEASONAL S OR W   1-HR TIMESHIFT MIDYEAR ⇦ OR ⇨   JAMMING / OR /\   EARLIEST HEARD ◁   LATEST HEARD ▷   NEW FOR 2001 †

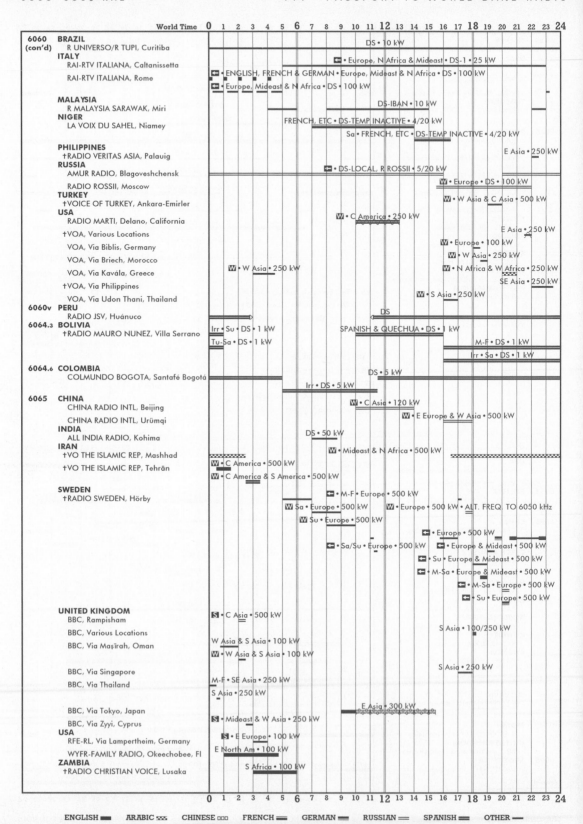

World Time 0 1 2 3 4 5 6 7 8 9 10 11 12 13 14 15 16 17 18 19 20 21 22 23 24

6060 BRAZIL (con'd)
R UNIVERSO/R TUPI, Curitiba — DS • 10 kW

ITALY
RAI-RTV ITALIANA, Caltanissetta — • Europe, N Africa & Mideast • DS-1 • 25 kW
RAI-RTV ITALIANA, Rome — • ENGLISH, FRENCH & GERMAN • Europe, Mideast & N Africa • DS • 100 kW
— • Europe, Mideast & N Africa • DS • 100 kW

MALAYSIA
R MALAYSIA SARAWAK, Miri — DS-IBAN • 10 kW

NIGER
LA VOIX DU SAHEL, Niamey — FRENCH, ETC • DS-TEMP INACTIVE • 4/20 kW
Sa • FRENCH, ETC • DS-TEMP INACTIVE • 4/20 kW

PHILIPPINES
†RADIO VERITAS ASIA, Palauig — E Asia • 250 kW

RUSSIA
AMUR RADIO, Blagoveshchensk — • DS-LOCAL, R ROSSII • 5/20 kW
RADIO ROSSII, Moscow — W • Europe • DS • 100 kW

TURKEY
†VOICE OF TURKEY, Ankara-Emirler — W • W Asia & C Asia • 500 kW

USA
RADIO MARTI, Delano, California — W • C America • 250 kW
†VOA, Various Locations — E Asia • 250 kW
VOA, Via Biblis, Germany — W • Europe • 100 kW
VOA, Via Briech, Morocco — W • W Asia • 250 kW
VOA, Via Kavála, Greece — W • W Asia • 250 kW / W • N Africa & W Africa • 250 kW
†VOA, Via Philippines — SE Asia • 250 kW
VOA, Via Udon Thani, Thailand — W • S Asia • 250 kW

6060v PERU
RADIO JSV, Huánuco — DS

6064.3 BOLIVIA
†RADIO MAURO NUNEZ, Villa Serrano — Irr • Su • DS • 1 kW / SPANISH & QUECHUA • DS • 1 kW
Tu-Sa • DS • 1 kW / M-F • DS • 1 kW
Irr • Sa • DS • 1 kW

6064.6 COLOMBIA
COLMUNDO BOGOTA, Santafé Bogotá — DS • 5 kW
Irr • DS • 5 kW

6065 CHINA
CHINA RADIO INTL, Beijing — W • C Asia • 120 kW
CHINA RADIO INTL, Urümqi — W • E Europe & W Asia • 500 kW

INDIA
ALL INDIA RADIO, Kohima — DS • 50 kW

IRAN
†VO THE ISLAMIC REP, Mashhad — W • Mideast & N Africa • 500 kW
†VO THE ISLAMIC REP, Tehrān — W • C America • 500 kW
W • C America & S America • 500 kW

SWEDEN
†RADIO SWEDEN, Hörby — • M-F • Europe • 500 kW
W • Sa • Europe • 500 kW / W • Europe • 500 kW • ALT. FREQ. TO 6050 kHz
W • Su • Europe • 500 kW
• Europe • 500 kW
• Sa/Su • Europe • 500 kW / • Europe & Mideast • 500 kW
• Su • Europe & Mideast • 500 kW
• M-Sa • Europe & Mideast • 500 kW
• M-Sa • Europe • 500 kW
• Su • Europe • 500 kW

UNITED KINGDOM
BBC, Rampisham — S • C Asia • 500 kW
BBC, Various Locations — S Asia • 100/250 kW
BBC, Via Maṣīrah, Oman — W Asia & S Asia • 100 kW
W • W Asia & S Asia • 100 kW
BBC, Via Singapore — S Asia • 250 kW
BBC, Via Thailand — M-F • SE Asia • 250 kW
S Asia • 250 kW
BBC, Via Tokyo, Japan — E Asia • 300 kW
BBC, Via Zyyi, Cyprus — S • Mideast & W Asia • 250 kW

USA
RFE-RL, Via Lampertheim, Germany — S • E Europe • 100 kW
WYFR-FAMILY RADIO, Okeechobee, Fl — E North Am • 100 kW

ZAMBIA
†RADIO CHRISTIAN VOICE, Lusaka — S Africa • 100 kW

0 1 2 3 4 5 6 7 8 9 10 11 12 13 14 15 16 17 18 19 20 21 22 23 24

ENGLISH ▬ ARABIC ▨ CHINESE ▢▢▢ FRENCH ▬ GERMAN ▬ RUSSIAN ═ SPANISH ▬ OTHER ▬

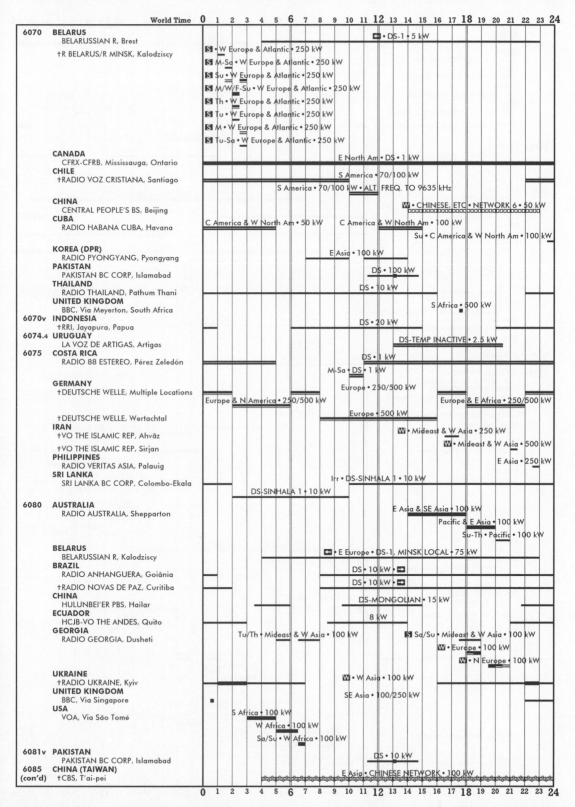

		World Time	0 1 2 3 4 5 6 7 8 9 10 11 12 13 14 15 16 17 18 19 20 21 22 23 24

6070 BELARUS
BELARUSSIAN R, Brest
• DS-1 • 5 kW

†R BELARUS/R MINSK, Kalodziscy
S • W Europe & Atlantic • 250 kW
S M-Sa • W Europe & Atlantic • 250 kW
S Su • W Europe & Atlantic • 250 kW
S M/W/F-Su • W Europe & Atlantic • 250 kW
S Th • W Europe & Atlantic • 250 kW
S Tu • W Europe & Atlantic • 250 kW
S M • W Europe & Atlantic • 250 kW
S Tu-Sa • W Europe & Atlantic • 250 kW

CANADA
CFRX-CFRB, Mississauga, Ontario — E North Am • DS • 1 kW

CHILE
†RADIO VOZ CRISTIANA, Santiago — S America • 70/100 kW
S America • 70/100 kW • ALT. FREQ. TO 9635 kHz

CHINA
CENTRAL PEOPLE'S BS, Beijing — W • CHINESE, ETC • NETWORK 6 • 50 kW

CUBA
RADIO HABANA CUBA, Havana — C America & W North Am • 50 kW   C America & W North Am • 100 kW
Su • C America & W North Am • 100 kW

KOREA (DPR)
RADIO PYONGYANG, Pyongyang — E Asia • 100 kW

PAKISTAN
PAKISTAN BC CORP, Islamabad — DS • 100 kW

THAILAND
RADIO THAILAND, Pathum Thani — DS • 10 kW

UNITED KINGDOM
BBC, Via Meyerton, South Africa — S Africa • 500 kW

6070v INDONESIA
†RRI, Jayapura, Papua — DS • 20 kW

6074.4 URUGUAY
LA VOZ DE ARTIGAS, Artigas — DS-TEMP INACTIVE • 2.5 kW

6075 COSTA RICA
RADIO 88 ESTEREO, Pérez Zeledón — DS • 1 kW
M-Sa • DS • 1 kW

GERMANY
†DEUTSCHE WELLE, Multiple Locations — Europe • 250/500 kW
Europe & N America • 250/500 kW   Europe & E Africa • 250/500 kW

†DEUTSCHE WELLE, Wertachtal — Europe • 500 kW

IRAN
†VO THE ISLAMIC REP, Ahvāz — W • Mideast & W Asia • 250 kW

†VO THE ISLAMIC REP, Sirjan — W • Mideast & W Asia • 500 kW

PHILIPPINES
RADIO VERITAS ASIA, Palauig — E Asia • 250 kW

SRI LANKA
SRI LANKA BC CORP, Colombo-Ekala — Irr • DS-SINHALA 1 • 10 kW
DS-SINHALA 1 • 10 kW

6080 AUSTRALIA
RADIO AUSTRALIA, Shepparton — E Asia & SE Asia • 100 kW
Pacific & E Asia • 100 kW
Su-Th • Pacific • 100 kW

BELARUS
BELARUSSIAN R, Kalodziscy — E Europe • DS-1, MINSK LOCAL • 75 kW

BRAZIL
RADIO ANHANGUERA, Goiânia — DS • 10 kW

†RADIO NOVAS DE PAZ, Curitiba — DS • 10 kW

CHINA
HULUNBEI'ER PBS, Hailar — DS-MONGOLIAN • 15 kW

ECUADOR
HCJB-VO THE ANDES, Quito — 8 kW

GEORGIA
RADIO GEORGIA, Dusheti — Tu/Th • Mideast & W Asia • 100 kW
S Sa/Su • Mideast & W Asia • 100 kW
W • Europe • 100 kW
W • N Europe • 100 kW

UKRAINE
†RADIO UKRAINE, Kyiv — W • W Asia • 100 kW

UNITED KINGDOM
BBC, Via Singapore — SE Asia • 100/250 kW

USA
VOA, Via São Tomé — S Africa • 100 kW
W Africa • 100 kW
Sa/Su • W Africa • 100 kW

6081v PAKISTAN
PAKISTAN BC CORP, Islamabad — DS • 10 kW

6085 CHINA (TAIWAN)
(con'd) †CBS, T'ai-pei — E Asia • CHINESE NETWORK • 100 kW

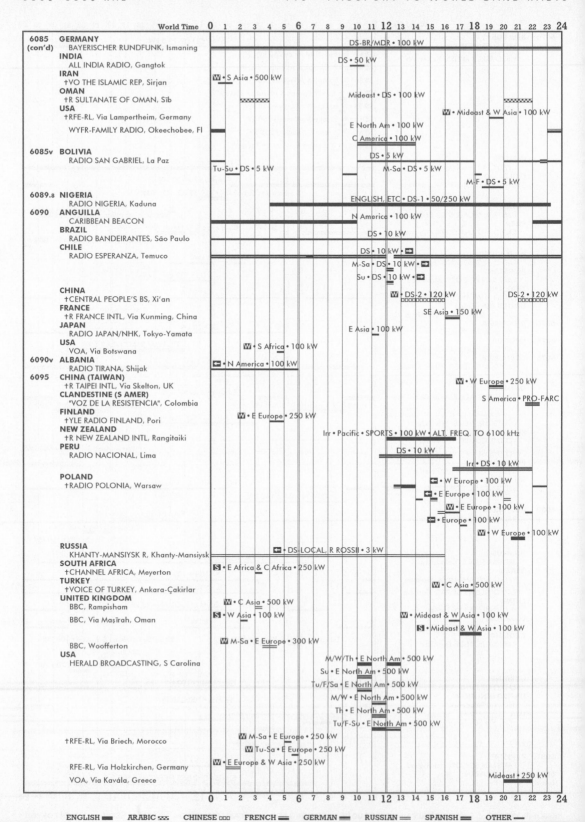

	World Time	0 1 2 3 4 5 6 7 8 9 10 11 12 13 14 15 16 17 18 19 20 21 22 23 24

6085 GERMANY
(con'd)   BAYERISCHER RUNDFUNK, Ismaning — DS-BR/MDR • 100 kW
INDIA
    ALL INDIA RADIO, Gangtok — DS • 50 kW
IRAN
    †VO THE ISLAMIC REP, Sirjan — W • S Asia • 500 kW
OMAN
    †R SULTANATE OF OMAN, Sīb — Mideast • DS • 100 kW
USA
    †RFE-RL, Via Lampertheim, Germany — W • Mideast & W Asia • 100 kW
    WYFR-FAMILY RADIO, Okeechobee, Fl — E North Am • 100 kW / C America • 100 kW

6085v BOLIVIA
    RADIO SAN GABRIEL, La Paz — DS • 5 kW / Tu-Su • DS • 5 kW / M-Sa • DS • 5 kW / M-F • DS • 5 kW

6089.8 NIGERIA
    RADIO NIGERIA, Kaduna — ENGLISH, ETC • DS-1 • 50/250 kW
6090 ANGUILLA
    CARIBBEAN BEACON — N America • 100 kW
BRAZIL
    RADIO BANDEIRANTES, São Paulo — DS • 10 kW
CHILE
    RADIO ESPERANZA, Temuco — DS • 10 kW • ▶ / M-Sa • DS • 10 kW • ▶ / Su • DS • 10 kW • ▶

CHINA
    †CENTRAL PEOPLE'S BS, Xi'an — W • DS-2 • 120 kW / DS-2 • 120 kW
FRANCE
    †R FRANCE INTL, Via Kunming, China — SE Asia • 150 kW
JAPAN
    RADIO JAPAN/NHK, Tokyo-Yamata — E Asia • 100 kW
USA
    VOA, Via Botswana — W • S Africa • 100 kW
6090v ALBANIA
    RADIO TIRANA, Shijak — ◀ • N America • 100 kW
6095 CHINA (TAIWAN)
    †R TAIPEI INTL, Via Skelton, UK — W • W Europe • 250 kW
CLANDESTINE (S AMER)
    "VOZ DE LA RESISTENCIA", Colombia — S America • PRO-FARC
FINLAND
    †YLE RADIO FINLAND, Pori — W • E Europe • 250 kW
NEW ZEALAND
    †R NEW ZEALAND INTL, Rangitaiki — Irr • Pacific • SPORTS • 100 kW • ALT. FREQ. TO 6100 kHz
PERU
    RADIO NACIONAL, Lima — DS • 10 kW / Irr • DS • 10 kW
POLAND
    †RADIO POLONIA, Warsaw — ◀ • W Europe • 100 kW / ◀ • E Europe • 100 kW / W • E Europe • 100 kW / ◀ • Europe • 100 kW / W • W Europe • 100 kW
RUSSIA
    KHANTY-MANSIYSK R, Khanty-Mansiysk — ◀ • DS-LOCAL, R ROSSII • 3 kW
SOUTH AFRICA
    †CHANNEL AFRICA, Meyerton — S • E Africa & C Africa • 250 kW
TURKEY
    †VOICE OF TURKEY, Ankara-Çakirlar — W • C Asia • 500 kW
UNITED KINGDOM
    BBC, Rampisham — W • C Asia • 500 kW
    BBC, Via Maşīrah, Oman — S • W Asia • 100 kW / W • Mideast & W Asia • 100 kW / S • Mideast & W Asia • 100 kW
    BBC, Woofferton — W M-Sa • E Europe • 300 kW
USA
    HERALD BROADCASTING, S Carolina — M/W/Th • E North Am • 500 kW / Su • E North Am • 500 kW / Tu/F/Sa • E North Am • 500 kW / M/W • E North Am • 500 kW / Th • E North Am • 500 kW / Tu/F-Su • E North Am • 500 kW
    †RFE-RL, Via Briech, Morocco — W M-Sa • E Europe • 250 kW / W Tu-Sa • E Europe • 250 kW
    RFE-RL, Via Holzkirchen, Germany — W • E Europe & W Asia • 250 kW
    VOA, Via Kavála, Greece — Mideast • 250 kW

	0 1 2 3 4 5 6 7 8 9 10 11 12 13 14 15 16 17 18 19 20 21 22 23 24

ENGLISH ▬ ARABIC ⌇⌇⌇ CHINESE ▫▫▫ FRENCH ▭▭ GERMAN ▬▬ RUSSIAN ══ SPANISH ▭ OTHER ▬

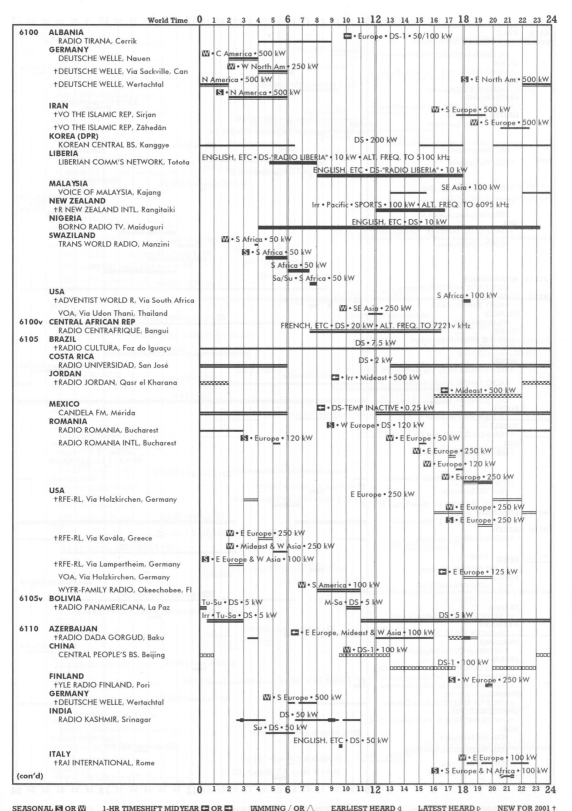

World Time: 0 1 2 3 4 5 6 7 8 9 10 11 12 13 14 15 16 17 18 19 20 21 22 23 24

6100 ALBANIA
RADIO TIRANA, Cerrik — ◨•Europe•DS-1•50/100 kW
GERMANY
DEUTSCHE WELLE, Nauen — W•C America•500 kW
— W•W North Am•250 kW
†DEUTSCHE WELLE, Via Sackville, Can — N America•500 kW — S•E North Am•500 kW
†DEUTSCHE WELLE, Wertachtal — S•N America•500 kW

IRAN
†VO THE ISLAMIC REP, Sirjan — W•S Europe•500 kW
†VO THE ISLAMIC REP, Zāhedān — W•S Europe•500 kW
KOREA (DPR)
KOREAN CENTRAL BS, Kanggye — DS•200 kW
LIBERIA
LIBERIAN COMM'S NETWORK, Totota — ENGLISH, ETC•DS-"RADIO LIBERIA"•10 kW•ALT. FREQ. TO 5100 kHz
— ENGLISH, ETC•DS-"RADIO LIBERIA"•10 kW

MALAYSIA
VOICE OF MALAYSIA, Kajang — SE Asia•100 kW
NEW ZEALAND
†R NEW ZEALAND INTL, Rangitaiki — Irr•Pacific•SPORTS•100 kW•ALT. FREQ. TO 6095 kHz
NIGERIA
BORNO RADIO TV, Maiduguri — ENGLISH, ETC•DS•10 kW
SWAZILAND
TRANS WORLD RADIO, Manzini — W•S Africa•50 kW
— S•S Africa•50 kW
— $ Africa•50 kW
— Sa/Su•S Africa•50 kW

USA
†ADVENTIST WORLD R, Via South Africa — S Africa•100 kW
VOA, Via Udon Thani, Thailand — W•SE Asia•250 kW
6100v CENTRAL AFRICAN REP
RADIO CENTRAFRIQUE, Bangui — FRENCH, ETC•DS•20 kW•ALT. FREQ. TO 7221v kHz
6105 BRAZIL
†RADIO CULTURA, Foz do Iguaçu — DS•7.5 kW
COSTA RICA
RADIO UNIVERSIDAD, San José — DS•2 kW
JORDAN
†RADIO JORDAN, Qasr el Kharana — ◨•Irr•Mideast•500 kW
— •Mideast•500 kW

MEXICO
CANDELA FM, Mérida — ◨•DS-TEMP INACTIVE•0.25 kW
ROMANIA
RADIO ROMANIA, Bucharest — S•W Europe•DS•120 kW
RADIO ROMANIA INTL, Bucharest — S•Europe•120 kW — W•E Europe•50 kW
— W•E Europe•250 kW
— W•Europe•120 kW
— W•Europe•250 kW
USA
†RFE-RL, Via Holzkirchen, Germany — E Europe•250 kW
— W•E Europe•250 kW
— S•E Europe•250 kW

†RFE-RL, Via Kavála, Greece — W•E Europe•250 kW
— W•Mideast & W Asia•250 kW
†RFE-RL, Via Lampertheim, Germany — S•E Europe & W Asia•100 kW
VOA, Via Holzkirchen, Germany — •E Europe•125 kW
WYFR-FAMILY RADIO, Okeechobee, Fl — W•S America•100 kW
6105v BOLIVIA
†RADIO PANAMERICANA, La Paz — Tu-Su•DS•5 kW — M-Sa•DS•5 kW
— Irr•Tu-Sa•DS•5 kW — DS•5 kW

6110 AZERBAIJAN
†RADIO DADA GORGUD, Baku — ◨•E Europe, Mideast & W Asia•100 kW
CHINA
CENTRAL PEOPLE'S BS, Beijing — W•DS-1•100 kW
— DS-1•100 kW

FINLAND
†YLE RADIO FINLAND, Pori — S•W Europe•250 kW
GERMANY
†DEUTSCHE WELLE, Wertachtal — W•S Europe•500 kW
INDIA
RADIO KASHMIR, Srinagar — DS•50 kW
— Su•DS•50 kW
— ENGLISH, ETC•DS•50 kW

ITALY
†RAI INTERNATIONAL, Rome — W•E Europe•100 kW
— S•S Europe & N Africa•100 kW

(con'd)

World Time: 0 1 2 3 4 5 6 7 8 9 10 11 12 13 14 15 16 17 18 19 20 21 22 23 24

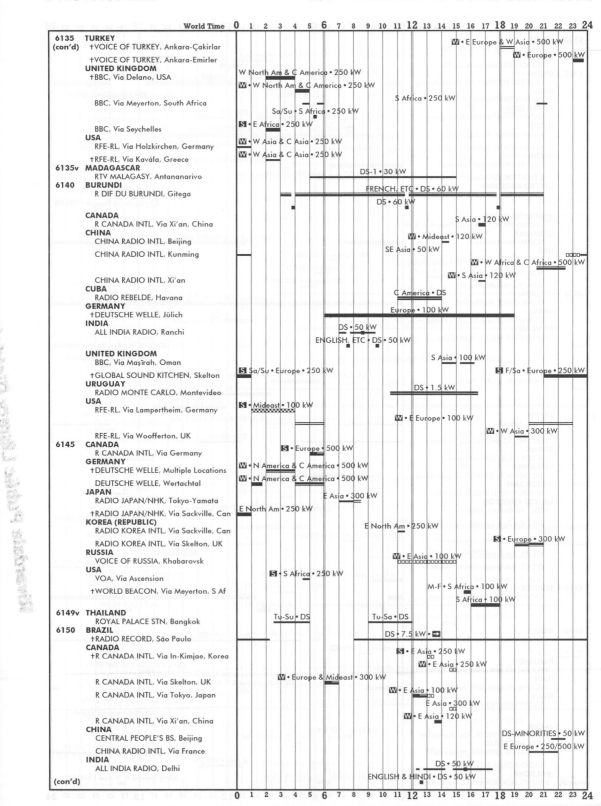

World Time 0 1 2 3 4 5 6 7 8 9 10 11 12 13 14 15 16 17 18 19 20 21 22 23 24

6135	**TURKEY**	
(con'd)	†VOICE OF TURKEY, Ankara-Çakirlar	W • E Europe & W Asia • 500 kW
	†VOICE OF TURKEY, Ankara-Emirler	W • Europe • 500 kW
	UNITED KINGDOM	
	†BBC, Via Delano, USA	W North Am & C America • 250 kW / W • W North Am & C America • 250 kW
	BBC, Via Meyerton, South Africa	S Africa • 250 kW / Sa/Su • S Africa • 250 kW
	BBC, Via Seychelles	S • E Africa • 250 kW
	USA	
	RFE-RL, Via Holzkirchen, Germany	W • W Asia & C Asia • 250 kW
	†RFE-RL, Via Kavála, Greece	W • W Asia & C Asia • 250 kW
6135v	**MADAGASCAR**	
	RTV MALAGASY, Antananarivo	DS-1 • 30 kW
6140	**BURUNDI**	
	R DIF DU BURUNDI, Gitega	FRENCH, ETC • DS • 60 kW / DS • 60 kW
	CANADA	
	R CANADA INTL, Via Xi'an, China	S Asia • 120 kW
	CHINA	
	CHINA RADIO INTL, Beijing	W • Mideast • 120 kW
	CHINA RADIO INTL, Kunming	SE Asia • 50 kW / W • W Africa & C Africa • 500 kW
	CHINA RADIO INTL, Xi'an	W • S Asia • 120 kW
	CUBA	
	RADIO REBELDE, Havana	C America • DS
	GERMANY	
	†DEUTSCHE WELLE, Jülich	Europe • 100 kW
	INDIA	
	ALL INDIA RADIO, Ranchi	DS • 50 kW / ENGLISH, ETC • DS • 50 kW
	UNITED KINGDOM	
	BBC, Via Maşīrah, Oman	S Asia • 100 kW
	†GLOBAL SOUND KITCHEN, Skelton	S Sa/Su • Europe • 250 kW / S F/Sa • Europe • 250 kW
	URUGUAY	
	RADIO MONTE CARLO, Montevideo	DS • 1.5 kW
	USA	
	RFE-RL, Via Lampertheim, Germany	S • Mideast • 100 kW / W • E Europe • 100 kW
	RFE-RL, Via Woofferton, UK	W • W Asia • 300 kW
6145	**CANADA**	
	R CANADA INTL, Via Germany	S • Europe • 500 kW
	GERMANY	
	†DEUTSCHE WELLE, Multiple Locations	W • N America & C America • 500 kW
	DEUTSCHE WELLE, Wertachtal	W • N America & C America • 500 kW
	JAPAN	
	RADIO JAPAN/NHK, Tokyo-Yamata	E Asia • 300 kW
	†RADIO JAPAN/NHK, Via Sackville, Can	E North Am • 250 kW
	KOREA (REPUBLIC)	
	RADIO KOREA INTL, Via Sackville, Can	E North Am • 250 kW
	RADIO KOREA INTL, Via Skelton, UK	S • Europe • 300 kW
	RUSSIA	
	VOICE OF RUSSIA, Khabarovsk	W • E Asia • 100 kW
	USA	
	VOA, Via Ascension	S • S Africa • 250 kW
	†WORLD BEACON, Via Meyerton, S Af	M-F • S Africa • 100 kW / S Africa • 100 kW
6149v	**THAILAND**	
	ROYAL PALACE STN, Bangkok	Tu-Su • DS / Tu-Sa • DS
6150	**BRAZIL**	
	†RADIO RECORD, São Paulo	DS • 7.5 kW • ⇨
	CANADA	
	†R CANADA INTL, Via In-Kimjae, Korea	S • E Asia • 250 kW / W • E Asia • 250 kW
	R CANADA INTL, Via Skelton, UK	W • Europe & Mideast • 300 kW
	R CANADA INTL, Via Tokyo, Japan	W • E Asia • 100 kW / E Asia • 300 kW
	R CANADA INTL, Via Xi'an, China	W • E Asia • 120 kW
	CHINA	
	CENTRAL PEOPLE'S BS, Beijing	DS-MINORITIES • 50 kW
	CHINA RADIO INTL, Via France	E Europe • 250/500 kW
	INDIA	
	ALL INDIA RADIO, Delhi	DS • 50 kW / ENGLISH & HINDI • DS • 50 kW
(con'd)		

0 1 2 3 4 5 6 7 8 9 10 11 12 13 14 15 16 17 18 19 20 21 22 23 24

ENGLISH ▬▬   ARABIC ⩘⩘⩘   CHINESE ▭▭▭   FRENCH ▭▭   GERMAN ▬▬   RUSSIAN ══   SPANISH ▬▬   OTHER ▬▬

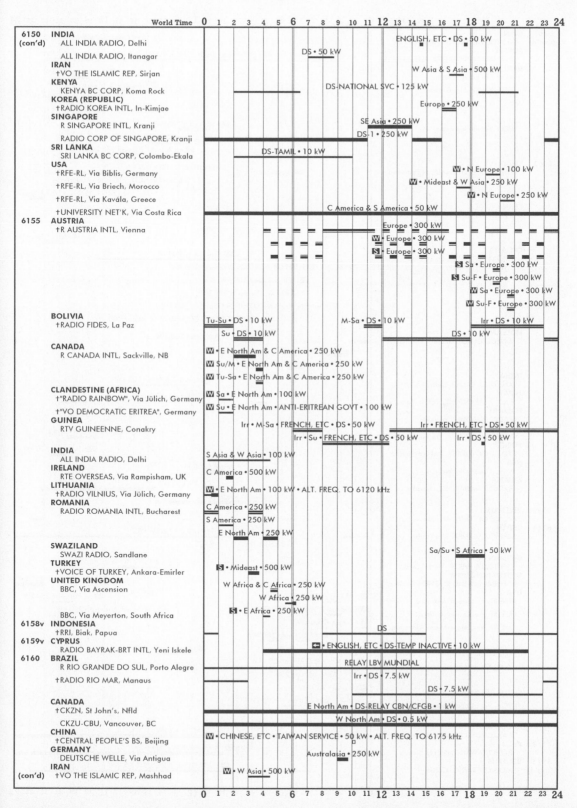

| | World Time | 0 | 1 | 2 | 3 | 4 | 5 | 6 | 7 | 8 | 9 | 10 | 11 | 12 | 13 | 14 | 15 | 16 | 17 | 18 | 19 | 20 | 21 | 22 | 23 | 24 |

6150 INDIA
(con'd) ALL INDIA RADIO, Delhi — ENGLISH, ETC • DS • 50 kW

ALL INDIA RADIO, Itanagar — DS • 50 kW

IRAN
†VO THE ISLAMIC REP, Sirjan — W Asia & S Asia • 500 kW

KENYA
KENYA BC CORP, Koma Rock — DS-NATIONAL SVC • 125 kW

KOREA (REPUBLIC)
†RADIO KOREA INTL, In-Kimjae — Europe • 250 kW

SINGAPORE
R SINGAPORE INTL, Kranji — SE Asia • 250 kW

RADIO CORP OF SINGAPORE, Kranji — DS-1 • 250 kW

SRI LANKA
SRI LANKA BC CORP, Colombo-Ekala — DS-TAMIL • 10 kW

USA
†RFE-RL, Via Biblis, Germany — W • N Europe • 100 kW

†RFE-RL, Via Briech, Morocco — W • Mideast & W Asia • 250 kW

†RFE-RL, Via Kavála, Greece — W • N Europe • 250 kW

†UNIVERSITY NET'K, Via Costa Rica — C America & S America • 50 kW

6155 AUSTRIA
†R AUSTRIA INTL, Vienna — Europe • 300 kW
W • Europe • 300 kW
S • Europe • 300 kW
S Sa • Europe • 300 kW
S Su-F • Europe • 300 kW
W Sa • Europe • 300 kW
W Su-F • Europe • 300 kW

BOLIVIA
†RADIO FIDES, La Paz — Tu-Su • DS • 10 kW   M-Sa • DS • 10 kW   Irr • DS • 10 kW
Su • DS • 10 kW   DS • 10 kW

CANADA
R CANADA INTL, Sackville, NB — W • E North Am & C America • 250 kW
W Su/M • E North Am & C America • 250 kW
W Tu-Sa • E North Am & C America • 250 kW

CLANDESTINE (AFRICA)
†"RADIO RAINBOW", Via Jülich, Germany — W Sa • E North Am • 100 kW
†"VO DEMOCRATIC ERITREA", Germany — W Su • E North Am • ANTI-ERITREAN GOVT • 100 kW

GUINEA
RTV GUINEENNE, Conakry — Irr • M-Sa • FRENCH, ETC • DS • 50 kW   Irr • FRENCH, ETC • DS • 50 kW
Irr • Su • FRENCH, ETC • DS • 50 kW   Irr • DS • 50 kW

INDIA
ALL INDIA RADIO, Delhi — S Asia & W Asia • 100 kW

IRELAND
RTE OVERSEAS, Via Rampisham, UK — C America • 500 kW

LITHUANIA
†RADIO VILNIUS, Via Jülich, Germany — W • E North Am • 100 kW • ALT. FREQ. TO 6120 kHz

ROMANIA
RADIO ROMANIA INTL, Bucharest — C America • 250 kW
S America • 250 kW
E North Am • 250 kW

SWAZILAND
SWAZI RADIO, Sandlane — Sa/Su • S Africa • 50 kW

TURKEY
†VOICE OF TURKEY, Ankara-Emirler — S • Mideast • 500 kW

UNITED KINGDOM
BBC, Via Ascension — W Africa & C Africa • 250 kW
W Africa • 250 kW

BBC, Via Meyerton, South Africa — S • E Africa • 250 kW

6158v INDONESIA
†RRI, Biak, Papua — DS

6159v CYPRUS
RADIO BAYRAK-BRT INTL, Yeni Iskele — ← • ENGLISH, ETC • DS-TEMP INACTIVE • 10 kW

6160 BRAZIL
R RIO GRANDE DO SUL, Porto Alegre — RELAY LBV MUNDIAL

†RADIO RIO MAR, Manaus — Irr • DS • 7.5 kW
DS • 7.5 kW

CANADA
†CKZN, St John's, Nfld — E North Am • DS-RELAY CBN/CFGB • 1 kW

CKZU-CBU, Vancouver, BC — W North Am • DS • 0.5 kW

CHINA
†CENTRAL PEOPLE'S BS, Beijing — W • CHINESE, ETC • TAIWAN SERVICE • 50 kW • ALT. FREQ. TO 6175 kHz

GERMANY
DEUTSCHE WELLE, Via Antigua — Australasia • 250 kW

IRAN
(con'd) †VO THE ISLAMIC REP, Mashhad — W • W Asia • 500 kW

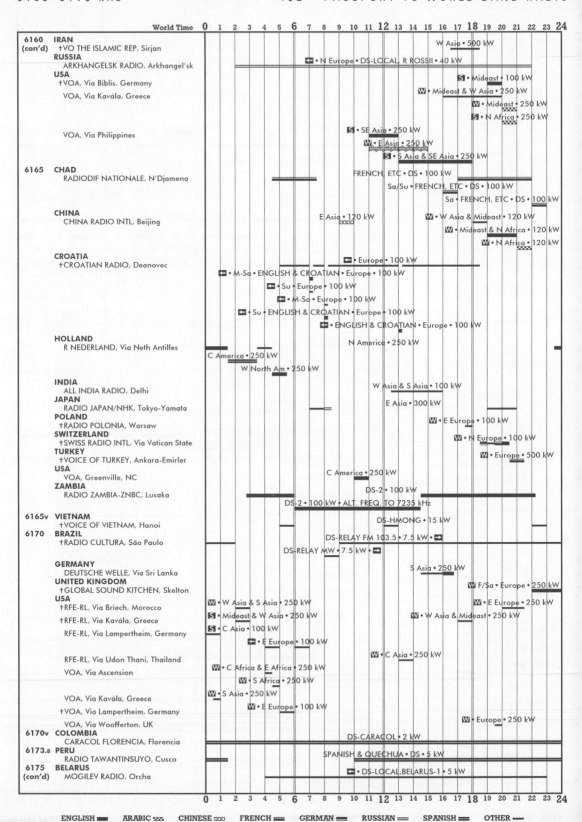

World Time 0 1 2 3 4 5 6 7 8 9 10 11 12 13 14 15 16 17 18 19 20 21 22 23 24

6160 IRAN
(con'd) †VO THE ISLAMIC REP, Sirjan — W Asia • 500 kW
         RUSSIA
            ARKHANGELSK RADIO, Arkhangel'sk — N Europe • DS-LOCAL, R ROSSII 40 kW
         USA
            †VOA, Via Biblis, Germany — S • Mideast • 100 kW
                                        W • Mideast & W Asia • 250 kW
            VOA, Via Kavála, Greece — W • Mideast • 250 kW
                                      S • N Africa • 250 kW
            VOA, Via Philippines — S • SE Asia • 250 kW
                                   W • E Asia • 250 kW
                                   S • S Asia & SE Asia • 250 kW

6165 CHAD
         RADIODIF NATIONALE, N'Djamena — FRENCH, ETC • DS • 100 kW
                                         Sa/Su • FRENCH, ETC • DS • 100 kW
                                         Sa • FRENCH, ETC • DS • 100 kW
      CHINA
         CHINA RADIO INTL, Beijing — E Asia • 120 kW
                                     W • W Asia & Mideast • 120 kW
                                     W • Mideast & N Africa • 120 kW
                                     W • N Africa • 120 kW
      CROATIA
         †CROATIAN RADIO, Deanovec — Europe • 100 kW
                                     • M-Sa • ENGLISH & CROATIAN • Europe • 100 kW
                                     • Su • Europe • 100 kW
                                     • M-Sa • Europe • 100 kW
                                     • Su • ENGLISH & CROATIAN • Europe • 100 kW
                                     • ENGLISH & CROATIAN • Europe • 100 kW
      HOLLAND
         R NEDERLAND, Via Neth Antilles — N America • 250 kW
                                          C America • 250 kW
                                          W North Am • 250 kW
      INDIA
         ALL INDIA RADIO, Delhi — W Asia & S Asia • 100 kW
      JAPAN
         RADIO JAPAN/NHK, Tokyo-Yamata — E Asia • 300 kW
      POLAND
         †RADIO POLONIA, Warsaw — W • E Europe • 100 kW
      SWITZERLAND
         †SWISS RADIO INTL, Via Vatican State — W • N Europe • 100 kW
      TURKEY
         †VOICE OF TURKEY, Ankara-Emirler — W • Europe • 500 kW
      USA
         VOA, Greenville, NC — C America • 250 kW
      ZAMBIA
         RADIO ZAMBIA-ZNBC, Lusaka — DS-2 • 100 kW
                                     DS-2 • 100 kW • ALT. FREQ. TO 7235 kHz

6165v VIETNAM
         †VOICE OF VIETNAM, Hanoi — DS-HMONG • 15 kW
6170 BRAZIL
         †RADIO CULTURA, São Paulo — DS-RELAY FM 103.5 • 7.5 kW •
                                     DS-RELAY MW • 7.5 kW •
      GERMANY
         DEUTSCHE WELLE, Via Sri Lanka — S Asia • 250 kW
      UNITED KINGDOM
         †GLOBAL SOUND KITCHEN, Skelton — W F/Sa • Europe • 250 kW
      USA
         †RFE-RL, Via Briech, Morocco — W • W Asia & S Asia • 250 kW
                                        W • E Europe • 250 kW
         †RFE-RL, Via Kavála, Greece — S • Mideast & W Asia • 250 kW
                                       W • W Asia & Mideast • 250 kW
         RFE-RL, Via Lampertheim, Germany — S • C Asia • 100 kW
                                            • E Europe • 100 kW
         RFE-RL, Via Udon Thani, Thailand — W • C Asia • 250 kW
         VOA, Via Ascension — W • C Africa & E Africa • 250 kW
                              W • S Africa • 250 kW
         VOA, Via Kavála, Greece — W • S Asia • 250 kW
         †VOA, Via Lampertheim, Germany — • E Europe • 100 kW
         VOA, Via Woofferton, UK — W • Europe • 250 kW
6170v COLOMBIA
         CARACOL FLORENCIA, Florencia — DS-CARACOL • 2 kW
6173.8 PERU
         RADIO TAWANTINSUYO, Cusco — SPANISH & QUECHUA • DS • 5 kW
6175 BELARUS
(con'd) MOGILEV RADIO, Orcha — DS-LOCAL, BELARUS-1 • 5 kW

World Time 0 1 2 3 4 5 6 7 8 9 10 11 12 13 14 15 16 17 18 19 20 21 22 23 24

ENGLISH ▬   ARABIC ▨   CHINESE □□□   FRENCH ══   GERMAN ▬   RUSSIAN ══   SPANISH ══   OTHER ▬

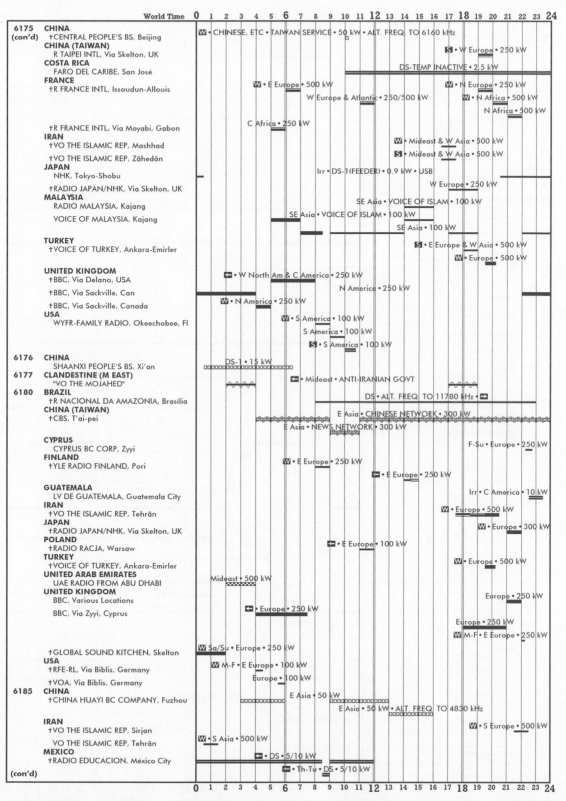

World Time 0 1 2 3 4 5 6 7 8 9 10 11 12 13 14 15 16 17 18 19 20 21 22 23 24

6175 (con'd)	**CHINA**	
	†CENTRAL PEOPLE'S BS, Beijing	W • CHINESE, ETC • TAIWAN SERVICE • 50 kW • ALT. FREQ. TO 6160 kHz
	CHINA (TAIWAN)	
	R TAIPEI INTL, Via Skelton, UK	S • W Europe • 250 kW
	COSTA RICA	
	FARO DEL CARIBE, San José	DS-TEMP INACTIVE • 2.5 kW
	FRANCE	
	†R FRANCE INTL, Issoudun-Allouis	W • E Europe • 500 kW W • N Europe • 250 kW
		W Europe & Atlantic • 250/500 kW W • N Africa • 500 kW
		N Africa • 500 kW
	†R FRANCE INTL, Via Moyabi, Gabon	C Africa • 250 kW
	IRAN	
	†VO THE ISLAMIC REP, Mashhad	W • Mideast & W Asia • 500 kW
	†VO THE ISLAMIC REP, Zāhedān	S • Mideast & W Asia • 500 kW
	JAPAN	
	NHK, Tokyo-Shobu	Irr • DS-1 (FEEDER) • 0.9 kW • USB
	†RADIO JAPAN/NHK, Via Skelton, UK	W Europe • 250 kW
	MALAYSIA	
	RADIO MALAYSIA, Kajang	SE Asia • VOICE OF ISLAM • 100 kW
	VOICE OF MALAYSIA, Kajang	SE Asia • VOICE OF ISLAM • 100 kW
		SE Asia • 100 kW
	TURKEY	
	†VOICE OF TURKEY, Ankara-Emirler	S • E Europe & W Asia • 500 kW
		W • Europe • 500 kW
	UNITED KINGDOM	
	†BBC, Via Delano, USA	⟷ • W North Am & C America • 250 kW
	†BBC, Via Sackville, Can	N America • 250 kW
	†BBC, Via Sackville, Canada	W • N America • 250 kW
	USA	
	WYFR-FAMILY RADIO, Okeechobee, Fl	W • S America • 100 kW
		S America • 100 kW
		S • S America • 100 kW
6176	**CHINA**	
	SHAANXI PEOPLE'S BS, Xi'an	DS-1 • 15 kW
6177	**CLANDESTINE (M EAST)**	
	"VO THE MOJAHED"	⟷ • Mideast • ANTI-IRANIAN GOVT
6180	**BRAZIL**	
	†R NACIONAL DA AMAZONIA, Brasilia	DS • ALT. FREQ. TO 11780 kHz • ⟷
	CHINA (TAIWAN)	
	†CBS, T'ai-pei	E Asia • CHINESE NETWORK • 300 kW
		E Asia • NEWS NETWORK • 300 kW
	CYPRUS	
	CYPRUS BC CORP, Zyyi	F-Su • Europe • 250 kW
	FINLAND	
	†YLE RADIO FINLAND, Pori	W • E Europe • 250 kW
		⟷ • E Europe • 250 kW
	GUATEMALA	
	LV DE GUATEMALA, Guatemala City	Irr • C America • 10 kW
	IRAN	
	†VO THE ISLAMIC REP, Tehrān	W • Europe • 500 kW
	JAPAN	
	†RADIO JAPAN/NHK, Via Skelton, UK	W • Europe • 300 kW
	POLAND	
	†RADIO RACJA, Warsaw	⟷ • E Europe • 100 kW
	TURKEY	
	†VOICE OF TURKEY, Ankara-Emirler	W • Europe • 500 kW
	UNITED ARAB EMIRATES	
	UAE RADIO FROM ABU DHABI	Mideast • 500 kW
	UNITED KINGDOM	
	BBC, Various Locations	Europe • 250 kW
	BBC, Via Zyyi, Cyprus	⟷ • Europe • 250 kW
		Europe • 250 kW
		W • M-F • E Europe • 250 kW
	†GLOBAL SOUND KITCHEN, Skelton	W Sa/Su • Europe • 250 kW
	USA	
	†RFE-RL, Via Biblis, Germany	W M-F • E Europe • 100 kW
	†VOA, Via Biblis, Germany	Europe • 100 kW
6185	**CHINA**	
	†CHINA HUAYI BC COMPANY, Fuzhou	E Asia • 50 kW
		E Asia • 50 kW • ALT. FREQ. TO 4830 kHz
	IRAN	
	†VO THE ISLAMIC REP, Sirjan	W • S Europe • 500 kW
	VO THE ISLAMIC REP, Tehrān	W • S Asia • 500 kW
	MEXICO	
	†RADIO EDUCACION, México City	⟷ • DS • 5/10 kW
(con'd)		⟷ • Th-Tu • DS • 5/10 kW

0 1 2 3 4 5 6 7 8 9 10 11 12 13 14 15 16 17 18 19 20 21 22 23 24

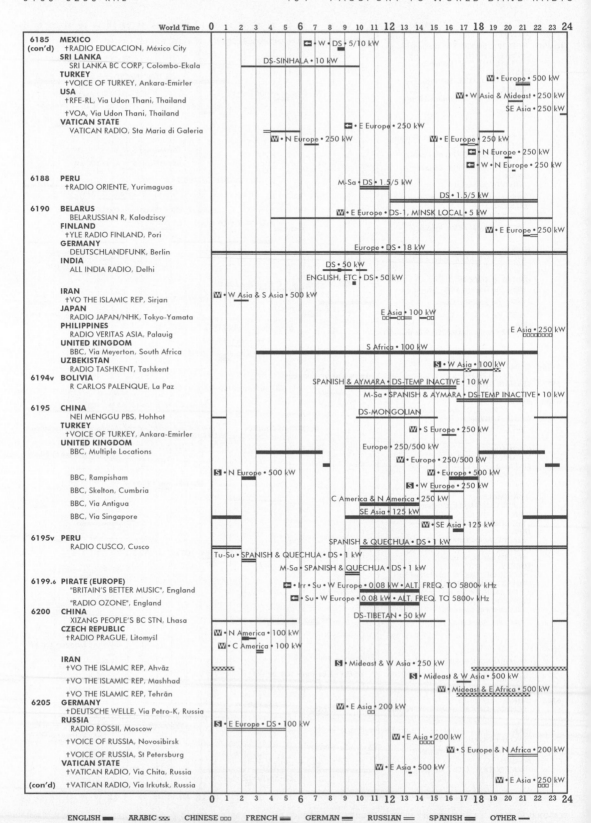

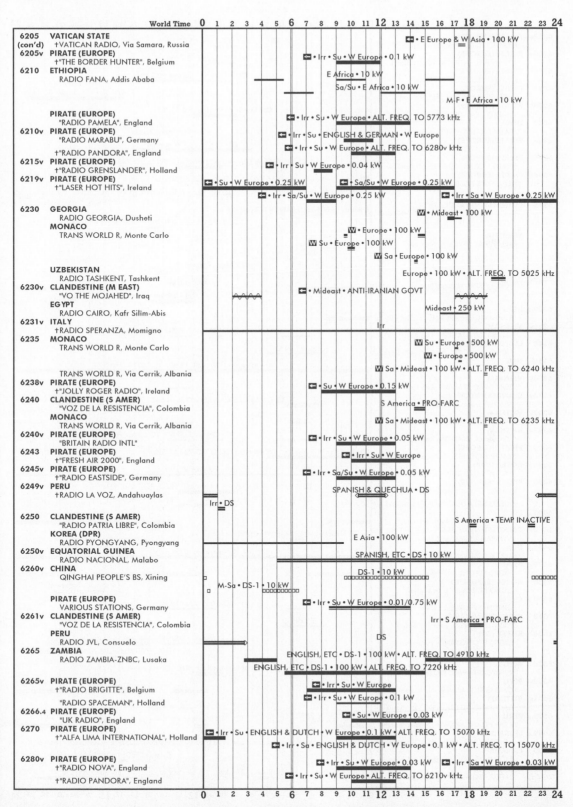

World Time 0 1 2 3 4 5 6 7 8 9 10 11 12 13 14 15 16 17 18 19 20 21 22 23 24

Freq	Station	Details
6205 (con'd)	VATICAN STATE †VATICAN RADIO, Via Samara, Russia	E Europe & W Asia • 100 kW
6205v	PIRATE (EUROPE) †"THE BORDER HUNTER", Belgium	• Irr • Su • W Europe • 0.1 kW
6210	ETHIOPIA RADIO FANA, Addis Ababa	E Africa • 10 kW / Sa/Su • E Africa • 10 kW / M-F • E Africa • 10 kW
	PIRATE (EUROPE) "RADIO PAMELA", England	• Irr • Su • W Europe • ALT. FREQ. TO 5773 kHz
6210v	PIRATE (EUROPE) "RADIO MARABU", Germany	• Irr • Su • ENGLISH & GERMAN • W Europe
	†"RADIO PANDORA", England	• Irr • Su • W Europe • ALT. FREQ. TO 6280v kHz
6215v	PIRATE (EUROPE) †"RADIO GRENSLANDER", Holland	• Irr • Su • W Europe • 0.04 kW
6219v	PIRATE (EUROPE) †"LASER HOT HITS", Ireland	• Su • W Europe • 0.25 kW / • Sa/Su • W Europe • 0.25 kW / • Irr • Sa/Su • W Europe • 0.25 kW / • Irr • Sa • W Europe • 0.25 kW
6230	GEORGIA RADIO GEORGIA, Dusheti	W • Mideast • 100 kW
	MONACO TRANS WORLD R, Monte Carlo	W • Europe • 100 kW / W Su • Europe • 100 kW / W Sa • Europe • 100 kW
	UZBEKISTAN RADIO TASHKENT, Tashkent	Europe • 100 kW • ALT. FREQ. TO 5025 kHz
6230v	CLANDESTINE (M EAST) "VO THE MOJAHED", Iraq	• Mideast • ANTI-IRANIAN GOVT
	EGYPT RADIO CAIRO, Kafr Silim-Abis	Mideast • 250 kW
6231v	ITALY †RADIO SPERANZA, Momigno	Irr
6235	MONACO TRANS WORLD R, Monte Carlo	W Su • Europe • 500 kW / W • Europe • 500 kW / W Sa • Mideast • 100 kW • ALT. FREQ. TO 6240 kHz
6238v	PIRATE (EUROPE) †"JOLLY ROGER RADIO", Ireland	• Su • W Europe • 0.15 kW
6240	CLANDESTINE (S AMER) "VOZ DE LA RESISTENCIA", Colombia	S America • PRO-FARC
	MONACO TRANS WORLD R, Via Cerrik, Albania	W Sa • Mideast • 100 kW • ALT. FREQ. TO 6235 kHz
6240v	PIRATE (EUROPE) "BRITAIN RADIO INTL"	• Irr • Su • W Europe • 0.05 kW
6243	PIRATE (EUROPE) †"FRESH AIR 2000", England	• Irr • Su • W Europe
6245v	PIRATE (EUROPE) †"RADIO EASTSIDE", Germany	• Irr • Sa/Su • W Europe • 0.05 kW
6249v	PERU †RADIO LA VOZ, Andahuaylas	SPANISH & QUECHUA • DS
6250	CLANDESTINE (S AMER) "RADIO PATRIA LIBRE", Colombia	Irr • DS / S America • TEMP INACTIVE
	KOREA (DPR) RADIO PYONGYANG, Pyongyang	E Asia • 100 kW
6250v	EQUATORIAL GUINEA RADIO NACIONAL, Malabo	SPANISH, ETC • DS • 10 kW
6260v	CHINA QINGHAI PEOPLE'S BS, Xining	DS-1 • 10 kW / M-Sa • DS-1 • 10 kW
	PIRATE (EUROPE) VARIOUS STATIONS, Germany	• Irr • Su • W Europe • 0.01/0.75 kW
6261v	CLANDESTINE (S AMER) "VOZ DE LA RESISTENCIA", Colombia	Irr • S America • PRO-FARC
	PERU RADIO JVL, Consuelo	DS
6265	ZAMBIA RADIO ZAMBIA-ZNBC, Lusaka	ENGLISH, ETC • DS-1 • 100 kW • ALT. FREQ. TO 4910 kHz / ENGLISH, ETC • DS-1 • 100 kW • ALT. FREQ. TO 7220 kHz
6265v	PIRATE (EUROPE) †"RADIO BRIGITTE", Belgium	• Irr • Su • W Europe
	"RADIO SPACEMAN", Holland	• Irr • Su • W Europe • 0.1 kW
6266.4	PIRATE (EUROPE) "UK RADIO", England	• Su • W Europe • 0.03 kW
6270	PIRATE (EUROPE) †"ALFA LIMA INTERNATIONAL", Holland	• Irr • Su • ENGLISH & DUTCH • W Europe • 0.1 kW • ALT. FREQ. TO 15070 kHz / • Irr • Sa • ENGLISH & DUTCH • W Europe • 0.1 kW • ALT. FREQ. TO 15070 kHz
6280v	PIRATE (EUROPE) †"RADIO NOVA", England	• Irr • Su • W Europe • 0.03 kW / • Irr • Sa • W Europe • 0.03 kW
	†"RADIO PANDORA", England	• Irr • Su • W Europe • ALT. FREQ. TO 6210v kHz

0 1 2 3 4 5 6 7 8 9 10 11 12 13 14 15 16 17 18 19 20 21 22 23 24

SEASONAL ⓈOR Ⓦ   1-HR TIMESHIFT MIDYEAR ⬅ OR ➡   JAMMING / OR ⋀   EARLIEST HEARD ◁   LATEST HEARD ▷   NEW FOR 2001 †

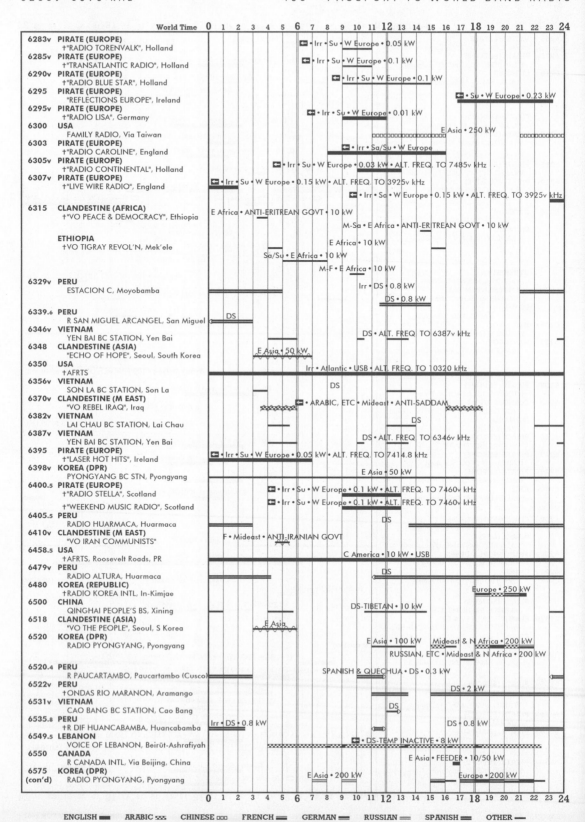

World Time 0 1 2 3 4 5 6 7 8 9 10 11 12 13 14 15 16 17 18 19 20 21 22 23 24

6283v PIRATE (EUROPE)
†"RADIO TORENVALK", Holland — Irr • Su • W Europe • 0.05 kW

6285v PIRATE (EUROPE)
†"TRANSATLANTIC RADIO", Holland — Irr • Su • W Europe • 0.1 kW

6290v PIRATE (EUROPE)
†"RADIO BLUE STAR", Holland — Irr • Su • W Europe • 0.1 kW

6295 PIRATE (EUROPE)
"REFLECTIONS EUROPE", Ireland — Su • W Europe • 0.23 kW

6295v PIRATE (EUROPE)
†"RADIO LISA", Germany — Irr • Su • W Europe • 0.01 kW

6300 USA
FAMILY RADIO, Via Taiwan — E Asia • 250 kW

6303 PIRATE (EUROPE)
†"RADIO CAROLINE", England — Irr • Sa/Su • W Europe

6305v PIRATE (EUROPE)
†"RADIO CONTINENTAL", Holland — Irr • Su • W Europe • 0.03 kW • ALT. FREQ. TO 7485v kHz

6307v PIRATE (EUROPE)
†"LIVE WIRE RADIO", England — Irr • Su • W Europe • 0.15 kW • ALT. FREQ. TO 3925v kHz / Irr • Sa • W Europe • 0.15 kW • ALT. FREQ. TO 3925v kHz

6315 CLANDESTINE (AFRICA)
†"VO PEACE & DEMOCRACY", Ethiopia — E Africa • ANTI-ERITREAN GOVT • 10 kW / M-Sa • E Africa • ANTI-ERITREAN GOVT • 10 kW

ETHIOPIA
†VO TIGRAY REVOL'N, Mek'ele — E Africa • 10 kW / Sa/Su • E Africa • 10 kW / M-F • E Africa • 10 kW

6329v PERU
ESTACION C, Moyobamba — Irr • DS • 0.8 kW / DS • 0.8 kW

6339.6 PERU
R SAN MIGUEL ARCANGEL, San Miguel — DS

6346v VIETNAM
YEN BAI BC STATION, Yen Bai — DS • ALT. FREQ. TO 6387v kHz

6348 CLANDESTINE (ASIA)
"ECHO OF HOPE", Seoul, South Korea — E Asia • 50 kW

6350 USA
†AFRTS — Irr • Atlantic • USB • ALT. FREQ. TO 10320 kHz

6356v VIETNAM
SON LA BC STATION, Son La — DS

6370v CLANDESTINE (M EAST)
"VO REBEL IRAQ", Iraq — ARABIC, ETC • Mideast • ANTI-SADDAM

6382v VIETNAM
LAI CHAU BC STATION, Lai Chau — DS

6387v VIETNAM
YEN BAI BC STATION, Yen Bai — DS • ALT. FREQ. TO 6346v kHz

6395 PIRATE (EUROPE)
†"LASER HOT HITS", Ireland — Irr • Su • W Europe • 0.05 kW • ALT. FREQ. TO 7414.8 kHz

6398v KOREA (DPR)
PYONGYANG BC STN, Pyongyang — E Asia • 50 kW

6400.5 PIRATE (EUROPE)
†"RADIO STELLA", Scotland — Irr • Su • W Europe • 0.1 kW • ALT. FREQ. TO 7460v kHz
†"WEEKEND MUSIC RADIO", Scotland — Irr • Su • W Europe • 0.1 kW • ALT. FREQ. TO 7460v kHz

6405.5 PERU
RADIO HUARMACA, Huarmaca — DS

6410v CLANDESTINE (M EAST)
"VO IRAN COMMUNISTS" — F • Mideast • ANTI-IRANIAN GOVT

6458.5 USA
†AFRTS, Roosevelt Roads, PR — C America • 10 kW • USB

6479v PERU
RADIO ALTURA, Huarmaca — DS

6480 KOREA (REPUBLIC)
†RADIO KOREA INTL, In-Kimjae — Europe • 250 kW

6500 CHINA
QINGHAI PEOPLE'S BS, Xining — DS-TIBETAN • 10 kW

6518 CLANDESTINE (ASIA)
"VO THE PEOPLE", Seoul, S Korea — E Asia

6520 KOREA (DPR)
RADIO PYONGYANG, Pyongyang — E Asia • 100 kW / Mideast & N Africa • 200 kW / RUSSIAN, ETC • Mideast & N Africa • 200 kW

6520.4 PERU
R PAUCARTAMBO, Paucartambo (Cusco) — SPANISH & QUECHUA • DS • 0.3 kW

6522v PERU
†ONDAS RIO MARANON, Aramango — DS • 2 kW

6531v VIETNAM
CAO BANG BC STATION, Cao Bang — DS

6535.8 PERU
†R DIF HUANCABAMBA, Huancabamba — Irr • DS • 0.8 kW / DS • 0.8 kW

6549.5 LEBANON
VOICE OF LEBANON, Beirūt-Ashrafiyah — DS-TEMP INACTIVE • 8 kW

6550 CANADA
R CANADA INTL, Via Beijing, China — E Asia • FEEDER • 10/50 kW

6575 KOREA (DPR)
(con'd) RADIO PYONGYANG, Pyongyang — E Asia • 200 kW / Europe • 200 kW

World Time 0 1 2 3 4 5 6 7 8 9 10 11 12 13 14 15 16 17 18 19 20 21 22 23 24

ENGLISH ■ ARABIC ⋙ CHINESE □□□ FRENCH ═ GERMAN ▬ RUSSIAN ═ SPANISH ━ OTHER —

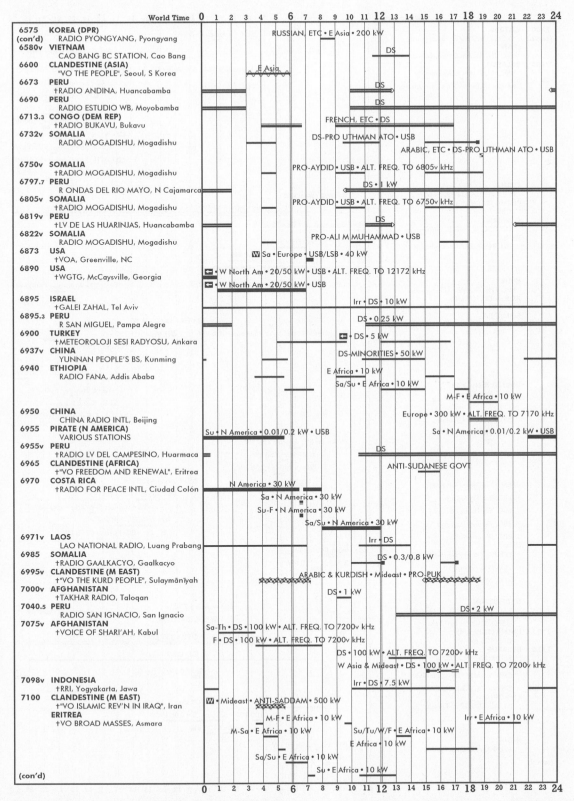

World Time		
6575 (con'd)	KOREA (DPR)	RUSSIAN, ETC • E Asia • 200 kW
	RADIO PYONGYANG, Pyongyang	
6580v	VIETNAM	DS
	CAO BANG BC STATION, Cao Bang	
6600	CLANDESTINE (ASIA)	E Asia
	"VO THE PEOPLE", Seoul, S Korea	
6673	PERU	DS
	†RADIO ANDINA, Huancabamba	
6690	PERU	DS
	RADIO ESTUDIO WB, Moyobamba	
6713.3	CONGO (DEM REP)	FRENCH, ETC • DS
	†RADIO BUKAVU, Bukavu	
6732v	SOMALIA	DS-PRO UTHMAN ATO • USB
	RADIO MOGADISHU, Mogadishu	ARABIC, ETC • DS-PRO UTHMAN ATO • USB
6750v	SOMALIA	PRO-AYDID • USB • ALT. FREQ. TO 6805v kHz
	†RADIO MOGADISHU, Mogadishu	
6797.7	PERU	DS • 1 kW
	R ONDAS DEL RIO MAYO, N Cajamarca	
6805v	SOMALIA	PRO-AYDID • USB • ALT. FREQ. TO 6750v kHz
	†RADIO MOGADISHU, Mogadishu	
6819v	PERU	DS
	†LV DE LAS HUARINJAS, Huancabamba	
6822v	SOMALIA	PRO-ALI M MUHAMMAD • USB
	RADIO MOGADISHU, Mogadishu	
6873	USA	W Sa • Europe • USB/LSB • 40 kW
	†VOA, Greenville, NC	
6890	USA	← • W North Am • 20/50 kW • USB • ALT. FREQ. TO 12172 kHz
	†WGTG, McCaysville, Georgia	← • W North Am • 20/50 kW • USB
6895	ISRAEL	Irr • DS • 10 kW
	†GALEI ZAHAL, Tel Aviv	
6895.3	PERU	DS • 0.25 kW
	R SAN MIGUEL, Pampa Alegre	
6900	TURKEY	← • DS • 5 kW
	†METEOROLOJI SESI RADYOSU, Ankara	
6937v	CHINA	DS-MINORITIES • 50 kW
	YUNNAN PEOPLE'S BS, Kunming	
6940	ETHIOPIA	E Africa • 10 kW
	RADIO FANA, Addis Ababa	Sa/Su • E Africa • 10 kW
		M-F • E Africa • 10 kW
6950	CHINA	Europe • 300 kW • ALT. FREQ. TO 7170 kHz
	CHINA RADIO INTL, Beijing	
6955	PIRATE (N AMERICA)	Su • N America • 0.01/0.2 kW • USB
	VARIOUS STATIONS	Sa • N America • 0.01/0.2 kW • USB
6955v	PERU	DS
	†RADIO LV DEL CAMPESINO, Huarmaca	
6965	CLANDESTINE (AFRICA)	ANTI-SUDANESE GOVT
	†"VO FREEDOM AND RENEWAL", Eritrea	
6970	COSTA RICA	N America • 30 kW
	†RADIO FOR PEACE INTL, Ciudad Colón	Sa • N America • 30 kW
		Su-F • N America • 30 kW
		Sa/Su • N America • 30 kW
6971v	LAOS	Irr • DS
	LAO NATIONAL RADIO, Luang Prabang	
6985	SOMALIA	DS • 0.3/0.8 kW
	†RADIO GAALKACYO, Gaalkacyo	
6995v	CLANDESTINE (M EAST)	ARABIC & KURDISH • Mideast • PRO-PUK
	†"VO THE KURD PEOPLE", Sulaymānīyah	
7000v	AFGHANISTAN	DS • 1 kW
	†TAKHAR RADIO, Taloqan	
7040.5	PERU	DS • 2 kW
	RADIO SAN IGNACIO, San Ignacio	
7075v	AFGHANISTAN	Sa-Th • DS • 100 kW • ALT. FREQ. TO 7200v kHz
	†VOICE OF SHARI'AH, Kabul	F • DS • 100 kW • ALT. FREQ. TO 7200v kHz
		DS • 100 kW • ALT. FREQ. TO 7200v kHz
		W Asia & Mideast • DS • 100 kW • ALT. FREQ. TO 7200v kHz
7098v	INDONESIA	Irr • DS • 7.5 kW
	†RRI, Yogyakarta, Jawa	
7100	CLANDESTINE (M EAST)	W • Mideast • ANTI-SADDAM • 500 kW
	†"VO ISLAMIC REV'N IN IRAQ", Iran	
	ERITREA	M-F • E Africa • 10 kW
	†VO BROAD MASSES, Asmara	Irr • E Africa • 10 kW
		M-Sa • E Africa • 10 kW
		Su/Tu/W/F • E Africa • 10 kW
		E Africa • 10 kW
		Sa/Su • E Africa • 10 kW
		Su • E Africa • 10 kW
(con'd)		

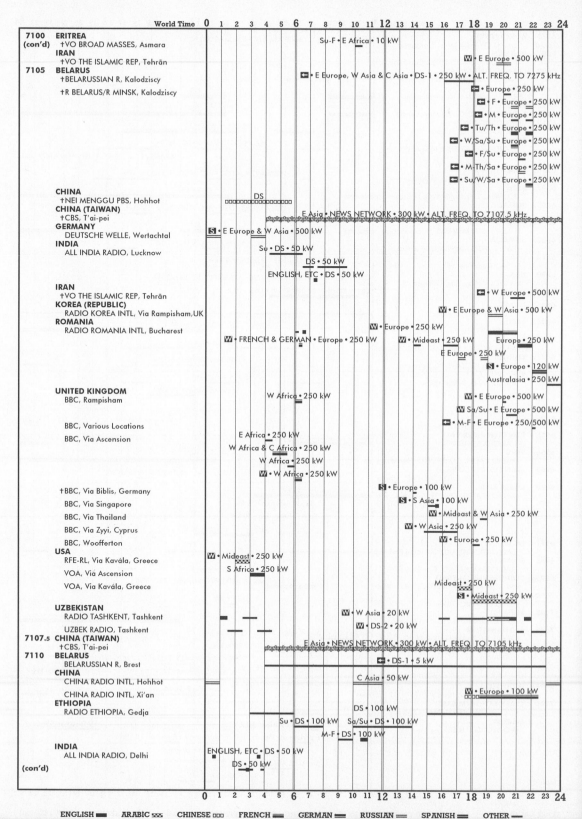

ENGLISH ▬▬   ARABIC ░░░   CHINESE ▫▫▫   FRENCH ▬▬   GERMAN ▬▬   RUSSIAN ══   SPANISH ══   OTHER ──

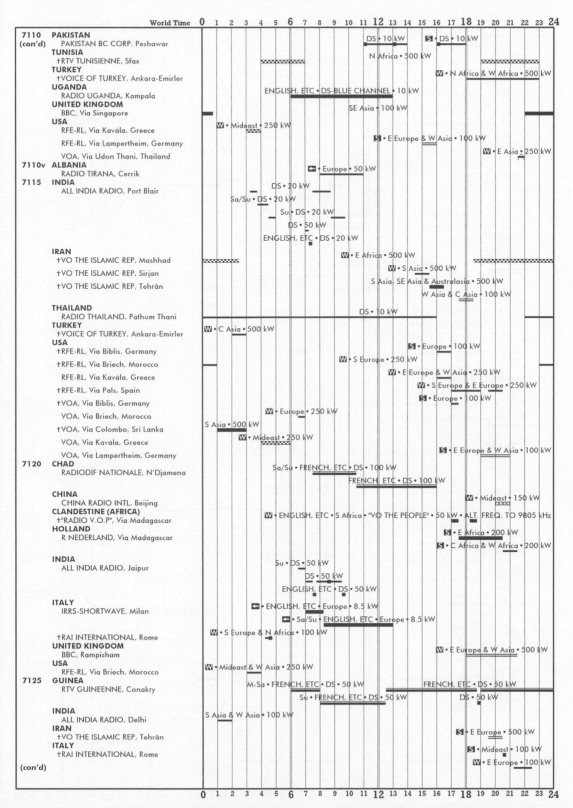

World Time 0 1 2 3 4 5 6 7 8 9 10 11 12 13 14 15 16 17 18 19 20 21 22 23 24

7110
(con'd) PAKISTAN
PAKISTAN BC CORP, Peshawar — DS • 10 kW / S • DS • 10 kW
TUNISIA
†RTV TUNISIENNE, Sfax — N Africa • 500 kW
TURKEY
†VOICE OF TURKEY, Ankara-Emirler — W • N Africa & W Africa • 500 kW
UGANDA
RADIO UGANDA, Kampala — ENGLISH, ETC • DS-BLUE CHANNEL • 10 kW
UNITED KINGDOM
BBC, Via Singapore — SE Asia • 100 kW
USA
RFE-RL, Via Kavála, Greece — W • Mideast • 250 kW
RFE-RL, Via Lampertheim, Germany — S • E Europe & W Asia • 100 kW
VOA, Via Udon Thani, Thailand — W • E Asia • 250 kW
7110v ALBANIA
RADIO TIRANA, Cerrik — • Europe • 50 kW
7115 INDIA
ALL INDIA RADIO, Port Blair — DS • 20 kW
Sa/Su • DS • 20 kW
Su • DS • 20 kW
DS • 50 kW
ENGLISH, ETC • DS • 20 kW
IRAN
†VO THE ISLAMIC REP, Mashhad — W • E Africa • 500 kW
†VO THE ISLAMIC REP, Sirjan — W • S Asia • 500 kW
†VO THE ISLAMIC REP, Tehrān — S Asia, SE Asia & Australasia • 500 kW
W Asia & C Asia • 100 kW
THAILAND
RADIO THAILAND, Pathum Thani — DS • 10 kW
TURKEY
†VOICE OF TURKEY, Ankara-Emirler — W • C Asia • 500 kW
USA
†RFE-RL, Via Biblis, Germany — S • Europe • 100 kW
†RFE-RL, Via Briech, Morocco — W • S Europe • 250 kW
RFE-RL, Via Kavála, Greece — W • E Europe & W Asia • 250 kW
†RFE-RL, Via Pals, Spain — W • S Europe & E Europe • 250 kW
†VOA, Via Biblis, Germany — S • Europe • 100 kW
VOA, Via Briech, Morocco — W • Europe • 250 kW
†VOA, Via Colombo, Sri Lanka — S Asia • 500 kW
VOA, Via Kavála, Greece — W • Mideast • 250 kW
VOA, Via Lampertheim, Germany — S • E Europe & W Asia • 100 kW
7120 CHAD
RADIODIF NATIONALE, N'Djamena — Sa/Su • FRENCH, ETC • DS • 100 kW
FRENCH, ETC • DS • 100 kW
CHINA
CHINA RADIO INTL, Beijing — W • Mideast • 150 kW
CLANDESTINE (AFRICA)
†"RADIO V.O.P", Via Madagascar — W • ENGLISH, ETC • S Africa • "VO THE PEOPLE" • 50 kW • ALT. FREQ. TO 9805 kHz
HOLLAND
R NEDERLAND, Via Madagascar — S • E Africa • 200 kW
S • C Africa & W Africa • 200 kW
INDIA
ALL INDIA RADIO, Jaipur — Su • DS • 50 kW
DS • 50 kW
ENGLISH, ETC • DS • 50 kW
ITALY
IRRS-SHORTWAVE, Milan — • ENGLISH, ETC • Europe • 8.5 kW
• Sa/Su • ENGLISH, ETC • Europe • 8.5 kW
†RAI INTERNATIONAL, Rome — W • S Europe & N Africa • 100 kW
UNITED KINGDOM
BBC, Rampisham — W • E Europe & W Asia • 500 kW
USA
RFE-RL, Via Briech, Morocco — W • Mideast & W Asia • 250 kW
7125 GUINEA
RTV GUINEENNE, Conakry — M-Sa • FRENCH, ETC • DS • 50 kW — FRENCH, ETC • DS • 50 kW
Su • FRENCH, ETC • DS • 50 kW — DS • 50 kW
INDIA
ALL INDIA RADIO, Delhi — S Asia & W Asia • 100 kW
IRAN
†VO THE ISLAMIC REP, Tehrān — S • E Europe • 500 kW
ITALY
†RAI INTERNATIONAL, Rome — S • Mideast • 100 kW
W • E Europe • 100 kW

(con'd)

0 1 2 3 4 5 6 7 8 9 10 11 12 13 14 15 16 17 18 19 20 21 22 23 24

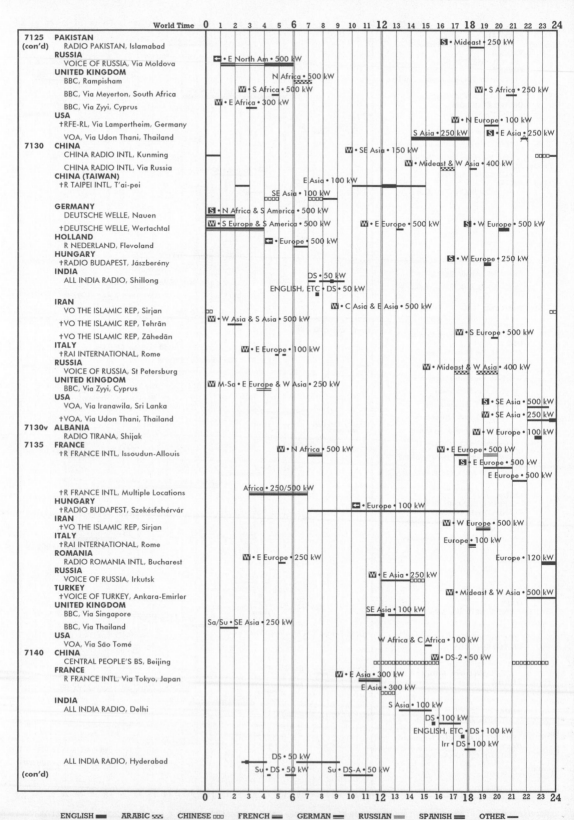

World Time		

7125 (con'd) **PAKISTAN**
RADIO PAKISTAN, Islamabad — S • Mideast • 250 kW
RUSSIA
VOICE OF RUSSIA, Via Moldova — E North Am • 500 kW
UNITED KINGDOM
BBC, Rampisham — N Africa • 500 kW
BBC, Via Meyerton, South Africa — W • S Africa • 500 kW / W • S Africa • 250 kW
BBC, Via Zyyi, Cyprus — W • E Africa • 300 kW
USA
†RFE-RL, Via Lampertheim, Germany — W • N Europe • 100 kW
VOA, Via Udon Thani, Thailand — S Asia • 250 kW / S • E Asia • 250 kW

7130 CHINA
CHINA RADIO INTL, Kunming — W • SE Asia • 150 kW
CHINA RADIO INTL, Via Russia — W • Mideast & W Asia • 400 kW
CHINA (TAIWAN)
†R TAIPEI INTL, T'ai-pei — E Asia • 100 kW
SE Asia • 100 kW
GERMANY
DEUTSCHE WELLE, Nauen — S • N Africa & S America • 500 kW
†DEUTSCHE WELLE, Wertachtal — W • S Europe & S America • 500 kW / W • E Europe • 500 kW / S • W Europe • 500 kW
HOLLAND
R NEDERLAND, Flevoland — Europe • 500 kW
HUNGARY
†RADIO BUDAPEST, Jászberény — S • W Europe • 250 kW
INDIA
ALL INDIA RADIO, Shillong — DS • 50 kW
ENGLISH, ETC • DS • 50 kW
IRAN
VO THE ISLAMIC REP, Sirjan — W • C Asia & E Asia • 500 kW
†VO THE ISLAMIC REP, Tehrän — W • W Asia & S Asia • 500 kW
†VO THE ISLAMIC REP, Zähedän — W • S Europe • 500 kW
ITALY
†RAI INTERNATIONAL, Rome — W • E Europe • 100 kW
RUSSIA
VOICE OF RUSSIA, St Petersburg — W • Mideast & W Asia • 400 kW
UNITED KINGDOM
BBC, Via Zyyi, Cyprus — W M-Sa • E Europe & W Asia • 250 kW
USA
VOA, Via Iranawila, Sri Lanka — S • SE Asia • 500 kW
†VOA, Via Udon Thani, Thailand — W • SE Asia • 250 kW

7130v ALBANIA
RADIO TIRANA, Shijak — W • W Europe • 100 kW
7135 FRANCE
†R FRANCE INTL, Issoudun-Allouis — W • N Africa • 500 kW / W • E Europe • 500 kW / S • E Europe • 500 kW / E Europe • 500 kW
†R FRANCE INTL, Multiple Locations — Africa • 250/500 kW
HUNGARY
†RADIO BUDAPEST, Szekésfehérvár — Europe • 100 kW
IRAN
†VO THE ISLAMIC REP, Sirjan — W • W Europe • 500 kW
ITALY
†RAI INTERNATIONAL, Rome — Europe • 100 kW
ROMANIA
RADIO ROMANIA INTL, Bucharest — W • E Europe • 250 kW / Europe • 120 kW
RUSSIA
VOICE OF RUSSIA, Irkutsk — W • E Asia • 250 kW
TURKEY
†VOICE OF TURKEY, Ankara-Emirler — W • Mideast & W Asia • 500 kW
UNITED KINGDOM
BBC, Via Singapore — SE Asia • 100 kW
BBC, Via Thailand — Sa/Su • SE Asia • 250 kW
USA
VOA, Via São Tomé — W Africa & C Africa • 100 kW
7140 CHINA
CENTRAL PEOPLE'S BS, Beijing — W • DS-2 • 50 kW
FRANCE
R FRANCE INTL, Via Tokyo, Japan — W • E Asia • 300 kW
E Asia • 300 kW
INDIA
ALL INDIA RADIO, Delhi — S Asia • 100 kW
DS • 100 kW
ENGLISH, ETC • DS • 100 kW
Irr • DS • 100 kW
ALL INDIA RADIO, Hyderabad — DS • 50 kW
Su • DS • 50 kW / Su • DS-A • 50 kW
(con'd)

ENGLISH ▬   ARABIC ▨▨▨   CHINESE □□□   FRENCH ═══   GERMAN ▬▬   RUSSIAN ══   SPANISH ═══   OTHER ▬▬

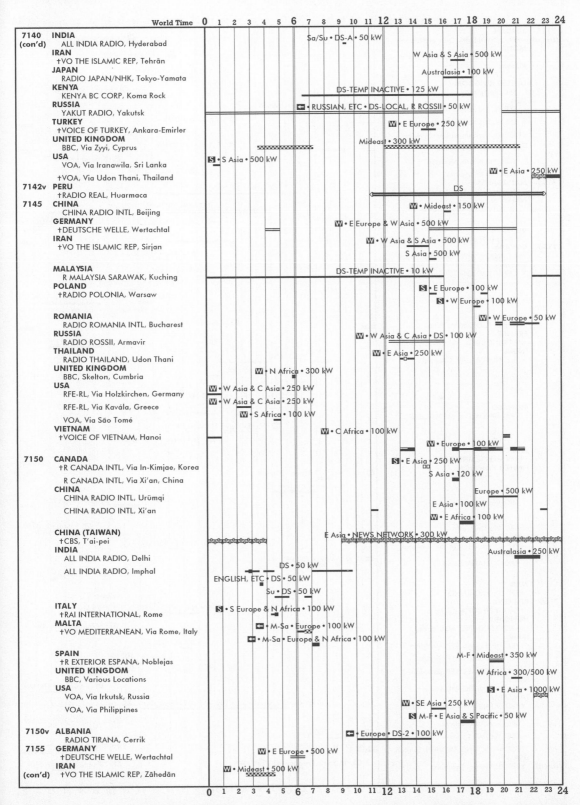

World Time	0 1 2 3 4 5 6 7 8 9 10 11 12 13 14 15 16 17 18 19 20 21 22 23 24

7140 **INDIA**
(con'd) ALL INDIA RADIO, Hyderabad — Sa/Su • DS-A • 50 kW
IRAN
†VO THE ISLAMIC REP, Tehrān — W Asia & S Asia • 500 kW
JAPAN
RADIO JAPAN/NHK, Tokyo-Yamata — Australasia • 100 kW
KENYA
KENYA BC CORP, Koma Rock — DS-TEMP INACTIVE • 125 kW
RUSSIA
YAKUT RADIO, Yakutsk — RUSSIAN, ETC • DS-LOCAL, R ROSSII • 50 kW
TURKEY
†VOICE OF TURKEY, Ankara-Emirler — W • E Europe • 250 kW
UNITED KINGDOM
BBC, Via Zyyi, Cyprus — Mideast • 300 kW
USA
VOA, Via Iranawila, Sri Lanka — S • S Asia • 500 kW

†VOA, Via Udon Thani, Thailand — W • E Asia • 250 kW
7142v **PERU**
†RADIO REAL, Huarmaca — DS
7145 **CHINA**
CHINA RADIO INTL, Beijing — W • Mideast • 150 kW
GERMANY
†DEUTSCHE WELLE, Wertachtal — W • E Europe & W Asia • 500 kW
IRAN
†VO THE ISLAMIC REP, Sirjan — W • W Asia & S Asia • 500 kW
S Asia • 500 kW

MALAYSIA
R MALAYSIA SARAWAK, Kuching — DS-TEMP INACTIVE • 10 kW
POLAND
†RADIO POLONIA, Warsaw — S • E Europe • 100 kW
S • W Europe • 100 kW

ROMANIA
RADIO ROMANIA INTL, Bucharest — W • W Europe • 50 kW
RUSSIA
RADIO ROSSII, Armavir — W • W Asia & C Asia • DS • 100 kW
THAILAND
RADIO THAILAND, Udon Thani — W • E Asia • 250 kW
UNITED KINGDOM
BBC, Skelton, Cumbria — W • N Africa • 300 kW
USA
RFE-RL, Via Holzkirchen, Germany — W • W Asia & C Asia • 250 kW

RFE-RL, Via Kavála, Greece — W • W Asia & C Asia • 250 kW

VOA, Via São Tomé — W • S Africa • 100 kW
VIETNAM
†VOICE OF VIETNAM, Hanoi — W • C Africa • 100 kW
W • Europe • 100 kW

7150 **CANADA**
†R CANADA INTL, Via In-Kimjae, Korea — S • E Asia • 250 kW

R CANADA INTL, Via Xi'an, China — S Asia • 120 kW
CHINA
CHINA RADIO INTL, Urümqi — Europe • 500 kW

CHINA RADIO INTL, Xi'an — E Asia • 100 kW
W • E Africa • 100 kW

CHINA (TAIWAN)
†CBS, T'ai-pei — E Asia • NEWS NETWORK • 300 kW
INDIA
ALL INDIA RADIO, Delhi — Australasia • 250 kW

ALL INDIA RADIO, Imphal — DS • 50 kW
ENGLISH, ETC • DS • 50 kW
Su • DS • 50 kW

ITALY
†RAI INTERNATIONAL, Rome — S • S Europe & N Africa • 100 kW
MALTA
†VO MEDITERRANEAN, Via Rome, Italy — M-Sa • Europe • 100 kW
M-Sa • Europe & N Africa • 100 kW

SPAIN
†R EXTERIOR ESPANA, Noblejas — M-F • Mideast • 350 kW
UNITED KINGDOM
BBC, Various Locations — W Africa • 300/500 kW
USA
VOA, Via Irkutsk, Russia — S • E Asia • 1000 kW

VOA, Via Philippines — W • SE Asia • 250 kW
S • M-F • E Asia & S Pacific • 50 kW

7150v **ALBANIA**
RADIO TIRANA, Cerrik — Europe • DS-2 • 100 kW
7155 **GERMANY**
†DEUTSCHE WELLE, Wertachtal — W • E Europe • 500 kW
IRAN
(con'd) †VO THE ISLAMIC REP, Zāhedān — W • Mideast • 500 kW

	0 1 2 3 4 5 6 7 8 9 10 11 12 13 14 15 16 17 18 19 20 21 22 23 24

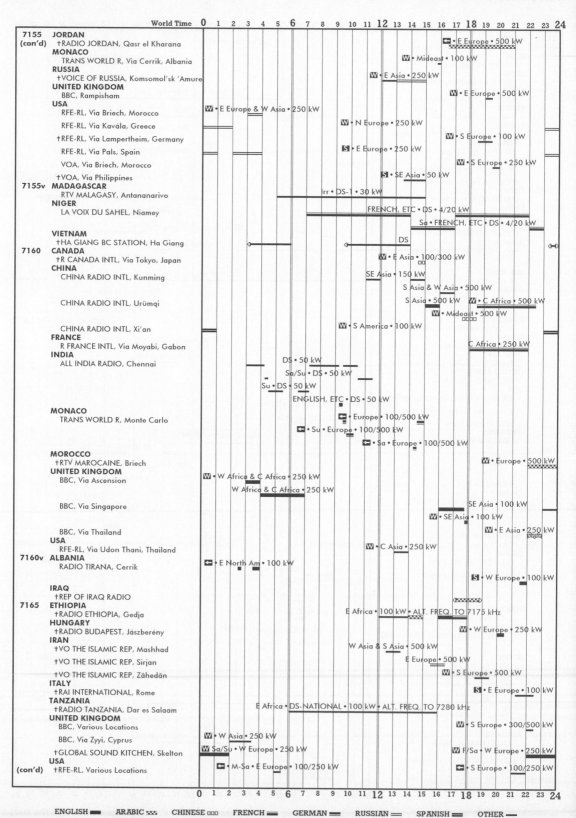

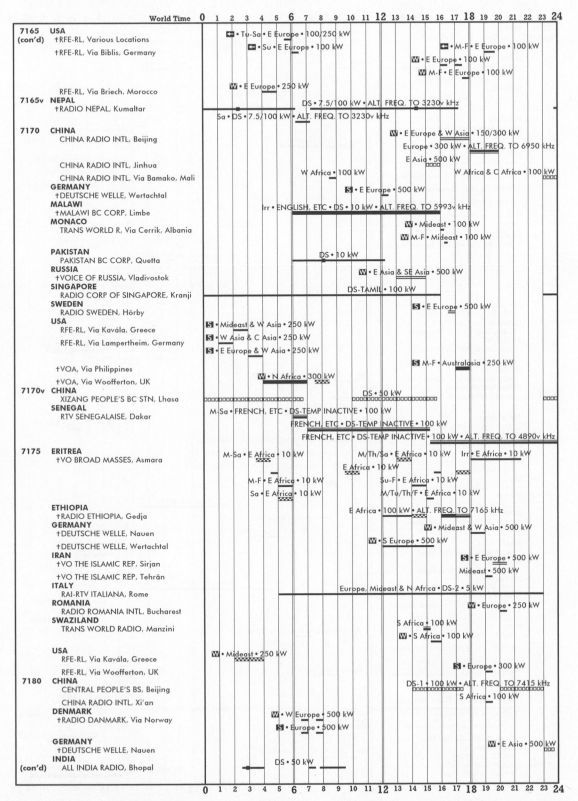

World Time   0 1 2 3 4 5 6 7 8 9 10 11 12 13 14 15 16 17 18 19 20 21 22 23 24

7165   **USA**
(con'd)   †RFE-RL, Various Locations   ⬅ • Tu-Sa • E Europe • 100/250 kW
           †RFE-RL, Via Biblis, Germany   ⬅ • Su • E Europe • 100 kW
                                                                                    ⬅ • M-F • E Europe • 100 kW
                                                                    ☒ • E Europe • 100 kW
                                                                    ☒ M-F • E Europe • 100 kW

           RFE-RL, Via Briech, Morocco   ☒ • E Europe • 250 kW
7165v **NEPAL**   DS • 7.5/100 kW • ALT. FREQ. TO 3230v kHz
           †RADIO NEPAL, Kumaltar
                                                Sa • DS • 7.5/100 kW • ALT. FREQ. TO 3230v kHz

7170   **CHINA**
           CHINA RADIO INTL, Beijing   ☒ • E Europe & W Asia • 150/300 kW
                                                                                Europe • 300 kW • ALT. FREQ. TO 6950 kHz
                                                                                E Asia • 500 kW
           CHINA RADIO INTL, Jinhua
           CHINA RADIO INTL, Via Bamako, Mali   W Africa • 100 kW   W Africa & C Africa • 100 kW
           GERMANY
           †DEUTSCHE WELLE, Wertachtal   ⓈS • E Europe • 500 kW
           MALAWI
           †MALAWI BC CORP, Limbe   Irr • ENGLISH, ETC • DS • 10 kW • ALT. FREQ. TO 5993v kHz
           MONACO
           TRANS WORLD R, Via Cerrik, Albania   ☒ • Mideast • 100 kW
                                                                  ☒ M-F • Mideast • 100 kW

           PAKISTAN
           PAKISTAN BC CORP, Quetta   DS • 10 kW
           RUSSIA
           †VOICE OF RUSSIA, Vladivostok   ☒ • E Asia & SE Asia • 500 kW
           SINGAPORE
           RADIO CORP OF SINGAPORE, Kranji   DS-TAMIL • 100 kW
           SWEDEN
           RADIO SWEDEN, Hörby   ⓈS • E Europe • 500 kW
           USA
           RFE-RL, Via Kavála, Greece   ⓈS • Mideast & W Asia • 250 kW
           RFE-RL, Via Lampertheim, Germany   ⓈS • W Asia & C Asia • 250 kW
                                                 ⓈS • E Europe & W Asia • 250 kW

           †VOA, Via Philippines   ⓈS M-F • Australasia • 250 kW
           †VOA, Via Woofferton, UK   ☒ • N Africa • 300 kW
7170v **CHINA**
           XIZANG PEOPLE'S BC STN, Lhasa   ▢▢▢▢▢▢▢▢ DS • 50 kW ▢▢▢▢▢▢▢▢▢▢▢▢▢▢▢▢▢
           SENEGAL
           RTV SENEGALAISE, Dakar   M-Sa • FRENCH, ETC • DS-TEMP INACTIVE • 100 kW
                                                 FRENCH, ETC • DS-TEMP INACTIVE • 100 kW
                                                 FRENCH, ETC • DS-TEMP INACTIVE • 100 kW • ALT. FREQ. TO 4890v kHz

7175   **ERITREA**
           †VO BROAD MASSES, Asmara   M-Sa • E Africa • 10 kW   M/Th/Sa • E Africa • 10 kW   Irr • E Africa • 10 kW
                                                                   E Africa • 10 kW
                                                 M-F • E Africa • 10 kW   Su-F • E Africa • 10 kW
                                                 Sa • E Africa • 10 kW   M/Tu/Th/F • E Africa • 10 kW

           ETHIOPIA
           †RADIO ETHIOPIA, Gedja   E Africa • 100 kW • ALT. FREQ. TO 7165 kHz
           GERMANY
           †DEUTSCHE WELLE, Nauen   ☒ • Mideast & W Asia • 500 kW
           †DEUTSCHE WELLE, Wertachtal   ☒ • S Europe • 500 kW
           IRAN
           †VO THE ISLAMIC REP, Sirjan   ⓈS • E Europe • 500 kW
           †VO THE ISLAMIC REP, Tehrān   Mideast • 500 kW
           ITALY
           RAI-RTV ITALIANA, Rome   Europe, Mideast & N Africa • DS-2 • 5 kW
           ROMANIA
           RADIO ROMANIA INTL, Bucharest   ☒ • Europe • 250 kW
           SWAZILAND
           TRANS WORLD RADIO, Manzini   S Africa • 100 kW
                                                 ☒ • S Africa • 100 kW

           USA
           RFE-RL, Via Kavála, Greece   ☒ • Mideast • 250 kW
           RFE-RL, Via Woofferton, UK
7180   **CHINA**   ⓈS • Europe • 300 kW
           CENTRAL PEOPLE'S BS, Beijing   DS-1 • 100 kW • ALT. FREQ. TO 7415 kHz
           CHINA RADIO INTL, Xi'an   S Africa • 100 kW
           DENMARK
           †RADIO DANMARK, Via Norway   ☒ • W Europe • 500 kW
                                                 ⓈS • Europe • 500 kW

           GERMANY
           †DEUTSCHE WELLE, Nauen   ☒ • E Asia • 500 kW
           INDIA
(con'd)   ALL INDIA RADIO, Bhopal   DS • 50 kW

0 1 2 3 4 5 6 7 8 9 10 11 12 13 14 15 16 17 18 19 20 21 22 23 24

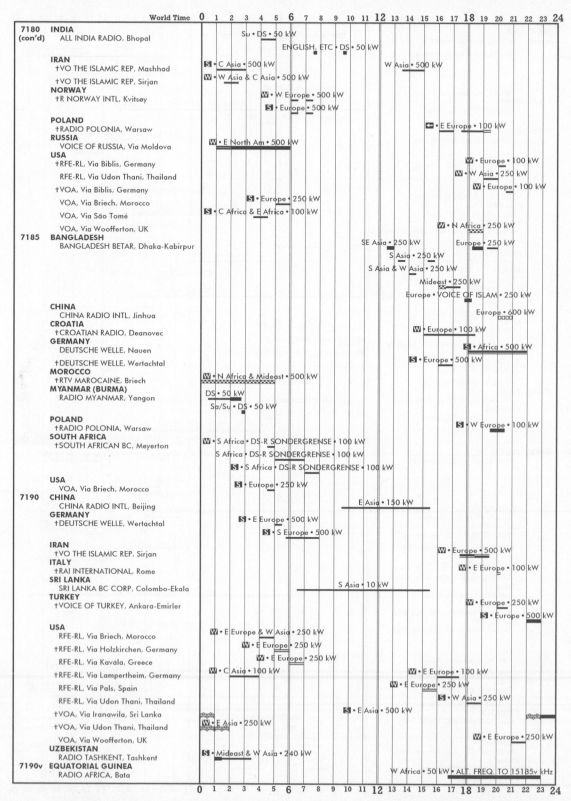

World Time 0 1 2 3 4 5 6 7 8 9 10 11 12 13 14 15 16 17 18 19 20 21 22 23 24

7180 INDIA
(con'd) ALL INDIA RADIO, Bhopal — Su • DS • 50 kW
— ENGLISH, ETC • DS • 50 kW

IRAN
†VO THE ISLAMIC REP, Mashhad — S • C Asia • 500 kW — W Asia • 500 kW
†VO THE ISLAMIC REP, Sirjan — W • W Asia & C Asia • 500 kW
NORWAY
†R NORWAY INTL, Kvitsøy — W • W Europe • 500 kW
— S • Europe • 500 kW

POLAND
†RADIO POLONIA, Warsaw — ⟵ • E Europe • 100 kW
RUSSIA
VOICE OF RUSSIA, Via Moldova — W • E North Am • 500 kW
USA
†RFE-RL, Via Biblis, Germany — W • Europe • 100 kW
RFE-RL, Via Udon Thani, Thailand — W • W Asia • 250 kW
†VOA, Via Biblis, Germany — W • Europe • 100 kW
VOA, Via Briech, Morocco — S • Europe • 250 kW
VOA, Via São Tomé — S • C Africa & E Africa • 100 kW
VOA, Via Woofferton, UK — W • N Africa • 250 kW

7185 BANGLADESH
BANGLADESH BETAR, Dhaka-Kabirpur — SE Asia • 250 kW — Europe • 250 kW
— S Asia • 250 kW
— S Asia & W Asia • 250 kW
— Mideast • 250 kW
— Europe • VOICE OF ISLAM • 250 kW

CHINA
CHINA RADIO INTL, Jinhua — Europe • 600 kW
CROATIA
†CROATIAN RADIO, Deanovec — W • Europe • 100 kW
GERMANY
DEUTSCHE WELLE, Nauen — S • Africa • 500 kW
†DEUTSCHE WELLE, Wertachtal — S • Europe • 500 kW
MOROCCO
†RTV MAROCAINE, Briech — W • N Africa & Mideast • 500 kW
MYANMAR (BURMA)
RADIO MYANMAR, Yangon — DS • 50 kW
— Sa/Su • DS • 50 kW

POLAND
†RADIO POLONIA, Warsaw — S • W Europe • 100 kW
SOUTH AFRICA
†SOUTH AFRICAN BC, Meyerton — W • S Africa • DS-R SONDERGRENSE • 100 kW
— S Africa • DS-R SONDERGRENSE • 100 kW
— S • S Africa • DS-R SONDERGRENSE • 100 kW

USA
VOA, Via Briech, Morocco — S • Europe • 250 kW
7190 CHINA
CHINA RADIO INTL, Beijing — E Asia • 150 kW
GERMANY
†DEUTSCHE WELLE, Wertachtal — S • E Europe • 500 kW
— S • S Europe • 500 kW

IRAN
†VO THE ISLAMIC REP, Sirjan — W • Europe • 500 kW
ITALY
†RAI INTERNATIONAL, Rome — W • E Europe • 100 kW
SRI LANKA
SRI LANKA BC CORP, Colombo-Ekala — S Asia • 10 kW
TURKEY
†VOICE OF TURKEY, Ankara-Emirler — W • Europe • 250 kW
— S • Europe • 500 kW

USA
RFE-RL, Via Briech, Morocco — W • E Europe & W Asia • 250 kW
†RFE-RL, Via Holzkirchen, Germany — W • E Europe • 250 kW
RFE-RL, Via Kavála, Greece — W • E Europe • 250 kW
†RFE-RL, Via Lampertheim, Germany — W • C Asia • 100 kW — W • E Europe • 100 kW
RFE-RL, Via Pals, Spain — W • E Europe • 250 kW
†RFE-RL, Via Udon Thani, Thailand — S • W Asia • 250 kW
†VOA, Via Iranawila, Sri Lanka — S • E Asia • 500 kW
†VOA, Via Udon Thani, Thailand — W • E Asia • 250 kW
VOA, Via Woofferton, UK — W • E Europe • 250 kW
UZBEKISTAN
RADIO TASHKENT, Tashkent — S • Mideast & W Asia • 240 kW
7190v EQUATORIAL GUINEA
RADIO AFRICA, Bata — W Africa • 50 kW • ALT. FREQ. TO 15185v kHz

0 1 2 3 4 5 6 7 8 9 10 11 12 13 14 15 16 17 18 19 20 21 22 23 24

ENGLISH ▬   ARABIC ▨▨   CHINESE ▫▫▫   FRENCH ══   GERMAN ▬▬   RUSSIAN ═   SPANISH ▬▬   OTHER ▬

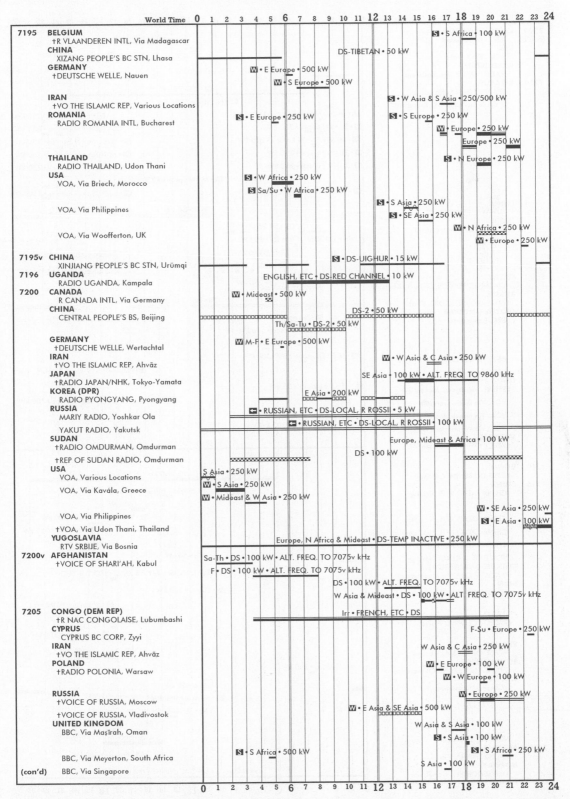

World Time   0 1 2 3 4 5 6 7 8 9 10 11 12 13 14 15 16 17 18 19 20 21 22 23 24

7195 BELGIUM
  †R VLAANDEREN INTL, Via Madagascar — S • S Africa • 100 kW
CHINA
  XIZANG PEOPLE'S BC STN, Lhasa — DS-TIBETAN • 50 kW
GERMANY
  †DEUTSCHE WELLE, Nauen — W • E Europe • 500 kW / W • S Europe • 500 kW
IRAN
  †VO THE ISLAMIC REP, Various Locations — S • W Asia & S Asia • 250/500 kW
ROMANIA
  RADIO ROMANIA INTL, Bucharest — S • E Europe • 250 kW / S • S Europe • 250 kW / W • Europe • 250 kW / Europe • 250 kW
THAILAND
  RADIO THAILAND, Udon Thani — N Europe • 250 kW
USA
  VOA, Via Briech, Morocco — S • W Africa • 250 kW / S Sa/Su • W Africa • 250 kW
  VOA, Via Philippines — S • S Asia • 250 kW / S • SE Asia • 250 kW
  VOA, Via Woofferton, UK — W • N Africa • 250 kW / W • Europe • 250 kW

7195v CHINA
  XINJIANG PEOPLE'S BC STN, Urümqi — S • DS-UIGHUR • 15 kW
7196 UGANDA
  RADIO UGANDA, Kampala — ENGLISH, ETC • DS-RED CHANNEL • 10 kW
7200 CANADA
  R CANADA INTL, Via Germany — W • Mideast • 500 kW
CHINA
  CENTRAL PEOPLE'S BS, Beijing — DS-2 • 50 kW / Th/Sa-Tu • DS-2 • 50 kW
GERMANY
  †DEUTSCHE WELLE, Wertachtal — W M-F • E Europe • 500 kW
IRAN
  †VO THE ISLAMIC REP, Ahvāz — W • W Asia & C Asia • 250 kW
JAPAN
  †RADIO JAPAN/NHK, Tokyo-Yamata — SE Asia • 100 kW • ALT. FREQ. TO 9860 kHz
KOREA (DPR)
  RADIO PYONGYANG, Pyongyang — E Asia • 200 kW
RUSSIA
  MARIY RADIO, Yoshkar Ola — • RUSSIAN, ETC • DS-LOCAL, R ROSSII • 5 kW
  YAKUT RADIO, Yakutsk — • RUSSIAN, ETC • DS-LOCAL, R ROSSII • 100 kW
SUDAN
  †RADIO OMDURMAN, Omdurman — Europe, Mideast & Africa • 100 kW
  †REP OF SUDAN RADIO, Omdurman — DS • 100 kW
USA
  VOA, Various Locations — S Asia • 250 kW
  VOA, Via Kavála, Greece — W • S Asia • 250 kW / W • Mideast & W Asia • 250 kW
  VOA, Via Philippines — W • SE Asia • 250 kW
  †VOA, Via Udon Thani, Thailand — S • E Asia • 100 kW
YUGOSLAVIA
  RTV SRBIJE, Via Bosnia — Europe, N Africa & Mideast • DS-TEMP INACTIVE • 250 kW
7200v AFGHANISTAN
  †VOICE OF SHARI'AH, Kabul — Sa-Th • DS • 100 kW • ALT. FREQ. TO 7075v kHz / F • DS • 100 kW • ALT. FREQ. TO 7075v kHz / DS • 100 kW • ALT. FREQ. TO 7075v kHz / W Asia & Mideast • DS • 100 kW • ALT. FREQ. TO 7075v kHz

7205 CONGO (DEM REP)
  †R NAC CONGOLAISE, Lubumbashi — Irr • FRENCH, ETC • DS
CYPRUS
  CYPRUS BC CORP, Zyyi — F-Su • Europe • 250 kW
IRAN
  †VO THE ISLAMIC REP, Ahvāz — W Asia & C Asia • 250 kW
POLAND
  †RADIO POLONIA, Warsaw — W • E Europe • 100 kW / W • W Europe • 100 kW
RUSSIA
  †VOICE OF RUSSIA, Moscow — W • Europe • 250 kW
  †VOICE OF RUSSIA, Vladivostok — W • E Asia & SE Asia • 500 kW
UNITED KINGDOM
  BBC, Via Maṣīrah, Oman — W Asia & S Asia • 100 kW / S • S Asia • 100 kW
  BBC, Via Meyerton, South Africa — S • S Africa • 500 kW / S • S Africa • 250 kW
(con'd) BBC, Via Singapore — S Asia • 100 kW

0 1 2 3 4 5 6 7 8 9 10 11 12 13 14 15 16 17 18 19 20 21 22 23 24

SEASONAL S OR W   1-HR TIMESHIFT MIDYEAR ← OR →   JAMMING / OR ∧   EARLIEST HEARD ◁   LATEST HEARD ▷   NEW FOR 2001 †

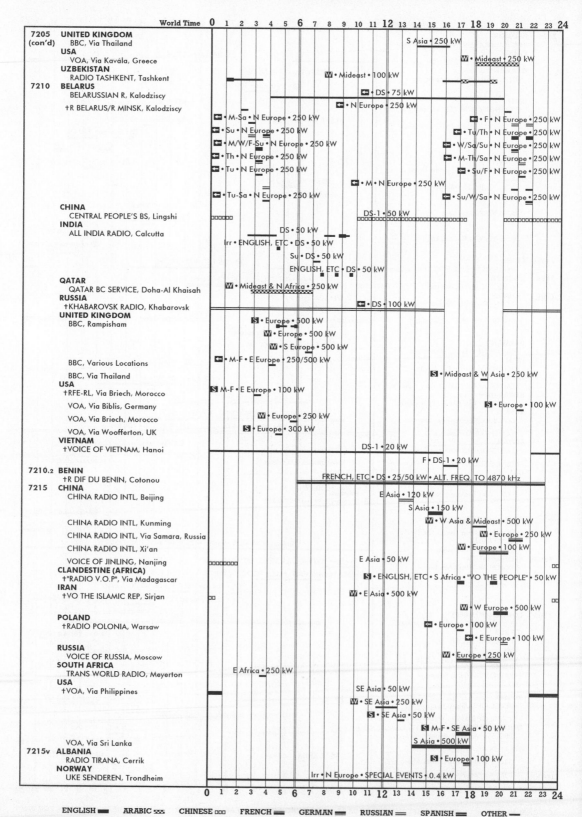

	World Time	0 1 2 3 4 5 6 7 8 9 10 11 12 13 14 15 16 17 18 19 20 21 22 23 24

7205 **UNITED KINGDOM**
(con'd)   BBC, Via Thailand — S Asia • 250 kW
USA
VOA, Via Kavála, Greece — W • Mideast • 250 kW
UZBEKISTAN
RADIO TASHKENT, Tashkent — W • Mideast • 100 kW
7210 **BELARUS**
BELARUSSIAN R, Kalodziscy — DS 75 kW
†R BELARUS/R MINSK, Kalodziscy — N Europe • 250 kW
— M-Sa • N Europe • 250 kW   F • N Europe • 250 kW
— Su • N Europe • 250 kW   Tu/Th • N Europe • 250 kW
— M/W/F-Su • N Europe • 250 kW   W/Sa/Su • N Europe • 250 kW
— Th • N Europe • 250 kW   M-Th/Sa • N Europe • 250 kW
— Tu • N Europe • 250 kW   Su/F • N Europe • 250 kW
— M • N Europe • 250 kW
— Tu-Sa • N Europe • 250 kW   Su/W/Sa • N Europe • 250 kW
CHINA
CENTRAL PEOPLE'S BS, Lingshi — DS-1 • 50 kW
INDIA
ALL INDIA RADIO, Calcutta — DS • 50 kW
Irr • ENGLISH, ETC • DS • 50 kW
Su • DS • 50 kW
ENGLISH, ETC • DS • 50 kW
QATAR
QATAR BC SERVICE, Doha-Al Khaisah — W • Mideast & N Africa • 250 kW
RUSSIA
†KHABAROVSK RADIO, Khabarovsk — DS • 100 kW
UNITED KINGDOM
BBC, Rampisham — S • Europe • 500 kW
W • Europe • 500 kW
W • S Europe • 500 kW
BBC, Various Locations — M-F • E Europe • 250/500 kW
BBC, Via Thailand — S • Mideast & W Asia • 250 kW
USA
†RFE-RL, Via Briech, Morocco — S M-F • E Europe • 100 kW
VOA, Via Biblis, Germany — S • Europe • 100 kW
VOA, Via Briech, Morocco — W • Europe • 250 kW
VOA, Via Woofferton, UK — S • Europe • 300 kW
VIETNAM
†VOICE OF VIETNAM, Hanoi — DS-1 • 20 kW
7210.2 **BENIN** — F • DS-1 • 20 kW
†R DIF DU BENIN, Cotonou — FRENCH, ETC • DS 25/50 kW • ALT. FREQ. TO 4870 kHz
7215 **CHINA**
CHINA RADIO INTL, Beijing — E Asia • 120 kW
S Asia • 150 kW
CHINA RADIO INTL, Kunming — W • W Asia & Mideast • 500 kW
CHINA RADIO INTL, Via Samara, Russia — W • Europe • 250 kW
CHINA RADIO INTL, Xi'an — W • Europe • 100 kW
VOICE OF JINLING, Nanjing — E Asia • 50 kW
CLANDESTINE (AFRICA)
†"RADIO V.O.P", Via Madagascar — S • ENGLISH, ETC • S Africa • "VO THE PEOPLE" • 50 kW
IRAN
†VO THE ISLAMIC REP, Sirjan — W • E Asia • 500 kW
POLAND
†RADIO POLONIA, Warsaw — W • W Europe • 500 kW
— Europe • 100 kW
— • E Europe • 100 kW
RUSSIA
VOICE OF RUSSIA, Moscow — W • Europe • 250 kW
SOUTH AFRICA
TRANS WORLD RADIO, Meyerton — E Africa • 250 kW
USA
†VOA, Via Philippines — SE Asia • 50 kW
W • SE Asia • 250 kW
S • SE Asia • 50 kW
S M-F • SE Asia • 50 kW
VOA, Via Sri Lanka — S Asia • 500 kW
7215v **ALBANIA**
RADIO TIRANA, Cerrik — S • Europe • 100 kW
NORWAY
UKE SENDEREN, Trondheim — Irr • N Europe • SPECIAL EVENTS • 0.4 kW

		0 1 2 3 4 5 6 7 8 9 10 11 12 13 14 15 16 17 18 19 20 21 22 23 24

ENGLISH ▬   ARABIC ⋙   CHINESE ▫▫▫   FRENCH ▬   GERMAN ▬   RUSSIAN ═   SPANISH ▬   OTHER ▬

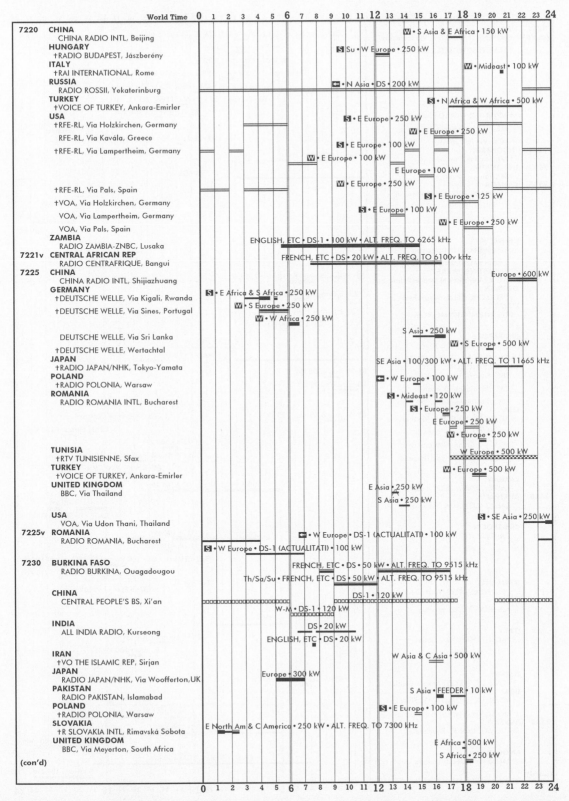

World Time   0 1 2 3 4 5 6 7 8 9 10 11 12 13 14 15 16 17 18 19 20 21 22 23 24

7220 CHINA
CHINA RADIO INTL, Beijing — W • S Asia & E Africa • 150 kW
HUNGARY
†RADIO BUDAPEST, Jászberény — S Su • W Europe • 250 kW
ITALY
†RAI INTERNATIONAL, Rome — W • Mideast • 100 kW
RUSSIA
RADIO ROSSII, Yekaterinburg — ⇦ • N Asia • DS • 200 kW
TURKEY
†VOICE OF TURKEY, Ankara-Emirler — S • N Africa & W Africa • 500 kW
USA
†RFE-RL, Via Holzkirchen, Germany — S • E Europe • 250 kW
RFE-RL, Via Kavála, Greece — W • E Europe • 250 kW
†RFE-RL, Via Lampertheim, Germany — S • E Europe • 100 kW
W • E Europe • 100 kW
E Europe • 100 kW
†RFE-RL, Via Pals, Spain — W • E Europe • 250 kW
†VOA, Via Holzkirchen, Germany — S • E Europe • 125 kW
VOA, Via Lampertheim, Germany — S • E Europe • 100 kW
VOA, Via Pals, Spain — W • E Europe • 250 kW
ZAMBIA
RADIO ZAMBIA-ZNBC, Lusaka — ENGLISH, ETC • DS-1 • 100 kW • ALT. FREQ. TO 6265 kHz
7221v CENTRAL AFRICAN REP
RADIO CENTRAFRIQUE, Bangui — FRENCH, ETC • DS • 20 kW • ALT. FREQ. TO 6100v kHz
7225 CHINA
CHINA RADIO INTL, Shijiazhuang — Europe • 600 kW
GERMANY
†DEUTSCHE WELLE, Via Kigali, Rwanda — S • E Africa & S Africa • 250 kW
W • S Europe • 250 kW
†DEUTSCHE WELLE, Via Sines, Portugal — W • W Africa • 250 kW
DEUTSCHE WELLE, Via Sri Lanka — S Asia • 250 kW
†DEUTSCHE WELLE, Wertachtal — W • S Europe • 500 kW
JAPAN
†RADIO JAPAN/NHK, Tokyo-Yamata — SE Asia • 100/300 kW • ALT. FREQ. TO 11665 kHz
POLAND
†RADIO POLONIA, Warsaw — ⇦ • W Europe • 100 kW
ROMANIA
RADIO ROMANIA INTL, Bucharest — S • Mideast • 120 kW
S • Europe • 250 kW
E Europe • 250 kW
W • Europe • 250 kW
TUNISIA
†RTV TUNISIENNE, Sfax — W Europe • 500 kW
TURKEY
†VOICE OF TURKEY, Ankara-Emirler — W • Europe • 500 kW
UNITED KINGDOM
BBC, Via Thailand — E Asia • 250 kW
S Asia • 250 kW
USA
VOA, Via Udon Thani, Thailand — S • SE Asia • 250 kW
7225v ROMANIA
RADIO ROMANIA, Bucharest — ⇦ • W Europe • DS-1 (ACTUALITATI) • 100 kW
S • W Europe • DS-1 (ACTUALITATI) • 100 kW
7230 BURKINA FASO
RADIO BURKINA, Ouagadougou — FRENCH, ETC • DS • 50 kW • ALT. FREQ. TO 9515 kHz
Th/Sa/Su • FRENCH, ETC • DS • 50 kW • ALT. FREQ. TO 9515 kHz
CHINA
CENTRAL PEOPLE'S BS, Xi'an — DS-1 • 120 kW
W-M • DS-1 • 120 kW
INDIA
ALL INDIA RADIO, Kurseong — DS • 20 kW
ENGLISH, ETC • DS • 20 kW
IRAN
†VO THE ISLAMIC REP, Sirjan — W Asia & C Asia • 500 kW
JAPAN
RADIO JAPAN/NHK, Via Woofferton, UK — Europe • 300 kW
PAKISTAN
RADIO PAKISTAN, Islamabad — S Asia • FEEDER • 10 kW
POLAND
†RADIO POLONIA, Warsaw — S • E Europe • 100 kW
SLOVAKIA
†R SLOVAKIA INTL, Rimavská Sobota — E North Am & C America • 250 kW • ALT. FREQ. TO 7300 kHz
UNITED KINGDOM
BBC, Via Meyerton, South Africa — E Africa • 500 kW
S Africa • 250 kW

(con'd)

0 1 2 3 4 5 6 7 8 9 10 11 12 13 14 15 16 17 18 19 20 21 22 23 24

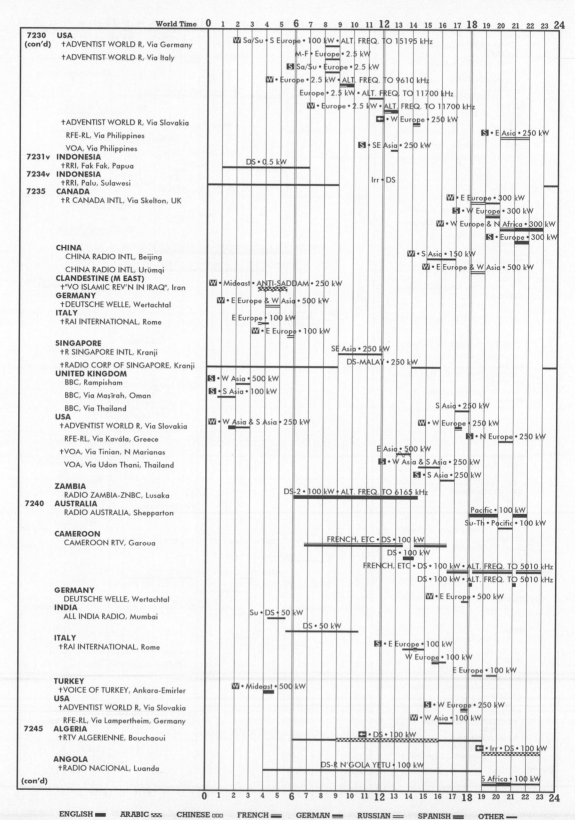

		World Time	0 1 2 3 4 5 6 7 8 9 10 11 12 13 14 15 16 17 18 19 20 21 22 23 24

7230 USA (con'd)
†ADVENTIST WORLD R, Via Germany — W Sa/Su • S Europe • 100 kW • ALT. FREQ. TO 15195 kHz
†ADVENTIST WORLD R, Via Italy — M-F • Europe • 2.5 kW
— S Sa/Su • Europe • 2.5 kW
— W • Europe • 2.5 kW • ALT. FREQ. TO 9610 kHz
— Europe • 2.5 kW • ALT. FREQ. TO 11700 kHz
— W • Europe • 2.5 kW • ALT. FREQ. TO 11700 kHz
†ADVENTIST WORLD R, Via Slovakia — W Europe • 250 kW
RFE-RL, Via Philippines — S • E Asia • 250 kW
VOA, Via Philippines — S • SE Asia • 250 kW

7231v INDONESIA
†RRI, Fak Fak, Papua — DS • 0.5 kW

7234v INDONESIA
†RRI, Palu, Sulawesi — Irr • DS

7235 CANADA
†R CANADA INTL, Via Skelton, UK — W • E Europe • 300 kW
— S • W Europe • 300 kW
— W • W Europe & N Africa • 300 kW
— S • Europe • 300 kW

CHINA
CHINA RADIO INTL, Beijing — W • S Asia • 150 kW
CHINA RADIO INTL, Urümqi — W • E Europe & W Asia • 500 kW

CLANDESTINE (M EAST)
†"VO ISLAMIC REV'N IN IRAQ", Iran — W • Mideast • ANTI-SADDAM • 250 kW

GERMANY
†DEUTSCHE WELLE, Wertachtal — W • E Europe & W Asia • 500 kW

ITALY
†RAI INTERNATIONAL, Rome — E Europe • 100 kW
— W • E Europe • 100 kW

SINGAPORE
†R SINGAPORE INTL, Kranji — SE Asia • 250 kW
†RADIO CORP OF SINGAPORE, Kranji — DS-MALAY • 250 kW

UNITED KINGDOM
BBC, Rampisham — S • W Asia • 500 kW
BBC, Via Maşīrah, Oman — S • S Asia • 100 kW
BBC, Via Thailand — S Asia • 250 kW

USA
†ADVENTIST WORLD R, Via Slovakia — W • W Asia & S Asia • 250 kW / W • W Europe • 250 kW
RFE-RL, Via Kavála, Greece — S • N Europe • 250 kW
†VOA, Via Tinian, N Marianas — E Asia • 500 kW
VOA, Via Udon Thani, Thailand — S • W Asia & S Asia • 250 kW / S • S Asia • 250 kW

ZAMBIA
RADIO ZAMBIA-ZNBC, Lusaka — DS-2 • 100 kW • ALT. FREQ. TO 6165 kHz

7240 AUSTRALIA
RADIO AUSTRALIA, Shepparton — Pacific • 100 kW / Su-Th • Pacific • 100 kW

CAMEROON
CAMEROON RTV, Garoua — FRENCH, ETC • DS • 100 kW / DS • 100 kW / FRENCH, ETC • DS • 100 kW • ALT. FREQ. TO 5010 kHz / DS • 100 kW • ALT. FREQ. TO 5010 kHz

GERMANY
DEUTSCHE WELLE, Wertachtal — W • E Europe • 500 kW

INDIA
ALL INDIA RADIO, Mumbai — Su • DS • 50 kW / DS • 50 kW

ITALY
†RAI INTERNATIONAL, Rome — S • E Europe • 100 kW / W Europe • 100 kW / E Europe • 100 kW

TURKEY
†VOICE OF TURKEY, Ankara-Emirler — W • Mideast • 500 kW

USA
†ADVENTIST WORLD R, Via Slovakia — S • W Europe • 250 kW
RFE-RL, Via Lampertheim, Germany — W • W Asia • 100 kW

7245 ALGERIA
†RTV ALGERIENNE, Bouchaoui — DS • 100 kW / Irr • DS • 100 kW

ANGOLA
†RADIO NACIONAL, Luanda — DS-R N'GOLA YETU • 100 kW / S Africa • 100 kW

(con'd)

	World Time	0 1 2 3 4 5 6 7 8 9 10 11 12 13 14 15 16 17 18 19 20 21 22 23 24

ENGLISH ▬   ARABIC ∽∽   CHINESE □□□   FRENCH ══   GERMAN ▭▭   RUSSIAN ══   SPANISH ══   OTHER ──

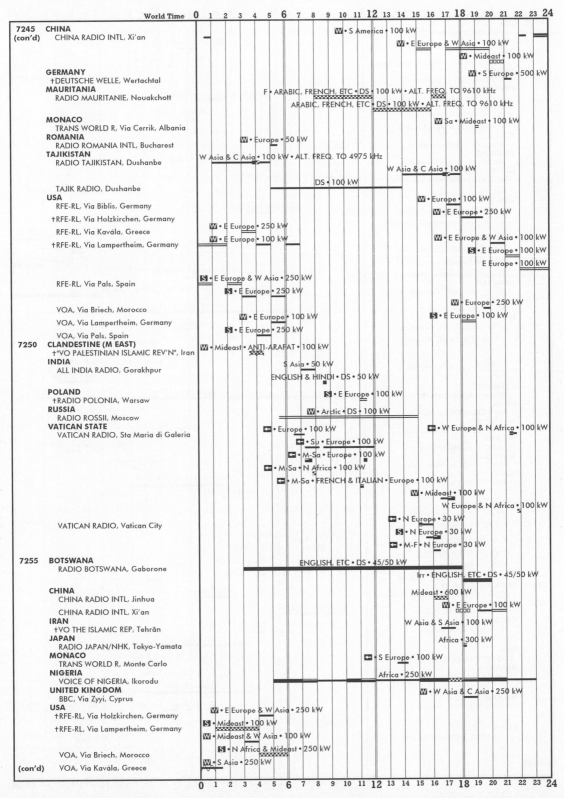

World Time 0 1 2 3 4 5 6 7 8 9 10 11 12 13 14 15 16 17 18 19 20 21 22 23 24

kHz	Country / Station	Schedule
7245 (con'd)	**CHINA**	
	CHINA RADIO INTL, Xi'an	[W] • S America • 100 kW
		[W] • E Europe & W Asia • 100 kW
		[W] • Mideast • 100 kW
	GERMANY	
	†DEUTSCHE WELLE, Wertachtal	[W] • S Europe • 500 kW
	MAURITANIA	
	RADIO MAURITANIE, Nouakchott	F • ARABIC, FRENCH, ETC • DS • 100 kW • ALT. FREQ. TO 9610 kHz
		ARABIC, FRENCH, ETC • DS • 100 kW • ALT. FREQ. TO 9610 kHz
	MONACO	
	TRANS WORLD R, Via Cerrik, Albania	[W] Sa • Mideast • 100 kW
	ROMANIA	
	RADIO ROMANIA INTL, Bucharest	[W] • Europe • 50 kW
	TAJIKISTAN	
	RADIO TAJIKISTAN, Dushanbe	W Asia & C Asia • 100 kW • ALT. FREQ. TO 4975 kHz
		W Asia & C Asia • 100 kW
	TAJIK RADIO, Dushanbe	DS • 100 kW
	USA	
	RFE-RL, Via Biblis, Germany	[W] • Europe • 100 kW
	†RFE-RL, Via Holzkirchen, Germany	[W] • E Europe • 250 kW
	RFE-RL, Via Kavála, Greece	[W] • E Europe • 250 kW
	†RFE-RL, Via Lampertheim, Germany	[W] • E Europe • 100 kW
		[W] • E Europe & W Asia • 100 kW
		[S] • E Europe • 100 kW
		E Europe • 100 kW
	RFE-RL, Via Pals, Spain	[S] • E Europe & W Asia • 250 kW
		[S] • E Europe • 250 kW
	VOA, Via Briech, Morocco	[W] • Europe • 250 kW
	VOA, Via Lampertheim, Germany	[W] • E Europe • 100 kW
		[S] • E Europe • 100 kW
	VOA, Via Pals, Spain	[S] • E Europe • 250 kW
7250	**CLANDESTINE (M EAST)**	
	†"VO PALESTINIAN ISLAMIC REV'N", Iran	[W] • Mideast • ANTI-ARAFAT • 100 kW
	INDIA	
	ALL INDIA RADIO, Gorakhpur	S Asia • 50 kW
		ENGLISH & HINDI • DS • 50 kW
	POLAND	
	†RADIO POLONIA, Warsaw	[S] • E Europe • 100 kW
	RUSSIA	
	RADIO ROSSII, Moscow	[W] • Arctic • DS • 100 kW
	VATICAN STATE	
	VATICAN RADIO, Sta Maria di Galeria	⬅ • Europe • 100 kW
		⬅ • W Europe & N Africa • 100 kW
		⬅ • Su • Europe • 100 kW
		⬅ • M-Sa • Europe • 100 kW
		⬅ • M-Sa • N Africa • 100 kW
		⬅ • M-Sa • FRENCH & ITALIAN • Europe • 100 kW
		[W] • Mideast • 100 kW
		W Europe & N Africa • 100 kW
	VATICAN RADIO, Vatican City	⬅ • N Europe • 30 kW
		[S] • N Europe • 30 kW
		⬅ • M-F • N Europe • 30 kW
7255	**BOTSWANA**	
	RADIO BOTSWANA, Gaborone	ENGLISH, ETC • DS • 45/50 kW
		Irr • ENGLISH, ETC • DS • 45/50 kW
	CHINA	
	CHINA RADIO INTL, Jinhua	Mideast • 600 kW
	CHINA RADIO INTL, Xi'an	[W] • E Europe • 100 kW
	IRAN	
	†VO THE ISLAMIC REP, Tehrān	W Asia & S Asia • 100 kW
	JAPAN	
	RADIO JAPAN/NHK, Tokyo-Yamata	Africa • 300 kW
	MONACO	
	TRANS WORLD R, Monte Carlo	⬅ • S Europe • 100 kW
	NIGERIA	
	VOICE OF NIGERIA, Ikorodu	Africa • 250 kW
	UNITED KINGDOM	
	BBC, Via Zyyi, Cyprus	[W] • W Asia & C Asia • 250 kW
	USA	
	†RFE-RL, Via Holzkirchen, Germany	[W] • E Europe & W Asia • 250 kW
	†RFE-RL, Via Lampertheim, Germany	[S] • Mideast • 100 kW
		[W] • Mideast & W Asia • 100 kW
	VOA, Via Briech, Morocco	[S] • N Africa & Mideast • 250 kW
(con'd)	VOA, Via Kavála, Greece	[W] • S Asia • 250 kW

0 1 2 3 4 5 6 7 8 9 10 11 12 13 14 15 16 17 18 19 20 21 22 23 24

SEASONAL [S] OR [W] 1-HR TIMESHIFT MIDYEAR ⬅ OR ➡ JAMMING / OR /\ EARLIEST HEARD ◁ LATEST HEARD ▷ NEW FOR 2001 †

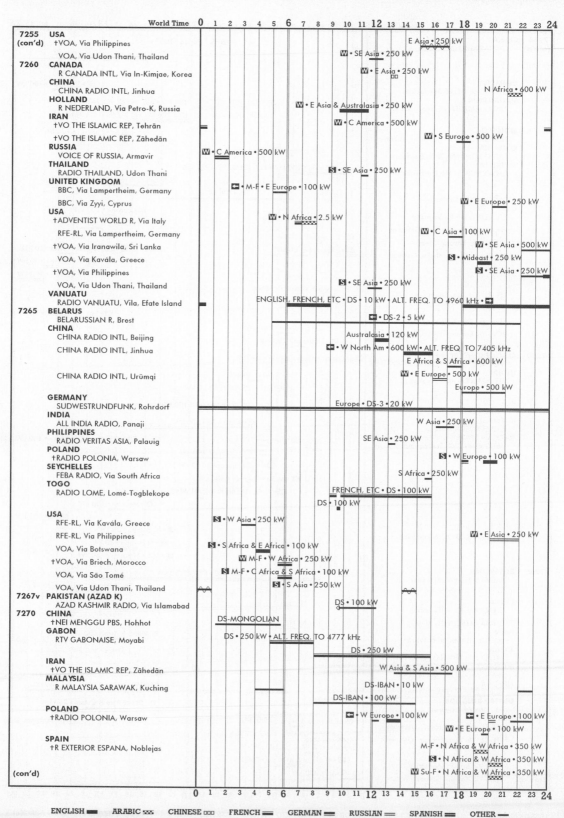

World Time 0 1 2 3 4 5 6 7 8 9 10 11 12 13 14 15 16 17 18 19 20 21 22 23 24

7255
(con'd) **USA**
†VOA, Via Philippines — E Asia • 250 kW
VOA, Via Udon Thani, Thailand — W • SE Asia • 250 kW
7260 **CANADA**
R CANADA INTL, Via In-Kimjae, Korea — W • E Asia • 250 kW
CHINA
CHINA RADIO INTL, Jinhua — N Africa • 600 kW
HOLLAND
R NEDERLAND, Via Petro-K, Russia — W • E Asia & Australasia • 250 kW
IRAN
†VO THE ISLAMIC REP, Tehrān — W • C America • 500 kW
†VO THE ISLAMIC REP, Zāhedān — W • S Europe • 500 kW
RUSSIA
VOICE OF RUSSIA, Armavir — W • C America • 500 kW
THAILAND
RADIO THAILAND, Udon Thani — S • SE Asia • 250 kW
UNITED KINGDOM
BBC, Via Lampertheim, Germany — M-F • E Europe • 100 kW
BBC, Via Zyyi, Cyprus — W • E Europe • 250 kW
USA
†ADVENTIST WORLD R, Via Italy — W • N Africa • 2.5 kW
RFE-RL, Via Lampertheim, Germany — W • C Asia • 100 kW
†VOA, Via Iranawila, Sri Lanka — W • SE Asia • 500 kW
VOA, Via Kavála, Greece — S • Mideast • 250 kW
†VOA, Via Philippines — S • SE Asia • 250 kW
VOA, Via Udon Thani, Thailand — S • SE Asia • 250 kW
VANUATU
RADIO VANUATU, Vila, Efate Island — ENGLISH, FRENCH, ETC • DS • 10 kW • ALT. FREQ. TO 4960 kHz •
7265 **BELARUS**
BELARUSSIAN R, Brest — DS-2 • 5 kW
CHINA
CHINA RADIO INTL, Beijing — Australasia • 120 kW
CHINA RADIO INTL, Jinhua — W North Am • 600 kW • ALT. FREQ. TO 7405 kHz
— E Africa & S Africa • 600 kW
CHINA RADIO INTL, Urümqi — W • E Europe • 500 kW
— Europe • 500 kW
GERMANY
SUDWESTRUNDFUNK, Rohrdorf — Europe • DS-3 • 20 kW
INDIA
ALL INDIA RADIO, Panaji — W Asia • 250 kW
PHILIPPINES
RADIO VERITAS ASIA, Palauig — SE Asia • 250 kW
POLAND
†RADIO POLONIA, Warsaw — S • W Europe • 100 kW
SEYCHELLES
FEBA RADIO, Via South Africa — S Africa • 250 kW
TOGO
RADIO LOME, Lomé-Togblekope — FRENCH, ETC • DS • 100 kW
— DS • 100 kW
USA
RFE-RL, Via Kavála, Greece — S • W Asia • 250 kW
RFE-RL, Via Philippines — W • E Asia • 250 kW
VOA, Via Botswana — S • S Africa & E Africa • 100 kW
†VOA, Via Briech, Morocco — W M-F • W Africa • 250 kW
VOA, Via São Tomé — S M-F • C Africa & S Africa • 100 kW
VOA, Via Udon Thani, Thailand — S • S Asia • 250 kW
7267v **PAKISTAN (AZAD K)**
AZAD KASHMIR RADIO, Via Islamabad — DS • 100 kW
7270 **CHINA**
†NEI MENGGU PBS, Hohhot — DS-MONGOLIAN
GABON
RTV GABONAISE, Moyabi — DS • 250 kW • ALT. FREQ. TO 4777 kHz
— DS • 250 kW
IRAN
†VO THE ISLAMIC REP, Zāhedān — W Asia & S Asia • 500 kW
MALAYSIA
R MALAYSIA SARAWAK, Kuching — DS-IBAN • 10 kW
— DS-IBAN • 100 kW
POLAND
†RADIO POLONIA, Warsaw — • W Europe • 100 kW — • E Europe • 100 kW
— W • E Europe • 100 kW
SPAIN
†R EXTERIOR ESPANA, Noblejas — M-F • N Africa & W Africa • 350 kW
— S • N Africa & W Africa • 350 kW
— W Su-F • N Africa & W Africa • 350 kW

(con'd)

0 1 2 3 4 5 6 7 8 9 10 11 12 13 14 15 16 17 18 19 20 21 22 23 24

ENGLISH ▬   ARABIC ▨   CHINESE ▢▢▢   FRENCH ═   GERMAN ▬   RUSSIAN ═   SPANISH ═   OTHER ▬

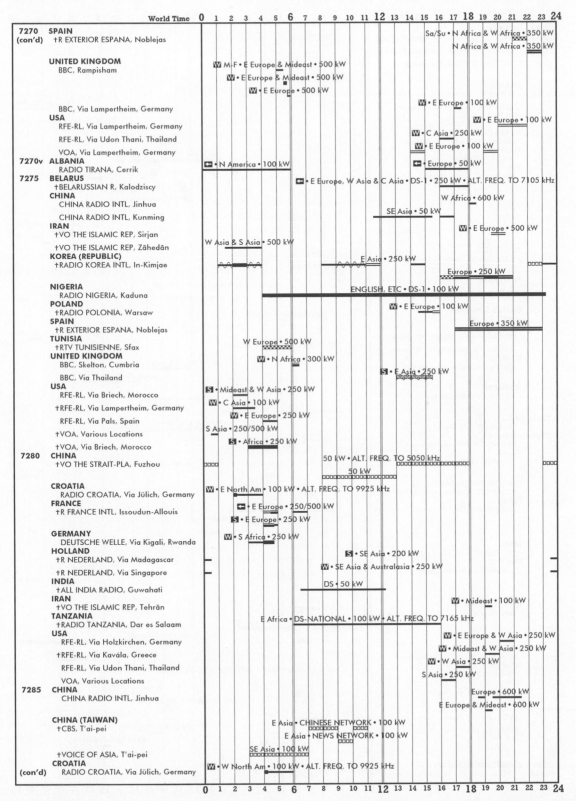

World Time 0 1 2 3 4 5 6 7 8 9 10 11 12 13 14 15 16 17 18 19 20 21 22 23 24

7270 SPAIN
(con'd) †R EXTERIOR ESPANA, Noblejas
Sa/Su • N Africa & W Africa • 350 kW
N Africa & W Africa • 350 kW

UNITED KINGDOM
BBC, Rampisham
W M-F • E Europe & Mideast • 500 kW
W • E Europe & Mideast • 500 kW
W • E Europe • 500 kW

BBC, Via Lampertheim, Germany
W • E Europe • 100 kW
USA
RFE-RL, Via Lampertheim, Germany
W • E Europe • 100 kW
RFE-RL, Via Udon Thani, Thailand
W • C Asia • 250 kW
VOA, Via Lampertheim, Germany
W • E Europe • 100 kW
7270v ALBANIA
RADIO TIRANA, Cerrik
⇦ • N America • 100 kW
⇦ • Europe • 50 kW
7275 BELARUS
†BELARUSSIAN R, Kalodziscy
⇦ • E Europe, W Asia & C Asia • DS-1 • 250 kW • ALT. FREQ. TO 7105 kHz
CHINA
CHINA RADIO INTL, Jinhua
W Africa • 600 kW

CHINA RADIO INTL, Kunming
SE Asia • 50 kW
IRAN
†VO THE ISLAMIC REP, Sirjan
W • E Europe • 500 kW
†VO THE ISLAMIC REP, Zāhedān
W Asia & S Asia • 500 kW
KOREA (REPUBLIC)
†RADIO KOREA INTL, In-Kimjae
E Asia • 250 kW
Europe • 250 kW

NIGERIA
RADIO NIGERIA, Kaduna
ENGLISH, ETC • DS-1 • 100 kW
POLAND
†RADIO POLONIA, Warsaw
W • E Europe • 100 kW
SPAIN
†R EXTERIOR ESPANA, Noblejas
Europe • 350 kW
TUNISIA
†RTV TUNISIENNE, Sfax
W Europe • 500 kW
UNITED KINGDOM
BBC, Skelton, Cumbria
W • N Africa • 300 kW

BBC, Via Thailand
S • E Asia • 250 kW
USA
RFE-RL, Via Briech, Morocco
S • Mideast & W Asia • 250 kW
†RFE-RL, Via Lampertheim, Germany
W • C Asia • 100 kW
RFE-RL, Via Pals, Spain
W • E Europe • 250 kW
†VOA, Various Locations
S Asia • 250/500 kW
†VOA, Via Briech, Morocco
S • Africa • 250 kW
7280 CHINA
†VO THE STRAIT-PLA, Fuzhou
50 kW • ALT. FREQ. TO 5050 kHz
50 kW

CROATIA
RADIO CROATIA, Via Jülich, Germany
W • E North Am • 100 kW • ALT. FREQ. TO 9925 kHz
FRANCE
†R FRANCE INTL, Issoudun-Allouis
⇦ • E Europe • 250/500 kW
S • E Europe • 250 kW
GERMANY
DEUTSCHE WELLE, Via Kigali, Rwanda
W • S Africa • 250 kW
HOLLAND
†R NEDERLAND, Via Madagascar
S • SE Asia • 200 kW
†R NEDERLAND, Via Singapore
W • SE Asia & Australasia • 250 kW
INDIA
†ALL INDIA RADIO, Guwahati
DS • 50 kW
IRAN
†VO THE ISLAMIC REP, Tehrān
W • Mideast • 100 kW
TANZANIA
†RADIO TANZANIA, Dar es Salaam
E Africa • DS-NATIONAL • 100 kW • ALT. FREQ. TO 7165 kHz
USA
RFE-RL, Via Holzkirchen, Germany
W • E Europe & W Asia • 250 kW
†RFE-RL, Via Kavála, Greece
W • Mideast & W Asia • 250 kW
RFE-RL, Via Udon Thani, Thailand
W • W Asia • 250 kW
VOA, Various Locations
S Asia • 250 kW
7285 CHINA
CHINA RADIO INTL, Jinhua
Europe • 600 kW
E Europe & Mideast • 600 kW

CHINA (TAIWAN)
†CBS, T'ai-pei
E Asia • CHINESE NETWORK • 100 kW
E Asia • NEWS NETWORK • 100 kW

†VOICE OF ASIA, T'ai-pei
SE Asia • 100 kW
CROATIA
(con'd) RADIO CROATIA, Via Jülich, Germany
W • W North Am • 100 kW • ALT. FREQ. TO 9925 kHz

0 1 2 3 4 5 6 7 8 9 10 11 12 13 14 15 16 17 18 19 20 21 22 23 24

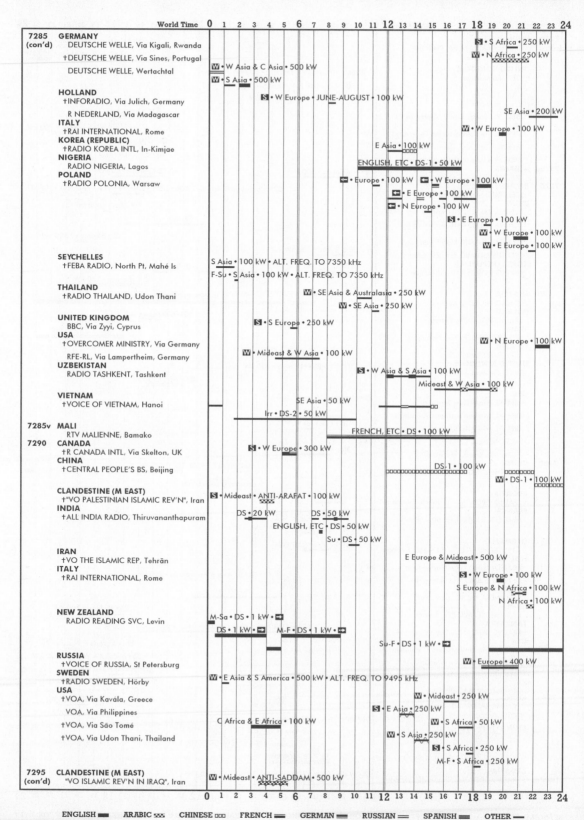

World Time 0 1 2 3 4 5 6 7 8 9 10 11 12 13 14 15 16 17 18 19 20 21 22 23 24

7285
(con'd) **GERMANY**
DEUTSCHE WELLE, Via Kigali, Rwanda — Ⓢ • S Africa • 250 kW
†DEUTSCHE WELLE, Via Sines, Portugal — Ⓦ • N Africa • 250 kW
DEUTSCHE WELLE, Wertachtal — Ⓦ • W Asia & C Asia • 500 kW
— Ⓦ • S Asia • 500 kW

HOLLAND
†INFORADIO, Via Julich, Germany — Ⓢ • W Europe • JUNE-AUGUST • 100 kW
R NEDERLAND, Via Madagascar — SE Asia • 200 kW
ITALY
†RAI INTERNATIONAL, Rome — Ⓦ • W Europe • 100 kW
KOREA (REPUBLIC)
†RADIO KOREA INTL, In-Kimjae — E Asia • 100 kW
NIGERIA
RADIO NIGERIA, Lagos — ENGLISH, ETC • DS-1 • 50 kW
POLAND
†RADIO POLONIA, Warsaw — 🔁 • Europe • 100 kW   🔁 • W Europe • 100 kW
— 🔁 • E Europe • 100 kW
— 🔁 • N Europe • 100 kW
— Ⓢ • E Europe • 100 kW
— Ⓦ • W Europe • 100 kW
— Ⓦ • E Europe • 100 kW

SEYCHELLES
†FEBA RADIO, North Pt, Mahé Is — S Asia • 100 kW • ALT. FREQ. TO 7350 kHz
— F-Su • S Asia • 100 kW • ALT. FREQ. TO 7350 kHz

THAILAND
†RADIO THAILAND, Udon Thani — Ⓦ • SE Asia & Australasia • 250 kW
— Ⓦ • SE Asia • 250 kW

UNITED KINGDOM
BBC, Via Zyyi, Cyprus — Ⓢ • S Europe • 250 kW
USA
†OVERCOMER MINISTRY, Via Germany — Ⓦ • N Europe • 100 kW
RFE-RL, Via Lampertheim, Germany — Ⓦ • Mideast & W Asia • 100 kW
UZBEKISTAN
RADIO TASHKENT, Tashkent — Ⓢ • W Asia & S Asia • 100 kW
— Mideast & W Asia • 100 kW

VIETNAM
†VOICE OF VIETNAM, Hanoi — SE Asia • 50 kW
— Irr • DS-2 • 50 kW

7285v MALI
RTV MALIENNE, Bamako — FRENCH, ETC • DS • 100 kW
7290 CANADA
†R CANADA INTL, Via Skelton, UK — Ⓢ • W Europe • 300 kW
CHINA
†CENTRAL PEOPLE'S BS, Beijing — DS-1 • 100 kW
— Ⓦ • DS-1 • 100 kW

CLANDESTINE (M EAST)
†"VO PALESTINIAN ISLAMIC REV'N", Iran — Ⓢ • Mideast • ANTI-ARAFAT • 100 kW
INDIA
†ALL INDIA RADIO, Thiruvananthapuram — DS • 20 kW   DS • 50 kW
— ENGLISH, ETC • DS • 50 kW
— Su • DS • 50 kW

IRAN
†VO THE ISLAMIC REP, Tehrān — E Europe & Mideast • 500 kW
ITALY
†RAI INTERNATIONAL, Rome — Ⓢ • W Europe • 100 kW
— S Europe & N Africa • 100 kW
— N Africa • 100 kW

NEW ZEALAND
RADIO READING SVC, Levin — M-Sa • DS • 1 kW • 🔁
— DS • 1 kW • 🔁   M-F • DS • 1 kW • 🔁
— Su-F • DS • 1 kW • 🔁

RUSSIA
†VOICE OF RUSSIA, St Petersburg — Ⓦ • Europe • 400 kW
SWEDEN
†RADIO SWEDEN, Hörby — Ⓦ • E Asia & S America • 500 kW • ALT. FREQ. TO 9495 kHz
USA
†VOA, Via Kavála, Greece — Ⓦ • Mideast • 250 kW
VOA, Via Philippines — Ⓢ • E Asia • 250 kW
†VOA, Via São Tomé — C Africa & E Africa • 100 kW   Ⓦ • S Africa • 50 kW
†VOA, Via Udon Thani, Thailand — Ⓦ • S Asia • 250 kW
— Ⓢ • S Africa • 250 kW
— M-F • S Africa • 250 kW

7295 CLANDESTINE (M EAST)
(con'd) "VO ISLAMIC REV'N IN IRAQ", Iran — Ⓦ • Mideast • ANTI-SADDAM • 500 kW

0 1 2 3 4 5 6 7 8 9 10 11 12 13 14 15 16 17 18 19 20 21 22 23 24

ENGLISH ▬   ARABIC ⨯⨯⨯   CHINESE ☐☐☐   FRENCH ═══   GERMAN ▬▬▬   RUSSIAN ═══   SPANISH ═══   OTHER ▬

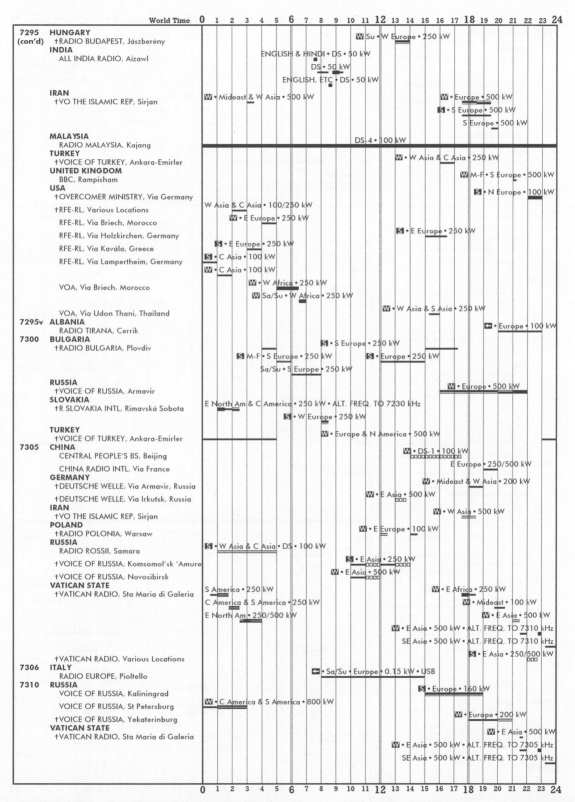

| World Time | 0 1 2 3 4 5 6 7 8 9 10 11 12 13 14 15 16 17 18 19 20 21 22 23 24 |

7295 **HUNGARY**
(con'd) †RADIO BUDAPEST, Jászberény — W Su • W Europe • 250 kW
INDIA
ALL INDIA RADIO, Aizawl — ENGLISH & HINDI • DS • 50 kW
— DS • 50 kW
— ENGLISH, ETC • DS • 50 kW
IRAN
†VO THE ISLAMIC REP, Sirjan — W • Mideast & W Asia • 500 kW
— W • Europe • 500 kW
— S • S Europe • 500 kW
— S Europe • 500 kW
MALAYSIA
RADIO MALAYSIA, Kajang — DS-4 • 100 kW
TURKEY
†VOICE OF TURKEY, Ankara-Emirler — W • W Asia & C Asia • 250 kW
UNITED KINGDOM
BBC, Rampisham — M-F • S Europe • 500 kW
USA
†OVERCOMER MINISTRY, Via Germany — S • N Europe • 100 kW
†RFE-RL, Various Locations — W Asia & C Asia • 100/250 kW
RFE-RL, Via Briech, Morocco — W • E Europe • 250 kW
RFE-RL, Via Holzkirchen, Germany — S • E Europe • 250 kW
RFE-RL, Via Kavála, Greece — S • E Europe • 250 kW
RFE-RL, Via Lampertheim, Germany — S • C Asia • 100 kW
— W • C Asia • 100 kW
VOA, Via Briech, Morocco — W • W Africa • 250 kW
— W Sa/Su • W Africa • 250 kW
VOA, Via Udon Thani, Thailand — W • W Asia & S Asia • 250 kW
7295v **ALBANIA**
RADIO TIRANA, Cerrik — ⇐ • Europe • 100 kW
7300 **BULGARIA**
†RADIO BULGARIA, Plovdiv — S • S Europe • 250 kW
— S M-F • S Europe • 250 kW
— S • Europe • 250 kW
— Sa/Su • S Europe • 250 kW
RUSSIA
†VOICE OF RUSSIA, Armavir — W • Europe • 500 kW
SLOVAKIA
†R SLOVAKIA INTL, Rimavská Sobota — E North Am & C America • 250 kW • ALT. FREQ. TO 7230 kHz
— S • W Europe • 250 kW
TURKEY
†VOICE OF TURKEY, Ankara-Emirler — W • Europe & N America • 500 kW
7305 **CHINA**
CENTRAL PEOPLE'S BS, Beijing — W • DS-1 • 100 kW
CHINA RADIO INTL, Via France — E Europe • 250/500 kW
GERMANY
†DEUTSCHE WELLE, Via Armavir, Russia — W • Mideast & W Asia • 200 kW
†DEUTSCHE WELLE, Via Irkutsk, Russia — W • E Asia • 500 kW
IRAN
†VO THE ISLAMIC REP, Sirjan — W • W Asia • 500 kW
POLAND
†RADIO POLONIA, Warsaw — W • E Europe • 100 kW
RUSSIA
RADIO ROSSII, Samara — S • W Asia & C Asia • DS • 100 kW
†VOICE OF RUSSIA, Komsomol'sk 'Amure — S • E Asia • 250 kW
†VOICE OF RUSSIA, Novosibirsk — W • E Asia • 500 kW
VATICAN STATE
†VATICAN RADIO, Sta Maria di Galeria — S America • 250 kW
— C America & S America • 250 kW
— E North Am • 250/500 kW
— W • E Africa • 250 kW
— W • Mideast • 100 kW
— W • E Asia • 500 kW
— W • E Asia • 500 kW • ALT. FREQ. TO 7310 kHz
— SE Asia • 500 kW • ALT. FREQ. TO 7310 kHz
— S • E Asia • 250/500 kW
†VATICAN RADIO, Various Locations
7306 **ITALY**
RADIO EUROPE, Pioltello — ⇐ • Sa/Su • Europe • 0.15 kW • USB
7310 **RUSSIA**
VOICE OF RUSSIA, Kaliningrad — S • Europe • 160 kW
VOICE OF RUSSIA, St Petersburg — W • C America & S America • 800 kW
†VOICE OF RUSSIA, Yekaterinburg — W • Europe • 200 kW
VATICAN STATE
†VATICAN RADIO, Sta Maria di Galeria — W • E Asia • 500 kW
— W • E Asia • 500 kW • ALT. FREQ. TO 7305 kHz
— SE Asia • 500 kW • ALT. FREQ. TO 7305 kHz

| 0 1 2 3 4 5 6 7 8 9 10 11 12 13 14 15 16 17 18 19 20 21 22 23 24 |

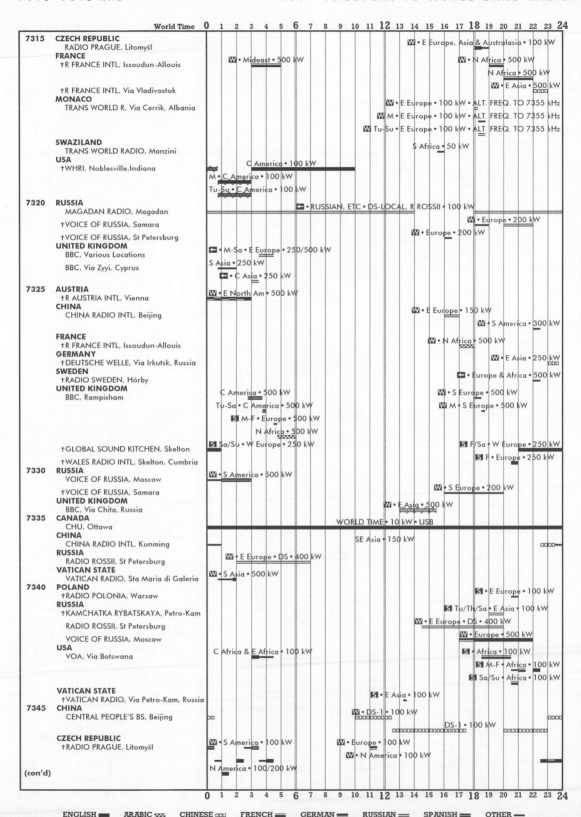

World Time 0 1 2 3 4 5 6 7 8 9 10 11 12 13 14 15 16 17 18 19 20 21 22 23 24

7315	**CZECH REPUBLIC**	
	RADIO PRAGUE, Litomyšl	W • E Europe, Asia & Australasia • 100 kW
	FRANCE	
	†R FRANCE INTL, Issoudun-Allouis	W • Mideast • 500 kW W • N Africa • 500 kW
		N Africa • 500 kW
		W • E Asia • 500 kW
	†R FRANCE INTL, Via Vladivostok	
	MONACO	
	TRANS WORLD R, Via Cerrik, Albania	W • E Europe • 100 kW • ALT. FREQ. TO 7355 kHz
		W M • E Europe • 100 kW • ALT. FREQ. TO 7355 kHz
		W Tu-Su • E Europe • 100 kW • ALT. FREQ. TO 7355 kHz
	SWAZILAND	
	TRANS WORLD RADIO, Manzini	S Africa • 50 kW
	USA	
	†WHRI, Noblesville, Indiana	C America • 100 kW
		M • C America • 100 kW
		Tu-Su • C America • 100 kW
7320	**RUSSIA**	
	MAGADAN RADIO, Magadan	• RUSSIAN, ETC • DS-LOCAL, R ROSSII • 100 kW
	†VOICE OF RUSSIA, Samara	W • Europe • 200 kW
	†VOICE OF RUSSIA, St Petersburg	W • Europe • 200 kW
	UNITED KINGDOM	
	BBC, Various Locations	• M-Sa • E Europe • 250/500 kW
		S Asia • 250 kW
	BBC, Via Zyyi, Cyprus	• C Asia • 250 kW
7325	**AUSTRIA**	
	†R AUSTRIA INTL, Vienna	W • E North Am • 500 kW
	CHINA	
	CHINA RADIO INTL, Beijing	W • E Europe • 150 kW
		W • S America • 300 kW
	FRANCE	
	†R FRANCE INTL, Issoudun-Allouis	W • N Africa • 500 kW
	GERMANY	
	†DEUTSCHE WELLE, Via Irkutsk, Russia	W • E Asia • 250 kW
	SWEDEN	
	†RADIO SWEDEN, Hörby	• Europe & Africa • 500 kW
	UNITED KINGDOM	
	BBC, Rampisham	C America • 500 kW W • S Europe • 500 kW
		Tu-Sa • C America • 500 kW W M • S Europe • 500 kW
		S M-F • Europe • 500 kW
		N Africa • 500 kW
	†GLOBAL SOUND KITCHEN, Skelton	S Sa/Su • W Europe • 250 kW S F/Sa • W Europe • 250 kW
	†WALES RADIO INTL, Skelton, Cumbria	S F • Europe • 250 kW
7330	**RUSSIA**	
	VOICE OF RUSSIA, Moscow	W • S America • 500 kW
	†VOICE OF RUSSIA, Samara	W • S Europe • 200 kW
	UNITED KINGDOM	
	BBC, Via Chita, Russia	W • E Asia • 500 kW
7335	**CANADA**	
	CHU, Ottawa	WORLD TIME • 10 kW • USB
	CHINA	
	CHINA RADIO INTL, Kunming	SE Asia • 150 kW
	RUSSIA	
	RADIO ROSSII, St Petersburg	W • E Europe • DS • 400 kW
	VATICAN STATE	
	VATICAN RADIO, Sta Maria di Galeria	W • S Asia • 500 kW
7340	**POLAND**	
	†RADIO POLONIA, Warsaw	S • E Europe • 100 kW
	RUSSIA	
	†KAMCHATKA RYBATSKAYA, Petro-Kam	S Tu/Th/Sa • E Asia • 100 kW
	RADIO ROSSII, St Petersburg	W • E Europe • DS • 400 kW
	VOICE OF RUSSIA, Moscow	W • Europe • 500 kW
	USA	
	VOA, Via Botswana	C Africa & E Africa • 100 kW S • Africa • 100 kW
		S M-F • Africa • 100 kW
		S Sa/Su • Africa • 100 kW
	VATICAN STATE	
	†VATICAN RADIO, Via Petro-Kam, Russia	S • E Asia • 100 kW
7345	**CHINA**	
	CENTRAL PEOPLE'S BS, Beijing	W • DS-1 • 100 kW
		DS-1 • 100 kW
	CZECH REPUBLIC	
	†RADIO PRAGUE, Litomyšl	W • S America • 100 kW W • Europe • 100 kW
		W • N America • 100 kW
		N America • 100/200 kW
(con'd)		

0 1 2 3 4 5 6 7 8 9 10 11 12 13 14 15 16 17 18 19 20 21 22 23 24

ENGLISH ▬   ARABIC ⋙   CHINESE □□□   FRENCH ▭   GERMAN ▬   RUSSIAN ═   SPANISH ▭   OTHER ▬

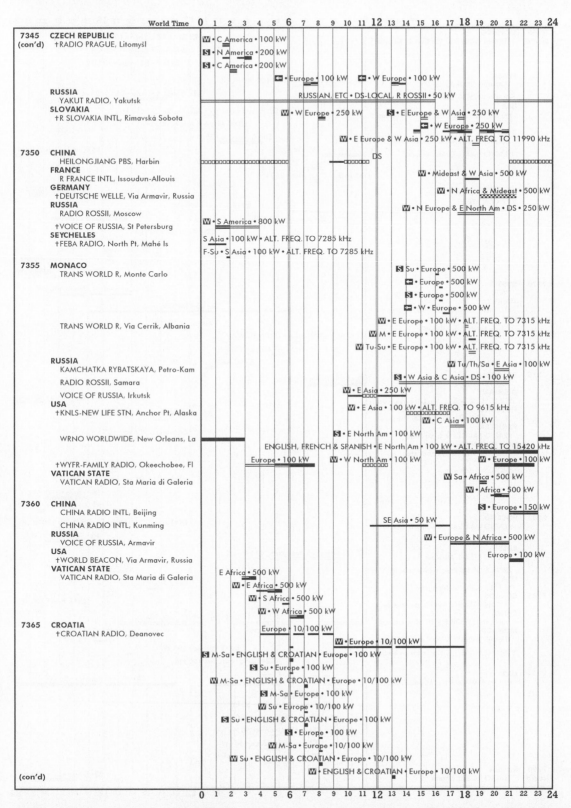

World Time　0　1　2　3　4　5　6　7　8　9　10　11　12　13　14　15　16　17　18　19　20　21　22　23　24

7345　CZECH REPUBLIC
(con'd)　　†RADIO PRAGUE, Litomyšl
　　　W • C America • 100 kW
　　　S • N America • 200 kW
　　　S • C America • 200 kW
　　　⇐ • Europe • 100 kW　⇐ • W Europe • 100 kW

　　　RUSSIA
　　　　YAKUT RADIO, Yakutsk
　　　RUSSIAN, ETC • DS-LOCAL, R ROSSII • 50 kW
　　　SLOVAKIA
　　　　†R SLOVAKIA INTL, Rimavská Sobota
　　　W • W Europe • 250 kW　S • E Europe & W Asia • 250 kW
　　　⇐ • W Europe • 250 kW
　　　W • E Europe & W Asia • 250 kW • ALT. FREQ. TO 11990 kHz

7350　CHINA
　　　HEILONGJIANG PBS, Harbin　　　　　DS
　　　FRANCE
　　　　R FRANCE INTL, Issoudun-Allouis
　　　W • Mideast & W Asia • 500 kW
　　　GERMANY
　　　　†DEUTSCHE WELLE, Via Armavir, Russia
　　　W • N Africa & Mideast • 500 kW
　　　RUSSIA
　　　　RADIO ROSSII, Moscow
　　　W • N Europe & E North Am • DS • 250 kW
　　　　†VOICE OF RUSSIA, St Petersburg
　　　W • S America • 800 kW
　　　SEYCHELLES
　　　　†FEBA RADIO, North Pt, Mahé Is
　　　S Asia • 100 kW • ALT. FREQ. TO 7285 kHz
　　　F-Su • S Asia • 100 kW • ALT. FREQ. TO 7285 kHz

7355　MONACO
　　　TRANS WORLD R, Monte Carlo
　　　S Su • Europe • 500 kW
　　　⇐ • Europe • 500 kW
　　　S • Europe • 500 kW
　　　⇐ • W Europe • 500 kW
　　　TRANS WORLD R, Via Cerrik, Albania
　　　W • E Europe • 100 kW • ALT. FREQ. TO 7315 kHz
　　　W M • E Europe • 100 kW • ALT. FREQ. TO 7315 kHz
　　　W Tu-Su • E Europe • 100 kW • ALT. FREQ. TO 7315 kHz
　　　RUSSIA
　　　　KAMCHATKA RYBATSKAYA, Petro-Kam
　　　W Tu/Th/Sa • E Asia • 100 kW
　　　　RADIO ROSSII, Samara
　　　S • W Asia & C Asia • DS • 100 kW
　　　　VOICE OF RUSSIA, Irkutsk
　　　W • E Asia • 250 kW
　　　USA
　　　　†KNLS-NEW LIFE STN, Anchor Pt, Alaska
　　　W • E Asia • 100 kW • ALT. FREQ. TO 9615 kHz
　　　W • C Asia • 100 kW
　　　　WRNO WORLDWIDE, New Orleans, La
　　　S • E North Am • 100 kW
　　　ENGLISH, FRENCH & SPANISH • E North Am • 100 kW • ALT. FREQ. TO 15420 kHz
　　　　†WYFR-FAMILY RADIO, Okeechobee, Fl
　　　Europe • 100 kW　W • W North Am • 100 kW　W • Europe • 100 kW
　　　VATICAN STATE
　　　　VATICAN RADIO, Sta Maria di Galeria
　　　W Sa • Africa • 500 kW
　　　W • Africa • 500 kW

7360　CHINA
　　　CHINA RADIO INTL, Beijing
　　　S • Europe • 150 kW
　　　CHINA RADIO INTL, Kunming
　　　SE Asia • 50 kW
　　　RUSSIA
　　　　VOICE OF RUSSIA, Armavir
　　　W • Europe & N Africa • 500 kW
　　　USA
　　　　†WORLD BEACON, Via Armavir, Russia
　　　Europe • 100 kW
　　　VATICAN STATE
　　　　VATICAN RADIO, Sta Maria di Galeria
　　　E Africa • 500 kW
　　　W • E Africa • 500 kW
　　　W • S Africa • 500 kW
　　　W • W Africa • 500 kW

7365　CROATIA
　　　†CROATIAN RADIO, Deanovec
　　　Europe • 10/100 kW
　　　W • Europe • 10/100 kW
　　　S M-Sa • ENGLISH & CROATIAN • Europe • 100 kW
　　　S Su • Europe • 100 kW
　　　W M-Sa • ENGLISH & CROATIAN • Europe • 10/100 kW
　　　S M-Sa • Europe • 100 kW
　　　W Su • Europe • 10/100 kW
　　　S Su • ENGLISH & CROATIAN • Europe • 100 kW
　　　S • Europe • 100 kW
　　　W M-Sa • Europe • 10/100 kW
　　　W Su • ENGLISH & CROATIAN • Europe • 10/100 kW
　　　W • ENGLISH & CROATIAN • Europe • 10/100 kW

(con'd)

0　1　2　3　4　5　6　7　8　9　10　11　12　13　14　15　16　17　18　19　20　21　22　23　24

SEASONAL **S** OR **W**　　1-HR TIMESHIFT MIDYEAR ⇐ OR ⇒　　JAMMING / OR /\　　EARLIEST HEARD ◁　　LATEST HEARD ▷　　NEW FOR 2001 †

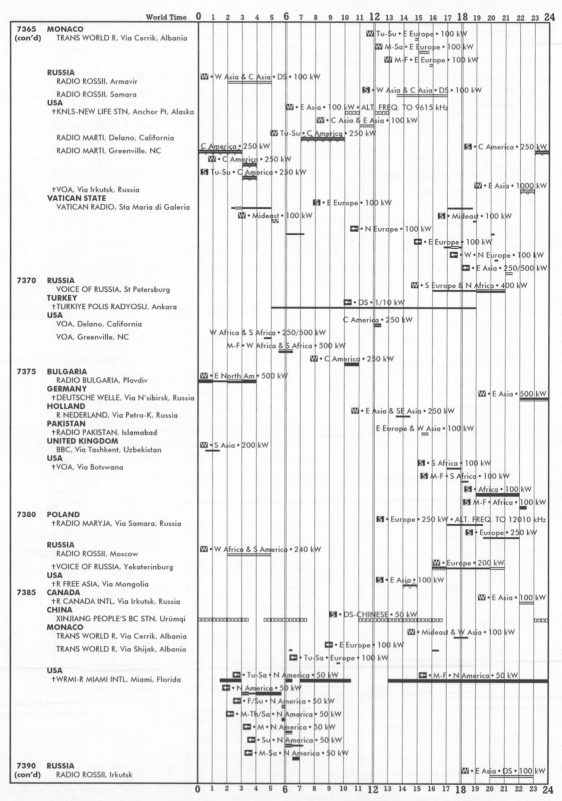

World Time 0 1 2 3 4 5 6 7 8 9 10 11 12 13 14 15 16 17 18 19 20 21 22 23 24

7365 MONACO
(con'd)   TRANS WORLD R, Via Cerrik, Albania
- W Tu-Su • E Europe • 100 kW
- W M-Sa • E Europe • 100 kW
- W M-F • E Europe • 100 kW

RUSSIA
 RADIO ROSSII, Armavir — W • W Asia & C Asia • DS • 100 kW
 RADIO ROSSII, Samara — S • W Asia & C Asia • DS • 100 kW
USA
 †KNLS-NEW LIFE STN, Anchor Pt, Alaska — W • E Asia • 100 kW • ALT. FREQ. TO 9615 kHz
 — W • C Asia & E Asia • 100 kW
 RADIO MARTI, Delano, California — W Tu-Su • C America • 250 kW
 RADIO MARTI, Greenville, NC — C America • 250 kW / S • C America • 250 kW
 — W • C America • 250 kW
 — S Tu-Su • C America • 250 kW

 †VOA, Via Irkutsk, Russia — W • E Asia • 1000 kW
VATICAN STATE
 VATICAN RADIO, Sta Maria di Galeria — S • E Europe • 100 kW
 — W • Mideast • 100 kW
 — S • Mideast • 100 kW
 — • N Europe • 100 kW
 — • E Europe • 100 kW
 — • W • N Europe • 100 kW
 — • E Asia • 250/500 kW

7370 RUSSIA
 VOICE OF RUSSIA, St Petersburg — W • S Europe & N Africa • 400 kW
TURKEY
 †TURKIYE POLIS RADYOSU, Ankara — • DS • 1/10 kW
USA
 VOA, Delano, California — C America • 250 kW
 — W Africa & S Africa • 250/500 kW
 VOA, Greenville, NC — M-F • W Africa & S Africa • 500 kW
 — W • C America • 250 kW

7375 BULGARIA
 RADIO BULGARIA, Plovdiv — W • E North Am • 500 kW
GERMANY
 †DEUTSCHE WELLE, Via N'sibirsk, Russia — W • E Asia • 500 kW
HOLLAND
 R NEDERLAND, Via Petro-K, Russia — W • E Asia & SE Asia • 250 kW
PAKISTAN
 †RADIO PAKISTAN, Islamabad — E Europe & W Asia • 100 kW
UNITED KINGDOM
 BBC, Via Tashkent, Uzbekistan — W • S Asia • 200 kW
USA
 †VOA, Via Botswana — S • S Africa • 100 kW
 — S M-F • S Africa • 100 kW
 — S • Africa • 100 kW
 — S M-F • Africa • 100 kW

7380 POLAND
 †RADIO MARYJA, Via Samara, Russia — S • Europe • 250 kW • ALT. FREQ. TO 12010 kHz
 — S • Europe • 250 kW
RUSSIA
 RADIO ROSSII, Moscow — W • W Africa & S America • 240 kW
 †VOICE OF RUSSIA, Yekaterinburg — W • Europe • 200 kW
USA
 †R FREE ASIA, Via Mongolia — S • E Asia • 100 kW
7385 CANADA
 †R CANADA INTL, Via Irkutsk, Russia — W • E Asia • 100 kW
CHINA
 XINJIANG PEOPLE'S BC STN, Urümqi — S • DS-CHINESE • 50 kW
MONACO
 TRANS WORLD R, Via Cerrik, Albania — W • Mideast & W Asia • 100 kW
 TRANS WORLD R, Via Shijak, Albania — • E Europe • 100 kW
 — • Tu-Sa • Europe • 100 kW

USA
 †WRMI-R MIAMI INTL, Miami, Florida — • Tu-Sa • N America • 50 kW
 — • M-F • N America • 50 kW
 — • N America • 50 kW
 — • F/Su • N America • 50 kW
 — • M-Th/Sa • N America • 50 kW
 — • M • N America • 50 kW
 — • Su • N America • 50 kW
 — • M-Sa • N America • 50 kW

7390 RUSSIA
(con'd)   RADIO ROSSII, Irkutsk — W • E Asia • DS • 100 kW

0 1 2 3 4 5 6 7 8 9 10 11 12 13 14 15 16 17 18 19 20 21 22 23 24

ENGLISH ▬ ARABIC ▨ CHINESE ▫▫▫ FRENCH ═ GERMAN ▬ RUSSIAN ═ SPANISH ▬ OTHER ▬

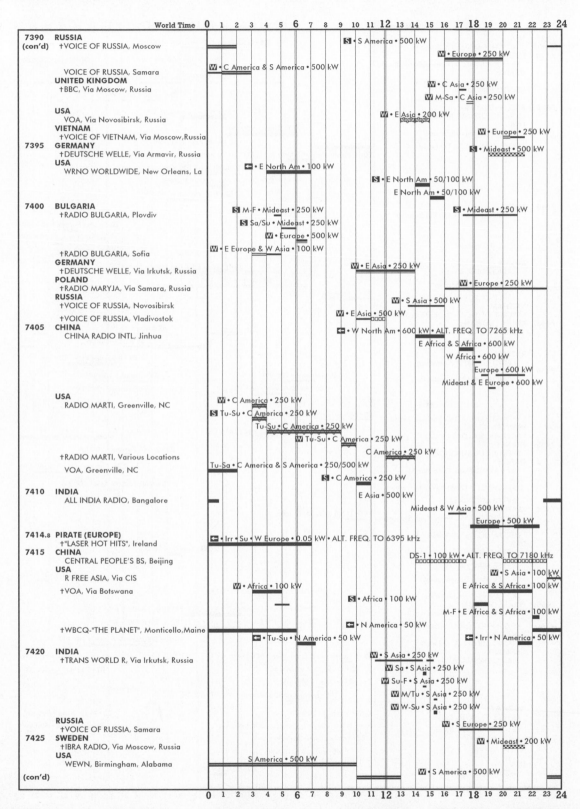

World Time																								

7390 RUSSIA
(con'd) †VOICE OF RUSSIA, Moscow
  VOICE OF RUSSIA, Samara
UNITED KINGDOM
  †BBC, Via Moscow, Russia
USA
  VOA, Via Novosibirsk, Russia
VIETNAM
  †VOICE OF VIETNAM, Via Moscow, Russia
7395 GERMANY
  †DEUTSCHE WELLE, Via Armavir, Russia
USA
  WRNO WORLDWIDE, New Orleans, La

7400 BULGARIA
  †RADIO BULGARIA, Plovdiv

  †RADIO BULGARIA, Sofia
GERMANY
  †DEUTSCHE WELLE, Via Irkutsk, Russia
POLAND
  †RADIO MARYJA, Via Samara, Russia
RUSSIA
  †VOICE OF RUSSIA, Novosibirsk
  †VOICE OF RUSSIA, Vladivostok
7405 CHINA
  CHINA RADIO INTL, Jinhua

USA
  RADIO MARTI, Greenville, NC

  †RADIO MARTI, Various Locations
  VOA, Greenville, NC

7410 INDIA
  ALL INDIA RADIO, Bangalore

7414.8 PIRATE (EUROPE)
  †"LASER HOT HITS", Ireland
7415 CHINA
  CENTRAL PEOPLE'S BS, Beijing
USA
  R FREE ASIA, Via CIS
  †VOA, Via Botswana

  †WBCQ-"THE PLANET", Monticello, Maine

7420 INDIA
  †TRANS WORLD R, Via Irkutsk, Russia

RUSSIA
  †VOICE OF RUSSIA, Samara
7425 SWEDEN
  †IBRA RADIO, Via Moscow, Russia
USA
  WEWN, Birmingham, Alabama

(con'd)

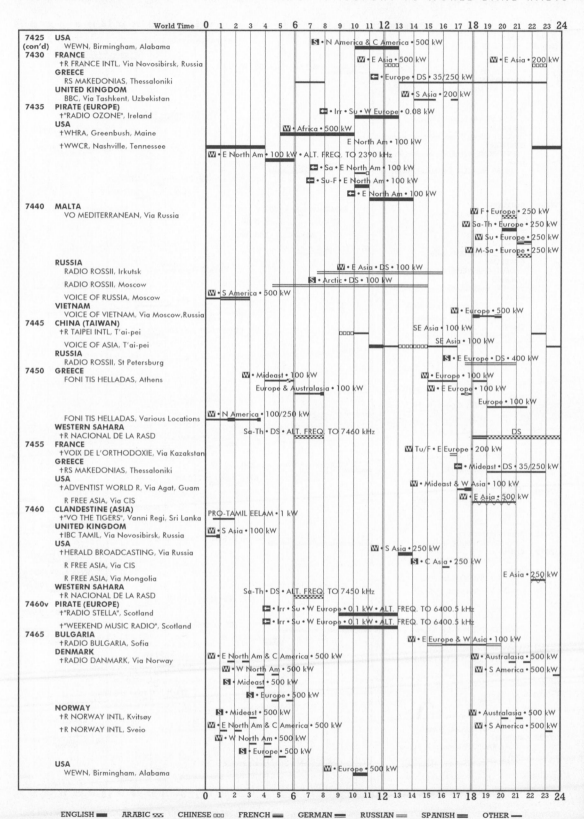

		World Time
7425 (con'd)	USA	WEWN, Birmingham, Alabama — N America & C America • 500 kW
7430	FRANCE	†R FRANCE INTL, Via Novosibirsk, Russia — W • E Asia • 500 kW / W • E Asia • 200 kW
	GREECE	RS MAKEDONIAS, Thessaloniki — Europe • DS • 35/250 kW
	UNITED KINGDOM	BBC, Via Tashkent, Uzbekistan — W • S Asia • 200 kW
7435	PIRATE (EUROPE)	†"RADIO OZONE", Ireland — Irr • Su • W Europe • 0.08 kW
	USA	†WHRA, Greenbush, Maine — W • Africa • 500 kW / E North Am • 100 kW
		†WWCR, Nashville, Tennessee — W • E North Am • 100 kW • ALT. FREQ. TO 2390 kHz / Sa • E North Am • 100 kW / Su-F • E North Am • 100 kW / E North Am • 100 kW
7440	MALTA	VO MEDITERRANEAN, Via Russia — W F • Europe • 250 kW / W Sa-Th • Europe • 250 kW / W Su • Europe • 250 kW / W M-Sa • Europe • 250 kW
	RUSSIA	RADIO ROSSII, Irkutsk — W • E Asia • DS • 100 kW
		RADIO ROSSII, Moscow — S • Arctic • DS • 100 kW
		VOICE OF RUSSIA, Moscow — W • S America • 500 kW
	VIETNAM	VOICE OF VIETNAM, Via Moscow, Russia — W • Europe • 500 kW
7445	CHINA (TAIWAN)	†R TAIPEI INTL, T'ai-pei — SE Asia • 100 kW
		VOICE OF ASIA, T'ai-pei — SE Asia • 100 kW
	RUSSIA	RADIO ROSSII, St Petersburg — S • E Europe • DS • 400 kW
7450	GREECE	FONI TIS HELLADAS, Athens — W • Mideast • 100 kW / Europe & Australasia • 100 kW / W • Europe • 100 kW / W • E Europe • 100 kW / Europe • 100 kW
		FONI TIS HELLADAS, Various Locations — W • N America • 100/250 kW
	WESTERN SAHARA	†R NACIONAL DE LA RASD — Sa-Th • DS • ALT. FREQ. TO 7460 kHz / DS
7455	FRANCE	†VOIX DE L'ORTHODOXIE, Via Kazakstan — W Tu/F • E Europe • 200 kW
	GREECE	†RS MAKEDONIAS, Thessaloniki — Mideast • DS • 35/250 kW
	USA	†ADVENTIST WORLD R, Via Agat, Guam — W • Mideast & W Asia • 100 kW
		R FREE ASIA, Via CIS — W • E Asia • 500 kW
7460	CLANDESTINE (ASIA)	†"VO THE TIGERS", Vanni Regi, Sri Lanka — PRO-TAMIL EELAM • 1 kW
	UNITED KINGDOM	†IBC TAMIL, Via Novosibirsk, Russia — W • S Asia • 100 kW
	USA	†HERALD BROADCASTING, Via Russia — W • S Asia • 250 kW
		R FREE ASIA, Via CIS — S • C Asia • 250 kW
		R FREE ASIA, Via Mongolia — E Asia • 250 kW
	WESTERN SAHARA	†R NACIONAL DE LA RASD — Sa-Th • DS • ALT. FREQ. TO 7450 kHz
7460v	PIRATE (EUROPE)	†"RADIO STELLA", Scotland — Irr • Su • W Europe • 0.1 kW • ALT. FREQ. TO 6400.5 kHz
		†"WEEKEND MUSIC RADIO", Scotland — Irr • Su • W Europe • 0.1 kW • ALT. FREQ. TO 6400.5 kHz
7465	BULGARIA	†RADIO BULGARIA, Sofia — W • E Europe & W Asia • 100 kW
	DENMARK	†RADIO DANMARK, Via Norway — W • E North Am & C America • 500 kW / W • Australasia • 500 kW / W • W North Am • 500 kW / W • S America • 500 kW / S • Mideast • 500 kW / S • Europe • 500 kW
	NORWAY	†R NORWAY INTL, Kvitsøy — S • Mideast • 500 kW / W • Australasia • 500 kW
		†R NORWAY INTL, Sveio — W • E North Am & C America • 500 kW / W • S America • 500 kW / W • W North Am • 500 kW / S • Europe • 500 kW
	USA	WEWN, Birmingham, Alabama — W • Europe • 500 kW

ENGLISH ■   ARABIC ▨▨▨   CHINESE ▫▫▫   FRENCH ▬   GERMAN ▬   RUSSIAN =   SPANISH ▬   OTHER —

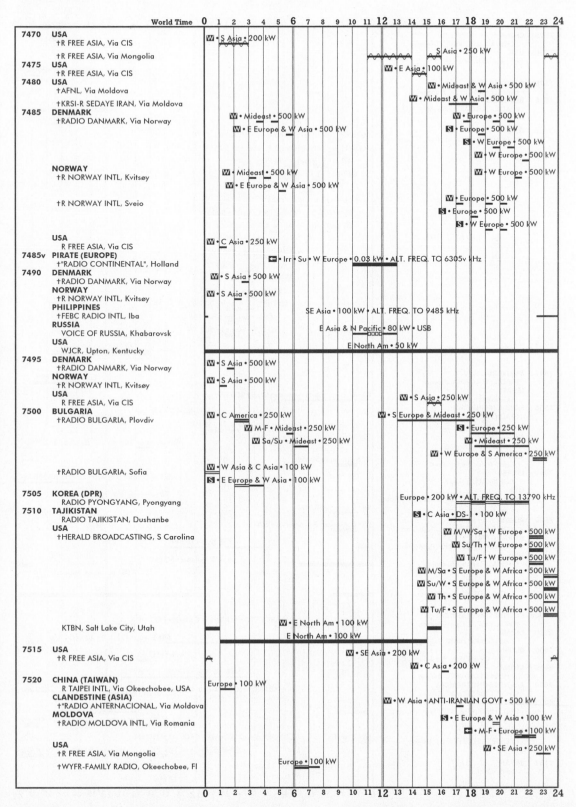

| | World Time | 0 | 1 | 2 | 3 | 4 | 5 | 6 | 7 | 8 | 9 | 10 | 11 | 12 | 13 | 14 | 15 | 16 | 17 | 18 | 19 | 20 | 21 | 22 | 23 | 24 |

7470 USA
†R FREE ASIA, Via CIS — W • S Asia • 200 kW
†R FREE ASIA, Via Mongolia — S Asia • 250 kW

7475 USA
†R FREE ASIA, Via CIS — W • E Asia • 100 kW

7480 USA
†AFNL, Via Moldova — W • Mideast & W Asia • 500 kW
†KRSI-R SEDAYE IRAN, Via Moldova — W • Mideast & W Asia • 500 kW

7485 DENMARK
†RADIO DANMARK, Via Norway — W • Mideast • 500 kW / W • E Europe & W Asia • 500 kW / W • Europe • 500 kW / S • Europe • 500 kW / S • W Europe • 500 kW / W • W Europe • 500 kW

NORWAY
†R NORWAY INTL, Kvitsøy — W • Mideast • 500 kW / W • E Europe & W Asia • 500 kW / W • W Europe • 500 kW

†R NORWAY INTL, Sveio — W • Europe • 500 kW / S • Europe • 500 kW / S • W Europe • 500 kW

USA
R FREE ASIA, Via CIS — W • C Asia • 250 kW

7485v PIRATE (EUROPE)
†"RADIO CONTINENTAL", Holland — ⇄ • Irr • Su • W Europe • 0.03 kW • ALT. FREQ. TO 6305v kHz

7490 DENMARK
†RADIO DANMARK, Via Norway — W • S Asia • 500 kW

NORWAY
†R NORWAY INTL, Kvitsøy — W • S Asia • 500 kW

PHILIPPINES
†FEBC RADIO INTL, Iba — SE Asia • 100 kW • ALT. FREQ. TO 9485 kHz

RUSSIA
VOICE OF RUSSIA, Khabarovsk — E Asia & N Pacific • 80 kW • USB

USA
WJCR, Upton, Kentucky — E North Am • 50 kW

7495 DENMARK
†RADIO DANMARK, Via Norway — W • S Asia • 500 kW

NORWAY
†R NORWAY INTL, Kvitsøy — W • S Asia • 500 kW

USA
R FREE ASIA, Via CIS — W • S Asia • 250 kW

7500 BULGARIA
†RADIO BULGARIA, Plovdiv — W • C America • 250 kW / W • S Europe & Mideast • 250 kW / W M-F • Mideast • 250 kW / S • Europe • 250 kW / W Sa/Su • Mideast • 250 kW / W • Mideast • 250 kW / W • W Europe & S America • 250 kW

†RADIO BULGARIA, Sofia — W • W Asia & C Asia • 100 kW / S • E Europe & W Asia • 100 kW

7505 KOREA (DPR)
RADIO PYONGYANG, Pyongyang — Europe • 200 kW • ALT. FREQ. TO 13790 kHz

7510 TAJIKISTAN
RADIO TAJIKISTAN, Dushanbe — S • C Asia • DS-1 • 100 kW

USA
†HERALD BROADCASTING, S Carolina — W M/W/Sa • W Europe • 500 kW / W Su/Th • W Europe • 500 kW / W Tu/F • W Europe • 500 kW / W M/Sa • S Europe & W Africa • 500 kW / W Su/W • S Europe & W Africa • 500 kW / W Th • S Europe & W Africa • 500 kW / W Tu/F • S Europe & W Africa • 500 kW

KTBN, Salt Lake City, Utah — W • E North Am • 100 kW / E North Am • 100 kW

7515 USA
†R FREE ASIA, Via CIS — W • SE Asia • 200 kW / W • C Asia • 200 kW

7520 CHINA (TAIWAN)
R TAIPEI INTL, Via Okeechobee, USA — Europe • 100 kW

CLANDESTINE (ASIA)
†"RADIO ANTERNACIONAL, Via Moldova — W • W Asia • ANTI-IRANIAN GOVT • 500 kW

MOLDOVA
†RADIO MOLDOVA INTL, Via Romania — S • E Europe & W Asia • 100 kW / ⇄ • M-F • Europe • 100 kW

USA
†R FREE ASIA, Via Mongolia — W • SE Asia • 250 kW

†WYFR-FAMILY RADIO, Okeechobee, Fl — Europe • 100 kW

| | 0 | 1 | 2 | 3 | 4 | 5 | 6 | 7 | 8 | 9 | 10 | 11 | 12 | 13 | 14 | 15 | 16 | 17 | 18 | 19 | 20 | 21 | 22 | 23 | 24 |

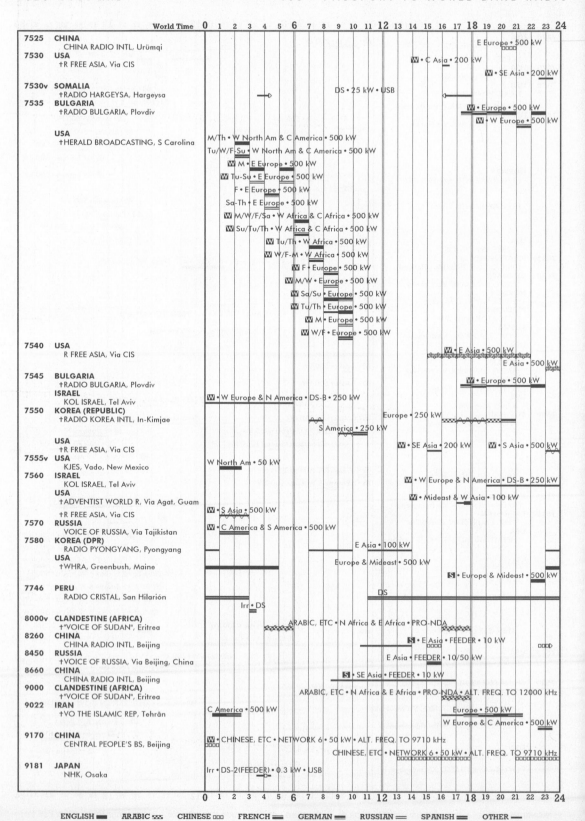

| World Time | 0 | 1 | 2 | 3 | 4 | 5 | 6 | 7 | 8 | 9 | 10 | 11 | 12 | 13 | 14 | 15 | 16 | 17 | 18 | 19 | 20 | 21 | 22 | 23 | 24 |

Freq	Country / Station	Details
7525	**CHINA** CHINA RADIO INTL, Urümqi	E Europe • 500 kW
7530	**USA** †R FREE ASIA, Via CIS	W • C Asia • 200 kW W • SE Asia • 200 kW
7530v	**SOMALIA** †RADIO HARGEYSA, Hargeysa	DS • 25 kW • USB
7535	**BULGARIA** †RADIO BULGARIA, Plovdiv	W • Europe • 500 kW W • W Europe • 500 kW
	USA †HERALD BROADCASTING, S Carolina	M/Th • W North Am & C America • 500 kW Tu/W/F-Su • W North Am & C America • 500 kW W M • E Europe • 500 kW W Tu-Su • E Europe • 500 kW F • E Europe • 500 kW Sa-Th • E Europe • 500 kW W M/W/F/Sa • W Africa & C Africa • 500 kW W Su/Tu/Th • W Africa & C Africa • 500 kW W Tu/Th • W Africa • 500 kW W W/F-M • W Africa • 500 kW W F • Europe • 500 kW W M/W • Europe • 500 kW W Sa/Su • Europe • 500 kW W Tu/Th • Europe • 500 kW W M • Europe • 500 kW W W/F • Europe • 500 kW
7540	**USA** R FREE ASIA, Via CIS	W • E Asia • 500 kW E Asia • 500 kW
7545	**BULGARIA** †RADIO BULGARIA, Plovdiv	W • Europe • 500 kW
	ISRAEL KOL ISRAEL, Tel Aviv	W • W Europe & N America • DS-B • 250 kW
7550	**KOREA (REPUBLIC)** †RADIO KOREA INTL, In-Kimjae	Europe • 250 kW S America • 250 kW
	USA †R FREE ASIA, Via CIS	W • SE Asia • 200 kW W • S Asia • 500 kW
7555v	**USA** KJES, Vado, New Mexico	W North Am • 50 kW
7560	**ISRAEL** KOL ISRAEL, Tel Aviv	W • W Europe & N America • DS-B • 250 kW
	USA †ADVENTIST WORLD R, Via Agat, Guam	W • Mideast & W Asia • 100 kW
	†R FREE ASIA, Via CIS	W • S Asia • 500 kW
7570	**RUSSIA** VOICE OF RUSSIA, Via Tajikistan	W • C America & S America • 500 kW
7580	**KOREA (DPR)** RADIO PYONGYANG, Pyongyang	E Asia • 100 kW
	USA †WHRA, Greenbush, Maine	Europe & Mideast • 500 kW S • Europe & Mideast • 500 kW
7746	**PERU** RADIO CRISTAL, San Hilarión	DS Irr • DS
8000v	**CLANDESTINE (AFRICA)** †"VOICE OF SUDAN", Eritrea	ARABIC, ETC • N Africa & E Africa • PRO-NDA
8260	**CHINA** CHINA RADIO INTL, Beijing	S • E Asia • FEEDER • 10 kW
8450	**RUSSIA** †VOICE OF RUSSIA, Via Beijing, China	E Asia • FEEDER • 10/50 kW
8660	**CHINA** CHINA RADIO INTL, Beijing	S • SE Asia • FEEDER • 10 kW
9000	**CLANDESTINE (AFRICA)** †"VOICE OF SUDAN", Eritrea	ARABIC, ETC • N Africa & E Africa • PRO-NDA • ALT. FREQ. TO 12000 kHz
9022	**IRAN** †VO THE ISLAMIC REP, Tehrān	C America • 500 kW Europe • 500 kW W Europe & C America • 500 kW
9170	**CHINA** CENTRAL PEOPLE'S BS, Beijing	W • CHINESE, ETC • NETWORK 6 • 50 kW • ALT. FREQ. TO 9710 kHz CHINESE, ETC • NETWORK 6 • 50 kW • ALT. FREQ. TO 9710 kHz
9181	**JAPAN** NHK, Osaka	Irr • DS-2(FEEDER) • 0.3 kW • USB

| | 0 | 1 | 2 | 3 | 4 | 5 | 6 | 7 | 8 | 9 | 10 | 11 | 12 | 13 | 14 | 15 | 16 | 17 | 18 | 19 | 20 | 21 | 22 | 23 | 24 |

ENGLISH ▬   ARABIC ⋙   CHINESE ▭▭▭   FRENCH ═   GERMAN ▬   RUSSIAN ═   SPANISH ═   OTHER ▬

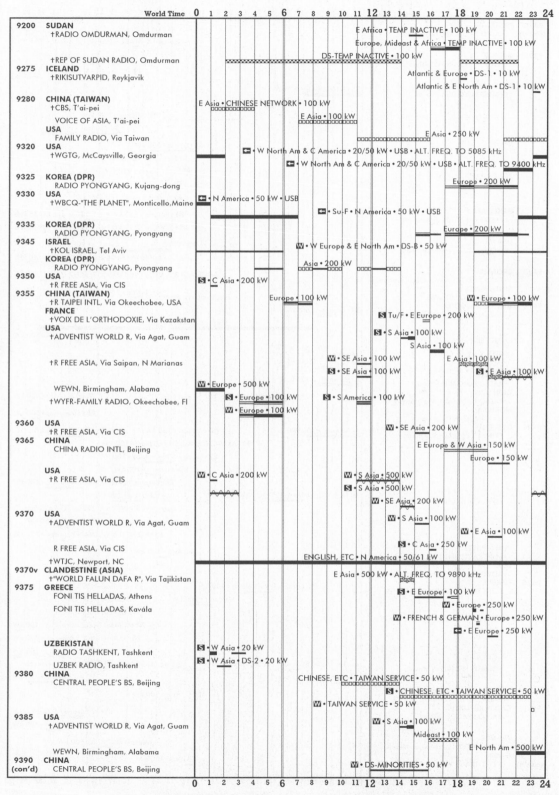

World Time	0 1 2 3 4 5 6 7 8 9 10 11 12 13 14 15 16 17 18 19 20 21 22 23 24
9200 SUDAN	
†RADIO OMDURMAN, Omdurman	E Africa • TEMP INACTIVE • 100 kW
	Europe, Mideast & Africa • TEMP INACTIVE • 100 kW
†REP OF SUDAN RADIO, Omdurman	DS-TEMP INACTIVE • 100 kW
9275 ICELAND	
†RIKISUTVARPID, Reykjavik	Atlantic & Europe • DS-1 • 10 kW
	Atlantic & E North Am • DS-1 • 10 kW
9280 CHINA (TAIWAN)	
†CBS, T'ai-pei	E Asia • CHINESE NETWORK • 100 kW
VOICE OF ASIA, T'ai-pei	E Asia • 100 kW
USA	
FAMILY RADIO, Via Taiwan	E Asia • 250 kW
9320 USA	
†WGTG, McCaysville, Georgia	⊡ W North Am & C America • 20/50 kW • USB • ALT. FREQ. TO 5085 kHz
	⊡ W North Am & C America • 20/50 kW • USB • ALT. FREQ. TO 9400 kHz
9325 KOREA (DPR)	
RADIO PYONGYANG, Kujang-dong	Europe • 200 kW
9330 USA	
†WBCQ-"THE PLANET", Monticello, Maine	⊡ N America • 50 kW • USB
	⊡ • Su-F • N America • 50 kW • USB
9335 KOREA (DPR)	
RADIO PYONGYANG, Pyongyang	Europe • 200 kW
9345 ISRAEL	
†KOL ISRAEL, Tel Aviv	W • W Europe & E North Am • DS-B • 50 kW
KOREA (DPR)	
RADIO PYONGYANG, Pyongyang	Asia • 200 kW
9350 USA	
†R FREE ASIA, Via CIS	S • C Asia • 200 kW
9355 CHINA (TAIWAN)	
†R TAIPEI INTL, Via Okeechobee, USA	Europe • 100 kW W • Europe • 100 kW
FRANCE	
†VOIX DE L'ORTHODOXIE, Via Kazakstan	S • Tu/F • E Europe • 200 kW
USA	
†ADVENTIST WORLD R, Via Agat, Guam	S • S Asia • 100 kW
	S Asia • 100 kW
†R FREE ASIA, Via Saipan, N Marianas	W • SE Asia • 100 kW E Asia • 100 kW
	S • SE Asia • 100 kW W • E Asia • 100 kW
WEWN, Birmingham, Alabama	W • Europe • 500 kW
†WYFR-FAMILY RADIO, Okeechobee, Fl	S • Europe • 100 kW S • S America • 100 kW
	W • Europe • 100 kW
9360 USA	
†R FREE ASIA, Via CIS	W • SE Asia • 200 kW
9365 CHINA	
CHINA RADIO INTL, Beijing	E Europe & W Asia • 150 kW
	Europe • 150 kW
USA	
†R FREE ASIA, Via CIS	W • C Asia • 200 kW W • S Asia • 500 kW
	S • S Asia • 500 kW
	W • SE Asia • 200 kW
9370 USA	
†ADVENTIST WORLD R, Via Agat, Guam	W • S Asia • 100 kW
	W • E Asia • 100 kW
R FREE ASIA, Via CIS	S • C Asia • 250 kW
†WTJC, Newport, NC	ENGLISH, ETC • N America • 50/61 kW
9370v CLANDESTINE (ASIA)	
†"WORLD FALUN DAFA R", Via Tajikistan	E Asia • 500 kW • ALT. FREQ. TO 9890 kHz
9375 GREECE	
FONI TIS HELLADAS, Athens	S • E Europe • 100 kW
FONI TIS HELLADAS, Kavála	W • Europe • 250 kW
	W • FRENCH & GERMAN • Europe • 250 kW
	⊡ • E Europe • 250 kW
UZBEKISTAN	
RADIO TASHKENT, Tashkent	S • W Asia • 20 kW
UZBEK RADIO, Tashkent	S • W Asia • DS-2 • 20 kW
9380 CHINA	
CENTRAL PEOPLE'S BS, Beijing	CHINESE, ETC • TAIWAN SERVICE • 50 kW
	S • CHINESE, ETC • TAIWAN SERVICE • 50 kW
	W • TAIWAN SERVICE • 50 kW
9385 USA	
†ADVENTIST WORLD R, Via Agat, Guam	W • S Asia • 100 kW
	Mideast • 100 kW
WEWN, Birmingham, Alabama	E North Am • 500 kW
9390 CHINA	
(con'd) CENTRAL PEOPLE'S BS, Beijing	W • DS-MINORITIES • 50 kW

0 1 2 3 4 5 6 7 8 9 10 11 12 13 14 15 16 17 18 19 20 21 22 23 24

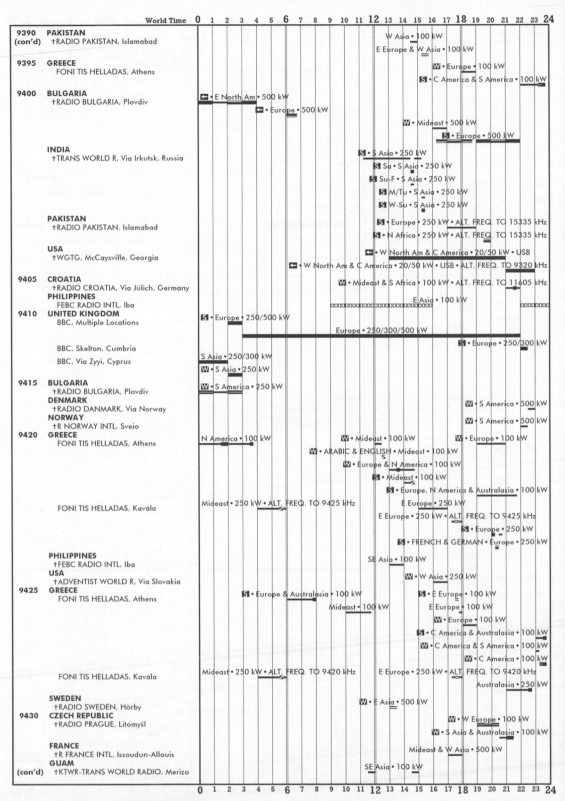

World Time 0 1 2 3 4 5 6 7 8 9 10 11 12 13 14 15 16 17 18 19 20 21 22 23 24

9390 PAKISTAN
(con'd) †RADIO PAKISTAN, Islamabad
    W Asia • 100 kW
    E Europe & W Asia • 100 kW

9395 GREECE
    FONI TIS HELLADAS, Athens
    W • Europe • 100 kW
    S • C America & S America • 100 kW

9400 BULGARIA
    †RADIO BULGARIA, Plovdiv
    E North Am • 500 kW
    • Europe • 500 kW
    W • Mideast • 500 kW
    S • Europe • 500 kW

    INDIA
    †TRANS WORLD R, Via Irkutsk, Russia
    S • S Asia • 250 kW
    S Sa • S Asia • 250 kW
    S Su-F • S Asia • 250 kW
    S M/Tu • S Asia • 250 kW
    S W-Su • S Asia • 250 kW

    PAKISTAN
    †RADIO PAKISTAN, Islamabad
    S • Europe • 250 kW • ALT. FREQ. TO 15335 kHz
    S • N Africa • 250 kW • ALT. FREQ. TO 15335 kHz

    USA
    †WGTG, McCaysville, Georgia
    W North Am & C America • 20/50 kW • USB
    W North Am & C America • 20/50 kW • USB • ALT. FREQ. TO 9320 kHz

9405 CROATIA
    †RADIO CROATIA, Via Jülich, Germany
    W • Mideast & S Africa • 100 kW • ALT. FREQ. TO 11605 kHz
    PHILIPPINES
    FEBC RADIO INTL, Iba
    E Asia • 100 kW

9410 UNITED KINGDOM
    BBC, Multiple Locations
    S • Europe • 250/500 kW
    Europe • 250/300/500 kW

    BBC, Skelton, Cumbria
    S • Europe • 250/300 kW
    BBC, Via Zyyi, Cyprus
    S Asia • 250/300 kW
    W • S Asia • 250 kW

9415 BULGARIA
    †RADIO BULGARIA, Plovdiv
    W • S America • 250 kW
    DENMARK
    †RADIO DANMARK, Via Norway
    W • S America • 500 kW
    NORWAY
    †R NORWAY INTL, Sveio
    W • S America • 500 kW

9420 GREECE
    FONI TIS HELLADAS, Athens
    N America • 100 kW
    W • Mideast • 100 kW
    W • Europe • 100 kW
    W • ARABIC & ENGLISH • Mideast • 100 kW
    W • Europe & N America • 100 kW
    S • Mideast • 100 kW
    W • Europe, N America & Australasia • 100 kW

    FONI TIS HELLADAS, Kavála
    Mideast • 250 kW • ALT. FREQ. TO 9425 kHz
    E Europe • 250 kW
    E Europe • 250 kW • ALT. FREQ. TO 9425 kHz
    S • Europe • 250 kW
    S • FRENCH & GERMAN • Europe • 250 kW

    PHILIPPINES
    †FEBC RADIO INTL, Iba
    SE Asia • 100 kW
    USA
    †ADVENTIST WORLD R, Via Slovakia
    W • W Asia • 250 kW

9425 GREECE
    FONI TIS HELLADAS, Athens
    S • Europe & Australasia • 100 kW
    S • E Europe • 100 kW
    Mideast • 100 kW
    E Europe • 100 kW
    W • Europe • 100 kW
    S • C America & Australasia • 100 kW
    W • C America & S America • 100 kW
    W • C America • 100 kW

    FONI TIS HELLADAS, Kavála
    Mideast • 250 kW • ALT. FREQ. TO 9420 kHz
    E Europe • 250 kW • ALT. FREQ. TO 9420 kHz
    Australasia • 250 kW

    SWEDEN
    †RADIO SWEDEN, Hörby
    W • E Asia • 500 kW
9430 CZECH REPUBLIC
    †RADIO PRAGUE, Litomyšl
    W • W Europe • 100 kW
    W • S Asia & Australasia • 100 kW

    FRANCE
    †R FRANCE INTL, Issoudun-Allouis
    Mideast & W Asia • 500 kW
    GUAM
(con'd) †KTWR-TRANS WORLD RADIO, Merizo
    SE Asia • 100 kW

0 1 2 3 4 5 6 7 8 9 10 11 12 13 14 15 16 17 18 19 20 21 22 23 24

ENGLISH ▬   ARABIC ⋙   CHINESE □□□   FRENCH ══   GERMAN ▬   RUSSIAN ══   SPANISH ══   OTHER ──

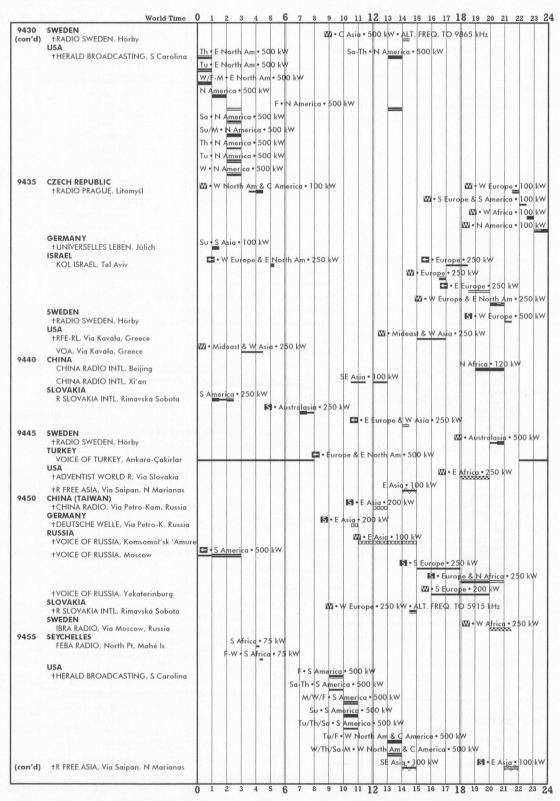

| | World Time | 0 1 2 3 4 5 6 7 8 9 10 11 12 13 14 15 16 17 18 19 20 21 22 23 24 |

9430 **SWEDEN**
(con'd) †RADIO SWEDEN, Hörby — W • C Asia • 500 kW • ALT. FREQ. TO 9865 kHz
USA
†HERALD BROADCASTING, S Carolina — Th • E North Am • 500 kW / Sa-Th • N America • 500 kW
Tu • E North Am • 500 kW
W/F-M • E North Am • 500 kW
N America • 500 kW
F • N America • 500 kW
Sa • N America • 500 kW
Su/M • N America • 500 kW
Th • N America • 500 kW
Tu • N America • 500 kW
W • N America • 500 kW

9435 **CZECH REPUBLIC**
†RADIO PRAGUE, Litomyšl — W • W North Am & C America • 100 kW
W • W Europe • 100 kW
W • S Europe & S America • 100 kW
W • W Africa • 100 kW
W • N America • 100 kW

GERMANY
†UNIVERSELLES LEBEN, Jülich — Su • S Asia • 100 kW
ISRAEL
KOL ISRAEL, Tel Aviv — ⇦ • W Europe & E North Am • 250 kW
⇦ • Europe • 250 kW
W • Europe • 250 kW
⇦ • E Europe • 250 kW
W • W Europe & E North Am • 250 kW

SWEDEN
†RADIO SWEDEN, Hörby — S • W Europe • 500 kW
USA
†RFE-RL, Via Kavála, Greece — W • Mideast & W Asia • 250 kW
VOA, Via Kavála, Greece — W • Mideast & W Asia • 250 kW
9440 **CHINA**
CHINA RADIO INTL, Beijing — N Africa • 120 kW
CHINA RADIO INTL, Xi'an — SE Asia • 100 kW
SLOVAKIA
R SLOVAKIA INTL, Rimavská Sobota — S America • 250 kW
S • Australasia • 250 kW
⇦ • E Europe & W Asia • 250 kW

9445 **SWEDEN**
†RADIO SWEDEN, Hörby — W • Australasia • 500 kW
TURKEY
VOICE OF TURKEY, Ankara-Çakirlar — ⇦ • Europe & E North Am • 500 kW
USA
†ADVENTIST WORLD R, Via Slovakia — W • E Africa • 250 kW
†R FREE ASIA, Via Saipan, N Marianas — E Asia • 100 kW
9450 **CHINA (TAIWAN)**
†CHINA RADIO, Via Petro-Kam, Russia — S • E Asia • 200 kW
GERMANY
†DEUTSCHE WELLE, Via Petro-K, Russia — S • E Asia • 200 kW
RUSSIA
†VOICE OF RUSSIA, Komsomol'sk 'Amure — W • E Asia • 100 kW
†VOICE OF RUSSIA, Moscow — ⇦ • S America • 500 kW
S • S Europe • 250 kW
S • Europe & N Africa • 250 kW
W • S Europe • 200 kW
†VOICE OF RUSSIA, Yekaterinburg
SLOVAKIA
†R SLOVAKIA INTL, Rimavská Sobota — W • W Europe • 250 kW • ALT. FREQ. TO 5915 kHz
SWEDEN
IBRA RADIO, Via Moscow, Russia — W • W Africa • 250 kW
9455 **SEYCHELLES**
FEBA RADIO, North Pt, Mahé Is — S Africa • 75 kW
F-W • S Africa • 75 kW

USA
†HERALD BROADCASTING, S Carolina — F • S America • 500 kW
Sa-Th • S America • 500 kW
M/W/F • S America • 500 kW
Su • S America • 500 kW
Tu/Th/Sa • S America • 500 kW
Tu/F • W North Am & C America • 500 kW
W/Th/Sa-M • W North Am & C America • 500 kW
(con'd) †R FREE ASIA, Via Saipan, N Marianas — SE Asia • 100 kW / S • E Asia • 100 kW

SEASONAL S OR W   1-HR TIMESHIFT MIDYEAR ⇦ OR ⇨   JAMMING / OR ∧   EARLIEST HEARD ◁   LATEST HEARD ▷   NEW FOR 2001 †

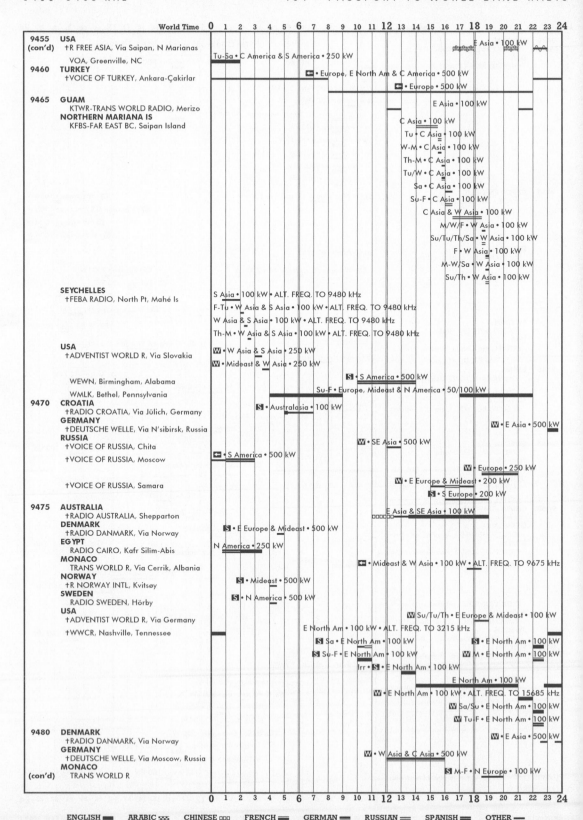

| | World Time | 0 | 1 | 2 | 3 | 4 | 5 | 6 | 7 | 8 | 9 | 10 | 11 | 12 | 13 | 14 | 15 | 16 | 17 | 18 | 19 | 20 | 21 | 22 | 23 | 24 |

9455
(con'd) **USA**
  †R FREE ASIA, Via Saipan, N Marianas — E Asia • 100 kW
  VOA, Greenville, NC — Tu-Sa • C America & S America • 250 kW
9460 **TURKEY**
  †VOICE OF TURKEY, Ankara-Çakirlar — • Europe, E North Am & C America • 500 kW; • Europe • 500 kW

9465 **GUAM**
  KTWR-TRANS WORLD RADIO, Merizo — E Asia • 100 kW
NORTHERN MARIANA IS
  KFBS-FAR EAST BC, Saipan Island — C Asia • 100 kW
    Tu • C Asia • 100 kW
    W-M • C Asia • 100 kW
    Th-M • C Asia • 100 kW
    Tu/W • C Asia • 100 kW
    Sa • C Asia • 100 kW
    Su-F • C Asia • 100 kW
    C Asia & W Asia • 100 kW
    M/W/F • W Asia • 100 kW
    Su/Tu/Th/Sa • W Asia • 100 kW
    F • W Asia • 100 kW
    M-W/Sa • W Asia • 100 kW
    Su/Th • W Asia • 100 kW

  SEYCHELLES
  †FEBA RADIO, North Pt, Mahé Is — S Asia • 100 kW • ALT. FREQ. TO 9480 kHz
    F-Tu • W Asia & S Asia • 100 kW • ALT. FREQ. TO 9480 kHz
    W Asia & S Asia • 100 kW • ALT. FREQ. TO 9480 kHz
    Th-M • W Asia & S Asia • 100 kW • ALT. FREQ. TO 9480 kHz

  USA
  †ADVENTIST WORLD R, Via Slovakia — W • W Asia & S Asia • 250 kW
    W • Mideast & W Asia • 250 kW

  WEWN, Birmingham, Alabama — S • S America • 500 kW
  WMLK, Bethel, Pennsylvania — Su-F • Europe, Mideast & N America • 50/100 kW
9470 **CROATIA**
  †RADIO CROATIA, Via Jülich, Germany — S • Australasia • 100 kW
  GERMANY
  †DEUTSCHE WELLE, Via N'sibirsk, Russia — W • E Asia • 500 kW
  RUSSIA
  †VOICE OF RUSSIA, Chita — W • SE Asia • 500 kW
  †VOICE OF RUSSIA, Moscow — • S America • 500 kW
    W • Europe • 250 kW
  †VOICE OF RUSSIA, Samara — W • E Europe & Mideast • 200 kW
    S • S Europe • 200 kW

9475 **AUSTRALIA**
  †RADIO AUSTRALIA, Shepparton — E Asia & SE Asia • 100 kW
  DENMARK
  †RADIO DANMARK, Via Norway — S • E Europe & Mideast • 500 kW
  EGYPT
  RADIO CAIRO, Kafr Silim-Abis — N America • 250 kW
  MONACO
  TRANS WORLD R, Via Cerrik, Albania — • Mideast & W Asia • 100 kW • ALT. FREQ. TO 9675 kHz
  NORWAY
  †R NORWAY INTL, Kvitsøy — S • Mideast • 500 kW
  SWEDEN
  RADIO SWEDEN, Hörby — S • N America • 500 kW
  USA
  †ADVENTIST WORLD R, Via Germany — W Su/Tu/Th • E Europe & Mideast • 100 kW
  †WWCR, Nashville, Tennessee — E North Am • 100 kW • ALT. FREQ. TO 3215 kHz
    S • Sa • E North Am • 100 kW; S • E North Am • 100 kW
    S Su-F • E North Am • 100 kW; W M • E North Am • 100 kW
    Irr • S • E North Am • 100 kW
    E North Am • 100 kW
    W • E North Am • 100 kW • ALT. FREQ. TO 15685 kHz
    W Sa/Su • E North Am • 100 kW
    W Tu-F • E North Am • 100 kW

9480 **DENMARK**
  †RADIO DANMARK, Via Norway — W • E Asia • 500 kW
  GERMANY
  †DEUTSCHE WELLE, Via Moscow, Russia — W • W Asia & C Asia • 500 kW
  MONACO
(con'd) TRANS WORLD R — S M-F • N Europe • 100 kW

| | 0 | 1 | 2 | 3 | 4 | 5 | 6 | 7 | 8 | 9 | 10 | 11 | 12 | 13 | 14 | 15 | 16 | 17 | 18 | 19 | 20 | 21 | 22 | 23 | 24 |

ENGLISH ■   ARABIC ⋙   CHINESE ⬚⬚⬚   FRENCH ══   GERMAN ══   RUSSIAN ══   SPANISH ══   OTHER ──

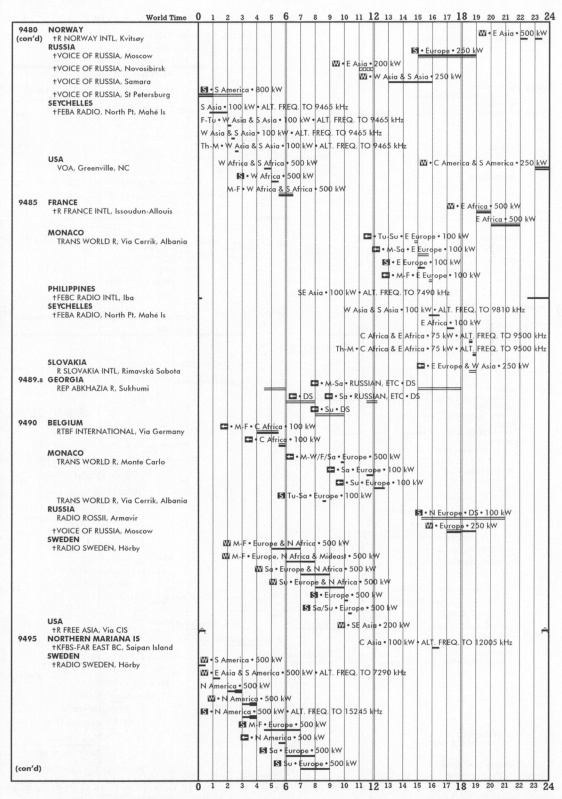

World Time   0 1 2 3 4 5 6 7 8 9 10 11 12 13 14 15 16 17 18 19 20 21 22 23 24

9480 NORWAY
(con'd) †R NORWAY INTL, Kvitsøy   W • E Asia • 500 kW
RUSSIA
  †VOICE OF RUSSIA, Moscow   S • Europe • 250 kW
  †VOICE OF RUSSIA, Novosibirsk   W • E Asia • 200 kW
  †VOICE OF RUSSIA, Samara   W • W Asia & S Asia • 250 kW
  †VOICE OF RUSSIA, St Petersburg   S • S America • 800 kW
SEYCHELLES
  †FEBA RADIO, North Pt, Mahé Is   S Asia • 100 kW • ALT. FREQ. TO 9465 kHz
     F-Tu • W Asia & S Asia • 100 kW • ALT. FREQ. TO 9465 kHz
     W Asia & S Asia • 100 kW • ALT. FREQ. TO 9465 kHz
     Th-M • W Asia & S Asia • 100 kW • ALT. FREQ. TO 9465 kHz
USA
  VOA, Greenville, NC   W Africa & S Africa • 500 kW   W • C America & S America • 250 kW
     S • W Africa • 500 kW
     M-F • W Africa & S Africa • 500 kW

9485 FRANCE
  †R FRANCE INTL, Issoudun-Allouis   W • E Africa • 500 kW
     E Africa • 500 kW
MONACO
  TRANS WORLD R, Via Cerrik, Albania   Tu-Su • E Europe • 100 kW
     M-Sa • E Europe • 100 kW
     S • E Europe • 100 kW
     M-F • E Europe • 100 kW
PHILIPPINES
  †FEBC RADIO INTL, Iba   SE Asia • 100 kW • ALT. FREQ. TO 7490 kHz
SEYCHELLES
  †FEBA RADIO, North Pt, Mahé Is   W Asia & S Asia • 100 kW • ALT. FREQ. TO 9810 kHz
     E Africa • 100 kW
     C Africa & E Africa • 75 kW • ALT. FREQ. TO 9500 kHz
     Th-M • C Africa & E Africa • 75 kW • ALT. FREQ. TO 9500 kHz
SLOVAKIA
  R SLOVAKIA INTL, Rimavská Sobota   S • E Europe & W Asia • 250 kW
9489.8 GEORGIA
  REP ABKHAZIA R, Sukhumi   M-Sa • RUSSIAN, ETC • DS
     DS   Sa • RUSSIAN, ETC • DS
     Su • DS

9490 BELGIUM
  RTBF INTERNATIONAL, Via Germany   M-F • C Africa • 100 kW
     C Africa • 100 kW
MONACO
  TRANS WORLD R, Monte Carlo   M-W/F/Sa • Europe • 500 kW
     Sa • Europe • 100 kW
     Su • Europe • 100 kW
  TRANS WORLD R, Via Cerrik, Albania   S Tu-Sa • Europe • 100 kW
RUSSIA
  RADIO ROSSII, Armavir   S • N Europe • DS • 100 kW
  †VOICE OF RUSSIA, Moscow   W • Europe • 250 kW
SWEDEN
  †RADIO SWEDEN, Hörby   W M-F • Europe & N Africa • 500 kW
     W M-F • Europe, N Africa & Mideast • 500 kW
     S Sa • Europe & N Africa • 500 kW
     W Su • Europe & N Africa • 500 kW
     S • Europe • 500 kW
     S Sa/Su • Europe • 500 kW
USA
  †R FREE ASIA, Via CIS   W • SE Asia • 200 kW
9495 NORTHERN MARIANA IS
  †KFBS-FAR EAST BC, Saipan Island   C Asia • 100 kW • ALT. FREQ. TO 12005 kHz
SWEDEN
  †RADIO SWEDEN, Hörby   W • S America • 500 kW
     W • E Asia & S America • 500 kW • ALT. FREQ. TO 7290 kHz
     N America • 500 kW
     W • N America • 500 kW
     S • N America • 500 kW • ALT. FREQ. TO 15245 kHz
     S M-F • Europe • 500 kW
     N America • 500 kW
     S Sa • Europe • 500 kW
     S Su • Europe • 500 kW

(con'd)

0 1 2 3 4 5 6 7 8 9 10 11 12 13 14 15 16 17 18 19 20 21 22 23 24

SEASONAL S OR W   1-HR TIMESHIFT MIDYEAR ⬅ OR ➡   JAMMING / OR ∧   EARLIEST HEARD ◁   LATEST HEARD ▷   NEW FOR 2001 †

World Time 0 1 2 3 4 5 6 7 8 9 10 11 12 13 14 15 16 17 18 19 20 21 22 2

kHz	Country / Station	Broadcasts
9495 (con'd)	USA †WHRI, Noblesville,Indiana	M-Sa • N America & C America • 100 kW Su • N America & C America • 100 kW N America & C America • 100 kW [S] • N America & C America • 100 kW
9500	AUSTRALIA †RADIO AUSTRALIA, Shepparton	E Asia & SE Asia • 100 kW
	BULGARIA †RADIO BULGARIA, Plovdiv	[S] • S America • 250 kW [W] Sa/Su • Mideast • 250 kW [W] Sa/Su • S Europe • 250 kW
	CHINA CENTRAL PEOPLE'S BS, Xi'an	DS-2 • 50 kW Th/Sa-Tu • DS-2 • 50 kW
	SEYCHELLES †FEBA RADIO, North Pt, Mahé Is	C Africa & E Africa • 75 kW • ALT. FREQ. TO 9485 Th-M • C Africa & E Africa • 75 kW • ALT. FREQ. TO 9485
	SWAZILAND TRANS WORLD RADIO, Manzini	E Africa • 100 kW Sa/Su • E Africa • 100 kW Su/F • E Africa • 100 kW
	VATICAN STATE VATICAN RADIO, Sta Maria di Galeria	[W] Su • E Europe • 100 kW [W] • SE Asia • 500 kW [W] • E Asia • 500 kW [W] • Australasia • 250 kW [W] • S Asia • 250 kW [W] Sa • S Asia • 250 kW
9504v	PERU RADIO TACNA, Tacna	DS • 0.18 kW
9505	BRAZIL †RADIO RECORD, São Paulo	DS • 7.5 kW • ➡
	CANADA †R CANADA INTL, Via Vienna, Austria	[W] • Mideast • 100/300 kW
	CHINA †VO THE STRAIT-PLA, Fuzhou	50 kW • ALT. FREQ. TO 4900 kHz 50 kW
	CUBA RADIO HABANA CUBA, Havana	S America • 250 kW
	GERMANY DEUTSCHE WELLE, Wertachtal	[W] • SE Asia • 500
	IRAN †VO THE ISLAMIC REP, Tehrān	[S] • S Asia • 500 kW
	JAPAN †RADIO JAPAN/NHK, Tokyo-Yamata	W North Am • 300 kW W North Am • 300 kW • ALT. FREQ. TO 9535 kHz
	PHILIPPINES RADIO VERITAS ASIA, Palauig	SE Asia • 250 kW
	USA †RFE-RL, Via Briech, Morocco	[S] M-F • E Europe • 250 kW
	RFE-RL, Via Holzkirchen, Germany	[W] • E Europe & W Asia • 250 kW
	RFE-RL, Via Kavála, Greece	[S] • E Europe & W Asia • 250 k
	†RFE-RL, Via Lampertheim, Germany	[W] • W Asia & Mideast • 100
	RFE-RL, Via Pals, Spain	[W] • N Europe • 250 kW
	†RFE-RL, Via Woofferton, UK	[S] • E Europe • 250 kW [S] M-F • E Europe • 250 kW
	†VOA, Via Iranawila, Sri Lanka	[S] • W Asia & S Asia • 500 kW [S] • SE Asia • 500 kW
	VOA, Via Udon Thani, Thailand	[W] • S Asia • 250 kW [S] • W Asia & S Asia • 250 kW
	VOA, Via Woofferton, UK	M-F • N Africa • 250/300 kW
	WYFR-FAMILY RADIO, Okeechobee, Fl	W North Am • 100 kW [S] • E North Am • 100 kW
9510	FINLAND †YLE RADIO FINLAND, Pori	[W] • Australasia • 500 kW
	ROMANIA RADIO ROMANIA INTL, Bucharest	E North Am • 250 kW [W] • Mideast • 250 kW [W] • Europe • 250 kW S America • 250 kW [S] • Europe • 120 kW [S] • Mideast • 250 kW [S] • Europe • 250 kW [S] • E Europe • 250 kW
	SOUTH AFRICA †TRANS WORLD RADIO, Meyerton	W Africa • 500 kW Sa • W Africa • 500 kW
(con'd)	UNITED KINGDOM BBC, Rampisham	[S] • Mideast & W Asia • 500 kW

0 1 2 3 4 5 6 7 8 9 10 11 12 13 14 15 16 17 18 19 20 21 22 2

ENGLISH ▬ ARABIC ▭ CHINESE ▫▫▫ FRENCH ═ GERMAN ═ RUSSIAN ═ SPANISH ═ OTHER —

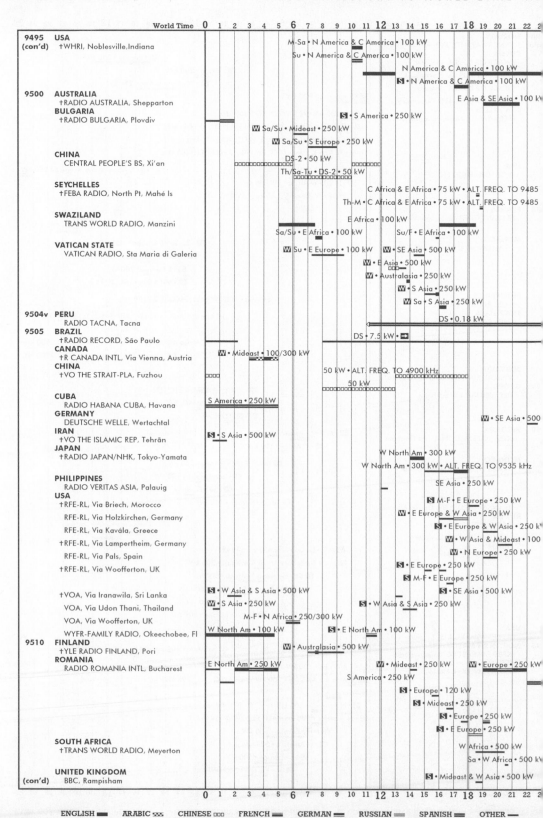

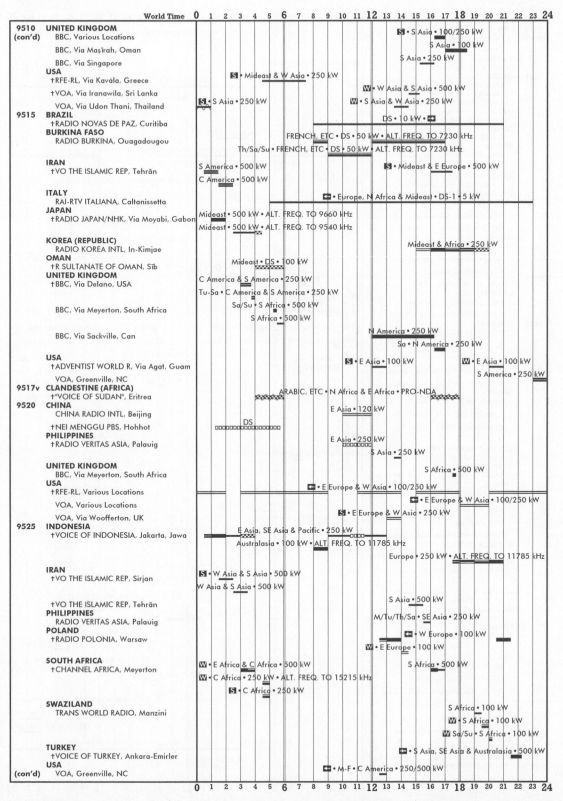

| World Time | 0 | 1 | 2 | 3 | 4 | 5 | 6 | 7 | 8 | 9 | 10 | 11 | 12 | 13 | 14 | 15 | 16 | 17 | 18 | 19 | 20 | 21 | 22 | 23 | 24 |

9510 (con'd) **UNITED KINGDOM**
BBC, Various Locations — 🅂 • S Asia • 100/250 kW
BBC, Via Maṣīrah, Oman — S Asia • 100 kW
BBC, Via Singapore — S Asia • 250 kW
USA
†RFE-RL, Via Kavála, Greece — 🅂 • Mideast & W Asia • 250 kW
†VOA, Via Iranawila, Sri Lanka — 🅆 • W Asia & S Asia • 500 kW
VOA, Via Udon Thani, Thailand — 🅂 • S Asia • 250 kW   🅆 • S Asia & W Asia • 250 kW

9515 BRAZIL
†RADIO NOVAS DE PAZ, Curitiba — DS • 10 kW • ⬅
BURKINA FASO
RADIO BURKINA, Ouagadougou — FRENCH, ETC • DS • 50 kW • ALT. FREQ. TO 7230 kHz
Th/Sa/Su • FRENCH, ETC • DS • 50 kW • ALT. FREQ. TO 7230 kHz
IRAN
†VO THE ISLAMIC REP, Tehrān — S America • 500 kW
C America • 500 kW   🅂 • Mideast & E Europe • 500 kW
ITALY
RAI-RTV ITALIANA, Caltanissetta — ➡ • Europe, N Africa & Mideast • DS-1 • 5 kW
JAPAN
†RADIO JAPAN/NHK, Via Moyabi, Gabon — Mideast • 500 kW • ALT. FREQ. TO 9660 kHz
Mideast • 500 kW • ALT. FREQ. TO 9540 kHz
KOREA (REPUBLIC)
RADIO KOREA INTL, In-Kimjae — Mideast & Africa • 250 kW
OMAN
†R SULTANATE OF OMAN, Sīb — Mideast • DS • 100 kW
UNITED KINGDOM
†BBC, Via Delano, USA — C America & S America • 250 kW
Tu-Sa • C America & S America • 250 kW
Sa/Su • S Africa • 500 kW
BBC, Via Meyerton, South Africa — S Africa • 500 kW
BBC, Via Sackville, Can — N America • 250 kW
Sa • N America • 250 kW
USA
†ADVENTIST WORLD R, Via Agat, Guam — 🅂 • E Asia • 100 kW   🅆 • E Asia • 100 kW
VOA, Greenville, NC — S America • 250 kW
9517v CLANDESTINE (AFRICA)
†"VOICE OF SUDAN", Eritrea — ARABIC, ETC • N Africa & E Africa • PRO-NDA
9520 CHINA
CHINA RADIO INTL, Beijing — E Asia • 120 kW
†NEI MENGGU PBS, Hohhot — DS
PHILIPPINES
†RADIO VERITAS ASIA, Palauig — E Asia • 250 kW
S Asia • 250 kW
UNITED KINGDOM
BBC, Via Meyerton, South Africa — S Africa • 500 kW
USA
†RFE-RL, Various Locations — ➡ • E Europe & W Asia • 100/250 kW
VOA, Various Locations — ➡ • E Europe & W Asia • 100/250 kW
VOA, Via Woofferton, UK — 🅂 • E Europe & W Asia • 250 kW
9525 INDONESIA
†VOICE OF INDONESIA, Jakarta, Jawa — E Asia, SE Asia & Pacific • 250 kW
Australasia • 100 kW • ALT. FREQ. TO 11785 kHz
Europe • 250 kW • ALT. FREQ. TO 11785 kHz
IRAN
†VO THE ISLAMIC REP, Sirjan — 🅂 • W Asia & S Asia • 500 kW
W Asia & S Asia • 500 kW
†VO THE ISLAMIC REP, Tehrān — S Asia • 500 kW
PHILIPPINES
RADIO VERITAS ASIA, Palauig — M/Tu/Th/Sa • SE Asia • 250 kW
POLAND
†RADIO POLONIA, Warsaw — ➡ • W Europe • 100 kW
🅆 • E Europe • 100 kW
SOUTH AFRICA
†CHANNEL AFRICA, Meyerton — 🅆 • E Africa & C Africa • 500 kW   S Africa • 500 kW
🅆 • C Africa • 250 kW • ALT. FREQ. TO 15215 kHz
🅂 • C Africa • 250 kW
SWAZILAND
TRANS WORLD RADIO, Manzini — S Africa • 100 kW
🅆 • S Africa • 100 kW
🅆 Sa/Su • S Africa • 100 kW
TURKEY
†VOICE OF TURKEY, Ankara-Emirler — ➡ • S Asia, SE Asia & Australasia • 500 kW
USA
(con'd) VOA, Greenville, NC — ➡ • M-F • C America • 250/500 kW

| 0 | 1 | 2 | 3 | 4 | 5 | 6 | 7 | 8 | 9 | 10 | 11 | 12 | 13 | 14 | 15 | 16 | 17 | 18 | 19 | 20 | 21 | 22 | 23 | 24 |

SEASONAL 🅂 OR 🅆   1-HR TIMESHIFT MIDYEAR ➡ OR ⬅   JAMMING / OR /\   EARLIEST HEARD ◁   LATEST HEARD ▷   NEW FOR 2001 †

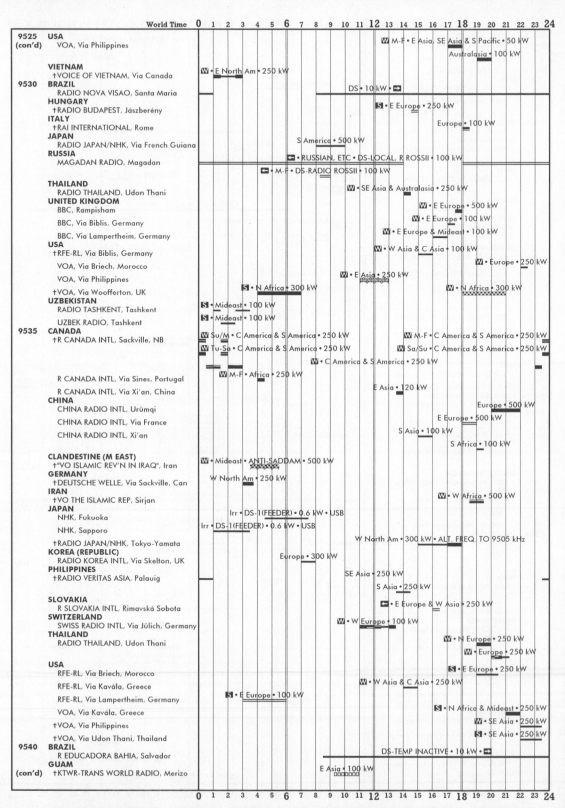

World Time 0 1 2 3 4 5 6 7 8 9 10 11 12 13 14 15 16 17 18 19 20 21 22 23 24

9525 (con'd)	**USA** VOA, Via Philippines
	W • M-F • E Asia, SE Asia & S Pacific • 50 kW
	Australasia • 100 kW
	VIETNAM †VOICE OF VIETNAM, Via Canada — W • E North Am • 250 kW
9530	**BRAZIL** RADIO NOVA VISAO, Santa Maria — DS • 10 kW • ▶
	HUNGARY †RADIO BUDAPEST, Jászberény — S • E Europe • 250 kW
	ITALY †RAI INTERNATIONAL, Rome — Europe • 100 kW
	JAPAN RADIO JAPAN/NHK, Via French Guiana — S America • 500 kW
	RUSSIA MAGADAN RADIO, Magadan — ◀ • RUSSIAN, ETC • DS-LOCAL, R ROSSII • 100 kW
	◀ • M-F • DS-RADIO ROSSII • 100 kW
	THAILAND RADIO THAILAND, Udon Thani — W • SE Asia & Australasia • 250 kW
	UNITED KINGDOM BBC, Rampisham — W • E Europe • 500 kW
	BBC, Via Biblis, Germany — W • E Europe • 100 kW
	BBC, Via Lampertheim, Germany — W • E Europe & Mideast • 100 kW
	USA †RFE-RL, Via Biblis, Germany — W • W Asia & C Asia • 100 kW
	VOA, Via Briech, Morocco — W • Europe • 250 kW
	VOA, Via Philippines — W • E Asia • 250 kW
	†VOA, Via Woofferton, UK — S • N Africa • 300 kW / W • N Africa • 300 kW
	UZBEKISTAN RADIO TASHKENT, Tashkent — S • Mideast • 100 kW
	UZBEK RADIO, Tashkent — S • Mideast • 100 kW
9535	**CANADA** †R CANADA INTL, Sackville, NB — W Su/M • C America & S America • 250 kW / W M-F • C America & S America • 250 kW
	W Tu-Sa • C America & S America • 250 kW / W Sa/Su • C America & S America • 250 kW
	W • C America & S America • 250 kW
	R CANADA INTL, Via Sines, Portugal — W M-F • Africa • 250 kW
	R CANADA INTL, Via Xi'an, China — E Asia • 120 kW
	CHINA CHINA RADIO INTL, Urümqi — Europe • 500 kW
	CHINA RADIO INTL, Via France — E Europe • 500 kW
	CHINA RADIO INTL, Xi'an — S Asia • 100 kW
	S Africa • 100 kW
	CLANDESTINE (M EAST) †"VO ISLAMIC REV'N IN IRAQ", Iran — W • Mideast • ANTI-SADDAM • 500 kW
	GERMANY †DEUTSCHE WELLE, Via Sackville, Can — W North Am • 250 kW
	IRAN †VO THE ISLAMIC REP, Sirjan — W • W Africa • 500 kW
	JAPAN NHK, Fukuoka — Irr • DS-1(FEEDER) • 0.6 kW • USB
	NHK, Sapporo — Irr • DS-1(FEEDER) • 0.6 kW • USB
	†RADIO JAPAN/NHK, Tokyo-Yamata — W North Am • 300 kW • ALT. FREQ. TO 9505 kHz
	KOREA (REPUBLIC) RADIO KOREA INTL, Via Skelton, UK — Europe • 300 kW
	PHILIPPINES †RADIO VERITAS ASIA, Palauig — SE Asia • 250 kW
	S Asia • 250 kW
	SLOVAKIA R SLOVAKIA INTL, Rimavská Sobota — ◀ • E Europe & W Asia • 250 kW
	SWITZERLAND SWISS RADIO INTL, Via Jülich, Germany — W • W Europe • 100 kW
	THAILAND RADIO THAILAND, Udon Thani — W • N Europe • 250 kW
	W • Europe • 250 kW
	USA RFE-RL, Via Briech, Morocco — S • E Europe • 250 kW
	RFE-RL, Via Kavála, Greece — W • W Asia & C Asia • 250 kW
	RFE-RL, Via Lampertheim, Germany — S • E Europe • 100 kW
	VOA, Via Kavála, Greece — S • N Africa & Mideast • 250 kW
	†VOA, Via Philippines — W • SE Asia • 250 kW
	†VOA, Via Udon Thani, Thailand — S • SE Asia • 250 kW
9540	**BRAZIL** R EDUCADORA BAHIA, Salvador — DS-TEMP INACTIVE • 10 kW • ▶
(con'd)	**GUAM** †KTWR-TRANS WORLD RADIO, Merizo — E Asia • 100 kW

0 1 2 3 4 5 6 7 8 9 10 11 12 13 14 15 16 17 18 19 20 21 22 23 24

ENGLISH ▬ ARABIC ⋙ CHINESE ▫▫▫ FRENCH ═ GERMAN ▬ RUSSIAN ═ SPANISH ═ OTHER ▬

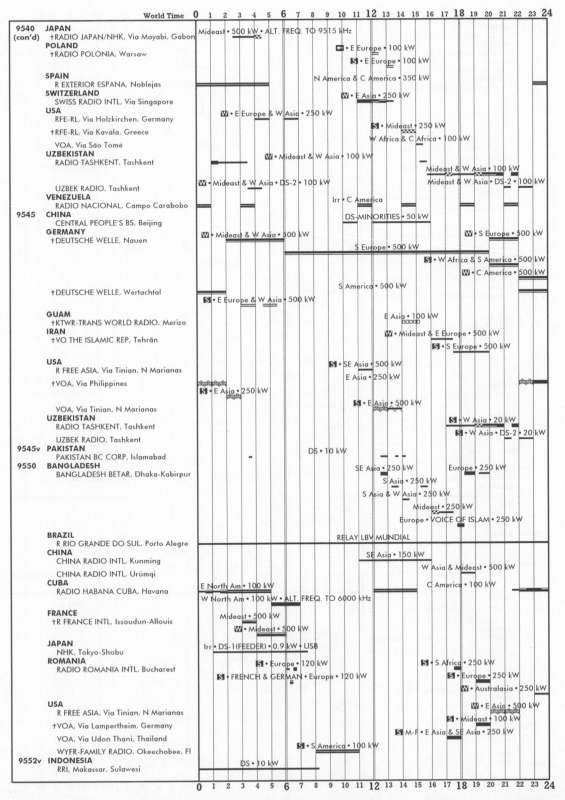

| World Time | 0 | 1 | 2 | 3 | 4 | 5 | 6 | 7 | 8 | 9 | 10 | 11 | 12 | 13 | 14 | 15 | 16 | 17 | 18 | 19 | 20 | 21 | 22 | 23 | 24 |

9540 (con'd)

JAPAN
†RADIO JAPAN/NHK, Via Moyabi, Gabon — Mideast • 500 kW • ALT. FREQ. TO 9515 kHz

POLAND
†RADIO POLONIA, Warsaw — ◧ • E Europe • 100 kW / ⑤ • E Europe • 100 kW

SPAIN
R EXTERIOR ESPANA, Noblejas — N America & C America • 350 kW

SWITZERLAND
SWISS RADIO INTL, Via Singapore — ☒ • E Asia • 250 kW

USA
RFE-RL, Via Holzkirchen, Germany — ☒ • E Europe & W Asia • 250 kW
†RFE-RL, Via Kavála, Greece — ⑤ • Mideast • 250 kW
VOA, Via São Tomé — W Africa & C Africa • 100 kW

UZBEKISTAN
RADIO TASHKENT, Tashkent — ☒ • Mideast & W Asia • 100 kW / Mideast & W Asia • 100 kW

UZBEK RADIO, Tashkent — ☒ • Mideast & W Asia • DS-2 • 100 kW / Mideast & W Asia • DS-2 • 100 kW

VENEZUELA
RADIO NACIONAL, Campo Carabobo — Irr • C America

9545 CHINA
CENTRAL PEOPLE'S BS, Beijing — DS-MINORITIES • 50 kW

GERMANY
†DEUTSCHE WELLE, Nauen — ☒ • Mideast & W Asia • 500 kW / ☒ • S Europe • 500 kW
S Europe • 500 kW
⑤ • W Africa & S America • 500 kW
☒ • C America • 500 kW

†DEUTSCHE WELLE, Wertachtal — ⑤ • E Europe & W Asia • 500 kW
S America • 500 kW

GUAM
†KTWR-TRANS WORLD RADIO, Merizo — E Asia • 100 kW

IRAN
†VO THE ISLAMIC REP, Tehrãn — ☒ • Mideast & E Europe • 500 kW / ⑤ • S Europe • 500 kW

USA
R FREE ASIA, Via Tinian, N Marianas — ⑤ • SE Asia • 500 kW
E Asia • 250 kW
†VOA, Via Philippines — ⑤ • E Asia • 250 kW

VOA, Via Tinian, N Marianas — ⑤ • E Asia • 500 kW

UZBEKISTAN
RADIO TASHKENT, Tashkent — ⑤ • W Asia • 20 kW

UZBEK RADIO, Tashkent — ⑤ • W Asia • DS-2 • 20 kW

9545v PAKISTAN
PAKISTAN BC CORP, Islamabad — DS • 10 kW

9550 BANGLADESH
BANGLADESH BETAR, Dhaka-Kabirpur — SE Asia • 250 kW / Europe • 250 kW
S Asia • 250 kW
S Asia & W Asia • 250 kW
Mideast • 250 kW
Europe • VOICE OF ISLAM • 250 kW

BRAZIL
R RIO GRANDE DO SUL, Porto Alegre — RELAY LBV MUNDIAL

CHINA
CHINA RADIO INTL, Kunming — SE Asia • 150 kW

CHINA RADIO INTL, Urümqi — W Asia & Mideast • 500 kW

CUBA
RADIO HABANA CUBA, Havana — E North Am • 100 kW / C America • 100 kW
W North Am • 100 kW • ALT. FREQ. TO 6000 kHz

FRANCE
†R FRANCE INTL, Issoudun-Allouis — Mideast • 500 kW
☒ • Mideast • 500 kW

JAPAN
NHK, Tokyo-Shobu — Irr • DS-1(FEEDER) • 0.9 kW • USB

ROMANIA
RADIO ROMANIA INTL, Bucharest — ⑤ • Europe • 120 kW / ⑤ • S Africa • 250 kW
⑤ • FRENCH & GERMAN • Europe • 120 kW / ⑤ • Europe • 250 kW
☒ • Australasia • 250 kW

USA
R FREE ASIA, Via Tinian, N Marianas — ☒ • E Asia • 500 kW
†VOA, Via Lampertheim, Germany — ⑤ • Mideast • 100 kW
VOA, Via Udon Thani, Thailand — ⑤ M-F • E Asia & SE Asia • 250 kW
WYFR-FAMILY RADIO, Okeechobee, Fl — ⑤ • S America • 100 kW

9552v INDONESIA
RRI, Makassar, Sulawesi — DS • 10 kW

| 0 | 1 | 2 | 3 | 4 | 5 | 6 | 7 | 8 | 9 | 10 | 11 | 12 | 13 | 14 | 15 | 16 | 17 | 18 | 19 | 20 | 21 | 22 | 23 | 24 |

SEASONAL ⑤ OR ☒   1-HR TIMESHIFT MIDYEAR ◧ OR ▣   JAMMING / OR ∧   EARLIEST HEARD ◁   LATEST HEARD ▷   NEW FOR 2001 †

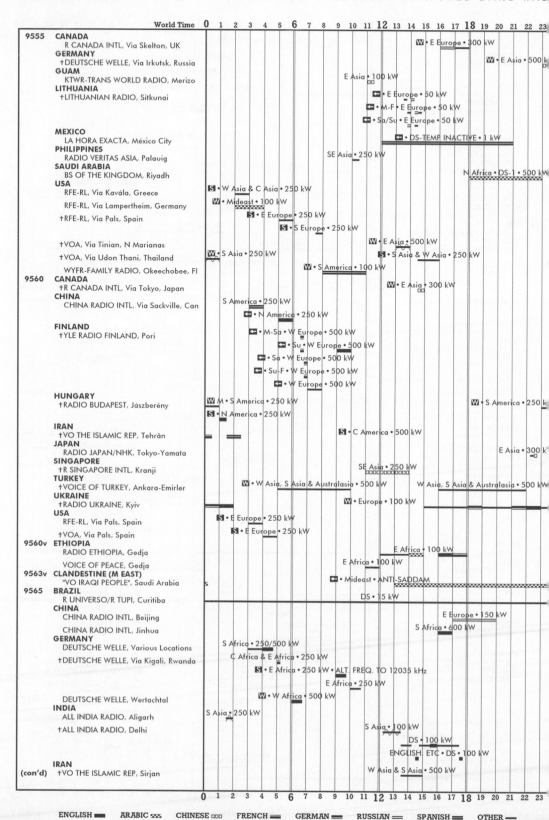

World Time — 0 1 2 3 4 5 6 7 8 9 10 11 12 13 14 15 16 17 18 19 20 21 22 23

9555 CANADA
R CANADA INTL, Via Skelton, UK — W • E Europe • 300 kW
GERMANY
†DEUTSCHE WELLE, Via Irkutsk, Russia — W • E Asia • 500 k
GUAM
KTWR-TRANS WORLD RADIO, Merizo — E Asia • 100 kW
LITHUANIA
†LITHUANIAN RADIO, Sitkunai — • E Europe • 50 kW / • M-F • E Europe • 50 kW / • Sa/Su • E Europe • 50 kW / • DS-TEMP INACTIVE • 1 kW
MEXICO
LA HORA EXACTA, México City
PHILIPPINES
RADIO VERITAS ASIA, Palauig — SE Asia • 250 kW
SAUDI ARABIA
BS OF THE KINGDOM, Riyadh — N Africa • DS-1 • 500 kW
USA
RFE-RL, Via Kavála, Greece — S • W Asia & C Asia • 250 kW
RFE-RL, Via Lampertheim, Germany — W • Mideast • 100 kW
†RFE-RL, Via Pals, Spain — S • E Europe • 250 kW / S • S Europe • 250 kW
†VOA, Via Tinian, N Marianas — W • E Asia • 500 kW
†VOA, Via Udon Thani, Thailand — W • S Asia • 250 kW / S • S Asia & W Asia • 250 kW
WYFR-FAMILY RADIO, Okeechobee, Fl — W • S America • 100 kW
9560 CANADA
†R CANADA INTL, Via Tokyo, Japan — W • E Asia • 300 kW
CHINA
CHINA RADIO INTL, Via Sackville, Can — S America • 250 kW / • N America • 250 kW
FINLAND
†YLE RADIO FINLAND, Pori — • M-Sa • W Europe • 500 kW / • Su • W Europe • 500 kW / • Sa • W Europe • 500 kW / • Su-F • W Europe • 500 kW / • W Europe • 500 kW
HUNGARY
†RADIO BUDAPEST, Jászberény — W M • S America • 250 kW / S • N America • 250 kW / W • S America • 250 k
IRAN
†VO THE ISLAMIC REP, Tehrān — S • C America • 500 kW
JAPAN
RADIO JAPAN/NHK, Tokyo-Yamata — E Asia • 300 k
SINGAPORE
†R SINGAPORE INTL, Kranji — SE Asia • 250 kW
TURKEY
†VOICE OF TURKEY, Ankara-Emirler — W • W Asia, S Asia & Australasia • 500 kW / W Asia, S Asia & Australasia • 500 kW
UKRAINE
†RADIO UKRAINE, Kyiv — W • Europe • 100 kW
USA
RFE-RL, Via Pals, Spain — S • E Europe • 250 kW
†VOA, Via Pals, Spain — S • E Europe • 250 kW
9560v ETHIOPIA
RADIO ETHIOPIA, Gedja — E Africa • 100 kW
VOICE OF PEACE, Gedja — E Africa • 100 kW
9563v CLANDESTINE (M EAST)
"VO IRAQI PEOPLE", Saudi Arabia — • Mideast • ANTI-SADDAM
9565 BRAZIL
R UNIVERSO/R TUPI, Curitiba — DS • 15 kW
CHINA
CHINA RADIO INTL, Beijing — E Europe • 150 kW
CHINA RADIO INTL, Jinhua — S Africa • 600 kW
GERMANY
DEUTSCHE WELLE, Various Locations — S Africa • 250/500 kW
†DEUTSCHE WELLE, Via Kigali, Rwanda — C Africa & E Africa • 250 kW / S • E Africa • 250 kW • ALT. FREQ. TO 12035 kHz / E Africa • 250 kW
DEUTSCHE WELLE, Wertachtal — W • W Africa • 500 kW
INDIA
ALL INDIA RADIO, Aligarh — S Asia • 250 kW
†ALL INDIA RADIO, Delhi — S Asia • 100 kW / DS • 100 kW / ENGLISH, ETC • DS • 100 kW
IRAN
(con'd) †VO THE ISLAMIC REP, Sirjan — W Asia & S Asia • 500 kW

0 1 2 3 4 5 6 7 8 9 10 11 12 13 14 15 16 17 18 19 20 21 22 23

ENGLISH ▬ ARABIC ⋙ CHINESE ▫▫▫ FRENCH ═ GERMAN ▬ RUSSIAN ═ SPANISH ▬ OTHER ▬

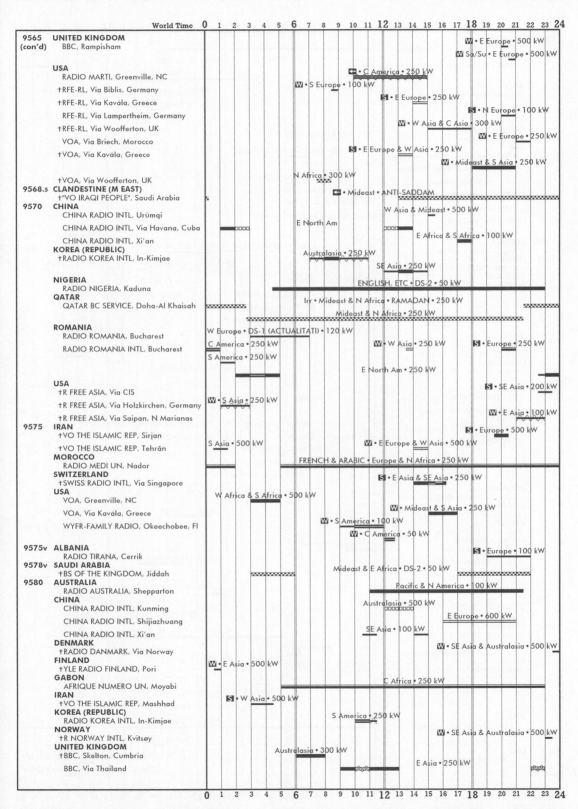

Frequency / Country / Station	Schedule
9565 **UNITED KINGDOM** (con'd) BBC, Rampisham	W • E Europe • 500 kW; W Sa/Su • E Europe • 500 kW
USA RADIO MARTI, Greenville, NC	⊡ • C America • 250 kW
†RFE-RL, Via Biblis, Germany	W • S Europe • 100 kW
†RFE-RL, Via Kavála, Greece	S • E Europe • 250 kW
RFE-RL, Via Lampertheim, Germany	S • N Europe • 100 kW
†RFE-RL, Via Woofferton, UK	W • W Asia & C Asia • 300 kW
VOA, Via Briech, Morocco	W • E Europe • 250 kW
†VOA, Via Kavála, Greece	S • E Europe & W Asia • 250 kW; W • Mideast & S Asia • 250 kW
†VOA, Via Woofferton, UK	N Africa • 300 kW
9568.5 CLANDESTINE (M EAST) †"VO IRAQI PEOPLE", Saudi Arabia	⊡ • Mideast • ANTI-SADDAM
9570 CHINA CHINA RADIO INTL, Urümqi	W Asia & Mideast • 500 kW
CHINA RADIO INTL, Via Havana, Cuba	E North Am
CHINA RADIO INTL, Xi'an	E Africa & S Africa • 100 kW
KOREA (REPUBLIC) †RADIO KOREA INTL, In-Kimjae	Australasia • 250 kW; SE Asia • 250 kW
NIGERIA RADIO NIGERIA, Kaduna	ENGLISH, ETC • DS-2 • 50 kW
QATAR QATAR BC SERVICE, Doha-Al Khaisah	Irr • Mideast & N Africa • RAMADAN • 250 kW; Mideast & N Africa • 250 kW
ROMANIA RADIO ROMANIA, Bucharest	W Europe • DS-1 (ACTUALITATI) • 120 kW
RADIO ROMANIA INTL, Bucharest	C America • 250 kW; W • W Asia • 250 kW; S • Europe • 250 kW; S America • 250 kW; E North Am • 250 kW
USA †R FREE ASIA, Via CIS	S • SE Asia • 200 kW
†R FREE ASIA, Via Holzkirchen, Germany	W • S Asia • 250 kW
†R FREE ASIA, Via Saipan, N Marianas	W • E Asia • 100 kW
9575 IRAN †VO THE ISLAMIC REP, Sirjan	S • Europe • 500 kW
†VO THE ISLAMIC REP, Tehrän	S Asia • 500 kW; W • E Europe & W Asia • 500 kW
MOROCCO RADIO MEDI UN, Nador	FRENCH & ARABIC • Europe & N Africa • 250 kW
SWITZERLAND †SWISS RADIO INTL, Via Singapore	S • E Asia & SE Asia • 250 kW
USA VOA, Greenville, NC	W Africa & S Africa • 500 kW
VOA, Via Kavála, Greece	W • Mideast & S Asia • 250 kW
WYFR-FAMILY RADIO, Okeechobee, Fl	W • S America • 100 kW; W • C America • 50 kW
9575v ALBANIA RADIO TIRANA, Cerrik	S • Europe • 100 kW
9578v SAUDI ARABIA †BS OF THE KINGDOM, Jiddah	Mideast & E Africa • DS-2 • 50 kW
9580 AUSTRALIA RADIO AUSTRALIA, Shepparton	Pacific & N America • 100 kW
CHINA CHINA RADIO INTL, Kunming	Australasia • 500 kW
CHINA RADIO INTL, Shijiazhuang	E Europe • 600 kW
CHINA RADIO INTL, Xi'an	SE Asia • 100 kW
DENMARK †RADIO DANMARK, Via Norway	W • SE Asia & Australasia • 500 kW
FINLAND †YLE RADIO FINLAND, Pori	W • E Asia • 500 kW
GABON AFRIQUE NUMERO UN, Moyabi	C Africa • 250 kW
IRAN †VO THE ISLAMIC REP, Mashhad	S • W Asia • 500 kW
KOREA (REPUBLIC) RADIO KOREA INTL, In-Kimjae	S America • 250 kW
NORWAY †R NORWAY INTL, Kvitsøy	W • SE Asia & Australasia • 500 kW
UNITED KINGDOM †BBC, Skelton, Cumbria	Australasia • 300 kW
BBC, Via Thailand	E Asia • 250 kW

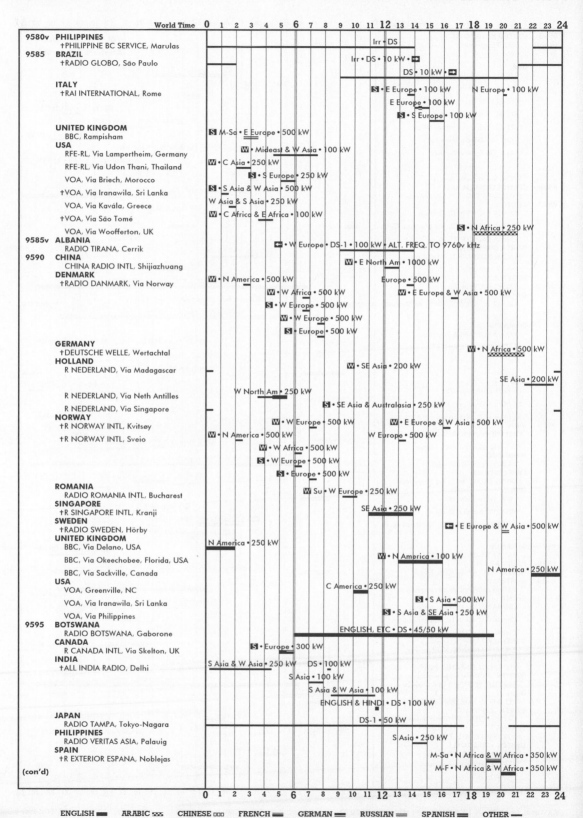

	World Time	0 1 2 3 4 5 6 7 8 9 10 11 12 13 14 15 16 17 18 19 20 21 22 23 24
9580v	**PHILIPPINES** †PHILIPPINE BC SERVICE, Marulas	Irr • DS
9585	**BRAZIL** †RADIO GLOBO, São Paulo	Irr • DS • 10 kW • ▭▶ DS • 10 kW • ▭▶
	ITALY †RAI INTERNATIONAL, Rome	⑤ • E Europe • 100 kW N Europe • 100 kW E Europe • 100 kW ⑤ • S Europe • 100 kW
	UNITED KINGDOM BBC, Rampisham	⑤ M-Sa • E Europe • 500 kW
	USA RFE-RL, Via Lampertheim, Germany	Ⓦ • Mideast & W Asia • 100 kW
	RFE-RL, Via Udon Thani, Thailand	Ⓦ • C Asia • 250 kW
	VOA, Via Briech, Morocco	⑤ • S Europe • 250 kW
	†VOA, Via Iranawila, Sri Lanka	⑤ • S Asia & W Asia • 500 kW
	VOA, Via Kavála, Greece	W Asia & S Asia • 250 kW
	†VOA, Via São Tomé	Ⓦ • C Africa & E Africa • 100 kW
	VOA, Via Woofferton, UK	⑤ • N Africa • 250 kW ▨▨▨▨
9585v	**ALBANIA** RADIO TIRANA, Cerrik	◀▭ • W Europe • DS-1 • 100 kW • ALT. FREQ. TO 9760v kHz
9590	**CHINA** CHINA RADIO INTL, Shijiazhuang	Ⓦ • E North Am • 1000 kW
	DENMARK †RADIO DANMARK, Via Norway	Ⓦ • N America • 500 kW Europe • 500 kW Ⓦ • W Africa • 500 kW Ⓦ • E Europe & W Asia • 500 kW ⑤ • W Europe • 500 kW Ⓦ • W Europe • 500 kW ⑤ • Europe • 500 kW
	GERMANY †DEUTSCHE WELLE, Wertachtal	Ⓦ • N Africa • 500 kW ▨▨▨
	HOLLAND R NEDERLAND, Via Madagascar	Ⓦ • SE Asia • 200 kW SE Asia • 200 kW
	R NEDERLAND, Via Neth Antilles	W North Am • 250 kW
	R NEDERLAND, Via Singapore	⑤ • SE Asia & Australasia • 250 kW
	NORWAY †R NORWAY INTL, Kvitsøy	Ⓦ • W Europe • 500 kW Ⓦ • E Europe & W Asia • 500 kW
	†R NORWAY INTL, Sveio	Ⓦ • N America • 500 kW W Europe • 500 kW Ⓦ • W Africa • 500 kW ⑤ • W Europe • 500 kW ⑤ • Europe • 500 kW
	ROMANIA RADIO ROMANIA INTL, Bucharest	Ⓦ Su • W Europe • 250 kW
	SINGAPORE †R SINGAPORE INTL, Kranji	SE Asia • 250 kW
	SWEDEN †RADIO SWEDEN, Hörby	◀▭ • E Europe & W Asia • 500 kW
	UNITED KINGDOM BBC, Via Delano, USA	N America • 250 kW
	BBC, Via Okeechobee, Florida, USA	Ⓦ • N America • 100 kW
	BBC, Via Sackville, Canada	N America • 250 kW
	USA VOA, Greenville, NC	C America • 250 kW
	VOA, Via Iranawila, Sri Lanka	⑤ • S Asia • 500 kW
	VOA, Via Philippines	⑤ • S Asia & SE Asia • 250 kW
9595	**BOTSWANA** RADIO BOTSWANA, Gaborone	ENGLISH, ETC • DS • 45/50 kW
	CANADA R CANADA INTL, Via Skelton, UK	⑤ • Europe • 300 kW
	INDIA †ALL INDIA RADIO, Delhi	S Asia & W Asia • 250 kW DS • 100 kW S Asia • 100 kW S Asia & W Asia • 100 kW ENGLISH & HINDI • DS • 100 kW
	JAPAN RADIO TAMPA, Tokyo-Nagara	DS-1 • 50 kW
	PHILIPPINES RADIO VERITAS ASIA, Palauig	S Asia • 250 kW
	SPAIN †R EXTERIOR ESPANA, Noblejas	M-Sa • N Africa & W Africa • 350 kW M-F • N Africa & W Africa • 350 kW
(con'd)		0 1 2 3 4 5 6 7 8 9 10 11 12 13 14 15 16 17 18 19 20 21 22 23 24

ENGLISH ▬▬ ARABIC ▨▨▨ CHINESE □□□ FRENCH ═══ GERMAN ▬▬ RUSSIAN ══ SPANISH ══ OTHER ──

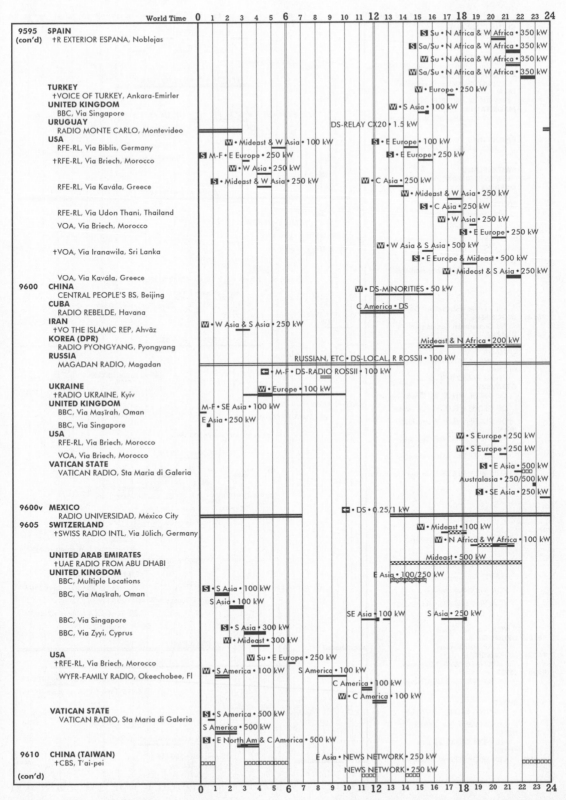

World Time | 0 1 2 3 4 5 6 7 8 9 10 11 12 13 14 15 16 17 18 19 20 21 22 23 24

9595 **SPAIN**
(con'd) †R EXTERIOR ESPANA, Noblejas
- S Su • N Africa & W Africa • 350 kW
- S Sa/Su • N Africa & W Africa • 350 kW
- W Su • N Africa & W Africa • 350 kW
- W Sa/Su • N Africa & W Africa • 350 kW

TURKEY
†VOICE OF TURKEY, Ankara-Emirler — W • Europe • 250 kW

UNITED KINGDOM
BBC, Via Singapore — W • S Asia • 100 kW

URUGUAY
RADIO MONTE CARLO, Montevideo — DS-RELAY CX20 • 1.5 kW

USA
RFE-RL, Via Biblis, Germany — W • Mideast & W Asia • 100 kW / S • E Europe • 100 kW
†RFE-RL, Via Briech, Morocco — S M-F • E Europe • 250 kW / S • E Europe • 250 kW
— W • W Asia • 250 kW
RFE-RL, Via Kavála, Greece — S • Mideast & W Asia • 250 kW / W • C Asia • 250 kW
— W • Mideast & W Asia • 250 kW
RFE-RL, Via Udon Thani, Thailand — S • C Asia • 250 kW
VOA, Via Briech, Morocco — W • W Asia • 250 kW
— S • E Europe • 250 kW
†VOA, Via Iranawila, Sri Lanka — W • W Asia & S Asia • 500 kW
— S • E Europe & Mideast • 500 kW
VOA, Via Kavála, Greece — W • Mideast & S Asia • 250 kW

9600 **CHINA**
CENTRAL PEOPLE'S BS, Beijing — W • DS-MINORITIES • 50 kW

CUBA
RADIO REBELDE, Havana — C America • DS

IRAN
†VO THE ISLAMIC REP, Ahvāz — W • W Asia & S Asia • 250 kW

KOREA (DPR)
RADIO PYONGYANG, Pyongyang — Mideast & N Africa • 200 kW

RUSSIA
MAGADAN RADIO, Magadan — RUSSIAN, ETC • DS-LOCAL, R ROSSII • 100 kW
— M-F • DS-RADIO ROSSII • 100 kW

UKRAINE
†RADIO UKRAINE, Kyiv — W • Europe • 100 kW

UNITED KINGDOM
BBC, Via Maşīrah, Oman — M-F • SE Asia • 100 kW
BBC, Via Singapore — E Asia • 250 kW

USA
RFE-RL, Via Briech, Morocco — W • S Europe • 250 kW
VOA, Via Briech, Morocco — W • S Europe • 250 kW

VATICAN STATE
VATICAN RADIO, Sta Maria di Galeria — S • E Asia • 500 kW
— Australasia • 250/500 kW
— S • SE Asia • 250 kW

9600v **MEXICO**
RADIO UNIVERSIDAD, México City — • DS • 0.25/1 kW

9605 **SWITZERLAND**
†SWISS RADIO INTL, Via Jülich, Germany — W • Mideast • 100 kW
— W • N Africa & W Africa • 100 kW

UNITED ARAB EMIRATES
†UAE RADIO FROM ABU DHABI — Mideast • 500 kW

UNITED KINGDOM
BBC, Multiple Locations — E Asia • 100/250 kW
BBC, Via Maşīrah, Oman — S • S Asia • 100 kW
— S Asia • 100 kW
— SE Asia • 100 kW / S Asia • 250 kW
BBC, Via Singapore — S • S Asia • 300 kW
BBC, Via Zyyi, Cyprus — W • Mideast • 300 kW

USA
†RFE-RL, Via Briech, Morocco — W Su • E Europe • 250 kW
WYFR-FAMILY RADIO, Okeechobee, Fl — W • S America • 100 kW / S America • 100 kW
— C America • 100 kW
— W • C America • 100 kW

VATICAN STATE
VATICAN RADIO, Sta Maria di Galeria — S • S America • 500 kW
— S America • 500 kW
— S • E North Am & C America • 500 kW

9610 **CHINA (TAIWAN)**
†CBS, T'ai-pei — E Asia • NEWS NETWORK • 250 kW
— NEWS NETWORK • 250 kW

(con'd)

0 1 2 3 4 5 6 7 8 9 10 11 12 13 14 15 16 17 18 19 20 21 22 23 24

SEASONAL S OR W   1-HR TIMESHIFT MIDYEAR ⟵ OR ⟶   JAMMING / OR /\   EARLIEST HEARD ◁   LATEST HEARD ▷   NEW FOR 2001 †

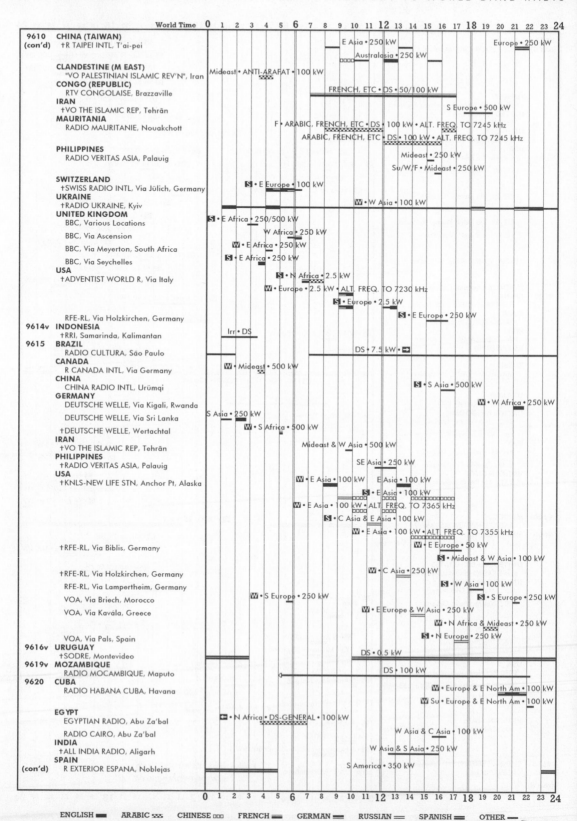

World Time 0 1 2 3 4 5 6 7 8 9 10 11 12 13 14 15 16 17 18 19 20 21 22 23 24

9610 CHINA (TAIWAN)
(con'd) †R TAIPEI INTL, T'ai-pei — E Asia • 250 kW — Australasia • 250 kW — Europe • 250 kW

CLANDESTINE (M EAST)
"VO PALESTINIAN ISLAMIC REV'N", Iran — Mideast • ANTI-ARAFAT • 100 kW
CONGO (REPUBLIC)
RTV CONGOLAISE, Brazzaville — FRENCH, ETC • DS • 50/100 kW
IRAN
†VO THE ISLAMIC REP, Tehrān — S Europe • 500 kW
MAURITANIA
RADIO MAURITANIE, Nouakchott — F • ARABIC, FRENCH, ETC • DS • 100 kW • ALT. FREQ. TO 7245 kHz — ARABIC, FRENCH, ETC • DS • 100 kW • ALT. FREQ. TO 7245 kHz

PHILIPPINES
RADIO VERITAS ASIA, Palauig — Mideast • 250 kW — Su/W/F • Mideast • 250 kW

SWITZERLAND
†SWISS RADIO INTL, Via Jülich, Germany — S • E Europe • 100 kW
UKRAINE
†RADIO UKRAINE, Kyiv — W • W Asia • 100 kW
UNITED KINGDOM
BBC, Various Locations — S • E Africa • 250/500 kW

BBC, Via Ascension — W Africa • 250 kW

BBC, Via Meyerton, South Africa — W • E Africa • 250 kW

BBC, Via Seychelles — S • E Africa • 250 kW
USA
†ADVENTIST WORLD R, Via Italy — S • N Africa • 2.5 kW

— W • Europe • 2.5 kW • ALT. FREQ. TO 7230 kHz

— S • Europe • 2.5 kW

RFE-RL, Via Holzkirchen, Germany — S • E Europe • 250 kW
9614v INDONESIA
†RRI, Samarinda, Kalimantan — Irr • DS
9615 BRAZIL
RADIO CULTURA, São Paulo — DS • 7.5 kW • ▶
CANADA
R CANADA INTL, Via Germany — W • Mideast • 500 kW
CHINA
CHINA RADIO INTL, Urümqi — S • S Asia • 500 kW
GERMANY
DEUTSCHE WELLE, Via Kigali, Rwanda — W • W Africa • 250 kW

DEUTSCHE WELLE, Via Sri Lanka — S Asia • 250 kW

— W • S Africa • 500 kW
†DEUTSCHE WELLE, Wertachtal
IRAN
†VO THE ISLAMIC REP, Tehrān — Mideast & W Asia • 500 kW
PHILIPPINES
†RADIO VERITAS ASIA, Palauig — SE Asia • 250 kW
USA
†KNLS-NEW LIFE STN, Anchor Pt, Alaska — W • E Asia • 100 kW — E Asia • 100 kW

— S • E Asia • 100 kW

— W • E Asia • 100 kW • ALT. FREQ. TO 7365 kHz

— S • C Asia & E Asia • 100 kW

— W • E Asia • 100 kW • ALT. FREQ. TO 7355 kHz

†RFE-RL, Via Biblis, Germany — W • E Europe • 50 kW

— S • Mideast & W Asia • 100 kW

†RFE-RL, Via Holzkirchen, Germany — W • C Asia • 250 kW

RFE-RL, Via Lampertheim, Germany — S • W Asia • 100 kW

VOA, Via Briech, Morocco — W • S Europe • 250 kW — S • S Europe • 250 kW

VOA, Via Kavála, Greece — W • E Europe & W Asia • 250 kW — W • N Africa & Mideast • 250 kW

VOA, Via Pals, Spain — S • N Europe • 250 kW
9616v URUGUAY
†SODRE, Montevideo — DS • 0.5 kW
9619v MOZAMBIQUE
RADIO MOCAMBIQUE, Maputo — DS • 100 kW
9620 CUBA
RADIO HABANA CUBA, Havana — W • Europe & E North Am • 100 kW — W Su • Europe & E North Am • 100 kW

EGYPT
EGYPTIAN RADIO, Abu Za'bal — ◀ • N Africa • DS-GENERAL • 100 kW

RADIO CAIRO, Abu Za'bal — W Asia & C Asia • 100 kW
INDIA
†ALL INDIA RADIO, Aligarh — W Asia & S Asia • 250 kW
SPAIN
(con'd) R EXTERIOR ESPANA, Noblejas — S America • 350 kW

0 1 2 3 4 5 6 7 8 9 10 11 12 13 14 15 16 17 18 19 20 21 22 23 24

ENGLISH ▬ ARABIC ⋙ CHINESE ⊡⊡⊡ FRENCH ▬ GERMAN ▬ RUSSIAN ═ SPANISH ▭ OTHER ▬

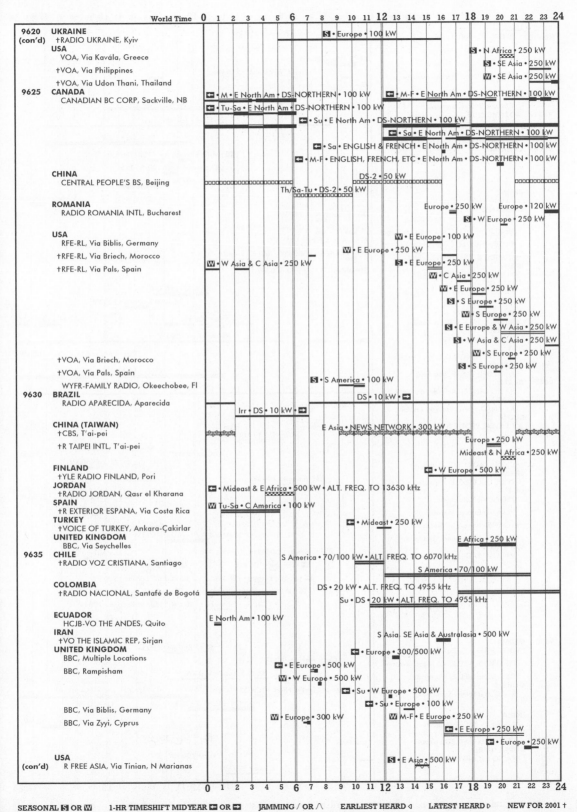

| World Time | 0 | 1 | 2 | 3 | 4 | 5 | 6 | 7 | 8 | 9 | 10 | 11 | 12 | 13 | 14 | 15 | 16 | 17 | 18 | 19 | 20 | 21 | 22 | 23 | 24 |

9620 **UKRAINE**
(con'd) †RADIO UKRAINE, Kyiv — S • Europe • 100 kW

USA
 VOA, Via Kavála, Greece — S • N Africa • 250 kW

 †VOA, Via Philippines — S • SE Asia • 250 kW

 †VOA, Via Udon Thani, Thailand — W • SE Asia • 250 kW

9625 **CANADA**
 CANADIAN BC CORP, Sackville, NB — M • E North Am • DS-NORTHERN • 100 kW · M-F • E North Am • DS-NORTHERN • 100 kW
 Tu-Sa • E North Am • DS-NORTHERN • 100 kW
 Su • E North Am • DS-NORTHERN • 100 kW
 Sa • E North Am • DS-NORTHERN • 100 kW
 Sa • ENGLISH & FRENCH • E North Am • DS-NORTHERN • 100 kW
 M-F • ENGLISH, FRENCH, ETC • E North Am • DS-NORTHERN • 100 kW

CHINA
 CENTRAL PEOPLE'S BS, Beijing — DS-2 • 50 kW
 Th/Sa-Tu • DS-2 • 50 kW

ROMANIA
 RADIO ROMANIA INTL, Bucharest — Europe • 250 kW · Europe • 120 kW
 S • W Europe • 250 kW

USA
 RFE-RL, Via Biblis, Germany — W • E Europe • 100 kW
 †RFE-RL, Via Briech, Morocco — W • E Europe • 250 kW
 †RFE-RL, Via Pals, Spain — W • W Asia & C Asia • 250 kW
 S • E Europe • 250 kW
 W • C Asia • 250 kW
 W • E Europe • 250 kW
 S • S Europe • 250 kW
 W • S Europe • 250 kW
 S • E Europe & W Asia • 250 kW
 S • W Asia & C Asia • 250 kW
 W • S Europe • 250 kW
 S • S Europe • 250 kW

 †VOA, Via Briech, Morocco
 †VOA, Via Pals, Spain
 WYFR-FAMILY RADIO, Okeechobee, Fl — S • S America • 100 kW

9630 **BRAZIL**
 RADIO APARECIDA, Aparecida — DS • 10 kW
 Irr • DS • 10 kW

CHINA (TAIWAN)
 †CBS, T'ai-pei — E Asia • NEWS NETWORK • 300 kW
 †R TAIPEI INTL, T'ai-pei — Europe • 250 kW
 Mideast & N Africa • 250 kW

FINLAND
 †YLE RADIO FINLAND, Pori — W Europe • 500 kW
JORDAN
 †RADIO JORDAN, Qasr el Kharana — Mideast & E Africa • 500 kW • ALT. FREQ. TO 13630 kHz
SPAIN
 †R EXTERIOR ESPANA, Via Costa Rica — W Tu-Sa • C America • 100 kW
TURKEY
 †VOICE OF TURKEY, Ankara-Çakirlar — Mideast • 250 kW
UNITED KINGDOM
 BBC, Via Seychelles — E Africa • 250 kW
9635 **CHILE**
 †RADIO VOZ CRISTIANA, Santiago — S America • 70/100 kW • ALT. FREQ. TO 6070 kHz
 S America • 70/100 kW

COLOMBIA
 †RADIO NACIONAL, Santafé de Bogotá — DS • 20 kW • ALT. FREQ. TO 4955 kHz
 Su • DS • 20 kW • ALT. FREQ. TO 4955 kHz

ECUADOR
 HCJB-VO THE ANDES, Quito — E North Am • 100 kW
IRAN
 †VO THE ISLAMIC REP, Sirjan — S Asia, SE Asia & Australasia • 500 kW
UNITED KINGDOM
 BBC, Multiple Locations — Europe • 300/500 kW
 BBC, Rampisham — E Europe • 500 kW
 W • W Europe • 500 kW
 Su • W Europe • 500 kW
 Su • Europe • 100 kW
 BBC, Via Biblis, Germany — W • Europe • 300 kW
 BBC, Via Zyyi, Cyprus — W M-F • E Europe • 250 kW
 E Europe • 250 kW
 Europe • 250 kW

USA
(con'd) R FREE ASIA, Via Tinian, N Marianas — S • E Asia • 500 kW

| World Time | 0 | 1 | 2 | 3 | 4 | 5 | 6 | 7 | 8 | 9 | 10 | 11 | 12 | 13 | 14 | 15 | 16 | 17 | 18 | 19 | 20 | 21 | 22 | 23 | 24 |

SEASONAL S OR W   1-HR TIMESHIFT MIDYEAR ⇐ OR ⇒   JAMMING / OR ∧   EARLIEST HEARD ◁   LATEST HEARD ▷   NEW FOR 2001 †

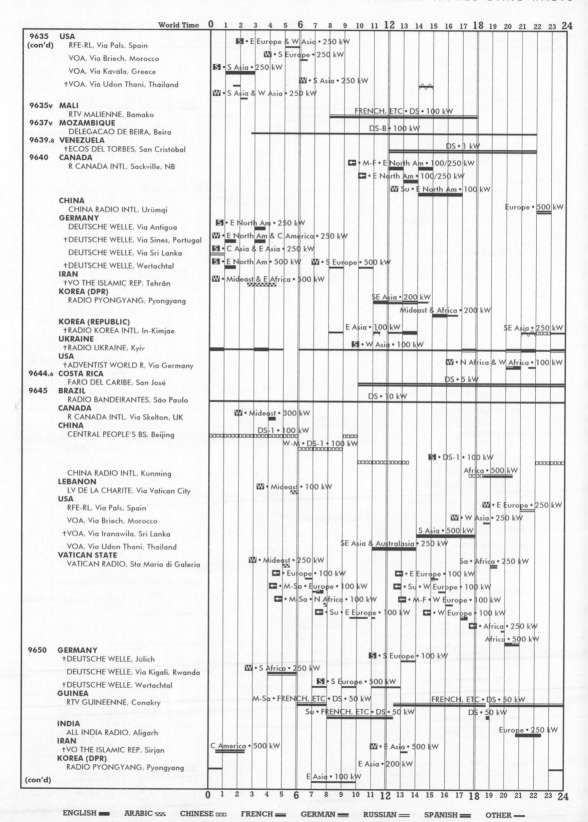

World Time 0 1 2 3 4 5 6 7 8 9 10 11 12 13 14 15 16 17 18 19 20 21 22 23 24

kHz	Country / Station	Schedule
9635 (con'd)	**USA**	
	RFE-RL, Via Pals, Spain	[S] • E Europe & W Asia • 250 kW
	VOA, Via Briech, Morocco	[W] • S Europe • 250 kW
	VOA, Via Kavála, Greece	[S] • S Asia • 250 kW
	†VOA, Via Udon Thani, Thailand	[W] • S Asia • 250 kW; [W] • S Asia & W Asia • 250 kW
9635v	**MALI**	
	RTV MALIENNE, Bamako	FRENCH, ETC • DS • 100 kW
9637v	**MOZAMBIQUE**	
	DELEGACAO DE BEIRA, Beira	DS-B • 100 kW
9639.8	**VENEZUELA**	
	†ECOS DEL TORBES, San Cristóbal	DS • 1 kW
9640	**CANADA**	
	R CANADA INTL, Sackville, NB	← • M-F • E North Am • 100/250 kW; ← • E North Am • 100/250 kW; [W] Su • E North Am • 100 kW
	CHINA	
	CHINA RADIO INTL, Urümqi	Europe • 500 kW
	GERMANY	
	DEUTSCHE WELLE, Via Antigua	[S] • E North Am • 250 kW
	†DEUTSCHE WELLE, Via Sines, Portugal	[W] • E North Am & C America • 250 kW
	DEUTSCHE WELLE, Via Sri Lanka	[S] • C Asia & E Asia • 250 kW
	†DEUTSCHE WELLE, Wertachtal	[S] • E North Am • 500 kW; [W] • S Europe • 500 kW
	IRAN	
	†VO THE ISLAMIC REP, Tehrān	[W] • Mideast & E Africa • 500 kW
	KOREA (DPR)	
	RADIO PYONGYANG, Pyongyang	SE Asia • 200 kW; Mideast & Africa • 200 kW
	KOREA (REPUBLIC)	
	†RADIO KOREA INTL, In-Kimjae	E Asia • 100 kW; SE Asia • 250 kW
	UKRAINE	
	†RADIO UKRAINE, Kyiv	[S] • W Asia • 100 kW
	USA	
	†ADVENTIST WORLD R, Via Germany	[W] • N Africa & W Africa • 100 kW
9644.6	**COSTA RICA**	
	FARO DEL CARIBE, San José	DS • 5 kW
9645	**BRAZIL**	
	RADIO BANDEIRANTES, São Paulo	DS • 10 kW
	CANADA	
	R CANADA INTL, Via Skelton, UK	[W] • Mideast • 300 kW
	CHINA	
	CENTRAL PEOPLE'S BS, Beijing	DS-1 • 100 kW; W-M • DS-1 • 100 kW; [S] • DS-1 • 100 kW
	CHINA RADIO INTL, Kunming	Africa • 500 kW
	LEBANON	
	LV DE LA CHARITE, Via Vatican City	[W] • Mideast • 100 kW
	USA	
	RFE-RL, Via Pals, Spain	[W] • E Europe • 250 kW
	VOA, Via Briech, Morocco	[W] • W Asia • 250 kW
	†VOA, Via Iranawila, Sri Lanka	S Asia • 500 kW
	VOA, Via Udon Thani, Thailand	SE Asia & Australasia • 250 kW
	VATICAN STATE	
	VATICAN RADIO, Sta Maria di Galeria	[W] • Mideast • 250 kW; Sa • Africa • 250 kW; ← • Europe • 100 kW; ← • E Europe • 100 kW; ← • M-Sa • Europe • 100 kW; ← • Su • W Europe • 100 kW; ← • M-Sa • N Africa • 100 kW; ← • M-F • W Europe • 100 kW; ← • Su • E Europe • 100 kW; ← • W Europe • 100 kW; ← • Africa • 250 kW; Africa • 500 kW
9650	**GERMANY**	
	†DEUTSCHE WELLE, Jülich	[S] • S Europe • 100 kW
	DEUTSCHE WELLE, Via Kigali, Rwanda	[W] • S Africa • 250 kW
	†DEUTSCHE WELLE, Wertachtal	[S] • S Europe • 500 kW
	GUINEA	
	RTV GUINEENNE, Conakry	M-Sa • FRENCH, ETC • DS • 50 kW; FRENCH, ETC • DS • 50 kW; Su • FRENCH, ETC • DS • 50 kW; DS • 50 kW
	INDIA	
	ALL INDIA RADIO, Aligarh	Europe • 250 kW
	IRAN	
	†VO THE ISLAMIC REP, Sirjan	C America • 500 kW; [W] • E Asia • 500 kW
	KOREA (DPR)	
	RADIO PYONGYANG, Pyongyang	E Asia • 200 kW; E Asia • 100 kW
(con'd)		

0 1 2 3 4 5 6 7 8 9 10 11 12 13 14 15 16 17 18 19 20 21 22 23 24

ENGLISH ▬ ARABIC ▭ CHINESE ▫▫▫ FRENCH ═ GERMAN ═ RUSSIAN ═ SPANISH ═ OTHER ─

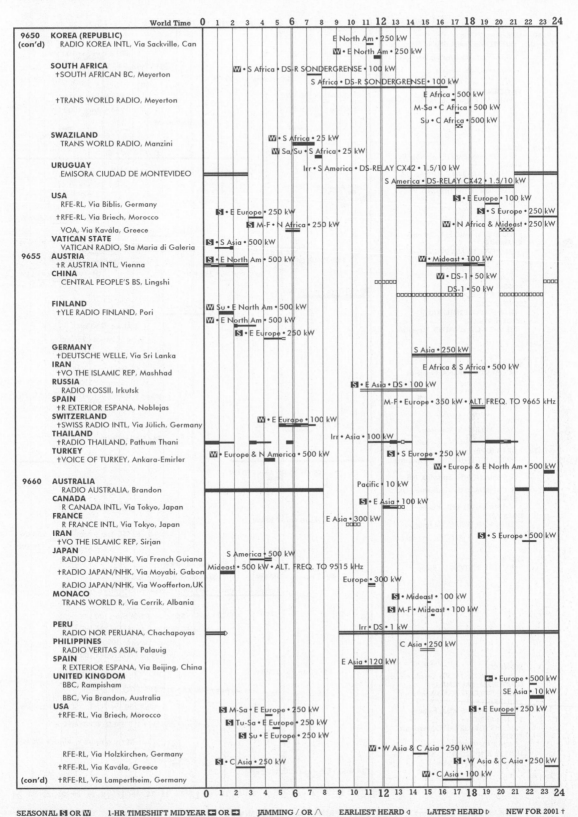

World Time   0 1 2 3 4 5 6 7 8 9 10 11 12 13 14 15 16 17 18 19 20 21 22 23 24

9650
(con'd)

KOREA (REPUBLIC)
RADIO KOREA INTL, Via Sackville, Can
- E North Am • 250 kW
- W • E North Am • 250 kW

SOUTH AFRICA
†SOUTH AFRICAN BC, Meyerton
- W • S Africa • DS-R SONDERGRENSE • 100 kW
- S Africa • DS-R SONDERGRENSE • 100 kW

†TRANS WORLD RADIO, Meyerton
- E Africa • 500 kW
- M-Sa • C Africa • 500 kW
- Su • C Africa • 500 kW

SWAZILAND
TRANS WORLD RADIO, Manzini
- W • S Africa • 25 kW
- W Sa/Su • S Africa • 25 kW

URUGUAY
EMISORA CIUDAD DE MONTEVIDEO
- Irr • S America • DS-RELAY CX42 • 1.5/10 kW
- S America • DS-RELAY CX42 • 1.5/10 kW

USA
RFE-RL, Via Biblis, Germany
- S • E Europe • 100 kW
- S • E Europe • 250 kW
†RFE-RL, Via Briech, Morocco
- S • S Europe • 250 kW
VOA, Via Kavála, Greece
- S M-F • N Africa • 250 kW
- W • N Africa & Mideast • 250 kW

VATICAN STATE
VATICAN RADIO, Sta Maria di Galeria
- S • S Asia • 500 kW

9655
AUSTRIA
†R AUSTRIA INTL, Vienna
- S • E North Am • 500 kW
- W • Mideast • 100 kW

CHINA
CENTRAL PEOPLE'S BS, Lingshi
- W • DS-1 • 50 kW
- DS-1 • 50 kW

FINLAND
†YLE RADIO FINLAND, Pori
- W Su • E North Am • 500 kW
- W • E North Am • 500 kW
- S • E Europe • 250 kW

GERMANY
†DEUTSCHE WELLE, Via Sri Lanka
- S Asia • 250 kW

IRAN
†VO THE ISLAMIC REP, Mashhad
- E Africa & S Africa • 500 kW

RUSSIA
RADIO ROSSII, Irkutsk
- S • E Asia • DS • 100 kW

SPAIN
†R EXTERIOR ESPANA, Noblejas
- M-F • Europe • 350 kW • ALT. FREQ. TO 9665 kHz

SWITZERLAND
†SWISS RADIO INTL, Via Jülich, Germany
- W • E Europe • 100 kW

THAILAND
†RADIO THAILAND, Pathum Thani
- Irr • Asia • 100 kW

TURKEY
†VOICE OF TURKEY, Ankara-Emirler
- W • Europe & N America • 500 kW
- S • S Europe • 250 kW
- W • Europe & E North Am • 500 kW

9660
AUSTRALIA
RADIO AUSTRALIA, Brandon
- Pacific • 10 kW

CANADA
R CANADA INTL, Via Tokyo, Japan
- S • E Asia • 100 kW

FRANCE
R FRANCE INTL, Via Tokyo, Japan
- E Asia • 300 kW

IRAN
†VO THE ISLAMIC REP, Sirjan
- S • S Europe • 500 kW

JAPAN
RADIO JAPAN/NHK, Via French Guiana
- S America • 500 kW
†RADIO JAPAN/NHK, Via Moyabi, Gabon
- Mideast • 500 kW • ALT. FREQ. TO 9515 kHz
RADIO JAPAN/NHK, Via Woofferton, UK
- Europe • 300 kW

MONACO
TRANS WORLD R, Via Cerrik, Albania
- S • Mideast • 100 kW
- S M-F • Mideast • 100 kW

PERU
RADIO NOR PERUANA, Chachapoyas
- Irr • DS • 1 kW

PHILIPPINES
RADIO VERITAS ASIA, Palauig
- C Asia • 250 kW

SPAIN
R EXTERIOR ESPANA, Via Beijing, China
- E Asia • 120 kW

UNITED KINGDOM
BBC, Rampisham
- • Europe • 500 kW
BBC, Via Brandon, Australia
- SE Asia • 10 kW

USA
†RFE-RL, Via Briech, Morocco
- S M-Sa • E Europe • 250 kW
- S • E Europe • 250 kW
- S Tu-Sa • E Europe • 250 kW
- S Su • E Europe • 250 kW

RFE-RL, Via Holzkirchen, Germany
- W • W Asia & C Asia • 250 kW
†RFE-RL, Via Kavála, Greece
- S • C Asia • 250 kW
- W • W Asia & C Asia • 250 kW

(con'd) †RFE-RL, Via Lampertheim, Germany
- W • C Asia • 100 kW

0 1 2 3 4 5 6 7 8 9 10 11 12 13 14 15 16 17 18 19 20 21 22 23 24

SEASONAL S OR W   1-HR TIMESHIFT MIDYEAR ⊏ OR ⊐   JAMMING / OR /\   EARLIEST HEARD ◁   LATEST HEARD ▷   NEW FOR 2001 †

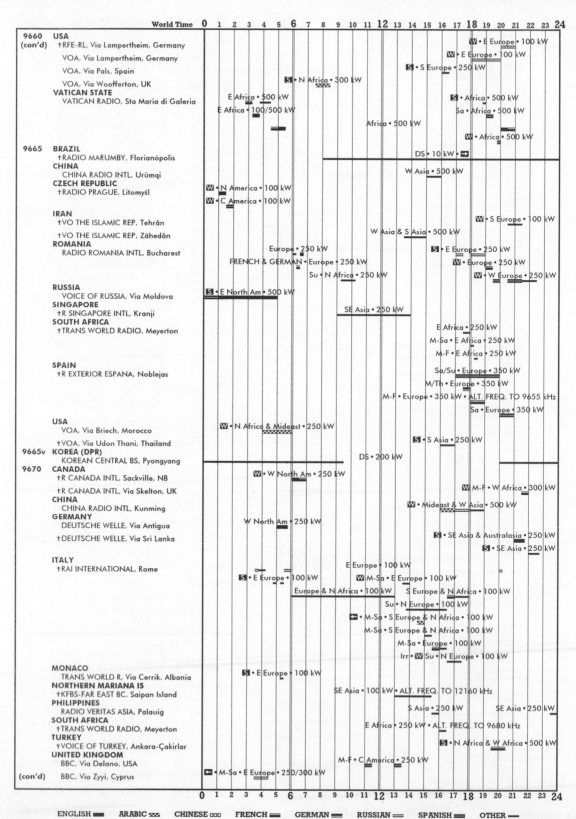

9660 **USA**	
(con'd) †RFE-RL, Via Lampertheim, Germany	
VOA, Via Lampertheim, Germany	
VOA, Via Pals, Spain	
VOA, Via Woofferton, UK	
VATICAN STATE	
VATICAN RADIO, Sta Maria di Galeria	
9665 **BRAZIL**	
†RADIO MARUMBY, Florianópolis	
CHINA	
CHINA RADIO INTL, Urümqi	
CZECH REPUBLIC	
†RADIO PRAGUE, Litomyšl	
IRAN	
†VO THE ISLAMIC REP, Tehrān	
†VO THE ISLAMIC REP, Zāhedān	
ROMANIA	
RADIO ROMANIA INTL, Bucharest	
RUSSIA	
VOICE OF RUSSIA, Via Moldova	
SINGAPORE	
†R SINGAPORE INTL, Kranji	
SOUTH AFRICA	
†TRANS WORLD RADIO, Meyerton	
SPAIN	
†R EXTERIOR ESPANA, Noblejas	
USA	
VOA, Via Briech, Morocco	
†VOA, Via Udon Thani, Thailand	
9665v KOREA (DPR)	
KOREAN CENTRAL BS, Pyongyang	
9670 CANADA	
†R CANADA INTL, Sackville, NB	
†R CANADA INTL, Via Skelton, UK	
CHINA	
CHINA RADIO INTL, Kunming	
GERMANY	
DEUTSCHE WELLE, Via Antigua	
†DEUTSCHE WELLE, Via Sri Lanka	
ITALY	
†RAI INTERNATIONAL, Rome	
MONACO	
TRANS WORLD R, Via Cerrik, Albania	
NORTHERN MARIANA IS	
†KFBS-FAR EAST BC, Saipan Island	
PHILIPPINES	
RADIO VERITAS ASIA, Palauig	
SOUTH AFRICA	
†TRANS WORLD RADIO, Meyerton	
TURKEY	
†VOICE OF TURKEY, Ankara-Çakirlar	
UNITED KINGDOM	
BBC, Via Delano, USA	
(con'd) BBC, Via Zyyi, Cyprus	

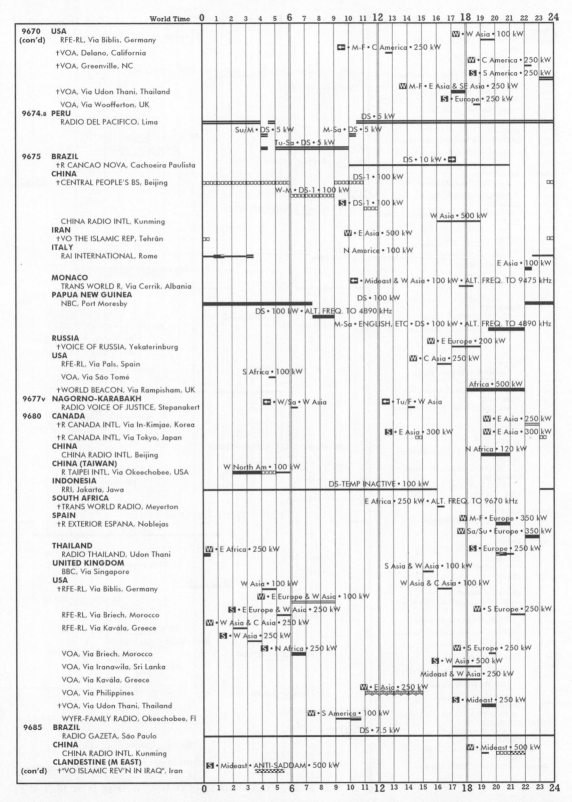

9670 **(con'd)**	**USA**	
	RFE-RL, Via Biblis, Germany	W • W Asia • 100 kW
	†VOA, Delano, California	M-F • C America • 250 kW
	†VOA, Greenville, NC	W • C America • 250 kW S • S America • 250 kW
	†VOA, Via Udon Thani, Thailand	W M-F • E Asia & SE Asia • 250 kW
	VOA, Via Woofferton, UK	S • Europe • 250 kW
9674.8	**PERU**	DS • 5 kW
	RADIO DEL PACIFICO, Lima	Su/M • DS • 5 kW M-Sa • DS • 5 kW Tu-Sa • DS • 5 kW
9675	**BRAZIL**	
	†R CANCAO NOVA, Cachoeira Paulista	DS • 10 kW •
	CHINA	
	†CENTRAL PEOPLE'S BS, Beijing	DS-1 • 100 kW W-M • DS-1 • 100 kW S • DS-1 • 100 kW
	CHINA RADIO INTL, Kunming	W Asia • 500 kW
	IRAN	
	†VO THE ISLAMIC REP, Tehrān	W • E Asia • 500 kW
	ITALY	
	RAI INTERNATIONAL, Rome	N America • 100 kW E Asia • 100 kW
	MONACO	
	TRANS WORLD R, Via Cerrik, Albania	• Mideast & W Asia • 100 kW • ALT. FREQ. TO 9475 kHz
	PAPUA NEW GUINEA	DS • 100 kW
	NBC, Port Moresby	DS • 100 kW • ALT. FREQ. TO 4890 kHz M-Sa • ENGLISH, ETC • DS • 100 kW • ALT. FREQ. TO 4890 kHz
	RUSSIA	
	†VOICE OF RUSSIA, Yekaterinburg	W • E Europe • 200 kW
	USA	
	RFE-RL, Via Pals, Spain	W • C Asia • 250 kW
	VOA, Via São Tomé	S Africa • 100 kW
	†WORLD BEACON, Via Rampisham, UK	Africa • 500 kW
9677v	**NAGORNO-KARABAKH**	
	RADIO VOICE OF JUSTICE, Stepanakert	• W/Sa • W Asia • Tu/F • W Asia
9680	**CANADA**	
	†R CANADA INTL, Via In-Kimjae, Korea	W • E Asia • 250 kW
	†R CANADA INTL, Via Tokyo, Japan	S • E Asia • 300 kW W • E Asia • 300 kW
	CHINA	
	CHINA RADIO INTL, Beijing	N Africa • 120 kW
	CHINA (TAIWAN)	
	R TAIPEI INTL, Via Okeechobee, USA	W North Am • 100 kW
	INDONESIA	
	RRI, Jakarta, Jawa	DS-TEMP INACTIVE • 100 kW
	SOUTH AFRICA	
	†TRANS WORLD RADIO, Meyerton	E Africa • 250 kW • ALT. FREQ. TO 9670 kHz
	SPAIN	
	†R EXTERIOR ESPANA, Noblejas	W M-F • Europe • 350 kW W Sa/Su • Europe • 350 kW
	THAILAND	S • Europe • 250 kW
	RADIO THAILAND, Udon Thani	W • E Africa • 250 kW
	UNITED KINGDOM	
	BBC, Via Singapore	S Asia & W Asia • 100 kW
	USA	
	†RFE-RL, Via Biblis, Germany	W Asia • 100 kW W Asia & C Asia • 100 kW W • E Europe & W Asia • 100 kW
	RFE-RL, Via Briech, Morocco	S • E Europe & W Asia • 250 kW W • S Europe • 250 kW
	RFE-RL, Via Kavála, Greece	W • W Asia & C Asia • 250 kW S • W Asia • 250 kW
	VOA, Via Briech, Morocco	S • N Africa • 250 kW W • S Europe • 250 kW
	VOA, Via Iranawila, Sri Lanka	S • W Asia • 500 kW
	VOA, Via Kavála, Greece	Mideast & W Asia • 250 kW
	VOA, Via Philippines	W • E Asia • 250 kW
	†VOA, Via Udon Thani, Thailand	S • Mideast • 250 kW
	WYFR-FAMILY RADIO, Okeechobee, Fl	W • S America • 100 kW
9685	**BRAZIL**	
	RADIO GAZETA, São Paulo	DS • 7.5 kW
	CHINA	
	CHINA RADIO INTL, Kunming	W • Mideast • 500 kW
	CLANDESTINE (M EAST)	
(con'd)	†"VO ISLAMIC REV'N IN IRAQ", Iran	S • Mideast • ANTI-SADDAM • 500 kW

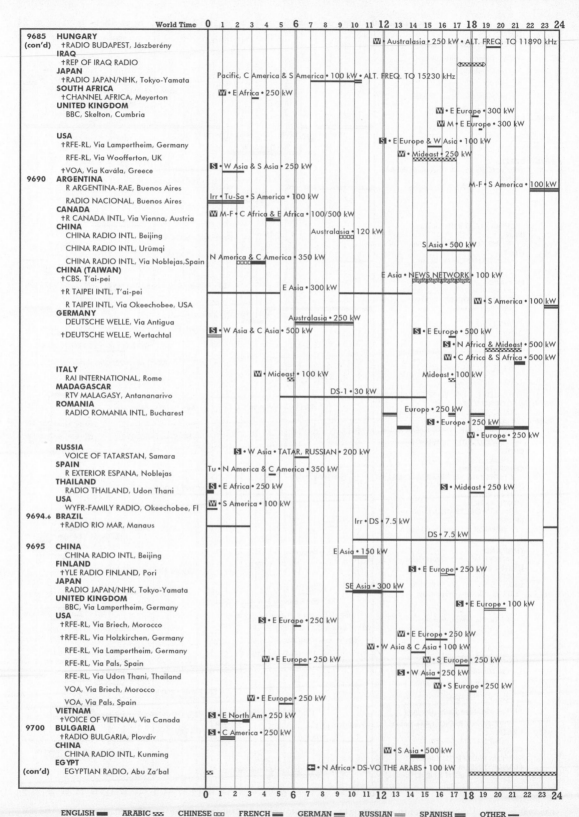

| World Time | 0 | 1 | 2 | 3 | 4 | 5 | 6 | 7 | 8 | 9 | 10 | 11 | 12 | 13 | 14 | 15 | 16 | 17 | 18 | 19 | 20 | 21 | 22 | 23 | 24 |

9685 HUNGARY
(con'd) †RADIO BUDAPEST, Jászberény — W • Australasia • 250 kW • ALT. FREQ. TO 11890 kHz

IRAQ
†REP OF IRAQ RADIO

JAPAN
†RADIO JAPAN/NHK, Tokyo-Yamata — Pacific, C America & S America • 100 kW • ALT. FREQ. TO 15230 kHz

SOUTH AFRICA
†CHANNEL AFRICA, Meyerton — W • E Africa • 250 kW

UNITED KINGDOM
BBC, Skelton, Cumbria — W • E Europe • 300 kW / W • M • E Europe • 300 kW

USA
†RFE-RL, Via Lampertheim, Germany — S • E Europe & W Asia • 100 kW

RFE-RL, Via Woofferton, UK — W • Mideast • 250 kW

†VOA, Via Kavála, Greece — S • W Asia & S Asia • 250 kW

9690 ARGENTINA
R ARGENTINA-RAE, Buenos Aires — M-F • S America • 100 kW

RADIO NACIONAL, Buenos Aires — Irr • Tu-Sa • S America • 100 kW

CANADA
†R CANADA INTL, Via Vienna, Austria — W • M-F • C Africa & E Africa • 100/500 kW

CHINA
CHINA RADIO INTL, Beijing — Australasia • 120 kW

CHINA RADIO INTL, Urümqi — S Asia • 500 kW

CHINA RADIO INTL, Via Noblejas, Spain — N America & C America • 350 kW

CHINA (TAIWAN)
†CBS, T'ai-pei — E Asia • NEWS NETWORK • 100 kW

†R TAIPEI INTL, T'ai-pei — E Asia • 300 kW

R TAIPEI INTL, Via Okeechobee, USA — W • S America • 100 kW

GERMANY
DEUTSCHE WELLE, Via Antigua — Australasia • 250 kW

†DEUTSCHE WELLE, Wertachtal — S • W Asia & C Asia • 500 kW / S • E Europe • 500 kW / S • N Africa & Mideast • 500 kW / W • C Africa & S Africa • 500 kW

ITALY
RAI INTERNATIONAL, Rome — W • Mideast • 100 kW / Mideast • 100 kW

MADAGASCAR
RTV MALAGASY, Antananarivo — DS-1 • 30 kW

ROMANIA
RADIO ROMANIA INTL, Bucharest — Europe • 250 kW / S • Europe • 250 kW / W • Europe • 250 kW

RUSSIA
VOICE OF TATARSTAN, Samara — S • W Asia • TATAR, RUSSIAN • 200 kW

SPAIN
R EXTERIOR ESPANA, Noblejas — Tu • N America & C America • 350 kW

THAILAND
RADIO THAILAND, Udon Thani — S • E Africa • 250 kW / S • Mideast • 250 kW

USA
WYFR-FAMILY RADIO, Okeechobee, Fl — W • S America • 100 kW

9694.6 BRAZIL
†RADIO RIO MAR, Manaus — Irr • DS 7.5 kW / DS • 7.5 kW

9695 CHINA
CHINA RADIO INTL, Beijing — E Asia • 150 kW

FINLAND
†YLE RADIO FINLAND, Pori — S • E Europe • 250 kW

JAPAN
RADIO JAPAN/NHK, Tokyo-Yamata — SE Asia • 300 kW

UNITED KINGDOM
BBC, Via Lampertheim, Germany — S • E Europe • 100 kW

USA
†RFE-RL, Via Briech, Morocco — S • E Europe • 250 kW

†RFE-RL, Via Holzkirchen, Germany — W • E Europe • 250 kW

RFE-RL, Via Lampertheim, Germany — W • W Asia & C Asia • 100 kW

RFE-RL, Via Pals, Spain — W • E Europe • 250 kW / W • S Europe • 250 kW

RFE-RL, Via Udon Thani, Thailand — S • W Asia • 250 kW

VOA, Via Briech, Morocco — W • S Europe • 250 kW

VOA, Via Pals, Spain — W • E Europe • 250 kW

VIETNAM
†VOICE OF VIETNAM, Via Canada — S • E North Am • 250 kW

9700 BULGARIA
†RADIO BULGARIA, Plovdiv — S • C America • 250 kW

CHINA
CHINA RADIO INTL, Kunming — W • S Asia • 500 kW

EGYPT
(con'd) EGYPTIAN RADIO, Abu Za'bal — N Africa • DS-VO THE ARABS • 100 kW

| | 0 | 1 | 2 | 3 | 4 | 5 | 6 | 7 | 8 | 9 | 10 | 11 | 12 | 13 | 14 | 15 | 16 | 17 | 18 | 19 | 20 | 21 | 22 | 23 | 24 |

ENGLISH ▬ ARABIC ⋙ CHINESE □□□ FRENCH ══ GERMAN ▬ RUSSIAN ═ SPANISH ▭ OTHER ▬

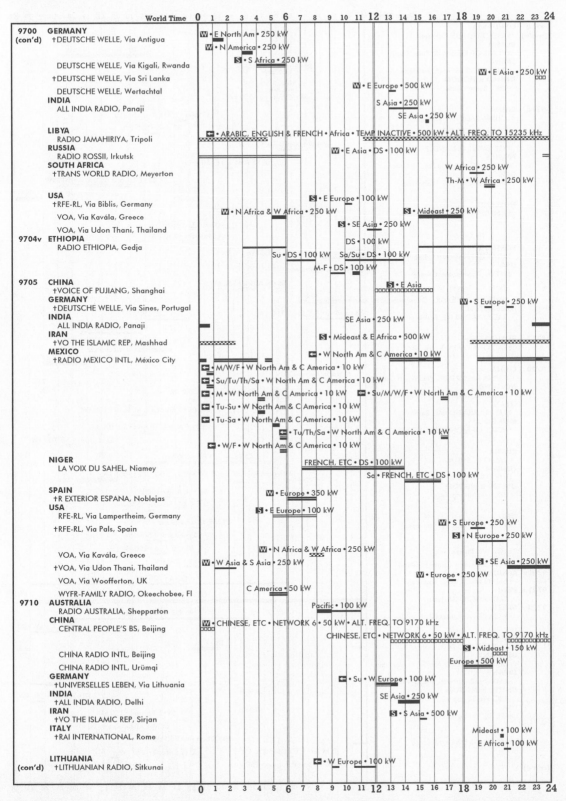

| | | | World Time | 0 1 2 3 4 5 6 7 8 9 10 11 12 13 14 15 16 17 18 19 20 21 22 23 24 |

9700 GERMANY
(con'd) †DEUTSCHE WELLE, Via Antigua — W • E North Am • 250 kW; W • N America • 250 kW; S • S Africa • 250 kW

DEUTSCHE WELLE, Via Kigali, Rwanda — W • E Asia • 250 kW

†DEUTSCHE WELLE, Via Sri Lanka — W • E Europe • 500 kW

DEUTSCHE WELLE, Wertachtal

INDIA
ALL INDIA RADIO, Panaji — S Asia • 250 kW; SE Asia • 250 kW

LIBYA
RADIO JAMAHIRIYA, Tripoli — • ARABIC, ENGLISH & FRENCH • Africa • TEMP INACTIVE • 500 kW • ALT. FREQ. TO 15235 kHz

RUSSIA
RADIO ROSSII, Irkutsk — W • E Asia • DS • 100 kW

SOUTH AFRICA
†TRANS WORLD RADIO, Meyerton — W Africa • 250 kW; Th-M • W Africa • 250 kW

USA
†RFE-RL, Via Biblis, Germany — S • E Europe • 100 kW

VOA, Via Kavála, Greece — W • N Africa & W Africa • 250 kW; S • Mideast • 250 kW

VOA, Via Udon Thani, Thailand — S • SE Asia • 250 kW

9704v ETHIOPIA
RADIO ETHIOPIA, Gedja — DS • 100 kW; Su • DS • 100 kW; Sa/Su • DS • 100 kW; M-F • DS • 100 kW

9705 CHINA
†VOICE OF PUJIANG, Shanghai — S • E Asia

GERMANY
†DEUTSCHE WELLE, Via Sines, Portugal — W • S Europe • 250 kW

INDIA
ALL INDIA RADIO, Panaji — SE Asia • 250 kW

IRAN
†VO THE ISLAMIC REP, Mashhad — S • Mideast & E Africa • 500 kW

MEXICO
†RADIO MEXICO INTL, México City — • W North Am & C America • 10 kW; • M/W/F • W North Am & C America • 10 kW; • Su/Tu/Th/Sa • W North Am & C America • 10 kW; • M • W North Am & C America • 10 kW; • Su/M/W/F • W North Am & C America • 10 kW; • Tu-Su • W North Am & C America • 10 kW; • Tu-Sa • W North Am & C America • 10 kW; • Tu/Th/Sa • W North Am & C America • 10 kW; • W/F • W North Am & C America • 10 kW

NIGER
LA VOIX DU SAHEL, Niamey — FRENCH, ETC • DS • 100 kW; Sa • FRENCH, ETC • DS • 100 kW

SPAIN
†R EXTERIOR ESPANA, Noblejas — W • Europe • 350 kW

USA
RFE-RL, Via Lampertheim, Germany — S • E Europe • 100 kW

†RFE-RL, Via Pals, Spain — W • S Europe • 250 kW; S • N Europe • 250 kW

VOA, Via Kavála, Greece — W • N Africa & W Africa • 250 kW

†VOA, Via Udon Thani, Thailand — W • W Asia & S Asia • 250 kW; S • SE Asia • 250 kW

VOA, Via Woofferton, UK — W • Europe • 250 kW

WYFR-FAMILY RADIO, Okeechobee, Fl — C America • 50 kW

9710 AUSTRALIA
RADIO AUSTRALIA, Shepparton — Pacific • 100 kW

CHINA
CENTRAL PEOPLE'S BS, Beijing — W • CHINESE, ETC • NETWORK 6 • 50 kW • ALT. FREQ. TO 9170 kHz; CHINESE, ETC • NETWORK 6 • 50 kW • ALT. FREQ. TO 9170 kHz

CHINA RADIO INTL, Beijing — S • Mideast • 150 kW

CHINA RADIO INTL, Urümqi — Europe • 500 kW

GERMANY
†UNIVERSELLES LEBEN, Via Lithuania — • Su • W Europe • 100 kW

INDIA
†ALL INDIA RADIO, Delhi — SE Asia • 250 kW

IRAN
†VO THE ISLAMIC REP, Sirjan — S • S Asia • 500 kW

ITALY
†RAI INTERNATIONAL, Rome — Mideast • 100 kW; E Africa • 100 kW

LITHUANIA
(con'd) †LITHUANIAN RADIO, Sitkunai — • W Europe • 100 kW

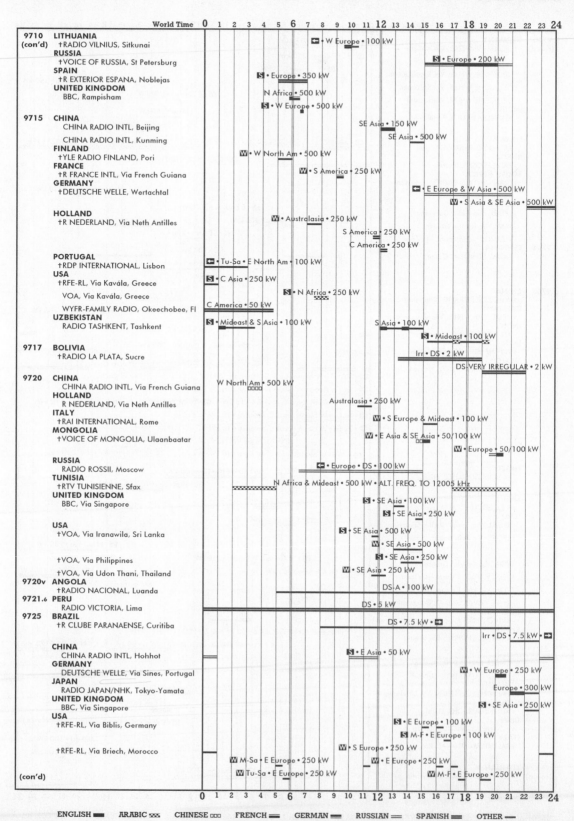

9710 (con'd)	
	†RADIO VILNIUS, Sitkunai — W Europe • 100 kW
RUSSIA	
	†VOICE OF RUSSIA, St Petersburg — S • Europe • 200 kW
SPAIN	
	†R EXTERIOR ESPANA, Noblejas — S • Europe • 350 kW
UNITED KINGDOM	
	BBC, Rampisham — N Africa • 500 kW; S • W Europe • 500 kW
9715 CHINA	
	CHINA RADIO INTL, Beijing — SE Asia • 150 kW
	CHINA RADIO INTL, Kunming — SE Asia • 500 kW
FINLAND	
	†YLE RADIO FINLAND, Pori — W • W North Am • 500 kW
FRANCE	
	†R FRANCE INTL, Via French Guiana — W • S America • 250 kW
GERMANY	
	†DEUTSCHE WELLE, Wertachtal — E Europe & W Asia • 500 kW; W • S Asia & SE Asia • 500 kW
HOLLAND	
	†R NEDERLAND, Via Neth Antilles — W • Australasia • 250 kW; S America • 250 kW; C America • 250 kW
PORTUGAL	
	†RDP INTERNATIONAL, Lisbon — Tu-Sa • E North Am • 100 kW
USA	
	†RFE-RL, Via Kavála, Greece — S • C Asia • 250 kW
	VOA, Via Kavála, Greece — S • N Africa • 250 kW
	WYFR-FAMILY RADIO, Okeechobee, Fl — C America • 50 kW
UZBEKISTAN	
	RADIO TASHKENT, Tashkent — S • Mideast & S Asia • 100 kW; S Asia • 100 kW; S • Mideast • 100 kW
9717 BOLIVIA	
	†RADIO LA PLATA, Sucre — Irr • DS • 2 kW; DS-VERY IRREGULAR • 2 kW
9720 CHINA	
	CHINA RADIO INTL, Via French Guiana — W North Am • 500 kW
HOLLAND	
	R NEDERLAND, Via Neth Antilles — Australasia • 250 kW
ITALY	
	†RAI INTERNATIONAL, Rome — W • S Europe & Mideast • 100 kW
MONGOLIA	
	†VOICE OF MONGOLIA, Ulaanbaatar — W • E Asia & SE Asia • 50/100 kW; W • Europe • 50/100 kW
RUSSIA	
	RADIO ROSSII, Moscow — Europe • DS • 100 kW
TUNISIA	
	†RTV TUNISIENNE, Sfax — N Africa & Mideast • 500 kW • ALT. FREQ. TO 12005 kHz
UNITED KINGDOM	
	BBC, Via Singapore — S • SE Asia • 100 kW; S • SE Asia • 250 kW
USA	
	†VOA, Via Iranawila, Sri Lanka — S • SE Asia • 500 kW; W • SE Asia • 500 kW
	†VOA, Via Philippines — S • SE Asia • 250 kW
	†VOA, Via Udon Thani, Thailand — W • SE Asia • 250 kW
9720v ANGOLA	
	†RADIO NACIONAL, Luanda — DS-A • 100 kW
9721.6 PERU	
	RADIO VICTORIA, Lima — DS • 5 kW
9725 BRAZIL	
	†R CLUBE PARANAENSE, Curitiba — DS • 7.5 kW • ; Irr • DS • 7.5 kW •
CHINA	
	CHINA RADIO INTL, Hohhot — S • E Asia • 50 kW
GERMANY	
	DEUTSCHE WELLE, Via Sines, Portugal — W • W Europe • 250 kW
JAPAN	
	RADIO JAPAN/NHK, Tokyo-Yamata — Europe • 300 kW
UNITED KINGDOM	
	BBC, Via Singapore — S • SE Asia • 250 kW
USA	
	†RFE-RL, Via Biblis, Germany — S • E Europe • 100 kW; S • M-F • E Europe • 100 kW; W • S Europe • 250 kW
	†RFE-RL, Via Briech, Morocco — W M-Sa • E Europe • 250 kW; W • E Europe • 250 kW; W Tu-Sa • E Europe • 250 kW; W M-F • E Europe • 250 kW
(con'd)	

World Time   0 1 2 3 4 5 6 7 8 9 10 11 12 13 14 15 16 17 18 19 20 21 22 23 24

ENGLISH ▬   ARABIC ⬚⬚⬚   CHINESE ⬚⬚⬚   FRENCH ═   GERMAN ▬   RUSSIAN ═   SPANISH ▬   OTHER ▬

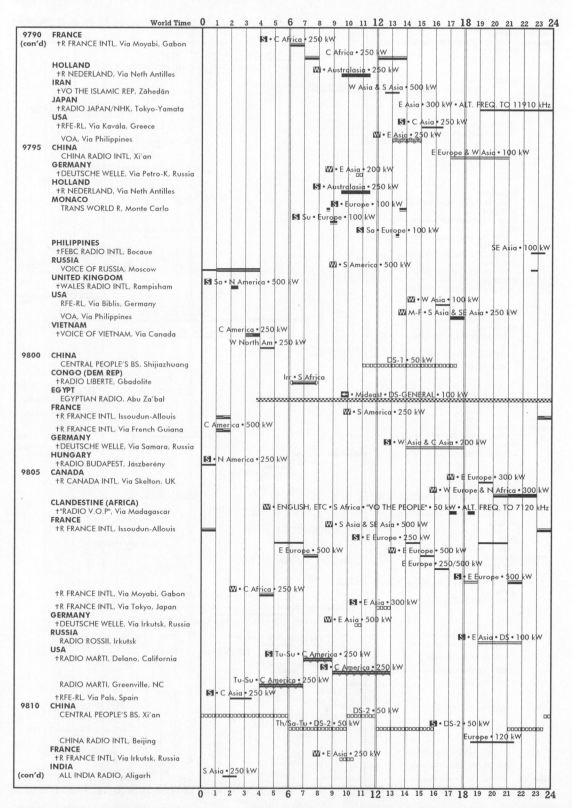

9790 **FRANCE**	
(con'd)	†R FRANCE INTL, Via Moyabi, Gabon
	HOLLAND
	†R NEDERLAND, Via Neth Antilles
	IRAN
	†VO THE ISLAMIC REP, Zāhedān
	JAPAN
	†RADIO JAPAN/NHK, Tokyo-Yamata
	USA
	†RFE-RL, Via Kavála, Greece
	VOA, Via Philippines
9795	**CHINA**
	CHINA RADIO INTL, Xi'an
	GERMANY
	†DEUTSCHE WELLE, Via Petro-K, Russia
	HOLLAND
	†R NEDERLAND, Via Neth Antilles
	MONACO
	TRANS WORLD R, Monte Carlo
	PHILIPPINES
	†FEBC RADIO INTL, Bocaue
	RUSSIA
	VOICE OF RUSSIA, Moscow
	UNITED KINGDOM
	†WALES RADIO INTL, Rampisham
	USA
	RFE-RL, Via Biblis, Germany
	VOA, Via Philippines
	VIETNAM
	†VOICE OF VIETNAM, Via Canada
9800	**CHINA**
	CENTRAL PEOPLE'S BS, Shijiazhuang
	CONGO (DEM REP)
	†RADIO LIBERTE, Gbadolite
	EGYPT
	EGYPTIAN RADIO, Abu Za'bal
	FRANCE
	†R FRANCE INTL, Issoudun-Allouis
	†R FRANCE INTL, Via French Guiana
	GERMANY
	†DEUTSCHE WELLE, Via Samara, Russia
	HUNGARY
	†RADIO BUDAPEST, Jászberény
9805	**CANADA**
	†R CANADA INTL, Via Skelton, UK
	CLANDESTINE (AFRICA)
	†"RADIO V.O.P", Via Madagascar
	FRANCE
	†R FRANCE INTL, Issoudun-Allouis
	†R FRANCE INTL, Via Moyabi, Gabon
	†R FRANCE INTL, Via Tokyo, Japan
	GERMANY
	†DEUTSCHE WELLE, Via Irkutsk, Russia
	RUSSIA
	RADIO ROSSII, Irkutsk
	USA
	†RADIO MARTI, Delano, California
	RADIO MARTI, Greenville, NC
	†RFE-RL, Via Pals, Spain
9810	**CHINA**
	CENTRAL PEOPLE'S BS, Xi'an
	CHINA RADIO INTL, Beijing
	FRANCE
	†R FRANCE INTL, Via Irkutsk, Russia
	INDIA
(con'd)	ALL INDIA RADIO, Aligarh

World Time   0 1 2 3 4 5 6 7 8 9 10 11 12 13 14 15 16 17 18 19 20 21 22 23 24

- S • C Africa • 250 kW
- C Africa • 250 kW
- W • Australasia • 250 kW
- W Asia & S Asia • 500 kW
- E Asia • 300 kW • ALT. FREQ. TO 11910 kHz
- S • C Asia • 250 kW
- W • E Asia • 250 kW
- E Europe & W Asia • 100 kW
- W • E Asia • 200 kW
- S • Australasia • 250 kW
- S • Europe • 100 kW
- S • Su • Europe • 100 kW
- S • Sa • Europe • 100 kW
- SE Asia • 100 kW
- W • S America • 500 kW
- S • Sa • N America • 500 kW
- W • W Asia • 100 kW
- W • M-F • S Asia & SE Asia • 250 kW
- C America • 250 kW
- W North Am • 250 kW
- DS-1 • 50 kW
- Irr • S Africa
- ⇐ • Mideast • DS-GENERAL • 100 kW
- W • S America • 250 kW
- C America • 500 kW
- S • W Asia & C Asia • 200 kW
- S • N America • 250 kW
- W • E Europe • 300 kW
- W • W Europe & N Africa • 300 kW
- W • ENGLISH, ETC • S Africa • "VO THE PEOPLE" • 50 kW • ALT. FREQ. TO 7120 kHz
- W • S Asia & SE Asia • 500 kW
- S • E Europe • 250 kW
- E Europe • 500 kW
- W • E Europe • 500 kW
- E Europe • 250/500 kW
- S • E Europe • 500 kW
- W • C Africa • 250 kW
- S • E Asia • 300 kW
- W • E Asia • 500 kW
- S • E Asia • DS • 100 kW
- S • Tu-Su • C America • 250 kW
- S • C America • 250 kW
- Tu-Su • C America • 250 kW
- S • C Asia • 250 kW
- DS-2 • 50 kW
- Th/Sa-Tu • DS-2 • 50 kW
- S • DS-2 • 50 kW
- Europe • 120 kW
- W • E Asia • 250 kW
- S Asia • 250 kW

0 1 2 3 4 5 6 7 8 9 10 11 12 13 14 15 16 17 18 19 20 21 22 23 24

SEASONAL S OR W   1-HR TIMESHIFT MIDYEAR ⇐ OR ⇒   JAMMING / OR /\   EARLIEST HEARD ◁   LATEST HEARD ▷   NEW FOR 2001 †

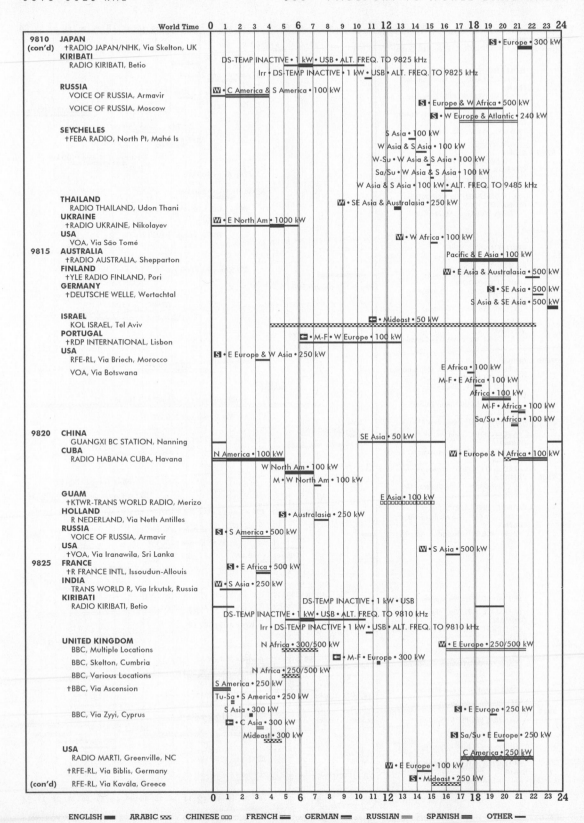

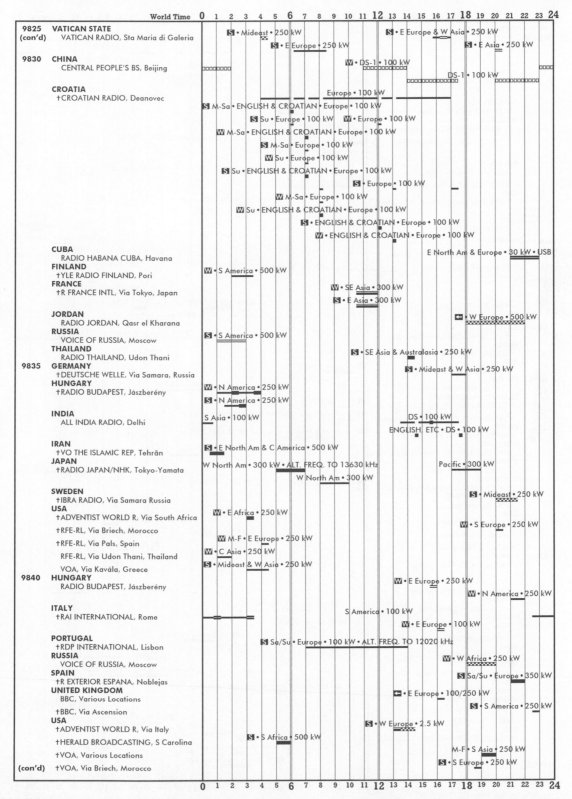

World Time																								

9825 VATICAN STATE
(con'd)   VATICAN RADIO, Sta Maria di Galeria
- S • Mideast • 250 kW
- S • E Europe • 250 kW
- S • E Europe & W Asia • 250 kW
- S • E Asia • 250 kW

9830 CHINA
CENTRAL PEOPLE'S BS, Beijing
- W • DS-1 • 100 kW
- DS-1 • 100 kW

CROATIA
†CROATIAN RADIO, Deanovec
- Europe • 100 kW
- S M-Sa • ENGLISH & CROATIAN • Europe • 100 kW
- S Su • Europe • 100 kW
- W • Europe • 100 kW
- W M-Sa • ENGLISH & CROATIAN • Europe • 100 kW
- S M-Sa • Europe • 100 kW
- W Su • Europe • 100 kW
- S Su • ENGLISH & CROATIAN • Europe • 100 kW
- S • Europe • 100 kW
- W M-Sa • Europe • 100 kW
- W Su • ENGLISH & CROATIAN • Europe • 100 kW
- S • ENGLISH & CROATIAN • Europe • 100 kW
- W • ENGLISH & CROATIAN • Europe • 100 kW

CUBA
RADIO HABANA CUBA, Havana
- E North Am & Europe • 30 kW • USB

FINLAND
†YLE RADIO FINLAND, Pori
- W • S America • 500 kW

FRANCE
†R FRANCE INTL, Via Tokyo, Japan
- W • SE Asia • 300 kW
- S • E Asia • 300 kW

JORDAN
RADIO JORDAN, Qasr el Kharana
- ☐ • W Europe • 500 kW

RUSSIA
VOICE OF RUSSIA, Moscow
- S • S America • 500 kW

THAILAND
RADIO THAILAND, Udon Thani
- S • SE Asia & Australasia • 250 kW

9835 GERMANY
†DEUTSCHE WELLE, Via Samara, Russia
- S • Mideast & W Asia • 250 kW

HUNGARY
†RADIO BUDAPEST, Jászberény
- W • N America • 250 kW
- S • N America • 250 kW

INDIA
ALL INDIA RADIO, Delhi
- S Asia • 100 kW
- DS • 100 kW
- ENGLISH, ETC • DS • 100 kW

IRAN
†VO THE ISLAMIC REP, Tehrān
- S • E North Am & C America • 500 kW

JAPAN
†RADIO JAPAN/NHK, Tokyo-Yamata
- W North Am • 300 kW • ALT. FREQ. TO 13630 kHz
- Pacific • 300 kW
- W North Am • 300 kW

SWEDEN
†IBRA RADIO, Via Samara Russia
- S • Mideast • 250 kW

USA
†ADVENTIST WORLD R, Via South Africa
- W • E Africa • 250 kW

†RFE-RL, Via Briech, Morocco
- W • S Europe • 250 kW

†RFE-RL, Via Pals, Spain
- W M-F • E Europe • 250 kW

RFE-RL, Via Udon Thani, Thailand
- W • C Asia • 250 kW

VOA, Via Kavála, Greece
- S • Mideast & W Asia • 250 kW

9840 HUNGARY
RADIO BUDAPEST, Jászberény
- W • E Europe • 250 kW
- W • N America • 250 kW

ITALY
†RAI INTERNATIONAL, Rome
- S America • 100 kW
- W • E Europe • 100 kW

PORTUGAL
†RDP INTERNATIONAL, Lisbon
- S Sa/Su • Europe • 100 kW • ALT. FREQ. TO 12020 kHz

RUSSIA
VOICE OF RUSSIA, Moscow
- W • W Africa • 250 kW

SPAIN
†R EXTERIOR ESPANA, Noblejas
- S Sa/Su • Europe • 350 kW

UNITED KINGDOM
BBC, Various Locations
- ☐ • E Europe • 100/250 kW

†BBC, Via Ascension
- S • S America • 250 kW

USA
†ADVENTIST WORLD R, Via Italy
- S • W Europe • 2.5 kW

†HERALD BROADCASTING, S Carolina
- S • S Africa • 500 kW

†VOA, Various Locations
- M-F • S Asia • 250 kW

(con'd)   †VOA, Via Briech, Morocco
- S • S Europe • 250 kW

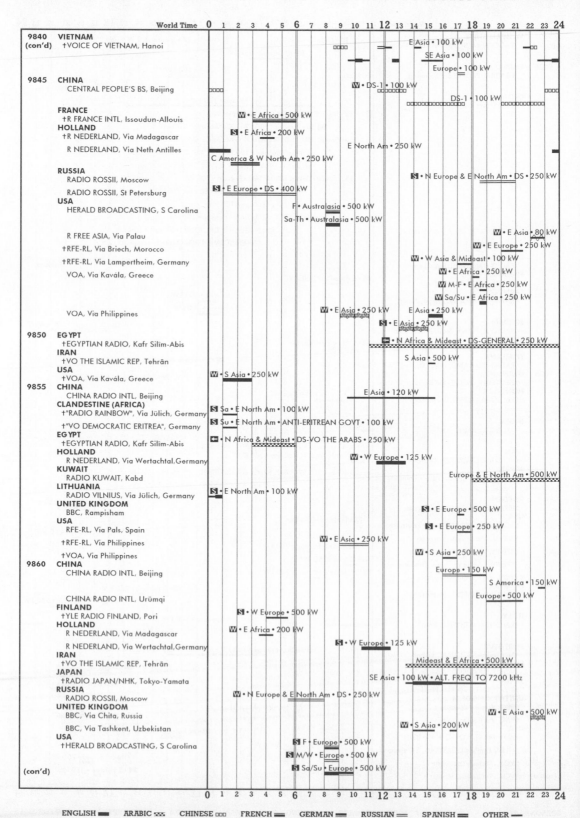

| World Time | 0 | 1 | 2 | 3 | 4 | 5 | 6 | 7 | 8 | 9 | 10 | 11 | 12 | 13 | 14 | 15 | 16 | 17 | 18 | 19 | 20 | 21 | 22 | 23 | 24 |

9840 VIETNAM
(con'd) †VOICE OF VIETNAM, Hanoi
- E Asia • 100 kW
- SE Asia • 100 kW
- Europe • 100 kW

9845 CHINA
CENTRAL PEOPLE'S BS, Beijing
- W • DS-1 • 100 kW
- DS-1 • 100 kW

FRANCE
†R FRANCE INTL, Issoudun-Allouis
- W • E Africa • 500 kW

HOLLAND
†R NEDERLAND, Via Madagascar
- S • E Africa • 200 kW

R NEDERLAND, Via Neth Antilles
- E North Am • 250 kW
- C America & W North Am • 250 kW

RUSSIA
RADIO ROSSII, Moscow
- S • N Europe & E North Am • DS • 250 kW

RADIO ROSSII, St Petersburg
- S • E Europe • DS • 400 kW

USA
HERALD BROADCASTING, S Carolina
- F • Australasia • 500 kW
- Sa-Th • Australasia • 500 kW

R FREE ASIA, Via Palau
- W • E Asia • 80 kW

†RFE-RL, Via Briech, Morocco
- W • E Europe • 250 kW

†RFE-RL, Via Lampertheim, Germany
- W • W Asia & Mideast • 100 kW

VOA, Via Kavála, Greece
- W • E Africa • 250 kW
- W M-F • E Africa • 250 kW
- W Sa/Su • E Africa • 250 kW

VOA, Via Philippines
- W • E Asia • 250 kW
- E Asia • 250 kW
- S • E Asia • 250 kW

9850 EGYPT
†EGYPTIAN RADIO, Kafr Silim-Abis
- N Africa & Mideast • DS-GENERAL • 250 kW

IRAN
†VO THE ISLAMIC REP, Tehrän
- S Asia • 500 kW

USA
†VOA, Via Kavála, Greece
- W • S Asia • 250 kW

9855 CHINA
CHINA RADIO INTL, Beijing
- E Asia • 120 kW

CLANDESTINE (AFRICA)
†"RADIO RAINBOW", Via Jülich, Germany
- S Sa • E North Am • 100 kW

†"VO DEMOCRATIC ERITREA", Germany
- S Su • E North Am • ANTI-ERITREAN GOVT • 100 kW

EGYPT
†EGYPTIAN RADIO, Kafr Silim-Abis
- N Africa & Mideast • DS-VO THE ARABS • 250 kW

HOLLAND
R NEDERLAND, Via Wertachtal, Germany
- W • W Europe • 125 kW

KUWAIT
RADIO KUWAIT, Kabd
- Europe & E North Am • 500 kW

LITHUANIA
RADIO VILNIUS, Via Jülich, Germany
- S • E North Am • 100 kW

UNITED KINGDOM
BBC, Rampisham
- S • E Europe • 500 kW

USA
RFE-RL, Via Pals, Spain
- S • E Europe • 250 kW

†RFE-RL, Via Philippines
- W • E Asia • 250 kW

†VOA, Via Philippines
- W • S Asia • 250 kW

9860 CHINA
CHINA RADIO INTL, Beijing
- Europe • 150 kW
- S America • 150 kW

CHINA RADIO INTL, Urümqi
- Europe • 500 kW

FINLAND
†YLE RADIO FINLAND, Pori
- S • W Europe • 500 kW

HOLLAND
R NEDERLAND, Via Madagascar
- W • E Africa • 200 kW

R NEDERLAND, Via Wertachtal, Germany
- S • W Europe • 125 kW

IRAN
†VO THE ISLAMIC REP, Tehrän
- Mideast & E Africa • 500 kW

JAPAN
†RADIO JAPAN/NHK, Tokyo-Yamata
- SE Asia • 100 kW • ALT. FREQ TO 7200 kHz

RUSSIA
RADIO ROSSII, Moscow
- W • N Europe & E North Am • DS • 250 kW

UNITED KINGDOM
BBC, Via Chita, Russia
- W • E Asia • 500 kW

BBC, Via Tashkent, Uzbekistan
- W • S Asia • 200 kW

USA
†HERALD BROADCASTING, S Carolina
- S F • Europe • 500 kW
- S M/W • Europe • 500 kW
- S Sa/Su • Europe • 500 kW

(con'd)

| | 0 | 1 | 2 | 3 | 4 | 5 | 6 | 7 | 8 | 9 | 10 | 11 | 12 | 13 | 14 | 15 | 16 | 17 | 18 | 19 | 20 | 21 | 22 | 23 | 24 |

ENGLISH ▬   ARABIC ▨   CHINESE □□□   FRENCH ═   GERMAN ▬   RUSSIAN ═   SPANISH ═   OTHER ▬

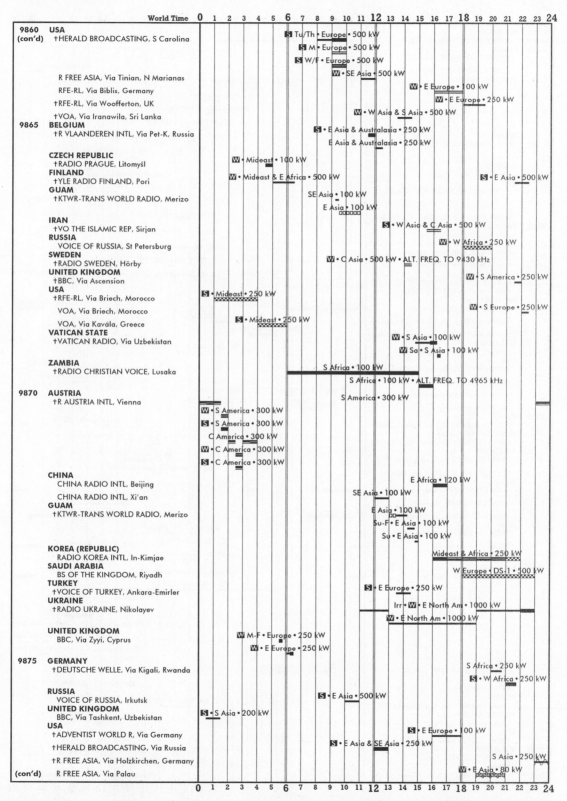

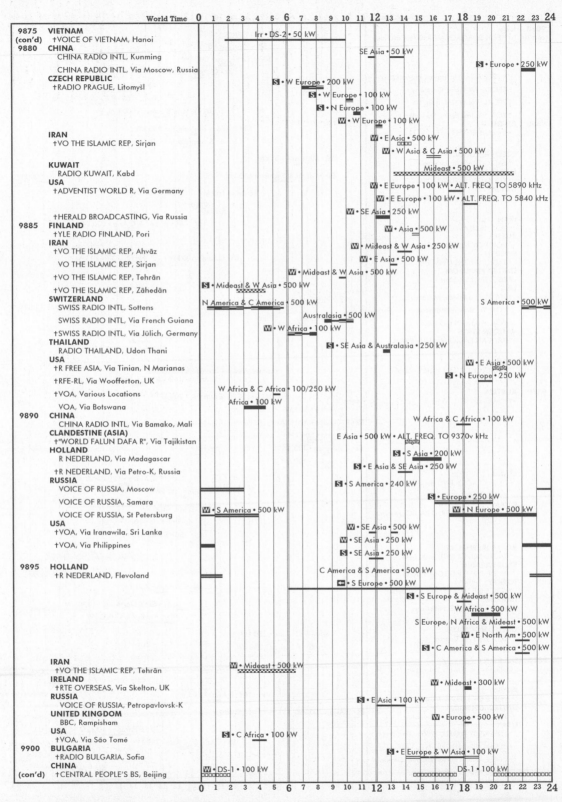

	World Time	0 1 2 3 4 5 6 7 8 9 10 11 12 13 14 15 16 17 18 19 20 21 22 23 24
9875 (con'd)	VIETNAM †VOICE OF VIETNAM, Hanoi	Irr • DS-2 • 50 kW
9880	CHINA CHINA RADIO INTL, Kunming	SE Asia • 50 kW
	CHINA RADIO INTL, Via Moscow, Russia	S • Europe • 250 kW
	CZECH REPUBLIC †RADIO PRAGUE, Litomyšl	S • W Europe • 200 kW
		S • W Europe • 100 kW
		S • N Europe • 100 kW
		W • W Europe • 100 kW
	IRAN †VO THE ISLAMIC REP, Sirjan	W • E Asia • 500 kW
		W • W Asia & C Asia • 500 kW
	KUWAIT RADIO KUWAIT, Kabd	Mideast • 500 kW
	USA †ADVENTIST WORLD R, Via Germany	W • E Europe • 100 kW • ALT. FREQ. TO 5890 kHz
		W • E Europe • 100 kW • ALT. FREQ. TO 5840 kHz
	†HERALD BROADCASTING, Via Russia	W • SE Asia • 250 kW
9885	FINLAND †YLE RADIO FINLAND, Pori	W • Asia • 500 kW
	IRAN †VO THE ISLAMIC REP, Ahvāz	W • Mideast & W Asia • 250 kW
	VO THE ISLAMIC REP, Sirjan	W • E Asia • 500 kW
	†VO THE ISLAMIC REP, Tehrān	W • Mideast & W Asia • 500 kW
	†VO THE ISLAMIC REP, Zāhedān	S • Mideast & W Asia • 500 kW
	SWITZERLAND SWISS RADIO INTL, Sottens	N America & C America • 500 kW S America • 500 kW
	SWISS RADIO INTL, Via French Guiana	Australasia • 500 kW
	†SWISS RADIO INTL, Via Jülich, Germany	W • W Africa • 100 kW
	THAILAND RADIO THAILAND, Udon Thani	S • SE Asia & Australasia • 250 kW
	USA †R FREE ASIA, Via Tinian, N Marianas	W • E Asia • 500 kW
	†RFE-RL, Via Woofferton, UK	S • N Europe • 250 kW
	†VOA, Various Locations	W Africa & C Africa • 100/250 kW
	VOA, Via Botswana	Africa • 100 kW
9890	CHINA CHINA RADIO INTL, Via Bamako, Mali	W Africa & C Africa • 100 kW
	CLANDESTINE (ASIA) †"WORLD FALUN DAFA R", Via Tajikistan	E Asia • 500 kW • ALT. FREQ. TO 9370v kHz
	HOLLAND R NEDERLAND, Via Madagascar	S • S Asia • 200 kW
	†R NEDERLAND, Via Petro-K, Russia	S • E Asia & SE Asia • 250 kW
	RUSSIA VOICE OF RUSSIA, Moscow	S • S America • 240 kW
	VOICE OF RUSSIA, Samara	S • Europe • 250 kW
	VOICE OF RUSSIA, St Petersburg	W • S America • 500 kW W • N Europe • 500 kW
	USA †VOA, Via Iranawila, Sri Lanka	W • SE Asia • 500 kW
	†VOA, Via Philippines	W • SE Asia • 250 kW
		S • SE Asia • 250 kW
9895	HOLLAND †R NEDERLAND, Flevoland	C America & S America • 500 kW
		← • S Europe • 500 kW
		S • S Europe & Mideast • 500 kW
		W Africa • 500 kW
		S Europe, N Africa & Mideast • 500 kW
		W • E North Am • 500 kW
		S • C America & S America • 500 kW
	IRAN †VO THE ISLAMIC REP, Tehrān	W • Mideast • 500 kW
	IRELAND †RTE OVERSEAS, Via Skelton, UK	W • Mideast • 300 kW
	RUSSIA VOICE OF RUSSIA, Petropavlovsk-K	S • E Asia • 100 kW
	UNITED KINGDOM BBC, Rampisham	W • Europe • 500 kW
	USA †VOA, Via São Tomé	S • C Africa • 100 kW
9900	BULGARIA †RADIO BULGARIA, Sofia	S • E Europe & W Asia • 100 kW
	CHINA	W • DS-1 • 100 kW DS-1 • 100 kW
(con'd)	†CENTRAL PEOPLE'S BS, Beijing	

ENGLISH ▬   ARABIC ▨   CHINESE ▱   FRENCH ═   GERMAN ▬   RUSSIAN ═   SPANISH ═   OTHER ─

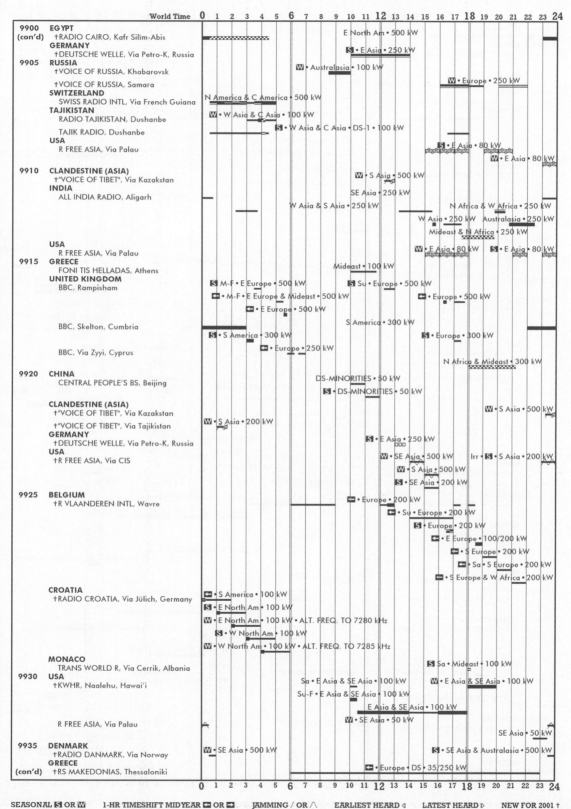

World Time 0 1 2 3 4 5 6 7 8 9 10 11 12 13 14 15 16 17 18 19 20 21 22 23 24

9900
(con'd) †RADIO CAIRO, Kafr Silim-Abis — E North Am • 500 kW
EGYPT
GERMANY †DEUTSCHE WELLE, Via Petro-K, Russia — ⑤ • E Asia • 250 kW
9905 RUSSIA †VOICE OF RUSSIA, Khabarovsk — Ⓦ • Australasia • 100 kW
  †VOICE OF RUSSIA, Samara — Ⓦ • Europe • 250 kW
SWITZERLAND SWISS RADIO INTL, Via French Guiana — N America & C America • 500 kW
TAJIKISTAN RADIO TAJIKISTAN, Dushanbe — Ⓦ • W Asia & C Asia • 100 kW
  TAJIK RADIO, Dushanbe — ⑤ • W Asia & C Asia • DS-1 • 100 kW
USA R FREE ASIA, Via Palau — ⑤ • E Asia • 80 kW / Ⓦ • E Asia • 80 kW

9910 CLANDESTINE (ASIA) †"VOICE OF TIBET", Via Kazakstan — Ⓦ • S Asia • 500 kW
INDIA ALL INDIA RADIO, Aligarh — SE Asia • 250 kW
  W Asia & S Asia • 250 kW
  N Africa & W Africa • 250 kW
  W Asia • 250 kW Australasia • 250 kW
  Mideast & N Africa • 250 kW
USA R FREE ASIA, Via Palau — Ⓦ • E Asia • 80 kW ⑤ • E Asia • 80 kW
9915 GREECE FONI TIS HELLADAS, Athens — Mideast • 100 kW
UNITED KINGDOM BBC, Rampisham — ⑤ • M-F • E Europe • 500 kW ⑤ • Su • Europe • 500 kW
  ⮐ • M-F • E Europe & Mideast • 500 kW ⮐ • Europe • 500 kW
  ⮐ • E Europe • 500 kW
  BBC, Skelton, Cumbria — S America • 300 kW ⑤ • Europe • 300 kW
  ⑤ • S America • 300 kW
  BBC, Via Zyyi, Cyprus — ⮐ • Europe • 250 kW
  N Africa & Mideast • 300 kW

9920 CHINA CENTRAL PEOPLE'S BS, Beijing — DS-MINORITIES • 50 kW
  ⑤ • DS-MINORITIES • 50 kW
CLANDESTINE (ASIA) †"VOICE OF TIBET", Via Kazakstan — Ⓦ • S Asia • 500 kW
  †"VOICE OF TIBET", Via Tajikistan — Ⓦ • S Asia • 200 kW
GERMANY †DEUTSCHE WELLE, Via Petro-K, Russia — ⑤ • E Asia • 250 kW
USA †R FREE ASIA, Via CIS — Ⓦ • SE Asia • 500 kW Irr • ⑤ • S Asia • 200 kW
  Ⓦ • S Asia • 500 kW
  ⑤ • SE Asia • 200 kW

9925 BELGIUM †R VLAANDEREN INTL, Wavre — ⮐ • Europe • 200 kW
  ⮐ • Su • Europe • 200 kW
  ⑤ • Europe • 200 kW
  ⮐ • E Europe • 100/200 kW
  ⮐ • S Europe • 200 kW
  ⮐ • Sa • S Europe • 200 kW
  ⑤ • S Europe & W Africa • 200 kW

CROATIA †RADIO CROATIA, Via Jülich, Germany — ⮐ • S America • 100 kW
  ⑤ • E North Am • 100 kW
  Ⓦ • E North Am • 100 kW • ALT. FREQ. TO 7280 kHz
  ⑤ • W North Am • 100 kW
  Ⓦ • W North Am • 100 kW • ALT. FREQ. TO 7285 kHz

MONACO TRANS WORLD R, Via Cerrik, Albania — ⑤ • Sa • Mideast • 100 kW
9930 USA †KWHR, Naalehu, Hawai'i — Sa • E Asia & SE Asia • 100 kW Ⓦ • E Asia & SE Asia • 100 kW
  Su-F • E Asia & SE Asia • 100 kW
  E Asia & SE Asia • 100 kW
  R FREE ASIA, Via Palau — Ⓦ • SE Asia • 50 kW
  SE Asia • 50 kW

9935 DENMARK †RADIO DANMARK, Via Norway — Ⓦ • SE Asia • 500 kW ⑤ • SE Asia & Australasia • 500 kW
GREECE
(con'd) †RS MAKEDONIAS, Thessaloniki — ⮐ • Europe • DS • 35/250 kW

0 1 2 3 4 5 6 7 8 9 10 11 12 13 14 15 16 17 18 19 20 21 22 23 24

SEASONAL ⑤ OR Ⓦ 1-HR TIMESHIFT MIDYEAR ⮐ OR ⮕ JAMMING / OR /\ EARLIEST HEARD ◁ LATEST HEARD ▷ NEW FOR 2001 †

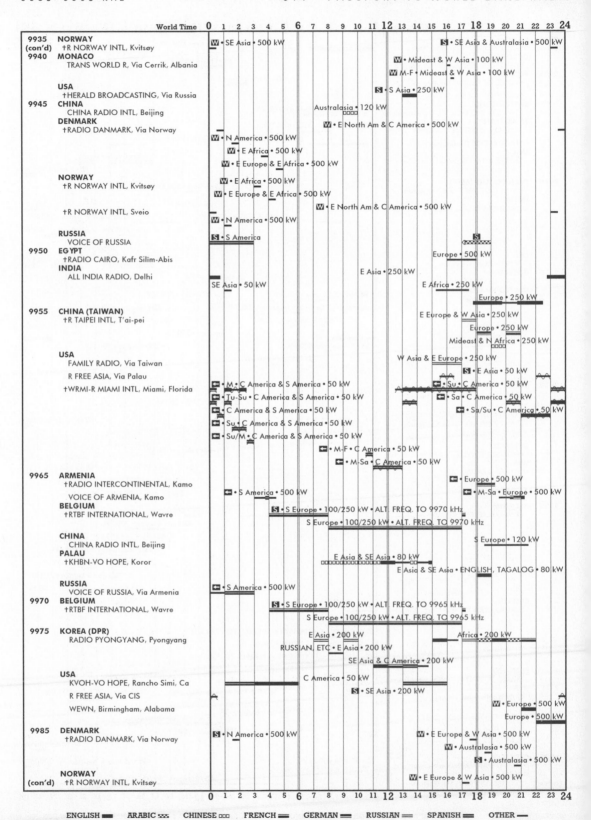

World Time 0 1 2 3 4 5 6 7 8 9 10 11 12 13 14 15 16 17 18 19 20 21 22 23 24

9935 **NORWAY**
(con'd) †R NORWAY INTL, Kvitsøy — W • SE Asia • 500 kW / S • SE Asia & Australasia • 500 kW
9940 **MONACO**
TRANS WORLD R, Via Cerrik, Albania — W • Mideast & W Asia • 100 kW / W • M-F • Mideast & W Asia • 100 kW

USA
†HERALD BROADCASTING, Via Russia — S • S Asia • 250 kW
9945 **CHINA**
CHINA RADIO INTL, Beijing — Australasia • 120 kW
DENMARK
†RADIO DANMARK, Via Norway — W • E North Am & C America • 500 kW
W • N America • 500 kW
W • E Africa • 500 kW
W • E Europe & E Africa • 500 kW

NORWAY
†R NORWAY INTL, Kvitsøy — W • E Africa • 500 kW
W • E Europe & E Africa • 500 kW

†R NORWAY INTL, Sveio — W • E North Am & C America • 500 kW
W • N America • 500 kW

RUSSIA
VOICE OF RUSSIA — S • S America
9950 **EGYPT**
†RADIO CAIRO, Kafr Silim-Abis — Europe • 500 kW
INDIA
ALL INDIA RADIO, Delhi — E Asia • 250 kW
SE Asia • 50 kW
E Africa • 250 kW
Europe • 250 kW

9955 **CHINA (TAIWAN)**
†R TAIPEI INTL, T'ai-pei — E Europe & W Asia • 250 kW
Europe • 250 kW
Mideast & N Africa • 250 kW

USA
FAMILY RADIO, Via Taiwan — W Asia & E Europe • 250 kW
R FREE ASIA, Via Palau — S • E Asia • 50 kW
†WRMI-R MIAMI INTL, Miami, Florida — M • C America & S America • 50 kW / Su • C America • 50 kW
Tu-Su • C America & S America • 50 kW / Sa • C America • 50 kW
C America & S America • 50 kW / Sa/Su • C America • 50 kW
Su • C America & S America • 50 kW
Su/M • C America & S America • 50 kW
M-F • C America • 50 kW
M-Sa • C America • 50 kW

9965 **ARMENIA**
†RADIO INTERCONTINENTAL, Kamo — Europe • 500 kW
VOICE OF ARMENIA, Kamo — S America • 500 kW / M-Sa • Europe • 500 kW
BELGIUM
†RTBF INTERNATIONAL, Wavre — S • S Europe • 100/250 kW • ALT. FREQ. TO 9970 kHz
S Europe • 100/250 kW • ALT. FREQ. TO 9970 kHz

CHINA
CHINA RADIO INTL, Beijing — S Europe • 120 kW
PALAU
†KHBN-VO HOPE, Koror — E Asia & SE Asia • 80 kW
E Asia & SE Asia • ENGLISH, TAGALOG • 80 kW

RUSSIA
VOICE OF RUSSIA, Via Armenia — S America • 500 kW
9970 **BELGIUM**
†RTBF INTERNATIONAL, Wavre — S • S Europe • 100/250 kW • ALT. FREQ. TO 9965 kHz
S Europe • 100/250 kW • ALT. FREQ. TO 9965 kHz

9975 **KOREA (DPR)**
RADIO PYONGYANG, Pyongyang — E Asia • 200 kW / Africa • 200 kW
RUSSIAN, ETC • E Asia • 200 kW
SE Asia & C America • 200 kW

USA
KVOH-VO HOPE, Rancho Simi, Ca — C America • 50 kW
R FREE ASIA, Via CIS — S • SE Asia • 200 kW
WEWN, Birmingham, Alabama — W • Europe • 500 kW
Europe • 500 kW

9985 **DENMARK**
†RADIO DANMARK, Via Norway — S • N America • 500 kW / W • E Europe & W Asia • 500 kW
W • Australasia • 500 kW
S • Australasia • 500 kW

NORWAY
(con'd) †R NORWAY INTL, Kvitsøy — W • E Europe & W Asia • 500 kW

0 1 2 3 4 5 6 7 8 9 10 11 12 13 14 15 16 17 18 19 20 21 22 23 24

ENGLISH ▬ ARABIC ▨ CHINESE □□□ FRENCH ▦ GERMAN ▬ RUSSIAN ═ SPANISH ▭ OTHER ▬

World Time 0 1 2 3 4 5 6 7 8 9 10 11 12 13 14 15 16 17 18 19 20 21 22 23 24

9985 (con'd)	**NORWAY** †R NORWAY INTL, Kvitsøy	W • Australasia • 500 kW S • Australasia • 500 kW
	USA †WYFR-FAMILY RADIO, Okeechobee, Fl	W • S America • 100 kW W • Europe • 100 kW S • Europe • 100 kW W • W Africa • 100 kW
9988	**EGYPT** †RADIO CAIRO, Kafr Silim-Abis	Europe • 500 kW
9990	**EGYPT** †RADIO CAIRO, Kafr Silim-Abis	Europe • 500 kW
10000	**USA** WWV, Fort Collins, Colorado	WEATHER/WORLD TIME • 10 kW
	WWVH, Kekaha, Hawai'i	WEATHER/WORLD TIME • 10 kW
10320	**USA** †AFRTS	Irr • Atlantic • USB • ALT. FREQ. TO 6350 kHz
10330	**INDIA** ALL INDIA RADIO, Multiple Locations	DS • 50/100 kW
10869	**USA** †VOA, Greenville, NC	S • Sa • Europe • USB/LSB • 40 kW
10940.5	**USA** †AFRTS, Via Sigonella, Italy	Europe & N Africa • USB • ALT. FREQ. TO 4993 kHz
11000	**CHINA** CENTRAL PEOPLE'S BS, Beijing	S • CHINESE, ETC • NETWORK 6 • 50 kW CHINESE, ETC • NETWORK 6 • 50 kW W-M • CHINESE, ETC • NETWORK 6 • 50 kW
11092.5	**ST HELENA** RADIO ST HELENA, Jamestown	Irr • SPECIAL EVENTS • 1.5 kW • USB
11100	**CHINA** CENTRAL PEOPLE'S BS, Beijing	CHINESE, ETC • TAIWAN SERVICE • 50 kW • ALT. FREQ. TO 11680 kHz S • CHINESE, ETC • TAIWAN SERVICE • 50 kW
11335	**KOREA (DPR)** RADIO PYONGYANG, Kujang-dong	N America • 200 kW SE Asia & C America • 200 kW
11402	**ICELAND** †RIKISUTVARPID, Reykjavik	Atlantic & E North Am • DS-1 • 10 kW • ALT. FREQ. TO 12115 kHz Atlantic & Europe • DS-1 • 10 kW • ALT. FREQ. TO 12115 kHz
11481	**PIRATE (EUROPE)** "RADIO BANDONICA", Holland	Irr • Su • W Europe • 0.1 kW
11485v	**PIRATE (EUROPE)** †"R EAST COAST HOLLAND", Holland	Irr • Su • 0.05 kW 　　　　Irr • Sa • 0.05 kW
11500	**RUSSIA** †VOICE OF RUSSIA, Via Tajikistan	S • S Asia • 500 kW
	†VOICE OF RUSSIA, Via Xi'an, China	SE Asia • 100 kW
	USA †R FREE ASIA	W • E Asia
11510	**USA** †R FREE ASIA, Via CIS	W • SE Asia • 200 kW S • SE Asia • 500 kW S • S Asia • 500 kW
11520	**USA** †R FREE ASIA, Via CIS	S • C Asia • 250 kW 　　SE Asia • 200/500 kW W • S Asia • 500 kW S • E Asia • 500 kW
11530	**USA** R FREE ASIA, Via CIS	S • SE Asia • 200 kW
11535	**USA** †R FREE ASIA, Via CIS	W • SE Asia • 100 kW 　　SE Asia • 100/200 kW
11540	**USA** †R FREE ASIA, Via CIS	S • SE Asia • 200 kW W • S Asia • 100 kW
11550	**AUSTRALIA** †RADIO AUSTRALIA, Via Taiwan	M-F • SE Asia • 250 kW　　　SE Asia • 250 kW Sa/Su • SE Asia • 250 kW
	CHINA (TAIWAN) †R TAIPEI INTL, T'ai-pei	E Asia • 100 kW　　　E Asia • 250 kW SE Asia • 100 kW
	USA †ADVENTIST WORLD R, Via Agat, Guam	W • Mideast • 100 kW
	FAMILY RADIO, Via Taiwan	S Asia • 250 kW
	†HERALD BROADCASTING, S Carolina	W M/W/Sa • W Europe • 500 kW W Su/Tu/F • W Europe • 500 kW W Th • W Europe • 500 kW W Tu/F • W Europe • 500 kW
(con'd)		

0 1 2 3 4 5 6 7 8 9 10 11 12 13 14 15 16 17 18 19 20 21 22 23 24

SEASONAL S OR W　　1-HR TIMESHIFT MIDYEAR ➡ OR ⬅　　JAMMING / OR /\　　EARLIEST HEARD ◁　　LATEST HEARD ▷　　NEW FOR 2001 †

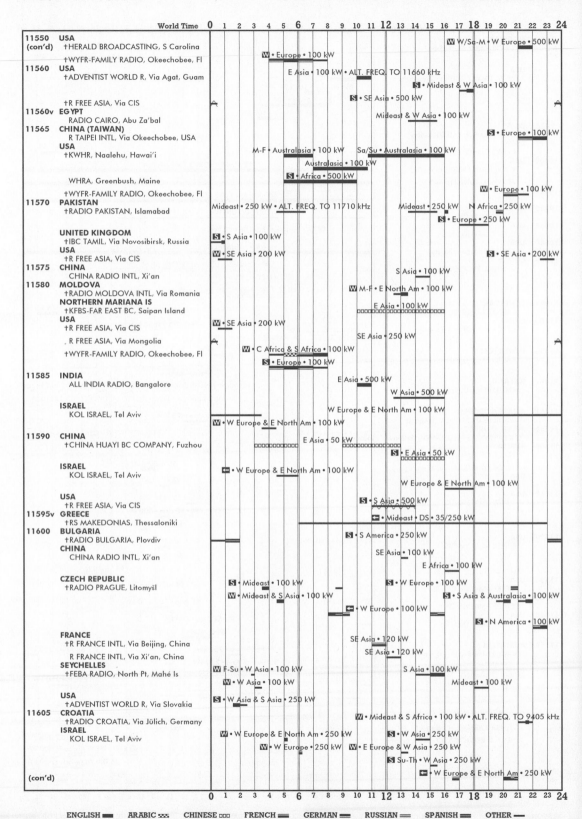

World Time	0 1 2 3 4 5 6 7 8 9 10 11 12 13 14 15 16 17 18 19 20 21 22 23 24

11550 USA
(con'd) †HERALD BROADCASTING, S Carolina — W • W/Sa-M • W Europe • 500 kW
         †WYFR-FAMILY RADIO, Okeechobee, Fl — W • Europe • 100 kW

11560 USA
         †ADVENTIST WORLD R, Via Agat, Guam — E Asia • 100 kW • ALT. FREQ. TO 11660 kHz
                                              S • Mideast & W Asia • 100 kW
         †R FREE ASIA, Via CIS — S • SE Asia • 500 kW

11560v EGYPT
         RADIO CAIRO, Abu Za'bal — Mideast & W Asia • 100 kW

11565 CHINA (TAIWAN)
         R TAIPEI INTL, Via Okeechobee, USA — S • Europe • 100 kW
         USA
         †KWHR, Naalehu, Hawai'i — M-F • Australasia • 100 kW   Sa/Su • Australasia • 100 kW
                                   Australasia • 100 kW
         WHRA, Greenbush, Maine — S • Africa • 500 kW
         †WYFR-FAMILY RADIO, Okeechobee, Fl — W • Europe • 100 kW

11570 PAKISTAN
         †RADIO PAKISTAN, Islamabad — Mideast • 250 kW • ALT. FREQ. TO 11710 kHz   Mideast • 250 kW   N Africa • 250 kW
                                      S • Europe • 250 kW
         UNITED KINGDOM
         †IBC TAMIL, Via Novosibirsk, Russia — S • S Asia • 100 kW
         USA
         †R FREE ASIA, Via CIS — W • SE Asia • 200 kW   S • SE Asia • 200 kW

11575 CHINA
         CHINA RADIO INTL, Xi'an — S Asia • 100 kW

11580 MOLDOVA
         †RADIO MOLDOVA INTL, Via Romania — W • M-F • E North Am • 100 kW
         NORTHERN MARIANA IS
         †KFBS-FAR EAST BC, Saipan Island — E Asia • 100 kW
         USA
         †R FREE ASIA, Via CIS — W • SE Asia • 200 kW
         R FREE ASIA, Via Mongolia — SE Asia • 250 kW
         †WYFR-FAMILY RADIO, Okeechobee, Fl — W • C Africa & S Africa • 100 kW
                                              S • Europe • 100 kW

11585 INDIA
         ALL INDIA RADIO, Bangalore — E Asia • 500 kW
                                      W Asia • 500 kW
         ISRAEL
         KOL ISRAEL, Tel Aviv — W Europe & E North Am • 100 kW
                                W • W Europe & E North Am • 100 kW

11590 CHINA
         †CHINA HUAYI BC COMPANY, Fuzhou — E Asia • 50 kW   S • E Asia • 50 kW
         ISRAEL
         KOL ISRAEL, Tel Aviv — • W Europe & E North Am • 100 kW
                                W Europe & E North Am • 100 kW
         USA
         †R FREE ASIA, Via CIS — S • S Asia • 500 kW

11595v GREECE
         †RS MAKEDONIAS, Thessaloniki — • Mideast • DS • 35/250 kW

11600 BULGARIA
         †RADIO BULGARIA, Plovdiv — S • S America • 250 kW
         CHINA
         CHINA RADIO INTL, Xi'an — SE Asia • 100 kW
                                   E Africa • 100 kW
         CZECH REPUBLIC
         †RADIO PRAGUE, Litomyšl — S • Mideast • 100 kW   S • W Europe • 100 kW
                                   W • Mideast & S Asia • 100 kW   S • S Asia & Australasia • 100 kW
                                                                • W Europe • 100 kW
                                                                S • N America • 100 kW
         FRANCE
         †R FRANCE INTL, Via Beijing, China — SE Asia • 120 kW
         R FRANCE INTL, Via Xi'an, China — SE Asia • 120 kW
         SEYCHELLES
         †FEBA RADIO, North Pt, Mahé Is — W • F-Su • W Asia • 100 kW   S Asia • 100 kW
                                          W • W Asia • 100 kW   Mideast • 100 kW
         USA
         †ADVENTIST WORLD R, Via Slovakia — S • W Asia & S Asia • 250 kW

11605 CROATIA
         †RADIO CROATIA, Via Jülich, Germany — W • Mideast & S Africa • 100 kW • ALT. FREQ. TO 9405 kHz
         ISRAEL
         KOL ISRAEL, Tel Aviv — W • W Europe & E North Am • 250 kW   S • W Asia • 250 kW
                                W • W Europe • 250 kW   W • E Europe & W Asia • 250 kW
                                                          S • Su-Th • W Asia • 250 kW
                                                          • W Europe & E North Am • 250 kW

(con'd)

0 1 2 3 4 5 6 7 8 9 10 11 12 13 14 15 16 17 18 19 20 21 22 23 24

ENGLISH ▬▬   ARABIC ▨▨   CHINESE □□□   FRENCH ══   GERMAN ▬▬   RUSSIAN ══   SPANISH ══   OTHER ──

World Time 0 1 2 3 4 5 6 7 8 9 10 11 12 13 14 15 16 17 18 19 20 21 22 23 24

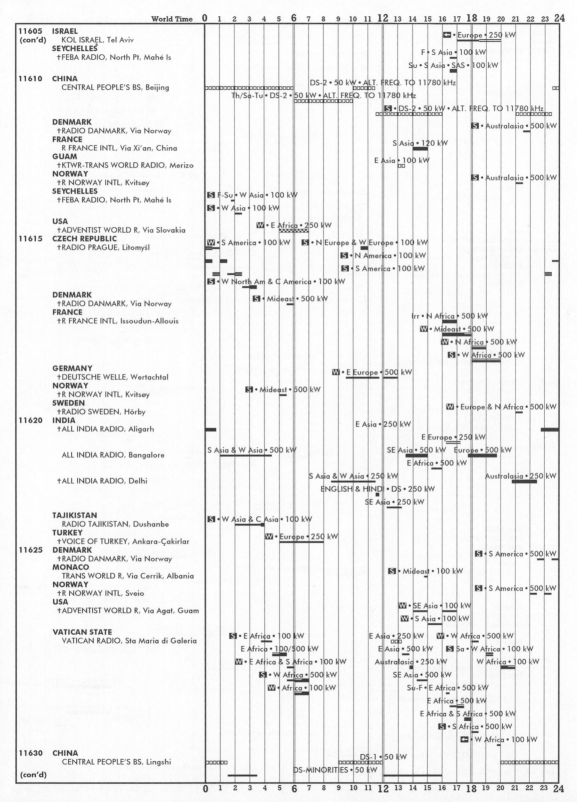

11605 ISRAEL
(con'd) KOL ISRAEL, Tel Aviv — ▰ • Europe • 250 kW
SEYCHELLES
†FEBA RADIO, North Pt, Mahé Is — F • S Asia • 100 kW
Su • S Asia • SAS • 100 kW

11610 CHINA
CENTRAL PEOPLE'S BS, Beijing — DS-2 • 50 kW • ALT. FREQ. TO 11780 kHz
Th/Sa-Tu • DS-2 • 50 kW • ALT. FREQ. TO 11780 kHz
S • DS-2 • 50 kW • ALT. FREQ. TO 11780 kHz
DENMARK
†RADIO DANMARK, Via Norway — S • Australasia • 500 kW
FRANCE
R FRANCE INTL, Via Xi'an, China — S Asia • 120 kW
GUAM
†KTWR-TRANS WORLD RADIO, Merizo — E Asia • 100 kW
NORWAY
†R NORWAY INTL, Kvitsøy — S • Australasia • 500 kW
SEYCHELLES
†FEBA RADIO, North Pt, Mahé Is — S • F-Su • W Asia • 100 kW
S • W Asia • 100 kW
USA
†ADVENTIST WORLD R, Via Slovakia — W • E Africa • 250 kW

11615 CZECH REPUBLIC
†RADIO PRAGUE, Litomyšl — W • S America • 100 kW   S • N Europe & W Europe • 100 kW
S • N America • 100 kW
S • S America • 100 kW
S • W North Am & C America • 100 kW
DENMARK
†RADIO DANMARK, Via Norway — S • Mideast • 500 kW
FRANCE
†R FRANCE INTL, Issoudun-Allouis — Irr • N Africa • 500 kW
W • Mideast • 500 kW
W • N Africa • 500 kW
S • W Africa • 500 kW
GERMANY
†DEUTSCHE WELLE, Wertachtal — W • E Europe • 500 kW
NORWAY
†R NORWAY INTL, Kvitsøy — S • Mideast • 500 kW
SWEDEN
†RADIO SWEDEN, Hörby — W • Europe & N Africa • 500 kW

11620 INDIA
†ALL INDIA RADIO, Aligarh — E Asia • 250 kW
E Europe • 250 kW
ALL INDIA RADIO, Bangalore — S Asia & W Asia • 500 kW   SE Asia • 500 kW   Europe • 500 kW
E Africa • 500 kW
†ALL INDIA RADIO, Delhi — S Asia & W Asia • 250 kW   Australasia • 250 kW
ENGLISH & HINDI • DS • 250 kW
SE Asia • 250 kW
TAJIKISTAN
RADIO TAJIKISTAN, Dushanbe — S • W Asia & C Asia • 100 kW
TURKEY
†VOICE OF TURKEY, Ankara-Çakirlar — W • Europe • 250 kW

11625 DENMARK
†RADIO DANMARK, Via Norway — S • S America • 500 kW
MONACO
TRANS WORLD R, Via Cerrik, Albania — S • Mideast • 100 kW
NORWAY
†R NORWAY INTL, Sveio — S • S America • 500 kW
USA
†ADVENTIST WORLD R, Via Agat, Guam — W • SE Asia • 100 kW
W • S Asia • 100 kW
VATICAN STATE
VATICAN RADIO, Sta Maria di Galeria — S • E Africa • 100 kW   E Asia • 250 kW   W • W Africa • 500 kW
E Africa • 100/500 kW   E Asia • 500 kW   S • Sa • W Africa • 100 kW
W • E Africa & S Africa • 100 kW   Australasia • 250 kW   W Africa • 100 kW
S • W Africa • 500 kW   SE Asia • 500 kW
W • Africa • 100 kW   Su-F • E Africa • 500 kW
E Africa • 500 kW
E Africa & S Africa • 500 kW
S • S Africa • 500 kW
▰ • W Africa • 100 kW

11630 CHINA
CENTRAL PEOPLE'S BS, Lingshi — DS-1 • 50 kW
(con'd) DS-MINORITIES • 50 kW

World Time 0 1 2 3 4 5 6 7 8 9 10 11 12 13 14 15 16 17 18 19 20 21 22 23 24

SEASONAL S OR W   1-HR TIMESHIFT MIDYEAR ▰ OR ▱   JAMMING / OR /\   EARLIEST HEARD ◁   LATEST HEARD ▷   NEW FOR 2001 †

World Time 0 1 2 3 4 5 6 7 8 9 10 11 12 13 14 15 16 17 18 19 20 21 22 23 24

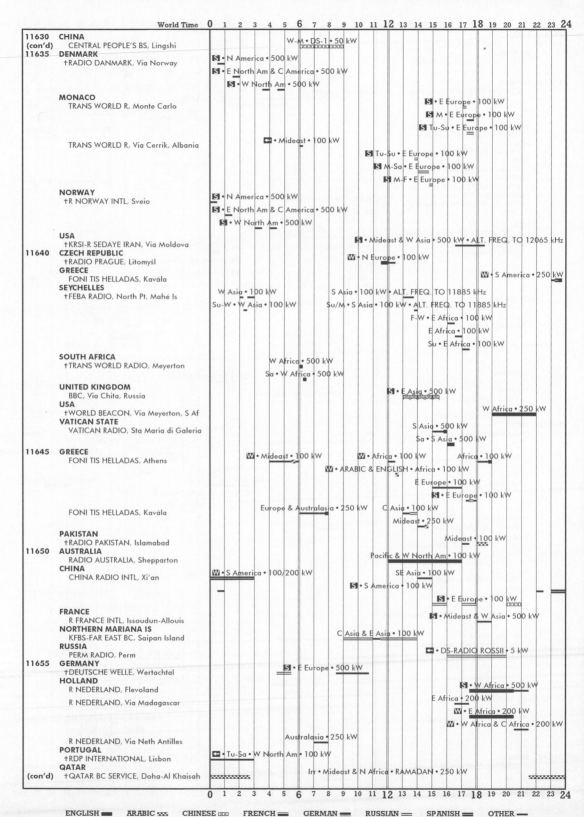

Frequency	Station	Schedule
11630 (con'd)	CHINA CENTRAL PEOPLE'S BS, Lingshi	W-M • DS-1 • 50 kW
11635	DENMARK †RADIO DANMARK, Via Norway	S • N America • 500 kW S • E North Am & C America • 500 kW S • W North Am • 500 kW
	MONACO TRANS WORLD R, Monte Carlo	S • E Europe • 100 kW S M • E Europe • 100 kW S Tu-Su • E Europe • 100 kW
	TRANS WORLD R, Via Cerrik, Albania	• Mideast • 100 kW S Tu-Su • E Europe • 100 kW S M-Sa • E Europe • 100 kW S M-F • E Europe • 100 kW
	NORWAY †R NORWAY INTL, Sveio	S • N America • 500 kW S • E North Am & C America • 500 kW S • W North Am • 500 kW
	USA †KRSI-R SEDAYE IRAN, Via Moldova	S • Mideast & W Asia • 500 kW • ALT. FREQ. TO 12065 kHz
11640	CZECH REPUBLIC †RADIO PRAGUE, Litomyšl	W • N Europe • 100 kW
	GREECE FONI TIS HELLADAS, Kavála	W • S America • 250 kW
	SEYCHELLES †FEBA RADIO, North Pt, Mahé Is	W Asia • 100 kW S Asia • 100 kW • ALT. FREQ. TO 11885 kHz Su-W • W Asia • 100 kW Su/M • S Asia • 100 kW • ALT. FREQ. TO 11885 kHz F-W • E Africa • 100 kW E Africa • 100 kW Su • E Africa • 100 kW
	SOUTH AFRICA †TRANS WORLD RADIO, Meyerton	W Africa • 500 kW Sa • W Africa • 500 kW
	UNITED KINGDOM BBC, Via Chita, Russia	S • E Asia • 500 kW
	USA †WORLD BEACON, Via Meyerton, S Af	W Africa • 250 kW
	VATICAN STATE VATICAN RADIO, Sta Maria di Galeria	S Asia • 500 kW Sa • S Asia • 500 kW
11645	GREECE FONI TIS HELLADAS, Athens	W • Mideast • 100 kW W • Africa • 100 kW Africa • 100 kW W • ARABIC & ENGLISH • Africa • 100 kW E Europe • 100 kW S • E Europe • 100 kW
	FONI TIS HELLADAS, Kavála	Europe & Australasia • 250 kW C Asia • 100 kW Mideast • 250 kW Mideast • 100 kW
	PAKISTAN †RADIO PAKISTAN, Islamabad	
11650	AUSTRALIA RADIO AUSTRALIA, Shepparton	Pacific & W North Am • 100 kW
	CHINA CHINA RADIO INTL, Xi'an	W • S America • 100/200 kW SE Asia • 100 kW S • S America • 100 kW S • E Europe • 100 kW S • Mideast & W Asia • 500 kW
	FRANCE R FRANCE INTL, Issoudun-Allouis	
	NORTHERN MARIANA IS KFBS-FAR EAST BC, Saipan Island	C Asia & E Asia • 100 kW
	RUSSIA PERM RADIO, Perm	• DS-RADIO ROSSII • 5 kW
11655	GERMANY †DEUTSCHE WELLE, Wertachtal	S • E Europe • 500 kW
	HOLLAND R NEDERLAND, Flevoland	S • W Africa • 500 kW E Africa • 200 kW W • E Africa • 200 kW W • W Africa & C Africa • 200 kW
	R NEDERLAND, Via Madagascar	
	R NEDERLAND, Via Neth Antilles	Australasia • 250 kW
	PORTUGAL †RDP INTERNATIONAL, Lisbon	• Tu-Sa • W North Am • 100 kW
	QATAR (con'd) †QATAR BC SERVICE, Doha-Al Khaisah	Irr • Mideast & N Africa • RAMADAN • 250 kW

0 1 2 3 4 5 6 7 8 9 10 11 12 13 14 15 16 17 18 19 20 21 22 23 24

ENGLISH ▬ ARABIC ▨ CHINESE ⬚⬚⬚ FRENCH ▭▭ GERMAN ▬ RUSSIAN ═ SPANISH ▭▭ OTHER ▬

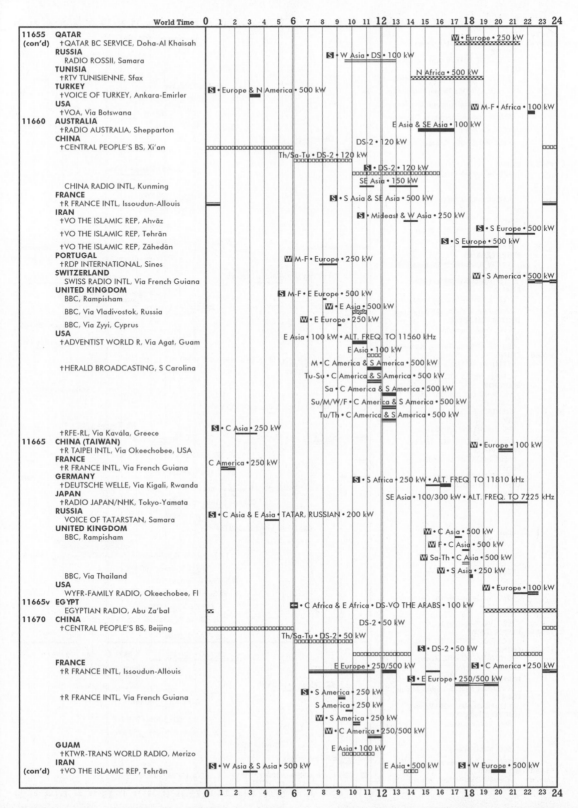

World Time 0 1 2 3 4 5 6 7 8 9 10 11 12 13 14 15 16 17 18 19 20 21 22 23 24

11655	QATAR
(con'd)	†QATAR BC SERVICE, Doha-Al Khaisah
	RUSSIA
	RADIO ROSSII, Samara
	TUNISIA
	†RTV TUNISIENNE, Sfax
	TURKEY
	†VOICE OF TURKEY, Ankara-Emirler
	USA
	†VOA, Via Botswana
11660	AUSTRALIA
	†RADIO AUSTRALIA, Shepparton
	CHINA
	†CENTRAL PEOPLE'S BS, Xi'an
	CHINA RADIO INTL, Kunming
	FRANCE
	†R FRANCE INTL, Issoudun-Allouis
	IRAN
	†VO THE ISLAMIC REP, Ahvāz
	†VO THE ISLAMIC REP, Tehrān
	†VO THE ISLAMIC REP, Zāhedān
	PORTUGAL
	†RDP INTERNATIONAL, Sines
	SWITZERLAND
	SWISS RADIO INTL, Via French Guiana
	UNITED KINGDOM
	BBC, Rampisham
	BBC, Via Vladivostok, Russia
	BBC, Via Zyyi, Cyprus
	USA
	†ADVENTIST WORLD R, Via Agat, Guam
	†HERALD BROADCASTING, S Carolina
	†RFE-RL, Via Kavála, Greece
11665	CHINA (TAIWAN)
	†R TAIPEI INTL, Via Okeechobee, USA
	FRANCE
	†R FRANCE INTL, Via French Guiana
	GERMANY
	†DEUTSCHE WELLE, Via Kigali, Rwanda
	JAPAN
	†RADIO JAPAN/NHK, Tokyo-Yamata
	RUSSIA
	VOICE OF TATARSTAN, Samara
	UNITED KINGDOM
	BBC, Rampisham
	BBC, Via Thailand
	USA
	WYFR-FAMILY RADIO, Okeechobee, Fl
11665v	EGYPT
	EGYPTIAN RADIO, Abu Za'bal
11670	CHINA
	†CENTRAL PEOPLE'S BS, Beijing
	FRANCE
	†R FRANCE INTL, Issoudun-Allouis
	†R FRANCE INTL, Via French Guiana
	GUAM
	†KTWR-TRANS WORLD RADIO, Merizo
	IRAN
(con'd)	†VO THE ISLAMIC REP, Tehrān

Program labels (as shown on the chart):

- QATAR: W • Europe • 250 kW
- RADIO ROSSII: S • W Asia • DS • 100 kW
- RTV TUNISIENNE: N Africa • 500 kW
- VOICE OF TURKEY: S • Europe & N America • 500 kW
- VOA: W M-F • Africa • 100 kW
- RADIO AUSTRALIA: E Asia & SE Asia • 100 kW
- CENTRAL PEOPLE'S BS, Xi'an: DS-2 • 120 kW / Th/Sa-Tu • DS-2 • 120 kW / S • DS-2 • 120 kW
- CHINA RADIO INTL, Kunming: SE Asia • 150 kW
- R FRANCE INTL, Issoudun: S • S Asia & SE Asia • 500 kW
- VO THE ISLAMIC REP, Ahvāz: S • Mideast & W Asia • 250 kW
- VO THE ISLAMIC REP, Tehrān: S • S Europe • 500 kW
- VO THE ISLAMIC REP, Zāhedān: S • S Europe • 500 kW
- RDP INTERNATIONAL: W M-F • Europe • 250 kW
- SWISS RADIO INTL: W • S America • 500 kW
- BBC, Rampisham: S M-F • E Europe • 500 kW
- BBC, Via Vladivostok: W • E Asia • 500 kW
- BBC, Via Zyyi: W • E Europe • 250 kW
- ADVENTIST WORLD R: E Asia • 100 kW • ALT. FREQ. TO 11560 kHz
- HERALD BROADCASTING: E Asia • 100 kW
- M • C America & S America • 500 kW
- Tu-Su • C America & S America • 500 kW
- Sa • C America & S America • 500 kW
- Su/M/W/F • C America & S America • 500 kW
- Tu/Th • C America & S America • 500 kW
- RFE-RL: S • C Asia • 250 kW
- R TAIPEI INTL: W • Europe • 100 kW
- R FRANCE INTL, Via French Guiana: C America • 250 kW
- DEUTSCHE WELLE: S • S Africa • 250 kW • ALT. FREQ. TO 11810 kHz
- RADIO JAPAN/NHK: SE Asia • 100/300 kW • ALT. FREQ. TO 7225 kHz
- VOICE OF TATARSTAN: S • C Asia & E Asia • TATAR, RUSSIAN • 200 kW
- BBC, Rampisham: W • C Asia • 500 kW / W F • C Asia • 500 kW / W Sa-Th • C Asia • 500 kW
- BBC, Via Thailand: W • S Asia • 250 kW
- WYFR-FAMILY RADIO: W • Europe • 100 kW
- EGYPTIAN RADIO: C Africa & E Africa • DS-VO THE ARABS • 100 kW
- CENTRAL PEOPLE'S BS, Beijing: DS-2 • 50 kW / Th/Sa-Tu • DS-2 • 50 kW / S • DS-2 • 50 kW
- R FRANCE INTL, Issoudun: E Europe • 250/500 kW / S • C America • 250 kW / S • E Europe • 250/500 kW
- R FRANCE INTL, Via French Guiana: S America • 250 kW / S America • 250 kW / W • S America • 250 kW / W • C America • 250/500 kW
- KTWR-TRANS WORLD RADIO: E Asia • 100 kW
- VO THE ISLAMIC REP, Tehrān: S • W Asia & S Asia • 500 kW / E Asia • 500 kW / S • W Europe • 500 kW

World Time 0 1 2 3 4 5 6 7 8 9 10 11 12 13 14 15 16 17 18 19 20 21 22 23 24

SEASONAL S OR W   1-HR TIMESHIFT MIDYEAR ⬅ OR ➡   JAMMING / OR ∧   EARLIEST HEARD ◁   LATEST HEARD ▷   NEW FOR 2001 †

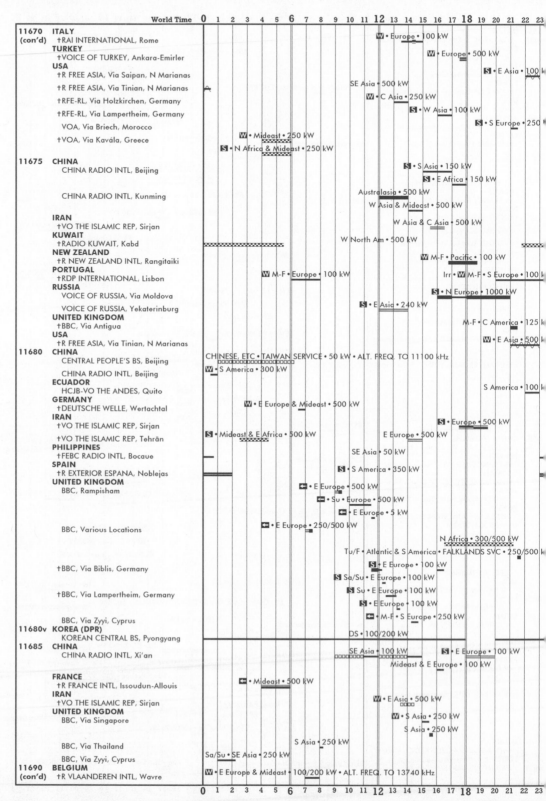

World Time	0 1 2 3 4 5 6 7 8 9 10 11 12 13 14 15 16 17 18 19 20 21 22 23

11670 ITALY
(con'd) †RAI INTERNATIONAL, Rome — W • Europe • 100 kW
TURKEY
  †VOICE OF TURKEY, Ankara-Emirler — W • Europe • 500 kW
USA
  †R FREE ASIA, Via Saipan, N Marianas — S • E Asia • 100
  †R FREE ASIA, Via Tinian, N Marianas — SE Asia • 500 kW
  †RFE-RL, Via Holzkirchen, Germany — W • C Asia • 250 kW
  †RFE-RL, Via Lampertheim, Germany — S • W Asia • 100 kW
  VOA, Via Briech, Morocco — S • S Europe • 250
  †VOA, Via Kavála, Greece — W • Mideast • 250 kW / S • N Africa & Mideast • 250 kW

11675 CHINA
  CHINA RADIO INTL, Beijing — S • S Asia • 150 kW / S • E Africa • 150 kW
  CHINA RADIO INTL, Kunming — Australasia • 500 kW / W Asia & Mideast • 500 kW
IRAN
  †VO THE ISLAMIC REP, Sirjan — W Asia & C Asia • 500 kW
KUWAIT
  †RADIO KUWAIT, Kabd — W North Am • 500 kW
NEW ZEALAND
  †R NEW ZEALAND INTL, Rangitaiki — W M-F • Pacific • 100 kW
PORTUGAL
  †RDP INTERNATIONAL, Lisbon — W M-F • Europe • 100 kW / Irr • W M-F • S Europe • 100 kW
RUSSIA
  VOICE OF RUSSIA, Via Moldova — S • N Europe • 1000 kW
  VOICE OF RUSSIA, Yekaterinburg — S • E Asia • 240 kW
UNITED KINGDOM
  †BBC, Via Antigua — M-F • C America • 125 k
USA
  †R FREE ASIA, Via Tinian, N Marianas — W • E Asia • 500

11680 CHINA
  CENTRAL PEOPLE'S BS, Beijing — CHINESE, ETC • TAIWAN SERVICE • 50 kW • ALT. FREQ. TO 11100 kHz
  CHINA RADIO INTL, Beijing — W • S America • 300 kW
ECUADOR
  HCJB-VO THE ANDES, Quito — S America • 100
GERMANY
  †DEUTSCHE WELLE, Wertachtal — W • E Europe & Mideast • 500 kW
IRAN
  †VO THE ISLAMIC REP, Sirjan — S • Europe • 500 kW
  †VO THE ISLAMIC REP, Tehrän — S • Mideast & E Africa • 500 kW / E Europe • 500 kW
PHILIPPINES
  †FEBC RADIO INTL, Bocaue — SE Asia • 50 kW
SPAIN
  †R EXTERIOR ESPANA, Noblejas — S • S America • 350 kW
UNITED KINGDOM
  BBC, Rampisham — • E Europe • 500 kW / • Su • Europe • 500 kW / • E Europe • 5 kW
  BBC, Various Locations — • E Europe • 250/500 kW / N Africa • 300/500 kW / Tu/F • Atlantic & S America • FALKLANDS SVC • 250/500 k
  †BBC, Via Biblis, Germany — S • E Europe • 100 kW / S Sa/Su • E Europe • 100 kW
  †BBC, Via Lampertheim, Germany — S Su • E Europe • 100 kW / S • E Europe • 100 kW
  BBC, Via Zyyi, Cyprus — • M-F • S Europe • 250 kW
11680v KOREA (DPR)
  KOREAN CENTRAL BS, Pyongyang — DS • 100/200 kW
11685 CHINA
  CHINA RADIO INTL, Xi'an — SE Asia • 100 kW / S • E Europe • 100 kW / Mideast & E Europe • 100 kW
FRANCE
  †R FRANCE INTL, Issoudun-Allouis — • Mideast • 500 kW
IRAN
  †VO THE ISLAMIC REP, Sirjan — W • E Asia • 500 kW
UNITED KINGDOM
  BBC, Via Singapore — W • S Asia • 250 kW / S Asia • 250 kW
  BBC, Via Thailand — S Asia • 250 kW
  BBC, Via Zyyi, Cyprus — Sa/Su • SE Asia • 250 kW
11690 BELGIUM
(con'd) †R VLAANDEREN INTL, Wavre — W • E Europe & Mideast • 100/200 kW • ALT. FREQ. TO 13740 kHz

	0 1 2 3 4 5 6 7 8 9 10 11 12 13 14 15 16 17 18 19 20 21 22 23

ENGLISH ▬ ARABIC ⁓ CHINESE ▭▭▭ FRENCH ══ GERMAN ▬ RUSSIAN ══ SPANISH ══ OTHER ─

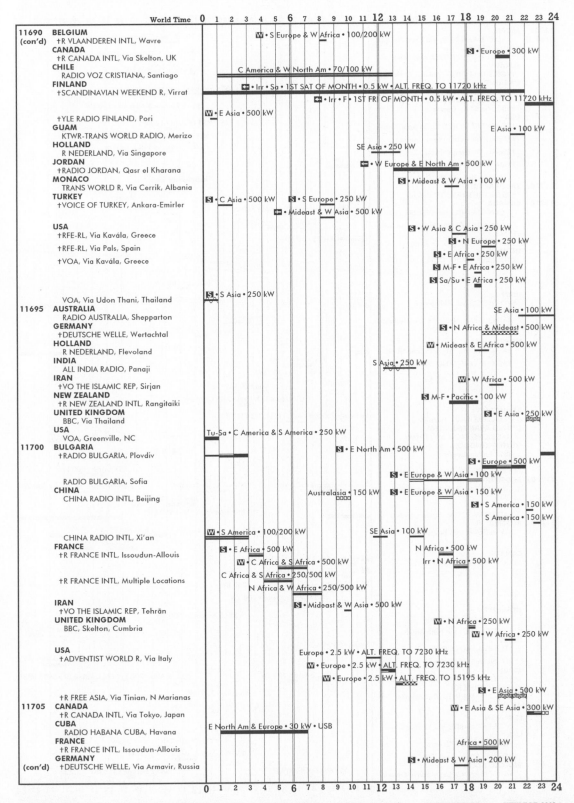

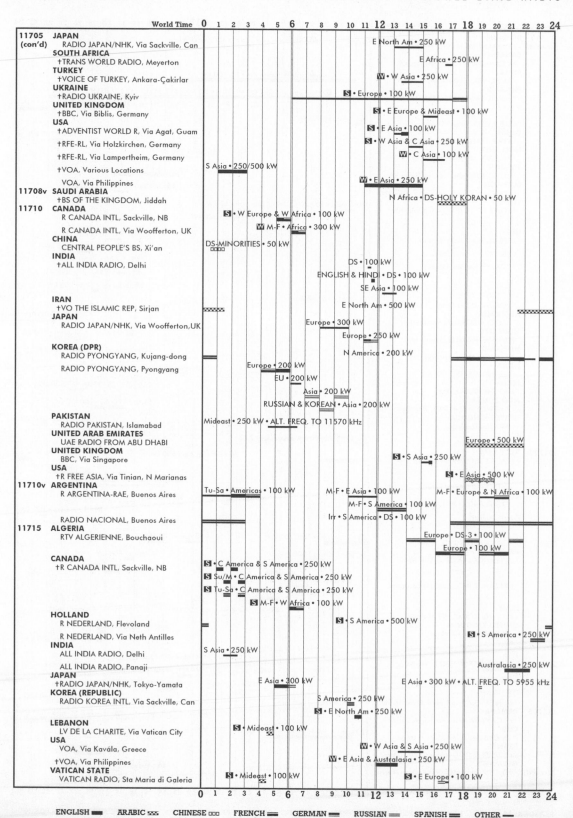

World Time	0 1 2 3 4 5 6 7 8 9 10 11 12 13 14 15 16 17 18 19 20 21 22 23 24

11705 JAPAN
(con'd)   RADIO JAPAN/NHK, Via Sackville, Can — E North Am • 250 kW
SOUTH AFRICA
†TRANS WORLD RADIO, Meyerton — E Africa • 250 kW
TURKEY
†VOICE OF TURKEY, Ankara-Çakirlar — W • W Asia • 250 kW
UKRAINE
†RADIO UKRAINE, Kyiv — S • Europe • 100 kW
UNITED KINGDOM
†BBC, Via Biblis, Germany — S • E Europe & Mideast • 100 kW
USA
†ADVENTIST WORLD R, Via Agat, Guam — S • E Asia • 100 kW
†RFE-RL, Via Holzkirchen, Germany — S • W Asia & C Asia • 250 kW
†RFE-RL, Via Lampertheim, Germany — W • C Asia • 100 kW
†VOA, Various Locations — S Asia • 250/500 kW
VOA, Via Philippines — W • E Asia • 250 kW
11708v SAUDI ARABIA
†BS OF THE KINGDOM, Jiddah — N Africa • DS-HOLY KORAN • 50 kW
11710 CANADA
R CANADA INTL, Sackville, NB — S • W Europe & W Africa • 100 kW
R CANADA INTL, Via Woofferton, UK — W M-F • Africa • 300 kW
CHINA
CENTRAL PEOPLE'S BS, Xi'an — DS-MINORITIES • 50 kW
INDIA
†ALL INDIA RADIO, Delhi — DS • 100 kW
ENGLISH & HINDI • DS • 100 kW
SE Asia • 100 kW
IRAN
†VO THE ISLAMIC REP, Sirjan — E North Am • 500 kW
JAPAN
RADIO JAPAN/NHK, Via Woofferton, UK — Europe • 300 kW
Europe • 250 kW
N America • 200 kW
KOREA (DPR)
RADIO PYONGYANG, Kujang-dong —
RADIO PYONGYANG, Pyongyang — Europe • 200 kW
EU • 200 kW
Asia • 200 kW
RUSSIAN & KOREAN • Asia • 200 kW
PAKISTAN
RADIO PAKISTAN, Islamabad — Mideast • 250 kW • ALT. FREQ. TO 11570 kHz
UNITED ARAB EMIRATES
UAE RADIO FROM ABU DHABI — Europe • 500 kW
UNITED KINGDOM
BBC, Via Singapore — S • S Asia • 250 kW
USA
†R FREE ASIA, Via Tinian, N Marianas — S • E Asia • 500 kW
11710v ARGENTINA
R ARGENTINA-RAE, Buenos Aires — Tu-Sa • Americas • 100 kW   M-F • E Asia • 100 kW   M-F • Europe & N Africa • 100 kW
M-F • S America • 100 kW
RADIO NACIONAL, Buenos Aires — Irr • S America • DS • 100 kW
11715 ALGERIA
RTV ALGERIENNE, Bouchaoui — Europe • DS-3 • 100 kW
Europe • 100 kW
CANADA
†R CANADA INTL, Sackville, NB — S • C America & S America • 250 kW
S • Su/M • C America & S America • 250 kW
S • Tu-Sa • C America & S America • 250 kW
S • M-F • W Africa • 100 kW
HOLLAND
R NEDERLAND, Flevoland — S • S America • 500 kW
R NEDERLAND, Via Neth Antilles — S • S America • 250 kW
INDIA
ALL INDIA RADIO, Delhi — S Asia • 250 kW
ALL INDIA RADIO, Panaji — Australasia • 250 kW
JAPAN
†RADIO JAPAN/NHK, Tokyo-Yamata — E Asia • 300 kW   E Asia • 300 kW • ALT. FREQ. TO 5955 kHz
KOREA (REPUBLIC)
RADIO KOREA INTL, Via Sackville, Can — S America • 250 kW
S • E North Am • 250 kW
LEBANON
LV DE LA CHARITE, Via Vatican City — S • Mideast • 100 kW
USA
VOA, Via Kavála, Greece — W • W Asia & S Asia • 250 kW
†VOA, Via Philippines — W • E Asia & Australasia • 250 kW
VATICAN STATE
VATICAN RADIO, Sta Maria di Galeria — S • Mideast • 100 kW   S • E Europe • 100 kW

0 1 2 3 4 5 6 7 8 9 10 11 12 13 14 15 16 17 18 19 20 21 22 23 24

ENGLISH ▬ ARABIC ░░░ CHINESE □□□ FRENCH ═══ GERMAN ▬ RUSSIAN ═══ SPANISH ═══ OTHER ▬

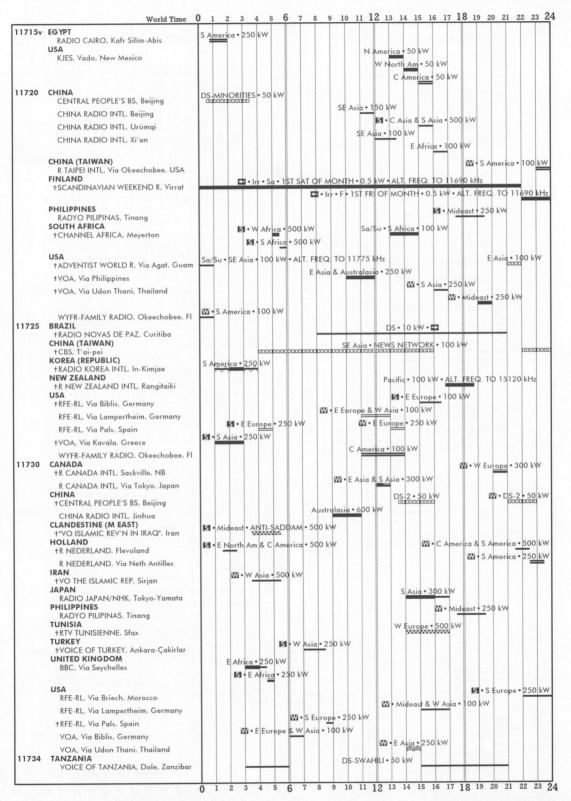

World Time	0 1 2 3 4 5 6 7 8 9 10 11 12 13 14 15 16 17 18 19 20 21 22 23 24

11715v EGYPT
RADIO CAIRO, Kafr Silim-Abis — S America • 250 kW
USA
KJES, Vado, New Mexico — N America • 50 kW / W North Am • 50 kW / C America • 50 kW

11720 CHINA
CENTRAL PEOPLE'S BS, Beijing — DS-MINORITIES • 50 kW
CHINA RADIO INTL, Beijing — SE Asia • 150 kW
CHINA RADIO INTL, Urümqi — S • C Asia & S Asia • 500 kW
CHINA RADIO INTL, Xi'an — SE Asia • 100 kW / E Africa • 100 kW
CHINA (TAIWAN)
R TAIPEI INTL, Via Okeechobee, USA — W • S America • 100 kW
FINLAND
†SCANDINAVIAN WEEKEND R, Virrat — ⇄ • Irr • Sa • 1ST SAT OF MONTH • 0.5 kW • ALT. FREQ. TO 11690 kHz / ⇄ • Irr • F • 1ST FRI OF MONTH • 0.5 kW • ALT. FREQ. TO 11690 kHz
PHILIPPINES
RADYO PILIPINAS, Tinang — S • Mideast • 250 kW
SOUTH AFRICA
†CHANNEL AFRICA, Meyerton — S • W Africa • 500 kW / Sa/Su • S Africa • 100 kW / S • S Africa • 500 kW
USA
†ADVENTIST WORLD R, Via Agat, Guam — Sa/Su • SE Asia • 100 kW • ALT. FREQ. TO 11775 kHz / E Asia • 100 kW
†VOA, Via Philippines — E Asia & Australasia • 250 kW
†VOA, Via Udon Thani, Thailand — W • S Asia • 250 kW / W • Mideast • 250 kW
WYFR-FAMILY RADIO, Okeechobee, Fl — W • S America • 100 kW
11725 BRAZIL
†RADIO NOVAS DE PAZ, Curitiba — DS • 10 kW • ⇄
CHINA (TAIWAN)
†CBS, T'ai-pei — SE Asia • NEWS NETWORK • 100 kW
KOREA (REPUBLIC)
†RADIO KOREA INTL, In-Kimjae — S America • 250 kW
NEW ZEALAND
†R NEW ZEALAND INTL, Rangitaiki — Pacific • 100 kW • ALT. FREQ. TO 15120 kHz
USA
†RFE-RL, Via Biblis, Germany — S • E Europe • 100 kW
RFE-RL, Via Lampertheim, Germany — W • E Europe & W Asia • 100 kW
RFE-RL, Via Pals, Spain — S • E Europe • 250 kW / W • E Europe • 250 kW
†VOA, Via Kavála, Greece — S • S Asia • 250 kW
WYFR-FAMILY RADIO, Okeechobee, Fl — C America • 100 kW
11730 CANADA
†R CANADA INTL, Sackville, NB — W • W Europe • 300 kW
R CANADA INTL, Via Tokyo, Japan — W • E Asia & S Asia • 300 kW
CHINA
†CENTRAL PEOPLE'S BS, Beijing — DS-2 • 50 kW / W • DS-2 • 50 kW
CHINA RADIO INTL, Jinhua — Australasia • 600 kW
CLANDESTINE (M EAST)
†"VO ISLAMIC REV'N IN IRAQ", Iran — S • Mideast • ANTI-SADDAM • 500 kW
HOLLAND
†R NEDERLAND, Flevoland — S • E North Am & C America • 500 kW / W • C America & S America • 500 kW
R NEDERLAND, Via Neth Antilles — W • S America • 250 kW
IRAN
†VO THE ISLAMIC REP, Sirjan — W • W Asia • 500 kW
JAPAN
RADIO JAPAN/NHK, Tokyo-Yamata — S Asia • 300 kW
PHILIPPINES
RADYO PILIPINAS, Tinang — W • Mideast • 250 kW
TUNISIA
†RTV TUNISIENNE, Sfax — W Europe • 500 kW
TURKEY
†VOICE OF TURKEY, Ankara-Çakirlar — S • W Asia • 250 kW
UNITED KINGDOM
BBC, Via Seychelles — E Africa • 250 kW / S • E Africa • 250 kW
USA
RFE-RL, Via Briech, Morocco — S • S Europe • 250 kW
RFE-RL, Via Lampertheim, Germany — W • Mideast & W Asia • 100 kW
†RFE-RL, Via Pals, Spain — W • S Europe • 250 kW
VOA, Via Biblis, Germany — W • E Europe & W Asia • 100 kW
VOA, Via Udon Thani, Thailand — W • E Asia • 250 kW
11734 TANZANIA
VOICE OF TANZANIA, Dole, Zanzibar — DS-SWAHILI • 50 kW

	0 1 2 3 4 5 6 7 8 9 10 11 12 13 14 15 16 17 18 19 20 21 22 23 24

SEASONAL ⑤ OR Ⓦ   1-HR TIMESHIFT MIDYEAR ⇄ OR ⇄   JAMMING / OR ∧   EARLIEST HEARD ◁   LATEST HEARD ▷   NEW FOR 2001 †

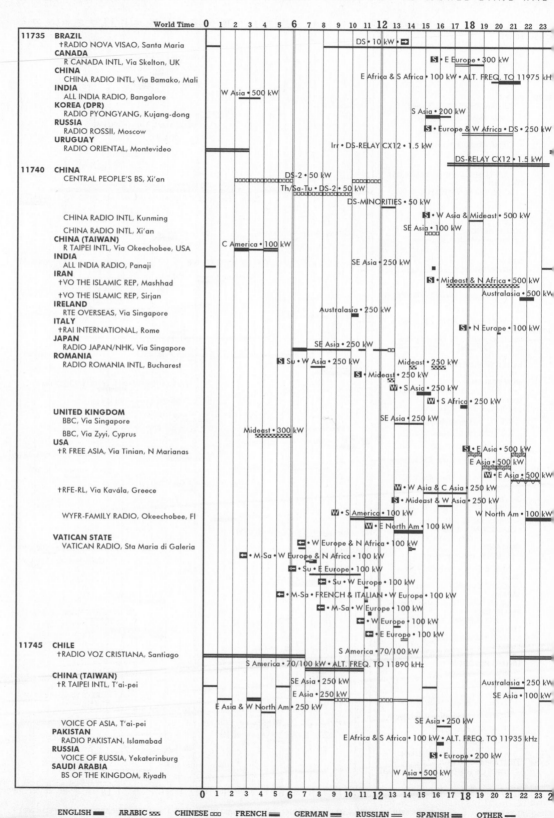

| World Time | 0 | 1 | 2 | 3 | 4 | 5 | 6 | 7 | 8 | 9 | 10 | 11 | 12 | 13 | 14 | 15 | 16 | 17 | 18 | 19 | 20 | 21 | 22 | 23 |

11735 BRAZIL
  †RADIO NOVA VISAO, Santa Maria — DS • 10 kW • ➡
CANADA
  R CANADA INTL, Via Skelton, UK — S • E Europe • 300 kW
CHINA
  CHINA RADIO INTL, Via Bamako, Mali — E Africa & S Africa • 100 kW • ALT. FREQ. TO 11975 kH
INDIA
  ALL INDIA RADIO, Bangalore — W Asia • 500 kW
KOREA (DPR)
  RADIO PYONGYANG, Kujang-dong — S Asia • 200 kW
RUSSIA
  RADIO ROSSII, Moscow — S • Europe & W Africa • DS • 250 kW
URUGUAY
  RADIO ORIENTAL, Montevideo — Irr • DS-RELAY CX12 • 1.5 kW
  DS-RELAY CX12 • 1.5 kW

11740 CHINA
  CENTRAL PEOPLE'S BS, Xi'an — DS-2 • 50 kW
  Th/Sa-Tu • DS-2 • 50 kW
  DS-MINORITIES • 50 kW
  CHINA RADIO INTL, Kunming — S • W Asia & Mideast • 500 kW
  CHINA RADIO INTL, Xi'an — SE Asia • 100 kW
CHINA (TAIWAN)
  R TAIPEI INTL, Via Okeechobee, USA — C America • 100 kW
INDIA
  ALL INDIA RADIO, Panaji — SE Asia • 250 kW
IRAN
  †VO THE ISLAMIC REP, Mashhad — S • Mideast & N Africa • 500 kW
  †VO THE ISLAMIC REP, Sirjan — Australasia • 500 kW
IRELAND
  RTE OVERSEAS, Via Singapore — Australasia • 250 kW
ITALY
  †RAI INTERNATIONAL, Rome — S • N Europe • 100 kW
JAPAN
  RADIO JAPAN/NHK, Via Singapore — SE Asia • 250 kW
ROMANIA
  RADIO ROMANIA INTL, Bucharest — S Su • W Asia • 250 kW
  Mideast • 250 kW
  S • Mideast • 250 kW
  W • S Asia • 250 kW
  W • S Africa • 250 kW
UNITED KINGDOM
  BBC, Via Singapore — SE Asia • 250 kW
  BBC, Via Zyyi, Cyprus — Mideast • 300 kW
USA
  †R FREE ASIA, Via Tinian, N Marianas — S • E Asia • 500 kW
  E Asia • 500 kW
  W • E Asia • 500 kW
  †RFE-RL, Via Kavála, Greece — W • W Asia & C Asia • 250 kW
  S • Mideast & W Asia • 250 kW
  WYFR-FAMILY RADIO, Okeechobee, Fl — W • S America • 100 kW
  W North Am • 100 kW
  W • E North Am • 100 kW
VATICAN STATE
  VATICAN RADIO, Sta Maria di Galeria — • W Europe & N Africa • 100 kW
  • M-Sa • W Europe & N Africa • 100 kW
  • Su • E Europe • 100 kW
  • Su • W Europe • 100 kW
  • M-Sa • FRENCH & ITALIAN • W Europe • 100 kW
  • M-Sa • W Europe • 100 kW
  • W Europe • 100 kW
  • E Europe • 100 kW

11745 CHILE
  †RADIO VOZ CRISTIANA, Santiago — S America • 70/100 kW
  S America • 70/100 kW • ALT. FREQ. TO 11890 kHz
CHINA (TAIWAN)
  †R TAIPEI INTL, T'ai-pei — SE Asia • 250 kW
  E Asia • 250 kW
  E Asia & W North Am • 250 kW
  Australasia • 250 kW
  SE Asia • 100 kW
  VOICE OF ASIA, T'ai-pei — SE Asia • 250 kW
PAKISTAN
  RADIO PAKISTAN, Islamabad — E Africa & S Africa • 100 kW • ALT. FREQ. TO 11935 kHz
RUSSIA
  VOICE OF RUSSIA, Yekaterinburg — S • Europe • 200 kW
SAUDI ARABIA
  BS OF THE KINGDOM, Riyadh — W Asia • 500 kW

| 0 | 1 | 2 | 3 | 4 | 5 | 6 | 7 | 8 | 9 | 10 | 11 | 12 | 13 | 14 | 15 | 16 | 17 | 18 | 19 | 20 | 21 | 22 | 23 | 2 |

ENGLISH ▬   ARABIC 〰   CHINESE □□□   FRENCH ━   GERMAN ▬   RUSSIAN ═   SPANISH ▬   OTHER ▬

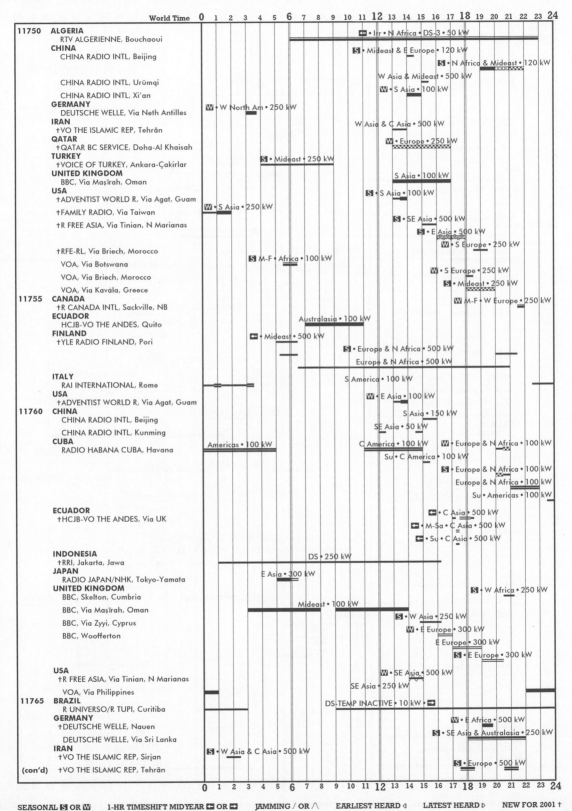

World Time

11750	**ALGERIA**
	RTV ALGERIENNE, Bouchaoui
	CHINA
	CHINA RADIO INTL, Beijing
	CHINA RADIO INTL, Urümqi
	CHINA RADIO INTL, Xi'an
	GERMANY
	DEUTSCHE WELLE, Via Neth Antilles
	IRAN
	†VO THE ISLAMIC REP, Tehrān
	QATAR
	†QATAR BC SERVICE, Doha-Al Khaisah
	TURKEY
	†VOICE OF TURKEY, Ankara-Çakirlar
	UNITED KINGDOM
	BBC, Via Maşīrah, Oman
	USA
	†ADVENTIST WORLD R, Via Agat, Guam
	†FAMILY RADIO, Via Taiwan
	†R FREE ASIA, Via Tinian, N Marianas
	†RFE-RL, Via Briech, Morocco
	VOA, Via Botswana
	VOA, Via Briech, Morocco
	VOA, Via Kavála, Greece
11755	**CANADA**
	†R CANADA INTL, Sackville, NB
	ECUADOR
	HCJB-VO THE ANDES, Quito
	FINLAND
	†YLE RADIO FINLAND, Pori
	ITALY
	RAI INTERNATIONAL, Rome
	USA
	†ADVENTIST WORLD R, Via Agat, Guam
11760	**CHINA**
	CHINA RADIO INTL, Beijing
	CHINA RADIO INTL, Kunming
	CUBA
	RADIO HABANA CUBA, Havana
	ECUADOR
	†HCJB-VO THE ANDES, Via UK
	INDONESIA
	†RRI, Jakarta, Jawa
	JAPAN
	RADIO JAPAN/NHK, Tokyo-Yamata
	UNITED KINGDOM
	BBC, Skelton, Cumbria
	BBC, Via Maşīrah, Oman
	BBC, Via Zyyi, Cyprus
	BBC, Woofferton
	USA
	†R FREE ASIA, Via Tinian, N Marianas
	VOA, Via Philippines
11765	**BRAZIL**
	R UNIVERSO/R TUPI, Curitiba
	GERMANY
	†DEUTSCHE WELLE, Nauen
	DEUTSCHE WELLE, Via Sri Lanka
	IRAN
	†VO THE ISLAMIC REP, Sirjan
(con'd)	†VO THE ISLAMIC REP, Tehrān

SEASONAL **S** OR **W**   1-HR TIMESHIFT MIDYEAR ⬅ OR ➡   JAMMING / OR ∧   EARLIEST HEARD ◁   LATEST HEARD ▷   NEW FOR 2001 †

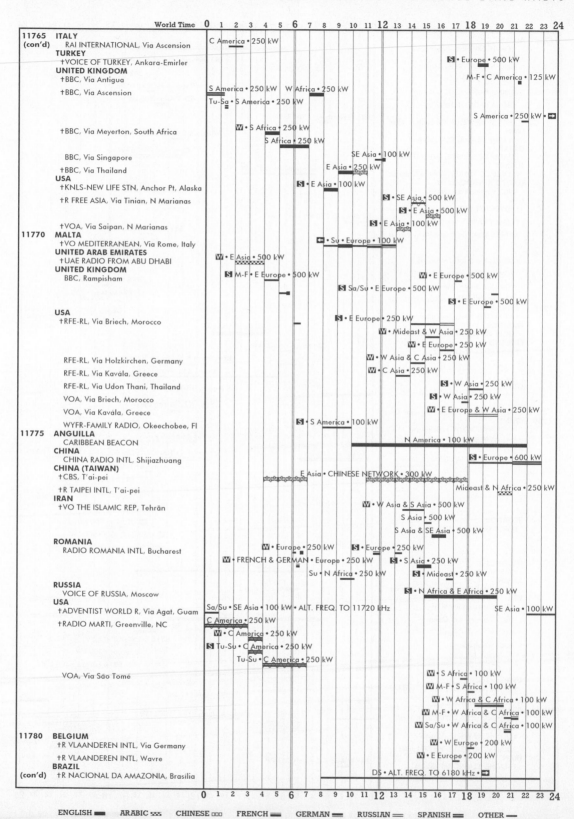

World Time 0 1 2 3 4 5 6 7 8 9 10 11 12 13 14 15 16 17 18 19 20 21 22 23 24

11765 **ITALY**
(con'd)   RAI INTERNATIONAL, Via Ascension — C America • 250 kW
            TURKEY
              †VOICE OF TURKEY, Ankara-Emirler — S • Europe • 500 kW
            UNITED KINGDOM
              †BBC, Via Antigua — M-F • C America • 125 kW
              †BBC, Via Ascension — S America • 250 kW   W Africa • 250 kW
                                     Tu-Sa • S America • 250 kW
                                     S America • 250 kW •
              †BBC, Via Meyerton, South Africa — W • S Africa • 250 kW
                                     S Africa • 250 kW
              BBC, Via Singapore — SE Asia • 100 kW
              †BBC, Via Thailand — E Asia • 250 kW
            USA
              †KNLS-NEW LIFE STN, Anchor Pt, Alaska — S • E Asia • 100 kW
              †R FREE ASIA, Via Tinian, N Marianas — S • SE Asia • 500 kW
                                     S • E Asia • 500 kW
              †VOA, Via Saipan, N Marianas — S • E Asia • 100 kW
11770 **MALTA**
              †VO MEDITERRANEAN, Via Rome, Italy — • Su • Europe • 100 kW
            UNITED ARAB EMIRATES
              †UAE RADIO FROM ABU DHABI — W • E Asia • 500 kW
            UNITED KINGDOM
              BBC, Rampisham — S • M-F • E Europe • 500 kW   W • E Europe • 500 kW
                                     S Sa/Su • E Europe • 500 kW
                                     S • E Europe • 500 kW
            USA
              †RFE-RL, Via Briech, Morocco — S • E Europe • 250 kW
                                     W • Mideast & W Asia • 250 kW
                                     W • E Europe • 250 kW
              RFE-RL, Via Holzkirchen, Germany — W • W Asia & C Asia • 250 kW
              RFE-RL, Via Kavála, Greece — W • C Asia • 250 kW
              RFE-RL, Via Udon Thani, Thailand — S • W Asia • 250 kW
              VOA, Via Briech, Morocco — S • W Asia • 250 kW
              VOA, Via Kavála, Greece — W • E Europe & W Asia • 250 kW
              WYFR-FAMILY RADIO, Okeechobee, Fl — S • S America • 100 kW
11775 **ANGUILLA**
              CARIBBEAN BEACON — N America • 100 kW
            CHINA
              CHINA RADIO INTL, Shijiazhuang — S • Europe • 600 kW
            CHINA (TAIWAN)
              †CBS, T'ai-pei — E Asia • CHINESE NETWORK • 300 kW
              †R TAIPEI INTL, T'ai-pei — Mideast & N Africa • 250 kW
            IRAN
              †VO THE ISLAMIC REP, Tehrān — W • W Asia & S Asia • 500 kW
                                     S Asia • 500 kW
                                     S Asia & SE Asia • 500 kW
            ROMANIA
              RADIO ROMANIA INTL, Bucharest — W • Europe • 250 kW   S • Europe • 250 kW
                                     W • FRENCH & GERMAN • Europe • 250 kW   S • S Asia • 250 kW
                                     Su • N Africa • 250 kW   S • Mideast • 250 kW
            RUSSIA
              VOICE OF RUSSIA, Moscow — S • N Africa & E Africa • 250 kW
            USA
              †ADVENTIST WORLD R, Via Agat, Guam — Sa/Su • SE Asia • 100 kW • ALT. FREQ. TO 11720 kHz   SE Asia • 100 kW
              †RADIO MARTI, Greenville, NC — C America • 250 kW
                                     W • C America • 250 kW
                                     S • Tu-Su • C America • 250 kW
                                     Tu-Su • C America • 250 kW
              VOA, Via São Tomé — W • S Africa • 100 kW
                                     W M-F • S Africa • 100 kW
                                     W • W Africa & C Africa • 100 kW
                                     W M-F • W Africa & C Africa • 100 kW
                                     W Sa/Su • W Africa & C Africa • 100 kW
11780 **BELGIUM**
              †R VLAANDEREN INTL, Via Germany — W • W Europe • 200 kW
              †R VLAANDEREN INTL, Wavre — W • E Europe • 200 kW
            BRAZIL
(con'd)   †R NACIONAL DA AMAZONIA, Brasilia — DS • ALT. FREQ. TO 6180 kHz •

0 1 2 3 4 5 6 7 8 9 10 11 12 13 14 15 16 17 18 19 20 21 22 23 24

ENGLISH ▬   ARABIC ∿∿∿   CHINESE □□□   FRENCH ═   GERMAN ━   RUSSIAN ═   SPANISH ═   OTHER —

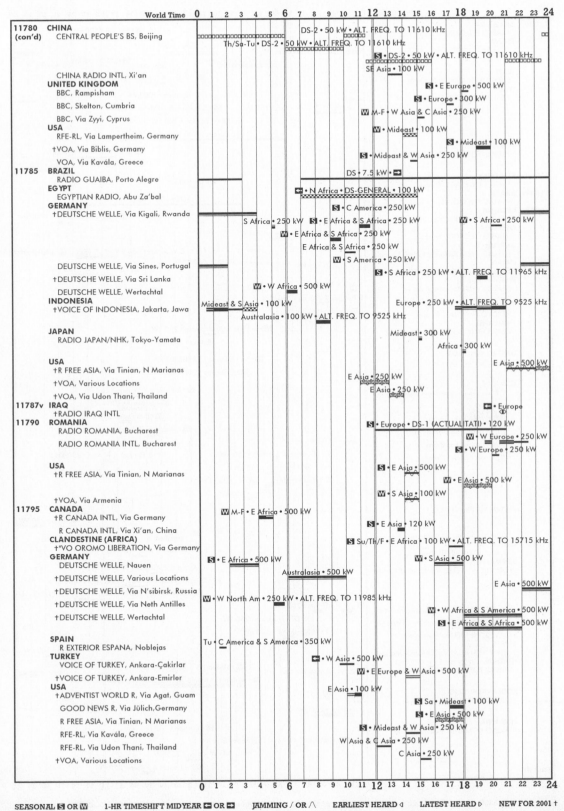

World Time 0 1 2 3 4 5 6 7 8 9 10 11 12 13 14 15 16 17 18 19 20 21 22 23 24

11780 CHINA
(con'd) CENTRAL PEOPLE'S BS, Beijing — DS-2 • 50 kW • ALT. FREQ. TO 11610 kHz
　Th/Sa-Tu • DS-2 • 50 kW • ALT. FREQ. TO 11610 kHz
　S • DS-2 • 50 kW • ALT. FREQ. TO 11610 kHz
　CHINA RADIO INTL, Xi'an — SE Asia • 100 kW
UNITED KINGDOM
　BBC, Rampisham — S • E Europe • 500 kW
　BBC, Skelton, Cumbria — S • Europe • 300 kW
　BBC, Via Zyyi, Cyprus — W • M-F • W Asia & C Asia • 250 kW
USA
　RFE-RL, Via Lampertheim, Germany — W • Mideast • 100 kW
　†VOA, Via Biblis, Germany — S • Mideast • 100 kW
　VOA, Via Kavála, Greece — S • Mideast & W Asia • 250 kW
11785 BRAZIL
　RADIO GUAIBA, Porto Alegre — DS • 7.5 kW •
EGYPT
　EGYPTIAN RADIO, Abu Za'bal — N Africa • DS-GENERAL • 100 kW
GERMANY
　†DEUTSCHE WELLE, Via Kigali, Rwanda — S • C America • 250 kW
　S Africa • 250 kW   S • E Africa & S Africa • 250 kW   W • S Africa • 250 kW
　W • E Africa & S Africa • 250 kW
　E Africa & S Africa • 250 kW
　W • S America • 250 kW
　DEUTSCHE WELLE, Via Sines, Portugal — S • S Africa • 250 kW • ALT. FREQ. TO 11965 kHz
　†DEUTSCHE WELLE, Via Sri Lanka — W • W Africa • 500 kW
　DEUTSCHE WELLE, Wertachtal
INDONESIA
　†VOICE OF INDONESIA, Jakarta, Jawa — Mideast & S Asia • 100 kW   Europe • 250 kW • ALT. FREQ. TO 9525 kHz
　Australasia • 100 kW • ALT. FREQ. TO 9525 kHz
JAPAN
　RADIO JAPAN/NHK, Tokyo-Yamata — Mideast • 300 kW
　Africa • 300 kW
USA
　†R FREE ASIA, Via Tinian, N Marianas — E Asia • 500 kW
　†VOA, Various Locations — E Asia • 250 kW
　†VOA, Via Udon Thani, Thailand — E Asia • 250 kW
11787v IRAQ
　†RADIO IRAQ INTL — • Europe
11790 ROMANIA
　RADIO ROMANIA, Bucharest — S • Europe • DS-1 (ACTUALITATI) • 120 kW
　RADIO ROMANIA INTL, Bucharest — W • W Europe • 250 kW
　S • W Europe • 250 kW
USA
　†R FREE ASIA, Via Tinian, N Marianas — S • E Asia • 500 kW
　W • E Asia • 500 kW
　†VOA, Via Armenia — W • S Asia • 100 kW
11795 CANADA
　†R CANADA INTL, Via Germany — W • M-F • E Africa • 500 kW
　R CANADA INTL, Via Xi'an, China — S • E Asia • 120 kW
CLANDESTINE (AFRICA)
　†"VO OROMO LIBERATION, Via Germany — S • Su/Th/F • E Africa • 100 kW • ALT. FREQ. TO 15715 kHz
GERMANY
　DEUTSCHE WELLE, Nauen — S • E Africa • 500 kW   W • S Asia • 500 kW
　†DEUTSCHE WELLE, Various Locations — Australasia • 500 kW
　†DEUTSCHE WELLE, Via N'sibirsk, Russia — E Asia • 500 kW
　†DEUTSCHE WELLE, Via Neth Antilles — W • W North Am • 250 kW • ALT. FREQ. TO 11985 kHz
　†DEUTSCHE WELLE, Via Neth Antilles — W • W Africa & S America • 500 kW
　†DEUTSCHE WELLE, Wertachtal — S • E Africa & S Africa • 500 kW
SPAIN
　R EXTERIOR ESPANA, Noblejas — Tu • C America & S America • 350 kW
TURKEY
　VOICE OF TURKEY, Ankara-Çakirlar — • W Asia • 500 kW
　†VOICE OF TURKEY, Ankara-Emirler — W • E Europe & W Asia • 500 kW
USA
　†ADVENTIST WORLD R, Via Agat, Guam — E Asia • 100 kW
　GOOD NEWS R, Via Jülich, Germany — S • Sa • Mideast • 100 kW
　R FREE ASIA, Via Tinian, N Marianas — S • E Asia • 500 kW
　RFE-RL, Via Kavála, Greece — S • Mideast & W Asia • 250 kW
　RFE-RL, Via Udon Thani, Thailand — W Asia & C Asia • 250 kW
　†VOA, Various Locations — C Asia • 250 kW

0 1 2 3 4 5 6 7 8 9 10 11 12 13 14 15 16 17 18 19 20 21 22 23 24

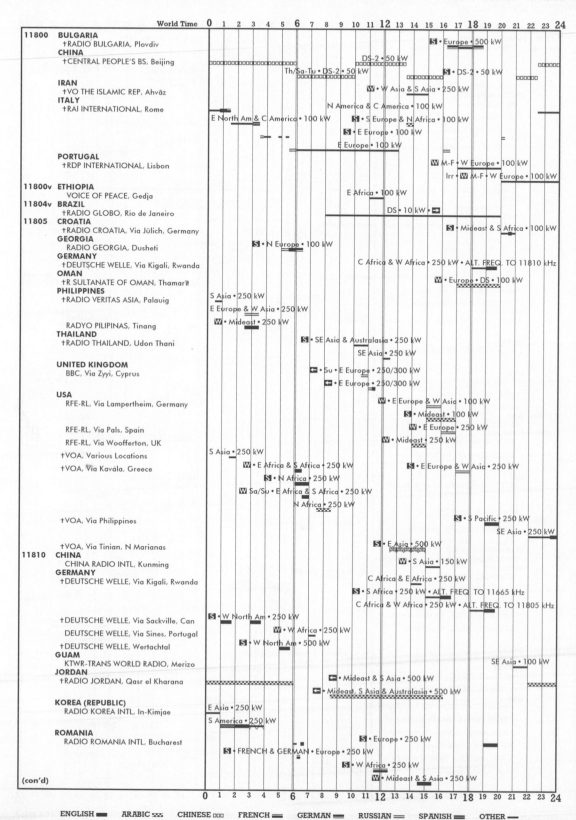

| | World Time | 0 | 1 | 2 | 3 | 4 | 5 | 6 | 7 | 8 | 9 | 10 | 11 | 12 | 13 | 14 | 15 | 16 | 17 | 18 | 19 | 20 | 21 | 22 | 23 | 24 |

11800
BULGARIA
†RADIO BULGARIA, Plovdiv — S • Europe • 500 kW
CHINA
†CENTRAL PEOPLE'S BS, Beijing — Th/Sa-Tu • DS-2 • 50 kW / DS-2 • 50 kW / S • DS-2 • 50 kW
IRAN
†VO THE ISLAMIC REP, Ahvāz — W • W Asia & S Asia • 250 kW
ITALY
†RAI INTERNATIONAL, Rome — N America & C America • 100 kW
E North Am & C America • 100 kW
S • S Europe & N Africa • 100 kW
S • E Europe • 100 kW
E Europe • 100 kW
PORTUGAL
†RDP INTERNATIONAL, Lisbon — W • M-F • W Europe • 100 kW
Irr • W • M-F • W Europe • 100 kW

11800v ETHIOPIA
VOICE OF PEACE, Gedja — E Africa • 100 kW
11804v BRAZIL
†RADIO GLOBO, Rio de Janeiro — DS • 10 kW
11805 CROATIA
†RADIO CROATIA, Via Jülich, Germany — S • Mideast & S Africa • 100 kW
GEORGIA
RADIO GEORGIA, Dusheti — S • N Europe • 100 kW
GERMANY
†DEUTSCHE WELLE, Via Kigali, Rwanda — C Africa & W Africa • 250 kW • ALT. FREQ. TO 11810 kHz
OMAN
†R SULTANATE OF OMAN, Thamarīt — W • Europe • DS • 100 kW
PHILIPPINES
†RADIO VERITAS ASIA, Palauig — S Asia • 250 kW
E Europe & W Asia • 250 kW
RADYO PILIPINAS, Tinang — W • Mideast • 250 kW
THAILAND
†RADIO THAILAND, Udon Thani — S • SE Asia & Australasia • 250 kW
SE Asia • 250 kW
UNITED KINGDOM
BBC, Via Zyyi, Cyprus — • Su • E Europe • 250/300 kW
• E Europe • 250/300 kW
USA
RFE-RL, Via Lampertheim, Germany — W • E Europe & W Asia • 100 kW
S • Mideast • 100 kW
RFE-RL, Via Pals, Spain — W • E Europe • 250 kW
RFE-RL, Via Woofferton, UK — W • Mideast • 250 kW
†VOA, Various Locations — S Asia • 250 kW
†VOA, Via Kavála, Greece — W • E Africa & S Africa • 250 kW
S • N Africa • 250 kW
S • E Europe & W Asia • 250 kW
W Sa/Su • E Africa & S Africa • 250 kW
N Africa • 250 kW
†VOA, Via Philippines — S • S Pacific • 250 kW
SE Asia • 250 kW
†VOA, Via Tinian, N Marianas — S • E Asia • 500 kW
11810 CHINA
CHINA RADIO INTL, Kunming — W • S Asia • 150 kW
GERMANY
†DEUTSCHE WELLE, Via Kigali, Rwanda — C Africa & E Africa • 250 kW
S • S Africa • 250 kW • ALT. FREQ. TO 11665 kHz
C Africa & W Africa • 250 kW • ALT. FREQ. TO 11805 kHz
†DEUTSCHE WELLE, Via Sackville, Can — S • W North Am • 250 kW
DEUTSCHE WELLE, Via Sines, Portugal — W • W Africa • 250 kW
†DEUTSCHE WELLE, Wertachtal — S • W North Am • 500 kW
GUAM
KTWR-TRANS WORLD RADIO, Merizo — SE Asia • 100 kW
JORDAN
†RADIO JORDAN, Qasr el Kharana — • Mideast & S Asia • 500 kW
• Mideast, S Asia & Australasia • 500 kW
KOREA (REPUBLIC)
RADIO KOREA INTL, In-Kimjae — E Asia • 250 kW
S America • 250 kW
ROMANIA
RADIO ROMANIA INTL, Bucharest — S • Europe • 250 kW
S • FRENCH & GERMAN • Europe • 250 kW
S • W Africa • 250 kW
W • Mideast & S Asia • 250 kW

(con'd)

| 0 | 1 | 2 | 3 | 4 | 5 | 6 | 7 | 8 | 9 | 10 | 11 | 12 | 13 | 14 | 15 | 16 | 17 | 18 | 19 | 20 | 21 | 22 | 23 | 24 |

ENGLISH ▬   ARABIC ⧄   CHINESE □□□   FRENCH ═   GERMAN ▬▬   RUSSIAN ═   SPANISH ═   OTHER ▬

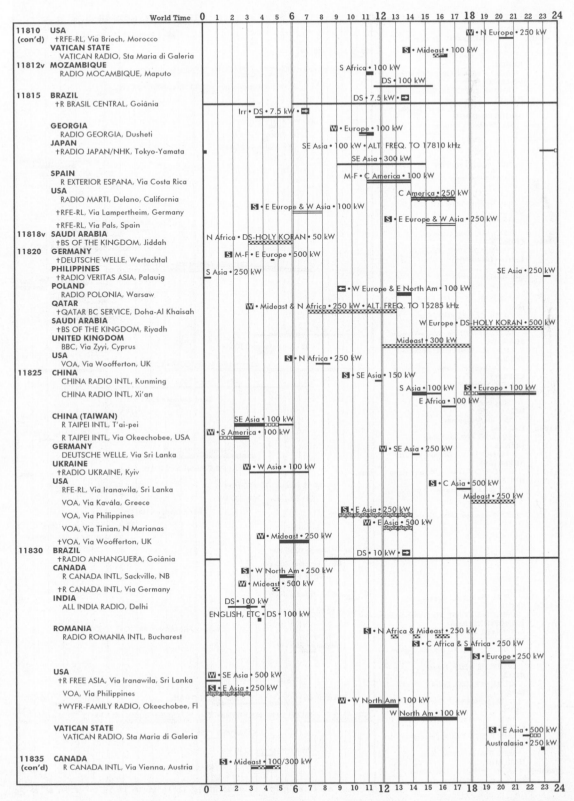

11810	**USA**
(con'd)	†RFE-RL, Via Briech, Morocco
	VATICAN STATE
	VATICAN RADIO, Sta Maria di Galeria
11812v	**MOZAMBIQUE**
	RADIO MOCAMBIQUE, Maputo
11815	**BRAZIL**
	†R BRASIL CENTRAL, Goiânia
	GEORGIA
	RADIO GEORGIA, Dusheti
	JAPAN
	†RADIO JAPAN/NHK, Tokyo-Yamata
	SPAIN
	R EXTERIOR ESPANA, Via Costa Rica
	USA
	RADIO MARTI, Delano, California
	†RFE-RL, Via Lampertheim, Germany
	†RFE-RL, Via Pals, Spain
11818v	**SAUDI ARABIA**
	†BS OF THE KINGDOM, Jiddah
11820	**GERMANY**
	†DEUTSCHE WELLE, Wertachtal
	PHILIPPINES
	†RADIO VERITAS ASIA, Palauig
	POLAND
	RADIO POLONIA, Warsaw
	QATAR
	†QATAR BC SERVICE, Doha-Al Khaisah
	SAUDI ARABIA
	†BS OF THE KINGDOM, Riyadh
	UNITED KINGDOM
	BBC, Via Zyyi, Cyprus
	USA
	VOA, Via Woofferton, UK
11825	**CHINA**
	CHINA RADIO INTL, Kunming
	CHINA RADIO INTL, Xi'an
	CHINA (TAIWAN)
	R TAIPEI INTL, T'ai-pei
	R TAIPEI INTL, Via Okeechobee, USA
	GERMANY
	DEUTSCHE WELLE, Via Sri Lanka
	UKRAINE
	†RADIO UKRAINE, Kyiv
	USA
	RFE-RL, Via Iranawila, Sri Lanka
	VOA, Via Kavála, Greece
	VOA, Via Philippines
	VOA, Via Tinian, N Marianas
	†VOA, Via Woofferton, UK
11830	**BRAZIL**
	†RADIO ANHANGUERA, Goiânia
	CANADA
	R CANADA INTL, Sackville, NB
	†R CANADA INTL, Via Germany
	INDIA
	ALL INDIA RADIO, Delhi
	ROMANIA
	RADIO ROMANIA INTL, Bucharest
	USA
	†R FREE ASIA, Via Iranawila, Sri Lanka
	VOA, Via Philippines
	†WYFR-FAMILY RADIO, Okeechobee, Fl
	VATICAN STATE
	VATICAN RADIO, Sta Maria di Galeria
11835	**CANADA**
(con'd)	R CANADA INTL, Via Vienna, Austria

World Time markings: 0 1 2 3 4 5 6 7 8 9 10 11 12 13 14 15 16 17 18 19 20 21 22 23 24

Transmission notes (as shown on chart):
- W • N Europe • 250 kW
- S • Mideast • 100 kW
- S Africa • 100 kW
- DS • 100 kW
- DS • 7.5 kW
- Irr • DS • 7.5 kW
- W • Europe • 100 kW
- SE Asia • 100 kW • ALT. FREQ. TO 17810 kHz
- SE Asia • 300 kW
- M-F • C America • 100 kW
- C America • 250 kW
- S • E Europe & W Asia • 100 kW
- S • E Europe & W Asia • 250 kW
- N Africa • DS-HOLY KORAN • 50 kW
- S • M-F • E Europe • 500 kW
- S Asia • 250 kW
- SE Asia • 250 kW
- W Europe & E North Am • 100 kW
- W • Mideast & N Africa • 250 kW • ALT. FREQ. TO 15285 kHz
- W Europe • DS-HOLY KORAN • 500 kW
- Mideast • 300 kW
- S • N Africa • 250 kW
- S • SE Asia • 150 kW
- S Asia • 100 kW
- S • Europe • 100 kW
- E Africa • 100 kW
- SE Asia • 100 kW
- W • S America • 100 kW
- W • SE Asia • 250 kW
- W • W Asia • 100 kW
- S • C Asia • 500 kW
- Mideast • 250 kW
- S • E Asia • 250 kW
- W • E Asia • 500 kW
- W • Mideast • 250 kW
- DS • 10 kW
- S • W North Am • 250 kW
- W • Mideast • 500 kW
- DS • 100 kW
- ENGLISH, ETC • DS • 100 kW
- S • N Africa & Mideast • 250 kW
- S • C Africa & S Africa • 250 kW
- S • Europe • 250 kW
- W • SE Asia • 500 kW
- S • E Asia • 250 kW
- W • W North Am • 100 kW
- W North Am • 100 kW
- S • E Asia • 500 kW
- Australasia • 250 kW
- S • Mideast • 100/300 kW

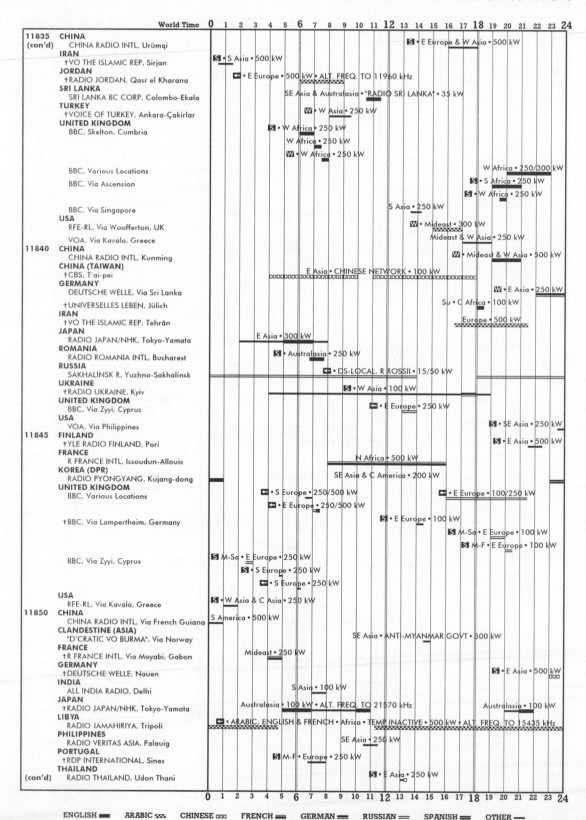

World Time 0 1 2 3 4 5 6 7 8 9 10 11 12 13 14 15 16 17 18 19 20 21 22 23 24

11835 CHINA
(con'd)   CHINA RADIO INTL, Urümqi — E Europe & W Asia • 500 kW
IRAN
†VO THE ISLAMIC REP, Sirjan — S Asia • 500 kW
JORDAN
†RADIO JORDAN, Qasr el Kharana — E Europe • 500 kW • ALT. FREQ. TO 11960 kHz
SRI LANKA
SRI LANKA BC CORP, Colombo-Ekala — SE Asia & Australasia • "RADIO SRI LANKA" • 35 kW
TURKEY
†VOICE OF TURKEY, Ankara-Çakirlar — W Asia • 250 kW
UNITED KINGDOM
BBC, Skelton, Cumbria — W Africa • 250 kW
W Africa • 250 kW
W Africa • 250 kW

BBC, Various Locations — W Africa • 250/300 kW
BBC, Via Ascension — S Africa • 250 kW
W Africa • 250 kW

BBC, Via Singapore — S Asia • 250 kW
USA
RFE-RL, Via Woofferton, UK — Mideast • 300 kW
VOA, Via Kavála, Greece — Mideast & W Asia • 250 kW
11840 CHINA
CHINA RADIO INTL, Kunming — Mideast & W Asia • 500 kW
CHINA (TAIWAN)
†CBS, T'ai-pei — E Asia • CHINESE NETWORK • 100 kW
GERMANY
DEUTSCHE WELLE, Via Sri Lanka — E Asia • 250 kW
†UNIVERSELLES LEBEN, Jülich — Su • C Africa • 100 kW
IRAN
†VO THE ISLAMIC REP, Tehrān — Europe • 500 kW
JAPAN
RADIO JAPAN/NHK, Tokyo-Yamata — E Asia • 300 kW
ROMANIA
RADIO ROMANIA INTL, Bucharest — Australasia • 250 kW
RUSSIA
SAKHALINSK R, Yuzhno-Sakhalinsk — DS-LOCAL, R ROSSII • 15/50 kW
UKRAINE
†RADIO UKRAINE, Kyiv — W Asia • 100 kW
UNITED KINGDOM
BBC, Via Zyyi, Cyprus — E Europe • 250 kW
USA
VOA, Via Philippines — SE Asia • 250 kW
11845 FINLAND
†YLE RADIO FINLAND, Pori — E Asia • 500 kW
FRANCE
R FRANCE INTL, Issoudun-Allouis — N Africa • 500 kW
KOREA (DPR)
RADIO PYONGYANG, Kujang-dong — SE Asia & C America • 200 kW
UNITED KINGDOM
BBC, Various Locations — S Europe • 250/500 kW — E Europe • 100/250 kW
E Europe • 250/500 kW
†BBC, Via Lampertheim, Germany — E Europe • 100 kW
M-Sa • E Europe • 100 kW
M-F • E Europe • 100 kW
BBC, Via Zyyi, Cyprus — M-Sa • E Europe • 250 kW
S Europe • 250 kW
S Europe • 250 kW
USA
RFE-RL, Via Kavála, Greece — W Asia & C Asia • 250 kW
11850 CHINA
CHINA RADIO INTL, Via French Guiana — S America • 500 kW
CLANDESTINE (ASIA)
"D'CRATIC VO BURMA", Via Norway — SE Asia • ANTI-MYANMAR GOVT • 500 kW
FRANCE
†R FRANCE INTL, Via Moyabi, Gabon — Mideast • 250 kW
GERMANY
†DEUTSCHE WELLE, Nauen — E Asia • 500 kW
INDIA
ALL INDIA RADIO, Delhi — S Asia • 100 kW
JAPAN
†RADIO JAPAN/NHK, Tokyo-Yamata — Australasia • 100 kW • ALT. FREQ. TO 21570 kHz — Australasia • 100 kW
LIBYA
RADIO JAMAHIRIYA, Tripoli — ARABIC, ENGLISH & FRENCH • Africa • TEMP INACTIVE • 500 kW • ALT. FREQ. TO 15435 kHz
PHILIPPINES
RADIO VERITAS ASIA, Palauig — SE Asia • 250 kW
PORTUGAL
†RDP INTERNATIONAL, Sines — M-F • Europe • 250 kW
THAILAND
(con'd)   RADIO THAILAND, Udon Thani — E Asia • 250 kW

0 1 2 3 4 5 6 7 8 9 10 11 12 13 14 15 16 17 18 19 20 21 22 23 24

ENGLISH ▬ ARABIC ⬚ CHINESE ⬚ FRENCH ═ GERMAN ▬ RUSSIAN ═ SPANISH ═ OTHER ▬

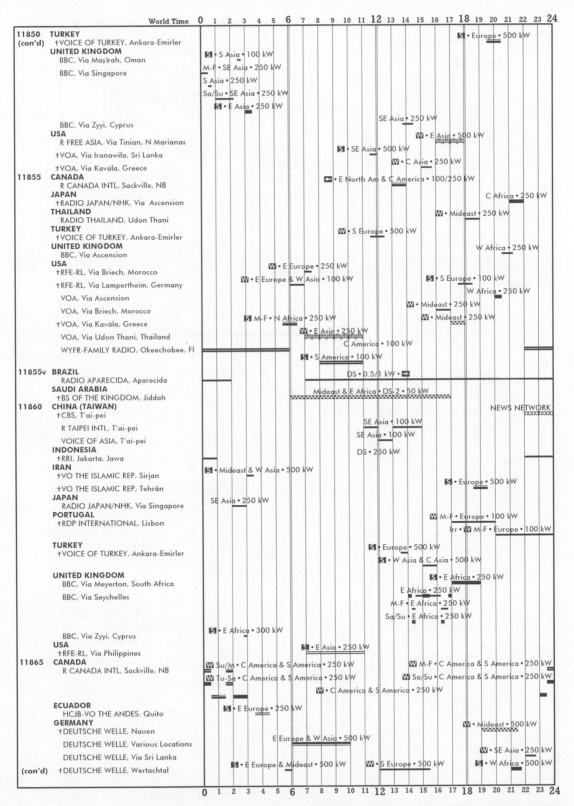

World Time 0 1 2 3 4 5 6 7 8 9 10 11 12 13 14 15 16 17 18 19 20 21 22 23 24

11850 TURKEY
(con'd) †VOICE OF TURKEY, Ankara-Emirler — **S** • Europe • 500 kW
UNITED KINGDOM
  BBC, Via Maşīrah, Oman — **S** • S Asia • 100 kW
  — M-F • SE Asia • 250 kW
  BBC, Via Singapore — S Asia • 250 kW
  — Sa/Su • SE Asia • 250 kW
  — **S** • E Asia • 250 kW
  BBC, Via Zyyi, Cyprus — SE Asia • 250 kW
USA
  R FREE ASIA, Via Tinian, N Marianas — **W** • E Asia • 500 kW
  †VOA, Via Iranawila, Sri Lanka — **S** • SE Asia • 500 kW
  †VOA, Via Kaválla, Greece — **W** • C Asia • 250 kW
11855 CANADA
  R CANADA INTL, Sackville, NB — **←** • E North Am & C America • 100/250 kW
JAPAN
  †RADIO JAPAN/NHK, Via Ascension — C Africa • 250 kW
THAILAND
  RADIO THAILAND, Udon Thani — **W** • Mideast • 250 kW
TURKEY
  †VOICE OF TURKEY, Ankara-Emirler — **W** • S Europe • 500 kW
UNITED KINGDOM
  BBC, Via Ascension — W Africa • 250 kW
USA
  †RFE-RL, Via Briech, Morocco — **W** • E Europe • 250 kW
  †RFE-RL, Via Lampertheim, Germany — **W** • E Europe & W Asia • 100 kW — **S** • S Europe • 100 kW
  VOA, Via Ascension — W Africa • 250 kW
  VOA, Via Briech, Morocco — **W** • Mideast • 250 kW
  †VOA, Via Kaválla, Greece — **S** M-F • N Africa • 250 kW — **W** • Mideast • 250 kW
  VOA, Via Udon Thani, Thailand — **W** • E Asia • 250 kW
  WYFR-FAMILY RADIO, Okeechobee, Fl — C America • 100 kW
  — **S** • S America • 100 kW
11855v BRAZIL
  RADIO APARECIDA, Aparecida — DS • 0.5/1 kW • **→**
SAUDI ARABIA
  †BS OF THE KINGDOM, Jiddah — Mideast & E Africa • DS-2 • 50 kW
11860 CHINA (TAIWAN)
  †CBS, T'ai-pei — NEWS NETWORK
  R TAIPEI INTL, T'ai-pei — SE Asia • 100 kW
  VOICE OF ASIA, T'ai-pei — SE Asia • 100 kW
INDONESIA
  †RRI, Jakarta, Jawa — DS • 250 kW
IRAN
  †VO THE ISLAMIC REP, Sirjan — **S** • Mideast & W Asia • 500 kW
  †VO THE ISLAMIC REP, Tehrān — **S** • Europe • 500 kW
JAPAN
  RADIO JAPAN/NHK, Via Singapore — SE Asia • 250 kW
PORTUGAL
  †RDP INTERNATIONAL, Lisbon — **W** M-F • Europe • 100 kW
  — Irr • **W** M-F • Europe • 100 kW
TURKEY
  †VOICE OF TURKEY, Ankara-Emirler — **S** • Europe • 500 kW
  — **S** • W Asia & C Asia • 500 kW
UNITED KINGDOM
  BBC, Via Meyerton, South Africa — **S** • E Africa • 250 kW
  BBC, Via Seychelles — E Africa • 250 kW
  — M-F • E Africa • 250 kW
  — Sa/Su • E Africa • 250 kW
  BBC, Via Zyyi, Cyprus — **S** • E Africa • 300 kW
USA
  †RFE-RL, Via Philippines — **S** • E Asia • 250 kW
11865 CANADA
  R CANADA INTL, Sackville, NB — **W** Su/M • C America & S America • 250 kW — **W** M-F • C America & S America • 250 kW
  — **W** Tu-Sa • C America & S America • 250 kW — **W** Sa/Su • C America & S America • 250 kW
  — **W** • C America & S America • 250 kW
ECUADOR
  HCJB-VO THE ANDES, Quito — **S** • E Europe • 250 kW
GERMANY
  †DEUTSCHE WELLE, Nauen — **W** • Mideast • 500 kW
  DEUTSCHE WELLE, Various Locations — E Europe & W Asia • 500 kW
  DEUTSCHE WELLE, Via Sri Lanka — **W** • SE Asia • 250 kW
(con'd) †DEUTSCHE WELLE, Wertachtal — **S** • E Europe & Mideast • 500 kW — **W** • S Europe • 500 kW — **S** • W Africa • 500 kW

0 1 2 3 4 5 6 7 8 9 10 11 12 13 14 15 16 17 18 19 20 21 22 23 24

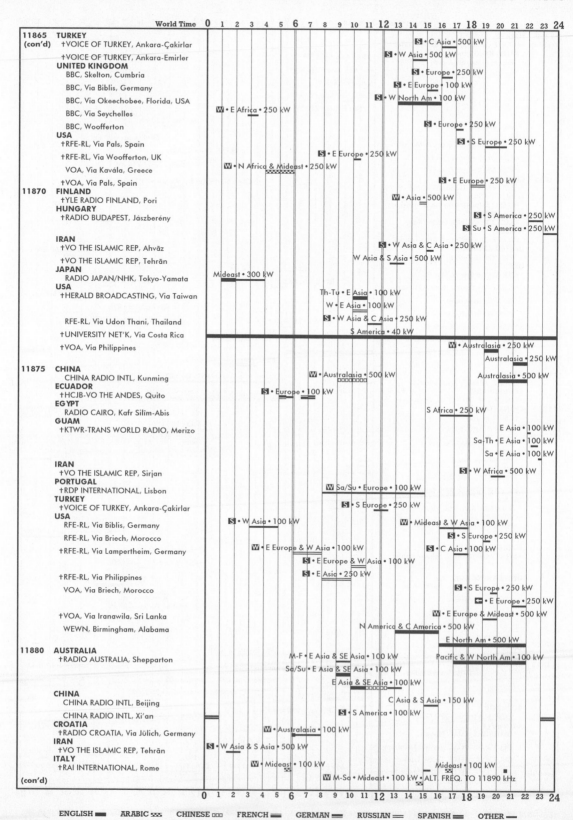

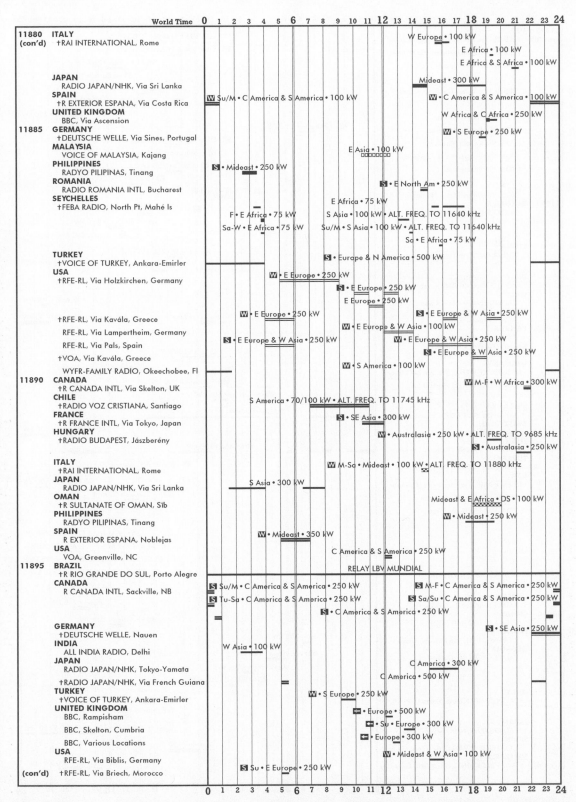

World Time   0 1 2 3 4 5 6 7 8 9 10 11 12 13 14 15 16 17 18 19 20 21 22 23 24

11880 ITALY
(con'd)   †RAI INTERNATIONAL, Rome
     W Europe • 100 kW
     E Africa • 100 kW
     E Africa & S Africa • 100 kW

JAPAN
   RADIO JAPAN/NHK, Via Sri Lanka   Mideast • 300 kW
SPAIN
   †R EXTERIOR ESPANA, Via Costa Rica   W Su/M • C America & S America • 100 kW   W • C America & S America • 100 kW
UNITED KINGDOM
   BBC, Via Ascension   W Africa & C Africa • 250 kW
11885 GERMANY
   †DEUTSCHE WELLE, Via Sines, Portugal   W • S Europe • 250 kW
MALAYSIA
   VOICE OF MALAYSIA, Kajang   E Asia • 100 kW
PHILIPPINES
   RADYO PILIPINAS, Tinang   S • Mideast • 250 kW
ROMANIA
   RADIO ROMANIA INTL, Bucharest   S • E North Am • 250 kW
SEYCHELLES
   †FEBA RADIO, North Pt, Mahé Is   E Africa • 75 kW
   F • E Africa • 75 kW   S Asia • 100 kW • ALT. FREQ. TO 11640 kHz
   Sa-W • E Africa • 75 kW   Su/M • S Asia • 100 kW • ALT. FREQ. TO 11640 kHz
   Sa • E Africa • 75 kW

TURKEY
   †VOICE OF TURKEY, Ankara-Emirler   S • Europe & N America • 500 kW
USA
   †RFE-RL, Via Holzkirchen, Germany   W • E Europe • 250 kW
   S • E Europe • 250 kW
   E Europe • 250 kW
   †RFE-RL, Via Kavála, Greece   W • E Europe • 250 kW   S • E Europe & W Asia • 250 kW
   RFE-RL, Via Lampertheim, Germany   W • E Europe & W Asia • 100 kW
   RFE-RL, Via Pals, Spain   S • E Europe & W Asia • 250 kW   W • E Europe & W Asia • 250 kW
   †VOA, Via Kavála, Greece   S • E Europe & W Asia • 250 kW
   WYFR-FAMILY RADIO, Okeechobee, Fl   W • S America • 100 kW
11890 CANADA
   †R CANADA INTL, Via Skelton, UK   W M-F • W Africa • 300 kW
CHILE
   †RADIO VOZ CRISTIANA, Santiago   S America • 70/100 kW • ALT. FREQ. TO 11745 kHz
FRANCE
   †R FRANCE INTL, Via Tokyo, Japan   S • SE Asia • 300 kW
HUNGARY
   †RADIO BUDAPEST, Jászberény   W • Australasia • 250 kW • ALT. FREQ. TO 9685 kHz
   S • Australasia • 250 kW
ITALY
   †RAI INTERNATIONAL, Rome   W M-Sa • Mideast • 100 kW • ALT. FREQ. TO 11880 kHz
JAPAN
   RADIO JAPAN/NHK, Via Sri Lanka   S Asia • 300 kW
OMAN
   †R SULTANATE OF OMAN, Sīb   Mideast & E Africa • DS • 100 kW
PHILIPPINES
   RADYO PILIPINAS, Tinang   W • Mideast • 250 kW
SPAIN
   R EXTERIOR ESPANA, Noblejas   W • Mideast • 350 kW
USA
   VOA, Greenville, NC   C America & S America • 250 kW
11895 BRAZIL
   †R RIO GRANDE DO SUL, Porto Alegre   RELAY LBV MUNDIAL
CANADA
   R CANADA INTL, Sackville, NB   S Su/M • C America & S America • 250 kW   S M-F • C America & S America • 250 kW
   S Tu-Sa • C America & S America • 250 kW   S Sa/Su • C America & S America • 250 kW
   S • C America & S America • 250 kW
GERMANY
   †DEUTSCHE WELLE, Nauen   S • SE Asia • 250 kW
INDIA
   ALL INDIA RADIO, Delhi   W Asia • 100 kW
JAPAN
   RADIO JAPAN/NHK, Tokyo-Yamata   C America • 300 kW
   †RADIO JAPAN/NHK, Via French Guiana   C America • 500 kW
TURKEY
   †VOICE OF TURKEY, Ankara-Emirler   W • S Europe • 250 kW
UNITED KINGDOM
   BBC, Rampisham   • Europe • 500 kW
   BBC, Skelton, Cumbria   • Su • Europe • 300 kW
   BBC, Various Locations   • Europe • 300 kW
USA
   RFE-RL, Via Biblis, Germany   W • Mideast & W Asia • 100 kW
(con'd)   †RFE-RL, Via Briech, Morocco   S Su • E Europe • 250 kW

0 1 2 3 4 5 6 7 8 9 10 11 12 13 14 15 16 17 18 19 20 21 22 23 24

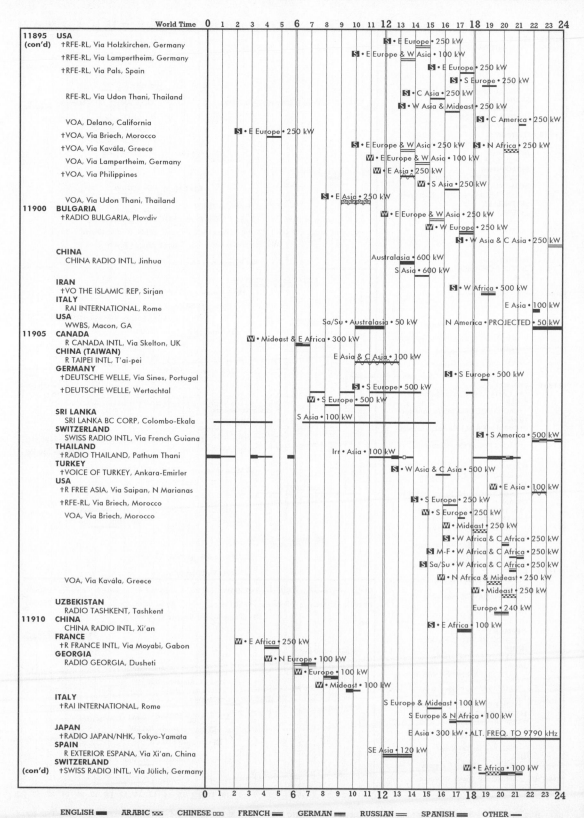

11895 **USA**	
(con'd) †RFE-RL, Via Holzkirchen, Germany	S • E Europe • 250 kW
†RFE-RL, Via Lampertheim, Germany	S • E Europe & W Asia • 100 kW
†RFE-RL, Via Pals, Spain	S • E Europe • 250 kW
	S • S Europe • 250 kW
RFE-RL, Via Udon Thani, Thailand	S • C Asia • 250 kW
	S • W Asia & Mideast • 250 kW
VOA, Delano, California	S • C America • 250 kW
†VOA, Via Briech, Morocco	S • E Europe • 250 kW
†VOA, Via Kavála, Greece	S • E Europe & W Asia • 250 kW S • N Africa • 250 kW
VOA, Via Lampertheim, Germany	W • E Europe & W Asia • 100 kW
†VOA, Via Philippines	W • E Asia • 250 kW
	W • S Asia • 250 kW
VOA, Via Udon Thani, Thailand	S • E Asia • 250 kW
11900 **BULGARIA**	
†RADIO BULGARIA, Plovdiv	W • E Europe & W Asia • 250 kW
	W • W Europe • 250 kW
	S • W Asia & C Asia • 250 kW
CHINA	
CHINA RADIO INTL, Jinhua	Australasia • 600 kW
	S Asia • 600 kW
IRAN	
†VO THE ISLAMIC REP, Sirjan	S • W Africa • 500 kW
ITALY	
RAI INTERNATIONAL, Rome	E Asia • 100 kW
USA	
WWBS, Macon, GA	Sa/Su • Australasia • 50 kW N America • PROJECTED • 50 kW
11905 **CANADA**	
R CANADA INTL, Via Skelton, UK	W • Mideast & E Africa • 300 kW
CHINA (TAIWAN)	
R TAIPEI INTL, T'ai-pei	E Asia & C Asia • 100 kW
GERMANY	
†DEUTSCHE WELLE, Via Sines, Portugal	S • S Europe • 500 kW
†DEUTSCHE WELLE, Wertachtal	S • S Europe • 500 kW
	W • S Europe • 500 kW
SRI LANKA	
SRI LANKA BC CORP, Colombo-Ekala	S Asia • 100 kW
SWITZERLAND	
SWISS RADIO INTL, Via French Guiana	S • S America • 500 kW
THAILAND	
†RADIO THAILAND, Pathum Thani	Irr • Asia • 100 kW
TURKEY	
†VOICE OF TURKEY, Ankara-Emirler	S • W Asia & C Asia • 500 kW
USA	
†R FREE ASIA, Via Saipan, N Marianas	W • E Asia • 100 kW
†RFE-RL, Via Briech, Morocco	S • S Europe • 250 kW
VOA, Via Briech, Morocco	W • S Europe • 250 kW
	W • Mideast • 250 kW
	S • W Africa & C Africa • 250 kW
	S M-F • W Africa & C Africa • 250 kW
	S Sa/Su • W Africa & C Africa • 250 kW
VOA, Via Kavála, Greece	W • N Africa & Mideast • 250 kW
	W • Mideast • 250 kW
UZBEKISTAN	
RADIO TASHKENT, Tashkent	Europe • 240 kW
11910 **CHINA**	
CHINA RADIO INTL, Xi'an	S • E Africa • 100 kW
FRANCE	
†R FRANCE INTL, Via Moyabi, Gabon	W • E Africa • 250 kW
GEORGIA	
RADIO GEORGIA, Dusheti	W • N Europe • 100 kW
	W • Europe • 100 kW
	W • Mideast • 100 kW
ITALY	
†RAI INTERNATIONAL, Rome	S Europe & Mideast • 100 kW
	S Europe & N Africa • 100 kW
JAPAN	
†RADIO JAPAN/NHK, Tokyo-Yamata	E Asia • 300 kW • ALT. FREQ. TO 9790 kHz
SPAIN	
R EXTERIOR ESPANA, Via Xi'an, China	SE Asia • 120 kW
SWITZERLAND	
(con'd) †SWISS RADIO INTL, Via Jülich, Germany	W • E Africa • 100 kW

World Time: 0 1 2 3 4 5 6 7 8 9 10 11 12 13 14 15 16 17 18 19 20 21 22 23 24

ENGLISH ▬   ARABIC ▨   CHINESE ▭▭▭   FRENCH ══   GERMAN ▬▬   RUSSIAN ══   SPANISH ══   OTHER ▬

World Time — 0 1 2 3 4 5 6 7 8 9 10 11 **12** 13 14 15 16 17 **18** 19 20 21 22 23 **24**

11910 TURKEY
(con'd) †VOICE OF TURKEY, Ankara-Çakirlar — S • Europe • 250 kW / W • Europe • 250 kW
  †VOICE OF TURKEY, Ankara-Emirler — S • Europe • 500 kW
  USA
  RFE-RL, Via Biblis, Germany — W • W Asia & C Asia • 100 kW
  †RFE-RL, Via Briech, Morocco — S • E Europe & W Asia • 250 kW
  †RFE-RL, Via Udon Thani, Thailand — W • C Asia • 250 kW

11913v SAUDI ARABIA
  †BS OF THE KINGDOM, Jiddah — W Asia • DS-1 • 50 kW • ALT. FREQ. TO 11948v kHz

11915 BRAZIL
  †RADIO GAUCHA, Porto Alegre — DS • 7.5 kW • ➡ / Irr • DS • 7.5 kW • ➡

  CANADA
  R CANADA INTL, Via Skelton, UK — W • E Europe • 300 kW
  CHINA
  CHINA RADIO INTL, Xi'an — SE Asia • 100 kW
  CHINA (TAIWAN)
  †R TAIPEI INTL, T'ai-pei — E Asia • 100 kW / SE Asia • 100 kW
  GERMANY
  DEUTSCHE WELLE, Via Sri Lanka — S • SE Asia & Australasia • 250 kW / S • SE Asia • 250 kW
  †DEUTSCHE WELLE, Wertachtal — S • E Europe & W Asia • 500 kW
  RUSSIA
  †VOICE OF TATARSTAN, Samara — W • N Europe • TATAR, RUSSIAN • 200 kW
  USA
  †RFE-RL, Via Briech, Morocco — W • E Europe • 250 kW
  RFE-RL, Via Holzkirchen, Germany — S • E Europe & W Asia • 250 kW
  RFE-RL, Via Kavála, Greece — S • W Asia & C Asia • 250 kW
  †VOA, Via São Tomé — W • C Africa • 100 kW / W M-F • N Africa & W Africa • 100 kW

11920 CANADA
  †R CANADA INTL, Sackville, NB — S • E North Am & C America • 250 kW
  ECUADOR
  HCJB-VO THE ANDES, Quito — S America • 100 kW
  ITALY
  †RAI INTERNATIONAL, Via Singapore — Australasia • 250 kW
  JAPAN
  †RADIO JAPAN/NHK, Via Singapore — Australasia • 250 kW / Australasia • 250 kW • ALT. FREQ. TO 6035 kHz
  MOROCCO
  †RTV MAROCAINE, Briech — S • N Africa & Mideast • 500 kW
  UNITED KINGDOM
  BBC, Via Maṣīrah, Oman — W Asia & S Asia • 100 kW
  BBC, Via Singapore — SE Asia • 250 kW
  USA
  †ADVENTIST WORLD R, Via Agat, Guam — SE Asia • 100 kW
  †VOA, Via Saipan, N Marianas — W • S Asia • 100 kW
  VOA, Via Udon Thani, Thailand — W • E Africa • 250 kW

11925 BRAZIL
  RADIO BANDEIRANTES, São Paulo — DS • 10 kW
  CHINA
  CENTRAL PEOPLE'S BS, Lingshi — W • DS-1 • 50 kW / DS-1 • 50 kW
  IRAN
  †VO THE ISLAMIC REP, Ahvāz — S • W Asia & C Asia • 250 kW
  RUSSIA
  VOICE OF TATARSTAN, Samara — S • N Europe • TATAR, RUSSIAN • 200 kW
  TURKEY
  †VOICE OF TURKEY, Ankara-Çakirlar — W • Mideast • 250 kW
  USA
  †RFE-RL, Via Briech, Morocco — S • S Europe • 250 kW / S • E Europe & W Asia • 250 kW
  †VOA, Greenville, NC — S M-F • C America • 250 kW / S • C America • 250 kW
  †VOA, Via Lampertheim, Germany — S • E Europe & Mideast • 100 kW
  VOA, Via Philippines — E Asia • 250 kW
  †VOA, Via Udon Thani, Thailand — E Asia • 250 kW

11930 IRAN
  †VO THE ISLAMIC REP, Sirjan — W Asia & C Asia • 500 kW
  JORDAN
  †RADIO JORDAN, Qasr el Kharana — ➡ • W Europe & E North Am • 500 kW
  PAKISTAN
  †RADIO PAKISTAN, Islamabad — S Asia • 100 kW • ALT. FREQ. TO 12015 kHz
  TURKEY
  †VOICE OF TURKEY, Ankara-Çakirlar — ➡ • E Europe • 250 kW / S • S Europe • 250 kW

(con'd)

World Time — 0 1 2 3 4 5 6 7 8 9 10 11 **12** 13 14 15 16 17 **18** 19 20 21 22 23 **24**

SEASONAL **S** OR **W**   1-HR TIMESHIFT MIDYEAR ➡ OR ➡   JAMMING / OR ∧   EARLIEST HEARD ◁   LATEST HEARD ▷   NEW FOR 2001 †

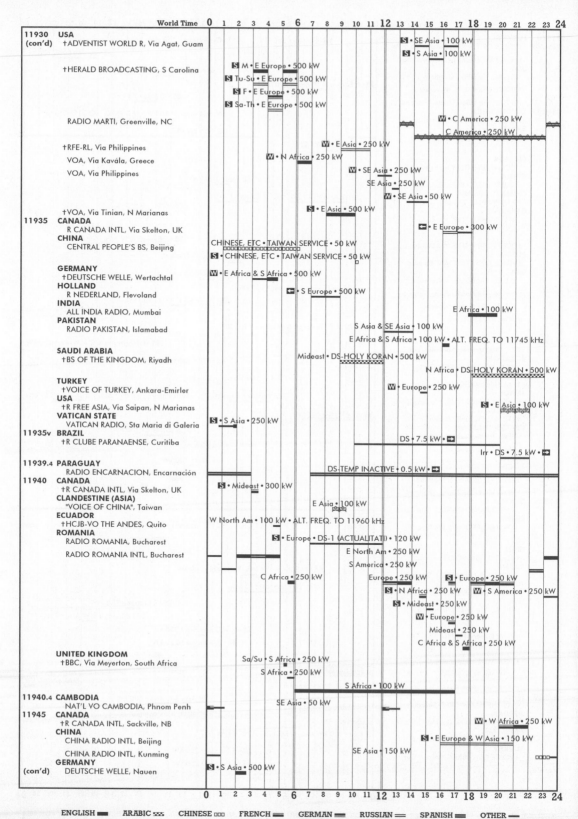

| World Time | 0 | 1 | 2 | 3 | 4 | 5 | 6 | 7 | 8 | 9 | 10 | 11 | 12 | 13 | 14 | 15 | 16 | 17 | 18 | 19 | 20 | 21 | 22 | 23 | 24 |

11930 USA
(con'd) †ADVENTIST WORLD R, Via Agat, Guam — S • SE Asia • 100 kW; S • S Asia • 100 kW

†HERALD BROADCASTING, S Carolina — S M • E Europe • 500 kW; S Tu-Su • E Europe • 500 kW; S F • E Europe • 500 kW; S Sa-Th • E Europe • 500 kW

RADIO MARTI, Greenville, NC — W • C America • 250 kW; C America • 250 kW

†RFE-RL, Via Philippines — W • E Asia • 250 kW
VOA, Via Kavála, Greece — W • N Africa • 250 kW
VOA, Via Philippines — W • SE Asia • 250 kW; SE Asia • 250 kW; W • SE Asia • 50 kW

†VOA, Via Tinian, N Marianas — S • E Asia • 500 kW

11935 CANADA
R CANADA INTL, Via Skelton, UK — E Europe • 300 kW

CHINA
CENTRAL PEOPLE'S BS, Beijing — CHINESE, ETC • TAIWAN SERVICE • 50 kW; S • CHINESE, ETC • TAIWAN SERVICE • 50 kW

GERMANY
†DEUTSCHE WELLE, Wertachtal — W • E Africa & S Africa • 500 kW

HOLLAND
R NEDERLAND, Flevoland — S Europe • 500 kW

INDIA
ALL INDIA RADIO, Mumbai — E Africa • 100 kW

PAKISTAN
RADIO PAKISTAN, Islamabad — S Asia & SE Asia • 100 kW; E Africa & S Africa • 100 kW • ALT. FREQ. TO 11745 kHz

SAUDI ARABIA
†BS OF THE KINGDOM, Riyadh — Mideast • DS-HOLY KORAN • 500 kW; N Africa • DS-HOLY KORAN • 500 kW

TURKEY
†VOICE OF TURKEY, Ankara-Emirler — W • Europe • 250 kW

USA
†R FREE ASIA, Via Saipan, N Marianas — S • E Asia • 100 kW

VATICAN STATE
VATICAN RADIO, Sta Maria di Galeria — S • S Asia • 250 kW

11935v BRAZIL
†R CLUBE PARANAENSE, Curitiba — DS • 7.5 kW; Irr • DS • 7.5 kW

11939.4 PARAGUAY
RADIO ENCARNACION, Encarnación — DS-TEMP INACTIVE • 0.5 kW

11940 CANADA
†R CANADA INTL, Via Skelton, UK — S • Mideast • 300 kW

CLANDESTINE (ASIA)
"VOICE OF CHINA", Taiwan — E Asia • 100 kW

ECUADOR
†HCJB-VO THE ANDES, Quito — W North Am • 100 kW • ALT. FREQ. TO 11960 kHz

ROMANIA
RADIO ROMANIA, Bucharest — S • Europe • DS-1 (ACTUALITATI) • 120 kW

RADIO ROMANIA INTL, Bucharest — E North Am • 250 kW; S America • 250 kW; C Africa • 250 kW; Europe • 250 kW; S • Europe • 250 kW; S • N Africa • 250 kW; W • S America • 250 kW; S • Mideast • 250 kW; W • Europe • 250 kW; Mideast • 250 kW; C Africa & S Africa • 250 kW

UNITED KINGDOM
†BBC, Via Meyerton, South Africa — Sa/Su • S Africa • 250 kW; S Africa • 250 kW; S Africa • 100 kW

11940.4 CAMBODIA
NAT'L VO CAMBODIA, Phnom Penh — SE Asia • 50 kW

11945 CANADA
†R CANADA INTL, Sackville, NB — W • W Africa • 250 kW

CHINA
CHINA RADIO INTL, Beijing — S • E Europe & W Asia • 150 kW

CHINA RADIO INTL, Kunming — SE Asia • 150 kW

GERMANY
(con'd) DEUTSCHE WELLE, Nauen — S • S Asia • 500 kW

| World Time | 0 | 1 | 2 | 3 | 4 | 5 | 6 | 7 | 8 | 9 | 10 | 11 | 12 | 13 | 14 | 15 | 16 | 17 | 18 | 19 | 20 | 21 | 22 | 23 | 24 |

ENGLISH ▬   ARABIC ▨   CHINESE ▢▢▢   FRENCH ▬   GERMAN ▬   RUSSIAN ▬   SPANISH ▬   OTHER ▬

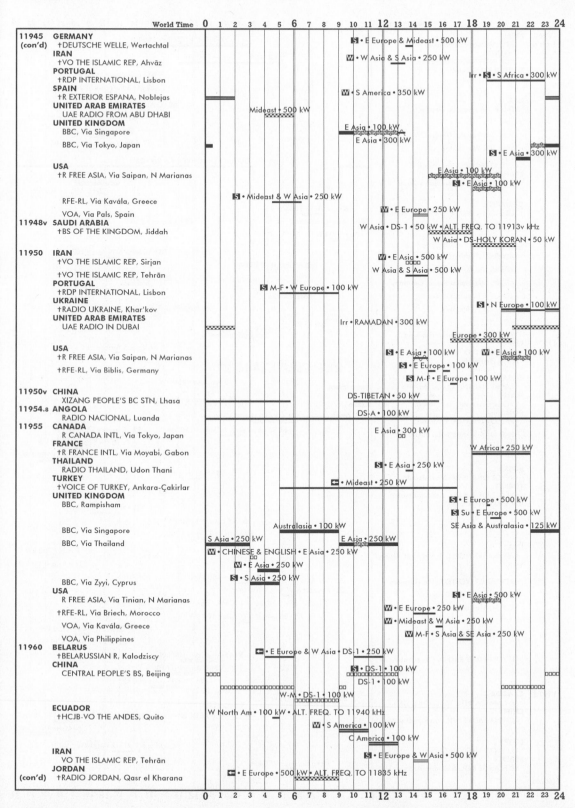

	World Time	0 1 2 3 4 5 6 7 8 9 10 11 12 13 14 15 16 17 18 19 20 21 22 23 24

11945 **GERMANY**
(con'd)   †DEUTSCHE WELLE, Wertachtal — **S** • E Europe & Mideast • 500 kW

IRAN
  †VO THE ISLAMIC REP, Ahvāz — **W** • W Asia & S Asia • 250 kW

PORTUGAL
  †RDP INTERNATIONAL, Lisbon — Irr • **S** • S Africa • 300 kW

SPAIN
  †R EXTERIOR ESPANA, Noblejas — **W** • S America • 350 kW

UNITED ARAB EMIRATES
  UAE RADIO FROM ABU DHABI — Mideast • 500 kW

UNITED KINGDOM
  BBC, Via Singapore — E Asia • 100 kW
                     E Asia • 300 kW

  BBC, Via Tokyo, Japan — **S** • E Asia • 300 kW

USA
  †R FREE ASIA, Via Saipan, N Marianas — E Asia • 100 kW
                                         S • E Asia • 100 kW

  RFE-RL, Via Kavála, Greece — **S** • Mideast & W Asia • 250 kW

  VOA, Via Pals, Spain — **W** • E Europe • 250 kW

11948v SAUDI ARABIA
  †BS OF THE KINGDOM, Jiddah — W Asia • DS-1 • 50 kW • ALT. FREQ. TO 11913v kHz
                               W Asia • DS-HOLY KORAN • 50 kW

11950 IRAN
  †VO THE ISLAMIC REP, Sirjan — **W** • E Asia • 500 kW

  †VO THE ISLAMIC REP, Tehrān — W Asia & S Asia • 500 kW

PORTUGAL
  †RDP INTERNATIONAL, Lisbon — **S** M-F • W Europe • 100 kW

UKRAINE
  †RADIO UKRAINE, Khar'kov — **S** • N Europe • 100 kW

UNITED ARAB EMIRATES
  UAE RADIO IN DUBAI — Irr • RAMADAN • 300 kW
                       Europe • 300 kW

USA
  †R FREE ASIA, Via Saipan, N Marianas — **S** • E Asia • 100 kW
                                         W • E Asia • 100 kW

  †RFE-RL, Via Biblis, Germany — **S** • E Europe • 100 kW
                                 S M-F • E Europe • 100 kW

11950v CHINA
  XIZANG PEOPLE'S BC STN, Lhasa — DS-TIBETAN • 50 kW

11954.8 ANGOLA
  RADIO NACIONAL, Luanda — DS-A • 100 kW

11955 CANADA
  R CANADA INTL, Via Tokyo, Japan — E Asia • 300 kW

FRANCE
  †R FRANCE INTL, Via Moyabi, Gabon — W Africa • 250 kW

THAILAND
  RADIO THAILAND, Udon Thani — **S** • E Asia • 250 kW

TURKEY
  †VOICE OF TURKEY, Ankara-Çakirlar — ◧ • Mideast • 250 kW

UNITED KINGDOM
  BBC, Rampisham — **S** • E Europe • 500 kW
                   S Su • E Europe • 500 kW

  BBC, Via Singapore — Australasia • 100 kW
                       SE Asia & Australasia • 125 kW

  BBC, Via Thailand — S Asia • 250 kW
                      E Asia • 250 kW
                      W • CHINESE & ENGLISH • E Asia • 250 kW
                      W • E Asia • 250 kW

  BBC, Via Zyyi, Cyprus — **S** • S Asia • 250 kW

USA
  R FREE ASIA, Via Tinian, N Marianas — **S** • E Asia • 500 kW

  †RFE-RL, Via Briech, Morocco — **W** • E Europe • 250 kW

  VOA, Via Kavála, Greece — **W** • Mideast & W Asia • 250 kW

  VOA, Via Philippines — **W** M-F • S Asia & SE Asia • 250 kW

11960 BELARUS
  †BELARUSSIAN R, Kalodziscy — ◧ • E Europe & W Asia • DS-1 • 250 kW

CHINA
  CENTRAL PEOPLE'S BS, Beijing — **S** • DS-1 • 100 kW
                                 DS-1 • 100 kW
                                 W-M • DS-1 • 100 kW

ECUADOR
  †HCJB-VO THE ANDES, Quito — W North Am • 100 kW • ALT. FREQ. TO 11940 kHz
                              W • S America • 100 kW
                              C America • 100 kW

IRAN
  VO THE ISLAMIC REP, Tehrān — **S** • E Europe & W Asia • 500 kW

JORDAN
(con'd)   †RADIO JORDAN, Qasr el Kharana — ◧ • E Europe • 500 kW • ALT. FREQ. TO 11835 kHz

	0 1 2 3 4 5 6 7 8 9 10 11 12 13 14 15 16 17 18 19 20 21 22 23 24

SEASONAL **S** OR **W**   1-HR TIMESHIFT MIDYEAR ◧ OR ◨   JAMMING / OR ∧   EARLIEST HEARD ◁   LATEST HEARD ▷   NEW FOR 2001 †

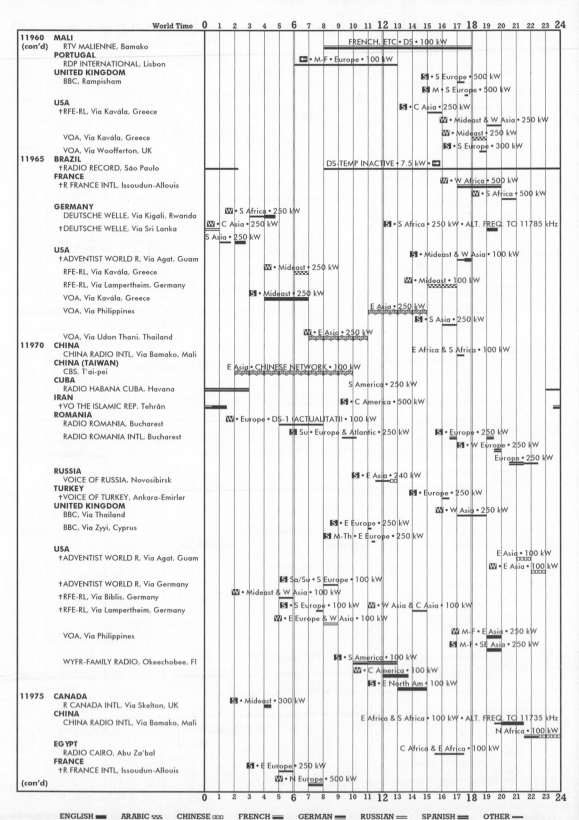

| | World Time | 0 | 1 | 2 | 3 | 4 | 5 | 6 | 7 | 8 | 9 | 10 | 11 | 12 | 13 | 14 | 15 | 16 | 17 | 18 | 19 | 20 | 21 | 22 | 23 | 24 |

11960 **MALI**
(con'd) RTV MALIENNE, Bamako — FRENCH, ETC • DS • 100 kW
PORTUGAL
RDP INTERNATIONAL, Lisbon — ◄ • M-F • Europe • 100 kW
UNITED KINGDOM
BBC, Rampisham — S • S Europe • 500 kW / S M • S Europe • 500 kW
USA
†RFE-RL, Via Kavála, Greece — S • C Asia • 250 kW
W • Mideast & W Asia • 250 kW
VOA, Via Kavála, Greece — W • Mideast • 250 kW
VOA, Via Woofferton, UK — S • S Europe • 300 kW

11965 **BRAZIL**
†RADIO RECORD, São Paulo — DS-TEMP INACTIVE • 7.5 kW • ►
FRANCE
†R FRANCE INTL, Issoudun-Allouis — W • W Africa • 500 kW / W • S Africa • 500 kW
GERMANY
DEUTSCHE WELLE, Via Kigali, Rwanda — W • S Africa • 250 kW
†DEUTSCHE WELLE, Via Sri Lanka — W • C Asia • 250 kW / S • S Africa • 250 kW • ALT. FREQ. TO 11785 kHz
S Asia • 250 kW
USA
†ADVENTIST WORLD R, Via Agat, Guam — S • Mideast & W Asia • 100 kW
RFE-RL, Via Kavála, Greece — W • Mideast • 250 kW
RFE-RL, Via Lampertheim, Germany — W • Mideast • 100 kW
VOA, Via Kavála, Greece — S • Mideast • 250 kW
VOA, Via Philippines — E Asia • 250 kW / S • S Asia • 250 kW
VOA, Via Udon Thani, Thailand — W • E Asia • 250 kW

11970 **CHINA**
CHINA RADIO INTL, Via Bamako, Mali — E Africa & S Africa • 100 kW
CHINA (TAIWAN)
CBS, T'ai-pei — E Asia • CHINESE NETWORK • 100 kW
CUBA
RADIO HABANA CUBA, Havana — S America • 250 kW
IRAN
†VO THE ISLAMIC REP, Tehrän — S • C America • 500 kW
ROMANIA
RADIO ROMANIA, Bucharest — W • Europe • DS-1 (ACTUALITATI) • 100 kW
RADIO ROMANIA INTL, Bucharest — S Su • Europe & Atlantic • 250 kW / S • Europe • 250 kW / S • W Europe • 250 kW
Europe • 250 kW
RUSSIA
VOICE OF RUSSIA, Novosibirsk — S • E Asia • 240 kW
TURKEY
†VOICE OF TURKEY, Ankara-Emirler — S • Europe • 250 kW
UNITED KINGDOM
BBC, Via Thailand — W • W Asia • 250 kW
BBC, Via Zyyi, Cyprus — S • E Europe • 250 kW / S M-Th • E Europe • 250 kW
USA
†ADVENTIST WORLD R, Via Agat, Guam — E Asia • 100 kW / W • E Asia • 100 kW
†ADVENTIST WORLD R, Via Germany — S Sa/Su • S Europe • 100 kW
†RFE-RL, Via Biblis, Germany — W • Mideast & W Asia • 100 kW
†RFE-RL, Via Lampertheim, Germany — S • S Europe • 100 kW / W • W Asia & C Asia • 100 kW
W • E Europe & W Asia • 100 kW
VOA, Via Philippines — W M-F • E Asia • 250 kW / S M-F • SE Asia • 250 kW
WYFR-FAMILY RADIO, Okeechobee, Fl — S • S America • 100 kW
W • C America • 100 kW
S • E North Am • 100 kW

11975 **CANADA**
R CANADA INTL, Via Skelton, UK — S • Mideast • 300 kW
CHINA
CHINA RADIO INTL, Via Bamako, Mali — E Africa & S Africa • 100 kW • ALT. FREQ. TO 11735 kHz
N Africa • 100 kW
EGYPT
RADIO CAIRO, Abu Za'bal — C Africa & E Africa • 100 kW
FRANCE
†R FRANCE INTL, Issoudun-Allouis — S • E Europe • 250 kW

(con'd) W • N Europe • 500 kW

| | World Time | 0 | 1 | 2 | 3 | 4 | 5 | 6 | 7 | 8 | 9 | 10 | 11 | 12 | 13 | 14 | 15 | 16 | 17 | 18 | 19 | 20 | 21 | 22 | 23 | 24 |

ENGLISH ▬   ARABIC ▨   CHINESE ▫▫▫   FRENCH ═   GERMAN ▬   RUSSIAN ═   SPANISH ▬   OTHER ▬

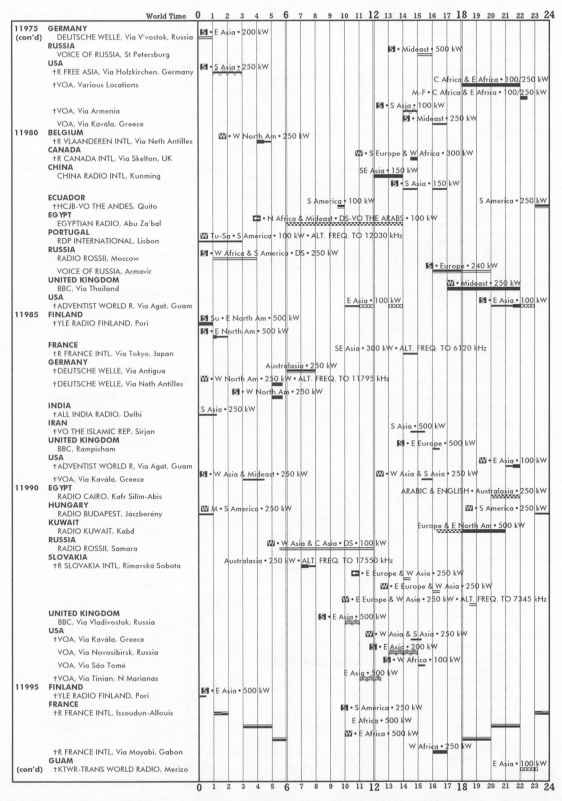

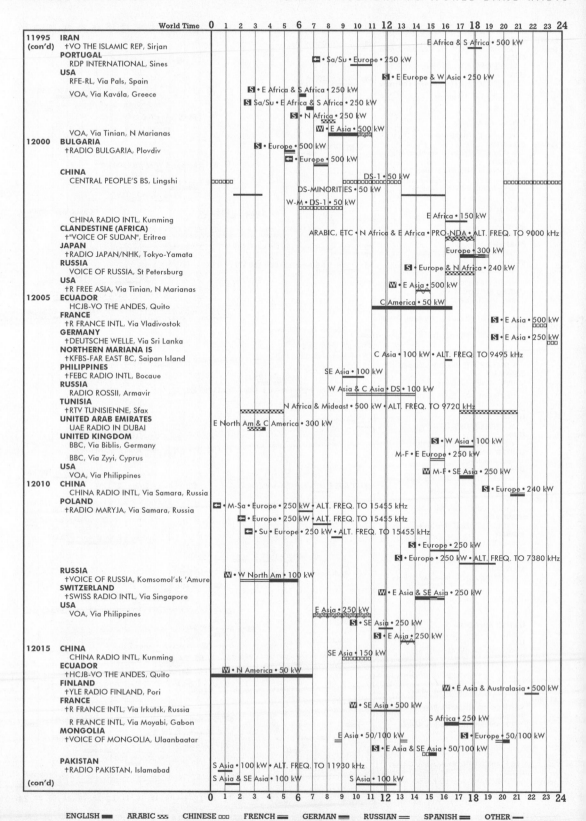

World Time 0 1 2 3 4 5 6 7 8 9 10 11 12 13 14 15 16 17 18 19 20 21 22 23 24

11995
(con'd) IRAN
†VO THE ISLAMIC REP, Sirjan — E Africa & S Africa • 500 kW
PORTUGAL
RDP INTERNATIONAL, Sines — Sa/Su • Europe • 250 kW
USA
RFE-RL, Via Pals, Spain — E Europe & W Asia • 250 kW
VOA, Via Kavála, Greece — S • E Africa & S Africa • 250 kW
— S • Sa/Su • E Africa & S Africa • 250 kW
— S • N Africa • 250 kW
VOA, Via Tinian, N Marianas — W • E Asia • 500 kW

12000 BULGARIA
†RADIO BULGARIA, Plovdiv — S • Europe • 500 kW
— Europe • 500 kW

CHINA
CENTRAL PEOPLE'S BS, Lingshi — DS-1 • 50 kW
— DS-MINORITIES • 50 kW
— W-M • DS-1 • 50 kW

CHINA RADIO INTL, Kunming — E Africa • 150 kW
CLANDESTINE (AFRICA)
†"VOICE OF SUDAN", Eritrea — ARABIC, ETC • N Africa & E Africa • PRO-NDA • ALT. FREQ. TO 9000 kHz
JAPAN
†RADIO JAPAN/NHK, Tokyo-Yamata — Europe • 300 kW
RUSSIA
VOICE OF RUSSIA, St Petersburg — S • Europe & N Africa • 240 kW
USA
†R FREE ASIA, Via Tinian, N Marianas — W • E Asia • 500 kW

12005 ECUADOR
HCJB-VO THE ANDES, Quito — C America • 50 kW
FRANCE
†R FRANCE INTL, Via Vladivostok — S • E Asia • 500 kW
GERMANY
†DEUTSCHE WELLE, Via Sri Lanka — S • E Asia • 250 kW
NORTHERN MARIANA IS
†KFBS-FAR EAST BC, Saipan Island — C Asia • 100 kW • ALT. FREQ TO 9495 kHz
PHILIPPINES
†FEBC RADIO INTL, Bocaue — SE Asia • 100 kW
RUSSIA
RADIO ROSSII, Armavir — W Asia & C Asia • DS • 100 kW
TUNISIA
†RTV TUNISIENNE, Sfax — N Africa & Mideast • 500 kW • ALT. FREQ. TO 9720 kHz
UNITED ARAB EMIRATES
UAE RADIO IN DUBAI — E North Am & C America • 300 kW
UNITED KINGDOM
BBC, Via Biblis, Germany — S • W Asia • 100 kW
BBC, Via Zyyi, Cyprus — M-F • E Europe • 250 kW
USA
VOA, Via Philippines — W M-F • SE Asia • 250 kW

12010 CHINA
CHINA RADIO INTL, Via Samara, Russia — S • Europe • 240 kW
POLAND
†RADIO MARYJA, Via Samara, Russia — M-Sa • Europe • 250 kW • ALT. FREQ. TO 15455 kHz
— Europe • 250 kW • ALT. FREQ. TO 15455 kHz
— Su • Europe • 250 kW • ALT. FREQ. TO 15455 kHz
— S • Europe • 250 kW
— S • Europe • 250 kW • ALT. FREQ. TO 7380 kHz

RUSSIA
†VOICE OF RUSSIA, Komsomol'sk 'Amure — W • W North Am • 100 kW
SWITZERLAND
†SWISS RADIO INTL, Via Singapore — W • E Asia & SE Asia • 250 kW
USA
VOA, Via Philippines — E Asia • 250 kW
— S • SE Asia • 250 kW
— S • E Asia • 250 kW

12015 CHINA
CHINA RADIO INTL, Kunming — SE Asia • 150 kW
ECUADOR
†HCJB-VO THE ANDES, Quito — W • N America • 50 kW
FINLAND
†YLE RADIO FINLAND, Pori — W • E Asia & Australasia • 500 kW
FRANCE
†R FRANCE INTL, Via Irkutsk, Russia — W • SE Asia • 500 kW
R FRANCE INTL, Via Moyabi, Gabon — S Africa • 250 kW
MONGOLIA
†VOICE OF MONGOLIA, Ulaanbaatar — E Asia • 50/100 kW
— S • Europe • 50/100 kW
— S • E Asia & SE Asia • 50/100 kW
PAKISTAN
†RADIO PAKISTAN, Islamabad — S Asia • 100 kW • ALT. FREQ. TO 11930 kHz
— S Asia & SE Asia • 100 kW
— S Asia • 100 kW

(con'd)

0 1 2 3 4 5 6 7 8 9 10 11 12 13 14 15 16 17 18 19 20 21 22 23 24

ENGLISH ▪▪ ARABIC ⋉⋉ CHINESE □□□ FRENCH ═ GERMAN ▬ RUSSIAN ═ SPANISH ═ OTHER ─

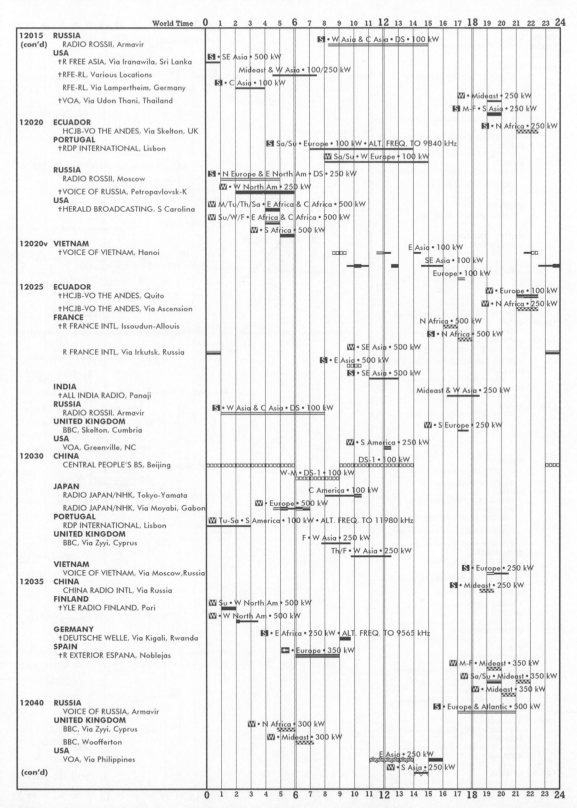

	World Time	0 1 2 3 4 5 6 7 8 9 10 11 12 13 14 15 16 17 18 19 20 21 22 23 24

12015 **RUSSIA**
(con'd)   RADIO ROSSII, Armavir — S • W Asia & C Asia • DS • 100 kW
USA
  †R FREE ASIA, Via Iranawila, Sri Lanka — S • SE Asia • 500 kW
  †RFE-RL, Various Locations — Mideast & W Asia • 100/250 kW
  RFE-RL, Via Lampertheim, Germany — S • C Asia • 100 kW
  †VOA, Via Udon Thani, Thailand — W • Mideast • 250 kW
    — S M-F • S Asia • 250 kW

12020 **ECUADOR**
  HCJB-VO THE ANDES, Via Skelton, UK — S • N Africa • 250 kW
PORTUGAL
  †RDP INTERNATIONAL, Lisbon — S Sa/Su • Europe • 100 kW • ALT. FREQ. TO 9840 kHz
    — W Sa/Su • W Europe • 100 kW
RUSSIA
  RADIO ROSSII, Moscow — S • N Europe & E North Am • DS • 250 kW
  †VOICE OF RUSSIA, Petropavlovsk-K — W • W North Am • 250 kW
USA
  †HERALD BROADCASTING, S Carolina — W M/Tu/Th/Sa • E Africa & C Africa • 500 kW
    — W Su/W/F • E Africa & C Africa • 500 kW
    — W • S Africa • 500 kW

12020v **VIETNAM**
  †VOICE OF VIETNAM, Hanoi — E Asia • 100 kW
    — SE Asia • 100 kW
    — Europe • 100 kW

12025 **ECUADOR**
  †HCJB-VO THE ANDES, Quito — W • Europe • 100 kW
  †HCJB-VO THE ANDES, Via Ascension — W • N Africa • 250 kW
FRANCE
  †R FRANCE INTL, Issoudun-Allouis — N Africa • 500 kW
    — S • N Africa • 500 kW
  R FRANCE INTL, Via Irkutsk, Russia — W • SE Asia • 500 kW
    — S • E Asia • 500 kW
    — S • SE Asia • 500 kW
INDIA
  †ALL INDIA RADIO, Panaji — Mideast & W Asia • 250 kW
RUSSIA
  RADIO ROSSII, Armavir — S • W Asia & C Asia • DS • 100 kW
UNITED KINGDOM
  BBC, Skelton, Cumbria — W • S Europe • 250 kW
USA
  VOA, Greenville, NC — W • S America • 250 kW

12030 **CHINA**
  CENTRAL PEOPLE'S BS, Beijing — DS-1 • 100 kW
    — W-M • DS-1 • 100 kW
JAPAN
  RADIO JAPAN/NHK, Tokyo-Yamata — C America • 100 kW
  RADIO JAPAN/NHK, Via Moyabi, Gabon — W • Europe • 500 kW
PORTUGAL
  RDP INTERNATIONAL, Lisbon — W Tu-Sa • S America • 100 kW • ALT. FREQ. TO 11980 kHz
UNITED KINGDOM
  BBC, Via Zyyi, Cyprus — F • W Asia • 250 kW
    — Th/F • W Asia • 250 kW
VIETNAM
  VOICE OF VIETNAM, Via Moscow, Russia — S • Europe • 250 kW

12035 **CHINA**
  CHINA RADIO INTL, Via Russia — S • Mideast • 250 kW
FINLAND
  †YLE RADIO FINLAND, Pori — W Su • W North Am • 500 kW
    — W • W North Am • 500 kW
GERMANY
  †DEUTSCHE WELLE, Via Kigali, Rwanda — S • E Africa • 250 kW • ALT. FREQ. TO 9565 kHz
SPAIN
  †R EXTERIOR ESPANA, Noblejas — ⇔ • Europe • 350 kW
    — W M-F • Mideast • 350 kW
    — W Sa/Su • Mideast • 350 kW
    — W • Mideast • 350 kW

12040 **RUSSIA**
  VOICE OF RUSSIA, Armavir — S • Europe & Atlantic • 500 kW
UNITED KINGDOM
  BBC, Via Zyyi, Cyprus — W • N Africa • 300 kW
  BBC, Woofferton — W • Mideast • 300 kW
USA
  VOA, Via Philippines — E Asia • 250 kW
    — W • S Asia • 250 kW
(con'd)

	0 1 2 3 4 5 6 7 8 9 10 11 12 13 14 15 16 17 18 19 20 21 22 23 24

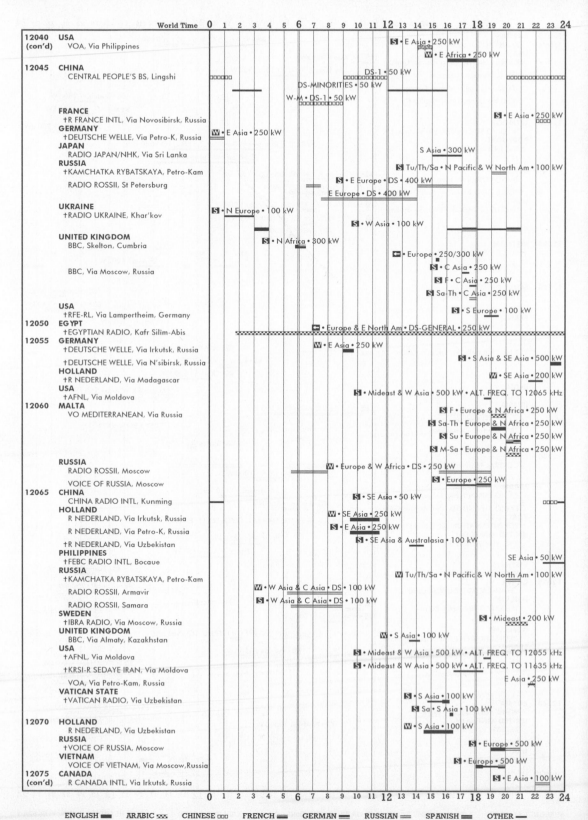

	World Time	0 1 2 3 4 5 6 7 8 9 10 11 12 13 14 15 16 17 18 19 20 21 22 23 24

12040
(con'd) USA
 VOA, Via Philippines — S • E Asia • 250 kW / W • E Africa • 250 kW

12045 CHINA
 CENTRAL PEOPLE'S BS, Lingshi — DS-1 • 50 kW / DS-MINORITIES • 50 kW / W-M • DS-1 • 50 kW

 FRANCE
 †R FRANCE INTL, Via Novosibirsk, Russia — S • E Asia • 250 kW
 GERMANY
 †DEUTSCHE WELLE, Via Petro-K, Russia — W • E Asia • 250 kW
 JAPAN
 RADIO JAPAN/NHK, Via Sri Lanka — S Asia • 300 kW
 RUSSIA
 †KAMCHATKA RYBATSKAYA, Petro-Kam — S • Tu/Th/Sa • N Pacific & W North Am • 100 kW

 RADIO ROSSII, St Petersburg — S • E Europe • DS • 400 kW / E Europe • DS • 400 kW

 UKRAINE
 †RADIO UKRAINE, Khar'kov — S • N Europe • 100 kW

 UNITED KINGDOM
 BBC, Skelton, Cumbria — S • N Africa • 300 kW / • Europe • 250/300 kW

 BBC, Via Moscow, Russia — S • C Asia • 250 kW / S F • C Asia • 250 kW / S Sa-Th • C Asia • 250 kW

 USA
 †RFE-RL, Via Lampertheim, Germany — S • S Europe • 100 kW
12050 EGYPT
 †EGYPTIAN RADIO, Kafr Silim-Abis — • Europe & E North Am • DS-GENERAL • 250 kW
12055 GERMANY
 †DEUTSCHE WELLE, Via Irkutsk, Russia — W • E Asia • 250 kW

 †DEUTSCHE WELLE, Via N'sibirsk, Russia — S • S Asia & SE Asia • 500 kW
 HOLLAND
 †R NEDERLAND, Via Madagascar — W • SE Asia • 200 kW
 USA
 †AFNL, Via Moldova — S • Mideast & W Asia • 500 kW • ALT. FREQ. TO 12065 kHz
12060 MALTA
 VO MEDITERRANEAN, Via Russia — S F • Europe & N Africa • 250 kW / S Sa-Th • Europe & N Africa • 250 kW / S Su • Europe & N Africa • 250 kW / S M-Sa • Europe & N Africa • 250 kW

 RUSSIA
 RADIO ROSSII, Moscow — W • Europe & W Africa • DS • 250 kW

 VOICE OF RUSSIA, Moscow — S • Europe • 250 kW
12065 CHINA
 CHINA RADIO INTL, Kunming — S • SE Asia • 50 kW
 HOLLAND
 R NEDERLAND, Via Irkutsk, Russia — W • SE Asia • 250 kW

 R NEDERLAND, Via Petro-K, Russia — S • E Asia • 250 kW

 †R NEDERLAND, Via Uzbekistan — S • SE Asia & Australasia • 100 kW
 PHILIPPINES
 †FEBC RADIO INTL, Bocaue — SE Asia • 50 kW
 RUSSIA
 †KAMCHATKA RYBATSKAYA, Petro-Kam — W Tu/Th/Sa • N Pacific & W North Am • 100 kW

 RADIO ROSSII, Armavir — W • W Asia & C Asia • DS • 100 kW

 RADIO ROSSII, Samara — S • W Asia & C Asia • DS • 100 kW
 SWEDEN
 †IBRA RADIO, Via Moscow, Russia — S • Mideast • 200 kW
 UNITED KINGDOM
 BBC, Via Almaty, Kazakhstan — W • S Asia • 100 kW
 USA
 †AFNL, Via Moldova — S • Mideast & W Asia • 500 kW • ALT. FREQ. TO 12055 kHz

 †KRSI-R SEDAYE IRAN, Via Moldova — S • Mideast & W Asia • 500 kW • ALT. FREQ. TO 11635 kHz

 VOA, Via Petro-Kam, Russia — E Asia • 250 kW
 VATICAN STATE
 †VATICAN RADIO, Via Uzbekistan — S • S Asia • 100 kW / S Sa • S Asia • 100 kW

12070 HOLLAND
 R NEDERLAND, Via Uzbekistan — W • S Asia • 100 kW
 RUSSIA
 †VOICE OF RUSSIA, Moscow — S • Europe • 500 kW
 VIETNAM
 VOICE OF VIETNAM, Via Moscow, Russia — S • Europe • 500 kW
12075 CANADA
(con'd) R CANADA INTL, Via Irkutsk, Russia — S • E Asia • 100 kW

	0 1 2 3 4 5 6 7 8 9 10 11 12 13 14 15 16 17 18 19 20 21 22 23 24

ENGLISH ▬▬   ARABIC ▨▨▨   CHINESE □□□   FRENCH ═══   GERMAN ▬▬▬   RUSSIAN ══   SPANISH ══   OTHER ──

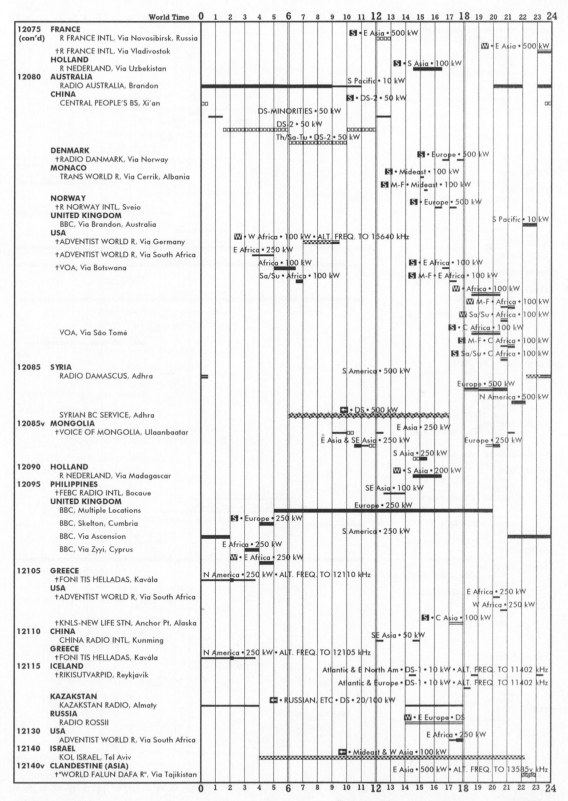

World Time   0 1 2 3 4 5 6 7 8 9 10 11 12 13 14 15 16 17 18 19 20 21 22 23 24

12075
(con'd) FRANCE
 R FRANCE INTL, Via Novosibirsk, Russia — S • E Asia • 500 kW
 †R FRANCE INTL, Via Vladivostok — W • E Asia • 500 kW
HOLLAND
 R NEDERLAND, Via Uzbekistan — S • S Asia • 100 kW
12080 AUSTRALIA
 RADIO AUSTRALIA, Brandon — S Pacific • 10 kW
CHINA
 CENTRAL PEOPLE'S BS, Xi'an — S • DS-2 • 50 kW
 DS-MINORITIES • 50 kW
 DS-2 • 50 kW
 Th/Sa-Tu • DS-2 • 50 kW
DENMARK
 †RADIO DANMARK, Via Norway — S • Europe • 500 kW
MONACO
 TRANS WORLD R, Via Cerrik, Albania — S • Mideast • 100 kW
 S • M-F • Mideast • 100 kW
NORWAY
 †R NORWAY INTL, Sveio — S • Europe • 500 kW
UNITED KINGDOM
 BBC, Via Brandon, Australia — S Pacific • 10 kW
USA
 †ADVENTIST WORLD R, Via Germany — W • W Africa • 100 kW • ALT. FREQ. TO 15640 kHz
 †ADVENTIST WORLD R, Via South Africa — E Africa • 250 kW
 †VOA, Via Botswana — Africa • 100 kW
 S • E Africa • 100 kW
 Sa/Su • Africa • 100 kW
 S • M-F • E Africa • 100 kW
 W • Africa • 100 kW
 W M-F • Africa • 100 kW
 W Sa/Su • Africa • 100 kW
 VOA, Via São Tomé — S • C Africa • 100 kW
 S • M-F • C Africa • 100 kW
 S • Sa/Su • C Africa • 100 kW
12085 SYRIA
 RADIO DAMASCUS, Adhra — S America • 500 kW
 Europe • 500 kW
 N America • 500 kW
 SYRIAN BC SERVICE, Adhra — ⇆ • DS • 500 kW
12085v MONGOLIA
 †VOICE OF MONGOLIA, Ulaanbaatar — E Asia • 250 kW
 E Asia & SE Asia • 250 kW
 Europe • 250 kW
 S Asia • 250 kW
12090 HOLLAND
 R NEDERLAND, Via Madagascar — W • S Asia • 200 kW
12095 PHILIPPINES
 †FEBC RADIO INTL, Bocaue — SE Asia • 100 kW
UNITED KINGDOM
 BBC, Multiple Locations — Europe • 250 kW
 BBC, Skelton, Cumbria — S • Europe • 250 kW
 BBC, Via Ascension — S America • 250 kW
 BBC, Via Zyyi, Cyprus — E Africa • 250 kW
 W • E Africa • 250 kW
12105 GREECE
 †FONI TIS HELLADAS, Kavála — N America • 250 kW • ALT. FREQ. TO 12110 kHz
USA
 †ADVENTIST WORLD R, Via South Africa — E Africa • 250 kW
 W Africa • 250 kW
 †KNLS-NEW LIFE STN, Anchor Pt, Alaska — S • C Asia • 100 kW
12110 CHINA
 CHINA RADIO INTL, Kunming — SE Asia • 50 kW
GREECE
 †FONI TIS HELLADAS, Kavála — N America • 250 kW • ALT. FREQ. TO 12105 kHz
12115 ICELAND
 †RIKISUTVARPID, Reykjavik — Atlantic & E North Am • DS-1 • 10 kW • ALT. FREQ. TO 11402 kHz
 Atlantic & Europe • DS-1 • 10 kW • ALT. FREQ. TO 11402 kHz
KAZAKSTAN
 KAZAKSTAN RADIO, Almaty — ⇆ • RUSSIAN, ETC • DS 20/100 kW
RUSSIA
 RADIO ROSSII — W • E Europe • DS
12130 USA
 ADVENTIST WORLD R, Via South Africa — E Africa • 250 kW
12140 ISRAEL
 KOL ISRAEL, Tel Aviv — ⇆ • Mideast & W Asia • 100 kW
12140v CLANDESTINE (ASIA)
 †"WORLD FALUN DAFA R", Via Tajikistan — E Asia • 500 kW • ALT. FREQ. TO 13585v kHz

0 1 2 3 4 5 6 7 8 9 10 11 12 13 14 15 16 17 18 19 20 21 22 23 24

SEASONAL S OR W   1-HR TIMESHIFT MIDYEAR ⇆ OR ⇆   JAMMING / OR ∧   EARLIEST HEARD ◁   LATEST HEARD ▷   NEW FOR 2001 †

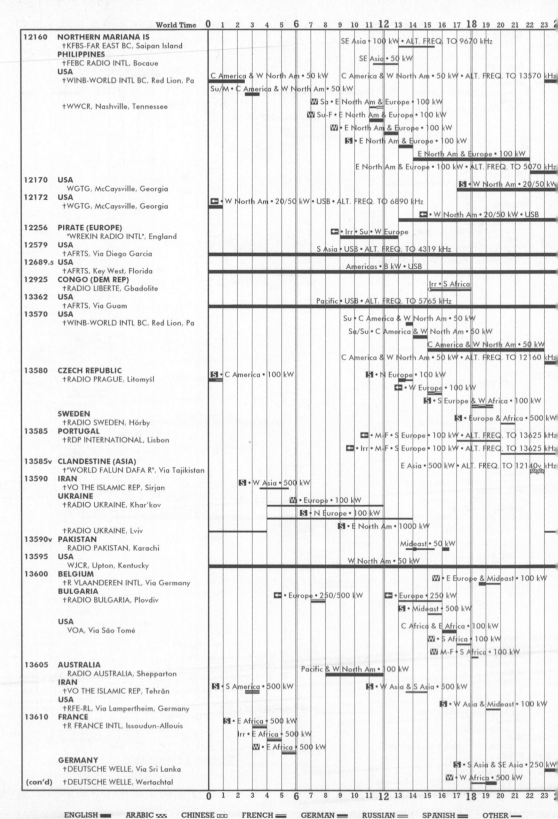

World Time	0 1 2 3 4 5 6 7 8 9 10 11 12 13 14 15 16 17 18 19 20 21 22 23
12160 NORTHERN MARIANA IS †KFBS-FAR EAST BC, Saipan Island	SE Asia • 100 kW • ALT. FREQ. TO 9670 kHz
PHILIPPINES †FEBC RADIO INTL, Bocaue	SE Asia • 50 kW
USA †WINB-WORLD INTL BC, Red Lion, Pa	C America & W North Am • 50 kW C America & W North Am • 50 kW • ALT. FREQ. TO 13570 kHz Su/M • C America & W North Am • 50 kW
†WWCR, Nashville, Tennessee	W Sa • E North Am & Europe • 100 kW W Su-F • E North Am & Europe • 100 kW W • E North Am & Europe • 100 kW S • E North Am & Europe • 100 kW E North Am & Europe • 100 kW E North Am & Europe • 100 kW • ALT. FREQ. TO 5070 kHz
12170 USA WGTG, McCaysville, Georgia	S • W North Am • 20/50 kW
12172 USA †WGTG, McCaysville, Georgia	← • W North Am • 20/50 kW • USB • ALT. FREQ. TO 6890 kHz ← • W North Am • 20/50 kW • USB
12256 PIRATE (EUROPE) "WREKIN RADIO INTL", England	← • Irr • Su • W Europe
12579 USA †AFRTS, Via Diego Garcia	S Asia • USB • ALT. FREQ. TO 4319 kHz
12689.5 USA †AFRTS, Key West, Florida	Americas • B kW • USB
12925 CONGO (DEM REP) †RADIO LIBERTE, Gbadolite	Irr • S Africa →
13362 USA †AFRTS, Via Guam	Pacific • USB • ALT. FREQ. TO 5765 kHz
13570 USA †WINB-WORLD INTL BC, Red Lion, Pa	Su • C America & W North Am • 50 kW Sa/Su • C America & W North Am • 50 kW C America & W North Am • 50 kW C America & W North Am • 50 kW • ALT. FREQ. TO 12160 kHz
13580 CZECH REPUBLIC †RADIO PRAGUE, Litomyšl	S • C America • 100 kW S • N Europe • 100 kW ← • W Europe • 100 kW S • S Europe & W Africa • 100 kW S • Europe & Africa • 500 kW
SWEDEN †RADIO SWEDEN, Hörby	
13585 PORTUGAL †RDP INTERNATIONAL, Lisbon	← • M-F • S Europe • 100 kW • ALT. FREQ. TO 13625 kHz ← • Irr • M-F • S Europe • 100 kW • ALT. FREQ. TO 13625 kHz
13585v CLANDESTINE (ASIA) †"WORLD FALUN DAFA R", Via Tajikistan	E Asia • 500 kW • ALT. FREQ. TO 12140v kHz
13590 IRAN †VO THE ISLAMIC REP, Sirjan	S • W Asia • 500 kW
UKRAINE †RADIO UKRAINE, Khar'kov	W • Europe • 100 kW S • N Europe • 100 kW
†RADIO UKRAINE, Lviv	S • E North Am • 1000 kW
13590v PAKISTAN RADIO PAKISTAN, Karachi	Mideast • 50 kW
13595 USA WJCR, Upton, Kentucky	W North Am • 50 kW
13600 BELGIUM †R VLAANDEREN INTL, Via Germany	W • E Europe & Mideast • 100 kW
BULGARIA †RADIO BULGARIA, Plovdiv	← • Europe • 250/500 kW ← • Europe • 250 kW S • Mideast • 500 kW
USA VOA, Via São Tomé	C Africa & E Africa • 100 kW W • S Africa • 100 kW W M-F • S Africa • 100 kW
13605 AUSTRALIA RADIO AUSTRALIA, Shepparton	Pacific & W North Am • 100 kW
IRAN †VO THE ISLAMIC REP, Tehrān	S • S America • 500 kW S • W Asia & S Asia • 500 kW
USA †RFE-RL, Via Lampertheim, Germany	S • W Asia & Mideast • 100 kW
13610 FRANCE †R FRANCE INTL, Issoudun-Allouis	S • E Africa • 500 kW Irr • E Africa • 500 kW W • E Africa • 500 kW
GERMANY †DEUTSCHE WELLE, Via Sri Lanka	S • S Asia & SE Asia • 250 kW
(con'd) †DEUTSCHE WELLE, Wertachtal	W • W Africa • 500 kW

0 1 2 3 4 5 6 7 8 9 10 11 12 13 14 15 16 17 18 19 20 21 22 23

ENGLISH ▬ ARABIC ⬚ CHINESE ▭ FRENCH ▬ GERMAN ▬ RUSSIAN ═ SPANISH ▬ OTHER ▬

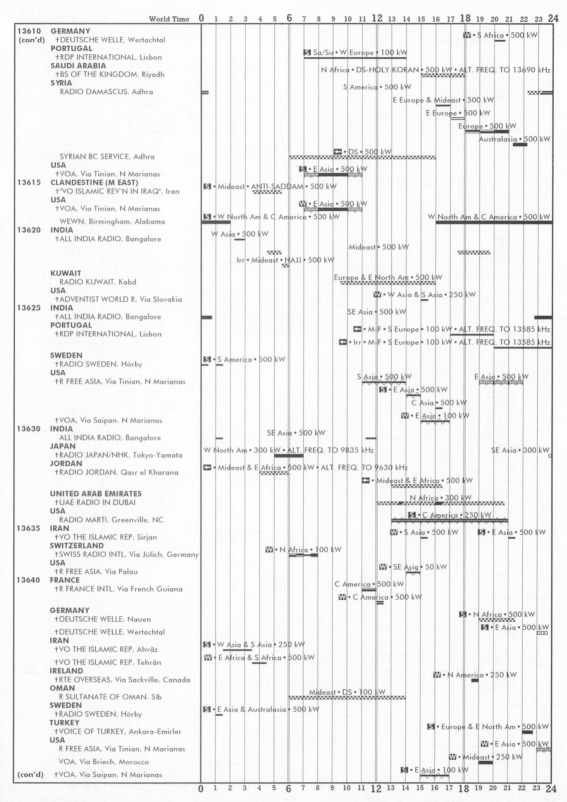

World Time 0 1 2 3 4 5 6 7 8 9 10 11 12 13 14 15 16 17 18 19 20 21 22 23 24

13610 **GERMANY**
(con'd)   †DEUTSCHE WELLE, Wertachtal — W • S Africa • 500 kW
      PORTUGAL
         †RDP INTERNATIONAL, Lisbon — S Sa/Su • W Europe • 100 kW
      SAUDI ARABIA
         †BS OF THE KINGDOM, Riyadh — N Africa • DS-HOLY KORAN • 500 kW • ALT. FREQ. TO 13690 kHz
      SYRIA
         RADIO DAMASCUS, Adhra — S America • 500 kW
                                   E Europe & Mideast • 500 kW
                                   E Europe • 500 kW
                                   Europe • 500 kW
                                   Australasia • 500 kW

         SYRIAN BC SERVICE, Adhra — ⊏⊐ • DS • 500 kW
      USA
         †VOA, Via Tinian, N Marianas — S • E Asia • 500 kW
13615 **CLANDESTINE (M EAST)**
         †"VO ISLAMIC REV'N IN IRAQ", Iran — S • Mideast • ANTI-SADDAM • 500 kW
      USA
         †VOA, Via Tinian, N Marianas — W • E Asia • 500 kW

         WEWN, Birmingham, Alabama — S • W North Am & C America • 500 kW   W North Am & C America • 500 kW
13620 **INDIA**
         †ALL INDIA RADIO, Bangalore — W Asia • 500 kW
                                        Mideast • 500 kW
                                        Irr • Mideast • HAJJ • 500 kW

      KUWAIT
         RADIO KUWAIT, Kabd — Europe & E North Am • 500 kW
      USA
         †ADVENTIST WORLD R, Via Slovakia — W • W Asia & S Asia • 250 kW
13625 **INDIA**
         †ALL INDIA RADIO, Bangalore — SE Asia • 500 kW
      PORTUGAL
         †RDP INTERNATIONAL, Lisbon — ⊏⊐ • M-F • S Europe • 100 kW • ALT. FREQ. TO 13585 kHz
                                        ⊏⊐ • Irr • M-F • S Europe • 100 kW • ALT. FREQ. TO 13585 kHz

      SWEDEN
         †RADIO SWEDEN, Hörby — S • S America • 500 kW
      USA
         †R FREE ASIA, Via Tinian, N Marianas — S Asia • 500 kW   E Asia • 500 kW
                                                 S • E Asia • 500 kW
                                                 C Asia • 500 kW

         †VOA, Via Saipan, N Marianas — W • E Asia • 100 kW
13630 **INDIA**
         ALL INDIA RADIO, Bangalore — SE Asia • 500 kW
      JAPAN
         †RADIO JAPAN/NHK, Tokyo-Yamata — W North Am • 300 kW • ALT. FREQ. TO 9835 kHz   SE Asia • 300 kW
      JORDAN
         †RADIO JORDAN, Qasr el Kharana — ⊏⊐ • Mideast & E Africa • 500 kW • ALT. FREQ. TO 9630 kHz
                                           ⊏⊐ • Mideast & E Africa • 500 kW

      UNITED ARAB EMIRATES
         †UAE RADIO IN DUBAI — N Africa • 300 kW
      USA
         RADIO MARTI, Greenville, NC — S • C America • 250 kW
13635 **IRAN**
         †VO THE ISLAMIC REP, Sirjan — W • S Asia • 500 kW   S • E Asia • 500 kW
      SWITZERLAND
         †SWISS RADIO INTL, Via Jülich, Germany — W • N Africa • 100 kW
      USA
         †R FREE ASIA, Via Palau — W • SE Asia • 50 kW
13640 **FRANCE**
         †R FRANCE INTL, Via French Guiana — C America • 500 kW
                                              W • C America • 500 kW

      GERMANY
         †DEUTSCHE WELLE, Nauen — S • N Africa • 500 kW
         †DEUTSCHE WELLE, Wertachtal — S • E Asia • 500 kW
      IRAN
         †VO THE ISLAMIC REP, Ahvāz — S • W Asia & S Asia • 250 kW
         †VO THE ISLAMIC REP, Tehrān — W • E Africa & S Africa • 500 kW
      IRELAND
         †RTE OVERSEAS, Via Sackville, Canada — W • N America • 250 kW
      OMAN
         R SULTANATE OF OMAN, Sīb — Mideast • DS • 100 kW
      SWEDEN
         †RADIO SWEDEN, Hörby — S • E Asia & Australasia • 500 kW
      TURKEY
         †VOICE OF TURKEY, Ankara-Emirler — S • Europe & E North Am • 500 kW
      USA
         R FREE ASIA, Via Tinian, N Marianas — W • E Asia • 500 kW
         VOA, Via Briech, Morocco — W • Mideast • 250 kW
(con'd) †VOA, Via Saipan, N Marianas — S • E Asia • 100 kW

0 1 2 3 4 5 6 7 8 9 10 11 12 13 14 15 16 17 18 19 20 21 22 23 24

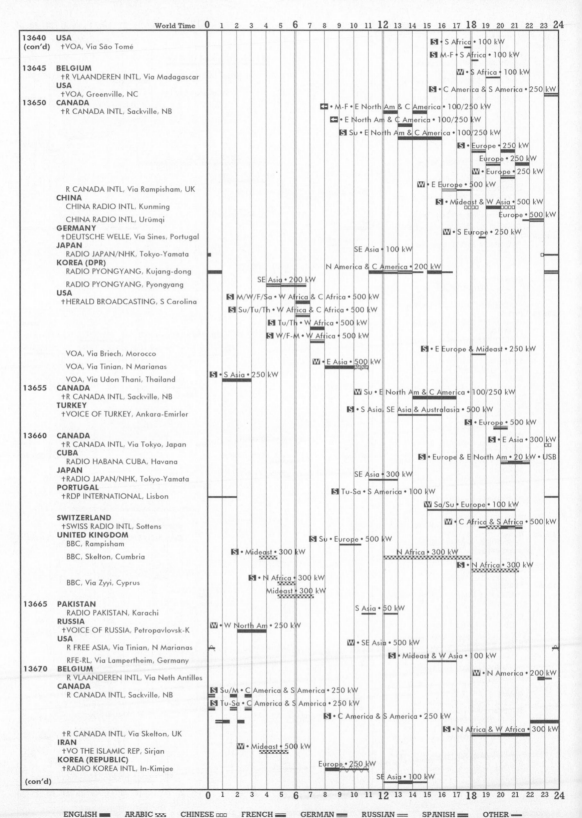

| World Time | 0 | 1 | 2 | 3 | 4 | 5 | 6 | 7 | 8 | 9 | 10 | 11 | 12 | 13 | 14 | 15 | 16 | 17 | 18 | 19 | 20 | 21 | 22 | 23 | 24 |

13640 USA (con'd)
†VOA, Via São Tomé — S • S Africa • 100 kW; S • M-F • S Africa • 100 kW

13645 BELGIUM
†R VLAANDEREN INTL, Via Madagascar — W • S Africa • 100 kW
USA
†VOA, Greenville, NC — S • C America & S America • 250 kW

13650 CANADA
†R CANADA INTL, Sackville, NB — • M-F • E North Am & C America • 100/250 kW; • E North Am & C America • 100/250 kW; S • Su • E North Am & C America • 100/250 kW; S • Europe • 250 kW; Europe • 250 kW; W • Europe • 250 kW

R CANADA INTL, Via Rampisham, UK — W • E Europe • 500 kW
CHINA
CHINA RADIO INTL, Kunming — S • Mideast & W Asia • 500 kW
CHINA RADIO INTL, Urümqi — Europe • 500 kW
GERMANY
†DEUTSCHE WELLE, Via Sines, Portugal — W • S Europe • 250 kW
JAPAN
RADIO JAPAN/NHK, Tokyo-Yamata — SE Asia • 100 kW
KOREA (DPR)
RADIO PYONGYANG, Kujang-dong — N America & C America • 200 kW

RADIO PYONGYANG, Pyongyang — SE Asia • 200 kW
USA
†HERALD BROADCASTING, S Carolina — S • M/W/F/Sa • W Africa & C Africa • 500 kW; S • Su/Tu/Th • W Africa & C Africa • 500 kW; S • Tu/Th • W Africa • 500 kW; S • W/F-M • W Africa • 500 kW

VOA, Via Briech, Morocco — S • E Europe & Mideast • 250 kW

VOA, Via Tinian, N Marianas — W • E Asia • 500 kW

VOA, Via Udon Thani, Thailand — S • S Asia • 250 kW
13655 CANADA
†R CANADA INTL, Sackville, NB — W • Su • E North Am & C America • 100/250 kW
TURKEY
†VOICE OF TURKEY, Ankara-Emirler — S • S Asia, SE Asia & Australasia • 500 kW; S • Europe • 500 kW

13660 CANADA
†R CANADA INTL, Via Tokyo, Japan — S • E Asia • 300 kW
CUBA
RADIO HABANA CUBA, Havana — S • Europe & E North Am • 20 kW • USB
JAPAN
†RADIO JAPAN/NHK, Tokyo-Yamata — SE Asia • 300 kW
PORTUGAL
†RDP INTERNATIONAL, Lisbon — S • Tu-Sa • S America • 100 kW; W • Sa/Su • Europe • 100 kW

SWITZERLAND
†SWISS RADIO INTL, Sottens — W • C Africa & S Africa • 500 kW
UNITED KINGDOM
BBC, Rampisham — S • Su • Europe • 500 kW
BBC, Skelton, Cumbria — S • Mideast • 300 kW; N Africa • 300 kW; S • N Africa • 300 kW

BBC, Via Zyyi, Cyprus — S • N Africa • 300 kW; Mideast • 300 kW

13665 PAKISTAN
RADIO PAKISTAN, Karachi — S Asia • 50 kW
RUSSIA
†VOICE OF RUSSIA, Petropavlovsk-K — W • W North Am • 250 kW
USA
R FREE ASIA, Via Tinian, N Marianas — W • SE Asia • 500 kW

RFE-RL, Via Lampertheim, Germany — S • Mideast & W Asia • 100 kW
13670 BELGIUM
R VLAANDEREN INTL, Via Neth Antilles — W • N America • 200 kW
CANADA
R CANADA INTL, Sackville, NB — S • Su/M • C America & S America • 250 kW; S • Tu-Sa • C America & S America • 250 kW; S • C America & S America • 250 kW

†R CANADA INTL, Via Skelton, UK — S • N Africa & W Africa • 300 kW
IRAN
†VO THE ISLAMIC REP, Sirjan — W • Mideast • 500 kW
KOREA (REPUBLIC)
†RADIO KOREA INTL, In-Kimjae — Europe • 250 kW; SE Asia • 100 kW

(con'd)

| | 0 | 1 | 2 | 3 | 4 | 5 | 6 | 7 | 8 | 9 | 10 | 11 | 12 | 13 | 14 | 15 | 16 | 17 | 18 | 19 | 20 | 21 | 22 | 23 | 24 |

ENGLISH ■■   ARABIC ⋙   CHINESE □□□   FRENCH ══   GERMAN ══   RUSSIAN ══   SPANISH ══   OTHER ──

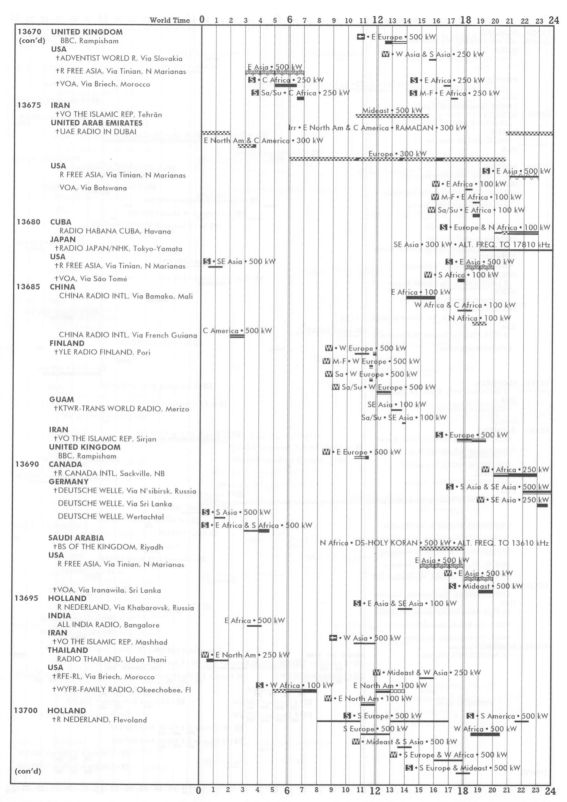

World Time   0 1 2 3 4 5 6 7 8 9 10 11 12 13 14 15 16 17 18 19 20 21 22 23 24

13670   **UNITED KINGDOM**
(con'd)   BBC, Rampisham   E Europe • 500 kW
   USA
    †ADVENTIST WORLD R, Via Slovakia   W • W Asia & S Asia • 250 kW
    †R FREE ASIA, Via Tinian, N Marianas   E Asia • 500 kW
    †VOA, Via Briech, Morocco   S • C Africa • 250 kW   S • E Africa • 250 kW
    S • Sa/Su • C Africa • 250 kW   S • M-F • E Africa • 250 kW

13675   **IRAN**
   †VO THE ISLAMIC REP, Tehrān   Mideast • 500 kW
   UNITED ARAB EMIRATES
    †UAE RADIO IN DUBAI   Irr • E North Am & C America • RAMADAN • 300 kW
    E North Am & C America • 300 kW
    Europe • 300 kW
   USA
    R FREE ASIA, Via Tinian, N Marianas   S • E Asia • 500 kW
    VOA, Via Botswana   W • E Africa • 100 kW
    W • M-F • E Africa • 100 kW
    W • Sa/Su • E Africa • 100 kW

13680   **CUBA**
   RADIO HABANA CUBA, Havana   S • Europe & N Africa • 100 kW
   JAPAN
    †RADIO JAPAN/NHK, Tokyo-Yamata   SE Asia • 300 kW • ALT. FREQ. TO 17810 kHz
   USA
    †R FREE ASIA, Via Tinian, N Marianas   S • SE Asia • 500 kW   S • E Asia • 500 kW
    †VOA, Via São Tomé   W • S Africa • 100 kW

13685   **CHINA**
   CHINA RADIO INTL, Via Bamako, Mali   E Africa • 100 kW
    W Africa & C Africa • 100 kW
    N Africa • 100 kW
   CHINA RADIO INTL, Via French Guiana   C America • 500 kW
   FINLAND
    †YLE RADIO FINLAND, Pori   W • W Europe • 500 kW
    W • M-F • W Europe • 500 kW
    W • Sa • W Europe • 500 kW
    W • Sa/Su • W Europe • 500 kW
   GUAM
    †KTWR-TRANS WORLD RADIO, Merizo   SE Asia • 100 kW
    Sa/Su • SE Asia • 100 kW
   IRAN
    †VO THE ISLAMIC REP, Sirjan   S • Europe • 500 kW
   UNITED KINGDOM
    BBC, Rampisham   W • E Europe • 500 kW

13690   **CANADA**
   †R CANADA INTL, Sackville, NB   W • Africa • 250 kW
   GERMANY
    †DEUTSCHE WELLE, Via N'sibirsk, Russia   S • S Asia & SE Asia • 500 kW
   DEUTSCHE WELLE, Via Sri Lanka   W • SE Asia • 250 kW
   DEUTSCHE WELLE, Wertachtal   S • S Asia • 500 kW
    S • E Africa & S Africa • 500 kW
   SAUDI ARABIA
    †BS OF THE KINGDOM, Riyadh   N Africa • DS-HOLY KORAN • 500 kW • ALT. FREQ. TO 13610 kHz
   USA
    R FREE ASIA, Via Tinian, N Marianas   E Asia • 500 kW
    W • E Asia • 500 kW
    †VOA, Via Iranawila, Sri Lanka   S • Mideast • 500 kW

13695   **HOLLAND**
   R NEDERLAND, Via Khabarovsk, Russia   S • E Asia & SE Asia • 100 kW
   INDIA
    ALL INDIA RADIO, Bangalore   E Africa • 500 kW
   IRAN
    †VO THE ISLAMIC REP, Mashhad   W Asia • 500 kW
   THAILAND
    RADIO THAILAND, Udon Thani   W • E North Am • 250 kW
   USA
    †RFE-RL, Via Briech, Morocco   W • Mideast & W Asia • 250 kW
    †WYFR-FAMILY RADIO, Okeechobee, Fl   S • W Africa • 100 kW   E North Am • 100 kW
    W • E North Am • 100 kW

13700   **HOLLAND**
   †R NEDERLAND, Flevoland   S • S Europe • 500 kW   S • S America • 500 kW
    S Europe • 500 kW   W Africa • 500 kW
    W • Mideast & S Asia • 500 kW
    W • S Europe & W Africa • 500 kW
(con'd)   S • S Europe & Mideast • 500 kW

0 1 2 3 4 5 6 7 8 9 10 11 12 13 14 15 16 17 18 19 20 21 22 23 24

World Time 0 1 2 3 4 5 6 7 8 9 10 11 12 13 14 15 16 17 18 19 20 21 22 23 24

13765
(con'd)   **SWEDEN**
　　　　†RADIO SWEDEN, Hörby — **W** • Mideast • 500 kW
　　　USA
　　　　†R FREE ASIA, Via Iranawila, Sri Lanka — **S** • SE Asia • 500 kW
　　　VATICAN STATE
　　　　VATICAN RADIO, Sta Maria di Galeria — **S** • E Africa • 500 kW
　　　　　S • S Africa • 500 kW
　　　　　S • W Africa • 500 kW
　　　　　S • E Asia • 500 kW　　**S** • W Africa • 250 kW
　　　　　S • Australasia • 500 kW

13770   **FINLAND**
　　　　†YLE RADIO FINLAND, Pori — **S** Su • W North Am • 500 kW
　　　　　S • W North Am • 500 kW
　　　INDIA
　　　　ALL INDIA RADIO, Bangalore — W Asia & Mideast • 500 kW
　　　PORTUGAL
　　　　†RDP INTERNATIONAL, Lisbon — **W** Tu-Sa • S America • 100 kW　　**S** Sa/Su • S Europe • 100 kW
　　　　　S • S Europe • 100 kW
　　　　　Irr • **S** • C America • 100 kW
　　　　　Irr • **W** • C America • 100 kW
　　　SWITZERLAND
　　　　SWISS RADIO INTL, Sottens — **S** • E Africa • 500 kW
　　　USA
　　　　†HERALD BROADCASTING, S Carolina — **S** M/W/Sa • W Europe • 500 kW
　　　　　S Su/Th • W Europe • 500 kW
　　　　　S Tu/F • W Europe • 500 kW
　　　　　S M • S Europe & W Africa • 500 kW
　　　　　S Su/W • S Europe & W Africa • 500 kW
　　　　　S Th • S Europe & W Africa • 500 kW
　　　　　S Tu/F • S Europe & W Africa • 500 kW
　　　　†R FREE ASIA, Via Tinian, N Marianas — **S** • SE Asia • 500 kW
　　　　VOA, Greenville, NC — C America • 250 kW

13775   **IRAN**
　　　　†VO THE ISLAMIC REP, Tehrān — **S** • Mideast • 500 kW
　　　RUSSIA
　　　　VOICE OF RUSSIA, Kenga — **S** • E Asia • 100 kW
　　　USA
　　　　R FREE ASIA, Via Palau — **S** • SE Asia • 80 kW
　　　　†VOA, Via Udon Thani, Thailand — **S** • E Asia • 250 kW

13780   **GERMANY**
　　　　DEUTSCHE WELLE, Nauen — **S** • Africa • 500 kW
　　　　†DEUTSCHE WELLE, Via Kigali, Rwanda — **W** • W Africa & C America • 250 kW
　　　　†DEUTSCHE WELLE, Via Sines, Portugal — **S** • S America • 250 kW
　　　　†DEUTSCHE WELLE, Via Sri Lanka — **S** • E North Am & C America • 250 kW
　　　　　S • S Africa • 250 kW • ALT. FREQ. TO 15425 kHz
　　　　†DEUTSCHE WELLE, Wertachtal — S Europe & Mideast • 500 kW
　　　　　S • S Europe & Mideast • 500 kW
　　　　　W • C Africa & S Africa • 500 kW

13785   **FINLAND**
　　　　†YLE RADIO FINLAND, Pori — **S** • E Asia • 500 kW
　　　IRAN
　　　　†VO THE ISLAMIC REP, Ahvāz — **S** • W Asia & S Asia • 250 kW
　　　USA
　　　　†VOA, Via Tinian, N Marianas — **W** • E Asia • 500 kW

13790   **GERMANY**
　　　　†DEUTSCHE WELLE, Via Sines, Portugal — **S** • W Africa • 250 kW　　**S** • N Africa • 250 kW　　**S** • S Europe • 250 kW
　　　　　N Africa • 250 kW
　　　　　W • N Africa • 250 kW
　　　　†DEUTSCHE WELLE, Via Sri Lanka — **W** • E Asia • 250 kW
　　　　†DEUTSCHE WELLE, Wertachtal — **S** • E Europe & Mideast • 500 kW
　　　IRAN
　　　　†VO THE ISLAMIC REP, Zāhedān — **S** • S Europe • 500 kW
　　　KOREA (DPR)
　　　　RADIO PYONGYANG, Pyongyang — Europe • 200 kW　　Europe • 200 kW • ALT. FREQ. TO 7505 kHz
　　　　　Asia • 200 kW
　　　　　RUSSIAN, ETC • Asia • 200 kW
　　　PORTUGAL
　　　　†RDP INTERNATIONAL, Lisbon — **W** Sa/Su • W Europe • 100 kW
　　　SWITZERLAND
　　　　SWISS RADIO INTL, Via French Guiana — **W** • S Africa • 500 kW
(con'd)   SWISS RADIO INTL, Via Jülich, Germany — **W** • Mideast • 100 kW

0 1 2 3 4 5 6 7 8 9 10 11 12 13 14 15 16 17 18 19 20 21 22 23 24

ENGLISH ▬   ARABIC ⋙   CHINESE ▫▫▫   FRENCH ═══   GERMAN ▬▬   RUSSIAN ══   SPANISH ═══   OTHER ▬▬

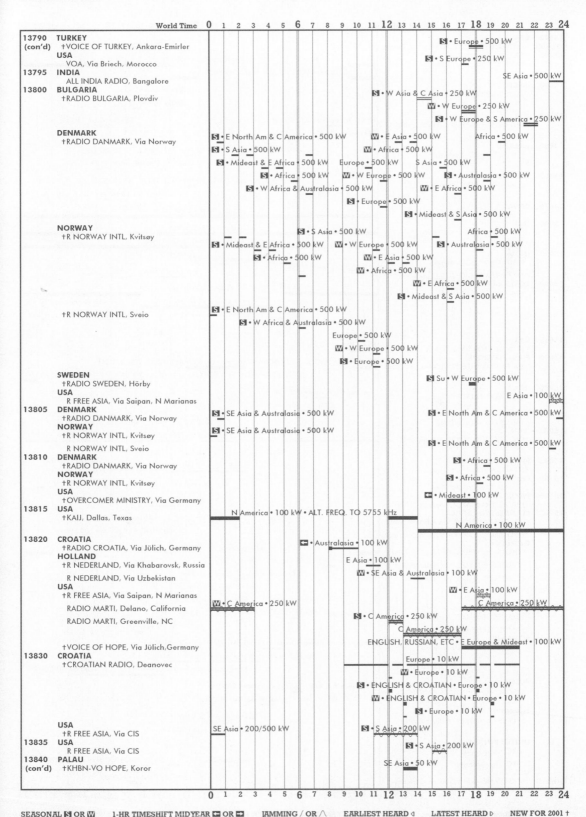

Freq	Country / Station	World Time 0-24 broadcast schedule
13790 (con'd)	**TURKEY** †VOICE OF TURKEY, Ankara-Emirler	S • Europe • 500 kW
	USA VOA, Via Briech, Morocco	S • S Europe • 250 kW
13795	**INDIA** ALL INDIA RADIO, Bangalore	SE Asia • 500 kW
13800	**BULGARIA** †RADIO BULGARIA, Plovdiv	S • W Asia & C Asia • 250 kW; W • W Europe • 250 kW; S • W Europe & S America • 250 kW
	DENMARK †RADIO DANMARK, Via Norway	S • E North Am & C America • 500 kW; W • E Asia • 500 kW; Africa • 500 kW; S • S Asia • 500 kW; W • Africa • 500 kW; S • Mideast & E Africa • 500 kW; Europe • 500 kW; S Asia • 500 kW; S • Africa • 500 kW; W • W Europe • 500 kW; S • Australasia • 500 kW; S • W Africa & Australasia • 500 kW; W • E Africa • 500 kW; S • Europe • 500 kW; S • Mideast & S Asia • 500 kW
	NORWAY †R NORWAY INTL, Kvitsøy	S • S Asia • 500 kW; Africa • 500 kW; S • Mideast & E Africa • 500 kW; W • W Europe • 500 kW; S • Australasia • 500 kW; S • Africa • 500 kW; W • E Asia • 500 kW; W • Africa • 500 kW; W • E Africa • 500 kW; S • Mideast & S Asia • 500 kW
	†R NORWAY INTL, Sveio	S • E North Am & C America • 500 kW; S • W Africa & Australasia • 500 kW; Europe • 500 kW; W • W Europe • 500 kW; S • Europe • 500 kW
	SWEDEN †RADIO SWEDEN, Hörby	S Su • W Europe • 500 kW
	USA R FREE ASIA, Via Saipan, N Marianas	E Asia • 100 kW
13805	**DENMARK** †RADIO DANMARK, Via Norway	S • SE Asia & Australasia • 500 kW; S • E North Am & C America • 500 kW
	NORWAY †R NORWAY INTL, Kvitsøy	S • SE Asia & Australasia • 500 kW
	R NORWAY INTL, Sveio	S • E North Am & C America • 500 kW
13810	**DENMARK** †RADIO DANMARK, Via Norway	S • Africa • 500 kW
	NORWAY †R NORWAY INTL, Kvitsøy	S • Africa • 500 kW
	USA †OVERCOMER MINISTRY, Via Germany	⇇ • Mideast • 100 kW
13815	**USA** †KAIJ, Dallas, Texas	N America • 100 kW • ALT. FREQ. TO 5755 kHz; N America • 100 kW
13820	**CROATIA** †RADIO CROATIA, Via Jülich, Germany	⇇ • Australasia • 100 kW
	HOLLAND †R NEDERLAND, Via Khabarovsk, Russia	E Asia • 100 kW
	R NEDERLAND, Via Uzbekistan	W • SE Asia & Australasia • 100 kW
	USA †R FREE ASIA, Via Saipan, N Marianas	W • E Asia • 100 kW
	RADIO MARTI, Delano, California	W • C America • 250 kW; C America • 250 kW
	RADIO MARTI, Greenville, NC	S • C America • 250 kW; C America • 250 kW
	†VOICE OF HOPE, Via Jülich, Germany	ENGLISH, RUSSIAN, ETC • E Europe & Mideast • 100 kW
13830	**CROATIA** †CROATIAN RADIO, Deanovec	Europe • 10 kW; W • Europe • 10 kW; S • ENGLISH & CROATIAN • Europe • 10 kW; W • ENGLISH & CROATIAN • Europe • 10 kW; S • Europe • 10 kW
	USA †R FREE ASIA, Via CIS	SE Asia • 200/500 kW; S • S Asia • 200 kW
13835	**USA** R FREE ASIA, Via CIS	S • S Asia • 200 kW
13840 (con'd)	**PALAU** †KHBN-VO HOPE, Koror	SE Asia • 50 kW

SEASONAL S OR W   1-HR TIMESHIFT MIDYEAR ⇇ OR ⇉   JAMMING / OR ∧   EARLIEST HEARD ◁   LATEST HEARD ▷   NEW FOR 2001 †

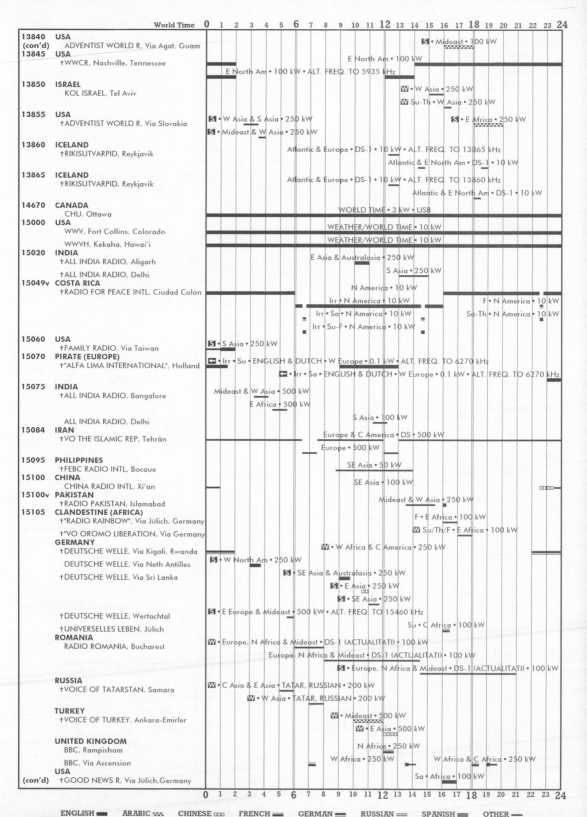

Freq	Country / Station	Schedule
13840 (con'd)	USA — ADVENTIST WORLD R, Via Agat, Guam	S • Mideast • 100 kW
13845	USA — †WWCR, Nashville, Tennessee	E North Am • 100 kW / E North Am • 100 kW • ALT. FREQ. TO 5935 kHz
13850	ISRAEL — KOL ISRAEL, Tel Aviv	W • W Asia • 250 kW / W Su–Th • W Asia • 250 kW
13855	USA — †ADVENTIST WORLD R, Via Slovakia	S • W Asia & S Asia • 250 kW / S • Mideast & W Asia • 250 kW / S • E Africa • 250 kW
13860	ICELAND — †RIKISUTVARPID, Reykjavik	Atlantic & Europe • DS-1 • 10 kW • ALT. FREQ. TO 13865 kHz / Atlantic & E North Am • DS-1 • 10 kW
13865	ICELAND — †RIKISUTVARPID, Reykjavik	Atlantic & Europe • DS-1 • 10 kW • ALT. FREQ. TO 13860 kHz / Atlantic & E North Am • DS-1 • 10 kW
14670	CANADA — CHU, Ottawa	WORLD TIME • 3 kW • USB
15000	USA — WWV, Fort Collins, Colorado	WEATHER/WORLD TIME • 10 kW
	WWVH, Kekaha, Hawai'i	WEATHER/WORLD TIME • 10 kW
15020	INDIA — †ALL INDIA RADIO, Aligarh	E Asia & Australasia • 250 kW
	†ALL INDIA RADIO, Delhi	S Asia • 250 kW
15049v	COSTA RICA — †RADIO FOR PEACE INTL, Ciudad Colón	N America • 10 kW / Irr • N America • 10 kW / F • N America • 10 kW / Irr • Sa • N America • 10 kW / Sa–Th • N America • 10 kW / Irr • Su–F • N America • 10 kW
15060	USA — †FAMILY RADIO, Via Taiwan	S • S Asia • 250 kW
15070	PIRATE (EUROPE) — †"ALFA LIMA INTERNATIONAL", Holland	• Irr • Su • ENGLISH & DUTCH • W Europe • 0.1 kW • ALT. FREQ. TO 6270 kHz / • Irr • Sa • ENGLISH & DUTCH • W Europe • 0.1 kW • ALT. FREQ. TO 6270 kHz
15075	INDIA — †ALL INDIA RADIO, Bangalore	Mideast & W Asia • 500 kW / E Africa • 500 kW
	ALL INDIA RADIO, Delhi	S Asia • 100 kW
15084	IRAN — †VO THE ISLAMIC REP, Tehrān	Europe & C America • DS • 500 kW / Europe • 500 kW
15095	PHILIPPINES — †FEBC RADIO INTL, Bocaue	SE Asia • 50 kW
15100	CHINA — CHINA RADIO INTL, Xi'an	SE Asia • 100 kW
15100v	PAKISTAN — †RADIO PAKISTAN, Islamabad	Mideast & W Asia • 250 kW
15105	CLANDESTINE (AFRICA) — †"RADIO RAINBOW", Via Jülich, Germany	F • E Africa • 100 kW
	†"VO OROMO LIBERATION", Via Germany	W Su/Th/F • E Africa • 100 kW
	GERMANY — †DEUTSCHE WELLE, Via Kigali, Rwanda	W • W Africa & C America • 250 kW
	DEUTSCHE WELLE, Via Neth Antilles	S • W North Am • 250 kW
	†DEUTSCHE WELLE, Via Sri Lanka	S • SE Asia & Australasia • 250 kW / S • E Asia • 250 kW / S • SE Asia • 250 kW
	†DEUTSCHE WELLE, Wertachtal	S • E Europe & Mideast • 500 kW • ALT. FREQ. TO 15460 kHz
	†UNIVERSELLES LEBEN, Jülich	Su • C Africa • 100 kW
	ROMANIA — RADIO ROMANIA, Bucharest	W • Europe, N Africa & Mideast • DS-1 (ACTUALITATI) • 100 kW / Europe, N Africa & Mideast • DS-1 (ACTUALITATI) • 100 kW / S • Europe, N Africa & Mideast • DS-1 (ACTUALITATI) • 100 kW
	RUSSIA — †VOICE OF TATARSTAN, Samara	W • C Asia & E Asia • TATAR, RUSSIAN • 200 kW / W • W Asia • TATAR, RUSSIAN • 200 kW
	TURKEY — †VOICE OF TURKEY, Ankara-Emirler	W • Mideast • 500 kW / W • E Asia • 500 kW
	UNITED KINGDOM — BBC, Rampisham	N Africa • 250 kW
	BBC, Via Ascension	W Africa • 250 kW / W Africa & C Africa • 250 kW
(con'd)	USA — †GOOD NEWS R, Via Jülich, Germany	Sa • Africa • 100 kW

World Time scale: 0 1 2 3 4 5 6 7 8 9 10 11 12 13 14 15 16 17 18 19 20 21 22 23 24

ENGLISH ▬   ARABIC ░░░   CHINESE ▭▭▭   FRENCH ═   GERMAN ▬   RUSSIAN ═   SPANISH ▬   OTHER ▬

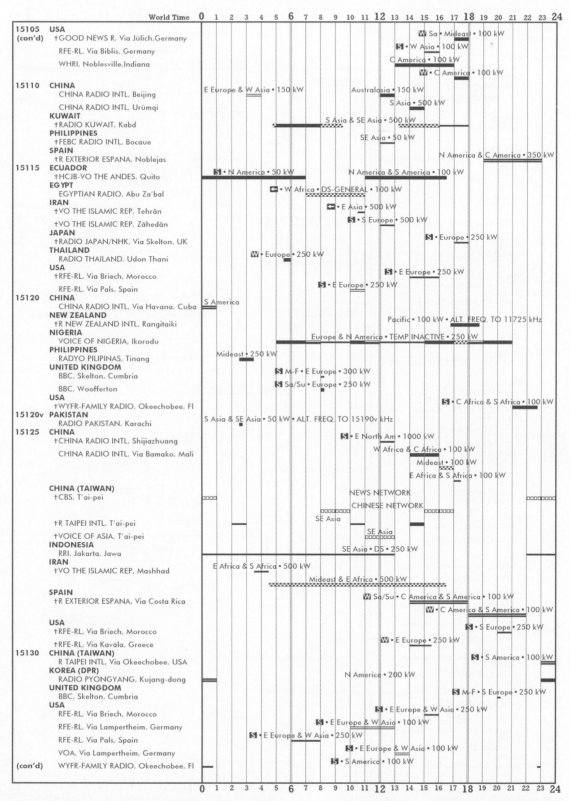

World Time 0 1 2 3 4 5 6 7 8 9 10 11 12 13 14 15 16 17 18 19 20 21 22 23 24

15105 USA
(con'd) †GOOD NEWS R, Via Jülich, Germany — W Sa • Mideast • 100 kW
RFE-RL, Via Biblis, Germany — S • W Asia • 100 kW
WHRI, Noblesville, Indiana — C America • 100 kW — W • C America • 100 kW

15110 CHINA
CHINA RADIO INTL, Beijing — E Europe & W Asia • 150 kW — Australasia • 150 kW
CHINA RADIO INTL, Urümqi — S Asia • 500 kW
KUWAIT
†RADIO KUWAIT, Kabd — S Asia & SE Asia • 500 kW
PHILIPPINES
†FEBC RADIO INTL, Bocaue — SE Asia • 50 kW
SPAIN
†R EXTERIOR ESPANA, Noblejas — N America & C America • 350 kW

15115 ECUADOR
†HCJB-VO THE ANDES, Quito — S • N America • 50 kW — N America & S America • 100 kW
EGYPT
EGYPTIAN RADIO, Abu Za'bal — W Africa • DS-GENERAL • 100 kW
IRAN
†VO THE ISLAMIC REP, Tehrān — E Asia • 500 kW
†VO THE ISLAMIC REP, Zāhedān — S • S Europe • 500 kW
JAPAN
†RADIO JAPAN/NHK, Via Skelton, UK — S • Europe • 250 kW
THAILAND
RADIO THAILAND, Udon Thani — W • Europe • 250 kW
USA
†RFE-RL, Via Briech, Morocco — S • E Europe • 250 kW
RFE-RL, Via Pals, Spain — S • E Europe • 250 kW

15120 CHINA
CHINA RADIO INTL, Via Havana, Cuba — S America
NEW ZEALAND
†R NEW ZEALAND INTL, Rangitaiki — Pacific • 100 kW • ALT. FREQ. TO 11725 kHz
NIGERIA
VOICE OF NIGERIA, Ikorodu — Europe & N America • TEMP INACTIVE • 250 kW
PHILIPPINES
RADYO PILIPINAS, Tinang — Mideast • 250 kW
UNITED KINGDOM
BBC, Skelton, Cumbria — S M-F • E Europe • 300 kW
BBC, Woofferton — S Sa/Su • Europe • 250 kW
USA
†WYFR-FAMILY RADIO, Okeechobee, Fl — S • C Africa & S Africa • 100 kW
15120v PAKISTAN
RADIO PAKISTAN, Karachi — S Asia & SE Asia • 50 kW • ALT. FREQ. TO 15190v kHz
15125 CHINA
†CHINA RADIO INTL, Shijiazhuang — S • E North Am • 1000 kW
CHINA RADIO INTL, Via Bamako, Mali — W Africa & C Africa • 100 kW — Mideast • 100 kW — E Africa & S Africa • 100 kW
CHINA (TAIWAN)
†CBS, T'ai-pei — NEWS NETWORK — CHINESE NETWORK
†R TAIPEI INTL, T'ai-pei — SE Asia
†VOICE OF ASIA, T'ai-pei — SE Asia
INDONESIA
RRI, Jakarta, Jawa — SE Asia • DS • 250 kW
IRAN
†VO THE ISLAMIC REP, Mashhad — E Africa & S Africa • 500 kW — Mideast & E Africa • 500 kW
SPAIN
†R EXTERIOR ESPANA, Via Costa Rica — W Sa/Su • C America & S America • 100 kW — W • C America & S America • 100 kW
USA
†RFE-RL, Via Briech, Morocco — S • S Europe • 250 kW
†RFE-RL, Via Kavála, Greece — W • E Europe • 250 kW
15130 CHINA (TAIWAN)
R TAIPEI INTL, Via Okeechobee, USA — S • S America • 100 kW
KOREA (DPR)
RADIO PYONGYANG, Kujang-dong — N America • 200 kW
UNITED KINGDOM
BBC, Skelton, Cumbria — S M-F • S Europe • 250 kW
USA
RFE-RL, Via Briech, Morocco — S • E Europe & W Asia • 250 kW
RFE-RL, Via Lampertheim, Germany — S • E Europe & W Asia • 100 kW
RFE-RL, Via Pals, Spain — S • E Europe & W Asia • 250 kW
VOA, Via Lampertheim, Germany — S • E Europe & W Asia • 100 kW
(con'd) WYFR-FAMILY RADIO, Okeechobee, Fl — S • S America • 100 kW

0 1 2 3 4 5 6 7 8 9 10 11 12 13 14 15 16 17 18 19 20 21 22 23 24

SEASONAL S OR W   1-HR TIMESHIFT MIDYEAR ⊡ OR ⊟   JAMMING / OR ∧   EARLIEST HEARD ◁   LATEST HEARD ▷   NEW FOR 2001 †

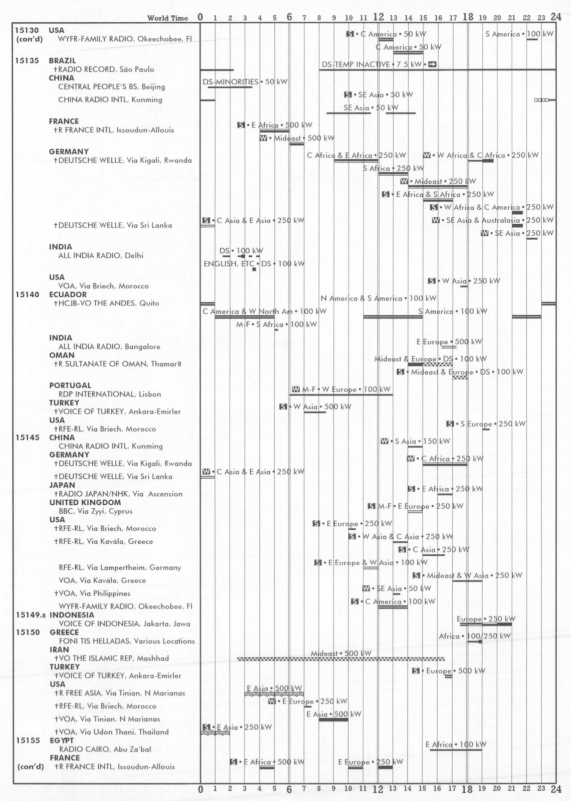

World Time | 0 1 2 3 4 5 6 7 8 9 10 11 12 13 14 15 16 17 18 19 20 21 22 23 24

15130 USA
(con'd) WYFR-FAMILY RADIO, Okeechobee, Fl
- S • C America • 50 kW
- C America • 50 kW
- S America • 100 kW

15135 BRAZIL
†RADIO RECORD, São Paulo
- DS-TEMP INACTIVE • 7.5 kW • ⇨

CHINA
CENTRAL PEOPLE'S BS, Beijing
- DS-MINORITIES • 50 kW

CHINA RADIO INTL, Kunming
- S • SE Asia • 50 kW
- SE Asia • 50 kW

FRANCE
†R FRANCE INTL, Issoudun-Allouis
- S • E Africa • 500 kW
- W • Mideast • 500 kW

GERMANY
†DEUTSCHE WELLE, Via Kigali, Rwanda
- C Africa & E Africa • 250 kW
- W • W Africa & C Africa • 250 kW
- S Africa • 250 kW
- W • Mideast • 250 kW
- S • E Africa & S Africa • 250 kW
- S • W Africa & C America • 250 kW

†DEUTSCHE WELLE, Via Sri Lanka
- S • C Asia & E Asia • 250 kW
- W • SE Asia & Australasia • 250 kW
- W • SE Asia • 250 kW

INDIA
ALL INDIA RADIO, Delhi
- DS • 100 kW
- ENGLISH, ETC • DS • 100 kW

USA
VOA, Via Briech, Morocco
- S • W Asia • 250 kW

15140 ECUADOR
†HCJB-VO THE ANDES, Quito
- N America & S America • 100 kW
- C America & W North Am • 100 kW
- S America • 100 kW
- M-F • S Africa • 100 kW

INDIA
ALL INDIA RADIO, Bangalore
- E Europe • 500 kW

OMAN
†R SULTANATE OF OMAN, Thamarīt
- Mideast & Europe • DS • 100 kW
- S • Mideast & Europe • DS • 100 kW

PORTUGAL
RDP INTERNATIONAL, Lisbon
- W • M-F • W Europe • 100 kW

TURKEY
†VOICE OF TURKEY, Ankara-Emirler
- S • W Asia • 500 kW

USA
†RFE-RL, Via Briech, Morocco
- S • S Europe • 250 kW

15145 CHINA
CHINA RADIO INTL, Kunming
- W • S Asia • 150 kW

GERMANY
†DEUTSCHE WELLE, Via Kigali, Rwanda
- W • C Africa • 250 kW

†DEUTSCHE WELLE, Via Sri Lanka
- W • C Asia & E Asia • 250 kW

JAPAN
†RADIO JAPAN/NHK, Via Ascension
- S • E Africa • 250 kW

UNITED KINGDOM
BBC, Via Zyyi, Cyprus
- S • M-F • E Europe • 250 kW

USA
†RFE-RL, Via Briech, Morocco
- S • E Europe • 250 kW

†RFE-RL, Via Kavála, Greece
- S • W Asia & C Asia • 250 kW
- S • C Asia • 250 kW

RFE-RL, Via Lampertheim, Germany
- S • E Europe & W Asia • 100 kW

VOA, Via Kavála, Greece
- S • Mideast & W Asia • 250 kW

†VOA, Via Philippines
- W • SE Asia • 50 kW

WYFR-FAMILY RADIO, Okeechobee, Fl
- S • C America • 100 kW

15149.8 INDONESIA
VOICE OF INDONESIA, Jakarta, Jawa
- Europe • 250 kW

15150 GREECE
FONI TIS HELLADAS, Various Locations
- Africa • 100/250 kW

IRAN
†VO THE ISLAMIC REP, Mashhad
- Mideast • 500 kW

TURKEY
†VOICE OF TURKEY, Ankara-Emirler
- S • Europe • 500 kW

USA
†R FREE ASIA, Via Tinian, N Marianas
- E Asia • 500 kW

†RFE-RL, Via Briech, Morocco
- W • E Europe • 250 kW

†VOA, Via Tinian, N Marianas
- E Asia • 500 kW

†VOA, Via Udon Thani, Thailand
- S • E Asia • 250 kW

15155 EGYPT
RADIO CAIRO, Abu Za'bal
- E Africa • 100 kW

FRANCE
(con'd) †R FRANCE INTL, Issoudun-Allouis
- S • E Africa • 500 kW
- E Europe • 250 kW

0 1 2 3 4 5 6 7 8 9 10 11 12 13 14 15 16 17 18 19 20 21 22 23 24

ENGLISH ▬   ARABIC ⌇⌇   CHINESE □□□   FRENCH ══   GERMAN ▭▭   RUSSIAN ⩵   SPANISH ══   OTHER ━

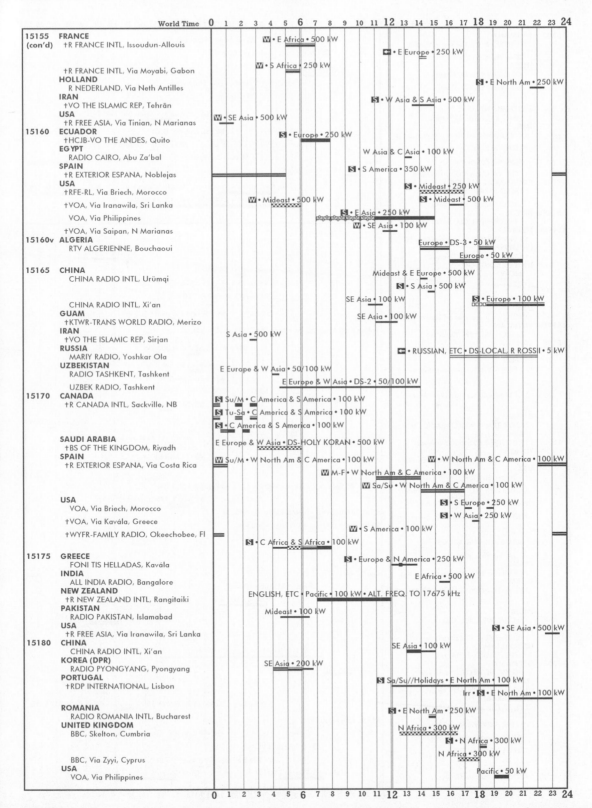

World Time																								

15155 **FRANCE**
(con'd) †R FRANCE INTL, Issoudun-Allouis — W • E Africa • 500 kW; S • E Europe • 250 kW

†R FRANCE INTL, Via Moyabi, Gabon — W • S Africa • 250 kW
HOLLAND
R NEDERLAND, Via Neth Antilles — S • E North Am • 250 kW
IRAN
†VO THE ISLAMIC REP, Tehrān — S • W Asia & S Asia • 500 kW
USA
†R FREE ASIA, Via Tinian, N Marianas — W • SE Asia • 500 kW

15160 **ECUADOR**
†HCJB-VO THE ANDES, Quito — S • Europe • 250 kW
EGYPT
RADIO CAIRO, Abu Za'bal — W Asia & C Asia • 100 kW
SPAIN
†R EXTERIOR ESPANA, Noblejas — S • S America • 350 kW
USA
†RFE-RL, Via Briech, Morocco — S • Mideast • 250 kW
†VOA, Via Iranawila, Sri Lanka — W • Mideast • 500 kW; S • Mideast • 500 kW
VOA, Via Philippines — S • E Asia • 250 kW
†VOA, Via Saipan, N Marianas — W • SE Asia • 100 kW

15160v **ALGERIA**
RTV ALGERIENNE, Bouchaoui — Europe • DS-3 • 50 kW; Europe • 50 kW

15165 **CHINA**
CHINA RADIO INTL, Urümqi — Mideast & E Europe • 500 kW; S • S Asia • 500 kW

CHINA RADIO INTL, Xi'an — SE Asia • 100 kW; S • Europe • 100 kW
GUAM
†KTWR-TRANS WORLD RADIO, Merizo — SE Asia • 100 kW
IRAN
†VO THE ISLAMIC REP, Sirjan — S Asia • 500 kW
RUSSIA
MARIY RADIO, Yoshkar Ola — RUSSIAN, ETC • DS-LOCAL, R ROSSII • 5 kW
UZBEKISTAN
RADIO TASHKENT, Tashkent — E Europe & W Asia • 50/100 kW

UZBEK RADIO, Tashkent — E Europe & W Asia • DS-2 • 50/100 kW

15170 **CANADA**
†R CANADA INTL, Sackville, NB — S • Su/M • C America & S America • 100 kW; S • Tu-Sa • C America & S America • 100 kW; S • C America & S America • 100 kW

SAUDI ARABIA
†BS OF THE KINGDOM, Riyadh — E Europe & W Asia • DS-HOLY KORAN • 500 kW
SPAIN
†R EXTERIOR ESPANA, Via Costa Rica — W • Su/M • W North Am & C America • 100 kW; W • W North Am & C America • 100 kW; W • M-F • W North Am & C America • 100 kW; W • Sa/Su • W North Am & C America • 100 kW

USA
VOA, Via Briech, Morocco — S • S Europe • 250 kW
†VOA, Via Kavála, Greece — S • W Asia • 250 kW
†WYFR-FAMILY RADIO, Okeechobee, Fl — W • S America • 100 kW; S • C Africa & S Africa • 100 kW

15175 **GREECE**
FONI TIS HELLADAS, Kavála — S • Europe & N America • 250 kW
INDIA
ALL INDIA RADIO, Bangalore — E Africa • 500 kW
NEW ZEALAND
†R NEW ZEALAND INTL, Rangitaiki — ENGLISH, ETC • Pacific • 100 kW • ALT. FREQ. TO 17675 kHz
PAKISTAN
RADIO PAKISTAN, Islamabad — Mideast • 100 kW
USA
†R FREE ASIA, Via Iranawila, Sri Lanka — S • SE Asia • 500 kW

15180 **CHINA**
CHINA RADIO INTL, Xi'an — SE Asia • 100 kW
KOREA (DPR)
RADIO PYONGYANG, Pyongyang — SE Asia • 200 kW
PORTUGAL
†RDP INTERNATIONAL, Lisbon — S • Sa/Su//Holidays • E North Am • 100 kW; Irr • S • E North Am • 100 kW

ROMANIA
RADIO ROMANIA INTL, Bucharest — S • E North Am • 250 kW
UNITED KINGDOM
BBC, Skelton, Cumbria — N Africa • 300 kW; S • N Africa • 300 kW

BBC, Via Zyyi, Cyprus — N Africa • 300 kW
USA
VOA, Via Philippines — Pacific • 50 kW

SEASONAL S OR W   1-HR TIMESHIFT MIDYEAR ⊡ OR ⊡   JAMMING / OR ∧   EARLIEST HEARD ◁   LATEST HEARD ▷   NEW FOR 2001 †

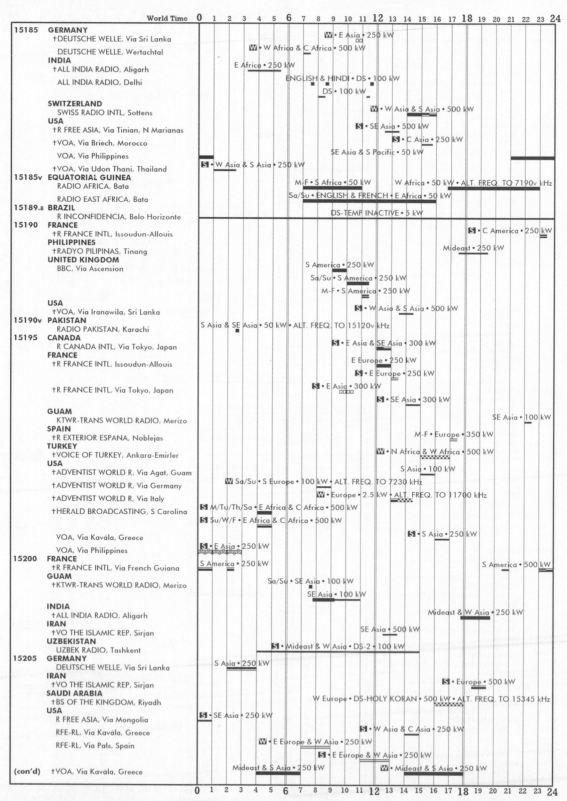

	World Time	0 1 2 3 4 5 6 7 8 9 10 11 12 13 14 15 16 17 18 19 20 21 22 23 24

15185 GERMANY
  †DEUTSCHE WELLE, Via Sri Lanka — **W** • E Asia • 250 kW
  DEUTSCHE WELLE, Wertachtal — **W** • W Africa & C Africa • 500 kW
INDIA
  †ALL INDIA RADIO, Aligarh — E Africa • 250 kW
  ALL INDIA RADIO, Delhi — ENGLISH & HINDI • DS • 100 kW
  DS • 100 kW
SWITZERLAND
  SWISS RADIO INTL, Sottens — **W** • W Asia & S Asia • 500 kW
USA
  †R FREE ASIA, Via Tinian, N Marianas — **S** • SE Asia • 500 kW
  †VOA, Via Briech, Morocco — **S** • C Asia • 250 kW
  VOA, Via Philippines — SE Asia & S Pacific • 50 kW
  †VOA, Via Udon Thani, Thailand — **S** • W Asia & S Asia • 250 kW
15185v EQUATORIAL GUINEA
  RADIO AFRICA, Bata — M-F • S Africa • 50 kW   W Africa • 50 kW • ALT. FREQ. TO 7190v kHz
  RADIO EAST AFRICA, Bata — Sa/Su • ENGLISH & FRENCH • E Africa • 50 kW
15189.8 BRAZIL
  R INCONFIDENCIA, Belo Horizonte — DS-TEMP INACTIVE • 5 kW
15190 FRANCE
  †R FRANCE INTL, Issoudun-Allouis — **S** • C America • 250 kW
PHILIPPINES
  †RADYO PILIPINAS, Tinang — Mideast • 250 kW
UNITED KINGDOM
  BBC, Via Ascension — S America • 250 kW
  Sa/Su • S America • 250 kW
  M-F • S America • 250 kW
USA
  †VOA, Via Iranawila, Sri Lanka — **S** • W Asia & S Asia • 500 kW
15190v PAKISTAN
  RADIO PAKISTAN, Karachi — S Asia & SE Asia • 50 kW • ALT. FREQ. TO 15120v kHz
15195 CANADA
  R CANADA INTL, Via Tokyo, Japan — **S** • E Asia & SE Asia • 300 kW
FRANCE
  †R FRANCE INTL, Issoudun-Allouis — E Europe • 250 kW
  S • E Europe • 250 kW
  †R FRANCE INTL, Via Tokyo, Japan — **S** • E Asia • 300 kW
  S • SE Asia • 300 kW
GUAM
  KTWR-TRANS WORLD RADIO, Merizo — SE Asia • 100 kW
SPAIN
  †R EXTERIOR ESPANA, Noblejas — M-F • Europe • 350 kW
TURKEY
  †VOICE OF TURKEY, Ankara-Emirler — **W** • N Africa & W Africa • 500 kW
USA
  †ADVENTIST WORLD R, Via Agat, Guam — S Asia • 100 kW
  †ADVENTIST WORLD R, Via Germany — **W** Sa/Su • S Europe • 100 kW • ALT. FREQ. TO 7230 kHz
  †ADVENTIST WORLD R, Via Italy — **W** • Europe • 2.5 kW • ALT. FREQ. TO 11700 kHz
  †HERALD BROADCASTING, S Carolina — **S** M/Tu/Th/Sa • E Africa & C Africa • 500 kW
  S Su/W/F • E Africa & C Africa • 500 kW
  VOA, Via Kavála, Greece — **S** • S Asia • 250 kW
  VOA, Via Philippines — **S** • E Asia • 250 kW
15200 FRANCE
  †R FRANCE INTL, Via French Guiana — S America • 250 kW   S America • 500 kW
GUAM
  †KTWR-TRANS WORLD RADIO, Merizo — Sa/Su • SE Asia • 100 kW
  SE Asia • 100 kW
INDIA
  †ALL INDIA RADIO, Aligarh — Mideast & W Asia • 250 kW
IRAN
  †VO THE ISLAMIC REP, Sirjan — SE Asia • 500 kW
UZBEKISTAN
  UZBEK RADIO, Tashkent — **S** • Mideast & W Asia • DS-2 • 100 kW
15205 GERMANY
  DEUTSCHE WELLE, Via Sri Lanka — S Asia • 250 kW
IRAN
  †VO THE ISLAMIC REP, Sirjan — **S** • Europe • 500 kW
SAUDI ARABIA
  †BS OF THE KINGDOM, Riyadh — W Europe • DS-HOLY KORAN • 500 kW • ALT. FREQ. TO 15345 kHz
USA
  R FREE ASIA, Via Mongolia — **S** • SE Asia • 250 kW
  RFE-RL, Via Kavála, Greece — **S** • W Asia & C Asia • 250 kW
  RFE-RL, Via Pals, Spain — **W** • E Europe & W Asia • 250 kW
  S • E Europe & W Asia • 250 kW
(con'd) †VOA, Via Kavála, Greece — Mideast & S Asia • 250 kW   **W** • Mideast & S Asia • 250 kW

	0 1 2 3 4 5 6 7 8 9 10 11 12 13 14 15 16 17 18 19 20 21 22 23 24

ENGLISH ▬   ARABIC ⋙   CHINESE ▫▫▫   FRENCH ═   GERMAN ▬   RUSSIAN ═   SPANISH ═   OTHER ▬

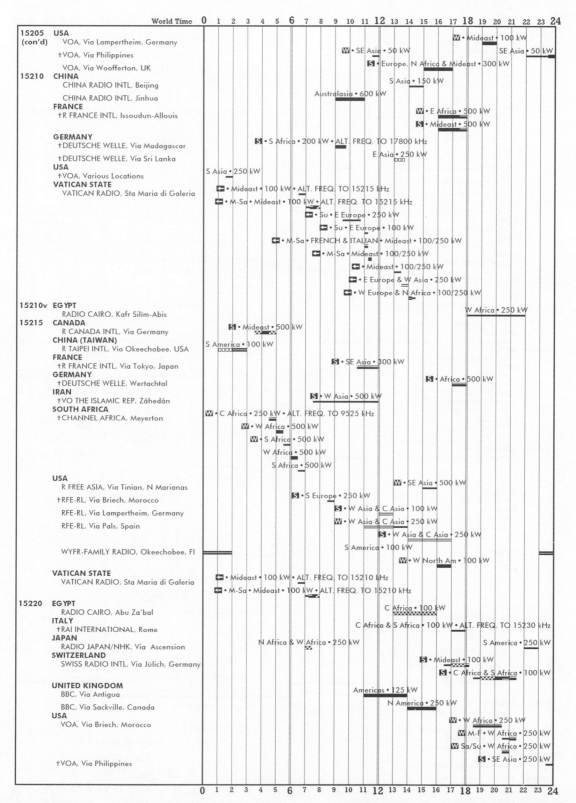

World Time

15205	USA	
(con'd)	VOA, Via Lampertheim, Germany	W • Mideast • 100 kW
	†VOA, Via Philippines	W • SE Asia • 50 kW SE Asia • 50 kW
	VOA, Via Woofferton, UK	S • Europe, N Africa & Mideast • 300 kW
15210	CHINA	
	CHINA RADIO INTL, Beijing	S Asia • 150 kW
	CHINA RADIO INTL, Jinhua	Australasia • 600 kW
	FRANCE	
	†R FRANCE INTL, Issoudun-Allouis	W • E Africa • 500 kW
		S • Mideast • 500 kW
	GERMANY	
	†DEUTSCHE WELLE, Via Madagascar	S • S Africa • 200 kW • ALT. FREQ. TO 17800 kHz
	†DEUTSCHE WELLE, Via Sri Lanka	E Asia • 250 kW
	USA	
	†VOA, Various Locations	S Asia • 250 kW
	VATICAN STATE	
	VATICAN RADIO, Sta Maria di Galeria	• Mideast • 100 kW • ALT. FREQ. TO 15215 kHz
		• M-Sa • Mideast • 100 kW • ALT. FREQ. TO 15215 kHz
		• Su • E Europe • 250 kW
		• Su • E Europe • 100 kW
		• M-Sa • FRENCH & ITALIAN • Mideast • 100/250 kW
		• M-Sa • Mideast • 100/250 kW
		• Mideast • 100/250 kW
		• E Europe & W Asia • 250 kW
		• W Europe & N Africa • 100/250 kW
15210v	EGYPT	
	RADIO CAIRO, Kafr Silim-Abis	W Africa • 250 kW
15215	CANADA	
	R CANADA INTL, Via Germany	S • Mideast • 500 kW
	CHINA (TAIWAN)	
	R TAIPEI INTL, Via Okeechobee, USA	S America • 100 kW
	FRANCE	
	†R FRANCE INTL, Via Tokyo, Japan	S • SE Asia • 300 kW
	GERMANY	
	†DEUTSCHE WELLE, Wertachtal	S • Africa • 500 kW
	IRAN	
	†VO THE ISLAMIC REP, Zähedän	S • W Asia • 500 kW
	SOUTH AFRICA	
	†CHANNEL AFRICA, Meyerton	W • C Africa • 250 kW • ALT. FREQ. TO 9525 kHz
		W • W Africa • 500 kW
		W • S Africa • 500 kW
		W Africa • 500 kW
		S Africa • 500 kW
	USA	
	R FREE ASIA, Via Tinian, N Marianas	W • SE Asia • 500 kW
	†RFE-RL, Via Briech, Morocco	S • S Europe • 250 kW
	RFE-RL, Via Lampertheim, Germany	S • W Asia & C Asia • 100 kW
	RFE-RL, Via Pals, Spain	W • W Asia & C Asia • 250 kW
		S • W Asia & C Asia • 250 kW
	WYFR-FAMILY RADIO, Okeechobee, Fl	S America • 100 kW
		W • W North Am • 100 kW
	VATICAN STATE	
	VATICAN RADIO, Sta Maria di Galeria	• Mideast • 100 kW • ALT. FREQ. TO 15210 kHz
		• M-Sa • Mideast • 100 kW • ALT. FREQ. TO 15210 kHz
15220	EGYPT	
	RADIO CAIRO, Abu Za'bal	C Africa • 100 kW
	ITALY	
	†RAI INTERNATIONAL, Rome	C Africa & S Africa • 100 kW • ALT. FREQ. TO 15230 kHz
	JAPAN	
	RADIO JAPAN/NHK, Via Ascension	N Africa & W Africa • 250 kW S America • 250 kW
	SWITZERLAND	
	SWISS RADIO INTL, Via Jülich, Germany	S • Mideast • 100 kW
		S • C Africa & S Africa • 100 kW
	UNITED KINGDOM	
	BBC, Via Antigua	Americas • 125 kW
	BBC, Via Sackville, Canada	N America • 250 kW
	USA	
	VOA, Via Briech, Morocco	W • W Africa • 250 kW
		W M-F • W Africa • 250 kW
		W Sa/Su • W Africa • 250 kW
	†VOA, Via Philippines	S • SE Asia • 250 kW

SEASONAL S OR W   1-HR TIMESHIFT MIDYEAR ⇐ OR ⇒   JAMMING / OR ∧   EARLIEST HEARD ◁   LATEST HEARD ▷   NEW FOR 2001 †

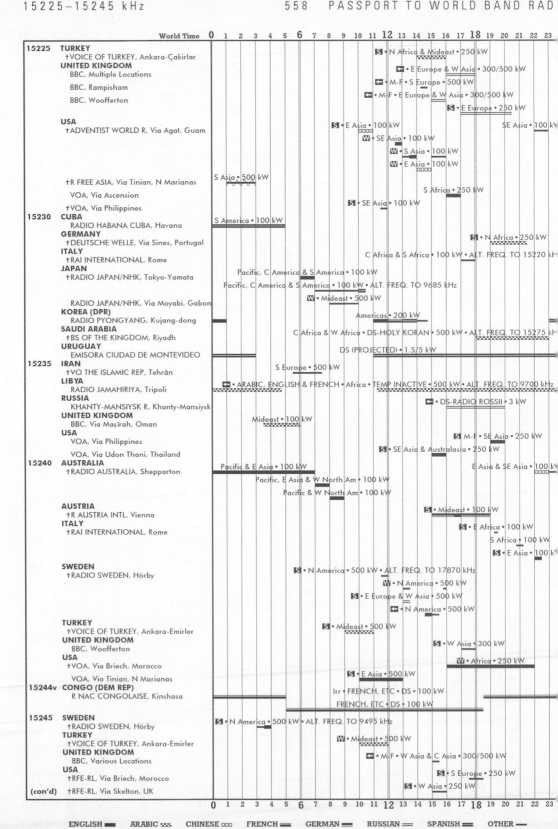

World Time 0 1 2 3 4 5 6 7 8 9 10 11 12 13 14 15 16 17 18 19 20 21 22 23

15225 TURKEY
†VOICE OF TURKEY, Ankara-Çakirlar — S • N Africa & Mideast • 250 kW
UNITED KINGDOM
BBC, Multiple Locations — E Europe & W Asia • 300/500 kW
BBC, Rampisham — M-F • S Europe • 500 kW
BBC, Woofferton — M-F • E Europe & W Asia • 300/500 kW
— S • E Europe • 250 kW
USA
†ADVENTIST WORLD R, Via Agat, Guam — S • E Asia • 100 kW / SE Asia • 100 kW
— W • SE Asia • 100 kW
— W • S Asia • 100 kW
— W • E Asia • 100 kW
†R FREE ASIA, Via Tinian, N Marianas — S Asia • 500 kW
VOA, Via Ascension — S Africa • 250 kW
†VOA, Via Philippines — S • SE Asia • 100 kW

15230 CUBA
RADIO HABANA CUBA, Havana — S America • 100 kW
GERMANY
†DEUTSCHE WELLE, Via Sines, Portugal — S • N Africa • 250 kW
ITALY
†RAI INTERNATIONAL, Rome — C Africa & S Africa • 100 kW • ALT. FREQ. TO 15220 kHz
JAPAN
†RADIO JAPAN/NHK, Tokyo-Yamata — Pacific, C America & S America • 100 kW
— Pacific, C America & S America • 100 kW • ALT. FREQ. TO 9685 kHz
RADIO JAPAN/NHK, Via Moyabi, Gabon — W • Mideast • 500 kW
KOREA (DPR)
RADIO PYONGYANG, Kujang-dong — Americas • 200 kW
SAUDI ARABIA
†BS OF THE KINGDOM, Riyadh — C Africa & W Africa • DS-HOLY KORAN • 500 kW • ALT. FREQ. TO 15275 kH
URUGUAY
EMISORA CIUDAD DE MONTEVIDEO — DS (PROJECTED) • 1.5/5 kW

15235 IRAN
†VO THE ISLAMIC REP, Tehrān — S Europe • 500 kW
LIBYA
RADIO JAMAHIRIYA, Tripoli — ARABIC, ENGLISH & FRENCH • Africa • TEMP INACTIVE • 500 kW • ALT. FREQ. TO 9700 kHz
RUSSIA
KHANTY-MANSIYSK R, Khanty-Mansiysk — DS-RADIO ROSSII • 3 kW
UNITED KINGDOM
BBC, Via Maṣīrah, Oman — Mideast • 100 kW
USA
VOA, Via Philippines — S • M-F • SE Asia • 250 kW
VOA, Via Udon Thani, Thailand — S • SE Asia & Australasia • 250 kW

15240 AUSTRALIA
†RADIO AUSTRALIA, Shepparton — Pacific & E Asia • 100 kW / E Asia & SE Asia • 100 kW
— Pacific, E Asia & W North Am • 100 kW
— Pacific & W North Am • 100 kW
AUSTRIA
†R AUSTRIA INTL, Vienna — S • Mideast • 100 kW
ITALY
†RAI INTERNATIONAL, Rome — S • E Africa • 100 kW
— S Africa • 100 kW
— S • E Asia • 100 kW
SWEDEN
†RADIO SWEDEN, Hörby — S • N America • 500 kW • ALT. FREQ. TO 17870 kHz
— W • N America • 500 kW
— S • E Europe & W Asia • 500 kW
— N America • 500 kW
TURKEY
†VOICE OF TURKEY, Ankara-Emirler — S • Mideast • 500 kW
UNITED KINGDOM
BBC, Woofferton — S • W Asia • 300 kW
USA
†VOA, Via Briech, Morocco — W • Africa • 250 kW
VOA, Via Tinian, N Marianas — S • E Asia • 500 kW

15244v CONGO (DEM REP)
R NAC CONGOLAISE, Kinshasa — Irr • FRENCH, ETC • DS • 100 kW
— FRENCH, ETC • DS • 100 kW

15245 SWEDEN
†RADIO SWEDEN, Hörby — S • N America • 500 kW • ALT. FREQ. TO 9495 kHz
TURKEY
†VOICE OF TURKEY, Ankara-Emirler — W • Mideast • 500 kW
UNITED KINGDOM
BBC, Various Locations — M-F • W Asia & C Asia • 300/500 kW
USA
†RFE-RL, Via Briech, Morocco — S • S Europe • 250 kW
(con'd) †RFE-RL, Via Skelton, UK — S • W Asia • 250 kW

0 1 2 3 4 5 6 7 8 9 10 11 12 13 14 15 16 17 18 19 20 21 22 23

ENGLISH ■ ARABIC ⋙ CHINESE ▫▫▫ FRENCH ═ GERMAN ▬ RUSSIAN ═ SPANISH ▬ OTHER —

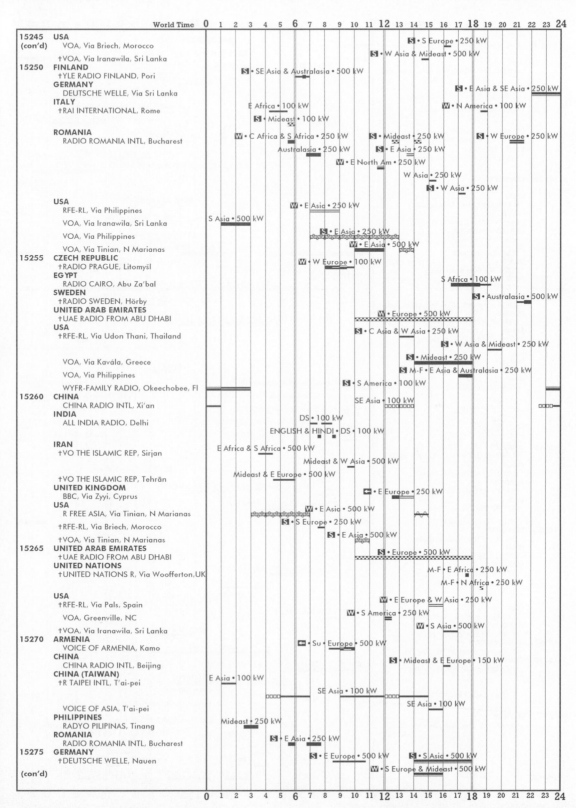

	World Time	0 1 2 3 4 5 6 7 8 9 10 11 12 13 14 15 16 17 18 19 20 21 22 23 24

15245 **USA**
(con'd) VOA, Via Briech, Morocco — **S** • S Europe • 250 kW
  †VOA, Via Iranawila, Sri Lanka — **S** • W Asia & Mideast • 500 kW
15250 **FINLAND**
  †YLE RADIO FINLAND, Pori — **S** • SE Asia & Australasia • 500 kW
  GERMANY
  DEUTSCHE WELLE, Via Sri Lanka — **S** • E Asia & SE Asia • 250 kW
  ITALY
  †RAI INTERNATIONAL, Rome — E Africa • 100 kW — **W** • N America • 100 kW
  — **S** • Mideast • 100 kW
  ROMANIA
  RADIO ROMANIA INTL, Bucharest — **W** • C Africa & S Africa • 250 kW — **S** • Mideast • 250 kW — **S** • W Europe • 250 kW
  Australasia • 250 kW — **S** • E Asia • 250 kW
  W • E North Am • 250 kW
  W Asia • 250 kW
  S • W Asia • 250 kW

  USA
  RFE-RL, Via Philippines — **W** • E Asia • 250 kW
  VOA, Via Iranawila, Sri Lanka — S Asia • 500 kW
  VOA, Via Philippines — **S** • E Asia • 250 kW
  VOA, Via Tinian, N Marianas — **W** • E Asia • 500 kW
15255 **CZECH REPUBLIC**
  †RADIO PRAGUE, Litomyšl — **W** • W Europe • 100 kW
  EGYPT
  RADIO CAIRO, Abu Za'bal — S Africa • 100 kW
  SWEDEN
  †RADIO SWEDEN, Hörby — **S** • Australasia • 500 kW
  UNITED ARAB EMIRATES
  †UAE RADIO FROM ABU DHABI — **W** • Europe • 500 kW
  USA
  †RFE-RL, Via Udon Thani, Thailand — **S** • C Asia & W Asia • 250 kW
  — **S** • W Asia & Mideast • 250 kW

  VOA, Via Kavála, Greece — **S** • Mideast • 250 kW
  VOA, Via Philippines — **S** • M-F • E Asia & Australasia • 250 kW
  WYFR-FAMILY RADIO, Okeechobee, Fl — **S** • S America • 100 kW
15260 **CHINA**
  CHINA RADIO INTL, Xi'an — SE Asia • 100 kW
  INDIA
  ALL INDIA RADIO, Delhi — DS • 100 kW
  ENGLISH & HINDI • DS • 100 kW
  IRAN
  †VO THE ISLAMIC REP, Sirjan — E Africa & S Africa • 500 kW
  Mideast & W Asia • 500 kW
  †VO THE ISLAMIC REP, Tehrān — Mideast & E Europe • 500 kW
  UNITED KINGDOM
  BBC, Via Zyyi, Cyprus — **→** • E Europe • 250 kW
  USA
  R FREE ASIA, Via Tinian, N Marianas — **W** • E Asia • 500 kW
  †RFE-RL, Via Briech, Morocco — **S** • S Europe • 250 kW
  †VOA, Via Tinian, N Marianas — **S** • E Asia • 500 kW
15265 **UNITED ARAB EMIRATES**
  †UAE RADIO FROM ABU DHABI — **S** • Europe • 500 kW
  UNITED NATIONS
  †UNITED NATIONS R, Via Woofferton, UK — M-F • E Africa • 250 kW
  M-F • N Africa • 250 kW
  USA
  †RFE-RL, Via Pals, Spain — **W** • E Europe & W Asia • 250 kW
  VOA, Greenville, NC — **W** • S America • 250 kW
  †VOA, Via Iranawila, Sri Lanka — **W** • S Asia • 500 kW
15270 **ARMENIA**
  VOICE OF ARMENIA, Kamo — **→** • Su • Europe • 500 kW
  CHINA
  CHINA RADIO INTL, Beijing — **S** • Mideast & E Europe • 150 kW
  CHINA (TAIWAN)
  †R TAIPEI INTL, T'ai-pei — E Asia • 100 kW
  VOICE OF ASIA, T'ai-pei — SE Asia • 100 kW
  SE Asia • 100 kW
  PHILIPPINES
  RADYO PILIPINAS, Tinang — Mideast • 250 kW
  ROMANIA
  RADIO ROMANIA INTL, Bucharest — **S** • E Asia • 250 kW
15275 **GERMANY**
  †DEUTSCHE WELLE, Nauen — **S** • E Europe • 500 kW — **S** • S Asia • 500 kW
  W • S Europe & Mideast • 500 kW
(con'd)

		0 1 2 3 4 5 6 7 8 9 10 11 12 13 14 15 16 17 18 19 20 21 22 23 24

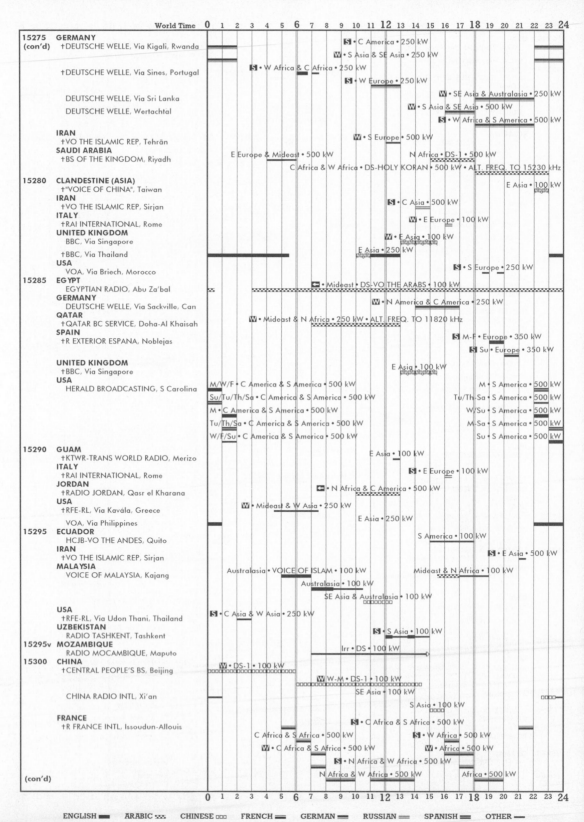

	World Time	0 1 2 3 4 5 6 7 8 9 10 11 12 13 14 15 16 17 18 19 20 21 22 23 24

15275 (con'd) **GERMANY**
†DEUTSCHE WELLE, Via Kigali, Rwanda — **S** • C America • 250 kW / **W** • S Asia & SE Asia • 250 kW

†DEUTSCHE WELLE, Via Sines, Portugal — **S** • W Africa & C Africa • 250 kW / **S** • W Europe • 250 kW

DEUTSCHE WELLE, Via Sri Lanka — **W** • SE Asia & Australasia • 250 kW

DEUTSCHE WELLE, Wertachtal — **W** • S Asia & SE Asia • 500 kW / **S** • W Africa & S America • 500 kW

IRAN
†VO THE ISLAMIC REP, Tehrān — **W** • S Europe • 500 kW

SAUDI ARABIA
†BS OF THE KINGDOM, Riyadh — E Europe & Mideast • 500 kW / N Africa • DS-1 • 500 kW / C Africa & W Africa • DS-HOLY KORAN • 500 kW • ALT. FREQ. TO 15230 kHz

15280 **CLANDESTINE (ASIA)**
†"VOICE OF CHINA", Taiwan — E Asia • 100 kW

IRAN
†VO THE ISLAMIC REP, Sirjan — **S** • C Asia • 500 kW

ITALY
†RAI INTERNATIONAL, Rome — **W** • E Europe • 100 kW

UNITED KINGDOM
BBC, Via Singapore — **W** • E Asia • 100 kW

†BBC, Via Thailand — E Asia • 250 kW

USA
VOA, Via Briech, Morocco — **S** • S Europe • 250 kW

15285 **EGYPT**
EGYPTIAN RADIO, Abu Za'bal — ◧ • Mideast • DS-VO THE ARABS • 100 kW

GERMANY
DEUTSCHE WELLE, Via Sackville, Can — **W** • N America & C America • 250 kW

QATAR
†QATAR BC SERVICE, Doha-Al Khaisah — **W** • Mideast & N Africa • 250 kW • ALT. FREQ. TO 11820 kHz

SPAIN
†R EXTERIOR ESPANA, Noblejas — **S** M-F • Europe • 350 kW / **S** Su • Europe • 350 kW

UNITED KINGDOM
†BBC, Via Singapore — E Asia • 100 kW

USA
HERALD BROADCASTING, S Carolina — M/W/F • C America & S America • 500 kW / M • S America • 500 kW
Su/Tu/Th/Sa • C America & S America • 500 kW / Tu/Th-Sa • S America • 500 kW
M • C America & S America • 500 kW / W/Su • S America • 500 kW
Tu/Th/Sa • C America & S America • 500 kW / M-Sa • S America • 500 kW
W/F/Su • C America & S America • 500 kW / Su • S America • 500 kW

15290 **GUAM**
†KTWR-TRANS WORLD RADIO, Merizo — E Asia • 100 kW

ITALY
†RAI INTERNATIONAL, Rome — **S** • E Europe • 100 kW

JORDAN
†RADIO JORDAN, Qasr el Kharana — ◧ • N Africa & C America • 500 kW

USA
†RFE-RL, Via Kavála, Greece — **W** • Mideast & W Asia • 250 kW

VOA, Via Philippines — E Asia • 250 kW

15295 **ECUADOR**
HCJB-VO THE ANDES, Quito — S America • 100 kW

IRAN
†VO THE ISLAMIC REP, Sirjan — **S** • E Asia • 500 kW

MALAYSIA
VOICE OF MALAYSIA, Kajang — Australasia • VOICE OF ISLAM • 100 kW / Mideast & N Africa • 100 kW
Australasia • 100 kW
SE Asia & Australasia • 100 kW

USA
†RFE-RL, Via Udon Thani, Thailand — **S** • C Asia & W Asia • 250 kW

UZBEKISTAN
RADIO TASHKENT, Tashkent — **S** • S Asia • 100 kW

15295v **MOZAMBIQUE**
RADIO MOCAMBIQUE, Maputo — Irr • DS • 100 kW

15300 **CHINA**
†CENTRAL PEOPLE'S BS, Beijing — **W** • DS-1 • 100 kW / **W** W-M • DS-1 • 100 kW

CHINA RADIO INTL, Xi'an — SE Asia • 100 kW / S Asia • 100 kW

FRANCE
†R FRANCE INTL, Issoudun-Allouis — **S** • C Africa & S Africa • 500 kW / **S** • W Africa • 500 kW
C Africa & S Africa • 500 kW / **S** • W Africa • 500 kW
W • C Africa & S Africa • 500 kW / **W** • Africa • 500 kW
S • N Africa & W Africa • 500 kW
N Africa & W Africa • 500 kW / Africa • 500 kW

(con'd)

	0 1 2 3 4 5 6 7 8 9 10 11 12 13 14 15 16 17 18 19 20 21 22 23 24

ENGLISH ▬▬   ARABIC ⋆⋆⋆   CHINESE ▫▫▫   FRENCH ▬   GERMAN ▬▬   RUSSIAN ══   SPANISH ▬   OTHER ▬

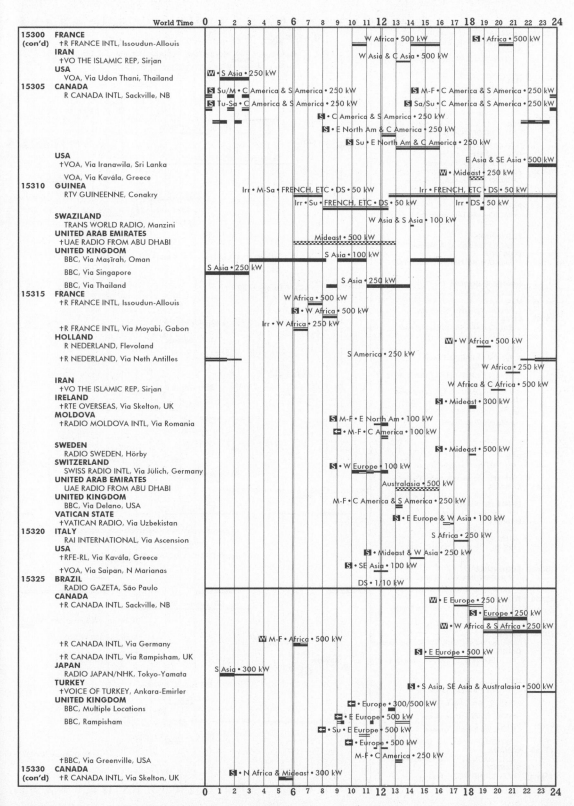

World Time 0 1 2 3 4 5 6 7 8 9 10 11 12 13 14 15 16 17 18 19 20 21 22 23 24

15300 **FRANCE**
(con'd) †R FRANCE INTL, Issoudun-Allouis — W Africa • 500 kW — S Africa • 500 kW
IRAN
†VO THE ISLAMIC REP, Sirjan — W Asia & C Asia • 500 kW
USA
VOA, Via Udon Thani, Thailand — W • S Asia • 250 kW
15305 **CANADA**
R CANADA INTL, Sackville, NB — S Su/M • C America & S America • 250 kW — S M-F • C America & S America • 250 kW
— S Tu-Sa • C America & S America • 250 kW — S Sa/Su • C America & S America • 250 kW
— S • C America & S America • 250 kW
— S • E North Am & C America • 250 kW
— S Su • E North Am & C America • 250 kW
USA
†VOA, Via Iranawila, Sri Lanka — E Asia & SE Asia • 500 kW
VOA, Via Kavála, Greece — W • Mideast • 250 kW
15310 **GUINEA**
RTV GUINEENNE, Conakry — Irr • M-Sa • FRENCH, ETC • DS • 50 kW — Irr • FRENCH, ETC • DS • 50 kW
— Irr • Su • FRENCH, ETC • DS • 50 kW — Irr • DS • 50 kW
SWAZILAND
TRANS WORLD RADIO, Manzini — W Asia & S Asia • 100 kW
UNITED ARAB EMIRATES
†UAE RADIO FROM ABU DHABI — Mideast • 500 kW
UNITED KINGDOM
BBC, Via Maşīrah, Oman — S Asia • 100 kW
BBC, Via Singapore — S Asia • 250 kW
BBC, Via Thailand — S Asia • 250 kW
15315 **FRANCE**
†R FRANCE INTL, Issoudun-Allouis — W Africa • 500 kW
— S • W Africa • 500 kW
†R FRANCE INTL, Via Moyabi, Gabon — Irr • W Africa • 250 kW
HOLLAND
R NEDERLAND, Flevoland — W • W Africa • 500 kW
†R NEDERLAND, Via Neth Antilles — S America • 250 kW
— W Africa • 250 kW
IRAN
†VO THE ISLAMIC REP, Sirjan — W Africa & C Africa • 500 kW
IRELAND
†RTE OVERSEAS, Via Skelton, UK — S • Mideast • 300 kW
MOLDOVA
†RADIO MOLDOVA INTL, Via Romania — S M-F • E North Am • 100 kW
— ⇦ • M-F • C America • 100 kW
SWEDEN
RADIO SWEDEN, Hörby — S • Mideast • 500 kW
SWITZERLAND
SWISS RADIO INTL, Via Jülich, Germany — S • W Europe • 100 kW
UNITED ARAB EMIRATES
UAE RADIO FROM ABU DHABI — Australasia • 500 kW
UNITED KINGDOM
BBC, Via Delano, USA — M-F • C America & S America • 250 kW
VATICAN STATE
†VATICAN RADIO, Via Uzbekistan — S • E Europe & W Asia • 100 kW
15320 **ITALY**
RAI INTERNATIONAL, Via Ascension — S Africa • 250 kW
USA
†RFE-RL, Via Kavála, Greece — S • Mideast & W Asia • 250 kW
†VOA, Via Saipan, N Marianas — S • SE Asia • 100 kW
15325 **BRAZIL**
RADIO GAZETA, São Paulo — DS • 1/10 kW
CANADA
†R CANADA INTL, Sackville, NB — W • E Europe • 250 kW
— S • Europe • 250 kW
— W • W Africa & S Africa • 250 kW
†R CANADA INTL, Via Germany — W M-F • Africa • 500 kW
†R CANADA INTL, Via Rampisham, UK — S • E Europe • 500 kW
JAPAN
RADIO JAPAN/NHK, Tokyo-Yamata — S Asia • 300 kW
TURKEY
†VOICE OF TURKEY, Ankara-Emirler — S • S Asia, SE Asia & Australasia • 500 kW
UNITED KINGDOM
BBC, Multiple Locations — ⇦ • Europe • 300/500 kW
BBC, Rampisham — ⇦ • E Europe • 500 kW
— ⇦ • Su • E Europe • 500 kW
— ⇦ • Europe • 500 kW
— M-F • C America • 250 kW
†BBC, Via Greenville, USA
15330 **CANADA**
(con'd) †R CANADA INTL, Via Skelton, UK — S • N Africa & Mideast • 300 kW

World Time 0 1 2 3 4 5 6 7 8 9 10 11 12 13 14 15 16 17 18 19 20 21 22 23 24

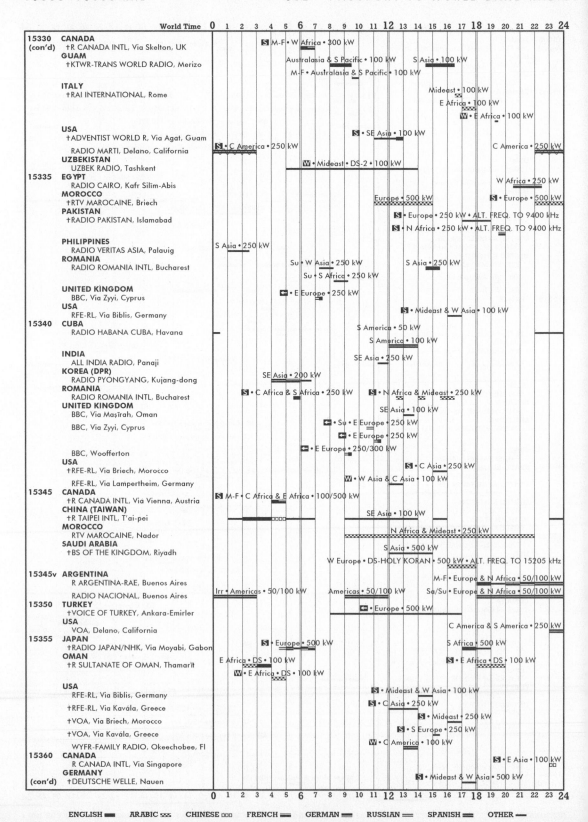

World Time 0 1 2 3 4 5 6 7 8 9 10 11 12 13 14 15 16 17 18 19 20 21 22 23 24

Freq	Country / Station	Details
15330 (con'd)	CANADA †R CANADA INTL, Via Skelton, UK	S • M-F • W Africa • 300 kW
	GUAM †KTWR-TRANS WORLD RADIO, Merizo	Australasia & S Pacific • 100 kW ● S Asia • 100 kW ● M-F • Australasia & S Pacific • 100 kW
	ITALY †RAI INTERNATIONAL, Rome	Mideast • 100 kW ● E Africa • 100 kW ● W • E Africa • 100 kW
	USA †ADVENTIST WORLD R, Via Agat, Guam	S • SE Asia • 100 kW
	RADIO MARTI, Delano, California	S • C America • 250 kW ● C America • 250 kW
	UZBEKISTAN UZBEK RADIO, Tashkent	W • Mideast • DS-2 • 100 kW
15335	EGYPT RADIO CAIRO, Kafr Silim-Abis	W Africa • 250 kW
	MOROCCO †RTV MAROCAINE, Briech	Europe • 500 kW ● S • Europe • 500 kW
	PAKISTAN †RADIO PAKISTAN, Islamabad	S • Europe • 250 kW • ALT. FREQ. TO 9400 kHz ● S • N Africa • 250 kW • ALT. FREQ. TO 9400 kHz
	PHILIPPINES RADIO VERITAS ASIA, Palauig	S Asia • 250 kW
	ROMANIA RADIO ROMANIA INTL, Bucharest	Su • W Asia • 250 kW ● S Asia • 250 kW ● Su • S Africa • 250 kW
	UNITED KINGDOM BBC, Via Zyyi, Cyprus	← • E Europe • 250 kW
	USA RFE-RL, Via Biblis, Germany	S • Mideast & W Asia • 100 kW
15340	CUBA RADIO HABANA CUBA, Havana	S America • 50 kW ● S America • 100 kW
	INDIA ALL INDIA RADIO, Panaji	SE Asia • 250 kW
	KOREA (DPR) RADIO PYONGYANG, Kujang-dong	SE Asia • 200 kW
	ROMANIA RADIO ROMANIA INTL, Bucharest	S • C Africa & S Africa • 250 kW ● S • N Africa & Mideast • 250 kW
	UNITED KINGDOM BBC, Via Maṣīrah, Oman	SE Asia • 100 kW
	BBC, Via Zyyi, Cyprus	← • Su • E Europe • 250 kW ● ← • E Europe • 250 kW
	BBC, Woofferton	← • E Europe • 250/300 kW
	USA †RFE-RL, Via Briech, Morocco	S • C Asia • 250 kW
	RFE-RL, Via Lampertheim, Germany	W • W Asia & C Asia • 100 kW
15345	CANADA †R CANADA INTL, Via Vienna, Austria	S • M-F • C Africa & E Africa • 100/500 kW
	CHINA (TAIWAN) †R TAIPEI INTL, T'ai-pei	SE Asia • 100 kW
	MOROCCO RTV MAROCAINE, Nador	N Africa & Mideast • 250 kW
	SAUDI ARABIA †BS OF THE KINGDOM, Riyadh	S Asia • 500 kW ● W Europe • DS-HOLY KORAN • 500 kW • ALT. FREQ. TO 15205 kHz
15345v	ARGENTINA R ARGENTINA-RAE, Buenos Aires	M-F • Europe & N Africa • 50/100 kW
	RADIO NACIONAL, Buenos Aires	Irr • Americas • 50/100 kW ● Americas • 50/100 kW ● Sa/Su • Europe & N Africa • 50/100 kW
15350	TURKEY †VOICE OF TURKEY, Ankara-Emirler	← • Europe • 500 kW
	USA VOA, Delano, California	C America & S America • 250 kW
15355	JAPAN †RADIO JAPAN/NHK, Via Moyabi, Gabon	S • Europe • 500 kW ● S Africa • 500 kW
	OMAN †R SULTANATE OF OMAN, Thamarit	E Africa • DS • 100 kW ● S • E Africa • DS • 100 kW ● W • E Africa • DS • 100 kW
	USA RFE-RL, Via Biblis, Germany	S • Mideast & W Asia • 100 kW
	†RFE-RL, Via Kavála, Greece	S • C Asia • 250 kW
	†VOA, Via Briech, Morocco	S • Mideast • 250 kW
	†VOA, Via Kavála, Greece	S • S Europe • 250 kW
	WYFR-FAMILY RADIO, Okeechobee, Fl	W • C America • 100 kW
15360	CANADA R CANADA INTL, Via Singapore	S • E Asia • 100 kW
	GERMANY (con'd) †DEUTSCHE WELLE, Nauen	S • Mideast & W Asia • 500 kW

0 1 2 3 4 5 6 7 8 9 10 11 12 13 14 15 16 17 18 19 20 21 22 23 24

ENGLISH ▬ ARABIC ▨ CHINESE □□□ FRENCH ▬ GERMAN ▬ RUSSIAN ═ SPANISH ▬ OTHER ▬

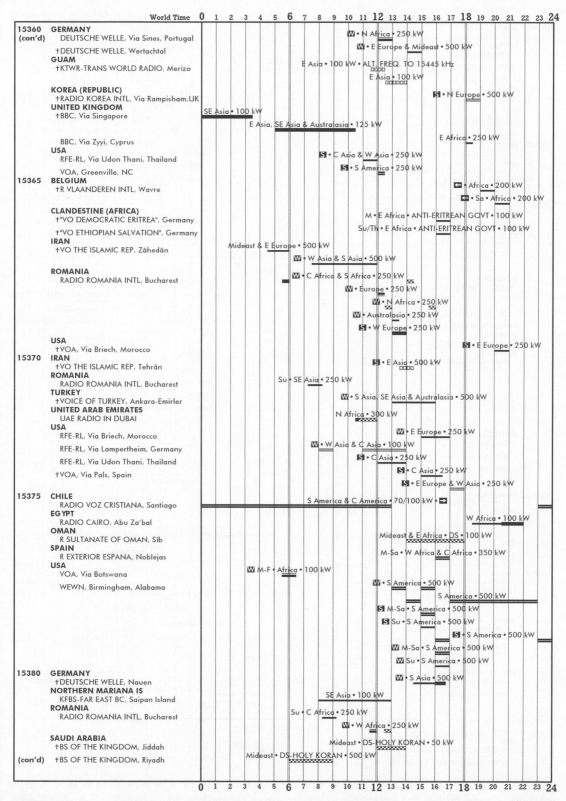

| | World Time | 0 | 1 | 2 | 3 | 4 | 5 | 6 | 7 | 8 | 9 | 10 | 11 | 12 | 13 | 14 | 15 | 16 | 17 | 18 | 19 | 20 | 21 | 22 | 23 | 24 |

15360 GERMANY
(con'd) DEUTSCHE WELLE, Via Sines, Portugal — W • N Africa • 250 kW
†DEUTSCHE WELLE, Wertachtal — W • E Europe & Mideast • 500 kW
GUAM
†KTWR-TRANS WORLD RADIO, Merizo — E Asia • 100 kW • ALT. FREQ. TO 15445 kHz
E Asia • 100 kW
KOREA (REPUBLIC)
†RADIO KOREA INTL, Via Rampisham, UK — S • N Europe • 500 kW
UNITED KINGDOM
†BBC, Via Singapore — SE Asia • 100 kW
E Asia, SE Asia & Australasia • 125 kW
BBC, Via Zyyi, Cyprus — E Africa • 250 kW
USA
RFE-RL, Via Udon Thani, Thailand — S • C Asia & W Asia • 250 kW
VOA, Greenville, NC — S • S America • 250 kW

15365 BELGIUM
†R VLAANDEREN INTL, Wavre — ⬅ • Africa • 200 kW
⬅ • Sa • Africa • 200 kW
CLANDESTINE (AFRICA)
†"VO DEMOCRATIC ERITREA", Germany — M • E Africa • ANTI-ERITREAN GOVT • 100 kW
†"VO ETHIOPIAN SALVATION", Germany — Su/Th • E Africa • ANTI-ERITREAN GOVT • 100 kW
IRAN
†VO THE ISLAMIC REP, Zāhedān — Mideast & E Europe • 500 kW
W • W Asia & S Asia • 500 kW
ROMANIA
RADIO ROMANIA INTL, Bucharest — W • C Africa & S Africa • 250 kW
W • Europe • 250 kW
W • N Africa • 250 kW
W • Australasia • 250 kW
S • W Europe • 250 kW
USA
†VOA, Via Briech, Morocco — S • E Europe • 250 kW
15370 IRAN
†VO THE ISLAMIC REP, Tehrān — S • E Asia • 500 kW
ROMANIA
RADIO ROMANIA INTL, Bucharest — Su • SE Asia • 250 kW
TURKEY
†VOICE OF TURKEY, Ankara-Emirler — W • S Asia, SE Asia & Australasia • 500 kW
UNITED ARAB EMIRATES
UAE RADIO IN DUBAI — N Africa • 300 kW
USA
RFE-RL, Via Briech, Morocco — W • E Europe • 250 kW
RFE-RL, Via Lampertheim, Germany — W • W Asia & C Asia • 100 kW
RFE-RL, Via Udon Thani, Thailand — S • C Asia • 250 kW
S • C Asia • 250 kW
†VOA, Via Pals, Spain — S • E Europe & W Asia • 250 kW

15375 CHILE
RADIO VOZ CRISTIANA, Santiago — S America & C America • 70/100 kW • ➡
EGYPT
RADIO CAIRO, Abu Za'bal — W Africa • 100 kW
OMAN
R SULTANATE OF OMAN, Sīb — Mideast & E Africa • DS • 100 kW
SPAIN
R EXTERIOR ESPANA, Noblejas — M-Sa • W Africa & C Africa • 350 kW
USA
VOA, Via Botswana — W M-F • Africa • 100 kW
WEWN, Birmingham, Alabama — W • S America • 500 kW
S America • 500 kW
S M-Sa • S America • 500 kW
S Su • S America • 500 kW
S • S America • 500 kW
W M-Sa • S America • 500 kW
W Su • S America • 500 kW

15380 GERMANY
†DEUTSCHE WELLE, Nauen — W • S Asia • 500 kW
NORTHERN MARIANA IS
KFBS-FAR EAST BC, Saipan Island — SE Asia • 100 kW
ROMANIA
RADIO ROMANIA INTL, Bucharest — Su • C Africa • 250 kW
W • W Africa • 250 kW
SAUDI ARABIA
†BS OF THE KINGDOM, Jiddah — Mideast • DS-HOLY KORAN • 50 kW
(con'd) †BS OF THE KINGDOM, Riyadh — Mideast • DS-HOLY KORAN • 500 kW

| | 0 | 1 | 2 | 3 | 4 | 5 | 6 | 7 | 8 | 9 | 10 | 11 | 12 | 13 | 14 | 15 | 16 | 17 | 18 | 19 | 20 | 21 | 22 | 23 | 24 |

SEASONAL S OR W   1-HR TIMESHIFT MIDYEAR ⬅ OR ➡   JAMMING / OR /\   EARLIEST HEARD ◁   LATEST HEARD ▷   NEW FOR 2001 †

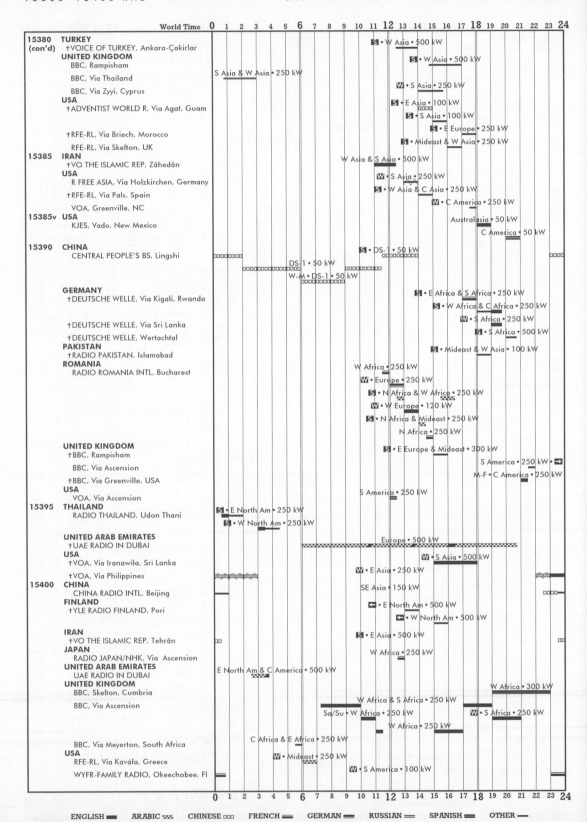

| World Time | | 0 | 1 | 2 | 3 | 4 | 5 | 6 | 7 | 8 | 9 | 10 | 11 | 12 | 13 | 14 | 15 | 16 | 17 | 18 | 19 | 20 | 21 | 22 | 23 | 24 |

15380 **TURKEY**
(con'd)   †VOICE OF TURKEY, Ankara-Çakirlar — S • W Asia • 500 kW
   UNITED KINGDOM
      BBC, Rampisham — S • W Asia • 500 kW
      BBC, Via Thailand — S Asia & W Asia • 250 kW
      BBC, Via Zyyi, Cyprus — W • S Asia • 250 kW
   USA
      †ADVENTIST WORLD R, Via Agat, Guam — S • E Asia • 100 kW / S • S Asia • 100 kW
      †RFE-RL, Via Briech, Morocco — S • E Europe • 250 kW
      RFE-RL, Via Skelton, UK — S • Mideast & W Asia • 250 kW
15385 **IRAN**
      †VO THE ISLAMIC REP, Zāhedān — W Asia & S Asia • 500 kW
   USA
      R FREE ASIA, Via Holzkirchen, Germany — W • S Asia • 250 kW
      †RFE-RL, Via Pals, Spain — S • W Asia & C Asia • 250 kW
      VOA, Greenville, NC — W • C America • 250 kW
15385v **USA**
      KJES, Vado, New Mexico — Australasia • 50 kW / C America • 50 kW

15390 **CHINA**
      CENTRAL PEOPLE'S BS, Lingshi — S • DS-1 • 50 kW / DS-1 • 50 kW / W-M • DS-1 • 50 kW
   GERMANY
      †DEUTSCHE WELLE, Via Kigali, Rwanda — S • E Africa & S Africa • 250 kW
      — S • W Africa & C Africa • 250 kW
      †DEUTSCHE WELLE, Via Sri Lanka — W • S Africa • 250 kW
      †DEUTSCHE WELLE, Wertachtal — S • S Africa • 500 kW
   PAKISTAN
      †RADIO PAKISTAN, Islamabad — S • Mideast & W Asia • 100 kW
   ROMANIA
      RADIO ROMANIA INTL, Bucharest — W Africa • 250 kW
      — W • Europe • 250 kW
      — S • N Africa & W Africa • 250 kW
      — W • W Europe • 120 kW
      — S • N Africa & Mideast • 250 kW
      — N Africa • 250 kW
   UNITED KINGDOM
      †BBC, Rampisham — S • E Europe & Mideast • 300 kW
      BBC, Via Ascension — S America • 250 kW • →
      †BBC, Via Greenville, USA — M-F • C America • 250 kW
   USA
      VOA, Via Ascension — S America • 250 kW
15395 **THAILAND**
      RADIO THAILAND, Udon Thani — S • E North Am • 250 kW / S • W North Am • 250 kW
   UNITED ARAB EMIRATES
      †UAE RADIO IN DUBAI — Europe • 500 kW
   USA
      †VOA, Via Iranawila, Sri Lanka — W • S Asia • 500 kW
      †VOA, Via Philippines — W • E Asia • 250 kW
15400 **CHINA**
      CHINA RADIO INTL, Beijing — SE Asia • 150 kW
   FINLAND
      †YLE RADIO FINLAND, Pori — ◄ • E North Am • 500 kW / ◄ • W North Am • 500 kW
   IRAN
      †VO THE ISLAMIC REP, Tehrān — S • E Asia • 500 kW
   JAPAN
      RADIO JAPAN/NHK, Via Ascension — W Africa • 250 kW
   UNITED ARAB EMIRATES
      UAE RADIO IN DUBAI — E North Am & C America • 500 kW
   UNITED KINGDOM
      BBC, Skelton, Cumbria — W Africa • 300 kW
      BBC, Via Ascension — W Africa & S Africa • 250 kW
      — Sa/Su • W Africa • 250 kW
      — W • S Africa • 250 kW
      — W Africa • 250 kW
      BBC, Via Meyerton, South Africa — C Africa & E Africa • 250 kW
   USA
      RFE-RL, Via Kavála, Greece — W • Mideast • 250 kW
      WYFR-FAMILY RADIO, Okeechobee, Fl — W • S America • 100 kW

| World Time | | 0 | 1 | 2 | 3 | 4 | 5 | 6 | 7 | 8 | 9 | 10 | 11 | 12 | 13 | 14 | 15 | 16 | 17 | 18 | 19 | 20 | 21 | 22 | 23 | 24 |

ENGLISH ▬   ARABIC ⁓⁓   CHINESE ▫▫▫   FRENCH ▬   GERMAN ▬   RUSSIAN ═   SPANISH ▬   OTHER ▬

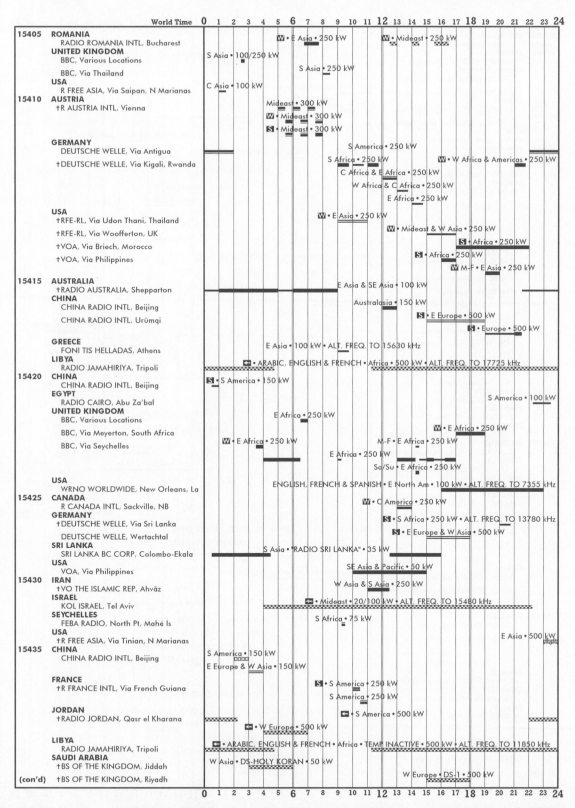

World Time	0 1 2 3 4 5 6 7 8 9 10 11 12 13 14 15 16 17 18 19 20 21 22 23 24
15405 **ROMANIA**	
RADIO ROMANIA INTL, Bucharest	W • E Asia • 250 kW W • Mideast • 250 kW
UNITED KINGDOM	
BBC, Various Locations	S Asia • 100/250 kW
BBC, Via Thailand	S Asia • 250 kW
USA	
R FREE ASIA, Via Saipan, N Marianas	C Asia • 100 kW
15410 **AUSTRIA**	
†R AUSTRIA INTL, Vienna	Mideast • 300 kW
	W • Mideast • 300 kW
	S • Mideast • 300 kW
GERMANY	
DEUTSCHE WELLE, Via Antigua	S America • 250 kW
†DEUTSCHE WELLE, Via Kigali, Rwanda	S Africa • 250 kW W • W Africa & Americas • 250 kW
	C Africa & E Africa • 250 kW
	W Africa & C Africa • 250 kW
	E Africa • 250 kW
USA	
†RFE-RL, Via Udon Thani, Thailand	W • E Asia • 250 kW
†RFE-RL, Via Woofferton, UK	W • Mideast & W Asia • 250 kW
†VOA, Via Briech, Morocco	S • Africa • 250 kW
†VOA, Via Philippines	S • Africa • 250 kW
	W • M-F • E Asia • 250 kW
15415 **AUSTRALIA**	
†RADIO AUSTRALIA, Shepparton	E Asia & SE Asia • 100 kW
CHINA	
CHINA RADIO INTL, Beijing	Australasia • 150 kW
CHINA RADIO INTL, Ürümqi	S • E Europe • 500 kW
	S • Europe • 500 kW
GREECE	
FONI TIS HELLADAS, Athens	E Asia • 100 kW • ALT. FREQ. TO 15630 kHz
LIBYA	
RADIO JAMAHIRIYA, Tripoli	⇆ • ARABIC, ENGLISH & FRENCH • Africa • 500 kW • ALT. FREQ. TO 17725 kHz
15420 **CHINA**	
CHINA RADIO INTL, Beijing	S • S America • 150 kW
EGYPT	
RADIO CAIRO, Abu Za'bal	S America • 100 kW
UNITED KINGDOM	
BBC, Various Locations	E Africa • 250 kW
BBC, Via Meyerton, South Africa	W • E Africa • 250 kW
BBC, Via Seychelles	W • E Africa • 250 kW
	E Africa • 250 kW
	M-F • E Africa • 250 kW
	Sa/Su • E Africa • 250 kW
USA	
WRNO WORLDWIDE, New Orleans, La	ENGLISH, FRENCH & SPANISH • E North Am • 100 kW • ALT. FREQ. TO 7355 kHz
15425 **CANADA**	
R CANADA INTL, Sackville, NB	W • C America • 250 kW
GERMANY	
†DEUTSCHE WELLE, Via Sri Lanka	S • S Africa • 250 kW • ALT. FREQ. TO 13780 kHz
DEUTSCHE WELLE, Wertachtal	S • E Europe & W Asia • 500 kW
SRI LANKA	
SRI LANKA BC CORP, Colombo-Ekala	S Asia • "RADIO SRI LANKA" • 35 kW
USA	
VOA, Via Philippines	SE Asia & Pacific • 50 kW
15430 **IRAN**	
†VO THE ISLAMIC REP, Ahvāz	W Asia & S Asia • 250 kW
ISRAEL	
KOL ISRAEL, Tel Aviv	⇆ • Mideast • 20/100 kW • ALT. FREQ. TO 15480 kHz
SEYCHELLES	
FEBA RADIO, North Pt, Mahé Is	S Africa • 75 kW
USA	
†R FREE ASIA, Via Tinian, N Marianas	E Asia • 500 kW
15435 **CHINA**	
CHINA RADIO INTL, Beijing	S America • 150 kW
	E Europe & W Asia • 150 kW
FRANCE	
†R FRANCE INTL, Via French Guiana	S • S America • 250 kW
	S America • 250 kW
JORDAN	
†RADIO JORDAN, Qasr el Kharana	⇆ • S America • 500 kW
	⇆ • W Europe • 500 kW
LIBYA	
RADIO JAMAHIRIYA, Tripoli	⇆ • ARABIC, ENGLISH & FRENCH • Africa • TEMP INACTIVE • 500 kW • ALT. FREQ. TO 11850 kHz
SAUDI ARABIA	
†BS OF THE KINGDOM, Jiddah	W Asia • DS-HOLY KORAN • 50 kW
(con'd) †BS OF THE KINGDOM, Riyadh	W Europe • DS-1 • 500 kW

	0 1 2 3 4 5 6 7 8 9 10 11 12 13 14 15 16 17 18 19 20 21 22 23 24

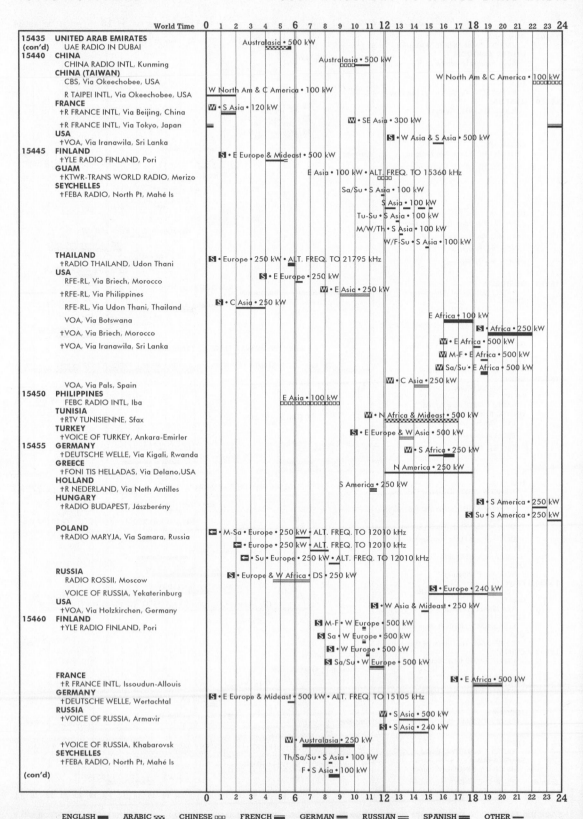

World Time   0 1 2 3 4 5 6 7 8 9 10 11 12 13 14 15 16 17 18 19 20 21 22 23 24

15435 **UNITED ARAB EMIRATES**
(con'd)   UAE RADIO IN DUBAI   Australasia • 500 kW
15440 **CHINA**
   CHINA RADIO INTL, Kunming   Australasia • 500 kW
   CHINA (TAIWAN)
   CBS, Via Okeechobee, USA   W North Am & C America • 100 kW
   R TAIPEI INTL, Via Okeechobee, USA   W North Am & C America • 100 kW
   FRANCE
   †R FRANCE INTL, Via Beijing, China   W • S Asia • 120 kW
   †R FRANCE INTL, Via Tokyo, Japan   W • SE Asia • 300 kW
   USA
   †VOA, Via Iranawila, Sri Lanka   S • W Asia & S Asia • 500 kW
15445 **FINLAND**
   †YLE RADIO FINLAND, Pori   S • E Europe & Mideast • 500 kW
   GUAM
   †KTWR-TRANS WORLD RADIO, Merizo   E Asia • 100 kW • ALT. FREQ. TO 15360 kHz
   SEYCHELLES
   †FEBA RADIO, North Pt, Mahé Is   Sa/Su • S Asia • 100 kW
   S Asia • 100 kW
   Tu-Su • S Asia • 100 kW
   M/W/Th • S Asia • 100 kW
   W/F-Su • S Asia • 100 kW

   THAILAND
   †RADIO THAILAND, Udon Thani   S • Europe • 250 kW • ALT. FREQ. TO 21795 kHz
   USA
   RFE-RL, Via Briech, Morocco   S • E Europe • 250 kW
   †RFE-RL, Via Philippines   W • E Asia • 250 kW
   RFE-RL, Via Udon Thani, Thailand   S • C Asia • 250 kW
   VOA, Via Botswana   E Africa • 100 kW
   †VOA, Via Briech, Morocco   S • Africa • 250 kW
   †VOA, Via Iranawila, Sri Lanka   W • E Africa • 500 kW
   W M-F • E Africa • 500 kW
   W Sa/Su • E Africa • 500 kW
   VOA, Via Pals, Spain   W • C Asia • 250 kW
15450 **PHILIPPINES**
   FEBC RADIO INTL, Iba   E Asia • 100 kW
   TUNISIA
   †RTV TUNISIENNE, Sfax   W • N Africa & Mideast • 500 kW
   TURKEY
   †VOICE OF TURKEY, Ankara-Emirler   S • E Europe & W Asia • 500 kW
15455 **GERMANY**
   †DEUTSCHE WELLE, Via Kigali, Rwanda   W • S Africa • 250 kW
   GREECE
   †FONI TIS HELLADAS, Via Delano, USA   N America • 250 kW
   HOLLAND
   †R NEDERLAND, Via Neth Antilles   S America • 250 kW
   HUNGARY
   †RADIO BUDAPEST, Jászberény   S • S America • 250 kW
   S Su • S America • 250 kW
   POLAND
   †RADIO MARYJA, Via Samara, Russia   • M-Sa • Europe • 250 kW • ALT. FREQ. TO 12010 kHz
   • Europe • 250 kW • ALT. FREQ. TO 12010 kHz
   • Su • Europe • 250 kW • ALT. FREQ. TO 12010 kHz
   RUSSIA
   RADIO ROSSII, Moscow   S • Europe & W Africa • DS • 250 kW
   VOICE OF RUSSIA, Yekaterinburg   S • Europe • 240 kW
   USA
   †VOA, Via Holzkirchen, Germany   S • W Asia & Mideast • 250 kW
15460 **FINLAND**
   †YLE RADIO FINLAND, Pori   S M-F • W Europe • 500 kW
   S Sa • W Europe • 500 kW
   S • W Europe • 500 kW
   S Sa/Su • W Europe • 500 kW
   FRANCE
   †R FRANCE INTL, Issoudun-Allouis   S • E Africa • 500 kW
   GERMANY
   †DEUTSCHE WELLE, Wertachtal   S • E Europe & Mideast • 500 kW • ALT. FREQ. TO 15105 kHz
   RUSSIA
   †VOICE OF RUSSIA, Armavir   W • S Asia • 500 kW
   S • S Asia • 240 kW
   †VOICE OF RUSSIA, Khabarovsk   W • Australasia • 250 kW
   SEYCHELLES
   †FEBA RADIO, North Pt, Mahé Is   Th/Sa/Su • S Asia • 100 kW
   F • S Asia • 100 kW
(con'd)

0 1 2 3 4 5 6 7 8 9 10 11 12 13 14 15 16 17 18 19 20 21 22 23 24

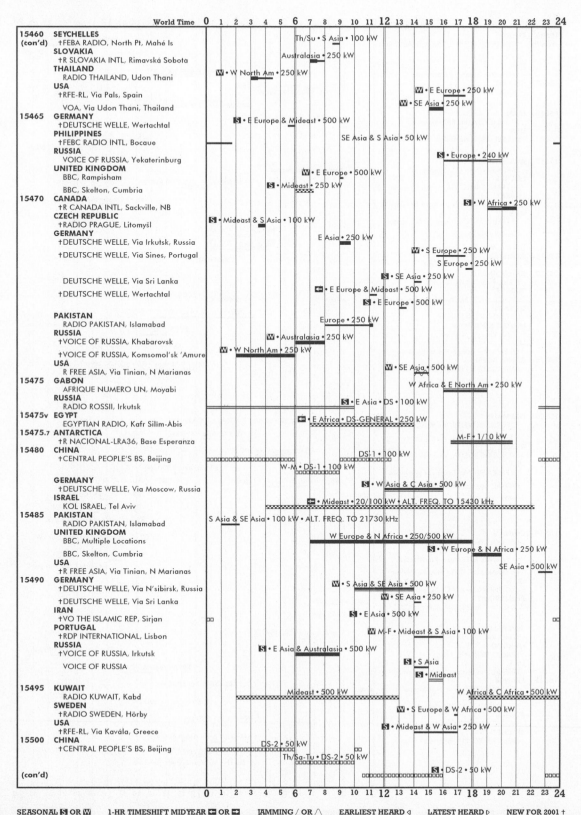

World Time 0 1 2 3 4 5 6 7 8 9 10 11 12 13 14 15 16 17 18 19 20 21 22 23 24

15460 (con'd)	**SEYCHELLES** †FEBA RADIO, North Pt, Mahé Is
	SLOVAKIA †R SLOVAKIA INTL, Rimavská Sobota
	THAILAND RADIO THAILAND, Udon Thani
	USA †RFE-RL, Via Pals, Spain
	VOA, Via Udon Thani, Thailand
15465	**GERMANY** †DEUTSCHE WELLE, Wertachtal
	PHILIPPINES †FEBC RADIO INTL, Bocaue
	RUSSIA VOICE OF RUSSIA, Yekaterinburg
	UNITED KINGDOM BBC, Rampisham
	BBC, Skelton, Cumbria
15470	**CANADA** †R CANADA INTL, Sackville, NB
	CZECH REPUBLIC †RADIO PRAGUE, Litomyšl
	GERMANY †DEUTSCHE WELLE, Via Irkutsk, Russia
	†DEUTSCHE WELLE, Via Sines, Portugal
	DEUTSCHE WELLE, Via Sri Lanka
	†DEUTSCHE WELLE, Wertachtal
	PAKISTAN RADIO PAKISTAN, Islamabad
	RUSSIA †VOICE OF RUSSIA, Khabarovsk
	†VOICE OF RUSSIA, Komsomol'sk 'Amure
	USA R FREE ASIA, Via Tinian, N Marianas
15475	**GABON** AFRIQUE NUMERO UN, Moyabi
	RUSSIA RADIO ROSSII, Irkutsk
15475v	**EGYPT** EGYPTIAN RADIO, Kafr Silim-Abis
15475.7	**ANTARCTICA** †R NACIONAL-LRA36, Base Esperanza
15480	**CHINA** †CENTRAL PEOPLE'S BS, Beijing
	GERMANY †DEUTSCHE WELLE, Via Moscow, Russia
	ISRAEL KOL ISRAEL, Tel Aviv
15485	**PAKISTAN** RADIO PAKISTAN, Islamabad
	UNITED KINGDOM BBC, Multiple Locations
	BBC, Skelton, Cumbria
	USA †R FREE ASIA, Via Tinian, N Marianas
15490	**GERMANY** †DEUTSCHE WELLE, Via N'sibirsk, Russia
	†DEUTSCHE WELLE, Via Sri Lanka
	IRAN †VO THE ISLAMIC REP, Sirjan
	PORTUGAL †RDP INTERNATIONAL, Lisbon
	RUSSIA †VOICE OF RUSSIA, Irkutsk
	VOICE OF RUSSIA
15495	**KUWAIT** RADIO KUWAIT, Kabd
	SWEDEN †RADIO SWEDEN, Hörby
	USA †RFE-RL, Via Kavála, Greece
15500	**CHINA** †CENTRAL PEOPLE'S BS, Beijing
(con'd)	

Th/Su • S Asia • 100 kW
Australasia • 250 kW
W • W North Am • 250 kW
W • E Europe • 250 kW
W • SE Asia • 250 kW
S • E Europe & Mideast • 500 kW
SE Asia & S Asia • 50 kW
S • Europe • 240 kW
W • E Europe • 500 kW
S • Mideast • 250 kW
S • W Africa • 250 kW
S • Mideast & S Asia • 100 kW
E Asia • 250 kW
W • S Europe • 250 kW
S Europe • 250 kW
S • SE Asia • 250 kW
• E Europe & Mideast • 500 kW
S • E Europe • 500 kW
Europe • 250 kW
W • Australasia • 250 kW
W • W North Am • 250 kW
W • SE Asia • 500 kW
W Africa & E North Am • 250 kW
S • E Asia • DS • 100 kW
• E Africa • DS-GENERAL • 250 kW
M-F • 1/10 kW
DS-1 • 100 kW
W-M • DS-1 • 100 kW
S • W Asia & C Asia • 500 kW
• Mideast • 20/100 kW • ALT. FREQ. TO 15430 kHz
S Asia & SE Asia • 100 kW • ALT. FREQ. TO 21730 kHz
W Europe & N Africa • 250/500 kW
S • W Europe & N Africa • 250 kW
SE Asia • 500 kW
W • S Asia & SE Asia • 500 kW
W • SE Asia • 250 kW
S • E Asia • 500 kW
W M-F • Mideast & S Asia • 100 kW
S • E Asia & Australasia • 500 kW
S • S Asia
S • Mideast
Mideast • 500 kW
W Africa & C Africa • 500 kW
W • S Europe & W Africa • 500 kW
S • Mideast & W Asia • 250 kW
DS-2 • 50 kW
Th/Sa-Tu • DS-2 • 50 kW
S • DS-2 • 50 kW

0 1 2 3 4 5 6 7 8 9 10 11 12 13 14 15 16 17 18 19 20 21 22 23 24

SEASONAL S OR W   1-HR TIMESHIFT MIDYEAR ⇦ OR ⇨   JAMMING / OR ∧   EARLIEST HEARD ◁   LATEST HEARD ▷   NEW FOR 2001 †

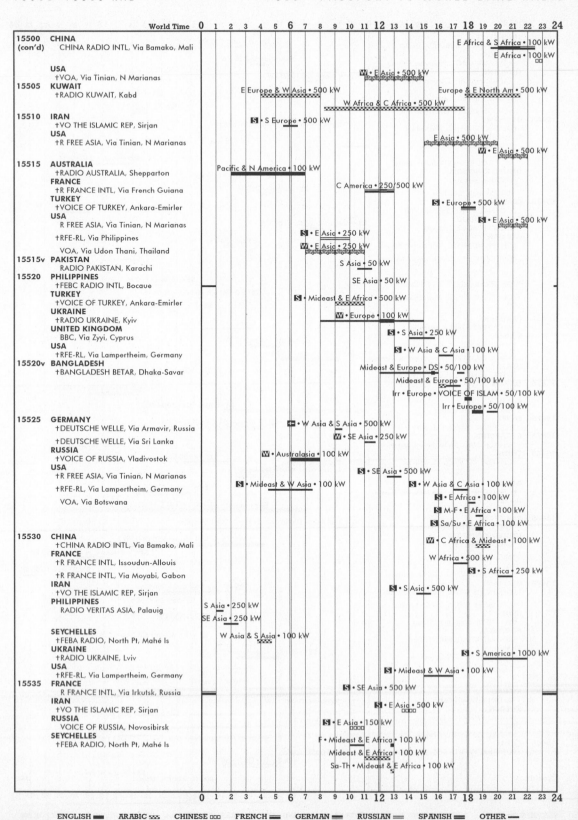

World Time	0 1 2 3 4 5 6 7 8 9 10 11 12 13 14 15 16 17 18 19 20 21 22 23 24
15500 **CHINA**	
(con'd) CHINA RADIO INTL, Via Bamako, Mali	E Africa & S Africa • 100 kW
	E Africa • 100 kW
USA	
†VOA, Via Tinian, N Marianas	W • E Asia • 500 kW
15505 KUWAIT	
†RADIO KUWAIT, Kabd	E Europe & W Asia • 500 kW Europe & E North Am • 500 kW
	W Africa & C Africa • 500 kW
15510 IRAN	
†VO THE ISLAMIC REP, Sirjan	S • S Europe • 500 kW
USA	
†R FREE ASIA, Via Tinian, N Marianas	E Asia • 500 kW
	W • E Asia • 500 kW
15515 AUSTRALIA	
†RADIO AUSTRALIA, Shepparton	Pacific & N America • 100 kW
FRANCE	
†R FRANCE INTL, Via French Guiana	C America • 250/500 kW
TURKEY	
†VOICE OF TURKEY, Ankara-Emirler	S • Europe • 500 kW
USA	
R FREE ASIA, Via Tinian, N Marianas	S • E Asia • 500 kW
†RFE-RL, Via Philippines	S • E Asia • 250 kW
VOA, Via Udon Thani, Thailand	W • E Asia • 250 kW
15515v PAKISTAN	
RADIO PAKISTAN, Karachi	S Asia • 50 kW
15520 PHILIPPINES	
†FEBC RADIO INTL, Bocaue	SE Asia • 50 kW
TURKEY	
†VOICE OF TURKEY, Ankara-Emirler	S • Mideast & E Africa • 500 kW
UKRAINE	
†RADIO UKRAINE, Kyiv	W • Europe • 100 kW
UNITED KINGDOM	
BBC, Via Zyyi, Cyprus	S • S Asia • 250 kW
USA	
†RFE-RL, Via Lampertheim, Germany	S • W Asia & C Asia • 100 kW
15520v BANGLADESH	
†BANGLADESH BETAR, Dhaka-Savar	Mideast & Europe • DS • 50/100 kW
	Mideast & Europe • 50/100 kW
	Irr • Europe • VOICE OF ISLAM • 50/100 kW
	Irr • Europe • 50/100 kW
15525 GERMANY	
†DEUTSCHE WELLE, Via Armavir, Russia	• W Asia & S Asia • 500 kW
†DEUTSCHE WELLE, Via Sri Lanka	W • SE Asia • 250 kW
RUSSIA	
†VOICE OF RUSSIA, Vladivostok	W • Australasia • 100 kW
USA	
†R FREE ASIA, Via Tinian, N Marianas	S • SE Asia • 500 kW
†RFE-RL, Via Lampertheim, Germany	S • Mideast & W Asia • 100 kW S • W Asia & C Asia • 100 kW
VOA, Via Botswana	S • E Africa • 100 kW
	S M-F • E Africa • 100 kW
	S Sa/Su • E Africa • 100 kW
15530 CHINA	
†CHINA RADIO INTL, Via Bamako, Mali	W • C Africa & Mideast • 100 kW
FRANCE	
†R FRANCE INTL, Issoudun-Allouis	W Africa • 500 kW
†R FRANCE INTL, Via Moyabi, Gabon	S • S Africa • 250 kW
IRAN	
†VO THE ISLAMIC REP, Sirjan	S • S Asia • 500 kW
PHILIPPINES	
RADIO VERITAS ASIA, Palauig	S Asia • 250 kW
	SE Asia • 250 kW
SEYCHELLES	
†FEBA RADIO, North Pt, Mahé Is	W Asia & S Asia • 100 kW
UKRAINE	
†RADIO UKRAINE, Lviv	S • S America • 1000 kW
USA	
†RFE-RL, Via Lampertheim, Germany	S • Mideast & W Asia • 100 kW
15535 FRANCE	
R FRANCE INTL, Via Irkutsk, Russia	S • SE Asia • 500 kW
IRAN	
†VO THE ISLAMIC REP, Sirjan	S • E Asia • 500 kW
RUSSIA	
VOICE OF RUSSIA, Novosibirsk	S • E Asia • 150 kW
SEYCHELLES	
†FEBA RADIO, North Pt, Mahé Is	F • Mideast & E Africa • 100 kW
	Mideast & E Africa • 100 kW
	Sa-Th • Mideast & E Africa • 100 kW

0 1 2 3 4 5 6 7 8 9 10 11 12 13 14 15 16 17 18 19 20 21 22 23 24

ENGLISH ▬   ARABIC ⠶⠶⠶   CHINESE ☐☐☐   FRENCH ▭▭   GERMAN ▬   RUSSIAN ═   SPANISH ▬   OTHER ▬

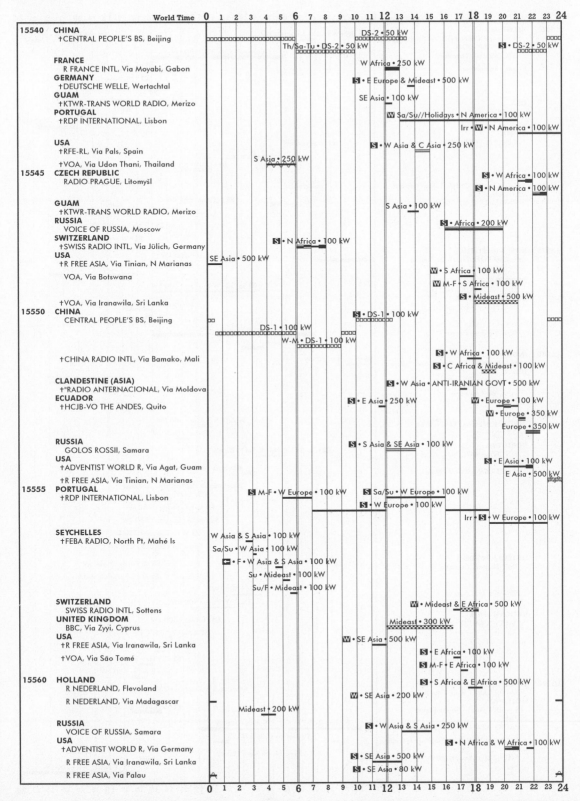

World Time 0 1 2 3 4 5 6 7 8 9 10 11 12 13 14 15 16 17 18 19 20 21 22 23 24

kHz	Country	Station	Schedule
15540	CHINA	†CENTRAL PEOPLE'S BS, Beijing	DS-2 • 50 kW; Th/Sa-Tu • DS-2 • 50 kW; [S] • DS-2 • 50 kW
	FRANCE	R FRANCE INTL, Via Moyabi, Gabon	W Africa • 250 kW
	GERMANY	†DEUTSCHE WELLE, Wertachtal	[S] • E Europe & Mideast • 500 kW
	GUAM	†KTWR-TRANS WORLD RADIO, Merizo	SE Asia • 100 kW
	PORTUGAL	†RDP INTERNATIONAL, Lisbon	[W] Sa/Su//Holidays • N America • 100 kW; Irr • [W] • N America • 100 kW
	USA	†RFE-RL, Via Pals, Spain	[S] • W Asia & C Asia • 250 kW
		†VOA, Via Udon Thani, Thailand	S Asia • 250 kW
15545	CZECH REPUBLIC	RADIO PRAGUE, Litomyšl	[S] • W Africa • 100 kW; [S] • N America • 100 kW
	GUAM	†KTWR-TRANS WORLD RADIO, Merizo	S Asia • 100 kW
	RUSSIA	VOICE OF RUSSIA, Moscow	[S] • Africa • 200 kW
	SWITZERLAND	†SWISS RADIO INTL, Via Jülich, Germany	[S] • N Africa • 100 kW
	USA	†R FREE ASIA, Via Tinian, N Marianas	SE Asia • 500 kW
		VOA, Via Botswana	[W] • S Africa • 100 kW; [W] M-F • S Africa • 100 kW
		†VOA, Via Iranawila, Sri Lanka	[S] • Mideast • 500 kW
15550	CHINA	CENTRAL PEOPLE'S BS, Beijing	[S] • DS-1 • 100 kW; DS-1 • 100 kW; W-M • DS-1 • 100 kW
		†CHINA RADIO INTL, Via Bamako, Mali	[S] • W Africa • 100 kW; [S] • C Africa & Mideast • 100 kW
	CLANDESTINE (ASIA)	†"RADIO ANTERNACIONAL, Via Moldova	[S] • W Asia • ANTI-IRANIAN GOVT • 500 kW
	ECUADOR	†HCJB-VO THE ANDES, Quito	[S] • E Asia • 250 kW; [W] • Europe • 100 kW; [W] • Europe • 350 kW; Europe • 350 kW
	RUSSIA	GOLOS ROSSII, Samara	[S] • S Asia & SE Asia • 100 kW
	USA	†ADVENTIST WORLD R, Via Agat, Guam	[S] • E Asia • 100 kW
		†R FREE ASIA, Via Tinian, N Marianas	E Asia • 500 kW
15555	PORTUGAL	†RDP INTERNATIONAL, Lisbon	[S] M-F • W Europe • 100 kW; [S] Sa/Su • W Europe • 100 kW; [S] • W Europe • 100 kW; Irr • [S] • W Europe • 100 kW
	SEYCHELLES	†FEBA RADIO, North Pt, Mahé Is	W Asia & S Asia • 100 kW; Sa/Su • W Asia • 100 kW; [←] • F • W Asia & S Asia • 100 kW; Su • Mideast • 100 kW; Su/F • Mideast • 100 kW
	SWITZERLAND	SWISS RADIO INTL, Sottens	[W] • Mideast & E Africa • 500 kW
	UNITED KINGDOM	BBC, Via Zyyi, Cyprus	Mideast • 300 kW
	USA	†R FREE ASIA, Via Iranawila, Sri Lanka	[W] • SE Asia • 500 kW
		†VOA, Via São Tomé	[S] • E Africa • 100 kW; [S] M-F • E Africa • 100 kW
15560	HOLLAND	R NEDERLAND, Flevoland	[S] • S Africa & E Africa • 500 kW
		R NEDERLAND, Via Madagascar	[W] • SE Asia • 200 kW; Mideast • 200 kW
	RUSSIA	VOICE OF RUSSIA, Samara	[S] • W Asia & S Asia • 250 kW
	USA	†ADVENTIST WORLD R, Via Germany	[S] • N Africa & W Africa • 100 kW
		R FREE ASIA, Via Iranawila, Sri Lanka	[S] • SE Asia • 500 kW
		R FREE ASIA, Via Palau	[S] • SE Asia • 80 kW

SEASONAL [S] OR [W] 1-HR TIMESHIFT MIDYEAR [←] OR [→] JAMMING / OR /\ EARLIEST HEARD ◁ LATEST HEARD ▷ NEW FOR 2001 †

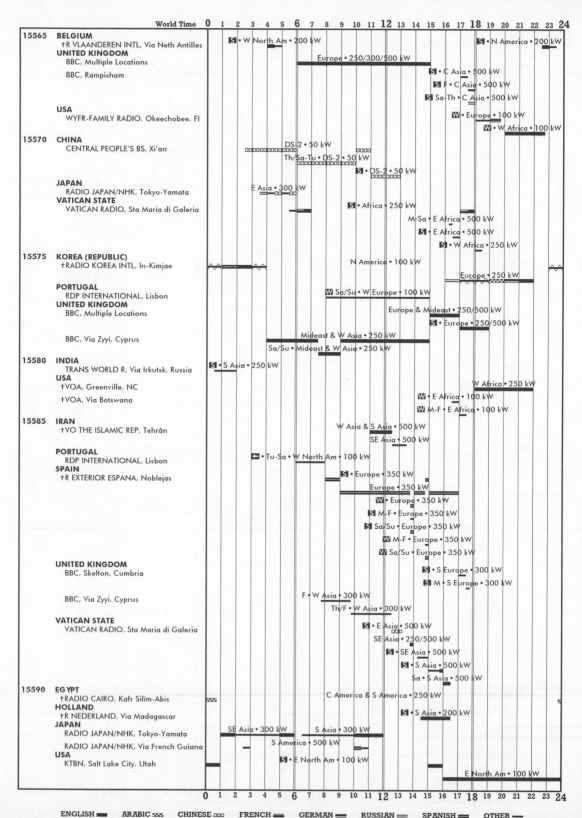

| | | World Time | 0 | 1 | 2 | 3 | 4 | 5 | 6 | 7 | 8 | 9 | 10 | 11 | 12 | 13 | 14 | 15 | 16 | 17 | 18 | 19 | 20 | 21 | 22 | 23 | 24 |

15565 BELGIUM
†R VLAANDEREN INTL, Via Neth Antilles — S • W North Am • 200 kW ; S • N America • 200 kW
UNITED KINGDOM
BBC, Multiple Locations — Europe • 250/300/500 kW
BBC, Rampisham — S • C Asia • 500 kW ; S F • C Asia • 500 kW ; Sa-Th • C Asia • 500 kW
USA
WYFR-FAMILY RADIO, Okeechobee, Fl — W • Europe • 100 kW ; W • W Africa • 100 kW

15570 CHINA
CENTRAL PEOPLE'S BS, Xi'an — DS-2 • 50 kW ; Th/Sa-Tu • DS-2 • 50 kW ; S • DS-2 • 50 kW
JAPAN
RADIO JAPAN/NHK, Tokyo-Yamata — E Asia • 300 kW
VATICAN STATE
VATICAN RADIO, Sta Maria di Galeria — S • Africa • 250 kW ; M-Sa • E Africa • 500 kW ; S • E Africa • 500 kW ; W • W Africa • 250 kW

15575 KOREA (REPUBLIC)
†RADIO KOREA INTL, In-Kimjae — N America • 100 kW ; Europe • 250 kW
PORTUGAL
RDP INTERNATIONAL, Lisbon — W Sa/Su • W Europe • 100 kW
UNITED KINGDOM
BBC, Multiple Locations — Europe & Mideast • 250/500 kW ; S • Europe • 250/500 kW
BBC, Via Zyyi, Cyprus — Mideast & W Asia • 250 kW ; Sa/Su • Mideast & W Asia • 250 kW

15580 INDIA
TRANS WORLD R, Via Irkutsk, Russia — S • S Asia • 250 kW
USA
†VOA, Greenville, NC — W Africa • 250 kW
†VOA, Via Botswana — W • E Africa • 100 kW ; W M-F • E Africa • 100 kW

15585 IRAN
†VO THE ISLAMIC REP, Tehrān — W Asia & S Asia • 500 kW ; SE Asia • 500 kW
PORTUGAL
RDP INTERNATIONAL, Lisbon — Tu-Sa • W North Am • 100 kW
SPAIN
†R EXTERIOR ESPANA, Noblejas — S • Europe • 350 kW ; Europe • 350 kW ; W • Europe • 350 kW ; S M-F • Europe • 350 kW ; S Sa/Su • Europe • 350 kW ; W M-F • Europe • 350 kW ; W Sa/Su • Europe • 350 kW
UNITED KINGDOM
BBC, Skelton, Cumbria — S • S Europe • 300 kW ; S M • S Europe • 300 kW
BBC, Via Zyyi, Cyprus — F • W Asia • 300 kW ; Th/F • W Asia • 300 kW
VATICAN STATE
VATICAN RADIO, Sta Maria di Galeria — S • E Asia • 500 kW ; SE Asia • 250/500 kW ; S • SE Asia • 500 kW ; S • S Asia • 500 kW ; Sa • S Asia • 500 kW

15590 EGYPT
†RADIO CAIRO, Kafr Silim-Abis — C America & S America • 250 kW
HOLLAND
†R NEDERLAND, Via Madagascar — S • S Asia • 200 kW
JAPAN
RADIO JAPAN/NHK, Tokyo-Yamata — SE Asia • 300 kW ; S Asia • 300 kW
RADIO JAPAN/NHK, Via French Guiana — S America • 500 kW
USA
KTBN, Salt Lake City, Utah — S • E North Am • 100 kW ; E North Am • 100 kW

| | | | 0 | 1 | 2 | 3 | 4 | 5 | 6 | 7 | 8 | 9 | 10 | 11 | 12 | 13 | 14 | 15 | 16 | 17 | 18 | 19 | 20 | 21 | 22 | 23 | 24 |

ENGLISH ▬   ARABIC ⌇⌇   CHINESE ▭▭▭   FRENCH ═   GERMAN ▬   RUSSIAN ═   SPANISH ═   OTHER ▬

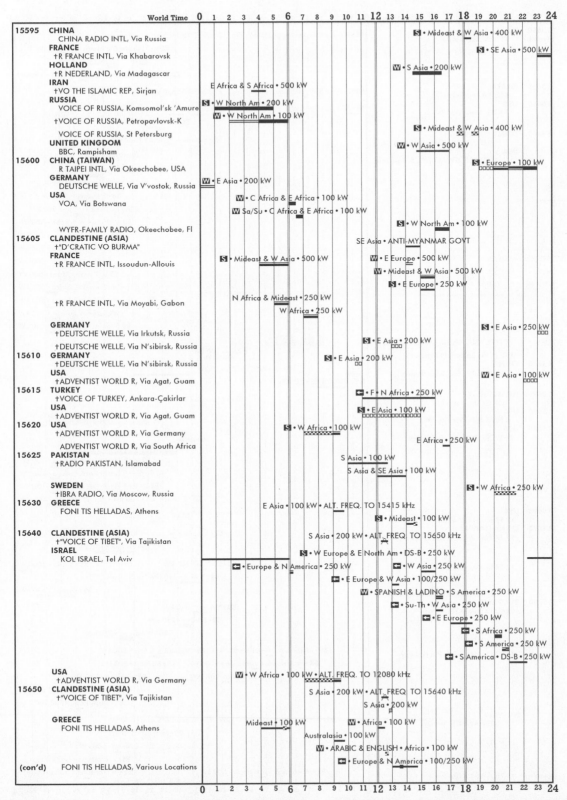

World Time | 0 1 2 3 4 5 6 7 8 9 10 11 12 13 14 15 16 17 18 19 20 21 22 23 24

15595 CHINA
CHINA RADIO INTL, Via Russia — S • Mideast & W Asia • 400 kW
FRANCE
†R FRANCE INTL, Via Khabarovsk — S • SE Asia • 500 kW
HOLLAND
†R NEDERLAND, Via Madagascar — W • S Asia • 200 kW
IRAN
†VO THE ISLAMIC REP, Sirjan — E Africa & S Africa • 500 kW
RUSSIA
VOICE OF RUSSIA, Komsomol'sk 'Amure — S • W North Am • 200 kW

†VOICE OF RUSSIA, Petropavlovsk-K — W • W North Am • 100 kW

VOICE OF RUSSIA, St Petersburg — S • Mideast & W Asia • 400 kW
UNITED KINGDOM
BBC, Rampisham — W • W Asia • 500 kW
15600 CHINA (TAIWAN)
R TAIPEI INTL, Via Okeechobee, USA — S • Europe • 100 kW
GERMANY
DEUTSCHE WELLE, Via V'vostok, Russia — W • E Asia • 200 kW
USA
VOA, Via Botswana — W • C Africa & E Africa • 100 kW

W Sa/Su • C Africa & E Africa • 100 kW

S • W North Am • 100 kW

WYFR-FAMILY RADIO, Okeechobee, Fl
15605 CLANDESTINE (ASIA)
†"D'CRATIC VO BURMA" — SE Asia • ANTI-MYANMAR GOVT
FRANCE
†R FRANCE INTL, Issoudun-Allouis — S • Mideast & W Asia • 500 kW   W • E Europe • 500 kW

W • Mideast & W Asia • 500 kW

S • E Europe • 250 kW

†R FRANCE INTL, Via Moyabi, Gabon — N Africa & Mideast • 250 kW

W Africa • 250 kW

GERMANY
†DEUTSCHE WELLE, Via Irkutsk, Russia — S • E Asia • 250 kW

†DEUTSCHE WELLE, Via N'sibirsk, Russia — S • E Asia • 200 kW
15610 GERMANY
†DEUTSCHE WELLE, Via N'sibirsk, Russia — S • E Asia • 200 kW
USA
†ADVENTIST WORLD R, Via Agat, Guam — W • E Asia • 100 kW
15615 TURKEY
†VOICE OF TURKEY, Ankara-Çakirlar — ⇆ • F • N Africa • 250 kW
USA
†ADVENTIST WORLD R, Via Agat, Guam — S • E Asia • 100 kW
15620 USA
†ADVENTIST WORLD R, Via Germany — S • W Africa • 100 kW

ADVENTIST WORLD R, Via South Africa — E Africa • 250 kW
15625 PAKISTAN
†RADIO PAKISTAN, Islamabad — S Asia • 100 kW

S Asia & SE Asia • 100 kW

SWEDEN
†IBRA RADIO, Via Moscow, Russia — S • W Africa • 250 kW
15630 GREECE
FONI TIS HELLADAS, Athens — E Asia • 100 kW • ALT. FREQ. TO 15415 kHz

S • Mideast • 100 kW

15640 CLANDESTINE (ASIA)
†"VOICE OF TIBET", Via Tajikistan — S Asia • 200 kW • ALT. FREQ. TO 15650 kHz
ISRAEL
KOL ISRAEL, Tel Aviv — S • W Europe & E North Am • DS-B • 250 kW

⇆ • Europe & N America • 250 kW   ⇆ • W Asia • 250 kW

⇆ • E Europe & W Asia • 100/250 kW

W • SPANISH & LADINO • S America • 250 kW

⇆ • Su-Th • W Asia • 250 kW

⇆ • E Europe • 250 kW

⇆ • S Africa • 250 kW

⇆ • S America • 250 kW

⇆ • S America • DS-B • 250 kW

USA
†ADVENTIST WORLD R, Via Germany — W • W Africa • 100 kW • ALT. FREQ. TO 12080 kHz
15650 CLANDESTINE (ASIA)
†"VOICE OF TIBET", Via Tajikistan — S Asia • 200 kW • ALT. FREQ. TO 15640 kHz

S Asia • 200 kW

GREECE
FONI TIS HELLADAS, Athens — Mideast • 100 kW   W • Africa • 100 kW

Australasia • 100 kW

W • ARABIC & ENGLISH • Africa • 100 kW

⇆ • Europe & N America • 100/250 kW

(con'd) FONI TIS HELLADAS, Various Locations

0 1 2 3 4 5 6 7 8 9 10 11 12 13 14 15 16 17 18 19 20 21 22 23 24

SEASONAL S OR W   1-HR TIMESHIFT MIDYEAR ⇆ OR ⇄   JAMMING / OR /\   EARLIEST HEARD ◁   LATEST HEARD ▷   NEW FOR 2001 †

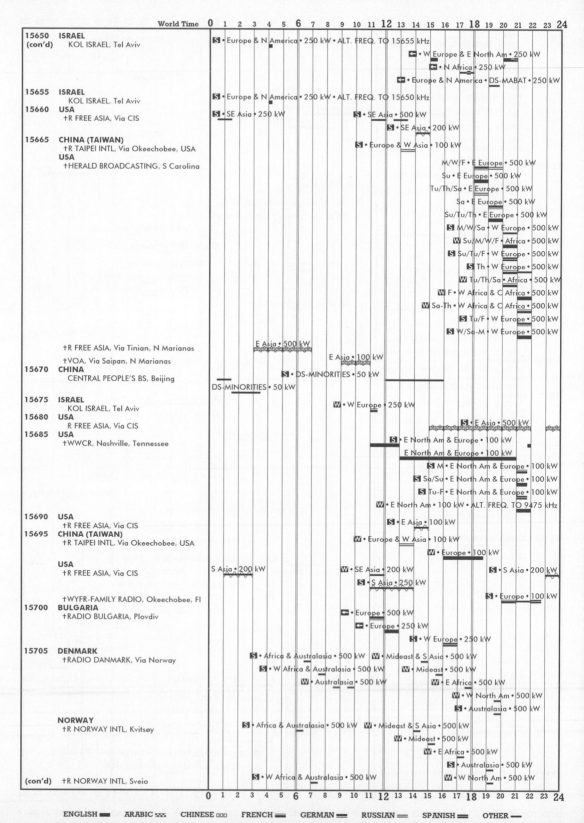

World Time 0 1 2 3 4 5 6 7 8 9 10 11 12 13 14 15 16 17 18 19 20 21 22 23 24

15650 ISRAEL
(con'd)   KOL ISRAEL, Tel Aviv
- S • Europe & N America • 250 kW • ALT. FREQ. TO 15655 kHz
- • W Europe & E North Am • 250 kW
- • N Africa • 250 kW
- • Europe & N America • DS-MABAT • 250 kW

15655 ISRAEL
KOL ISRAEL, Tel Aviv
- S • Europe & N America • 250 kW • ALT. FREQ. TO 15650 kHz

15660 USA
†R FREE ASIA, Via CIS
- S • SE Asia • 250 kW
- S • SE Asia • 500 kW
- S • SE Asia • 200 kW

15665 CHINA (TAIWAN)
†R TAIPEI INTL, Via Okeechobee, USA
- S • Europe & W Asia • 100 kW

USA
†HERALD BROADCASTING, S Carolina
- M/W/F • E Europe • 500 kW
- Su • E Europe • 500 kW
- Tu/Th/Sa • E Europe • 500 kW
- Sa • E Europe • 500 kW
- Su/Tu/Th • E Europe • 500 kW
- S M/W/Sa • W Europe • 500 kW
- W Su/M/W/F • Africa • 500 kW
- S Su/Tu/F • W Europe • 500 kW
- S Th • W Europe • 500 kW
- W Tu/Th/Sa • Africa • 500 kW
- W F • W Africa & C Africa • 500 kW
- W Sa-Th • W Africa & C Africa • 500 kW
- S Tu/F • W Europe • 500 kW
- S W/Sa-M • W Europe • 500 kW

†R FREE ASIA, Via Tinian, N Marianas
- E Asia • 500 kW

†VOA, Via Saipan, N Marianas
- E Asia • 100 kW

15670 CHINA
CENTRAL PEOPLE'S BS, Beijing
- S • DS-MINORITIES • 50 kW
- DS-MINORITIES • 50 kW

15675 ISRAEL
KOL ISRAEL, Tel Aviv
- W • W Europe • 250 kW

15680 USA
R FREE ASIA, Via CIS
- S • E Asia • 500 kW

15685 USA
†WWCR, Nashville, Tennessee
- S • E North Am & Europe • 100 kW
- E North Am & Europe • 100 kW
- S M • E North Am & Europe • 100 kW
- S Sa/Su • E North Am & Europe • 100 kW
- S Tu-F • E North Am & Europe • 100 kW
- W • E North Am • 100 kW • ALT. FREQ. TO 9475 kHz

15690 USA
†R FREE ASIA, Via CIS
- S • E Asia • 100 kW

15695 CHINA (TAIWAN)
†R TAIPEI INTL, Via Okeechobee, USA
- W • Europe & W Asia • 100 kW
- W • Europe • 100 kW

USA
†R FREE ASIA, Via CIS
- S Asia • 200 kW
- W • SE Asia • 200 kW
- S • S Asia • 200 kW
- S • S Asia • 250 kW
- S • Europe • 100 kW

†WYFR-FAMILY RADIO, Okeechobee, Fl

15700 BULGARIA
†RADIO BULGARIA, Plovdiv
- • Europe • 500 kW
- • Europe • 250 kW
- W • W Europe • 250 kW

15705 DENMARK
†RADIO DANMARK, Via Norway
- S • Africa & Australasia • 500 kW
- W • Mideast & S Asia • 500 kW
- S • W Africa & Australasia • 500 kW
- W • Mideast • 500 kW
- W • Australasia • 500 kW
- W • E Africa • 500 kW
- W • W North Am • 500 kW
- S • Australasia • 500 kW

NORWAY
†R NORWAY INTL, Kvitsøy
- S • Africa & Australasia • 500 kW
- W • Mideast & S Asia • 500 kW
- W • Mideast • 500 kW
- W • E Africa • 500 kW
- S • Australasia • 500 kW
- S • W Africa & Australasia • 500 kW
- W • W North Am • 500 kW

(con'd)   †R NORWAY INTL, Sveio

0 1 2 3 4 5 6 7 8 9 10 11 12 13 14 15 16 17 18 19 20 21 22 23 24

ENGLISH ■■   ARABIC ⸰⸰⸰   CHINESE □□□   FRENCH ══   GERMAN ▬▬   RUSSIAN ══   SPANISH ══   OTHER ▬

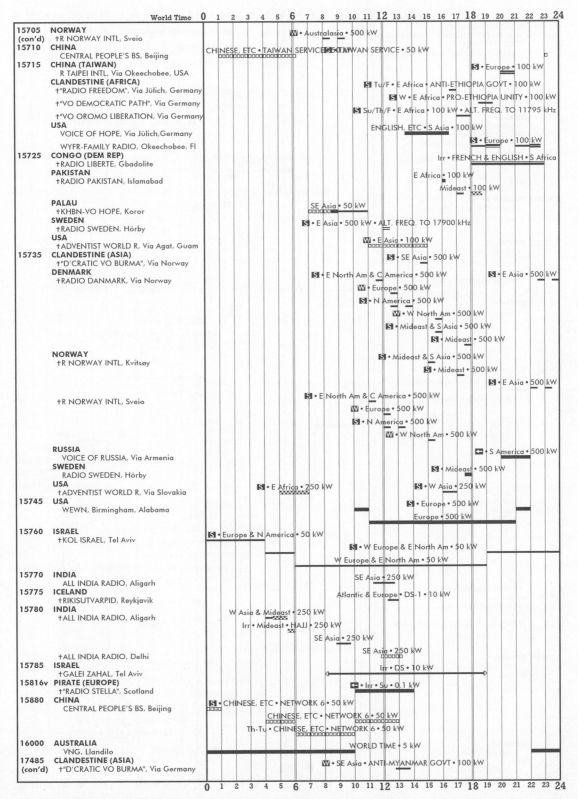

	World Time	0 1 2 3 4 5 6 7 8 9 10 11 12 13 14 15 16 17 18 19 20 21 22 23 24
15705 (con'd)	NORWAY †R NORWAY INTL, Sveio	W • Australasia • 500 kW
15710	CHINA CENTRAL PEOPLE'S BS, Beijing	CHINESE, ETC • TAIWAN SERVICE • 50 kW / TAIWAN SERVICE • 50 kW
15715	CHINA (TAIWAN) R TAIPEI INTL, Via Okeechobee, USA	S • Europe • 100 kW
	CLANDESTINE (AFRICA) †"RADIO FREEDOM", Via Jülich, Germany	S Tu/F • E Africa • ANTI-ETHIOPIA GOVT • 100 kW
	†"VO DEMOCRATIC PATH", Via Germany	S W • E Africa • PRO-ETHIOPIA UNITY • 100 kW
	†"VO OROMO LIBERATION, Via Germany	S Su/Th/F • E Africa • 100 kW • ALT. FREQ. TO 11795 kHz
	USA VOICE OF HOPE, Via Jülich, Germany	ENGLISH, ETC • S Asia • 100 kW
	WYFR-FAMILY RADIO, Okeechobee, Fl	S • Europe • 100 kW
15725	CONGO (DEM REP) †RADIO LIBERTE, Gbadolite	Irr • FRENCH & ENGLISH • S Africa
	PAKISTAN †RADIO PAKISTAN, Islamabad	E Africa • 100 kW
		Mideast • 100 kW
	PALAU †KHBN-VO HOPE, Koror	SE Asia • 50 kW
	SWEDEN †RADIO SWEDEN, Hörby	S • E Asia • 500 kW • ALT. FREQ. TO 17900 kHz
	USA †ADVENTIST WORLD R, Via Agat, Guam	W • E Asia • 100 kW
15735	CLANDESTINE (ASIA) †"D'CRATIC VO BURMA", Via Norway	S • SE Asia • 500 kW
	DENMARK †RADIO DANMARK, Via Norway	S • E North Am & C America • 500 kW S • E Asia • 500 kW
		W • Europe • 500 kW
		S • N America • 500 kW
		W • W North Am • 500 kW
		S • Mideast & S Asia • 500 kW
		S • Mideast • 500 kW
	NORWAY †R NORWAY INTL, Kvitsøy	S • Mideast & S Asia • 500 kW
		S • Mideast • 500 kW
		S • E Asia • 500 kW
	†R NORWAY INTL, Sveio	S • E North Am & C America • 500 kW
		W • Europe • 500 kW
		S • N America • 500 kW
		W • W North Am • 500 kW
	RUSSIA VOICE OF RUSSIA, Via Armenia	⬅ • S America • 500 kW
	SWEDEN RADIO SWEDEN, Hörby	S • Mideast • 500 kW
	USA †ADVENTIST WORLD R, Via Slovakia	S • E Africa • 250 kW S • W Asia • 250 kW
15745	USA WEWN, Birmingham, Alabama	S • Europe • 500 kW
		Europe • 500 kW
15760	ISRAEL †KOL ISRAEL, Tel Aviv	S • Europe & N America • 50 kW
		S • W Europe & E North Am • 50 kW
		W Europe & E North Am • 50 kW
15770	INDIA ALL INDIA RADIO, Aligarh	SE Asia • 250 kW
15775	ICELAND †RIKISUTVARPID, Reykjavik	Atlantic & Europe • DS-1 • 10 kW
15780	INDIA †ALL INDIA RADIO, Aligarh	W Asia & Mideast • 250 kW
		Irr • Mideast • HAJJ • 250 kW
		SE Asia • 250 kW
		SE Asia • 250 kW
	†ALL INDIA RADIO, Delhi	
15785	ISRAEL †GALEI ZAHAL, Tel Aviv	Irr • DS • 10 kW
15816v	PIRATE (EUROPE) †"RADIO STELLA", Scotland	⬅ • Irr • Su • 0.1 kW
15880	CHINA CENTRAL PEOPLE'S BS, Beijing	S • CHINESE, ETC • NETWORK 6 • 50 kW
		CHINESE, ETC • NETWORK 6 • 50 kW
		Th-Tu • CHINESE, ETC • NETWORK 6 • 50 kW
16000	AUSTRALIA VNG, Llandilo	WORLD TIME • 5 kW
17485 (con'd)	CLANDESTINE (ASIA) †"D'CRATIC VO BURMA", Via Germany	W • SE Asia • ANTI-MYANMAR GOVT • 100 kW

World Time	0 1 2 3 4 5 6 7 8 9 10 11 12 13 14 15 16 17 18 19 20 21 22 23 24

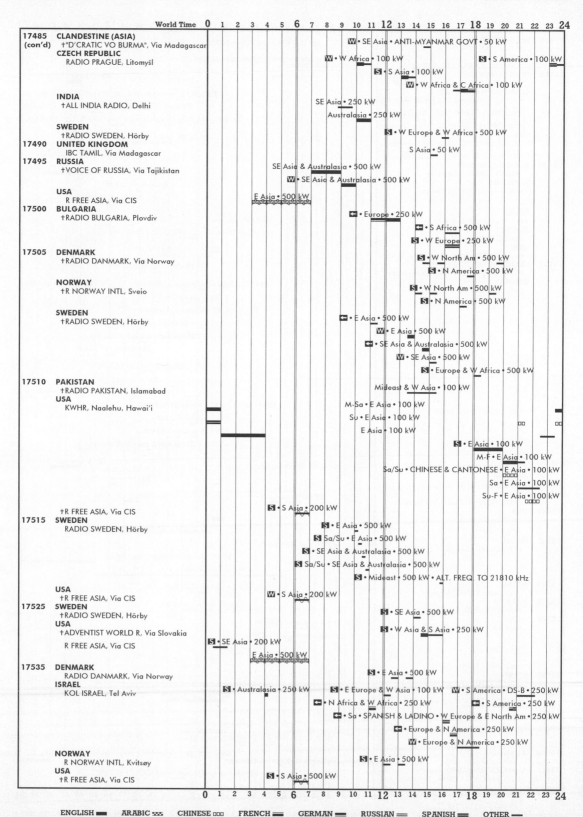

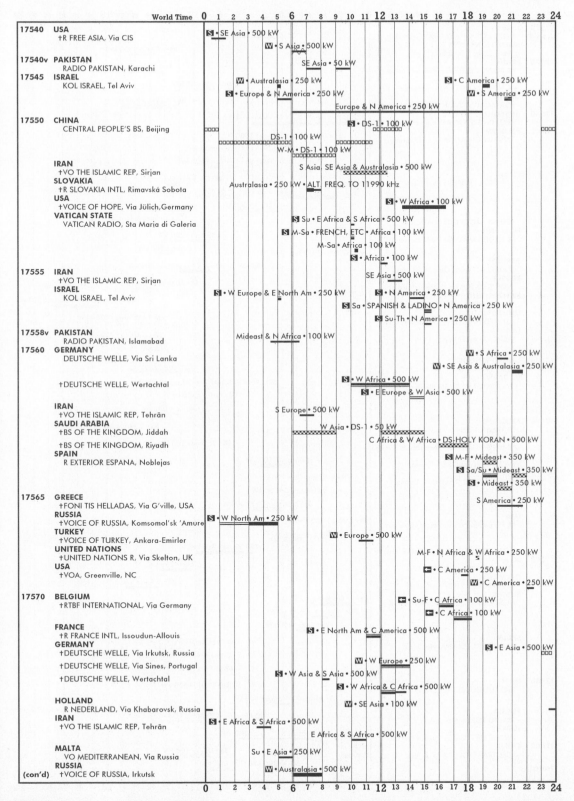

| | World Time | 0 | 1 | 2 | 3 | 4 | 5 | 6 | 7 | 8 | 9 | 10 | 11 | 12 | 13 | 14 | 15 | 16 | 17 | 18 | 19 | 20 | 21 | 22 | 23 | 24 |

17540 USA
†R FREE ASIA, Via CIS
S • SE Asia • 500 kW
W • S Asia • 500 kW

17540v PAKISTAN
RADIO PAKISTAN, Karachi
SE Asia • 50 kW

17545 ISRAEL
KOL ISRAEL, Tel Aviv
W • Australasia • 250 kW
S • C America • 250 kW
S • Europe & N America • 250 kW
W • S America • 250 kW
Europe & N America • 250 kW

17550 CHINA
CENTRAL PEOPLE'S BS, Beijing
S • DS-1 • 100 kW
DS-1 • 100 kW
W-M • DS-1 • 100 kW

IRAN
†VO THE ISLAMIC REP, Sirjan
S Asia, SE Asia & Australasia • 500 kW

SLOVAKIA
†R SLOVAKIA INTL, Rimavská Sobota
Australasia • 250 kW • ALT. FREQ. TO 11990 kHz

USA
†VOICE OF HOPE, Via Jülich, Germany
S • W Africa • 100 kW

VATICAN STATE
VATICAN RADIO, Sta Maria di Galeria
S • Su • E Africa & S Africa • 500 kW
S • M-Sa • FRENCH, ETC • Africa • 100 kW
M-Sa • Africa • 100 kW
S • Africa • 100 kW

17555 IRAN
†VO THE ISLAMIC REP, Sirjan
SE Asia • 500 kW

ISRAEL
KOL ISRAEL, Tel Aviv
S • W Europe & E North Am • 250 kW
S • N America • 250 kW
S • Sa • SPANISH & LADINO • N America • 250 kW
S • Su-Th • N America • 250 kW

17558v PAKISTAN
RADIO PAKISTAN, Islamabad
Mideast & N Africa • 100 kW

17560 GERMANY
DEUTSCHE WELLE, Via Sri Lanka
W • S Africa • 250 kW
W • SE Asia & Australasia • 250 kW
†DEUTSCHE WELLE, Wertachtal
S • W Africa • 500 kW
S • E Europe & W Asia • 500 kW

IRAN
†VO THE ISLAMIC REP, Tehrān
S Europe • 500 kW

SAUDI ARABIA
†BS OF THE KINGDOM, Jiddah
W Asia • DS-1 • 50 kW
†BS OF THE KINGDOM, Riyadh
C Africa & W Africa • DS-HOLY KORAN • 500 kW

SPAIN
R EXTERIOR ESPANA, Noblejas
S • M-F • Mideast • 350 kW
S • Sa/Su • Mideast • 350 kW
S • Mideast • 350 kW

17565 GREECE
†FONI TIS HELLADAS, Via G'ville, USA
S America • 250 kW

RUSSIA
†VOICE OF RUSSIA, Komsomol'sk 'Amure
S • W North Am • 250 kW

TURKEY
†VOICE OF TURKEY, Ankara-Emirler
W • Europe • 500 kW

UNITED NATIONS
†UNITED NATIONS R, Via Skelton, UK
M-F • N Africa & W Africa • 250 kW

USA
†VOA, Greenville, NC
← • C America • 250 kW
W • C America • 250 kW

17570 BELGIUM
†RTBF INTERNATIONAL, Via Germany
← • Su-F • C Africa • 100 kW
← • C Africa • 100 kW

FRANCE
†R FRANCE INTL, Issoudun-Allouis
S • E North Am & C America • 500 kW

GERMANY
†DEUTSCHE WELLE, Via Irkutsk, Russia
S • E Asia • 500 kW
†DEUTSCHE WELLE, Via Sines, Portugal
W • W Europe • 250 kW
†DEUTSCHE WELLE, Wertachtal
S • W Asia & S Asia • 500 kW
S • W Africa & C Africa • 500 kW

HOLLAND
R NEDERLAND, Via Khabarovsk, Russia
W • SE Asia • 100 kW

IRAN
†VO THE ISLAMIC REP, Tehrān
S • E Africa & S Africa • 500 kW
E Africa & S Africa • 500 kW

MALTA
VO MEDITERRANEAN, Via Russia
Su • E Asia • 250 kW

RUSSIA
(con'd) †VOICE OF RUSSIA, Irkutsk
W • Australasia • 500 kW

| | 0 | 1 | 2 | 3 | 4 | 5 | 6 | 7 | 8 | 9 | 10 | 11 | 12 | 13 | 14 | 15 | 16 | 17 | 18 | 19 | 20 | 21 | 22 | 23 | 24 |

SEASONAL S OR W   1-HR TIMESHIFT MIDYEAR ← OR →   JAMMING / OR ∧   EARLIEST HEARD ◁   LATEST HEARD ▷   NEW FOR 2001 †

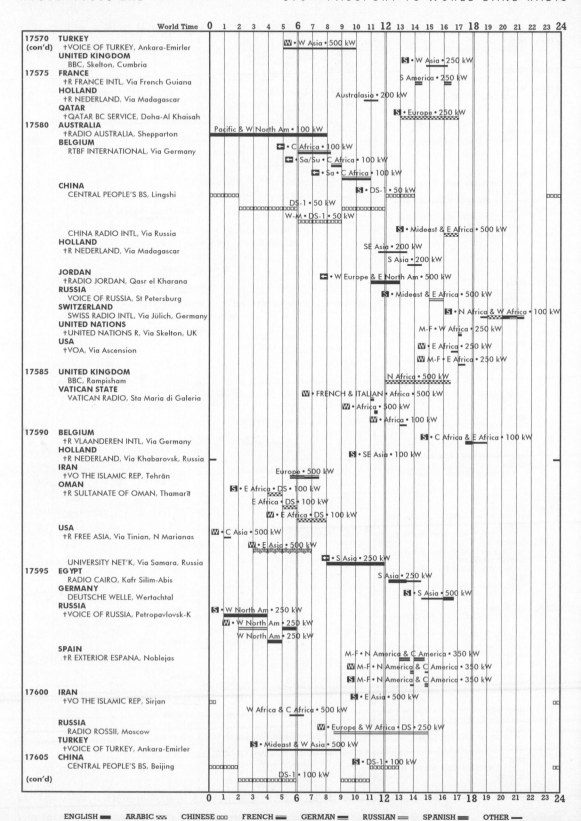

World Time 0 1 2 3 4 5 6 7 8 9 10 11 12 13 14 15 16 17 18 19 20 21 22 23 24

17570 TURKEY
(con'd)   †VOICE OF TURKEY, Ankara-Emirler — W • W Asia • 500 kW
      UNITED KINGDOM
          BBC, Skelton, Cumbria — S • W Asia • 250 kW
17575 FRANCE
          †R FRANCE INTL, Via French Guiana — S America • 250 kW
      HOLLAND
          †R NEDERLAND, Via Madagascar — Australasia • 200 kW
      QATAR
          †QATAR BC SERVICE, Doha-Al Khaisah — S • Europe • 250 kW
17580 AUSTRALIA
          †RADIO AUSTRALIA, Shepparton — Pacific & W North Am • 100 kW
      BELGIUM
          RTBF INTERNATIONAL, Via Germany — C Africa • 100 kW
                                          Sa/Su • C Africa • 100 kW
                                          Sa • C Africa • 100 kW
      CHINA
          CENTRAL PEOPLE'S BS, Lingshi — DS-1 • 50 kW
                                         DS-1 • 50 kW
                                         W-M • DS-1 • 50 kW
          CHINA RADIO INTL, Via Russia — S • Mideast & E Africa • 500 kW
      HOLLAND
          †R NEDERLAND, Via Madagascar — SE Asia • 200 kW
                                         S Asia • 200 kW
      JORDAN
          †RADIO JORDAN, Qasr el Kharana — W Europe & E North Am • 500 kW
      RUSSIA
          VOICE OF RUSSIA, St Petersburg — S • Mideast & E Africa • 500 kW
      SWITZERLAND
          SWISS RADIO INTL, Via Jülich, Germany — S • N Africa & W Africa • 100 kW
      UNITED NATIONS
          †UNITED NATIONS R, Via Skelton, UK — M-F • W Africa • 250 kW
      USA
          †VOA, Via Ascension — W • E Africa • 250 kW
                                W M-F • E Africa • 250 kW
17585 UNITED KINGDOM
          BBC, Rampisham — N Africa • 500 kW
      VATICAN STATE
          VATICAN RADIO, Sta Maria di Galeria — W • FRENCH & ITALIAN • Africa • 500 kW
                                                W • Africa • 500 kW
                                                W • Africa • 100 kW
17590 BELGIUM
          †R VLAANDEREN INTL, Via Germany — S • C Africa & E Africa • 100 kW
      HOLLAND
          †R NEDERLAND, Via Khabarovsk, Russia — S • SE Asia • 100 kW
      IRAN
          †VO THE ISLAMIC REP, Tehrān — Europe • 500 kW
      OMAN
          †R SULTANATE OF OMAN, Thamarīt — S • E Africa • DS • 100 kW
                                            E Africa • DS • 100 kW
                                            W • E Africa • DS • 100 kW
      USA
          †R FREE ASIA, Via Tinian, N Marianas — W • C Asia • 500 kW
                                                 W • E Asia • 500 kW
          UNIVERSITY NET'K, Via Samara, Russia — S Asia • 250 kW
17595 EGYPT
          RADIO CAIRO, Kafr Silīm-Abis — S Asia • 250 kW
      GERMANY
          DEUTSCHE WELLE, Wertachtal — S • S Asia • 500 kW
      RUSSIA
          †VOICE OF RUSSIA, Petropavlovsk-K — S • W North Am • 250 kW
                                              W • W North Am • 250 kW
                                              W North Am • 250 kW
      SPAIN
          †R EXTERIOR ESPANA, Noblejas — M-F • N America & C America • 350 kW
                                         W M-F • N America & C America • 350 kW
                                         S M-F • N America & C America • 350 kW
17600 IRAN
          †VO THE ISLAMIC REP, Sirjan — S • E Asia • 500 kW
                                        W Africa & C Africa • 500 kW
      RUSSIA
          RADIO ROSSII, Moscow — W • Europe & W Africa • DS • 250 kW
      TURKEY
          †VOICE OF TURKEY, Ankara-Emirler — S • Mideast & W Asia • 500 kW
17605 CHINA
          CENTRAL PEOPLE'S BS, Beijing — S • DS-1 • 100 kW
                                         DS-1 • 100 kW
(con'd)

0 1 2 3 4 5 6 7 8 9 10 11 12 13 14 15 16 17 18 19 20 21 22 23 24

ENGLISH ▬ ARABIC ⧉ CHINESE □□□ FRENCH ═ GERMAN ▬ RUSSIAN ═ SPANISH ═ OTHER ▬

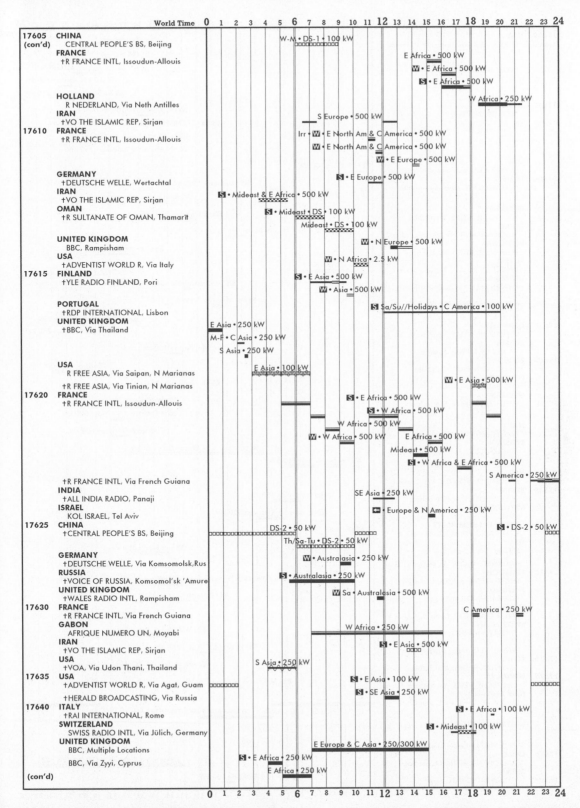

World Time

17605	**CHINA**
(con'd)	CENTRAL PEOPLE'S BS, Beijing — W-M • DS-1 • 100 kW
	FRANCE
	†R FRANCE INTL, Issoudun-Allouis — E Africa • 500 kW
	W • E Africa • 500 kW
	S • E Africa • 500 kW
	HOLLAND
	R NEDERLAND, Via Neth Antilles — W Africa • 250 kW
	IRAN
	†VO THE ISLAMIC REP, Sirjan — S Europe • 500 kW
17610	**FRANCE**
	†R FRANCE INTL, Issoudun-Allouis — Irr • W • E North Am & C America • 500 kW
	W • E North Am & C America • 500 kW
	W • E Europe • 500 kW
	GERMANY
	†DEUTSCHE WELLE, Wertachtal — S • E Europe • 500 kW
	IRAN
	†VO THE ISLAMIC REP, Sirjan — S • Mideast & E Africa • 500 kW
	OMAN
	†R SULTANATE OF OMAN, Thamarit — S • Mideast • DS • 100 kW
	Mideast • DS • 100 kW
	UNITED KINGDOM
	BBC, Rampisham — W • N Europe • 500 kW
	USA
	†ADVENTIST WORLD R, Via Italy — W • N Africa • 2.5 kW
17615	**FINLAND**
	†YLE RADIO FINLAND, Pori — S • E Asia • 500 kW
	W • Asia • 500 kW
	PORTUGAL
	†RDP INTERNATIONAL, Lisbon — S • Sa/Su//Holidays • C America • 100 kW
	UNITED KINGDOM
	†BBC, Via Thailand — E Asia • 250 kW
	M-F • C Asia • 250 kW
	S Asia • 250 kW
	USA
	R FREE ASIA, Via Saipan, N Marianas — E Asia • 100 kW
	†R FREE ASIA, Via Tinian, N Marianas — W • E Asia • 500 kW
17620	**FRANCE**
	†R FRANCE INTL, Issoudun-Allouis — S • E Africa • 500 kW
	S • W Africa • 500 kW
	W Africa • 500 kW
	W • W Africa • 500 kW
	E Africa • 500 kW
	Mideast • 500 kW
	S • W Africa & E Africa • 500 kW
	†R FRANCE INTL, Via French Guiana — S America • 250 kW
	INDIA
	†ALL INDIA RADIO, Panaji — SE Asia • 250 kW
	ISRAEL
	KOL ISRAEL, Tel Aviv — Europe & N America • 250 kW
17625	**CHINA**
	†CENTRAL PEOPLE'S BS, Beijing — DS-2 • 50 kW
	S • DS-2 • 50 kW
	Th/Sa-Tu • DS-2 • 50 kW
	GERMANY
	†DEUTSCHE WELLE, Via Komsomolsk,Rus — W • Australasia • 250 kW
	RUSSIA
	†VOICE OF RUSSIA, Komsomol'sk 'Amure — S • Australasia • 250 kW
	UNITED KINGDOM
	†WALES RADIO INTL, Rampisham — W Sa • Australasia • 500 kW
17630	**FRANCE**
	†R FRANCE INTL, Via French Guiana — C America • 250 kW
	GABON
	AFRIQUE NUMERO UN, Moyabi — W Africa • 250 kW
	IRAN
	†VO THE ISLAMIC REP, Sirjan — S • E Asia • 500 kW
	USA
	†VOA, Via Udon Thani, Thailand — S Asia • 250 kW
17635	**USA**
	†ADVENTIST WORLD R, Via Agat, Guam — S • E Asia • 100 kW
	S • SE Asia • 250 kW
	†HERALD BROADCASTING, Via Russia
17640	**ITALY**
	†RAI INTERNATIONAL, Rome — S • E Africa • 100 kW
	SWITZERLAND
	SWISS RADIO INTL, Via Jülich, Germany — S • Mideast • 100 kW
	UNITED KINGDOM
	BBC, Multiple Locations — E Europe & C Asia • 250/300 kW
	BBC, Via Zyyi, Cyprus — S • E Africa • 250 kW
	E Africa • 250 kW
(con'd)	

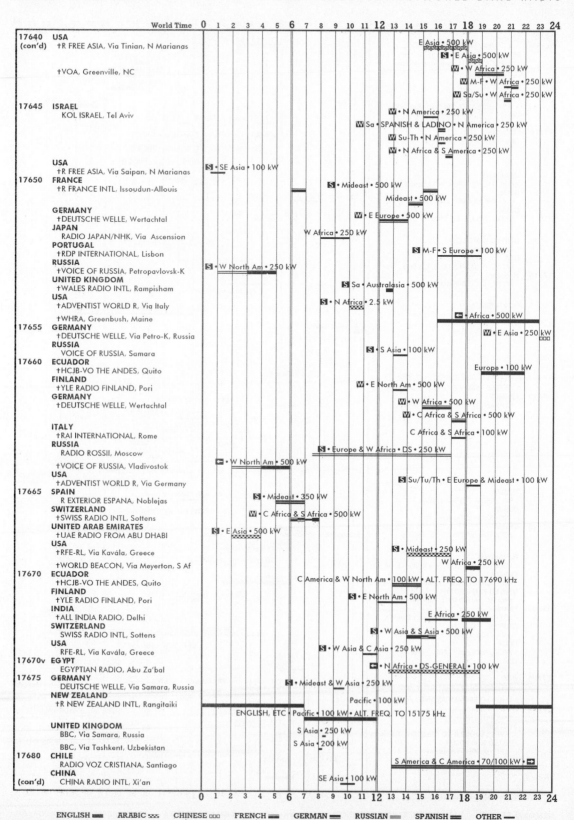

World Time 0 1 2 3 4 5 6 7 8 9 10 11 12 13 14 15 16 17 18 19 20 21 22 23 24

17640 USA
(con'd) †R FREE ASIA, Via Tinian, N Marianas — E Asia • 500 kW — S • E Asia • 500 kW
    †VOA, Greenville, NC — W • W Africa • 250 kW — W • M-F • W Africa • 250 kW — W • Sa/Su • W Africa • 250 kW

17645 ISRAEL
    KOL ISRAEL, Tel Aviv — W • N America • 250 kW — W Sa • SPANISH & LADINO • N America • 250 kW — W • Su-Th • N America • 250 kW — W • N Africa & S America • 250 kW

USA
    †R FREE ASIA, Via Saipan, N Marianas — S • SE Asia • 100 kW
17650 FRANCE
    †R FRANCE INTL, Issoudun-Allouis — S • Mideast • 500 kW — Mideast • 500 kW

GERMANY
    †DEUTSCHE WELLE, Wertachtal — W • E Europe • 500 kW
JAPAN
    RADIO JAPAN/NHK, Via Ascension — W Africa • 250 kW
PORTUGAL
    †RDP INTERNATIONAL, Lisbon — S • M-F • S Europe • 100 kW
RUSSIA
    †VOICE OF RUSSIA, Petropavlovsk-K — S • W North Am • 250 kW
UNITED KINGDOM
    †WALES RADIO INTL, Rampisham — S Sa • Australasia • 500 kW
USA
    †ADVENTIST WORLD R, Via Italy — S • N Africa • 2.5 kW
    †WHRA, Greenbush, Maine — Africa • 500 kW
17655 GERMANY
    †DEUTSCHE WELLE, Via Petro-K, Russia — W • E Asia • 250 kW
RUSSIA
    VOICE OF RUSSIA, Samara — S • S Asia • 100 kW
17660 ECUADOR
    †HCJB-VO THE ANDES, Quito — Europe • 100 kW
FINLAND
    †YLE RADIO FINLAND, Pori — W • E North Am • 500 kW
GERMANY
    †DEUTSCHE WELLE, Wertachtal — W • W Africa • 500 kW — W • C Africa & S Africa • 500 kW

ITALY
    †RAI INTERNATIONAL, Rome — C Africa & S Africa • 100 kW
RUSSIA
    RADIO ROSSII, Moscow — S • Europe & W Africa • DS • 250 kW
    †VOICE OF RUSSIA, Vladivostok — W North Am • 500 kW
USA
    †ADVENTIST WORLD R, Via Germany — S • Su/Tu/Th • E Europe & Mideast • 100 kW
17665 SPAIN
    R EXTERIOR ESPANA, Noblejas — S • Mideast • 350 kW
SWITZERLAND
    †SWISS RADIO INTL, Sottens — W • C Africa & S Africa • 500 kW
UNITED ARAB EMIRATES
    †UAE RADIO FROM ABU DHABI — S • E Asia • 500 kW
USA
    †RFE-RL, Via Kavála, Greece — S • Mideast • 250 kW
    †WORLD BEACON, Via Meyerton, S Af — W Africa • 250 kW
17670 ECUADOR
    †HCJB-VO THE ANDES, Quito — C America & W North Am • 100 kW • ALT. FREQ. TO 17690 kHz
FINLAND
    †YLE RADIO FINLAND, Pori — S • E North Am • 500 kW
INDIA
    †ALL INDIA RADIO, Delhi — E Africa • 250 kW
SWITZERLAND
    SWISS RADIO INTL, Sottens — S • W Asia & S Asia • 500 kW
USA
    RFE-RL, Via Kavála, Greece — S • W Asia & C Asia • 250 kW
17670v EGYPT
    EGYPTIAN RADIO, Abu Za'bal — N Africa • DS-GENERAL • 100 kW
17675 GERMANY
    DEUTSCHE WELLE, Via Samara, Russia — S • Mideast & W Asia • 250 kW
NEW ZEALAND
    †R NEW ZEALAND INTL, Rangitaiki — Pacific • 100 kW — ENGLISH, ETC • Pacific • 100 kW • ALT. FREQ. TO 15175 kHz

UNITED KINGDOM
    BBC, Via Samara, Russia — S Asia • 250 kW
    BBC, Via Tashkent, Uzbekistan — S Asia • 200 kW
17680 CHILE
    RADIO VOZ CRISTIANA, Santiago — S America & C America • 70/100 kW
CHINA
(con'd) CHINA RADIO INTL, Xi'an — SE Asia • 100 kW

0 1 2 3 4 5 6 7 8 9 10 11 12 13 14 15 16 17 18 19 20 21 22 23 24

ENGLISH ▬   ARABIC ⋙   CHINESE ⬚⬚⬚   FRENCH ▬   GERMAN ▬   RUSSIAN ═   SPANISH ▬   OTHER ─

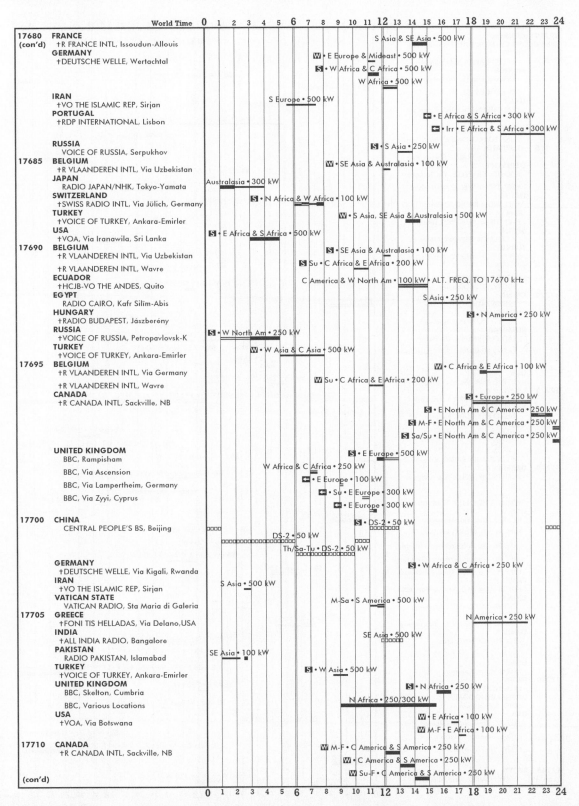

World Time   0 1 2 3 4 5 6 7 8 9 10 11 12 13 14 15 16 17 18 19 20 21 22 23 24

Freq	Country / Station	Details
17680 (con'd)	**FRANCE** †R FRANCE INTL, Issoudun-Allouis	S Asia & SE Asia • 500 kW
	GERMANY †DEUTSCHE WELLE, Wertachtal	W • E Europe & Mideast • 500 kW
		S • W Africa & C Africa • 500 kW
		W Africa • 500 kW
	IRAN †VO THE ISLAMIC REP, Sirjan	S Europe • 500 kW
	PORTUGAL †RDP INTERNATIONAL, Lisbon	• E Africa & S Africa • 300 kW
		• Irr • E Africa & S Africa • 300 kW
	RUSSIA VOICE OF RUSSIA, Serpukhov	S • S Asia • 250 kW
17685	**BELGIUM** †R VLAANDEREN INTL, Via Uzbekistan	W • SE Asia & Australasia • 100 kW
	JAPAN RADIO JAPAN/NHK, Tokyo-Yamata	Australasia • 300 kW
	SWITZERLAND †SWISS RADIO INTL, Via Jülich, Germany	S • N Africa & W Africa • 100 kW
	TURKEY †VOICE OF TURKEY, Ankara-Emirler	W • S Asia, SE Asia & Australasia • 500 kW
	USA †VOA, Via Iranawila, Sri Lanka	S • E Africa & S Africa • 500 kW
17690	**BELGIUM** †R VLAANDEREN INTL, Via Uzbekistan	S • SE Asia & Australasia • 100 kW
	†R VLAANDEREN INTL, Wavre	S Su • C Africa & E Africa • 200 kW
	ECUADOR †HCJB-VO THE ANDES, Quito	C America & W North Am • 100 kW • ALT. FREQ. TO 17670 kHz
	EGYPT RADIO CAIRO, Kafr Silim-Abis	S Asia • 250 kW
	HUNGARY †RADIO BUDAPEST, Jászberény	S • N America • 250 kW
	RUSSIA †VOICE OF RUSSIA, Petropavlovsk-K	S • W North Am • 250 kW
	TURKEY †VOICE OF TURKEY, Ankara-Emirler	W • W Asia & C Asia • 500 kW
17695	**BELGIUM** †R VLAANDEREN INTL, Via Germany	W • C Africa & E Africa • 100 kW
	†R VLAANDEREN INTL, Wavre	W Su • C Africa & E Africa • 200 kW
	CANADA †R CANADA INTL, Sackville, NB	S • Europe • 250 kW
		S • E North Am & C America • 250 kW
		S M-F • E North Am & C America • 250 kW
		S Sa/Su • E North Am & C America • 250 kW
	UNITED KINGDOM BBC, Rampisham	S • E Europe • 500 kW
	BBC, Via Ascension	W Africa & C Africa • 250 kW
	BBC, Via Lampertheim, Germany	• E Europe • 100 kW
	BBC, Via Zyyi, Cyprus	• Su • E Europe • 300 kW
		• E Europe • 300 kW
17700	**CHINA** CENTRAL PEOPLE'S BS, Beijing	S • DS-2 • 50 kW
		DS-2 • 50 kW
		Th/Sa-Tu • DS-2 • 50 kW
	GERMANY †DEUTSCHE WELLE, Via Kigali, Rwanda	S • W Africa & C Africa • 250 kW
	IRAN †VO THE ISLAMIC REP, Sirjan	S Asia • 500 kW
	VATICAN STATE VATICAN RADIO, Sta Maria di Galeria	M-Sa • S America • 500 kW
17705	**GREECE** †FONI TIS HELLADAS, Via Delano, USA	N America • 250 kW
	INDIA †ALL INDIA RADIO, Bangalore	SE Asia • 500 kW
	PAKISTAN RADIO PAKISTAN, Islamabad	SE Asia • 100 kW
	TURKEY †VOICE OF TURKEY, Ankara-Emirler	S • W Asia • 500 kW
	UNITED KINGDOM BBC, Skelton, Cumbria	S • N Africa • 250 kW
	BBC, Various Locations	N Africa • 250/300 kW
	USA †VOA, Via Botswana	W • E Africa • 100 kW
		W M-F • E Africa • 100 kW
17710	**CANADA** †R CANADA INTL, Sackville, NB	W M-F • C America & S America • 250 kW
		W • C America & S America • 250 kW
(con'd)		W Su-F • C America & S America • 250 kW

0 1 2 3 4 5 6 7 8 9 10 11 12 13 14 15 16 17 18 19 20 21 22 23 24

SEASONAL **S** OR **W**   1-HR TIMESHIFT MIDYEAR ⬅ OR ➡   JAMMING / OR /\   EARLIEST HEARD ◁   LATEST HEARD ▷   NEW FOR 2001 †

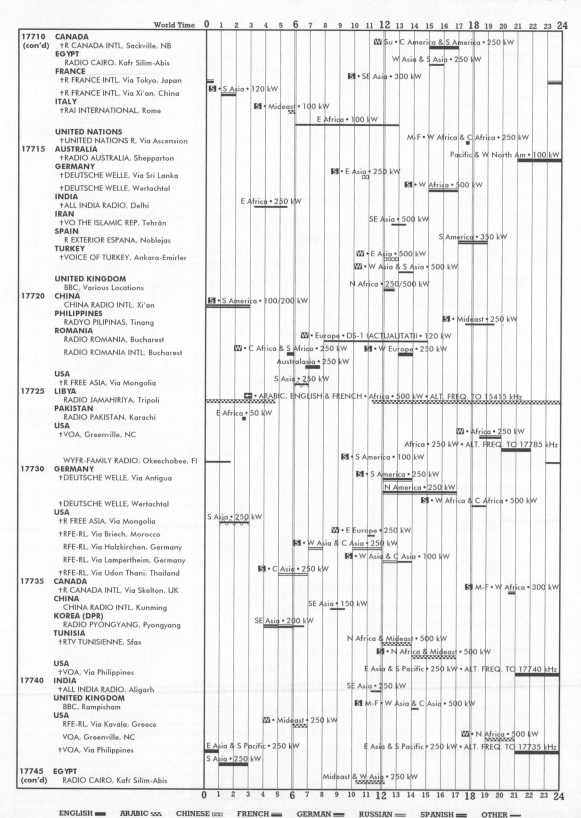

World Time 0 1 2 3 4 5 6 7 8 9 10 11 12 13 14 15 16 17 18 19 20 21 22 23 24

17710 CANADA
(con'd) †R CANADA INTL, Sackville, NB
W • Su • C America & S America • 250 kW
W Asia & S Asia • 250 kW

EGYPT
  RADIO CAIRO, Kafr Silīm-Abis

FRANCE
  †R FRANCE INTL, Via Tokyo, Japan
S • SE Asia • 300 kW

  †R FRANCE INTL, Via Xi'an, China
S • S Asia • 120 kW

ITALY
  †RAI INTERNATIONAL, Rome
S • Mideast • 100 kW
E Africa • 100 kW

  †UNITED NATIONS R, Via Ascension
M-F • W Africa & C Africa • 250 kW

17715 AUSTRALIA
  †RADIO AUSTRALIA, Shepparton
Pacific & W North Am • 100 kW

GERMANY
  †DEUTSCHE WELLE, Via Sri Lanka
S • E Asia • 250 kW

  †DEUTSCHE WELLE, Wertachtal
S • W Africa • 500 kW

INDIA
  †ALL INDIA RADIO, Delhi
E Africa • 250 kW

IRAN
  †VO THE ISLAMIC REP, Tehrān
SE Asia • 500 kW

SPAIN
  R EXTERIOR ESPANA, Noblejas
S America • 350 kW

TURKEY
  †VOICE OF TURKEY, Ankara-Emirler
W • E Asia • 500 kW
W • W Africa & S Asia • 500 kW
N Africa • 250/500 kW

UNITED KINGDOM
  BBC, Various Locations

17720 CHINA
  CHINA RADIO INTL, Xi'an
S • S America • 100/200 kW

PHILIPPINES
  RADYO PILIPINAS, Tinang
S • Mideast • 250 kW

ROMANIA
  RADIO ROMANIA, Bucharest
W • Europe • DS-1 (ACTUALITATI) • 120 kW

  RADIO ROMANIA INTL, Bucharest
W • C Africa & S Africa • 250 kW   W • W Europe • 250 kW
Australasia • 250 kW

USA
  †R FREE ASIA, Via Mongolia
S Asia • 250 kW

17725 LIBYA
  RADIO JAMAHIRIYA, Tripoli
• ARABIC, ENGLISH & FRENCH • Africa • 500 kW • ALT. FREQ. TO 15415 kHz

PAKISTAN
  RADIO PAKISTAN, Karachi
E Africa • 50 kW

USA
  †VOA, Greenville, NC
W • Africa • 250 kW
Africa • 250 kW • ALT. FREQ. TO 17785 kHz

  WYFR-FAMILY RADIO, Okeechobee, Fl
S • S America • 100 kW

17730 GERMANY
  †DEUTSCHE WELLE, Via Antigua
S • S America • 250 kW
N America • 250 kW

  †DEUTSCHE WELLE, Wertachtal
S • W Africa & C Africa • 500 kW

USA
  †R FREE ASIA, Via Mongolia
S Asia • 250 kW

  †RFE-RL, Via Briech, Morocco
W • E Europe • 250 kW

  RFE-RL, Via Holzkirchen, Germany
S • W Asia & C Asia • 250 kW

  RFE-RL, Via Lampertheim, Germany
S • W Asia & C Asia • 100 kW

  †RFE-RL, Via Udon Thani, Thailand
S • C Asia • 250 kW

17735 CANADA
  †R CANADA INTL, Via Skelton, UK
S M-F • W Africa • 300 kW

CHINA
  CHINA RADIO INTL, Kunming
SE Asia • 150 kW

KOREA (DPR)
  RADIO PYONGYANG, Pyongyang
SE Asia • 200 kW

TUNISIA
  †RTV TUNISIENNE, Sfax
N Africa & Mideast • 500 kW
S • N Africa & Mideast • 500 kW

USA
  †VOA, Via Philippines
E Asia & S Pacific • 250 kW • ALT. FREQ. TO 17740 kHz

17740 INDIA
  †ALL INDIA RADIO, Aligarh
SE Asia • 250 kW

UNITED KINGDOM
  BBC, Rampisham
S M-F • W Asia & C Asia • 500 kW

USA
  RFE-RL, Via Kavála, Greece
W • Mideast • 250 kW

  VOA, Greenville, NC
W • N Africa • 500 kW

  †VOA, Via Philippines
E Asia & S Pacific • 250 kW   E Asia & S Pacific • 250 kW • ALT. FREQ. TO 17735 kHz
S Asia • 250 kW

17745 EGYPT
(con'd) RADIO CAIRO, Kafr Silīm-Abis
Mideast & W Asia • 250 kW

0 1 2 3 4 5 6 7 8 9 10 11 12 13 14 15 16 17 18 19 20 21 22 23 24

ENGLISH ▬   ARABIC ░░   CHINESE ▭▭▭   FRENCH ▬   GERMAN ▬   RUSSIAN ═   SPANISH ▬   OTHER ▬

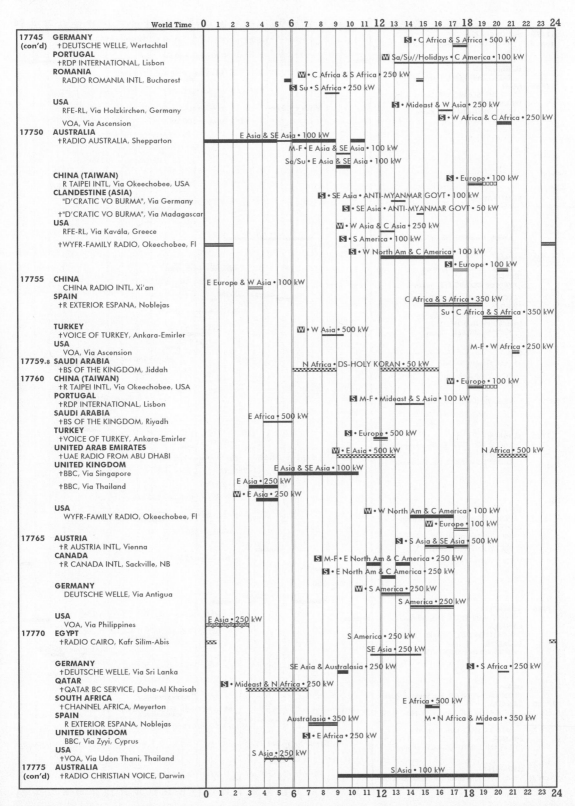

World Time 0 1 2 3 4 5 6 7 8 9 10 11 12 13 14 15 16 17 18 19 20 21 22 23 24

17745
(con'd) **GERMANY**
    †DEUTSCHE WELLE, Wertachtal — 🅂 • C Africa & S Africa • 500 kW
    PORTUGAL
    †RDP INTERNATIONAL, Lisbon — 🅆 • Sa/Su//Holidays • C America • 100 kW
    ROMANIA
    RADIO ROMANIA INTL, Bucharest — 🅆 • C Africa & S Africa • 250 kW
        🅂 • Su • S Africa • 250 kW
    USA
    RFE-RL, Via Holzkirchen, Germany — 🅂 • Mideast & W Asia • 250 kW
    VOA, Via Ascension — 🅂 • W Africa & C Africa • 250 kW
17750 **AUSTRALIA**
    †RADIO AUSTRALIA, Shepparton — E Asia & SE Asia • 100 kW
        M-F • E Asia & SE Asia • 100 kW
        Sa/Su • E Asia & SE Asia • 100 kW
    CHINA (TAIWAN)
    R TAIPEI INTL, Via Okeechobee, USA — 🅂 • Europe • 100 kW
    CLANDESTINE (ASIA)
    "D'CRATIC VO BURMA", Via Germany — 🅂 • SE Asia • ANTI-MYANMAR GOVT • 100 kW
    †"D'CRATIC VO BURMA", Via Madagascar — 🅂 • SE Asia • ANTI-MYANMAR GOVT • 50 kW
    USA
    RFE-RL, Via Kavála, Greece — 🅆 • W Asia & C Asia • 250 kW
    †WYFR-FAMILY RADIO, Okeechobee, Fl — 🅂 • S America • 100 kW
        🅂 • W North Am & C America • 100 kW
        🅂 • Europe • 100 kW
17755 **CHINA**
    CHINA RADIO INTL, Xi'an — E Europe & W Asia • 100 kW
    SPAIN
    †R EXTERIOR ESPANA, Noblejas — C Africa & S Africa • 350 kW
        Su • C Africa & S Africa • 350 kW
    TURKEY
    †VOICE OF TURKEY, Ankara-Emirler — 🅆 • W Asia • 500 kW
    USA
    VOA, Via Ascension — M-F • W Asia • 250 kW
17759.8 **SAUDI ARABIA**
    †BS OF THE KINGDOM, Jiddah — N Africa • DS-HOLY KORAN • 50 kW
17760 **CHINA (TAIWAN)**
    †R TAIPEI INTL, Via Okeechobee, USA — 🅆 • Europe • 100 kW
    PORTUGAL
    †RDP INTERNATIONAL, Lisbon — 🅂 M-F • Mideast & S Asia • 100 kW
    SAUDI ARABIA
    †BS OF THE KINGDOM, Riyadh — E Africa • 500 kW
    TURKEY
    †VOICE OF TURKEY, Ankara-Emirler — 🅂 • Europe • 500 kW
    UNITED ARAB EMIRATES
    †UAE RADIO FROM ABU DHABI — 🅆 • E Asia • 500 kW   N Africa • 500 kW
    UNITED KINGDOM
    †BBC, Via Singapore — E Asia & SE Asia • 100 kW
    †BBC, Via Thailand — E Asia • 250 kW
        🅆 • E Asia • 250 kW
    USA
    WYFR-FAMILY RADIO, Okeechobee, Fl — 🅆 • W North Am & C America • 100 kW
        🅆 • Europe • 100 kW
17765 **AUSTRIA**
    †R AUSTRIA INTL, Vienna — 🅂 • S Asia & SE Asia • 500 kW
    CANADA
    †R CANADA INTL, Sackville, NB — 🅂 M-F • E North Am & C America • 250 kW
        🅂 • E North Am & C America • 250 kW
    GERMANY
    DEUTSCHE WELLE, Via Antigua — 🅆 • S America • 250 kW
        S America • 250 kW
    USA
    VOA, Via Philippines — E Asia • 250 kW
17770 **EGYPT**
    †RADIO CAIRO, Kafr Silim-Abis — S America • 250 kW
        SE Asia • 250 kW
    GERMANY
    †DEUTSCHE WELLE, Via Sri Lanka — SE Asia & Australasia • 250 kW   🅂 • S Africa • 250 kW
    QATAR
    †QATAR BC SERVICE, Doha-Al Khaisah — 🅂 • Mideast & N Africa • 250 kW
    SOUTH AFRICA
    †CHANNEL AFRICA, Meyerton — E Africa • 500 kW
    SPAIN
    R EXTERIOR ESPANA, Noblejas — Australasia • 350 kW   M • N Africa & Mideast • 350 kW
    UNITED KINGDOM
    BBC, Via Zyyi, Cyprus — 🅂 • E Africa • 250 kW
    USA
    †VOA, Via Udon Thani, Thailand — S Asia • 250 kW
17775 **AUSTRALIA**
(con'd) †RADIO CHRISTIAN VOICE, Darwin — S Asia • 100 kW

0 1 2 3 4 5 6 7 8 9 10 11 12 13 14 15 16 17 18 19 20 21 22 23 24

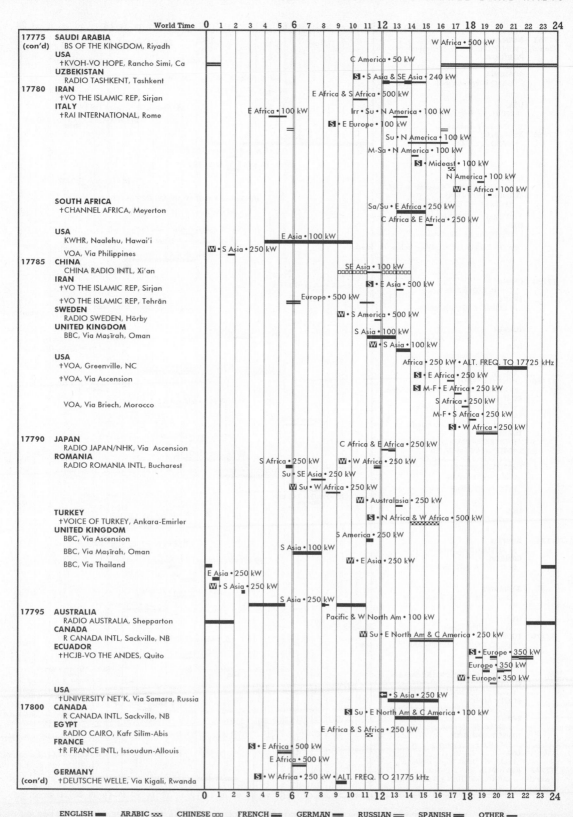

World Time 0 1 2 3 4 5 6 7 8 9 10 11 12 13 14 15 16 17 18 19 20 21 22 23 24

17775 **SAUDI ARABIA**
(con'd)   BS OF THE KINGDOM, Riyadh — W Africa • 500 kW
           USA
           †KVOH-VO HOPE, Rancho Simi, Ca — C America • 50 kW
           UZBEKISTAN
           RADIO TASHKENT, Tashkent — S • S Asia & SE Asia • 240 kW
17780 **IRAN**
           †VO THE ISLAMIC REP, Sirjan — E Africa & S Africa • 500 kW
           ITALY
           †RAI INTERNATIONAL, Rome — E Africa • 100 kW
                                      Irr • Su • N America • 100 kW
                                      S • E Europe • 100 kW
                                      Su • N America • 100 kW
                                      M-Sa • N America • 100 kW
                                      S • Mideast • 100 kW
                                      N America • 100 kW
                                      W • E Africa • 100 kW
           SOUTH AFRICA
           †CHANNEL AFRICA, Meyerton — Sa/Su • E Africa • 250 kW
                                      C Africa & E Africa • 250 kW
           USA
           KWHR, Naalehu, Hawai'i — E Asia • 100 kW
           VOA, Via Philippines — W • S Asia • 250 kW
17785 **CHINA**
           CHINA RADIO INTL, Xi'an — SE Asia • 100 kW
           IRAN
           †VO THE ISLAMIC REP, Sirjan — S • E Asia • 500 kW
           †VO THE ISLAMIC REP, Tehrān — Europe • 500 kW
           SWEDEN
           RADIO SWEDEN, Hörby — W • S America • 500 kW
           UNITED KINGDOM
           BBC, Via Maşīrah, Oman — S Asia • 100 kW
                                    W • S Asia • 100 kW
           USA
           †VOA, Greenville, NC — Africa • 250 kW • ALT. FREQ. TO 17725 kHz
           †VOA, Via Ascension — S • E Africa • 250 kW
                                 S • M-F • E Africa • 250 kW
                                 S Africa • 250 kW
           VOA, Via Briech, Morocco — M-F • S Africa • 250 kW
                                      S • W Africa • 250 kW
17790 **JAPAN**
           RADIO JAPAN/NHK, Via Ascension — C Africa & E Africa • 250 kW
           ROMANIA
           RADIO ROMANIA INTL, Bucharest — S Africa • 250 kW   W • W Africa • 250 kW
                                           Su • SE Asia • 250 kW
                                           W Su • W Africa • 250 kW
                                           W • Australasia • 250 kW
           TURKEY
           †VOICE OF TURKEY, Ankara-Emirler — S • N Africa & W Africa • 500 kW
           UNITED KINGDOM
           BBC, Via Ascension — S America • 250 kW
           BBC, Via Maşīrah, Oman — S Asia • 100 kW
           BBC, Via Thailand — W • E Asia • 250 kW
                               E Asia • 250 kW
                               W • S Asia • 250 kW
                               S Asia • 250 kW
17795 **AUSTRALIA**
           RADIO AUSTRALIA, Shepparton — Pacific & W North Am • 100 kW
           CANADA
           R CANADA INTL, Sackville, NB — W Su • E North Am & C America • 250 kW
           ECUADOR
           †HCJB-VO THE ANDES, Quito — S • Europe • 350 kW
                                       Europe • 350 kW
                                       W • Europe • 350 kW
           USA
           †UNIVERSITY NET'K, Via Samara, Russia — S Asia • 250 kW
17800 **CANADA**
           R CANADA INTL, Sackville, NB — S • Su • E North Am & C America • 100 kW
           EGYPT
           RADIO CAIRO, Kafr Silim-Abis — E Africa & S Africa • 250 kW
           FRANCE
           †R FRANCE INTL, Issoudun-Allouis — S • E Africa • 500 kW
                                              E Africa • 500 kW
           GERMANY
(con'd)   †DEUTSCHE WELLE, Via Kigali, Rwanda — S • W Africa • 250 kW • ALT. FREQ. TO 21775 kHz

0 1 2 3 4 5 6 7 8 9 10 11 12 13 14 15 16 17 18 19 20 21 22 23 24

ENGLISH ▬▬ ARABIC ▨▨ CHINESE ▫▫▫ FRENCH ═══ GERMAN ▭▭ RUSSIAN ══ SPANISH ══ OTHER ▬

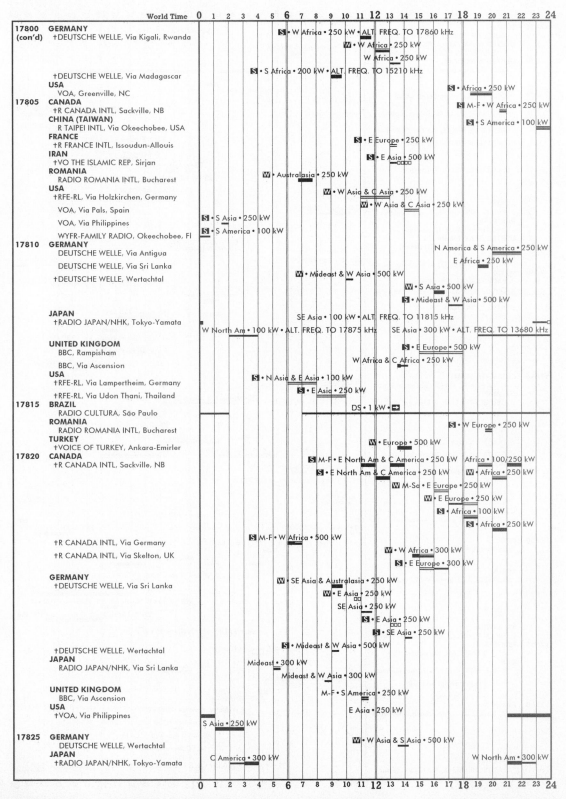

World Time 0 1 2 3 4 5 **6** 7 8 9 10 11 **12** 13 14 15 16 17 **18** 19 20 21 22 23 **24**

17800	**GERMANY**
(con'd)	†DEUTSCHE WELLE, Via Kigali, Rwanda
	†DEUTSCHE WELLE, Via Madagascar
	USA
	VOA, Greenville, NC
17805	**CANADA**
	†R CANADA INTL, Sackville, NB
	CHINA (TAIWAN)
	R TAIPEI INTL, Via Okeechobee, USA
	FRANCE
	†R FRANCE INTL, Issoudun-Allouis
	IRAN
	†VO THE ISLAMIC REP, Sirjan
	ROMANIA
	RADIO ROMANIA INTL, Bucharest
	USA
	†RFE-RL, Via Holzkirchen, Germany
	VOA, Via Pals, Spain
	VOA, Via Philippines
	WYFR-FAMILY RADIO, Okeechobee, Fl
17810	**GERMANY**
	DEUTSCHE WELLE, Via Antigua
	DEUTSCHE WELLE, Via Sri Lanka
	†DEUTSCHE WELLE, Wertachtal
	JAPAN
	†RADIO JAPAN/NHK, Tokyo-Yamata
	UNITED KINGDOM
	BBC, Rampisham
	BBC, Via Ascension
	USA
	†RFE-RL, Via Lampertheim, Germany
	†RFE-RL, Via Udon Thani, Thailand
17815	**BRAZIL**
	RADIO CULTURA, São Paulo
	ROMANIA
	RADIO ROMANIA INTL, Bucharest
	TURKEY
	†VOICE OF TURKEY, Ankara-Emirler
17820	**CANADA**
	†R CANADA INTL, Sackville, NB
	†R CANADA INTL, Via Germany
	†R CANADA INTL, Via Skelton, UK
	GERMANY
	†DEUTSCHE WELLE, Via Sri Lanka
	†DEUTSCHE WELLE, Wertachtal
	JAPAN
	RADIO JAPAN/NHK, Via Sri Lanka
	UNITED KINGDOM
	BBC, Via Ascension
	USA
	†VOA, Via Philippines
17825	**GERMANY**
	DEUTSCHE WELLE, Wertachtal
	JAPAN
	†RADIO JAPAN/NHK, Tokyo-Yamata

Program annotations (read left to right within the grid):

17800 GERMANY — 🆂 • W Africa • 250 kW • ALT. FREQ. TO 17860 kHz; 🆆 • W Africa • 250 kW; W Africa • 250 kW; 🆂 • S Africa • 200 kW • ALT. FREQ. TO 15210 kHz
USA / VOA, Greenville — 🆂 • Africa • 250 kW
17805 CANADA — 🆂 M-F • W Africa • 250 kW
CHINA (TAIWAN) — 🆂 • S America • 100 kW
FRANCE — 🆂 • E Europe • 250 kW
IRAN — 🆂 • E Asia • 500 kW
ROMANIA — 🆆 • Australasia • 250 kW
RFE-RL, Via Holzkirchen — 🆆 • W Asia & C Asia • 250 kW; 🆆 • W Asia & C Asia • 250 kW
VOA, Via Pals — 🆂 • S Asia • 250 kW
VOA, Via Philippines — 🆂 • S America • 100 kW
17810 GERMANY / Via Antigua — N America & S America • 250 kW
Via Sri Lanka — E Africa • 250 kW
Wertachtal — 🆆 • Mideast & W Asia • 500 kW; 🆆 • S Asia • 500 kW; 🆂 • Mideast & W Asia • 500 kW
JAPAN — SE Asia • 100 kW • ALT. FREQ. TO 11815 kHz; W North Am • 100 kW • ALT. FREQ. TO 17875 kHz; SE Asia • 300 kW • ALT. FREQ. TO 13680 kHz
BBC, Rampisham — 🆂 • E Europe • 500 kW
BBC, Via Ascension — W Africa & C Africa • 250 kW
RFE-RL, Via Lampertheim — 🆂 • N Asia & E Asia • 100 kW
RFE-RL, Via Udon Thani — 🆂 • E Asia • 250 kW
17815 BRAZIL — DS • 1 kW • ➡
ROMANIA — 🆂 • W Europe • 250 kW
TURKEY — 🆆 • Europe • 500 kW
17820 CANADA, Sackville — 🆂 M-F • E North Am & C America • 250 kW; Africa • 100/250 kW; 🆂 • E North Am & C America • 250 kW; 🆆 • Africa • 250 kW; 🆆 M-Sa • E Europe • 250 kW; 🆆 • E Europe • 250 kW; 🆂 • Africa • 100 kW; 🆂 • Africa • 250 kW
Via Germany — 🆂 M-F • W Africa • 500 kW
Via Skelton — 🆆 • W Africa • 300 kW; 🆂 • E Europe • 300 kW
GERMANY, Via Sri Lanka — 🆆 • SE Asia & Australasia • 250 kW; 🆆 • E Asia • 250 kW; SE Asia • 250 kW; 🆂 • E Asia • 250 kW; 🆂 • SE Asia • 250 kW
Wertachtal — 🆂 • Mideast & W Asia • 500 kW
JAPAN, Via Sri Lanka — Mideast • 300 kW; Mideast & W Asia • 300 kW
BBC, Via Ascension — M-F • S America • 250 kW
VOA, Via Philippines — E Asia • 250 kW
17825 GERMANY — S Asia • 250 kW; 🆆 • W Asia & S Asia • 500 kW
JAPAN — C America • 300 kW; W North Am • 300 kW

0 1 2 3 4 5 **6** 7 8 9 10 11 **12** 13 14 15 16 17 **18** 19 20 21 22 23 **24**

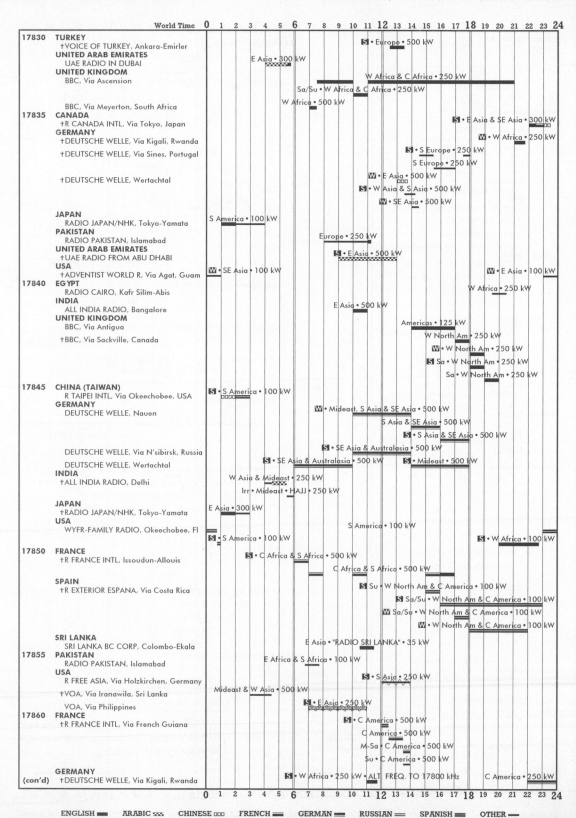

| World Time | 0 | 1 | 2 | 3 | 4 | 5 | 6 | 7 | 8 | 9 | 10 | 11 | 12 | 13 | 14 | 15 | 16 | 17 | 18 | 19 | 20 | 21 | 22 | 23 | 24 |

17830 TURKEY
  †VOICE OF TURKEY, Ankara-Emirler — S • Europe • 500 kW
UNITED ARAB EMIRATES
  UAE RADIO IN DUBAI — E Asia • 300 kW
UNITED KINGDOM
  BBC, Via Ascension — W Africa & C Africa • 250 kW
       — Sa/Su • W Africa & C Africa • 250 kW
  BBC, Via Meyerton, South Africa — W Africa • 500 kW
17835 CANADA
  †R CANADA INTL, Via Tokyo, Japan — S • E Asia & SE Asia • 300 kW
GERMANY
  †DEUTSCHE WELLE, Via Kigali, Rwanda — W • W Africa • 250 kW
  †DEUTSCHE WELLE, Via Sines, Portugal — S • S Europe • 250 kW
       — S Europe • 250 kW
  †DEUTSCHE WELLE, Wertachtal — W • E Asia • 500 kW
       — S • W Asia & S Asia • 500 kW
       — W • SE Asia • 500 kW
JAPAN
  RADIO JAPAN/NHK, Tokyo-Yamata — S America • 100 kW
PAKISTAN
  RADIO PAKISTAN, Islamabad — Europe • 250 kW
UNITED ARAB EMIRATES
  †UAE RADIO FROM ABU DHABI — S • E Asia • 500 kW
USA
  †ADVENTIST WORLD R, Via Agat, Guam — W • SE Asia • 100 kW   W • E Asia • 100 kW
17840 EGYPT
  RADIO CAIRO, Kafr Silim-Abis — W Africa • 250 kW
INDIA
  ALL INDIA RADIO, Bangalore — E Asia • 500 kW
UNITED KINGDOM
  BBC, Via Antigua — Americas • 125 kW
       — W North Am • 250 kW
  †BBC, Via Sackville, Canada — W • W North Am • 250 kW
       — S Sa • W North Am • 250 kW
       — Sa • W North Am • 250 kW
17845 CHINA (TAIWAN)
  R TAIPEI INTL, Via Okeechobee, USA — S • S America • 100 kW
GERMANY
  DEUTSCHE WELLE, Nauen — W • Mideast, S Asia & SE Asia • 500 kW
       — S Asia & SE Asia • 500 kW
       — S • S Asia & SE Asia • 500 kW
  DEUTSCHE WELLE, Via N'sibirsk, Russia — S • SE Asia & Australasia • 500 kW
  DEUTSCHE WELLE, Wertachtal — S • SE Asia & Australasia • 500 kW   S • Mideast • 500 kW
INDIA
  †ALL INDIA RADIO, Delhi — W Asia & Mideast • 250 kW
       — Irr • Mideast • HAJJ • 250 kW
JAPAN
  †RADIO JAPAN/NHK, Tokyo-Yamata — E Asia • 300 kW
USA
  WYFR-FAMILY RADIO, Okeechobee, Fl — S America • 100 kW
       — S • S America • 100 kW   S • W Africa • 100 kW
17850 FRANCE
  †R FRANCE INTL, Issoudun-Allouis — S • C Africa & S Africa • 500 kW
       — C Africa & S Africa • 500 kW
SPAIN
  †R EXTERIOR ESPANA, Via Costa Rica — S Su • W North Am & C America • 100 kW
       — S Sa/Su • W North Am & C America • 100 kW
       — W Sa/Su • W North Am & C America • 100 kW
       — W • W North Am & C America • 100 kW
SRI LANKA
  SRI LANKA BC CORP, Colombo-Ekala — E Asia • "RADIO SRI LANKA" • 35 kW
17855 PAKISTAN
  RADIO PAKISTAN, Islamabad — E Africa & S Africa • 100 kW
USA
  R FREE ASIA, Via Holzkirchen, Germany — S • S Asia • 250 kW
  †VOA, Via Iranawila, Sri Lanka — Mideast & W Asia • 500 kW
  VOA, Via Philippines — S • E Asia • 250 kW
17860 FRANCE
  †R FRANCE INTL, Via French Guiana — S • C America • 500 kW
       — C America • 500 kW
       — M-Sa • C America • 500 kW
       — Su • C America • 500 kW
(con'd) GERMANY
  †DEUTSCHE WELLE, Via Kigali, Rwanda — S • W Africa • 250 kW • ALT FREQ. TO 17800 kHz   C America • 250 kW

| | 0 | 1 | 2 | 3 | 4 | 5 | 6 | 7 | 8 | 9 | 10 | 11 | 12 | 13 | 14 | 15 | 16 | 17 | 18 | 19 | 20 | 21 | 22 | 23 | 24 |

ENGLISH ▬▬   ARABIC ▨▨▨   CHINESE □□□   FRENCH ▭▭▭   GERMAN ▬▬   RUSSIAN ══   SPANISH ▬▬   OTHER ▬▬

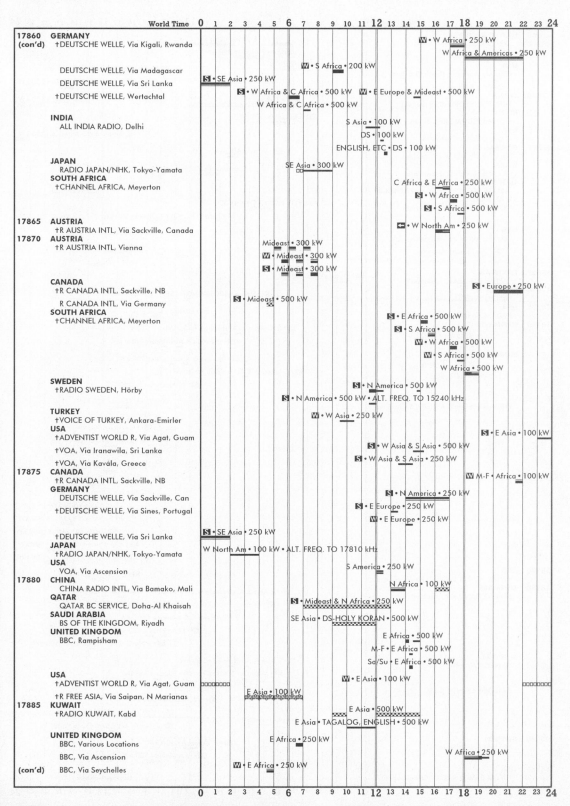

World Time	0 1 2 3 4 5 6 7 8 9 10 11 12 13 14 15 16 17 18 19 20 21 22 23 24
17860 **GERMANY**	
(con'd) †DEUTSCHE WELLE, Via Kigali, Rwanda	W • W Africa • 250 kW
	W Africa & Americas • 250 kW
DEUTSCHE WELLE, Via Madagascar	W • S Africa • 200 kW
DEUTSCHE WELLE, Via Sri Lanka	S • SE Asia • 250 kW
†DEUTSCHE WELLE, Wertachtal	S • W Africa & C Africa • 500 kW W • E Europe & Mideast • 500 kW
	W Africa & C Africa • 500 kW
INDIA	
ALL INDIA RADIO, Delhi	S Asia • 100 kW
	DS • 100 kW
	ENGLISH, ETC • DS • 100 kW
JAPAN	
RADIO JAPAN/NHK, Tokyo-Yamata	SE Asia • 300 kW
SOUTH AFRICA	
†CHANNEL AFRICA, Meyerton	C Africa & E Africa • 250 kW
	S • W Africa • 500 kW
	S • S Africa • 500 kW
17865 AUSTRIA	
†R AUSTRIA INTL, Via Sackville, Canada	⇨ • W North Am • 250 kW
17870 AUSTRIA	
†R AUSTRIA INTL, Vienna	Mideast • 300 kW
	W • Mideast • 300 kW
	S • Mideast • 300 kW
CANADA	
†R CANADA INTL, Sackville, NB	S • Europe • 250 kW
R CANADA INTL, Via Germany	S • Mideast • 500 kW
SOUTH AFRICA	
†CHANNEL AFRICA, Meyerton	S • E Africa • 500 kW
	S • S Africa • 500 kW
	W • W Africa • 500 kW
	W • S Africa • 500 kW
	W Africa • 500 kW
SWEDEN	
†RADIO SWEDEN, Hörby	S • N America • 500 kW
	S • N America • 500 kW • ALT. FREQ. TO 15240 kHz
TURKEY	
†VOICE OF TURKEY, Ankara-Emirler	W • W Asia • 250 kW
USA	
†ADVENTIST WORLD R, Via Agat, Guam	S • E Asia • 100 kW
†VOA, Via Iranawila, Sri Lanka	S • W Asia & S Asia • 500 kW
†VOA, Via Kavála, Greece	S • W Asia & S Asia • 250 kW
17875 CANADA	
†R CANADA INTL, Sackville, NB	W • M-F • Africa • 100 kW
GERMANY	
DEUTSCHE WELLE, Via Sackville, Can	S • N America • 250 kW
†DEUTSCHE WELLE, Via Sines, Portugal	S • E Europe • 250 kW
	W • E Europe • 250 kW
†DEUTSCHE WELLE, Via Sri Lanka	S • SE Asia • 250 kW
JAPAN	
†RADIO JAPAN/NHK, Tokyo-Yamata	W North Am • 100 kW • ALT. FREQ. TO 17810 kHz
USA	
VOA, Via Ascension	S America • 250 kW
17880 CHINA	
CHINA RADIO INTL, Via Bamako, Mali	N Africa • 100 kW
QATAR	
QATAR BC SERVICE, Doha-Al Khaisah	S • Mideast & N Africa • 250 kW
SAUDI ARABIA	
BS OF THE KINGDOM, Riyadh	SE Asia • DS-HOLY KORAN • 500 kW
UNITED KINGDOM	
BBC, Rampisham	E Africa • 500 kW
	M-F • E Africa • 500 kW
	Sa/Su • E Africa • 500 kW
USA	
†ADVENTIST WORLD R, Via Agat, Guam	W • E Asia • 100 kW
†R FREE ASIA, Via Saipan, N Marianas	E Asia • 100 kW
17885 KUWAIT	
†RADIO KUWAIT, Kabd	E Asia • 500 kW
	E Asia • TAGALOG, ENGLISH • 500 kW
UNITED KINGDOM	
BBC, Various Locations	E Africa • 250 kW
BBC, Via Ascension	W Africa • 250 kW
(con'd) BBC, Via Seychelles	W • E Africa • 250 kW

SEASONAL **S** OR **W**   1-HR TIMESHIFT MIDYEAR ⇦ OR ⇨   JAMMING / OR /\   EARLIEST HEARD ◁   LATEST HEARD ▷   NEW FOR 2001 †

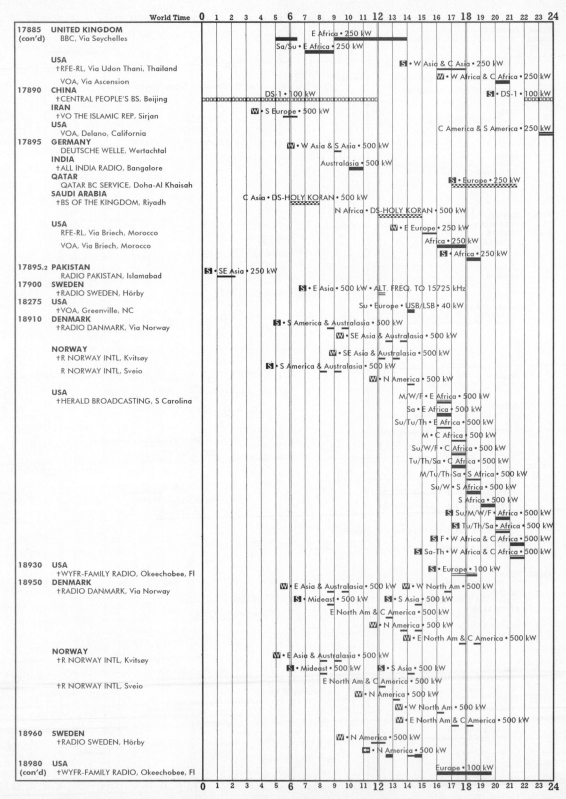

World Time 0 1 2 3 4 5 6 7 8 9 10 11 12 13 14 15 16 17 18 19 20 21 22 23 24

17885 (con'd) **UNITED KINGDOM**
BBC, Via Seychelles — E Africa • 250 kW; Sa/Su • E Africa • 250 kW

USA
†RFE-RL, Via Udon Thani, Thailand — [S] • W Asia & C Asia • 250 kW
VOA, Via Ascension — [W] • W Africa & C Africa • 250 kW

17890 **CHINA**
†CENTRAL PEOPLE'S BS, Beijing — DS-1 • 100 kW; [S] • DS-1 • 100 kW

IRAN
†VO THE ISLAMIC REP, Sirjan — [W] • S Europe • 500 kW

USA
VOA, Delano, California — C America & S America • 250 kW

17895 **GERMANY**
DEUTSCHE WELLE, Wertachtal — [W] • W Asia & S Asia • 500 kW

INDIA
†ALL INDIA RADIO, Bangalore — Australasia • 500 kW

QATAR
QATAR BC SERVICE, Doha-Al Khaisah — [S] • Europe • 250 kW

SAUDI ARABIA
†BS OF THE KINGDOM, Riyadh — C Asia • DS-HOLY KORAN • 500 kW; N Africa • DS-HOLY KORAN • 500 kW

USA
RFE-RL, Via Briech, Morocco — [W] • E Europe • 250 kW
VOA, Via Briech, Morocco — Africa • 250 kW; [S] • Africa • 250 kW

17895.2 **PAKISTAN**
RADIO PAKISTAN, Islamabad — [S] • SE Asia • 250 kW

17900 **SWEDEN**
†RADIO SWEDEN, Hörby — [S] • E Asia • 500 kW • ALT. FREQ. TO 15725 kHz

18275 **USA**
†VOA, Greenville, NC — Su • Europe • USB/LSB • 40 kW

18910 **DENMARK**
†RADIO DANMARK, Via Norway — [S] • S America & Australasia • 500 kW; [W] • SE Asia & Australasia • 500 kW

NORWAY
†R NORWAY INTL, Kvitsøy — [W] • SE Asia & Australasia • 500 kW
R NORWAY INTL, Sveio — [S] • S America & Australasia • 500 kW; [W] • N America • 500 kW

USA
†HERALD BROADCASTING, S Carolina — M/W/F • E Africa • 500 kW; Sa • E Africa • 500 kW; Su/Tu/Th • E Africa • 500 kW; M • C Africa • 500 kW; Su/W/F • C Africa • 500 kW; Tu/Th/Sa • C Africa • 500 kW; M/Tu/Th-Sa • S Africa • 500 kW; Su/W • S Africa • 500 kW; S Africa • 500 kW; [S] Su/M/W/F • Africa • 500 kW; [S] Tu/Th/Sa • Africa • 500 kW; [S] F • W Africa & C Africa • 500 kW; [S] Sa-Th • W Africa & C Africa • 500 kW

18930 **USA**
†WYFR-FAMILY RADIO, Okeechobee, Fl — [S] • Europe • 100 kW

18950 **DENMARK**
†RADIO DANMARK, Via Norway — [W] • E Asia & Australasia • 500 kW; [W] • W North Am • 500 kW; [S] • Mideast • 500 kW; [S] • S Asia • 500 kW; E North Am & C America • 500 kW; [W] • N America • 500 kW; [W] • E North Am & C America • 500 kW

NORWAY
†R NORWAY INTL, Kvitsøy — [W] • E Asia & Australasia • 500 kW; [S] • Mideast • 500 kW; [S] • S Asia • 500 kW
†R NORWAY INTL, Sveio — E North Am & C America • 500 kW; [W] • N America • 500 kW; [W] • W North Am • 500 kW; [W] • E North Am & C America • 500 kW

18960 **SWEDEN**
†RADIO SWEDEN, Hörby — [W] • N America • 500 kW; ← • N America • 500 kW

18980 (con'd) **USA**
†WYFR-FAMILY RADIO, Okeechobee, Fl — Europe • 100 kW

0 1 2 3 4 5 6 7 8 9 10 11 12 13 14 15 16 17 18 19 20 21 22 23 24

ENGLISH ARABIC CHINESE FRENCH GERMAN RUSSIAN SPANISH OTHER

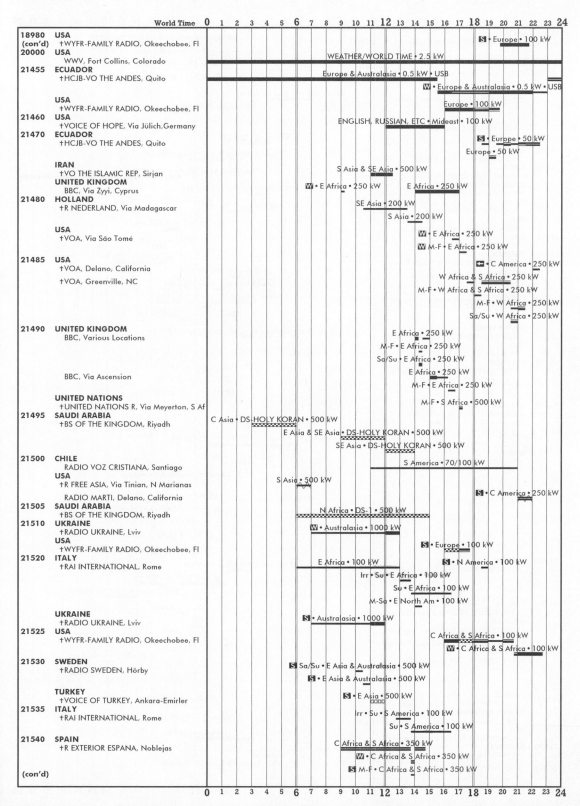

| | World Time | 0 | 1 | 2 | 3 | 4 | 5 | 6 | 7 | 8 | 9 | 10 | 11 | 12 | 13 | 14 | 15 | 16 | 17 | 18 | 19 | 20 | 21 | 22 | 23 | 24 |

18980 (con'd) USA
†WYFR-FAMILY RADIO, Okeechobee, Fl — S • Europe • 100 kW

20000 USA
WWV, Fort Collins, Colorado — WEATHER/WORLD TIME • 2.5 kW

21455 ECUADOR
†HCJB-VO THE ANDES, Quito — Europe & Australasia • 0.5 kW • USB
W • Europe & Australasia • 0.5 kW • USB

USA
†WYFR-FAMILY RADIO, Okeechobee, Fl — Europe • 100 kW

21460 USA
†VOICE OF HOPE, Via Jülich, Germany — ENGLISH, RUSSIAN, ETC • Mideast • 100 kW

21470 ECUADOR
†HCJB-VO THE ANDES, Quito — S • Europe • 50 kW
Europe • 50 kW

IRAN
†VO THE ISLAMIC REP, Sirjan — S Asia & SE Asia • 500 kW

UNITED KINGDOM
BBC, Via Zyyi, Cyprus — W • E Africa • 250 kW
E Africa • 250 kW

21480 HOLLAND
†R NEDERLAND, Via Madagascar — SE Asia • 200 kW
S Asia • 200 kW

USA
†VOA, Via São Tomé — W • E Africa • 250 kW
W M-F • E Africa • 250 kW

21485 USA
†VOA, Delano, California — C America • 250 kW
†VOA, Greenville, NC — W Africa & S Africa • 250 kW
M-F • W Africa & S Africa • 250 kW
M-F • W Africa • 250 kW
Sa/Su • W Africa • 250 kW

21490 UNITED KINGDOM
BBC, Various Locations — E Africa • 250 kW
M-F • E Africa • 250 kW
Sa/Su • E Africa • 250 kW

BBC, Via Ascension — E Africa • 250 kW
M-F • E Africa • 250 kW

UNITED NATIONS
†UNITED NATIONS R, Via Meyerton, S Af — M-F • S Africa • 500 kW

21495 SAUDI ARABIA
†BS OF THE KINGDOM, Riyadh — C Asia • DS-HOLY KORAN • 500 kW
E Asia & SE Asia • DS-HOLY KORAN • 500 kW
SE Asia • DS-HOLY KORAN • 500 kW

21500 CHILE
RADIO VOZ CRISTIANA, Santiago — S America • 70/100 kW

USA
†R FREE ASIA, Via Tinian, N Marianas — S Asia • 500 kW

RADIO MARTI, Delano, California — S • C America • 250 kW

21505 SAUDI ARABIA
†BS OF THE KINGDOM, Riyadh — N Africa • DS-1 • 500 kW

21510 UKRAINE
†RADIO UKRAINE, Lviv — W • Australasia • 1000 kW

USA
†WYFR-FAMILY RADIO, Okeechobee, Fl — S • Europe • 100 kW

21520 ITALY
†RAI INTERNATIONAL, Rome — E Africa • 100 kW
S • N America • 100 kW
Irr • Su • E Africa • 100 kW
Su • E Africa • 100 kW
M-Sa • E North Am • 100 kW

UKRAINE
†RADIO UKRAINE, Lviv — S • Australasia • 1000 kW

21525 USA
†WYFR-FAMILY RADIO, Okeechobee, Fl — C Africa & S Africa • 100 kW
W • C Africa & S Africa • 100 kW

21530 SWEDEN
†RADIO SWEDEN, Hörby — S Sa/Su • E Asia & Australasia • 500 kW
S • E Asia & Australasia • 500 kW

TURKEY
†VOICE OF TURKEY, Ankara-Emirler — S • E Asia • 500 kW

21535 ITALY
†RAI INTERNATIONAL, Rome — Irr • Su • S America • 100 kW
Su • S America • 100 kW

21540 SPAIN
†R EXTERIOR ESPANA, Noblejas — C Africa & S Africa • 350 kW
W • C Africa & S Africa • 350 kW
S M-F • C Africa & S Africa • 350 kW

(con'd)

| | World Time | 0 | 1 | 2 | 3 | 4 | 5 | 6 | 7 | 8 | 9 | 10 | 11 | 12 | 13 | 14 | 15 | 16 | 17 | 18 | 19 | 20 | 21 | 22 | 23 | 24 |

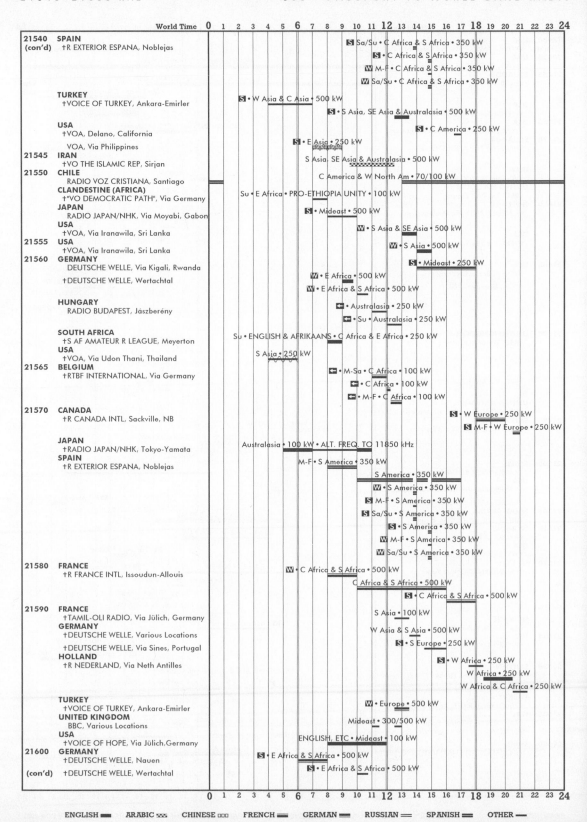

| | World Time | 0 | 1 | 2 | 3 | 4 | 5 | 6 | 7 | 8 | 9 | 10 | 11 | 12 | 13 | 14 | 15 | 16 | 17 | 18 | 19 | 20 | 21 | 22 | 23 | 24 |

21540   SPAIN
(con'd)   †R EXTERIOR ESPANA, Noblejas
    S • Sa/Su • C Africa & S Africa • 350 kW
    S • C Africa & S Africa • 350 kW
    W • M-F • C Africa & S Africa • 350 kW
    W • Sa/Su • C Africa & S Africa • 350 kW

    TURKEY
    †VOICE OF TURKEY, Ankara-Emirler
    S • W Asia & C Asia • 500 kW
    S • S Asia, SE Asia & Australasia • 500 kW

    USA
    †VOA, Delano, California
    S • C America • 250 kW
    VOA, Via Philippines
    S • E Asia • 250 kW

21545   IRAN
    †VO THE ISLAMIC REP, Sirjan
    S Asia, SE Asia & Australasia • 500 kW

21550   CHILE
    RADIO VOZ CRISTIANA, Santiago
    C America & W North Am • 70/100 kW
    CLANDESTINE (AFRICA)
    †"VO DEMOCRATIC PATH", Via Germany
    Su • E Africa • PRO-ETHIOPIA UNITY • 100 kW
    JAPAN
    RADIO JAPAN/NHK, Via Moyabi, Gabon
    S • Mideast • 500 kW
    USA
    †VOA, Via Iranawila, Sri Lanka
    W • S Asia & SE Asia • 500 kW

21555   USA
    †VOA, Via Iranawila, Sri Lanka
    W • S Asia • 500 kW
21560   GERMANY
    DEUTSCHE WELLE, Via Kigali, Rwanda
    S • Mideast • 250 kW
    †DEUTSCHE WELLE, Wertachtal
    W • E Africa • 500 kW
    W • E Africa & S Africa • 500 kW

    HUNGARY
    RADIO BUDAPEST, Jászberény
    • Australasia • 250 kW
    • Su • Australasia • 250 kW

    SOUTH AFRICA
    †S AF AMATEUR R LEAGUE, Meyerton
    Su • ENGLISH & AFRIKAANS • C Africa & E Africa • 250 kW
    USA
    †VOA, Via Udon Thani, Thailand
    S Asia • 250 kW

21565   BELGIUM
    †RTBF INTERNATIONAL, Via Germany
    • M-Sa • C Africa • 100 kW
    • C Africa • 100 kW
    • M-F • C Africa • 100 kW

21570   CANADA
    †R CANADA INTL, Sackville, NB
    S • W Europe • 250 kW
    S • M-F • W Europe • 250 kW

    JAPAN
    †RADIO JAPAN/NHK, Tokyo-Yamata
    Australasia • 100 kW • ALT. FREQ. TO 11850 kHz
    SPAIN
    †R EXTERIOR ESPANA, Noblejas
    M-F • S America • 350 kW
    S America • 350 kW
    W • S America • 350 kW
    S • M-F • S America • 350 kW
    S • Sa/Su • S America • 350 kW
    S • S America • 350 kW
    W • M-F • S America • 350 kW
    W • Sa/Su • S America • 350 kW

21580   FRANCE
    †R FRANCE INTL, Issoudun-Allouis
    W • C Africa & S Africa • 500 kW
    C Africa & S Africa • 500 kW
    S • C Africa & S Africa • 500 kW

21590   FRANCE
    †TAMIL-OLI RADIO, Via Jülich, Germany
    S Asia • 100 kW
    GERMANY
    †DEUTSCHE WELLE, Various Locations
    W Asia & S Asia • 500 kW
    †DEUTSCHE WELLE, Via Sines, Portugal
    S • S Europe • 250 kW
    HOLLAND
    †R NEDERLAND, Via Neth Antilles
    S • W Africa • 250 kW
    W Africa • 250 kW
    W Africa & C Africa • 250 kW

    TURKEY
    †VOICE OF TURKEY, Ankara-Emirler
    W • Europe • 500 kW
    UNITED KINGDOM
    BBC, Various Locations
    Mideast • 300/500 kW
    USA
    †VOICE OF HOPE, Via Jülich, Germany
    ENGLISH, ETC • Mideast • 100 kW
21600   GERMANY
    †DEUTSCHE WELLE, Nauen
    S • E Africa & S Africa • 500 kW
(con'd)   †DEUTSCHE WELLE, Wertachtal
    S • E Africa & S Africa • 500 kW

| | 0 | 1 | 2 | 3 | 4 | 5 | 6 | 7 | 8 | 9 | 10 | 11 | 12 | 13 | 14 | 15 | 16 | 17 | 18 | 19 | 20 | 21 | 22 | 23 | 24 |

ENGLISH ▬   ARABIC ⬚⬚⬚   CHINESE □□□   FRENCH ▬   GERMAN ▬   RUSSIAN ═   SPANISH ▬   OTHER ▬

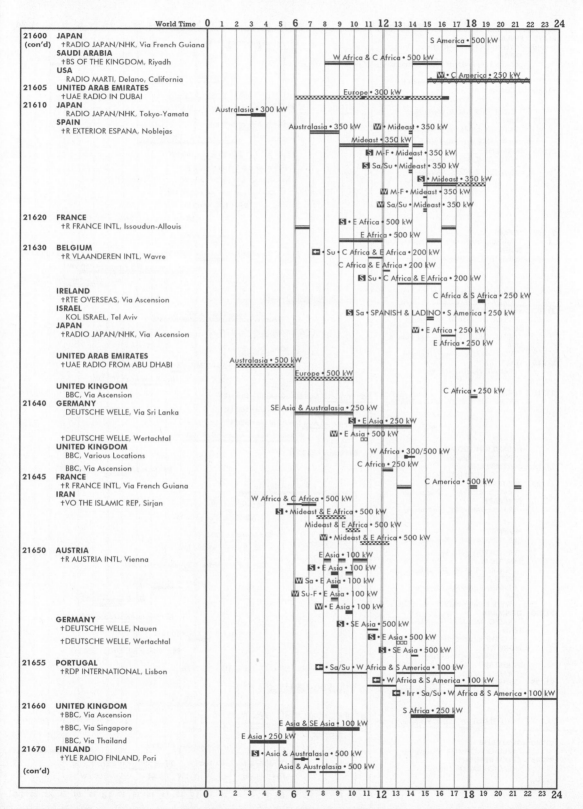

World Time

21600 **JAPAN**
(con'd) †RADIO JAPAN/NHK, Via French Guiana — S America • 500 kW
SAUDI ARABIA
†BS OF THE KINGDOM, Riyadh — W Africa & C Africa • 500 kW
USA
RADIO MARTI, Delano, California — W • C America • 250 kW
21605 **UNITED ARAB EMIRATES**
†UAE RADIO IN DUBAI — Europe • 300 kW
21610 **JAPAN**
RADIO JAPAN/NHK, Tokyo-Yamata — Australasia • 300 kW
SPAIN
†R EXTERIOR ESPANA, Noblejas — Australasia • 350 kW / W • Mideast • 350 kW
Mideast • 350 kW
S M-F • Mideast • 350 kW
Sa/Su • Mideast • 350 kW
S • Mideast • 350 kW
W M-F • Mideast • 350 kW
W Sa/Su • Mideast • 350 kW
21620 **FRANCE**
†R FRANCE INTL, Issoudun-Allouis — S • E Africa • 500 kW
E Africa • 500 kW
21630 **BELGIUM**
†R VLAANDEREN INTL, Wavre — ⇦ • Su • C Africa & E Africa • 200 kW
C Africa & E Africa • 200 kW
S Su • C Africa & E Africa • 200 kW
IRELAND
†RTE OVERSEAS, Via Ascension — C Africa & S Africa • 250 kW
ISRAEL
KOL ISRAEL, Tel Aviv — S Sa • SPANISH & LADINO • S America • 250 kW
JAPAN
†RADIO JAPAN/NHK, Via Ascension — W • E Africa • 250 kW
E Africa • 250 kW
UNITED ARAB EMIRATES
†UAE RADIO FROM ABU DHABI — Australasia • 500 kW
Europe • 500 kW
UNITED KINGDOM
BBC, Via Ascension — C Africa • 250 kW
21640 **GERMANY**
DEUTSCHE WELLE, Via Sri Lanka — SE Asia & Australasia • 250 kW
S • E Asia • 250 kW
†DEUTSCHE WELLE, Wertachtal — W • E Asia • 500 kW
UNITED KINGDOM
BBC, Various Locations — W Africa • 300/500 kW
BBC, Via Ascension — C Africa • 250 kW
21645 **FRANCE**
†R FRANCE INTL, Via French Guiana — C America • 500 kW
IRAN
†VO THE ISLAMIC REP, Sirjan — W Africa & C Africa • 500 kW
S • Mideast & E Africa • 500 kW
Mideast & E Africa • 500 kW
W • Mideast & E Africa • 500 kW
21650 **AUSTRIA**
†R AUSTRIA INTL, Vienna — E Asia • 100 kW
S • E Asia • 100 kW
W Sa • E Asia • 100 kW
W Su-F • E Asia • 100 kW
W • E Asia • 100 kW
GERMANY
†DEUTSCHE WELLE, Nauen — S • SE Asia • 500 kW
†DEUTSCHE WELLE, Wertachtal — S • E Asia • 500 kW
S • SE Asia • 500 kW
21655 **PORTUGAL**
†RDP INTERNATIONAL, Lisbon — ⇦ • Sa/Su • W Africa & S America • 100 kW
⇦ • W Africa & S America • 100 kW
⇦ • Irr • Sa/Su • W Africa & S America • 100 kW
21660 **UNITED KINGDOM**
†BBC, Via Ascension — S Africa • 250 kW
†BBC, Via Singapore — E Asia & SE Asia • 100 kW
BBC, Via Thailand — E Asia • 250 kW
21670 **FINLAND**
†YLE RADIO FINLAND, Pori — S • Asia & Australasia • 500 kW
Asia & Australasia • 500 kW
(con'd)

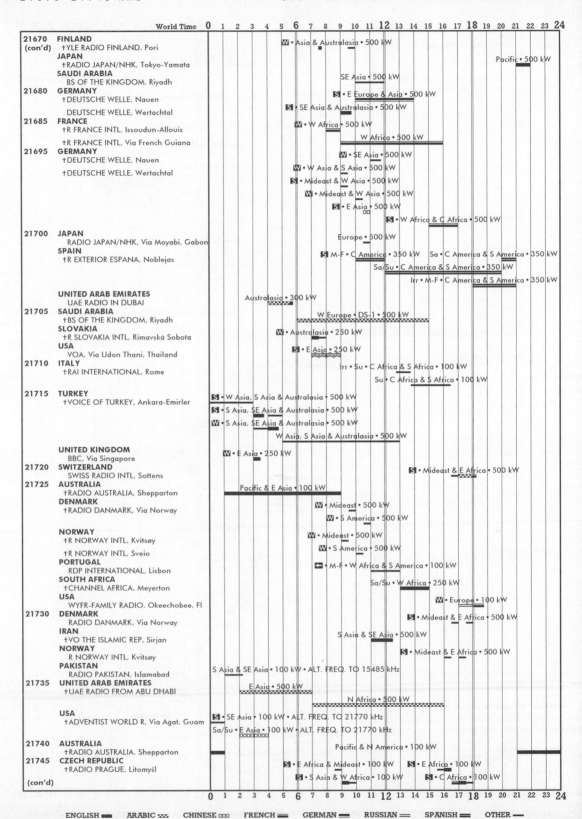

World Time | 0 1 2 3 4 5 6 7 8 9 10 11 12 13 14 15 16 17 18 19 20 21 22 23 24

21670
(con'd) **FINLAND**
   †YLE RADIO FINLAND, Pori — W • Asia & Australasia • 500 kW
JAPAN
   †RADIO JAPAN/NHK, Tokyo-Yamata — Pacific • 500 kW
SAUDI ARABIA
   BS OF THE KINGDOM, Riyadh — SE Asia • 500 kW
21680 GERMANY
   †DEUTSCHE WELLE, Nauen — S • E Europe & Asia • 500 kW
   DEUTSCHE WELLE, Wertachtal — S • SE Asia & Australasia • 500 kW
21685 FRANCE
   †R FRANCE INTL, Issoudun-Allouis — W • W Africa • 500 kW
   †R FRANCE INTL, Via French Guiana — W Africa • 500 kW
21695 GERMANY
   †DEUTSCHE WELLE, Nauen — W • SE Asia • 500 kW
   †DEUTSCHE WELLE, Wertachtal — W • W Asia & S Asia • 500 kW
      — S • Mideast & W Asia • 500 kW
      — W • Mideast & W Asia • 500 kW
      — S • E Asia • 500 kW
      — S • W Africa & C Africa • 500 kW
21700 JAPAN
   RADIO JAPAN/NHK, Via Moyabi, Gabon — Europe • 500 kW
SPAIN
   †R EXTERIOR ESPANA, Noblejas — S • M-F • C America • 350 kW   Sa • C America & S America • 350 kW
      — Sa/Su • C America & S America • 350 kW
      — Irr • M-F • C America & S America • 350 kW
UNITED ARAB EMIRATES
   UAE RADIO IN DUBAI — Australasia • 300 kW
21705 SAUDI ARABIA
   †BS OF THE KINGDOM, Riyadh — W Europe • DS-1 • 500 kW
SLOVAKIA
   †R SLOVAKIA INTL, Rimavská Sobota — W • Australasia • 250 kW
USA
   VOA, Via Udon Thani, Thailand — S • E Asia • 250 kW
21710 ITALY
   †RAI INTERNATIONAL, Rome — Irr • Su • C Africa & S Africa • 100 kW
      — Su • C Africa & S Africa • 100 kW
21715 TURKEY
   †VOICE OF TURKEY, Ankara-Emirler — S • W Asia, S Asia & Australasia • 500 kW
      — S • S Asia, SE Asia & Australasia • 500 kW
      — W • S Asia, SE Asia & Australasia • 500 kW
      — W Asia, S Asia & Australasia • 500 kW
UNITED KINGDOM
   BBC, Via Singapore — W • E Asia • 250 kW
21720 SWITZERLAND
   SWISS RADIO INTL, Sottens — S • Mideast & E Africa • 500 kW
21725 AUSTRALIA
   †RADIO AUSTRALIA, Shepparton — Pacific & E Asia • 100 kW
DENMARK
   †RADIO DANMARK, Via Norway — W • Mideast • 500 kW
      — W • S America • 500 kW
NORWAY
   †R NORWAY INTL, Kvitsøy — W • Mideast • 500 kW
   †R NORWAY INTL, Sveio — W • S America • 500 kW
PORTUGAL
   RDP INTERNATIONAL, Lisbon — M-F • W Africa & S America • 100 kW
SOUTH AFRICA
   †CHANNEL AFRICA, Meyerton — Sa/Su • W Africa • 250 kW
USA
   WYFR-FAMILY RADIO, Okeechobee, Fl — W • Europe • 100 kW
21730 DENMARK
   RADIO DANMARK, Via Norway — S • Mideast & E Africa • 500 kW
IRAN
   †VO THE ISLAMIC REP, Sirjan — S Asia & SE Asia • 500 kW
NORWAY
   R NORWAY INTL, Kvitsøy — S • Mideast & E Africa • 500 kW
PAKISTAN
   RADIO PAKISTAN, Islamabad — S Asia & SE Asia • 100 kW • ALT. FREQ. TO 15485 kHz
21735 UNITED ARAB EMIRATES
   †UAE RADIO FROM ABU DHABI — E Asia • 500 kW
      — N Africa • 500 kW
USA
   †ADVENTIST WORLD R, Via Agat, Guam — S • SE Asia • 100 kW • ALT. FREQ. TO 21770 kHz
      — Sa/Su • E Asia • 100 kW • ALT. FREQ. TO 21770 kHz
21740 AUSTRALIA
   †RADIO AUSTRALIA, Shepparton — Pacific & N America • 100 kW
21745 CZECH REPUBLIC
   †RADIO PRAGUE, Litomyšl — S • E Africa & Mideast • 100 kW   S • E Africa • 100 kW
      — S • S Asia & W Africa • 100 kW   S • C Africa • 100 kW

(con'd)

0 1 2 3 4 5 6 7 8 9 10 11 12 13 14 15 16 17 18 19 20 21 22 23 24

ENGLISH ■■ ARABIC ⋙ CHINESE □□□ FRENCH ══ GERMAN ▬▬ RUSSIAN ══ SPANISH ══ OTHER ──

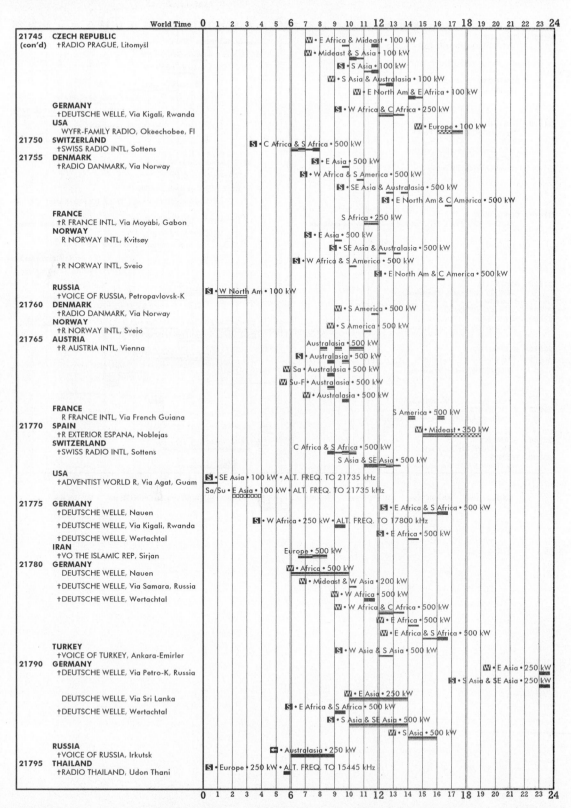

	World Time	0 1 2 3 4 5 6 7 8 9 10 11 12 13 14 15 16 17 18 19 20 21 22 23 24
21745	**CZECH REPUBLIC**	
(con'd)	†RADIO PRAGUE, Litomyšl	W • E Africa & Mideast • 100 kW
		W • Mideast & S Asia • 100 kW
		S • S Asia • 100 kW
		W • S Asia & Australasia • 100 kW
		W • E North Am & E Africa • 100 kW
	GERMANY	
	†DEUTSCHE WELLE, Via Kigali, Rwanda	S • W Africa & C Africa • 250 kW
	USA	
	WYFR-FAMILY RADIO, Okeechobee, Fl	W • Europe • 100 kW
21750	**SWITZERLAND**	
	†SWISS RADIO INTL, Sottens	S • C Africa & S Africa • 500 kW
21755	**DENMARK**	
	†RADIO DANMARK, Via Norway	S • E Asia • 500 kW
		S • W Africa & S America • 500 kW
		S • SE Asia & Australasia • 500 kW
		S • E North Am & C America • 500 kW
	FRANCE	
	†R FRANCE INTL, Via Moyabi, Gabon	S Africa • 250 kW
	NORWAY	
	R NORWAY INTL, Kvitsøy	S • E Asia • 500 kW
		S • SE Asia & Australasia • 500 kW
	†R NORWAY INTL, Sveio	S • W Africa & S America • 500 kW
		S • E North Am & C America • 500 kW
	RUSSIA	
	†VOICE OF RUSSIA, Petropavlovsk-K	S • W North Am • 100 kW
21760	**DENMARK**	
	†RADIO DANMARK, Via Norway	W • S America • 500 kW
	NORWAY	
	†R NORWAY INTL, Sveio	W • S America • 500 kW
21765	**AUSTRIA**	
	†R AUSTRIA INTL, Vienna	Australasia • 500 kW
		S • Australasia • 500 kW
		W Sa • Australasia • 500 kW
		W Su-F • Australasia • 500 kW
		W • Australasia • 500 kW
	FRANCE	
	R FRANCE INTL, Via French Guiana	S America • 500 kW
21770	**SPAIN**	
	†R EXTERIOR ESPANA, Noblejas	W • Mideast • 350 kW
	SWITZERLAND	
	†SWISS RADIO INTL, Sottens	C Africa & S Africa • 500 kW
		S Asia & SE Asia • 500 kW
	USA	
	†ADVENTIST WORLD R, Via Agat, Guam	S • SE Asia • 100 kW • ALT. FREQ. TO 21735 kHz
		Sa/Su • E Asia • 100 kW • ALT. FREQ. TO 21735 kHz
21775	**GERMANY**	
	†DEUTSCHE WELLE, Nauen	S • E Africa & S Africa • 500 kW
	†DEUTSCHE WELLE, Via Kigali, Rwanda	S • W Africa • 250 kW • ALT. FREQ. TO 17800 kHz
	†DEUTSCHE WELLE, Wertachtal	S • E Africa • 500 kW
	IRAN	
	†VO THE ISLAMIC REP, Sirjan	Europe • 500 kW
21780	**GERMANY**	
	DEUTSCHE WELLE, Nauen	W • Africa • 500 kW
	†DEUTSCHE WELLE, Via Samara, Russia	W • Mideast & W Asia • 200 kW
	†DEUTSCHE WELLE, Wertachtal	W • W Africa • 500 kW
		W • W Africa & C Africa • 500 kW
		W • E Africa • 500 kW
		W • E Africa & S Africa • 500 kW
	TURKEY	
	†VOICE OF TURKEY, Ankara-Emirler	S • W Asia & S Asia • 500 kW
21790	**GERMANY**	
	†DEUTSCHE WELLE, Via Petro-K, Russia	W • E Asia • 250 kW
		S • S Asia & SE Asia • 250 kW
	DEUTSCHE WELLE, Via Sri Lanka	S • E Africa & S Africa • 500 kW
	†DEUTSCHE WELLE, Wertachtal	S • S Asia & SE Asia • 500 kW
		W • S Asia • 500 kW
	RUSSIA	
	†VOICE OF RUSSIA, Irkutsk	⮂ • Australasia • 250 kW
21795	**THAILAND**	
	†RADIO THAILAND, Udon Thani	S • Europe • 250 kW • ALT. FREQ. TO 15445 kHz

	0 1 2 3 4 5 6 7 8 9 10 11 12 13 14 15 16 17 18 19 20 21 22 23 24

SEASONAL **S** OR **W**   1-HR TIMESHIFT MIDYEAR **⮂** OR **⮀**   JAMMING / OR ∧   EARLIEST HEARD ◁   LATEST HEARD ▷   NEW FOR 2001 †

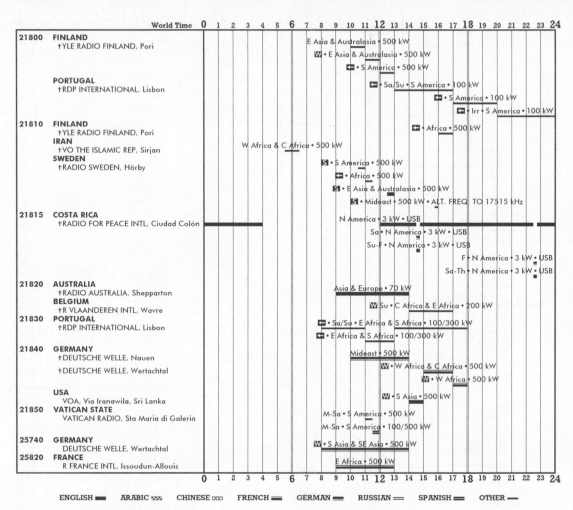

| World Time | 0 | 1 | 2 | 3 | 4 | 5 | 6 | 7 | 8 | 9 | 10 | 11 | 12 | 13 | 14 | 15 | 16 | 17 | 18 | 19 | 20 | 21 | 22 | 23 | 24 |

21800 **FINLAND**
　†YLE RADIO FINLAND, Pori — E Asia & Australasia • 500 kW
　W • E Asia & Australasia • 500 kW
　• S America • 500 kW

　PORTUGAL
　†RDP INTERNATIONAL, Lisbon — • Sa/Su • S America • 100 kW
　• S America • 100 kW
　• Irr • S America • 100 kW

21810 **FINLAND**
　†YLE RADIO FINLAND, Pori — • Africa • 500 kW
　IRAN
　†VO THE ISLAMIC REP, Sirjan — W Africa & C Africa • 500 kW
　SWEDEN
　†RADIO SWEDEN, Hörby — S • S America • 500 kW
　• Africa • 500 kW
　S • E Asia & Australasia • 500 kW
　S • Mideast • 500 kW • ALT. FREQ. TO 17515 kHz

21815 **COSTA RICA**
　†RADIO FOR PEACE INTL, Ciudad Colón — N America • 3 kW • USB
　Sa • N America • 3 kW • USB
　Su-F • N America • 3 kW • USB
　F • N America • 3 kW • USB
　Sa-Th • N America • 3 kW • USB

21820 **AUSTRALIA**
　†RADIO AUSTRALIA, Shepparton — Asia & Europe • 70 kW
　BELGIUM
　†R VLAANDEREN INTL, Wavre — W Su • C Africa & E Africa • 200 kW
21830 **PORTUGAL**
　†RDP INTERNATIONAL, Lisbon — • Sa/Su • E Africa & S Africa • 100/300 kW
　• E Africa & S Africa • 100/300 kW

21840 **GERMANY**
　†DEUTSCHE WELLE, Nauen — Mideast • 500 kW
　†DEUTSCHE WELLE, Wertachtal — W • W Africa & C Africa • 500 kW
　W • W Africa • 500 kW

　USA
　VOA, Via Iranawila, Sri Lanka — W • S Asia • 500 kW
21850 **VATICAN STATE**
　VATICAN RADIO, Sta Maria di Galeria — M-Sa • S America • 500 kW
　M-Sa • S America • 100/500 kW

25740 **GERMANY**
　DEUTSCHE WELLE, Wertachtal — W • S Asia & SE Asia • 500 kW
25820 **FRANCE**
　R FRANCE INTL, Issoudun-Allouis — E Africa • 500 kW

| | 0 | 1 | 2 | 3 | 4 | 5 | 6 | 7 | 8 | 9 | 10 | 11 | 12 | 13 | 14 | 15 | 16 | 17 | 18 | 19 | 20 | 21 | 22 | 23 | 24 |

ENGLISH ▬ ARABIC ⫶⫶⫶ CHINESE ☐☐☐ FRENCH ▬ GERMAN ▬ RUSSIAN ═ SPANISH ▬ OTHER ▬

Printed in Canada